EIGHTH EDITION

ECONOMICS

PARKIN POWELL MATTHEWS

EUROPEAN EDITION

Addison Wesley
is an imprint of

PEARSON

Harlow, England • London • New York • Boston • San Francisco • Toronto • Sydney • Singapore • Hong Kong
Tokyo • Seoul • Taipei • New Delhi • Cape Town • Madrid • Mexico City • Amsterdam • Munich • Paris • Milan

Pearson Education Limited
Edinburgh Gate
Harlow
Essex CM20 2JE
England

and Associated Companies throughout the world

Visit us on the World Wide Web at:
www.pearson.com/uk

Original edition entitled *Economics* published by Addison-Wesley Publishing
Company, Inc. – A Pearson Education company

This edition published by Pearson Education Limited 2012

ISBN 978-0-273-73575-5

British Library Cataloguing-in-Publication Data
A catalogue record for this book is available from the British Library

10 9 8 7 6 5 4 3 2 1
14 13 12 11

Typeset in 10/12.5 Times by 35
Printed and bound by Rotolito Lombarda, Italy

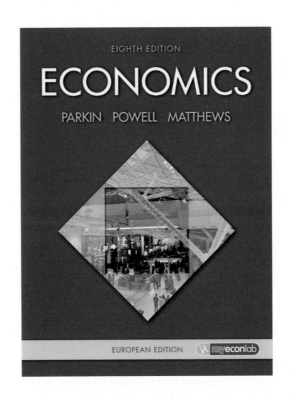

EIGHTH EDITION

ECONOMICS

PARKIN POWELL MATTHEWS

EUROPEAN EDITION   myeconlab

To Our Students

About the Authors

Michael Parkin is Professor Emeritus in the Department of Economics at the University of Western Ontario, Canada, where he teaches the principles course to around 900 students each year. He studied economics at the University of Leicester but received his real training in the subject from an extraordinary group of economists at the University of Essex during the early 1970s. Professor Parkin has held faculty appointments at the Universities of Sheffield, Leicester, Essex and Manchester and visiting appointments at Brown University, Bond University, the Reserve Bank of Australia and the Bank of Japan. He is a past president of the Canadian Economics Association and has served on the editorial boards of the *American Economic Review* and the *Journal of Monetary Economics* and as managing editor of the *Manchester School* and the *Canadian Journal of Economics*. Professor Parkin's economic research has resulted in over 160 publications in journals and edited volumes, including the *American Economic Review*, the *Journal of Political Economy*, the *Review of Economic Studies*, the *Economic Journal*, *Economica*, the *Manchester School*, the *Journal of Monetary Economics* and the *Journal of Money, Credit and Banking*, and edited volumes. He became visible to the public through his work on inflation that discredited the use of prices and incomes policies.

Melanie Powell took her first degree at Kingston University and her MSc in economics at Birkbeck College, London University. She has been a research fellow in health economics at York University, a principal lecturer in economics at Leeds Metropolitan University, and the director of economic studies and part-time MBAs at the Leeds University Business School. She is now a Reader at the University of Derby, Derbyshire Business School. Her main interests as a microeconomist are in applied welfare economics, and she has many publications in the area of health economics and decision making. Her current research uses the experimental techniques of psychology applied to economic decision making.

Kent Matthews received his training as an economist at the London School of Economics, Birkbeck College University of London and the University of Liverpool. He is currently the Sir Julian Hodge Professor of Banking and Finance at the Cardiff Business School. He has held research appointments at the London School of Economics, the National Institute of Economic and Social Research, the Bank of England and Lombard Street Research Ltd, and faculty positions at the Universities of Liverpool, Western Ontario, Leuven, Liverpool John Moores and Humboldt Berlin. He is the author of eight books and over 60 papers in scholarly journals and edited volumes. His research interest is in applied macroeconomics and the economics of banking.

Brief Contents

Alternative Pathways through the Micro Chapters

Micro Flexibility

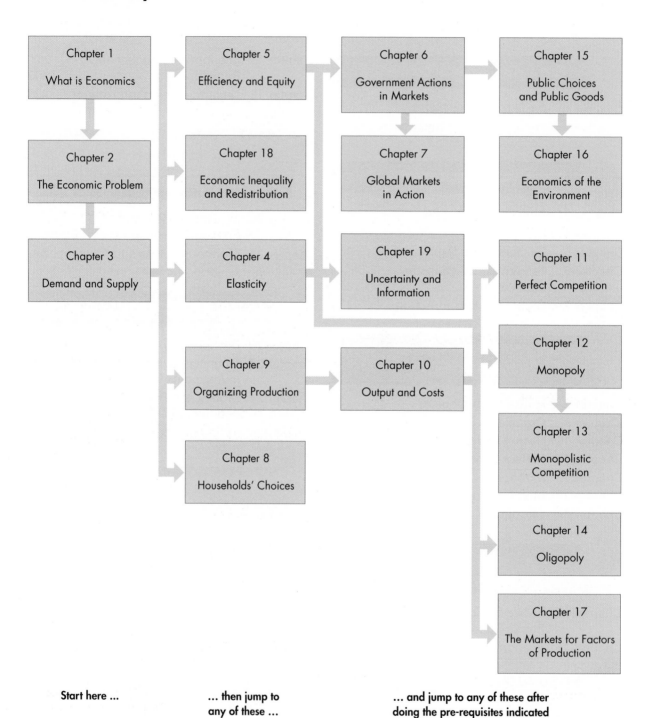

Chapter 1 What is Economics	**Chapter 5** Efficiency and Equity	**Chapter 6** Government Actions in Markets	**Chapter 15** Public Choices and Public Goods
Chapter 2 The Economic Problem	**Chapter 18** Economic Inequality and Redistribution	**Chapter 7** Global Markets in Action	**Chapter 16** Economics of the Environment
Chapter 3 Demand and Supply	**Chapter 4** Elasticity	**Chapter 19** Uncertainty and Information	**Chapter 11** Perfect Competition
	Chapter 9 Organizing Production	**Chapter 10** Output and Costs	**Chapter 12** Monopoly
	Chapter 8 Households' Choices		**Chapter 13** Monopolistic Competition
			Chapter 14 Oligopoly
			Chapter 17 The Markets for Factors of Production

Start here …   … then jump to any of these …   … and jump to any of these after doing the pre-requisites indicated

Alternative Pathways through the Macro Chapters

Macro Flexibility

Chapter 20

Measuring GDP and
Economic Growth

Chapter 21

Monitoring Jobs
and Inflation

Chapter 22

Economic Growth

Chapter 23

Finance, Saving
and Investment

Chapter 26

Aggregate Supply and
Aggregate Demand

Chapter 24

Money, the Price Level
and Inflation

Chapter 25

International Finance

Chapter 27

Expenditure Multipliers

Chapter 29

Fiscal Policy

Chapter 28

Inflation and
Output Cycles

Chapter 30

Monetary Policy

Start here ...

... then jump to
any of these ...

... and jump to any of these after
doing the pre-requisites indicated

Contents

Part 6 Monitoring Macroeconomic Performance — 457
The Big Picture — 457

Part 7 Macroeconomic Trends — 505
Expanding the Frontier — 505

Guided Tour for Students

Setting the Scene

The book is divided into nine parts. **Part Openers** clearly explain why a group of chapters are linked and how they relate to the previous and following parts, ensuring that you understand the connections among topics.

Chapter Openers motivate the topic and set the scene. We carry the introductory story into the main body of the chapter and return to it in the *Reading Between the Lines* or the *Business Case Study* at the end of the chapter.

Learning Objectives enable you to see exactly where the chapter is going and to set your goals before you begin the chapter. We link these goals directly to the chapter's major headings.

Using the Study Tools

Highlighted **Key Terms** within the text simplify your task of learning the vocabulary of economics. Each term appears in a list of **Key Terms** at the end of the chapter and in the **Glossary** at the end of the book. The terms are also highlighted in the index and can be found online in the MyEconLab glossary and Flashcards.

A government regulation that makes it illegal to charge a price higher than a specified level is called a **price ceiling** or **price cap**.

The effects of a price ceiling or crucially on whether the ceiling is that is above or below the equilibriu

Price ceiling A government regulation that sets the maximum price that may legally be charged. (p. 128)

Price discrimination The practice of selling different units of a good or service for different prices or of charging one customer different prices for different quantities bought. (p. 277)

Key Terms

Black market, 128
Minimum wage, 131
Price cap, 128
Price ceiling, 128
Price floor, 131
Price support, 141
Production quota, 139
Production subsidy, 140
Rent ceiling, 128
Search activity, 128
Tax incidence, 133

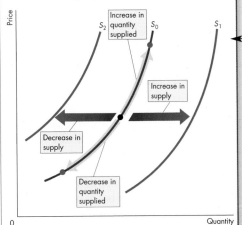

Figure 3.6 A Change in the Quantity Supplied versus a Change in Supply

When the price of the good changes, there is a movement along the supply curve and a change in the quantity supplied, shown by the blue arrows on supply curve S_0.

When any other influence on selling plans changes, there is a shift of the supply curve and a change in supply. An increase in supply shifts the supply curve rightward (from S_0 to S_1), and a decrease in supply shifts the supply curve leftward (from S_0 to S_2).

myeconlab Animation

Diagrams show where the economic action is! Graphical analysis is the most powerful tool available for teaching and learning economics. We have developed the diagrams with the study and review needs of students in mind. Our diagrams feature:

◆ Original curves consistently shown in blue
◆ Shifted curves consistently shown in red
◆ Colour-blended arrows to suggest movement
◆ Other important features highlighted in red
◆ Graphs often paired with data tables
◆ Graphs labelled with boxed notes
◆ Extended captions that make each diagram and its caption a self-contained object for study and review
◆ Every diagram can be found with a step-by-step animation in MyEconLab.

A **Review Quiz** at the end of every major section is tied to the chapter's learning objectives and enables you to go over the material again to reinforce your understanding of a topic before moving on. More practice on the topics can be found in the **MyEconLab Study Plan**.

Review Quiz

1 Define the quantity supplied of a good or service.
2 What is the law of supply and how do we illustrate it?
3 What does the supply curve tell us about the price at which firms will supply a given quantity of a good?
4 List all the influences on selling plans and for each influence say whether it changes supply.
5 What happens to the quantity of mobile phones supplied and the supply of mobile phones if the price of a mobile phone falls?

You can work these questions in Study Plan 3.3 and get instant feedback.

Connecting with Reality

***Economics in Action* Boxes** show you the connections between theory and real-world data or events. Tables and figures put the real-world flesh on the bones of the models and help you learn how to apply your newly gained knowledge of economic principles to the economic world around you.

ECONOMICS IN ACTION

Global Market for Crude Oil

The demand and supply model provides insights into all competitive markets. Here, we apply what you've learned about the effects of an increase in demand to the global market for crude oil.

Crude oil is like the life-blood of the global economy. It is used to fuel our cars, trucks, aeroplanes, trains and buses, to generate electricity and to produce a wide range of plastics. When the price of crude oil rises, the cost of transport, electricity and materials all increase.

In 2001, the price of a barrel of oil was $20 (using the value of money in 2010). In 2008, before the global financial crisis ended a long period of economic expansion, the price peaked at $127 a barrel. While the price of oil was rising, the quantity of oil produced and consumed also increased. In 2001, the world produced 65 million barrels of oil a day. By 2008, that quantity was 72 million barrels.

Who or what has been raising the price of oil? Oil producers might be greedy, and some of them might be big enough to withhold supply and raise the price. But it wouldn't be in their self-interest to do so for long. The higher price would soon bring forth a greater quantity supplied from other producers and the profit of the producer limiting supply would fall.

Oil producers could try to cooperate and jointly withhold supply. The Organization of Petroleum Exporting Countries, OPEC, is such a group of producers. But OPEC doesn't control the *world* supply and its members' self-interest is to produce the quantities that give them the maximum attainable profit.

constant along supply curve S. The demand for oil in 2001 was D_{2001}, so in 2001 the price was $20 a barrel and the quantity was 65 million barrels per day. The demand for oil increased and by 2008 it had reached D_{2008}. The price of oil increased to $127 a barrel and the quantity increased to 72 million barrels a day. The increase in the quantity is an *increase in the quantity supplied*, not an increase in supply.

Figure 1 The Global Market for Crude Oil

Reading Between the Lines

Demand and Supply: The Price of Coffee

The Financial Times, 30 July 2010

Coffee Surges on Poor Colombian Harvests

Javier Blas

Coffee prices hit a 12-year high on Friday on the back of low supplies of premium Arabica coffee from Colombia after a string of poor crops in the Latin American country.

The strong fundamental picture has also encouraged hedge funds to reverse their previous bearish views on coffee prices.

In New York, ICE September Arabica coffee jumped 3.2 per cent to 178.75 cents per pound, the highest since February 1998. It traded later at 177.25 cents, up 6.8 per cent on the week.

The London-based International Coffee Organisation on Friday warned that the 'current tight demand and supply situation'

was 'likely to persist in the near to medium term'.

Coffee industry executives believe prices could rise towards 200 cents per pound in New York before the arrival of the new Brazilian crop later this year.

'Until October it is going to be tight on high quality coffee,' said a senior executive at one of Europe's largest coffee roasters. He said: The industry has been surprised by the scarcity of high quality beans'.

Colombia coffee production, key for supplies of premium beans, last year plunged to a 33-year low of 7.8m bags, each of 60kg, down nearly a third from 11.1m bags in 2006, tightening supplies worldwide.

© The Financial Times Ltd. Reprinted with permission.

The Essence of the Story

● The price of premium Arabica coffee increased by 3.2 per cent to almost 180 cents per pound in July 2010, the highest price since February 1998.

● A sequence of poor crops in Columbia cut the production of premium Arabica coffee to a 33-year low of 7.8 million 60 kilogram bags, down from 11.1 million bags in 2008.

● The International Coffee Organisation expec the 'current tight demand and supply' 'persist in the near to medium term'.

● Coffee industry executives say prices mig approach 200 cents per pound before th new Brazilian crop arrives later this year.

● Hedge funds previously expected the price coffee to fall but now expect it to rise furthe

---

Economic Analysis

● This news article reports two sources of changes in supply and demand that changed the price of coffee.

● The first source is the sequence of poor harvests in Columbia. These events decreased the world supply of Arabica coffee.

● Before the reported events, the world production of Arabica was 120 million bags per year and its price was 174 cents per pound.

● The decrease in the Columbian harvest decreased world production to about 116 million bags – a decrease of about 3 per cent of world production.

● Figure 1 shows the situation before the poor Columbian harvests and the effects of those poor harvests. The demand curve is D_0 and initially, the supply curve was S_0. The market equilibrium is at 120 million bags per year and a price of 174 cents per pound.

● The poor Columbian harvests decreased supply and the supply curve shifted leftward to S_1. The price rose to 180 cents per pound and the quantity decreased to 116 million bags.

● The second source of change influenced both supply and demand. It is a change in the expected future price of coffee.

● The hedge funds are speculators who try to profit from buying at a low price and selling at a high price.

● With the supply of coffee expected to remain low, the price was expected to rise further – a rise in the expected future price of coffee.

● When the expected future price of coffee rises, some people want to buy more coffee (so they can sell it later) – an increase in demand. And some people offer less coffee for sale (so they can sell it later for a higher price) – a decrease in supply.

● Figure 2 shows the effects of these changes in demand and supply. Demand increased from D_0 to D_1 and supply decreased from S_0 to S_1.

Figure 1 The effects of the Columbian crop

Figure 2 The effects of the expected future price

● Because demand increases and supply decreases, the price rises. In this example, it rises to 200 cents per pound.

● Also, because demand increases and supply decreases, the change in the equilibrium quantity can go in either direction.

● In this example, the increase in demand equals the decrease in supply, so the equilibrium quantity remains constant at 116 million bags per year.

Reading Between the Lines and **Business Case Study**

This Parkin, Powell and Matthews hallmark helps students think like economists by connecting chapter tools and concepts to the world around them. At the end of each chapter in Reading Between the Lines or a Business Case Study, students apply the tools they have just learned by analysing an article from a newspaper or news website or a real-world case. Each article or case sheds additional light on the questions first raised in the Chapter Opener. Questions about the article or case also appear with the end-of-chapter problems and applications.

Each chapter closes with a concise **Summary** organized by major topics, a list of **Key Terms** (with page references), **Study Plan Problems and Applications** and **Additional Problems and Applications**. All Study Plan problems are available in MyEconLab with instant feedback. All Additional problems are available in MyEconLab if assigned by your lecturer.

Using MyEconLab

MyEconLab puts you in control of your study. By using MyEconLab, you can *test* your knowledge and *practise* to improve your understanding.

To register, go to **www.myeconlab.com** and follow the instructions on-screen using the code in your Student Access Kit. If you don't have an Access Kit, you can buy one online.

Sample Tests (two for each chapter) are preloaded in MyEconLab and enable you to test your understanding and identify the areas in which you need to do further work. Your lecturer might also create custom tests or quizzes.

MyEconLab creates a personal **Study Plan** for you based on your performance on the sample tests. The Study Plan diagnoses weaknesses and consists of a series of additional exercises with detailed feedback and 'Help Me Solve This' explanations for topics in which you need further help. The Study Plan is also linked to other study tools.

From the Study Plan exercises, you can link to **Help Me Solve This** (step-by-step explanations) and an **electronic version of your textbook** with all the **figures animated**.

Note on MyEconLab for Lecturers

 Why MyEconLab?

MyEconLab provides you with a low-cost means of monitoring and testing your students.

 Lecturer Support

You can use MyEconLab in a wide variety of ways and spend no time or invest a great deal of time in tailoring it to your personal needs.

Pearson Education offers you personalized support for MyEconLab through its dedicated team of technology specialists. Their job is to support you in your use of all Pearson Education's media products, including MyEconLab.

To contact your technology specialist please go to **www.pearsoned.co.uk/replocator**.

 What Do I Need to Do?

Nothing! Once your students have registered, they automatically have access to MyEconLab. Review the Guided Tour for Students on p. xxiii. Students have access to Sample Tests, Study Plan and other resources, but you may choose:

- ◆ To monitor your students' performance
- ◆ To set assignments
- ◆ To create your own self-author exercises

Monitor Your Students

To monitor your students' activity on MyEconLab you will need to set up a class group. Then MyEconLab's Gradebook automatically records each student's time spent and performance on the Tests and Study Plan and generates reports that you can organize either by student or by chapter. You can easily export data from the Gradebook into your own spreadsheet for combining with your exam and paper test marks.

Set Assignments

You can use MyEconLab to build your own tests, quizzes or homework assignments from the question base provided. The questions include multiple choice, graph drawing and free response questions. Many of the questions are generated algorithmically so that they present differently each time they are used.

If you set assignments, you need to be aware of the distinction between a Test, Quiz and Homework.

A Test and a Quiz play like an examination with no help and no feedback. Use this format when you want to test your students and give credit for their performance.

Homework plays like the Study Plan exercises. It gives the student detailed feedback and links to Help Me Solve This, e-text and animated figures. Use this format when you want to check that your students have done some practice questions.

Self-author Exercises

If you want to devote the time, you can create your own exercises by using the Econ Exercise Builder.

 Special Versions of MyEconLab

MyEconLab with CourseCompass places the resources inside a course management system. To find out more about the CourseCompass version go to **www.coursecompass.com**.

A MyEconLab Institutional Site licence is also available. Please contact your local Academic Sales Representative at **www.pearsoned.co.uk/replocator** for further details of these options.

Preface

The future is always uncertain. But at some times, and now is one of them, the range of possible near-future events is enormous. The major source of this great uncertainty is economic policy. There is uncertainty about the way international trade policy will evolve as protectionism is returning to the political agenda. There is uncertainty about exchange rate policy as competitive devaluation rears its head. There is extraordinary uncertainty about monetary policy with the central banks of many countries having exploded the quantity of bank reserves and continuing to create more money in an attempt to stimulate their fragile economies. And there is uncertainty about fiscal policy as unprecedented deficits interact with ageing populations to create national debt time bombs.

After the first tremors of financial crisis hit the global economy in August 2007, economics moved from the business report to the front page and justified fear gripped producers, consumers, financial institutions and governments. Even the idea that the market is an efficient mechanism for allocating scarce resources came into question as some political leaders trumpeted the end of capitalism and the dawn of a new economic order in which tighter regulation reigned in unfettered greed.

Rarely do teachers of economics have such a rich feast on which to draw. And rarely are the principles of economics more surely needed to provide the solid foundation on which to think about economic events and navigate the turbulence of economic life.

Although thinking like an economist can bring a clearer perspective to and deeper understanding of today's events, students don't find the economic way of thinking easy or natural.

Economics seeks to put clarity and understanding in the grasp of the student through its careful and vivid exploration of the tension between self-interest and the social interest, the role and power of incentives – of opportunity cost and marginal benefit – and demonstrating the possibility that markets supplemented by other mechanisms might allocate resources efficiently.

Students who use this text thoughtfully begin to think about issues the way economists do and learn how to explore difficult policy problems and make more informed decisions in their own economic lives.

The Eighth Edition Revision

Simpler where possible, stripped of some technical detail, more copiously illustrated with well-chosen photographs, reinforced with improved chapter summaries and problem sets, and even more tightly integrated with MyEconLab: These are the hallmarks of this eighth edition of *Economics*.

This comprehensive revision also incorporates and responds to the detailed suggestions for improvements made by reviewers and users, both in the broad architecture of the text and each chapter. The revision builds on the improvements achieved in previous editions and retains its thorough and detailed presentation of the principles of economics, its emphasis on real-world examples and applications, its development of critical thinking skills, its diagrams renowned for pedagogy and precision, and its path-breaking technology.

Most chapters have been fine-tuned to achieve even greater clarity and to present the material in a more straightforward, visual and intuitive way.

Some chapters have been thoroughly reworked to cover new issues, particularly those that involve current policy problems. These changes are aimed at better enabling students to learn how to use the economic toolkit to analyse their own decisions and understand the events and issues they are confronted with in the media and at the ballot box.

Current issues organize each chapter. News stories about today's major economic events tie each chapter together, from new chapter-opening vignettes to end-of-chapter problems and online practice. Each chapter includes a discussion of a critical issue of our time to demonstrate how economic theory can be applied to explore a particular debate or question.

Among the many issues covered are:

◆ The gains from trade, globalization and protectionism in Chapters 2 and 8
◆ How ethanol competes with food and drives its price up in Chapter 2
◆ Healthcare in Chapter 16
◆ Climate change in Chapter 17

◆ The carbon tax debate in Chapter 17

◆ Increasing inequality in the UK and decreasing inequality across the nations in Chapter 18

◆ The Bank of England's extraordinary actions and their impact on the balance sheets of banks in Chapter 24

◆ Fragile recovery from recession in Chapters 21, 26 and 28

◆ Currency fluctuations and the managed Chinese yuan in Chapter 25

◆ Fiscal stimulus and the debate about the fiscal stimulus multipliers in Chapter 29

◆ Extraordinary monetary stimulus in Chapter 30

◆ Real-world examples and applications appear in the body of each chapter and in the end-of-chapter problems and applications

A selection of questions that appear weekly in MyEconLab in *Economics in the News* are also available for assignment as homework, quizzes or tests.

Highpoints of the Micro Revision

In addition to being thoroughly updated and revised to include the topics and features just described, the microeconomics chapters feature the following **nine notable changes**.

1. What Is Economics? (Chapter 1)

We have reworked the explanation of the economic way of thinking around six key ideas, all illustrated with student-relevant choices. The graphing appendix to this chapter has an increased focus on scatter diagrams and their interpretation and on understanding shifts of curves.

2. Households' Choices (Chapter 8)

Students find the analysis of the income effect and the substitution effect difficult and we have reworked this material to make the explanation clearer. We have omitted the work-leisure choice coverage of earlier editions and given the chapter a student-friendly application to choices about films to see and cola to buy. The dramatic changes in the market for recorded music illustrate the theory in action. The chapter now includes an explanation of developments in behavioural economics and neuroeconomics as an alternative way of understanding human choices.

3. Monopoly (Chapter 12)

The final section of this chapter now covers the regulation of natural monopoly, which was previously found in a separate chapter. This change makes it easier to teach monopoly regulation when the material on unregulated natural monopoly and its inefficiency is fresh in the student's mind.

4. Monopolistic Competition (Chapter 13)

This market type now has its own full chapter treatment. Product differentiation and its consequences: excess capacity, markup over cost and high selling costs are explained with student-friendly examples.

5. Oligopoly (Chapter 14)

This market type also has its own full chapter treatment with a new final section on UK and EU antitrust laws. As with the monopoly chapter, this change makes it easier to teach antitrust law and its effects while the coverage of cartels and the temptation to fix prices is fresh in the student's mind.

6. Public Choices and Public Goods (Chapter 15)

The topics in the previous edition's chapters on externalities and public goods and common resources have been reorganized to achieve an issue focus rather than a technical focus. Chapter 15 is about public provision of both public goods and mixed goods with positive externalities.

This new chapter begins with an overview of public choice theory, a classification of goods and externalities, and an identification of the market failures that give rise to public choices. The chapter then goes on to explain the free-rider problem and the underprovision of public goods, the bureaucracy problem and overprovision, and the underprovision of mixed goods with external benefits, illustrated by education and healthcare. The chapter explains how education and healthcare vouchers provide an effective way of achieving efficiency in the provision of these two vital services.

7. Economics of the Environment (Chapter 16)

This new chapter brings all the environmental damage issues together by combining material on negative externalities and common resources. Covering all this material in the same chapter (the previous edition split them between two chapters) enables their common solutions – property rights (Coase) or individual transferable quotas – to be explained and emphasized.

8. Economic Inequality and Redistribution (Chapter 18)

This chapter now includes a section on inequality in the world economy and compares UK and US inequality with that in nations at the two extremes of equality and inequality. The new section also looks at the trend in global inequality. The discussion of the sources of inequality now includes an explanation of the superstar contest idea.

9. Uncertainty and Information (Chapter 19)

This chapter contains a heavily revised explanation of the 'lemon' problem and trading risk in credit and insurance markets. The dramatic rise in the price of credit risk during the global financial crisis illustrates the working of the market for risky loans.

Highpoints of the Macro Revision

All the macro chapters have been updated to incorporate data through the third quarter of 2010 (later for some variables) and the news and policy situation through to the winter of 2010–2011.

The thoroughly updated coverage of macroeconomics is now organized in four parts: monitoring macroeconomic performance, macroeconomic trends, macroeconomic fluctuations and macroeconomic policy. The introductory chapter of previous editions is now redistributed across the other chapters as needed. The content of the previous edition's chapter on the classical model is distributed between the economic growth chapter and a new chapter on financial markets. In addition to these organizational changes, the macroeconomics chapters feature the following **nine major revisions**.

1. Measuring GDP and Economic Growth (Chapter 20)

This chapter now includes a description and discussion of the recent history of real GDP growth and fluctuations found in the previous edition's introductory macro chapter. The explanation of the real GDP calculation has been simplified, and the chain volume measure of real GDP calculation is presented in a new Mathematical Note at the end of the chapter. We have revised the section on cross-country comparisons and the limitations of GDP to make the material clearer and we have added photo illustrations of PPP and items omitted from GDP.

2. Monitoring Jobs and Inflation (Chapter 21)

This substantially revised chapter has a simplified coverage of the anatomy and types of unemployment but a more comprehensive explanation of the sources of unemployment. As today's unemployment is compared with that of the Great Depression, the empirical relationship between cyclical unemployment and the output gap is more clearly illustrated. The measurement of the price level and inflation is motivated with a discussion of inflation and why it is a problem. The chapter also includes new material on alternative price indexes including the GDP deflator. The chapter concludes with a brief new section on the general use of real variables in macroeconomics.

3. Economic Growth (Chapter 22)

This relocated and now early chapter on economic growth begins with an explanation of what determines potential GDP (adapted from the previous edition's classical model chapter) and then explains what makes potential GDP grow. The sources of labour productivity growth are thoroughly explored but we have simplified this material by omitting the technical details on growth accounting and replaced them with an intuitive discussion of the crucial role of human capital and intellectual property rights. We illustrate the role played by these key factors in the *Industrial Revolution*. We have made the chapter more relevant and empirical by including a summary of the correlations between the growth rate and the positive and negative influences on it.

4. Finance, Saving and Investment (Chapter 23)

New to the eighth edition, this chapter provides a thorough and extensive explanation of financial markets and institutions and their role in providing the funds for investment – an engine of economic growth. The circular flow model of Chapter 20 is extended to include the flows in the market for loanable funds that finance investment. The chapter explains the role of government in the market for loanable funds and explains crowding out and the role of debt and the government budget deficit. The chapter also includes a discussion of borrowing and lending in the global loanable funds market and the events in the credit crisis of 2008.

5. Money, the Price Level and Inflation (Chapter 24)

This chapter is heavily revised to simplify the explanation of the money creation process. A Mathematical Note at the end of the chapter provides a more comprehensive analysis of this process. The chapter records and explains the Bank of England's extraordinary injection of monetary base following the financial panic of 2008.

We have redrawn the line between this 'money and banking' chapter, and the later 'monetary policy' chapter by including in this chapter a complete explanation of how an open market operation works. We have also provided clearer and more thorough explanations of the money multiplier and money market equilibrium in the short and the long run and in the transition to the long run. The quantity theory of money is explained in this chapter.

6. International Finance (Chapter 25)

We have relocated and restructured this chapter to emphasize the crucial role of the exchange rate as an influence on macroeconomic performance. The revised chapter better explains the distinction between the fundamentals and the role of expectations. It also includes an explanation of how arbitrage works in the foreign exchange market.

7. Aggregate Supply and Aggregate Demand (Chapter 26)

This chapter is a streamlined version of the previous edition's content, but with a new and more detailed explanation and illustration of the UK business cycle. The added clarity and focus of this chapter reflects the tone and goals of the eighth edition.

8. Fiscal Policy (Chapter 29)

The topic of this chapter is front-page news almost every day and is likely to remain so. The revision describes the deficit and the accumulating debt and explains the consequences of the uncertainty they engender. An entirely new section examines the fiscal stimulus measures taken over the past year, channels through which stimulus works, its unwanted side effects, its potentially limited power and its short comings. The controversy about and range of views on the magnitude of fiscal stimulus multiplier is examined.

9. Monetary Policy (Chapter 30)

This chapter describes and explains the dramatic monetary policy responses to the 2008–2009 recession and the fragile recovery of 2010. It also contains an improved description of the MPC's decision-making process. Technical details about alternative monetary policy strategies have been replaced with a new section on the extraordinary policy actions of 2008–2010.

 Features to Enhance Teaching and Learning

Reading Between the Lines and Case Study

This Parkin, Powell and Matthews hallmark helps students think like economists by connecting chapter tools and concepts to the world around them. In *Reading Between the Lines* and *Case Study*, which appears at the end of each chapter, students apply the tools they have just learned by analysing an article from a newspaper or news website or a real-world case. Each article or case sheds additional light on the questions first raised in the Chapter Opener. Questions about the article or case also appear with the end-of-chapter problems and applications.

Each *Reading Between the Lines* and *Case Study* in the Seventh edition has been replaced with a new one.

Economics in Action Boxes

The boxes in the Seventh edition have been replaced with *Economics in Action* boxes, which address current events and economic occurrences that highlight and amplify the topics covered in the chapter.

Instead of simply reporting the current events, the material in the boxes applies the event to an economics lesson, enabling students to see how economics plays a part in the world around them as they read through the chapter.

Some of the many issues covered in these boxes include the global market for crude oil, the best affordable choice of seeing films at cinemas or at home on DVDs, the cost of selling a pair of shoes, how Apple doesn't make the iPhone, intellectual property rights propel economic growth, the UK business cycle and the size of the fiscal stimulus multipliers.

For the Lecturer

This book enables you to achieve three objectives in your principles course:

◆ Focus on the economic way of thinking
◆ Explain the issues and problems of our time
◆ Choose your own course structure

Focus on the Economic Way of Thinking

You know how hard it is to encourage a student to think like an economist, but that is your goal. Consistent with this goal, the text focuses on and repeatedly uses the central ideas: choice; trade-off; opportunity cost; the margin; incentives; the gains from voluntary exchange; the forces of demand, supply and equilibrium; the pursuit of economic rent; the tension between self-interest and the social interest; and the scope and limitations of government actions.

Explain the Issues and Problems of Our Time

Students must *use* the central ideas and tools if they are to begin to *understand* them. There is no better way to motivate students than by using the tools of economics to explain the issues that confront today's world. Issues such as globalization and the emergence of China as a major economic force; the new economy with new near-monopolies such as eBay and the widening income gap between rich and poor; climate change; the challenge that the tragedy of the commons creates; the persistent unemployment; the challenges of fiscal policy that face many EU nations; and the challanges of monetary policy that face the Bank of England and the ECB.

Choose Your Own Course Structure

You want to teach your own course. We have organized this book to enable you to do so. We demonstrate the book's flexibility in the flexibliity charts that show the alternative pathways through the micro and macro chapters on pp. viii–ix. By following the arrows through the charts you can select the path that best fits your preference for course structure. Whether you want to teach a traditional course that blends theory and policy, or one that takes a fast-track through either theory or policy issues, *Economics* gives you the choice.

Lecturer's Support Tools

The eighth edition has the following support tools:

◆ Lecturer's manual
◆ Test banks
◆ PowerPoint resources
◆ MyEconLab

Lecturer's Manual

Nicola Lynch and Eugen Mihaita of the University of Derby have created a Lecturer's Manual. Each chapter contains an outline, what's new in the Eighth Edition, teaching suggestions, a look at where we have been and where we are going, a description of the electronic supplements, and additional discussion questions.

Test Banks

Andrew Hunt of Durham University has reviewed and edited all our Test Bank questions and created many new questions to ensure their clarity and consistency with the Eighth Edition.

An electronic Test Bank provides 3,500 multiple-choice questions. This Test Bank is available in Test Generator Software (TestGen with QuizMaster). Fully networkable, it is available for Windows and Macintosh. TestGen's graphical interface enables lecturers to view, edit and add questions; transfer questions to tests; and print different forms of tests. Tests can be formatted with varying fonts and styles, margins and headers and footers, as in any word-processing document. Search and sort features let the lecturer quickly locate questions and arrange them in a preferred order. QuizMaster, working with your university's computer network, automatically marks the exams, stores the results on disk and allows the lecturer to view or print a variety of reports.

A pdf Test Bank provides a further 1,500 true-false and numerical questions.

Both Test Banks are available online to download from **www.myeconlab.com**

PowerPoint Resources

Robin Bade has developed a Microsoft PowerPoint Lecture Presentation for each chapter that includes all the figures from the text, animated graphs, and speaking notes. The lecture notes in the Lecturer's Manual and the slide outlines are correlated, and the speaking notes are based on the Lecturer's Manual Teaching suggestions.

The PowerPoint resources also include a separate set of files that contain large-scale versions of all the text's figures (most of them animated). Use these to make your own presentations.

PowerPoint slides are available for Macintosh and Windows.

Clicker-Questions in PowerPoint

Andrew Hunt of Durham University has created clicker-ready questions in PowerPoint. These slides are available in both Turning Point and PRS. The slides contain ten multiple-choice questions for each chapter that test the concepts introduced. Lecturers can use these questions as assignments or review quizzes during a lecture. The system also enables student responses to be captured in a gradebook.

MyEconLab

MyEconLab is an online resource for your economics course. Its central features are a powerful graphing engine and large bank of questions for student study and lecturer testing. Lecturers can create and assign tests, quizzes or homework that incorporate graphing questions. MyEconLab saves lecturers time by automatically marking all questions and tracking results in an online gradebook.

Questions include multiple-choice, free response (usually numerical) and draw-graph. Many questions are generated algorithmically, so there is lots of variety and practice opportunity.

Every week during the academic year, we post a new *Economics in the News* item, with a news headline and a link to a news article. We also provide links to websites where further information about the topic in the article can be found. We also provide a number of questions that can be assigned as topics for essays or as discussion during lectures. These news questions are available in MyEconLab.

The electronic Test Bank is preloaded into MyEconLab, which gives lecturers ample material from which they can create assignments, tests and quizzes.

The Lecturer's Manual and the PowerPoint Resources are available on MyEconLab. 'Ask the Authors' feature gives lecturers the opportunuity to communicate with the authors via email.

A Note on MyEconLab for Lecturers on p. xxiv provides additional information. To request an Instructor Access Code for MyEconLab, visit **www.myeconlab.com**

 # For the Student

Two outstanding support tools for the student are:

◆ MyEconLab
◆ PowerPoint Notes

MyEconLab

Optimize your study time with MyEconLab, our online assessment and tutorial system. When you take a sample test online, MyEconLab gives you targeted feedback and a personalized Study Plan to identify the topics that you need to review.

The Study Plan consists of practice problems taken directly from the end-of-chapter Study Plan Problems and Applications and the Review Quiz in the textbook.

The Study Plan gives you unlimited opportunity to practise. And as you work each exercise, instant feedback helps you understand and apply the concepts. Many Study Plan exercises contain algorithmically generated values to ensure that you get as much practice as you need.

Study Plan exercises link to the following learning resources:

1. Step-by-step *Help Me Solve This* help you to break down a problem much the same way as a lecturer would during a class. These are available for selected problems.

2. Links to the *Pearson e-Text* promote reading of the text when you need to revisit a concept or explanation.

3. *Animated graphs* appeal to a variety of learning styles.

4. A *graphing tool* enables you to build and manipulate graphs to better understand how concepts, numbers and graphs connect.

For more details on how to use MyEconLab, see the Guided Tour for Students on pp. xx–xxiii.

PowerPoint Notes

Robin Bade has prepared a set of Microsoft PowerPoint Notes for students. These notes contain an outline of each chapter with the textbook figures animated. Students can download these PowerPoint Notes from MyEconLab, print them, bring them to the lecture and use them to create their own set of study notes.

◆ Acknowledgements

We extend our gratitude and thanks to the many people who have contributed to this new edition of our text and to all those who made such important contributions to the previous editions on which this one is based. So many people have provided help and encouragement either directly or indirectly that it is impossible to name them all.

We particularly thank our colleagues, present and past, who have helped to shape our understanding of economics and who have provided help in the creation of this new edition. We thank our reviewers who have read and commented on our work and provided countless good ideas that we have eagerly accepted. We also thank our families for their input and patience.

We especially acknowledge and express our deep gratitude to Robin Bade whose innovative work on the most recent Canadian edition has been invaluable to us. We also thank Robin for her meticulous reading of this edition and for the uncountable, some detailed and some major, improvements she has brought to it.

We thank Richard Parkin for his work on the graphics, both in the text and on MyEconLab.

We thank Nicola Lynch and Eugen Mihaita of the University of Derby for their work (with Melanie) on the Lecturer's Manual and Andrew Hunt of Durham University for his work on the Test Banks.

We thank Jeannie Gillmore and Laurel Davies for their work on MyEconLab test questions.

We could not have produced this book without the help of the people for whom it is written, our students. We thank the several thousand students we have been privileged to teach over many years. Their comments on previous editions (and on our teaching) whether in complaint or praise have been invaluable.

Nor could we have produced this book without the help of our publisher. We thank the many outstanding editors, media specialists, and others at Pearson Education who contributed to the concerted publishing effort that brought this edition to completion. They are: Rachel Gear, Editorial Director; Kate Brewin, Publisher; Joe Vella, Managing Editor; Philippa Fiszzon, Senior Editor; Kevin Ancient, Design Manager; Kay Holman, Senior Production Controller; Summa Verbeek, Marketing Manager; and Katie Eyles, Media Development Editor and Louise Hammond, Media Producer, who managed the development of the online resources.

Finally, we want to thank our reviewers. A good textbook is the distillation of the collective wisdom of a generation of dedicated teachers. We have been privileged to tap into this wisdom. We extend our thanks to Douglas Chalmers, Glasgow Caledonian University; Gary Cook, University of Liverpool; Steve Cook, Swansea University; Adrian Darnell, Durham University; Valerie Dickie, Heriot-Watt University; M. J. McCrostie, University of Buckingham; Maria Gil Molto, Loughborough University; Karen Jackson, University of Bradford; Gorm Jacobsen, Agder University, Norway; Chris Reid, University of Portsmouth; Kevin Reilly, Leeds University; Cillian Ryan, University of Birmingham; Jen Snowball, Rhodes University, South Africa; Phil Tomlinson, University of Bath; Gonzolo Varela, University of Sussex; and Robert Wright, Strathclyde University. We also thank other reviewers who have asked to remain anonymous.

As always, the proof of the pudding is in the eating! The value of this book will be decided by its users and whether you are a student or a teacher, we encourage you to send us your comments and suggestions.

Michael Parkin,
University of Western Ontario,
michael.parkin@uwo.ca

Melanie Powell
University of Derby,
m.j.powell@derby.ac.uk

Kent Matthews,
Cardiff University,
MatthewsK@Cardiff.ac.uk

Talking with Xavier Sala-i-Martin

Xavier Sala-i-Martin is Professor of Economics at Columbia University. He is also Senior Economic Advisor to the World Economic Forum, Associate Editor of the Journal of Economic Growth, *founder and CEO of Umbele Foundation: A Future for Africa and President of the Economic Commission of the Barcelona football club. Professor Sala-i-Martin was an undergraduate at Universitat Autonoma de Barcelona and a graduate student at Harvard University, where he obtained his PhD in 1990. In 2004, he was awarded the Premio Juan Carlos I de Economía, a biannual prize given by the Bank of Spain to the best economist in Spain and Latin America.*

Michael Parkin talked with Xavier Sala-i-Martin about his research and the challenges of lifting people from poverty.

PART

1

The Scope of Economics

What attracted you to economics?

It was a random event. I wanted to be rich, so I asked my mom, "In my family, who is the richest guy?" She said, "Your uncle John." And I asked, "What did he study?" And she said, "Economics." So I went into economics! In Spain, there are no liberal arts colleges where you can study lots of things. At age 18, you must decide what career you will follow. If you choose economics, you go to economics school and take economics five years in a row. So you have to make a decision in a crazy way, like I did.

We hear a lot about the rich getting richer and the poor getting poorer, but you say that poverty is going down. What is happening to the global distribution of income?

There are two issues: poverty and inequality. When in 2001 I said poverty is going down, everyone said I was crazy. The United Nations Development Report, which uses World Bank data, was saying the exact opposite. I said the World Bank methodology was flawed. After a big public argument that you can read in *The Economist*, the World Bank revised its poverty numbers and now agrees with me that poverty rates are falling.

Now, why is poverty falling? In 1970, 80 per cent of the world's poor were in Asia – in China, India, Bangladesh and Indonesia. China's 'Great Leap Forward' was a great leap backward. People were starving to death. Now, the growth of these countries has been spectacular and the global poverty rate has fallen. Yet, if you look at Africa, Africa is going backwards. But Africa has 700 million people. China has 1.3 billion. India has 1.1 billion. Indonesia has 300 million. Asia has 4 billion of the world's 6 billion people. These big guys are growing. It's impossible that global poverty is not going down.

But what we care about is poverty in different regions of the world. Asia has been doing very well, but Africa has not. Unfortunately, Africa is still going in the wrong direction.

You've made a big personal commitment to Africa. What is the Africa problem? Why does this continent lag behind Asia? Why, as you've just put it, is Africa going in the wrong direction?

Number one, Africa is a very violent continent. There are 22 wars in Africa as we speak. Two, nobody will invest in Africa. Three, we in the rich world – the US, Europe and Japan – won't let them trade. Because we have agricultural subsidies, trade barriers and tariffs for their products, they can't sell to us.

Africans should globalize themselves. They should open, and we should let them open. They should introduce markets. But to get markets, you need legal systems, police, transparency, less red tape. You need a lot of the things we have now. They have corrupt economies, very bureaucratic, with no property rights, the judiciary is corrupt. All of that has to change. They need female education. One of the biggest rates of return that we have is educating girls. To educate girls, we'll need to build schools, we need to pay teachers, we need to buy uniforms, we need to provide the incentives for girls to go to school, which usually is like a string. You pull it, you don't push it. Pushing education doesn't work. What you need is: let the girls know that the rate of return on education is very high by providing jobs after they leave school. So you need to change the incentives of the girls to go to school and educate themselves. That's going to increase the national product, but it will also increase health, and it will also reduce fertility.

Returning to the problems of poverty and inequality, how can inequality be increasing within countries but decreasing globally – across countries?

Because most inequality comes from the fact that some people live in rich countries and some people live in poor countries. The big difference across people is not that there are rich Americans and poor Americans. Americans are very close to each other relative to the difference between Americans and people from Senegal. What is closing today is the gap across countries – and for the first time in history. Before the Industrial Revolution, everybody was equal. Equal and poor. Equally poor. People were living at subsistence levels, which means you eat, you're clothed, you have a house, you die. No films, no travel, no music, no toothbrush. Just subsist. And if the weather is not good, one third of the population dies. That was the history of the world between 10,000 BC and today.

Yes, there was a king, there was Caesar, but the majority of the population were peasants.

All of a sudden, the Industrial Revolution means that one small country, England, takes off and there is 2 per cent growth every year. The living standard of the workers of England goes up and up and up. Then the US, then France, then the rest of Europe, then Canada all begin to grow.

In terms of today's population, one billion people become rich and five billion remain poor. Now for the first time in history, these five billion people are growing more rapidly than the rich guys. They're catching up quickly. The incomes of the majority of poor citizens of the world are growing faster than those of Americans.

Question!
Question everything!

What advice do you have for someone who is just beginning to study economics?

Question! Question everything! Take some courses in history and mathematics. And read my latest favorite book, Bill Easterly's *The White Man's Burden*.* It shows why we have not been doing the right thing in the aid business. I'm a little bit less dramatic than he is. He says that nothing has worked. I think some things have worked, and we have to take advantage of what has worked to build on it. But I agree with the general principle that being nice, being good, doesn't necessarily mean doing good. Lots of people with good intentions do harm. Economic science teaches us that incentives are the key.

---

* William Easterly, *The White Man's Burden: Why the West's Efforts to Aid the Rest Have Done So Much Ill and So Little Good*, New York, Penguin Books, 2006.

CHAPTER
1

What Is Economics?

After studying this chapter you will be able to:

- ◆ Define economics and distinguish between microeconomics and macroeconomics
- ◆ Explain the big questions of economics
- ◆ Explain the key ideas that define the economic way of thinking
- ◆ Describe how economists go about their work as social scientists and policy advisers

You are studying economics at a time when the world's richest nations are recovering from a deep recession in which incomes shrank and millions of jobs were lost. At the same time some poorer nations, Brazil, China, India and Russia, are growing rapidly and playing ever-greater roles in an expanding global economy. In these turbulent times, new businesses are born and old ones die, new jobs are created and old ones disappear.

To face these challenges and seize new opportunities, you need to understand the powerful forces at play. The economics that you're about to learn will be your most reliable guide. In this chapter you will find out about the questions economists ask, the way they think and the way they search for answers.

◆ A Definition of Economics

All economic questions arise because we want more than we can get. We want a peaceful and secure world. We want clean air and rivers. We want long and healthy lives. We want good schools and universities. We want space and comfort in our homes. We want a huge range of sports and recreational gear from running shoes to motor bikes. We want the time to enjoy sports and games, read books and magazines, see films, listen to music, travel and so on.

What each one of us can get is limited by time, by the income we earn and by the prices we must pay. Everyone ends up with some unsatisfied wants. As a society, what we can get is limited by our productive resources. These resources include the gifts of nature, human labour and ingenuity and tools and equipment that we have produced.

Our inability to satisfy all our wants is called **scarcity**. The poor and the rich alike face scarcity. A child in Tanzania is hungry and thirsty because her parents can't afford food and the well in her village is dirty and almost empty. The scarcity that she faces is clear and disturbing. But even David Beckham, a multi-millionaire, faces scarcity. He wants to spend the weekend playing football *and* filming an advert, but he can't do both. We face scarcity as a society. We want to provide better healthcare *and* better education *and* a cleaner environment and so on. Scarcity is everywhere. Even parrots face scarcity!

Faced with scarcity, we must *choose* among the available alternatives. The child in Tanzania must *choose* dirty water and scraps of bread or go thirsty and hungry. David Beckham must *choose* the football *or* the filming. As a society, we must *choose* among healthcare, education and the environment.

The choices that we make depend on the incentives that we face. An **incentive** is a reward that encourages or a penalty that discourages an action. If heavy rain fills the well, the child in Tanzania has an *incentive* to choose more water. If the fee received from filming is £1 million, David Beckham has an incentive to skip the football and make the advert. If computer prices tumble, we have an *incentive* as a society to connect more schools to the Internet.

Economics is the social science that studies the *choices* that individuals, businesses, governments and entire societies make as they cope with *scarcity* and the *incentives* that influence and reconcile those choices. The subject divides into two main parts:

◆ Microeconomics
◆ Macroeconomics

Microeconomics

Microeconomics is the study of the choices that individuals and businesses make, the way these choices interact in markets and the influence of governments. Some examples of microeconomic questions are: Why are people buying more mobile phones? How would a tax on downloading music affect the sales of CDs?

Macroeconomics

Macroeconomics is the study of the performance of the national economy and the global economy. Some examples of macroeconomic questions are: Why did unemployment increase in 2008 and 2009? Why did Japan's economy stagnate during the 1990s? Can the Bank of England bring prosperity by keeping interest rates low?

Not only do I want a cracker – we all want a cracker!

Review Quiz

1   List some examples of scarcity that you face.
2   Find examples of scarcity in today's headlines.
3   Find an illustration of the distinction between microeconomics and macroeconomics in today's headlines.

You can work these questions in Study Plan 1.1 and get instant feedback.

Two Big Economic Questions

Two big questions summarize the scope of economics:

◆ How do choices end up determining *what*, *how* and *for whom* goods and services get produced?

◆ When do choices made in the pursuit of *self-interest* also promote the *social interest*?

What, How and For Whom?

Goods and services are the objects that people value and produce to satisfy wants. Goods are physical objects such as golf balls. Services are actions performed such as cutting hair and filling teeth. By far the largest part of what people in the rich industrial countries produce today are services such as retail and wholesale services, health services and education. Goods are a small and decreasing part of what we produce.

What?

What we produce changes over time. Every year, new technologies allow us to build better equipped homes, higher-performance sporting equipment and even deliver a more pleasant experience in the dentist's chair. And technological advance makes us incredibly more productive at producing food and manufacturing goods.

Figure 1.1 shows some trends in what we produce in the UK. It highlights five items that have expanded and three that have shrunk since 2001. What are the forces that bring these changes in what we produce? Why are we producing more construction output and services such as health, education, finance and transport? Why are we producing fewer manufactured goods and doing less mining?

How?

Goods and services get produced by using productive resources that economists call **factors of production**. Factors of production are grouped into four categories:

◆ Land

◆ Labour

◆ Capital

◆ Entrepreneurship

Land

The 'gifts of nature' that we use to produce goods and services are called **land**. In economics, land is what in

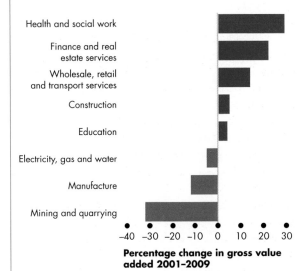

Figure 1.1 Changes in What We Produce

The production of many services has expanded, while mining and manufacture have shrunk.

Source of data: Office for National Statistics, *Change in Gross Value Added by Industry*.

myeconlab Animation

everyday language we call *natural resources*. It includes land in the everyday sense together with metal ores, oil, gas and coal, water, air, wind and sunshine.

Our land surface and water resources are renewable and some of our mineral resources can be recycled. But the resources that we use to create energy are non-renewable – they can be used only once.

Labour

The work time and work effort that people devote to producing goods and services is called **labour**. Labour includes the physical and the mental efforts of all the people who work on farms and construction sites and in factories, shops and offices.

The *quality* of labour depends on **human capital**, which is the knowledge and skill that people obtain from education, on-the-job training and work experience. You are building your own human capital today as you work on your economics course, and your human capital will continue to grow as you become better at your job.

Human capital expands over time and varies between countries. Figure 1.2 shows the proportion of young people entering post-secondary education and the growth in this measure since 2000 as a measure of human capital in different countries.

Figure 1.2   A Measure of Human Capital

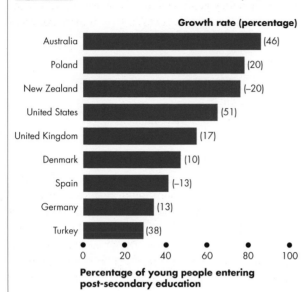

Growth rate (percentage)

Australia (46)
Poland (20)
New Zealand (–20)
United States (51)
United Kingdom (17)
Denmark (10)
Spain (–13)
Germany (13)
Turkey (38)

0   20   40   60   80   100

Percentage of young people entering post-secondary education

College and university education is a major source of human capital. The figure shows the percentage of young people entering post-secondary education in nine countries in 2007 and its growth rate since 2000. Although Australia has the highest entry rate at 86 per cent and Turkey the lowest at 29 per cent, both countries have a high growth rate of human capital, while New Zealand and Spain have a falling rate.

Source of data: OECD, *Education at a Glance 2009*, Table A2.5.

myeconlab Animation ──────────────────◆

Capital

The tools, instruments, machines, buildings and other constructions that businesses now use to produce goods and services are called **capital**.

In everyday language, we talk about money, shares and bonds as being capital. These items are *financial capital*. Financial capital plays an important role in enabling businesses to borrow the funds that they use to buy capital. But financial capital is not used to produce goods and services – it is not a factor of production.

Entrepreneurship

The human resource that organizes labour, land and capital is called **entrepreneurship**. Entrepreneurs come up with new ideas about what and how to produce, make business decisions and bear the risks that arise from these decisions.

How are the quantities of factors of production that get used to produce the many different goods and services determined?

For Whom?

Who gets the goods and services that are produced depends on the incomes that people earn. A large income enables a person to buy large quantities of goods and services. A small income leaves a person with few options and small quantities of goods and services.

People earn their incomes by selling the services of the factors of production they own:

1 Land earns **rent**.
2 Labour earns **wages**.
3 Capital earns **interest**.
4 Entrepreneurship earns **profit**.

Which factor of production earns the most income? The answer is labour. Wages and fringe benefits are around 70 per cent of total income. Land, capital and entrepreneurship share the rest. These percentages have been remarkably constant over time.

Knowing how income is shared among the factors of production doesn't tell us how it is shared among individuals. You know of lots of people who earn very large incomes. J. K. Rowling earns more than £20 million a year and David Beckham will make $US250 million over five years.

You know of even more people who earn very small incomes. People who serve fast food earn £5 an hour.

Some differences in income are persistent. On average, men earn more than women and whites earn more than ethnic minorities. Europeans earn more on average than Asians who in turn earn more than Africans. A typical annual income in the poorest countries of the world is just a few hundred pounds, less than the equivalent of a typical weekly wage in the richest countries of the world.

Why is the distribution of income so unequal? Why do women earn less than men? Why do J. K. Rowling and David Beckham earn such huge incomes? Why do university graduates earn more than people with only a few GCSEs? Why do Europeans earn more than Africans? Why are the incomes of Asians rising so rapidly?

Economics provides answers to all these questions about what, how and for whom goods and services get produced. And you will discover these answers as you progress with your study of the subject.

The second big question of economics that we'll now examine is a harder question both to appreciate and to answer.

When Is the Pursuit of Self-interest in the Social Interest?

Every day, you and 465 million other EU citizens, along with 6.9 billion people in the rest of the world, make economic choices that result in *what*, *how* and *for whom* goods and services get produced.

Self-interest

A choice is in your **self-interest** if you think that choice is the best one available for you. You make most of your choices in your self-interest. You use your time and other resources in the ways that make the most sense to you, and you don't think too much about how your choices affect other people. Think about when you order a pizza to be delivered to your home. You order the pizza because you are hungry and you don't order it thinking that the delivery person needs an income. When the pizza arrives, the delivery person is not doing you a favour but is working in his or her self-interest.

Social Interest

A choice is in the **social interest** if it leads to an outcome that is the best for society as a whole. The social interest has two dimensions: efficiency and equity (or fairness). What is best for society is an efficient and fair use of resources.

Economists say that **efficiency** is achieved when the available resources are used to produce goods and services at the lowest possible cost and in the quantities that will give the greatest possible value or benefit. You will study the concept of efficiency in more detail in Chapter 5. For now, just think of efficiency as a situation in which resources are put to their best possible use.

Equity or fairness doesn't have a precise definition. Reasonable people, including economists, have a variety of views about what is fair. There is always room for some disagreement and a need to be careful and clear about which notion of fairness is being used.

The Big Question

Now let's ask whether we can organize our economic lives so that when each one of us makes a choice in our self-interest, we actually promote the social interest? Can trading in free markets achieve this social interest? Do we need government action to help achieve the social interest? Do we need international cooperation and treaties to help achieve the social interest?

Questions about the social interest are hard ones to answer and they generate a lot of discussion, debate and disagreement. Let's take a closer look at these questions with four examples:

◆ Globalization
◆ The information-age economy
◆ Climate change
◆ Economic stability and financial crisis

Globalization

The term *globalization* means the expansion of international trade, borrowing and lending and investment.

Globalization is in the self-interest of consumers because they can buy low-cost goods and services produced in other countries. It is also in the self-interest of the multinational firms that produce in low-cost regions and sell in high-price regions. But is globalization in the self-interest of the low-wage workers in India who are sewing the sequins on your low-cost top or in the interest of displaced clothing workers in London? Is it in the social interest?

ECONOMICS IN ACTION

Life in a Small and Ever-shrinking World

When high-street fashion shops produce this season's clothes, people in India get low-paid work; and when China Airlines buys new aeroplanes, British workers at Rolls Royce in Derby build their engines. While globalization brings expanded production and job opportunities for some workers, it also destroys jobs. New jobs in India means workers in Europe's clothing manufacturing industries must learn new skills, take lower-paid service jobs or retire earlier than previously planned.

The Information-age Economy

The technological change of the past 40 years has been called the *Information Revolution*.

The Information Revolution has clearly served your self-interest: it has provided your mobile phone, laptop, the latest applications and the Internet. It has also served the self-interest of Bill Gates of Microsoft and Gordon Moore of Intel, both of whom have seen their wealth soar.

But did the information revolution best serve the social interest? Did Microsoft produce the best possible Windows operating system and sell it at a price that was in the social interest? Did Intel make the right quality of microchips and sell them in the right quantities at the right prices? Was the quality too low and the prices too high? Would the social interest have been better served if Microsoft and Intel had faced competition from other firms?

Climate Change

Climate change is a huge political issue today. Every serious political leader is acutely aware of the problem and of the popularity of having proposals that might lower carbon emissions to reduce the impact of climate change. Every day you make self-interested choices to use electricity, petrol and diesel, but you also create carbon emissions; you leave your carbon footprint. You can lessen your carbon footprint by walking, riding a bike, taking a cold shower, or planting a tree. But can we rely upon the self-interested decisions of every individual to make decisions that affect the earth's carbon-dioxide concentration in the social interest? Should governments change the incentives we face so that our self-interested choices are also in the social interest? How can governments change incentives? How can we discourage the use of fossil fuels and encourage the use of alternatives such as wind and solar power?

ECONOMICS IN ACTION

Microchips and Windows

Gordon Moore, who founded the chip-maker Intel, and Bill Gates, a co-founder of Microsoft, held privileged positions in the *Information Revolution*.

For many years, Intel chips were the only available chips and Windows was the only available operating system for the original IBM PC and its clones. The PC and Apple's Mac competed, but the PC has a huge market share.

An absence of competition gave Intel and Microsoft the power and ability to sell their products at prices far above the cost of production. If the prices of microchips and Windows had been lower, more people would have been able to afford a computer and would have chosen to buy one.

ECONOMICS IN ACTION

Greenhouse Gas Emissions

Burning fossil fuels to generate electricity and to power aeroplanes and motor vehicles pours a staggering 28 billion tonnes – 4 tonnes per person – of carbon dioxide into the atmosphere each year.

Two thirds of the world's carbon emissions are produced in the US, China, the EU, Russia and India. The fastest growing emissions are from India and China. The amount of global warming caused by economic activity and its effects are uncertain, but the emissions continue to grow and pose huge risks for climate change and our future.

Economic Stability and Financial Crisis

The years between 1993 and 2007 were a period of remarkable economic stability, so much so that they've been called the Great Moderation. During those years, European and global economies were booming. Incomes in the US increased by 30 per cent and incomes in China tripled. Even the economic shock waves of 9/11 emissions brought only a small dip in the strong pace of US and global economic growth. But in August 2007, a period of financial stress began. A bank in France was the first to feel the pain that soon would grip the entire global financial system.

ECONOMICS IN ACTION

Financial Crisis

Flush with funds and offering record low interest rates, banks went on a lending spree to home buyers. Rapidly rising home prices made home owners feel well off and they were happy to borrow and spend. Banks then bundled their home loans into new assets or securities that were sold and resold to other banks around the world to generate cash for more loans.

In 2006, interest rates began to rise and the rate of rise in home prices slowed and some borrowers defaulted on their loans. What started as a trickle became a flood. As more people defaulted, banks faced losses totalling billions of pounds by mid-2007.

Global credit markets stopped working as banks would not lend to each other or to businesses. Some retail banks faced collapse as depositors raced to withdraw their cash. People began to fear the financial crisis would lead to a prolonged slowdown in economic activity like the Great Depression of the 1930s. Central banks, including the Bank of England, determined to avoid a catastrophe, started lending on a very large scale to the troubled banks.

northern rock

Banks take in people's deposits and get more funds by borrowing from each other and from other firms. Banks use these funds to make loans. All the banks' choices to borrow and lend and the choices of people and businesses to lend to and borrow from banks are made in self-interest. But does this lending and borrowing serve the social interest? Is there too much borrowing and lending that needs to be reined in, or is there too little and a need to stimulate more?

When the banks got into trouble, the Bank of England and the European Central Bank bailed them out with big loans backed by the taxpayers. Did the Bank of England's bailout of troubled banks like Lloyds TSB serve the social interest? Did the Bank of England's rescue action just allow banks to repeat their dangerous lending in the future?

Banks weren't the only recipients of public funds. Some European governments supported their motor industries with a 'scrappage' scheme to encourage the purchase of new cars. Government support of the motor industry served the European motor industry self-interest. Did the scheme also serve the social interest?

Review Quiz

1 Describe the broad facts about **what, how** and **for whom** goods and services are produced.
2 Define the four factors of production and give an example of each one. What is the income earned by the people who sell the services of each of these factors of production?
3 Distinguish between self-interest and the social interest.
4 Use headlines from the recent news stories to illustrate the potential for conflict between self-interest and social interest.

You can work these questions in Study Plan 1.2 and get instant feedback.

We've looked at four topics and asked many questions that illustrate the big question: Can choices made in the pursuit of self-interest also promote the social interest? We've asked questions but not answered them because we've not yet explained the economic principles needed to do so.

By working through this book, you will discover the economic principles that help economists figure out when the social interest is being served, when it is not and what might be done when it is not being served. We will return to each of these questions in future chapters.

The Economic Way of Thinking

The questions that economics tries to answer tell us about the scope of economics, but they don't tell us how economists think and go about seeking answers to these questions. You're now going to see how economists go about their work.

We're going to look at six key ideas that define the economic way of thinking. These ideas are:

◆ A choice is a *trade-off*.

◆ People make *rational choices* by comparing benefits and costs.

◆ *Benefit* is what you gain from something.

◆ Cost is what you *must give up* to get something.

◆ Most choices are 'how-much' choices made at the *margin*.

◆ Choices respond to *incentives*.

A Choice Is a Trade-off

Because we face scarcity, we must make choices. And when we make a choice, we select from the available alternatives. For example, you can spend Saturday night studying for your next economics test or having fun with your friends, but you can't do both of these activities at the same time. You must choose how much time to devote to each. Whatever choice you make, you could have chosen something else.

You can think about your choice as a trade-off. A **trade-off** is an exchange – giving up one thing to get something else. When you choose how to spend your Saturday night, you face a trade-off between studying and hanging out with your friends.

Making a Rational Choice

Economists view the choices that people make as rational. A **rational choice** is one that compares costs and benefits and achieves the greatest benefit over cost for the person making the choice.

Only the wants of the person making a choice are relevant to determine its rationality. For example, you might like your coffee black and strong but your friend prefers his milky and sweet. So it is rational for you to choose espresso and for your friend to choose cappuccino.

The idea of rational choice provides an answer to the first question: What goods and services will be produced and in what quantities? The answer is those that people rationally choose to buy!

But how do people choose rationally? Why do more people choose an iPod rather than a Creative? Why has the UK government chosen to improve the A1 and M1 motorways joining the North and the South rather than build a new rail track? The answers turn on comparing benefits and costs.

Benefit: What You Gain

The **benefit** of something is the gain or pleasure that it brings and is determined by **preferences** – by what a person likes and dislikes and the intensity of those feelings. If you get a huge kick out of updating your Facebook page every day, that activity brings you a large benefit. If you have little interest in listening to a news pod cast, that activity brings you a small benefit.

Some benefits are large and easy to identify, such as the benefit that you get from being at university. A big piece of that benefit is the goods and services that you will be able to enjoy with the boost to your earning power when you graduate. Some benefits are small, such as the benefit you get from a slice of pizza.

Economists measure benefit as the most that a person is willing to give up to get something. You are willing to give up a lot to be at university but you would give up only an iTunes download for a slice of pizza.

Cost: What You *Must* Give Up

The **opportunity cost** of something is the highest-valued alternative that must be given up to get it.

To make the idea of opportunity cost clear, think about your opportunity cost of being at university. It has two components: the things you can't afford to buy and the things you can't do with your time.

Start with the things you can't afford to buy. You've spent all your available income on tuition, residence fees, books and a laptop. If you weren't at university, you would have spent this money on going to clubs and films and all the other things that you enjoy. But that's only the start of your opportunity cost. You've also given up the opportunity to get a job. Suppose that the best job you could get if you weren't at university is working at HSBC as a trainee earning £18,000 a year. Another part of your opportunity cost of being at university is all the things that you could buy with the extra £18,000 you would have.

As you well know, being a student eats up many hours in class time, doing homework assignments, preparing for tests and so on. To do all these school activities, you must give up many hours of what would otherwise be leisure time spent with your friends. So the opportunity cost of being at university is all the good things that you can't afford and don't have the spare time to enjoy. You might want to put a value on that cost or you might just list all the items that make up the opportunity cost.

The examples of opportunity cost that we've just considered are all-or-nothing costs – you're either at university or not at university. Most situations are not like this one. They involve choosing *how much* of an activity to do.

How Much? Choosing at the Margin

You can allocate the next hour between studying and e-mailing your friends. But the choice is not all or nothing. You must decide how many minutes to allocate to each activity. To make this decision, you compare the benefit of a little bit more study time with its cost – you make your choice at the **margin**.

The benefit that arises from an increase in an activity is called **marginal benefit**. For example, your marginal benefit from one more night of study before a test is the boost it gives to your grade. Your marginal benefit doesn't include the grade you're already achieving without that extra night of work.

The *opportunity cost* of an *increase* in an activity is called **marginal cost**. For you, the marginal cost of studying one more night is the cost of not spending that night on your favourite leisure activity.

To make your decisions, you compare marginal benefit against the marginal cost. If the marginal benefit from an extra night of study exceeds its marginal cost, you study the extra night. If the marginal cost exceeds the marginal benefit, you don't study the extra night.

Choices Respond to Incentives

Economists take human nature as given and view people as acting in their self-interest. All people – consumers, producers, politicians and civil servants – pursue their self-interest.

Self-interested actions are not necessarily *selfish* actions. You might decide to use your resources in ways that bring pleasure to others as well as to yourself. But a self-interested act gets the most value for *you* based on *your* view about benefit.

The central idea of economics is that we can predict the self-interested choices that people make by looking at the *incentives* they face. People undertake those activities for which marginal benefit exceeds marginal cost and reject those for which marginal cost exceeds marginal benefit.

For example, your economics lecturer gives you a problem set and tells you these problems will be on the next test. Your marginal benefit from working on these problems is large, so you work hard on them. In contrast, your statistics lecturer gives you a problem set on a topic that she says will never be on a test. You get little marginal benefit from working on these problems, so you decide to skip most of them.

Economists see incentives as the key to reconciling self-interest and social interest. When our choices are not in the social interest, it is because of the incentives we face. One of the challenges for economists is to figure out when the incentives that result in self-interested choices are also in the social interest.

Economists emphasize the crucial role that institutions play in influencing the incentives that people face as they pursue their self-interest. Private property protected by a system of laws and markets that enable voluntary exchange are the fundamental institutions. You will learn as you progress with your study of economics that where these institutions exist, self-interest can indeed promote the social interest.

Review Quiz

1 Explain the idea of a trade-off and think of three trade-offs that you made today.
2 Explain what economists mean by rational choice and think of three choices that you've made today that are rational.
3 Explain why opportunity cost is the best forgone alternative and provide examples of some opportunity costs that you have faced today.
4 Explain what it means to choose at the margin and illustrate with three choices at the margin that you have made today.
5 Explain why choices respond to incentives and think of three incentives to which you have responded today.

You can work these questions in Study Plan 1.3 and get instant feedback.

Economics as a Social Science and Policy Tool

Economics is a social science and a toolkit for advising on policy decisions.

Economist as Social Scientist

As social scientists, economists seek to discover how the economic world works. In pursuit of this goal, like all scientists, economists distinguish between positive and normative statements.

Positive Statements

A *positive* statement is about what is. It says what is currently believed about the way the world operates. A positive statement might be right or wrong, but we can test it by checking it against the facts. 'Our planet is warming because of the amount of coal that we're burning' is a positive statement. We can test whether it is right or wrong.

A central task of economists is to test positive statements about how the economic world works and to weed out those that are wrong. Economics first got off the ground in the late 1700s, so it is a young science compared with, for example, physics, and much remains to be discovered.

Normative Statements

A normative statement is about *what ought to be*. It depends on values and cannot be tested. Policy goals are normative statements. For example, 'We ought to cut our use of coal by 50 per cent' is a normative policy statement. You may agree or disagree with it, but you can't test it. It doesn't assert a fact that can be checked.

Unscrambling Cause and Effect

Economists are particularly interested in positive statements about cause and effect. Are computers getting cheaper because people are buying them in greater quantities? Or are people buying computers in greater quantities because they are getting cheaper? Or is some third factor causing both the price of a computer to fall and the quantity of computers bought to increase?

To answer such questions, economists create and test economic models. An **economic model** is a description of some aspect of the economic world that includes only those features that are needed for the purpose at hand.

For example, an economic model of a mobile-phone network might include features such as the prices of calls, the number of mobile phone users and the volume of calls. But the model would ignore mobile-phone colours and ringtones.

A model is tested by comparing its predictions with the facts. However, testing an economic model is difficult because we observe the outcomes of the simultaneous change of many factors. To cope with this problem, economists look for natural experiments (situations in the ordinary course of economic life in which the one factor of interest is different and other things are equal or similar); conduct statistical investigations to find correlations; and perform economic experiments by putting people in decision-making situations and varying the influence of one factor at a time to discover how they respond.

Economist as Policy Adviser

Economics is useful. It is a toolkit for advising governments and businesses and for making personal decisions. Some of the most famous economists work partly as policy advisers.

For example, Sir Alan Budd, who was Provost of The Queen's College, Oxford University until 2008, was the first Chair of the UK government's new Office for Budget Responsibility in 2010. He has also been an economic adviser to the UK Treasury, Barclays Bank and Credit Suisse First Boston as well as many other economic organizations.

All the policy questions on which economists provide advice involve a blend of the positive and the normative. Economics can't help with the normative part – the policy goal. But for a given goal, economics provides a method of evaluating alternative solutions – comparing marginal benefits and marginal costs and finding the solution that makes the best use of available resources.

Review Quiz

1   Distinguish between a positive statement and a normative statement and provide examples.
2   What is an economic model? Can you think of a model that you might use in your everyday life? Describe it.
3   How do economists try to disentangle cause and effect?
4   How is economics used as a policy tool?

You can work these questions in Study Plan 1.4 and get instant feedback.

SUMMARY

Key Points

A Definition of Economics (p. 4)

◆ All economic questions arise from scarcity – from the fact that wants exceed the resources available to satisfy them.

◆ Economics is the social science that studies the choices people make as they cope with scarcity.

◆ The subject divides into microeconomics and macroeconomics.

Working Problem 1 will give you a better understanding of the definition of economics.

Two Big Economic Questions (pp. 5–9)

◆ Two big questions summarize the scope of economics:

1 How do choices end up determining what, how and for whom goods and services get produced?

2 When do choices made in the pursuit of self-interest also promote the social interest?

Working Problems 2 and 3 will give you a better understanding of the two big questions of economics.

The Economic Way of Thinking

(pp. 10–11)

◆ Every choice is a trade-off – exchanging more of something for less of something else.

◆ People make rational choices by comparing benefit and cost.

◆ Cost – opportunity cost – is what you must give up to get something.

◆ Most choices are 'how much' choices made at the *margin* by comparing marginal benefit and marginal cost.

◆ Choices respond to incentives.

Working Problems 4 and 5 will give you a better understanding of the economic way of thinking.

Economics as a Social Science and Policy Tool (p. 12)

◆ Economists distinguish between positive statements – what is – and normative statements – what ought to be.

◆ To explain the economic world, economists create and test economic models.

◆ Economics is a tool-kit used to provide advice on government, business and personal economic decisions.

Working Problem 6 will give you a better understanding of economics as a social science and policy tool.

Key Terms

Benefit, 10
Capital, 6
Economic model, 12
Economics, 4
Efficiency, 7
Entrepreneurship, 6
Factors of production, 5
Goods and services, 5
Human capital, 5
Incentive, 4
Interest, 6
Labour, 5
Land, 5
Macroeconomics, 4
Margin, 11
Marginal benefit, 11
Marginal cost, 11
Microeconomics, 4
Opportunity cost, 10
Preferences, 10
Profit, 6
Rational choice, 10
Rent, 6
Scarcity, 4
Self-interest, 7
Social interest, 7
Trade-off, 10
Wages, 6

STUDY PLAN PROBLEMS AND APPLICATIONS

 You can work Problems 1 to 6 in MyEconLab Chapter 1 Study Plan and get instant feedback.

A Definition of Economics (Study Plan 1.1)

1 Apple decides to make iTunes freely available in unlimited quantities.

   a Does Apple's decision change the incentives that people face?

   b Is Apple's decision an example of a microeconomic or a macroeconomic issue?

Two Big Economic Questions
(Study Plan 1.2)

2 Which of the following pairs does not match?

   a Labour and wages

   b Land and rent

   c Entreprenuership and profit

   d Capital and profit

3 Explain how the following news headlines concern self-interest and the social interest:

   a Tesco Expands in Europe

   b McDonald's Moves into Salads

   c Food Must Be Labelled with Nutrition Data

The Economic Way of Thinking
(Study Plan 1.3)

4 The night before an economics exam, you go to the cinema instead of working your MyEconLab study plan. You get 50 per cent on your exam compared with the 70 per cent that you normally score.

   a Did you face a trade-off?

   b What was the opportunity cost of your evening at the cinema?

5 **Costs Soar for London Olympics**

   The regeneration of East London, the site of the 2012 Olympic Games, is set to add an extra £1.5 billion to taxpayers' bill.

            Source: *The Times*, 6 July 2006

   Is the cost of regenerating East London an opportunity cost of hosting the 2012 Olympic Games? Explain.

Economics as a Social Science and Policy Tool (Study Plan 1.4)

6 Which of the following statements is positive, which is normative and which can be tested?

   a The EU should cut its imports.

   b China is the EU's largest trading partner.

   c If the price of antiretroviral drugs increases, HIV/AIDS sufferers will consume fewer of the drugs.

ADDITIONAL PROBLEMS AND APPLICATIONS

 You can work these problems in MyEconLab if assigned by your lecturer.

A Definition of Economics

7 **Hundreds Line up for 5p.m. Ticket Giveaway**

   By noon, hundreds of Eminem fans had lined up for a chance to score free tickets to the concert.

            Source: *Detroit Free Press*, 18 May 2009

   When Eminem gave away tickets, what was free and what was scarce? Explain your answer.

Two Big Economic Questions

8 How does the creation of a successful film influence what, how and for whom goods and services are produced?

9 How does a successful film illustrate self-interested choices that are also in the social interest?

The Economic Way of Thinking

10 Before starring in *Iron Man*, Robert Downey Jr. had appeared in 45 films that grossed an average of $5 million on the opening weekend. In contrast, *Iron Man* grossed $102 million.

   a How do you expect *Iron Man*'s success to affect the opportunity cost of hiring Robert Downey Jr.?

   b How have the incentives for a film producer to hire Robert Downey Jr. changed?

11 What might be an incentive for you to take an extra university course during the summer break? List some of the benefits and costs involved in your decision. Would your choice be rational?

Economics as a Social Science and Policy Tool

12 Look at today's *Financial Times*. What is the leading economic news story? With which big economic questions does it deal? What trade-offs does it discuss?

13 Give two microeconomic and two macroeconomic statements and classify them as positive or normative.

Chapter 1 Appendix

Graphs in Economics

After studying this appendix, you will be able to:

◆ Make and interpret a scatter diagram

◆ Identify linear and non-linear relationships and relationships that have a maximum and a minimum

◆ Define and calculate the slope of a line

◆ Graph relationships among more than two variables

Graphing Data

A graph represents a quantity as a distance. Figure A1.1 shows two examples. A distance on the horizontal line represents temperature. A movement from left to right shows an increase in temperature. The point marked 0 represents zero degrees. To the right of 0, the temperature is positive and to the left of 0, it is negative. A distance on the vertical line represents height. The point marked 0 represents sea level. Points above 0 represent metres above sea level. Points below 0 (indicated by a minus sign) represent metres below sea level.

In Figure A1.1, the scale lines are perpendicular to each other and are called *axes*. The vertical line is the *y*-axis, and the horizontal line is the *x*-axis. Each axis has a zero point, which is shared by the two axes. This common zero point is called the *origin*.

To show something in a two-variable graph, we need two pieces of information: the value of the *x* variable and the value of the *y* variable. For example, off the coast of Norway on a winter's day, the temperature is 0 degrees – the value of *x*. A fishing boat is located 0 metres above sea level – the value of *y*. This information appears at the origin at point *A* in Figure A1.1. In the heated cabin of the boat, the temperature is a comfortable 24 degrees. Point *B* represents this information. The same 24 degrees in the cabin of an airliner 9,000 metres above sea level is at point *C*.

Finally, the temperature of the ice cube in the drink of the airline passenger is shown by the point marked *D*. This point represents 9,000 metres above sea level at a temperature of 0 degrees.

We can draw two lines, called *coordinates*, from point *C*. One, called the *y*-coordinate, runs from *C*

Figure A1.1 Making a Graph

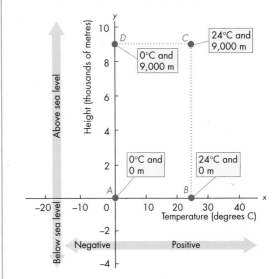

Graphs have axes that measure quantities as distances. Here, the horizontal axis (*x*-axis) measures temperature, and the vertical axis (*y*-axis) measures height.

Point *A* represents a fishing boat at sea level (0 on the *y*-axis) on a day when the temperature is 0°C. Point *B* represents inside the cabin of the boat at a temperature of 24°C.

Point *C* represents inside the cabin of an airliner 9,000 metres above sea level at a temperature of 24°C. Point *D* represents an ice cube in an airliner 9,000 metres above sea level.

myeconlab Animation ───────────────────────────────◆

to the horizontal axis. Its length is the same as the value marked off on the *y*-axis. The other, called the *x*-coordinate, runs from *C* to the vertical axis. Its length is the same as the value marked off on the *x*-axis. We describe a point in a graph by the values of its *x*-coordinate and its *y*-coordinate. For example, at point *C*, *x* is 24 degrees and *y* is 9,000 metres.

Graphs like that in Figure A1.1 can show any type of quantitative data on two variables. The graph can show just a few points, like Figure A1.1, or many points. Before we look at graphs with many points, let's reinforce what you've just learned by looking at two graphs made with economic data.

Economists measure variables that describe *what*, *how* and *for whom* goods and services are produced. These variables are quantities produced and prices. Figure A1.2 shows two examples of economic graphs.

Figure A1.2(a) is a graph about iTunes song downloads in January 2010. The *x*-axis measures the quantity

Figure A1.2   Two Graphs of Economic Data

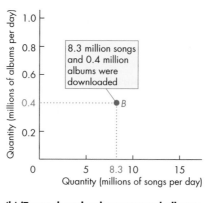

The graph in part (a) tells us that in January 2010, 8.3 million songs per day were downloaded from the iTunes store at a price of 99 cents a song.

The graph in part (b) tells us that in January 2010, 8.3 million songs per day and 0.4 million albums per day were downloaded from the iTunes store.

(a) iTunes downloads: quantity and price   **(b) iTunes downloads: songs and albums**

myeconlab Animation

---

of songs downloaded per day and the *y*-axis measures the price of a song. Point *A* tells us what the quantity and price were. You can 'read' this graph as telling you that in January 2010, 8.3 million songs a day were downloaded at a price of 99¢ per song.

Figure A1.2(b) is a graph about iTunes song and album downloads in January 2010. The *x*-axis measures the quantity of songs downloaded per day and the *y*-axis measures the quantity of albums downloaded per day. Point *B* tells us what these quantities were. You can 'read' this graph as telling you that in January 2010, 8.3 million songs a day and 0.4 million albums a day were downloaded.

The three graphs that you've just seen tell you how to make a graph and how to read a data point on a graph, but they don't improve on the raw data. Graphs become interesting and revealing when they contain a number of data points because then you can visualize the data.

Economists create graphs based on the principles in Figures A1.1 and A1.2 to reveal, describe and visualize the relationships among variables. We're now going to look at some examples. These graphs are called *scatter diagrams*.

Scatter Diagrams

A **scatter diagram** plots the value of one variable against the value of another variable for a number of different values of each variable. Such a graph reveals whether a relationship exists between two variables and describes their relationship.

The table in Figure A1.3 shows some data on two variables: the number of tickets sold at the box office and the number of DVDs sold for eight of the most popular films in 2009.

What is the relationship between these two variables? Does a big box office success generate a large volume of DVD sales? Or does a box office success mean that fewer DVDs are sold?

We can answer these questions by making a scatter diagram. We do so by graphing the data in the table. Each point in the graph shows the number of box office tickets sold (the *x* variable) and the number of DVDs sold (the *y* variable) of one of the films. With eight films, eight points are 'scattered' within the graph.

The point labelled *A* tells us that Star Trek sold 34 million tickets at the box office and 6 million DVDs.

The points in the graph form a pattern, which reveals that larger box office sales are associated with larger DVD sales. But the points also tell us that this association is weak. You can't predict DVD sales with any confidence by knowing only the number of tickets sold at the box office.

Figure A1.4 shows two scatter diagrams of economic variables. Part (a) shows the relationship between expenditure and income on average. Each dot shows expenditure per person and income per person in a given year from 1999 to 2009. The dots are 'scattered' within the graph. The red dot tells us that in 2007, income per person was £14,000 and expenditure per person was £13,700. The dots in this graph form a pattern, which reveals that as income increases, expenditure increases.

Figure A1.3   A Scatter Diagram

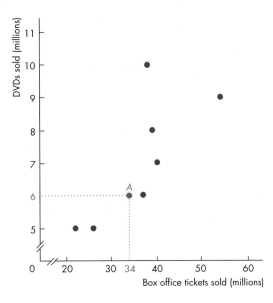

Film	Tickets	DVDs
	(millions)	
Twilight	38	10
Transformers: Revenge of the Fallen	54	9
Up	39	8
Harry Potter and the Half-Blood Prince	40	7
Star Trek	34	6
The Hangover	37	6
Ice Age: Dawn of the Dinosaurs	26	5
The Proposal	22	5

The table lists the number of tickets sold at the box office and the number of DVDs sold for eight popular films. The scatter diagram reveals the relationship between these two variables. Each point shows the values of the two variables for a specific film. For example, point *A* shows the point for *Star Trek*, which sold 34 million tickets at the box office and 6 million DVDs. The pattern formed by the points shows that there is a tendency for large box office sales to bring greater DVD sales. But you couldn't predict how many DVDs a film would sell just by knowing its box office sales.

myeconlab Animation

Figure A1.4(b) shows a scatter diagram of UK unemployment and inflation from 1999 to 2009. The points show no close relationship between the two variables. Movements in the inflation rate are not related to those in the unemployment rate in any simple way.

You can see that a scatter diagram conveys a wealth of information, and it does so in much less space than we have used to describe only some of its features. But you do have to 'read' the graph to obtain all this information.

Figure A1.4   Scatter Diagrams

(a) Expenditure and income

(b) Unemployment and inflation

A scatter diagram in part (a) shows the relationship between income and expenditure from 1999 to 2009. The red dot shows that in 2007, income was £14,000 and expenditure was £13,700. The dots form a pattern that shows that as income increases so too does expenditure.

The scatter diagram in part (b) shows a weak relationship between UK unemployment and inflation during most of the 2000s.

myeconlab Animation

Breaks in the Axes

Figure A1.4(a) and Figure A1.4(b) have breaks in their axes, as shown by the small gaps. The breaks indicate that there are jumps from the origin, 0, to the first values recorded.

In Figure A1.4(a), the breaks are used because the lowest values exceed £11,000. With no breaks in the axes, there would be a lot of empty space, all the points would be crowded into the top right corner and it would be hard to see the relationship between these two variables. By breaking the axes, we bring the relationship into view.

Putting a break in the axes is like using a zoom lens to bring the relationship into the centre of the graph and magnify it so that it fills the graph.

Misleading Graphs

Breaks can be used to highlight a relationship. But they can also be used to mislead – to make a graph that lies. The most common way of making a graph lie is to use axis breaks and either to stretch or compress a scale. For example, suppose that in Figure A1.4(a), the *y*-axis that measures expenditure ran from zero to £15,000 while the *x*-axis was the same as the one shown, running from £12,000 to £15,000. The graph would now create the impression that despite a huge increase in income, expenditure had barely changed.

To avoid being misled, it is a good idea to get into the habit of looking closely at the values and the labels on the axes of a graph before you start trying to interpret it.

Correlation and Causation

A scatter diagram that shows a clear relationship between two variables, such as Figure A1.4(a), tells us that the two variables have a high correlation. When a high correlation is present, we can predict the value of one variable from the value of the other variable. But correlation does not imply causation.

Sometimes a high correlation is a coincidence, but sometimes it does arise from a causal relationship. It is likely, for example, that rising income causes rising expenditure (Figure A1.4a).

You've now seen how we can use graphs in economics to show economic data and to reveal relationships between variables. Next, we'll learn how economists use graphs to construct and display economic models.

Graphs Used in Economic Models

The graphs used in economics are not always designed to show real-world data. Often they are used to show general relationships among the variables in an economic model.

An *economic model* is a stripped down, simplified description of an economy or of a component of an economy such as a business or a household. It consists of statements about economic behaviour that can be expressed as equations or as curves in a graph. Economists use models to explore the effects of different policies or other influences on the economy in ways that are similar to the use of model aeroplanes in wind tunnels and models of the climate.

You will encounter many different kinds of graphs in economic models, but there are some repeating patterns. Once you've learned to recognize these patterns, you will instantly understand the meaning of a graph. Here, we'll look at the different types of curves that are used in economic models, and we'll see some everyday examples of each type of curve. The patterns to look for in graphs are the four cases in which:

◆ Variables move in the same direction

◆ Variables move in opposite directions

◆ Variables have a maximum or a minimum

◆ Variables are unrelated

Variables That Move in the Same Direction

A relationship in which two variables move in the same direction is called a **positive relationship** or a **direct relationship**. Figure A1.5 shows some examples of positive relationships. Notice that the line that shows such a relationship slopes upward.

Figure A1.5 shows three types of relationships, one that has a straight line and two that have curved lines. But all the lines in these three graphs are called curves. Any line on a graph – no matter whether it is straight or curved – is called a *curve*.

A relationship shown by a straight line is called a **linear relationship**. Figure A1.5(a) shows a linear relationship between the number of kilometres travelled in 5 hours and speed. For example, point *A* shows that if

Figure A1.5 Positive (Direct) Relationships

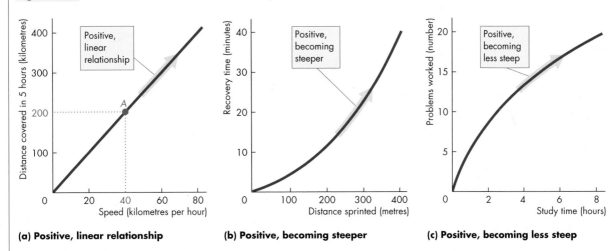

(a) Positive, linear relationship   **(b) Positive, becoming steeper**   **(c) Positive, becoming less steep**

Each part of this figure shows a positive (direct) relation-ship between two variables. That is, as the value of the variable measured on the x-axis increases, so does the value of the variable measured on the y-axis. Part (a) shows a linear relationship – as the two variables increase together, we move along a straight line.

Part (b) shows a positive relationship such that as the two variables increase together, we move along a curve that becomes steeper.

Part (c) shows a positive relationship such that as the two variables increase together, we move along a curve that becomes less steep.

myeconlab Animation

◆

our speed is 40 kms per hour, we will travel 200 kilo-metres in 5 hours. If we double our speed to 80 kms per hour, we will travel 400 kilometres in 5 hours.

Figure A1.5(b) shows the relationship between dis-tance sprinted and recovery time (the time it takes the heart rate to return to its normal resting rate). This rela-tionship is an upward-sloping one that starts out quite flat but then becomes steeper as we move along the curve away from the origin. The reason this curve slopes upward and becomes steeper is because the additional recovery time needed from sprinting an additional 100 metres increases. It takes less than 5 minutes to recover from the first 100 metres but more than 10 minutes to recover from the third 100 metres.

Figure A1.5(c) shows the relationship between the number of problems worked by a student and the amount of study time. This relationship is an upward-sloping one that starts out quite steep and becomes flatter as we move away from the origin. Study time becomes less productive as you increase the hours spent studying and become more tired.

Variables That Move in Opposite Directions

A relationship between variables that move in opposite directions is called a **negative relationship** or an **inverse relationship**. Figure A1.6 shows some examples. Figure A1.6(a) shows the relationship between the number of hours available for playing squash and for playing tennis when the total is 5 hours. One extra hour spent playing tennis means one hour less playing squash and vice versa. This relationship is negative and linear.

Figure A1.6(b) shows the relationship between the cost per kilometre travelled and the length of a journey. The longer the journey, the lower is the cost per kilo-metre. But as the journey length increases, the cost per kilometre decreases, but the fall in the cost is smaller, the longer the journey. This feature of the relationship is shown by the fact that the curve slopes downward, starting out steep at a short journey length and then becoming flatter as the journey length increases. This relationship arises because some of the costs are fixed.

Figure A1.6 Negative (Inverse) Relationships

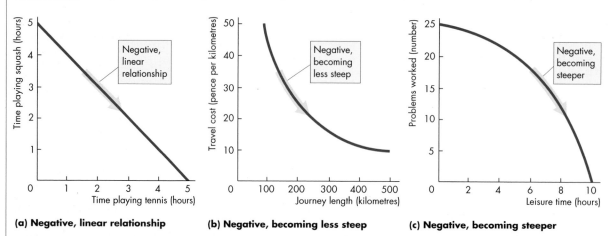

(a) Negative, linear relationship   **(b) Negative, becoming less steep**   **(c) Negative, becoming steeper**

Each part of this figure shows a negative (inverse) relationship between two variables. That is, as the value of the variable measured on the x-axis increases, the value of the variable measured on the y-axis decreases.

Part (a) shows a linear relationship. The total time spent playing tennis and squash is 5 hours. As the time spent playing tennis increases, the time spent playing squash decreases and we move along a straight line.

Part (b) shows a negative relationship such that as the journey length increases, the travel cost decreases as we move along a curve that becomes less steep.

Part (c) shows a negative relationship such that as leisure time increases, the number of problems worked decreases as we move along a curve that becomes steeper.

Figure A1.6(c) shows the relationship between the amount of leisure time and the number of problems worked by a student. Increasing leisure time produces an increasingly large reduction in the number of problems worked. This relationship is a negative one that starts out with a gentle slope at a small number of leisure hours and becomes steeper as the number of leisure hours increases. This relationship is a different view of the idea shown in Figure A1.5(c).

Variables That Have a Maximum or a Minimum

Many relationships in economic models have a maximum or a minimum. For example, firms try to make the largest possible profit and to produce at the lowest possible cost. Figure A1.7 shows relationships that have a maximum or a minimum.

Figure A1.7(a) shows the relationship between rainfall and wheat yield. When there is no rainfall, wheat will not grow, so the yield is zero. As the rainfall increases up to 10 days a month, the wheat yield increases. With 10 rainy days each month, the wheat yield reaches its maximum at 2.0 tonnes per hectare (point A). Rain in excess of 10 days a month starts to lower the yield of wheat. If every day is rainy, the wheat suffers from a lack of sunshine and the yield decreases to zero. This relationship is one that starts out sloping upward, reaches a maximum and then slopes downward.

Figure A1.7(b) shows the reverse case – a relationship that begins sloping downward, falls to a minimum and then slopes upward. Most economic costs are like this relationship. An example is the relationship between the travel cost per kilometre and the speed of a car. At low speeds, the car is creeping in a traffic jam. The number of kilometres per litre is low, so the cost per kilometre is high. At high speeds, the car is travelling faster than its efficient speed, using a large quantity of petrol, and again the number of kilometres per litre is low and the cost per kilometre is high. At a speed of 85 kms per hour, the cost per kilometre is at its minimum (point B). This relationship is one that starts out sloping downward, reaches a minimum and then slopes upward.

Figure A1.7 Maximum and Minimum Points

(a) Relationship with a maximum

(b) Relationship with a minimum

Part (a) shows a relationship that has a maximum point, *A*. The curve slopes upward as it rises to its maximum point, is flat at its maximum and then slopes downward.

Part (b) shows a relationship with a minimum point, *B*. The curve slopes downward as it falls to its minimum point, is flat at its minimum and then slopes upward.

Variables That Are Unrelated

There are many situations in which no matter what happens to the value of one variable, the other variable remains constant. Sometimes we want to show the independence between two variables in a graph, and Figure A1.8 shows two ways of achieving this.

In describing the graphs in Figures A1.5 to Figure A1.8, we have talked about curves that slope upward or slope downward and curves that become steeper and less steep. Let's spend a little time discussing exactly what we mean by slope and how we measure the slope of a curve.

Figure A1.8 Variables That Are Unrelated

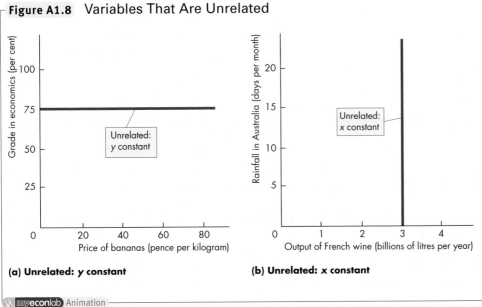

(a) Unrelated: *y* constant

(b) Unrelated: *x* constant

This figure shows how we can graph two variables that are unrelated. In part (a), a student's grade in economics is plotted at 75 per cent on the *y*-axis regardless of the price of bananas on the *x*-axis. The curve is horizontal.

In part (b), the output of the vineyards of France on the *x*-axis does not vary with the rainfall in Australia on the *y*-axis. The curve is vertical.

The Slope of a Relationship

We can measure the influence of one variable on another by the slope of the relationship. The **slope** of a relationship is the change in the value of the variable measured on the y-axis divided by the change in the value of the variable measured on the x-axis. We use the Greek letter Δ (*delta*) to represent 'change in'. So Δy means the change in the value of the variable measured on the y-axis, and Δx means the change in the value of the variable measured on the x-axis. The slope of the relationship is:

$$\frac{\Delta y}{\Delta x}$$

If a large change in the variable measured on the y-axis (Δy) is associated with a small change in the variable measured on the x-axis (Δx), the slope is large and the curve is steep. If a small change in the variable measured on the y-axis (Δy) is associated with a large change in the variable measured on the x-axis (Δx), the slope is small and the curve is flat.

We can make the idea of slope sharper by doing some calculations.

The Slope of a Straight Line

The slope of a straight line is the same regardless of where on the line you calculate it. The slope of a straight line is constant.

Figure A1.9   The Slope of a Straight Line

(a) Positive slope

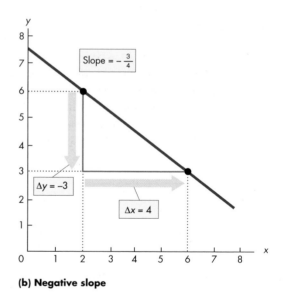

(b) Negative slope

To calculate the slope of a straight line, we divide the change in the value of the variable measured on the y-axis (Δy) by the change in the value of the variable measured on the x-axis (Δx), as we move along the curve.

Part (a) shows the calculation of a positive slope. When x increases from 2 to 6, Δx equals 4. That change in x brings about an increase in y from 3 to 6, so Δy equals 3. The slope ($\Delta y/\Delta x$) equals 3/4.

Part (b) shows the calculation of a negative slope. When x increases from 2 to 6, Δx equals 4. That increase in x brings about a decrease in y from 6 to 3, so Δy equals –3. The slope ($\Delta y/\Delta x$) equals –3/4.

Let's calculate the slopes of the lines in Figure A1.9. In part (a), when x increases from 2 to 6, y increases from 3 to 6. The change in x is +4: that is, Δx is 4. The change in y is +3: that is, Δy is 3. The slope of that line is:

$$\frac{\Delta y}{\Delta x} = \frac{3}{4}$$

In part (b), when x increases from 2 to 6, y decreases from 6 to 3. The change in y is *minus* 3: that is, Δy is –3. The change in x is *plus* 4: that is, Δx is 4. The slope of the curve is:

$$\frac{\Delta y}{\Delta x} = \frac{-3}{4}$$

Notice that the two slopes have the same magnitude (3/4), but the slope of the line in part (a) is positive (3/4), while the slope in part (b) is negative (–3/4). The slope of a positive relationship is positive; the slope of a negative relationship is negative.

The Slope of a Curved Line

The slope of a curved line is trickier. The slope of a curved line is not constant. Its slope depends on where on the line we calculate it. There are two ways to calculate the slope of a curved line: you can calculate the slope at a point, or you can calculate the slope across an arc of the curve. Let's look at the two alternatives.

Slope at a Point

To calculate the slope at a point on a curve, you need to construct a straight line that has the same slope as the curve at the point in question. Figure A1.10 shows how this is done. Suppose you want to calculate the slope of the curve at point A. Place a ruler on the graph so that it touches point A and no other point on the curve, then draw a straight line along the edge of the ruler. The straight red line is this line, and it is the *tangent* to the curve at point A. If the ruler touches the curve only at point A, then the slope of the curve at point A must be the same as the slope of the edge of the ruler. If the curve and the ruler do not have the same slope, the line along the edge of the ruler will cut the curve instead of just touching it.

Now that you have found a straight line with the same slope as the curve at point A, you can calculate the slope of the curve at point A by calculating the slope of the straight line. Along the straight line, as x increases from

Figure A1.10   Slope at a Point

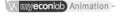

To calculate the slope of the curve at point A, draw the red line that just touches the curve at A – the tangent. The slope of this straight line is calculated by dividing the change in y by the change in x along the line. When x increases from 0 to 4, Δx equals 4. That change in x is associated with an increase in y from 2 to 5, so Δy equals 3. The slope of the red line is 3/4. So the slope of the curve at point A is 3/4.

⟨**myeconlab**⟩ Animation ────────────────◆

0 to 4 ($\Delta x = 4$) y increases from 2 to 5 ($\Delta y = 3$). The slope of the line is:

$$\frac{\Delta y}{\Delta x} = \frac{3}{4}$$

So the slope of the curve at point A is 3/4.

Slope Across an Arc

An arc of a curve is a piece of a curve. In Figure A1.11, you are looking at the same curve as in Figure A1.10. But instead of calculating the slope at point A, we are going to calculate the slope across the arc from B to C. You can see that the slope is greater at B than at C. When we calculate the slope across an arc, we are calculating the average slope between two points. As we move along the arc from B to C, x increases from 3 to 5 and y increases from 4 to 5.5. The change in x is 2 ($\Delta x = 2$), and the change in y is 1.5 ($\Delta y = 1.5$).

Figure A1.11   Slope Across an Arc

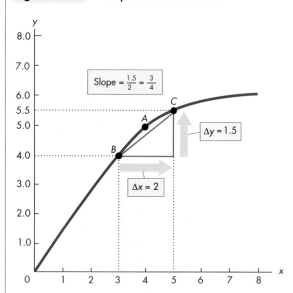

To calculate the average slope of the curve along the arc *BC*, draw a straight line from point *B* to point *C*. The slope of the line *BC* is calculated by dividing the change in *y* by the change in *x*. In moving from *B* to *C*, Δ*x* equals 2 and Δ*y* equals 1.5. The slope of the line *BC* is 1.5 divided by 2, or 3/4. So the slope of the curve across the arc *BC* is 3/4.

myeconlab Animation ◆

The slope of the red line *BC* is:

$$\frac{\Delta y}{\Delta x} = \frac{1.5}{2} = \frac{3}{4}$$

So the slope of the curve across the arc *BC* is 3/4.

This calculation gives us the slope of the curve between points *B* and *C*. The actual slope calculated is the slope of the straight line from *B* to *C*. This slope approximates the average slope of the curve along the arc *BC*. In this particular example, the slope across the arc *BC* is identical to the slope of the curve at point *A*. But the calculation of the slope of a curve does not always work out so neatly. You might have some fun constructing some more examples and some counter examples.

You now know how to make and interpret a graph. But so far, we've limited our attention to graphs of two variables. We're now going to learn how to graph more than two variables.

Graphing Relationships Among More Than Two Variables

We have seen that we can graph the relationship between two variables as a point formed by the *x*- and *y*-coordinates in a two-dimensional graph. You may be thinking that although a two-dimensional graph is informative, most of the things in which you are likely to be interested involve relationships among many variables, not just two. For example, the amount of ice cream consumed depends on the price of ice cream and the temperature. If ice cream is expensive and the temperature is low, people eat a lot less ice cream than when ice cream is inexpensive and the temperature is high. For any given price of ice cream, the quantity consumed varies with the temperature; and for any given temperature, the quantity of ice cream consumed varies with its price.

Figure A1.12 shows a relationship among three variables. The table shows the number of litres of ice cream consumed each day at various temperatures and ice cream prices. How can we graph these numbers?

To graph a relationship that involves more than two variables, we use the *ceteris paribus* assumption.

Ceteris Paribus

Ceteris paribus (often shortened to *cet. par.*) means 'if all other relevant things remain the same'. To isolate the relationship of interest in a laboratory experiment, a scientist holds everything constant except for the variable whose effect is being studied. Economists use the same method to graph a relationship that has more than two variables.

Figure A1.12(a) shows an example. There, you can see what happens to the quantity of ice cream consumed as the price of ice cream varies when the temperature is held constant.

The curve labelled 20°C shows the relationship between ice cream consumption and the price of a scoop if the temperature remains at 20°C. The numbers used to plot that curve are those in the first two columns of the table. For example, if the temperature is 20°C, 10 litres are consumed when the price is £1.20 a scoop and 6 litres are consumed when the price is £1.60 a scoop.

The curve labelled 25°C shows the relationship between ice cream consumption and the price of a scoop when the temperature remains at 25°C. The numbers used to plot the curve are those in the first and third

Figure A1.12 Graphing a Relationship Among Three Variables

Price (pounds per scoop)	Ice cream consumption (litres per day)	
	20°C	25°C
0.40	52	91
0.80	18	32
1.20	**10**	**17**
1.60	6	10
2.00	5	8
2.40	4	6

Ice cream consumption depends on its price and the temperature. The table tells us how many litres of ice cream are consumed each day at different prices and two different temperatures. For example, if the price is £1.20 a scoop and the temperature is 20°C, 10 litres of ice cream are consumed.

To graph a relationship among three variables, the value of one variable is held constant. The graph shows the relationship between price and consumption when temperature is held constant. One curve holds temperature at 20°C and the other at 25°C.

A change in the price of ice cream brings a *movement along* one of the curves – along the blue curve at 20°C and along the red curve at 25°C.

When the temperature rises from 20°C to 25°C, the curve that shows the relationship between consumption and price *shifts* rightward from the blue curve to the red curve.

columns of the table. For example, if the temperature is 25°C, 17 litres of ice cream are consumed when the price is £1.20 a scoop and 32 litres when the price is £0.80 a scoop.

When the price of ice cream changes but the temperature is constant, you can think of what happens in the graph as a movement along one of the curves. At 20°C there is a movement along the blue curve and at 25°C there is a movement along the red curve.

When Other Things Change

The temperature is held constant along each of the curves in Figure A1.12, but in reality the temperature changes. When that event occurs, you can think of what happens in the graph as a shift of the curve.

When the temperature rises from 20°C to 25°C, the curve that shows the relationship between ice cream consumption and the price of ice cream shifts rightward from the blue curve to the red curve.

You will encounter these ideas of movements along and shifts of curves at many points in your study of economics. Think carefully about what you've just learned and make up some examples (with assumed numbers) about other relationships.

With what you have learned about graphs, you can move forward with your study of economics. There are no graphs in this book that are more complicated than those that have been explained in this appendix. Use this appendix as a refresher if you find that you're having difficulty interpreting or making a graph.

Equations of Straight Lines

If a straight line in a graph describes the relationship between two variables, we call it a *linear relationship*. Figure 1 shows the linear relationship between Cathy's expenditure and income. Cathy spends £100 a week (by borrowing or spending her past savings) when income is zero. And out of each pound earned, Cathy spends 50 pence (and saves 50 pence).

All linear relationships are described by the same general equation. We call the quantity that is measured on the horizontal (or *x*-axis) *x* and we call the quantity that is measured on the vertical (or *y*-axis) *y*. In the case of Figure 1, *x* is income and *y* is expenditure.

A Linear Equation

The equation that describes a linear relationship between *x* and *y* is:

$$y = a + bx$$

In this equation, *a* and *b* are fixed numbers and they are called constants. The values of *x* and *y* vary so these numbers are called variables. Because the equation describes a straight line, it is called a *linear equation*.

The equation tells us that when the value of *x* is zero, the value of *y* is *a*. We call the constant *a* the *y-axis intercept*. The reason is that on the graph the straight line hits the *y*-axis at a value equal to *a*. Figure 1 illustrates the *y*-axis intercept.

For positive values of *x*, the value of *y* exceeds *a*. The constant *b* tells us by how much *y* increases above *a* as *x* increases. The constant *b* is the slope of the line.

Slope of a Line

As we explain on p. 22, the slope of a relationship is the change in the value of *y* divided by the change in the value of *x*. We use the Greek letter Δ (delta) to represent 'change in'. So Δ*y* means the change in the value of the variable measured on the *y*-axis, and Δ*x* means the change in the value of the variable measured on the *x*-axis. Therefore the slope of the relationship is:

$$\Delta y / \Delta x$$

To see why the slope is *b*, suppose that initially the value of *x* is x_1, or £200 in Figure 2. The corresponding value of *y* is y_1, also £200 in Figure 2. The equation of the line tells us that:

$$y_1 = a + bx_1 \tag{1}$$

Now the value of *x* increases by Δ*x* to $x_1 + \Delta x$ (or £400 in Figure 2). And the value of *y* increases by Δ*y* to $y_1 + \Delta y$ (or £300 in Figure 2).

The equation of the line now tells us that:

$$y_1 + \Delta y = a + b(x_1 + \Delta x) \tag{2}$$

Figure 1 Linear relationship

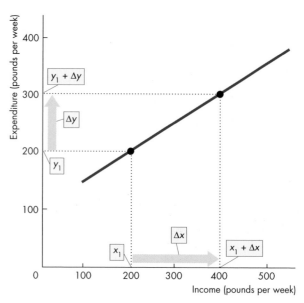

Figure 2 Calculating slope

To calculate the slope of the line, subtract equation (1) from equation (2) to obtain:

$$\Delta y = b\Delta x \qquad (3)$$

and now divide equation (3) by Δx to obtain:

$$\Delta y/\Delta x = b$$

So the slope of the line is b.

We can calculate the slope of the line in Figure 2. When x increases from 200 to 400, y increases from 200 to 300, so Δx is 200 and Δy is 100. The slope, b, equals:

$$\Delta y/\Delta x = 100/200 = 0.5$$

Position of the Line

The y-axis intercept determines the position of the line on the graph. Figure 3 illustrates the relationship between the y-axis intercept and the position of the line on the graph. In this graph, the y-axis measures saving and the x-axis measures income.

When the y-axis intercept, a, is positive, the line hits the y-axis at a positive value of y – as the blue line does. Its y-axis intercept is 100.

When the y-axis intercept, a, is zero, the line hits the y-axis at the origin – as the purple line does. Its y-axis intercept is 0.

When the y-axis intercept, a, is negative, the line hits the y-axis at a negative value of y – as the red line does. Its y-axis intercept is –100.

As the equations of the three lines show, the value of the y-axis intercept does *not* influence the slope of the line. All three lines have a slope equal to 0.5.

Positive Relationships

Figures 1 and 2 show a positive relationship – the two variables x and y move in the same direction. All positive relationships have a slope that is *positive*. In the equation of the line, the constant b is positive.

In the example in Figure 1, the y-axis intercept, a, is 100. The slope b equals 0.5. The equation of the line is:

$$y = 100 + 0.5x$$

Negative Relationships

Figure 4 shows a negative relationship – the variables x and y move in opposite directions. All negative relationships have a slope that is *negative*. In the equation of the line, the constant b is negative.

In the example in Figure 4, the y-axis intercept, a, is 30. The slope, b, equals $\Delta y/\Delta x$ as we move along the line. When x increases from 0 to 2, y decreases from 30 to 10, so Δx is 2 and Δy is –20. The slope equals $\Delta y/\Delta x$, which is –20/2 or –10. The equation of the line is:

$$y = 30 + (-10)x$$

or

$$y = 30 - 10x$$

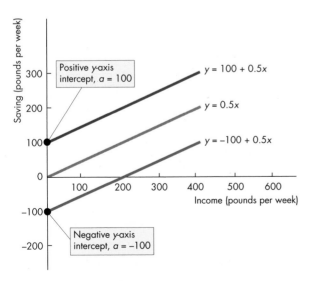

Figure 3 The *y*-axis intercept

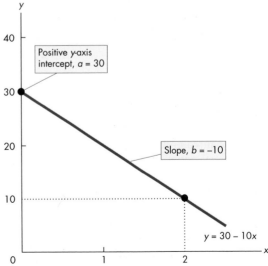

Figure 4 Negative relationship

Review Quiz

1 Explain how we 'read' the three graphs in Figures A1.1 and A1.2.
2 Explain what scatter diagrams show and why we use them.
3 Explain how we 'read' the three scatter diagrams in Figure A1.3 and A1.4.
4 Draw a graph to show the relationship between two variables that move in the same direction.
5 Draw a graph to show the relationship between two variables that move in opposite directions.
6 Draw a graph to show the relationship between two variables that have a maximum and a minimum.

7 Which of the relationships in Questions 4 and 5 is a positive relationship and which is a negative relationship?
8 What are the two ways of calculating the slope of a curved line?
9 How do we graph a relationship among more than two variables?
10 Explain what change will bring a movement along a curve.
11 Explain what change will bring a shift of a curve.

You can work these questions in Study Plan 1.A and get instant feedback.

SUMMARY

Key Points

Graphing Data (pp. 15–18)

◆ A graph is made by plotting the values of two variables x and y at a point that corresponds to their values measured along the x-axis and y-axis.

◆ A scatter diagram is a graph that plots the values of two variables for a number of different values of each.

◆ A scatter diagram shows the relationship between two variables. It shows whether two variables are positively related, negatively related, or unrelated.

Graphs Used in Economic Models (pp. 18–21)

◆ Graphs are used to show relationships among variables in economic models.

◆ Relationships can be positive (an upward-sloping curve), negative (a downward-sloping curve), positive and then negative (have a maximum point), negative and then positive (have a minimum point), or unrelated (a horizontal or vertical curve).

The Slope of a Relationship (pp. 22–24)

◆ The slope of a relationship is calculated as the change in the value of the variable measured on the y-axis divided by the change in the value of the variable measured on the x-axis, that is, $\Delta y/\Delta x$.

◆ A straight line has a constant slope.

◆ A curved line has a varying slope. To calculate the slope of a curved line, we calculate the slope at a point or across an arc.

Graphing Relationships Among More Than Two Variables (pp. 24–25)

◆ To graph a relationship among more than two variables, we hold constant the values of all the variables except two.

◆ We then plot the value of one of the variables against the value of another.

◆ A *cet. par.* change in the value of a variable on an axis of a graph brings a movement along the curve.

◆ A change in the value of a variable held constant along the curve brings a shift of the curve.

Key Terms

Ceteris paribus, 24
Direct relationship, 18
Inverse relationship, 19
Linear relationship, 18
Negative relationship, 19
Positive relationship, 18
Scatter diagram, 16
Slope, 22

STUDY PLAN PROBLEMS AND APPLICATIONS

myeconlab You can work Problems 1 to 11 in MyEconLab Chapter 1A Study Plan and get instant feedback.

Use this spreadsheet to answer Problems 1 to 3. The spreadsheet gives data on the US economy: column A is the year, column B is the inflation rate, column C is the interest rate, column D is the growth rate and column E is the unemployment rate.

	A	B	C	D	E
1	1999	2.2	4.6	4.8	4.2
2	2000	3.4	5.8	4.1	4.0
3	2001	2.8	3.4	1.1	4.7
4	2002	1.6	1.6	1.8	5.8
5	2003	2.3	1.0	2.5	6.0
6	2004	2.7	1.4	3.6	5.5
7	2005	3.4	3.2	3.1	5.1
8	2006	3.2	4.7	2.7	4.6
9	2007	2.8	4.4	2.1	4.6
10	2008	3.8	1.4	0.4	5.8
11	2009	-0.4	0.2	-2.4	9.3

1 Draw a scatter diagram to show the relationship between the inflation rate and the interest rate. Describe the relationship.

2 Draw a scatter diagram to show the relationship between the growth rate and the unemployment rate. Describe the relationship.

3 Draw a scatter diagram to show the relationship between the interest rate and the unemployment rate. Describe the relationship.

Use the following news clip to work Problems 4 to 6.

***Clash of the Titans* Tops Box Office With Sales of $61.2 million:**

Film	Cinemas (number)	Revenue (dollars per cinema)
Clash of the Titans	3,777	16,213
Tyler Perry's Why Did I Get Married	2,155	13,591
How To Train Your Dragon	4,060	7,145
The Last Song	2,673	5,989

Source: Bloomberg, 5 April 2010

4 Draw a graph of the relationship between the revenue per cinema on the *y*-axis and the number of cinemas on the *x*-axis. Describe the relationship.

5 Calculate the slope of the relationship between 4,060 and 2,673 cinemas.

6 Calculate the slope of the relationship between 2,155 and 4,060 cinemas.

7 Calculate the slope of the following relationship:

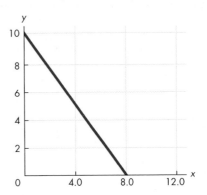

Use the following relationship to work Problems 8 and 9.

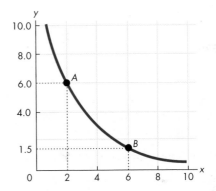

8 Calculate the slope of the relationship at point *A* and at point *B*.

9 Calculate the slope across the arc *AB*.

Use the following table, which gives the price of a balloon ride, the temperature and the number of rides per day, to work Problems 10 and 11.

Price (pounds per ride)	Balloon rides (number per day)		
	10°C	20°C	30°C
5.00	32	40	50
10.00	27	32	40
15.00	18	27	32
20.00	10	18	27

10 Draw a graph of the relationships between the price and the number of rides, holding the temperature constant at 20°C.

11 What happens in the graph in Problem 10 if the temperature rises to 30°C?

ADDITIONAL PROBLEMS AND APPLICATIONS

myeconlab   You can work these problems in MyEconLab if assigned by your lecturer.

Use the following spreadsheet to work Problems 12 to 14. The spreadsheet provides data on oil and petrol: column A is the year, column B is the price of oil (dollars per barrel), column C is the price of petrol (pence per litre), column D is oil production and column E is the quantity of petrol refined (both in millions of barrels per day).

	A	B	C	D	E
1	1999	24	118	5.9	8.1
2	2000	30	152	5.8	8.2
3	2001	17	146	5.8	8.3
4	2002	24	139	5.7	8.4
5	2003	27	160	5.7	8.5
6	2004	37	190	5.4	8.7
7	2005	49	231	5.2	8.7
8	2006	56	262	5.1	8.9
9	2007	86	284	5.1	9.0
10	2008	43	330	5.0	8.9
11	2009	76	241	4.9	8.9

12 Draw a scatter diagram of the price of oil and the quantity of oil produced. Describe the relationship.

13 Draw a scatter diagram of the price of petrol and the quantity of petrol refined. Describe the relationship.

14 Draw a scatter diagram of the quantities of oil produced and petrol refined. Describe the relationship.

Use the following data to work Problems 15 to 17.

Draw a graph that shows the relationship between the two variables *x* and *y*:

x	0	1	2	3	4	5
y	25	24	22	18	12	0

15 a Is the relationship positive or negative?

   b Does the slope of the relationship become steeper or flatter as the value of *x* increases?

   c Think of some economic relationships that might be similar to this one.

16 Calculate the slope of the relationship between *x* and *y* when *x* equals 3.

17 Calculate the slope of the relationship across the arc as *x* increases from 4 to 5.

18 In the following graph, calculate the slope of the relationship at point *A*.

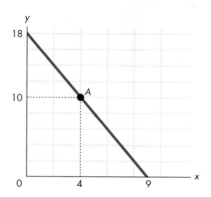

Use the following graph to work Problems 19 and 20.

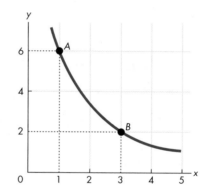

19 Calculate the slope at points *A* and *B*.

20 Calculate the slope across the arc *AB*.

Use the following table, which gives the price of an umbrella, the amount of rainfall and the number of umbrellas purchased, to work Problems 21 to 23.

Price	Umbrellas (number purchased per day)		
(pounds per umbrella)	0	200	400
		(mm of rainfall)	
5.00	7	8	12
10.00	4	7	8
15.00	2	4	7
20.00	1	2	4

21 Draw a graph of the relationship between the price and the number of umbrellas purchased, holding the amount of rainfall constant at 200 mm. Describe the relationship.

22 What happens in the graph in Problem 21 if the price rises and rainfall is constant?

23 What happens in the graph in Problem 21 if the rainfall increases from 200 mm to 400 mm?

Grown
for
Biofuel

The Economic Problem

Why does food cost much more today than it did a few years ago? One reason is that we now use part of our food crop to produce biofuel as a substitute for petrol and diesel. Another reason is that droughts have decreased global grain production.

In this chapter, you will study an economic model – the production possibilities frontier – and you will learn why biofuel production and drought have increased the cost of producing food. You will also learn how to assess whether it is a good idea to increase maize production to produce fuel and how we gain by trading with others.

At the end of the chapter, in *Reading Between the Lines*, we'll apply what you've learned to understanding why biofuel production is raising the cost of food.

Production Possibilities and Opportunity Cost

Every working day, in mines and factories, shops and offices, on farms and construction sites, 200 million European workers produce a vast variety of goods and services valued at €50 billion. But the quantities of goods and services that we can produce are limited by both our available resources and technology. And if we want to increase our production of one good, we must decrease our production of something else – we face trade-offs.

You are going to learn about the production possibilities frontier, which describes the limit to what we can produce and provides a neat way of thinking about and illustrating the idea of a trade-off.

The **production possibilities frontier** (*PPF*) is the boundary between those combinations of goods and services that can be produced and those that cannot. To illustrate the *PPF*, we focus on two goods at a time and hold the quantities produced of all the other goods and services constant. That is, we look at a *model* economy in which everything remains the same (*ceteris paribus*) except for the production of the two goods we are considering.

Let's look at the production possibilities frontier for CDs and pizza, which stand for *any* pair of goods or services.

Production Possibilities Frontier

The *production possibilities frontier* for CDs and pizza shows the limits to the production of these two goods, given the total resources available to produce them. Figure 2.1 shows this production possibilities frontier. The table lists some combinations of the quantities of pizzas and CDs that can be produced in a month given the resources available. The figure graphs these combinations. The *x*-axis shows the quantity of pizzas produced and the *y*-axis shows the quantity of CDs produced.

The *PPF* illustrates *scarcity* because we cannot attain the points outside the frontier. They are points that describe wants that can't be satisfied. We can produce at all the points *inside* the *PPF* and *on* the *PPF*. These points are attainable. Suppose that in a typical month, we produce 4 million pizzas and 5 million CDs. Figure 2.1 shows this combination as point *E* and as possibility *E* in the table. The figure also shows other production possibilities.

Figure 2.1 The Production Possibilities Frontier

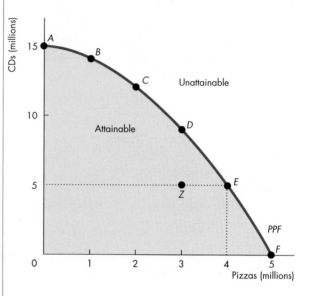

Possibility	Pizzas (millions)		CDs (millions)
A	0	and	15
B	1	and	14
C	2	and	12
D	3	and	9
E	4	and	5
F	5	and	0

The table lists six points on the production possibilities frontier for CDs and pizza. Row *A* tells us that if we produce no pizza, the maximum quantity of CDs we can produce is 15 million. Points *A*, *B*, *C*, *D*, *E* and *F* in the figure represent the rows of the table. The line passing through these points is the production possibilities frontier (*PPF*).

The *PPF* separates the attainable from the unattainable. Production is possible at any point inside the orange area or on the frontier. Points outside the frontier are unattainable. Points inside the frontier such as point *Z* are inefficient because resources are either wasted or misallocated. At such points, it is possible to use the available resources to produce more of either or both goods.

myeconlab Animation

For example, we might stop producing pizza and move all the people who produce it into producing CDs. Point *A* in Figure 2.1 and possibility *A* in the table show this case. The quantity of CDs produced increases to 15 million, and pizza production dries up. Alternatively, we might close the CD factories and switch all the resources into producing pizza. In this situation, we produce 5 million pizzas. Point *F* in the figure and possibility *F* in the table show this case.

Production Efficiency

We achieve **production efficiency** if we cannot produce more of one good without producing less of some other good. When production is efficient, we are at a point *on* the *PPF*. If we are at a point *inside* the *PPF*, such as point *Z*, production is *inefficient* because we have some *unused* resources or we have some *misallocated* resources or both.

Resources are unused when they are idle but could be working. For example, we might leave some of the factories idle or some workers unemployed.

Resources are *misallocated* when they are assigned to tasks for which they are not the best match. For example, we might assign skilled pizza makers to work in a CD factory and skilled CD makers to work in a pizza shop. We could get more pizza *and* more CDs from these same workers if we reassigned them to the tasks that more closely match their skills.

If we produce at a point inside the *PPF* such as *Z* in Figure 2.1, we can use our resources more efficiently to produce more pizzas, more CDs, or more of *both* pizzas and CDs. But if we produce at a point *on* the *PPF*, we are using our resources efficiently and we can produce more of one good only if we produce less of the other. That is, along the *PPF*, we face a *trade-off*.

Trade-off Along the *PPF*

Every choice *along* the *PPF* involves a *trade-off* – we must give up something to get something else. On the *PPF* in Figure 2.1, we must give up some CDs to get more pizza or give up some pizza to get more CDs.

Trade-offs arise in every imaginable real-world situation, and you reviewed several of them in Chapter 1. At any given point in time, we have a fixed amount of labour, land, capital and entrepreneurship. By using our available technologies, we can employ these resources to produce goods and services. But we are limited in what we can produce. This limit defines a boundary between what we can attain and what we cannot attain.

This boundary is the real world's production possibilities frontier, and it defines the trade-offs that we must make. On our real-world *PPF*, we can produce more of any one good or service only if we produce less of some other goods or services.

When doctors say that we must spend more on AIDS and cancer research, they are suggesting a trade-off: more medical research for less of some other things. When a politician says that she wants to spend more on education and healthcare, she is suggesting a trade-off: more education and healthcare for less defence expenditure or less private spending (because of higher taxes). When an environmental group argues for less logging in tropical rainforests, it is suggesting a trade-off: greater conservation of endangered wildlife for less hardwood. When your parents say that you should study more, they are suggesting a trade-off: more study time for less leisure or sleep.

All trade-offs involve a cost – an opportunity cost.

Opportunity Cost

The **opportunity cost** of an action is the highest-valued alternative forgone. The *PPF* helps us to make the concept of opportunity cost precise and enables us to calculate it. Along the *PPF*, there are only two goods, so there is only one alternative forgone: some quantity of the other good. Given our current resources and technology, we can produce more pizzas only if we produce fewer CDs. The opportunity cost of producing an additional pizza is the number of CDs we *must* forgo. Similarly, the opportunity cost of producing an additional CD is the quantity of pizzas we *must* forgo.

For example, at point *C* in Figure 2.1, we produce fewer pizzas and more CDs than at point *D*. If we choose point *D* over point *C*, the additional 1 million pizzas *cost* 3 million CDs. One pizza costs 3 CDs.

We can also work out the opportunity cost of choosing point *C* over point *D* in Figure 2.1. If we move from point *D* to point *C*, the quantity of CDs produced increases by 3 million and the quantity of pizzas produced decreases by 1 million. So if we choose point *C* over point *D*, the additional 3 million CDs *cost* 1 million pizzas. So 1 CD costs 1/3 of a pizza.

Opportunity Cost Is a Ratio

Opportunity cost is a ratio. It is the decrease in the quantity produced of one good divided by the increase in the quantity produced of another good as we move along the production possibilities frontier.

Because opportunity cost is a ratio, the opportunity cost of producing an additional CD is equal to the *inverse* of the opportunity cost of producing an additional pizza. Check this proposition by returning to the calculations we've just worked through. When we move along the *PPF* from *C* to *D*, the opportunity cost of a pizza is 3 CDs. The inverse of 3 is 1/3, so if we decrease the production of pizzas and increase the production of CDs by moving from *D* to *C*, the opportunity cost of a CD must be 1/3 of a pizza. You can check that this number is correct. If we move from *D* to *C*, we produce 3 million more CDs and 1 million fewer pizzas. Because 3 million CDs cost 1 million pizzas, the opportunity cost of 1 CD is 1/3 of a pizza.

Increasing Opportunity Cost

The opportunity cost of a pizza increases as the quantity of pizzas produced increases. Also, the opportunity cost of a CD increases as the quantity of CDs produced increases. This phenomenon of increasing opportunity cost is reflected in the shape of the *PPF* – it is bowed outward.

When a large quantity of CDs and a small quantity of pizzas are produced – between points *A* and *B* in Figure 2.1 – the frontier has a gentle slope. A given increase in the quantity of pizzas *costs* a small decrease in the quantity of CDs, so the opportunity cost of a pizza is a small quantity of CDs.

When a large quantity of pizzas and a small quantity of CDs are produced – between points *E* and *F* in Figure 2.1 – the frontier is steep. A given increase in the quatity of pizzas *costs* a large decrease in the quantity of CDs, so the opportunity cost of a pizza is a large quantity of CDs.

The *PPF* is bowed outward because resources are not all equally productive in all activities. People with several years of experience working for Philips are good at producing CDs but not very good at making pizzas. So if we move some of these people from Philips to Domino's, we get a small increase in the quantity of pizzas but a large decrease in the quantity of CDs. Similarly, people who have spent years working at Domino's are good at producing pizzas, but they have no idea how to produce CDs. So if we move some of these people from Domino's to Philips, we get a small increase in the quantity of CDs but a large decrease in the quantity of pizzas. The more of either good we try to produce, the less productive are the additional resources we use to produce that good and the larger is the opportunity cost of a unit of that good.

Increasing Opportunity Costs Are Everywhere

Just about every activity that you can think of is one with an increasing opportunity cost. We allocate the most skilful farmers and the most fertile land to the production of food. And we allocate the best doctors and the least fertile land to the production of healthcare services. If we shift fertile land and tractors away from farming to hospitals and ambulances and ask farmers to become hospital porters, the production of food drops drastically and the increase in the production of healthcare services is small. The opportunity cost of a unit of healthcare services rises. Similarly, if we shift our resources away from healthcare towards farming, we must use more doctors and nurses as farmers and more hospitals as hydroponic tomato factories. The decrease in the production of healthcare services is large, but the increase in food production is small. The opportunity cost of a unit of food rises. This example is extreme and unlikely, but these same considerations apply to most pairs of goods.

There may be some rare situations in which opportunity cost is constant. Switching resources from bottling ketchup to bottling mayonnaise is a possible example. But in general, when resources are reallocated, they must be assigned to tasks for which they are an increasingly poor match. Increasing opportunity costs are a general fact of life.

Review Quiz

1 How does the production possibilities frontier illustrate scarcity?
2 How does the production possibilities frontier illustrate production efficiency?
3 How does the production possibilities frontier show that every choice involves a trade-off?
4 How does the production possibilities frontier illustrate opportunity cost?
5 Why is opportunity cost a ratio?
6 Why does the *PPF* for most goods bow outward and what does that imply about the relationship between opportunity cost and the quantity produced?

You can work these questions in Study Plan 2.1 and get instant feedback.

We've seen that what we can produce is limited by the production possibilities frontier. We've also seen that production on the *PPF* is efficient. But we can produce many different quantities on the *PPF*. How do we choose among them? How do we know which point on the *PPF* is the best one?

◈ Using Resources Efficiently

We achieve *production efficiency* at every point on the *PPF*, but which point is best? The answer is the point on the *PPF* at which goods and services are produced in the quantities that provide the greatest possible benefit. When goods and services are produced at the lowest possible cost and in the quantities that provide the greatest possible benefit, we have achieved **allocative efficiency**.

The questions that we raised when we reviewed the four big issues in Chapter 1 are questions about allocative efficiency. To answer such questions, we must measure and compare costs and benefits.

The *PPF* and Marginal Cost

Marginal cost is the opportunity cost of producing *one more unit*. We can calculate marginal cost from the slope of the *PPF*. As the quantity of pizzas produced increases, the *PPF* gets steeper and marginal cost of a pizza increases. Figure 2.2 illustrates the calculation of the marginal cost of a pizza.

Begin by finding the opportunity cost of pizza in blocks of 1 million pizzas. The first million pizzas cost 1 million CDs, the second million pizzas cost 2 million CDs, the third million pizzas cost 3 million CDs, and so on. The bars in part (a) illustrate these calculations.

The bars in part (b) show the cost of an average pizza in each of the 1 million pizza blocks. Focus on the third million pizzas – the move from *C* to *D* in part (a). Over this range, because the 1 million pizzas cost 3 million CDs, one of these pizzas, on the average, costs 3 CDs – the height of the bar in part (b).

Next, find the opportunity cost of each additional pizza – the marginal cost of a pizza. The marginal cost of a pizza increases as the quantity of pizzas produced increases. The marginal cost at point *C* is less than it is at point *D*. On the average over the range from *C* to *D*, the marginal cost of a pizza is 3 CDs. But it exactly equals 3 CDs only in the middle of the range between *C* and *D*.

The red dot in part (b) indicates that the marginal cost of a pizza is 3 CDs when 2.5 million pizzas are produced. Each black dot in part (b) is interpreted in the same way. The red curve that passes through these dots, labelled *MC*, is the marginal cost curve. It shows the marginal cost of a pizza at each quantity of pizza as we move along the *PPF*.

Figure 2.2   The PPF and Marginal Cost

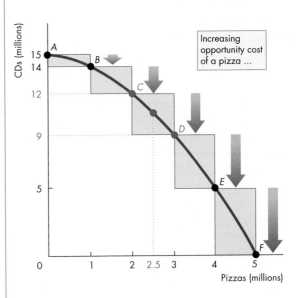

(a) PPF and opportunity cost

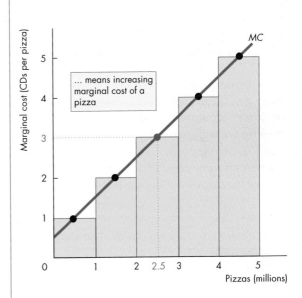

(b) Marginal cost

Marginal cost is calculated from the slope of the *PPF* in part (a). As the quantity of pizzas produced increases, the *PPF* gets steeper and the marginal cost of a pizza increases. The bars in part (a) show the opportunity cost of pizza in blocks of 1 million pizzas. The bars in part (b) show the cost of an average pizza in each of these 1 million blocks. The red curve, *MC*, shows the marginal cost of a pizza at each point along the *PPF*. This curve passes through the centre of each of the bars in part (b).

 myeconlab Animation ——————————————— ◆

Preferences and Marginal Benefit

The **marginal benefit** from a good or service is the benefit received from consuming one more unit of it. This benefit is subjective. It depends on people's **preferences** – people's likes and dislikes and the intensity of those feelings.

Marginal benefit and *preferences* stand in sharp contrast to *marginal cost* and *production possibilities*. Preferences describe what people like and want and the production possibilities describe the limits or constraints on what is feasible.

We need a concrete way of illustrating preferences that parallels the way we illustrate the limits to production using the *PPF*.

The device that we use to illustrate preferences is the **marginal benefit curve**, which is a curve that shows the relationship between the marginal benefit from a good and the quantity consumed of that good. Note that the *marginal benefit curve* is unrelated to the *PPF* and cannot be derived from it.

We measure the marginal benefit from a good or service by the most that people are willing to pay for an additional unit of it. The idea is that you are willing to pay less for a good than it is worth to you but you are not willing to pay more: the most you are willing to pay for something is its marginal benefit.

It is a general principle that the more we have of any good or service, the smaller is its marginal benefit and the less we are willing to pay for another unit of it. This tendency is so widespread and strong that we call it a principle – the *principle of decreasing marginal benefit*.

The basic reason why the marginal benefit of a good or service decreases as we consume more of it is that we like variety. The more we consume of any one good or service, the more we tire of it and would prefer to switch to something else.

Think about your willingness to pay for pizza (or any other item). If pizza is hard to come by and you can buy only a few slices a year, you might be willing to pay a high price to get an additional slice. But if pizza is all you've eaten for the past few days, you are willing to pay almost nothing for another slice.

You've learned to think about cost as opportunity cost, not pounds or euros. You can think about marginal benefit and willingness to pay in the same terms. The marginal benefit, measured by what you are willing to pay for something, is the quantity of other goods and services that you are willing to forgo. Let's continue with the example of CDs and pizza and illustrate preferences this way.

Figure 2.3 Preferences and the Marginal Benefit Curve

Possibility	Pizzas (millions)	Willingness to pay (CDs per pizza)
A	0.5	5
B	1.5	4
C	2.5	3
D	3.5	2
E	4.5	1

The smaller the quantity of pizzas produced, the more CDs people are willing to give up for an additional pizza. If pizza production is 0.5 million, people are willing to pay 5 CDs per pizza. But if pizza production is 4.5 million, people are willing to pay only 1 CD per pizza. Willingness to pay measures marginal benefit. A universal feature of people's preferences is that marginal benefit decreases.

myeconlab Animation

Figure 2.3 illustrates preferences as the willingness to pay for pizza in terms of CDs. In row *A*, pizza production is 0.5 million, and at that quantity people are willing to pay 5 CDs per pizza. As the quantity of pizzas produced increases, the amount that people are willing to pay for a pizza falls. When pizza production is 4.5 million, people are willing to pay only 1 CD per pizza.

Let's now use the concepts of marginal cost and marginal benefit to describe the efficient quantity of pizzas to produce.

Figure 2.4   Efficient Use of Resources

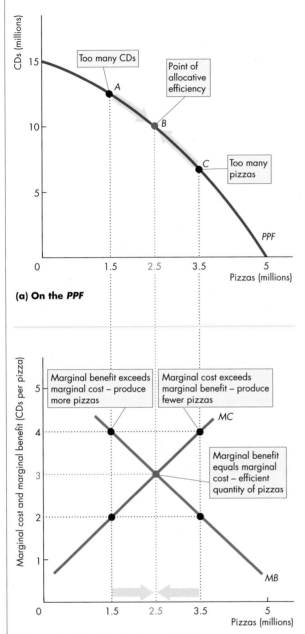

(a) On the PPF

(b) Marginal benefit equals marginal cost

The greater the quantity of pizzas produced, the smaller is the marginal benefit (*MB*) from pizza – the fewer CDs people are willing to give up to get an additional pizza. But the greater the quantity of pizzas produced, the greater is the marginal cost (*MC*) of pizza – the more CDs people must give up to get an additional pizza. When marginal benefit equals marginal cost, resources are being used efficiently.

myeconlab Animation

Efficient Use of Resources

At any point on the *PPF*, we cannot produce more of one good without giving up some other good. At the best point on the *PPF*, we cannot produce more of one good without giving up some other good that provides greater benefit. We are producing at the point of allocative efficiency – the point on the *PPF* that we prefer above all other points.

Suppose in Figure 2.4, we produce 1.5 million pizzas. The marginal cost of a pizza is 2 CDs and the marginal benefit from a pizza is 4 CDs. Because someone values an additional pizza more highly than it costs to produce, we can get more value from our resources by moving some of them out of producing CDs and into producing pizzas.

Now suppose we produce 3.5 million pizzas. The marginal cost of a pizza is now 4 CDs, but the marginal benefit from a pizza is only 2 CDs. Because the additional pizza costs more to produce than anyone thinks it is worth, we can get more value from our resources by moving some of them away from producing pizzas and into producing CDs.

But suppose we produce 2.5 million pizzas. Marginal cost and marginal benefit are now equal at 3 CDs. This allocation of resources between pizzas and CDs is efficient. If more pizzas are produced, the forgone CDs are worth more than the additional pizzas. If fewer pizzas are produced, the forgone pizzas are worth more than the additional CDs.

Review Quiz

1 What is marginal cost? How is it measured?
2 What is marginal benefit? How is it measured?
3 How does the marginal benefit from a good change as the quantity of that good increases?
4 What is allocative efficiency and how does it relate to the production possibilites frontier?
5 What conditions must be satisfied if resources are used efficiently?

You can work these questions in Study Plan 2.2 and get instant feedback.

You now understand the limits to production and the conditions under which resources are used efficiently. Your next task is to study the expansion of production possibilities.

Economic Growth

During the past 30 years, production per person in the EU has doubled. An expansion of production possibilities is called **economic growth**. Economic growth increases our *standard of living,* but it does not overcome scarcity and avoid opportunity cost. To make our economy grow, we face a trade-off – the faster we make production grow, the greater is the opportunity cost of economic growth.

The Cost of Economic Growth

Economic growth comes from technological change and capital accumulation. **Technological change** is the development of new goods and of better ways of producing goods and services. **Capital accumulation** is the growth of capital resources, which includes *human capital.*

Technological change and capital accumulation have vastly expanded our production possibilities. We can produce automobiles that provide us with more transportation than was available when we had only horses and carriages. We can produce satellites that provide global communications on a much larger scale than that available with the earlier cable technology. But if we use our resources to develop new technologies and produce capital, we must decrease our production of consumption goods and services. New technologies and new capital have an opportunity cost. Let's look at this opportunity cost.

Instead of studying the *PPF* of pizzas and CDs, we'll hold the quantity of CDs produced constant and examine the *PPF* for pizzas and pizza ovens. Figure 2.5 shows this *PPF* as the blue curve *ABC*. If we devote no resources to producing pizza ovens, we produce at point *A*. If we produce 3 million pizzas, we can produce 6 pizza ovens at point *B*. If we produce no pizza, we can produce 10 ovens at point *C*.

The amount by which our production possibilities expand depends on the resources we devote to technological change and capital accumulation. If we devote no resources to this activity (point *A*), our *PPF* remains the blue curve PPF_0 in Figure 2.5. If we cut the current production of pizza and produce 6 ovens (point *B*), then in the future, we'll have more capital and our *PPF* will rotate outward to the position shown by the red curve PPF_1. The fewer resources we devote to producing pizza and the more resources we devote to producing ovens, the greater is the future expansion of our production possibilities.

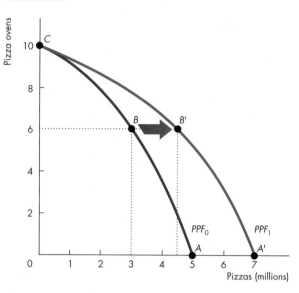

Figure 2.5 Economic Growth

PPF_0 shows the limits to the production of pizza and pizza ovens, with the production of all other goods and services remaining the same. If we allocate no resources to producing pizza ovens and produce 5 million pizzas, our production possibilities will remain the same, PPF_0.

But if we decrease pizza production to 3 million and produce 6 ovens, our production possibilities will expand. After one period, the *PPF* rotates outward to PPF_1 and we can produce at point *B'*, a point outside the original PPF_0.

We can rotate the *PPF* outward, but we cannot avoid opportunity cost. The opportunity cost of producing more pizzas in the future is fewer pizzas today.

myeconlab Animation ━━━━━━━━━━◆

Economic growth brings enormous benefit in the form of increased consumption, but it is not free and does not abolish scarcity.

In Figure 2.5, to make economic growth happen we must use some resources to produce new ovens, which leaves fewer resources to produce pizza. To move to *B'* in the future, we must move from *A* to *B* today. The opportunity cost of more pizzas in the future is fewer pizzas today. Also, on the new *PPF*, we continue to face a trade-off and opportunity cost.

The ideas about economic growth that we have explored in the setting of the pizza industry also apply to nations. Hong Kong and the EU provide a striking case study.

Economic Growth in the EU and Hong Kong

The experience of the EU and Hong Kong are a striking example of the effects of our choices on the rate of economic growth.

Figure 1 shows that, in 1970, the production possibilities per person in the EU were more than double those in Hong Kong. In 1970, the EU was at point *A* on its *PPF* and Hong Kong was at point *A* on its *PPF*. Since 1970, the EU has devoted one-fifth of it resources to accumulating capital and the other four-fifths to consumption. Hong Kong has devoted one-third of its resources to accumulating capital and two-thirds to consumption.

By 2010, the production possibilities per person in Hong Kong had reached a similar level to those in the EU. If Hong Kong continues to devote more resources to accumulating capital than the EU does (at point *B* on its 2010 *PPF*), Hong Kong will continue to grow more rapidly. But if Hong Kong increases consumption and decreases capital accumulation (moving to point *C* on its 2010 *PPF*), then its economic growth rate will slow.

The EU is typical of the rich industrial countries and Hong Kong is typical of the fast-growing Asian economies. Countries like China, India and Taiwan have expanded

Figure 1 Economic Growth in the EU and Hong Kong

their production possibilities by between 5 and 10 per cent a year.

If such high growth rates are maintained, these other Asian countries will continue to close the gap between themselves and the EU, as Hong Kong has done.

A Nation's Economic Growth

The experiences of the EU and Hong Kong make a striking example of the effects of our choices about consumption and capital goods on the rate of economic growth.

If a nation devotes all its factors of production to producing consumption goods and services and none to advancing technology and accumulating capital, its production possibilities in the future will be the same as they are today.

To expand production possibilities in the future, a nation must devote fewer resources to producing current consumption goods and services and some resources to accumulating capital and developing new technologies. As production possibilities expand, consumption in the future can increase. The decrease in consumption today is the opportunity cost of an increase in consumption in the future.

Review Quiz

1 What are the two key factors that generate economic growth?
2 How does economic growth influence the *PPF*?
3 What is the opportunity cost of economic growth?
4 Why has Hong Kong experienced faster economic growth than the EU?

You can work these questions in Study Plan 2.3 and get instant feedback.

We have seen that we can increase our production possibilities by accumulating capital and developing new technology. Next, we'll study another way in which we can expand our production possibilities – the amazing fact that *both* buyers and sellers gain from specialization and trade.

Gains from Trade

People can produce for themselves all the goods and services that they consume, or they can produce one good or a few goods and trade with others. Producing only one good or a few goods is called *specialization*.

We are going to discover how people gain by specializing in the production of the good in which they have a *comparative advantage* and trading with each other.

Comparative Advantage and Absolute Advantage

A person has a **comparative advantage** in an activity if that person can perform the activity at a lower opportunity cost than anyone else. Differences in opportunity costs arise from differences in individual abilities and from differences in the characteristics of other resources.

No one excels at everything. One person is an outstanding batter but a poor catcher; another person is a brilliant lawyer but a poor teacher. In almost all human endeavours, what one person does easily, someone else finds difficult. The same applies to land and capital. One plot of land is fertile but has no mineral deposits; another plot of land has outstanding views but is infertile. One machine has great precision but is difficult to operate; another is fast but often breaks down.

Although no one excels at everything, some people excel and can outperform others in many activities – perhaps all activities. A person who is more productive than others has an **absolute advantage**.

Absolute advantage involves comparing productivities – production per hour – whereas comparative advantage involves comparing opportunity cost.

A person who has an absolute advantage does not have a *comparative* advantage in every activity. Maria Sharapova can run faster and play tennis better than most people. She has an absolute advantage in these two activities. But compared with other people, she is a better tennis player than runner, so her *comparative* advantage is in playing tennis.

Because people's abilities and the quality of their resources differ, they have different opportunity costs of producing various goods and services. Such differences give rise to comparative advantage.

To explore the idea of comparative advantage, and its astonishing implications, we'll look at the production process in two smoothie bars: one operated by Erin and the other operated by Jack.

Erin's Smoothie Bar

Erin produces smoothies and salads. In Erin's high-tech bar, she can turn out either a smoothie or a salad every 2 minutes – see Table 2.1.

If Erin spends all her time making smoothies, she can produce 30 an hour. And if she spends all her time making salads, she can also produce 30 an hour. If she splits her time equally between the two, she can produce 15 smoothies and 15 salads an hour. For each additional smoothie Erin produces, she must decrease her production of salads by one, and for each additional salad she produces, she must decrease her production of smoothies by one. So

> **Erin's opportunity cost of producing 1 smoothie is 1 salad,**

and

> **Erin's opportunity cost of producing 1 salad is 1 smoothie.**

Erin's customers buy smoothies and salads in equal quantities, so she splits her time equally between the items and produces 15 smoothies and 15 salads an hour.

Jack's Smoothie Bar

Jack also produces both smoothies and salads. But Jack's bar is smaller than Erin's. Also, Jack has only one blender, and it's a slow old machine. Even if Jack uses all his resources to produce smoothies, he can produce only 6 an hour – see Table 2.2. But Jack is good in the salad department, so if he uses all his resources to make salads, he can produce 30 an hour.

Jack's ability to make smoothies and salads is the same regardless of how he splits an hour between the two tasks. He can make a salad in 2 minutes or a smoothie in 10 minutes. For each additional smoothie Jack produces, he must decrease his production of salads by 5. And for each additional salad he produces, he

Table 2.1		
Erin's Production Possibilities		
Item	**Minutes to produce 1**	**Quantity per hour**
Smoothies	2	30
Salads	2	30

Table 2.2

Jack's Production Possibilities

Item	Minutes to produce 1	Quantity per hour
Smoothies	10	6
Salads	2	30

must decrease his production of smoothies by 1/5 of a smoothie. So

> **Jack's opportunity cost of producing 1 smoothie is 5 salads,**

and

> **Jack's opportunity cost of producing 1 salad is 1/5 of a smoothie.**

Jack's customers, like Erin's, buy smoothies and salads in equal quantities. So Jack spends 50 minutes of each hour making smoothies and 10 minutes of each hour making salads. With this division of his time, Jack produces 5 smoothies and 5 salads an hour.

Erin's Comparative Advantage

In which of the two activities does Erin have a comparative advantage? Recall that comparative advantage is a situation in which one person's opportunity cost of producing a good is lower than another person's opportunity cost of producing that same good. Erin has a comparative advantage in producing smoothies. Her opportunity cost of a smoothie is 1 salad, whereas Jack's opportunity cost of a smoothie is 5 salads.

Jack's Comparative Advantage

If Erin has a comparative advantage in producing smoothies, Jack must have a comparative advantage in producing salads. His opportunity cost of a salad is 1/5 of a smoothie, whereas Erin's opportunity cost of a salad is 1 smoothie.

Achieving the Gains from Trade

Erin and Jack run into each other one evening in a singles bar. After a few minutes of getting acquainted, Erin tells Jack about her amazing smoothie business. Her only problem, she tells Jack, is that she wishes she

could produce more because potential customers leave when the queue gets too long.

Jack is hesitant to risk spoiling his chances by telling Erin about his own struggling business, but he takes the risk. Jack explains to Erin that he spends 50 minutes of every hour making 5 smoothies and 10 minutes making 5 salads. Erin's eyes pop. "Have I got a deal for you!" she exclaims.

Here's the deal that Erin sketches on a serviette. Jack stops making smoothies and allocates all his time to producing salads. Erin stops making salads and allocates all her time to producing smoothies. That is, they both specialize in producing the good in which they have a comparative advantage. Together they produce 30 smoothies and 30 salads – see Table 2.3(b).

They then trade. Erin sells Jack 10 smoothies and Jack sells Erin 20 salads – the price of a smoothie is 2 salads – see Table 2.3(c).

After the trade, Jack has 10 salads – the 30 he produces minus the 20 he sells to Erin. He also has the 10 smoothies that he buys from Erin. So Jack now has increased the quantities of smoothies and salads that he can sell to his customers – see Table 2.3(d).

Table 2.3

Erin and Jack Gain from Trade

(a) Before trade	Erin	Jack
Smoothies	15	5
Salads	15	5

(b) Production	Erin	Jack
Smoothies	30	0
Salads	0	30

(c) Trade	Erin	Jack
Smoothies	sell 10	buy 10
Salads	buy 20	sell 20

(d) After trade	Erin	Jack
Smoothies	20	10
Salads	20	10

(e) Gains from trade	Erin	Jack
Smoothies	+5	+5
Salads	+5	+5

Erin has 20 smoothies – the 30 she produces minus the 10 she sells to Jack. And she has the 20 salads she buys from Jack – see Table 2.3(d). Both Erin and Jack gain 5 smoothies and 5 salads – see Table 2.3(e).

To illustrate her idea, Erin grabs a fresh serviette and draws the graphs in Figure 2.6. The blue *PPF* in part (a) shows Jack's production possibilities. Before trade, he is producing 5 smoothies and 5 salads an hour at point *A*. The blue *PPF* in part (b) shows Erin's production possibilities. Before trade, she is producing 15 smoothies and 15 salads an hour at point *A*.

Erin's proposal is that they each specialize in producing the good in which they have a comparative advantage. Jack produces 30 salads and no smoothies at point *B* on his *PPF*. Erin produces 30 smoothies and no salads at point *B* on her *PPF*.

Erin and Jack then trade smoothies and salads at a price of 2 salads per smoothie or 1/2 of a smoothie per salad. Jack buys smoothies from Erin for 2 salads each, which is less than the 5 salads it costs him to produce a smoothie. Erin buys salads from Jack for 1/2 a smoothie each, which is less than the 1 smoothie that it costs her to produce a salad.

With trade, Jack has 10 smoothies and 10 salads at point *C* – a gain of 5 smoothies and 5 salads. Jack moves to a point *outside his PPF*.

With trade, Erin has 20 smoothies and 20 salads at point *C* – a gain of 5 smoothies and 5 salads. Erin moves to a point *outside* her *PPF*.

Despite Erin being more productive than Jack, both Erin and Jack gain from producing more of the good in which they have a comparative advantage and trading.

Figure 2.6   The Gains from Trade

(a) Jack

(b) Erin

Jack initially produces at point *A* on his *PPF* in part (a), and Erin initially produces at point *A* on her *PPF* in part (b). Jack's opportunity cost of producing a salad is less than Erin's, so Jack has a comparative advantage in producing salads. Erin's opportunity cost of producing a smoothie is less than Jack's, so Erin has a comparative advantage in producing smoothies.

If Jack specializes in salad, he produces 30 salads and no smoothies at point *B* on his *PPF*. If Erin produces

30 smoothies and no salads, she produces at point *B* on her *PPF*.

They exchange salads for smoothies along the red 'Trade line'. Erin buys salads from Jack for less than her opportunity cost of producing them. And Jack buys smoothies from Erin for less than his opportunity cost of producing them. Each goes to point *C* – a point outside his or her *PPF*. Both Jack and Erin increase production by 5 smoothies and 5 salads with no change in resources.

The EU and China Gain from Trade

In Chapter 1 (see p. 7), we asked whether globalization is in the social interest. What you have just learned about the gains from trade provides a big part of the answer. We gain from specialization and trade.

The gains that we achieve from *international trade* are similar to those achieved by Jack and Erin. When Europeans buy clothes that are manufactured in China and when China buys Airbus aircraft manufactured in the EU, people in both countries gain.

We could slide along our *PPF* producing fewer aircraft and more jackets. Similarly, China could slide along its *PPF* producing more aircraft and fewer jackets. But everyone would lose. The opportunity cost of our jackets and China's opportunity cost of aircraft would rise.

By specializing in aircraft and trading with China, we get our jackets at a lower cost than that at which we can produce them, and China gets its aircraft at a lower cost than that at which it can produce them.

Review Quiz

1 What gives a person a comparative advantage?
2 Distinguish between comparative advantage and absolute advantage.
3 Why do people specialize and trade?
4 What are the gains from specialization and trade?
5 What is the source of the gains from trade?

You can work these questions in Study Plan 2.4 and get instant feedback.

Economic Coordination

People gain by specializing in the production of those goods and services in which they have a comparative advantage and trading with each other. Erin and Jack, whose production of salads and smoothies we studied earlier in this chapter, can get together and make a deal that enables them to enjoy the gains from specialization and trade. But for billions of individuals to specialize and produce millions of different goods and services, their choices must somehow be coordinated.

Two competing economic coordination systems have been used: central economic planning and decentralized markets.

Central economic planning might appear to be the best system because it can express national priorities. But when this system was tried, as it was for 60 years in Russia and for 30 years in China, it was a miserable failure. Today, these and most other previously planned economies are adopting a decentralized market system.

Decentralized coordination works best, but for it to do so it needs four complementary social institutions:

◆ Firms
◆ Markets
◆ Property rights
◆ Money

Firms

A **firm** is an economic unit that employs factors of production and organizes them to produce and sell goods and services. Tesco and Virgin Atlantic are examples of firms.

Firms coordinate a huge amount of economic activity. A Starbucks coffee shop, for example, might buy the machines and labour services of Erin and Jack and start to produce salads and smoothies at all its outlets.

But Tesco would not have become Britian's largest retailer if it had produced all the things that it sells. It became the largest UK retailer by specializing in providing retail services and buying the goods and services it sells from other firms that specialize in their production (just like Erin and Jack did). This trade between Tesco and the producers of the goods and services it sells takes place in markets.

Markets

In ordinary speech, the word *market* means a place where people buy and sell goods such as fish, meat, fruits and vegetables. In economics, a *market* has a more general meaning. A **market** is any arrangement that enables buyers and sellers to get information and to do business with each other. An example is the market in which oil is bought and sold – the world oil market. The world oil market is not a place. It is the network of oil producers, oil users, wholesalers and brokers who buy and sell oil. In the world oil market, decision makers do not meet physically. They make deals throughout the world by telephone, fax and direct computer link.

Markets have evolved because they facilitate trade. Without organized markets, we would miss out on a substantial part of the potential gains from trade. Enterprising individuals and firms, each pursuing their own self-interest, have profited from making markets – standing ready to buy or sell the items in which they specialize. But markets can work only when property rights exist.

Property Rights

The social arrangements that govern the ownership, use and disposal of anything that people value are called **property rights**. *Real property* includes land and buildings – the things we call property in ordinary speech – and durable goods such as plant and equipment. *Financial property* includes shares and bonds and money in the bank. *Intellectual property* is the intangible product of creative effort. This type of property includes books, music, computer programs and inventions of all kinds and is protected by copyrights and patents.

Where property rights are enforced, people have the incentive to specialize and produce the goods and services in which they have a comparative advantage. Where people can steal the production of others, resources are devoted not to production but to protecting possessions. Without property rights, we would still be hunting and gathering like our Stone Age ancestors.

Money

Money is any commodity or token that is generally acceptable as a means of payment. Erin and Jack didn't use money; they exchanged salads and smoothies. In principle, trade in markets can exchange any item for any other item. But you can perhaps imagine how complicated life would be if we exchanged goods for other goods. The 'invention' of money makes trading in markets much more efficient.

Circular Flows Through Markets

Figure 2.7 shows the flows that result from the choices that households and firms make. Households specialize and choose the quantities of labour, land, capital and entrepreneurship to sell or rent to firms. Firms choose the quantities of factors of production to hire. These (red) flows go through the *factor markets*. Households choose the quantities of goods and services to buy, and firms choose the quantities to produce. These (red) flows go through the *goods markets*. Households receive incomes from firms and make expenditures on goods and services (the green flows).

How do markets coordinate all these decisions?

Coordinating Decisions

Markets coordinate decisions through price adjustments. To see how, think about the market for fresh-baked bread. Suppose that some people who want to buy fresh-baked bread are not able to do so. To make the choices of buyers and sellers compatible, buyers must switch to prepackaged bread or more fresh-baked bread must be offered for sale (or both). A rise in the price of fresh-baked bread produces this outcome. A higher price encourages bakers to offer more fresh-baked bread for sale. It also encourages some people to change the bread they buy. Fewer people buy fresh-baked bread, and more buy prepackaged bread. More fresh-baked bread (and more prepackaged bread) are offered for sale.

Alternatively, suppose that more fresh-baked bread is available than people want to buy. In this case, to make the choices of buyers and sellers compatible, more fresh-baked bread must be bought or less fresh-baked bread must be offered for sale (or both). A fall in the price of fresh-baked bread achieves this outcome. A lower price encourages bakers to produce a smaller quantity of, and encourages people to buy more fresh-baked bread.

Figure 2.7   Circular Flows in the Market Economy

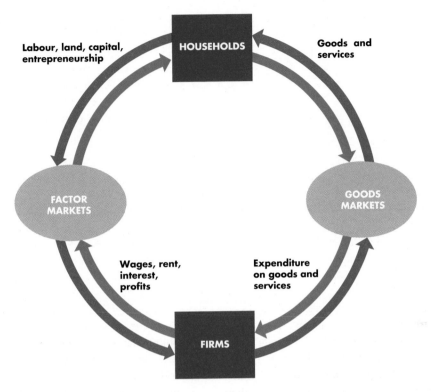

Households and firms make economic choices and markets coordinate these choices.

Households choose the quantities of labour, land, capital and entrepreneurship to sell or rent to firms in exchange for wages, rent, interest and profit. Households also choose how to spend their incomes on the various types of goods and services available.

Firms choose the quantities of factors of production to hire and the quantities of the various goods and services to produce.

Goods markets and factor markets coordinate these choices of households and firms.

The counterclockwise red flows are real flows – the flow of factors of production from households to firms and the flow of goods and services from firms to households.

The clockwise green flows are the payments for the red flows. They are the flow of incomes from firms to households and the flow of expenditure on goods and services from households to firms.

 Animation

Review Quiz

1   Why are social institutions such as firms, markets, property rights and money necessary?
2   What are the main functions of markets?
3   What are the flows in the market economy that go from firms to households and from households to firms?
4   In the circular flows of the market economy, which flows are real flows? Which flows are money flows?

You can work these questions in Study Plan 2.5 and get instant feedback.   myeconlab

You have now begun to see how economists approach economic questions. Scarcity, choice and divergent opportunity costs explain why we specialize and trade and why firms, markets, property rights and money have developed. You can see all around you the lessons you've learned in this chapter.

Reading Between the Lines on pp. 46–47 provides an opportunity to apply the *PPF* model to deepen your understanding of the reasons for the increase in the cost of food associated with the increase in maize production.

Reading Between the Lines

The Rising Opportunity Cost of Food

The Guardian, 5 April 2008

Crop Switch Worsens Global Food Price Crisis

John Vidal

Two years ago the UN's Food and Agriculture Organization expected biofuels to help eradicate hunger and poverty. . . . Yesterday the UN secretary general, Ban Ki-moon raised real doubt over that policy amid signs that the world was facing its worst food crisis in a generation.

Since . . . 2006 tens of thousands of farmers have switched from food to fuel production. . . . Spurred by generous subsidies and an EU commitment to increase the use of biofuels to counter climate change, at least 8m hectares (20m acres) of maize, wheat, soya and other crops which once provided animal feed and food have been taken out of production in the US. In addition, large areas of Brazil, Argentina, Canada and eastern Europe are diverting . . . crops to biofuels. The result, exacerbated by . . . shortages because of severe weather, has been big increases of all global food commodity prices.

Lester Brown, director of the Earth Policy Institute in Washington, said . . . 'the US has diverted 60m tonnes of food to fuel. On the heels of seven years of consumption of world grains exceeding supply, this has put a great strain on the world's grain supplies'.

Robert Zoellick, president of the World Bank, said this week that prices of all staple food had risen 80% in three years, and that 33 countries faced unrest because of the price rises. . . . In Bangladesh . . . a government source said: 'One reason is that the overall drop in food production because of biofuels has prevented food being exported.' . . .

Last month the UK's chief scientist and food expert, Professor John Beddington, said the prospect of food shortages over the next 20 years was so acute that politicians, scientists and farmers must tackle it immediately.

The Essence of the Story

◆ In 2006, the UN's Food and Agriculture Organization expected biofuel to reduce poverty and the EU promoted the use of biofuels to counter climate change.

◆ Farmers around the world switched from producing crops for food to crops for biofuel.

◆ World food prices rose 80 per cent in 3 years and policy advisers say the switch to growing crops for biofuels has reduced the amount of food available, adding to the pressure for food price rises.

◆ The UK's chief scientist said the prospect of food shortages must be tackled immediately by politicians, scientists and farmers.

Economic Analysis

- Biofuel is made from maize (and several other crops), so biofuel and food compete to use the same resources.

- To produce more biofuel under UN and EU policy, farmers increased the number of acres devoted to biofuel crop production.

- Increasing the production of crops for biofuel means decreasing the production of crops for food and decreasing the production of other crops.

- Figure 1 shows the EU production possibilities frontier, *PPF*, for one of the biofuel crops, maize, and other goods and services.

- A movement along the *PPF* in Figure 1 from point *A* to point *B* illustrates the increase in the production of maize and decrease in the production of other goods and services.

- In moving from point *A* to point *B*, the EU incurs a higher opportunity cost of producing maize, as the greater slope of the *PPF* at point *B* indicates.

- In other regions of the world, despite the fact that more land was devoted to maize production, the amount of maize produced didn't change in 2007 and 2008.

- The reason is that bad weather lowered the crop yield per hectare in those regions.

- Figure 2 shows the rest of the world's *PPF* for maize and other goods and services in 2007 and 2008.

- The increase in the amount of land devoted to producing maize is illustrated by a movement along PPF_{07}.

- With a decrease in the crop yield, production possibilities decreased and the *PPF* rotated inward.

- The rotation from PPF_{07} to PPF_{08} illustrates this decrease in production possibilities.

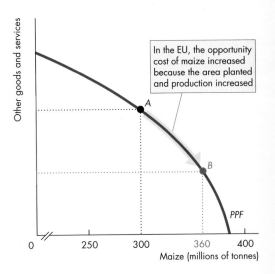

In the EU, the opportunity cost of maize increased because the area planted and production increased

Figure 1 EU *PPF*

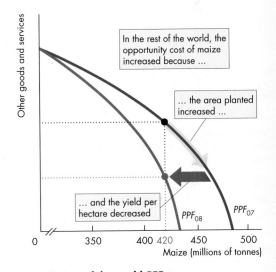

In the rest of the world, the opportunity cost of maize increased because …

… the area planted increased …

… and the yield per hectare decreased

Figure 2 Rest of the world *PPF*

- The opportunity cost of producing maize in the rest of the world increased for two reasons: the movement along its *PPF* and the inward rotation of the *PPF*.

- With a higher opportunity cost of producing maize, the cost of both biofuel and food increases.

SUMMARY

Key Points

Production Possibilities and Opportunity Cost (pp. 32–34)

◆ The production possibilities frontier is the boundary between production levels that are attainable and those that are unattainable when all available resources are used to their limit.

◆ Production efficiency occurs at points on the production possibilities frontier.

◆ Along the production possibilities frontier, the opportunity cost of producing more of one good is the amount of the other good that must be given up.

◆ The opportunity cost of all goods increases as production of the good increases.

Working Problems 1 to 3 will give you a better understanding of production possibilities and opportunity cost.

Using Resources Efficiently (pp. 35–37)

◆ Allocative efficiency occurs when goods and services are produced at the least possible cost and in the quantities that bring the greatest possible benefit.

◆ The marginal cost of a good is the opportunity cost of producing one more unit of it.

◆ The marginal benefit from a good is the benefit received from consuming one more unit of it and is measured by the willingness to pay for it.

◆ The marginal benefit of a good decreases as the amount of the good available increases.

◆ Resources are used efficiently when the marginal cost of each good is equal to its marginal benefit.

Working Problems 4 to 10 will give you a better understanding of using resources efficiently.

Economic Growth (pp. 38–39)

◆ Economic growth, which is the expansion of production possibilities, results from capital accumulation and technological change.

◆ The opportunity cost of economic growth is forgone current consumption.

◆ The benefit of economic growth is increased future consumption.

Working Problem 11 will give you a better understanding of economic growth.

Gains from Trade (pp. 40–43)

◆ A person has a comparative advantage in producing a good if that person can produce the good at a lower opportunity cost than everyone else.

◆ People gain by specializing in the activity in which they have a comparative advantage and trading.

Working Problems 12 and 13 will give you a better understanding of the gains from trade.

Economic Coordination (pp. 43–45)

◆ Firms coordinate a large amount of economic activity, but there is a limit to the efficient size of a firm.

◆ Markets coordinate the economic choices of people and firms.

◆ Markets can work efficiently only when property rights exist and money makes trading in markets more efficient.

Working Problem 14 will give you a better understanding of economic coordination.

Key Terms

Absolute advantage, 40
Allocative efficiency, 35
Capital accumulation, 38
Comparative advantage, 40
Economic growth, 38
Firm, 43
Marginal benefit, 36
Marginal benefit curve, 36
Marginal cost, 35
Market, 44
Money, 44
Opportunity cost, 33
Preferences, 36
Production efficiency, 33
Production possibilities frontier, 32
Property rights, 44
Technological change, 38

STUDY PLAN PROBLEMS AND APPLICATIONS

 You can work Problems 1 to 20 in MyEconLab Chapter 2 Study Plan and get instant feedback.

Production Possibilities and Opportunity Cost (Study Plan 2.1)

Use the following information to work Problems 1 to 3.

Brazil produces ethanol from sugar, and the land used to grow sugar can be used to grow food crops. Suppose that Brazil's production possibilities for ethanol and food crops are as follows:

Ethanol (barrels per day)		Food crops (tonnes per day)
70	and	0
64	and	1
54	and	2
40	and	3
22	and	4
0	and	5

1 a Draw a graph of Brazil's *PPF* and explain how your graph illustrates scarcity.

b If Brazil produces 40 barrels of ethanol a day, how much food must it produce to achieve production efficiency?

c Why does Brazil face a trade-off on its *PPF*?

2 a If Brazil increases its production of ethanol from 40 barrels per day to 54 barrels per day, what is the opportunity cost of the additional ethanol?

b If Brazil increases its production of food crops from 2 tonnes per day to 3 tonnes per day, what is the opportunity cost of the additional food?

c What is the relationship between your answers to parts (a) and (b)?

3 Does Brazil face an increasing opportunity cost of ethanol? What feature of Brazil's *PPF* illustrates increasing opportunity cost?

Using Resources Efficiently

(Study Plan 2.2)

Use the table in Problem 1 to work Problems 4 and 5.

4 Define marginal cost and calculate Brazil's marginal cost of producing a tonne of food when the quantity produced is 2.5 tonnes per day.

5 Define marginal benefit, explain how it is measured, and explain why the data in the table does not enable you to calculate Brazil's marginal benefit from food.

6 Distinguish between production efficiency and allocative efficiency. Explain why many production possibilities achieve production efficiency but only one achieves allocative efficiency.

Use the following graphs to work Problems 7 to 10.

Harry enjoys tennis but wants a high grade in his economics course. The graphs show his *PPF* for these two 'goods' and his *MB* curve for tennis.

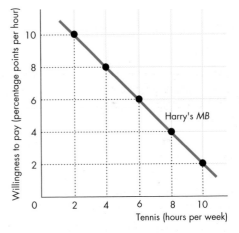

7 What is Harry's marginal cost of tennis if he plays for (i) 3 hours a week, (ii) 5 hours a week and (iii) 7 hours a week?

8 a If Harry uses his time to achieve allocative efficiency, what is his economics mark and how many hours of tennis does he play?

b Explain why Harry would be worse off getting a higher mark than your answer in part (a).

9 If Harry becomes a tennis superstar with big earnings from tennis, what happens to his *PPF*, his *MB* curve and his efficient time allocation?

10 If Harry suddenly finds high marks in economics easier to attain, what happens to his *PPF*, his *MB* curve and his efficient time allocation.

Economic Growth (Study Plan 2.3)

11 A farm grows wheat and produces pork. The marginal cost of producing each of these products increases as more of it is produced.

  a Make a graph that illustrates the farm's *PPF*.

  b The farm adopts a new technology that allows it to use fewer resources to fatten pigs. On a graph show the impact of the new technology on the farm's *PPF*.

  c With the farm using the new technology described in part (b), has the opportunity cost of producing a tonne of wheat increased, decreased or remained the same? Explain and illustrate your answer.

  d Is the farm more efficient with the new technology than it was with the old one? Why?

Gains from Trade (Study Plan 2.4)

12 In an hour, Sue can produce 40 caps or 4 jackets and Tessa can produce 80 caps or 4 jackets.

  a Calculate Sue's opportunity cost of producing a cap.

  b Calculate Tessa's opportunity cost of producing a cap.

  c Who has a comparative advantage in producing caps?

  d If Sue and Tessa specialize in producing the good in which each of them has a comparative advantage, and they trade 1 jacket for 15 caps, who gains from the specialization and trade?

13 Suppose that Tessa buys a new machine for making jackets that enables her to make 20 jackets an hour. (She can still make only 80 caps per hour.)

  a Who now has a comparative advantage in producing jackets?

  b Can Sue and Tessa still gain from trade?

  c Would Sue and Tessa still be willing to trade 1 jacket for 15 caps? Explain your answer.

Economic Coordination (Study Plan 2.5)

14 For 50 years, Cuba has had a centrally planned economy in which the government makes the big decisions on how resources will be allocated.

  a Why would you expect Cuba's production possibilities (per person) to be smaller than those of the EU?

  b What are the social institutions that Cuba might lack that help the EU to achieve allocative efficiency?

Economics in the News (Study Plan 2.N)

Use the following data to work Problems 15 to 17.

Brazil produces ethanol from sugar at a cost of 83 cents per gallon. The US produces ethanol from corn at a cost of $1.14 per gallon. Sugar grown on one acre of land produces twice the quantity of ethanol as the corn grown on an acre. The US imports 5 per cent of the ethanol it uses and produces the rest itself. Since 2003, US ethanol production has more than doubled and US corn production has increased by 45 per cent.

15 **a** Does Brazil or the US have a comparative advantage in producing ethanol?

  b Sketch the *PPF* for ethanol and other goods and services for the US.

  c Sketch the *PPF* for ethanol and other goods and services for Brazil.

16 **a** Do you expect the opportunity cost of producing ethanol in the US to have increased since 2003? Explain why.

  b Do you think the US has achieved production efficiency in its manufacture of ethanol? Explain why or why not.

  c Do you think the US has achieved allocative efficiency in its manufacture of ethanol? Explain why or why not.

17 Make a graph similar to Figure 2.6 to show how both the US and Brazil gain from specialization and trade.

Use this news clip to work Problems 18 to 20.

Time For Tea

Americans are switching to loose-leaf tea for its health benefits. Tea could be grown in the US, but picking tea leaves would be costly because it can only be done by workers and not by machine.

Source: *The Economist*, 8 July 2005

18 **a** Sketch *PPF*s for the production of tea and other goods and services in India and the US.

  b Sketch marginal cost curves for the production of tea in India and the US.

19 **a** Sketch the marginal benefit curves for tea in the US before and after Americans began to appreciate the health benefits of loose tea.

  b Explain how the quantity of loose tea that achieves allocative efficiency has changed.

  c Does the change in preferences towards tea affect the opportunity cost of producing tea?

20 Explain why the US does not produce tea and instead imports it from India.

ADDITIONAL PROBLEMS AND APPLICATIONS

 You can work these problems in MyEconLab if assigned by your lecturer.

Production Possibilities and Opportunity Cost

Use the following information to work Problems 21 and 22.

Sunland's production possibilities are:

Food (kilograms per month)		Sunscreen (litres per month)
300	and	0
200	and	50
100	and	100
0	and	150

21 **a** Draw a graph of Sunland's production possibilities frontier.

  b If Sunland produces 150 kilograms of food how much sunscreen must it produce if it achieves production efficiency?

  c What is Sunland's opportunity cost of producing 1 kilogram of food?

  d What is Sunland's opportunity cost of producing 1 litre of sunscreen?

  e What is the relationship between your answers to parts (c) and (d)?

22 What feature of a *PPF* illustrates increasing opportunity cost? Explain why Sunland's opportunity cost does or does not increase.

Using Resources Efficiently

23 In Problem 21, what is the marginal cost of a kilogram of food in Sunland when the quantity produced is 150 kilograms per month? What is special about the marginal cost of food in Sunland?

24 The table describes the preferences in Sunland:

Sunscreen (litres per month)		Willingness to pay (kilograms per litre)
25	and	3
75	and	2
125	and	1

  a What is the marginal benefit from sunscreen and how is it measured?

  b Draw a graph of Sunland's marginal benefit from sunscreen.

Economic Growth

25 Capital accumulation and technological change bring economic growth, which means that the *PPF* keeps shifting outward: production that was unattainable yesterday becomes attainable today; production that is unattainable today will become attainable tomorrow. Why doesn't this process of economic growth mean that scarcity is being defeated and will one day be gone?

Gains from Trade

Use the following data to work Problems 26 and 27.

Kim can produce 40 pies or 400 cakes an hour. Liam can produce 100 pies or 200 cakes an hour.

26 **a** Calculate Kim's opportunity cost of a pie and Liam's opportunity cost of a pie.

  b If each spends 30 minutes of each hour producing pies and 30 minutes producing cakes, how many pies and cakes does each produce?

  c Who has a comparative advantage in producing pies? Who has a comparative advantage in producing cakes?

27 **a** Draw a graph of Kim's *PPF* and Liam's *PPF*.

  b On your graph, show a point at which each produces when they spend 30 minutes of each hour producing pies and 30 minutes producing cakes.

  c On your graph, show what Kim produces and what Liam produces when they specialize.

  d When they specialize and trade, what are the total gains from trade?

  e If Kim and Liam share the total gains equally, what trade takes place between them?

Economic Coordination

28 Indicate on a graph of the circular flows in the market economy, the real and money flows in which the following items belong:

  a You buy an iPad from the Apple Store.

  b Apple Inc. pays the designers of the iPad.

  c Apple Inc. decides to expand and rents an adjacent building.

  d You buy a new e-book from Amazon.

  e Apple Inc. hires a student as an intern during the summer.

Economics in the News

29 After you have studied *Reading Between the Lines* on pp. 46–47 answer the following questions.

a Why might EU climate change policy increase US production of maize?

b Why would you expect an increase in the quantity of US or EU maize production to raise the opportunity cost of maize?

c Why did the cost of producing maize increase in the rest of the world?

d Is it possible that the increased quantity of maize produced, despite the higher cost of production, moves the US closer to allocative efficiency?

30 Malaria Eradication Back on the Table

In response to the Gates Malaria Forum in October 2007, countries are debating the pros and cons of eradication. Dr. Arata Kochi of the World Health Organization believes that with enough money malaria cases could be cut by 90 per cent, but he believes that it would be very expensive to eliminate the remaining 10 per cent of cases. He concluded that countries should not strive to eradicate malaria.

Source: *The New York Times*, 4 March 2008

a Is Dr. Kochi talking about production efficiency or allocative efficiency or both?

b Make a graph with the percentage of malaria cases eliminated on the *x*-axis and the marginal cost and marginal benefit of driving down malaria cases on the *y*-axis. On your graph:

(i) Draw a marginal cost curve that is consistent with Dr. Kochi's opinion.

(ii) Draw a marginal benefit curve that is consistent with Dr. Kochi's opinion.

(iii) Identify the quantity of malaria eradicated that achieves allocative efficiency.

Use the following news clip to work Problem 31.

31 Lots of Little Screens

Inexpensive broadband access has created a generation of television producers for whom the Internet is their native medium. As they redirect the focus from TV to computers, mobile phones, and iPods, the video market is developing into an open digital network.

Source: *The New York Times*, 2 December 2007

a How has inexpensive broadband changed the production possibilities of video entertainment and other goods and services?

b Sketch a *PPF* for video entertainment and other goods and services before broadband.

c Show how the arrival of inexpensive broadband has changed the *PPF*.

d Sketch a marginal benefit curve for video entertainment.

e Show how the new generation of TV producers for whom the Internet is their native medium might have changed the marginal benefit from video entertainment.

f Explain how the efficient quantity of video entertainment has changed.

Use the following news clip to work Problems 32 and 34.

Britain's Music Stores Squeezed off the High Street

The article describes trends in music retailing: Sony Music and Amazon selling online, supermarkets selling at low prices, and traditional high street music retailers HMV, Music Zone, and Virgin Megastores all struggling.

Source: *The Economist*, 20 January 2007

32 Draw the *PPF* curves for high street music retailers and online music retailers before and after the Internet became available.

33 Draw the marginal cost and marginal benefit curves for high street music retailers and online music retailers before and after the Internet became available.

34 Explain how changes in production possibilities, preferences or both have changed the way in which recorded music is retailed.

Use the following news clip to work Problems 35 and 36.

He Shoots! He Scores! He Makes Films!

All-star basketball player Baron Davis and his school friend, Cash Warren, premiered their first film *Made in America* at the Sundance Festival in January 2008. The film, based on gang activity in South Central Los Angeles, received good reviews.

Source: *The New York Times*, 24 February 2008

35 a Does Baron Davis have an absolute advantage in basketball and film directing and is this the reason for his success in both activities?

b Does Baron Davis have a comparative advantage in basketball or film directing or both and is this the reason for his success in both activities?

36 a Sketch a *PPF* between playing basketball and producing other goods and services for Baron Davis and for yourself.

b How do you (and people like you) and Baron Davis (and people like him) gain from specialization and trade?

How Markets Work

The Amazing Market

The five chapters that you will study in this part explain how markets work. Markets are amazing. They enable people who have never met and who know nothing about each other to interact and do business. Markets determine prices and allocate our scarce resources to the uses that we value most highly.

You will begin in Chapter 3 by learning about the laws of demand and supply. You will discover the market forces that make prices adjust to coordinate the plans of buyers and the plans of sellers.

In Chapter 4, you will meet the handy concept of elasticity and learn how to calculate, interpret and use it to predict how prices and quantities respond to changes in supply and demand.

In Chapter 5, you will discover what Adam Smith called 'the invisible hand'. You will see that when people pursue their self-interest in competitive markets, the outcome is in the social interest – resources go to their most highly valued uses.

In Chapter 6, you will learn about markets in action when governments intervene to fix the minimum price or the maximum price, impose taxes or production quotas, or make some goods illegal.

Finally, in Chapter 7, you will study global markets in action. You will see how globalization brings gains from international trade and why restrictions on international trade are not in the social interest.

THE AMAZING MARKET

The market is an amazing instrument. It enables people who have never met and who know nothing about each other to interact and do business. It also enables us to allocate our scarce resources to the uses that we value most highly. Markets can be very simple or highly organized. Markets are ancient and they are modern.

A simple and ancient market is one that the American historian Daniel J. Boorstin describes in *The Discoverers* (p. 161). In the late fourteenth century:

> *The Muslim caravans that went southward from Morocco across the Atlas Mountains arrived after twenty days at the shores of the Senegal River. There the Moroccan traders laid out separate piles of salt, of beads from Ceutan coral, and cheap manufactured goods. Then they retreated out of sight. The local tribesmen, who lived in the strip mines where they dug their gold, came to the shore and put a heap of gold beside each pile of Moroccan goods. Then they, in turn, went out of view, leaving the Moroccan traders either to take the gold offered for a particular pile or to reduce the pile of their merchandise to suit the offered price in gold. Once again the Moroccan traders withdrew, and the process went on. By this system of commercial etiquette, the Moroccans collected their gold.*

An organized and modern market is an auction at which the EU government sells rights to mobile phone companies for the use of the airwaves.

Everything and anything that can be exchanged is traded in markets to the benefit of both buyers and sellers – goods, services and resources; pounds, euros, dollars and yen; goods to be delivered now and goods to be delivered in the future. Only the imagination limits what can be traded in markets.

Alfred Marshall (1842–1924) grew up in an England that was being transformed by the railways and by the expansion of manufacturing. Mary Paley was one of Marshall's students at Cambridge, and when Alfred and Mary married, in 1877, celibacy rules barred Alfred from continuing to teach at Cambridge. By 1884, with more liberal rules, the Marshalls returned to Cambridge, where Alfred became Professor of Political Economy.

Many economists had a hand in refining the demand and supply model, but the first thorough and complete statement of the model as we know it today was set out by Alfred Marshall, with the help of Mary Paley Marshall.

Published in 1890, this monumental treatise, *The Principles of Economics*, became the textbook on economics on both sides of the Atlantic for almost half a century.

'The forces to be dealt with are . . . so numerous, that it is best to take a few at a time. . . . Thus we begin by isolating the primary relations of supply, demand, and price.'

ALFRED MARSHALL,
The Principles of Economics

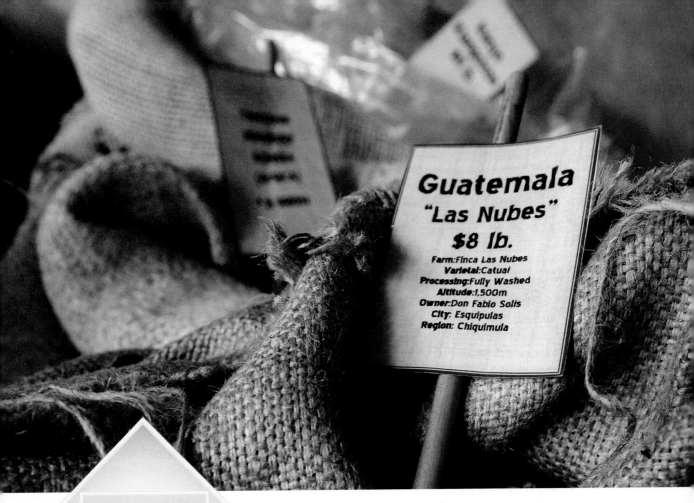

Guatemala
"Las Nubes"
$8 lb.
Farm:Finca Las Nubes
Varietal:Catuai
Processing:Fully Washed
Altitude:1,500m
Owner:Don Fabio Solis
City: Esquipulas
Region: Chiquimula

CHAPTER 3

Demand and Supply

After studying this chapter you will be able to:

◆ Describe a competitive market and think about a price as an opportunity cost

◆ Explain the influences on demand

◆ Explain the influences on supply

◆ Explain how demand and supply determine prices and quantities bought and sold

◆ Use demand and supply to make predictions about changes in prices and quantities

What makes the price of coffee hit a 12-year high, the price of oil double in a year and the price of wheat nearly double in three months? Will these prices come down? This chapter enables you to answer these and similar questions about why prices rise, fall or just fluctuate.

In this chapter, you will see how people make choices about scarce resources by responding to prices and how prices are determined by demand and supply. The demand and supply model is the main tool of economics. It helps us to answer the big economic question: What, how and for whom goods and services are produced?

At the end of the chapter, in *Reading Between the Lines*, we'll apply the model to the market for coffee and explain why its price increased sharply in 2010.

Markets and Prices

When you want to buy a new pair of running shoes, or a sandwich, or an energy drink, or a bottle of water, or decide to upgrade your CD player, you must find a place where people sell those items. The place in which you find them is a *market*. You learned in Chapter 2 (p. 44) that a market is any arrangement that enables buyers and sellers to get information and to do business with each other.

A market has two sides: buyers and sellers. There are markets for *goods* such as apples and hiking boots, for *services* such as haircuts and tennis lessons, for *resources* such as computer programmers and earth-movers, and for other manufactured *inputs* such as memory chips and car parts. There are also markets for money, such as the euro and the dollar, and for financial securities such as BP shares and Yahoo! shares. Only our imagination limits what can be traded in markets.

Some markets are physical places where buyers and sellers meet and where an auctioneer or a broker helps to determine the prices. Examples of this type of market are the London Stock Exchange and the Billingsgate fish market.

Some markets are groups of people spread around the world who never meet and know little about each other but are connected through the Internet or by telephone and fax. Examples are the e-commerce markets and currency markets.

But most markets are unorganized collections of buyers and sellers. You do most of your trading in this type of market. An example is the market for football boots. The buyers in this multi-million pound a year market are the several million people who play football (or who want to make an exotic fashion statement). The sellers are the tens of thousands of retail sports equipment and footwear stores. Each buyer can visit several different stores and each seller knows that the buyer has a choice of stores.

A Competitive Market

Markets vary in the intensity of competition that buyers and sellers face. In this chapter, we're going to study a **competitive market** – a market that has many buyers and many sellers, so no single buyer or seller can influence the price.

Producers offer items for sale only if the price is high enough to cover their opportunity cost. And consumers respond to changing opportunity cost by seeking cheaper alternatives to expensive items.

We are going to study the way people respond to *prices* and the forces that determine prices. But to pursue these tasks, we need to understand the relationship between a price and an opportunity cost.

In everyday life, the *price* of an object is the number of pounds or euros that must be given up in exchange for it. Economists refer to this price as the **money price**.

The *opportunity cost* of an action is the highest-valued alternative forgone. If, when you buy a coffee, the highest-valued thing you forgo is some chocolate, then the opportunity cost of the coffee is the *quantity* of chocolate forgone. We can calculate the quantity of chocolate forgone from the money prices of coffee and chocolate.

If the money price of coffee is £3 a cup and the money price of a chocolate bar is £1, then the opportunity cost of 1 cup of coffee is 3 chocolate bars. To calculate this opportunity cost, we divide the price of a cup of coffee by the price of a chocolate bar and find the *ratio* of one price to the other. The ratio of one price to another is called a **relative price** and a *relative price is an opportunity cost*.

We can express the relative price of coffee in terms of chocolate or any other good. The normal way of expressing a relative price is in terms of a 'basket' of all goods and services. To calculate this relative price, we divide the money price of a good by the money price of a 'basket' of all goods (called a *price index*). The resulting relative price tells us the opportunity cost of the good in terms of how much of the 'basket' we must give up to buy it.

The theory of demand and supply that we are about to study determines *relative prices* and the word 'price' means *relative* price. When we predict that a price will fall, we do not mean that its *money* price will fall – although it might. We mean that its *relative* price will fall. That is, its price will fall *relative* to the average price of other goods and services.

Review Quiz

1 What is the distinction between a money price and a relative price?
2 Explain why a relative price is an opportunity cost.
3 Think of examples of goods whose relative price has risen or has fallen by a large amount.

You can work these questions in Study Plan 3.1 and get instant feedback. myeconlab

Let's begin our study of demand and supply, starting with demand.

Demand

If you demand something, then you

1 Want it,

2 Can afford it and

3 Plan to buy it.

Wants are the unlimited desires or wishes that people have for goods and services. How many times have you thought that you would like something 'if only you could afford it' or 'if it weren't so expensive'? Scarcity guarantees that many – perhaps most – of our wants will never be satisfied. Demand reflects a decision about which wants to satisfy.

The **quantity demanded** of a good or service is the amount that consumers plan to buy during a given time period at a particular price. The quantity demanded is not necessarily the same as the quantity actually bought. Sometimes the quantity demanded exceeds the amount of goods available, so the quantity bought is less than the quantity demanded.

The quantity demanded is measured as an amount per unit of time. For example, suppose that you buy one cup of coffee a day. The quantity of coffee that you demand can be expressed as 1 cup per day, 7 cups per week, or 365 cups per year.

Many factors influence buying plans and one of them is price. We look first at the relationship between the quantity demanded of a good and its price. To study this relationship, we make a *ceteris paribus* assumption. That is, we keep all other influences on buying plans the same and we ask: How, other things remaining the same, does the quantity demanded of a good change as its price changes?

The law of demand provides the answer.

The Law of Demand

The **law of demand** states:

> **Other things remaining the same, the higher the price of a good, the smaller is the quantity demanded; and the lower the price of a good, the greater is the quantity demanded.**

Why does a higher price reduce the quantity demanded? For two reasons:

◆ Substitution effect

◆ Income effect

Substitution Effect

When the price of a good rises, other things remaining the same, its *relative* price – its opportunity cost – rises. Although each good is unique, it has *substitutes* – other goods that can be used in its place. As the opportunity cost of a good rises, people buy less of that good and more of its substitutes.

Income Effect

When the price of a good rises and other influences on buying plans remain unchanged, the price rises relative to incomes. Faced with a higher price and unchanged income, people cannot afford to buy all the things they previously bought. They must decrease the quantities demanded of at least some goods and services and normally the good whose price has increased will be one of the goods that people buy less of.

To see the substitution effect and the income effect at work, think about the effects of a change in the price of an energy drink. Many goods are substitutes for an energy drink. For example, an energy bar or an energy gel could be consumed in place of an energy drink.

Suppose that an energy drink initially sells for £3 and then its price falls to £1.50. People now substitute energy drinks for energy bars – the substitution effect. And with a budget that now has some slack from the lower price of an energy drink, people buy more energy drinks – the income effect. The quantity of energy drinks demanded increases for these two reasons.

Now suppose that an energy drink sells for £3 and its price rises to £4. People now substitute energy bars for energy drinks – the substitution effect. Faced with tighter budgets, people buy even fewer energy drinks – the income effect. The quantity of energy drinks demanded decreases for these two reasons.

Demand Curve and Demand Schedule

You are now about to study one of the two most used curves in economics: the demand curve. And you are going to encounter one of the most critical distinctions: the distinction between *demand* and *quantity demanded*.

The term **demand** refers to the entire relationship between the price of the good and the quantity demanded of the good. Demand is illustrated by the demand curve and the demand schedule. The term *quantity demanded* refers to a point on a demand curve – the quantity demanded at a particular price.

Figure 3.1 shows the demand curve for energy drinks. A **demand curve** shows the relationship between the quantity demanded of a good and its price when all other influences on consumers' planned purchases remain the same.

The table in Figure 3.1 is the *demand schedule*, which lists the quantity demanded at each price when all the other influences on consumers' planned purchases remain the same. For example, if the price of an energy drink is 50 pence, the quantity demanded is 9 million a week. If the price is £2.50, the quantity demanded is 2 million a week. The other rows of the table show the quantities demanded at prices of £1.00, £1.50 and £2.00.

We graph the demand schedule as a demand curve with the quantity demanded on the *x*-axis and the price on the *y*-axis. The points on the demand curve labelled *A* to *E* correspond to the rows of the demand schedule. For example, point *A* on the graph shows a quantity demanded of 9 million energy drinks a week at a price of 50 pence a drink.

Willingness and Ability to Pay

We can also view a demand curve as a willingness-and-ability-to-pay curve. And the willingness and ability to pay is a measure of *marginal benefit*.

If a small quantity is available, the highest price that someone is willing and able to pay for one more unit is high. As the quantity available increases, the marginal benefit falls and the highest price that someone is willing and able to pay falls along the demand curve.

In Figure 3.1, if only 2 million energy drinks are available each week, the highest price that someone is willing to pay for the 2 millionth drink is £2.50. But if 9 million energy drinks are available each week, someone is willing to pay 50 pence for the last drink bought.

A Change in Demand

When any factor that influences buying plans other than the price of the good changes, there is a **change in demand**. Figure 3.2 illustrates an increase in demand. When demand increases, the demand curve shifts rightward and the quantity demanded is greater at each and every price. For example, at a price of £2.50, on the original (blue) demand curve, the quantity demanded is 2 million energy drinks a week. On the new (red) demand curve, the quantity demanded is 6 million energy drinks a week. Look closely at the numbers in the table in Figure 3.2 and check that the quantity demanded at each price is greater.

Figure 3.1 The Demand Curve

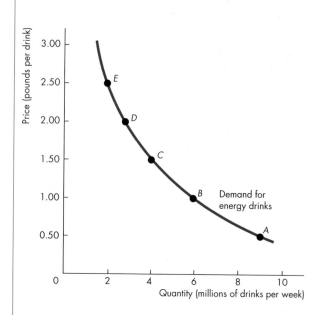

	Price (pounds per drink)	Quantity demanded (millions of energy drinks per week)
A	0.50	9
B	1.00	6
C	1.50	4
D	2.00	3
E	2.50	2

The table shows a demand schedule for energy drinks. At a price of 50 pence an energy drink, 9 million a week are demanded; at a price of £1.50 an energy drink, 4 million a week are demanded. The demand curve shows the relationship between quantity demanded and price, everything else remaining the same. The demand curve slopes downward: as price decreases, the quantity demanded increases.

The demand curve can be read in two ways. For a given price, the demand curve tells us the quantity that people plan to buy. For example, at a price of £1.50 an energy drink, the quantity demanded is 4 million energy drinks a week. For a given quantity, the demand curve tells us the maximum price that consumers are willing and able to pay for the last energy drink available. For example, the maximum price that consumers will pay for the 6 millionth drink is £1.00.

myeconlab Animation

Figure 3.2   An Increase in Demand

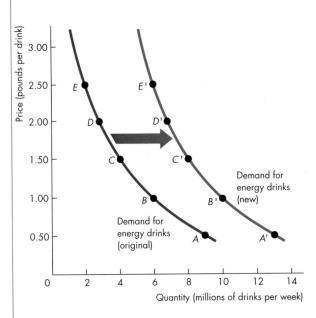

Original demand schedule Original income			New demand schedule New higher income		
	Price (pounds per drink)	Quantity demanded (millions of drinks per week)		Price (pounds per drink)	Quantity demanded (millions of drinks per week)
A	0.50	9	A'	0.50	13
B	1.00	6	B'	1.00	10
C	1.50	4	C'	1.50	8
D	2.00	3	D'	2.00	7
E	2.50	2	E'	2.50	6

A change in any influence on buyers' plans other than the price of the good itself results in a new demand schedule and a shift of the demand curve. A change in income changes the demand for energy drinks.

At a price of £1.50 an energy drink, 4 million drinks a week are demanded at the original income (row C of the table) and 8 million energy drinks a week are demanded at the new higher income. A rise in income increases the demand for energy drinks. The demand curve shifts *rightward*, as shown by the shift arrow and the resulting red curve.

Six main factors bring changes in demand. They are changes in:

◆ Prices of related goods
◆ Expected future prices
◆ Income
◆ Expected future income or credit
◆ Population
◆ Preferences

Prices of Related Goods

The quantity of energy drinks that consumers plan to buy depends in part on the prices of its substitutes. A **substitute** is a good that can be used in place of another good. For example, a bus ride is a substitute for a train ride and an energy bar is a substitute for an energy drink. If the price of an energy bar rises, people buy fewer energy bars and more energy drinks. The demand for energy drinks increases.

The quantity of a good that people plan to buy also depends on the prices of its complements. A **complement** is a good that is used in conjunction with another good. For example, fish and chips are complements and so are energy drinks and exercise. If the price of an hour at the gym falls, people buy more gym time *and more* energy drinks.

Expected Future Prices

If the price of a good is expected to rise in the future and if the good can be stored, the opportunity cost of obtaining the good for future use is lower today than it will be when the price has increased. So people retime their purchases – they substitute over time. They buy more of the good now before its price is expected to rise (and less later), so the demand for the good increases.

For example, suppose that Spain is hit by a frost that damages the season's orange crop. You expect the price of orange juice to rise in the future, so you fill your freezer with enough frozen juice to get you through the next six months. Your current demand for frozen orange juice has increased and your future demand has decreased.

Similarly, if the expected future price of a good falls, the opportunity cost of buying the good today is high relative to what it is expected to be in the future. So people retime their purchases. They buy less of the good now before its price is expected to fall, so the demand for the good decreases today and increases in the future.

Computer prices are constantly falling and this fact poses a dilemma. Will you buy a new computer now, in time for the start of the academic year, or will you wait until the price has fallen some more? Because people expect computer prices to keep falling, the current demand for computers is less (the future demand is greater) than it otherwise would be.

Income

Consumers' income influences demand. When income increases, consumers buy more of most goods; and when income decreases, consumers buy less of most goods. Although an increase in income leads to an increase in the demand for *most* goods, it does not lead to an increase in the demand for *all* goods.

A **normal good** is one for which demand increases as income increases. An **inferior good** is one for which demand decreases as income increases. As income increases, the demand for air travel (a normal good) increases and the demand for long-distance bus trips (an inferior good) decreases.

Expected Future Income or Credit

When expected future income increases or credit becomes easier to get, demand for the good might increase now. For example, a bank worker gets the news that she will receive a big bonus at the end of the year, so she decides to buy a new car right now.

Population

Demand also depends on the size and the age structure of the population. The larger the population, the greater is the demand for all goods and services; the smaller the population, the smaller is the demand.

For example, the demand for parking spaces or cinema seats or energy drinks or just about anything that you can imagine is much greater in London than it is in Leeds.

Also, the larger the proportion of the population in a given age group, the greater is the demand for the goods and services used by that age group. For example, the number of older people is increasing relative to the number of babies. As a result, the demand for walking frames is increasing at a faster pace than that at which the demand for prams is increasing.

Preferences

Demand depends on preferences. *Preferences* are an individual's attitudes towards goods and services.

Table 3.1

The Demand for Energy Drinks

The Law of Demand

The quantity of energy drinks demanded

Decreases if:	*Increases if*:
◆ The price of an energy drink rises	◆ The price of an energy drink falls

Changes in Demand

The demand for energy drinks

Decreases if:	*Increases if*:
◆ The price of a substitute falls	◆ The price of a substitute rises
◆ The price of a complement rises	◆ The price of a complement falls
◆ The expected future price of an energy drink falls	◆ The expected future price of an energy drink rises
◆ Income falls*	◆ Income rises*
◆ Expected future income falls or credit becomes harder to get*	◆ Expected future income rises or credit becomes easier to get*
◆ The population decreases	◆ The population increases

* An energy drink is a normal good.

Preferences depend on such things as the weather, information and fashion. For example, greater health and fitness awareness has shifted preferences in favour of energy drinks, so the demand for energy drinks has increased.

Table 3.1 summarizes the influences on demand and the direction of those influences.

A Change in the Quantity Demanded versus a Change in Demand

Changes in the factors that influence buyers' plans cause either a change in the quantity demanded or a change in demand. Equivalently, they cause either a movement along the demand curve or a shift of the demand curve. The distinction between a change in the quantity demanded and a change in demand is the same as that between a movement along the demand curve and a shift of the demand curve.

A point on the demand curve shows the quantity demanded at a given price. So a movement along the demand curve shows a **change in the quantity demanded**. The entire demand curve shows demand. So a shift of the demand curve shows a *change in demand*. Figure 3.3 illustrates and summarizes these distinctions.

Movement Along the Demand Curve

If the price of the good changes but no other influence on buying plans changes, we illustrate this as a movement along the demand curve.

A fall in the price of a good increases the quantity demanded of it. In Figure 3.3, we illustrate the effect of a fall in price as a movement down along the blue demand curve D_0.

A rise in the price of a good decreases the quantity demanded of it. In Figure 3.3, we illustrate the effect of a rise in price as a movement up along the blue demand curve D_0.

A Shift of the Demand Curve

If the price of a good remains constant but some other influence on buyers' plans changes, there is a change in demand for that good. We illustrate a change in demand as a shift of the demand curve. For example, if more people work out at the gym, consumers buy more energy drinks regardless of the price of a drink. That is what a rightward shift of the demand curve shows – more energy drinks are bought at each and every price.

In Figure 3.3, when any influence on buyers' planned purchases changes, other than the price of the good, there is a *change in demand* and the demand curve shifts. Demand *increases* and the demand curve *shifts rightward* (to the red demand curve D_1) if income increases (for a normal good), the price of a substitute rises, the price of a complement falls, expected future income increases, the expected future price of the good rises, or the population increases.

Demand *decreases* and the demand curve *shifts leftward* (to the red demand curve D_2) if income decreases (for a normal good), the price of a substitute falls, the price of a complement rises, expected future income decreases, the expected future price of the good falls, or the population decreases. (For an inferior good, the effects of changes in income are in the direction opposite to those described above.)

Figure 3.3 A Change in the Quantity Demanded versus a Change in Demand

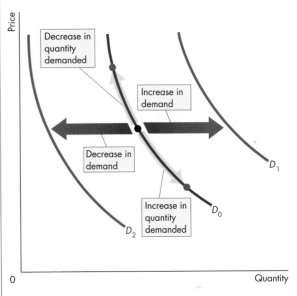

When the price of the good changes, there is a movement along the demand curve and a change in the quantity demanded, shown by the blue arrows on demand curve D_0.

When any other influence on buyers' plans changes, there is a shift of the demand curve and a change in demand. An increase in demand shifts the demand curve rightward (from D_0 to D_1). A decrease in demand shifts the demand curve leftward (from D_0 to D_2).

 Animation

Review Quiz

1 Define the quantity demanded of a good or service.
2 What is the law of demand and how do we illustrate it?
3 What does the demand curve tell us about the price that consumers are willing to pay?
4 List all the influences on buying plans that change demand and for each influence say whether it increases or decreases demand.
5 Distinguish between the quantity demanded of a good and demand for the good.
6 Why does the demand not change when the price of a good changes with no change in the other influences on buying plans?

You can work these questions in Study Plan 3.2 and get instant feedback.

◈ Supply

If a firm supplies a good or a service, the firm

1   Has the resources and technology to produce it,

2   Can profit from producing it and

3   Plans to produce it and sell it.

A supply is more than just having the *resources* and the *technology* to produce something. *Resources and technology* are the constraints that limit what is possible.

Many useful things can be produced, but they are not produced unless it is profitable to do so. (No one produces electric bed-making machines, for example!) Supply reflects a decision about which technologically feasible items to produce.

The **quantity supplied** of a good or service is the amount that producers plan to sell during a given time period at a particular price. The quantity supplied is not necessarily the same amount as the quantity actually sold. Sometimes the quantity supplied is greater than the quantity demanded, so the quantity sold is less than the quantity supplied.

Like the quantity demanded, the quantity supplied is measured as an amount per unit of time. For example, suppose that Ford produces 1,000 cars a day. The quantity of cars supplied by Ford can be expressed as 1,000 a day, 7,000 a week, or 365,000 a year. Without the time dimension, we cannot tell whether a particular number is large or small.

Many factors influence selling plans and, again, one of them is price. We look first at the relationship between the quantity supplied of a good and its price. And again, as we did when we studied demand, to isolate this relationship, we keep all other influences on selling plans the same and we ask: How, other things remaining the same, does the quantity supplied of a good change as its price changes?

The law of supply provides the answer.

The Law of Supply

The **law of supply** states:

> **Other things remaining the same, the higher the price of a good, the greater is the quantity supplied; and the lower the price of a good, the smaller is the quantity supplied.**

Why does a higher price increase the quantity supplied? It is because *marginal cost increases*. As the quantity produced of any good increases, the marginal cost of producing the good increases. (You can refresh your memory of increasing marginal cost in Chapter 2, p. 35.)

It is never worth producing a good if the price received for it does not at least cover the marginal cost of producing it. So when the price of a good rises, other things remaining the same, producers are willing to incur a higher marginal cost and increase production. The higher price brings forth an increase in the quantity supplied.

Let's now illustrate the law of supply with a supply curve and a supply schedule.

Supply Curve and Supply Schedule

You are now going to study the second of the two most used curves in economics: the supply curve. And you're going to learn about the critical distinction between *supply* and *quantity supplied*.

The term **supply** refers to the entire relationship between the quantity supplied and the price of a good. Supply is illustrated by the supply curve and the supply schedule. The term *quantity supplied* refers to a point on a supply curve – the quantity supplied at a particular price.

Figure 3.4 shows the supply curve of energy drinks. A **supply curve** shows the relationship between the quantity supplied of a good and its price when all other influences on producers' planned sales remain the same. The supply curve is a graph of a supply schedule.

The table in Figure 3.4 sets out the supply schedule for energy drinks. A *supply schedule* lists the quantities supplied at each price when all the other influences on producers' planned sales remain the same. For example, if the price of an energy drink is 50 pence, the quantity supplied is zero – in row *A* of the table. If the price of an energy drink is £1.00, the quantity supplied is 3 million drinks a week – in row *B*. The other rows of the table show the quantities supplied at prices of £1.50, £2.00 and £2.50.

To make a supply curve, we graph the quantity supplied on the *x*-axis and the price on the *y*-axis. The points on the supply curve labelled *A* to *E* correspond to the rows of the supply schedule. For example, point *A* on the graph shows a quantity supplied of zero at a price of 50 pence an energy drink. Point *E* shows a quantity supplied of 6 million drinks at £2.50 an energy drink.

Figure 3.4   The Supply Curve

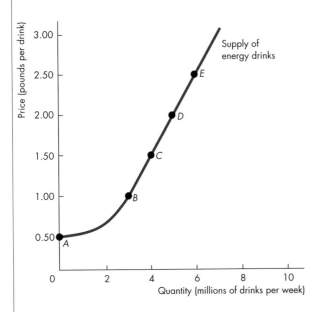

	Price (pounds per energy drink)	Quantity supplied (millions of energy drinks per week)
A	0.50	0
B	1.00	3
C	1.50	4
D	2.00	5
E	2.50	6

The table shows the supply schedule of energy drinks. For example, at a price of £1.00, 3 million energy drinks a week are supplied; at a price of £2.50, 6 million energy drinks a week are supplied. The supply curve shows the relationship between the quantity supplied and price, other things remaining the same. The supply curve usually slopes upward. As the price of a good increases, the quantity supplied increases.

A supply curve can be read in two ways. For a given price, it tells us the quantity that producers plan to sell at that price. For example, at a price of £1.50 a drink, producers are willing to supply 4 million drinks a week. For a given quantity, the supply curve tells us the minimum price at which producers are willing to sell one more drink. For example, if 6 million drinks are produced each week, the lowest price at which someone is willing to sell the 6 millionth drink is £2.50.

Minimum Supply Price

The supply curve, like the demand curve, has two interpretations. It is the minimum-supply-price curve. It tells us the lowest price at which someone is willing to sell another unit. This lowest price is *marginal cost*.

If a small quantity is produced, the lowest price at which someone is willing to sell one more unit is low. But as the quantity produced increases, the lowest price at which someone is willing to sell one more unit rises along the supply curve.

In Figure 3.4, if 6 million energy drinks are produced each week, the lowest price that a producer is willing to accept for the 6 millionth drink is £2.50. But if only 4 million energy drinks are produced each week, a producer is willing to accept £1.50 for the last drink sold.

A Change in Supply

When any factor that influences selling plans other than the price of the good changes, there is a **change in supply**. Six main factors bring changes in supply. They are changes in:

◆ Prices of factors of production
◆ Prices of related goods produced
◆ Expected future prices
◆ Number of suppliers
◆ Technology
◆ The state of nature

Prices of Factors of Production

The prices of factors of production used to produce a good influence the supply of the good. The easiest way to see this influence is to think about the supply curve as a minimum-supply-price curve. If the price of a factor of production rises, the lowest price a producer is willing to accept rises, so supply decreases. For example, during 2009, as the price of jet fuel increased, the supply of air transportation decreased. Similarly, a rise in the minimum wage decreases the supply of energy drinks.

Prices of Related Goods Produced

The prices of related goods and services that firms produce influence supply. For example, if the price of soft drinks rises, the supply of energy drinks decreases. Energy drinks and soft drinks are *substitutes in production* – goods that can be produced by using the same resources. If the price of beef rises, the supply of leather increases. Beef and leather are *complements in production* – goods that must be produced together.

Expected Future Prices

If the expected future price of a good rises, the return from selling it in the future is higher than it is today. So supply decreases today and increases in the future.

Number of Suppliers

The larger the number of firms that produce a good, the greater is the supply of the good. As firms enter an industry, the supply of the good produced increases. As firms leave an industry, the supply decreases.

Technology

The term 'technology' is used broadly to mean the way that factors of production are used to produce a good. A technology change occurs when a new method is discovered that lowers the cost of producing a good. For example, new methods used in the factories that produce computer chips have lowered the cost and increased the supply of computer chips.

The State of Nature

The state of nature includes all the natural forces that influence production, including the state of the weather. Good weather can increase the supply of many crops and bad weather can decrease their supply. Extreme natural events such as insect plagues also influence supply.

Figure 3.5 illustrates an increase in supply. When supply increases, the supply curve shifts *rightward* and the quantity supplied is larger at each and every price. For example, at a price of £1.00, on the original (blue) supply curve, the quantity supplied is 3 million energy drinks a week. On the new (red) supply curve, the quantity supplied is 6 million energy drinks a week. Look closely at the numbers in the table in Figure 3.5 and check that the quantity supplied at each price is larger.

Table 3.2 summarizes the influences on supply and the directions of those influences.

A Change in the Quantity Supplied versus a Change in Supply

Changes in the influences on selling plans brings either a change in the quantity supplied or a change in supply. Equivalently, they bring either a movement along the supply curve or a shift of the supply curve.

Figure 3.5 An Increase in Supply

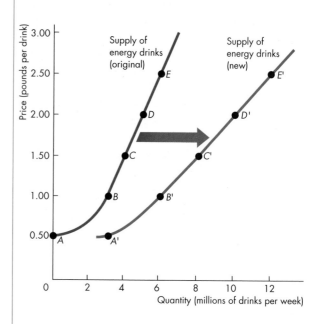

Original supply schedule		New supply schedule	
Original technology		**New technology**	
Price (pounds per drink)	**Quantity supplied (millions of drinks per week)**	**Price (pounds per drink)**	**Quantity supplied (millions of drinks per week)**
A 0.50	0	A' 0.50	3
B 1.00	3	B' 1.00	6
C 1.50	4	C' 1.50	8
D 2.00	5	D' 2.00	10
E 2.50	6	E' 2.50	12

A change in any influence on sellers' plans other than the price of the good itself results in a new supply schedule and a shift of the supply curve. For example, with a new cost-saving technology for producing energy drinks, the supply of energy drinks changes.

At a price of £1.50 a drink, 4 million energy drinks a week are supplied when producers use the old technology (row *C* of the table) and 8 million energy drinks a week are supplied when producers use the new technology. An advance in technology increases the supply of energy drinks. The supply curve shifts rightward, as shown by the shift arrow and the resulting red curve.

myeconlab Animation

A point on the supply curve shows the quantity supplied at a given price. A movement along the supply curve shows a **change in the quantity supplied**. The entire supply curve shows supply. A shift of the supply curve shows a *change in supply*.

Figure 3.6 illustrates and summarizes these distinctions. If the price of a good changes and other things remain the same, there is a *change in the quantity supplied* of the good. If the price of the good falls, the quantity supplied decreases and there is a movement down the supply curve S_0. If the price of a good rises, the quantity supplied increases and there is a movement up the supply curve S_0. When any other influence on selling plans changes, the supply curve shifts and there is a *change in supply*. If the supply curve is S_0 and if production costs fall, supply increases and the supply curve shifts to the red supply curve S_1. If production costs rise, supply decreases and the supply curve shifts to the red supply curve S_2.

Figure 3.6 A Change in the Quantity Supplied versus a Change in Supply

When the price of the good changes, there is a movement along the supply curve and a change in the quantity supplied, shown by the blue arrows on supply curve S_0.

When any other influence on selling plans changes, there is a shift of the supply curve and a change in supply. An increase in supply shifts the supply curve rightward (from S_0 to S_1), and a decrease in supply shifts the supply curve leftward (from S_0 to S_2).

 Animation

Table 3.2

The Supply of Energy Drinks

The Law of Supply

The quantity of energy drinks supplied

Decreases if:	*Increases if:*
◆ The price of an energy drink falls	◆ The price of an energy drink rises

Changes in Supply

The supply of energy drinks

Decreases if:	*Increases if:*
◆ The price of a factor of production used to produce energy drinks rises	◆ The price of a factor of production used to produce energy drinks falls
◆ The price of a substitute in production rises	◆ The price of a substitute in production falls
◆ The price of a complement in production falls	◆ The price of a complement in production rises
◆ The expected future price of an energy drink rises	◆ The expected future price of an energy drink falls
◆ The number of suppliers of energy drinks decreases	◆ The number of suppliers of energy drinks increases
◆ A technology change or natural event decreases energy drink production	◆ A technology change or natural event increases energy drink production

Review Quiz

1 Define the quantity supplied of a good or service.
2 What is the law of supply and how do we illustrate it?
3 What does the supply curve tell us about the price at which firms will supply a given quantity of a good?
4 List all the influences on selling plans and for each influence say whether it changes supply.
5 What happens to the quantity of mobile phones supplied and the supply of mobile phones if the price of a mobile phone falls?

You can work these questions in Study Plan 3.3 and get instant feedback.

Your next task is to use what you've learned about demand and supply and see how prices and quantities are determined.

Market Equilibrium

We have seen that when the price of a good rises, the quantity demanded *decreases* and the quantity supplied *increases*. We are now going to see how prices coordinate the plans of buyers and sellers and achieve equilibrium.

Equilibrium is a situation in which opposing forces balance each other. Equilibrium in a market occurs when the price balances the plans of buyers and sellers. The **equilibrium price** is the price at which the quantity demanded equals the quantity supplied. The **equilibrium quantity** is the quantity bought and sold at the equilibrium price. A market moves towards its equilibrium because:

◆ Price regulates buying and selling plans.

◆ Price adjusts when plans don't match.

Price as a Regulator

The price of a good regulates the quantities demanded and supplied. If the price is too high, the quantity supplied exceeds the quantity demanded. If the price is too low, the quantity demanded exceeds the quantity supplied. There is one price at which the quantity demanded equals the quantity supplied. Let's work out what that price is.

Figure 3.7 shows the market for energy drinks. The table shows the demand schedule (from Figure 3.1) and the supply schedule (from Figure 3.4). If the price of an energy drink is 50 pence, the quantity demanded is 9 million drinks a week, but no drinks are supplied. There is a shortage of 9 million drinks a week. This shortage is shown in the final column of the table. At a price of £1.00 a drink, there is still a shortage, but only of 3 million drinks a week. If the price is £2.50 a drink, the quantity supplied is 6 million drinks a week, but the quantity demanded is only 2 million. There is a surplus of 4 million drinks a week. The one price at which there is neither a shortage nor a surplus is £1.50 a drink. At that price, the quantity demanded equals the quantity supplied: 4 million drinks a week. The equilibrium price is £1.50 a drink and the equilibrium quantity is 4 million drinks a week.

Figure 3.7 shows that the demand curve and the supply curve intersect at the equilibrium price of £1.50 a drink. At each price *above* £1.50 a drink, there is a surplus. For example, at £2.00 a drink, the surplus is 2 million drinks a week, as shown by the blue arrow. At each price *below* £1.50 a drink, there is a shortage of drinks.

Figure 3.7 Equilibrium

Price (pounds per drink)	Quantity demanded	Quantity supplied	Shortage (−) or surplus (+)
	(millions of drinks per week)		
0.50	9	0	−9
1.00	6	3	−3
1.50	4	4	0
2.00	3	5	+2
2.50	2	6	+4

The table lists the quantities demanded and quantities supplied as well as the shortage or surplus of drinks at each price. If the price is £1.00 an energy drink, 6 million drinks a week are demanded and 3 million are supplied. There is a shortage of 3 million drinks a week and the price rises.

If the price is £2.00 an energy drink, 3 million drinks a week are demanded and 5 million are supplied. There is a surplus of 2 million drinks a week and the price falls.

If the price is £1.50 an energy drink, 4 million drinks a week are demanded and 4 million are supplied. There is neither a shortage nor a surplus. Neither buyers nor sellers have any incentive to change the price. The price at which the quantity demanded equals the quantity supplied is the equilibrium price. The equilibrium quantity is 4 million drinks a week.

For example, at £1.00 a drink, the shortage is 3 million drinks a week, as shown by the red arrow.

Price Adjustments

You've seen that if the price is below equilibrium, there is a shortage and that if the price is above equilibrium, there is a surplus. But can we count on the price to change and eliminate a shortage or surplus? We can, because such price changes are beneficial to both buyers and sellers. Let's see why the price changes when there is a shortage or a surplus.

A Shortage Forces the Price Up

Suppose the price of an energy drink is £1. Consumers plan to buy 6 million drinks a week and producers plan to sell 3 million drinks a week. Consumers can't force producers to sell more than they plan, so the quantity that is actually offered for sale is 3 million drinks a week. In this situation, powerful forces operate to increase the price and move it towards the equilibrium price. Some producers, noticing many unsatisfied consumers, raise the price. Some producers increase their output. As producers push the price up, the price rises towards its equilibrium. The rising price reduces the shortage because it decreases the quantity demanded and increases the quantity supplied. When the price has increased to the point at which there is no longer a shortage, the forces moving the price stop operating and the price comes to rest at its equilibrium.

A Surplus Forces the Price Down

Suppose the price is £2 a drink. Producers plan to sell 5 million drinks a week and consumers plan to buy 3 million drinks a week. Producers cannot force consumers to buy more than they plan, so the quantity bought is 3 million drinks a week. In this situation, powerful forces operate to lower the price and move it towards the equilibrium price. Some producers, unable to sell the quantities of drinks they planned to sell, cut their prices. In addition, some producers scale back production. As producers cut the price, the price falls towards its equilibrium. The falling price decreases the surplus because it increases the quantity demanded and decreases the quantity supplied. When the price has fallen to the point at which there is no longer a surplus, the forces moving the price stop operating and the price comes to rest at its equilibrium.

The Best Deal Available for Buyers and Sellers

When the price is below equilibrium, it is forced up towards the equilibrium. Why don't buyers resist the increase and refuse to buy at the higher price? Because they value the good more highly than the current price and they cannot satisfy all their demands at the current price. In some markets – for example, the auction markets that operate on eBay – the buyers might even be the ones who force the price up by offering to pay higher prices.

When the price is above equilibrium, it is bid down towards the equilibrium. Why don't sellers resist this decrease and refuse to sell at the lower price? Because their minimum supply price is below the current price and they cannot sell all they would like to at the current price. Normally, it is the sellers who force the price down by offering lower prices to gain market share.

At the price at which the quantity demanded equals the quantity supplied neither buyers nor sellers can do business at a better price. Buyers pay the highest price they are willing to pay for the last unit bought and sellers receive the lowest price at which they are willing to supply the last unit sold.

When people freely make offers to buy and sell and when buyers try to buy at the lowest possible price and sellers try to sell at the highest possible price, the price at which trade takes place is the equilibrium price – the price at which the quantity demanded equals the quantity supplied. The price coordinates the plans of buyers and sellers and no one has an incentive to change the price.

Review Quiz

1 What is the equilibrium price of a good or service?
2 Over what range of prices does a shortage arise? What happens to the price when there is a shortage?
3 Over what range of prices does a surplus arise? What happens to the price when there is a surplus?
4 Why is the price at which the quantity demanded equals the quantity supplied the equilibrium price?
5 Why is the equilibrium price the best deal available for both buyers and sellers?

You can work these questions in Study Plan 3.4 and get instant feedback.

Predicting Changes in Price and Quantity

The demand and supply theory that we have just studied provides us with a powerful way of analyzing influences on prices and the quantities bought and sold. According to the theory, a change in price stems from a change in demand, a change in supply, or a change in both demand and supply. Let's look first at the effects of a change in demand.

An Increase in Demand

If more people join health clubs, the demand for energy drinks increases. The table in Figure 3.8 shows the original and new demand schedules for energy drinks (the same as those in Figure 3.2) as well as the supply schedule of energy drinks.

The increase in demand creates a shortage at the original price of £1.50 a drink and to eliminate the shortage, the price must rise.

Figure 3.8 shows what happens. The figure shows the original demand for and supply of energy drinks. The original equilibrium price is £1.50 a drink and the quantity is 4 million drinks a week. When demand increases, the demand curve shifts rightward. The equilibrium price rises to £2.50 a drink and the quantity supplied increases to 6 million drinks a week, as highlighted in the figure. There is an *increase in the quantity supplied* but *no change in supply* – a movement along, but no shift of, the supply curve.

A Decrease in Demand

We can reverse this change in demand. Start at a price of £2.50 a drink with 6 million drinks a week, and then work out what happens if demand decreases to its original level. Such a decrease in demand might arise from a fall in the price of an energy bar (a substitute for energy drinks).

The decrease in demand shifts the demand curve *leftward*. The equilibrium price falls to £1.50 a drink and the equilibrium quantity decreases to 4 million drinks a week.

We can now make our first two predictions:

1 **When demand increases, both the price and the quantity increase.**

2 **When demand decreases, both the price and the quantity decrease.**

Figure 3.8   The Effects of a Change in Demand

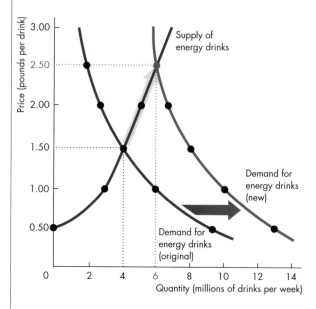

Price (pounds per drink)	Quantity demanded (millions of drinks per week)		Quantity supplied (millions of drinks per week)
	Original	New	
0.50	9	13	0
1.00	6	10	3
1.50	**4**	**8**	**4**
2.00	3	7	5
2.50	2	6	6

Initially, the demand for energy drinks is the blue demand curve. The equilibrium price is £1.50 an energy drink and the equilibrium quantity is 4 million drinks a week. With more health-conscious people doing more exercise, the demand for energy drinks increases and the demand curve shifts rightward to become the red curve.

At £1.50 an energy drink, there is now a shortage of 4 million drinks a week. The price of an energy drink rises to a new equilibrium of £2.50. As the price rises to £2.50, the quantity supplied increases – shown by the blue arrow on the supply curve – to the new equilibrium quantity of 6 million drinks a week. Following an increase in demand, the quantity supplied increases but supply does not change – the supply curve does not shift.

Global Market for Crude Oil

The demand and supply model provides insights into all competitive markets. Here, we apply what you've learned about the effects of an increase in demand to the global market for crude oil.

Crude oil is like the life-blood of the global economy. It is used to fuel our cars, trucks, aeroplanes, trains and buses, to generate electricity and to produce a wide range of plastics. When the price of crude oil rises, the cost of transport, electricity and materials all increase.

In 2001, the price of a barrel of oil was $20 (using the value of money in 2010). In 2008, before the global financial crisis ended a long period of economic expansion, the price peaked at $127 a barrel. While the price of oil was rising, the quantity of oil produced and consumed also increased. In 2001, the world produced 65 million barrels of oil a day. By 2008, that quantity was 72 million barrels.

Who or what has been raising the price of oil? Oil producers might be greedy, and some of them might be big enough to withhold supply and raise the price. But it wouldn't be in their self-interest to do so for long. The higher price would soon bring forth a greater quantity supplied from other producers and the profit of the producer limiting supply would fall.

Oil producers could try to cooperate and jointly withhold supply. The Organization of Petroleum Exporting Countries, OPEC, is such a group of producers. But OPEC doesn't control the *world* supply and its members' self-interest is to produce the quantities that give them the maximum attainable profit.

So even though the global oil market has some big players, they don't fix the price. Instead, the actions of thousands of buyers and sellers and the forces of demand and supply determine the price of oil.

So how have demand and supply changed? Because both the price and the quantity have increased, the demand for oil must have increased. Supply might have changed too, but here we'll suppose that supply has remained the same.

The global demand for oil has increased for one major reason: world income has increased. The increase has been particularly large in the emerging economies of Brazil, China and India. Increased world income has increased the demand for oil-using goods such as electricity, gasoline and plastics, which in turn has increased the demand for oil.

The figure illustrates the effects of the increase in demand on the global oil market. The supply of oil remained

constant along supply curve S. The demand for oil in 2001 was D_{2001}, so in 2001 the price was $20 a barrel and the quantity was 65 million barrels per day. The demand for oil increased and by 2008 it had reached D_{2008}. The price of oil increased to $127 a barrel and the quantity increased to 72 million barrels a day. The increase in the quantity is an *increase in the quantity supplied*, not an increase in supply.

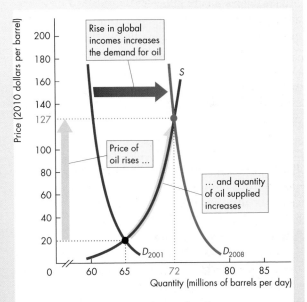

Figure 1 The Global Market for Crude Oil

An Increase in Supply

When the producers of energy drinks switch to new cost-saving technology, the supply of energy drinks increases. The table in Figure 3.9 shows the new supply schedule (the same as that in Figure 3.5). What are the new equilibrium price and quantity? The answer is highlighted in the table: the price falls to £1.00 a drink and the quantity increases to 6 million a week. You can see why by looking at the quantities demanded and supplied at the original price of £1.50 a drink. The quantity supplied at that price is 8 million drinks a week and there is a surplus of drinks. The price falls. Only when the price is £1.00 a drink does the quantity supplied equal the quantity demanded.

Figure 3.9 illustrates the effect of an increase in supply. It shows the demand curve and the original and new supply curves. The initial equilibrium price is £1.50 a drink and the quantity is 4 million drinks a week. When the supply increases, the supply curve shifts rightward. The equilibrium price falls to £1.00 a drink and the quantity demanded increases to 6 million drinks a week, highlighted in the figure. There is an *increase in the quantity demanded* but *no change in demand* – a movement along, but no shift of, the demand curve.

A Decrease in Supply

Start out at a price of £1.00 a drink with 6 million drinks a week being bought and sold. Then suppose that the cost of labour or raw materials rises and the supply of energy drinks decreases. The decrease in supply shifts the supply curve *leftward*. The equilibrium price rises to £1.50 a drink and the quantity demanded decreases. The equilibrium quantity decreases to 4 million drinks a week.

We can now make two more predictions:

1 **When supply increases, the quantity increases and the price falls.**

2 **When supply decreases, the quantity decreases and the price rises.**

You've now seen what happens to the price and the quantity when either demand or supply changes while the other one remains unchanged. In real markets, both demand and supply can change together. When this happens, to predict the changes in price and quantity, we must combine the effects that you've just seen. That is your final task in this chapter.

Figure 3.9 The Effects of a Change in Supply

Price (pounds per drink)	Quantity demanded (millions of drinks per week)	Quantity supplied (millions of drinks per week)	
		Original	New
0.50	9	0	3
1.00	6	3	6
1.50	4	4	8
2.00	3	5	10
2.50	2	6	12

Initially, the supply of energy drinks is shown by the blue supply curve. The equilibrium price is £1.50 a drink and the equilibrium quantity is 4 million drinks a week. When the new cost-saving technology is adopted, the supply of energy drinks increases and the supply curve shifts rightward to become the red curve.

At £1.50 a drink, there is now a surplus of 4 million drinks a week. The price of an energy drink falls to a new equilibrium of £1.00 a drink. As the price falls to £1.00 a drink, the quantity demanded increases – shown by the blue arrow on the demand curve – to the new equilibrium quantity of 6 million drinks a week. Following an increase in supply, the quantity demanded increases but demand does not change – the demand curve does not shift.

The World Market for Wheat

We can use the demand and supply model to explain why the price of wheat has rocketed. The global market for wheat is a competitive market. Russia is the fourth largest producer of wheat in the world behind the European Union, China and India. In most years, Russian farmers produce far more wheat than Russia needs so Russia has become one of the world's top three exporters of wheat.

But 2010 was not a normal year. Russia experienced one of the worst droughts in its history in 2010. Temperatures soared to over 35°C in the summer months in western Russia. The extreme heat fanned forest fires, which killed many people and destroyed farms and crops covering an area the size of Portugal.

In August 2010, Russia announced a ban on the export of Russian wheat for the rest of the year. Countries that import a lot of Russian wheat, such as Egypt, suddenly had to find wheat from other exporting countries. There are plentiful stores of wheat from earlier harvests, but Russia is one of the biggest holders of those stores.

Other European wheat producers also suffered drought and Pakistan and Canada produced less wheat because of flooding in 2010. Over the summer, world wheat prices doubled from the year low in June to a year high in July. When Russia announced the export ban, prices jumped again.

The figure shows what was happening in the world market for wheat. Demand, shown by the demand curve, D, didn't change in June and July 2010. In June before the fires, wheat stocks were plentiful, fields were full and the price was low at £90 per tonne. The supply curve was S_{June} and the quantity of wheat available was 500 million tonnes.

By July, drought and flooding destroyed crops and decreased world supply to S_{July}. With excess demand of 50 million tonnes at the June price, the price began to rise. In July, the price hit £150 per tonne and the quantity of wheat fell to 470 million tonnes. The decrease in supply raised the price and decreased the quantity demanded – a movement along the demand curve – to 470 million tonnes.

When Russia announced the ban on wheat exports in August, the supply of wheat in the global market decreased further to S_{August}. The world price increased to £175 per tonne and the quantity demanded decreased to 460 million tonnes.

The events we've described here in the market for wheat illustrate the effects of a change in supply with no change in demand.

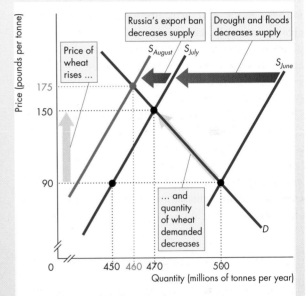

Figure 1 The World Wheat Market

All the Possible Changes in Demand and Supply

Figure 3.10 brings together and summarizes the effects of all the possible changes in demand and supply. With what you've learned about the effects of a change in either demand or supply, you can predict what happens if both demand and supply change together. Let's begin by reviewing what you already know.

Change in Demand with No Change in Supply

The first row of Figure 3.10, parts (a), (b) and (c), summarizes the effects of a change in demand with no change in supply. In part (a), with no change in either demand or supply, neither the price nor the quantity changes. With an *increase* in demand and no change in supply in part (b), both the price and quantity increase. And with a *decrease* in demand and no change in supply in part (c), both the price and the quantity decrease.

Change in Supply with No Change in Demand

The first column of Figure 3.10, parts (a), (d) and (g), summarizes the effects of a change in supply with no change in demand. With an *increase* in supply and no change in demand in part (d), the price falls and quantity increases. And with a *decrease* in supply and no change in demand in part (g), the price rises and the quantity decreases.

Increase in Both Demand and Supply

You've seen that an increase in demand raises the price and increases the quantity. And you've seen that an increase in supply lowers the price and increases the quantity. Figure 3.10(e) combines these two changes. Because either an increase in demand or an increase in supply increases the quantity, the quantity also increases when both demand and supply increase. But the effect on the price is uncertain. An increase in demand raises the price and an increase in supply lowers the price, so we can't say whether the price will rise or fall when both demand and supply increase. We need to know the magnitudes of the changes in demand and supply to predict the effects on price. In the example in Figure 3.10(e), the price does not change. But notice that if demand increases by slightly more than the amount shown in the figure, the price will rise. And if supply increases by slightly more than the amount shown in the figure, the price will fall.

Decrease in Both Demand and Supply

Figure 3.10(i) shows the case in which demand and supply *both decrease*. For the same reasons as those we've just reviewed, when both demand and supply decrease, the quantity decreases and, again, the direction of the price change is uncertain.

Decrease in Demand and Increase in Supply

You've seen that a decrease in demand lowers the price and decreases the quantity. You've also seen that an increase in supply lowers the price and increases the quantity. Figure 3.10(f) combines these two changes. Both the decrease in demand and the increase in supply lower the price. So the price falls. But a decrease in demand decreases the quantity and an increase in supply increases the quantity, so we can't predict the direction in which the quantity will change unless we know the magnitudes of the changes in demand and supply. In Figure 3.10(f), the quantity does not change. But notice that if demand decreases by slightly more than the amount shown in the figure, the quantity will decrease. And if supply increases by slightly more than the amount shown in the figure, the quantity will increase.

Increase in Demand and Decrease in Supply

Figure 3.10(h) shows the case in which demand increases and supply decreases. Now, the price rises and, again, the direction of the quantity change is uncertain.

Review Quiz

What is the effect on the price and quantity of MP3 players (such as the iPod) if:

1   The price of a PC falls or the price of an MP3 download rises? (Draw the diagrams!)
2   More firms produce MP3 players or electronics workers' wages rise? (Draw the diagrams!)
3   Any two of these events in questions 1 and 2 occur together? (Draw the diagrams!)

You can work these questions in Study Plan 3.5 and get instant feedback.

To complete your study of demand and supply, take a look at *Reading Between the Lines* on pp. 74–75, which explains why the price of coffee increased in 2010 and is expected to rise again. Try to get into the habit of using the demand and supply model to understand movements in prices in your everyday life.

Figure 3.10   The Effects of All the Possible Changes in Demand and Supply

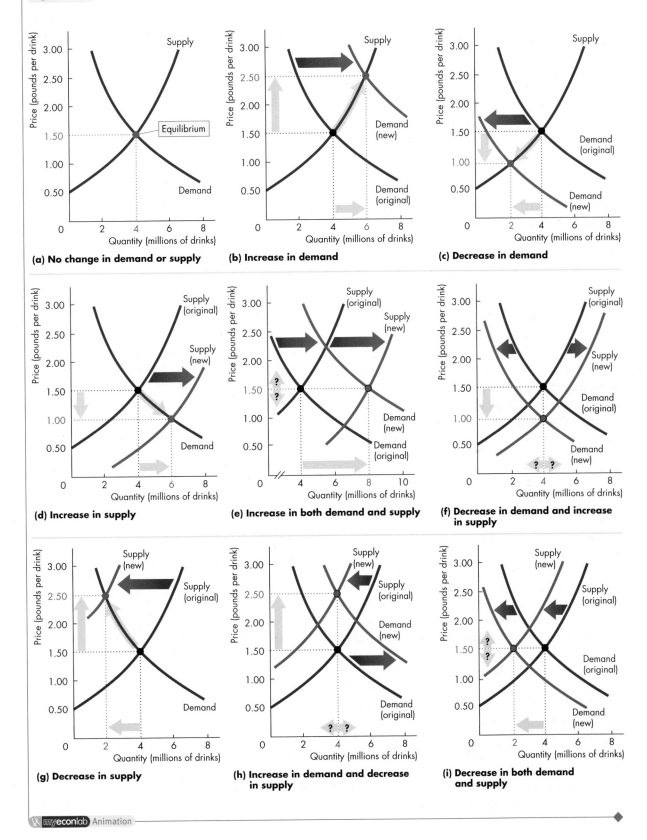

(a) **No change in demand or supply**

(b) **Increase in demand**

(c) **Decrease in demand**

(d) **Increase in supply**

(e) **Increase in both demand and supply**

(f) **Decrease in demand and increase in supply**

(g) **Decrease in supply**

(h) **Increase in demand and decrease in supply**

(i) **Decrease in both demand and supply**

myeconlab Animation

Reading Between the Lines

Demand and Supply: The Price of Coffee

The Financial Times, 30 July 2010

Coffee Surges on Poor Colombian Harvests

Javier Blas

Coffee prices hit a 12-year high on Friday on the back of low supplies of premium Arabica coffee from Colombia after a string of poor crops in the Latin American country.

The strong fundamental picture has also encouraged hedge funds to reverse their previous bearish views on coffee prices.

In New York, ICE September Arabica coffee jumped 3.2 per cent to 178.75 cents per pound, the highest since February 1998. It traded later at 177.25 cents, up 6.8 per cent on the week.

The London-based International Coffee Organisation on Friday warned that the 'current tight demand and supply situation'

was 'likely to persist in the near to medium term'.

Coffee industry executives believe prices could rise towards 200 cents per pound in New York before the arrival of the new Brazilian crop later this year.

'Until October it is going to be tight on high quality coffee,' said a senior executive at one of Europe's largest coffee roasters. He said: 'The industry has been surprised by the scarcity of high quality beans'.

Colombia coffee production, key for supplies of premium beans, last year plunged to a 33-year low of 7.8m bags, each of 60kg, down nearly a third from 11.1m bags in 2008, tightening supplies worldwide. . . .

The Essence of the Story

- ◆ The price of premium Arabica coffee increased by 3.2 per cent to almost 180 cents per pound in July 2010, the highest price since February 1998.

- ◆ A sequence of poor crops in Columbia cut the production of premium Arabica coffee to a 33-year low of 7.8 million 60 kilogram bags, down from 11.1 million bags in 2008.

- ◆ The International Coffee Organisation expects the 'current tight demand and supply' to 'persist in the near to medium term'.

- ◆ Coffee industry executives say prices might approach 200 cents per pound before the new Brazilian crop arrives later this year.

- ◆ Hedge funds previously expected the price of coffee to fall but now expect it to rise further.

Economic Analysis

◆ This news article reports two sources of changes in supply and demand that changed the price of coffee.

◆ The first source is the sequence of poor harvests in Columbia. These events decreased the world supply of Arabica coffee.

◆ Before the reported events, the world production of Arabica was 120 million bags per year and its price was 174 cents per pound.

◆ The decrease in the Columbian harvest decreased world production to about 116 million bags – a decrease of about 3 per cent of world production.

◆ Figure 1 shows the situation before the poor Columbian harvests and the effects of those poor harvests. The demand curve is D_0 and initially, the supply curve was S_0. The market equilibrium is at 120 million bags per year and a price of 174 cents per pound.

◆ The poor Columbian harvests decreased supply and the supply curve shifted leftward to S_1. The price rose to 180 cents per pound and the quantity decreased to 116 million bags.

◆ The second source of change influenced both supply and demand. It is a change in the expected future price of coffee.

◆ The hedge funds are speculators who try to profit from buying at a low price and selling at a high price.

◆ With the supply of coffee expected to remain low, the price was expected to rise further – a rise in the expected future price of coffee.

◆ When the expected future price of coffee rises, some people want to buy more coffee (so they can sell it later) – an increase in demand. And some people offer less coffee for sale (so they can sell it later for a higher price) – a decrease in supply.

◆ Figure 2 shows the effects of these changes in demand and supply. Demand increased from D_0 to D_1 and supply decreased from S_0 to S_2.

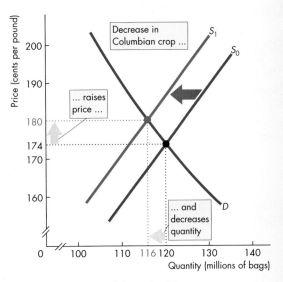

Figure 1 The effects of the Columbian crop

Figure 2 The effects of the expected future price

◆ Because demand increases and supply decreases, the price rises. In this example, it rises to 200 cents per pound.

◆ Also, because demand increases and supply decreases, the change in the equilibrium quantity can go in either direction.

◆ In this example, the increase in demand equals the decrease in supply, so the equilibrium quantity remains constant at 116 million bags per year.

Demand, Supply and Equilibrium

Demand Curve

The law of demand states that as the price of a good or service falls, the quantity demanded of it increases. We illustrate the law of demand by setting out a demand schedule, drawing a graph of the demand curve, or writing down an equation. When the demand curve is a straight line, the following linear equation describes it:

$$P = a - bQ_D$$

where P is the price and Q_D is the quantity demanded. The a and b are positive constants. Figure 1 illustrates this demand curve.

The demand equation tells us three things:

1 The price at which no one is willing to buy the good (Q_D is zero). That is, if the price is a, then the quantity demanded is zero. You can see the price a on Figure 1. It is the price at which the demand curve hits the y-axis – what we call the demand curve's 'intercept on the y-axis'.

2 As the price falls, the quantity demanded increases. If Q_D is a positive number, then the price P must be less than a. And as Q_D gets larger, the price P becomes smaller. That is, as the quantity increases, the maximum price that buyers are willing to pay for the good falls.

3 The constant b tells us how fast the maximum price that someone is willing to pay for the good falls as the quantity increases. That is, the constant b tells us about the steepness of the demand curve. The equation tells us that the slope of the demand curve is $-b$.

Supply Curve

The law of supply states that as the price of a good or service rises, the quantity supplied of it increases. We illustrate the law of supply by setting out a supply schedule, drawing a graph of the supply curve, or writing down an equation. When the supply curve is a straight line, the following linear equation describes it:

$$P = c + dQ_S$$

where P is the price and Q_S the quantity supplied. The c and d are positive constants. Figure 2 illustrates this supply curve.

The supply equation tells us three things:

1 The price at which no one is willing to sell the good (Q_S is zero). If the price is c, then the quantity supplied is zero. You can see the price c on Figure 2. It is the price at which the supply curve hits the y-axis – what we call the supply curve's 'intercept on the y-axis'.

2 As the price rises, the quantity supplied increases. If Q_S is a positive number, then the price P must be greater than c. And as Q_S increases, the price P gets larger. That is, as the quantity increases, the minimum price that sellers are willing to accept rises.

3 The constant d tells us how fast the minimum price at which someone is willing to sell the good rises as the quantity increases. That is, the constant d tells us about the steepness of the supply curve. The equation tells us that the slope of the supply curve is d.

Figure 1 The demand curve

Figure 2 The supply curve

Market Equilibrium

Demand and supply determine market equilibrium. Figure 3 shows the equilibrium price (P^*) and equilibrium quantity (Q^*) at the intersection of the demand curve and the supply curve.

We can use the equations to find the equilibrium price and equilibrium quantity. The price of a good will adjust until the quantity demanded equals the quantity supplied. That is:

$$Q_D = Q_S$$

So at the equilibrium price (P^*) and equilibrium quantity (Q^*):

$$Q_D = Q_S = Q^*$$

To find the equilibrium price and equilibrium quantity: first substitute Q^* for Q_D in the demand equation and Q^* for Q_S in the supply equation. Then the price is the equilibrium price (P^*), which gives:

$$P^* = a - bQ^*$$

$$P^* = c + dQ^*$$

Notice that:

$$a - bQ^* = c + dQ^*$$

Now solve for Q^*:

$$a - c = bQ^* + dQ^*$$

$$a - c = (b + d)Q^*$$

$$Q^* = \frac{a - c}{b + d}$$

To find the equilibrium price (P^*) substitute for Q^* in either the demand equation or the supply equation.

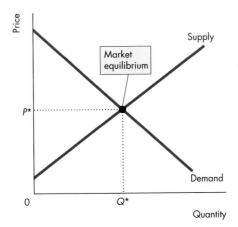

Figure 3 Market equilibrium

Using the demand equation:

$$P^* = a - b\left(\frac{a - c}{b + d}\right)$$

$$P^* = \frac{a(b + d) - b(a - c)}{b + d}$$

$$P^* = \frac{ad + bc}{b + d}$$

Alternatively, using the supply equation:

$$P^* = c + d\left(\frac{a - c}{b + d}\right)$$

$$P^* = \frac{c(b + d) + d(a - c)}{b + d}$$

$$P^* = \frac{ad + bc}{b + d}$$

An Example

The demand for ice cream is:

$$P = 400 - 2Q_D$$

The supply of ice cream is:

$$P = 100 + 1Q_S$$

The price of an ice cream is expressed in pence and the quantities are expressed in ice creams per day.

To find the equilibrium price (P^*) and equilibrium quantity (Q^*), substitute Q^* for Q_D and Q_S and substitute P^* for P. That is:

$$P^* = 400 - 2Q^*$$

$$P^* = 100 + 1Q^*$$

Now solve for Q^*:

$$400 - 2Q^* = 100 + 1Q^*$$

$$300 = 3Q^*$$

$$Q^* = 100$$

And:

$$P^* = 400 - 2(100) = 200$$

The equilibrium price is £2 an ice cream, and the equilibrium quantity is 100 ice creams per day.

◆◆◆◆◆◆ SUMMARY

Key Points

Markets and Prices (p. 56)

◆ A competitive market is one that has so many buyers and sellers that no one can influence the price.

◆ Opportunity cost is a relative price.

◆ Demand and supply determine relative prices.

Working Problem 1 will give you a better understanding of markets and prices.

Demand (pp. 57–61)

◆ Demand is the relationship between the quantity demanded of a good and its price when all other influences on buying plans remain the same.

◆ The higher the price of a good, other things remaining the same, the smaller is the quantity demanded – the law of demand.

◆ Demand depends on the prices of related goods (substitutes and complements), expected future prices, income, expected future income and credit, population and preferences.

Working Problems 2 to 5 will give you a better understanding of demand.

Supply (pp. 62–65)

◆ Supply is the relationship between the quantity supplied of a good and its price when all other influences on selling plans remain the same.

◆ The higher the price of a good, other things remaining the same, the greater is the quantity supplied – the law of supply.

◆ Supply depends on the prices of factors of production used to produce a good, the prices of related goods produced, expected future prices, the number of suppliers, technology and the state of nature.

Working Problems 6 to 9 will give you a better understanding of supply.

Market Equilibrium (pp. 66–67)

◆ At the equilibrium price, the quantity demanded equals the quantity supplied.

◆ At any price above the equilibrium price, there is a surplus and the price falls.

◆ At any price below the equilibrium price, there is a shortage and the price rises.

Working Problems 10 and 11 will give you a better understanding of market equilibrium.

Predicting Changes in Price and Quantity (pp. 68–73)

◆ An increase in demand brings a rise in the price and an increase in the quantity supplied. A decrease in demand brings a fall in the price and a decrease in the quantity supplied.

◆ An increase in supply brings a fall in the price and an increase in the quantity demanded. A decrease in supply brings a rise in the price and a decrease in the quantity demanded.

◆ An increase in demand and an increase in supply bring an increased quantity but an uncertain price change. An increase in demand and a decrease in supply bring a higher price but an uncertain change in quantity.

Working Problems 12 and 13 will give you a better understanding of predicting changes in price and quantity.

Key Terms

Change in demand, 58
Change in supply, 63
Change in the quantity demanded, 61
Change in the quantity supplied, 65
Competitive market, 56
Complement, 59
Demand, 57
Demand curve, 58
Equilibrium price, 66
Equilibrium quantity, 66
Inferior good, 60
Law of demand, 57
Law of supply, 62
Money price, 56
Normal good, 60
Quantity demanded, 57
Quantity supplied, 62
Relative price, 56
Substitute, 59
Supply, 62
Supply curve, 62

STUDY PLAN PROBLEMS AND APPLICATIONS

myeconlab   You can work Problems 1 to 17 in MyEconLab Chapter 3 Study Plan and get instant feedback.

Markets and Prices (Study Plan 3.1)

1 A notice in the *Edgehill Advertiser* in 1862 offered the following exchanges:

1 yard of cloth for 1 pound of bacon
2 yards of cloth for 1 pound of butter
4 yards of cloth for 1 pound of wool
8 yards of cloth for 1 bushel of salt

a What is the price of butter in terms of wool?

b If the money price of bacon was 20 pence per pound, what do you predict was the money price of butter?

c If the money price of bacon was 20 pence per pound and the money price of salt was £2.00 per bushel, do you think anyone would be willing to trade cloth for salt on the terms advertised above?

Demand (Study Plan 3.2)

2 The price of food increased during the past year.

a Explain why the law of demand applies to food just as it does to all other goods and services.

b Explain how the substitution effect influences food purchases and provide some examples of substitutions that people might make when the price of food rises and other things remain the same.

c Explain how the income effect influences food purchases and provide some examples of the income effect that might occur when the price of food rises and other things remain the same.

3 Classify the following goods and services as pairs of likely substitutes and as pairs of likely complements. (You may use an item in more than one pair.) The goods and services are:

coal, oil, natural gas, wheat, maize, rye, pasta, pizza, sausage, skateboard, roller blades, video game, laptop, iPod, mobile phone, text message, e-mail, phone call, voice mail

4 During 2010, the average income in China increased by 10 per cent. Compared to 2009, how do you expect the following would change:

a The demand for beef? Explain your answer.

b The demand for rice? Explain your answer.

5 In January 2010, the price of petrol in the US was $2.70 a gallon. By spring 2010, the price had increased to $3.00 a gallon. Assume that there were no changes in average income, population, or any other influence on buying plans.

Explain how the rise in the price of petrol would affect

a The demand for petrol.

b The quantity of petrol demanded.

Supply (Study Plan 3.3)

6 In 2008, the price of corn increased by 35 per cent and some cotton farmers stopped growing cotton and started to grow corn.

a Does this fact illustrate the law of demand or the law of supply? Explain your answer.

b Why would a cotton farmer grow corn?

Use the following information to work to Problems 7 to 9.

Dairies make low-fat milk from full-cream milk. In the process of making low-fat milk, the dairies produce cream, which is made into ice cream. In the market for low-fat milk, the following events occur one at a time:

(i) The wage rate of dairy workers rises.

(ii) The price of cream rises.

(iii) The price of low-fat milk rises.

(iv) With the period of low rainfall extending, dairies raise their expected price of low-fat milk next year.

(v) With advice from healthcare experts, dairy farmers decide to switch from producing full-cream milk to growing vegetables.

(vi) A new technology lowers the cost of producing ice cream.

7 Explain the effect of each event on the supply of low-fat milk.

8 Use a graph to illustrate the effect of each event.

9 Does any event (or events) illustrate the law of supply?

Market Equilibrium (Study Plan 3.4)

10 As more people buy computers, the demand for Internet service increases and the price of Internet service decreases. The fall in the price of Internet service decreases the supply of Internet service. Is this statement true or false? Explain your answer.

11 The table sets out the demand and supply schedules for chewing gum.

Price (pence per packet)	Quantity demanded	Quantity supplied
	(millions of packets a week)	
20	180	60
40	140	100
60	100	140
80	60	180
100	20	220

a Draw a graph of the chewing gum market and mark in the equilibrium price and quantity.

b Suppose that chewing gum is 70 pence a packet. Describe the situation in the chewing gum market and explain how the price of chewing gum adjusts.

c Suppose that the price of chewing gum is 30 pence a packet. Describe the situation in the chewing gum market and explain how the price adjusts.

Predicting Changes in Price and Quantity (Study Plan 3.5)

12 The following events occur one at a time:

(i) The price of crude oil rises.

(ii) The price of a car rises.

(iii) All speed limits on motorways are abolished.

(iv) Robots cut car production costs.

Explain which of these events will increase or decrease (and state which occurs).

a The demand for petrol.

b The supply of petrol.

c The quantity of petrol demanded.

d The quantity of petrol supplied.

13 In Problem 11, a fire destroys some chewing-gum factories and the quantity of chewing gum supplied decreases by 40 million packets a week at each price.

a Explain what happens in the market for chewing gum and draw a graph to illustrate the changes in the chewing gum market.

b If at the time the fire occurs, there is an increase in the teenage population, which increases the quantity of chewing gum demanded by 40 million packs a week at each price, what are the new equilibrium price and quantity of chewing gum? Illustrate these changes in your graph.

Economics in the News (Study Plan 3.N)

14 **Airline Fares Soar as Oil Cost Bites**

Fuel bills may lead to higher charges. Ryanair increased its airport check-in charges from £5 to £6 per person return and its baggage charges from £20 to £24 per bag return.

Source: Telegraph.co.uk, 9 February 2008

a According to the news clip, what is the influence on the supply of Ryanir flights?

b Explain how supply changes.

15 **Of Gambling, Grannies and Good Sense**

Nevada has plenty of jobs for the over 50s and its elderly population is growing faster than that in other states.

Source: *The Economist*, 26 July 2006

Explain how grannies have influenced:

a The demand in some Las Vegas markets.

b The supply in other Las Vegas markets.

16 **Frigid Winter is Bad News for Tomato Lovers**

An unusually cold January in Florida destroyed entire fields of tomatoes and forced many farmers to delay their harvest. Florida's growers are shipping only a quarter of their usual 5 million pounds a week. The price has risen from $6.50 for a 25-pound box a year ago to $30 now.

Source: *USA Today*, 3 March 2010

a Make a graph to illustrate the market for tomatoes in January 2009 and January 2010.

b On the graph, show how the events in the news clip influence the market for tomatoes.

c Why is the news 'bad for tomato lovers'?

17 **Petrol Prices to Top the 2009 High by Weekend**

The cost of filling up the car is rising as the crude oil price soars and petrol prices may exceed the peak price of 2009.

Source: *USA Today*, 7 January 2010

a Does demand for petrol or the supply of petrol or both change when the price of oil soars?

b Use a demand–supply graph to illustrate what happens to the equilibrium price of petrol and the equilibrium quantity of petrol bought when the price of oil soars.

ADDITIONAL PROBLEMS AND APPLICATIONS

 You can work these problems in MyEconLab if assigned by your lecturer.

Markets and Prices

18 What features of the world market for crude oil make it a competitive market?

19 The money price of a mobile phone is £90 and the money price of the Wii game Super Mario Galaxy is £45.

   a What is the opportunity cost of a mobile phone in terms of the Wii game?

   b What is the relative price of the Wii game in terms of mobile phones?

Demand

20 The price of petrol has increased during the past year.

   a Explain why the law of demand applies to petrol just as it does to all other goods and services.

   b Explain how the substitution effect influences petrol purchases and provide some examples of substitutions that people might make when the price of petrol rises and other things remain the same.

   c Explain how the income effect influences petrol purchases and provide some examples of the income effects that might occur when the price of petrol rises and other things remain the same.

21 Think about the demand for the three game consoles: Xbox, PS3 and Wii. Explain the effect of the following events on the demand for Xbox games and the quantity of Xbox games demanded, other things remaining the same.

   a The price of an Xbox falls.

   b The prices of a PS3 and a Wii fall.

   c The number of people writing and producing Xbox games increases.

   d Consumers' incomes increase.

   e Programmers who write code for Xbox games become more costly to hire.

   f The expected future price of an Xbox game falls.

   g A new game console that is a close substitute for Xbox comes onto the market.

Supply

22 Classify the following pairs of goods as substitutes in production, complements in production, or neither.

   a Bottled water and health club memberships.

   b Potato crisps and baked potatoes.

   c Leather purses and leather shoes.

   d Hybrids and SUVs.

   e Diet coke and regular coke.

23 As the prices of homes fell across the UK in 2008, the number of homes offered for sale decreased.

   a Does this fact illustrate the law of demand or the law of supply? Explain your answer.

   b Why would home owners decide not to sell?

24 **G.M. Cuts Production for Quarter**

General Motors cut its fourth-quarter production schedule by 10 per cent because Ford Motor, Chrysler and Toyota sales declined in August.

           Source: *The New York Times*, 5 September 2007

Explain whether this news clip illustrates a change in the supply of cars or a change in the quantity supplied of cars.

Market Equilibrium

Use the following figure to work Problems 25 and 26.

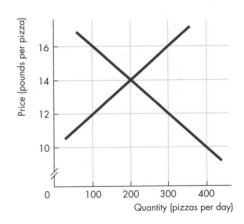

25 **a** Label the curves. Which curve shows the willingness to pay for pizza?

   b If the price is £16 a pizza, is there a shortage or a surplus of pizza and does the price rise or fall?

   c Sellers want to receive the highest possible price, so why would they be willing to accept less than £16 a pizza?

26 **a** If the price of a pizza is £12, is there a shortage or a surplus and does the price rise or fall?

   b Buyers want to pay the lowest possible price, so why would they be willing to pay more than £12 for a pizza?

27 The table sets out demand and supply schedules for crisps.

Price (pence per bag)	Quantity demanded	Quantity supplied
	(millions of bags per week)	
50	160	130
60	150	140
70	140	150
80	130	160
90	120	170
100	110	180

a Draw a graph of the crisps market and mark in the equilibrium price and quantity.

b Describe the situation in the market for crisps and explain how the price adjusts if crisps are 60 pence a bag.

Predicting Changes in Price and Quantity

28 In Problem 27, a new dip increases the quantity of crisps demanded by 30 million bags per week at each price.

a How does the demand and/or supply of crisps change?

b How does the price and quantity of crisps change?

29 If a virus destroys potato crops and the quantity of crisps supplied decreases by 40 million bags a week at each price, how does the equilibrium price and quantity of crisps change?

30 If the virus in Problem 29 hits just as the new dip comes onto the market, how does the equilibrium price and quantity of crisps change?

Economics in the News

31 After you have studied *Reading Between the Lines* on pp. 74–75, answer the following questions.

a What happened to the price of coffee in 2010?

b What substitutions do you expect might have been made to decrease the quantity of coffee demanded?

c What influenced the demand for coffee in 2010 and what influenced the quantity of coffee demanded?

d What influenced the supply of coffee during 2010 and how did supply change?

e How did the combination of the factors you have noted in parts (c) and (d) influence the price and quantity of coffee?

f Was the change in quantity of coffee a change in the quantity demanded or a change in the quantity supplied?

32 **Eurostar Boosted by *Da Vinci Code***

Eurostar, the train service linking London to Paris, said on Wednesday that first-half year sales rose 6 per cent, boosted by devotees of the blockbuster *Da Vinci Code*.

Source: CNN, 26 July 2006

a Explain how *Da Vinci Code* fans helped to raise Eurostar's sales.

b CNN commented on the 'fierce competition from budget airlines'. Explain the effect of this competition on Eurostar's sales.

c What markets in Paris do you think these fans influenced? Explain the influence on three markets.

33 **'Popcorn Cinema' Experience Gets Pricier**

Cinemas are raising the price of popcorn. Demand for field corn, which is used for animal feed, corn syrup and biofuel, has increased and its price has exploded. That's caused some farmers to shift from growing popcorn to easier-to-grow field corn.

Source: *USA Today*, 24 May 2008

Explain and illustrate graphically the events described in the news clip in the market for

a Popcorn.

b Cinema tickets.

Use the following news clip to work Problems 34 and 35.

Sony's Blu-Ray Wins High-Definition War

Toshiba Corp. yesterday withdrew from the race to be the next-generation home movie format, leaving Sony Corp.'s Blu-ray technology the winner. The move could finally jump-start a high-definition home DVD market.

Source: *The Washington Times*, 20 February 2008

34 a How would you expect the price of a used Toshiba player on eBay to change? Will the price change result from a change in demand, supply or both, and in which directions?

b How would you expect the price of a Blu-ray player to change?

35 Explain how the market for Blu-ray format films will change.

36 **Oil Soars to New Record – Over $135 a Barrel**

The price of oil hit a record high, above $135 a barrel, on Thursday – more than twice what it cost a year ago. OPEC has so far blamed price rises on speculators and says there is no shortage of oil.

Source: BBC News, 22 May 2008

a Explain how the price of oil can rise even though there is no shortage of oil.

b If a shortage of oil does occur, what does that imply about price adjustments and the role of price as a regulator in the market for oil?

c If OPEC is correct, what factors might have changed demand and/or supply and shifted the demand curve and/or the supply curve to cause the price to rise?

Elasticity

What will you do if the price of your favourite smoothie doubles next year? You will probably decide to find a cheaper alternative. But what if the price of petrol doubles or the price of a staple food like bread or rice doubles? Will your reaction be the same?

This chapter introduces elasticity, a tool that will help you answer questions like these. In *Reading Between the Lines* at the end of the chapter we will apply the tool to find out how Russian consumers reacted to a price hike in their staple food, buckwheat, in 2010.

After studying this chapter you will be able to:

◆ Define, calculate and explain the factors that influence the price elasticity of demand

◆ Define, calculate and explain the factors that influence the cross elasticity of demand and the income elasticity of demand

◆ Define, calculate and explain the factors that influence the elasticity of supply

Price Elasticity of Demand

You know that when supply increases, the equilibrium price falls and the equilibrium quantity increases. But does the price fall by a large amount and the quantity increase by a little? Or does the price barely fall and the quantity increase by a large amount?

The answer depends on the responsiveness of the quantity demanded to a change in price. You can see why by studying Figure 4.1, which shows two possible scenarios in a local smoothie market. Figure 4.1(a) shows one scenario and Figure 4.1(b) shows the other.

In both cases, supply is initially S_0. In part (a), the demand for smoothies is shown by the demand curve D_A. In part (b), the demand for smoothies is shown by the demand curve D_B. Initially, in both cases, the price is £3 a smoothie and the quantity of smoothies produced and consumed is 10 smoothies an hour.

Now three new juice bars open and the supply of smoothies increases. The supply curve shifts rightward to S_1. In case (a), the price falls by £2 to £1 a smoothie, and the quantity increases by only 5 to 15 smoothies an hour. In contrast, in case (b), the price falls by only £1 to £2 a smoothie and the quantity doubles to 20 smoothies an hour.

The different outcomes arise from differing degrees of responsiveness of the quantity demanded to a change in price. But what do we mean by responsiveness? One answer is slope. The slope of demand curve D_A is steeper than the slope of demand curve D_B.

In this example, we can compare the slopes of the two demand curves. But we can't always do so. The reason is that the slope of a demand curve depends on the units in which we measure the price and quantity. And we often must compare the demand curves for different goods and services that are measured in unrelated units. For example, a juice bar operator might want to compare the demand for smoothies with the demand for sandwiches. Which quantity demanded is more responsive to a price change?

This question can't be answered by comparing the slopes of two demand curves. The units of measurement of smoothies and sandwiches are unrelated. But the question *can* be answered with a measure of responsiveness that is independent of units of measurement. Elasticity is such a measure.

The **price elasticity of demand** is a units-free measure of the responsiveness of the quantity demanded of a good to a change in its price, when all other influences on buyers' plans remain the same.

Figure 4.1 How a Change in Supply Changes Price and Quantity

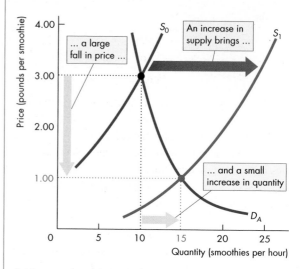

(a) Large price change and small quantity change

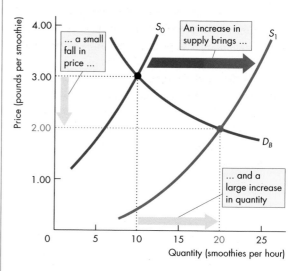

(b) Small price change and large quantity change

Initially, the price is £3 a smoothie and the quantity sold is 10 smoothies an hour. Then supply increases from S_0 to S_1. In part (a), the price falls by £2 to £1 a smoothie, and the quantity increases by 5 to 15 smoothies an hour.

In part (b), the price falls by only £1 to £2 a smoothie, and the quantity increases by 10 to 20 smoothies an hour. The price change is smaller and the quantity change is larger in case (b) than in case (a). The quantity demanded is more responsive to the price change in case (b) than in case (a).

myeconlab Animation

Calculating Price Elasticity of Demand

We calculate the *price elasticity of demand* by using the formula:

$$\text{Price elasticity of demand} = \frac{\text{Percentage change in quantity demanded}}{\text{Percentage change in price}}$$

To calculate the price elasticity of demand for smoothies, we need to know the quantities demanded at two different prices, when all other influences on buying plans remain the same. Suppose we have the data on prices and quantities demanded of smoothies.

Figure 4.2 zooms in on the demand curve for smoothies and shows how the quantity demanded responds to a small change in price. Initially, the price is £3.10 a smoothie and 9 smoothies an hour are sold – the original point in the figure. The price then falls to £2.90 a smoothie, and the quantity demanded increases to 11 smoothies an hour – the new point in the figure. When the price falls by 20 pence a smoothie, the quantity demanded increases by 2 smoothies an hour.

To calculate the price elasticity of demand, we express the changes in price and quantity as percentages of the *average price* and *average quantity*. By using the average price and average quantity, we calculate the elasticity at a point on the demand curve midway between the original point and the new point.

The original price is £3.10 and the new price is £2.90, so the average price is £3. Call the percentage change in the price, $\%\Delta P$, then:

$$\%\Delta P = \Delta P/P_{AVE} = (£0.20/£3.00) \times 100 = 6.67\%$$

The original quantity demanded is 9 smoothies and the new quantity demanded is 11 smoothies, so the average quantity demanded is 10 smoothies. Call the percentage change in the quantity demanded, $\%\Delta Q$, then:

$$\%\Delta Q = \Delta Q/Q_{AVE} = (2/10) \times 100 = 20\%$$

The price elasticity of demand equals the percentage change in the quantity demanded (20 per cent) divided by the percentage change in price (6.67 per cent) and is 3. That is:

$$\text{Price elasticity of demand} = \frac{\%\Delta Q}{\%\Delta P}$$

$$= \frac{20\%}{6.67\%}$$

$$= 3$$

Figure 4.2 Calculating the Elasticity of Demand

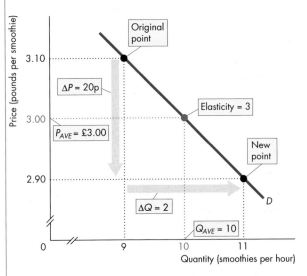

The elasticity of demand is calculated by using the formula:*

$$\text{Price elasticity of demand} = \frac{\text{Percentage change in quantity demanded}}{\text{Percentage change in price}}$$

$$= \frac{\%\Delta Q}{\%\Delta P} = \frac{\Delta Q/Q_{AVE}}{\Delta P/P_{AVE}}$$

$$= \frac{2/10}{0.20/3.00}$$

$$= 3$$

This calculation measures the elasticity at an average price of £3.00 a smoothie and an average quantity of 10 smoothies an hour.

* In the formula, the Greek letter delta (Δ) stands for 'change in' and %Δ stands for 'percentage change in'.

Average Price and Quantity

We use the *average* price and *average* quantity because it gives the most precise measurement of elasticity – midway between the original and new point. If the price falls from £3.10 to £2.90, the 20 pence price change is 6.45 per cent of £3.10. The 2 smoothies change in quantity is 22.2 per cent of 9 smoothies, the original quantity. So if we use these numbers, the price elasticity of demand is 22.2 divided by 6.45, which equals 3.44. If the price *rises* from £2.90 to £3.10, the 20 pence price change is 6.9 per cent of £2.90. The 2 smoothies change in quantity is 18.2 per cent of 11 smoothies, the original quantity. If we use these numbers, the price elasticity of demand is 18.2 divided by 6.9, which equals 2.64.

By using percentages of the *average* price and *average* quantity, we get the same value for the elasticity regardless of whether the price falls from £3.10 to £2.90 or rises from £2.90 to £3.10.

Percentages and Proportions

When we divide the percentage change in quantity by the percentage change in price, the 100s cancel. A percentage change is a *proportionate* change multiplied by 100. The proportionate change in price is $\Delta P/P_{AVE}$, and the proportionate change in quantity demanded is $\Delta Q/Q_{AVE}$. So if we divide $\Delta Q/Q_{AVE}$ by $\Delta P/P_{AVE}$, we get the same answer as we get by using percentage changes.

A Units-free Measure

Elasticity is a *units-free measure* because the percentage change in each variable is independent of the units in which the variable is measured. And the ratio of the two percentages is a number without units.

Minus Sign and Elasticity

When the price of a good *rises*, the quantity demanded *decreases* along the demand curve. Because a *positive* change in price brings a *negative* change in the quantity demanded, the price elasticity of demand is a negative

number. But it is the magnitude, or *absolute value*, of the price elasticity of demand that tells us how responsive – how elastic – demand is. To compare price elasticities of demand, we use the magnitude of the elasticity and ignore the minus sign.

Inelastic and Elastic Demand

Figure 4.3 shows three demand curves that cover the entire range of possible elasticities of demand. In Figure 4.3(a), the quantity demanded is constant regardless of the price. If the quantity demanded remains constant when the price changes, then the price elasticity of demand is zero and the good is said to have a **perfectly inelastic demand**. One good that has a very low price elasticity of demand (perhaps zero over some price range) is insulin. Insulin is of such importance to some diabetics that if the price rises or falls, they do not change the quantity they buy.

If the percentage change in the quantity demanded equals the percentage change in price, then the price elasticity equals 1 and the good is said to have a **unit elastic demand**. The demand in Figure 4.3(b) is an example of unit elastic demand.

Between the cases shown in Figure 4.3(a) and Figure 4.3(b) is the general case in which the percentage change in the quantity demanded is less than the percentage change in price. In this case, the price elasticity of demand is between zero and 1 and the

Figure 4.3 Inelastic and Elastic Demand

(a) Perfectly inelastic demand   **(b) Unit elastic demand**   **(c) Perfectly elastic demand**

Each demand illustrated here has a constant elasticity. The demand curve in part (a) illustrates the demand for a good that has a zero price elasticity of demand. The demand curve in part (b) illustrates the demand for a good with a unit price elasticity of demand. And the demand curve in part (c) illustrates the demand for a good with an infinite price elasticity of demand.

good is said to have an **inelastic demand**. Food and housing are examples of goods with inelastic demand.

If the quantity demanded changes by an infinitely large percentage in response to a tiny price change, then the price elasticity of demand is infinity and the good is said to have a **perfectly elastic demand**. Figure 4.3(c) shows a perfectly elastic demand. An example of a good that has a very high elasticity of demand (almost infinite) is a salad from two campus machines located side by side. If the two machines offer the same salads for the same price, some people buy from one machine and some from the other. But if one machine's price is higher than the other's, by even a small amount, no one will buy from the machine with the higher price. Salads from the two machines are perfect substitutes.

Between the cases in Figure 4.3(b) and Figure 4.3(c) is the general case in which the percentage change in the quantity demanded exceeds the percentage change in price. In this case, the price elasticity of demand is greater than 1 and the good is said to have an **elastic demand**. Cars and furniture are examples of goods that have elastic demand.

Elasticity Along a Linear Demand Curve

Elasticity and slope are not the same, but they are related. To understand how they are related, let's look at elasticity along a straight-line demand curve – a demand curve that has a constant slope.

Figure 4.4 illustrates the calculation of elasticity along a straight-line demand curve. First, suppose the price falls from £5 to £3 a smoothie. The quantity demanded increases from zero to 10 smoothies an hour. The average price is £4 a smoothie, and the average quantity is 5 smoothies. So:

$$\text{Price elasticity of demand} = \frac{\Delta Q/Q_{AVE}}{\Delta P/P_{AVE}}$$

$$= \frac{10/5}{2/4}$$

$$= 4$$

That is, the price elasticity of demand at an average price of £4 a smoothie is 4.

Next, suppose that the price falls from £3 to £2 a smoothie. The quantity demanded increases from 10 to 15 smoothies an hour. The average price is now £2.50 a smoothie, and the average quantity is 12.5 smoothies an hour.

So:

$$\text{Price elasticity of demand} = \frac{5/12.5}{1/2.5}$$

$$= 1$$

That is, the price elasticity of demand at an average price of £2.50 a smoothie is 1.

Finally, suppose that the price falls from £2 to zero. The quantity demanded increases from 15 to 25 smoothies an hour. The average price is now £1 and the average quantity is 20 smoothies an hour. So:

$$\text{Price elasticity of demand} = \frac{10/20}{2/1}$$

$$= 1/4$$

That is, the price elasticity of demand at an average price of £1 a smoothie is 1/4.

You've now seen how elasticity changes along a straight-line demand curve. At the mid-point of the curve, demand is unit elastic. At prices above the mid-point, demand is elastic. At prices below the mid-point, demand is inelastic.

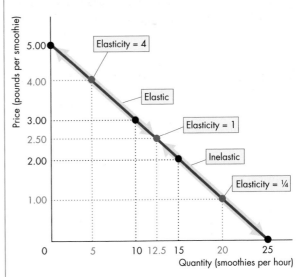

Figure 4.4 Elasticity Along a Linear Demand Curve

On a linear demand curve, elasticity decreases as the price falls and the quantity demanded increases. Demand is unit elastic at the mid-point of the demand curve (elasticity is 1). At prices above the mid-point, demand is elastic; at prices below the mid-point, demand is inelastic.

myeconlab Animation

Total Revenue and Elasticity

The **total revenue** from the sale of a good equals the price of the good multiplied by the quantity sold. When a price changes, total revenue also changes. But a rise in the price does not always increase total revenue. The change in total revenue depends on the elasticity of demand in the following way:

1   If demand is elastic, a 1 per cent price cut increases the quantity sold by more than 1 per cent and total revenue increases.

2   If demand is inelastic, a 1 per cent price cut increases the quantity sold by less than 1 per cent and total revenue decreases.

3   If demand is unit elastic, a 1 per cent price cut increases the quantity sold by 1 per cent and so total revenue does not change.

In Figure 4.5(a), over the price range from £5 to £2.50, demand is elastic. Over the price range from £2.50 to zero, demand is inelastic. At a price of £2.50, demand is unit elastic.

Figure 4.5(b) shows total revenue. At a price of £5, the quantity sold is zero (part a), so total revenue is zero (part b). At a price of zero, the quantity demanded is 25 smoothies an hour and total revenue is again zero.

A price cut in the elastic range brings an increase in total revenue – the percentage increase in the quantity demanded is greater than the percentage decrease in price.

A price cut in the inelastic range brings a decrease in total revenue – the percentage increase in the quantity demanded is less than the percentage decrease in price. When demand is unit elastic, total revenue is at a maximum.

Figure 4.5 shows how we can use this relationship between elasticity and total revenue to estimate elasticity using the total revenue test. The **total revenue test** is a method of estimating the price elasticity of demand by observing the change in total revenue that results from a change in the price, when all other influences on the quantity sold remain the same.

1   If a price cut increases total revenue, demand is elastic.

2   If a price cut decreases total revenue, demand is inelastic.

3   If a price cut leaves total revenue unchanged, demand is unit elastic.

Figure 4.5   Elasticity and Total Revenue

(a) Demand

(b) Total revenue

When demand is elastic, in the price range from £5 to £2.50, a decrease in price in part (a) brings an increase in total revenue in part (b). When demand is inelastic, in the price range from £2.50 to zero, a decrease in price in part (a) brings a decrease in total revenue in part (b). When demand is unit elastic, at a price of £2.50 in part (a), total revenue is at a maximum in part (b).

 Animation

Your Expenditure and Your Elasticity

When a price changes, the change in your expenditure on the good depends on *your* elasticity of demand.

1 If your demand is elastic, a 1 per cent price cut increases the quantity you buy by more than 1 per cent and your expenditure on the item increases.

2 If your demand is inelastic, a 1 per cent price cut increases the quantity you buy by less than 1 per cent and your expenditure on the item decreases.

3 If your demand is unit elastic, a 1 per cent price cut increases the quantity you buy by 1 per cent and your expenditure on the item does not change.

So if you spend more on an item when its price falls, your demand for that item is elastic; if you spend the same amount, your demand is unit elastic; and if you spend less, your demand is inelastic.

The Factors That Influence the Elasticity of Demand

What makes the demand for some goods elastic and the demand for others inelastic? The magnitude of the elasticity of demand depends on:

◆ Closeness of substitutes

◆ Proportion of income spent on the good

◆ Time elapsed since a price change

Closeness of Substitutes

The closer the substitutes for a good or service, the more elastic is the demand for it. For example, oil has substitutes but none that are currently very close (imagine a steam-driven, coal-fuelled aircraft). So the demand for oil is inelastic.

The degree of substitutability between two goods also depends on how narrowly (or broadly) we define them. For example, a personal computer has no really close substitutes, but a Dell PC is a close substitute for a Gateway PC. So the elasticity of demand for personal computers is lower than that for a Dell or a Gateway.

In everyday language we call some goods, such as food and housing, *necessities* and other goods, such as exotic vacations, *luxuries*. A necessity is a good that has poor substitutes and that is crucial for our well-being, so a necessity has an inelastic demand. A luxury is a good that usually has many substitutes, so a luxury has an elastic demand. *Economics in Action* lists and discusses some UK price elasticities of demand.

ECONOMICS IN ACTION

Some Real-world Price Elasticities of Demand

The table shows some estimates of price elasticities of demand in the UK. These values range from 1.4 for fresh meat, the most elastic demand in the table, to 0.5 for beer, the least elastic demand in the table. Fresh meat has many substitutes such as frozen meat and fish, so the demand for fresh meat is elastic. Green vegetables don't have many substitutes, so the demand for green vegetables is inelastic. But a particular green vegetable such as green beans has close substitutes such as green peas and broccoli. The elasticity of demand for green vegetables is smaller than the elasticity of demand for green beans.

You can see that the items with an elastic demand include luxuries (wine and spirits) while items with an inelastic demand include necessities (fruit juice and green vegetables).

The unit elasticity of demand for services is an average of the elasticities for many different services and hides wide variation across them.

Table 1

UK Price Elasticities of Demand

Good or service	Elasticity
Elastic demand	
Fresh meat	1.4
Spirits	1.3
Wine	1.2
Unit elasticity	
Services	1.0
Cereals	1.0
Inelastic demand	
Durable goods	0.9
Fruit juice	0.8
Green vegetables	0.6
Tobacco	0.5
Beer	0.5

Sources of data: Ministry of Agriculture, Food and Fisheries, *Household Food Consumption and Expenditure*, 1992, London, HMSO; C. Godfrey, 'Modelling Demand', *Preventing Alcohol and Tobacco Problems*, Vol. 1 (A. Maynard and P. Tether, eds), Avebury, 1990; J. Muellbauer, 'Testing the Barten Model of Household Composition Effects and the Cost of Children', *Economic Journal*, September 1977.

Proportion of Income Spent on the Good

Other things remaining the same, the greater the proportion of income spent on a good, the more elastic is the demand for it.

Price Elasticity of Demand for Food

Figure 1 shows the proportion of income spent on food and the price elasticity of demand for food in 10 countries. This figure confirms the general tendency that the larger the proportion of income spent on food, the more price elastic is the demand for food.

In a very poor country like Tanzania, where 62 per cent of income is spent on food, the price elasticity of demand for food is 0.77. In contrast, in Germany where 15 per cent of income is spent on food, the elasticity of demand for food is just 0.23.

In a country that spends a large proportion of its income on food, an increase in the price of food forces people to make a bigger adjustment to the quantity of food they buy than in a country in which only a small proportion of income is spent on food.

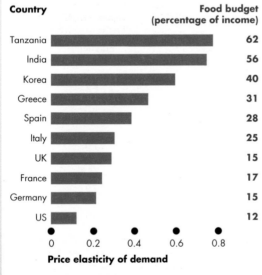

Figure 1 Price Elasticities in 10 Countries

Source of data: Henri Theil, Ching-Fan Chung and James L. Seale Jr, *Advances in Econometrics, Supplement 1, International Evidence on Consumption Patterns*. Greenwich, Connecticut, JAI Press Inc., 1989.

Think about your own demand for toothpaste and housing. If the price of toothpaste doubles, you consume almost as much as before. Your demand for toothpaste is inelastic. If the rent you pay doubles, you shriek and look for more students to share your accommodation. Your demand for housing is elastic. Why the difference? Housing takes a large proportion of your budget, and toothpaste takes only a tiny proportion. You don't like either price increase, but you hardly notice the higher price of toothpaste, while the higher rent puts your budget under severe strain.

Time Elapsed Since Price Change

The longer the time that has elapsed since a price change, the more elastic is demand. When the price of oil increased by 400 per cent during the 1970s, people barely changed the quantity of oil and petrol they bought. But gradually, as more efficient car and aeroplane engines were developed, the quantity used decreased. The demand for oil has become more elastic as more time has elapsed since that huge price hike. Similarly, when the price of a PC fell, the quantity of PCs demanded increased only slightly at first. But as more people have become better informed about the variety of ways of using a PC, the quantity of PCs bought has increased sharply. The demand for PCs has become more elastic.

You've now completed your study of the *price* elasticity of demand. Two other elasticity concepts tell us about the effects of other influences on demand. Let's look at these other elasticities of demand.

More Elasticities of Demand

Andy, who operates a juice bar, wants to know how a rise in the price of coffee at the café next door will affect the demand for his smoothies. He knows that smoothies and coffee are substitutes and that when the price of coffee rises, the demand for smoothies increases. But by how much?

Andy also wants to know how a rise in the price of his salads will affect the demand for his smoothies. He knows that smoothies and salads are complements and that when the price of a complement of smoothies rises, the demand for smoothies decreases. But again, by how much?

To answer these questions, Andy uses the cross elasticity of demand. Let's examine this elasticity measure.

Cross Elasticity of Demand

We measure the influence of a change in the price of a substitute or complement by using the concept of the cross elasticity of demand. The **cross elasticity of demand** is a measure of the responsiveness of the demand for a good to a change in the price of a substitute or complement, other things remaining the same. We calculate the *cross elasticity of demand* by using the formula:

$$\text{Cross elasticity of demand} = \frac{\text{Percentage change in quantity demanded}}{\text{Percentage change in price of substitute or complement}}$$

The cross elasticity of demand can be positive or negative. It is *positive* for a *substitute* and *negative* for a *complement*.

Substitutes

Suppose when the price of a coffee is £1.50, Andy sells 9 smoothies an hour. Now the price of a coffee rises to £2.50. With no change in the price of a smoothie or any other influence on buying plans, the quantity of smoothies sold increases to 11 an hour.

We use the same method that you learned when you studied the price elasticity of demand (p. 85). The change in the quantity demanded is +2 smoothies and the average quantity is 10 smoothies. So the quantity of smoothies demanded changes by 20 per cent. That is:

$$\Delta Q/Q_{AVE} = (+2/10) \times 100 = +20\%$$

The change in the price of a coffee, a substitute for a smoothie, is £1 – the new price, £2.50, minus the original price, £1.50. The average price is £2. So the price of a coffee rises by 50 per cent. That is:

$$\Delta P/P_{AVE} = (£1/£2) \times 100 = +50\%$$

So the cross elasticity of demand for smoothies with respect to the price of a coffee is:

$$\frac{+20\%}{+50\%} = 0.4$$

Because a *rise* in the price of coffee brings an *increase* in the demand for smoothies, the cross elasticity of demand for smoothies with respect to the price of coffee is *positive*. Both the price of the substitute and the quantity of the good change in the same direction. Figure 4.6 illustrates the cross elasticity of demand. Smoothies and coffees are substitutes. Because they are substitutes, when the price of a coffee *rises*, the demand for smoothies *increases*. The demand curve for smoothies shifts rightward from D_0 to D_1.

Figure 4.6   Cross Elasticity of Demand

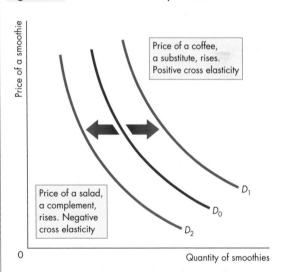

A coffee is a substitute for a smoothie. When the price of a coffee rises, the demand for smoothies increases and the demand curve for smoothies shifts rightward from D_0 to D_1. The cross elasticity of demand is positive.

A salad is a complement of a smoothie. When the price of a salad rises, the demand for smoothies decreases and the demand curve for smoothies shifts leftward from D_0 to D_2. The cross elasticity of demand is negative.

 Animation

Complements

Now suppose that the price of smoothie is constant and 11 smoothies an hour are sold. Then the price of a salad rises from £1.50 to £2.50. No other influence on buying plans changes and the quantity of smoothies sold decreases to 9 an hour.

The change in the quantity demanded is the opposite of what we've just calculated (again as percentages of the average quantity and average price): the quantity of smoothies demanded decreases by 20 per cent (−20%).

The change in the price of a salad, a complement of smoothie, is the same as the percentage change in the price of a coffee that we've just calculated: the price of a salad rises by 50 per cent (+50%). So the cross elasticity of demand for smoothies with respect to the price of a salad is:

$$\frac{-20\%}{+50\%} = -0.4$$

Because smoothies and salads are complements, when the price of a salad *rises*, the demand for smoothies *decreases*. The demand curve for smoothies shifts leftward from D_0 to D_2. Because a *rise* in the price of a salad brings an *decrease* in the demand for smoothies, the cross elasticity of demand for smoothies with respect to the price of a salad is *negative*. The price and quantity change in *opposite* directions.

The magnitude of the cross elasticity of demand determines how far the demand curve shifts. The larger the cross elasticity (absolute value), the greater is the change in demand and the larger is the shift in the demand curve.

If two items are close substitutes, such as two brands of spring water, the cross elasticity is large. If two items are close complements, such as fish and chips, the cross elasticity is large.

If two items are somewhat unrelated to each other, such as newspapers and smoothies, the cross elasticity is small – perhaps even zero.

Income Elasticity of Demand

Suppose that the economy is expanding and people are enjoying rising incomes. This prosperity is bringing an increase in the demand for most types of goods and services. But by how much will the demand for smoothies increase? The answer depends on the **income elasticity of demand**, which is a measure of the responsiveness of the demand for a good or service to a change in income, other things remaining the same.

The income elasticity of demand is calculated by using the formula:

$$\text{Income elasticity of demand} = \frac{\text{Percentage change in quantity demanded}}{\text{Percentage change in income}}$$

Income elasticities of demand can be positive or negative and fall into three interesting ranges:

◆ Greater than 1 (*normal* good, income elastic)
◆ Positive and less than 1 (*normal* good, income inelastic)
◆ Negative (*inferior* good)

Income Elastic Demand

Suppose that the price of a smoothie is constant and 9 smoothies an hour are sold. Then incomes rise from £475 to £525 a week and the quantity of smoothies sold increases to 11 an hour. The change in the quantity demanded is 2 smoothies. The average quantity is 10 smoothies, so the quantity demanded increases by 20 per cent. The change in income is £50 and the average income is £500, so incomes increase by 10 per cent. The income elasticity of demand for smoothies is:

$$\frac{20\%}{10\%} = 2$$

Because the income elasticity of demand is greater than 1, the demand for smoothies is income elastic. *When the demand for a good is income elastic, as income increases, the percentage of income spent on that good increases.*

Income Inelastic Demand

If the percentage increase in the quantity demanded is positive and less than the percentage increase in income, demand is income inelastic. *When the demand for a good is income inelastic, as income increases, the percentage of income spent on that good decreases.*

Inferior Goods

If the quantity demanded decreases as income increases, the income elasticity of demand is negative, and the good is an inferior good. The amount spent on an inferior good decreases as income increases. Goods in this category include small motorcycles, potatoes and rice. Low-income consumers buy most of these goods.

Real-world Income Elasticities of Demand

Table 1 shows some estimates of the income elasticities of demand in the UK. The demand for a necessity such as fresh meat and green vegetables is income inelastic, while the demand for luxury goods such as wines and spirits is income elastic. The demand for some goods such as tobacco and bread have negative income elasticities, so they are classified as inferior goods.

What is a necessity or a luxury depends on the level of income. For people with low income, food and clothing can be luxuries. So the *level* of income has a big effect on income elasticities of demand.

Figure 1 shows this effect on the income elasticity of demand for food in 10 countries. In countries with low incomes, such as Tanzania and India, the income elasticity of demand for food is high, while in the high-income countries of Europe and North America, the income elasticity of demand for food is much lower.

The numbers in the figure tell us that a 10 per cent increase in income leads to about a 7.5 per cent increase in demand for food in India, a 3 per cent increase in France, and a less than 2 per cent increase in the United States.

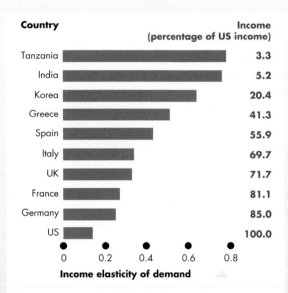

Country	Income (percentage of US income)
Tanzania	3.3
India	5.2
Korea	20.4
Greece	41.3
Spain	55.9
Italy	69.7
UK	71.7
France	81.1
Germany	85.0
US	100.0

Income elasticity of demand

Figure 1 Income Elasticities in 10 Countries

Source of data: Henri Theil, Ching-Fan Chung and James L. Seale Jr, *Advances in Econometrics, Supplement 1, International Evidence on Consumption Patterns*. Greenwich, Connecticut, JAI Press Inc., 1989.

Table 1

Some UK Income Elasticities

Good or service	Elasticity
Income elastic demand	
Wine	2.6
Services	1.8
Spirits	1.7
Durable goods	1.5
Income inelastic demand	
Fruit juice	0.9
Beer	0.6
Green vegetables	0.1
Fresh meat	0.0
Cereals	0.0
Inferior goods	
Tobacco	−0.1
Bread	−0.3

Sources of data: Ministry of Agriculture, Food and Fisheries, *Household Food Consumption and Expenditure*, 1992, London, HMSO; C. Godfrey, 'Modelling Demand', *Preventing Alcohol and Tobacco Problems*, Vol. 1 (A. Maynard and P. Tether, eds), Avebury, 1990; J. Muellbauer 'Testing the Barten Model of Household Composition Effects and the Cost of Children', *Economic Journal*, September 1977.

Review Quiz

1   What does the cross elasticity of demand measure?
2   What does the sign (positive versus negative) of the cross elasticity of demand tell us about the relationship between two goods?
3   What does the income elasticity of demand measure?
4   What does the sign (positive versus negative) of the income elasticity of demand tell us about a good?
5   Why does the level of income influence the magnitude of the income elasticity of demand?

You can work these questions in Study Plan 4.2 and get instant feedback.

You've now completed your study of the *price elasticity* of demand, the *cross elasticity* of demand and the *income elasticity* of demand. Let's now look at the other side of a market and examine the elasticity of supply.

Elasticity of Supply

You know that when demand increases, the equilibrium price rises and the equilibrium quantity increases. But does the price rise by a large amount and the quantity increase by a little? Or does the price barely rise and the quantity increase by a large amount?

The answer depends on the responsiveness of the quantity supplied to a change in price. You can see why by studying Figure 4.7, which shows two possible scenarios in a local smoothie market. Figure 4.7(a) shows one scenario, and Figure 4.7(b) shows the other.

In both cases, demand is initially D_0. In part (a), the supply of smoothies is shown by the supply curve S_A. In part (b), the supply of smoothies is shown by the supply curve S_B. Initially, in both cases, the price is £3 a smoothie and the quantity produced and consumed is 10 smoothies an hour.

Now increases in incomes and population increase the demand for smoothies. The demand curve shifts rightward to D_1. In case (a), the price rises by £2 to £5 a smoothie and the quantity increases by only 5 to 15 an hour. In contrast, in case (b), the price rises by only 20 pence to £3.20 a smoothie and the quantity increases by 10 to 20 smoothies an hour.

The different outcomes arise from differing degrees of responsiveness of the quantity supplied to a change in price. We measure the degree of responsiveness by using the concept of the elasticity of supply.

Calculating the Elasticity of Supply

The **elasticity of supply** measures the responsiveness of the quantity supplied to a change in the price of a good when all other influences on selling plans remain the same. It is calculated by using the formula:

$$\text{Price elasticity of supply} = \frac{\text{Percentage change in quantity supplied}}{\text{Percentage change in price}}$$

We again use the same method that you learned when you studied the elasticity of demand. (Refer back to p. 85 to check this method.) Let's calculate the elasticity of supply along the supply curves in Figure 4.7.

In Figure 4.7(a), when the price rises from £3 to £5, the price rise is £2 and the average price is £4, so the price rises by 50 per cent of the average price.

Figure 4.7 How a Change in Demand Changes Price and Quantity

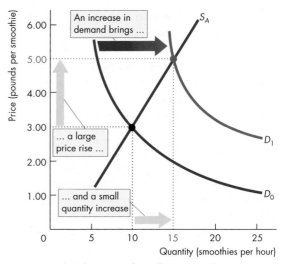

(a) Large price change and small quantity change

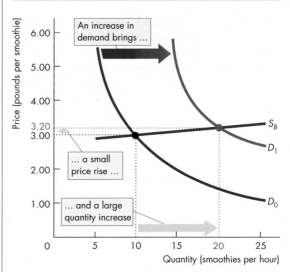

(b) Small price change and large quantity change

Initially, the price is £3 a smoothie and the quantity sold is 10 smoothies an hour. Then increases in incomes and population increase the demand for smoothies. The demand curve shifts rightward to D_1. In part (a) the price rises by £2 to £5 a smoothie, and the quantity increases by 5 to 15 smoothies an hour. In part (b), the price rises by only 20 pence to £3.20 a smoothie and the quantity increases by 10 to 20 smoothies an hour. The price change is smaller and the quantity change is larger in case (b) than in case (a). The quantity supplied is more responsive to a price change in case (b) than in case (a).

myeconlab Animation

The quantity increases from 10 to 15 smoothies an hour, so the increase is 5 smoothies, the average quantity is 12.5 smoothies an hour, and the quantity increases by 40 per cent.

The elasticity of supply is equal to 40 per cent divided by 50 per cent, which equals 0.8.

In Figure 4.7(b), when the price rises from £3 to £3.20, the price rise is 20 pence and the average price is £3.10, so the price rises by 6.45 per cent of the average price. The quantity increases from 10 to 20 smoothies an hour, so the increase is 10 smoothies, the average quantity is 15 smoothies, and the quantity increases by 66.67 per cent. The elasticity of supply equals 66.67 per cent divided by 6.45 per cent, which equals 10.34.

Figure 4.8 shows the range of elasticities of supply. If the quantity supplied is fixed regardless of the price, the supply curve is vertical and the elasticity of supply is zero. Supply is perfectly inelastic. This case is shown in Figure 4.8(a). A special intermediate case occurs when the percentage change in price equals the percentage change in quantity. Supply is then unit elastic. This case is shown in Figure 4.8(b). No matter how steep the supply curve is, if it is linear and passes through the origin, supply is unit elastic. If there is a price at which sellers are willing to offer any quantity for sale, the supply curve is horizontal and the elasticity of supply is infinite. Supply is perfectly elastic. This case is shown in Figure 4.8(c).

The Factors That Influence the Elasticity of Supply

The magnitude of the elasticity of supply depends on:

◆ Resource substitution possibilities
◆ Time frame for the supply decision

Resource Substitution Possibilities

Some goods and services can be produced only by using unique or rare productive resources. These items have a low, even perhaps a zero, elasticity of supply. Other goods and services can be produced by using commonly available resources that could be allocated to a wide variety of alternative tasks. Such items have a high elasticity of supply.

A Van Gogh painting is an example of a good with a vertical supply curve and a zero elasticity of supply. At the other extreme, wheat can be grown on land that is almost equally good for growing corn. So it is just as easy to grow wheat as corn, and the opportunity cost of wheat in terms of forgone corn is almost constant. As a result, the supply curve of wheat is almost horizontal and its elasticity of supply is very large. Similarly, when a good is produced in many different countries (for example, wheat, sugar and beef), the supply of the good is highly elastic.

Figure 4.8 Inelastic and Elastic Supply

(a) Perfectly inelastic supply   **(b) Unit elastic supply**   **(c) Perfectly elastic supply**

Each supply illustrated here has a constant elasticity. The supply curve in part (a) illustrates the supply of a good that has a zero elasticity of supply. The supply curve in part (b) illustrates the supply of a good with a unit elasticity of supply. All linear supply curves that pass through the origin illustrate supplies that are unit elastic. The supply curve in part (c) illustrates the supply of a good with an infinite elasticity of supply.

The supply of most goods and services lies between these two extremes. The quantity produced can be increased but only by incurring a higher cost. If a higher price is offered, the quantity supplied increases. Such goods and services have an elasticity of supply between zero and infinity.

Time Frame for Supply Decisions

To study the influence of the length of time elapsed since a price change we distinguish three time frames of supply:

1   Momentary supply
2   Short-run supply
3   Long-run supply

The *momentary supply curve* shows the response of the quantity supplied immediately following a price change.

Some goods, such as fruits and vegetables, have a perfectly inelastic momentary supply – a vertical supply curve. The quantities supplied depend on crop planting decisions made earlier. In the case of oranges, for example, planting decisions have to be made many years in advance of the crop being available.

The momentary supply curve is vertical because, on a given day, no matter what the price of oranges, producers cannot change their output. They have picked, packed and shipped their crop to market, and the quantity available for that day is fixed.

In contrast, some goods have a perfectly elastic momentary supply. Long-distance phone calls are an example. When many people simultaneously make a call, there is a big surge in the demand for telephone cables, computer switching and satellite time, and the quantity bought increases. But the price remains constant. Long-distance carriers monitor fluctuations in demand and reroute calls to ensure that the quantity supplied equals the quantity demanded without changing the price.

The *short-run supply curve* shows how the quantity supplied responds to a price change when only *some* of the technologically possible adjustments to production have been made. The short-run response to a price change is a sequence of adjustments. The first adjustment that is usually made is in the amount of labour employed. To increase output in the short run, firms work their labour force overtime and perhaps hire additional workers. To decrease their output in the short run, firms either lay off workers or reduce their hours of

work. With the passage of time, firms can make additional adjustments, perhaps training additional workers or buying additional tools and other equipment.

The short-run supply curve slopes upward because producers can take actions quite quickly to change the quantity supplied in response to a price change. For example, if the price of oranges falls, growers can stop picking and leave oranges to rot on the trees. Or if the price rises, they can use more fertilizer and improved irrigation to increase the yields of their existing trees. In the long run, they can plant more trees and increase the quantity supplied even more in response to a given price rise.

The *long-run supply curve* shows the response of the quantity supplied to a change in price after all the technologically possible ways of adjusting supply have been exploited. In the case of oranges, the long run is the time it takes new plantings to grow to full maturity – about 15 years. In some cases, the long-run adjustment occurs only after a completely new production plant has been built and workers have been trained to operate it – typically a process that might take several years.

You have now learned about the elasticities of demand and supply. Table 4.1 summarizes all the elasticities that you've met in this chapter.

In the next chapter, we study the efficiency of competitive markets. But before leaving elasticity, *Reading Between the Lines* on pp. 98–99 applies elasticity to the choices Russians faced when the price of their staple food, buckwheat, shot up during the fires of 2010.

Table 4.1

A Compact Glossary of Elasticities

Price Elasticity of Demand

A relationship is described as	When its magnitude is	Which means that
Perfectly elastic	Infinity	The smallest possible increase in price causes an infinitely large decrease in the quantity demanded*
Elastic	Less than infinity but greater than 1	The percentage decrease in the quantity demanded exceeds the percentage increase in price
Unit elastic	1	The percentage decrease in the quantity demanded equals the percentage increase in price
Inelastic	Greater than zero but less than 1	The percentage decrease in the quantity demanded is less than the percentage increase in price
Perfectly inelastic	Zero	The quantity demanded is the same at all prices

Cross Elasticity of Demand

A relationship is described as	When its magnitude is	Which means that
Close substitutes	Large	The smallest possible increase in the price of one good causes an infinitely large increase in the quantity demanded of the other good
Substitutes	Positive, less than infinity	If the price of one good increases the quantity demanded of the other good also increases
Unrelated	Zero	The quantity demanded of one good remains constant regardless of the price of the other good
Complements	Less than zero	The quantity demanded of one good decreases when the price of the other good increases

Income Elasticity of Demand

A relationship is described as	When its magnitude is	Which means that
Income elastic (normal good)	Greater than 1	The percentage increase in the quantity demanded is greater than the percentage increase in income
Income inelastic (normal good)	Less than 1 but greater than zero	The percentage increase in the quantity demanded is less than the percentage increase in income
Negative income elastic (inferior good)	Less than zero	When income increases, quantity demanded decreases

Price Elasticity of Supply

A relationship is described as	When its magnitude is	Which means that
Perfectly elastic	Infinity	The smallest possible increase in price causes an infinitely large increase in the quantity supplied
Elastic	Less than infinity but greater than 1	The percentage increase in the quantity supplied exceeds the percentage increase in the price
Unit elastic	1	The percentage increase in the quantity supplied equals the percentage increase in price
Inelastic	Greater than zero but less than 1	The percentage increase in the quantity supplied is less than the percentage increase in the price
Perfectly inelastic	Zero	The quantity supplied is the same at all prices

* In each description, the directions of change may be reversed. For example, in this case: the smallest possible decrease in the price causes an infinitely large increase in the quantity demanded.

Reading Between the Lines

Elasticity: Demand for Buckwheat

The Independent, 27 August 2010

Fears of Social Unrest When Harvest Fails

Shaun Walker

As prices for buckwheat and other basic foodstuffs rise sharply in Russia after one of the worst droughts in the country's history, . . . [t]he authorities, wary of potential social discontent if prices rise too high, have already banned grain exports to protect domestic supplies.

The shortage comes after one of the most punishing summers in Russian history, with temperatures well over 35C. . . . Forest fires raged across western Russia, leaving devastation. . . .

At least a quarter of the harvest [was] destroyed. . . . The most dramatic price rises have been for grechka, or buckwheat – a staple of the Russian diet. Russians eat grechka as a porridge for breakfast, or as a side dish with almost anything.

According to the state statistics service, the price for a kilo of grechka has risen 39 per cent since the start of the year. . . .

The Russian Grain Union said the buckwheat harvest this year is expected to be between 400 and 450 tonnes, compared to 566 tonnes last year and around 1 million tonnes in 2008.

The Essence of the Story

◆ Drought and fires across western Russia have destroyed a quarter of the buckwheat crop.

◆ Buckwheat, or grechka, is the staple food of the Russian diet.

◆ By August 2010, the price of buckwheat in Russia had risen by 39 per cent since the start of the year.

◆ The quantity of buckwheat produced from the summer harvest will be about 450 tonnes compared to 566 tonnes last year.

Economic Analysis

◆ Figure 1 shows the impact of the damaged harvest on the Russian buckwheat market.

◆ Before the fires, supply is S_0 and demand is D_0, the market quantity is 566 tonnes per year and the equilibrium price is 23 rubles per kilogram.

◆ After the fires, supply decreases to S_1 in Figure 1. At the price of 23 rubles, the quantity demanded exceeds the quantity supplied and the shortage (excess demand) forces the price up.

◆ As the price rises the quantity demanded decreases along the demand curve.

◆ The equilibrium price is 32 rubles per kilogram, 39 per cent higher than 23 rubles per kilogram and the new equilibrium quantity is 450 tonnes.

◆ Assuming no change in other influences on the demand for buckwheat, we can estimate its price elasticity of demand.

◆ Figure 2 shows the changes in price and quantity demanded and the elasticity calculation.

◆ Using the mid-point method, the percentage change in the quantity demanded equals (116 tonnes/508 tonnes) × 100, which equals 22.83 per cent.

◆ The percentage change in the price equals (9 rubles/27.5 rubles) × 100, which equals 32.73 per cent.

◆ The price elasticity of demand equals the percentage change in the quantity demanded (22.83) divided by the percentage change in the price (32.73), which equals 0.7.

◆ The estimated price elasticity of demand for buckwheat in Russia is 0.7, which means that the demand for buckwheat is inelastic. A large percentage change in the price brings a small percentage change in the quantity of buckwheat demanded.

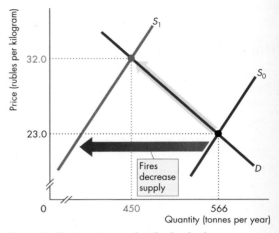

Figure 1 The Russian market for buckwheat

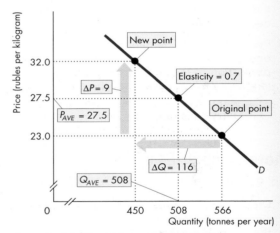

Figure 2 Elasticity of demand for buckwheat

◆ Because demand is inelastic, a decrease in supply brings a large rise in price.

◆ Russian consumers are reluctant to find or cannot find alternative grain substitutes for buckwheat despite the high price.

◆◆◆◆◆ S U M M A R Y

Key Points

Price Elasticity of Demand (pp. 84–90)

◆ Elasticity is a measure of the responsiveness of the quantity demanded of a good to a change in its price, other things remaining the same.

◆ Price elasticity of demand equals the percentage change in the quantity demanded divided by the percentage change in price.

◆ The larger the magnitude of the price elasticity of demand, the greater is the responsiveness of the quantity demanded to a given change in price.

◆ If demand is elastic, a fall in the price leads to an increase in total revenue. If demand is unit elastic, a fall in the price leaves total revenue unchanged. If demand is inelastic, a fall in the price leads to a decrease in total revenue.

◆ Price elasticity of demand depends on how easily one good serves as a substitute for another, the proportion of income spent on the good and the length of time elapsed since the price change

Working Problems 1 to 7 will give you a better understanding of price elasticity of demand.

More Elasticities of Demand
(pp. 91–93)

◆ Cross elasticity of demand measures the responsiveness of demand for one good to a change in the price of a substitute or a complement, other things remaining the same.

◆ The cross elasticity of demand with respect to the price of a substitute is positive. The cross elasticity of demand with respect to the price of a complement is negative.

◆ Income elasticity of demand measures the responsiveness of demand to a change in income, other things remaining the same. For a normal good, the income elasticity of demand is positive. For an inferior good, the income elasticity of demand is negative.

◆ When the income elasticity of demand is greater than 1 (income elastic), the percentage of income spent on the good increases as income increases.

◆ When the income elasticity of demand is less than 1 but greater than zero (income elastic and inferior), the percentage of income spent on the good decreases as income increases.

Working Problems 8 to 16 will give you a better understanding of more elasticities of demand.

Elasticity of Supply (pp. 94–97)

◆ Elasticity of supply measures the responsiveness of the quantity supplied of a good to a change in its price.

◆ The elasticity of supply is usually positive and ranges between zero (vertical supply curve) and infinity (horizontal supply curve).

◆ Supply decisions have three time frames: momentary, short run and long run.

◆ Momentary supply refers to the response of sellers to a price change at the instant that the price changes.

◆ Short-run supply refers to the response of sellers to a price change after some of the technologically feasible adjustments in production have been made

◆ Long-run supply refers to the response of sellers to a price change when all the technologically feasible adjustments in production have been made.

Working Problems 17 to 21 will give you a better understanding of elasticity of supply.

Key Terms

Cross elasticity of demand, 91
Elastic demand, 87
Elasticity of supply, 94
Income elasticity of demand, 92
Inelastic demand, 87
Perfectly elastic demand, 87
Perfectly inelastic demand, 86
Price elasticity of demand, 84
Total revenue, 88
Total revenue test, 88
Unit elastic demand, 86

STUDY PLAN PROBLEMS AND APPLICATIONS

myeconlab You can work Problems 1 to 21 in MyEconLab Chapter 4 Study Plan and get instant feedback.

Price Elasticity of Demand

(Study Plan 4.1)

1 Rain spoils the strawberry crop. As a result, the price rises from £2 to £3 a box and the quantity demanded decreases from 1,000 to 600 boxes a week. Over this price range:

   a What is the price elasticity of demand?

   b Describe the demand for strawberries.

2 If the quantity of dental services demanded increases by 10 per cent when the price of dental services falls by 10 per cent, is the demand for dental service inelastic, elastic, or unit elastic?

3 The demand schedule for hotel rooms is

Price (euros per room)	Quantity demanded (millions of rooms per year)
200	1,000
250	80
400	50
500	40
800	25

   a What happens to total revenue when the price falls from €400 to €250 and from €250 to €200 a night?

   b Is the demand for hotel rooms elastic, inelastic or unit elastic?

4 The figure shows the demand for pens.

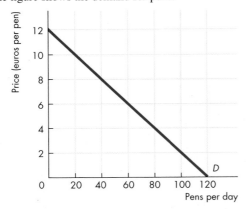

Calculate the elasticity of demand when the price rises from €4 to €6 a pen. Over what price range is the demand for pens elastic?

5 In 2003, when music downloading first took off, Universal Music slashed the average price of a CD from $21 to $15. The company said that it expected the price cut to boost the quantity of CDs sold by 30 per cent.

   a What was Universal Music's estimate of the price elasticity of demand for CDs?

   b Given your answer to part (a), if you were making the pricing decision at Universal Music, would you cut the price, raise the price, or leave the price unchanged? Explain your decision.

6 The demand for illegal drugs is inelastic. Much of the expenditure on illegal drugs comes from crime. Assuming these statements to be correct:

   a How will a successful campaign that decreases the supply of drugs influence the price of illegal drugs and the amount spent on them?

   b What will happen to the amount of crime?

   c What is the most effective way of decreasing the quantity of illegal drugs bought and decreasing the amount of drug-related crime?

7 **The Grip of Petrol**

   Drivers in the US are ranked as the least sensitive to changes in the price of petrol. For example, if the price rose from $3 to $4 per gallon and stayed there for a year US purchases of petrol would fall by only about 5 per cent.

   Source: *Slate*, 27 September 2005

   a Calculate the US price elasticity of demand for petrol. Is the US demand for petrol elastic, unit elastic or inelastic?

   b Explain how the price rise from $3 to $4 a gallon changes the total revenue from petrol sales.

More Elasticities of Demand

(Study Plan 4.2)

8 **Spam Sales Rise as Food Costs Soar**

   Sales of Spam are rising as consumers realize that Spam and other lower-cost foods can be substituted for costlier cuts of meat as a way of controlling their already stretched food budgets.

   Source: *AOL Money & Finance*, 28 May 2008

   a Is Spam a normal good or inferior good? Explain.

   b Would the income elasticity of demand for Spam be negative or positive? Explain.

9 If a 12 per cent rise in the price of orange juice decreases the quantity of orange juice demanded by 22 per cent and increases the quantity of apple juice demanded by 14 per cent, calculate the

   a Price elasticity of demand for orange juice.

   b Cross elasticity of demand for apple juice with respect to the price of orange juice.

10 When Judy's income increased from €130 to €170 a week, she increased her demand for concert tickets by 15 per cent and decreased her demand for bus rides by 10 per cent. Calculate Judy's income elasticity of demand for (a) concert tickets and (b) bus rides.

11 If a 5 per cent rise in the price of sushi increases the quantity of soy sauce demanded by 2 per cent and decreases the quantity of sushi demanded by 1 per cent, calculate:

a The price elasticity of demand for sushi.

b The cross elasticity of demand for soy sauce with respect to the price of sushi.

12 **Higher Textbook Prices Have Students Saying 'Pass'**

Textbook prices have doubled and risen faster than average prices for the past two decades. Sixty per cent of students do not buy textbooks. Some students hunt for used copies and sell them back at the end of the semester; some buy online, which is often cheaper than the campus store; some use the library copy and wait till it's free; some share the book with a friend.

Source: *Washington Post*, 23 January 2006

Explain what this news clip implies about

a The price elasticity of demand for textbooks.

b The income elasticity of demand for textbooks.

c The cross elasticity of demand for textbooks from the local bookstore with respect to the online price of a textbook.

Use the following information to work Problems 13 to 15.

As Petrol Prices Soar, Buyers Flock to Small Cars

Faced with high petrol prices, Americans are substituting smaller cars for SUVs. In April 2008, Toyota Yaris sales increased 46 per cent and Ford Focus sales increased 32 per cent from a year earlier. Sales of SUVs decreased by more than 25 per cent in 2008 and Chevrolet Tahoe sales fell 35 per cent. Truck sales decreased more than 15 per cent in 2008 and Ford F-series trucks sales decreased by 27 per cent in April 2008. The effect of a downsized vehicle fleet on fuel consumption is unknown. Petrol consumption decreased by 4 per cent in January 2008 from a year earlier. The price of petrol in January 2008 increased by about 30 per cent from a year earlier.

Source: *The New York Times*, 2 May 2009

13 Calculate the price elasticity of demand for petrol.

14 Calculate the cross elasticity of demand for:

a Toyota Yaris with respect to the price of petrol.

b Ford Focus with respect to the price of petrol.

15 Calculate the cross elasticity of demand for:

a Chevrolet Tahoe with respect to the price of petrol.

b A truck with respect to the price of petrol.

16 In 2008, as petrol and food prices increased and home prices slumped, people had less extra income to spend on home improvements. And the improvements that they made were on small inexpensive types of repairs and not major big-ticket items.

a What does this information imply about the income elasticity of demand for big-ticket home-improvement items?

b Would the income elasticity of demand be greater or less than 1? Explain.

Elasticity of Supply (Study Plan 4.3)

17 The table gives the supply schedule of jeans.

Price (euros per pair)	Quantity supplied (pairs per year)
10	240
20	280
30	320
40	360
50	400

Calculate the elasticity of supply when:

a The price falls from €50 to €30 per pair.

b The average price is €30 a pair.

18 A study ranks Paris number 3 in Europe for the most unaffordable housing market in urban locations, behind London and Berlin, and it is deemed severely unaffordable. With significant constraints on the supply of land for residential development, housing inflation has resulted.

a Would the supply of housing in Paris be elastic or inelastic?

b Explain how the elasticity of supply plays an important role in influencing how rapidly housing prices in Paris rise.

19 If a 10 per cent rise in the price of bread increases the quantity of bread supplied by 20 per cent, calculate the elasticity of supply of bread.

20 The elasticity of supply of blue jeans is 4. If the price of a pair of jeans rises by 5 per cent, what is the percentage change in quantity of jeans supplied.

21 A 10 per cent increase in the price of a good has led to a 1 per cent increase in the quantity supplied of the good after one month and to a 25 per cent increase in the quantity supplied after one year.

a Is the supply of this good elastic, unit elastic or inelastic after one month?

b What is the elasticity of supply after one year? Has the supply of this good become more or less elastic? Why?

ADDITIONAL PROBLEMS AND APPLICATIONS

 myeconlab You can work these problems in MyEconLab if assigned by your lecturer.

Price Elasticity of Demand

22 With higher fuel costs, airlines raised their average fare from 75 cents to €1.25 per passenger mile and the number of passenger miles decreased from 2.5 million a day to 1.5 million a day.

  a What is the price elasticity of demand for air travel over this price range?

  b Describe the demand for air travel.

23 The figure shows the demand for DVD rentals.

  a Calculate the elasticity of demand when the price of a DVD rental rises from £3 to £5.

  b At what price is the elasticity of demand for DVD rentals equal to 1?

Use the following table to work Problems 24 to 26.

The demand schedule for computer chips is

Price (euros per chip)	Quantity demanded (millions of chips per year)
200	50
250	45
300	40
350	35
400	30
450	25
500	20

24 **a** What happens to total revenue if the price falls from €400 to €350 a chip and from €350 to €300 a chip?

  b At what price is total revenue at a maximum?

25 At an average price of €350, is the demand for chips elastic, inelastic, or unit elastic? Use the total revenue test to answer this question.

26 At €250 a chip, is the demand for chips elastic or inelastic? Use the total revenue test to answer this question.

27 Your price elasticity of demand for bananas is 4. If the price of bananas rises by 5 per cent, what is

  a The percentage change in the quantity of bananas you buy?

  b The change in your expenditure on bananas?

28 **As Petrol Prices Soar, Americans Slowly Adapt**

As petrol prices rose in March 2008, Americans drove 11 billion fewer miles than in March 2007. Realizing that prices are not going down, Americans are adapting to higher energy costs. Americans spend 3.7 per cent of their disposable income on transportation fuels. How much we spend on petrol depends on the choices we make: what car we drive, where we live, how much time we spend driving, and where we choose to go. For many people, higher energy costs mean fewer restaurant meals, deferred weekend outings, less air travel, and more time closer to home.

Source: *International Herald Tribune,*
23 May 2008

  a List and explain the elasticities of demand that are implicitly referred to in the news clip.

  b Why, according to the news clip, is the demand for petrol inelastic?

More Elasticities of Demand

Use this information to work Problems 29 and 30.

This year people are taking fewer exotic holidays by air and instead are visiting local scenic places by car. The global financial crisis has encouraged many people to cut their holiday budgets.

29 Given the prices of the two holidays, is the income elasticity of demand for exotic holidays positive or negative? Are exotic holidays a normal good or an inferior good? Are local holidays a normal good or an inferior good?

30 Are exotic holidays and local holidays substitutes? Explain your answer.

31 When Alex's income was €3,000, he bought 4 cakes and 12 sandwiches a month. Now his income is €5,000 and he buys 8 cakes and 6 sandwiches a month. Calculate Alex's income elasticity of demand for

  a Cakes.

  b Sandwiches.

32 Wal-Mart's Recession-time Pet Project

During the recession, Wal-Mart moved its pet food and supplies to in front of its other fast-growing business, baby products. Retail experts point out that kids and pets tend to be fairly recession-resistant businesses – even in a recession, dogs will be fed and kids will get their toys.

Source: CNN, 13 May 2008

a What does this news clip imply about the income elasticity of demand for pet food and baby products?

b Would the income elasticity of demand be greater or less than 1? Explain.

33 If a 5 per cent fall in the price of chocolate sauce increases the quantity of chocolate sauce demanded by 10 per cent and increases the quantity of ice cream demanded by 15 per cent, calculate the

a Price elasticity of demand for chocolate sauce.

b Cross elasticity of demand for ice cream with respect to the price of chocolate sauce.

34 Netflix to Offer Online Films

Netflix has introduced a feature to allow customers to watch films on their personal computers. Netflix competes with video rental retailer Blockbuster, which has added an online rental service to its in-store rental service.

Source: CNN, 16 January 2007

a How will watching films online influence the price elasticity of demand for in-store DVD rentals?

b Would the cross elasticity of demand for online films and in-store DVD rentals be negative or positive? Explain.

c Would the cross elasticity of demand for online films with respect to high-speed Internet service be negative or positive? Explain.

35 To Love, Honour and Save Money

In a survey of caterers and event planners, nearly half of them said that they were seeing declines in wedding spending in response to the economic slowdown; 12 per cent even reported wedding cancellations because of financial concerns.

Source: *Time*, 2 June 2008

a Based upon this news clip, are wedding events a normal good or inferior good? Explain.

b Are wedding events more a necessity or a luxury? Would the income elasticity of demand be greater than 1, less than 1, or equal to 1? Explain.

Elasticity of Supply

36 The supply schedule for long-distance phone calls is

Price (pence per minute)	Quantity supplied (millions of mintes per day)
10	200
20	400
30	600
40	800

Calculate the elasticity of supply when:

a The price falls from 40 pence to 30 pence a minute.

b The average price is 20 pence a minute.

37 Weak Coal Prices Hit China's Third-largest Coal Miner

The chairman of Yanzhou Coal Mining reported that the recession had decreased the demand for coal, with its sales falling by 11.9 per cent to 7.92 million tons from 8.99 million tons a year earlier, despite a 10.6 per cent cut in the price.

Source: Dow Jones, 27 April 2009

Calculate the price elasticity of supply of coal. Is the supply of coal elastic or inelastic?

Economics in the News

38 After you have studied *Reading Between the Lines* on pp. 98–99 answer the following questions.

a Which demand is more price elastic and why: grains in general or buckwheat?

b When hot weather destroyed the Russian buckwheat crop and more buckwheat was imported, explain what happened to the supply of buckwheat and to the quantity of buckwheat supplied.

c What factors might increase the demand for buckwheat over time?

d Why can we assume that the demand for buckwheat did not increase over the summer period and how is this related to income elasticity of demand for buckwheat?

Efficiency and Equity

After studying this chapter you will be able to:

◆ Describe the alternative methods of allocating scarce resources

◆ Explain how marginal benefit and marginal cost determine demand and supply

◆ Explain the conditions under which markets are efficient

◆ Explain the main ideas about fairness and evaluate claims that markets result in unfair outcomes

Every time you decide to buy something, whether it's a bunch of roses or an everyday pizza, you express your view about how resources should be used and you make choices in your self-interest. Markets coordinate these choices. But do they allocate resources between roses and pizza and everything else efficiently?

Markets generate huge inequality: is that fair?

Efficiency and fairness (equity) are the two dimensions of the social interest. So our central question is: do markets operate in the social interest?

At the end of the chapter, in *Reading Between the Lines*, we see whether markets coped efficiently with the volcanic ash cloud that shut down Europe's airports in 2010.

Resource Allocation Methods

The goal of this chapter is to evaluate the ability of markets to allocate resources efficiently and fairly. But to see whether the market does a good job, we must compare it with its alternatives. Resources are scarce, so they must be allocated somehow. And trading in markets is just one of several alternative methods.

Resources might be allocated by

◆ Market price

◆ Command

◆ Majority rule

◆ Contest

◆ First-come, first-served

◆ Lottery

◆ Personal characteristics

◆ Force

Let's briefly examine each method.

Market Price

When a market price allocates a scarce resource, the people who are willing and able to pay that price get the resource. Two kinds of people decide not to pay the market price: those who can afford to pay but choose not to buy and those who are too poor and simply can't afford to buy.

For many goods and services, distinguishing between those who choose not to buy and those who can't afford to buy does not matter. But for some goods and services, it does matter. For example, poor people can't afford to pay school fees, pay for healthcare, or save to provide a pension when they retire. Because poor people can't afford these items that most people consider to be essential, in most societies, they are allocated by one of the other methods.

Command

A **command system** allocates resources by the order (command) of someone in authority. A command system is used extensively inside firms, public organizations and government departments. For example, if you have a job, most likely someone tells you what to do. Your labour is allocated to specific tasks by a command.

Command systems work well in organizations in which the lines of authority and responsibility are clear and it is easy to monitor the activities being performed. But a command system works badly when the range of activities to be monitored is large and when these activities are difficult to monitor.

A manager might be able to monitor several employees but a government department cannot monitor every firm in the economy. The system works so badly in North Korea, where it is used in place of markets, that it fails even to deliver an adequate supply of food.

Majority Rule

Majority rule allocates resources in the way that a majority of voters choose. Societies use majority rule to elect representative governments that make some of the biggest decisions. For example, majority rule in each member state of the EU determines the tax rates that eventually allocate scarce resources between private use and public use. Majority rule also determines how tax revenues are allocated among competing uses such as education and healthcare.

Majority rule works well when the decisions being made affect large numbers of people and self-interest must be suppressed to use resources most effectively.

Contest

A contest allocates resources to a winner (or a group of winners). Sporting events use this method.

Manchester United competes with Chelsea to end up at the top of the Premier League and the winner gets the biggest payoff. Andy Murray competes to win tennis matches and get the biggest prize. But contests are more general than those in a sports arena, though we don't normally call them contests. For example, there is a contest among Nokia, Motorola and Sony Ericsson in the mobile phone market. Managers often create contests inside their firms among employees for special bonuses.

Contests work well when the efforts of the 'players' are hard to monitor and reward directly. If everyone is offered the same wage, there is no incentive for anyone to make a special effort. But if a manager offers everyone in the company the opportunity to win a big prize, people are motivated to work hard and try to become the winner. Only a few people win the prize, but many people work harder in the process of trying to win. So total output produced by the workers of the firm is much greater than it would be without the contest.

First-come, First-served

A first-come, first-served method allocates resources to those who are first in line. Many restaurants won't accept reservations. They use first-come, first-served to allocate their scarce tables. Scarce space on congested motorways is allocated in this way too: the first to arrive on the slip-road gets the road space. If too many vehicles enter the motorway, the speed slows and people wait on the slip-road for space to become available.

First-come, first-served works best when a scarce resource can serve just one user at a time in a sequence. By serving the user who arrives first, this method minimizes the time spent waiting for the resource to become available.

Lottery

Lotteries allocate resources to those who pick the winning number, draw the lucky cards, or who pick the winning ticket in a gamble. National lotteries throughout Europe reallocate millions of euros worth of goods and services every year.

But lotteries are more widespread than jackpots and roulette wheels in casinos. Lotteries are used to allocate licensed taxi permits, landing slots to airlines at some airports, fishing rights and the electromagnetic spectrum used by mobile phones.

Lotteries work best when there is no effective way to distinguish among potential users of a scarce resource.

Personal Characteristics

When resources are allocated on the basis of personal characteristics, people with the 'right' characteristics get the resources. Some of the resources that matter most to you are allocated in this way. For example, you will choose a marriage partner on the basis of personal characteristics. But this method is also used in unfair ways: for example, allocating the best jobs to white, able-bodied males and discriminating against minorities, older people, people with disabilities and females.

Force

Force plays a crucial role, for both good and ill, in allocating scarce resources. Let's start with the ill.

War, the use of military force by one nation against another, has played an enormous role historically in allocating resources. The economic supremacy of European settlers in the Americas and Australia owes much to the use of this method.

Theft, the taking of the property of others without their consent, also plays a large role. Local crime and international crime throughout Europe allocate billions of euros worth of resources annually.

But force plays a crucial positive role in allocating resources. It provides the state with an effective method of transferring wealth from the rich to the poor. It also provides the legal framework in which voluntary exchange in markets can take place.

A legal system is the foundation on which our market economy functions. Without courts to enforce contracts, it would not be possible to do business. But the courts could not enforce contracts without the ability to apply force if necessary. The state provides the ultimate force that enables the courts to do their work.

More broadly, the force of the state is essential to uphold the principle of the rule of law. This principle is the bedrock of civilized economic (and social and political) life. With the rule of law upheld, people can go about their daily economic lives with the assurance that their property will be protected – that they can sue for violations against their property (and be sued if they violate the property of others).

Free from the burden of protecting their property and confident in the knowledge that those with whom they trade will honour their agreements, people can get on with focusing on the activity at which they have a comparative advantage and trading for mutual gain.

Review Quiz

1 Why do we need methods of allocating scarce resources?
2 Describe the alternative methods of allocating scarce resources.
3 Provide an example of each allocation method that illustrates when it works well.
4 Provide an example of each allocation method that illustrates when it works badly.

You can work these questions in Study Plan 5.1 and get instant feedback.

In the next sections, we're going to see how a market can achieve an efficient use of resources and serve the social interest. We will also examine the obstacles to efficiency and see how sometimes an alternative method might improve on the market. After looking at efficiency, we'll turn our attention to the more difficult issue of fairness.

Benefit, Cost and Surplus

Resources are allocated efficiently and in the *social interest* when they are used in the ways that people value most highly. You saw in Chapter 2 that this outcome occurs when the quantities produced are at the point on the *PPF* at which marginal benefit equals marginal cost (Chapter 2, pp. 35–37). We're now going to see whether competitive markets produce the efficient quantities. We begin on the demand side of a market.

Demand, Willingness to Pay and Value

In everyday life, we talk about 'getting value for money'. When we use this expression, we are distinguishing between *value* and *price*. Value is what we get and the price is what we pay.

The value of one more unit of a good or service is its marginal benefit. We measure marginal benefit by the maximum price that is willingly paid for another unit of the good or service. But willingness to pay determines demand. *A demand curve is a marginal benefit curve.*

In Figure 5.1(a), Lisa is willing to pay €1 for the 30th slice of pizza and €1 is her marginal benefit from that slice. In Figure 5.1(b), Nick is willing to pay €1 for the 10th slice and €1 is his marginal benefit from that slice. But for what quantity is the economy willing to pay €1? The answer is provided by the market demand curve.

Individual Demand and Market Demand

The relationship between the price of a good and the quantity demanded by one person is called *individual demand*. And the relationship between the price of a good and the quantity demanded by all buyers is called *market demand*.

> **The market demand curve is the horizontal sum of the individual demand curves and is formed by adding the quantities demanded by all the individuals at each price.**

Figure 5.1(c) illustrates the market demand for pizza if Lisa and Nick are the only people. Lisa's demand curve in part (a) and Nick's demand curve in part (b) sum horizontally to the market demand curve in part (c).

Figure 5.1   Individual Demand, Market Demand and Marginal Social Benefit

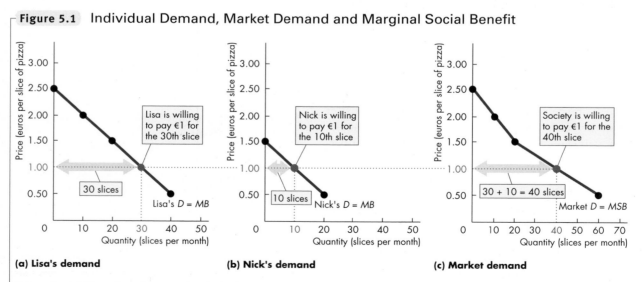

(a) Lisa's demand   **(b) Nick's demand**   **(c) Market demand**

At a price of €1 a slice, the quantity demanded by Lisa is 30 slices and the quantity demanded by Nick is 10 slices, so the quantity demanded by the market is 40 slices.

Lisa's demand curve in part (a) and Nick's demand curve in part (b) sum horizontally to the market demand curve in part (c).

The market demand curve is also the marginal social benefit curve (*MSB*).

At a price of €1 a slice, Lisa demands 30 slices and Nick demands 10 slices, so the quantity demanded by the market at €1 a slice is 40 slices.

For Lisa and Nick, their demand curves are their marginal benefit curves. For society, the market demand curve is the marginal benefit curve. We call the marginal benefit to the entire society marginal social benefit. So the market demand curve is also the *marginal social benefit curve (MSB)*.

Consumer Surplus

We don't always have to pay what we are willing to pay – we get a bargain. When people buy something for less than it is worth to them, they receive a consumer surplus. A **consumer surplus** is the excess of the benefit received from a good over the amount paid for it. We calculate consumer surplus as the marginal benefit (or value) of a good minus its price, summed over the quantity bought.

Figure 5.2(a) shows Lisa's consumer surplus from pizza when the price is €1 a slice. At this price, she buys 30 slices a month because the 30th slice is worth only €1 to her. But Lisa is willing to pay €2 for the 10th slice, so her marginal benefit from this slice is €1 more than she pays for it – she receives a *consumer surplus* of €1 on the 10th slice.

Lisa's consumer surplus is the sum of the surpluses on *all of the slices she buys*. This sum is the area of the green triangle – the area below the demand curve and above the market price line. The area of this triangle is equal to its base (30 slices) multiplied by its height (€1.50) divided by 2, which is €22.50. The area of the blue rectangle in Figure 5.2(a) shows what Lisa pays for 30 slices of pizza.

Figure 5.2(b) shows Nick's consumer surplus. Part (c) shows the consumer surplus for the economy, which is the sum of the consumer surpluses of Lisa and Nick.

All goods and services, like pizza, have decreasing marginal benefit, so people receive more benefit from consumption than the amount they pay.

Supply and Marginal Cost

Your next task is to see how market supply reflects marginal cost. The connection between supply and cost closely parallels the related ideas about demand and benefit that you've just studied. Firms are in business to

---

Figure 5.2   Demand and Consumer Surplus

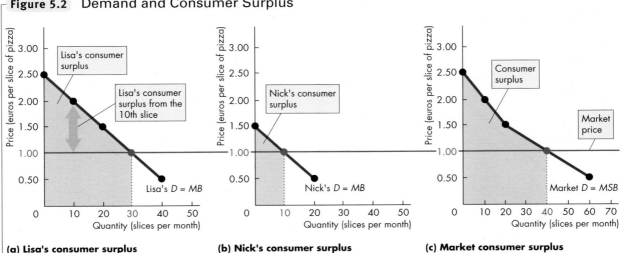

(a) Lisa's consumer surplus

(b) Nick's consumer surplus

(c) Market consumer surplus

Lisa is willing to pay €2.00 for her 10th slice of pizza (part a). At a market price of €1 a slice, Lisa receives a consumer surplus of €1 on the 10th slice. The green triangle shows her consumer surplus on the 30 slices she buys at €1 a slice.

The green triangle in part (b) shows Nick's consumer surplus on the 10 slices he buys at €1 a slice.

The green area in part (c) shows the consumer surplus for the economy. The blue rectangles show the amounts spent on pizza.

make a profit. To do so, they must sell their output for a price that exceeds the cost of production. Let's investigate the relationship between cost and price.

Supply, Cost and Minimum Supply-price

Firms make a profit when they receive more from the sale of a good than the cost of producing it. Just as consumers distinguish between value and price, so producers distinguish between *cost* and *price*. Cost is what a producer gives up and price is what a producer receives.

The cost of producing one more unit of a good or service is its marginal cost. Marginal cost is the minimum price that producers must receive to induce them to offer to sell another unit of the good or service. But the minimum supply-price determines supply. *A supply curve is a marginal cost curve.*

In Figure 5.3(a), Maria is willing to produce the 100th pizza for €15, her marginal cost of that pizza. In Figure 5.3(b), Mario is willing to produce the 50th pizza for €15, his marginal cost of that pizza. But what quantity is the economy willing to produce for €15 a pizza? The answer is provided by the *market supply curve*.

Individual Supply and Market Supply

The relationship between the price of a good and the quantity supplied by one producer is called *individual supply*. And the relationship between the price of a good and the quantity supplied by all producers is called *market supply*.

> The market supply curve is the horizontal sum of the individual supply curves and is formed by adding the quantities supplied by all the producers at each price.

Figure 5.3(c) illustrates the market supply if Maria and Mario are the only producers. Maria's supply curve in part (a) and Mario's supply curve in part (b) sum horizontally to the market supply curve in part (c).

At a price of €15 a pizza, Maria supplies 100 pizzas and Mario supplies 50 pizzas, so the quantity supplied by the market at €15 a pizza is 150 pizzas.

For Maria and Mario, their supply curves are their marginal cost curves. For society, the market supply curve is the society's marginal cost curve. We call the society's marginal cost the *marginal social cost*. So the market supply curve is also the *marginal social cost curve (MSC)*.

Figure 5.3 Individual Supply, Market Supply and Marginal Social Cost

(a) Maria's supply

(b) Mario's supply

(c) Market supply

At a price of €15 a pizza, the quantity supplied by Maria is 100 pizzas and the quantity supplied by Mario is 50 pizzas, so the quantity supplied by the market is 150 pizzas.

Maria's supply curve in part (a) and Mario's supply curve in part (b) sum horizontally to the market supply curve in part (c).

The market supply curve is also the marginal social cost curve (*MSC*).

myeconlab Animation

Producer Surplus

When price exceeds marginal cost, the firm receives a producer surplus. A **producer surplus** is the excess of the amount received from the sale of a good or service over the cost of producing it. Producer surplus is calculated as the price received for a good minus its minimum supply-price (or marginal cost), summed over the quantity sold.

Figure 5.4(a) shows Maria's producer surplus from pizzas when the price is €15 a pizza. At this price, she sells 100 pizzas a month because the 100th pizza costs her €15 to produce. But Maria is willing to produce the 50th pizza for her marginal cost, which is €10. So she receives a *producer surplus* of €5 on this pizza.

Maria's producer surplus is the sum of the surpluses on each pizza she sells. This sum is the area of the blue triangle – the area below the market price and above the supply curve. The area of this triangle is equal to its base (100) multiplied by its height (€10) divided by 2, which is €500. The red area in Figure 5.4(a) below the supply curve shows what it costs Maria to produce 100 pizzas.

The area of the blue triangle in Figure 5.4(b) shows Mario's producer surplus and the blue area in Figure

5.4(c) shows the producer surplus for the market. The producer surplus for the market is the sum of the producer surpluses of Maria and Mario.

Consumer surplus and producer surplus can be used to measure the efficiency of a market. Let's see how we can use these concepts to study the efficiency of a competitive market.

> ### Review Quiz
>
> 1 What is the relationship between the marginal benefit, value and demand?
> 2 What is the relationship between individual demand and market demand?
> 3 What is consumer surplus? How is it measured?
> 4 What is the relationship between the marginal cost, minimum supply-price and supply?
> 5 What is the relationship between individual supply and market supply?
> 6 What is producer surplus? How is it measured?
>
> You can work these questions in Study Plan 5.2 and get instant feedback.

Figure 5.4 Supply and Producer Surplus

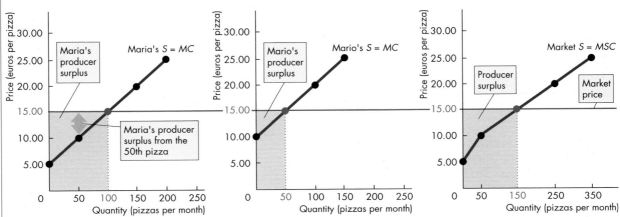

(a) Maria's producer surplus   **(b) Mario's producer surplus**   **(c) Market producer surplus**

Maria is willing to produce the 50th pizza for €10 in part (a). At a market price of €15 a pizza, Maria gets a producer surplus of €5 on the 50th pizza. The blue triangle shows her producer surplus on the 100 pizzas that she sells at €15 each.

The blue triangle in part (b) shows Mario's producer surplus on the 50 pizzas that he sells at €15 each.

The blue area in part (c) shows the producer surplus for the market. The red areas show the costs of producing the pizzas sold.

myeconlab Animation

Is the Competitive Market Efficient?

Figure 5.5(a) shows the market for pizza. The market forces that you studied in Chapter 3 (pp. 66–67) will pull the pizza market to its equilibrium price of €15 a pizza and equilibrium quantity of 10,000 pizzas a day. Buyers enjoy a consumer surplus (green area) and sellers enjoy a producer surplus (blue area). But is this competitive equilibrium efficient?

Efficiency of Competitive Equilibrium

You've seen that the market demand curve for a good or service tells us the marginal social benefit from it. You've also seen that the market supply of a good or service tells us the marginal social cost of producing it.

Equilibrium in a competitive market occurs when the quantity demanded equals the quantity supplied at the intersection of the demand curve and the supply curve. At this intersection point, marginal social benefit on the demand curve equals marginal social cost on the supply curve. This equality is the condition for allocative efficiency. So in equilibrium, a competitive market achieves allocative efficiency.

Figure 5.5 illustrates the efficiency of the competitive equilibrium. The demand curve and the supply curve intersect in part (a) and marginal social benefit equals marginal social cost in part (b). This condition delivers an efficient use of resources for the society.

If production is less than 10,000 pizzas a day, the marginal pizza is valued more highly than it costs to produce it. If production exceeds 10,000 pizzas a day, it costs more to produce the marginal pizza than the value consumers place on it. Only when 10,000 pizzas a day are produced is the marginal pizza worth what it costs to produce.

The competitive market pushes the quantity of pizzas produced to its efficient level of 10,000 a day. If production is less than 10,000 pizzas a day, a shortage raises the price of a pizza, which increases production. If production exceeds 10,000 pizzas a day, a surplus lowers the price of a pizza, which decreases production. So a competitive pizza market is efficient.

Figure 5.5(a) also shows the consumer surplus and the producer surplus. The sum of consumer surplus and producer surplus is called **total surplus**. When the efficient quantity is produced, total surplus is maximized. Buyers and sellers acting in their self-interest end up promoting the social interest.

Figure 5.5 An Efficient Market for Pizza

(a) Equilibrium and surpluses

(b) Efficiency

Competitive equilibrium in part (a) occurs when the quantity demanded equals the quantity supplied. Resources are used efficiently in part (b) when marginal social benefit, *MSB*, equals marginal social cost, *MSC*. Total surplus, which is the sum of consumer surplus (green triangle) and producer surplus (blue triangle) is maximized.

The efficient quantity in part (b) is the same as the equilibrium quantity in part (a). The competitive pizza market produces the efficient quantity of pizza.

myeconlab Animation

◆ ECONOMICS IN ACTION

The Invisible Hand

Writing in his book, *The Wealth of Nations*, in 1776, Adam Smith was the first to suggest that competitive markets send resources to the uses in which they have the highest value. Smith believed that each participant in a competitive market is 'led by an invisible hand to promote an end [the efficient use of resources] which was no part of his intention'.

You can see the invisible hand at work in the cartoon and in the world today.

Umbrella for Sale

The cold drinks vendor has both cold drinks and shade and he has a marginal cost and a minimum supply-price of each. The reader on the park bench has a marginal benefit and a willingness to pay for each.

The reader's marginal benefit from shade exceeds the vendor's marginal cost; but the vendor's marginal cost of a cold drink exceeds the reader's marginal benefit. They trade the umbrella. The vendor gets a producer surplus from selling the shade for more than its marginal cost and the reader gets a consumer surplus from buying the shade for less than its marginal benefit. Both are better off and the umbrella has moved to its highest-valued use.

The Invisible Hand at Work Today

The market economy relentlessly performs the activity illustrated in the cartoon to achieve an efficient allocation of resources.

A European frost cuts the supply of grapes. With fewer grapes available, the marginal social benefit increases. A shortage of grapes raises their price, so the market allocates the smaller quantity available to the people who value them most highly.

A new technology cuts the cost of producing a laptop. With a lower production cost, the supply of laptops increases and the price falls. The lower price encourages an increase in the quantity demanded. The marginal social benefit from a laptop is brought to equality with its marginal social cost.

© Mike Twohy/The New Yorker Collection/
www.cartoonbank.com

Market Failure

Markets do not always achieve an efficient outcome. We call a situation in which a market delivers an inefficient outcome one of **market failure**. Market failure can occur because too little of a good or service is produced (underproduction) or too much is produced (overproduction). We'll describe these two market failure outcomes and then see why they arise.

Underproduction

Figure 5.6(a) shows that the quantity of pizzas produced is 5,000 a day. At this quantity, consumers are willing to pay €20 for a pizza that costs only €10 to produce. The total surplus from pizza is smaller than its maximum possible. The quantity produced is inefficient – there is underproduction.

We measure the scale of inefficiency by **deadweight**

Figure 5.6   Underproduction and Overproduction

(a) Underproduction

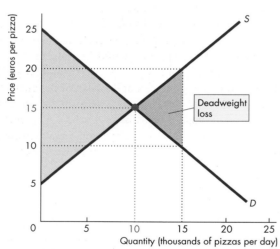

(b) Overproduction

If pizza production is cut to only 5,000 a day, a deadweight loss (the grey triangle) arises in part (a). Consumer surplus and producer surplus (the green and blue areas) are reduced. At 5,000 pizzas, the benefit of one more pizza exceeds its cost. The same is true for all levels of production up to 10,000 pizzas a day.

If production increases to 15,000 pizzas a day, a deadweight loss arises in part (b). At 15,000 pizzas a day, the cost of the 15,000th pizza exceeds its benefit. The cost of each pizza above 10,000 exceeds its benefit. Consumer surplus plus producer surplus equals the sum of the green and blue areas minus the deadweight loss triangle.

loss, which is the decrease in total surplus that results from an inefficient level of production. The grey triangle in Figure 5.6(a) shows the deadweight loss.

Overproduction

In Figure 5.6(b), the quantity of pizzas produced is 15,000 a day. At this quantity, consumers are willing to pay only €10 for a pizza that costs €20 to produce. By producing the 15,000th pizza, €10 of resources are wasted. Again, the grey triangle shows the deadweight loss, which reduces the total surplus to less than its maximum.

Inefficient production creates a deadweight loss that is borne by the entire society: it is a *social* loss.

Sources of Market Failure

Obstacles to efficiency that bring market failure and create deadweight loss are:

◆ Price and quantity regulations
◆ Taxes and subsidies
◆ Externalities
◆ Public goods and common resources
◆ Monopoly
◆ High transactions costs

Price and Quantity Regulations

Price regulations that put a cap on the rent a landlord can charge and laws that require employers to pay a minimum wage sometimes block the price adjustments that balance the quantity demanded and the quantity supplied and lead to underproduction. *Quantity regulations* that limit the amount that a farm is permitted to produce also lead to underproduction.

Taxes and Subsidies

Taxes increase the prices paid by buyers and lower the prices received by sellers. So taxes decrease the quantity produced and lead to underproduction. *Subsidies*, which are payments by the government to producers, decrease the prices paid by buyers and increase the prices received by sellers. So subsidies increase the quantity produced and lead to overproduction.

Externalities

An *externality* is a cost or a benefit that affects someone other than the seller or the buyer of a good or service.

An electric power utility creates an external cost by burning coal that brings acid rain and crop damage. The utility doesn't consider the cost of pollution when it decides how much power to produce. The result is overproduction. An apartment owner would provide an *external benefit* if she installed a smoke detector. But she doesn't consider her neighbour's marginal benefit when she is deciding whether to install a smoke detector. There is underproduction.

Public Goods and Common Resources

A *public good* is a good or service that is consumed simultaneously by everyone even if they don't pay for it. Examples are national defence and law enforcement. Competitive markets would underproduce a public good because of the *free-rider problem*: it is in each person's interest to free ride on everyone else and avoid paying for her or his share of a public good.

A *common resource* is owned by no one but used by everyone. Atlantic cod is an example. It is in everyone's self-interest to ignore the costs of their own use of a common resource that fall on others (called the *tragedy of the commons*), which leads to overproduction.

Monopoly

A *monopoly* is a firm that is the sole provider of a good or service. Local water supply and cable television are supplied by firms that are monopolies. The self-interest of a monopoly is to maximize its profit. The monopoly has no competitors, so it can set the price to achieve its self-interested goal. To achieve its goal, a monopoly produces too little and charges too high a price. It leads to underproduction.

High Transactions Costs

Retail markets employ enormous quantities of scarce labour and capital resources. It is costly to operate any market. Economists call the opportunity costs of making trades in a market **transactions costs**.

To use market price to allocate scarce resources, it must be worth bearing the opportunity cost of establishing a market. Some markets are just too costly to operate. For example, when you want to play tennis on your local 'free' court, you don't pay a market price for use of the court. You wait until the court becomes vacant and you 'pay' with your waiting time. When transactions costs are high, the market might underproduce.

You now know the conditions under which resource allocation is efficient. You've seen how a competitive market can be efficient and you've seen some impediments to efficiency.

Alternatives to the Market

When a market is inefficient, can one of the alternative non-market methods that we described at the beginning of this chapter do a better job? Sometimes it can.

Often, majority rule might be used but majority rule has its own shortcomings. A group that pursues the self-interest of its members can become the majority. For example, a price or quantity regulation that creates a deadweight loss is almost always the result of a self-interested group becoming the majority and imposing costs on the minority. Also, with majority rule, votes must be translated into actions by bureaucrats who have their own agendas based on their self-interest.

Managers in firms issue commands and avoid the transactions costs which would arise if they went to a market every time they needed a job done.

First-come, first-served saves a lot of hassle. A queue could have markets in which people trade their place in the queue – but someone would have to enforce the agreements. Can you imagine the hassle at a busy ATM if you had to buy your spot at the head of the queue?

There is no one efficient mechanism for allocating resources efficiently. But markets, when supplemented by majority rule, command systems inside firms and occasionally by first-come, first-served work well.

Review Quiz

1   Do competitive markets use resources efficiently? Explain why or why not.
2   What is deadweight loss and under what conditions does it occur?
3   What are the obstacles to achieving an efficient allocation of resources in the market economy?

You can work these questions in Study Plan 5.3 and get instant feedback.

Is an efficient allocation of resources also a fair allocation? Does the competitive market provide people with fair incomes and do people always pay a fair price? Don't we need the government to step into some competitive markets to prevent the price from falling too low or rising too high? Let's now study these questions.

Is the Competitive Market Fair?

When a natural disaster strikes, such as a severe winter storm or a major flood, the prices of many essential items jump. The reason the prices jump is that some people have a greater demand and greater willingness to pay when the items are in limited supply. So the higher prices achieve an efficient allocation of scarce resources. News reports of these price hikes almost never talk about efficiency. Instead, they talk about equity or fairness. The claim often made is that it is unfair for profit-seeking dealers to cheat the victims of natural disaster.

Similarly, when low-skilled people work for a wage that is below what most would regard as a 'living wage', the media and politicians talk of employers taking unfair advantage of their workers.

How do we decide whether something is fair or unfair? You know when *you* think something is unfair. But how do you know? What are the *principles* of fairness?

Philosophers have tried for centuries to answer this question. Economists have offered their answers too. But before we look at the proposed answers, you should know that there is no universally agreed upon answer.

Economists agree about efficiency. That is, they agree that it makes sense to make the economic pie as large as possible and to bake it at the lowest possible cost. But they do not agree about equity. That is, they do not agree about what are fair shares of the economic pie for all the people who make it. The reason is that ideas about fairness are not exclusively economic ideas. They touch on politics, ethics and religion. Nevertheless, economists have thought about these issues and have a contribution to make. So let's examine the views of economists on this topic.

To think about fairness, think of economic life as a game – a serious game. All ideas about fairness can be divided into two broad groups. They are:

◆ It's not fair if the *result* isn't fair.
◆ It's not fair if the *rules* aren't fair.

It's Not Fair if the *Result* Isn't Fair

The earliest efforts to establish a principle of fairness were based on the view that the result is what matters. The general idea was that it is unfair if people's incomes are too unequal. It is unfair that bank presidents earn millions of pounds a year while bank tellers earn only thousands of pounds a year. It is unfair that a shop owner enjoys a large profit and her customers pay higher prices in the aftermath of a flood.

There was a lot of excitement during the nineteenth century when economists thought they had made the incredible discovery that efficiency requires equality of incomes. To make the economic pie as large as possible, it must be cut into equal pieces, one for each person. This idea turns out to be wrong, but there is a lesson in the reason that it is wrong. So this nineteenth century idea is worth a closer look.

Utilitarianism

The nineteenth-century idea that only equality brings efficiency is called *utilitarianism*. **Utilitarianism** is a principle that states that we should strive to achieve 'the greatest happiness for the greatest number'. The people who developed this idea were known as utilitarians. They included some famous thinkers, such as Jeremy Bentham and John Stuart Mill.

Utilitarianism argues that to achieve 'the greatest happiness for the greatest number', income must be transferred from the rich to the poor up to the point of complete equality – to the point that there are no rich and no poor.

They reasoned in the following way: first, everyone has the same basic wants and are similar in their capacity to enjoy life. Second, the greater a person's income, the smaller is the marginal benefit of a pound. The millionth pound spent by a rich person brings a smaller marginal benefit to that person than the marginal benefit of the thousandth pound spent by a poorer person. So by transferring a pound from the millionaire to the poorer person, more is gained than is lost and the two people added together are better off.

Figure 5.7 illustrates this utilitarian idea. Tom and Jerry have the same marginal benefit curve, *MB*. (Marginal benefit is measured on the same scale of 1 to 3 for both Tom and Jerry.) Tom is at point *A*. He earns €5,000 a year and his marginal benefit of a pound is 3. Jerry is at point *B*. He earns €45,000 a year and his marginal benefit of a pound is 1. If a euro is transferred from Jerry to Tom, Jerry loses 1 unit of marginal benefit and Tom gains 3 units. So together, Tom and Jerry are better off. They are sharing the economic pie more efficiently. If a second euro is transferred, the same thing happens: Tom gains more than Jerry loses. And the same is true for every euro transferred until they both reach point *C*. At point *C*, Tom and Jerry have €25,000 each and each has a marginal benefit of 2 units. Now they are sharing the economic pie in the most efficient way. It is bringing the greatest attainable happiness to Tom and Jerry.

Figure 5.7   Utilitarian Fairness

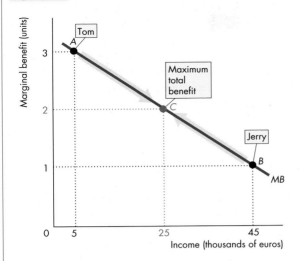

Tom earns €5,000 and has 3 units of marginal benefit at point A. Jerry earns €45,000 and has 1 unit of marginal benefit at point B. If income is transferred from Jerry to Tom, Jerry's loss is less than Tom's gain. Only when they have €25,000 each and 2 units of marginal benefit (at point C) can the sum of their total benefits increase no further.

myeconlab Animation ────────────────◆

The Big Trade-off

One big problem with the utilitarian ideal of complete equality is that it ignores the costs of making income transfers. The economist, Arthur Okun, in his book *Equality and Efficiency: The Big Tradeoff*, says the process of redistributing income is like trying to transfer water from one barrel to another with a leaky bucket. The more we try to increase equity by redistributing income, the more we reduce efficiency. Recognizing the cost of making income transfers leads to what is called the **big trade-off** – a trade-off between efficiency and fairness.

The big trade-off is based on the following facts. Income can be transferred from people with high incomes to people with low incomes only by taxing the high incomes. Taxing people's income from employment makes them work less. It results in the quantity of labour being less than the efficient quantity. Taxing people's income from capital makes them save less. It results in the quantity of capital being less than the efficient quantity. With smaller quantities of both labour and capital, the quantity of goods and

services produced is less than the efficient quantity. The economic pie shrinks.

The trade-off is between the size of the economy and the degree of equality with which its produce is shared. The greater the amount of income redistribution through income taxes, the greater the inefficiency – the smaller is the economic pie.

A second source of inefficiency arises because a euro taken from a rich person does not end up as a euro in the hands of a poorer person. Some of it is spent on administration of the tax and transfer system. The cost of the tax-collection agency, Revenue & Customs, and the welfare administering agency, Department of Work and Pensions, must be paid with some of the taxes collected.

Also, taxpayers hire accountants, auditors and lawyers to help ensure that they pay the correct amount of taxes. These activities use skilled labour and capital resources that could otherwise be used to produce goods and services that people value.

You can see that when all these costs are taken into account, taking a euro from a rich person does not give a euro to a poor person. It is even possible that with high taxes, those with low incomes end up being worse off. Suppose, for example, that highly taxed entrepreneurs decide to work less hard and shut down some of their businesses. Low-income workers get fired and must seek other, perhaps even lower-paid, work.

Because of the big trade-off, those who say that fairness is equality propose a modified version of utilitarianism.

Make the Poorest as Well Off as Possible

A Harvard philosopher, John Rawls, proposed a modified version of utilitarianism in a classic book entitled *A Theory of Justice*, published in 1971. Rawls says that, taking all the costs of income transfers into account, the fair distribution of the economic pie is the one that makes the poorest person as well off as possible.

The incomes of rich people should be taxed and, after paying the costs of administering the tax and transfer system, what is left should be transferred to the poor. But the taxes must not be so high that they make the economic pie shrink to the point that the poorest person ends up with a smaller piece. A bigger share of a smaller pie can be less than a smaller share of a bigger pie. The goal is to make the piece enjoyed by the poorest person as big as possible. Most likely this piece will not be an equal share.

The 'fair results' idea requires a change in the results after the game is over. Some economists say these changes are themselves unfair and they propose a different way of thinking about fairness.

It's Not Fair if the *Rules* Aren't Fair

The idea that it's not fair if the rules aren't fair is based on a fundamental principle that seems to be hard-wired into the human brain. It is the **symmetry principle**. The symmetry principle is the requirement that people in similar situations be treated similarly. It is the moral principle that lies at the centre of all the big religions. It says, in some form or other, 'behave towards others in the way you expect them to behave towards you'.

In economic life, this principle translates into *equality of opportunity*. But equality of opportunity to do what? This question is answered by the Harvard philosopher, Robert Nozick, in a book entitled *Anarchy, State and Utopia*, published in 1974. Nozick argues that the idea of fairness as an outcome or result cannot work and that fairness must be based on the fairness of the rules. He suggests that fairness obeys two rules:

1 The state must enforce laws that establish and protect private property.

2 Private property may be transferred from one person to another only by voluntary exchange.

The first rule says that everything that is valuable must be owned by individuals and that the state must ensure that theft is prevented. The second rule says that the only legitimate way a person can acquire property is to buy it in exchange for something else that the person owns. If these rules, which are fair rules, are followed, then the result is fair. It doesn't matter how unequally the economic pie is shared, provided that the pie is baked by people, each one of whom voluntarily provides services in exchange for a share of the pie offered in compensation.

These rules satisfy the symmetry principle. And if these rules are not followed, the symmetry principle is broken. You can see these facts by imagining a world in which the laws are not followed.

First, suppose that some resources or goods are not owned. They are common property. Then everyone is free to participate in a grab to use these resources or goods. The strongest will prevail. But when the strongest prevails, the strongest effectively *owns* the resources or goods in question and prevents others from enjoying them.

Second, suppose that we do not insist on voluntary exchange for transferring ownership of resources from one person to another. The alternative is *involuntary* transfer. In simple language, the alternative is theft.

Both of these situations violate the symmetry principle. Only the strong get to acquire what they want.

The weak end up with only the resources and goods that the strong don't want.

In contrast, if the two rules of fairness are followed, everyone, strong and weak, is treated in a similar way. All individuals are free to use their resources and human skills to create things that are valued by themselves and others and to exchange the fruits of their efforts with all others. This is the only set of arrangements that obeys the symmetry principle.

Fairness and Efficiency

If private property rights are enforced and if voluntary exchange takes place in a competitive market, resources will be allocated efficiently if there are no:

1 Price and quantity regulations

2 Taxes and subsidies

3 Externalities

4 Public goods and common resources

5 Monopolies

6 High transactions costs

And according to the Nozick rules, the resulting distribution of income and wealth will be fair. Let's study a concrete example to examine the claim that if resources are allocated efficiently, they are also allocated fairly.

Case Study: A Water Shortage in a Natural Disaster

A severe winter storm has broken the pipes that deliver drinking water to a city. Bottled water is available, but there is no tap water. What is the fair way to allocate the bottled water?

Market Price

Suppose that if the water is allocated by market price, the price jumps to €8 a bottle – five times its normal price. At this price, the people who own water can make a large profit by selling it. People who are willing and able to pay €8 a bottle get the water. And because most people can't afford the €8 price, they end up either without water or consuming just a few drops a day.

You can see that the water is being used efficiently. There is a fixed amount available, some people are willing to pay €8 to get a bottle and the water goes to those people. The people who own and sell water receive a large producer surplus. Total surplus (the sum of consumer surplus and producer surplus) is maximized.

In the rules view, the outcome is also fair. No one is denied the water they are willing to pay for. In the results view, the outcome would most likely be regarded as unfair. The lucky owners of water make a killing and the poorest end up the thirstiest.

Non-market Methods

Suppose that by a majority vote, the citizens decide that the government will buy all the water, pay for it with a tax and use one of the non-market methods to allocate the water to the citizens. The possibilities now are:

Command

Someone decides who is the most deserving. Perhaps everyone is given an equal share or perhaps government officials and their families get most of the water.

Contest

Bottles of water are prizes that go to those who are best at a particular contest.

First-come, first-served

Water goes to the first off the mark or to those who place the lowest value on their time and can afford to queue for it.

Lottery

Water goes to those in luck.

Personal characteristics

Water goes to those with the 'right' characteristics. For example, the old, the young or pregnant women.

These non-market methods deliver an allocation of water that is fair and efficient only by chance. In the rules view they are unfair because the distribution involves involuntary transfers of resources among citizens. In the results view they are unfair because the poorest don't end up being made as well off as possible.

The allocation is inefficient for two reasons. First, resources are used to operate the allocation scheme. Second, some people are willing to pay for more water than they have been allocated and others have been allocated more water than they are willing to pay for.

The second source of inefficiency can be overcome if, after the non-market allocation, people are permitted to trade water at its market price. Those who value water below the market price will sell and those who are willing to pay the market price will buy. Those who value the water most highly are the ones who consume it.

Market Price with Taxes

Another approach is to allocate the scarce water using the market price but then to alter the redistribution of buying power by taxing the sellers of water and providing benefits to the poor.

Suppose water owners are taxed on each bottle sold and the revenue from these taxes is given to the poorest people. People are then free, starting from this new distribution of buying power, to trade water at the market price. Because the owners of water are taxed on what they sell, they have a weaker incentive to offer water for sale and the supply decreases. The equilibrium price rises to more than €8 a bottle. There is now a deadweight loss in the market for water – similar to the loss that arises from underproduction on p. 113. (We study the effects of a tax and show its inefficiency in Chapter 6 on pp. 133–137.)

So the tax is inefficient. In the rules view, the tax is also unfair because it forces the owners of water to make a transfer to others. In the results view, the outcome might be regarded as being fair.

This brief case study illustrates the complexity of ideas about fairness. Economists have a clear criterion of efficiency but no comparably clear criterion of fairness. Most economists regard Nozick as being too extreme and want a fair tax in the rules. But there is no consensus about what would be a fair tax.

Review Quiz

1   What are the two big approaches to fairness?
2   Explain the utilitarian idea of fairness and what is wrong with it.
3   Explain the big trade-off and the idea of fairness developed to deal with it.
4   What is the main idea of fairness based on fair rules? Explain your answer.

You can work these questions in Study Plan 5.4 and get instant feedback.

You've now studied efficiency and equity, or fairness, the two biggest issues that run right through the whole of economics. *Reading Between the Lines* on pp. 120–121 looks at an example of an efficient market in our economy today. At many points throughout this book – and in your life – you will return to and use the ideas about efficiency and fairness that you've learned in this chapter. In the next chapter, we study some sources of *in*efficiency and *un*fairness.

Reading Between the Lines

Efficiency in Ash Cloud

The Associated Press, 19 April 2010

Volcano Cloud Hangs Over European Economy

Tom Odula

The ash cloud from Iceland's volcanic eruption is battering airlines. . . . Each new day of closed airspace is costing jobs or revenues for those dealing in perishables such as roses and mozzarella.

But the volcano disruption is also creating some winners, such as fully booked Scandinavian ferries, hotel owners charging $800 a night and taxi drivers pocketing $5,000 fares. . . .

Some 5,000 workers have been temporarily laid off in Kenya following $12 million in losses in flowers. . . . Still, express delivery services Federal Express and DHL said they have shifted many deliveries onto trucks and rail to limit their losses. . . . And most international commerce remained unaffected, since it is largely routed by sea, said Keith Rockwell, spokesman for the World Trade Organization.

'I wouldn't envision this affecting high-tech or other services trade, but it is terrible for those sectors that are affected,' Rockwell said, citing tourism and exports of fresh produce and flowers.

While travellers managed as best they could within Europe, those waiting for long-haul connections had less options. Rising hotel prices weren't making it easier.

'Yesterday, we had a hotel room at 250 euros. At midday, it was 460 euros, and in the evening, the price was 800 euros for a room – we can't pay that,' said Daniel, a 39-year-old French tourist, as he waited at Hong Kong's airport.

The Essence of the Story

◆ The ash cloud from an active Icelandic volcano closed airspace and disrupted air transport in Europe.

◆ The volcano disruption created both losers and winners.

◆ Among the winners were Scandinavian ferries, hotel owners and taxi drivers, who sold more and for higher prices.

◆ Among the losers were flower growers in Kenya, Federal Express and DHL and people stranded and facing higher hotel prices.

Economic Analysis

◆ On a normal day, growers around the world send 20 million flowers for auction in Holland. These flowers are then distributed around the world to their buyers. All this transport is done by air.

◆ When an ash cloud closed Holland's airports, alternative but more costly arrangements were quickly made to fly flowers in and out of Athens and Madrid and transport them by truck to Holland.

◆ Figure 1 illustrates the effects of the ash cloud. The demand curve (marginal benefit curve) shifted leftward from D_0 to D_1; the supply curve (marginal cost curve) also shifted leftward from S_0 to S_1; and the flower auction found the new equilibrium and efficient outcome.

◆ In Figure 1, the quantity of flowers traded decreased, but the price did not change. Both demand and supply were influenced by the loss of air transportation and decreased by the same amount.

◆ Consumer surplus (green) and producer surplus (blue) decreased, but total surplus was at its maximum given the situation.

◆ In the market for hotel rooms, there were winners as well as losers.

◆ Figure 2 illustrates the effects of the ash cloud in the market for hotel rooms. The demand curve (marginal benefit curve) shifted rightward from D_0 to D_1 but the supply curve didn't change. The price and the quantity increased.

◆ Consumer surplus (green) shrank and producer surplus (blue) expanded.

◆ Because at the new quantity and price marginal socal cost equalled marginal social benefit, the outcome was efficient.

Figure 1 **Dutch flower market: 19 April 2010**

Traders at the daily flower auction in Holland

Figure 2 **Market for hotel rooms: 19 April 2010**

SUMMARY

Key Points

Resource Allocation Methods
(pp. 106–107)

◆ Because resources are scarce, some mechanism must allocate them.

◆ The alternative allocation methods are market price; command; majority rule; contest; first-come, first-served; lottery; personal characteristics; and force.

Working Problems 1 and 2 will give you a better understanding of resource allocation methods.

Benefit, Cost and Surplus
(pp. 108–111)

◆ The maximum price willingly paid is marginal benefit, so a demand curve is a marginal benefit curve.

◆ The market demand curve is the horizontal sum of the individual demand curves and is the marginal social benefit curve.

◆ Value is what people are *willing to* pay; price is what people *must* pay.

◆ Consumer surplus is the excess of the benefit received from a good or service over the amount paid for it.

◆ The minimum supply-price is the marginal cost, so a supply curve is also a marginal cost curve.

◆ The market supply curve is the horizontal sum of the individual supply curves and is the marginal social cost curve.

◆ Cost is what producers pay; price is what producers receive.

◆ Producer surplus is the excess of the amount received from the sale of a good or service over the cost of producing it.

Working Problems 3 to 10 will give you a better understanding of benefit, cost and surplus.

Is the Competitive Market Efficient?
(pp. 112–115)

◆ In a competitive equilibrium, marginal social benefit equals marginal social cost and resource allocation is efficient.

◆ Buyers and sellers acting in their self-interest end up promoting the social interest.

◆ The sum of consumer surplus and producer surplus is maximized. Producing less than or more than the efficient quantity creates deadweight loss.

◆ Price and quantity regulations; taxes and subsidies; externalities; public goods and common resources; monopoly; and high transactions costs can create inefficiency and deadweight loss.

Working Problems 11 to 13 will give you a better understanding of the efficiency of competitive markets.

Is the Competitive Market Fair?
(pp. 116–119)

◆ Ideas about fairness divide into two groups: fair results and fair rules.

◆ Fair-results ideas require income transfers from the rich to the poor.

◆ Fair-rules ideas require property rights and voluntary exchange.

Working Problems 14 and 15 will give you a better understanding of the fairness of competitive markets.

Key Terms

Big trade-off, 117
Command system, 106
Consumer surplus, 109
Deadweight loss, 113
Market failure, 113
Producer surplus, 111
Symmetry principle, 118
Total surplus, 112
Transactions costs, 115
Utilitarianism, 116

STUDY PLAN PROBLEMS AND APPLICATIONS

 You can work Problems 1 to 17 in MyEconLab Chapter 5 Study Plan and get instant feedback.

Resource Allocation Methods

(Study Plan 5.1)

Use the following information to work Problems 1 and 2.

At Fifteen, the Jamie Oliver restaurant in London, reservations are essential. At Square, a restaurant in Leeds, reservations are recommended. At Maddisons, a restaurant in York, reservations are not accepted.

1 **a** Describe the method of allocating scarce table resources at these three restaurants.

   b Why do you think restaurants have different reservations policies?

2 Why do you think restaurants don't use the market price to allocate their tables?

Benefit, Cost and Surplus (Study Plan 5.2)

Use the following table to work Problems 3 to 5.

The table gives the demand schedules for train travel for the only buyers in the market: Ann, Beth and Cathy.

Price (euros per kilometre)	Quantity demanded (kilometres)		
	Ann	**Beth**	**Cathy**
3	30	25	20
4	25	20	15
5	20	15	10
6	15	10	5
7	10	5	0
8	5	0	0
9	0	0	0

3 Construct the market demand schedule. What is the maximum price that Ann, Beth and Cathy are willing to pay to travel 20 kilometres? Why?

4 When the total distance travelled is 60 kilometres,

   a What is the marginal social benefit? Why?

   b What is the marginal private benefit for each person and how many kilometres does each person travel?

5 When the price is €4 a kilometre,

   a What is each traveller's consumer surplus?

   b What is the market consumer surplus?

Use the following news clip to work Problems 6 and 7.

eBay Saves Billions for Bidders

If you think you would save money by bidding on eBay auctions, you would probably be right. Two Maryland researchers calculated the difference between the actual purchase price paid for auction items and the top price bidders stated they were willing to pay. They found that the difference averaged at least €4 per auction.

Source: *Information Week*, 28 January 2008

6 What method is used to allocate goods on eBay? How does the allocation method used by eBay auctions influence consumer surplus?

7 **a** Can an eBay auction give the seller a surplus?

   b On a graph show the consumer surplus and producer surplus from an eBay auction.

Use the following table to work Problems 8 to 10.

The table gives the supply schedules of hot air balloon rides for the only sellers in the market: Xavier, Yasmin and Zack.

Price (euros per ride)	Quantity supplied (rides)		
	Xavier	**Yasmin**	**Zack**
100	30	25	20
90	25	20	15
80	20	15	10
70	15	10	5
60	10	5	0
50	5	0	0
40	0	0	0

8 Construct the market supply schedule. What are the minimum prices that Xavier, Yasmin and Zack are willing to accept to supply 20 rides? Why?

9 When the total number of rides is 30,

   a What is the marginal social cost of a ride?

   b What is the marginal cost for each supplier and how many rides does each of the firms supply?

10 When the price is €70 a ride,

   a What is each firm's producer surplus?

   b What is the market producer surplus?

Is the Competitive Market Efficient?
(Study Plan 5.3)

11 The figure shows the demand for and supply of mobile phones.

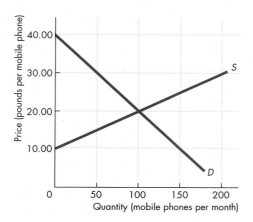

a What are the equilibrium price and equilibrium quantity of mobile phones?

b Shade in and label the consumer surplus at the competitive equilibrium.

c Shade in and label the producer surplus at the competitive equilibrium.

d Calculate the total surplus at the competitive equilibrium.

e Is the competitive market for mobile phones efficient?

12 The table gives the demand and supply schedules of sunscreen.

Price (euros per bottle)	Quantity demanded	Quantity supplied
	(bottles per day)	
0	400	0
5	300	100
10	200	200
15	100	300
20	0	400

Factories producing sunscreen are required to limit production to 100 bottles per day.

a What is the maximum price that consumers are willing to pay for the 100th bottle?

b What is the minimum price that producers are willing to accept for the 100th bottle?

c Describe the situation in the market for sunscreen.

13 Explain why each restaurant in Problem 1 might be using an efficient allocation method.

Is the Competitive Market Fair?
(Study Plan 5.4)

14 Explain why the allocation method used by each restaurant in Problem 1 is fair or not fair.

15 In problem 12, how can the 100 bottles available be allocated to beach-goers? Which possible methods would be fair and which would be unfair?

Economics in the News (Study Plan 5.N)

16 **The World's Largest Tulip and Flower Market**

Every day 20 million tulips, roses and other cut flowers are auctioned at the Dutch market called the Bloemenveiling. Each day 55,000 Dutch auctions take place, matching buyers and sellers.

Source: Tulip-Bulbs.com

A Dutch auction is one in which the auctioneer starts by announcing the highest price. If no one offers to buy the flowers, the auctioneer lowers the price until a buyer is found.

a What method is used to allocate flowers at the Bloemenveiling?

b How does a Dutch flower auction influence consumer surplus and producer surplus?

c Are the flower auctions at the Bloemenveiling efficient?

17 **Wii Sells Out Across Japan**

After a two-month TV-ad blitz for Wii in Japan, demand was expected to be much higher than supply. Yodobashi Camera was selling Wii games on a first-come, first-served basis. Eager customers showed up early so as not to miss out on their favourite titles. Those who tried to join the queue after 6 or 7 a.m. were turned away – many could be spotted rushing off to the smaller Akihabara stores that were holding raffles to decide who got a Wii.

Source: *Gamespot News*, 1 December 2006

a Why was the quantity demanded of Wii expected to exceed the quantity supplied?

b Did Nintendo produce the efficient quantity of Wii? Explain.

c Can you think of reasons why Nintendo might want to underproduce and leave the market with fewer Wii than people want to buy?

d What are the two methods of resource allocation described in the news clip? Is either method of allocating Wii efficient?

e What do you think some of the people who managed to buy a Wii did with it?

f Explain which is the fairer method of allocating the Wii: the market price or the two methods described in the news clip.

ADDITIONAL PROBLEMS AND APPLICATIONS

  You can work these problems in MyEconLab if assigned by your lecturer.

Resource Allocation Methods

18 At McDonald's, no reservations are accepted; at the Rex Whistler Restaurant at Tate Britain, reservations are accepted; at Zaffrano in Knightsbridge, reservations are essential.

  a Describe the method of allocating table resources in these three restaurants.

  b Why do you think restaurants have different reservations policies?

Benefit, Cost and Surplus

Use the following table to work Problems 19 to 22.

The table gives the demand schedules for jet-ski rides by the only suppliers: Rick, Sam and Tom.

Price	Quantity demanded (rides per day)		
(euros per ride)	Rick	Sam	Tom
10.00	0	0	0
12.50	5	0	0
15.00	10	5	0
17.50	15	10	5
20.00	20	15	10

19 What is each owner's minimum supply-price of 10 rides a day?

20 Which owner has the largest producer surplus when the price of a ride is €17.50? Explain why.

21 What is the marginal social cost of producing 45 rides a day?

22 Construct the market supply schedule of jet-ski rides.

Use the following table to work Problems 23 and 24.

The table gives the demand and supply schedules of sandwiches.

Price	Quantity demanded	Quantity supplied
(pounds per sandwich)	(sandwiches per hour)	
0	300	0
1	250	50
2	200	100
3	150	150
4	100	200
5	50	250
6	0	300

23 **a** What is the maximum price that consumers are willing to pay for the 200th sandwich?

  b What is the minimum price that producers are willing to accept for the 200th sandwich?

  c Are 200 sandwiches a day less than or greater than the efficient quantity?

Is the Competitive Market Efficient?

24 **a** If the sandwich market is efficient, what is the consumer surplus, the producer surplus and the total surplus?

  b If the demand for sandwiches increases and the sandwich makers continue to produce the efficient quantity, describe the change in producer surplus and the deadweight loss.

Use the following figure, which illlustrates the market for CDs to work Problems 25 and 26.

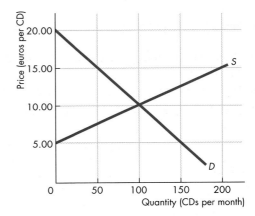

25 **a** What are the equilibrium price and equilibrium quantity of CDs?

  b Calculate the consumer surplus at the competitive equilibrium.

  c Calculate the producer surplus at the competitive equilibrium.

  d Calculate the total surplus at the competitive equilibrium.

  e Is the competitive market for CDs efficient?

26 If the demand for CDs decreases by 50 per month at each price, but CD producers continue to produce the previously efficient quantity, show on the graph:

  a The change in total surplus from CDs.

  b The deadweight loss created.

Use the following news clip to work Problems 27 to 29.

The Right Price for Digital Music

Apple's $1.29-for-the-latest-songs model isn't perfect and isn't it too much to pay for music that appeals to just a few people? What we need is a system that will be profitable but yet fair to music lovers. The solution: price song downloads according to demand. The more people who download a particular song, the higher will be the price of that song; the fewer people who buy a particular song, the lower will be the price of that song. That is a free-market solution – the market would determine the price.

Source: *Slate*, 5 December 2005

Assume that the marginal social cost of downloading a song from the iTunes Store is zero. (This assumption means that the cost of operating the iTunes Store doesn't change if people download more songs.)

27 **a** Draw a graph of the market for downloadable music with a price of $1.29 for all the latest songs. On your graph, show consumer surplus and producer surplus.

  b With a price of $1.29 for all the latest songs, is the market efficient or inefficient? If it is inefficient, show the deadweight loss on your graph.

28 If the pricing scheme described in the news clip were adopted, how would consumer surplus, producer surplus and the deadweight loss change?

29 **a** If the pricing scheme described in the news clip were adopted, would the market be efficient or inefficient? Explain.

  b Is the pricing scheme described in the news clip a 'free-market solution'? Explain.

Is the Competitive Market Fair?

30 The winner of the men's and women's tennis singles at the US Open is paid twice as much as the runner-up, but it takes two players to have a singles final. Is the compensation arrangement fair?

Use the following information to work Problems 31 and 32.

A winter storm cuts the power supply and isolates a small town in the mountains. The people rush to buy candles from the town store, which is the only source of candles. The store owner decides to ration the candles to one per family but to keep the price of a candle unchanged.

31 Who gets to use the candles? Who receives the consumer surplus and who receives the producer surplus on candles?

32 Is the allocation efficient? Is the allocation fair?

Economics in the News

33 After you have studied Reading Between the Lines on pp. 120–121 answer the following questions.

  a What is the method used to allocate the world's cut flowers and local hotel rooms?

  b Who benefits from this method of resource allocation: buyers, sellers or both? Explain your answer using the ideas of marginal social benefit, marginal social cost, consumer surplus and producer surplus.

  c After the ash cloud closed European airports, when the equilibrium quantity of cut flowers decreased, why was the outcome still efficient? Why was there not underproduction and a deadweight loss?

  d If the government of Holland placed a limit of 15 million a day on the quantity of flowers traded in the flower market in Holland, would there be underproduction and a deadweight loss created? Explain your answer.

34 **Fight over Water Rates; Escondido Farmers Say Increase would Put Them out of Business**

Agricultural users of water pay less than residential and business users. Since 1993, water rates have increased by more than 90 per cent for residential customers and by only 50 per cent for agricultural users.

Source: *The San Diego Union-Tribune*, 14 June 2006

  a Do you think that the allocation of water between agricultural and residential users is likely to be efficient? Explain your answer.

  b If agricultural users paid a higher price, would the allocation of resources be more efficient?

  c If agricultural users paid a higher price, what would happen to consumer surplus and producer surplus from water?

  d Is the difference in price paid by agricultural and residential users fair?

35 **New Zealand's Private Forests**

In the early 1990s, the New Zealand government auctioned half the national forests, converting these forests from public ownership to private ownership. The government's decision was an incentive to get the owners to operate like farmers – that is, take care of the resource and to use it to make a profit.

Source: *Reuters*, 7 September 2007

  a When all forests in New Zealand were government owned, was the New Zealand timber industry efficient? Did logging companies operate in the social interest or self-interest?

  b Since the early 1990s, has the New Zealand timber industry been efficient? Have logging companies operated in the social interest or self-interest?

  c What incentive do private timber companies have to ensure that they take care of the resource?

Government Actions in Markets

When people can't afford to buy houses, more people must rent and rental prices shoot up! Should the government cap the rents that landlords charge in difficult times? Perhaps the answer is increasing the minimum wage? Wouldn't that help the low paid?

We all pay taxes and some taxes are rising, so who really pays a tax: buyers or sellers? In the markets for many food items producers receive a subsidy. Who benefits from the subsidy: farmers or consumers? Some goods are illegal, yet they are still traded. How do markets for illegal goods work? This chapter answers these questions. In *Reading Between the Lines* at the end of the chapter, we explore the scale and effect of government support payments to farmers.

A Housing Market with a Rent Ceiling

We spend more of our income on housing than on any other good or service, so it isn't surprising that rents can be a political issue. When rents are high, or when they jump by a large amount, renters might lobby the government for limits on rents.

A government regulation that makes it illegal to charge a price higher than a specified level is called a **price ceiling** or **price cap**.

The effects of a price ceiling on a market depend crucially on whether the ceiling is imposed at a level that is above or below the equilibrium price.

A price ceiling set *above the equilibrium price* has no effect. The reason is that the price ceiling does not constrain the market forces. The force of the law and the market forces are not in conflict.

But a price ceiling *below the equilibrium price* has powerful effects on a market. The reason is that the price ceiling attempts to prevent the price from regulating the quantities demanded and supplied. The force of the law and the market forces are in conflict.

When a price ceiling is applied to a housing market, it is called a **rent ceiling** – the maximum rent that may be legally charged.

A rent ceiling set below the equilibrium rent creates:

◆ A housing shortage
◆ Increased search activity
◆ A black market

A Housing Shortage

At the equilibrium price, the quantity demanded equals the quantity supplied. In a housing market, when the rent is at the equilibrium level, the quantity of housing supplied equals the quantity of housing demanded and there is neither a shortage nor a surplus of housing.

But at a rent set below the equilibrium rent, the quantity of housing demanded exceeds the quantity of housing supplied – there is a shortage. So if a rent ceiling is set below the equilibrium rent, there will be a shortage of housing.

When there is a shortage, the quantity available is the quantity supplied and when there is no price ceiling the price would rise. But when there is a price ceiling, the quantity supplied must somehow be allocated among the frustrated demanders. One way in which this allocation occurs is through increased search activity.

Increased Search Activity

The time spent looking for someone with whom to do business is called **search activity**. We spend some time in search activity almost every time we make a purchase. When you're shopping for the latest hot new mobile phone, and you know four stores that stock it, how do you find which store has the best deal? You spend a few minutes on the Internet, checking out the various prices. In some markets, such as the housing market, people spend a lot of time checking the alternatives available before making a choice.

When a price is regulated and there is a shortage, search activity increases. In the case of a rent-controlled housing market, frustrated would-be renters scan the newspapers, not only for housing adverts but also for death notices! Any information about newly available housing is useful, and apartment seekers race to be first on the scene when news of a possible supplier breaks.

The *opportunity cost* of a good is equal not only to its price but also to the value of the search time spent finding the good. So the opportunity cost of housing is equal to the rent (a regulated price) plus the time and other resources spent searching for the restricted quantity available. Search activity is costly. It uses time and other resources, such as phone calls and car journeys that could have been used in other productive ways.

A rent ceiling controls only the rent portion of the cost of housing. The cost of increased search activity might end up making the full cost of housing higher than it would be without a rent ceiling.

Black Market

A rent ceiling also encourages illegal trading in a **black market**, an illegal market in which the equilibrium price exceeds the price ceiling. Black markets occur in rent-controlled housing markets. They also occur in the market for tickets to big sporting events and rock concerts, where 'ticket touts' (or 'scalpers') operate.

When a rent ceiling is in force, frustrated renters and landlords constantly seek ways of increasing rents. One common way is for a new tenant to pay a high price for worthless fittings, such as charging €2,000 for threadbare curtains. Another is for the tenant to pay an exorbitant price for new locks and keys called 'key money'.

The level of a black market rent depends on how tightly the rent ceiling is enforced. With loose enforcement, the black market rent is close to the unregulated rent. But with strict enforcement, the black market rent is equal to the maximum price that a renter is willing to pay.

Figure 6.1 illustrates the effects of a rent ceiling. The demand curve for housing is *D* and the supply curve is *S*. A rent ceiling is imposed at €1,000 a month. Rents that exceed €1,000 a month are in the grey-shaded illegal region in the figure. You can see that the equilibrium rent, where the demand and supply curves intersect, is in the illegal region.

At a rent of €1,000 a month, the quantity of housing supplied is 4,400 units and the quantity demanded is 10,000 units. So with a rent of €1,000 a month, there is a shortage of 5,600 units.

To rent the 4,400th unit, someone is willing to pay €1,200 a month. They might pay this amount by incurring search costs that bring the total cost of housing to €1,200 a month, or they might pay a black market price of €1,200 a month. Either way, the renter ends up incurring a cost that exceeds what the equilibrium rent would be in an unregulated market.

Inefficiency of Rent Ceilings

A rent ceiling set below the equilibrium rent results in an inefficient underproduction of housing services. The *marginal social benefit* of housing exceeds its *marginal social cost* and a deadweight loss shrinks the producer surplus and consumer surplus (see Chapter 5, pp. 109–111).

Figure 6.2 shows this inefficiency. The rent ceiling (€1,000 per month) is below the equilibrium rent (€1,100 per month) and the quantity of housing supplied (4,400 units) is less than the efficient quantity (7,400 units).

Because the quantity of housing supplied (the quantity available) is less than the efficient quantity, there is a deadweight loss, shown by the grey triangle. Producer surplus shrinks to the blue triangle and consumer surplus shrinks to the green triangle. The red rectangle represents the potential loss from increased search activity. This loss is borne by consumers and the full loss from the rent ceiling is the sum of the deadweight loss and the increased cost of search.

Figure 6.1   A Rent Ceiling

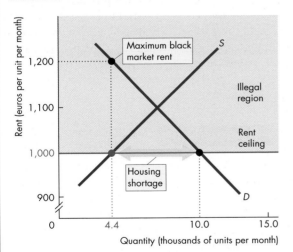

A rent above the rent ceiling of €1,000 a month is illegal (in the grey-shaded region). At a rent of €1,000 a month, the quantity of housing supplied is 4,400 units and the quantity demanded is 10,000 units. There is a housing shortage of 5,600 units.

Frustrated renters spend time searching for housing and they make deals with landlords in a black market. Someone is willing to pay €1,200 a month for the 4,400th unit. This is the maximum black market rent.

myeconlab Animation

Figure 6.2   The Inefficiency of a Rent Ceiling

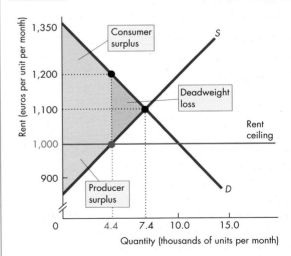

Without a rent ceiling, the market produces an efficient 7,400 units of housing at a rent of €1,100 a month. A rent ceiling of €1,000 a month decreases the quantity of housing supplied to 4,400 units. Producer surplus and consumer surplus shrink and a deadweight loss arises. The red rectangle represents the cost of resources used in increased search activity. The full loss from the rent ceiling equals the sum of the red rectangle and grey triangle.

myeconlab Animation

Are Rent Ceilings Fair?

Rent ceilings might be inefficient, but don't they achieve a fairer allocation of scarce housing? Let's explore this question.

The Two Views of Fairness

Chapter 5 (pp. 116–118) reviews two key ideas about fairness. According to the *fair rules* view, anything that blocks voluntary exchange is unfair, so rent ceilings are unfair. But according to the *fair result* view, a fair outcome is one that benefits the less well off. So according to this view, the fairest outcome is the one that allocates scarce housing to the poorest. To see whether rent ceilings help to achieve a fairer outcome in this sense, we need to consider how the market allocates scarce housing resources in the face of a rent ceiling.

Allocating Housing Among Demanders

Blocking rent adjustments doesn't eliminate scarcity. Rather, because it decreases the quantity of housing available, it creates an even bigger challenge for the housing market. Somehow, the market must ration a smaller quantity of housing and allocate that housing among the people who demand it. When the rent is not permitted to allocate scarce housing, what other mechanisms are available and are they fair? Three possible mechanisms are:

◆ A lottery

◆ First-come, first-served

◆ Discrimination

A lottery allocates housing to those who are lucky, not to those who are poor. First-come, first-served allocated housing in England after the Second World War to those with the foresight to get their names on a list first, not to the poorest. Discrimination allocates scarce housing based on the views and self-interest of owners. Discrimination based on friendship, family ties and criteria such as race, ethnicity or sex is more likely to enter the equation. We might make such discrimination illegal, but we cannot prevent it from occurring.

In principle, self-interested owners and bureaucrats could allocate housing to satisfy some criterion of fairness, but they are not likely to do so. It is hard, then, to make a case for rent ceilings on the basis of fairness. Non-price methods of allocation do not produce a fair outcome.

Is there a Case for Rent Ceilings?

The economic case against rent ceilings is now widely accepted, so new rent ceiling laws are rare. But when governments try to repeal rent control laws, current renters lobby politicians to maintain the ceilings. Also, other people would be happy if they were lucky enough to find a rent-controlled apartment. So there is usually plenty of political support for rent ceilings.

A Chartered Institute of Housing Report[1] in August 2010 argued that UK housing policy needs to target the lower paid workers who have been priced out of the private home ownership market, who cannot afford private rented property but will not be offered local authority housing. They argue that housing associations should offer below market rent housing (housing with a rent ceiling) to this group.

Because more people support rent ceilings than oppose them, politicians are sometimes willing to support them too. Local authority spending on housing is being cut in the UK and so local and central government politicians are likely to support charitable groups such as housing associations introducing rent ceilings.

The outcome is inefficient because scarce housing resources don't get allocated to the people who value them most highly.

[1] guardian.co.uk/society/2010/aug/15/renting-buying-home

Review Quiz

1 What is a rent ceiling and what are its effects if it is set above the equilibrium rent?
2 What are the effects of a rent ceiling that is set below the equilibrium rent?
3 How are scarce housing resources allocated when a rent ceiling is in place?
4 Why does a rent ceiling create an inefficient and unfair outcome in the housing market?

You can work these questions in Study Plan 6.1 and get instant feedback.

You now know how a price ceiling (rent ceiling) works. Next, we'll learn about the effects of a price floor by studying a minimum wage in a labour market.

A Labour Market with a Minimum Wage

For each of us, the labour market is the market that influences the jobs we get and the wages we earn. Firms decide how much labour to demand, and the lower the wage rate, the greater is the quantity of labour demanded. Households decide how much labour to supply, and the higher the wage rate, the greater is the quantity of labour supplied. The wage rate adjusts to make the quantity of labour demanded equal to the quantity supplied.

When wage rates fail to keep up with rising prices, labour unions might lobby the government for a higher wage rate. A government imposed regulation that makes it illegal to charge a price lower than a specified level is called a **price floor**.

The effects of a price floor on a market depend crucially on whether the floor is imposed at a level that is above or below the equilibrium price.

A price floor set *below the equilibrium price* has no effect. The reason is that the price floor does not constrain the market forces. The force of the law and the market forces are not in conflict. But a price floor *above the equilibrium price* has powerful effects on a market. The reason is that the price floor attempts to prevent the price from regulating the quantities demanded and supplied. The force of the law and the market forces are in conflict.

When a price floor is applied to a labour market, it is called a **minimum wage**. A minimum wage imposed at a level that is above the equilibrium wage creates unemployment. Let's look at the effects of a minimum wage.

Minimum Wage Brings Unemployment

At the equilibrium price, the quantity demanded equals the quantity supplied. In a labour market, when the wage rate is at the equilibrium level, the quantity of labour supplied equals the quantity of labour demanded. But at a wage rate above the equilibrium wage, the quantity of labour supplied exceeds the quantity of labour demanded – there is a surplus of labour. So when a minimum wage is set above the equilibrium wage, there is a surplus of labour. The demand for labour determines the level of employment, and the surplus of labour is unemployed.

Figure 6.3 illustrates the effect of the minimum wage on unemployment. The demand for labour curve is *D*

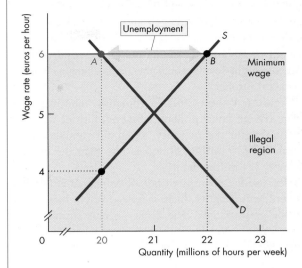

Figure 6.3 Minimum Wage and Unemployment

The minimum wage is set at €6 an hour. Any wage below €6 an hour is illegal (in the grey-shaded illegal region). At a minimum wage of €6 an hour, 20 million hours are hired but 22 million hours are available. Unemployment – *AB* – of 2 million hours a week is created. With only 20 million hours demanded, someone is willing to supply the 20 millionth hour for €4.

 myeconlab Animation

and the supply of labour curve is *S*. The horizontal red line shows the minimum wage set at €6 an hour. A wage rate below this level is illegal, in the grey-shaded illegal region of the figure. At the minimum wage rate, 20 million hours of labour are demanded (point *A*) and 22 million hours of labour are supplied (point *B*), so 2 million hours of available labour are unemployed.

With only 20 million hours demanded, someone is willing to supply that 20 millionth hour for €4. Frustrated unemployed workers spend time and other resources searching for hard-to-find jobs.

Inefficiency of a Minimum Wage

In the labour market, the supply curve measures the marginal social cost of labour to workers. This cost is leisure forgone. The demand curve measures the marginal social benefit from labour. This benefit is the value of the goods and services produced. An unregulated labour market allocates the economy's scarce labour resources to the jobs in which they are valued most highly. The market is efficient.

The minimum wage frustrates the market mechanism and results in unemployment and increased job search. At the quantity of labour employed, the marginal social benefit of labour exceeds its marginal social cost and a deadweight loss shrinks the firms' surplus and the workers' surplus.

Figure 6.4 shows this inefficiency. The minimum wage (€6 an hour) is above the equilibrium wage (€5 an hour) and the quantity of labour demanded and employed (20 million hours) is less than the efficient quantity (21 million hours).

Because the quantity of labour employed is less than the efficient quantity, there is a deadweight loss, shown by the grey triangle. The firms' surplus shrinks to the blue triangle and the workers' surplus shrinks to the green triangle. The red rectangle shows the potential loss from increased job search, which is borne by workers. The full loss from the minimum wage is the sum of the deadweight loss and the increased cost of job search.

Is there a Case for the Minimum Wage?

Minimum wage policies are widespread in Europe. The highest rates are paid in Luxembourg and France and the lowest in Romania and Bulgaria. The UK national minimum wage rate for people over 21 years was raised to £5.93 an hour in October 2010, a 2.2 per cent rise. In contrast to the UK decision to increase the minimum wage, 18 EU countries have frozen or reduced the minimum wage in 2010.

Although the minimum wage is inefficient, not everyone loses from it. The people who find jobs at the minimum wage gain. Supporters of the minimum wage believe that the elasticities of demand and supply in the labour market are low, so not much unemployment results. The consensus is that a 10 per cent rise in the minimum wage decreases teenage employment by between 1 and 3 per cent.

Figure 6.4 The Inefficiency of a Minimum Wage

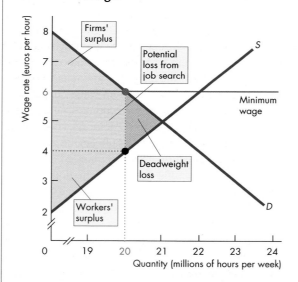

A minimum wage decreases employment. Firms' surplus (blue) and workers' surplus (green) shrink and a deadweight loss (grey area) arises. Job search increases and the red area shows the loss from this activity.

Is the Minimum Wage Fair?

The minimum wage is unfair on both views of fairness. It delivers an unfair *result* and it imposes unfair *rules*.

The *result* is unfair because only those people who have jobs and keep them benefit from the minimum wage. The unemployed end up worse off than they would be with no minimum wage. Some of them who search for jobs and find them end up worse off because they incur an increased cost of job search. In addition those who find jobs are not always the least well off. When the wage rate doesn't allocate labour, other mechanisms determine who finds a job. One such mechanism is discrimination, another source of unfairness.

The minimum wage imposes an unfair *rule* because it blocks voluntary exchange. Firms looking for workers are willing to hire more labour and people who are looking for work or are willing to work more hours, but they are not permitted by the minimum wage law to do so.

This view is challenged by David Card of the University of California at Berkeley and Alan Krueger of Princeton University who say that increases in the minimum wage can *increase* teenage employment and actually *decrease* unemployment. They argue that the employment rate of low-income workers *increases* following a wage increase. The higher wage rate makes workers more conscientious and productive and less likely to quit, which lowers unproductive labour turnover. They also argue that a higher wage rate makes managers seek ways to increase labour productivity.

Most economists are sceptical about Card and Krueger's argument. Why, economists ask, don't firms freely pay wage rates above the equilibrium wage to encourage more productive work habits? Also, they point to other explanations for the employment responses. One such explanation is that firms cut employment before the minimum wage is increased in *anticipation* of the increase.

Another effect of the minimum wage is an increase in the quantity of labour supplied. If this effect occurs, it might show up as an increase in the number of people who leave education early to look for work. Some economists say that this response does occur.

Review Quiz

1 What is a minimum wage and what are its effects if it is set above the equilibrium wage?
2 What are the effects of a minimum wage set below the equilibrium wage?
3 Explain how scarce jobs are allocated when a minimum wage is in place.
4 Explain why a minimum wage creates an inefficient allocation of labour resources.
5 Explain why a minimum wage is unfair.

You can work these questions in Study Plan 6.2 and get instant feedback.

Next we're going to study a more widespread government action in markets: taxes. We'll see how taxes change the prices and quantities of the things taxed. You will discover the surprising fact that while the government can impose a tax, it cannot decide who will pay the tax! You will also see that a tax is inefficient and creates a deadweight loss.

Taxes

Everything you earn and almost everything you buy is taxed. The income tax and a National Insurance contribution are deducted from your earnings. The prices of most of the things you buy include VAT and the prices of a few goods such as cigarettes, alcoholic drinks and petrol include a heavy excise tax. Firms also pay some taxes, one of which is a National Insurance contribution for every person they employ.

Who *really* pays these taxes? Because the income tax and National Insurance contribution are deducted from your pay, isn't it obvious that *you* pay these taxes? And isn't it equally obvious that you pay the VAT, that smokers pay the tax on cigarettes and that your employer pays the employer's National Insurance contribution?

You're going to discover that it isn't obvious who *really* pays a tax and that lawmakers don't make that decision. We begin with a definition of tax incidence.

Tax Incidence

Tax incidence is the division of the burden of a tax between buyers and sellers. When the government imposes a tax on the sale of a good,[1] the price paid by buyers might rise by the full amount of the tax, by a lesser amount, or not at all. If the price paid by buyers rises by the full amount of the tax, then the burden of the tax falls entirely on buyers – buyers pay the tax. If the price paid by buyers rises by a lesser amount than the tax, then the burden of the tax falls partly on buyers and partly on sellers. And if the price paid by buyers doesn't change at all, then the burden of the tax falls entirely on sellers.

Tax incidence does not depend on the tax law. The law might impose a tax on sellers or on buyers, but the outcome is the same in either case. To see why, let's look at the tax on cigarettes.

A Tax on Sellers

During 2003, the government of France increased the tax on the sale of cigarettes three times. We'll assume the tax was €1.50 a pack. To work out the effects of this tax on the sellers of cigarettes, we begin by examining the effects on demand and supply in the market for cigarettes.

---

[1] These propositions also apply to services and factors of production (land, labour and capital).

In Figure 6.5, the demand curve is D, and the supply curve is S. With no tax, the equilibrium price is €3 per pack and 350 million packs a year are bought and sold.

A tax on sellers is like an increase in cost, so it decreases supply. To determine the position of the new supply curve, we add the tax to the minimum price that sellers are willing to accept for each quantity sold. You can see that without the tax, sellers are willing to offer 350 million packs a year for €3 a pack. So with a €1.50 tax, they will offer 350 million packs a year only if the price is €4.50 a pack. The supply curve shifts to the red curve labelled S + *tax on sellers*.

Equilibrium occurs where the new supply curve intersects the demand curve at 325 million packs a year. The price paid by buyers rises by €1 to €4 a pack. The price received by sellers falls by 50 cents to €2.50 a pack. So buyers pay €1 of the tax and sellers pay the other 50 cents.

A Tax on Buyers

Suppose that instead of taxing sellers, the French government taxes cigarette buyers €1.50 a pack.

A tax on buyers lowers the amount they are willing to pay sellers, so it decreases demand and shifts the demand curve leftward. To determine the position of this new demand curve, we subtract the tax from the maximum price that buyers are willing to pay for each quantity bought.

You can see in Figure 6.6 that with no tax, buyers are willing to buy 350 million packs a year for €3 a pack. So with a €1.50 tax, they will buy 350 packs a year only if the price including the tax is €3 a pack, which means that they're willing to pay sellers only €1.50 a pack. The demand curve shifts to become the red curve labelled D – *tax on buyers*.

Equilibrium occurs where the new demand curve intersects the supply curve at a quantity of 325 million packs a year. The price received by sellers is €2.50 a pack, and the price paid by buyers is €4.

Equivalence of Tax on Buyers and Sellers

You can see that the tax on buyers in Figure 6.6 has the same effects as the tax on sellers in Figure 6.5. The quantity decreases to 325 million packs a year, the price paid by buyers rises to €4 a pack and the price received by sellers falls to €2.50 a pack. Buyers pay €1 of the €1.50 tax. Sellers pay the other 50 cents of the tax.

Figure 6.5   A Tax on Sellers

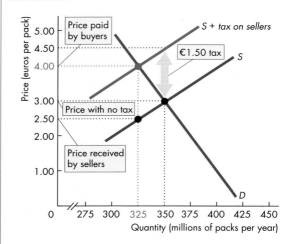

With no tax, 350 million packs a year are bought and sold at €3 a pack. A tax on sellers of €1.50 a pack decreases the supply of cigarettes and shifts the supply curve leftward to S + *tax on sellers*. The equilibrium quantity decreases to 325 million packs a year, the price paid by buyers rises to €4 a pack, and the price received by sellers falls to €2.50 a pack. The tax raises the price paid by buyers by less than the tax and lowers the price received by sellers, so buyers and sellers share the burden of the tax.

myeconlab Animation ━━━━━━━━━━━━━━━━━◆

Can We Share the Burden Equally?

Suppose that the government wants the burden of the cigarette tax to fall equally on buyers and sellers and declares that a 75 cents tax be imposed on each. Is the burden of the tax then shared equally?

You can see that it is not. The tax is still €1.50 a pack. You've seen that the tax has the same effect regardless of whether it is imposed on sellers or buyers. So imposing half the tax on one and half on the other is like an average of the two cases you've examined. In this case, the demand curve shifts downward by 75 cents and the supply curve shifts upward by 75 cents. The equilibrium quantity is still 325 million packs. Buyers pay €4 a pack, of which €1 is tax. Sellers receive €2.50 a pack (€3 from buyers minus the 50 cents tax).

When a transaction is taxed, there are two prices: the price paid by buyers, which includes the tax; and the price received by sellers, which excludes the tax. Buyers respond only to the price that includes the tax because

Figure 6.6   A Tax on Buyers

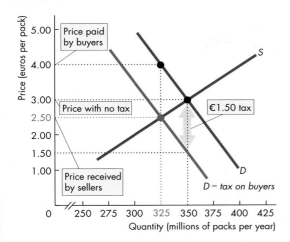

With no tax, 350 million packs a year are bought and sold at €3 a pack. A tax on buyers of €1.50 a pack decreases the demand for cigarettes and shifts the demand curve leftward to *D – tax on buyers*. The equilibrium quantity decreases to 325 million packs a year. The price paid by buyers rises to €4 a pack and the price received by sellers falls to €2.50 a pack. The tax raises the price paid by buyers by less than the tax and lowers the price received by sellers, so buyers and sellers share the burden of the tax.

myeconlab Animation

that is the price they pay. Sellers respond only to the price that excludes the tax because that is the price they receive.

A tax is like a wedge between the price buyers pay and the price sellers receive. The size of the wedge determines the effects of the tax, not the side of the market – demand side or supply side – on which the government imposes the tax.

Payroll Taxes

Some governments impose payroll taxes and share the tax equally between both employers (buyers) and workers (sellers). But the principles you've just learned apply to this tax too. The market for labour, not the government, determines how the burden of the tax is divided between firms and workers.

In the cigarette tax example, buyers pay twice as much of the tax as sellers pay. In general, the division of the tax between buyers and sellers depends on the elasticities of demand and supply, as you will now see.

Tax Incidence and Elasticity of Demand

The division of the tax between buyers and sellers depends partly on the elasticity of demand. There are two extreme cases:

◆ Perfectly inelastic demand – buyers pay
◆ Perfectly elastic demand – sellers pay

Perfectly Inelastic Demand

Figure 6.7 shows the UK market for insulin. Demand is perfectly inelastic at 100,000 bottles a day, regardless of the price, as shown by the vertical curve *D*. That is, a diabetic would sacrifice all other goods and services rather than not consume the quantity of insulin that provides good health. The supply curve of insulin is *S*. With no tax, the price is £2 a bottle and the quantity is 100,000 bottles a day.

If insulin is taxed at 20 pence a bottle, we must add the tax to the minimum price at which drug companies are willing to sell insulin. The result is the new supply curve *S + tax*. The price rises to £2.20 a bottle, but the quantity does not change. Buyers pay the entire tax of 20 pence a bottle.

Figure 6.7   Tax with Perfectly Inelastic Demand

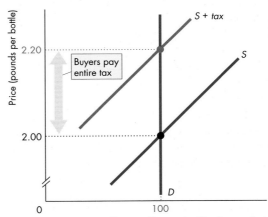

In the market for insulin, demand is perfectly inelastic. With no tax, the price is £2 a bottle and the quantity is 100,000 bottles a day. A tax of 20 pence a bottle decreases supply and shifts the supply curve to *S + tax*. The price rises to £2.20 a bottle, but the quantity bought does not change. Buyers pay the entire tax.

myeconlab Animation

Perfectly Elastic Demand

Figure 6.8 shows the market for pink marker pens. Demand is perfectly elastic at £1 a pen, as shown by the horizontal curve *D*. If pink markers are less expensive than the other pens, everyone uses pink. If pink pens are more expensive than the others, no one uses pink. The supply curve is *S*. With no tax, the price of a pink marker pen is £1 and the quantity is 4,000 a week.

Suppose that the government imposes a tax of 20 pence on pink marker pens but not on other colours. The new supply curve is *S + tax*. The price remains at £1 a pen and the quantity decreases to 1,000 a week. The tax leaves the price paid by buyers unchanged but lowers the amount received by sellers by the full amount of the tax. Sellers pay the entire tax of 20 pence a pink pen.

We've seen that when demand is perfectly inelastic, buyers pay the entire tax and when demand is perfectly elastic, sellers pay the entire tax. In the usual case, demand is neither perfectly inelastic nor perfectly elastic and the tax is split between buyers and sellers. But the division depends on the elasticity of demand: the more inelastic the demand for a good, the larger is the amount of the tax paid by buyers.

Figure 6.8 Tax with Perfectly Elastic Demand

In this market for pink marker pens, demand is perfectly elastic. With no tax, the price of a pen is £1 and the quantity is 4,000 pens a week. A tax of 20 pence a pink pen decreases supply and shifts the supply curve to *S + tax*. The price remains at £1 a pen, and the quantity of pink pens sold decreases to 1,000 a week. Sellers pay the entire tax.

Tax Incidence and Elasticity of Supply

The division of the tax between buyers and sellers depends, in part, on the elasticity of supply. There are two extreme cases:

◆ Perfectly inelastic supply – sellers pay
◆ Perfectly elastic supply – buyers pay

Perfectly Inelastic Supply

Figure 6.9(a) shows the market for water from a spring which flows at a constant rate that can't be controlled. The quantity supplied is 100,000 bottles a week, as shown by the supply curve *S*. The demand curve for the water from this spring is *D*. With no tax, the price is 50 pence a bottle and the quantity is 100,000 bottles.

Suppose this spring water is taxed at 5 pence a bottle. The supply curve does not change because the spring owners still produce 100,000 bottles a week even though the price has fallen. But buyers are willing to buy the 100,000 bottles only if the price is 50 pence a bottle. So the price remains at 50 pence a bottle. The tax reduces the price received by sellers to 45 pence a bottle and sellers pay the entire tax.

Perfectly Elastic Supply

Figure 6.9(b) illustrates the market for sand from which computer-chip makers extract silicon. The supply of sand is perfectly elastic at 10 pence a kilogram. The supply curve is *S*. The demand curve is *D*. With no tax, the price is 10 pence a kilogram and 5,000 kilograms a week are bought.

If sand is taxed at 1 penny a kilogram, we add the tax to the minimum supply-price. Sellers are now willing to offer any quantity at 11 pence a kilogram along the curve *S + tax*. The price rises to 11 pence a kilogram and 3,000 kilograms a week are bought. The price paid by buyers increases by the full amount of the tax. Buyers pay the entire tax.

We've seen that when supply is perfectly inelastic, sellers pay the entire tax and when supply is perfectly elastic, buyers pay the entire tax. In the usual case, supply is neither perfectly inelastic nor perfectly elastic and the tax is split between sellers and buyers. But how the tax is split depends on the elasticity of supply. The more elastic the supply, the larger is the amount of the tax paid by buyers.

Figure 6.9 Tax and the Elasticity of Supply

(a) Inelastic supply

(b) Elastic supply

Part (a) shows the market for water from a mineral spring. Supply is perfectly inelastic. With no tax, the price is 50 pence a bottle. With a tax of 5 pence a bottle, the price remains at 50 pence a bottle. The number of bottles bought remains the same, but the price received by sellers decreases to 45 pence a bottle. Sellers pay the entire tax.

Part (b) shows the market for sand. Supply is perfectly elastic. With no tax, the price of sand is 10 pence a kilogram. A tax of 1 penny a kilogram increases the minimum supply-price to 11 pence a kilogram. The supply curve shifts to *S + tax*. The price increases to 11 pence a kilogram. Buyers pay the entire tax.

Taxes and Efficiency

A tax drives a wedge between the price buyers pay and the price sellers receive and results in inefficient under-production. The price buyers pay is also the buyers' willingness to pay or *marginal social benefit*. The price sellers receive is also the sellers' minimum supply price, which equals *marginal social cost*.

Figure 6.10 shows the inefficiency of a tax on CD players. The demand curve, *D*, shows marginal social benefit, and the supply curve, *S*, shows marginal social cost. With no tax on CD players, the market produces the efficient quantity (5,000 CD players a week).

With a tax, the sellers' minimum supply-price rises by the amount of the tax and the supply curve shifts to *S + tax*. This supply curve does not show marginal social cost. The tax component isn't a social cost of production. It is a transfer of resources to the government.

At the new equilibrium quantity (4,000 CDs a week), both consumer surplus and producer surplus shrink. Part

Figure 6.10 Taxes and Efficiency

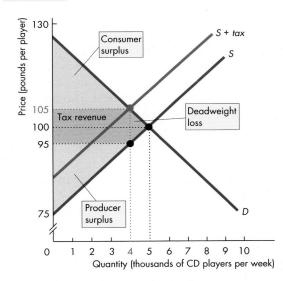

With no tax on CD players, 5,000 CD players are produced. With a tax of £10 a CD player, the buyers' price rises to £105 a player, the sellers' price falls to £95 a player, and the quantity decreases to 4,000 CD players a week. Consumer surplus shrinks to the green area and the producer surplus shrinks to the blue area. Part of the loss of consumer surplus and producer surplus goes to the government as tax revenue, (the purple area) and part becomes a deadweight loss (the grey area).

of each surplus goes to the government in tax revenue – the purple area; part becomes a deadweight loss – the grey area.

Only in the extreme cases of perfectly inelastic demand and perfectly inelastic supply does a tax not change the quantity bought and sold so that no deadweight loss arises.

Taxes and Fairness

We've examined the incidence and the efficiency of taxes, but when political leaders debate tax issues, it is fairness, not incidence and efficiency, that gets the most attention. Some politicians complain that tax cuts are unfair because they give the benefits of lower taxes to the rich. Others say it is fair that the rich get most of the tax cuts because they pay most of the taxes. No easy answers are available to questions about the fairness of taxes.

Economists have proposed two conflicting principles of fairness to apply to a tax system:

◆ The benefits principle
◆ The ability-to-pay principle

The Benefits Principle

The *benefits principle* is the proposition that people should pay taxes equal to the benefits they receive from the services provided by government. This arrangement is fair because it means that those who benefit most pay most taxes. It makes tax payments and the consumption of government-provided services similar to private consumption expenditures.

The benefits principle can justify high petrol taxes to pay for motorways, high taxes on alcoholic beverages and tobacco products to pay for public healthcare services, and high income tax rates on high incomes to pay for the benefits from law and order and living in a secure environment, from which the rich might benefit more than the poor.

The Ability-to-Pay Principle

The *ability-to-pay principle* is the proposition that people should pay taxes according to how easily they can bear the burden of the tax. A rich person can more easily bear the burden than a poor person can, so the ability-to-pay principle can reinforce the benefits principle to justify high rates of income tax on high incomes.

ECONOMICS IN ACTION

Workers and Consumers Pay Most Tax

A low elasticity of supply of labour and a high elasticity of demand for labour means that workers pay most of the income taxes and most of the National Insurance taxes. Because the elasticities of demand for alcohol, tobacco and petrol are low and the elasticities of supply are high, the burden of these (excise) taxes falls more on buyers than on sellers.

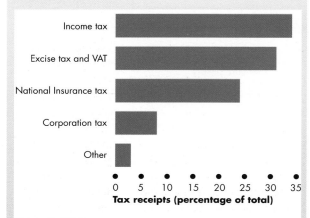

Figure 1 UK Taxes

Source of data: HM Revenue and Customs Annual Tax Receipts Table 1.2.

Review Quiz

1 How does the elasticity of demand influence the incidence of a tax, the tax revenue and the deadweight loss?
2 How does the elasticity of supply influence the incidence of a tax, the tax revenue and the deadweight loss?
3 Why is a tax inefficient?
4 When would a tax be efficient?
5 What are the two principles of fairness that are applied to a tax system?

You can work these questions in Study Plan 6.3 and get instant feedback.

Next, we look at agricultural markets and see how governments intervene in these markets to try to stabilize and boost farm revenues.

Production Quotas and Subsidies and Price Supports

Fluctuations in the weather bring fluctuations in farm output and prices and sometimes leave farmers with low incomes. To help farmers avoid low prices and low incomes, governments intervene in the markets for farm products. The three main methods of intervention in the markets for farm products are:

◆ Production quotas

◆ Production subsidies

◆ Price supports

Production Quotas

The markets for sugar beet, milk and cotton (among others) have, from time to time, been regulated with production quotas. A **production quota** is an upper limit to the quantity of a good that may be produced in a specified period. To discover the effects of a production quota, we'll look at the market for sugar beet.

Suppose that the sugar beet growers want to limit total production to get a higher price. They persuade the government to introduce a production quota on sugar beet.

The effect of a production quota depends on whether it is set below or above the equilibrium quantity. If the government introduced a production quota above the equilibrium quantity, nothing would change because sugar beet growers are already producing less than the quota. But a production quota *below the equilibrium quantity* has big effects, which are:

◆ A decrease in supply

◆ A rise in the price

◆ A decrease in marginal cost

◆ Inefficient underproduction

◆ An incentive to cheat and overproduce

Figure 6.11 illustrates these effects.

A Decrease in Supply

A production quota on sugar beet decreases the supply of sugar beet. Each grower is assigned a production limit that is less than the amount that would be produced – and supplied – without the quota. The total of the growers' limits equals the quota, and any production in excess of the quota is illegal.

The quantity supplied becomes the amount permitted by the production quota, and this quantity is fixed. The

Figure 6.11   The Effects of a Production Quota

With no quota, 60 million tonnes a year are produced at €30 a tonne. A quota of 40 million tonnes a year restricts total production to that amount. The equilibrium quantity decreases to 40 million tonnes a year, the price rises to €50 a tonne, and the farmers' marginal cost falls to €20 a tonne. In the new equilibrium, marginal social cost (on the supply curve) is less than marginal social benefit (on the demand curve) and a deadweight loss arises from underproduction.

myeconlab Animation

supply of sugar beet becomes perfectly inelastic at the quantity permitted under the quota.

In Figure 6.11, with no quota, growers would produce 60 million tonnes of sugar beet a year – the market equilibrium quantity. With a production quota set at 40 million tonnes a year, the grey shaded area shows the illegal region. As in the case of price ceilings and price floors, market forces and political forces are in conflict in this illegal region. The vertical red line labelled 'Quota' becomes the supply curve of sugar beet at prices above €20 a tonne.

A Rise in Price

The production quota raises the price of sugar beet. When the government sets a production quota, it leaves market forces free to determine the price. Because the quota decreases the supply of sugar beet, it raises the price. In Figure 6.11, with no quota, the price is €30 a tonne. With a quota of 40 million tonnes, the price rises to €50 a tonne.

A Decrease in Marginal Cost

The production quota lowers the marginal cost of growing sugar beet. Marginal cost decreases because growers produce less and stop using the resources with the highest marginal cost. Sugar beet growers slide down their supply (and marginal cost) curves. In Figure 6.11, marginal cost decreases to €20 a tonne.

Inefficiency

The production quota results in inefficient underproduction. Marginal social benefit at the quantity produced is equal to the market price, which has increased. Marginal social cost at the quantity produced has decreased and is less than the market price. So marginal social benefit exceeds marginal social cost and a deadweight loss arises.

An Incentive to Cheat and Overproduce

The production quota creates an incentive for growers to cheat and produce more than their individual production limit. With the quota, the price exceeds marginal cost, so the grower can get a larger profit by producing one more unit. But if all growers produce more than their assigned limit, the production quota becomes ineffective, and the price falls to the equilibrium (no quota) price.

To make the production quota effective, growers must set up a monitoring system to ensure that no one cheats and overproduces. But it is costly to set up and operate a monitoring system and it is difficult to detect and punish producers who violate their quotas. Because of the difficulty of operating a quota, producers often lobby governments to establish a quota and provide the monitoring and punishment systems that make it work.

Production Subsidies

A **production subsidy** is a payment made by the government to a producer for each unit produced. The effects of a production subsidy are opposite to the effects of a tax and they are:

◆ An increase in supply

◆ A fall in the price and an increase in quantity

◆ An increase in marginal cost

◆ Payments by government to farmers

◆ Inefficient *over*production

An Increase in Supply

In Figure 6.12, with no subsidy, the demand curve *D* and the supply curve *S* determine the price of sugar beet at €40 a tonne and the quantity of sugar beet at 40 million tonnes a year.

Suppose that the government introduces a subsidy of €20 a tonne to sugar beet farmers. A subsidy is like a negative tax or a decrease in cost, so the subsidy brings an increase in supply.

To determine the position of the new supply curve, we subtract the subsidy from the farmers' minimum supply-price. In Figure 6.12, with no subsidy, farmers are willing to offer 40 million tonnes a year at a price of €40 a tonne. With a production subsidy of €20 a tonne, farmers will offer 40 million tonnes a year if the price is as low as €20 a tonne. The supply curve shifts to the red curve labelled *S – subsidy*.

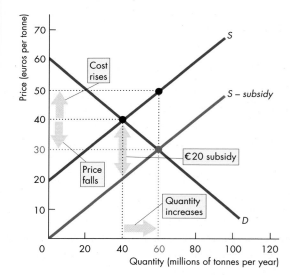

Figure 6.12 The Effects of a Production Subsidy

With no subsidy, 40 million tonnes a year are produced at €40 a tonne. A production subsidy of €20 a tonne shifts the supply curve rightward to *S – subsidy*. The equilibrium quantity increases to 60 million tonnes a year, the price falls to €30 a tonne, and the price plus subsidy received by farmers rises to €50 a tonne. In the new equilibrium, marginal social cost (on the blue supply curve) exceeds marginal social benefit (on the demand curve) and a deadweight loss arises from overproduction.

A Fall in Price and an Increase in Quantity

The subsidy lowers the price of sugar beet and increases the quantity produced. In Figure 6.12, equilibrium occurs where the new supply curve intersects the demand curve at a price of €30 a tonne and a quantity of 60 million tonnes a year.

An Increase in Marginal Cost

The subsidy lowers the price paid by consumers but increases the marginal cost of producing sugar beet. Marginal cost increases because farmers grow more sugar beet, which means that they must begin to use some resources that are less ideal for growing sugar beet. Farmers slide up their supply (and marginal cost) curves. In Figure 6.12, marginal cost increases to €50 a tonne.

Payments by Government to Farmers

The government pays a subsidy to sugar beet farmers on each tonne produced. In this example, farmers increase production to 60 million tonnes a year and receive a subsidy of €20 a tonne. So sugar beet farmers receive a subsidy payment from the government that totals €1,200 million a year.

Inefficient Overproduction

The production subsidy results in inefficient overproduction. At the quantity produced with the subsidy, marginal social benefit is equal to the market price, which has fallen. Marginal social cost has increased and it exceeds the market price. Because marginal social cost exceeds marginal social benefit, the increased production brings inefficiency.

Subsidies spill over to the rest of the world. Because a subsidy lowers the domestic market price, subsidized farmers will offer some of their output for sale on the world market. The increase in supply on the world market lowers the price in the rest of the world. Faced with lower prices, farmers in other countries decrease production and receive smaller revenues.

Price Supports

A **price support** is a government guaranteed minimum price for a good. The EU Common Agricultural Policy (CAP) is the world's most extensive farm support programme. Every year, the EU sets the target price *above*

the equilibrium price for many agricultural products. A price support in an agricultural market operates in a similar way to a price floor in a labour market, but there is a crucial difference between them. The main effects of a price support are:

◆ A rise in the price

◆ An increase in marginal cost

◆ Payments by government to farmers

◆ Inefficient overproduction

Figure 6.13 illustrates the effects of a price support in the market for wheat.

A Rise in the Price

Without price support, the competitive equilibrium price of wheat is €130 a tonne and 4 million tonnes are produced. If the EU sets a target price of €135 a tonne, the market price increases to €135 a tonne and the quantity demanded decreases to 2 million tonnes.

Figure 6.13   The Effects of a Price Support

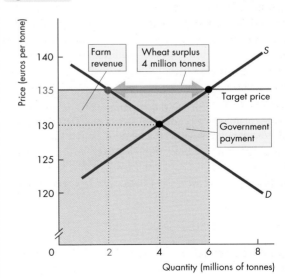

With no price support, 4 million tonnes are produced at €130 a tonne. A price support of €135 a tonne raises the price to €135 a tonne, increases the quantity produced to 6 million tonnes, decreases the quantity sold to 2 million tonnes, and creates a surplus of 4 million tonnes. To maintain the price support, the government buys the surplus for €540 million a year. If the government does not buy the surplus, the price will return to €130 a tonne.

myeconlab Animation

An Increase in Marginal Cost

A higher price encourages farmers to increase the quantity supplied to 6 million tonnes. But as they grow more wheat, they use more resources that are less suited to growing wheat. The marginal cost of production increases.

Payments by Government to Farmers

At the guaranteed price, there is a surplus of 4 million tonnes which the EU must buy to avoid the price falling below the target price. In Figure 6.13, this payment to farmers is €540 million a year.

Inefficient Overproduction

The EU price support system is inefficient because marginal social cost exceeds marginal social benefit. The overproduction or surpluses must be bought and stored at high cost to maintain the target price.

In 2009, the EU spent €55 billion under the CAP to buy and store surplus agricultural produce and more than €120 billion in support payments to farmers.

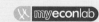

Review Quiz

1 Summarize the effects of a production quota on the market price and quantity produced.
2 Explain why a production quota is inefficient.
3 Summarize the effects of a production subsidy on the market price and the quantity produced.
4 Explain why a production subsidy is inefficient.
5 Summarize the effects of a price support on the market price and the quantity produced.
6 Explain why a price support is inefficient.

You can work these questions in Study Plan 6.4 and get instant feedback.

myeconlab

You've now seen the effects of a wide range of government interventions in markets and how these interventions bring inefficiency.

We're now going to examine markets that the government would like to close down – markets for illegal goods and services. Some examples of illegal goods are drugs, such as cannabis, Ecstasy, cocaine and heroin. Despite the fact that these drugs are illegal, trade in them is a multi-billion pound business. This trade can be understood by using the same economic model and principles that explain trade in legal goods. Let's see how.

Markets for Illegal Goods

Figure 6.14 shows a market for a drug. With demand curve, D and supply curve, S, if drugs are not illegal, the quantity bought and sold is Q_C and the price is P_C.

When a good is illegal, the cost of trading in it increases. By how much the cost increases and on whom the cost falls depend on the penalties for breaking the law and the effectiveness with which the law is enforced. The larger the penalties and the more effective the policing, the higher are the costs of trading the drug. Penalties might be imposed on sellers or buyers or both sellers and buyers.

If selling drugs is illegal, sellers will face fines and prison sentences if their activities are detected. Penalties for selling illegal drugs are part of the cost of supplying those drugs. These penalties lead to a decrease in supply and shift the supply curve of the drug leftward. To determine the new supply curve, we add the cost of breaking the law to the minimum price that drug dealers are willing to accept. In Figure 6.14, the cost of breaking the law by selling drugs (CBL) is added to the minimum price that dealers will accept and the supply curve shifts leftward to $S + CBL$. If penalties are imposed only on sellers, the market moves from point E to point F. The price rises and the quantity bought decreases.

If buying drugs is illegal, buyers face fines and prison sentences if their activities are detected. Penalties for buying the illegal drugs fall on buyers and the cost of breaking the law must be subtracted from the value of the good to determine the maximum price that buyers are willing to pay. Demand decreases and the demand curve shifts leftward. In Figure 6.14, the demand curve shifts to $D - CBL$. If penalties are imposed only on buyers, the market moves from point E to point G. The market price falls and the quantity bought decreases.

If penalties are imposed on sellers *and* buyers, both supply and demand decrease. In Figure 6.14, the costs of breaking the law are the same for both buyers and sellers, so the demand and supply curves shift leftward by the same amounts. The market moves to point H. The market price remains at the competitive market price, but the quantity bought decreases to Q_P. Buyers pay P_C plus the cost of breaking the law, which is P_B. And sellers receive P_C minus the cost of breaking the law, which is P_S.

The larger the penalty and the greater the degree of law enforcement, the larger is the decrease in demand and/or supply and the greater is the shift of the demand and/or supply curve. If the penalties are heavier on

Figure 6.14   A Market for an Illegal Good

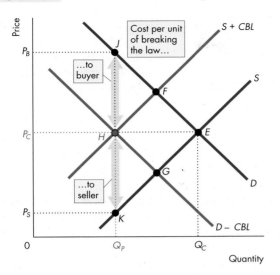

The demand curve for drugs is *D* and the supply curve is *S*. If drugs are not illegal, the quantity bought and sold is Q_C at a price of P_C at point *E*.

If selling drugs is illegal, the cost of breaking the law by selling drugs (*CBL*) is added to the minimum supply-price and supply decreases to *S + CBL*. The market moves to point *F*. If buying drugs is illegal, the cost of breaking the law is subtracted from the maximum price that buyers are willing to pay, and demand decreases to *D – CBL*. The market moves to point *G*.

With both buying and selling illegal, the supply curve and the demand curve shift and the market moves to point *H*. The market price remains at P_C, but the market price plus the penalty for buying rises to P_B (point *J*) and the market price minus the penalty for sellers falls to P_S (point *K*).

myeconlab Animation ─────────────── ◆

sellers, the supply curve shifts further than the demand curve and the market price rises above P_C. If the penalties are heavier on buyers, the demand curve shifts further than the supply curve and the price falls below P_C. In many European countries, the penalties on sellers of illegal drugs are larger than those on buyers. As a result, the decrease in supply is much larger than the decrease in demand. The quantity of drugs traded decreases and the price is higher than in a free market.

With high enough penalties and effective law enforcement, it is possible to reduce the quantity bought to zero. But in reality, such an outcome is unusual as law enforcement is too costly.

Because of this situation, some people suggest that drugs and other illegal goods should be legalized and sold openly but should also be taxed at a high rate in the

same way that legal drugs such as alcohol are taxed. How would such an arrangement work?

From your study of the effects of taxes, you can see that the quantity of drugs bought would decrease if they were taxed. A sufficiently high tax could be imposed to decrease supply, raise the price and achieve the same decrease in the quantity bought as with a prohibition on drugs. The government would collect tax revenue. Such a debate in the UK concerning cannabis led the government to reduce penalties on the illegal trade in 2003 but not to legalize the trade.

It is likely that a very high tax rate would be needed to cut the quantity of drugs bought to the level prevailing with a prohibition. It is also likely that many drug dealers and consumers would try to cover up their activities to evade the tax. If they did act in this way, they would face the cost of breaking the law – the tax law. If the penalty for tax law violation is as severe and as effectively policed as drug-dealing laws, the analysis we've already conducted applies also to this case. The quantity of drugs bought would depend on the penalties for law breaking and on the way in which the penalties are assigned to buyers and sellers.

Which is more effective: prohibition or taxes? In favour of taxes and against prohibition is the fact that the tax revenue can be used to make law enforcement more effective. It can also be used to run a more effective education campaign against illegal drug use. In favour of prohibition and against taxes is the fact that prohibition sends a signal that might influence preferences, decreasing the demand for illegal drugs. Also, some people intensely dislike the idea of the government profiting from trade in harmful substances.

Review Quiz

1   How does a penalty on sellers of an illegal good influence demand, supply, price and the quantity consumed?

2   How does a penalty on buyers of an illegal good influence demand, supply, price and the quantity consumed?

3   How does a penalty on both sellers and buyers of an illegal good influence demand, supply, price and the quantity consumed?

4   What is the case for legalizing drugs?

You can work these questions in Study Plan 6.4 and get instant feedback.

Reading Between the Lines on pp. 144–145 looks at why farm subsidies increased in 2009.

Reading Between the Lines

Increase in Farm Subsidies

The OECD, 1 July 2010

Government Support to Farmers Rises Slightly in OECD Countries

The share of farm receipts provided by government programmes rose slightly in OECD countries last year, reversing a declining trend in state support since 2004, according to a new OECD report. . . .

The latest rise in support across the OECD countries was due to the easing back of agricultural commodity prices after they hit record highs in 2008. The falls triggered government programmes aimed at propping up domestic prices or farm income.

The sharpest rises in support to farmers ... last year occurred in Canada, . . . Korea, . . . Norway, . . . and Switzerland. . . . In each of these countries the main cause was increased price support for dairy products. In the US, support to farmers rose to 10% of total farm receipts from 8% last year while in the EU the rise was to 24% from 22%. . . .

The report . . . says . . . policy makers should reduce subsidies which distort markets and cut the link between government payments and agricultural production.

Compensating farmers for low prices or insulating consumers from price fluctuations through export controls merely contributes to higher volatility in world prices, the report says.

Ken Ash, the OECD's Director of Trade and Agriculture, said: 'More focus should be placed on improving risk management while better functioning and more transparent global markets could reduce price volatility'.

The Essence of the Story

◆ Governments around the world make income support payments to farmers.

◆ As food prices increased between 2004 and 2008, the percentage of farm incomes from subsidies decreased.

◆ In 2009, a fall in food prices triggered an increase in subsidies as a percentage of farm income.

◆ In the EU, the increase was from 22 per cent of income to 24 per cent of income.

Economic Analysis

◆ The news article reports an increase in government payments to farmers triggered by lower prices for farm products.

◆ In this chapter, you've seen two ways in which governments support farmers: *production subsidies* and *price supports*.

◆ Figure 1 shows the effect of a production subsidy on wheat. Demand curve is *D*, supply curve is *S* and with no subsidy, the price would be €150 per tonne and the quantity produced would be 15 million tonnes.

◆ With a production subsidy of €20 per tonne, the supply curve is *S − subsidy*. The market price is €140 and the quantity demanded is 20 million tonnes. Farmers receive €2,800 million in the market and €400 million, which is 12.5 per cent of their total revenue, from the government.

◆ If the demand for wheat decreases, the market price falls, the quantity sold decreases, total revenue falls and the total subsidy payment falls. But the subsidy payment *increases as a percentage of total revenue*.

◆ Figure 2 shows the effect of the EU-style price support for wheat. As before, with no intervention the price is €150 a tonne and 15 million tonnes are produced.

◆ With a target price €160, 20 million tonnes are produced but only 10 million tonnes are purchased by consumers for which farmers receive €1,600 million. There is a surplus of 10 million tonnes a year.

◆ To maintain the target price the EU must buy the 10 million tonnes surplus at the target price of €160 a tonne. The government's total payment to farmers is €1,600 million or 50 per cent of their total receipts.

◆ If the target price remains the same and the demand for wheat decreases, the quantity sold decreases, surplus production and the government payment increase and the total government payment to farmers increases.

Figure 1 Production subsidy

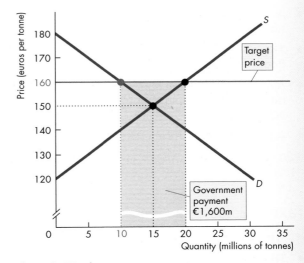

Figure 2 EU price support payments

◆ Both systems are inefficient and result in overproduction.

◆ The scale of government support for farmers in the EU is much higher than in most other large countries. (The news article reports the EU at 24 per cent compared to the US at 10 per cent.)

◆ EU farm support is among the most inefficient in the world.

◆ SUMMARY

Key Points

A Housing Market with a Rent Ceiling (pp. 128–130)

◆ A rent ceiling set above the equilibrium rent has no effect.

◆ If a rent ceiling is set below the equilibrium rent it creates a housing shortage, increases search activity and creates a black market.

◆ A rent ceiling that is set below the equilibrium rent is inefficient and unfair.

Working Problems 1 to 6 will give you a better understanding of a housing market with a rent ceiling.

A Labour Market with a Minimum Wage (pp. 131–133)

◆ A price floor set below the equilibrium price has no effect.

◆ The minimum wage is an example of a price floor.

◆ A minimum wage set above the equilibrium wage rate creates unemployment and increases search activity.

◆ A price floor is inefficient and unfair.

Working Problems 7 to 12 will give you a better understanding of a labour market with a minimum wage.

Taxes (pp. 133–138)

◆ A tax raises price but usually by less than the tax.

◆ The share of tax paid by buyers and sellers depend on the elasticity of demand and the elasticity of supply.

◆ The less elastic the demand and more elastic the supply, the greater is the price increase, the smaller is the quantity decrease, and the larger is the portion of the tax paid by buyers.

◆ If demand is perfectly elastic or supply is perfectly inelastic, sellers pay the entire tax. And if demand is perfectly inelastic or supply is perfectly elastic, buyers pay the entire tax.

Working Problems 13 to 15 will give you a better understanding of taxes.

Production Quotas and Subsidies and Price Supports (pp. 139–142)

◆ A production quota leads to inefficient underproduction, which raises price.

◆ A production subsidy is like a negative tax. It lowers the price and leads to inefficient overproduction.

◆ A price support leads to inefficient overproduction.

◆ The Common Agricultural Policy uses costly price supports.

Working Problems 16 to 18 will give you a better understanding of production quotas, subsidies and price supports.

Markets for Illegal Goods (pp. 142–143)

◆ Penalties on sellers of an illegal good increase the cost of selling the good and decrease its supply. Penalties on buyers decrease their willingness to pay and decrease demand for the good.

◆ The higher the penalties and the more effective the law enforcement, the smaller is the quantity bought.

◆ A tax that is set at a sufficiently high rate will decrease the quantity of a drug consumed, but there will be a tendency for the tax to be evaded.

Working Problem 19 will give you a better understanding of markets for illegal goods.

Key Terms

Black market, 128
Minimum wage, 131
Price cap, 128
Price ceiling, 128
Price floor, 131
Price support, 141
Production quota, 139
Production subsidy, 140
Rent ceiling, 128
Search activity, 128
Tax incidence, 133

STUDY PLAN PROBLEMS AND APPLICATIONS

 myeconlab   You can work Problems 1 to 19 in MyEconlab Study Plan Chapter 6 and get instant feedback.

A Housing Market with a Rent Ceiling
(Study Plan 6.1)

Use the following graph of the market for rental housing in Townsville to work Problems 1 and 2.

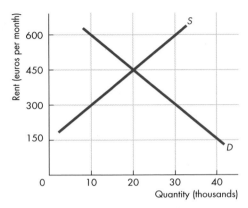

1 a What are the equilibrium rent and equilibrium quantity of rented housing?

b If a rent ceiling is set at €600 a month, what is the quantity of housing rented and what is the shortage of housing?

2 If a rent ceiling is set at €300 a month, what is the quantity of housing rented, the shortage of housing and the maximum price that someone is willing to pay for the last unit available?

Use the following news clip to work Problems 3 to 6.

Capping Petrol Prices

As petrol prices rise, many people are calling for price caps, but price caps generate a distorted reflection of reality, which leads buyers and suppliers to act in ways inconsistent with the price cap. By masking reality, price caps only make matters worse.

Source: *Pittsburgh Tribune-Review*,
12 September 2005

Suppose that a price ceiling is set below the equilibrium price.

3 How does the price cap influence the quantity of petrol supplied and the quantity demanded?

4 How does the price cap influence:

a The quantity of petrol sold and the shortage or surplus of petrol?

b The maximum price that someone is willing to pay for the last litre of petrol available on a black market?

5 Draw a graph to illustrate the effects of a price ceiling set below the equilibrium price in the market for petrol.

6 Explain the various ways in which a price ceiling on petrol that is set below the equilibrium price would make buyers and sellers of petrol better off or worse off. What would happen to total surplus and deadweight loss in this market?

A Labour Market with a Minimum Wage (Study Plan 6.2)

Use the following data to work Problems 7 to 9.

The table gives the demand and supply schedules of teenage labour.

Wage rate (pounds per hour)	Quantity demanded	Quantity supplied
	(hours per month)	
4	3,000	1,000
5	2,500	1,500
6	2,000	2,000
7	1,500	2,500
8	1,000	3,000

7 Calculate the equilibrium wage rate, the number of hours worked and the quantity of unemployment.

8 If a minimum wage for teenagers is £5 an hour, how many hours do they work and how many hours of teenage labour are unemployed?

9 If a minimum wage for teenagers is £7 an hour,

a How many hours do teenagers work and how many hours are unemployed?

b Demand for teenage labour increases by 500 hours a month. What is the wage rate paid to teenagers and how many hours of teenage labour are unemployed?

Use the following news clip to work Problems 10 to 12.

India Steps Up Pressure for Minimum Wage for Its Workers in the Gulf.

Oil-rich countries in the Persian Gulf, already confronted by strong labour protests, are facing renewed pressure from India to pay minimum wages for unskilled workers. With five million immigrant workers in the region, India is trying to win better conditions for their citizens.

Source: *International Herald Tribune*,
27 March 2008

Suppose that the Gulf countries paid a minimum wage above the equilibrium wage to Indian workers.

10 How would the market for labour be affected in the Gulf countries? Draw a supply and demand graph to illustrate your answer.

11 How would the market for labour be affected in India? Draw a supply and demand graph to illustrate your answer. [Be careful: the minimum wage is in the Gulf countries, not in India.]

12 Would migrant Indian workers be better off or worse off or unaffected by this minimum wage?

Taxes (Study Plan 6.3)

13 The table shows the demand and supply schedules for chocolate brownies in the UK.

Price (pence per brownie)	Quantity demanded	Quantity supplied
	(millions per day)	
50	5	3
60	4	4
70	3	5
80	2	6
90	1	7

a If brownies are not taxed, what is the price of a brownie and how many are consumed?

b If sellers are taxed at 20 pence a brownie, what is the price and how many brownies are sold? Who pays the tax?

c If buyers are taxed at 20 pence a brownie, what is the price and how many brownies are bought? Who pays the tax?

14 Imagine the UK government introduces a new tax on luxury items. The government anticipates that the tax will generate £30 million in revenue, but it generated only £16 million in revenue.

a Explain whether buyers or sellers of luxury items would pay more of the luxury tax.

b Explain why the luxury tax generated less tax revenue than was originally anticipated.

15 Suppose the tax on petrol is reduced by 18 pence a litre during August. Despite the cut in tax, high petrol prices are predicted to keep UK residents at home this summer.

Would the price of petrol that UK consumers pay fall by 18 pence a litre? How would consumer surplus change? Explain your answers.

Production Quotas and Subsidies and Price Supports (Study Plan 6.4)

Use the following data to work Problems 16 to 18.

The demand and supply schedules for rice are:

Price (pounds per box)	Quantity demanded	Quantity supplied
	(boxes per week)	
1.00	3,500	500
1.10	3,250	1,000
1.20	3,000	1,500
1.30	2,750	2,000
1.40	2,500	2,500
1.50	2,250	3,000
1.60	2,000	3,500

16 Calculate the price, the marginal cost of producing rice, and the quantity produced if the government sets a production quota of 2,000 boxes a week.

17 Calculate the price, the marginal cost of producing rice, and the quantity produced if the government introduces a production subsidy of £0.30 a box.

18 Calculate the price, the marginal cost of producing rice, the quantity produced and the surplus created if the government introduces a price support of £1.50 a box.

Markets for Illegal Goods (Study Plan 6.5)

19 The figure shows the market for a banned substance.

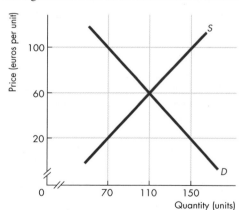

What are the equilibrium price and quantity if a penalty of €20 a unit is imposed on:

a Sellers only?

b Buyers only?

c Both sellers and buyers?

ADDITIONAL PROBLEMS AND APPLICATIONS

 You can work these problems in MyEconlab if assigned by your lecturer.

A Housing Market with a Rent Ceiling

Use the news clip to work Problems 20 and 21.

Why Rent Control Won't Go Away

Once in place, rent control usually proves extremely difficult to undo. London and Paris still have rent controls adopted as temporary measures during the First World War. 'Nelson's Third Law' – the contention by the late economist Arthur Nelson that the worse a government regulation is, the more difficult it is to get rid of – seems to apply here.

Source: William Tucker, Heartland Institute, 1 September 1997

20 a Who are the people who gain from rent controls?

   b Why are rent controls inefficient?

21 a Are the rent controls in London that remain from the First World War fair?

   b Explain 'Nelson's Third Law'. Why does it seem to apply to the rental market in London?

A Labour Market with a Minimum Wage

Use the news clip to work Problems 22 and 23.

Labour's Manifesto

The proposal for a 'living wage' of £7.60 an hour for employees in some parts of the public sector apply to low-skilled workers in the private sector.

Source: *The Financial Times*, 28 September 2010

22 On a graph of the market for low-skilled labour, show the effect of the introduction of a living wage on the quantity of labour employed.

23 Explain the effects of the high living wage on the workers' surplus and the firms' surplus. Will a living wage make the labour market more efficient or less efficient? Explain.

Taxes

24 The demand and supply schedules for roses are:

Price (pounds per bunch)	Quantity demanded	Quantity supplied
	(bunches per week)	
10	100	40
12	90	60
14	80	80
16	70	100
18	60	120

   a If there is no tax on roses, what is the price and how many bunches of roses are bought?

   b If roses are taxed at £6 a bunch, what is the price and quantity bought? Who pays the tax?

Use the following news clip to work Problems 25 to 27.

Cigarette Smuggling Ring Smashed

Customs officers have cracked a multimillion-euro cigarette smuggling operation. About 28 million illegally-imported cigarettes – worth 11.8 million euros – were seized. The potential loss to the exchequer is 9.4 million euro.

Source: *Belfast Telegraph*, 23 February 2010

25 How has the market for cigarettes in the UK responded to the high tax on cigarettes?

26 What effect does the emergence of a black market have on the elasticity of demand in the legal market for cigarettes?

27 Why might an increase in the tax rate actually cause a decrease in the tax revenue?

Production Quotas and Subsidies and Price Supports

Use the following figure to work Problems 28 to 30.

The figure shows the market for tomatoes. The government introduces a price support for tomatoes at €8 per pound.

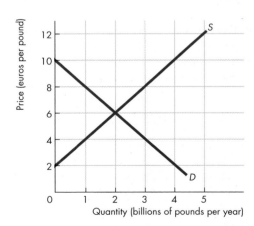

28 Before the price support is introduced, what are the equilibrium price and quantity of tomatoes? Is the market for tomatoes efficient?

29 After the government introduces a price support, what is the quantity of tomatoes produced, the quantity demanded, and the payment received by tomato farmers?

30 With the price support, is the market for tomatoes efficient? Who gains and who loses from the price support and is it efficient? Could the price support be regarded as being fair?

31 **French Farmers Man the Blockades in Brussels**

Farmers want the dairy industry to guarantee a minimum milk price of €300 per tonne – against €210 per tonne this month. Max Bottier, a dairy farmer in Normandy said that he needed €300 per tonne to break even.

Source: *The Times*, 26 May 2009

If a support price for milk is introduced and set at €300 per tonne, how will such a support price change the quantity of milk produced and the quantity bought by consumers. Who buys the excess supply? Will the European milk market be more or less efficient than it is today?

Markets for Illegal Goods

32 The table sets out the demand and supply schedules for an illegal drug.

Price (euros per unit)	Quantity demanded	Quantity supplied
	(units per day)	
50	500	300
60	400	400
70	300	500
80	200	600
90	100	700

a If there are no penalties on buying or selling the drug, what is the price and how many units a day are consumed?

b If the penalty on sellers is €20 per unit, what is the price and quantity consumed?

c If the penalty on buyers is €20 per unit, what is the price and quantity consumed?

Economics in the News

33 After you have studied *Reading Between the Lines* on pp. 144–145 answer the following questions.

a Compare and contrast the effects of a production subsidy with a price support system like that of the EU.

b Draw a graph to illustrate the effects of an increase in demand with a production subsidy and show why the percentage of farm income received from the government decreases.

c Draw a graph to illustrate the effects of an increase in demand with a price support and show why farm income received from the government decreases unless the support price is increased.

d Explain why both farm income support schemes are inefficient and why the EU system is even more inefficient than a production subsidy.

Use the following news clip for Problems 34 to 36.

Coal Shortage at China Plants

Chinese power plants have run short of coal, an unintended effect of government-mandated price controls designed to shield the public from rising global energy costs. Beijing has also frozen retail prices of petrol and diesel. That helped farmers and the urban poor, but it has spurred sales of big luxury cars and propelled double-digit annual growth in petrol consumption. At the same time, oil refiners are suffering heavy losses and some have begun cutting production, causing fuel shortages.

Source: CNN, 20 May 2008

34 **a** Are China's price controls described in the news clip price floors or price ceilings?

b Explain how China's price controls have created shortages or surpluses in the markets for coal, petrol and diesel.

c Illustrate your answer to part (b) graphically by using the supply and demand model.

35 Explain how China's price controls have changed consumer surplus, producer surplus, total surplus, and the deadweight loss in the markets for coal, petrol and diesel.

36 Show on a graph the change in consumer surplus, producer surplus, total surplus, and the deadweight loss in the markets for coal, petrol and diesel.

37 On 31 December 1776, Rhode Island established wage controls to limit wages to 70 cents a day for carpenters and 42 cents a day for tailors.

a Are these wage controls a price ceiling or a price floor? Why might they have been introduced?

b If these wage controls are effective, would you expect to see a surplus or a shortage of carpenters and tailors?

38 **Motorway Protest Over Rising Fuel Prices**

After fuel prices have soared to an all-time high, hundreds of bikers and motorists are expected to stage a go-slow protest along one of the North of England's main motorways. The AA said a two-car family had seen its monthly fuel costs rise from £233.32 to £254.60.

Source: *The Yorkshire Post*, 27 September 2010

Explain to protesting drivers why a price cap on the price of fuel would hurt families more than the high price of fuel.

Global Markets in Action

After studying this chapter you will be able to:

◆ Explain how markets work with international trade

◆ Explain the gains from international trade and identify its winners and losers

◆ Explain the effects of international trade barriers

◆ Explain and assess the arguments used to justify international trade barriers

Cheap fashion, banking services, iPhones and cars are all examples of the benefits of trade in global markets. Today, cargo jets and container ships carry billions of pounds worth of goods around the globe. Why go to such lengths to trade with others in far away places?

All these activities are part of the globalization process that is having a profound effect on our lives. Globalization is controversial and generates heated debate. Can EU companies compete with Asian companies where wages are much lower? Shouldn't governments restrict international trade and protect local producers?

In *Reading Between the Lines* at the end of the chapter you can apply what you have learned and see why EU car makers want to keep tariffs on cars from South Korea.

How Global Markets Work

Because we trade with people in other countries, the goods and services that we can buy and consume are not limited by what we can produce. The goods and services that we buy from other countries are our **imports**; and the goods and services that we sell to people in other countries are our **exports**.

International Trade Today

Global trade today is vast. In 2009, global exports and imports were over $31 trillion which is half the value of global production. The US is by far the world's largest international trader, with Germany ranked second and China ranked third.

The EU of 27 member states is the world's main exporting region. EU trade with countries outside the member states comprises 20 per cent of global trade. EU countries trade both goods and services with the rest of the world. About 70 per cent of UK international trade is trade in goods such as cars and chemicals and 30 per cent is trade in services such as tourism and finance.

Some EU member states, such as Germany, Finland and the Netherlands export more in value than they import, whereas others such as the UK, Ireland and Spain import more than they export.

What Drives International Trade?

Comparative advantage is the fundamental force that drives international trade. Comparative advantage (see Chapter 2, p. 40) is a situation in which a person can perform an activity or produce a good or service at a lower opportunity cost than anyone else. This same idea applies to nations. We can define *national comparative advantage* as a situation in which a nation can perform an activity or produce a good or service at a lower opportunity cost than any other nation.

The opportunity cost of producing a car is lower in Japan than in the UK, so Japan has a comparative advantage in producing cars. The opportunity cost of producing chemicals is lower in the UK than in Japan, so the UK has a comparative advantage in producing chemicals.

You saw in Chapter 2 how Erin and Jack reap gains from trade by specializing in the production of the good at which they have a comparative advantage and then trading with each other. Both are better off.

This same principle applies to trade among nations. Because Japan has a comparative advantage at producing

ECONOMICS IN ACTION

EU Trade Focus

The figure shows the four main areas of EU exports and EU imports. The EU exported goods and services worth €1,095,680 million and imported €1,199,807 million in 2009. Manufactured goods made up 59.4 per cent of imports but 80 per cent of exports. The second main import was fuel. Agricultural goods and others (including services) comprise about 8 per cent of imports and exports.

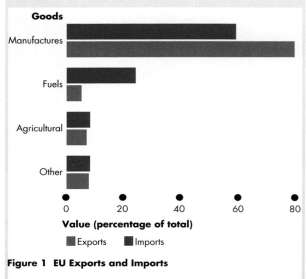

Figure 1 EU Exports and Imports

Source of data: Europa

cars and the UK has a comparative advantage at producing chemicals, the people of both countries can gain from specialization and trade. Japan can buy chemicals from the UK at a lower opportunity cost than that at which Japanese firms can produce them. People in the UK can buy cars from Japan for a lower opportunity cost than that at which UK firms can produce them. Also, through international trade, Japanese producers can get higher prices for their cars and Blue Circle can sell cement powder for a higher price. Both countries gain from international trade.

Let's now illustrate the gains from trade that we've just described by studying demand and supply in the global markets for cars and chemicals.

Why the UK Imports Cars

The UK imports cars because the rest of the world has a comparative advantage in producing cars. Figure 7.1 illustrates how this comparative advantage generates international trade and how trade influences the price of a car and the quantities produced and bought.

The demand curve D_{UK} and the supply curve S_{UK} show the demand and supply in the UK domestic market with no international trade. The demand curve tells us the quantity of cars that UK consumers are willing to buy at various prices. The supply curve tells us the quantity of cars that UK car makers are willing to sell at various prices – that is, the quantity supplied at each price when all cars sold in the UK are produced in the UK.

Figure 7.1(a) shows what the UK car market would be like with no international trade. The price of a car

would be £20,000 and 1 million cars a year would be produced by UK car makers and bought by UK consumers.

Figure 7.1(b) shows the market for cars with international trade. Now the price of a car is determined in the world market, not the UK domestic market. The world price is less than £20,000 a car, which means that the rest of the world has a comparative advantage in producing cars. The world price line shows the world price at £15,000 a car.

The UK demand curve, D_{UK}, tells us that at £15,000 a car, UK consumers buy 1.4 million cars a year. The UK supply curve, S_{UK}, tells us that at £15,000 a car, UK car makers produce 0.4 million cars a year. To buy 1.4 million cars when only 0.4 million are produced in the UK, we must import cars from the rest of the world. The quantity of cars imported is 1 million a year.

Figure 7.1   A Market with Imports

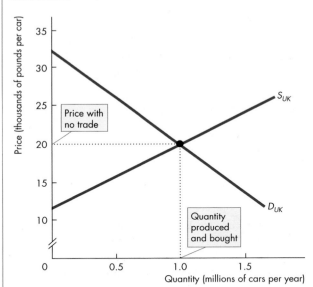

(a) Equilibrium without international trade

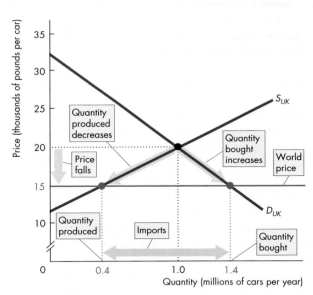

(b) Equilibrium in a market with imports

The supply of cars produced by UK car makers is S_{UK} and the demand for cars by UK consumers is D_{UK}. With no international trade, in part (a), the equilibrium price of a car in the UK is £20,000 and 1 million cars a year are produced and bought.

In part (b), the world price of a car is £15,000 and the rest of the world has a comparative advantage in

producing cars. With international trade, the price of a car in the UK falls to the world price.

The quantity of cars bought in the UK increases to 1.4 million a year and the quantity produced in the UK decreases to 0.4 million a year. The quantity imported equals the quantity bought minus the quantity produced in the UK, which is 1 million cars a year.

Why the UK Exports Chemicals

Figure 7.2 illustrates international trade in chemicals. The demand curve D_{UK} and the supply curve S_{UK} show the demand and supply in the UK domestic market only. The demand curve tells us the quantity of chemicals that UK buyers are willing to buy at various prices. The supply curve tells us the quantity of chemicals that UK chemical makers are willing to sell at various prices.

Figure 7.2(a) shows what the UK chemicals market would be like with no international trade. The price would be £40 per tonne and 100 million tonnes of chemicals a year would be produced by UK makers and bought by UK buyers.

Figure 7.2(b) shows the UK chemicals market with international trade. Now the price of chemicals is determined in the world market and the world price is higher than £40 per tonne, which means that the UK has a comparative advantage in producing chemicals. The world price line shows the world price at £75 a tonne.

The UK demand curve, D_{UK}, tells us that at £75 a tonne, 40 million tonnes of chemicals are bought by UK buyers a year. The UK supply curve, S_{UK}, tells us that at £75 a tonne, UK chemical makers produce 300 million tonnes a year. The quantity produced in the UK (300 million tonnes a year) minus the quantity purchased by UK buyers (40 million tonnes a year) is the quantity of chemicals exported, which is 260 million tonnes a year.

Review Quiz

1 Describe the situation in the market for a good or service that the UK imports.
2 Describe the situation in the market for a good or service that the UK exports.

You can work these questions in Study Plan 7.1 and get instant feedback.

myeconlab

Figure 7.2 A Market with Exports

(a) Equilibrium without international trade

(b) Equilibrium in a market with exports

In part (a), the UK market with no international trade, the UK domestic demand curve D_{UK} and the UK domestic supply curve S_{UK} determine the price at £40 a tonne and 100 million tonnes a year are produced and bought.

In part (b), the UK market with international trade, world demand and world supply determine the world price, which is £75 a tonne. The price in the UK market rises. UK chemical production increases to 300 million tonnes a year, UK purchases of chemicals decrease to 40 million tonnes a year and the UK exports 260 million tonnes of chemicals a year.

Winners, Losers and the Net Gain from Trade

In Chapter 1 (see p. 7), we asked whether globalization is in the self-interest of the low-wage worker in India who sews sequins on a T-shirt or a displaced clothing worker in London – whether it is in the social interest. We're now going to answer these questions. You will learn why producers complain about cheap foreign imports and why consumers of imported goods and services never complain.

Gains and Losses from Imports

We measure the gains and losses from imports by examining their effect on consumer surplus, producer surplus and total surplus. In the importing country the winners are those whose surplus increases and the losers are those whose surplus decreases.

Figure 7.3(a) shows what consumer surplus and producer surplus would be with no international trade in cars. UK domestic demand, D_{UK}, and UK domestic supply, S_{UK}, determine the price and quantity. The green area shows consumer surplus and the blue area shows producer surplus. Total surplus is the sum of consumer surplus and producer surplus.

Figure 7.3(b) shows how these surpluses change when the UK market opens to imports. The UK price falls to the world price. The quantity bought increases to the quantity demanded at the world price and consumer surplus expands from A to the larger green area $A + B + D$. The quantity produced in the UK decreases to the quantity supplied at the world price and producer surplus shrinks to the smaller blue area C.

Part of the gain in consumer surplus, the area B, is a loss of producer surplus – a redistribution of total surplus. But the other part of the increase in consumer surplus, the area D, is a net gain. This increase in total surplus results from the lower price and increased purchases and is the gain from imports.

Figure 7.3   Gains and Losses in a Market with Imports

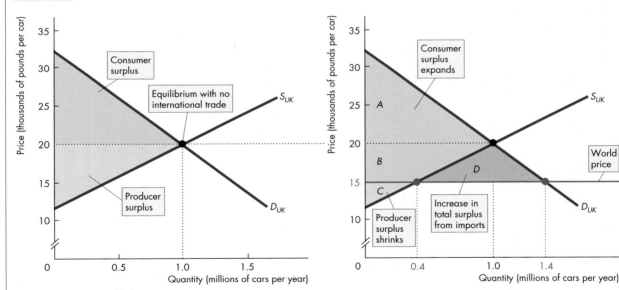

(a) Consumer and producer surplus without international trade

(b) The gains and losses from imports

In part (a), with no international trade, the green area shows the consumer surplus and the blue area shows the producer surplus.

In part (b), with international trade, the price of a car falls to the world price of £15,000. Consumer surplus expands to area $A + B + D$. Producer surplus shrinks to the area C. Area B is a transfer of surplus from producers to consumers. Area D is an increase in total surplus.

Gains and Losses from Exports

We measure the gains and losses from exports just like we measured those from imports, by their effect on consumer surplus, producer surplus and total surplus.

Figure 7.4(a) shows the situation with no international trade. The UK demand, D_{UK}, and UK supply, S_{UK}, determine the price and quantity. The green area shows the consumer surplus and the blue area shows the producer surplus. The two surpluses sum to the total surplus.

Figure 7.4(b) shows how the consumer surplus and producer surplus change when the good is exported. The price rises to the world price. The quantity bought decreases to the quantity demanded at the world price and the consumer surplus shrinks to the green area A. The quantity produced increases to the quantity supplied at the world price and the producer surplus expands to the blue area $B + C + D$.

Part of the gain in producer surplus, the area B, is a loss in consumer surplus – a redistribution of the total surplus. But the other part of the increase in producer

surplus, the area D, is a net gain. This increase in total surplus results from the higher price and increased production and is the gain from exports.

Gains for All

You've seen that both imports and exports bring gains. Because one country's exports are other countries' imports, international trade brings gain for all countries. International trade is a win–win game.

Figure 7.4 Gains and Losses in a Market with Exports

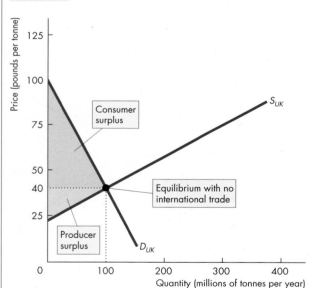

(a) Consumer and producer surplus without international trade

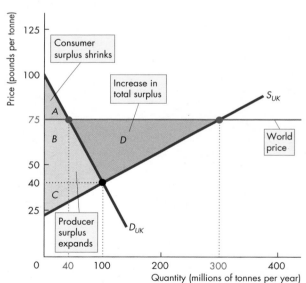

(b) The gains and losses from exports

In part (a), the UK market with no international trade, the green area shows the consumer surplus and the blue area shows the producer surplus. In part (b), the UK market with international trade, the price rises to the world price.

Consumer surplus shrinks to area A. Producer surplus expands to area $B + C + D$. Area B is a transfer of surplus from consumers to producers. Area D is an increase in total surplus – the gains from exports.

International Trade Restrictions

Governments use four main tools to restrict international trade and to protect domestic industries from foreign competition. They are:

◆ Tariffs
◆ Import quotas
◆ Export subsidies
◆ Other import barriers

Tariffs

A **tariff** is a tax that is imposed by the importing country when an imported good crosses its international boundary. For example, the EU imposed a new tariff of 20 per cent at its border on imported leather shoes from China in 2006. So when an EU citizen imports a pair of Chinese leather shoes costing €50 they pay the EU administration an import duty of €10.

Tariffs raise revenue for governments and serve the self-interest of people who earn their incomes in import-competing industries. But as you will see, restrictions on free international trade decrease the gains from trade and are not in the social interest.

The Effects of a Tariff

To see the effects of a tariff, let's return to the example in which the UK imports cars. With free trade, cars are imported and sold at the world price. Then under pressure from UK car producers, the UK government imposes a tariff on imported cars. Buyers of cars must now pay the world price plus the tariff. Several consequences follow and Figure 7.5 illustrates them.

In Figure 7.5(a) with no international trade, the world price is £15,000 per car, UK car makers produce 0.4 million cars per year and the UK imports 1 million cars a year. Figure 7.5(b) shows what happens with a tariff set at £4,000 per car.

Figure 7.5   The Effects of a Tariff

(a) Free trade

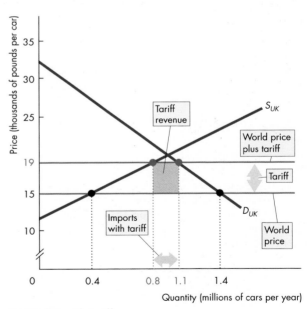

(b) Market with tariff

The world price of a car is £15,000. With free international trade in part (a), 1.4 million cars a year are bought by UK citizens. UK car makers produce 0.4 million cars a year and the UK imports 1 million cars a year.

With a tariff of £4,000 a car in part (b), the price in the UK rises to £19,000 a car. UK production increases, UK purchases decrease and UK imports decrease. The UK government collects a tariff revenue of £4,000 on each car imported (the purple rectangle).

The following changes occur in the UK car market:

◆ The price of a car rises

◆ The quantity of cars bought decreases

◆ The quantity of cars produced increases

◆ The quantity of cars imported decreases

◆ The UK government collects a tariff revenue

The Price of a Car Rises

To buy a car, UK citizens must pay the world price plus the tariff, so the price of a car rises by the £4,000 tariff to £19,000. Figure 7.5(b) shows the new domestic price line, which lies £4,000 above the world price line. The price rises by the full amount of the tariff. The buyer pays the entire tariff because supply from the rest of the world is perfectly elastic (see Chapter 6, pp. 136–137).

The Quantity of Cars Bought Decreases

The higher price of a car brings a decrease in the quantity demanded along the demand curve. Figure 7.5(b) shows the decrease from 1.4 million cars a year at £15,000 a car to 1.1 million a year at £19,000 a car.

The Quantity of Cars Produced Increases

The higher price of a car stimulates domestic production and UK car makers increase the quantity supplied along the supply curve. Figure 7.5(b) shows the increase from 0.4 million cars at £15,000 a car to 0.8 million a year at £19,000 a car.

The Quantity of Cars Imported Decreases

UK imports of cars decrease by 0.7 million, from 1 million to 0.3 million a year. Both the decrease in UK purchases and the increase in UK production contribute to this decrease in UK imports.

Tariff Revenue

The government's tariff revenue is £1,200 million – £4,000 per car on 0.3 million imported cars – and is shown by the purple rectangle of Figure 7.5(b).

Winners, Losers and the Social Loss from a Tariff

A tariff on an imported good creates winners and losers and a social loss. When the UK government imposes a tariff on an imported good,

◆ UK consumers of the good lose

◆ UK producers of the good gain

◆ UK consumers lose more than UK producers gain

◆ Society loses: a deadweight loss arises

ECONOMICS IN ACTION

Free Trade and EU Tariffs

The EU Single European Market has created the largest tariff-free area in the world. The EU has also cut other non-tariff barriers to internal trade and created some free trade areas with non-EU countries.

EU buyers of agricultural products face prices that are on the average 40 per cent above world prices. These higher prices result from the Common Agricultural Policy price support programme for farmers (see Chapter 6 p. 141). To keep EU prices higher than world prices, the EU imposes tariffs on non-EU imports of agricultural products. The higher the price support for farm income, the higher the import tariffs.

Figure 1 shows how EU support to farm incomes has changed over the past 30 years. As the level of farm support has fallen, so too has the average level of tariffs on farm products.

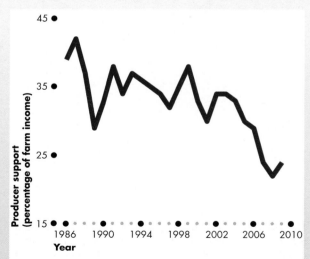

Figure 1 EU Agricultural Support

Source of data: OECD.

UK Consumers of the Good Lose

Because the UK price of a car rises, the quantity of cars demanded decreases. The combination of a higher price and smaller quantity bought decreases consumer surplus – the loss to UK consumers that arises from a tariff.

UK Producers of the Good Gain

Because the price of an imported car rises by the amount of the tariff, UK car makers are now able to sell their cars for the world price plus the tariff. At the higher price, the quantity of cars supplied by UK car makers increases. The combination of a higher price and larger quantity produced increases producer surplus – the gain to UK producers from the tariff.

UK Consumers Lose More than UK Producers Gain

Consumer surplus decreases for four reasons: some becomes producer surplus, some is lost in a higher cost of production (UK production costs are higher than foreign costs), some is lost because imports decrease and some goes to the UK government as tariff revenue.

Figure 7.6 shows these sources of lost consumer surplus. Part (a) shows the consumer surplus and producer surplus with free international trade in cars. Part (b)

shows these surpluses with a £4,000 tariff on imported cars. By comparing the two parts of the figure, you can see how a tariff changes the surpluses.

Consumer surplus – the green area – shrinks for the four reasons just discussed. First, the higher price transfers surplus from consumers to producers. The blue area *B* represents this transfer. Second, UK production costs are higher than foreign production costs. The supply curve S_{UK} shows the higher cost and the grey area *E* shows this loss. Third, some of the consumer surplus is transferred to the government as tariff revenue. The purple area *D* shows this transfer. Fourth, some consumer surplus is lost because imports decrease. The grey area *F* shows this loss.

Society Loses: a Deadweight Loss Arises

Some of the loss of consumer surplus is transferred to producers and some to the government and spent on government programmes that people value. But the increase in production cost and the loss from decreased imports is transferred to no one: it is a social loss – a deadweight loss. The grey areas labelled *E* and *F* represent this deadweight loss. Total surplus decreases by the area *E* + *F*.

Figure 7.6 The Effects of a Tariff

(a) Free trade

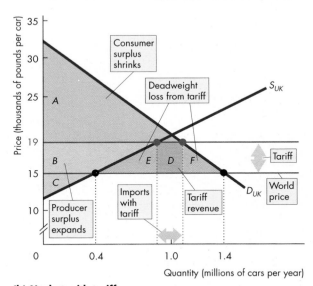

(b) Market with tariff

The world price of a car is £15,000. In part (a), with free trade, the UK imports 1 million cars a year. Consumer surplus, producer surplus and the gains from free trade are as large as possible.

In part (b), a tariff of £4,000 a car raises the UK price to

£19,000 per car. The quantity imported decreases. Consumer surplus shrinks by the areas *B*, *E*, *D* and *F*. Producer surplus increases by the area *B*. The government's tariff revenue is area *D* and the tariff creates a deadweight loss equal to the area *E* + *F*.

Import Quotas

An **import quota** is a restriction that limits the maximum quantity of a good that may be imported in a given period. Many countries impose import quotas and the UK imposed them on Japanese cars during the 1990s.

When the UK imposes a quota on imported cars, the UK price rises, the quantity bought decreases and the quantity produced in the UK increases. Figure 7.7 illustrates the effects.

Figure 7.7(a) shows what happens with an import quota of 0.3 million cars a year. The UK supply curve of cars becomes the domestic supply curve, S_{UK}, plus the import quota. So the supply curve becomes $S_{UK} + quota$. The price rises to £19,000, the quantity of cars bought decreases, the quantity of cars produced in the UK increases and car imports decrease to the quota. All the effects of this quota are identical to those of a £4,000 per car tariff, as you can check in Figure 7.5(b).

An import quota creates winners and losers that are similar to those of a tariff but with an interesting difference. Figure 7.7 shows these gains and losses. By comparing Figure 7.7(b) with a quota and Figure 7.7(a) with free trade, you can see how an import quota changes the consumer and producer surpluses.

Consumer surplus – the green area – shrinks. This decrease is the loss to consumers from the import quota. The decrease in consumer surplus is made up of four parts. First, some of the consumer surplus is transferred to producers. The blue area B represents this loss of consumer surplus (and gain of producer surplus). Second, part of the consumer surplus is lost because the domestic cost of production is higher than the world price. The grey area C represents this loss. Third, part of the consumer surplus is transferred to importers who buy cars for £15,000 (the world price) and sell them for £19,000 (the UK domestic price). The two purple areas D represent this loss of consumer surplus and profit for importers. Fourth, part of the consumer surplus is lost because imports decrease. The grey area E represents this loss.

The losses of consumer surplus from the higher cost of production and the decrease in imports is a social loss – a deadweight loss. The grey areas labelled C and E represent this deadweight loss. Total surplus decreases by the area $C + E$.

Figure 7.7 The Effects of an Import Quota

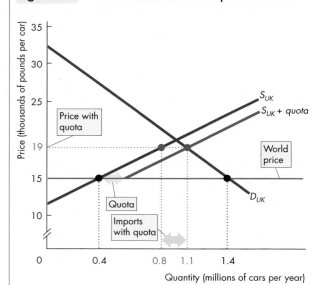

(a) Market with import quota

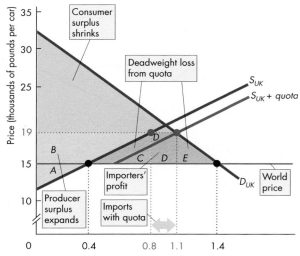

(b) Inefficiency of import quota

An import quota is set at 0.3 million cars a year. In part (a), the curve $S_{UK} + quota$ shows the supply of cars in the UK. The UK price rises to £19,000 a car, UK purchases decrease, UK production increases and imports decrease.

In part (b), consumer surplus shrinks by the areas B, C, D and E. Producer surplus expands by area B. Importers' profit is the two areas D and the quota creates a deadweight loss equal to area $C + E$.

Export Subsidies

An **export subsidy** is a payment made by a government to a domestic producer of an exported good. Examples of subsidies are payments made by the EU to sugar producers. You saw in Chapter 6 (pp. 140–141) that a subsidy shifts the domestic supply curve rightward, lowers the domestic price and increases the quantity bought and produced. But when the item that receives a subsidy is an export or an import, the subsidy also changes the amount of international trade. We can illustrate the effects of agricultural subsidies using the example of the market for sugar and African farmers.

Figure 7.8 shows the African market for sugar. Demand for sugar in Africa is D_A and the supply of sugar in Africa is S_A. With no EU and US subsidies, the world price of sugar is €4 a kilogram. At this price, African consumers buy 1 million tonnes a year and African farmers produce 14 million tonnes a year. African sugar exports are 13 million tonnes a year.

The subsidies reduce the cost of producing sugar in the EU and the US and increase the supply of sugar. The world supply increases and the world price falls.

┌───
Figure 7.8   The Effects of EU and US Export Subsidies

With EU and US subsidies, the world price falls from €4 to €2 per kilogram. In an African economy, people buy more sugar, farmers produce less sugar and exports decrease. Consumer surplus expands from A to A + B, producer surplus shrinks from B + C + D to C and a deadweight loss D arises.

In Figure 7.8 the world price falls to €2 a kilogram. The quantity bought by Africans increases to 3 million tonnes a year, but the quantity produced by African farmers decreases to 6 million tonnes a year. Exports fall from 13 million tonnes to 3 million tonnes a year.

A subsidy on an exported good creates winners and losers and a social loss. Figure 7.8 shows the gains and losses from an export subsidy. Consumer surplus in Africa increases from the green area A to the area $A + B$ as Africans purchase more sugar at the lower world price. Producer surplus shrinks from the area $B + C + D$ to the area C. Part of the loss, area D, arises because Africans produce less sugar and receive a lower price for it. Part of the loss of producer surplus, area B, is transferred to African consumers.

The total loss to producers, area $D + B$, exceeds the gains to consumers, area B. Total surplus decreases by the grey area D. The deadweight losses created by EU and US farm subsidies is a social loss for Africa.

Other Import Barriers

Two sets of policies that influence imports are health, safety and regulation barriers and voluntary export restraints. Thousands of detailed health, safety and other regulations restrict international trade. For example, the EU bans imports of most genetically modified foods such as US-produced soya beans. Although such regulations are not designed to limit international trade, they have that effect.

A voluntary export restraint is like a quota allocated to a foreign exporter of a good. This type of trade barrier isn't common, but was used in Japan in the 1980s.

Review Quiz

1 What are the tools that a country can use to restrict international trade?
2 Explain the effects of tariffs on domestic production, the quantity bought and the price.
3 Explain who gains and who loses from a tariff and why the losses exceed the gains.
4 Explain the effects of an import quota on domestic production, consumption and price.
5 Explain who gains and who loses from an import quota and why losses exceed the gains.

You can work these questions in Study Plan 7.3 and get instant feedback.   myeconlab

Let's now look at some commonly heard arguments for restricting international trade and see why they are never correct.

The Case Against Protection

For as long as countries and international trade have existed, people have debated whether a country is better off with free international trade or with protection from foreign competition. The debate continues, but for most economists a verdict has been delivered and it is the one you have just explored. Protectionism is inefficient. It creates deadweight losses.

We've seen the most powerful case for free trade in the example of how the UK (and all countries) benefit from specializing in production of the good in which they have a comparative advantage and trading with each other.

But there is a broader range of issues in the free trade versus protection debate. Let's review these issues.

Two classical arguments for restricting international trade are that protection is needed to:

◆ Establish an infant industry

◆ Counteract dumping

The Infant-industry Argument

An infant industry is a new industry. The **infant-industry argument** is that a new industry must be protected from foreign competition to enable it to grow into a mature industry and compete in world markets. The argument is based on the idea that comparative advantage changes or is dynamic and that on-the-job experience – *learning-by-doing* – is an important source of changes in comparative advantage. The fact that learning-by-doing can change comparative advantage does not justify protecting an infant industry.

First, the infant-industry argument is not valid if the benefits of learning-by-doing accrue *only* to the firms in the infant industry. The reason is that these firms will anticipate and reap the benefits of learning-by-doing without the additional incentive of protection from foreign competition.

For example, there are huge productivity gains from learning-by-doing in the manufacture of aircraft, but these gains benefit Airbus and other aircraft producers. Because the people making the decisions are the ones who benefit, they take the future gains into account when they decide on the scale of their activities. No benefits accrue to firms in other industries or other parts of the economy, so there is no need for government assistance to achieve an efficient outcome.

Second, even if the case is made for protecting an infant industry, it is more efficient to do so by a subsidy to firms in the industry, which is financed out of taxes.

The Dumping Argument

Dumping occurs when a foreign firm sells its exports at a lower price than its cost of production. The *dumping argument* is that domestic firms must be protected from dumping because if they are driven out of business, foreign firms will then charge higher prices.

There are powerful reasons to resist the dumping argument for protection. First, it is virtually impossible to detect dumping because it is hard to determine a firm's costs. As a result, the test for dumping is whether a firm's export price is below its domestic price. But this test is a weak one because it can be rational for a firm to charge a low price in markets in which the quantity demanded is highly sensitive to price and a higher price in markets in which demand is less price-sensitive.

Second, it is hard to think of a good that is produced by a natural global monopoly. So even if all the domestic firms in some industry were driven out of business, it would always be possible to find many alternative foreign sources of supply and to buy at prices determined in competitive markets.

Third, if a good or service were produced by a truly global natural monopoly, the best way of dealing with it would be by regulation – just as in the case of domestic monopolies. Such regulation would require international cooperation.

The two main arguments for protection that you have just studied have an element of credibility but there are other arguments. You may read newspaper stories that mention the following arguments for protectionism:

◆ Saves jobs

◆ Allows us to compete with cheap foreign labour

◆ Penalizes lax environmental standards

◆ Prevents rich countries from exploiting developing countries

Let's look at these in more detail.

Saves Jobs

Free trade does cost some jobs, but it also creates other jobs. Free trade brings about a global rationalization of labour and allocates labour resources to their highest-value activities. For example, protection of the textile industry has decreased, many workers have lost jobs in the UK textile industry but many textile jobs have been created in other countries such as Turkey and Malaysia. And many of the UK workers who lost textile jobs now have better-paying jobs in other industries, which have expanded. In total, more jobs have been created than have been destroyed in the textile industry.

Second, imports create jobs. They create jobs for retailers which sell imported goods and for firms which service these goods. They also create jobs by raising incomes in the rest of the world, some of which are spent on UK-produced goods and services.

Protectionism doesn't save jobs. It changes the mix of jobs but at the cost of a deadweight loss. Removing protectionism does impose costs of adjustment on people who previously worked in the protected industry and can have political costs and policy-making implications.

Allows Us to Compete with Cheap Foreign Labour

The relatively high wages in the UK and other EU member states doesn't imply that the EU cannot compete. Wages are higher, other things remaining the same, the higher is the productivity of labour. EU workers are more productive, on average, than lower-paid workers in China or India. For example, the productivity of EU labour is higher in financial services, biotechnology products and business computer systems than in assembling cars or televisions. These activities are ones in which the EU has a comparative advantage.

By engaging in free trade, the EU can increase production and exports of the goods in which it has a comparative advantage and increase the imports of goods in which our trading partners have a comparative advantage. We can make ourselves and our trading partners better off.

Penalizes Lax Environmental Standards

Another argument for protection is that many low-income countries keep costs low by having poor environmental standards. So we should put a tariff on the goods that we import from them.

In reply, it is not true that all poorer countries have significantly lower environmental standards than EU member states. Many poor countries do have a bad environmental record – including India and China – but some poorer countries have strict environmental laws and do enforce them. Also, the demand for higher environmental standards in poorer economies increases with income. Developing countries have the means to match environmental aspirations as their incomes rise. Rapid growth in income will most likely lead to rapid improvements in environmental standards. Free trade can generate rapid income growth and higher environmental standards in the long run.

Prevents Rich Countries from Exploiting Developing Countries

Another argument is that international trade must be restricted to prevent the people of the rich industrial world from exploiting the poorer people of the developing countries, forcing them to work for slave wages.

Wage rates in some developing countries are very low. But by trading with developing countries, we increase the demand for the goods that they produce and, more significantly, we increase the demand for their labour. When the demand for labour in developing countries increases, the wage rate also increases. So, far from exploiting people in developing countries, international trade improves their opportunities and increases their incomes.

The arguments for protection that we've reviewed leave free trade unscathed. But a new phenomenon is at work in our economy: offshore outsourcing. Surely this new source of foreign competition needs protection. Let's see if it does.

Offshoring and Outsourcing

BT, HSBC, Lloyds TSB, Burberry, Aviva and Tesco are just a few of the many UK firms which have sent jobs that were previously done in the UK to countries such as India, Sri Lanka, China, Thailand and to Eastern European countries such as Romania. These firms are outsourcing and offshoring. What exactly are these activities?

What are Offshoring and Outsourcing?

A UK company can source and produce its output in four main ways:

1   Hire UK labour and produce in the UK
2   Hire foreign labour and produce in other countries
3   Buy its output from other UK companies
4   Buy its output from foreign companies

Activities 3 and 4 are **outsourcing** and activities 2 and 4 are **offshoring**. Activity 4 is offshore outsourcing. Notice that offshoring includes activities that take place inside UK companies. If a UK company opens its own facilities in another country, then it is offshoring.

Offshoring has been going on for hundreds of years. But the activity expanded rapidly and became a source of concern during the 1990s when it began to cover activities that went beyond manufacturing to include information technology services and general office services such as finance, accounting and human resources management.

Why Did Offshoring Services Boom?

A dramatic fall in the cost of telecommunication generated the offshoring services boom of the 1990s. The gains from specialization and trade that you saw in the previous section must be large enough to make it worth incurring the costs of communication and transport. If the cost of producing a shirt in China isn't lower than the cost in the UK by an amount that exceeds the cost of transporting the shirt from China to the UK, then it is more efficient to produce shirts in the UK.

If services are to be produced offshore, then the cost of delivering those services must be low enough to leave the buyer with an overall lower cost. Until the 1990s, the cost of communicating across large distances was too high to make the offshoring of business services efficient. But when satellites, fibre-optic cables and computers cut the cost of a phone call between the UK and India to less than a few pence an hour, a huge base of offshore resources became competitive with similar resources in the UK.

What are the Benefits of Offshoring?

Offshoring brings gains from trade in the same way as any other type of international trade. A UK bank can export banking services to Indian companies and Indians might provide call centre services to UK companies. This trade benefits both UK citizens and Indian citizens provided the UK has a comparative advantage in banking services and India has a comparative advantage in call centre services.

Why is Offshoring a Concern?

Despite the gains from trade that offshoring brings, some people believe that it also brings costs that outweigh the gains. Why?

The concerns arise because offshoring is taking jobs in services. The loss of UK manufacturing jobs to other countries has been going on for decades. But the UK service sector has always expanded by enough to create new jobs to replace the lost manufacturing jobs. Now that UK service sector jobs are going overseas, the fear is that there will not be enough jobs in the UK. This fear is misplaced.

It is true that some service jobs are going overseas. But many service jobs are expanding. The UK imports call centre services, but it exports education, healthcare, legal, financial and a host of other types of services. Jobs in these sectors are expanding and will continue to expand. The numbers reinforce this view that the fear of job loss is misplaced. The exact number of jobs that have moved to lower-cost offshore locations is not known and estimates vary. But the number is likely to be small compared with the normal rate of job creation.

Winners and Losers from Offshoring

The trade gains from offshoring do not bring benefits to every person.

People who export the outsourced offshore services are clearly among the winners. They face an increased demand for their services, receive a higher price for them and sell a greater quantity. Given that most of these people are among the world's poorest, this gain must be considered a very important positive outcome from outsourcing and offshoring.

People who import outsourced offshore services, such as UK and EU citizens win *on average* but some lose. The winners are the consumers of the many goods and services that become available at a lower price. The winners also include the owners and investors in the firms that enjoy lower costs and increased profits. The losers are those who have invested in human capital to do a specific job that has now gone offshore. For them, finding a new job of any kind can be difficult. And finding a new job in a preferred location at a wage similar to that for the job that has gone abroad is often impossible.

Unemployment benefits provide short-term relief for these displaced workers. But this relief is not sufficient to fully compensate them for their loss.

The long-term solution to becoming redundant and losing a job is retraining and the acquisition of new skills. Providing educational facilities for repeated bouts of training and retraining is a task for governments that will become increasingly important as the twenty-first century progresses and technology advances.

Avoiding Trade Wars

There is one counter-argument to protection that is overwhelming. Protection invites retaliation and can trigger a trade war. The best example of a trade war occurred during the Great Depression of the 1930s when the US raised its tariffs. Country after country retaliated with its own tariff and in a short time world trade had almost disappeared. The costs to all countries were large and led to a renewed international resolve to avoid such self-defeating moves in the future. They also led to the creation of the GATT and eventually of the WTO, the EU and APEC (Asia Pacific Economic Cooperation).

Why Is International Trade Restricted?

Why, despite all the arguments against protection, is trade restricted? There are two key reasons.

First, government revenue is costly to collect and for some governments, especially those in developing countries, a tariff is easier to collect than other types of tax.

Second, and more important, tariffs benefit the domestic producers of import-competing goods and services. You saw in the example that we worked through earlier in this chapter that UK car makers lose from free trade (Figure 7.3, p. 155) and gain from a tariff (Figure 7.6, p. 159).

The number of people who stand to gain from protection is small but each one of them has a lot at stake. In contrast, the number of people who stand to lose from protection is large but each one of them has a small amount at stake. Think about the market for sugar. A small number of farmers stand to gain a few million pounds each from protection and a few million consumers stand to lose just a few pence a day. Add up all the losses and they exceed the gains. But each losing consumer barely notices the extra expenditure on sugar while the gain for each winning producer is a big deal.

This lopsided balance between winners and losers has powerful political consequences. The winners are willing to spend substantial amounts to persuade politicians to support a protectionist policy. They have a strong, well-organized political voice. They never argue that protection is needed for their own benefit. They dress up their cause by finding arguments that appear to make protection serve the social interest, even though it clearly does not. The losers, who support free trade, are a weak, ill-organized group that is barely heard. So the political outcome favours the protectionists.

Compensating Losers

If, in total, the gains from free international trade exceed the losses, why don't those who gain compensate those who lose so that everyone is in favour of free trade?

First, the cost of identifying the losers from free trade and of estimating the value of their losses would be enormous.

Second, it would never be clear whether a person who has fallen on hard times is suffering because of free trade or for other reasons, perhaps reasons that are largely under the control of the individual.

Third, some people who look like losers at one point in time may, in fact, end up gaining. The young textile worker who loses his job and becomes a Webmaster resents the loss of work and the need to move. But a year or two later, looking back on events, he counts himself fortunate. He's made a move that has increased his income and given him greater job security.

Because we do not explicitly compensate the losers from free international trade, protectionism remains a popular and permanent feature of our national economic and political life.

Review Quiz

1   What are the infant-industry and dumping arguments for protection? Are they correct?
2   Can protection save jobs, compensate for low foreign wages, compensate for costly environmental policies and prevent developing countries from being exploited?
3   What is offshore outsourcing? Who benefits from it and who loses?
4   What are the main reasons for imposing a tariff?
5   Why don't the winners from free trade win the political argument?

You can work these questions in Study Plan 7.4 and get instant feedback.

You've now seen how free international trade enables people to gain from increased specialization and trade and how barriers to international trade bring gains for some, but greater losses for all.

Reading Between the Lines on pp. 166–167 shows how the losses to EU car makers generate opposition to the new EU agreement with Korea to cut tariffs and why non-tariff barriers to trade persist.

Reading Between the Lines

EU Free Trade Deal

The Financial Times, 16 September 2010

EU Agrees Trade Deal with South Korea

FT

Italy has dropped its resistance to a European Union trade agreement with South Korea, putting the highly touted deal on track to come into force next year. . . .

The EU has touted the agreement as the most ambitious of its kind and a model for bilateral trade agreements it is pursuing elsewhere in Asia and Latin America. The accord, which will wipe out €1.6bn ($2bn) in annual duties on EU exports, has taken on added significance at a time when the economic crisis has sapped popular enthusiasm for trade liberalisation. ...

All 27 EU member states initialled the text of the agreement last October, an act that was supposed to rule out further negotiation. But Italy, under pressure from car maker Fiat, last week surprised foreign ministers at a meeting in Brussels by refusing to approve the deal and demanding additional concessions.

The Italians argued that the agreement, which eliminates European duties on South Korean cars, would put undue pressure on its own automakers at a time when they were already ailing. Privately, several European diplomats fumed that Italian posturing risked damaging the bloc's prestige.

The compromise struck on Thursday calls for a safeguard mechanism that would allow member states to reinstate tariffs if the deal results in a surge in Korean car imports. The roughly six-month delay it includes is less than the 15 months the Italians had originally sought.

. . .

© The Financial Times Ltd.

The Essence of the Story

- The EU has made a free trade agreement with South Korea.

- The agreement will eliminate €1.6bn in annual duties on EU exports.

- Car producer Fiat said eliminating import duties on South Korean cars would put it under undue pressure.

- Italy negotiated a safeguard mechanism that allows it to reinstate a tariff if the deal results in a surge in Korean car imports.

Economic Analysis

◆ Figure 1 shows the EU market for small cars (like those produced by South Korea and Fiat). EU demand and supply of cars are D_{EU} and S_{EU}.

◆ Cars can be imported. The world price is €9,091 and the EU tariff on car imports is 10 per cent.

◆ EU car makers produce a small proportion of world production and the EU faces a perfectly elastic supply of cars at the world price. The EU price is €10,000 – the world price plus the 10 per cent tariff.

◆ In Figure 1, the quantity of EU-produced cars is 7 million a year and the quantity of cars bought is 10 million a year. So 3 million cars a year are imported (20 per cent from South Korea).

◆ Consumer surplus is the green area A, producer surplus is the blue area B, tariff revenue is the purple area C and the deadweight loss from the tariff is the grey area, $D + E$.

◆ The new agreement related only to trade with South Korea, but the EU wants similar agreements with other countries.

◆ Figure 2 shows the effects in the EU car market if the tariff on cars from all countries is removed.

◆ The EU price falls to the world price of €9,091. The quantity of EU-produced cars decreases to 6 million a year and the quantity purchased increases to 12 million a year. Imports increase to 6 million a year.

◆ EU consumer surplus expands as consumers gain back the deadweight loss and tariff revenue. But EU producer surplus shrinks as EU car makers sell fewer cars at the lower price.

◆ EU car makers can regain some of the lost producer surplus by increasing exports of premium brand cars (different from the small

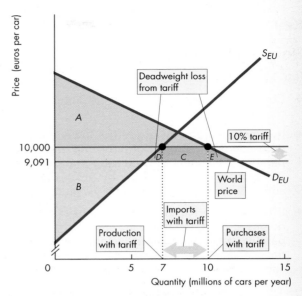

Figure 1 The EU car market with a 10 per cent tariff

Figure 2 The EU car market with free trade

cars in Figures 1 and 2) to South Korea and other countries with lower tariffs.

◆ Italian car makers argued against the new agreement because they believe South Korea will use regulatory restriction to block increased imports of premium EU cars.

SUMMARY

Key Points

How Global Markets Work
(pp. 152–154)

◆ Comparative advantage drives international trade.

◆ If the world price of a good is lower than the domestic price, the rest of the world has a comparative advantage in producing that good and the domestic country gains by producing less, consuming more and importing the good.

◆ If the world price of a good is higher than the domestic price, the domestic country has a comparative advantage in producing that good and the domestic country gains by producing more, consuming less and exporting the good.

Working Problems 1 to 6 will give you a better understanding of how global markets work.

Winners, Losers and the Net Gain from Trade (pp. 155–156)

◆ Compared to a no-trade situation, in a market with imports, consumer surplus is larger, producer surplus is smaller and total surplus is larger with free international trade.

◆ Compared to a no-trade situation, in a market with exports, consumer surplus is smaller, producer surplus is larger and total surplus is larger with free international trade

Working Problems 7 and 8 will give you a better understanding of winners, losers and the net gains from trade.

International Trade Restrictions
(pp. 157–161)

◆ Countries restrict international trade by imposing tariffs, export subsidies, import quotas or other import barriers.

◆ Trade restrictions raise the domestic price, decreases the quantity imported, decrease consumer surplus, increase producer surplus and create a deadweight loss.

Working Problems 9 to 20 will give you a better understanding of international trade restrictions.

The Case Against Protection
(pp. 162–165)

◆ Arguments that protection is necessary for infant industries and to prevent dumping are weak.

◆ Arguments that protection is necessary to save jobs, allow us to compete with cheap foreign labour, penalize lax environmental standards and prevent exploitation of developing countries are flawed.

◆ Offshore outsourcing is just a new way of reaping gains from trade and does not justify protection.

◆ Trade restrictions are popular because protection brings a small loss per person to a large number of people and a large gain per person to a small number of people. Those who gain have a stronger political voice than those who lose and it is too costly to identify and compensate losers.

Working Problem 21 will give you a better understanding of the case against protection.

Key Terms

Dumping, 162
Export subsidy, 161
Exports, 152
Import quota, 160
Imports, 152
Infant-industry argument, 162
Offshoring, 164
Outsourcing, 164
Tariff, 157

STUDY PLAN PROBLEMS AND APPLICATIONS

myeconlab You can work Problems 1 to 21 in MyEconLab Chapter 7 Study Plan and get instant feedback.

How Global Markets Work
(Study Plan 7.1)

Use the following information to work Problems 1 to 3.

Wholesalers of roses (the firms that supply your local flower shop with roses for Valentine's Day) buy and sell roses in containers that hold 120 stems. The table provides information about the wholesale market for roses in the UK. The demand schedule is the wholesalers' demand and the supply schedule is the UK rose growers' supply.

Price (pounds per container)	Quantity demanded	Quantity supplied
	(millions of containers per year)	
100	15	0
125	12	2
150	9	4
175	6	6
200	3	8
225	0	10

Wholesalers can buy roses at auction in Aalsmeer, Holland, for £125 per container.

1 **a** Without international trade, what would be the price of a container of roses and how many containers of roses a year would be bought and sold in the UK?

   b At the price in your answer to part (a), does the UK or the rest of the world have a comparative advantage in producing roses?

2 If UK wholesalers buy roses at the lowest possible price, how many do they buy from UK growers and how many do they import?

3 Draw a graph to illustrate the UK wholesale market for roses. Show the equilibrium in that market with no international trade and the equilibrium with free trade. Mark the quantity of roses produced in the UK, the quantity imported and the total quantity bought.

Use the following news clip to work Problems 4 and 5.

Underwater Oil Discovery to Transform Brazil into a Major Exporter

A huge underwater oil field discovered late last year has the potential to transform Brazil into a sizable exporter. Fifty years ago, Petrobras was formed as a trading company to import oil to support Brazil's growing economy. Two years ago, Brazil reached its long-sought goal of energy self-sufficiency.

Source: *International Herald Tribune*, 11 January 2008

4 Describe Brazil's comparative advantage in producing oil and explain why it has changed.

5 **a** Draw a graph to illustrate the Brazilian market for oil and explain why Brazil was an importer of oil until a few years ago.

   b Draw a graph to illustrate the Brazilian market for oil and explain why Brazil may become an exporter of oil in the near future.

6 **Postcard: Bangalore. Hearts Set on Joining the Global Economy, Indian IT Workers are Brushing Up on Their Interpersonal Skills**

The huge number of Indian workers staffing the world's tech firms and call centres possess cutting-edge technical knowledge, but their interpersonal and communication skills lag far behind. Enter Bangalore's finishing schools.

Source: *Time*, 5 May 2008

   a What comparative advantages does this news clip identify?

   b Using the information in this news clip, what services do you predict Bangalore (India) exports and what services do you predict it imports?

Winners, Losers and the Net Gain from Trade (Study Plan 7.2)

7 In the news clip in Problem 6, who will gain and who will lose from the trade in services that the news clip predicts?

8 Use the information on the UK wholesale market for roses in Problem 1 to:

   a Explain who gains and who loses from free international trade in roses compared to a situation in which UK citizens buy only roses grown in the UK.

   b Draw a graph to illustrate the gains and losses from free trade.

   c Calculate the gain from international trade.

International Trade Restrictions

(Study Plan 7.3)

Use the following news clip to work Problems 9 and 10.

Steel Tariffs Appear to Have Backfired on Bush

President Bush set aside his free-trade principles last year and imposed heavy tariffs on imported steel to help out struggling mills in Pennsylvania and West Virginia. Some economists say the tariffs may have cost more jobs than they saved, by driving up costs for car makers and other steel users.

Source: The Washington Post, 19 September 2003

9 **a** Explain how a high tariff on steel imports can help US domestic steel producers.

b Explain how a high tariff on steel imports can harm steel users.

10 Draw a graph of the US market for steel to show how a high tariff on steel imports helps US steel producers, harms US steel users and creates a deadweight loss.

Use the information on the UK wholesale market for roses in Problem 1 to work Problems 11 to 16.

11 If the UK puts a tariff of £25 per container on imports of roses, what happens to the UK price of roses, the quantity of roses bought, the quantity produced in the UK and the quantity imported?

12 Who gains and who loses from this tariff?

13 Draw a graph to illustrate the gains and losses from the tariff and on the graph identify the gains and losses, the tariff revenue and the deadweight loss.

14 If the UK puts an import quota on roses of 5 million containers, what happens to the UK price of roses, the quantity of roses bought and the quantity produced in the UK and the quantity imported?

15 Who gains and who loses from this quota?

16 Draw a graph to illustrate the gains and losses from the import quota and on the graph identify the gains and losses, the importers' profit and the deadweight loss created.

Use the following news clip to work Problems 17 and 18.

Car Sales Go Up as Prices Tumble

Car affordability in Australia is now at its best in 20 years, fuelling a surge in sales as prices tumble. In 2000, Australia cut the tariff to 15 per cent and on 1 January 2005, it cut the tariff to 10 per cent.

Source: The Courier Mail, 26 February 2005

17 Explain who gains and who loses from the lower tariff on imported cars.

18 Draw a graph to show how the price of a car, the quantity of cars bought, the quantity of cars produced in Australia and the quantity of cars imported into Australia changed.

Use the following news clip to work Problems 19 and 20.

Why the World Can't Afford Food

As food stocks dwindled, some countries placed export restrictions on food to protect their own supplies. This in turn drove up prices, punishing countries – especially poor ones – that depend on imports for much of their food.

Source: Time, 19 May 2008

19 **a** What are the benefits to a country from importing food?

b What costs might arise from relying on imported food?

20 If a country restricts food exports, what effect does this restriction have in that country on the price of food, the quantity of food it produces, the quantity of food it consumes and the quantity of food it exports?

The Case Against Protection

(Study Plan 7.4)

21 **Chinese Tyre Maker Rejects US Charge of Defects**

US regulators ordered the recall of more than 450,000 faulty tyres. The Chinese producer of the tyres disputed the allegations and hinted that the recall might be an effort by foreign competitors to hamper Chinese exports to the US. Mounting scrutiny of Chinese-made goods has become a source of new trade frictions between the US and China and fuelled worries among regulators, corporations and consumers about the risks associated with many products imported from China.

Source: International Herald Tribune, 26 June 2007

a What does the information in the news clip imply about the comparative advantage of producing tyres in the US and China?

b Could product quality be a valid argument against free trade?

c How would the product-quality argument against free trade be open to abuse by domestic producers of the imported good?

ADDITIONAL PROBLEMS AND APPLICATIONS

myeconlab You can work these problems in MyEconLab if assigned by your lecturer.

How Global Markets Work

22 Suppose that the world price of sugar is 10 pence a pound, the UK does not trade internationally and the equilibrium price of sugar in the UK is 20 pence a pound. The UK then begins to trade internationally.

   a How does the price of sugar in the UK change?

   b Do UK consumers buy more or less sugar?

   c Do UK sugar growers produce more or less sugar?

   d Does the UK export or import sugar and why?

23 Suppose that the world price of steel is $100 a tonne, India does not trade internationally and the equilibrium price of steel in India is $60 a tonne. India then begins to trade internationally.

   a How does the price of steel in India change?

   b How does the quantity of steel produced in India change?

   c How does the quantity of steel bought by India change?

   d Does India export or import steel and why?

24 A semiconductor is a key component in your laptop, mobile phone and iPod. The table provides information about the market for semiconductors in the EU.

Price (euros per unit)	Quantity demanded	Quantity supplied
	(billions of units per year)	
10	25	0
12	20	20
14	15	40
16	10	60
18	5	80
20	0	100

Producers of semiconductors get €18 a unit on the world market.

   a With no international trade, what would be the price of a semiconductor and how many semiconductors a year would be bought and sold in the EU?

   b Does the EU have a comparative advantage in producing semiconductors?

25 **Act Now, Eat Later**

The hunger crisis in poor countries has its roots in EU and US policies of subsidizing the diversion of food crops such as soya beans to produce biofuels such as ethanol. That is, doling out subsidies to put the world's dinner into the petrol tank.

Source: *Time*, 5 May 2008

   a What is the effect on the world price of soya beans of the increased use of soya beans to produce ethanol in the EU and US?

   b How does the change in the world price of soya beans affect the quantity of soya beans produced in a poor developing country with a comparative advantage in producing soya beans, the quantity the poor country consumes and the quantity that it either exports or imports?

Winners, Losers and the Net Gain from Trade

26 Use the news clip in Problem 25. Draw a graph of the market for soya beans in a poor developing country to show the changes in consumer surplus, producer surplus and deadweight loss.

Use the following news clip to work Problems 27 and 28.

South Korea to Resume US Beef Imports

South Korea will reopen its market to most US beef. South Korea banned imports of US beef in 2003 amid concerns over a case of mad cow disease in the US. The ban closed what was then the third-largest market for US beef exporters.

Source: CNN, 29 May 2008

27 **a** Explain how South Korea's import ban on US beef affected beef producers and consumers in South Korea.

   b Draw a graph of the market for beef in South Korea to illustrate your answer to part (a). Identify the changes in consumer surplus, producer surplus and deadweight loss.

28 **a** Assuming that South Korea is the only importer of US beef, explain how South Korea's import ban on US beef affected beef producers and consumers in the US.

   b Draw a graph of the market for beef in the US to illustrate your answer to part (a). Identify the changes in consumer surplus, producer surplus and deadweight loss.

International Trade Restrictions

Use the following information to work Problems 29 to 31.

Before 1995, trade between the US and Mexico was subject to tariffs. In 1995, Mexico joined NAFTA and all US and Mexican tariffs have gradually been removed.

29 Explain how the price that US consumers pay for goods from Mexico and the quantity of US imports from Mexico have changed. Who are the winners and who are the losers from this free trade?

30 Explain how the quantity of US exports to Mexico and the US government's tariff revenue from trade with Mexico have changed.

31 Suppose that in 2008, tomato growers in Florida lobby the US government to impose an import quota on Mexican tomatoes. Explain who in the US would gain and who would lose from such a quota.

Use the following information to work Problems 32 and 33.

Suppose that in response to huge job losses in the EU textile industry, the EU imposes a 100 per cent tariff on imports of textiles from China.

32 Explain how the tariff on textiles will change the price that EU buyers pay for textiles, the quantity of textiles imported and the quantity of textiles produced in the EU.

33 Explain how the EU and Chinese gains from trade will change. Who in the EU will lose and who will gain?

Use the following information to work Problems 34 and 35.

With free trade between Australia and the US, Australia would export beef to the US. But the US imposes an import quota on Australian beef.

34 Explain how this quota influences the price that US consumers pay for beef, the quantity of beef produced in the US and the US and the Australian gains from trade.

35 Explain who in the US gains from the quota on beef imports and who loses.

The Case Against Protection

36 **Trading Up**

The cost of protecting jobs in uncompetitive sectors through tariffs is high. For example, saving a job in the sugar industry costs US consumers $826,000 in higher prices a year; saving a dairy industry job costs $685,000 per year; and saving a job in the manufacturing of women's handbags costs $263,000.

Source: *The New York Times*, 26 June 2006

a What are the arguments for saving the jobs mentioned in this news clip?

b Explain why these arguments are faulty.

c Is there any merit to saving these jobs?

37 **Gulf Louvre Deal Riles French Art World**

The Louvre in Paris will benefit from the deal, officials insist, but a storm is raging in France over the government's decision to build a branch of the Louvre in Abu Dhabi – the first-ever foreign annex of the world-famous art gallery. The controversy is not over public spending on culture but on the fact that France stands to make money from the deal.

Source: BBC News, 6 March 2007

a Is the Louvre deal outsourcing, offshoring, both or neither?

b Who will gain and who will lose from the deal?

Economics in the News

38 After you have studied *Reading Between the Lines* on pp. 166–167 answer the following questions.

a What is a free trade agreement and what is its aim?

b Explain how a tariff on EU car imports changes EU production of cars, purchases of cars and imports of cars.

c Illustrate your answer to part (b) with an appropriate graphical analysis.

d Explain how removing the 10 per cent tariff on EU car imports changes consumer surplus and producer surplus.

e Illustrate your answer to part (d) with an appropriate graphical analysis.

f Explain why EU producers oppose cuts in car import tariffs.

Households, Firms and Markets

Choices and the Pursuit of Profit

Every day the powerful forces of demand and supply shape your choices and the fortunes of families, businesses, nations and empires in the same way as the tides and winds shape rocks and coastlines.

You've seen in Chapters 3 to 7 how market forces raise and lower prices, increase and decrease quantities bought and sold and send resources to their most valued uses at home and abroad. In the next seven chapters we will explore in more depth how these forces affect households' choices, the choices of firms and how both interact in markets.

The power of the market begins quietly and privately with the choices that each one of us makes. We choose how to allocate our budgets and our time to get the most we can out of our own scarce resources. Chapter 8 probes these choices and shows you the neat idea of mapping people's preferences and predicting how our choices respond to changing price incentives and affordable opportunities.

We make our choices against the backdrop of ever-changing technology. Every year, new goods appear and old ones disappear. New firms are born and old ones die. This process of change is managed by firms chasing profits in markets.

We begin our study of firms in Chapter 9 by learning about their costs and the relationship between technology and cost. Then we look at the relationship between output and the costs of production in Chapter 10.

Firms operate in different types of markets. Some markets, like the ones we've studied so far, are competitive. The most extreme competition, called perfect competition, is the topic of Chapter 11. At the other extreme is monopoly, a single firm with no competitors, which we study in Chapter 12.

In Chapter 13, we look at a blend of competition and monopoly where we study the behaviour of the firms that produce the huge variety of brands that confront us every day. Finally, in Chapter 14 we explore situations in which firms, like armies, act strategically, guessing the effects of their choices on the choices of others.

INSIDE THE BLACK BOXES

Jeremy Bentham's insight, that people maximize utility, revolutionized thinking about human choices. His insight was superseded by the idea of mapping preferences, which you'll meet in Chapter 8; and today, economists are using the tools of neuroscience to understand consumer choices.

John von Neumann's big idea was to think of strategies as moves in a game. He invented game theory as a tool to understand how decision makers interact when their choices are mutually interdependent: when the profit of each depends on the choices of both. You will learn in Chapter 14 how game theory is used to understand the actions of firms in markets with a small number of producers.

Jeremy Bentham (1748–1832), who lived in London, was the son and grandson of a lawyer and was himself trained as a barrister. But Bentham rejected the opportunity to maintain the family tradition and, instead, spent his life as a writer, an activist and a Member of Parliament in the pursuit of rational laws that would bring the greatest happiness to the greatest number of people.

Bentham, whose embalmed body is preserved to this day in a glass cabinet in the University of London, was the first person to use the concept of utility to explain human choices. But in Bentham's day, the distinction between explaining and prescribing was not a sharp one, and Bentham was ready to use his ideas to tell people how they ought to behave. He was one of the first to propose pensions for the retired, guaranteed employment, minimum wages and social benefits such as free education and free medical care.

'. . . It is the greatest happiness of the greatest number that is the measure of right and wrong.'

JEREMY BENTHAM
Fragment on Government

John von Neumann was one of the great minds of the twentieth century. Born in Budapest, Hungary, in 1903, Johnny, as he was known, showed early mathematical brilliance. He was 25 when he published the article that changed the social sciences and began a flood of research on game theory – a flood that has not subsided.

In that article, von Neumann proved that in a zero-sum game (such as sharing a pie), there exists a best strategy for each player.

Von Neumann did more than invent game theory: he also invented and built the first practical computer, and he worked on the Manhattan Project, which developed the atomic bomb during the Second World War.

Von Neumann believed that the social sciences would progress only if they used their own mathematical tools, not those of the physical sciences.

'Real life consists of bluffing, of little tactics of deception, of asking yourself what is the other man going to think I mean to do.'

JOHN VON NEUMANN, told to Jacob Bronowski (in a London taxi) and reported in *The Ascent of Man*

CHAPTER

8

Households' Choices

After studying this chapter you will be able to:

◆ Describe a household's budget line and show how it changes when a price or income changes

◆ Use indifference curves to map preferences and explain the principle of diminishing marginal rate of substitution

◆ Predict the effects of changes in prices and income on consumption choices

◆ Describe some new ways of explaining households' choices

We spend a lot of our time making choices about how to spend our income. What determines our choices, what makes our choices change and how do we make the best affordable choice?

The price of a DVD rental has fallen and we are renting ever more of them, but we're also going to the cinema more often. Why?

We are happy to download DVDs but why haven't e-books replaced paper books? In this chapter we study a model of choice that helps answer these questions. In *Reading Between the Lines* at the end of the chapter, we'll use the model to explain why e-books are only slowly replacing printed books.

◆ Consumption Possibilities

Consumption choices are limited by income and by the prices of goods and services. A household has a given amount of income to spend and cannot influence the prices of the goods and services it buys. It takes the prices as given. A household's **budget line** describes the limits to a household's consumption choices.

The Budget Line

Let's look at Lisa's budget line. Lisa is the only person in her household and she has £30 a month to spend. She buys two goods: films and cola. The price to see a film is £6 and the price of cola is £3 for a pack of 6 cans.

Figure 8.1 shows the alternative affordable ways for Lisa to see films and buy cola. In Row *A* she buys 10 packs of cola and sees no films. In Row *F* she sees 5 films and drinks no cola. Both of these combinations of films and packs of cola exhaust Lisa's income of £30 a month. Check that each of the other rows also exhausts Lisa's £30. The rows of the table define Lisa's consumption possibilities, given her income (£30 a month), and the prices of cola (£3 a pack) and a cinema ticket (£6).

Divisible and Indivisible Goods

Some goods – called divisible goods – can be bought in any quantity desired. Examples are petrol and electricity. We can best understand the household choice we're about to study if we assume that all goods and services are divisible. For example, Lisa can see half a film a month *on average* by seeing one film every two months. When we think of goods as being divisible, the consumption possibilities are not just the points *A* to *F* shown in Figure 8.1, but includes all the points that form the line from *A* to *F*. This line is Lisa's budget line.

Affordable and Unaffordable Quantities

Lisa's budget line is a constraint on her choices. It marks the boundary between what she can afford and what she cannot afford. Lisa can afford any point on the line and inside it. She cannot afford any point outside the budget line. The constraint on her consumption depends on the prices of the two goods (cinema tickets and packs of cola) and her income. This constraint changes when either price or her income changes. Let's see how by studying an equation that describes her consumption possibilities.

Figure 8.1 The Budget Line

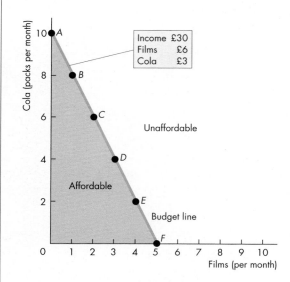

Consumption possibility	Films (per month)	Cola (packs per month)
A	0	10
B	1	8
C	2	6
D	3	4
E	4	2
F	5	0

Lisa's budget line is the boundary between what she can and cannot afford. The rows of the table are Lisa's affordable combinations of films and cola when her income is £30, the price of a cinema ticket is £6 and the price of cola is £3 a pack. For example, row *A* tells us that Lisa spends her £30 income when she buys 10 packs of cola and sees no films.

The graph shows Lisa's budget line. Points *A* to *F* on the graph represent the rows of the table. For divisible goods, the budget line is the continuous line *AF*.

To calculate the equation of Lisa's budget line, start from the fact that expenditure equals income. If the quantity of films that Lisa sees is Q_F and the quantity of cola she buys is Q_C, then:

$$£3Q_C + £6Q_F = £30$$

Divide by £3 to obtain:

$$Q_C + 2Q_F = 10$$

Subtract $2Q_F$ from both sides to obtain:

$$Q_C = 10 - 2Q_F$$

The Budget Equation

We can describe the budget line by using a *budget equation*. The budget equation starts with the fact that:

$$\text{Expenditure} = \text{Income}$$

Expenditure is equal to the sum of the price of each good multiplied by the quantity bought. For Lisa:

Expenditure = (Price of cola × Quantity of cola)
+ (Price to see a film × Quantity of films)

Call the price of cola P_C, the quantity of cola Q_C, the price to see a film P_F, the quantity of films Q_F and income Y. We can write Lisa's budget equation as:

$$P_C Q_C + P_F Q_F = Y$$

Using the prices Lisa faces, £3 a pack for cola and £6 to see a film, and Lisa's income, £30, we get:

$$£3Q_C + £6Q_F = £30$$

Lisa can choose any quantities of cola (Q_C) and films (Q_F) that satisfy this equation. To find the relationship between these quantities, divide both sides of the equation by the price of cola (P_C) to get:

$$Q_C + \frac{P_F}{P_C} \times Q_F = \frac{Y}{P_C}$$

Now subtract the term $(P_F/P_C) \times Q_F$ from both sides of this equation to give:

$$Q_C = \frac{Y}{P_C} - \frac{P_F}{P_C} \times Q_F$$

For Lisa, income (Y) is £30, the price to see a film (P_F) is £6 and the price of cola (P_C) is £3 a pack. So Lisa must choose the quantities of films and cola to satisfy the equation:

$$Q_C = \frac{£30}{£3} - \frac{£6}{£3} \times Q_F$$

$$Q_C = 10 - 2Q_F$$

To interpret the equation, look at the budget line in Figure 8.1 and check that the equation delivers that budget line. First, set Q_F equal to zero. The budget equation tells us that Q_C, the quantity of cola, equals Y/P_C, which is 10 packs. This combination of Q_F and Q_C is the one in row A of the table in Figure 8.1. Next, set Q_F equal to 5. Now Q_C equals zero (the combination in row F). Check that you can derive the other rows.

The budget equation contains two variables chosen by the household $(Q_F$ and $Q_C)$ and two variables $(Y/P_C$ and $P_F/P_C)$ that the household takes as given. Let's look more closely at these variables.

Real Income

A household's **real income** is its income expressed as the quantity of goods that the household can afford to buy. Lisa's real income in terms of cola is Y/P_C. This quantity is the maximum number of packs that Lisa can buy. It is equal to her money income divided by the price of cola. Lisa's income is £30 and the price of cola is £3 a pack, so her real income is 10 packs of cola. In Figure 8.1, real income is the point at which the budget line intersects the y-axis.

Relative Price

A **relative price** is the price of one good divided by the price of another good. In Lisa's budget equation, the variable (P_F/P_C) is the relative price of a film in terms of cola. For Lisa, P_F is £6 a film and P_C is £3 a pack of cola, so P_F/P_C is equal to 2 packs per film. That is, to see one more film, Lisa must give up 2 packs of cola.

You've just calculated Lisa's opportunity cost of seeing a film. Recall that the opportunity cost of an action is the best alternative forgone. For Lisa to see 1 more film a month, she must forgo 2 packs of cola. You've also calculated Lisa's opportunity cost of cola. For Lisa to buy 2 more packs a month, she must give up seeing 1 film. So her opportunity cost of 2 packs of cola is 1 film.

The relative price of a film in terms of cola is the magnitude of the slope of Lisa's budget line. To calculate the slope of the budget line, recall the formula (see the Chapter 1 Appendix): slope equals the change in the variable measured on the y-axis divided by the change in the variable measured on the x-axis as we move along the line. In Lisa's case (Figure 8.1), the variable measured on the y-axis is the quantity of cola and the variable measured on the x-axis is the quantity of films. Along Lisa's budget line, as cola decreases from 10 to 0 packs, films increase from 0 to 5. So the slope of the budget line is 10 packs divided by 5 films, or 2 packs per film. The magnitude of this slope is the same as the relative price of a film we've just calculated. It is also the opportunity cost of a film.

A Change in Prices

When prices change, so does the budget line. The lower the price of the good measured on the x-axis, other things remaining the same, the flatter is the budget

Figure 8.2 Changes in Prices and Income

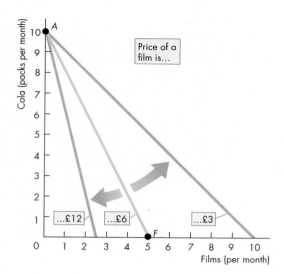

(a) A change in price

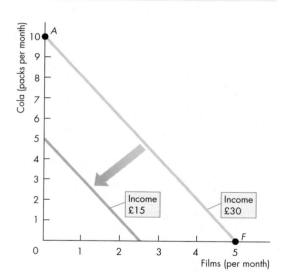

(b) A change in income

In part (a), the price to see a film changes. A fall in the price from £6 to £3 increases the number of films that Lisa can see for £30, so her budget line rotates outward and becomes flatter. A rise in the price from £6 to £12 rotates the budget line inward and makes it steeper.

In part (b), income falls from £30 to £15 while the prices of cola and seeing a film remain constant. The budget line shifts leftward but its slope does not change.

 Animation

line. For example, if the price to see a film falls from £6 to £3, real income in terms of cola does not change but the relative price to see a film falls. The budget line rotates *outward* and becomes flatter as shown in Figure 8.2(a). The higher the price of the good measured on the *x*-axis, other things remaining the same, the steeper is the budget line. For example, if the price to see a film rises from £6 to £12, the relative price to see a film increases. The budget line rotates *inward* and becomes steeper as shown in Figure 8.2(a).

A Change in Income

A change in *money* income changes real income but does not change the relative price. The budget line shifts, but its slope does not change. An increase in money income increases real income and shifts the budget line rightward. A decrease in money income decreases real income and shifts the budget line leftward.

Figure 8.2(b) shows the effect of a change in income on Lisa's budget line. The initial budget line when Lisa's income is £30 is the same one that we began with in Figure 8.1. The new budget line shows what Lisa can consume if her income falls to £15 a month. The two budget lines have the same slope because the relative price is the same. The new budget line is closer to the origin than the initial one because Lisa's real income has decreased.

Review Quiz

1   What does a household's budget line show?
2   How does the relative price and a household's real income influence its budget line?
3   If a European household has an income of €40 and buys only bus rides at €2 each and magazines at €4 each, what is the equation that describes the household's budget line?
4   If the price of one good changes, what happens to the relative price and to the slope of the household's budget line?
5   If a household's money income changes and prices do not change, what happens to the household's real income and budget line?

You can work these questions in Study Plan 8.1 and get instant feedback. **myeconlab**

We've studied the limits to what a household can consume. Let's now learn how we can describe the household's preferences and make a map that contains a lot of information about a household's preferences.

Preferences and Indifference Curves

Preferences are your likes and dislikes. You are going to discover a neat idea: that of drawing a map of a person's preferences. A preference map is based on the intuitively appealing assumption that people can sort all the possible combinations of goods they might consume into three groups: preferred, not preferred and indifferent. To make this idea more concrete, we asked Lisa to rank various combinations of films and cola.

Figure 8.3(a) shows part of Lisa's answer. She tells us that she currently sees 2 films and drinks 6 packs of cola a month at point C. She then lists all the combinations of films and cola that she thinks are just as good as her current combination. When we plot these combinations of films and cola, we get the green curve shown in Figure 8.3(a). This curve is the key element in a map of preferences and is called an indifference curve.

An **indifference curve** is a line that shows combinations of goods among which a consumer is *indifferent*. The indifference curve in Figure 8.3(a) tells us that Lisa is just as happy to see 2 films and drink 6 packs of cola a month at point C as she is to have the combination of films and cola at point G or at any other point along the curve.

Lisa also says she prefers any of the combinations of films and cola above the indifference curve in Figure 8.3(a) – the yellow area – to any combination on the indifference curve. And she prefers any combination on the indifference curve to any combination in the grey area below the indifference curve.

The indifference curve in Figure 8.3(a) is just one of a family of such curves. This indifference curve appears again in Figure 8.3(b). It is labelled I_1 and it passes through points C and G. The curves labelled I_0 and I_2 are two other indifference curves. Lisa prefers any point on indifference curve I_2 to any point on indifference curve I_1 and she prefers any point on I_1 to any point on I_0. We refer to I_2 as being a higher indifference curve than I_1 and I_1 as being higher than I_0. Because Lisa prefers I_2 to I_1 and I_1 to I_0, indifference curves do not intersect.

A *preference map* is a series of indifference curves that look like the contour lines on a map. By looking at a map, we can draw some conclusions about the terrain. Similarly, by looking at the shape of the indifference curves, we can draw conclusions about a person's preferences.

Let's see how to 'read' a preference map.

Figure 8.3 A Preference Map

(a) An indifference curve

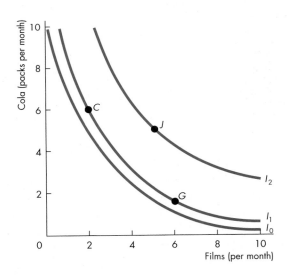

(b) Lisa's preference map

In part (a), Lisa consumes 6 packs of cola and sees 2 films a month at point C. She is indifferent between all the points on the green indifference curve such as C and G. She prefers any point above the indifference curve (yellow area) to any point on it, and she prefers any point on the indifference curve to any point below it (grey area).

Part (b) shows three indifference curves – I_0, I_1 and I_2 – that are part of Lisa's preference map. She prefers point J to point C or G, so she prefers any point on I_2 to any point on I_1.

 myeconlab Animation

Marginal Rate of Substitution

The **marginal rate of substitution** (or *MRS*) is the rate at which a person will give up good *y* (the good measured on the *y*-axis) to get an additional unit of good *x* (the good measured on the *x*-axis) and at the same time remain indifferent (remain on the same indifference curve). The magnitude of the slope of an indifference curve measures the marginal rate of substitution.

1 If the indifference curve is *steep*, the marginal rate of substitution is *high*. The person is willing to give up a large quantity of good *y* in exchange for a small quantity of good *x* while remaining indifferent

2 If the indifference curve is *flat*, the marginal rate of substitution is *low*. The person is willing to give up only a small amount of good *y* in exchange for a large amount of good *x* to remain indifferent

Figure 8.4 shows you how to calculate the marginal rate of substitution. Suppose that Lisa drinks 6 packs of cola and sees 2 films at point *C* on indifference curve I_1. To calculate her marginal rate of substitution, we measure the magnitude of the slope of the indifference curve at point *C*. To measure this magnitude, place a straight line against, or tangent to, the indifference curve at point *C*. Along that line, as the quantity of cola decreases by 10 packs, the number of films increases by 5 – an average of 2 packs per film. So at point *C*, Lisa is willing to give up cola for films at the rate of 2 packs per film – a marginal rate of substitution of 2.

Now, suppose that Lisa sees 6 films and drinks 1.5 packs of cola at point *G* on indifference curve I_1 in Figure 8.4. Her marginal rate of substitution is now measured by the magnitude of the slope of the indifference curve at point *G*. That slope is the same as the slope of the tangent to the indifference curve at point *G*. Here, as cola consumption decreases by 4.5 packs, film consumption increases by 9 – an average of 1/2 packs per film. So at point *G*, Lisa is willing to give up cola for films at the rate of 1/2 packs per film – a marginal rate of substitution of 1/2.

As Lisa sees more films and drinks less cola, her marginal rate of substitution diminishes. Diminishing marginal rate of substitution is the key assumption of consumer theory. The assumption of **diminishing marginal rate of substitution** is a general tendency for a person to be willing to give up less of good *y* to get one more unit of good *x*, while at the same time remaining indifferent as the quantity of *x* increases. In Lisa's case, she is less willing to give up cola to see one more film as the number of films she sees increases.

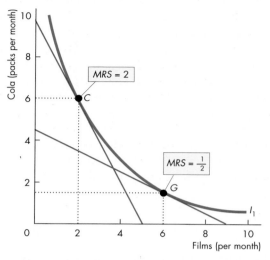

Figure 8.4 The Marginal Rate of Substitution

The magnitude of the slope of an indifference curve is called the marginal rate of substitution (*MRS*). The red line at point *C* tells us that Lisa is willing to give up 10 packs to see 5 films. Her marginal rate of substitution at point *C* is 10 divided by 5, which equals 2. The red line at point *G* tells us that Lisa is willing to give up 4.5 packs to see 9 films. Her marginal rate of substitution at point *G* is 4.5 divided by 9, which equals 1/2.

myeconlab Animation

Your Own Diminishing Marginal Rate of Substitution

Think about your own diminishing marginal rate of substitution. Suppose that in one month you drink 10 packs of cola and see no films. You would probably be happy to give up lots of cola just to see one film. But now suppose that in a month, you see 6 films and drink only 1 pack of cola. Most likely, you will probably not now be willing to give up much cola to see a seventh film. As a general rule, the greater the number of films you see, the smaller is the quantity of cola you are willing to give up to see an additional film.

The shape of the indifference curves incorporates the principle of the diminishing marginal rate of substitution because the curves are bowed towards the origin. The tightness of the bend of an indifference curve tells us how willing a person is to substitute one good for another while remaining indifferent. The examples that follow will make this point clear.

Degree of Substitutability

Most of us would not regard films and cola as being *close* substitutes for each other. Substitutes are goods that can be used in place of each other. But to some degree, we are willing to substitute between these two goods. No matter how enthusiastic you are about cola, there is surely some increase in the number of films you can see that will compensate you for being deprived of a can of cola. Similarly, no matter how addicted you are to films, surely some amount of cola will compensate you for being deprived of seeing one film. A person's indifference curves for films and cola might look something like those shown in Figure 8.5(a).

Close Substitutes

Some goods substitute so easily for each other that most of us do not even notice which we are consuming. There are different brands of marker pens and roller-ball pens. Most of us don't care whether we use a marker pen from the university bookshop or the local supermarket. When two goods are perfect substitutes, their indifference curves are straight lines that slope downward, as Figure 8.5(b) illustrates. The marginal rate of substitution between perfect substitutes is constant.

Complements

Some goods cannot substitute for each other at all. Instead, they are complements. The complements in Figure 8.5(c) are left and right running shoes. Indifference curves of perfect complements are L-shaped. For most of us, one left running shoe and one right running shoe are as good as one left running shoe and two right ones. Having two of each is preferred to having one of each, but two of one and one of the other is no better than one of each.

The extreme cases of perfect substitutes and perfect complements shown here don't often happen in reality. But they do illustrate that the shape of the indifference

Figure 8.5 The Degree of Substitutability

(a) Ordinary goods

(b) Perfect substitutes

(c) Perfect complements

The shape of the indifference curves reveals the degree of substitutability between two goods. Part (a) shows the indifference curves for two ordinary goods: films and cola. To consume less cola and remain indifferent, one must see more films. The number of films that compensates for a reduction in cola increases as less cola is consumed.

Part (b) shows the indifference curves for two perfect substitutes. For the consumer to remain indifferent, one fewer marker pen from the local supermarket must be replaced by one extra marker pen from the university bookshop.

Part (c) shows two perfect complements – goods that cannot be substituted for each other at all. One left running shoe with two right running shoes is no better than one of each. But having two of each is preferred to having one of each.

*"With the pork I'd recommend
an Alsatian white or a Coke."*

© Robert Weber/The New Yorker Collection/
www.cartoonbank.com

curve shows the degree of substitutability between two goods. The more perfectly substitutable the two goods, the more nearly are their indifference curves straight lines and the less quickly does the marginal rate of substitution diminish. Poor substitutes for each other have tightly curved indifference curves, approaching the shape of those shown in Figure 8.5(c).

As you can see in the cartoon, according to the waiter's preferences, Alsatian white and Coke are perfect substitutes and each is a complement of pork. We hope the customers agree with him.

1   What is an indifference curve and how does an indifference map show preferences?
2   Why does an indifference curve slope downward, and why is it bowed towards the origin?
3   What do we call the magnitude of the slope of an indifference curve?
4   What is the key assumption about a consumer's marginal rate of substitution?

You can work these questions in Study Plan 8.2 and get instant feedback.   myeconlab

The two components of the model of household choice are now in place: the budget line and the preference map. We will use these components to work out the consumer's choice and to predict how choices change when prices and income change.

Predicting Consumer Behaviour

We are now going to develop a model to predict the quantities of films and cola that Lisa chooses to buy. We're also going to see how these quantities change when a price changes or when Lisa's income changes. Finally, we're going to see how the substitution effect and the income effect, two ideas that you met in Chapter 3 (see p. 57), guarantee that for a normal good, the demand curve slopes downward.

Best Affordable Choice

When Lisa makes her best affordable choice of films and cola, she spends all her income and is on her highest attainable indifference curve. Figure 8.6 illustrates this choice: the budget line is from Figure 8.1 and her indifference curves are from Figure 8.3(b). Lisa's best affordable choice is 2 films and 6 packs of cola at point C – the *best affordable point.*

Figure 8.6   The Best Affordable Point

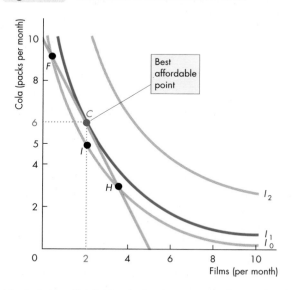

Lisa's best affordable choice is at point C, the point on her budget line and on her highest attainable indifference curve. At point C, Lisa's marginal rate of substitution between films and cola (the magnitude of the slope of the indifference curve I_1) equals the relative price of films and cola (the slope of the budget line).

myeconlab Animation

On the Budget Line

The best affordable point is on the budget line. For every point inside the budget line such as point I, there are points on the budget line that Lisa prefers. For example, she prefers all the points on the budget line between *F* and *H* to point *I*. So she chooses a point *on* the budget line.

On the Highest Attainable Indifference Curve

Every point on the budget line lies on an indifference curve. For example, points *F* and *H* lie on the indifference curve I_0. By moving along her budget line from either *F* or *H* towards *C*, Lisa reaches points on ever higher indifference curves that she prefers to points *F* or *H*. When Lisa gets to point *C*, she is on the highest attainable indifference curve.

Marginal Rate of Substitution Equals Relative Price

At point *C*, Lisa's marginal rate of substitution between films and cola (the magnitude of the slope of the indifference curve) is equal to the relative price of films and cola (the magnitude of the slope of the budget line). Lisa's willingness to pay for a film equals her opportunity cost of a film.

Let's now see how Lisa's choices change when a price changes.

A Change in Price

The effect of a change in the price of a good on the quantity of the good consumed is called the **price effect**. We will use Figure 8.7(a) to work out the price effect of a fall in the price of seeing a film. We start with the price at £6, the price of cola at £3 a pack and with Lisa's income at £30 a month. In this situation, Lisa chooses 6 packs of cola and sees 2 films a month at point *C*.

Now suppose that the price of a film falls to £3. With a lower price of film, the budget line rotates outward and becomes flatter. The new budget line is the darker orange line in Figure 8.7(a). To check how a price change affects the budget line, see Figure 8.2(a).

Lisa's best affordable point is now *J*, where she sees 5 films and buys 5 packs of cola. When the price of a film falls and the price of cola and her income remain constant, Lisa cuts her cola purchases from 6 to 5 packs and increases the number of films she sees from 2 to 5 a month. Lisa substitutes films for cola.

Figure 8.7 Price Effect and Demand Curve

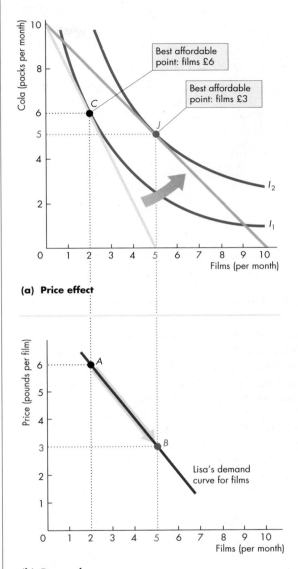

(a) Price effect

(b) Demand curve

Initially, Lisa consumes at point *C* in part (a). If the price to see a film falls from £6 to £3, Lisa chooses point *J*. Lisa increases the number of films she sees from 2 to 5 a month and decreases the cola she drinks from 6 to 5 packs. The move from point *C* to point *J* is the price effect.

At a price of £6 a film, Lisa sees 2 films a month at point *A* in part (b). At a price of £3 a film, Lisa sees 5 films a month, at point *B* in part (b). Lisa's demand curve for films passes through points *A* and *B* and traces out her best affordable quantity of films as the price of a film varies.

 Animation

ECONOMICS IN ACTION

Best Affordable Choice of Cinema Films and DVD Rentals

Between 2005 and 2010, box-office receipts increased by more than 20 per cent and during that same period, the average price of a cinema ticket increased by 6 per cent. So most of the increase in box-office receipts occurred because people went to the cinema more often.

Why is film-going booming? One answer is that the consumer's experience has improved. Films in 3-D such as *Avatar* and *Alice in Wonderland* play much better on the big screen than at home. Also, cinemas are able to charge a higher price for 3-D films, which further boosts receipts. But there is another answer, and at first thought an unlikely one: events in the market for DVD rentals have affected cinema going. To see why, let's look at the recent history of the DVD rentals market.

Back in 2005, Blockbuster was the main player in the UK DVD rental market, with Amazon second. Blockbuster had 720 shops in the UK. The price of a DVD rental was around £4 a night. LoveFilm and Video Island were the up and coming online order and postal return competition with a tiny share of the market. In 2006, the two small companies merged, and in 2008, they took over Amazon's UK and German rental business. They had 1 million subscribers by 2010 and 20 per cent of the market. LoveFilm now charges just over £1.00 per rental. Easy access to DVDs at £1 per rental transformed the market for film watching and Figure 1 shows why.

A student has a budget of £40 a month to allocate to films. To keep the story clear, we'll suppose that it cost £8 to go to the cinema in both 2005 and 2010. The price of a DVD rental in 2005 was £4, so the student's budget line is the one that runs from 5 cinema films on the *y*-axis to 10 DVD rentals on the *x*-axis.

The student's best affordable point is 2 cinema films and 6 rentals a month.

In 2010, the price of a rental falls to £1 a film but the price of a cinema ticket remains at £8. So the budget line rotates outward. The student's best affordable point is now at 3 cinema films and 16 rentals a month. (This student loves films!)

Many other things changed between 2005 and 2010 that influenced the markets for films and DVD rentals, but the fall in the price of a DVD rental was the biggest influence.

Figure 1   Best Affordable Films and DVD Rentals

The Demand Curve

In Chapter 3, we asserted that the demand curve slopes downward and that it shifts when the consumer's income changes or when the price of another good changes. We can now derive a demand curve from a consumer's budget line and indifference curves. By doing so, we can see that the law of demand and the downward-sloping demand curve are consequences of the consumer choosing his or her best affordable combination of goods.

To derive Lisa's demand curve for films, we lower the price to see a film and find her best affordable point at different prices, holding all other things constant. We've just done this for two film prices in Figure 8.7(a). Figure 8.7(b) highlights these two prices and two points that lie on Lisa's demand curve for films. When the price to see a film is £6, Lisa sees 2 films a month at point A. When the price falls to £3, she increases the number of films she sees to 5 films a month at point B. Lisa's demand curve for films is made up of these two points plus all the other points of Lisa's best affordable consumption of films at each film price, provided the price of cola and Lisa's income remain the same. As you can see, Lisa's demand curve for films slopes downward – the lower the price to see a film, the more films she sees each month. This is the law of demand.

Next, let's see how Lisa adjusts her purchases of films and cola when her income changes.

A Change in Income

The effect of a change in income on buying plans is called the **income effect**. Figure 8.8(a) shows the income effect when Lisa's income falls. With an income of £30, the price of a film £3 and the price of cola £3 a pack, Lisa's best affordable point is J – she sees 5 films and buys 5 packs of cola a month. If her income falls to £21, her best affordable point is K – she sees 4 films and buys 3 packs of cola a month. When Lisa's income falls, she buys less of both goods. Films and cola are normal goods.

The Demand Curve and the Income Effect

A change in income leads to a shift in the demand curve, as shown in Figure 8.8(b). With an income of £30, Lisa's demand curve is D_0, the same as in Figure 8.7. But when her income falls to £21, she plans to see fewer films at each price, so her demand curve for films shifts leftward to D_1.

Figure 8.8 Income Effect and Change in Demand

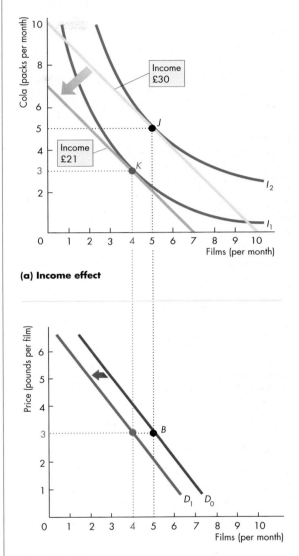

(a) Income effect

(b) Demand curve

A change in income shifts the budget line, changes the best affordable point and shifts the demand curve.

When Lisa's income is £30, the price of a film is £3 and the price of cola is £3 a pack, her best affordable point is J in part (a). When her income decreases from £30 to £21, her best affordable point is K. She sees fewer films and buys less cola.

When Lisa's income is £30, her demand curve for films is D_0 in part (b). When her income decreases to £21, her demand curve for films shifts leftward to D_1. For Lisa, seeing films is a normal good. Her demand for films decreases because she now sees fewer films at each price.

 Animation

Substitution Effect and Income Effect

For a normal good, a fall in price *always* increases the quantity bought. We can prove this assertion by dividing the price effect into two parts:

◆ The substitution effect
◆ The income effect

Figure 8.9(a) shows the price effect and Figures 8.9(b) and 8.9(c) divide the price effect into its two parts.

Substitution Effect

The **substitution effect** is the effect of a change in price on the quantities bought when the consumer (hypothetically) remains indifferent between the original and the new combinations of goods consumed. To work out Lisa's substitution effect, when the price of a film falls, we cut her income by enough to leave her on the same indifference curve as before.

Figure 8.9(a) shows the price effect of a fall in price of seeing a film from £6 to £3. The number of films increases from 2 to 5 a month. When the price falls, suppose (hypothetically) that we cut Lisa's income to £21. What's special about £21? It is the income that is just enough, at the new price of seeing a film, to keep Lisa's best affordable point on the same indifference curve as her original consumption point C. Lisa's budget line is now the medium orange line in Figure 8.9(b). With the lower price of a film and less income, Lisa's best affordable point is K on indifference curve I_1. The move from C to K is the substitution effect of the price change. The substitution effect of the fall in the price of a film is an increase in the films she sees from 2 to 4 a month. The direction of the substitution effect never varies: when the relative price of a good falls, the consumer substitutes more of that good for the other good.

Income Effect

To calculate the substitution effect, we gave Lisa a £9 pay cut. To calculate the income effect, we give Lisa back her £9. The £9 increase in income shifts Lisa's budget line outward, as shown in Figure 8.9(c). The

---

Figure 8.9   Substitution Effect and Income Effect

(a) Price effect

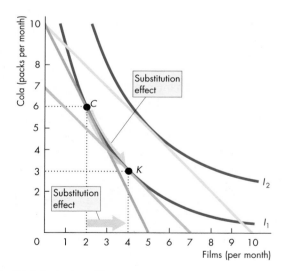

(b) Substitution effect

When the price of a film falls from £6 to £3, Lisa moves from point C to point J in part (a). The price effect is an increase in the number of films from 2 to 5 a month. This price effect is separated into a substitution effect in part (b) and an income effect in part (c).

To isolate the substitution effect, we confront Lisa with the new price of films but keep her on her original indifference curve, I_1. The substitution effect is the move from C to K along indifference curve I_1 – an increase from 2 to 4 films a month.

slope of the budget line does not change because both prices remain constant. This change in Lisa's budget line is similar to the one illustrated in Figure 8.8. As Lisa's budget line shifts outward, her consumption possibilities expand and her best affordable point becomes *J* on indifference curve I_2 in Figure 8.9(c). The move from *K* to *J* is the income effect of the price change.

As Lisa's income increases, she sees more films. For Lisa, films are a normal good. For a normal good, the income effect *reinforces* the substitution effect. Because the two effects work in the same direction, we can be sure that the demand curve slopes downward. But some goods are inferior goods. What can we say about the demand for an inferior good?

Inferior Goods

Recall that an inferior good is a good for which *demand decreases* when *income increases*. For an inferior good, the income effect is negative, which means that a lower price does not inevitably lead to an increase in the quantity demanded. The substitution effect of a fall in the price increases the quantity demanded, but the negative income effect works in the opposite direction and offsets the substitution effect to some degree. The key question is to what degree?

If the negative income effect *equals* the positive substitution effect, a fall in the price leaves the quantity bought the same. When a fall in the price leaves the quantity demanded unchanged, the demand curve is vertical and demand is perfectly inelastic.

If the negative income effect *is smaller than* the positive substitution effect, a fall in the price increases the quantity bought and the demand curve slopes downward like that for a normal good. But demand for an inferior good might be less elastic than that for a normal good.

If the negative income effect *exceeds* the positive substitution effect, a fall in the price *decreases* the quantity bought and the demand curve *slopes upward*. This case does not appear to occur in the real world.

You can apply the indifference curve model to explain the changes in the way we buy recorded music, see films, and make all our other consumption choices. We allocate our budgets to make our best affordable choices. Changes in prices and incomes change our best affordable choices and change consumption patterns.

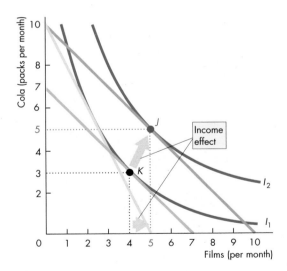

(c) Income effect

To isolate the income effect, we confront Lisa with the new price of films but increase her income so that she can move from the original indifference curve, I_1, to the new one, I_2. The income effect is the move from *K* to *J* – an increase from 4 to 5 films a month.

Review Quiz

1   When a consumer chooses the combination of goods and services to buy, what is she or he trying to achieve?
2   Explain the conditions that are met when a consumer has found the best affordable combination of goods and services to buy. (Use the terms *budget line*, *marginal rate of substitution* and *relative price* in your explanation.)
3   If the price of a normal good falls, what happens to the quantity demanded of that good?
4   Into what two effects can we divide the effect of a price change?
5   For a normal good, does the income effect reinforce the substitution effect or does it partly offset the substitution effect?

You can work these questions in Study Plan 8.3 and get instant feedback.

We're going to end this chapter by looking at some new ways of studying individual economic choices and consumer behaviour.

New Ways of Explaining Households' Choices

When William Stanley Jevons developed a theory in the 1860s, he would have loved to look inside people's brains and 'see' what he called 'utility'. But he believed that the human brain was the ultimate black box that could never be observed directly. For Jevons, and for most economists today, the purpose of consumer choice theory is to explain our *actions*, not what goes on inside our brains.

Economics has developed over the past 150 years with little help from and paying little attention to advances being made in psychology. Both economics and psychology seek to explain human behaviour, but they have developed different ways of attacking the challenge.

A few researchers *have* paid attention to the potential payoff from exploring economic problems by using the tools of psychology. These researchers, some economists and some psychologists, think that consumer theory is based on a view of how people make choices that attributes too much to reason and rationality. They propose an alternative approach based on the methods of psychology.

Other researchers, some economists and some neuroscientists, are using new tools to look inside the human brain and open up Jevons' 'black box'.

This section provides a very brief introduction to these new and exciting areas of economics. We'll explore the two related research agendas:

◆ Behavioural economics
◆ Neuroeconomics

Behavioural Economics

Behavioural economics studies the ways in which limits on the human brain's ability to compute and implement rational decisions influences economic behaviour – both the decisions that people make and the consequences of those decisions for the way markets work.

Behavioural economics starts with observed behaviour. It looks for anomalies – choices that do not seem to be rational. It then tries to account for the anomalies by using ideas developed by psychologists that emphasize features of the human brain that limit rational choice.

In behavioural economics, instead of being rational, people are assumed to have three impediments that prevent rational choice: bounded rationality, bounded willpower and bounded self-interest.

Bounded Rationality

Bounded rationality is rationality that is limited by the computing power of the human brain. We can't always work out the rational choice.

For Lisa, choosing between films and cola, it seems unlikely that she would have much trouble figuring out what to buy. But toss Lisa some uncertainty and the task becomes harder. She's read the reviews of *Ironman 2* on Fandango, but does she really want to see that film? How much marginal utility will it give her? Faced with uncertainty, people might use rules of thumb, listen to the views of others, and make decisions based on gut instinct rather than on rational calculation.

Bounded Willpower

Bounded willpower is the less than perfect willpower that prevents us from making a decision that we know, at the time of implementing the decision, we will later regret.

Lisa might be feeling particularly thirsty when she passes a cola vending machine. Under Lisa's rational best affordable buying plan, she buys her cola at the discount shop, where she gets it for the lowest possible price. Lisa has already bought her cola for this month, but it is at home. Spending 50 pence on a can now means giving up a film later this month.

Lisa's rational choice is to ignore the temporary thirst and stick to her plan. But she might not possess the willpower to do so – sometimes she will and sometimes she won't.

Bounded Self-interest

Bounded self-interest is the limited self-interest that results in sometimes suppressing our own interests to help others.

A winter storm hits Wales and Lisa, feeling sorry for the victims, donates £10 to a fund-raiser. She now has only £20 to spend on films and cola this month. The quantities that she buys are not, according to her indifference curve, the ones at her best affordable point.

The main applications of behavioural economics are in two areas: finance, where uncertainty is a key factor in decision making; and savings, where the future is a key factor.

But one behaviour observed by behavioural economists is more general and might affect your choices. It is called the endowment effect.

The Endowment Effect

The *endowment effect* is the tendency for people to value something more highly simply because they own it. If you are at your best affordable point, then the price you would be willing to accept to give up something that you own (for example, your coffee mug) should be the same as the price you are willing to pay for an identical one.

In experiments, students seem to display the endowment effect: the price they are willing to pay for a coffee mug that is identical to the one they own is *less* than the price they would be willing to accept to give up the coffee mug that they own. Behavioural economists say that this behaviour contradicts consumer theory.

Neuroeconomics

Neuroeconomics is the study of the activity of the human brain when a person makes an economic decision. The discipline uses the observational tools and ideas of neuroscience to obtain a better understanding of economic decisions.

Neuroeconomics is an experimental discipline. In an experiment, a person makes an economic decision and the electrical or chemical activity of the person's brain is observed and recorded using the same type of equipment that neurosurgeons use to diagnose brain disorders.

The observations provide information about which regions of the brain are active at different points in the process of making an economic decision.

Observations show that some economic decisions generate activity in the area of the brain (called the prefrontal cortex) where we store memories, analyse data and anticipate the consequences of our actions. If people make rational decisions, it is in this region of the brain that the decision occurs.

But observations also show that some economic decisions generate activity in the region of the brain (called the hippocampus) where we store memories of anxiety and fear. Decisions that are influenced by activity in this part of the brain might not be rational and be driven by fear or panic.

Neuroeconomists are also able to observe the amount of a brain hormone (called dopamine), the quantity of which increases in response to pleasurable events and

decreases in response to disappointing events. These observations might one day enable neuroeconomists to actually measure 'utility' and shine a bright light inside what was once believed to be the ultimate black box.

Controversy

The new ways of studying consumer choice that we've briefly described here are being used more widely to study business decisions and decisions in financial markets, and this type of research is surely going to become more popular.

But behavioural economics and neuroeconomics generate controversy. Most economists hold the view of Jevons that the goal of economics is to explain the decisions that we observe people making and not to explain what goes on inside people's heads.

Most economists would prefer to probe apparent anomalies more deeply and figure out why they are not anomalies after all.

Review Quiz

1 Define behavioural economics.
2 What are the three limitations on human rationality that behavioural economics emphasizes?
3 Define neuroeconomics.
4 What do behavioural economics and neuroeconomics seek to achieve?

You can work these questions in Study Plan 8.4 and get instant feedback.

You have now completed your study of households' choices and some new ideas about how people make economic choices.

Reading Between the Lines on pp. 190–191 shows you how the theory of households' choices explains why e-books have taken off, and how people choose to buy their books in electronic or paper format.

In the chapters that follow, we study the choices that firms make in their pursuit of profit and how those choices determine the supply of goods and services and the demand for productive resources.

Reading Between the Lines

Paper Books versus e-Books

Bloomberg.com, 19 July 2010

Amazon.com E-Book Sales Exceed Hardcovers for First Time

by
Joseph Galante

Amazon.com Inc., the largest Internet retailer, said growth in sales of its Kindle digital reader accelerated every month in the second quarter and that it's selling more electronic books than hardcover editions.

The pace of Kindle sales also has tripled since the company cut the price to $189 from $259, Amazon.com Chief Executive Officer Jeff Bezos said in a statement. . . .

Amazon.com sold more than triple the number of Kindle books in the first half of the year as it did in the same period last year, Seattle-based Amazon.com said. More than 81 percent of its 630,000 electronic books are $9.99 or less.

"We've reached a tipping point with the new price of Kindle," Bezos said in the statement. "Amazon.com customers now purchase more Kindle books than hardcover books -- astonishing when you consider that we've been selling hardcover books for 15 years, and Kindle books for 33 months." . . .

In the past three months, Amazon.com has sold 143 Kindle books for every 100 hardcover books, the company said. In July, sales of e-books accelerated to 180 sold for every 100 hardcover versions. Kindle book sales this year have also exceeded broader e-book sales growth, pegged by the Association of American Publishers at 207 percent through May, Amazon.com said.

The Essence of the Story

◆ Amazon sold 143 Kindle e-books for every 100 hardcover paper books.

◆ The Kindle store lists 630,000 e-books, and 81 per cent of them are priced at less than $10.

◆ Amazon has cut the price of its Kindle reader from $259 to $189 and the quantity sold has tripled.

◆ The quantity sold might explode if the Kindle was cheaper still.

Economic Analysis

◆ Print books and e-books are substitutes, but for most people, though, e-books and print books are extremely poor substitutes.

◆ For a committed print-book lover, no quantity of e-books can compensate for a print book – the marginal rate of substitution between print books and e-books is zero.

◆ Beth is a print-book lover and Figure 1 shows her indifference curves. With print books on the x-axis, Beth's indifference curves are steep – she is willing to forgo a large number of e-books to get one more print book.

◆ Beth's annual book budget is $340. The price of an e-book reader is $190, the price of an e-book is $10 and the price of a print book is $20.

◆ We'll assume that an e-book reader has only a one-year life. (Buyers know they will want the next-generation reader next year.)

◆ The orange line is Beth's budget line if she buys a reader. She can afford 15 e-books if she buys no print books [$190 + (15 × $10) = $340] and along this line, by forgoing 2 e-books she can buy 1 print book.

◆ If Beth doesn't buy an e-book reader, she buys no e-books and can afford 17 print books ($340 ÷ $20 = 17) – the red dot.

◆ The red dot is also the best affordable choice because this choice gets her onto her highest attainable indifference curve, I_2.

◆ Andy differs from Beth. He thinks that print books and e-books are perfect substitutes. But he also likes music and buys albums. Figure 2 shows Andy's indifference curves for books (all types) and albums.

◆ Andy's annual budget for albums and books is $550. The price of an album is $10 and the prices of a reader, an e-book, and a print book are the same as those that Beth faces.

◆ Figure 2 shows Andy's two budget lines: one if he buys only e-books and albums and another if he buys only print books and albums.

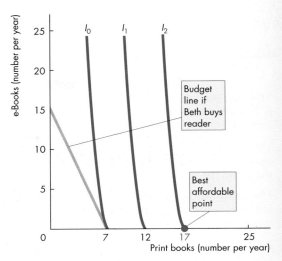

Figure 1 Print books versus e-books for a print-book lover

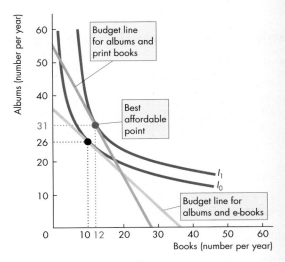

Figure 2 Books versus albums

◆ If Andy buys print books and albums, he can afford 12 print books and 31 albums [(12 × $20) + (31 × $10) = $550]. His best affordable choice is 12 print books and 31 albums.

◆ So even Andy, who thinks that e-books and print books are perfect substitutes, doesn't buy e-books. But he probably would if he had a larger budget.

> SUMMARY

Key Points

Consumption Possibilities
(pp. 176–178)

◆ The budget line is the boundary between what a household can and cannot afford given its income and the prices of goods.

◆ The point at which the budget line intersects the y-axis is the household's real income in terms of the good measured on that axis.

◆ The magnitude of the slope of the budget line is the relative price of good x (on the x-axis) in terms of good y (on the y-axis).

◆ A change in price changes the slope of the budget line. A change in income shifts the budget line but does not change its slope.

Working Problems 1 to 10 will give you a better understanding of consumption possibilities.

Preferences and Indifference Curves
(pp. 179–182)

◆ A consumer's preferences can be represented by indifference curves. An indifference curve joins all the combinations of goods among which the consumer is indifferent.

◆ A consumer prefers any point above an indifference curve to any point on it and any point on an indifference curve to any point below it.

◆ The magnitude of the slope of an indifference curve is called the marginal rate of substitution.

◆ The marginal rate of substitution diminishes as consumption of the good measured on the y-axis decreases and consumption of the good measured on the x-axis increases.

Working Problems 11 to 15 will give you a better understanding of preferences and indifference curves.

Predicting Consumer Behaviour
(pp. 182–187)

◆ A household consumes at its best affordable point. This point is on the budget line and on the highest attainable indifference curve and has a marginal rate of substitution equal to the relative price.

◆ The effect of a price change (the price effect) can be divided into a substitution effect and an income effect.

◆ The change in quantity when the price changes but the consumer (hypothetically) remains on the initial indifference curve is the substitution effect.

◆ The substitution always results in an increase in consumption of the good whose relative price has decreased.

◆ The income effect is the effect of a change in income on consumption.

◆ For a normal good, the income effect reinforces the substitution effect. For an inferior good, the income effect works in the opposite direction to the substitution effect.

Working Problems 16 to 20 will give you a better understanding of predicting consumer behaviour.

New Ways of Explaining Households' Choices (pp. 188–189)

◆ Behavioural economics studies limits on the ability of the human brain to compute and implement rational decisions.

◆ Bounded rationality, bounded willpower, and bounded self-interest are believed to explain some choices.

◆ Neuroeconomics uses the ideas and tools of neuroscience to study the effects of economic events and choices inside the human brain.

Working Problems 21 and 22 will give you a better understanding of the new ways of explaining households' choices.

Key Terms

Budget line, 176
Diminishing marginal rate of substitution, 180
Income effect, 185
Indifference curve, 179
Marginal rate of substitution, 180
Price effect, 183
Real income, 177
Relative price, 177
Substitution effect, 186

STUDY PLAN PROBLEMS AND APPLICATIONS

  You can work Problems 1 to 22 in MyEconLab Chapter 8 Study Plan and get instant feedback.

Consumption Possibilities

(Study Plan 8.1)

Use the following information to work Problems 1 to 4.

Sara has an income of £12 a week. The price of popcorn is £3 a bag, and the price of a smoothie is £3.

1 Calculate Sara's real income in terms of smoothies. Calculate her real income in terms of popcorn.

2 What is the relative price of smoothies in terms of popcorn? What is the opportunity cost of a smoothie?

3 Calculate the equation for Sara's budget line (with bags of popcorn on the left side).

4 Draw a graph of Sara's budget line with the quantity of smoothies on the x-axis. What is the slope of Sara's budget line? What determines its value?

Use the following information to work Problems 5 to 8.

Sara's income falls from £12 to £9 a week, while the price of popcorn is unchanged at £3 a bag and the price of a smoothie is unchanged at £3.

5 What is the effect of the fall in Sara's income on her real income in terms of smoothies?

6 What is the effect of the fall in Sara's income on her real income in terms of popcorn?

7 What is the effect of the fall in Sara's income on the relative price of a smoothie in terms of popcorn?

8 What is the slope of Sara's new budget line if it is drawn with smoothies on the x-axis?

Use the following information to work Problems 9 and 10.

Sara's income is £12 a week. The price of popcorn rises from £3 to £6 a bag, and the price of a smoothie is unchanged at £3.

9 What is the effect of the rise in the price of popcorn on Sara's real income in terms of smoothies and her real income in terms of popcorn?

10 What is the effect of the rise in the price of popcorn on the relative price of a smoothie in terms of popcorn? What is the slope of Sara's new budget line if it is drawn with smoothies on the x-axis?

Preferences and Indifference Curves

(Study Plan 8.2)

11 Draw figures that show your indifference curves for the following pairs of goods. For each pair, explain whether the goods are perfect substitutes, perfect complements or unrelated. The pairs of goods are:

a Right gloves and left gloves

b Coca-Cola and Pepsi

c Neurofen and ibuprofen (the generic form of Neurofen)

d Desktop computers and laptop computers

e Strawberries and cream

12 Discuss the shape of the indifference curve for each of the following pairs of goods. Explain the relationship between the shape of the indifference curve and the marginal rate of substitution as the quantities of the two goods change. The pairs of goods are:

a Orange juice and smoothies

b Cricket balls and bats

c Left shoe and right shoe

d Eye glasses and contact lenses

Use the following news clip to work Problems 13 and 14.

The Year in Medicine

Sudafed, used by allergy sufferers, contains as the active ingredient pseudoephedrine, which is widely used to make home-made methamphetamine. Allergy sufferers looking to buy Sudafed must now show photo ID, and sign a logbook. The most common alternative, phenylephrine, isn't as effective as pseudoephedrine.

Source: *Time*, 4 December 2006

13 Sketch an indifference curve for Sudafed and phenylephrine that is consistent with this news clip. On your graph, identify combinations that allergy sufferers prefer, do not prefer, and are indifferent among.

14 Explain how the marginal rate of substitution changes as an allergy sufferer increases the consumption of Sudafed.

Use the following information to work Problems 15 and 16.

With high petrol prices, 12 per cent of the people surveyed say that they have cancelled their Bank Holiday car trip and 11 per cent will take a shorter trip near home. That may save consumers some money, but it will also probably hurt service centres, which will sell less petrol and fewer snacks and hurt hotels, which will have fewer rooms used and serve fewer casual meals.

15 Describe the degree of substitutability between Bank Holiday trips and other trip-related goods and services and sketch a consumer's preference map that illustrates your description.

Predicting Consumer Behaviour
(Study Plan 8.3)

16 a Sketch a consumer's preference map between Bank Holiday trips and other goods and services. Draw a consumer's budget line prior to the rise in the price of petrol and mark the consumer's best affordable point.

   b On your graph, show how the best affordable point changes when the price of petrol rises.

Use the following information to work Problems 17 and 18.

Pam has chosen her best affordable combination of biscuits and cereal bars. She spends all of her weekly income on 30 biscuits at £1 each and 5 cereal bars at £2 each. Next week, people expect the price of a biscuit to fall to 50p and the price of a cereal bar to rise to £5.

17 a Will Pam be able to buy and want to buy 30 biscuits and 5 cereal bars next week?

   b Which situation does Pam prefer: biscuits at £1 and cereal bars at £2 or biscuits at 50p and cereal bars at £5?

18 a If Pam changes how she spends her weekly income, will she buy more or fewer biscuits and more or fewer cereal bars?

   b When the prices change next week, will there be an income effect, a substitution effect or both at work?

Use the following news clip to work Problems 19 and 20.

Boom Time For 'Gently Used' Clothes
Most retailers are blaming the economy for their poor sales, but one store chain that sells used brand name children's

clothes, toys, and furniture is boldly declaring that an economic downturn can actually be a boon for its business. Last year, the company took in $20 million in sales, up 5 per cent from the previous year. Sales are already up 5 per cent this year.

Source: CNN, 17 April 2008

19 a According to the news clip, is used clothing a normal good or an inferior good?

   b If the price of used clothing falls and income remains the same, explain how the quantity of used clothing bought changes.

   c If the price of used clothing falls and income remains the same, describe the substitution effect and the income effect that occur.

20 a Use a graph to illustrate a family's indifference curves for used clothing and other goods and services.

   b In your graph in part (a), draw two budget lines to show the effect of a fall in income on the quantity of used clothing purchased.

New Ways of Explaining Households' Choices (Study Plan 8.4)

Use the following news clip to work Problems 21 and 22.

Eating Away the Innings in Baseball's Cheap Seats
Baseball and gluttony, two of America's favourite pastimes, are merging and taking hold at Major League Baseball stadiums: all-you-can-eat seats. Some fans try to 'set personal records' during their first game in the section, but by their second or third time in such seats they eat normally, just as they would at a game.

Source: USA Today, 6 March 2008

21 a What conflict might exist between the best affordable point and setting 'personal records' for eating?

   b What does the fact that fans eat less at subsequent games indicate about the shape of the consumer's indifference curves as the quantity of food consumed increases?

22 a How can setting personal records for eating be reconciled with consumer theory?

   b Which ideas of behavioural economics are consistent with the information in the news clip?

ADDITIONAL PROBLEMS AND APPLICATIONS

myeconlab You can work these problems in MyEconLab if assigned by your lecturer.

Consumption Possibilities

Use the following information to work Problems 23 to 26.

Marc has a budget of £20 a month to spend on pizza and DVDs. The price of a pizza is £5, and the price of a DVD is £10.

23 What is the relative price of pizza in terms of DVDs and what is the opportunity cost of a pizza?

24 Calculate Marc's real income in terms of pizza. Calculate his real income in terms of DVDs.

25 Calculate the equation for Marc's budget line (with the quantity of pizza on the left side).

26 Draw a graph of Marc's budget line with the quantity of DVDs on the *x*-axis. What is the slope of Marc's budget line? What determines its value?

Use the following information to work Problems 27 to 30.

Amy has £20 a week to spend on coffee and cake. The price of coffee is £4 a cup, and the price of cake is £2 a slice.

27 Calculate the relative price of cake in terms of coffee.

28 Calculate the equation for Amy's budget line (with cups of coffee on the left side).

29 If Amy's income increases to £24 a week and the prices of coffee and cake remain unchanged, describe the change in her budget line.

30 If the price of a cake slice doubles while the price of coffee remains at £4 a cup and Amy's income remains at £20, describe the change in her budget line.

Use the following news clip to work Problems 31 and 32.

Petrol Prices Straining Budgets

With petrol prices rising, many people say they are staying in and scaling back spending to try to keep within their budget. They are driving as little as possible, cutting back on shopping and eating out, and reducing other discretionary spending.

Source: CNN, 29 February 2008

31 **a** Sketch a budget line for a household that spends its income on only two goods: petrol and restaurant meals. Identify the combinations of petrol and restaurant meals that are affordable and those that are unaffordable.

   b Sketch a second budget line to show how a rise in the price of petrol changes the affordable and unaffordable combinations of petrol and restaurant meals. Describe how the household's consumption possibilities change.

32 How does a rise in the price of petrol change the relative price of a restaurant meal? How does a rise in the price of petrol change real income in terms of restaurant meals?

Preferences and Indifference Curves

Use the following information to work Problems 33 and 34.

Rashid buys only books and CDs and the figure shows his preference map.

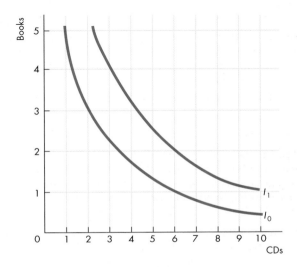

33 **a** If Rashid chooses 3 books and 2 CDs, what is his marginal rate of substitution?

   b If Rashid chooses 2 books and 6 CDs, what is his marginal rate of substitution?

34 Do Rashid's indifference curves display diminishing marginal rate of substitution? Explain why or why not.

35 **You May Be Paid More (or Less) Than You Think**

It's so hard to put a price on happiness, isn't it? But if you've ever had to choose between a job you like and a better-paying one that you like less, you probably wished some economist would tell you how much job satisfaction is worth. Trust in management is by far the biggest component to consider. Say you get a new boss and your trust in management goes up a bit (say, up 1 point on a 10-point scale). That's like getting a 36 per cent pay raise. In other words, that increased level of trust will boost your level of overall satisfaction in life by about the same amount as a 36 per cent raise would.

Source: CNN, 29 March 2006

a Measure trust in management on a 10-point scale, measure pay on the same 10-point scale, and think of them as two goods. Sketch an indifference curve (with trust on the *x*-axis) that is consistent with the news clip.

b What is the marginal rate of substitution between trust in management and pay according to this news clip?

c What does the news clip imply about the principle of diminishing marginal rate of substitution? Is that implication likely to be correct?

Predicting Consumer Behaviour

Use the following information to work Problems 36 and 37.

Jim has made his best affordable choice of muffins and coffee. He spends all of his income on 10 muffins at £1 each and 20 cups of coffee at £2 each. Now the price of a muffin rises to £1.50 and the price of coffee falls to £1.75 a cup.

36 a Will Jim now be able and want to buy 10 muffins and 20 coffees?

b Which situation does Jim prefer: muffins at £1 and coffee at £2 a cup or muffins at £1.50 and coffee at £1.75 a cup?

37 a If Jim changes the quantities that he buys, will he buy more or fewer muffins and more or less coffee?

b When the prices change, will there be an income effect, a substitution effect, or both at work?

Use the following information to work Problems 38 to 40.

Sara's income is £12 a week. The price of popcorn is £3 a bag, and the price of cola is £1.50 a can. The figure shows Sara's preference map for popcorn and cola.

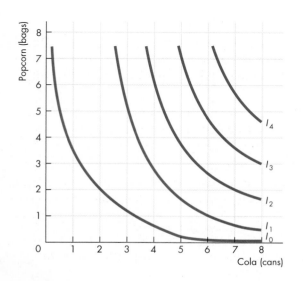

38 What quantities of popcorn and cola does Sara buy? What is Sara's marginal rate of substitution at the point at which she consumes?

39 Suppose that the price of cola rises to £3.00 a can and the price of popcorn and Sara's income remain the same. What quantities of cola and popcorn does Sara now buy? What are two points on Sara's demand curve for cola? Draw Sara's demand curve.

40 Suppose that the price of cola rises to £3.00 a can and the price of popcorn and Sara's income remain the same.

a What is the substitution effect of this price change and what is the income effect of the price change?

b Is cola a normal good or an inferior good? Explain.

New Ways of Explaining Consumer Choices

Use the following news clip to work Problems 41 to 43.

Putting a Price on Human Life

Researchers at Stanford and the University of Pennsylvania estimated that a healthy human life is worth about $129,000. Using government records on treatment costs for kidney dialysis as a benchmark, the authors tried to pinpoint the threshold beyond which ensuring another 'quality' year of life was no longer financially worthwhile. The study comes amid debate over whether the government should start rationing healthcare on the basis of cost effectiveness.

Source: *Time*, 9 June 2008

41 Why might the government ration healthcare according to treatment that is 'financially worthwhile' as opposed to providing as much treatment as is needed by a patient, regardless of costs?

42 What conflict might exist between a person's valuation of his or her own life and the rest of society's valuation of that person's life?

43 How does the potential conflict between self-interest and the social interest complicate setting a financial threshold for healthcare treatments?

Economics in the News

44 After you have studied *Reading Between the Lines* on pp. 190–191 answer the following questions.

a How do you buy books?

b Sketch your budget line for books and other goods.

c Sketch your indifference curves for books and other goods.

d Explain why Andy would buy e-books if the price of a reader fell to $100.

CHAPTER 9

Organizing Production

After studying this chapter you will be able to:

◆ Explain what a firm is and describe the economic problems that all firms face

◆ Distinguish between technological efficiency and economic efficiency

◆ Define and explain the principal–agent problem and describe how different types of business organizations cope with this problem

◆ Describe and distinguish between the types of markets in which firms operate

◆ Explain why firms coordinate some economic activities and markets coordinate others

When Tim Berners-Lee invented the World Wide Web in 1990, he paved the way for the creation of thousands of profitable businesses such as Facebook, Google and Microsoft.

The Internet has also created new ways for businesses to organize and new choices such as whether to outsource computing to cloud services. How do businesses operate efficiently? Why do firms produce some things but outsource or buy them from other firms?

In this chapter, you're going to learn about firms and the choices they make. In *Reading Between the Lines* at the end of the chapter, we'll apply what you've learned and look at the impact of cloud computing on firms' choices.

The Firm and Its Economic Problem

The 20 million or so firms in the EU differ in their size and in the scope of what they do. But they all perform the same basic economic functions. Each **firm** is an institution that hires factors of production and organizes those factors to produce and sell goods and services. Our goal is to predict how firms behave. To do so, we need to know a firm's goals and the constraints it faces. We begin with the goals.

The Firm's Goal

When economists ask entrepreneurs what they are trying to achieve, they get many different answers. Some talk about making a high-quality product, others about business growth, others about market share, others about the job satisfaction of their workforce and an increasing number today talk about social and environmental responsibility. All of these goals are pursued by firms, but they are not the fundamental goal. They are the means to that goal.

A firm's goal is to *maximize profit*. A firm that does not seek to maximize profit will either go out of business or be bought by a firm that does seek to maximize profit.

What is the profit that a firm seeks to maximize? To answer this question, we're going to look at Fashion First, a small firm that makes knitted jumpers. It is owned and operated by Norma.

Accounting Profit

In 2010, Fashion First received £400,000 a year for the jumpers sold and paid out £80,000 for wool, £20,000 for utilities, £120,000 for wages, £5,000 for lease of a computer from Dell, Inc. and £5,000 in interest on a bank loan. These expenses total £230,000, so the firm had a cash surplus of £170,000.

To measure the profit made by Fashion First, Norma's accountant subtracted £20,000 for depreciation of the firm's buildings and knitting machines from the £170,000 cash surplus. Depreciation is the fall in the value of the firm's capital. To calculate depreciation, accountants use standard rules set by accounting professionals. Using these rules, Norma's accountant calculated that Fashion First made a profit of £150,000 in 2010.

Economic Accounting

Accountants measure a firm's profit to ensure that a firm pays the correct amount of income tax and to show the bank how its loan has been used.

Economists measure a firm's profit to enable them to predict the firm's decisions, and the goal of these decisions is to maximize *economic profit*. **Economic profit** is equal to total revenue minus total cost, with total cost measured as the *opportunity cost of production*.

Opportunity Cost of Production

The *opportunity cost* of any action is the highest-valued alternative forgone. The *opportunity cost of production* is the value of the best alternative use of the resources that a firm uses in production.

A firm's opportunity cost of production is the value of *real* alternatives forgone. We express opportunity cost in money units so that we can compare and add up the value of the alternatives forgone. A firm's opportunity cost of production is the sum of the cost of using resources that are:

◆ Bought in the market

◆ Owned by the firm

◆ Supplied by the firm's owner

Resources Bought in the Market

A firm incurs an opportunity cost when it buys resources in the market. The amount spent on these resources is an opportunity cost of production because the firm could have bought different resources to produce some other good or service. For Fashion First, the resources bought in the market are wool, utilities, labour, a leased computer and a bank loan. The £230,000 spent on these items in 2010 could have been spent on other things, so it is an opportunity cost of producing jumpers.

Resources Owned by the Firm

A firm incurs an opportunity cost when it uses its own capital. The cost of using capital owned by the firm is an opportunity cost of production because the firm could sell the capital that it owns and rent capital from another firm. When a firm uses its own capital, it implicitly rents it from itself. In this case, the firm's opportunity cost of using the capital it owns is called the **implicit rental rate** of capital. The implicit rental rate has two components: economic depreciation and forgone interest.

Economic Depreciation

Accountants measure depreciation, the fall in the value of a firm's capital, using formulas that are unrelated to the change in the market value of capital. **Economic depreciation** is the fall in the *market value* of a firm's capital over a given period. It equals the market price of the capital at the beginning of the period minus the market price of the capital at the end of the period.

Suppose that Fashion First could have sold its buildings and knitting machines on 1 January 2010 for £400,000 and that it can sell the same capital on 31 December 2010 for £375,000. The firm's economic depreciation during 2010 is £25,000 (£400,000 – £375,000). This forgone £25,000 is an opportunity cost of production.

Forgone Interest

The funds used to buy capital could have been used for some other purpose, and in their next best use they would have earned interest. This forgone interest is an opportunity cost of production. Suppose that Fashion First used £300,000 of its own funds to buy capital. If the firm invested its £300,000 in bonds instead of a knitting factory (and rented the capital it needs to produce jumpers), it would have earned £15,000 a year in interest. This forgone interest is an opportunity cost of production.

Resources Supplied by the Firm's Owner

A firm's owner might supply *both* entrepreneurship and labour. The factor of production that organizes a firm and makes its business decisions might be supplied by the firm's owner or by a hired entrepreneur. The return to entrepreneurship is profit, and the return that an entrepreneur can expect to receive *on average* is called **normal profit**. Normal profit is the cost of entrepreneurship and is an opportunity cost of production.

If Norma supplies entrepreneurial services herself, and if the normal profit she can earn on these services is £45,000 a year, this amount is an opportunity cost of production at Fashion First.

In addition to supplying entrepreneurship, the owner of a firm might supply labour but not take a wage. The opportunity cost of the owner's labour is the wage income that the owner forgoes by not taking the best alternative job. If Norma supplies labour to Fashion First and if the wage she can earn on this labour at another firm is £55,000 a year, this amount of wages forgone is an opportunity cost of production at Fashion First.

Economic Accounting: a Summary

Table 9.1 summarizes economic accounting. Fashion First's total revenue is £400,000, its opportunity cost of production is £370,000 and its economic profit is £30,000.

Norma's personal income is the £30,000 of economic profit plus the £100,000 that she earns by supplying resources to Fashion First.

The Firm's Decisions

To achieve the objective of maximum economic profit, a firm must make five basic decisions:

1   What to produce and in what quantities.

2   How to produce.

3   How to organize and compensate its managers and workers.

4   How to market and price its products.

5   What to produce itself and what to buy from others.

In all these decisions, a firm's actions are limited by the constraints that it faces. Our next task is to learn about these constraints.

Table 9.1

Economic Accounting

Item	Amount (pounds)	Total (pounds)
Total revenue		**400,000**
Cost of resources bought in the market		
Wool	80,000	
Utilities	20,000	
Wages paid	120,000	
Computer lease	5,000	
Bank interest paid	5,000	230,000
Cost of resources owned by firm		
Forgone interest	15,000	
Economic depreciation	25,000	40,000
Cost of resources supplied by owner		
Normal profit	45,000	
Norma's forgone wages	55,000	100,000
Opportunity cost of production		**370,000**
Economic profit		**30,000**

The Firm's Constraints

Three features of a firm's environment limit the maximum profit it can make. They are:

◆ Technology constraints
◆ Information constraints
◆ Market constraints

Technology Constraints

Economists define technology broadly. A **technology** is any method of producing a good or service. Technology includes the detailed designs of machines. It also includes the layout of the workplace and the organization of the firm. For example, the shopping centre is a technology for producing retail services. It is a different technology from catalogue shopping, which in turn is different from the high street stores.

It might seem surprising that a firm's profits are limited by technology. Every year we learn about the latest technological advances that will revolutionize future production and consumption. Technology is advancing, but to produce more output and gain more revenue with current technology, a firm must hire more resources and incur greater costs. At any point in time, the increase in profit that the firm can achieve is limited by the technology currently available. For example, using its current plant and workforce, BMW can produce some maximum number of cars per day. To produce more cars per day, BMW must hire more resources, which increases BMW's costs and limits the increase in profit that BMW can make by selling the additional cars.

Information Constraints

A business manager can never possess all the information needed to make decisions. Businesses lack information about the present and the future – uncertainty. For example, suppose you plan to buy a new computer for your business. When should you buy it? The answer depends on how the price is going to change in the future. Where should you buy it? The answer depends on the prices at many different suppliers. To get the best deal, you must compare the quality and price in all the different shops. The opportunity cost of actually getting all this information and making all these comparisons will exceed the cost of the computer!

Similarly, a firm is constrained by limited information about the quality and effort of its workforce, the current and future plans of its customers and the plans of its competitors. Workers may slacken off while managers believe they are working hard. Customers may switch to competing suppliers. Firms must face competition from new firms and the new products and services they offer.

Firms try to create incentive systems for workers to ensure they work hard even when no one is monitoring their efforts. Firms also spend billions every year on market research and product development. But none of these efforts and expenditures eliminates the problems of incomplete information and uncertainty. Again, the cost of coping with limited information and uncertainty itself limits profit.

Market Constraints

What each firm can sell and the price it can obtain is constrained by the willingness of customers to pay and by the prices and marketing efforts of other firms. Similarly, the resources that each firm can buy and the prices it must pay are limited by the willingness of people to work for and invest in the firm. Firms spend billions every year marketing and selling their products. Some of the most creative minds strive to find the right message that will produce a knockout television advertisement. Market constraints and the expenditures firms make to overcome them limit the profit a firm can make.

Review Quiz

1 What is a firm's fundamental goal and what happens if the firm does not pursue this goal?
2 Why do accountants and economists calculate a firm's cost and profit in different ways?
3 What are the items that make opportunity cost different from the accountants' measure of cost?
4 Why is normal profit an opportunity cost?
5 What are the constraints that each firm faces? How does each constraint limit the firm's profit?

You can work these questions in Study Plan 9.1 and get instant feedback.

In the rest of this chapter and in Chapters 10 to 13, we study the decisions that firms make. You will learn how to predict a firm's behaviour as the response to both the constraints that it faces and the changes in those constraints. We begin by taking a closer look at the technology constraints that firms face.

Technological and Economic Efficiency

Microsoft employs a large workforce and most Microsoft workers possess a large amount of human capital. But the firm also uses a small amount of physical capital. In contrast, an oil extraction company employs a huge amount of drilling equipment (physical capital) and relatively little labour. Why? The answer lies in the concept of efficiency. There are two concepts of production efficiency: technological efficiency and economic efficiency. **Technological efficiency** occurs when the firm produces a given output by using the least amount of inputs. **Economic efficiency** occurs when the firm produces a given output at least cost. Let's explore the two concepts of efficiency by studying an example.

Suppose that there are four alternative techniques for making TV sets:

A   *Robot production.* One person monitors the entire computer-driven process.

B   *Production line.* Workers specialize in a small part of the job as the emerging TV set passes them on a production line.

C   *Hand-tool production.* A single worker uses a few hand tools to make a TV set.

D   *Bench production.* Workers specialize in a small part of the job but walk from bench to bench to perform their tasks.

Table 9.2 sets out the amounts of labour and capital required by each of these four methods to make 10 TV sets a day.

Which of these alternative methods are technologically efficient?

Technological Efficiency

Recall that *technological efficiency* occurs when the firm produces a given output by using the least amount of inputs. Inspect the numbers in Table 9.2 and notice that method A uses the most capital but the least labour. Method C uses the most labour but the least capital. Method B and method D use less capital but more labour than method A and less labour but more capital than method C.

Compare methods B and D. Method D requires 100 workers and 10 units of capital to produce 10 TV sets.

Table 9.2

Four Ways of Making 10 TV Sets a Day

Method	Quantities of inputs	
	Labour	Capital
A Robot production	1	1,000
B Production line	10	10
C Hand-tool production	1,000	1
D Bench production	100	10

Those same 10 TV sets can be produced by method B with 10 workers and the same 10 units of capital. Because method D uses the same amount of capital and more labour than method B, method D is not technologically efficient.

Are any of the other methods not technologically efficient? The answer is no. Each of the other three methods is technologically efficient. Method A uses more capital but less labour than method B, and method C uses more labour but less capital than method B.

Which of these methods are economically efficient?

Economic Efficiency

Recall that *economic efficiency* occurs when the firm produces a given output at least cost. Method D, which is technologically inefficient, is also economically inefficient. It uses the same amount of capital as method B but 10 times as much labour, so it costs more. A technologically inefficient method is never economically efficient.

One of the three technologically efficient methods is economically efficient. But which method is economically efficient depends on factor prices.

In Table 9.3(a), the wage rate is £75 per day and the rental rate of capital is £250 per day. By studying Table 9.3(a), you can see that method B has the lowest cost and is the economically efficient method.

In Table 9.3(b), the wage rate is £150 per day and the rental rate of capital is £1 per day. Looking at Table 9.3(b), you can see that method A has the lowest cost and is the economically efficient method. In this case, capital is cheap relative to labour, so the method that uses the most capital is the economically efficient method.

Table 9.3

The Costs of Different Ways of Making 10 TV Sets a Day

(a) Wage rate £75 per day. Capital rental rate £250 per day

Method	Inputs Labour	Inputs Capital	Labour cost (£75 per day)		Capital cost (£250 per day)		Total cost
A	1	1,000	£75	+	£250,000	=	£250,075
B	10	10	750	+	2,500	=	3,250
C	1,000	1	75,000	+	2,500	=	75,250

(b) Wage rate £150 per day. Capital rental rate £1 per day

Method	Inputs Labour	Inputs Capital	Labour cost (£150 per day)		Capital cost (£1 per day)		Total cost
A	1	1,000	£150	+	£1,000	=	£1,150
B	10	10	1,500	+	10	=	1,510
C	1,000	1	150,000	+	1	=	150,001

(c) Wage rate £1 per day. Capital rental rate £1,000 per day

Method	Inputs Labour	Inputs Capital	Labour cost (£1 per day)		Capital cost (£1,000 per day)		Total cost
A	1	1,000	1	+	£1,000,000	=	£1,000,001
B	10	10	10	+	10,000	=	10,010
C	1,000	1	1,000	+	1,000	=	2,000

In Table 9.3(c), the wage rate is £1 per day and the rental rate of capital is £1,000 per day. You can see that method *C* has the lowest cost and is economically efficient. In this case, labour is so cheap relative to capital that the method that uses the most labour is the economically efficient method.

From these examples, you can see that while technological efficiency depends only on what is feasible; economic efficiency depends on the relative costs of resources. The economically efficient method is the one that uses the smaller amount of a more expensive resource and a larger amount of a less expensive resource.

A firm that is not economically efficient does not maximize profit. Natural selection favours efficient firms and inefficient firms disappear. Inefficient firms go out of business or are taken over by firms that produce with lower costs.

Review Quiz

1   Is a firm technologically efficient if it uses the latest technology? Why or why not?
2   Is a firm economically inefficient if it can cut costs by producing less? Why or why not?
3   Explain the key distinction between technological efficiency and economic efficiency.
4   Why do some firms use lots of capital and not much labour, while others use very little capital and lots of labour?

You can work these questions in Study Plan 9.2 and get instant feedback.

Next we will study information constraints that firms face and the diversity of organizational structures these constraints generate.

Information and Organization

Each firm organizes the production of goods and services by combining and coordinating the factors of production it hires. But there is variety across firms in how they organize production. Firms use a mixture of two systems:

◆ Command systems
◆ Incentive systems

Command Systems

A **command system** is a method of organizing production that uses a managerial hierarchy. Commands pass downward through the managerial hierarchy and information passes upward. Managers collect and process information about the performance of the people under their control, make decisions about commands to issue and report to their own superiors.

The military uses the purest form of command system. Command systems in firms are less rigid than those in the military but share similar features. A chief executive officer (CEO) sits at the top of a firm's command system. Executives report to and receive commands from the CEO and pass their own commands down to middle managers who in turn supervise the day-to-day operations of the business.

Small-scale firms have one or two layers of managers while large-scale firms have several layers. As production processes have become ever more complex, management ranks have swollen. Today, more people have management jobs than ever before. But the information revolution of the 1990s slowed the growth of management and, in some industries, it decreased the number of layers of managers and brought a shake-out of middle managers.

Managers always have incomplete information about the efforts of those for whom they are responsible. It is for this reason that firms use incentive systems.

Incentive Systems

An **incentive system** is a method of organizing production that uses a market-like mechanism inside the firm. Instead of issuing commands, managers create compensation schemes that induce workers to perform in ways that maximize the firm's profit.

Selling organizations use incentive systems most extensively. Sales representatives who spend most of their working time alone and unsupervised are induced to work hard by being paid a small salary and a large performance-related bonus.

But incentive systems operate at all levels in a firm. CEOs share in the firm's profit, and factory floor workers receive wages based on the quantity they produce.

Mixed Systems

Firms will use both commands and incentives in a mixed system if it will help to maximize profit. They use commands when it is easy to monitor performance. They use incentives when monitoring performance is either not possible or too costly to be worth doing.

For example, it is easy and costs little to monitor the performance of workers on a production line. If one person works too slowly, the entire line slows. So a production line is organized with a command system.

In contrast, it is costly for shareholders to monitor the efforts of a CEO. So CEOs are rewarded with profit-related bonus payments.

Incentives systems are an attempt to cope with a general problem that we'll now examine.

The Principal–agent Problem

The **principal–agent problem** is the problem of devising compensation rules that induce an *agent* to act in the best interest of a *principal*. The principal might be the firm's shareholders, in which case the managers are the *agents*. The shareholders (the principals) want to induce the managers (agents) to act in the shareholders' interest. Or the principals might be the managers, in which case, the agents are the workers below the managers. There is a chain of principal–agent relationships throughout a firm.

Agents pursue their own goals and often impose costs on a principal. For example, the goal of a shareholder of the HSBC Bank (a principal) is to maximize the bank's profit. But the bank's profit depends on the actions of its managers (agents) who have their own goals. A manager might want to expand the size of her workforce to gain status when this action is inefficient.

Issuing commands does not solve the principal–agent problem. In most firms, the shareholders can't monitor the managers and often the managers can't monitor workers. Each principal must create incentives that induce each agent to work in the interests of the principal.

Three ways of coping with the principal–agent problem are:

◆ Ownership
◆ Incentive pay
◆ Long-term contracts

Ownership

By assigning the part-ownership of a business to a manager or a worker, the principal seeks to induce a better job performance that increases a firm's profit.

Share-ownership schemes for senior managers are common but share-ownership schemes for workers are less common.

Ownership schemes work best when the firm's profit is directly influenced by the efforts of the agent. If a CEO or manager does a poor job, the firm's profits will suffer. So providing CEOs and managers with compensation in the form of shares might be an effective way to reduce the principal–agent problem.

Ownership schemes work badly when the efforts of the agent have a negligible impact on the firm's profit. With or without shares in the company, a lazy worker has the same incentive to shirk and be unproductive. In these cases, other methods of coping with the principal–agent problem must be found.

The cartoon is a comment on the use of share ownership to address the principal–agent problem. The employee says he is happy to be compensated with shares but that as a shareholder he wouldn't employ himself!

Incentive Pay

Incentive pay schemes – pay related to performance – are very common. They are based on a variety of performance criteria such as profits, production or sales targets. Promoting an employee for good performance is another example of an incentive pay scheme. Like share ownership, incentive pay induces greater effort by an agent and increases the profit.

Long-term Contracts

Long-term contracts tie the long-term fortunes of managers and workers (agents) to the success of the principal(s) – the owner(s) of the firm. For example, a multi-year employment contract for a CEO encourages that person to take a long-term view and devise strategies that achieve maximum profit over a sustained period.

These three ways of coping with the principal–agent problem give rise to different types of business organization. Each type of business organization is a different response to the principal–agent problem. Each type uses a different combination of ownership, incentives and long-term contracts. Let's look at the main types of business organization.

Types of Business Organization

The three main types of business organization are:

◆ Proprietorship
◆ Partnership
◆ Company

Proprietorship

A *proprietorship* is a firm with a single owner who has unlimited liability. *Unlimited liability* is the legal responsibility for all the debts of a firm up to an amount equal to the entire wealth of the owner including the personal property of the owner. The proprietor makes management decisions, receives the firm's profits and is

Financial Times, Weekend, 13.11.99, p. xxvi.

responsible for its losses. Profits are taxed at the same rate as other sources of the proprietor's income.

Partnership

A *partnership* is a firm with two or more owners who have unlimited liability. Partners must agree on an appropriate management structure and on how to divide the firm's profits among themselves. The profits of a partnership are taxed as the personal income of the owners. But each partner is legally liable for all the debts of the partnership (limited only by the wealth of an individual partner). Liability for the full debts of the partnership is called *joint unlimited liability*.

Company

A *company* is a firm owned by one or more limited liability shareholders. *Limited liability* means that the owners have legal liability only for the value of their initial investment. This limitation of liability means that if the company becomes bankrupt, its owners are not required to use their personal wealth to pay the company's debts.

Company profits are taxed independently of shareholders' incomes. Because shareholders pay taxes on the income they receive as dividends on shares, corporate profits are taxed twice. Shareholders also pay capital gains tax when they sell a share for a higher price than they paid for it. Company shares generate capital gains when a company retains some of its profit and reinvests it in profitable activities. So even retained earnings are taxed twice because of the capital gains they generate.

Pros and Cons of Different Types of Firms

The different types of business organization that you have looked at arise as different ways of trying to cope with the principal–agent problem. Each type of business has advantages in particular situations. Because of its special advantages, each type continues to exist. Each type also has its disadvantages, which explains why it has not driven out the other two types.

Table 9.4 summarizes these and other pros and cons of the different types of firms.

Table 9.4

The Pros and Cons of Different Types of Firms

Type of firm	Pros	Cons
Proprietorship	◆ Easy to set up ◆ Simple decision making ◆ Profits taxed only once as owner's income	◆ Bad decisions not checked by need for consensus ◆ Owner's entire wealth at risk ◆ Firm dies with owner ◆ Capital is expensive ◆ Labour is expensive
Partnership	◆ Easy to set up ◆ Diversified decision making ◆ Can survive withdrawal of partner ◆ Profits taxed only once as owners' incomes	◆ Achieving consensus may be slow and expensive ◆ Owners' entire wealth at risk ◆ Withdrawal of a partner may create capital shortage ◆ Capital is expensive
Company	◆ Owners have limited liability ◆ Large-scale, low-cost capital available ◆ Professional management not restricted by ability of owners ◆ Perpetual life ◆ Long-term labour contracts cut labour costs	◆ Complex management structure can make decisions slow and expensive ◆ Profits taxed twice as company profit and as shareholders' income

> ## ECONOMICS IN ACTION

Types of Firms in the UK Economy

Proprietorships Most Common

In 2008, about 4.8 million firms in the UK employed 23 million people and made £3 billion of revenue. Figure 1 shows that nearly two-thirds of all firms are proprietorships – small businesses – over a quarter are companies and one-tenth are partnerships.

Companies Produce Most

Ninety-nine per cent of UK firms are small businesses that employ fewer than 50 people. They employ about half of all private sector employees and account for about one-third of private sector revenue. Large firms with more than 250 employees make up just 0.1 per cent of firms. Large firms are companies.

Variety Across Industries

Figure 2 shows how the total revenue is related to the firm's size in various industries. In agriculture, forestry and fishing,

small firms generate 86 per cent of sector revenue. Small firms also dominate private health, education and construction industries. Medium-sized companies are a small share of all industries. Large companies dominate in transport, manufacturing and mining industries. Companies dominate in industries that use a large amount of capital and proprietorships dominate where flexibility is critical.

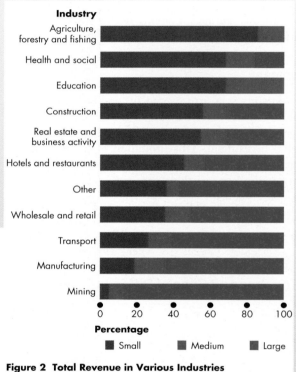

Figure 2 Total Revenue in Various Industries

Figure 1 Types of UK Firms

Source of data: BIS Department for Innovation, Business and Skills, October 2009.

> ### Review Quiz

1 Explain the distinction between a command system and an incentive system.
2 What is the principal–agent problem? What are three ways in which firms try to cope with it?
3 What are the three types of firms? Explain their advantages and disadvantages.
4 Why do all three types of firms survive and in which sectors is each type most prominent?

You can work these questions in Study Plan 9.3 and get instant feedback.

You've now seen how technological constraints and information constraints influence the way firms operate. You've seen why some firms operate with a large amount of labor and human capital and a small amount of physical capital. You've also seen how firms use a mixture of command and incentive systems and employ different types of business organization to cope with the principal–agent problem.

Your next task is to look at the variety of market situations in which firms operate and classify the different market environments in which firms do business.

Markets and the Competitive Environment

The markets in which firms operate vary a great deal. Some markets are highly competitive and profits are hard to come by. Some appear to be almost free from competition and firms in these markets earn large profits. Some markets are dominated by fierce advertising campaigns in which each firm seeks to persuade buyers that it has the best products. Some markets display a war-like character.

Economists identify four market types:

◆ Perfect competition
◆ Monopolistic competition
◆ Oligopoly
◆ Monopoly

Perfect Competition

Perfect competition arises when there are many firms that sell an identical product, many buyers and no restrictions on the entry of new firms into the industry. The many firms and buyers are all well informed about the prices of the products of each firm in the industry. The worldwide markets for wheat, rice and other grain crops are examples of perfect competition.

Monopolistic Competition

Monopolistic competition is a market structure in which a large number of firms compete by making similar but slightly different products. Making a product slightly different from the product of a competing firm is called **product differentiation**.

Firms in monopolistic competition are in fierce competition with each other. But product differentiation gives each monopolistically competitive firm an element of monopoly power. The firm is the sole producer of the particular version of the good in question.

For example, in the market for running shoes, Nike, Reebok, Fila, Asics and many other firms compete, but all make their own version of the perfect shoe. Each of these firms is the sole producer of a particular brand and so has a monopoly on that particular brand of shoe.

Differentiated products need not be different products. What matters is that consumers perceive the products to be different. For example, different brands of ibuprofen tablets are chemically identical and differ only in their packaging.

Oligopoly

Oligopoly is a market structure in which a small number of firms compete. Aeroplane manufacture, international air transport and computer software are examples of oligopolistic industries. Oligopolies might produce almost identical products, such as the colas produced by Coca-Cola and Pepsi Co; or they might produce differentiated products such as the Airbus A380 and the Boeing 747.

Monopoly

Monopoly arises when there is one firm which produces a good or service for which no close substitute exists and in which the firm is protected from competition by a barrier preventing the entry of new firms. In some places, the phone, gas, electricity and water suppliers are local monopolies – monopolies restricted to a given location. Microsoft, the software developer that created Windows, the operating system used by the vast majority of PCs, is an example of a global monopoly.

Perfect competition is the most extreme form of competition. Monopoly is the most extreme absence of competition. The other two market types fall between these extremes.

We've described the four types of market. But how do we recognize these market types? You would probably have little difficulty recognizing the difference between a perfectly competitive market and a monopoly market. But how would you distinguish between monopolistic competition and oligopoly?

Identifying a Market Structure

Many factors must be taken into account to determine which market structure describes a particular real-world market. One of these factors is the extent to which the market is dominated by a small number of firms. To measure this feature of markets, economists use indexes called measures of concentration.

Measures of Concentration

The most common measure of concentration uses total revenue and puts five firms in the group of largest firms. The result is the **five-firm concentration ratio**, which is the percentage of total revenue (or the value of sales) in an industry accounted for by the five firms with the largest value of sales. The range of the concentration ratio is from almost zero for perfect competition to 100 for monopoly.

Table 9.5 shows two hypothetical calculations of the five-firm concentration ratio, one for shoe manufacturing and one for egg farming. In this example, there are 15 firms in the shoe manufacturing industry. The largest five have 81 per cent of the sales, so the five-firm concentration ratio for that industry is 81 per cent. In the egg industry, with 1,005 firms, the top five firms account

---

Table 9.5

Concentration Ratio Calculations

Shoemakers		Egg farmers	
Firm	**Sales (millions of pounds)**	**Firm**	**Sales (millions of pounds)**
Lace-up plc	250	Bills's	0.9
Finefoot plc	200	Sue's	0.7
Easyfit plc	180	Jane's	0.5
Comfy plc	120	Tom's	0.4
Loafers plc	70	Jill's	0.3
Top 5 sales	820	Top 5 sales	2.8
Other 10 firms	190	Other 1,000 firms	349.2
Industry sales	1,010	Industry sales	352.0

Five-firm concentration ratios:

$$\text{Shoemakers:} \frac{820}{1,010} = 81 \text{ per cent}$$

$$\text{Egg farmers:} \frac{2.8}{352} = 0.8 \text{ per cent}$$

for only 0.8 per cent of total industry sales. In this case, the five-firm concentration ratio is 0.8 per cent.

The five-firm concentration ratio helps us measure the degree of competitiveness of a market. A low concentration ratio indicates a high degree of competition and a high concentration ratio indicates an absence of competition. In the extreme case of monopoly, the concentration ratio is 100 per cent because the largest (and only) firm makes the entire industry sales. Between these extremes, the five-firm concentration ratio is regarded as being a useful indicator of the likelihood of collusion among firms in an oligopoly. If the concentration ratio exceeds 60 per cent, it is likely that firms have a high degree of market power and may collude and behave like a monopoly.

If the concentration ratio is less than 40 per cent, the industry is regarded as competitive. A concentration ratio between 40 and 60 per cent indicates that the market structure is oligopoly.

Limitations of Concentration Measures

Concentration ratios are useful, but they have some limitations. They must be supplemented by other information to determine the market structure of an industry and the degree of market power of firms in that industry. The three key problems are:

◆ The geographical scope of the market

◆ Barriers to entry and firm turnover

◆ Market and industry correspondence

Geographical Scope of the Market

Concentration ratio data are based on a *national* view of the market. Many goods are sold in a national market, and for these goods, the concentration measures are useful.

But some goods are sold in a *regional* market. There are many national firms but few firms in each regional market. In this type of market, the national concentration ratios underestimate the true degree of concentration. The brewing industry is an example of a good in which the local market is more relevant than the national market. So although the national concentration ratio for brewers is in the middle range, there is a high degree of concentration in the brewing industry in most regions.

Other industries operate in a *global* market. So although the largest five car producers in the United

Kingdom account for 80 per cent of all cars sold by UK producers, they account for a smaller percentage of the total UK car market, which includes imports. In the global market for cars, UK producers account for an even smaller percentage of total sales. In this case, the national concentration ratios overestimate the true degree of concentration.

Barriers to Entry and Firm Turnover

Measures of concentration do not measure the severity of barriers to entry in a market. Some industries are highly concentrated but their markets have virtually free entry and a high turnover of firms. For example, many small towns have few restaurants, but there are few restrictions on opening a restaurant. Many firms enter and exit with great regularity.

Even if the turnover of new firms in a market is limited, an industry might be competitive because of *potential entry* – because a few firms in the market face competition from many firms that can easily enter the market and will do so if economic profits are available.

Market and Industry Correspondence

The classifications used to calculate concentration ratios allocate every firm in the economy to a particular industry. But markets for particular goods do not usually correspond to these industries for three reasons.

First, markets are often narrower than industries. For example, the pharmaceutical industry, which has a low concentration ratio, operates in many separate markets for individual products – for example, measles vaccine and AIDS-fighting drugs. These drugs do not compete with each other, so this industry, which looks competitive, includes firms that are monopolies (or near monopolies) in markets for individual drugs.

Second, most firms make many products. For example, the tobacco firms also operate in the food and insurance industries. The privatized water companies operate hotels and printing works. The value of sales for each firm show up in the industry to which the firm has been assigned. So their contribution to the industry to which they have been assigned might be overestimated.

Third, firms switch from one market to another depending on profit opportunities. Virgin, which today produces air transport services, train services and other products, has diversified from being a retail record shop and recording studio. Virgin no longer produces albums. Today, the Virgin group's products include credit cards and home loans, soft drinks, mobile phones, wines, balloon rides and more.

Publishers of newspapers, magazines and textbooks are today rapidly diversifying into Internet and multimedia products. These switches among industries show that there is much scope for entering and exiting an industry, and so measures of concentration have limited usefulness in describing the true degree of competition in a market.

Despite their limitations, concentration measures do provide a basis for determining the degree of competition in a market provided they are supplemented with other information about the geographical scope of a market, barriers to entry and the extent to which large, multi-product firms straddle a variety of markets. The less concentrated an industry and the lower its barriers

ECONOMICS IN ACTION

UK Concentration Ratios

Concentration ratios in the UK are derived from the Census of Production. This census is undertaken by the UK government and it provides information on the sales, employment and structure of every UK manufacturing firm.

Figure 1 shows some five-firm concentration ratios. Plastics, printing and publishing, hotels, catering and pubs

and jewellery have low concentration ratios, which indicates that they are competitive industries. Tobacco products, confectionery, soft drinks and mineral waters have high concentration ratios, which indicates that they are industries with a high degree of market power. Soap and toilet preparations, motor vehicles, leather goods and agricultural machinery have intermediate concentration ratios, which indicates limited market power.

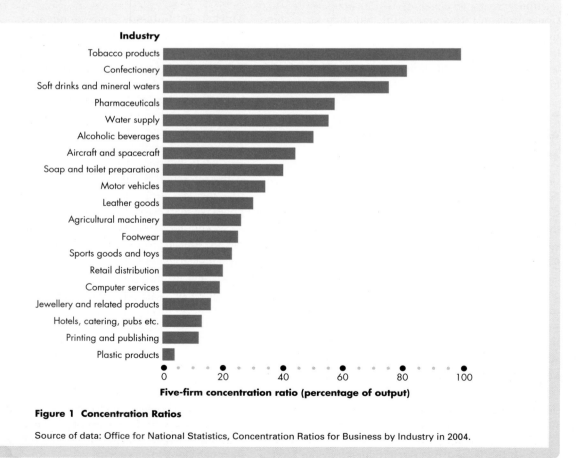

Figure 1 Concentration Ratios

Source of data: Office for National Statistics, Concentration Ratios for Business by Industry in 2004.

Table 9.6

Market Structure

Characteristics	Perfect competition	Monopolistic competition	Oligopoly	Monopoly
Number of firms in industry	Many	Many	Few	One
Product	Identical	Differentiated	Either identical or differentiated	No close substitutes
Barriers to entry	None	None	Moderate	High
Firm's control over price	None	Some	Considerable	Considerable or regulated
Concentration ratio	0	Low	High	100
Examples	Agricultural products	Cosmetics, bread, clothing	Washing powders, cereals	Local water utility, postal letter service

to entry, the more closely it approximates perfect competition. The more concentrated an industry and the higher the barriers to entry, the more it approximates oligopoly or even monopoly.

Table 9.6 summarizes the characteristics of different market structures and their concentration ratios.

UK Market Structures

The majority of markets for goods and services in Europe are highly competitive and only a few markets are monopolies. For example, more than 70 per cent by value of goods and services bought and sold in the UK are traded in highly competitive markets. Where monopoly does arise, it is usually in the public services although with privatization, public services have become more competitive.

But market power can still be strong in markets where privatization attracts few new entrants such as in the telecommunications industry. Less than 6 per cent of goods and services traded in the UK markets are essentially uncompetitive. Oligopoly is more common in manufacturing than in the services sector, but more than 55 per cent of UK manufacturing industries have a concentration ratio of less than 40 per cent.

The overall level of concentration in an economy can be measured by the proportion of total output accounted for by the largest 100 firms. The UK aggregate concentration ratio in manufacturing increased in the post-war period, indicating an increase

in market power, but it levelled off in the 1970s and 1980s and has fallen in recent years. The increase in concentration resulted from several waves of merger activity and the growth of transnational companies serving new global markets. But given the growth in world trade and advances in telecommunications and low-cost transport, many UK firms operate in global markets, which are highly competitive.

Review Quiz

1　What are the four market types? Explain the distinguishing characteristics of each.
2　Describe the five-firm concentration ratio.
3　Under what conditions do measures of concentration give a good indication of the degree of competition in the market?
4　Is our economy competitive? Is it becoming more competitive or less competitive?

You can work these questions in Study Plan 9.4 and get instant feedback.

You now know the variety of market types and the way we classify firms and industries into the different market types. Our final question in this chapter is what determines which items firms decide to buy from other firms rather than produce for themselves?

Produce or Outsource? Firms and Markets

To produce a good or service, even a simple one such as a shirt, factors of production must be hired and their activities coordinated. To produce a good as complicated as an iPhone, an enormous range of specialist factors of production must be coordinated.

Factors of production can be coordinated either by firms or markets. We'll describe these two ways of organizing production and then see why firms play a crucial role in achieving an efficient use of resources.

Firm Coordination

Firms hire labour, capital and land, and by using a mixture of command systems and incentive systems (see p. 203) organize and coordinate their activities to produce goods and services.

Firm coordination occurs when you take your car to the garage for an oil change, brake check and service. The garage owner hires a mechanic and tools and coordinates all the activities that get your car serviced. Firms also coordinate the production of cornflakes, golf clubs and a host of other items.

Market Coordination

Markets coordinate production by adjusting prices and making the decisions of buyers and sellers of factors of production and components consistent. Markets can coordinate production.

Market coordination occurs to produce a rock concert. A promoter books a stadium, rents some stage equipment, hires some audio and video recording engineers and technicians, engages some rock groups, a superstar, a publicity agent and a ticket agent. The promoter sells tickets to thousands of rock fans, audio rights to a recording company and video and broadcasting rights to a television network. All these transactions take place in markets that coordinate this huge variety of factors of production.

Outsourcing, buying parts or products from other firms, is another example of market coordination. Car makers outsource the production of windshields, windows, transmission systems, engines, tyres and many other auto parts. Apple outsources the entire production of iPods and iPhones.

What determines whether a firm or a market coordinates a particular set of activities?

Why Firms?

How does a firm decide whether to buy an item from another firm or manufacture it itself? The answer is cost. Taking account of the opportunity cost of time as well as the costs of the other inputs, a firm uses the method that costs least. In other words, it uses the economically efficient method.

If a task can be performed at a lower cost by markets than by a firm, markets will do the job and any attempt to set up a firm to replace such market activity will be doomed to failure.

Firms coordinate economic activity when a task can be performed more efficiently by a firm than by markets. Firms are often more efficient than markets as coordinators of economic activity because they can achieve:

◆ Lower transactions costs
◆ Economies of scale
◆ Economies of scope
◆ Economies of team production

Lower Transactions Costs

Firms eliminate transactions costs. **Transactions costs** are the costs arising from finding someone with whom to do business, of reaching an agreement about the price and other aspects of the exchange, and of ensuring that the terms of the agreement are fulfilled. *Market* transactions require buyers and sellers to get together and to negotiate the terms and conditions of their trading. Sometimes lawyers have to be hired to draw up contracts. A broken contract leads to still more expenses. A *firm* can lower such transactions costs by reducing the number of individual transactions undertaken.

Imagine getting your car fixed using market coordination. You hire a mechanic to diagnose the problems and make a list of the parts and tools needed to fix them. You buy the parts from several dealers, rent the tools, hire a car mechanic, return the tools and pay your bills. You can avoid all these transactions and the time they cost you by letting your local garage fix the car.

Economies of Scale

When the cost of producing a unit of a good falls as its output rate increases, **economies of scale** exist. A car maker experiences economies of scale because as the scale of production increases, the firm can use cost-saving equipment and highly specialized labour. A car

Apple Doesn't Make the iPhone

Apple designed the iPhone and markets it, but Apple doesn't manufacture it. Why? Apple wants to produce the iPhone at the lowest possible cost. Apple achieves its goal by assigning the production task to more than 30 firms, some of which are listed in the table opposite. These 30 firms produce the components in Asia, Europe and North America and then the components are assembled in the familiar case by Foxconn and Quanta in Taiwan. Most electronic products – TV sets, DVD players, iPods and iPads and personal computers – are produced in a similar way to the iPhone with a combination of firm and market coordination. Hundreds of little-known firms compete fiercely to get their components into well-known consumer products.

Altus-Tech	Taiwan
Balda	Germany
Broadcom	US
Cambridge Silicon Radio	UK
Catcher	Taiwan
Cyntec	Taiwan
Delta Electronics	Taiwan
Epson	Japan
Foxconn	Taiwan
Infineon Technology	Germany
Intel	US
Largan Precision	Taiwan
Lite On	Taiwan
Marvell	US
Micron	US
Novatek	Taiwan
Primax	Taiwan
Quanta	Taiwan
Samsung	Korea
Sanyo	Japan
Sharp	Japan
Taiwan Semiconductor	Taiwan
TMD	Japan

maker that produces only a few cars a year must use hand-tool methods that are costly. Economies of scale arise from specialization and the division of labour and firm coordination can reap these economies of scale more effectively than can market coordination.

Economies of Scope

A firm experiences **economies of scope** when it uses its specialized and often expensive resources to produce a *range of goods and services*. For example, Toshiba uses its designers and specialized equipment to make the hard drive for the iPod. But it makes many different types of hard drives and other related products. As a result, Toshiba produces the iPod hard drive at a lower cost than a firm making only the iPod hard drive could achieve.

Economies of Team Production

A production process in which the individuals in a group specialize in mutually supportive tasks is team production. Sports provide the best examples of team activity. In football, some team members specialize in defence and others in striking. The production of goods and services offers many examples of team activity. For example, production lines in a car plant work most efficiently when individual activity is organized in teams,

with each worker specializing in a few tasks. You can also think of an entire firm as being a team. The team has buyers of raw materials and other inputs, production workers and salespeople. Each individual member of the team specializes, but the value of the output of the team and the profit that it earns depend on the coordinated activities of all the team's members.

Because firms can economize on transactions costs, reap economies of scale and economies of scope and organize efficient team production, it is firms rather than markets that coordinate most economic activity.

Review Quiz

1 Describe the two ways in which economic activity can be coordinated.
2 What determines whether a firm or markets coordinate production?
3 What are the main reasons why firms can often coordinate production at lower cost than markets?

You can work these questions in Study Plan 9.5 and get instant feedback. myeconlab

Reading Between the Lines on pp. 214–215 looks at the latest Internet technology called 'cloud computing' and shows how it affects the constraints, efficiency, organization, competition and market coordination of firms.

Reading Between the Lines

Competition and Coordination

Telegraph.co.uk 2 October 2010

Cloud Computing: Will Microsoft and its Rivals Find a Silver Lining?

Richard Blackden

... The era in which companies pay to have software installed on computers is drawing to an end. . . . Services such as sending emails, using documents, managing calendars and updating spreadsheets will no longer be tied to an individual computer but be accessible everywhere via the Internet, and . . . companies will only pay for how much they use. . . . Many businesses will no longer bother having their own computer networks at all. Welcome, then, to the world of cloud computing.

The phrase, in which the word cloud is used as a metaphor for the Internet, has been generating . . . excitement . . . for the past three years. The best analogy . . . is to consider how homes get their electricity. Few have their own generators on the premises – instead people call on an electricity provider to power up a microwave, turn on a kettle or light a room as they need to.

In the era of cloud computing, businesses will treat computing services in the same way, sharing networks with other companies and paying only for what they use. Technology watchers say it's as fundamental a change as the advent of mainframe computers in the 1960s, the development of servers and the arrival of the Internet itself.

By next year, . . . [Microsoft] plans to be spending 90pc of its annual $9.5bn research and development budget on cloud computing. . . . 'The prevailing wisdom is that Microsoft has been dragged kicking and screaming into the cloud by Google,' said David Smith, who tracks the industry for Gartner. Google's web-based drive into Microsoft's heartland of e-mail and word processing has been aggressive, and the search engine says it can provide it at less than half the price

The Essence of the Story

- Firms no longer have to buy, maintain and run their own computer hardware and software to run their businesses.

- Cloud computing uses the Internet to share available computing power so firms can buy it like electricity .

- Cloud computing may be as big a shift in technology as mainframe computers and the Internet.

- Competition from Google and other cloud providers has dented Microsoft's dominance of software markets and forced it to develop similar services.

Economic Analysis

◆ Computing services play a crucial role in the production activity of almost every firm.

◆ In its pursuit of maximum profit a firm must decide whether to buy its own computers (and software) and hire labour to operate them, or buy cloud computing services.

◆ Also, using the same cloud technologies, a firm that buys its own computers must decide whether to sell computing services to other firms.

◆ Cloud computing has brought an increase in computer productivity and created an active market in computing services.

◆ Table 1 shows the names of some of the providers (large and small) of computing services using the cloud.

◆ Amazon, Google and Microsoft use their massive scale (Amazon in retailing and the other two in Internet search) to generate economies of scale in leasing computing time.

◆ Elance and other small-scale operators provide niche cloud services, some to freelancers around the world who are able then to work together and reap economies of team production.

◆ Table 2 names some of the firms that have found it more efficient to buy cloud computing services rather than install their own computers.

◆ Rentokil has cut its e-mail costs dramatically by using Google cloud services.

◆ Call centres have cut costs by using oDesk's cloud computing, which enables their employees to work from home without creating a principal–agent problem.

◆ The market in cloud computing services is becoming highly competitive and the price of cloud service fluctuates from minute to minute as Figure 1 shows.

Table 1

Cloud Service Providers

Large-scale providers	Small-scale providers
Amazon	Outsourcery
Google	Venda
Microsoft	Elance
Oracle	oDesk
Salesforce.com	LivOps

Table 2

Cloud Users, Providers and Impact

Cloud user	Cloud provider	Cloud service	Impact
Rentokil	Google	Outsourced e-mail	70 per cent cut in e-mail cost
Call centres	oDesk	Home worker monitoring	No call centre building
Barclays Visa	Hadoop	Data processing 73 billion transactions	Processing time cut from 1 month to 10 minutes

Figure 1 Price of cloud computing service

Source of data: cloudexchange.org

SUMMARY

Key Points

The Firm and Its Economic Problem
(pp. 198–200)

◆ Firms hire and organize factors of production to produce and sell goods and services.

◆ A firm's goal is to maximize economic profit, which is total revenue minus total cost measured as the opportunity cost of production.

◆ A firm's opportunity cost of production is the sum of the cost of the resources bought in the market, owned by the firm and supplied by the firm's owner.

◆ Normal profit is the opportunity cost of entrepreneurship and is part of the firm's opportunity cost.

◆ Technology, information and markets limit the economic profit that the firm can make.

Working Problems 1 and 2 will give you a better understanding of the firm and its economic problem.

Technological and Economic Efficiency (pp. 201–202)

◆ A method of production is technologically efficient when a firm produces a given output by using the least amount of resources.

◆ A method of production is economically efficient when the cost of producing a given output is as low as possible.

Working Problems 3 and 4 will give you a better understanding of technological and economic efficiency.

Information and Organization
(pp. 203–206)

◆ Firms use a combination of command systems and incentive systems to organize production.

◆ Faced with incomplete information and uncertainty, firms induce managers and workers to perform in ways that are consistent with the firm's goals.

◆ Proprietorships, partnerships and companies use ownership, incentives and long-term contracts to cope with the principal–agent problem.

Working Problems 5 to 8 will give you a better understanding of information and organization.

Markets and the Competitive Environment (pp. 207–211)

◆ In perfect competition, many sellers offer an identical product to many buyers.

◆ In monopolistic competition, many sellers offer slightly different products to many buyers and entry is free.

◆ In oligopoly, a small number of firms compete.

◆ In monopoly, one firm produces a good or service that has no close substitutes and the firm is protected by a barrier that prevents the entry of competitors.

Working Problems 9 and 10 will give you a better understanding of markets and the competitive environment.

Produce or Outsource? Firms and Markets (pp. 212–213)

◆ Firms coordinate economic activities when they can perform a task more efficiently – at lower cost – than markets can.

◆ Firms economize on transactions costs and achieve the benefits of economies of scale, economies of scope and of team production.

Working Problems 11 and 12 will give you a better understanding of firms and markets.

Key Terms

Command system, 203
Economic depreciation, 199
Economic efficiency, 201
Economic profit, 198
Economies of scale, 212
Economies of scope, 213
Firm, 198
Five-firm concentration ratio, 208
Implicit rental rate, 198
Incentive system, 203
Monopolistic competition, 207
Monopoly, 208
Normal profit, 199
Oligopoly, 207
Perfect competition, 207
Principal–agent problem, 203
Product differentiation, 207
Technological efficiency, 201
Technology, 200
Transactions costs, 212

STUDY PLAN PROBLEMS AND APPLICATIONS

 You can work Problems 1 to 13 in MyEconlab Study Plan Chapter 9 and get instant feedback.

The Firm and Its Economic Problem
(Study Plan 9.1)

1 One year ago, Jack and Jill set up a vinegar bottling firm (called JJVB). Use the following information to calculate JJVB's opportunity cost of production during its first year of operation:

◆ Jack and Jill put €50,000 of their own money into the firm.

◆ They bought equipment for €30,000.

◆ They hired one employee to help them for an annual wage of €20,000.

◆ Jack gave up his previous job, at which he earned €30,000 and spent all his time working for JJVB.

◆ Jill kept her old job, which paid €30 an hour, but gave up 10 hours of leisure each week (for 50 weeks) to work for JJVB.

◆ JJVB bought €10,000 of goods and services from other firms.

◆ The market value of the equipment at the end of the year was €28,000.

◆ Jack and Jill have a €100,000 home loan on which they pay an interest rate of 6 per cent a year.

2 Joe, who has no skills, no job experience and no alternative employment, runs a shoeshine stand at the airport. Operators of other shoeshine stands earn €10,000 a year. Joe pays rent to the airport of €2,000 a year, and his total revenue from shining shoes is €15,000 a year. Joe spent €1,000 on a chair, polish and brushes, using his credit card to buy them. The interest on a credit card balance is 20 per cent a year. At the end of the year, Joe was offered €500 for his business and all its equipment. Calculate Joe's opportunity cost of production and his economic profit.

Technological and Economic Efficiency (Study Plan 9.2)

3 Alternative ways of laundering 100 shirts are:

Method	Labour (hours)	Capital (machines)
A	1	10
B	5	8
C	20	4
D	50	1

a Which methods are technologically efficient?

b Which method is economically efficient if the hourly wage rate and the implicit rental rate of capital are:
  (i) Wage rate €1, rental rate €100?
  (ii) Wage rate €5, rental rate €50?
  (iii) Wage rate €50, rental rate €5?

4 John Deere's Farm Team

Deere opened up the Pune [India] centre in 2001. Deere's move was unexpected: Deere is known for its heavy-duty farm equipment and big construction gear whereas many of India's 300 million farmers still use oxen-pulled ploughs.

Source: *Fortune*, 14 April 2008

a Why do many Indian farmers still use oxen-pulled ploughs? Are they efficient or inefficient? Explain.

b How might making John Deere farm equipment available to Indian farmers change the technology constraint they face?

Information and Organization
(Study Plan 9.3)

5 Here It Is. Now, You Design It!

The idea is that the most successful companies no longer invent new products and services on their own. They create them along with their customers, and they do it in a way that produces a unique experience for each customer. The important corollary is that no company owns enough resources – or can possibly own enough – to furnish unique experiences for each customer, so companies must organize a constantly shifting global web of suppliers and partners to do the job.

Source: *Fortune*, 26 May 2008

a To organize and coordinate production, do successful companies use a command system or an incentive system?

b How does this method of organizing and coordinating production help firms achieve lower costs?

6 Rewarding Failure

Over the past 25 years CEO pay has risen faster than company profits, economic growth or average wages. A more sensible alternative to the current compensation system would require CEOs to own a lot of company shares. If shares are given to the boss, his or her salary and bonus should be docked to reflect its value. As for bonuses, they should be based on improving a company's cash earnings relative to its cost of capital, not to more easily manipulated earnings per share. Bonuses should not be capped, but they should be unavailable to the CEO for some period of years.

Source: *Fortune*, 28 April 2008

a What is the economic problem that CEO compensation schemes are designed to solve?

b How do the proposed changes to CEO compensation outlined in the news clip address the problem you described in part (a)?

Use the following news clip to work Problems 7 and 8.

Steps to Creating a Super Startup

Starting a business is a complicated and risky task. Just two thirds of new small businesses survive at least two years, and only 44 per cent survive at least four years. Most entrepreneurs start their businesses by dipping into their savings, borrowing from the family and using the founder's credit cards. Getting a bank loan is tough unless you have assets – and that often means using your home as security.

Source: CNN, 18 October 2007

7 When starting a business, what are the risks and potential rewards identified in the news clip that are associated with a proprietorship?

8 How might (i) a partnership and (ii) a company help to overcome the risks identified in the news clip?

Markets and the Competitive Environment (Study Plan 9.4)

9 Sales of the firms in the tattoo industry are:

Firm	Sales (euros)
Bright Spots plc	450
Freckles plc	325
Love Galore plc	250
Native Birds plc	200
Tiny Tattoo plc	175
Other 15 firms	800

a Calculate the five-firm concentration ratio.

b What is the structure of the tattoo industry on the basis of just the concentration ratio data?

c What other information would you need to determine whether the tattoo industry is competitive?

10 **GameStops Racks Up the Points**

No retailer has more cachet among gamers than GameStop. For now, only Wal-Mart has a larger market share – 21.3 per cent last year. GameStop's share was 21.1 per cent last year, and may well overtake Wal-Mart this year. But if new women gamers prefer shopping at Target to GameStop, Wal-Mart and Target might erode GameStop's market share.

Source: *Fortune*, 9 June 2008

a According to the news clip, what is the structure of the US retail video-game market?

b Estimate a range for a five-firm concentration ratio based on the information provided in this news clip.

Produce or Outsource? Firms and Markets (Study Plan 9.5)

11 Car makers buy parts from independent suppliers rather than produce the parts themselves. In the 1980s, Chrysler got about 70 per cent of its parts from independent suppliers, while Ford got about 60 per cent and General Motors got 25 per cent. A decade earlier, the proportions were 50 per cent at Chrysler, 5 per cent at Ford and 20 per cent at General Motors.

Source: The Cato Institute Policy Analysis, 1987

a Why did car makers decide to outsource most of their parts production?

b Explain why independent producers of car parts are more efficient than the car makers.

12 Federal Express enters into contracts with independent truck operators who offer FedEx service and who are rewarded by the volume of packages they carry. Why doesn't FedEx buy more trucks and hire more drivers? What incentive problems might arise from this arrangement?

Economics in the News (Study Plan 9.N)

13 Lego, the Danish toymaker, incurred economic losses in 2003 and 2004. Lego faced competition from low-cost copiers of its products and a fall in demand. In 2004, to restore profits, Lego fired 3,500 of its 8,000 workers; closed factories in Switzerland and the US; opened factories in Eastern Europe and Mexico; and introduced performance-based pay for its managers. Lego returned to profit in 2005.

Source: *The Economist*, 28 October 2006

a Describe the problems that Lego faced in 2003 and 2004, using the concepts of the three types of constraints that all firms face

b Which of the actions that Lego took to restore profits addressed an inefficiency? How did Lego seek to achieve economic efficiency?

c Which of Lego's actions addressed an information and organization problem? How did Lego change the way in which it coped with the principal–agent problem?

d In what type of market does Lego operate?

ADDITIONAL PROBLEMS AND APPLICATIONS

myeconlab   You can work these problems in MyEconlab if assigned by your lecturer.

The Firm and Its Economic Problem

Use the following data to work Problems 14 and 15.

Lee is a computer programmer who earned £35,000 in 2009. But on 1 January 2010, Lee opened a body board manufacturing business. At the end of the first year of operation, he submitted the following information to his accountant:

- He stopped renting out his cottage for £3,500 a year and used it as his factory. The market value of the cottage increased from £70,000 to £71,000.

- He spent £50,000 on materials, phone, etc.

- He leased machines for £10,000 a year.

- He paid £15,000 in wages.

- He used £10,000 from his savings account, which earns 5 per cent a year interest.

- He borrowed £40,000 at 10 per cent a year.

- He sold £160,000 worth of body boards.

- Normal profit is £25,000 a year.

14   Calculate Lee's opportunity cost of production and his economic profit.

15   Lee's accountant recorded the depreciation on his cottage during 2010 as £7,000. According to the accountant, what profit did Lee make?

16   In 2009, Toni taught music and earned £20,000. She also earned £4,000 by renting out her basement. On 1 January 2010, she quit teaching, stopped renting out her basement and began to use it as the office for her new website design business. She took £2,000 from her savings account to buy a computer. During 2010, she paid £1,500 for the lease of a Web server and £1,750 for a high-speed Internet service. She received a total revenue from website designing of £45,000 and earned interest at 5 per cent a year on her savings account balance. Normal profit is £55,000 a year. At the end of 2010, Toni could have sold her computer for £500. Calculate Toni's opportunity cost of production and her economic profit in 2010.

17   **The Colvin Interview: Chrysler**

The key driver of profitability will be that the focus of the company isn't on profitability. Our focus is on the customer. If we can find a way to give customers what they want better than anybody else, then what can stop us?

Source: *Fortune*, 14 April 2008

a   In spite of what Chrysler's vice chairman and co-president claims, why is Chrysler's focus actually on profitability?

b   What would happen to Chrysler if it didn't focus on maximizing profit, but instead focused its production and pricing decisions to 'give customers what they want'?

18   **Must Watches**

Stocks too volatile? Bonds too boring? Then try an alternative investment—one you can wear on your wrist. The typical return on a watch over five to ten years is roughly 10 per cent. One could do better in an index fund, but what other investment is so wearable?

Source: *Fortune*, 14 April 2008

a   What is the cost of buying a watch?

b   What is the opportunity cost of owning a watch?

c   Does owning a watch create an economic profit opportunity?

Technological and Economic Efficiency

Use the following data to work Problems 19 and 20.

Four methods of completing a tax return are: a personal computer (PC), a pocket calculator, a pocket calculator with pencil and paper, a pencil and paper. With a PC, the job takes an hour; with a pocket calculator, it takes 12 hours; with a pocket calculator and pencil and paper, it takes 12 hours; and with a pencil and paper, it takes 16 hours. The PC and its software cost €1,000, the pocket calculator costs €10 and the pencil and paper cost €1.

19   Which, if any, of the methods is technologically efficient?

20   Which method is economically efficient if the wage rate is

(i)   €5 an hour?
(ii)   €50 an hour?
(iii) €500 an hour?

21 **A Medical Sensation**

Hospitals are buying da Vinci surgical robots. Surgeons, sitting comfortably at a da Vinci console, can use various robotic attachments to perform even the most complex procedures.

Source: *Fortune*, 28 April 2008

a Assume that performing surgery with a surgical robot requires fewer surgeons and nurses. Is using the surgical robot technologically efficient?

b What additional information would you need to be able to say that switching to surgical robots is economically efficient for a hospital?

Information and Organization

22 Tesco plc has more than 2,700 stores, more than a quarter of a million employees and total revenues of about £40 million a year. Sarah runs the family-owned Frey Farms and supplies Tesco plc with mushrooms and other fresh produce.

a How do you think Tesco plc coordinates its activities? Is it likely to use mainly a command system or also to use incentive systems?

b How do you think Sarah coordinates the activities of Frey Farms? Is she likely to use mainly a command system or also to use incentive systems? Why?

c Describe, compare and contrast the principal–agent problems faced by Tesco plc and Frey Farms. How might each firm cope with its principal–agent problems?

23 Public sector workers in all areas are now subject to appraisal and bonus payments based on performance rather than their years on the job and coursework completed. In the education sector, some argue that improving teacher instruction and paying bonuses for raising student achievement encourages efforts to raise teaching quality. How could 'merit pay' attempt to cope with the principal–agent problem in education?

24 **Where Does Google Go Next?**

Google gives its engineers one day a week to work on whatever project they want. A couple of colleagues did what many of the young geniuses do at Google: They came up with a cool idea. At Google, you often end up with a laissez-faire mess instead of resource allocation.

Source: *Fortune*, 26 May 2008

a Describe Google's method of organizing production with its software engineers.

b What are the potential gains and opportunity costs associated with this method?

Markets and the Competitive Environment

25 Market shares of chocolate makers are:

Firm	Market share (per cent)
Mayfair plc	15
Bond plc	10
Magic plc	20
All Natural plc	15
Truffles plc	25
Gold plc	15

a Calculate the five-firm concentration ratio.

b What is the structure of the chocolate industry on the basis of just the concentration ratio data?

Produce or Outsource? Firms and Markets

Use the following information to work Problems 26 to 28.

Two leading design firms, Astro Studios of San Francisco and Hers Experimental Design Laboratory, Inc. of Osaka, Japan, worked with Microsoft to design the Xbox 360 video game console. IBM, ATI and SiS designed the Xbox 360's hardware. Two firms, Flextronics & Wistron and Celestica, manufacture the Xbox 360 at their plants in China.

26 Describe the roles of market coordination and coordination by firms in the design, manufacture and marketing of the Xbox 360.

27 Why do you think Microsoft works with a large number of other firms rather than performing all the tasks required to bring the Xbox to market at its headquarters in Seattle?

28 What are the roles of transactions costs, economies of scale, economies of scope and economies of team production in the design, manufacture and marketing of the Xbox?

Economics in the News

29 After you have studied *Reading Between the Lines* on pp. 214–215 answer the following questions.

a What is cloud computing?

b Amazon is known for its retailing business. Why does Amazon benefit from providing cloud services?

c How can cloud computing reduce the constraints on a firm's profits? Give an example.

d How might cloud computing services reduce the market power of Microsoft?

e How does cloud computing provide markets for services that were previously produced within a firm? Give an example.

f Why might cloud computing be as big a technological development as basic computing and the invention of the Internet?

Output and Costs

After studying this chapter you will be able to:

◆ Distinguish between the short run and the long run

◆ Explain the relationship between a firm's output and labour employed in the short run

◆ Explain the relationship between a firm's output and costs in the short run and derive a firm's short-run cost curves

◆ Explain the relationship between a firm's output and costs in the long run and derive a firm's long-run average cost curve

What do one of the largest European airlines and a small-scale woollen jumper maker have in common? Each firm must decide how much to produce, how many people to employ and how much capital to use. Is being bigger always better for a firm? Why do some firms, such as car makers, have plenty of slack and wish they could sell more whereas others operate flat out all the time? We will answer these questions by looking at the types of decisions firms make and their impact on costs.

In the *Business Case Study* at the end of the chapter, you can see how Europe's second largest airline, easyJet, makes decisions that affect the firm's costs, output and size.

Time Frames for Decisions

People who operate firms make many decisions. All of these decisions are aimed at one overriding objective: maximum attainable profit. But the decisions are not all equally critical. Some of the decisions are big ones. Once made, they are costly (or impossible) to reverse. If such a decision turns out to be incorrect, it might lead to the failure of the firm. Some of the decisions are small ones. They are easily changed. If one of these decisions turns out to be incorrect, the firm can change its actions and survive.

The biggest decision that any firm makes is what industry to enter. For most entrepreneurs, their background knowledge and interests drive this decision. But the decision also depends on profit prospects. No one sets up a firm without believing it will be profitable. And profit depends on total revenue and total cost (see Chapter 9, pp. 198–199).

The firm that we'll study has already chosen the industry in which to operate. It has also chosen its most effective method of organization. But it has not decided the quantity to produce, the quantities of factors of production to hire or the price at which to sell its output.

Decisions about the quantity to produce and the price to charge depend on the type of market in which the firm operates. Perfect competition, monopolistic competition, oligopoly and monopoly all confront the firm with their own special problems.

But decisions about *how* to produce a given output do not depend on the type of market in which the firm operates. These decisions are similar for *all* types of firms in *all* types of markets.

The actions that a firm can take to influence the relationship between output and cost depend on how soon the firm wants to act. A firm that plans to change its output rate tomorrow has fewer options than one that plans to change its output rate six months from now.

To study the relationship between a firm's output decision and its costs, we distinguish between two decision time frames:

◆ The short run
◆ The long run

The Short Run

The **short run** is a time frame in which the quantity of at least one factor of production is fixed. For most firms, capital, land and entrepreneurship are fixed factors of production and labour is the variable factor of production.

We call the fixed factors of production the firm's *plant*. So in the short run, a firm's plant is fixed. Fashion First's fixed plant is its factory building and its knitting machines. For an electric power utility, the fixed plant is its buildings, generators, computers and control systems.

To increase output in the short run, a firm must increase the quantity of a variable factor of production, which is usually labour. So to produce more output, Fashion First must hire more labour and operate its knitting machines for more hours per day. Similarly, an electric power utility must hire more labour and operate its generators for more hours per day.

Short-run decisions are easily reversed. The firm can increase or decrease output in the short run by increasing or decreasing the labour it hires.

The Long Run

The **long run** is a time frame in which the quantities of *all* factors of production can be varied. That is, the long run is a period in which the firm can change its *plant*.

To increase output in the long run, a firm is able to choose whether to change its plant as well as whether to increase the quantity of labour it hires. Fashion First can decide whether to install some additional knitting machines, use a new type of machine, reorganize its management or hire more labour. An electric power utility can decide whether to install more generators. And an airport can decide whether to build more runways, terminals and traffic-control facilities.

Long-run decisions are *not* easily reversed. Once a plant decision is made, the firm must live with it for some time. To emphasize this fact, we call the *past* expenditure on a plant that has no resale value a **sunk cost**. A sunk cost is irrelevant to the firm's current decisions. The only costs that influence its current decisions are the short-run cost of changing the quantity of labour and the long-run cost of changing its plant.

Review Quiz

1   Distinguish between the short run and the long run.
2   Why is a sunk cost irrelevant to a firm's current decisions?

You can work these questions in Study Plan 10.1 and get instant feedback.

We're going to study costs in the short run and the long run. We begin with the short run and describe the technology constraint the firm faces.

Short-run Technology Constraint

To increase output in the short run, a firm must increase the quantity of labour employed. We describe the relationship between output and the quantity of labour employed by using three related concepts:

1 Total product
2 Marginal product
3 Average product

These product concepts can be illustrated either by product schedules or by product curves. We'll look first at the product schedules.

Product Schedules

Table 10.1 shows some data that describe Fashion First's total product, marginal product and average product. The numbers tell us how Fashion First's production changes as more workers are employed, for a fixed level of plant and machines. They also tell us about the productivity of Fashion First's workforce.

Look first at the columns headed 'Labour' and 'Total product'. **Total product** is the maximum output that a given quantity of labour can produce. The table shows how total product increases as Fashion First employs more labour. For example, when Fashion First employs 1 worker, total product is 4 jumpers a day and when Fashion First employs 2 workers, total product is 10 jumpers a day. Each increase in employment brings an increase in total product.

The **marginal product** of labour is the increase in total product resulting from a one-unit increase in the quantity of labour employed with all other inputs remaining the same. For example, in Table 10.1, when Fashion First increases employment from 2 to 3 workers and does not change its capital, the marginal product of the third worker is 3 jumpers – total product increases from 10 to 13 jumpers.

The **average product** tells how productive workers are on the average. The average product of labour is equal to total product divided by the quantity of labour employed. For example, in Table 10.1, 3 workers can knit 13 jumpers a day, so the average product of labour is 13 divided by 3, which is 4.33 jumpers per worker.

If you look closely at the numbers in Table 10.1, you can see some patterns. For example, as Fashion First employs more workers, marginal product at first increases and then begins to decrease. For example, marginal product increases from 4 jumpers a day for the

first worker to 6 jumpers a day for the second worker and then decreases to 3 jumpers a day for the third worker. Also average product at first increases and then decreases. You can see the relationships between the number of workers employed and the three product concepts more clearly by looking at the product curves.

Product Curves

The product curves are graphs of the relationships between employment and the three product concepts you've just studied. They show how total product, marginal product and average product change as employment changes. They also show the relationships among the three concepts. Let's look at the three product curves.

Table 10.1

Total Product, Marginal Product and Average Product

	Labour (workers per day)	Total product (jumpers per day)	Marginal product (jumpers per worker)	Average product (jumpers per worker)
A	0	0		
			 4	
B	1	4		4.00
			 6	
C	2	10		5.00
			 3	
D	3	13		4.33
			 2	
E	4	15		3.75
			 1	
F	5	16		3.20

Total product is the total amount produced. Marginal product is the change in total product resulting from a one-unit increase in labour. For example, when labour increases from 2 to 3 workers a day (row C to row D), total product increases from 10 to 13 jumpers a day. The marginal product of going from 2 to 3 workers is 3 jumpers. (Marginal product is shown between the rows because it is the result of a change in the quantity of labour.) Average product of labour is total product divided by the quantity of labour employed. For example, 3 workers produce 13 jumpers a day, so the average product of 3 workers is 4.33 jumpers per worker.

Total Product Curve

Figure 10.1 shows Fashion First's total product curve, *TP*. As employment increases, so does the number of jumpers knitted. Points *A* to *F* on the curve correspond to the same rows in Table 10.1. These points show total product at various quantities of labour per day. But labour is divisible into hours and even minutes. By varying the amount of labour in the smallest units possible, we can draw the total product curve shown in Figure 10.1.

Look carefully at the shape of the total product curve. As employment increases from zero to 1 worker a day, the curve becomes steeper. Then, as employment continues to increase to 3, 4 and 5 workers per day, the curve becomes less steep.

The total product curve is similar to the *production possibilities frontier* (explained in Chapter 2). It separates the attainable output levels from those that are unattainable. All the points that lie above the curve are unattainable. Points that lie below the curve, in the orange area, are attainable. But they are inefficient – they use more labour than is necessary to produce a given output. Only the points *on* the total product curve are technologically efficient.

Figure 10.1 Total Product Curve

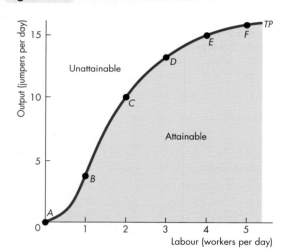

The total product curve (*TP*), is based on the data in Table 10.1. The total product curve shows how the quantity of jumpers changes as the quantity of labour employed changes. For example, using 1 knitting machine, 2 workers can produce 10 jumpers a day (row *C*). Points *A* to *F* on the curve correspond to the rows of Table 10.1. The total product curve separates the attainable output from the unattainable output. Points on the *TP* curve are efficient.

myeconlab Animation

Marginal Product Curve

Figure 10.2 shows Fashion First's marginal product of labour with 1 knitting machine. Part (a) reproduces the total product curve from Figure 10.1. Part (b) shows the marginal product curve, *MP*.

In Figure 10.2(a), the orange bars illustrate the marginal product of labour. The height of each bar measures marginal product. Marginal product is also measured by the slope of the total product curve. Recall that the slope of a curve is the change in the value of the variable measured on the *y*-axis – output – divided by the change in the variable measured on the *x*-axis – labour – as we move along the curve. A one-unit increase in labour, from 2 to 3 workers, increases output from 10 to 13 jumpers, so the slope from point *C* to point *D* is 3 jumpers per worker, the same as the marginal product that we've just calculated.

By varying the amount of labour in the smallest imaginable units, we can draw the marginal product curve shown in Figure 10.2(b). The *height* of this curve measures the *slope* of the total product curve at a point. The total product curve in part (a) shows that an increase in employment from 2 to 3 workers increases output from 10 to 13 jumpers (an increase of 3). The increase in output of 3 jumpers appears on the *y*-axis of part (b) as the marginal product of going from 2 to 3 workers. We plot that marginal product at the mid-point between 2 and 3 workers. Notice that marginal product in Figure 10.2(b) reaches a peak at 1.5 workers and at that point marginal product is 6 jumpers. The peak occurs at 1.5 workers because the total product curve is steepest when employment increases from 1 to 2 workers.

The total product and marginal product curves differ across firms and types of goods. An airline's product curves are different from those of your local supermarket, which in turn are different from those of Fashion First. But the shapes of the product curves are similar because almost every production process has two features:

◆ Increasing marginal returns initially
◆ Diminishing marginal returns eventually

Increasing Marginal Returns

Increasing marginal returns occur when the marginal product of an additional worker exceeds the marginal product of the previous worker. Increasing marginal returns arise from increased specialization and division of labour in the production process.

Figure 10.2 Total Product and Marginal Product

(a) Total product

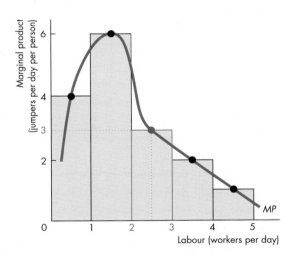

(b) Marginal product

Marginal product is illustrated in both parts of the figure by the orange bars. For example, when labour increases from 2 to 3 workers a day, marginal product is the orange bar whose height is 3 jumpers. (Marginal product is shown midway between the quantities of labour to emphasize that it is the result of changing the quantity of labour.)

The steeper the slope of the total product curve (*TP*) in part (a), the larger is marginal product (*MP*) in part (b). Marginal product increases to a maximum (in this example when the second worker is employed) and then declines – diminishing marginal product.

For example, if Fashion First employs just 1 worker, that person has to learn all the different aspects of jumper production: running the knitting machines, fixing breakdowns, packaging and mailing jumpers and buying and checking the type and colour of the wool. All of these tasks have to be done by that one person.

If Fashion First employs a second person, the 2 workers can specialize in different parts of the production process. As a result, 2 workers produce more than twice as much as 1. The marginal product of the second worker is greater than the marginal product of the first worker. Marginal returns are increasing.

Diminishing Marginal Returns

Most product processes experience increasing marginal returns initially, but all production processes eventually reach a point of diminishing marginal returns. **Diminishing marginal returns** occur when the marginal product of an additional worker is less than the marginal product of the previous worker.

Diminishing marginal returns arise from the fact that more and more workers are using the same capital and working in the same space. As more workers are added, there is less and less for the additional workers to do that is productive. For example, if Fashion First employs a third worker, output increases but not by as much as it did when it added the second worker. In this case, after two workers are employed, all the gains from specialization and the division of labour have been exhausted. By employing a third worker, the factory produces more jumpers, but the equipment is being operated closer to its limits. There are even times when the third worker has nothing to do because the machine is running without the need for further attention. Adding more and more workers continues to increase output but by successively smaller amounts. Marginal returns are diminishing. This phenomenon is such a pervasive one that it is called 'the law of diminishing returns'.

The **law of diminishing returns** states that:

> **As a firm uses more of a variable factor of production, with a given quantity of the fixed factor of production, the marginal product of the variable factor eventually diminishes.**

You will return to the law of diminishing returns when we study a firm's costs. But before we do, let's look at average product and the average product curve.

Average Product Curve

Figure 10.3 illustrates Fashion First's average product of labour, *AP*, and the relationship between the average and marginal product. Points *B* to *F* on the average product curve correspond to those same rows in Table 10.1.

Average product increases from 1 to 2 workers (its maximum value is at point *C*) but then decreases as yet more workers are employed. Also average product is largest when average product and marginal product are equal. That is, the marginal product curve cuts the average product curve at the point of maximum average product. For the number of workers at which the marginal product exceeds average product, average product is *increasing*. For the number of workers at which marginal product is less than average product, average product is *decreasing*.

The relationship between the average product and marginal product curves is a general feature of the relationship between the average and marginal values of any variable. Let's look at a familiar example.

Figure 10.3 Average Product

The figure shows the average product of labour and the connection between the average product and marginal product. With 1 worker a day, marginal product exceeds average product, so average product is increasing. With 2 workers a day, marginal product equals average product, so average product is at its maximum. With more than 2 workers a day, marginal product is less than average product, so average product is decreasing.

myeconlab Animation ◆

How to Pull Up Your Average

Do you want to pull up your average mark? Then make sure that your mark on this test is better than your current average! This test is your marginal test. If your marginal mark exceeds your average mark (like the second test in the graph), your average will rise. If your marginal mark equals your average mark (like the third test in the graph), your average won't change. If your marginal mark is below your average mark (like the fourth test in the figure), your average will fall.

The relationship between your marginal and average grades is exactly the same as that between marginal product and average product.

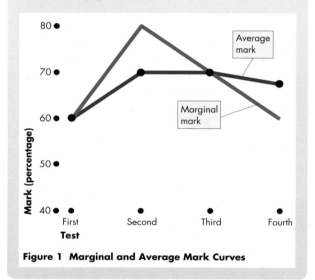

Figure 1 Marginal and Average Mark Curves

1   Explain how the marginal product and the average product change as the labour employed increases (a) initially and (b) eventually.
2   What is the law of diminishing returns? Why does marginal product eventually diminish?
3   Explain the relationship between marginal product and average product.

You can work these questions in Study Plan 10.2 and get instant feedback.

Norma, the owner of Fashion First, cares about Fashion First's product curves because they influence its costs. Let's look at Fashion First's costs.

To produce more output in the short run, a firm must employ more labour, which means it must increase its costs. We describe the relationship between output and costs by using three concepts:

◆ Total cost
◆ Marginal cost
◆ Average cost

Total Cost

A firm's **total cost** (*TC*) is the cost of *all* the factors of production it uses. We separate total cost into total *fixed* cost and total *variable* cost.

Total fixed cost (*TFC*) is the cost of the firm's fixed factors. For Fashion First, total fixed cost includes the cost of renting knitting machines and *normal profit*, which is the opportunity cost of Norma's entrepreneurship (see Chapter 9, p. 199). The quantities of a fixed factor don't change as output changes, so total fixed cost is the same at all outputs.

Total variable cost (*TVC*) is the cost of the firm's variable inputs. For Fashion First, labour is the variable factor, so this component of cost is its wage bill. Total variable cost changes as total product changes.

Total cost is the sum of total fixed cost and total variable cost. That is:

$$TC = TFC + TVC$$

The table in Figure 10.4 shows Fashion First's total costs. With one knitting machine that Fashion First rents for £25 a day, *TFC* is £25 a day. To produce jumpers, Fashion First hires labour, which costs £25 a day. *TVC* is the number of workers multiplied by £25. For example, to produce 13 jumpers a day, Fashion First hires 3 workers and its *TVC* is £75. *TC* is the sum of *TFC* and *TVC*, so to produce 13 jumpers a day, Fashion First's total cost, *TC*, is £100. Check the calculation in each row of the table.

Figure 10.4 shows Fashion First's total cost curves, which graph total cost against output. The green total fixed cost curve (*TFC*) is horizontal because total fixed cost is constant at £25. It does not change when output changes. The purple total variable cost curve (*TVC*) and the blue total cost curve (*TC*) both slope upward because total variable cost increases as output increases. The arrows highlight total fixed cost as the vertical distance between the *TVC* and *TC* curves.

Figure 10.4 Short-run Total Cost

	Labour (workers per day)	Output (jumpers per day)	Total fixed cost (*TFC*)	Total variable cost (*TVC*)	Total cost (*TC*)
			(pounds per day)		
A	0	0	25	0	25
B	1	4	25	25	50
C	2	10	25	50	75
D	3	13	25	75	100
E	4	15	25	100	125
F	5	16	25	125	150

Fashion First rents a knitting machine for £25 a day. This amount is Fashion First's total fixed cost. Fashion First hires workers at a wage rate of £25 a day, and this cost is Fashion First's total variable cost. For example, if Fashion First employs 3 workers, its total variable cost is (3 × £25), which equals £75.

Total cost is the sum of total fixed cost and total variable cost. For example, when Fashion First employs 3 workers, its total cost is £100: total fixed cost of £25 plus total variable cost of £75. The graph shows Fashion First's total cost curves.

Total fixed cost (*TFC*) is constant – it graphs as a horizontal line – and total variable cost (*TVC*) increases as output increases. Total cost (*TC*) also increases as output increases. The vertical distance between the total cost curve and the total variable cost curve is total fixed cost, as illustrated by the two arrows.

 myeconlab Animation

Marginal Cost

In Figure 10.4, total variable cost and total cost increase at a decreasing rate at small outputs and begin to increase at an increasing rate as output increases. To understand these patterns in the changes in total cost, we need to use the concept of *marginal cost*.

A firm's **marginal cost** is the change in total cost resulting from a one-unit increase in output. Marginal cost (MC) is calculated as the change in total cost (ΔTC) divided by the change in output (ΔQ). That is:

$$MC = \frac{\Delta TC}{\Delta Q}$$

The table in Figure 10.5 shows this calculation. For example, an increase in output from 10 to 13 jumpers increases total cost from £75 to £100. The change in output is 3 jumpers, and the change in total cost is £25. The marginal cost of one of those 3 jumpers is (£25 ÷ 3), which equals £8.33.

Figure 10.5 graphs the marginal cost as the red marginal cost curve, MC. This curve is U-shaped because when Fashion First hires a second worker, marginal cost decreases, but when it hires a third, a fourth and a fifth worker, marginal cost successively increases.

Marginal cost decreases at low outputs because of economies from greater specialization. It eventually increases because of *the law of diminishing returns*. The law of diminishing returns means that each additional worker produces a successively smaller addition to output. So to get an additional unit of output, ever more workers are required. Because more workers are required to produce one additional unit of output, the cost of the additional output – marginal cost – must eventually increase.

Marginal cost tells us how total cost changes as output changes. The final cost concept tells us what it costs, on the average, to produce a unit of output. Let's now look at Fashion First's average costs.

Average Cost

Average cost is cost per unit of output. There are three average costs:

1   Average fixed cost
2   Average variable cost
3   Average total cost

Average fixed cost (AFC) is total fixed cost per unit of output. **Average variable cost** (AVC) is total variable

cost per unit of output. **Average total cost** (ATC) is total cost per unit of output. The average cost concepts are calculated from the total cost concepts as follows:

$$TC = TFC + TVC$$

Divide each total cost term by the quantity produced, Q, to give:

$$\frac{TC}{Q} = \frac{TFC}{Q} + \frac{TVC}{Q}$$

or:

$$ATC = AFC + AVC$$

The table in Figure 10.5 shows the calculation of average total costs. For example, in the third row when output is 10 jumpers, average fixed cost is (£25 ÷ 10), which equals £2.50, average variable cost is (£50 ÷ 10), which equals £5.00, and average total cost is (£75 ÷ 10), which equals £7.50. Note average total cost is equal to average fixed cost (£2.50) plus average variable cost (£5.00).

Figure 10.5 shows the average cost curves. The green average fixed cost curve (AFC) slopes downward. As output increases, the same constant fixed cost is spread over a larger output. The blue average total cost curve (ATC) and the purple average variable cost curve (AVC) are U-shaped. The vertical distance between the average total cost and average variable cost curves is equal to average fixed cost – as indicated by the arrows. That distance between the ATC and AVC curves shrinks as output increases because average fixed cost decreases as output increases.

Marginal Cost and Average Cost

The red marginal cost curve (MC) intersects the average variable cost curve and the average total cost curve *at their minimum point*. When marginal cost is less than average cost, average cost is decreasing, and when marginal cost exceeds average cost, average cost is increasing. This relationship holds for both the ATC and the AVC curves and is another example of the relationship you saw in Figure 10.3 between average product and marginal product and your marginal and average test marks.

Why the Average Total Cost Curve Is U-shaped

Average total cost, ATC, is the sum of average fixed cost, AFC, and average variable cost, AVC. So the shape

Figure 10.5 Marginal Cost and Average Costs

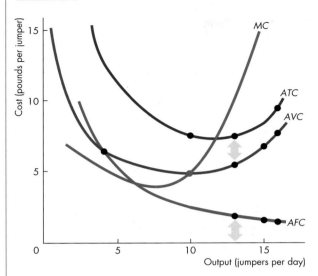

Marginal cost is calculated as the change in total cost divided by the change in output. When output increases from 4 to 10, an increase of 6, total cost increases by £25 and marginal cost is £25 ÷ 6, which equals £4.17. Each average cost concept is calculated by dividing the related total cost by output. When 10 jumpers are produced, AFC is £2.50 (£25 ÷ 10), AVC is £5 (£50 ÷ 10), and ATC is £7.50 (£75 ÷ 10).

The graph shows the marginal cost curve and the average cost curves. The marginal cost curve (*MC*) is U-shaped and intersects the average variable cost curve and the average total cost curve at their minimum points. Average fixed cost (*AFC*) decreases as output increases. The average total cost curve (*ATC*) and average variable cost curve (*AVC*) are U-shaped. The vertical distance between these two curves is equal to average fixed cost, as illustrated by the two arrows.

Labour (workers per day)	Output (jumpers per day)	Total fixed cost (*TFC*)	Total variable cost (*TVC*)	Total cost (*TC*)	Marginal cost (*MC*)	Average fixed cost (*AFC*)	Average variable cost (*AVC*)	Average total cost (*ATC*)
		(pounds per day)				(pounds per jumper)		
0	0	25		25				
					.... 6.25			
1	4	25	25	50		6.25	6.25	12.50
					.... 4.17			
2	10	25	50	75		2.50	5.00	7.50
					.... 8.33			
3	13	25	75	100		1.92	5.77	7.69
					.... 12.50			
4	15	25	100	125		1.67	6.67	8.33
					.... 25.00			
5	16	25	125	150		1.56	7.81	9.38

of the *ATC* curve combines the shapes of the *AFC* and *AVC* curves. The U-shape of the average total cost curve arises from the influence of two opposing forces:

1 Spreading fixed cost over a larger output

2 Eventually diminishing returns

When output increases, the firm spreads its total fixed costs over a larger output and its average fixed cost decreases – its *AFC* curve slopes downward.

Diminishing returns means that as output increases, ever-larger amounts of labour are needed to produce an additional unit of output. So as output increases, average variable cost decreases initially but eventually increases

and the firm's *AVC* curve eventually slopes upward. The *AVC* curve is U-shaped.

The shape of the *ATC* curve combines these two effects. Initially, as output increases, both average fixed cost and average variable cost decrease, so average total cost decreases and the *ATC* curve slopes downward.

But as output increases further and diminishing returns set in, average variable cost begins to increase. With average fixed cost decreasing more quickly than average variable cost is increasing, the *ATC* curve continues to slope downward. Eventually, average variable cost increases more quickly than average fixed cost decreases, so average total cost increases and the *ATC* curve slopes upward.

Cost Curves and Product Curves

The technology that a firm uses determines its costs. Figure 10.6 shows the links between the firm's technology constraint (its product curves) and its cost curves. The upper part of the figure shows the average product curve and the marginal product curve – like those in Figure 10.3. The lower part of the figure shows the average variable cost curve and the marginal cost curve – like those in Figure 10.5.

As labour increases up to 1.5 workers a day (upper graph), output increases to 6.5 jumpers a day (lower graph). Marginal product and average product rise and marginal cost and average variable cost fall. At the point of maximum marginal product, marginal cost is at a minimum.

As labour increases from 1.5 workers to 2 workers a day (upper graph), output increases from 6.5 jumpers to 10 jumpers a day (lower graph). Marginal product falls and marginal cost rises, but average product continues to rise and average variable cost continues to fall. At the point of maximum average product, average variable cost is at a minimum. As labour increases further, output increases. Average product diminishes and average variable cost increases.

Shifts in the Cost Curves

The position of a firm's short-run cost curves depends on two factors:

◆ Technology
◆ Prices of factors of production

Technology

A technological change that increases productivity shifts the total product curve upward. It also shifts the marginal product curve and the average product curve upward. With better technology, the same factors of production can produce more output. So technological change lowers cost and shifts the cost curves downward.

For example, advances in robotic production techniques have increased productivity in the car industry. As a result, the product curves of BMW, Renault and Volvo have shifted upward and their cost curves have shifted downward. But the relationships between their product curves and cost curves have not changed. The curves are still linked in the way shown in Figure 10.6.

Often, a technological advance results in a firm using more capital (a fixed factor) and less labour (a variable

Figure 10.6 Product Curves and Cost Curves

A firm's *MP* curve is linked to its *MC* curve. If, as the firm increases its labour from 0 to 1.5 workers a day, the firm's marginal product rises, its marginal cost falls. If marginal product is at a maximum, marginal cost is at a minimum. If, as the firm hires more labour, its marginal product diminishes, its marginal cost rises.

A firm's *AP* curve is linked to its *AVC* curve. If, as the firm increases its labour to 2 workers a day, its average product rises, its average variable cost falls. If average product is at a maximum, average variable cost is at a minimum. If, as the firm hires more labour, its average product diminishes, its average variable cost rises.

Table 10.2

A Compact Glossary of Costs

Term	Symbol	Definition	Equation
Fixed cost		Cost that is independent of the output level; cost of a fixed factor of production	
Variable cost		Cost that varies with the output level; cost of a variable factor of production	
Total fixed cost	TFC	Cost of the fixed factors of production (equals their number times their unit price)	
Total variable cost	TVC	Cost of the variable factors of production (equals their number times their unit price)	
Total cost	TC	Cost of all factors of production	$TC = TFC + TVC$
Total product (output)	TP	Total quantity produced (Q)	
Marginal cost	MC	Change in total cost resulting from a one-unit increase in total product	$MC = \Delta TC \div \Delta Q$
Average fixed cost	AFC	Total fixed cost per unit of output	$AFC = TFC \div Q$
Average variable cost	AVC	Total variable cost per unit of output	$AVC = TVC \div Q$
Average total cost	ATC	Total cost per unit of output	$ATC = AFC \div AVC$

factor). For example, today the telephone companies use computers to provide directory assistance in place of the human operators they used in the 1980s. When such a technological change occurs, total cost decreases, but fixed costs increase and variable costs decrease. This change in the mix of fixed cost and variable cost means that at low output levels, average total cost might increase, while at high output levels, average total cost decreases.

Prices of Factors of Production

An increase in the price of a factor of production increases costs and shifts the cost curves. But the way the curves shift depends on which factor price changes. An increase in rent or some other component of *fixed* cost shifts the fixed cost curves (*TFC* and *AFC*) upward and the total cost curve (*TC*) upward, but leaves the variable cost curves (*AVC* and *TVC*) and the marginal cost curve (*MC*) unchanged. An increase in the wage rate or some other component of *variable* cost shifts the variable curves (*TVC* and *AVC*) upward, the total cost curve (*TC*) and the marginal cost curve (*MC*) upward, but leaves the fixed cost curves (*AFC* and *TFC*)

unchanged. So for example, if the wage rate of lorry drivers increases, the variable cost and marginal cost of transportation services increase. If the interest expense paid by a trucking company increases, the fixed cost of transportation services increases.

You've now completed your study of short-run costs. All the concepts that you've met are summarized in a compact glossary in Table 10.2.

Review Quiz

1 What relationships do a firm's short-run cost curves show?
2 How does marginal cost change as output increases (a) initially, and (b) eventually?
3 What does the law of diminishing returns imply for the shape of the marginal cost curve?
4 What is the shape of the *AFC* curve and why?
5 What are the shapes of the *AVC* curve and *ATC* curve and why?

You can work these questions in Study Plan 10.3 and get instant feedback.

Long-run Cost

In the short run, a firm can vary the quantity of labour but the quantity of capital is fixed. So the firm has variable costs of labour and fixed costs of capital. In the long run, a firm can vary both the quantity of labour and the quantity of capital. So in the long run, all the firm's costs are variable. We are now going to study the firm's costs in the long run, when *all* costs are variable costs and when the quantity of labour and capital vary.

The behaviour of long-run costs depends on the firm's production function. The *production function* is the relationship between the maximum output attainable and the quantities of both labour and capital.

The Production Function

Table 10.3 shows Fashion First's production function. The table lists the total product for four different quantities of capital. The quantity of capital is defined as the plant size. Plant 1 represents a factory with 1 knitting machine – the case we have just studied. The other three plants have 2, 3 and 4 knitting machines. If Fashion First doubles its plant size from 1 to 2 knitting machines, the various amounts of labour can produce the outputs shown in the column under Plant 2 of the table. The next two columns show the outputs of yet larger plants. Each column in the table could be graphed as a total product curve for each plant size.

Diminishing Returns

Diminishing returns occur in each of the four plants as the quantity of labour increases. You can check that fact by calculating the marginal product of labour in plants with 2, 3 and 4 knitting machines. At each plant size, as the quantity of labour increases, the marginal product of labour (eventually) decreases.

Diminishing Marginal Product of Capital

Diminishing returns also occur as the quantity of capital increases. You can check that fact by calculating the marginal product of capital at a given quantity of labour. The *marginal product of capital* is the change in total product divided by the change in capital employed when the amount of labour employed is constant. It is the change in output resulting from a one-unit increase in the quantity of capital employed.

Table 10.3

The Production Function

Labour (workers per day)	Output (jumpers per day)			
	Plant 1	Plant 2	Plant 3	Plant 4
1	4	10	13	15
2	10	15	18	20
3	13	18	22	24
4	15	20	24	26
5	16	21	25	27
Knitting machines (number)	1	2	3	4

The table shows the total product data for four quantities of capital – four plant sizes. The bigger the plant size, the larger is the total product for any given amount of labour employed. But for a given plant size, the marginal product of labour diminishes as more labour is employed. For a given quantity of labour, the marginal product of capital diminishes as the quantity of capital used increases.

For example, if Fashion First employs 3 workers and increases its capital from 1 machine to 2 machines, output increases from 13 to 18 jumpers a day. The marginal product of capital is 5 jumpers a day. If with 3 workers, Fashion First increases its capital from 2 machines to 3 machines, output increases from 18 to 22 jumpers a day. The marginal product of the third machine is 4 jumpers a day, down from 5 jumpers a day for the second machine.

We can now see what the production function implies for long-run costs.

Short-run Cost and Long-run Cost

Continue to assume that labour costs £25 per worker per day and capital costs £25 per machine per day. Using these factor prices and the data in Table 10.3, we can calculate and graph the average total cost curves for factories with 1, 2, 3 and 4 knitting machines. We've already studied the costs of a factory with 1 knitting machine in Figures 10.5 and 10.6. In Figure 10.7, the average total cost curve for that case is ATC_1. Figure 10.7 also shows the average total cost curve for a factory with 2 machines, ATC_2, with 3 machines, ATC_3, and with 4 machines, ATC_4.

Figure 10.7   Short-run Costs of Four Different Plants

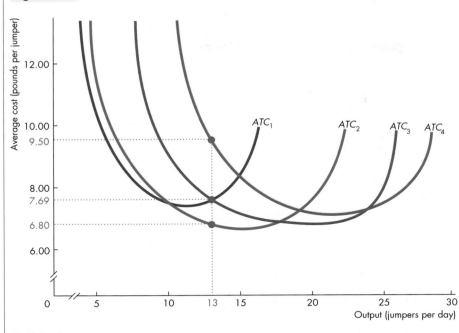

The figure shows short-run average total cost curves for four different quantities of capital.

Fashion First can produce 13 jumpers a day with 1 knitting machine on ATC_1, or with 3 knitting machines on ATC_3 for an average cost of £7.69 per jumper. Fashion First can produce the same number of jumpers by using 2 knitting machines on ATC_2 for £6.80 per jumper or with 4 machines on ATC_4 for £9.50 per jumper.

If Fashion First produces 13 jumpers a day, the least-cost method of production (the long-run method) is to use 2 machines on ATC_2.

 myeconlab Animation

You can see, in Figure 10.7, that plant size has a big effect on the firm's average total cost. Two things stand out.

1   Each short-run *ATC* curve is U-shaped.

2   For each short-run *ATC* curve, the larger the plant, the greater is the output at which average total cost is a minimum.

Each short-run average total cost curve is U-shaped because, as the quantity of labour increases, its marginal product at first increases and then diminishes. This pattern in the marginal product of labour, which we examined in some detail for the plant with 1 knitting machine on pp. 224–225, occurs at all plant sizes.

The minimum average total cost for a larger plant occurs at a greater output than it does for a smaller plant because the larger plant has a higher fixed cost and therefore, for any given output level, a higher average fixed cost.

Which short-run average cost curves Fashion First operates on depends on its plant size. But in the long run, Fashion First chooses its plant size. Its choice of plant size depends on the output that it plans to produce. The reason is that the average total cost of producing a given output depends on the plant size.

To see why, suppose that Fashion First plans to produce 13 jumpers a day. With 1 machine, the average total cost curve is ATC_1 (in Figure 10.7) and the average total cost of 13 jumpers a day is £7.69 per jumper. With 2 machines, on ATC_2, average total cost is £6.80 per jumper. With 3 machines on ATC_3, average total cost is £7.69 per jumper, the same as with 1 machine. Finally, with 4 machines, on ATC_4, average total cost is £9.50 per jumper.

The economically efficient plant size for producing a given output is the one that has the lowest average total cost. For Fashion First, the economically efficient plant to use to produce 13 jumpers a day is the one with 2 machines. In the long run, Fashion First chooses the plant size that minimizes average total cost. When a firm is producing a given output at the least possible cost, it is operating on its *long-run average cost curve.*

The **long-run average cost curve** is the relationship between the lowest attainable average total cost and output when both the plant size and labour are varied. The long-run average cost curve is a planning curve. It tells the firm the plant size and the quantity of labour to use at each output to minimize cost. Once the plant size is chosen, the firm operates on the short-run cost curves that apply to that plant size.

The Long-run Average Cost Curve

Figure 10.8 shows how the long-run average cost curve is derived. The long-run average cost curve *LRAC* consists of pieces of the four short-run *ATC* curves. For output up to 10 jumpers a day, the average total cost is lowest on ATC_1. For output rates between 10 and 18 jumpers a day, average total cost is lowest on ATC_2. For output rates between 18 and 24 jumpers a day, average total cost is lowest on ATC_3. For output rates in excess of 24 jumpers a day, average total cost is lowest on ATC_4. The piece of each *ATC* curve with the lowest average total cost is shown as dark blue in Figure 10.8. The dark blue scallop-shaped curve made up of the four pieces is Fashion First's *LRAC* curve.

Economies and Diseconomies of Scale

Economies of scale are features of a firm's technology that make average total cost *fall* as output increases. When economies of scale are present, the *LRAC* curve slopes downward. The *LRAC* in Figure 10.8 shows that Fashion First experiences economies of scale for outputs up to 15 jumpers a day.

Greater specialization of both labour and capital is the main source of economies of scale. For example, if

BMW produces only 100 cars a week, each worker must be capable of performing many different tasks and the capital must be general-purpose machines and tools. But if BMW produces 10,000 cars a week, each worker specializes in a small number of tasks, uses task-specific tools and becomes highly proficient.

Diseconomies of scale are features of a firm's technology that make average total cost *rise* as output increases. When diseconomies of scale are present, the *LRAC* curve slopes upward. In Figure 10.8, Fashion First experiences diseconomies of scale at outputs greater than 15 jumpers a day.

The challenge of managing a large enterprise is the main source of diseconomies of scale.

Constant returns to scale are features of a firm's technology that keep average total costs constant as output increases. When constant returns to scale are present, the *LRAC* curve is horizontal.

The economies of scale and diseconomies of scale at Fashion First arise from the firm's production function in Table 10.3. With 1 worker and 1 machine, the firm produces 4 jumpers a day. With 2 workers and 2 machines, total cost doubles but output more than doubles to 15 jumpers a day, so average total cost decreases and Fashion First experiences economies of scale.

Figure 10.8 The Long-run Average Cost Curve

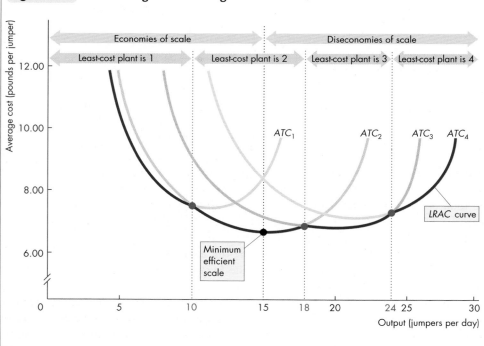

The long-run average cost curve traces the lowest attainable *ATC* when both labour and capital change. The green arrows highlight the output range over which each plant achieves the lowest *ATC*. Within each range, to change the quantity produced, the firm changes the quantity of labour it employs.

Along the *LRAC* curve economies of scale occur if average cost falls as output increases; diseconomies of scale occur if average cost rises as output increases.

Minimum efficient scale is the output at which average cost is lowest, 15 jumpers a day.

Produce More to Cut Cost

Why do BMW, Citroen and other car makers have expensive equipment lying around that isn't fully used? You can now answer this question with what you have learned in this chapter.

The basic answer is that car production faces economies of scale. A larger output rate brings a lower long-run average cost – the firm's *LRAC* curve slopes downward.

A car producer's average total cost curves look like those in Figure 1. To produce 20 vehicles an hour, the firm installs the plant with the short-run average total cost curve ATC_1. The average cost of producing a vehicle is £20,000.

Producing 20 vehicles an hour doesn't use the plant at its lowest possible average total cost. If the firm could sell enough cars for it to produce 40 vehicles an hour, the firm could use its current plant and produce at an average cost of £15,000 a vehicle.

But if the firm planned to produce 40 vehicles an hour, it would not use its current plant. The firm would install a bigger plant with the short-run average total cost curve ATC_2, and produce 40 vehicles an hour for £10,000 a car.

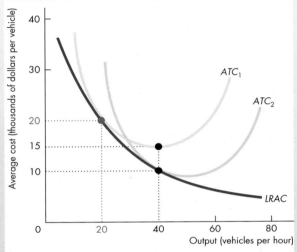

Figure 1   Car Plant's Average Cost Curves

With 4 workers and 4 machines, total cost doubles again, but output less than doubles to 26 jumpers a day, so average total cost increases and Fashion First experiences diseconomies of scale.

Minimum Efficient Scale

A firm's **minimum efficient scale** is the *smallest* quantity of output at which long-run average cost reaches its lowest level. At Fashion First, the minimum efficient scale is 15 jumpers per day.

The minimum efficient scale plays a role in determining market structure. In a market in which the minimum efficient scale is small relative to the market demand, the market has room for many firms. The market is competitive. In a market in which the minimum efficient scale is large relative to market demand, only a small number of firms, and sometimes only one firm, can make a profit. The market is an oligopoly or monopoly. We will look at these ideas in the next three chapters.

Review Quiz

1   What does a firm's production function show and how is it related to a total product curve?
2   Does the law of diminishing returns apply to capital as well as labour? Explain why or why not.
3   What does a firm's *LRAC* curve show? How is it related to the firm's short-run *ATC* curve?
4   What are economies and diseconomies of scale? How do they arise? What do they imply for the shape of the *LRAC* curve?
5   What is a firm's minimum efficient scale?

You can work these questions in Study Plan 10.4 and get instant feedback.   myeconlab

You have now studied how a firm's costs vary as it changes its output. The *Business Case Study* on pp. 236–237 applies what you have learned about a firm's cost curves to Europe's second largest airline, easyJet. The appendix presents an alternative analysis of costs.

Business Case Study

Airline Costs: The No Frills Approach

EasyJet Cuts Costs in Europe

EasyJet: The Company, Product and Market

EasyJet is a UK airline and ranks as Europe's second largest behind Ryanair. EasyJet competes with 200 other carriers and provides low cost flights to main airports with frequent services. In 2010, easyJet operated over 400 routes in 27 countries and carried over 48 million passengers. The company has a fleet of 180 aircraft, 6,660 staff, and a UK headquarters. European market demand for flights fell by 5 per cent in 2009 but easyJet passenger numbers grew

EasyJet's Rapid Growth

EasyJet has grown from an airline with just two aircraft (Boeing 737s) and two routes in 1995 to its current size by buying new aircraft and by acquiring airlines such as Go and GB airways. These buyouts provided second-hand aircraft and additional routes to increase output capacity alongside new planes.

EasyJet's Rising Costs

EasyJet's total costs increased by 15 per cent from 2008 to 2009. EasyJet's fuel costs increased by £86 million and other costs including airport charges and staff costs also increased. In addition, easyJet bought additional aircraft.

EasyJet's Costs

Item	2008	2009
Passengers (millions)	43.7	45.2
Seats flown	51.9	52.8
Aircraft	150.0	174.0
Total cost (£ million)	2,239.7	2,623.1
Average total cost (cost per seat)	43.15	49.67

Source of data: easyJet PLC, Reports and Accounts 2009, Interim Statement, 2010.

EasyJet Looks for Cost Cuts

In the past, easyJet has introduced on-line booking, purchase and check-in systems to cut costs alongside charging for baggage and extra services. EasyJet now aims to cut operating costs by £190 million by 2012 – saving £1 per seat. Of this, £20 million will be saved from cutting fuel burn through improved pilot techniques, fuel reporting systems and flight plan systems. £35 million will be saved from crew costs by increased efficiency and new work rostas. Other savings will come from buying new A320 airbus aircraft to replace 737s and other smaller aircraft. A320s are cheaper to own and maintain, have more seats and a cost per seat that is 6 per cent lower than other aircraft.

Economic Analysis

◆ In 2009, the demand for air travel in Europe fell, but easyJet increased its output (measured by passenger numbers and the number of seats flown) and increased its share of the market.

◆ Other things remaining the same, the expansion of easyJet's output would have lowered its average total cost.

◆ But other things didn't remain the same: the price of fuel increased and easyJet's average total cost increased.

◆ Figures 1 and 2 analyse these two sources of change in total cost by showing what happened to easyJet's ATC curve.

◆ Figure 1 shows what would have happened with no change in the price of fuel.

◆ In 2008, easyJet's output was 51.9 million seats flown at an average total cost of £43.45 per seat at point A on ATC curve ATC_{08}.

◆ In 2009, easyJet's output increased to 52.8 million seats flown. With no change in plant size (number of aircraft), the firm would have been able to produce its 2009 output at £40.00 per seat (an assumed value) at point B on ATC_{08}.

◆ But by buying more aircraft, the firm can lower its costs even more to move to £38.00 per seat (another assumed value) at point C on its LRAC curve and on ATC_{09}.

◆ EasyJet was not able to move to point C because the price of fuel increased and Figure 2 shows the consequences.

◆ The higher fuel price shifted the ATC curve upward from ATC_{09} to ATC'_{09} and easyJet's average total cost increased to £49.67 per seat at point D.

◆ With more (and newer) aircraft, easyJet increased passenger numbers and benefitted from economies of scale.

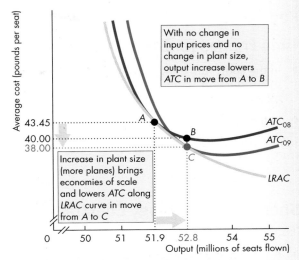

Figure 1   Changes in output and average cost: constant input prices

Figure 2   The effect of an increase in input prices

◆ By carrying more passengers, easyJet is able to get better deals from fuel suppliers, and from the suppliers of other services.

◆ EasyJet is seeking greater production efficiency by using a new technology to monitor fuel consumption and by introducing a new staff rota system. These changes will shift ATC'_{09} downward.

SUMMARY

Key Points

Time Frames for Decisions (p. 222)

◆ In the short run, the quantity of at least one factor of production is fixed and the quantities of the other factors can be varied.

◆ In the long run, the quantities of all factors of production can be varied.

Working Problems 1 and 2 will give you a better understanding of a firm's decision time frames.

Short-run Technology Constraint (pp. 223–226)

◆ A total product curve shows the quantity of output that a firm can produce using a given quantity of capital and different quantities of labour.

◆ Initially, the marginal product of labour increases as the quantity of labour increases because of increased specialization and the division of labour.

◆ Eventually, marginal product diminishes because an increased quantity of labour must share a fixed quantity of capital – the law of diminishing marginal returns.

◆ Initially, average product increases as the quantity of labour increases, but eventually average product diminishes.

Working Problems 3 to 8 will give you a better understanding of a firm's short-run technology constraint.

Short-run Cost (pp. 227–231)

◆ As output increases, total fixed cost is constant, and total variable cost and total cost increase.

◆ As output increases, average variable cost, average total cost and marginal cost decrease at small outputs and increase at large outputs. These cost curves are U-shaped.

Working Problems 9 to 14 will give you a better understanding of a firm's short-run cost.

Long-run Cost (pp. 232–235)

◆ Long-run cost is the cost of production when all factors of production – labour and plant – have been adjusted to their economically efficient levels.

◆ The firm has a set of short-run cost curves for each different plant. For each output, the firm has one least-cost plant. The larger the output, the larger is the plant that will minimize average total cost.

◆ The long-run average cost curve traces the relationship between the lowest attainable average total cost and output when both capital and labour can be varied.

◆ With economies of scale, the long-run average cost curve slopes downward. With diseconomies of scale, the long-run average cost curve slopes upward.

Working Problems 15 to 20 will give you a better understanding of a firm's long-run cost.

Key Terms

Average fixed cost, 228
Average product, 223
Average total cost, 228
Average variable cost, 228
Constant returns to scale, 234
Diminishing marginal returns, 225
Diseconomies of scale, 234
Economies of scale, 234
Law of diminishing returns, 225
Long run, 222
Long-run average cost curve, 233
Marginal cost, 228
Marginal product, 223
Minimum efficient scale, 235
Short run, 222
Sunk cost, 222
Total cost, 227
Total fixed cost, 227
Total product, 223
Total variable cost, 227

STUDY PLAN PROBLEMS AND APPLICATIONS

 You can work Problems 1 to 21 in MyEconLab Chapter 10 Study Plan and get instant feedback.

Decision Time Frames (Study Plan 10.1)

1 Which of the following news items involve a short-run decision and which involve a long-run decision? Explain.

18 April 2009: By next March, Tesco plans to open more than 100 shops in the UK, selling mobile and land-line packages in its largest stores.

6 October 2009: Tesco said that it would 'mothball' 13 stores in Nevada, Arizona and California – by boarding them up or subletting them, with a plan to reopen them in four to five years once the US economy recovers.

22 August 2010: Tesco is lauching its first drive-through supermarket this week. Customers order online and at the supermarket drive-through staff pack the shopping into the boot.

1 September 2010: Tesco plans to open 80 vast shopping malls in China by 2016.

2 **Farmers Turn from Tobacco to Flowers**

US tobacco farmers will be subsidized if they switch from growing tobacco to growing crops such as flowers and organic vegetables.

Source: *The New York Times*, 25 February 2001

a How does offering farmers a payment to exit tobacco growing influence the opportunity cost of growing tobacco?

b What is the opportunity cost of using the equipment owned by a tobacco farmer?

Short-run Technology Constraint
(Study Plan 10.2)

Use the following table to work Problems 3 to 7.

The table sets out Sue's Snowboards' total product schedule:

Labour (workers per week)	Output (snowboards per week)
1	30
2	70
3	120
4	160
5	190
6	210
7	220

3 Draw the total product curve.

4 Calculate the average product of labour and draw the average product curve.

5 Calculate the marginal product of labour and draw the marginal product curve.

6 a Over what output range does the firm enjoy the benefits of increased specialization and division of labour?

b Over what output range does the firm experience diminishing marginal product of labour?

c Over what range of output does the firm experience an increasing average product of labour but a diminishing marginal product of labour?

7 Explain how it is possible for a firm to experience simultaneously an increasing *average* product but a diminishing *marginal* product.

8 Sales at a footwear company rose from €160,000 in 2006 to €2.3 million in 2007, but in 2008 sales dipped to €1.5 million. Priscilla, the owner, blames the decline partly on a flood that damaged the firm's office and sapped morale. Assume that the prices of footwear didn't change.

a Explain the effect of the flood on the company's total product curve and marginal product curve.

b Draw a graph to show the effect of the flood on the company's total product curve and marginal product curve.

Short-run Cost (Study Plan 10.3)

Use the following data to work Problems 9 to 13.

Sue's Snowboards in Problem 3 employs workers at €500 a week and its total fixed cost is €1,000 a week.

9 Calculate total cost, total variable cost, and total fixed cost for each output and draw the short-run total cost curves.

10 Calculate average total cost, average fixed cost, average variable cost, and marginal cost at each output and draw the short-run average and marginal cost curves.

11 Illustrate the connection between Sue's *AP*, *MP*, *AVC* and *MC* curves like those in Figure 10.6.

12 Sue's Snowboards rents a factory building. If the rent is increased by €200 a week and other things remain the same, how do Sue's Snowboards' short-run average cost curves and marginal cost curve change?

13 Workers at Sue's Snowboards negotiate a wage increase of €100 a week for each worker. If other things remain the same, explain how Sue's Snowboards' short-run average cost curves and marginal cost curve change.

14 Grain Prices Go the Way of the Oil Price

Every morning millions of Americans confront the latest trend in commodities markets at their kitchen table. Rising prices for crops have begun to drive up the cost of breakfast.

Source: *The Economist*, 21 July 2007

Explain how the rising price of crops affects the average total cost and marginal cost of producing breakfast cereals.

Long-run Cost (Study Plan 10.4)

Use the table in Problem 3 and the following information to work Problems 15 and 16.

Sue's Snowboards buys a second plant and the output produced by each worker increases by 50 per cent. The total fixed cost of operating each plant is €1,000 a week. Each worker is paid €500 a week.

15 Calculate the average total cost of producing 180 and 240 snowboards a week when Sue's Snowboards operates two plants. Graph these points and sketch the *ATC* curve.

16 a To produce 180 snowboards a week, is it efficient to operate one or two plants?

b To produce 160 snowboards a week, is it efficient for Sue's to operate one or two plants?

Use the following table to work Problems 17 to 20.

The table shows the production function of Jackie's Canoe Rides.

Labour (workers per day)	Output (rides per day)			
	Plant 1	Plant 2	Plant 3	Plant 4
10	20	40	55	65
20	40	60	75	85
30	65	75	90	100
40	75	85	100	110
Canoes (number)	10	20	30	40

Jackie pays €100 a day for each canoe she rents and €50 a day for each canoe operator she hires.

17 Graph the *ATC* curves for Plant 1 and Plant 2. Explain why these *ATC* curves differ from each other.

18 Graph the *ATC* curves for Plant 3 and Plant 4. Explain why these *ATC* curves differ from each other.

19 a On Jackie's *LRAC* curve, what is the average cost of producing 40, 75 and 85 rides a week?

b What is Jackie's minimum efficient scale?

20 a Explain how Jackie's uses her *LRAC* curve to decide how many canoes to rent.

b Does Jackie's production function feature economies of scale or diseconomies of scale?

Economics in the News (Study Plan 10.N)

21 Airlines Seek Out New Ways to Save on Fuel as Costs Soar

The financial pain of higher fuel prices is particularly acute for airlines because it is their single biggest expense. Airlines pump about 7,000 gallons into a Boeing 737 and about 60,000 gallons into the bigger 747 jet. Each generation of aircraft is more efficient: an Airbus A330 long-range jet uses 38 per cent less fuel than the DC-10 it replaced, while the Airbus A319 medium-range jet is 27 per cent more efficient than the DC-9 it replaced.

Source: *The New York Times*, 11 June 2008

a Is the price of fuel a fixed cost or a variable cost for an airline?

b Explain how an increase in the price of fuel changes an airline's total costs, average costs and marginal cost.

c Draw a graph to show the effects of an increase in the price of fuel on an airline's *TFC*, *TVC*, *AFC*, *AVC* and *MC* curves.

d Explain how a technological advance that makes an airplane engine more fuel efficient changes an airline's total product, marginal product and average product.

e Draw a graph to illustrate the effects of a more fuel-efficient aircraft on an airline's *TP*, *MP* and *AP* curves.

f Explain how a technological advance that makes an airplane engine more fuel efficient changes an airline's average variable cost, marginal cost and average total cost.

g Draw a graph to illustrate how a technological advance that makes an airplane engine more fuel efficient changes an airline's *AVC*, *MC* and *ATC* curves.

ADDITIONAL PROBLEMS AND APPLICATIONS

 You can work these problems in MyEconLab if assigned by your lecturer.

Decision Time Frames

22   A Bakery on the Rise

Some 500 customers a day line up to buy Avalon's breads, scones, muffins and coffee. Staffing and management are worries. Avalon now employs 35 and plans to hire 15 more. Its payroll will climb by 30 per cent to 40 per cent. The new CEO has executed an ambitious agenda that includes the move to a larger space, which will increase the rent from $3,500 to $10,000 a month.

Source: *CNN*, 24 March 2008

a Which of Avalon's decisions described in the news clip is a short-run decision and which is a long-run decision?

b Why is Avalon's long-run decision riskier than its short-run decision?

23   The Sunk-Cost Fallacy

You have good tickets to a football game an hour's drive away. There's a storm raging outside, and the game is being televised. You can sit warm and safe at home and watch it on TV, or you can bundle up and go to the game. What do you do?

Source: *Slate*, 9 September 2005

a What type of cost is your expenditure on tickets?

b Why is the cost of the ticket irrelevant to your current decision about whether to stay at home or go to the game?

Short-run Technology Constraint

24 Terri runs a rose farm. One worker produces 1,000 roses a week; hiring a second worker doubles her total product; hiring a third worker doubles her output again; hiring a fourth worker increases her total product but by only 1,000 roses. Construct Terri's marginal product and average product schedules. Over what range of workers do marginal returns increase?

Short-run Cost

25 Use the events described in the news clip in Problem 22. By how much will Avalon's short-run decision increase its total variable cost? By how much will Avalon's long-run decision increase its monthly total fixed cost? Sketch Avalon's short-run *ATC* curve before and after the events described in the news clip.

26   Coffee King Starbucks Raises Its Prices

Starbucks is raising its prices because the wholesale price of milk has risen 70 per cent and there's a lot of milk in Starbucks' lattes.

Source: *USA Today*, 24 July 2007

Is milk a fixed factor of production or a variable factor of production? Describe how the increase in the price of milk changes Starbucks' short-run cost curves.

27 Bill's Bakery has a fire and Bill loses some of his cost data. The bits of paper that he recovers after the fire provide the data in the following table (all the cost numbers are euros).

TP	AFC	AVC	ATC	MC
10	120	100	220	
				80
20	*A*	*B*	150	
				90
30	40	90	130	
				130
40	30	*C*	*D*	
				E
50	24	108	132	

Bill asks you to come to his rescue and provide the missing data in the five spaces identified as *A*, *B*, *C*, *D* and *E*.

Use the following table to work Problems 28 and 29.

ProPainters hires students at €250 a week to paint houses. It leases equipment at €500 a week. The table sets out its total product schedule.

Labour (workers per week)	Output (houses painted per week)
1	2
2	5
3	9
4	12
5	14
6	15

28 If ProPainters paints 12 houses a week, calculate its total cost, average total cost and marginal cost. At what output is average total cost a minimum?

29 Explain why the gap between ProPainters' total cost and total variable cost is the same no matter how many houses are painted.

Long-run Cost

Use the table in Problem 28 and the following information to work Problems 30 and 31.

If ProPainters doubles the number of students it hires and doubles the amount of equipment it leases, it experiences diseconomies of scale.

30 Explain how the *ATC* curve with one unit of equipment differs from that when ProPainters uses double the amount of equipment.

31 Explain what might be the source of the diseconomies of scale that ProPainters experiences.

Use the following information to work Problems 32 and 33.

The table shows the production function of Bonnie's Balloon Rides. Bonnie's pays $500 a day for each balloon it rents and $25 a day for each balloon operator it hires.

Labour (workers per day)	Output (rides per day)			
	Plant 1	Plant 2	Plant 3	Plant 4
1	6	10	13	15
2	10	15	18	21
3	13	18	22	24
4	15	20	24	26
5	16	21	25	27
Balloons (number)	1	2	3	4

32 Graph the *ATC* curves for Plant 1 and Plant 2. Explain why these *ATC* curves differ.

33 Graph the *ATC* curves for Plant 3 and Plant 4. Explain why these *ATC* curves differ.

34 **a** On Bonnie's *LRAC* curve, what is the average cost of producing 18 rides and 15 rides a day?

   b Explain how Bonnie's uses its long-run average cost curve to decide how many balloons to rent.

Use the following news clip to work Problems 35 and 36.

Gap Will Focus on Smaller Scale Stores

Gap has too many stores that are 12,500 square feet. The target store size is 6,000 square feet to 10,000 square feet, so Gap plans to combine previously separate concept stores. Some Gap body, adult, maternity, baby and kids stores will be combined in one store.

Source: CNN, 10 June 2008

35 Thinking of a Gap store as a production plant, explain why Gap is making a decision to reduce the size of its stores. Is Gap's decision a long-run decision or a short-run decision?

36 How might combining Gap's concept stores into one store help better take advantage of economies of scale?

Economics in the News

37 After you have studied the *Business Case Study* on pp. 236–237 answer the following questions.

   a For each of the costs described in the news article, explain whether the cost is fixed or variable.

   b Explain how introducing the new A320 aircraft is likely to affect *AFC*, *AVC*, *ATC* and *MC* for easyJet. Sketch a graph to illustrate your answer.

   c Use the concepts of *AVC*, *MC* and *ATC* to explain why low cost carriers like easyJet can sell some tickets for prices as low as £10.

38 **Self-serve Espresso Bars**

Automated, self-service espresso kiosks are now being introduced in some stores. The machines can grind beans and deliver latte and espresso coffee and take credit and debit cards and cash. The kiosks cost €40,000 per unit, but must be installed and maintained. Self-service kiosks remove the labour costs for service. The kiosks must be refilled by store staff with coffee beans and milk.

Source: MSNBC, 1 June 2008

   a What is the total fixed cost of operating one self-service kiosk?

   b What are the variable costs of providing coffee at a self-service kiosk?

   c Assume that a coffee machine in a traditional service cafe costs less than €40,000. Explain how the fixed costs, variable costs and total costs of traditionally served and self-served coffee differ.

   d Sketch the marginal cost and average cost curves implied by your answer to part (c).

39 The cost of producing electricity using hydro power is about one-third of the cost of using coal, oil or nuclear power plants and is less than one-quarter the cost of using gas turbine plants. Most of the cost differences come from differences in fuel costs. But part of the cost difference comes from differences in plant costs. It costs less to build a hydroelectric plant than a coal, oil or nuclear plant. Gas turbine plants cost the least to build but are the most expensive to operate.

(Based on *Projected Costs of Generating Electricity*, International Energy Agency, 2005)

   a Use the above information to sketch the *AFC*, *AVC* and *ATC* curves for electricity production using three technologies: (i) hydro, (ii) coal, oil or nuclear and (iii) gas turbine.

   b Use the above information to sketch the marginal cost curves for electricity production using three technologies: (i) hydro, (ii) coal, oil or nuclear and (iii) gas turbine.

   c Given the cost differences among the three methods of generating electricity, why do we use more than one?

Chapter 10 Appendix

Producing at Least Cost

After studying this appendix, you will be able to:

◆ Make an isoquant map and explain the law of diminishing marginal rate of substitution

◆ Describe an isocost line and explain how a change in factor price shifts it

◆ Calculate the least-cost technique of production

Isoquants and Factor Substitution

A firm's long-run production function describes all the technically feasible combinations of labour and capital that can produce given output levels. Whatever goods it produces, a firm can choose between labour-intensive or capital-intensive production techniques. To move from one technique to another, a firm must change the combination of labour and capital it uses – a change called factor substitution.

In this appendix, you are going to use a new model to find the best combination of factors.

Figure A10.1 shows Fashion First's production function. The figure shows that in the long run, Fashion First can use three different combinations of labour and capital to produce 15 jumpers a day, and two different combinations to produce 10 and 21 jumpers a day. So to maximize profit, Fashion First uses the least-cost combination of labour and capital that minimizes its total cost.

An Isoquant Map

An **isoquant** is a curve that shows the different combinations of labour and capital required to produce a given quantity of output. The word isoquant means 'equal quantity'. There is an isoquant for each output level. A series of isoquants is called an **isoquant map**. Figure A10.2 shows an isoquant map for Fashion First with three isoquants: one for 10 jumpers a day, one for 15 jumpers a day and one for 21 jumpers a day. Each isoquant shown is based on the production function in Figure A10.1.

Although all goods and services can be produced using a variety of alternative production techniques, the ease with which labour and capital can be substituted for each other varies from industry to industry.

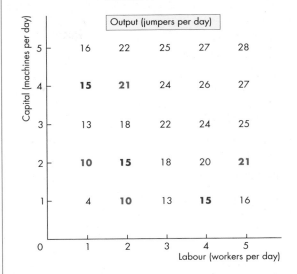

Figure A10.1 Fashion First's Production Function

The figure shows how many jumpers can be produced each day using different combinations of labour and capital. For example, Fashion First can produce 15 jumpers a day using 1 worker and 4 machines, or 2 workers and 2 machines, or 4 workers and 1 machine.

myeconlab Animation ◆

The production function reflects the ease of factor substitution and can be used to calculate the degree of substitutability between factors. This calculation involves the marginal rate of substitution of labour for capital. The **marginal rate of substitution of labour for capital** is the increase in labour needed per unit decrease in capital to allow output to remain constant. Let's look at this in more detail.

The Marginal Rate of Substitution

The marginal rate of substitution is the magnitude of the slope of an isoquant. Figure A10.3 shows the isoquant for 13 jumpers a day. Pick any point on this isoquant and imagine decreasing capital by the smallest conceivable amount and increasing labour by the amount necessary to keep output constant at 13 jumpers. As we decrease the quantity of capital and increase the quantity of labour to keep output constant at 13 jumpers a day, we travel down along the isoquant.

Figure A10.2 An Isoquant Map

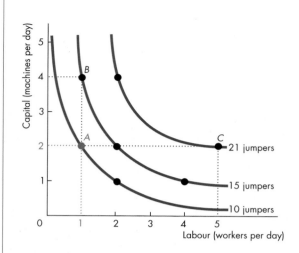

The figure shows three isoquants that are part of Fashion First's isoquant map. Along each isoquant, the output produced by labour and capital is constant. These isoquants correspond to the production function for 10, 15 and 21 jumpers a day in Figure A10.1.

If Fashion First uses 2 machines and 1 worker (at point *A*), it produces 10 jumpers a day. If Fashion First uses 4 machines and 1 worker (at point *B*), it produces 15 jumpers a day. If Fashion First uses 2 machines and 5 workers (at point *C*), it produces 21 jumpers a day.

myeconlab Animation

Figure A10.3 The Marginal Rate of Substitution

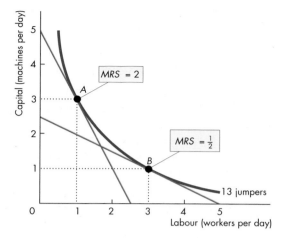

The marginal rate of substitution is measured by the magnitude of the slope of the isoquant. For example, to find the slope of the isoquant at point *A*, calculate the slope of the red line tangential to the isoquant at point *A*. The magnitude of the slope at point *A* is 2 (5 ÷ 2.5), so the marginal rate of substitution of labour for capital at point *A* is 2. Similarly, the magnitude of the marginal rate of substitution at point *B* equals the magnitude of the slope of the red tangential line at point *B* and is 1/2. So the marginal rate of substitution of labour for capital at point *B* is 1/2.

myeconlab Animation

In Figure A10.3, the marginal rate of substitution at point *A* is the magnitude of the slope of the red line tangential to the isoquant at point *A*. The slope of the isoquant at point *A* equals the slope of the line. To calculate the slope, move along the red line from 5 knitting machines and no workers to 2.5 workers and no knitting machines. Capital decreases by 5 knitting machines and labour increases by 2.5 workers. The magnitude of the slope is 5 divided by 2.5, which equals 2. So when using technique *A* to produce 13 jumpers a day, the marginal rate of substitution of labour for capital is 2.

The marginal rate of substitution at point *B* is the magnitude of the slope of the red line tangential to the isoquant at point *B*. Along this red line, if capital decreases by 2.5 knitting machines, labour increases by 5 workers. The magnitude of the slope is 2.5 knitting machines divided by 5, which equals 1/2. So when using technique *B* to produce 13 jumpers a day, the marginal rate of substitution of labour for capital is 1/2.

The marginal rates of substitution we have just calculated obey the **law of diminishing marginal rate of substitution** which states that:

The marginal rate of substitution of labour for capital diminishes as the amount of labour increases and the amount of capital decreases.

The law of diminishing marginal rate of substitution determines the shape of the isoquant. When the quantity of capital is large and the quantity of labour is small, the isoquant is steep and the marginal rate of substitution of labour for capital is large. As the quantity of capital decreases and the quantity of labour increases, the isoquant becomes flatter and the marginal rate of substitution of labour for capital diminishes. Isoquants bow towards the origin.

We are going to use Fashion First's isoquant map to work out the firm's least-cost technique of production, but first we must add the firm's costs to the model.

Isocost Lines

An **isocost line** shows the combinations of labour and capital that can be bought for a given total cost and given factor prices. Suppose that a knitting-machine worker can be hired for £25 a day and that a knitting machine can be rented for £25 a day. Figure A10.4 shows five possible combinations of labour and capital (A, B, C, D and E) that Fashion First can employ for a total cost of £100 a day. For example, point B shows that Fashion First can use 3 machines (for a cost of £75) and 1 worker (for a cost of £25). If Fashion First can employ workers and machines for fractions of a day, then any combination along the line AE will cost Fashion First £100 a day. This line is Fashion First's isocost line for a total cost of £100.

The Isocost Equation

An isocost equation describes an isocost line. The variables that affect a firm's total cost (TC) are the price of labour (P_L), the price of capital (P_K), the quantity of labour (L) and the quantity of capital (K).

The cost of the labour is ($P_L \times L$). The cost of capital is ($P_K \times K$). Total cost is the sum of these two costs.

Equation 1 shows a firm's total cost:

$$P_L L + P_K K = TC \qquad (1)$$

Equation 2 shows the total cost for Fashion First using the numbers in our example. The wage rate is £25 a day and the capital rental rate is also £25 a day, so Fashion First's total cost is:

$$£25L + £25K = £100 \qquad (2)$$

Now rearrange equation (1) by dividing by the price of capital and then subtract (P_L/P_K)L from both sides of the equation. The resulting equation is the equation of the isocost line:

$$K = \frac{TC}{P_K} - \frac{P_L}{P_K} \times L \qquad (3)$$

Equation 3 tells us how the firm can vary the quantity of capital as it changes the quantity of labour, holding total cost constant. Fashion First's isocost line is:

$$K = 4 - L \qquad (4)$$

Equation 4 corresponds to the isocost line in Figure A10.4.

Figure A10.4   An Isocost Line

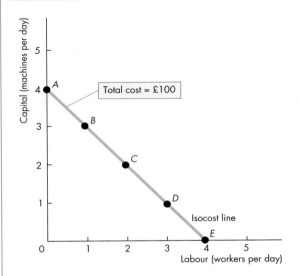

If labour is £25 a day and a knitting machine rents for £25 a day, Fashion First can employ the combinations of labour and capital shown by points A to E for a total cost of £100. The line through these points is an isocost line. It shows all possible combinations of labour and capital that Fashion First can hire for a total cost of £100 when labour is £25 a day and capital can be rented for £25 a day.

myeconlab Animation

The Isocost Map

An **isocost map** is a series of isocost lines, each one of which represents a different total cost but for given prices of labour and capital.

The larger the total cost, the greater are the quantities of labour and capital that can be employed. Figure A10.5 shows an isocost map. The middle isocost is the one you've seen before for a total cost of £100, when labour and capital cost £25 a day each. The other two isocost lines are for a total cost of £125 and £75, holding constant the factor prices at £25 a day each. The larger the total cost, the further is the isocost line from the origin.

The Effect of Factor Prices

The magnitude of the slope of the isocost lines shown in Figure A10.5 is 1. The slope tells us that 1 unit of labour costs 1 unit of capital. To decrease its capital by 1 unit and keep its total cost at £100 a day, Fashion First must increase the quantity of labour by 1 unit.

Figure A10.5 An Isocost Map

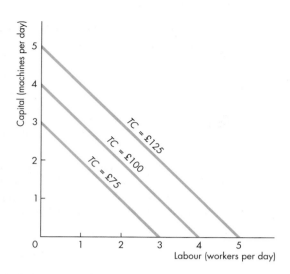

An isocost map shows the set of isocost lines, each for a different total cost. This isocost map shows three isocost lines, one for a total cost of £75 a day, one for £100 a day and one for £125 a day. Along the isocost lines, the prices of labour and capital are constant. For each isocost line shown here, the prices of labour and capital are £25 a day. The slope of an isocost line is equal to the relative price of labour to capital. The larger the total cost, the farther is the isocost line from the origin.

myeconlab Animation

Figure A10.6 Factor Prices and the Isocost Line

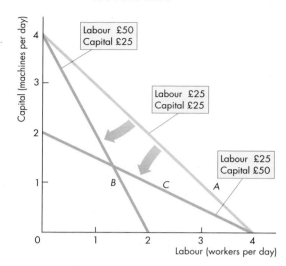

The slope of the isocost line depends on the relative factor price. Each of the isocost lines shown here has a total cost of £100 a day. If the prices of labour and capital are £25 a day, the isocost line is the line labelled *A*. If the price of labour rises to £50 a day but the price of capital remains at £25 a day, the isocost line becomes steeper and is the line labelled *B*. If the price of capital rises to £50 a day and the price of labour remains at £25 a day, the isocost line becomes flatter and is the line labelled *C*.

myeconlab Animation

If factor prices change, the slope of the isocost line changes. To see the effect of factor prices on the slope of the isocost line, start with the isocost equation:

$$K = \frac{TC}{P_K} - \frac{P_L}{P_K} \times L \qquad (3)$$

If the wage rate rises to £50 a day and the rental rate of a machine remains at £25 a day, then 1 unit of labour costs 2 units of capital. The relative price of labour to capital is £50 ÷ £25, which is 2. The isocost line becomes the steeper line *B* in Figure A10.6.

If the capital rental rate rises to £50 a day and the wage rate remains at £25 a day, then 1 unit of capital costs 2 units of labour. The relative price of labour to capital becomes £25 ÷ £50, which is 0.5. The isocost line becomes the flatter line *C* in Figure A10.6.

The higher the relative price of labour, the steeper is the isocost line. The magnitude of the slope of the isocost line measures the relative price of labour in terms of capital – the price of labour divided by the price of capital.

The Least-cost Technique

The **least-cost technique** is the combination of labour and capital that minimizes the total cost of producing a given level of output.

Suppose Fashion First plans to produce 15 jumpers a day, given the prices of capital and labour at £25 a day. What is the least-cost technique that Fashion First can use? Figure A10.7 shows the isoquant for an output of 15 jumpers and two isocost lines. One isocost is for a total cost of £125 a day and the other for £100 a day.

At point *A* in Figure A10.7, Fashion First can produce 15 jumpers using 1 worker and 4 machines. With this technique, the total cost is £125 a day. Point *C*, which uses 4 workers and 1 machine, is another technique that produces 15 jumpers for the same cost of £125 a day. At point *B*, Fashion First can use 2 machines and 2 workers to produce 15 jumpers, but the cost is £100 a day. So point *B* is the least-cost technique or the economically efficient technique for producing 15 jumpers, when machines and workers cost £25 a day each.

Figure A10.7 The Least-Cost Technique of Production

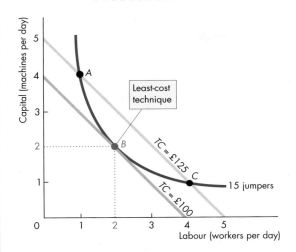

Fashion First can produce 15 jumpers a day by using 4 machines and 1 worker at point *A* or 1 machine and 4 workers at point *C*. The total cost using either of these techniques is £125 a day.

Fashion First can also use 2 machines and 2 workers at point *B* to produce 15 jumpers a day. The total cost using this technique is £100 a day. Point *B* is the least-cost technique of producing 15 jumpers.

At point *B*, the isoquant for 15 jumpers is tangential to the isocost line. The slope of the isoquant (the marginal rate of substitution) and the slope of the isocost line (the relative price of the factors) are the same.

myeconlab Animation ———————————◆

Figure A10.7 shows that there is only one way for Fashion First to produce 15 jumpers for £100 a day, but several ways to produce 15 jumpers for more than £100 a day. Techniques shown by points *A*, *B* and *C* are just examples. The points between *A*, *B* and *C* are also possible ways of producing 15 jumpers but for a total cost between £100 and £125 a day. Isocost lines exist between those shown which cut the isoquant for 15 jumpers at points between *A*, *B* and *C*. Fashion First could also produce 15 jumpers for a total cost of more than £125 a day by moving to a point on the isoquant outside the isocost line shown.

The least-cost technique for producing 15 jumpers a day is at point *B* in Figure A10.7. Fashion First cannot produce 15 jumpers for less than £100 a day. An isocost line for a total cost of less than £100 a day would not touch the isoquant for 15 jumpers because at the given prices of capital and labour, the total cost will not buy the factors needed to produce 15 jumpers.

Marginal Rate of Substitution and Marginal Products

The marginal rate of substitution and the marginal products are linked by an interesting formula:

The marginal rate of substitution of labour for capital equals the marginal product of labour divided by the marginal product of capital.

A few steps of reasoning are needed to establish this proposition.

First, we know that output changes when a firm changes the quantities of labour and capital employed. The change in output that results from a change in one of the factors is determined by the marginal product of the factor. So:

$$\text{Change in output} = (MP_L \times \Delta L) + (MP_K \times \Delta K) \quad (4)$$

Equation 4 shows a change in output equals the marginal product of labour, MP_L, multiplied by the change in labour, ΔL, plus the marginal product of capital, MP_K, multiplied by the change in capital, ΔK.

Suppose that Fashion First wants to change the quantities of labour and capital but continue to produce the same number of jumpers. That is, Fashion First wants to stay on the same isoquant, so the change in output must be zero. We can make the change in output zero in equation (4) to give equation (5):

$$MP_L \times \Delta L = -(MP_K \times \Delta K) \quad (5)$$

To stay on an isoquant when labour increases, capital must decrease. That is, when labour increases by ΔL, capital must decrease by:

$$MP_L \times \Delta L = MP_K \times -\Delta K \quad (6)$$

Equation 6 states that the marginal product of labour multiplied by the increase in labour equals the marginal product of capital multiplied by the decrease in capital. Dividing both sides of equation 6 by the increase in labour, ΔL, and then dividing both sides by the marginal product of capital, MP_K, gives equation 7:

$$\frac{MP_L}{MP_K} = -\frac{\Delta K}{\Delta L} \quad (7)$$

Equation 7 shows that when Fashion First remains on an isoquant, the decrease in its capital, $-\Delta K$, divided by the increase in its labour, ΔL, is equal to the marginal product of labour, MP_L, divided by the marginal product of capital, MP_K.

The decrease in capital divided by the increase in labour when the firm remains on a given isoquant is the *marginal rate of substitution of labour for capital*. What we have shown is that the marginal rate of substitution of labour for capital equals the ratio of the marginal product of labour to the marginal product of capital.

Marginal Cost

We can use the fact that the marginal rate of substitution of labour for capital equals the ratio of the marginal product of labour to the marginal product of capital to examine marginal cost.

We know that when the least-cost technique is used, the slope of the isoquant and the isocost line are equal as shown in equation 8:

$$\frac{MP_L}{MP_K} = \frac{P_L}{P_K} \tag{8}$$

We can now show that the total cost is minimized when the marginal product of labour per pound spent on labour equals the marginal product of capital per pound spent on capital.

Rearrange equation 8 by multiplying both sides by the marginal product of capital and then dividing both sides by the price of labour, to get equation 9:

$$\frac{MP_L}{P_L} = \frac{MP_K}{P_K} \tag{9}$$

Equation 9 says that the marginal product of labour per pound spent on labour is equal to the marginal product of capital per pound spent on capital. In other words, the extra output produced by the last pound spent on labour equals the extra output produced by the last pound spent on capital.

If the extra output produced by the last pound spent on labour exceeds the extra output produced by the last pound spent on capital, it pays a firm to use less capital and more labour. The firm can produce the same output at a lower total cost. Conversely, if the extra output produced by the last pound spent on capital exceeds the extra output produced by the last pound spent on labour, the firm can lower its cost of producing a given output by using less labour and more capital. A firm achieves the least-cost technique of production only when the extra output produced by the last pound spent on all the factors of production is the same.

Finally, we can show that the marginal cost of producing a unit of output with fixed capital and variable labour equals the marginal cost with fixed labour and variable capital. To see why, invert equation 9 to give:

$$\frac{P_L}{MP_L} = \frac{P_K}{MP_K} \tag{10}$$

Equation 10 shows that the price of labour divided by its marginal product equals the price of capital divided by its marginal product. The price of labour divided by the marginal product of labour is marginal cost of producing a unit of output when the quantity of capital is constant. Remember that marginal cost is the change in total cost resulting from a unit increase in output.

If output increases when one more unit of labour is employed, total output increases by the marginal product of labour. So marginal cost is the price of labour divided by the marginal product of labour. For example, if labour costs £25 a day and the marginal product of labour is 2 jumpers, then the marginal cost of a jumper is £12.50 (£25 ÷ 2).

The price of capital divided by the marginal product of capital has a similar interpretation. The price of capital divided by the marginal product of capital is marginal cost when the quantity of labour is constant.

You can see from equation 10 that with the least-cost technique, the marginal cost of producing a unit of output is the same regardless of whether the quantity of capital is constant and more labour is used or the quantity of labour is constant and more capital is used.

Making Connections

You're probably thinking that what you've learned in this Appendix looks a lot like what you learned in Chapter 8 about a consumer's decision. You are right. In a graph, an isoquant is like an indifference curve; an isocost line is like a budget line; and the least-cost production technique is like the consumer's best affordable point.

But there is an important difference between the two models. The consumer's goal is to get to the *highest* attainable indifference curve with a given budget. The firm's goal is to get to the *lowest* attainable isocost line for a given output. Nonetheless, the two models share similar techniques of analysis.

Key Terms

CHAPTER 11

Perfect Competition

You might be relaxing over a cup of coffee, but coffee shops operate in a fiercely competitive market with lean pickings for most owners. Competition is also fierce in other markets that affect your life, such as personal computers and mobile phones where prices have tumbled. Agricultural markets, such as the market for tea that you will encounter in *Reading Between the Lines*, are also competitive. What determines prices and profits of firms that operate in a competitive market? Why do firms enter or leave a competitive market? Why do firms sometimes shut down and lay off their workers? Is fierce competition efficient? We answer these questions in this chapter.

What Is Perfect Competition?

The firms that you study in this chapter face the force of raw competition. This type of extreme competition is called perfect competition. **Perfect competition** is a market in which:

1 Many firms sell identical products to many buyers.
2 There are no restrictions on entry into the market.
3 Established firms have no advantage over new ones.
4 Sellers and buyers are well informed about prices.

Farming, fishing, paper milling, the manufacture of paper cups, grocery retailing, plumbing and dry cleaning are examples of highly competitive industries.

How Perfect Competition Arises

Perfect competition arises if the firm's minimum efficient scale is small relative to the market demand for the good. In this situation, there is room for many firms in the industry. A firm's *minimum efficient scale* is the smallest quantity of output at which long-run average cost reaches its lowest level. (See Chapter 10, p. 235.)

In perfect competition, each firm produces a good or service that has no unique characteristics, so consumers don't care which firm's good they buy.

Price Takers

Firms in perfect competition are price takers. A **price taker** is a firm that cannot influence the market price because its production is an insignificant part of the total market.

Imagine you are a wheat farmer with a hundred hectares under cultivation, which sounds like a lot. But when compared to the millions of hectares in Ukraine, Canada, Australia, Argentina and the US, your hundred hectares is a drop in the ocean. Nothing makes your wheat any better than any other farmer's and all the buyers of wheat know the price at which they can do business.

If the market price of wheat is £85 a tonne and you ask £90 a tonne, no one will buy from you. People can go to the next farmer and the next and the one after that and buy all they need for £85 a tonne. If you set your price at £84 a tonne, you'll have lots of buyers. But you can sell all your output for £85 a tonne, so you're just giving away £1 a tonne. You can do no better than sell for the market price – you are a *price taker*.

Economic Profit and Revenue

A firm's goal is to maximize *economic profit*, which is equal to total revenue minus total cost. Total cost is the *opportunity cost* of production, which includes *normal profits* (see Chapter 9, p. 199).

A firm's **total revenue** equals the price of its output multiplied by the quantity sold (price × quantity). **Marginal revenue** is the change in total revenue that results from a one-unit increase in the quantity sold. Marginal revenue is calculated by dividing the change in total revenue by the change in the quantity sold.

Figure 11.1 illustrates these concepts in the market for jumpers. In part (a), the market demand curve, *D*, and the market supply curve, *S*, determine the market price. The market price is £25 a jumper. Fashion First is just one of many producers of jumpers, so the best that it can do is to sell its jumpers for £25 each.

Total Revenue

Total revenue is equal to the price multiplied by the quantity sold. In the table in Figure 11.1, if Fashion First sells 9 jumpers, the firm's total revenue is 9 × £25, which equals £225.

Figure 11.1(b) shows the firm's total revenue curve (*TR*), which graphs the relationship between total revenue and quantity sold. At point *A* on the *TR* curve, Fashion First sells 9 jumpers and has total revenue of £225. Because each additional jumper sold brings in a constant amount – £25 – the total revenue curve is an upward-sloping straight line.

Marginal Revenue

Marginal revenue is the change in total revenue that results from a one-unit increase in quantity sold. In the table in Figure 11.1, when the quantity sold increases from 8 to 9 jumpers, total revenue increases from £200 to £225, so marginal revenue is £25 a jumper.

Because the firm in perfect competition is a price taker, the change in total revenue that results from a one-unit increase in the quantity sold equals market price. In *perfect competition, the firm's marginal revenue equals the market price*. Figure 11.1(c) shows Fashion First's marginal revenue curve (*MR*), which is a horizontal line at the market price.

Demand for the Firm's Product

The firm can sell any quantity it chooses at the market price. So the demand curve for the firm's product is a

Figure 11.1 Demand, Price and Revenue in Perfect Competition

(a) Jumper industry

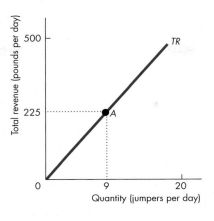

(b) Fashion First's total revenue

(c) Fashion First's marginal revenue

Quantity sold (*Q*) (jumpers per day)	Price (*P*) (pounds per jumper)	Total revenue (*TR = P × Q*) (pounds)	Marginal revenue (*MR = ΔTR/ΔQ*) (pounds per jumper)
8	25	200	
			25
9	25	225	
			25
10	25	250	

In part (a), market demand and market supply determine the market price (and quantity). Part (b) shows Fashion First's total revenue curve (*TR*). Point *A* corresponds to the second row of the table – Fashion First sells 9 jumpers at £25 a jumper, so total revenue is £225. Part (c) shows Fashion First's marginal revenue curve (*MR*). This curve is the demand curve for jumpers produced by Fashion First. Fashion First faces a perfectly elastic demand for its jumpers at the market price of £25 a jumper.

myeconlab Animation

horizontal line at the market price, the same as the firm's marginal revenue curve.

A horizontal demand curve illustrates a perfectly elastic demand, so the demand for the firm's output is perfectly elastic. One of Fashion First's jumpers is a *perfect substitute* for jumpers from the factory next door or from any other factory. But the *market* demand for jumpers is *not* perfectly elastic. Its elasticity depends on the substitutability of jumpers for other goods and services.

The Firm's Decisions

The goal of the competitive firm is to maximize economic profit, given the constraints it faces. To achieve its goal, a firm must decide:

1   How to produce at minimum cost
2   What quantity to produce
3   Whether to enter or exit a market

You've already seen how a firm makes the first decision. It does so by operating with the plant that minimizes long-run average cost – by being on its long-run average cost curve. We'll now see how the firm makes the other two decisions. We start by looking at the firm's output decision.

The Firm's Output Decision

A firm's cost curves (total cost, average cost, and marginal cost) describe the relationship between its output and costs (see Chapter 10, pp. 227–231). And a firm's revenue curves (total revenue and marginal revenue) describe the relationship between its output and revenue (p. 251). From the firm's cost curves and revenue curves, we can find the output that maximizes the firm's economic profit.

Figure 11.2 shows you how to do this for Fashion First. The table lists Fashion First's total revenue and total cost at different outputs, and part (a) of the figure shows its total revenue curve (*TR*) and total cost curve

(*TC*). These curves are graphs of the numbers shown in the first three columns of the table.

Economic profit equals total revenue minus total cost. The fourth column of the table in Figure 11.2 shows economic profit made by Fashion First and part (b) of the figure graphs these numbers as its economic profit curve (*EP*).

Fashion First maximizes economic profit by producing 9 jumpers a day. Total revenue is £225, total cost is £183 and economic profit is £42. No other output rate achieves a larger profit. At outputs of less than 4 jumpers and more than 12 jumpers a day, Fashion First would incur an economic loss. At either 4 or 12 jumpers a day, Fashion First would make zero economic profit, called a *break-even* point.

Figure 11.2 Total Revenue, Total Cost and Economic Profit

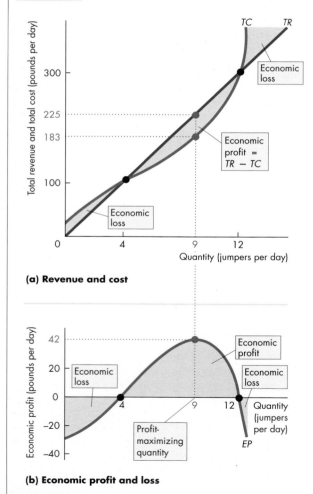

(a) Revenue and cost

(b) Economic profit and loss

Quantity (Q) (jumpers per day)	Total revenue (TR) (pounds)	Total cost (TC) (pounds)	Economic profit (TR – TC) (pounds)
0	0	22	−22
1	25	45	−20
2	50	66	−16
3	75	85	−10
4	100	100	0
5	125	114	11
6	150	126	24
7	175	141	34
8	200	160	40
9	**225**	**183**	**42**
10	250	210	40
11	275	245	30
12	300	300	0
13	325	360	−35

The table lists Fashion First's total revenue, total cost and economic profit. Part (a) graphs the total revenue and total cost curves and part (b) graphs economic profit. Fashion First makes maximum economic profit, £42 a day (£225 – £183), when it produces 9 jumpers. At outputs of 4 jumpers a day and 12 jumpers a day, Fashion First makes zero economic profit – these are break-even points. At outputs less than 4 and greater than 12 jumpers a day, Fashion First incurs an economic loss.

Marginal Analysis

Another way of finding the profit-maximizing output is to use *marginal analysis*, by comparing marginal revenue, *MR*, with marginal cost, *MC*. As output increases, marginal revenue remains constant but marginal cost changes. At low output levels, marginal cost decreases as output increases but eventually marginal cost increases.

If marginal revenue exceeds marginal cost (if *MR* > *MC*), then the extra revenue from selling one more unit exceeds the extra cost incurred to produce it. The firm makes an economic profit on the marginal unit, so economic profit increases if output *increases*.

If marginal revenue is less than marginal cost (if *MR* < *MC*), then the extra revenue from selling one more unit is less than the extra cost incurred to produce it. The firm incurs an economic loss on the marginal unit, so its economic profit decreases if output increases and its economic profit increases if output *decreases*.

If marginal revenue equals marginal cost (*MR* = *MC*), the firm makes maximum economic profit. The rule *MR* = *MC* is an example of marginal analysis.

Figure 11.3 illustrates these propositions. If Fashion First increases output from 8 jumpers to 9 jumpers, marginal revenue (£25) exceeds marginal cost (£23), so by producing the ninth jumper economic profit increases by £2 from £40 to £42 a day.The blue area in the figure shows the increase in economic profit when the firm increases production from 8 to 9 jumpers a day.

If Fashion First increases output from 9 jumpers to 10 jumpers, marginal revenue (£25) is less than marginal cost (£27), so by producing the tenth jumper, economic profit decreases. The red area in the figure shows the economic loss that arises from increasing production from 9 to 10 jumpers a day.

Fashion First maximizes economic profit by producing 9 jumpers a day, the quantity at which marginal revenue equals marginal cost.

A firm's profit-maximizing output is its quantity supplied at the market price. The quantity supplied at a price of £25 a jumper is 9 jumpers a day. If the price were higher than £25 a jumper, the firm would increase production. If the price were lower than £25 a jumper, the firm would decrease production. These profit-maximizing responses to different market prices are the foundation of the law of supply:

Other things remaining the same, the higher the market price of a good, the greater is the quantity supplied of that good.

Figure 11.3   Profit-maximizing Output

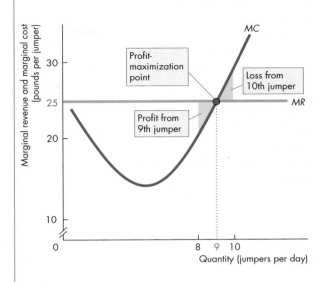

Quantity (*Q*) (jumpers per day)	Total revenue (*TR*) (pounds)	Marginal revenue (*MR*) (pounds per jumper)	Total cost (*TC*) (pounds)	Marginal cost (*MC*) (pounds per jumper)	Economic profit (*TR* – *TC*) (pounds)
7	175		141		34
		 25		 19	
8	200		160		40
		 25		 23	
9	225		183		42
		 25		 27	
10	250		210		40
		 25		 35	
11	275		245		30

Another way of finding the profit-maximizing output is to determine the output at which marginal revenue equals marginal cost. The table and figure show that marginal cost and marginal revenue are equal when Fashion First produces 9 jumpers a day. The table shows that if output increases from 8 to 9 jumpers, marginal cost is £23, which is less than the marginal revenue of £25. If output increases from 9 to 10 jumpers, marginal cost is £27, which exceeds the marginal revenue of £25. If marginal revenue exceeds marginal cost, an increase in output increases economic profit. If marginal revenue is less than marginal cost, an increase in output decreases economic profit. If marginal revenue equals marginal cost, economic profit is maximized.

 myeconlab Animation

Temporary Shutdown Decision

You've seen that a firm maximizes profit by producing the quantity at which marginal revenue (price) equals marginal cost. But suppose that at this quantity, price is less than average total cost. In this case, the firm incurs an economic loss. Maximum profit is a loss (a minimum loss). What does the firm do?

If the firm expects the loss to be permanent, it goes out of business. But if it expects the loss to be temporary, the firm must decide whether to shut down temporarily and produce no output, or to keep producing. To make this decision, the firm compares the loss from shutting down with the loss from producing and takes the action that minimizes its loss.

Loss Comparisons

A firm's economic loss equals total fixed cost, TFC, plus total variable cost minus total revenue. Total variable cost equals average variable cost, AVC, multiplied by the quantity produced, Q, and total revenue equals price, P, multiplied by the quantity Q. So

$$\text{Economic loss} = TFC + (AVC - P) \times Q.$$

If the firm shuts down, it produces no output ($Q = 0$). The firm has no variable costs and no revenue, but it must pay its fixed costs, so its economic loss equals total fixed cost.

If the firm produces, then in addition to its fixed costs, it incurs variable costs. But it also receives revenue. Its economic loss equals total fixed cost – the loss when shut down – plus total variable cost minus total revenue. If total variable cost exceeds total revenue, this loss exceeds total fixed cost and the firm shuts down. Equivalently, if average variable cost *exceeds* price, this loss exceeds total fixed cost and the firm *shuts down*.

The Shutdown Point

A firm's **shutdown point** is the price and quantity at which it is indifferent between producing and shutting down. The shutdown point occurs at the price and the quantity at which average variable cost is a minimum. At the shutdown point, the firm is minimizing its loss and its loss equals total fixed cost. If the price falls below minimum average variable cost, the firm shuts down temporarily and incurs a loss equal to total fixed cost. At prices above minimum average variable cost but below average total cost, the firm produces the loss-minimizing output and incurs a loss that is less than total fixed cost.

Figure 11.4 illustrates the firm's shutdown decision and the shutdown point that we've just described for Fashion First.

The firm's average variable cost curve is AVC and the marginal cost curve is MC. Average variable cost has a minimum of £17 a jumper when output is 7 jumpers a day. The MC curve intersects the AVC curve at its minimum. (We explained this relationship between marginal cost and average cost in Chapter 10; see p. 228.)

The figure shows the marginal revenue curve MR when the price is £17 a jumper, a price equal to minimum average variable cost.

Marginal revenue equals marginal cost at 7 jumpers a day, so this quantity maximizes economic profit (minimizes economic loss). The ATC curve shows that the firm's average total cost of producing 7 jumpers a day is £20.14 a jumper. The firm incurs a loss equal to £3.14 a jumper on 7 jumpers a day, so its loss is £22 a day, which equals total fixed cost.

Figure 11.4 The Shutdown Decision

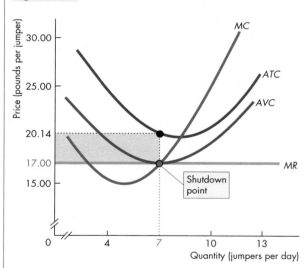

The shutdown point is at minimum average variable cost. At a price below minimum average variable cost, the firm shuts down and produces no output. At a price equal to minimum average variable cost, the firm is indifferent between shutting down and producing no output or producing the output at minimum average variable cost. Either way, the firm minimizes its economic loss. The area of the red rectangle shows that at the shutdown point the economic loss equals total fixed cost.

myeconlab Animation

The Firm's Short-run Supply Curve

A perfectly competitive firm's supply curve shows how its profit-maximizing output varies as the market price varies, other things remaining the same. The supply curve is derived from the firm's marginal cost curve and average variable cost curves. Figure 11.5 illustrates the derivation of the supply curve.

When the price *exceeds* minimum average variable cost (more than £17), the firm maximizes profit by producing the output at which marginal cost equals price. If the price rises, the firm increases its output – it moves up along its marginal cost curve.

When the price is *less* than minimum average variable cost (less than £17 a jumper), the firm maximizes profit by temporarily shutting down and producing no output. The firm produces zero output at all prices below minimum average variable cost.

When the price *equals* minimum average variable cost, the firm maximizes profit either by temporarily shutting down and producing no output or by producing the output at which average variable cost is a minimum – the shutdown point, T. The firm never produces a quantity between zero and the quantity at the shutdown point T (a quantity greater than zero and less than 7 jumpers a day).

The firm's supply curve in Figure 11.5(b) runs along the y-axis from a price of zero to a price equal to minimum average variable cost, jumps to point T, and then, as the price rises above minimum average variable cost, follows the marginal cost curve.

So far, we've studied a single firm in isolation. We've seen that the firm's profit-maximizing decision depends on the market price, which it takes as given. How is the market price determined? Let's find out.

Figure 11.5   A Firm's Supply Curve

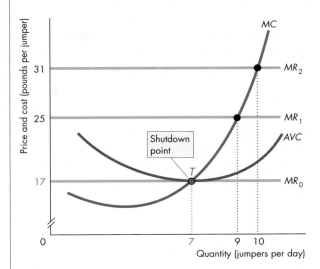

(a) Marginal cost and average variable cost

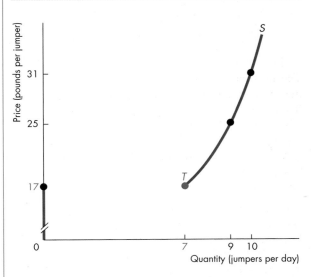

(b) Fashion First's supply curve

Part (a) shows Fashion First's profit-maximizing output at each market price. At £25 a jumper, Fashion First produces 9 jumpers. At £17 a jumper, Fashion First produces 7 jumpers. At any price below £17 a jumper, Fashion First produces nothing. Fashion First's shutdown point is T.

Part (b) shows Fashion First's supply curve – the quantity of jumpers it will produce at each price. It is made up of the marginal cost curve at all points above minimum average variable cost and the y-axis at all prices below minimum average variable cost.

 Animation

Output, Price and Profit in the Short Run

To determine the price and quantity in a perfectly competitive market, we need to know how market demand and market supply interact. We start by studying a perfectly competitive market in the short run. The short run is a situation in which the number of firms is fixed.

Market Supply in the Short Run

The **short-run market supply curve** shows the quantity supplied by all the firms in the market at each price when each firm's plant and the number of firms in the market remain the same.

You've seen how an individual firm's supply curve is determined. The market supply curve is derived from the supply curves of all the individual firms. The quantity supplied by the market at a given price is the sum of the quantities supplied by all the firms in the market at that price.

Figure 11.6 shows the supply curve for the competitive jumper industry. In this example, the industry consists of 1,000 firms exactly like Fashion First. At each price, the quantity supplied by the industry is 1,000 times the quantity supplied by a single firm.

The table in Figure 11.6 shows Fashion First's and the market's supply schedules and how the market supply curve is constructed. At prices below £17 a jumper, every firm in the market shuts down and produces nothing. The quantity supplied by the market is zero. At a price of £17 a jumper, each firm is indifferent between shutting down and producing nothing or producing 7 jumpers a day. Some firms will shut down and others will produce 7 jumpers a day. The quantity supplied by each firm is *either* 0 or 7 jumpers, but the quantity supplied by the market is *between* 0 (all firms shut down) and 7,000 (all firms produce 7 jumpers a day each).

The market supply curve is a graph of the market supply schedule and the points A to D on the supply curve represent the rows of the table.

To construct the market supply curve, we sum the quantities supplied by all firms at each price. Each of the 1,000 firms in the market has a supply schedule like Fashion First's.

At prices below £17 a jumper, the market supply curve runs along the y-axis. At a price of £17 a jumper, the market supply curve is horizontal – supply is perfectly elastic. As the price rises above £17 a jumper,

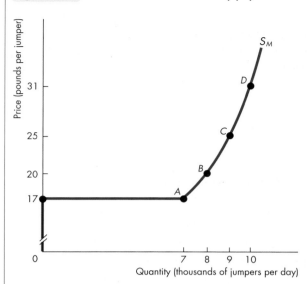

Figure 11.6   Short-run Market Supply Curve

	Price (pounds per jumper)	Quantity supplied by Fashion First (jumpers per day)	Quantity supplied by market (jumpers per day)
A	17	0 or 7	0 to 7,000
B	20	8	8,000
C	25	9	9,000
D	31	10	10,000

The market supply schedule is the sum of the supply schedules of all individual firms. A market that consists of 1,000 identical firms has a supply schedule similar to that of the individual firm, but the quantity supplied by the market is 1,000 times as large as that of the individual firm (see the table).

The market supply curve is S_M. Points A, B, C and D correspond to the rows of the table. At the shutdown price of £17, each firm produces either 0 or 7 jumpers per day. The market produces between 0 and 7,000 jumpers a day. The market supply is perfectly elastic at the shutdown price.

myeconlab Animation

each firm increases its quantity supplied and the quantity supplied by the market increases by 1,000 times that of an individual firm. Figure 11.6 shows the market supply curve S_M.

Short-run Equilibrium

Market demand and market supply determine market price and market output. Figure 11.7 shows the short-run equilibrium. The short-run supply curve, S, is the same as S_M in Figure 11.6. If the market demand curve is D_1, the equilibrium price is £20 a jumper. Each firm takes this price as given and produces its profit-maximizing output, which is 8 jumpers a day. Because the market has 1,000 firms, the market output is 8,000 jumpers a day.

A Change in Demand

Changes in market demand bring changes to short-run market equilibrium. Figure 11.7 shows these changes.

If the market demand increases and the demand curve shifts rightward to D_2, the price rises to £25 a jumper. At this price, each firm maximizes profit by increasing its output. The new output is 9 jumpers a day for each firm and 9,000 jumpers a day for the industry.

If demand decreases and the demand curve shifts leftward to D_3, the price falls to £17. At this price, each firm maximizes profit by decreasing its output. If each firm produces 7 jumpers a day, the market output decreases to 7,000 jumpers a day.

If the demand curve shifts further leftward than D_3, the market price remains constant at £17 because the market supply curve is horizontal at that price. Some firms continue to produce 7 jumpers a day and others temporarily shut down. Firms are indifferent between these two activities, and whichever they choose, they incur an economic loss equal to total fixed cost. The number of firms continuing to produce is just enough to satisfy the market demand at a price of £17 a jumper.

Profits and Losses in the Short Run

In short-run equilibrium, although the firm produces the profit-maximizing output, it does not necessarily end up making an economic profit. It might do so, but it might alternatively break even (make zero economic profit) or incur an economic loss.

Economic profit (or loss) per jumper is price, P, minus average total cost, ATC. So the firm's economic profit (loss) is $(P - ATC) \times Q$. If price equals average

---

Figure 11.7 Short-run Equilibrium

(a) Equilibrium

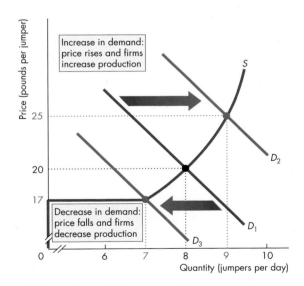

(b) Change in equilibrium

In part (a), the market supply curve is S, the market demand curve is D_1 and the market price is £20 a jumper. At this price, each firm produces 8 jumpers a day and the market produces 8,000 jumpers a day.

In part (b), when the market demand increases to D_2, the price rises to £25. Each firm increases its output to 9 jumpers a day and the market output is 9,000 jumpers a day. If demand decreases to D_3, the price falls to £17 and each firm decreases its output to 7 jumpers a day. The market output is 7,000 jumpers a day.

total cost, a firm breaks even – makes zero economic profit. The entrepreneur makes normal profit. If price exceeds average total cost, a firm makes an economic profit. If price is less than average total cost, the firm incurs an economic loss. Figure 11.8 shows these three possible short-run profit outcomes for Fashion First. These outcomes correspond to the three levels of market demand that we've just examined.

Three Possible Short-run Outcomes

Figure 11.8(a) corresponds to the situation in Figure 11.7(b) where the market demand is D_1. The equilibrium price of a jumper is £20 and Fashion First produces 8 jumpers a day. Average total cost is £20 a jumper. Price equals average total cost (ATC), so Fashion First breaks even (makes zero economic profit).

Figure 11.8(b) corresponds to the situation in Figure 11.7(b) where the market demand is D_2. The equilibrium price of a jumper is £25. Fashion First maximizes profit by producing 9 jumpers a day. Here, price exceeds average total cost, so Fashion First makes an economic profit. Economic profit is £42 a day. It is made up of £4.67 a jumper (£25.00 − £20.33), multiplied by 9, the profit-maximizing number of jumpers produced. The

blue rectangle shows this economic profit. The height of the rectangle is profit per jumper, £4.67, and the length is the quantity of jumpers produced, 9 a day, so the area of the rectangle measures Fashion First's economic profit of £42 a day.

Figure 11.8(c) corresponds to the situation in Figure 11.7(b) where the market demand is D_3. The equilibrium price of a jumper is £17. Here, price is less than average total cost and Fashion First incurs an economic loss. Price and marginal revenue are £17 a jumper, and the profit-maximizing (in this case, loss-minimizing) output is 7 jumpers a day. Total revenue is £119 a day (7 × £17). Fashion First's average total cost is £20.14 a jumper, so its economic loss per jumper is £3.14 (£20.14 − £17.00). Fashion First's economic loss equals this loss per jumper multiplied by the number of jumpers (£3.14 × 7), which equals £22 a day. The red rectangle shows this economic loss. The height of that rectangle is economic loss per jumper, £3.14, and the length is the quantity of jumpers produced, 7 a day, so the area of the rectangle is Fashion First's economic loss of £22 a day. If the price dips below £17 a jumper, the firm temporarily shuts down and incurs an economic loss equal to total fixed cost.

Figure 11.8 Three Short-run Outcomes for the Firm

(a) Break even

(b) Economic profit

(c) Economic loss

In the short run, the firm might break even (make zero economic profit), make an economic profit or incur an economic loss. In part (a), the price equals minimum average total cost. At the profit-maximizing output, the firm breaks even and makes zero economic profit. In part (b), the market price is £25 a jumper. At the profit-

maximizing output, the price exceeds the average total cost and the firm makes an economic profit equal to the area of the blue rectangle. In part (c), the market price is £17 a jumper. At the profit-maximizing output, the price is below minimum average total cost and the firm incurs an economic loss equal to the area of the red rectangle.

Production Cutback and Temporary Shutdown

The high price of petrol and anxiety about unemployment and future incomes brought a decrease in the demand for luxury goods including large luxury cars made by Honda in the UK.

Honda's profit-maximizing response to the decrease in demand was to cut production and lay off workers. Some of the production cuts and layoffs were temporary and some were permanent.

Honda's UK production plant in Swindon was temporarily shut down for four months in 2009 because total revenue was insufficient to cover total variable cost.

The firm also cut its workforce by 1,300 people. This cut was like that at Fashion First when the market demand for jumpers decreased from D_1 to D_3 in Figure 11.7(b).

Review Quiz

1 How do we derive the short-run market supply curve in perfect competition?
2 In perfect competition, when market demand increases, explain how the price of the good and the output and profit of each firm change in the short run.
3 In perfect competition, when market demand decreases, explain how the price of the good and the output and profit of each firm change in the short run.

You can work these questions in Study Plan 11.3 and get instant feedback.

Output, Price and Profit in the Long Run

In short-run equilibrium, a firm might make an economic profit, incur an economic loss or break even. Although each of these three situations is a short-run equilibrium, only one of them is a long-run equilibrium. To see why, we need to examine the forces at work in a competitive market in the long run. The reason is that in the long run, firms can enter or exit the market.

Entry and Exit

Entry occurs in a market when new firms come into the market and the number of firms increases. Exit occurs when existing firms leave a market and the number of firms decreases.

Firms respond to economic profit and economic loss by either entering or exiting a market. New firms enter a market in which existing firms are making an economic profit. Firms exit a market in which they are incurring an economic loss. Temporary economic profit and temporary economic loss don't trigger entry and exit. It's the prospect of persistent economic profit or loss that triggers entry and exit.

Entry and exit change the market supply, which influences the market price, the quantity produced by each firm, and its economic profit (or loss).

If firms enter a market, supply increases and the market supply curve shifts rightward. The increase in supply lowers the market price and eventually eliminates economic profit. When economic profit reaches zero, entry stops.

If firms exit a market, supply decreases and the market supply curve shifts leftward. The market price rises and economic loss decreases. Eventually, economic loss is eliminated and exit stops.

To summarize:

◆ New firms enter a market in which existing firms are making an economic profit.

◆ As new firms enter a market, the market price falls and the economic profit of each firm decreases.

◆ Firms exit a market in which they are incurring an economic loss.

◆ As firms exit a market, the market price rises and the economic loss incurred by the remaining firms decreases.

◆ Entry and exit stop when firms make zero economic profit.

A Closer Look at Entry

The jumper market has 800 firms with cost curves like those in Figure 11.9(a). The market demand curve is D, the market supply curve is S_1, and the price is £25 a jumper in Figure 11.9(b). Each firm produces 9 jumpers a day and makes an economic profit.

This economic profit is a signal for new firms to enter the market. As entry takes place, supply increases and the market supply curve shifts rightward towards S^*. As supply increases with no change in demand, the market price gradually falls from £25 to £20 a jumper. At this lower price, each firm makes zero economic profit and entry stops.

Entry results in an increase in market output, but each firm's output decreases. Because the price falls, each firm moves down its supply curve and produces less. Because the number of firms increases, the market produces more.

A Closer Look at Exit

The jumper market has 1,200 firms with cost curves like those in Figure 11.9(a). The market demand curve is D, the market supply curve is S_2, and the price is £17 a jumper in Figure 11.9(b). Each firm produces 7 jumpers a day and incurs an economic loss.

This economic loss is a signal for firms to exit the market. As exit takes place, supply decreases and the market supply curve shifts leftward towards S^*. As supply decreases with no change in demand, the market price gradually rises from £17 to £20 a jumper. At this higher price, losses are eliminated, each firm makes zero economic profit and exit stops.

Exit results in a decrease in market output, but each firm's output increases. Because the price rises, each firm moves up its supply curve and produces more. Because the number of firms decreases, the market produces less.

Figure 11.9   Entry, Exit and Long-run Equilibrium

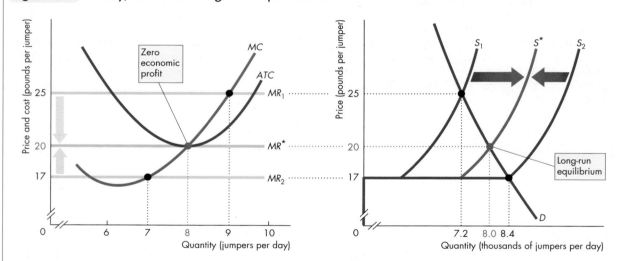

(a) Fashion First

(b) The jumper market

Each firm has cost curves like those of Fashion First in part (a). The market demand curve is D in part (b).

When the market supply curve in part (b) is S_1, the price is £25 a jumper. In part (a), each firm produces 9 jumpers a day and makes an economic profit. Profit triggers the entry of new firms and as new firms enter, the market supply curve shifts rightward, from S_1 towards S^*. The price falls from £25 to £20 a jumper, and the quantity produced increases from 7,200 to 8,000 jumpers. Each

firm's output decreases to 8 jumpers a day and economic profit falls to zero.

When the market supply curve is S_2, the price is £17 a jumper. In part (a), each firm produces 7 jumpers a day and incurs an economic loss. Loss triggers exit and as firms exit, the market supply curve shifts leftward, from S_2 towards S^*. The price rises from £17 to £20 a jumper, and the quantity produced decreases from 8,400 to 8,000 jumpers. Each firm's output increases from 7 to 8 jumpers a day and economic profit rises to zero.

ECONOMICS IN ACTION

Entry and Exit

An example of entry and falling prices occurred during the 1980s and 1990s in the personal computer market. When IBM introduced its first PC in 1981, IBM had little competition. The price was $7,000 (about $16,850 in today's money) and IBM made a large economic profit selling the new machine.

Observing IBM's huge success, new firms such as Gateway, NEC, Dell and a host of others entered the market with machines that were technologically identical to IBM's. In fact, they were so similar that they came to be called 'clones'. The massive wave of entry into the personal computer market increased the market supply and lowered the price. The economic profit for all firms decreased.

Today, a £300 computer is vastly more powerful than its 1981 ancestor that cost 42 times as much. The same PC market that saw entry during the 1980s and 1990s has experienced some exit more recently.

In 2001, IBM, the firm that first launched the PC, announced that it was exiting the market. The intense competition from Gateway, NEC, Dell and others that entered the market following IBM's lead has lowered the price and eliminated the economic profit. So IBM now concentrates on servers and other parts of the computer market.

IBM exited the PC market because it was incurring economic losses. Its exit decreased market supply and made it possible for the remaining firms in the market to make zero economic profit.

Whitbread, which built the first mass brewery in the UK in 1750, is another example of exit. For 250 years, people associated the name Whitbread with brewing beer. But the brewing market became globally competitive, and UK brewing firms suffered economic losses. Whitbread Group plc doesn't make beer any more. After years of shrinking revenues, Whitbread got out of the brewing and pub business in 2001 and is now a profitable hotel and restaurant business with a global coffee brand, Costa Coffee. Whitbread's expansion into its other new business areas increased its profits.

Whitbread exited brewing because it was facing an economic loss. Its exit decreased supply and made it possible for the remaining brewing firms in the market to break even.

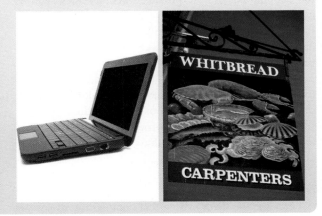

Long-run Equilibrium

You've now seen how economic profit induces entry, which in turn eliminates the profit. You've also seen how economic loss induces exit, which in turn eliminates the loss.

When economic profit and economic loss have been eliminated and entry and exit have stopped, a competitive market is in *long-run equilibrium*.

You've seen how a competitive market adjusts towards its long-run equilibrium. But a competitive market is rarely *in* a state of long-run equilibrium. Instead, it is constantly and restlessly evolving towards long-run equilibrium. The reason is that the market is constantly bombarded with events that change the constraints that firms face.

Markets are constantly adjusting to keep up with changes in tastes, which change demand, and changes in technology, which change costs.

In the next sections, we're going to see how a competitive market reacts to changing tastes and technology and how it guides resources to their highest-valued use.

Review Quiz

1   What triggers entry in a competitive market? Describe the process that ends further entry.
2   What triggers exit in a competitive market? Describe the process that ends further exit.

You can work these questions in Study Plan 11.4 and get instant feedback.

Changing Tastes and Advancing Technology

Increased awareness of the health hazard of smoking has decreased the demand for cigarettes. The development of inexpensive cars and air travel has decreased the demand for long-distance trains and buses. Solid-state electronics have decreased the demand for TV and radio repair services. The development of good-quality inexpensive clothing has decreased the demand for sewing machines. What happens in a competitive market when there is a permanent decrease in the market demand for its products?

Advances in video technology have brought a huge increase in the demand for flat panel TV sets. Advances in wireless communication have brought an explosion in the demand for mobile phones. Web services such as MySpace and YouTube have brought a big increase in the demand for broadband Internet service. What happens in a competitive market if the demand for its product increases?

Advances in technology are constantly lowering the costs of production. New biotechnologies have dramatically lowered the costs of producing many food and pharmaceutical products. New electronic technologies have lowered the cost of producing just about every good and service. What happens in a competitive industry when technological change lowers its production costs?

Let's use the theory of perfect competition to answer these questions.

A Permanent Change in Demand

Figure 11.10(a) shows a market that initially is in long-run competitive equilibrium. The demand curve is D_0, the supply curve is S_0, the market price is P_0 and market output is Q_0. Figure 11.10(b) shows a single firm in this initial long-run equilibrium. The firm produces q_0 and makes zero economic profit.

Now suppose that demand decreases and the demand curve shifts leftward to D_1, as shown in Figure 11.10(a). The market price falls to P_1 and the quantity supplied by the market decreases from Q_0 to Q_1 as the market slides down its short-run supply curve S_0.

Figure 11.10(b) shows the situation facing a firm. Price is now below minimum average total cost so the firm incurs an economic loss. But to keep its loss to a minimum, the firm adjusts its output to keep marginal

cost equal to the market price. At a price of P_1, each firm produces an output of q_1.

The market is now in short-run equilibrium but not long-run equilibrium. It is in short-run equilibrium because each firm is maximizing profit. But it is not in long-run equilibrium because each firm is incurring an economic loss – its average total cost exceeds the market price.

The economic loss is a signal for some firms to exit the market. As they do so, short-run market supply decreases and the supply curve shifts leftward.

As the market supply decreases, the market price rises – as shown by the arrows along the market demand curve D_1 in Figure 11.10(a).

At each higher price, a firm's profit-maximizing output is greater, so the firms remaining in the market increase their output as the price rises. Each firm slides up its marginal cost or supply curve in Figure 11.10(b), as shown by the arrows along the MC curve. That is, as some firms exit the market, the output of the market decreases but the output of each firm that remains in the market increases.

Eventually, enough firms exit the market for the market supply curve to have shifted to S_1 in Figure 11.10(a). At this time, the price has returned to its original level, P_0. At this price, the firms remaining in the market produce q_0 in part (b), the same quantity that they produced before the decrease in the market demand. Because firms are now making zero economic profit, no firm wants to enter or exit the market. The market supply curve remains at S_1, and the market produces Q_2. The market is again in long-run equilibrium.

The difference between the initial long-run equilibrium and the final long-run equilibrium is the number of firms in the market. A permanent decrease in demand has decreased the number of firms. Each remaining firm produces the same output in the new long-run equilibrium as it did initially and makes zero economic profit. In the process of moving from the initial equilibrium to the new one, firms incur economic losses.

We've just worked out how a competitive market responds to a permanent *decrease* in the market demand. A permanent increase in the market demand triggers a similar response, but in the opposite direction. The increase in demand brings a higher market price, increased economic profit and entry. Entry increases the market supply and eventually lowers the price to its original level and economic profit falls to zero.

The demand for Internet services increased permanently during the 1990s and huge profit opportunities

Figure 11.10   A Decrease in Demand

(a) Industry

(b) Firm

A market starts in long-run competitive equilibrium. Part (a) shows the market demand curve D_0, the market supply curve S_0, the equilibrium quantity Q_0 and the market price P_0. Each firm sells at the price P_0, so its marginal revenue curve is MR_0 in part (b). Each firm produces q_0 and makes zero economic profit.

Market demand decreases from D_0 to D_1 in part (a). The market price falls to P_1, each firm decreases its output to q_1 in part (b), and the market output decreases to Q_1 in part (a).

In this situation, firms incur economic losses. Some firms exit the market, and as they do so, the market supply curve gradually shifts leftward, from S_0 to S_1. This shift gradually raises the market price from P_1 back to P_0. While the price is below P_0, firms continue to incur economic losses and more firms exit the market. Once the price has returned to P_0, each firm makes zero economic profit. Firms have no further incentive to exit the market. Each firm produces q_0 and market output is Q_2.

myeconlab Animation

---

arose in this market. The result was a massive rate of entry of Internet service providers. The process of competition and change in the Internet service market is similar to what we have just studied but with an increase in demand rather than a decrease in demand.

We've now studied the effects of a permanent change in demand for a good. In doing so, we began and ended in a long-run equilibrium and examined the process that takes a market from one long-run equilibrium to another. It is this process, not the equilibrium points, that describes the real world.

One feature of the predictions that we have just generated seems odd. In the long run, regardless of whether the change in demand is a permanent increase or a permanent decrease, the market price returns to its original level. Is this outcome inevitable? In fact, it is not. It is possible for the market price in long-run equilibrium to remain the same, rise or fall.

External Economies and Diseconomies

The change in the long-run equilibrium price depends on external economies and external diseconomies. **External economies** are factors beyond the control of an individual firm that lower its costs as *market* output increases. **External diseconomies** are factors outside the control of a firm that raise its costs as *market* output increases. With no external economies or external diseconomies, a firm's costs remain constant as market output changes.

Figure 11.11 illustrates these three cases and introduces a new supply concept, the long-run market supply curve.

A **long-run market supply curve** shows how the quantity supplied by a market varies as the market price varies, after all the possible adjustments have been made, including changes in plant size and changes in the number of firms in the market.

Figure 11.11(a) shows the case we have just studied – no external economies or external diseconomies. The long-run market supply curve (LS_A) is perfectly elastic. In this case, a permanent increase in demand from D_0 to D_1 has no effect on the price in the long run. The increase in demand brings a temporary increase in price to P_S and a short-run quantity increase from Q_0 to Q_S. Entry increases short-run supply from S_0 to S_1, which lowers the price to its original level, P_0, and increases the quantity to Q_1.

Figure 11.11(b) shows the case of external diseconomies. The long-run market supply curve (LS_B) slopes upward. A permanent increase in demand from D_0 to D_1 increases the price in both the short run and the long run. As in the previous case, the increase in demand brings a temporary increase in price to P_S, and a short-run quantity increase from Q_0 to Q_S. Entry increases short-run supply from S_0 to S_2, which lowers the price from P_S to P_2 and increases the quantity to Q_2.

One source of external diseconomies is congestion. The airline market in recent years provides a good illustration. With bigger airline market output, there is more congestion of both airports and airspace, which results in longer delays and extra waiting time for passengers and aircraft. These external diseconomies mean that as the output of air travel services increases (in the absence of technological advances), the airline's average cost increases. As a result, the long-run supply curve is upward-sloping. So a permanent increase in demand brings an increase in quantity and a rise in the price. Technological advances decrease average costs and *shift* the long-run supply curve downward. So even a market that experiences external diseconomies might have falling prices over the long run.

Figure 11.11(c) shows the case of external economies. In this case, the long-run market supply curve (LS_C) slopes downward. A permanent increase in demand from D_0 to D_1 increases the price in the short run and lowers it in the long run. Again, the increase in demand brings a temporary increase in price to P_S and a short-run increase in the quantity from Q_0 to Q_S. Entry increases short-run supply from S_0 to S_3, which lowers the price from P_S to P_3 and increases the quantity to Q_3.

One of the best examples of external economies is the growth of specialist support services for a market as it expands. As farm output increased in the nineteenth

Figure 11.11 Long-run Changes in Price and Quantity

(a) Constant-cost industry

(b) Increasing-cost industry

(c) Decreasing-cost industry

Three possible changes in price and quantity occur in the long run. When demand increases from D_0 to D_1, entry occurs and the market supply curve shifts rightward.

In part (a), the long-run supply curve LS_A is horizontal. The quantity increases from Q_0 to Q_1 and the price remains constant at P_0.

In part (b), the long-run supply curve is LS_B; the price increases to P_2 and the quantity increases to Q_2. This case occurs in industries with external diseconomies.

In part (c), the long-run supply curve is LS_C; the price decreases to P_3 and the quantity increases to Q_3. This case occurs in a market with external economies.

myeconlab Animation

and early twentieth centuries, the services available to farmers expanded and their costs fell. New firms specialized in the development and marketing of farm machinery and fertilizers. As a result, average farm costs decreased. Farms enjoyed the benefits of external economies. As a consequence, as the demand for farm products increased, the output increased but the price fell.

Over the long term, the prices of many goods and services have fallen, not because of external economies but because of technological change. Let's now study this influence on a competitive market.

Technological Change

Industries are constantly discovering lower-cost techniques of production. Most cost-saving production techniques cannot be implemented, however, without investing in new plant and equipment. As a consequence, it takes time for a technological advance to spread through a market. Some firms whose plants are on the verge of being replaced will be quick to adopt the new technology, while other firms whose plants have recently been replaced will continue to operate with an old technology until they can no longer cover their average variable cost. Once average variable cost cannot be covered, a firm will scrap even a relatively new plant (embodying an old technology) in favour of a plant with a new technology.

New technology allows firms to produce at a lower cost. As a result, as firms adopt a new technology, their average total cost and marginal cost fall and the *ATC* and *MC* curves shift downward. With lower costs, firms are willing to supply a given quantity at a lower price or, equivalently, they are willing to supply a larger quantity at a given price. In other words, the market supply increases and the market supply curve shifts rightward. With a given demand, the quantity produced increases and the price falls.

Two forces are at work in a market undergoing technological change. Firms that adopt the new technology make an economic profit, so there is entry by new-technology firms. Firms that stick with the old technology incur economic losses; they either exit the market or switch to the new technology.

As old-technology firms disappear and new-technology firms enter, the price falls and the quantity produced increases. Eventually, the market arrives at a long-run equilibrium in which all the firms use the new technology and make zero economic profit. Because in the long run, competition eliminates economic profit,

technological change brings only temporary gains to producers. But the lower prices and better products that technological advances bring are permanent gains for consumers.

The process that we've just described is one in which some firms experience economic profits and others experience economic losses. It is a period of dynamic change for a market. Some firms do well, and others do badly. Often, the process has a geographical dimension – the expanding new-technology firms bring prosperity to what was once a backwater and traditional industrial regions decline. Sometimes, the new-technology firms are in another country, while the old-technology firms are in the domestic economy.

The information revolution of the 1990s produced many examples of changes like these. Commercial banking, which was traditionally concentrated in large cities such as London and Frankfurt, has decentralized with data processing centres in small Yorkshire towns. Scotland's 'silicon glen' has displaced traditional agricultural production.

Technological advances are not confined to the information market. Even in the agricultural sector, bio-technological advances are revolutionizing milk and crop production.

Review Quiz

1 Describe the course of events in a competitive market following a permanent decrease in the market demand. What happens to output, market price and economic profit in the short run and in the long run?

2 Describe the course of events in a competitive market following a permanent increase in the market demand. What happens to output, market price and economic profit in the short run and in the long run?

3 Describe the course of events in a competitive market following the adoption of a new technology. What happens to output, market price and economic profit in the short run and in the long run?

You can work these questions in Study Plan 11.5 and get instant feedback.

We've seen how a competitive market works in the short run and the long run. But does a competitive market achieve an efficient use of resources?

Competition and Efficiency

A competitive market can achieve an efficient use of resources. You first studied efficiency in Chapter 2. Then in Chapter 5, using only the concepts of demand, supply, consumer surplus and producer surplus, you saw how a competitive market achieves efficiency. Now that you have learned what lies behind demand and supply curves in a competitive market, you can gain a deeper understanding of the efficiency of a competitive market.

Efficient Use of Resources

Resource use is efficient when we produce the goods and services that people value most highly (see Chapter 2, pp. 35–37 and Chapter 5, p. 112). If someone can become better off without anyone else becoming worse off, resources are *not* being used efficiently. For example, suppose we produce a computer that no one wants and no one will ever use and, at the same time, some people are clamouring for more video games. If we produce one less computer and reallocate the unused resources to produce more video games, some people will become better off and no one will be worse off. So the initial resource allocation was inefficient.

In the more technical language that you have learned, resource use is efficient when marginal social benefit equals marginal social cost. In the computer and video games example, the marginal social benefit of a video game exceeds its marginal social cost. And the marginal social cost of a computer exceeds its marginal social benefit. So by producing fewer computers and more video games, we move resources towards a higher-valued use.

Choices, Equilibrium and Efficiency

We can use what you have learned about the decisions made by consumers and competitive firms and market equilibrium to describe an efficient use of resources.

Choices

Consumers allocate their budgets to get the most value possible out of them. We derive a consumer's demand curve by finding how the best budget allocation changes as the price of a good changes. So consumers get the most value out of their resources at all points along their demand curves. If the people who consume a good or service are the only ones who benefit from it, then the market demand curve measures the benefit to the entire society and is the marginal social benefit curve.

Competitive firms produce the quantity that maximizes profit. We derive the firm's supply curve by finding the profit-maximizing quantity at each price. So firms get the most value out of their resources at all points along their supply curves. If the firms that produce a good or service bear all the costs of producing it, then the market supply curve measures the marginal cost to the entire society and the market supply curve is the marginal social cost curve.

Equilibrium and Efficiency

Resources are used efficiently when marginal social benefit equals marginal social cost. Competitive equilibrium achieves this efficient outcome because, with no externalities, price equals marginal social benefit for consumers and price equals marginal social cost for producers.

The gains from trade are the consumer surplus plus the producer surplus. The gains from trade for consumers are measured by *consumer surplus*, which is the area below the demand curve and above the price paid (see Chapter 5, p. 109). The gains from trade for producers are measured by *producer surplus*, which is the area above the supply curve and below the price received (see Chapter 5, p. 111). The total gains from trade are the sum of consumer surplus and producer surplus. When the market for a good or service is in equilibrium, the gains from trade are maximized.

Illustrating an Efficient Allocation

Figure 11.12 illustrates an efficient allocation in perfect competition in long-run equilibrium. Part (a) shows the situation of an individual firm, and part (b) shows the market. The equilibrium market price is P^*. At that price, each firm makes zero economic profit. Each firm has the plant that enables it to produce at the lowest possible average total cost. Consumers are as well off as possible because the good cannot be produced at a lower cost and the price equals that least possible cost.

In part (b), consumers get the most out of their resources at all points on the market demand curve, $D = MSB$. Consumer surplus is the green area. Producers get the most out of their resources at all points on the market supply curve, $S = MSC$. Producer surplus is the blue area. Resources are used efficiently at the quantity Q^* and price P^*. At this point, marginal social benefit

Figure 11.12 Efficiency of Perfect Competition

(a) A single firm

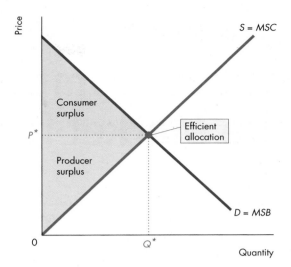

(b) A market

Demand, *D*, and supply, *S*, determine the equilibrium price, *P**. A firm in perfect competition in part (a) produces *q** at the lowest possible long-run average total cost.

In part (b), consumers have made the best available choices and are on the market demand curve, and firms

are producing at least cost and are on the market supply curve. With no externalities, marginal social benefit equals marginal social cost, so resources are used efficiently at the quantity *Q**.

myeconlab Animation

---

equals marginal social cost, and total surplus (the sum of producer surplus and consumer surplus) is maximized.

When firms in perfect competition are away from long-run equilibrium, either entry into the market or exit from the market is taking place and the market is moving towards the situation depicted in Figure 11.12. But the competitive market is still efficient. As long as marginal social benefit (on the market demand curve) equals marginal social cost (on the market supply curve), the market is efficient. But it is only in long-run equilibrium that consumers pay the lowest possible price.

You've now completed your study of perfect competition. *Reading Between the Lines* on pp. 268–269 gives you an opportunity to use what you have learned to understand recent events in the competitive market for Kenyan tea.

Although many markets approximate the model of perfect competition, many do not. In Chapter 12, we study markets at the opposite extreme of market power:

monopoly. Then we study markets that lie between perfect competition and monopoly. In Chapter 13, we study monopolistic competition and in Chapter 14, we study oligopoly. When you have completed this study, you'll have a tool kit that will enable you to understand the variety of real-world markets.

Review Quiz

1 State the conditions that must be met for resources to be allocated efficiently.
2 Describe the choices that consumers make and explain why consumers are efficient on the market demand curve.
3 Describe the choices that producers make and explain why producers are efficient on the market supply curve.
4 Explain why resources are used efficiently in a competitive market.

You can work these questions in Study Plan 11.6 and get instant feedback.

Reading Between the Lines

Perfect Competition: The Market for Kenyan Tea

Reuters, 22 October 2010

Kenyan Tea Growers say Strike has Little Impact

Mark Denge

A week-long strike by some workers in Kenyan tea farms is unlikely to affect auction prices and export volumes. . . .

On Monday . . . workers in the east Africa nation's tea farms went on strike over the use of tea plucking machines which they claimed could cost them their jobs.

Tea Board of Kenya (TBK) Managing Director Sicily Kariuki said . . . 'The small-holder sub-sector, which accounts for about 60 per cent of the total production and is the largest supplier of tea to the auction, is operating without interruptions.'

A bulk of Kenya's tea is produced by Kenya Tea Development Agency (KTDA) that caters for the more than 500,000 smallholder farmers. The agency manages 65 tea factories spread across tea growing zones in the country.

The average price for Kenya's top tea rose slightly to $3.49 per kg at this week's auction from $3.31 per kg last week, while volumes offered were also up.

'The decision of using machines for the picking or not, is purely a business decision motivated by . . . cost-efficiency.' (Kariuki said) . . .

Projected production volumes for 2010 will go beyond the 350 million kg mark . . . output in 2009 was about 315 million kg. . . . Output rose . . . driven by good rains and strong demand from the Indian and Chinese markets.

The Essence of the Story

◆ Some Kenyan tea farm workers are on strike over the introduction of tea plucking machines.

◆ The machines are being introduced to lower costs.

◆ The strike has not affected the bulk of Kenyan tea picked on 500,000 small farms and so will have little effect.

◆ With good harvests and strong world demand, 2010 will be a good year for Kenyan tea farmers. Both the market price and output are rising.

Economic Analysis

- The market for Kenyan tea is an example of perfect competition. Kenyan tea is sold at auction and growers are price takers.

- In 2010, Kenya produced about 350 million kg of tea, of which 210 million kg (60 per cent) was from small farms. So each month, 29 million kg of tea was produced and on average, a small farm produced 35 kg.

- Figure 1 shows the market for Kenyan tea in October 2010. Demand is D_0 and supply is S. The market price is $3.31 per kg and market quantity is 29 million kg.

- An increase in world demand shifts the demand curve rightward to D_1. The market price rises to $3.49 per kg and the market quantity increases to 31 million kg.

- Figure 2 shows the response of a small tea farm where marginal cost is MC and average total cost is ATC. At a price of $3.31 per kg, marginal revenue is MR_0 and the farm maximizes profit by producing 35 kg. Economic profit is zero in a long-run equilibrium.

- The rise in price to $3.49 per kg increases marginal revenue to MR_1, so each small farm increases output to 37 kg a month and makes an economic profit.

- Figure 3 shows the long-run effects of introducing tea plucking machines. As more and more large tea farms become mechanized, their marginal cost falls and market supply increases.

- In the long run, holding demand constant at D_1, the expansion of large farms increases supply. The price falls and the quantity demanded increases further. On the small farm in Figure 2, production returns to 35 kg per month and economic profit returns to zero.

- If mechanization drives the price below $3.31 per kg, some small farmers go out of business and exit the market.

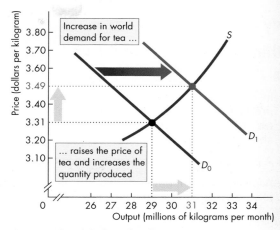

Figure 1 **The global market for Kenyan tea in the short run**

Figure 2 **Output decisions on a small Kenyan tea farm**

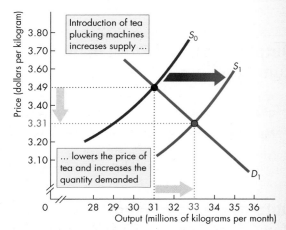

Figure 3 **The global market for Kenyan tea in the long run**

Key Points

What Is Perfect Competition?
(pp. 250–251)

◆ In perfect competition, many firms sell identical products to many buyers; there are no restrictions on entry; sellers and buyers are well informed about prices.

◆ A perfectly competitive firm is a price taker.

◆ A perfectly competitive firm's marginal revenue always equals the market price.

Working Problems 1 to 3 will give you a better understanding of perfect competition.

The Firm's Output Decision (pp. 252–255)

◆ The firm produces the output at which marginal revenue (price) equals marginal cost.

◆ In short-run equilibrium, a firm can make an economic profit, incur an economic loss or break even.

◆ If price is less than minimum average variable cost, the firm temporarily shuts down.

◆ At prices below minimum average variable cost, a firm's supply curve runs along the y-axis; at prices above minimum average variable cost, a firm's supply curve is its marginal cost curve.

Working Problems 4 to 7 will give you a better understanding of a firm's output decision.

Output, Price and Profit in the Short Run (pp. 256–259)

◆ A market supply curve shows the sum of the quantities supplied by each firm at each price.

◆ Market demand and market supply determine price.

Working Problems 8 and 9 will give you a better understanding of output, price and profit in the short run.

Output, Price and Profit in the Long Run (pp. 259–261)

◆ Economic profit induces entry and economic loss induces exit.

◆ Entry increases supply and lowers the market price and economic profit. Exit decreases supply and raises the market price and economic profit.

◆ In long-run equilibrium, economic profit is zero. There is no entry or exit.

Working Problems 10 and 11 will give you a better understanding of output, price and profit in the long run.

Changing Tastes and Advancing Technology (pp. 262–265)

◆ A permanent decrease in demand leads to a smaller market output and a smaller number of firms. A permanent increase in the demand leads to a larger market output and a larger number of firms.

◆ The long-run effect of a change in demand on market price depends on whether there are external economies (the price falls), external diseconomies (the price rises) or neither (the price remains constant).

◆ New technologies increase supply and in the long run lower the price and increase the quantity.

Working Problems 12 to 16 will give you a better understanding of changing tastes and advancing technologies.

Competition and Efficiency
(pp. 266–267)

◆ Resources are used efficiently when we produce goods and services in the quantities that everyone values most highly.

◆ Perfect competition achieves an efficient allocation. In long-run equilibrium, consumers pay the lowest possible price and marginal social benefit equals marginal social cost.

Key Terms

External diseconomies, 263
External economies, 263
Long-run market supply curve, 263
Marginal revenue, 250
Perfect competition, 250
Price taker, 250
Short-run market supply curve, 256
Shutdown point, 254
Total revenue, 250

STUDY PLAN PROBLEMS AND APPLICATIONS

myeconlab   You can work Problems 1 to 18 in MyEconLab Chapter 11 Study Plan and get instant feedback.

What Is Perfect Competition?
(Study Plan 11.1)

Use the following information to work Problems 1 to 3.

Leo's makes amaretto biscuits that are identical to those made by dozens of other firms, and there is free entry in the amaretto biscuit market. Buyers and sellers are well informed about prices.

1 In what type of market does Leo's operate? What determines the price of amaretto biscuits and what determines Leo's marginal revenue?

2 **a** If amaretto biscuits sell for €10 a box and Leo offers his biscuits for sale at €10.50 a box, how many boxes does he sell?

  b If amaretto biscuits sell for €10 a box and Leo offers his biscuit for sale at €9.50 a box, how many boxes does he sell?

3 What is the elasticity of demand for Leo's amaretto biscuits and how does it differ from the elasticity of the market demand for amaretto biscuits?

The Firm's Output Decision
(Study Plan 11.2)

Use the following information to work Problems 4 to 6.

Pat's Pizza Restaurant is a price taker and its costs are:

Output (pizzas per hour)	Total cost (euros per hour)
0	10
1	21
2	30
3	41
4	54
5	69

4 What is Pat's profit-maximizing output and economic profit if the market price is (i) €14 a pizza, (ii) €12 a pizza and (iii) €10 a pizza?

5 What is Pat's shutdown point and what is its economic profit if it shuts down temporarily?

6 Derive Pat's supply curve.

7 The market for paper is perfectly competitive and there are 1,000 firms that produce paper. The table in the next column sets out the market demand schedule for paper.

Price (euros per box)	Quantity demanded (thousands of boxes per week)
3.65	500
5.20	450
6.80	400
8.40	350
10.00	300
11.60	250
13.20	200

Each paper producer has the same costs when it uses its least-cost plant. The following table sets out those costs.

Output (boxes per week)	Marginal cost	Average variable cost	Average total cost
	(euros per box)		
200	4.60	7.80	11.80
250	7.00	7.00	11.00
300	7.65	7.10	10.43
350	8.40	7.20	10.06
400	10.00	7.50	10.00
450	12.40	8.00	10.22
500	20.70	9.00	11.00

  a What is the market price?
  b What is the market's output?
  c What is the output produced by each firm?
  d What is the economic profit made or economic loss incurred by each firm?

Output, Price and Profit in the Short Run (Study Plan 11.3)

8 In Problem 7, as more and more computer users read documents online rather than print them out, the market demand for paper decreases and in the short run the demand schedule becomes:

Price (euros per box)	Quantity demanded (thousands of boxes per week)
2.95	500
4.13	450
5.30	400
6.48	350
7.65	300
8.83	250
10.00	200
11.18	150

If each paper producer has the costs set out in Problem 7, what is the market price and the economic profit or loss of each firm in the short run?

9 British Airways Ups Fuel Surcharges

British Airways announced it would increase the fuel surcharge on all its flights starting on June 3, the third hike since the start of the year. On long-haul flights of more than 9 hours the fuel surcharge will rise by £30 to £109 per flight, whereas on short haul flights it will increase by £3 to £16.

Source: Forbes.com, 29 May 2008

a Explain how an increase in fuel prices might cause an airline to change its output (number of flights) in the short run.

b Draw a graph to show the increase in fuel prices on an airline's output in the short run.

c Explain why an airline might incur an economic loss in the short run as fuel prices rise.

Output, Price and Profit in the Long Run (Study Plan 11.4)

10 The pizza market is perfectly competitive, and all pizza producers have the same costs as Pat's Pizza Restaurant in Problem 4.

a At what price will some firms exit the pizza market in the long run?

b At what price will firms enter the pizza market in the long run?

11 In Problem 7, in the long run,

a Do firms have an incentive to enter or exit the paper market?

b If firms do enter or exit the market, explain how the economic profit or loss of the remaining paper producers will change.

c What is the long-run equilibrium market price and the quantity of paper produced? What is the number of firms in the market?

Changing Tastes and Advancing Technology (Study Plan 11.5)

12 If in the long run, the market demand for paper remains the same as in Problem 8,

a What is the long-run equilibrium price of paper, the market output, and the economic profit or loss of each firm?

b Does this market experience external economies, external diseconomies, or constant cost? Illustrate by drawing the long-run supply curve.

Use the following news clip to work Problems 13 and 14.

Coors Brewing Expanding Plant

Coors Brewing Company will expand its Virginia packaging plant at a cost of $24 million. The addition will accommodate a new production line, which will bottle beer faster. Coors Brewing employs 470 people at its Virginia plant. The expanded packaging line will add another eight jobs.

Source: Denver Business Journal, 6 January 2006

13 a How will Coors' expansion change its marginal cost curve and short-run supply curve?

b What does this expansion decision imply about the point on Coors' *LRAC* curve at which the firm was before the expansion?

14 a If other breweries follow the lead of Coors, what will happen to the market price of beer?

b How will the adjustment that you have described in part (a) influence the economic profit of Coors and other beer producers?

15 Explain and illustrate graphically how the growing world population is influencing the world market for wheat and a representative individual wheat farmer.

16 Explain and illustrate graphically how the nappy service market has been affected by the decrease in the birth rate and the development of disposable nappies.

Competition and Effiency (Study Plan 11.6)

17 In a perfectly competitive market in long-run equilibrium, can consumer surplus be increased? Can producer surplus be increased? Can a consumer become better off by making a substitution away from this market?

18 Never Pay Retail Again

Not only has scouring the Web for the best possible price become standard protocol before buying a big-ticket item, but more consumers are employing creative strategies for scoring hot deals. Comparison shopping and haggling are all becoming mainstream marks of savvy shoppers. Online shoppers can check a comparison service like Price Grabber before making a purchase.

Source: CNN, 30 May 2008

a Explain the effect of the Internet on the degree of competition in the market.

b Explain how the Internet influences market efficiency.

You can work these problems in MyEconLab if assigned by your lecturer.

What Is Perfect Competition?

Use the following information to work Problems 19 to 21.

Two service stations stand on opposite sides of the road: Rutter's and Sheetz's. Rutter's doesn't even have to look across the road to know when Sheetz's changes its petrol price. When Sheetz's raises the price, Rutter's pumps are busy. When Sheetz's lowers prices, there's not a car in sight. Both service stations survive but each has no control over the price.

19 In what type of market do these service stations operate? What determines the price of petrol and what determines the marginal revenue from petrol?

20 Describe the elasticity of demand for petrol that each of these service stations faces.

21 Why does each of these service stations have so little control over the price of the petrol it sells?

The Firm's Output Decision

22 The figure shows the costs of Quick Copy, one of the many copy shops in London.

If the market price of copying one page is 10 pence, calculate Quick Copy's

a Profit-maximizing output.

b Economic profit.

23 The market for smoothies is perfectly competitive and the table in the next column sets out the market demand for smoothies.

Price (euros per smoothie)	Quantity demanded (smoothies per hour)
1.90	1,000
2.00	950
2.20	800
2.91	700
4.25	550
5.25	400
5.50	300

Each of the 100 producers of smoothies has the following costs when it uses its least-cost plant.

Output (smoothies per hour)	Marginal cost	Average variable cost	Average total cost
	(euros per smoothie)		
3	2.50	4.00	7.33
4	2.20	3.53	6.03
5	1.90	3.24	5.24
6	2.00	3.00	4.67
7	2.91	2.91	4.34
8	4.25	3.00	4.25
9	8.00	3.33	4.44

a What is the market price of a smoothie?

b What is the market output?

c How many smoothies does each firm sell?

d What is the economic profit made or economic loss incurred by each firm?

24 **Honda Workers Return after Four Month Shutdown**

Honda shut down its UK Swindon car plant for four months in 2009, cutting annual production by 50 per cent to 11,300 vehicles and shedding 1,300 workers through voluntary redundancies. Workers were paid 2 months full pay and 2 months on 60 per cent of pay during the shutdown.

Source: Independent online, 17 February 2009

a Explain how the shutdown decision will affect the company's *TFC*, *TVC* and *TC*.

b Under what conditions would this shutdown decision maximize the company's economic profit (or minimize its loss)?

c Under what conditions did Honda start producing again?

25 Mini Announces 850 Lay-offs

Mini announced 850 redundancies at the Cowley car plant in Oxfordshire. The company is blaming 'volatile market conditions' for the need to change from three shifts a day to two shifts a day, which means closing production altogether at weekends.

Source: *The Independent*, 17 February 2009

Explain why 'volatile market conditions' created a situation in which Mini's profit-maximizing decision was to switch from three to two shifts.

Output, Price and Profit in the Short Run

26 Wheat Prices Down 40 per cent from Peak

Wheat prices in April have fallen more than 40 per cent from their peak in February. Farmers planted more wheat as prices increased and this year's harvest may be a record crop.

Source: BBC online, 25 April 2008

Why did wheat prices fall in 2008? Draw a graph to show that short-run effect on an individual farmer's economic profit.

Output, Price and Profit in the Long Run

27 In Problem 23, do firms enter or exit the market in the long run? What is the market price and the equilibrium quantity in the long run?

28 In Problem 24, under what conditions will Honda exit the car market?

Changing Tastes and Advancing Technology

29 Another DVD Format, but It's Cheaper

New Medium Enterprises claims the quality of its new system, HD VMD, is equal to Blu-ray's but it costs only $199 – cheaper than the $300 cost of a Blu-ray player. Chairman of the Blu-ray Disc Association says New Medium will fail because it believes that Blu-ray technology will always be more expensive. But mass production will cut the cost of a Blu-ray player to $90.

Source: *The New York Times*, 10 March 2008

a Explain how technological change in Blu-ray production might lead to lower prices in the long run. Illustrate your explanation with a graph.

b Even if Blu-ray prices do drop to $90 in the long run, why might the HD VMD still end up being less expensive at that time?

Competition and Efficiency

30 In a perfectly competitive market, each firm maximizes its profit by choosing only the quantity to produce. Regardless of whether the firm makes an economic profit or incurs an economic loss, the short-run equilibrium is efficient. Is the statement true? Explain why or why not.

Economics in the News

31 After you have studied *Reading Between the Lines* on pp. 268–269 answer the following questions.

a What are the features of the global market for Kenyan tea that make it competitive?

b Given that the strike was not expected to affect price or quantity to any great extent, why did the market price and quantity of Kenyan tea rise?

c If the market price were to fall below $3 a kilogram, what would happen to an individual small tea farmer's marginal revenue, marginal cost, average total cost, and economic profit?

d If large tea farms are successful in introducing mechanized picking, what is likely to happen to the marginal cost, average total cost and economic profit of a large tea farm?

32 Mobile Phone Sales Hit 1 Billion Mark

More than 1.15 billion mobile phones were sold worldwide in 2007, a 16 per cent increase in a year. Emerging markets, especially China and India, provided much of the growth as many people bought their first phone. In mature markets, such as Japan and Western Europe, consumers' appetite for feature-laden phones was met with new models packed with TV tuners, touch screens and cameras.

Source: CNET News, 27 February 2008

a Explain the effects of the increase in global demand for mobile phones on the market for mobile phones and on an individual mobile phone producer in the short run.

b Draw a graph to illustrate your answer in part (a).

c Explain the long-run effects of the increase in global demand for mobile phones on the market for mobile phones.

d What factors will determine whether the price of a mobile phone will rise, fall, or stay the same in the new long-run equilibrium?

CHAPTER
12

Monopoly

After studying this chapter you will be able to:

◆ Explain how monopoly arises and distinguish between single-price and price-discriminating monopolies

◆ Explain how a single-price monopoly determines its output and price

◆ Compare the performance and efficiency of single-price monopoly and competition

◆ Explain how a price-discriminating monopoly increases profit

◆ Explain the effects of monopoly regulation

Google, Microsoft and eBay are dominant players in the markets they serve. They are obviously not like firms in perfect competition. How do firms like these behave? How do they choose the quantities to produce and the prices to charge? How does their behaviour compare with perfectly competitive firms? Do they charge too much and produce too little? Would more competition among search engines or satellite broadcasters bring greater efficiency? Find out in this chapter.

Reading Between the Lines, at the end of the chapter, looks at whether Google may have abused its market power in Europe.

Monopoly and How It Arises

A **monopoly** is a market with a single firm that produces a good or service for which no close substitute exists and which is protected by a barrier that prevents other firms from selling that good or service.

How Monopoly Arises

Monopoly has two key features:

◆ No close substitute
◆ Barriers to entry

No Close Substitute

If a good has a close substitute, even though only one firm produces it, that firm effectively faces competition from the producer of the substitute. A monopoly sells a good or service that has no good close substitute. Water supplied by a local water board and bottled spring water are close substitutes for drinking, but not for showering or washing a car. A local water board is a monopoly.

Barriers to Entry

A constraint that protects a firm from potential competitors is called a **barrier to entry**. Three types of barrier to entry are

◆ Natural
◆ Ownership
◆ Legal

Natural Barriers to Entry
Natural barriers to entry create **natural monopoly**, a market in which economies of scale enable one firm to supply the entire market at the lowest possible cost.

In Figure 12.1, the market demand curve for electric power is *D*, and the long-run average cost curve is *LRAC*. Economies of scale prevail over the entire length of the *LRAC* curve.

One firm can produce 4 million kilowatt-hours at 5 pence a kilowatt-hour. At this price, the quantity demanded is 4 million kilowatt-hours. So if the price were 5 pence, one firm could supply the entire market. If two firms shared the market, it would cost each of them 10 pence a kilowatt-hour to produce a total of 4 million kilowatt-hours. In conditions like those shown in Figure 12.1, one firm can supply the entire market at

Figure 12.1 Natural Monopoly

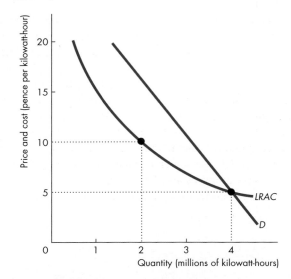

The market demand curve for electric power is *D*, and the long-run average cost curve is *LRAC*. Economies of scale exist over the entire *LRAC* curve. One firm can distribute 4 million kilowatt-hours at a cost of 5 pence a kilowatt-hour. This same total output costs 10 pence a kilowatt-hour with two firms. So one firm can meet the market demand at a lower cost than two or more firms can, and the market is a natural monopoly.

 myeconlab Animation

a lower cost than two or more firms can. The market is a natural monopoly.

Ownership Barriers to Entry
An ownership barrier to entry occurs if one firm owns a significant portion of a resource. An example of this type of monopoly occurred during the last century when De Beers controlled up to 90 per cent of the world's supply of diamonds. (Today, its share is only 65 per cent.)

Legal Barriers to Entry
Legal barriers to entry create legal monopoly. A **legal monopoly** is a market in which competition and entry are restricted by the granting of a monopoly franchise, a government licence, a patent or a copyright.

A *monopoly franchise* is an exclusive right granted to a firm to supply a good or service. An example in the UK is the Post Office, which has the exclusive right to carry first-class mail.

A *government licence* controls entry into particular occupations and professions. This type of barrier to entry occurs in medicine, law, dentistry and many other professional services. A government licence doesn't always create a monopoly, but it does restrict competition.

A *patent* is an exclusive right granted to the inventor of a product or service. A *copyright* is an exclusive right granted to the author or composer of a literary, musical, dramatic or artistic work. Patents and copyrights are valid for a limited time period. In the UK, a patent is valid for 16 years. Patents encourage the *invention* of new products and production methods. Patents also stimulate *innovation* – the use of new inventions – by encouraging inventors to publicize their discoveries and offer them for use under licence. Patents have stimulated innovations in areas as diverse as tomato seeds, pharmaceuticals, memory chips and video games.

ECONOMICS IN ACTION

Information-age Monopolies

Information-age technologies have created four big natural monopolies. These firms have large plant costs but almost zero marginal cost, so they experience economies of scale.

Microsoft has captured 90 per cent of the personal computer operating system market with Windows and 73 per cent of the Web browser market with Internet Explorer. eBay has captured 85 per cent of the consumer-to-consumer Internet auction market and Google has 78 per cent of the search engine market.

New technologies also destroy monopoly. Firms can now gain access to free software and Linux systems via the Internet from innovations in Cloud computing, weakening Microsoft's monopoly. FedEx and e-mail have weakened the monopoly of the Post Office.

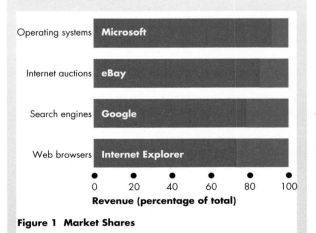

Figure 1 Market Shares

Monopoly Price-setting Strategies

A major difference between monopoly and competition is that a monopoly sets its own price. In doing so, the monopoly faces a market constraint: to sell a larger quantity, the monopoly must charge a lower price. But there are two monopoly situations that create two pricing strategies:

◆ Single price
◆ Price discrimination

Single Price

A **single-price monopoly** is a monopoly that must sell each unit of its output for the same price to all its customers. De Beers sells diamonds (of a given size and quality) for the same price to all its customers. If it tried to sell at a low price to some customers and at a higher price to others, only the low-price customers would buy from De Beers. Others would buy from De Beers' low-price customers. De Beers is a *single-price* monopoly.

Price Discrimination

When a firm practises **price discrimination**, it sells different units of a good or service for different prices. Many firms price discriminate. Microsoft sells Windows and Office software at different prices to different buyers. Computer manufacturers who install the software on new machines, students, teachers, governments and businesses all pay different prices. Airlines offer a dizzying array of different prices for the same trip. Pizza producers often charge one price for a single pizza and almost give away a second pizza. These are all examples of *price discrimination*.

When a firm price discriminates, it looks as though it is doing its customers a favour. In fact, it is charging the highest possible price for each unit that it sells and making the largest possible profit.

Review Quiz

1 How does monopoly arise?
2 How does a natural monopoly differ from a legal monopoly?
3 Distinguish between a price-discriminating monopoly and a single-price monopoly.

You can work these questions in Study Plan 12.1 and get instant feedback.

◆ A Single-price Monopoly's Output and Price Decision

To understand how a single-price monopoly makes its output and price decision, we must first study the link between price and marginal revenue.

Price and Marginal Revenue

Because in a monopoly there is only one firm, the demand curve facing the firm is the market demand curve. Let's look at Gina's Cut and Dry, the only hair-dressing salon within a 15 mile radius of a North Yorkshire town. The table in Figure 12.2 shows the market demand schedule. At a price of £20, she sells no haircuts. The lower the price, the more haircuts per hour Gina can sell. For example, at £12, consumers demand 4 haircuts per hour (row *E*).

Total revenue (*TR*) is the price (*P*) multiplied by the quantity sold (*Q*). For example, in row *D*, Gina sells 3 haircuts at £14 each, so total revenue is £42. *Marginal revenue* (*MR*) is the change in total revenue (*ΔTR*) resulting from a one-unit increase in the quantity sold. For example, if the price falls from £16 (row *C*) to £14 (row *D*), the quantity sold increases from 2 to 3 haircuts. Total revenue rises from £32 to £42, so the change in total revenue is £10. Because the quantity sold increases by 1 haircut, marginal revenue equals the change in total revenue and is £10. Marginal revenue is placed between the two rows to emphasize that marginal revenue relates to the *change* in the quantity sold.

Figure 12.2 shows the market demand curve and marginal revenue curve (*MR*) and also illustrates the calculation we've just made. Notice that at each level of output, marginal revenue is less than price – the marginal revenue curve lies below the demand curve.

Why is marginal revenue *less* than price? It is because when the price is lowered to sell one more unit, two opposing forces affect total revenue. The lower price results in a revenue loss and the increased quantity sold results in a revenue gain. For example, at a price of £16, Gina sells 2 haircuts (point *C*). If she lowers the price to £14, she sells 3 haircuts and has a revenue gain of £14 on the third haircut. But she now receives only £14 on the first two – £2 less than before. She loses £4 of revenue on the first 2 haircuts. To calculate marginal revenue, she must deduct this amount from the revenue gain of £14. So her marginal revenue is £10, which is less than the price.

Figure 12.2 Demand and Marginal Revenue

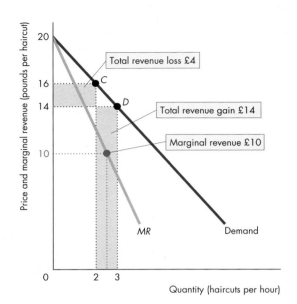

Price (P) (pounds per haircut)	Quantity demanded (Q) (haircuts per hour)	Total revenue (TR = P × Q) (pounds)	Marginal revenue (MR = ΔTR/ΔQ) (pounds per haircut)
A	20	0	0	
				 18
B	18	1	18	
				 14
C	**16**	**2**	**32**	
				.... **10**
D	**14**	**3**	**42**	
				 6
E	12	4	48	
				 2
F	10	5	50	

The table shows the demand schedule. Total revenue (*TR*) is price multiplied by quantity sold. For example, in row *C*, the price is £16 a haircut. Cut and Dry sells 2 haircuts and its total revenue is £32. Marginal revenue (*MR*) is the change in total revenue that results from a one-unit increase in the quantity sold. For example, when the price falls from £16 to £14 a haircut, the quantity sold increases by 1 haircut and total revenue increases by £10. Marginal revenue is £10. The demand curve and the marginal revenue curve, *MR*, are based on the numbers in the table and illustrate the calculation of marginal revenue when the price falls from £16 to £14 a haircut.

Marginal Revenue and Elasticity

A single-price monopoly's marginal revenue is related to the *elasticity of demand* for its good. The demand for a good can be *elastic* (the elasticity of demand is greater than 1), *inelastic* (the elasticity of demand is less than 1), or *unit elastic* (the elasticity of demand is equal to 1). Demand is *elastic* if a 1 per cent fall in the price brings a greater than 1 per cent increase in the quantity demanded. Demand is *inelastic* if a 1 per cent fall in the price brings a less than 1 per cent increase in the quantity demanded. And demand is *unit elastic* if a 1 per cent fall in the price brings a 1 per cent increase in the quantity demanded. (See Chapter 4, pp. 86–87.)

If demand is elastic, a fall in price brings an increase in total revenue – the increase in revenue from the increase in quantity sold outweighs the decrease in revenue from the lower price – and marginal revenue is *positive*. If demand is inelastic, a fall in the price brings a decrease in total revenue – the increase in revenue from the increase in quantity sold is outweighed by the decrease in revenue from the lower price – and marginal revenue is *negative*. If demand is unit elastic, total revenue does not change – the increase in revenue from the increase in quantity sold offsets the decrease in revenue from the lower price – and marginal revenue is *zero*. (The relationship between total revenue and elasticity is explained in Chapter 4, p. 88.)

Figure 12.3 illustrates the relationship between marginal revenue, total revenue and elasticity. As the price of a haircut gradually falls from £20 to £10, the quantity of haircuts demanded increases from 0 to 5 an hour, marginal revenue is positive in part (a), total revenue increases in part (b) and the demand for haircuts is elastic. As the price falls from £10 to £0, the quantity of haircuts demanded increases from 5 to 10 an hour, marginal revenue is negative in part (a), total revenue decreases in part (b) and the demand for haircuts is inelastic. When the price is £10 a haircut, marginal revenue is zero in part (a), total revenue is a maximum in part (b) and the demand for haircuts is unit elastic.

In Monopoly, Demand Is Always Elastic

The relationship between marginal revenue and elasticity that you've just discovered implies that a profit-maximizing monopoly never produces an output in the inelastic range of its demand curve. If it did so, it could produce a smaller quantity, charge a higher price and increase its economic profit. Let's now look at a monopoly's price and output decision.

Figure 12.3 Marginal Revenue and Elasticity

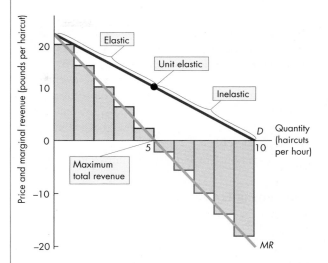

(a) Demand and marginal revenue curves

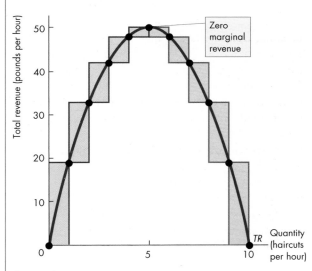

(b) Total revenue curve

In part (a), the demand curve is *D* and the marginal revenue curve is *MR*. In part (b), the total revenue curve is *TR*. Over the range from 0 to 5 haircuts an hour, a price cut increases total revenue, so marginal revenue is positive – as shown by the blue bars. Demand is elastic. Over the range from 5 to 10 haircuts an hour, a price cut decreases total revenue, so marginal revenue is negative – as shown by the red bars. Demand is inelastic. At 5 haircuts an hour, total revenue is maximized and marginal revenue is zero. Demand is unit elastic.

myeconlab Animation

Price and Output Decision

A monopoly sets its price and output at the levels that maximize economic profit. To determine this price and output level, we need to study the behaviour of both cost and revenue as output varies. A monopoly faces the same types of technology and cost constraints as a competitive firm, so its costs (total cost, average cost and marginal cost) behave just like those of a firm in perfect competition. And a monopoly's revenues (total revenue, price and marginal revenue) behave in the way we've just described.

Let's see how Cut and Dry maximizes its profit.

Maximizing Economic Profit

You can see in Table 12.1 and Figure 12.4(a) that total cost (*TC*) and total revenue (*TR*) both rise as output increases, but *TC* rises at an increasing rate and *TR* rises at a decreasing rate.

Economic profit, which equals *TR* minus *TC*, increases at small output levels, reaches a maximum and then decreases. The maximum profit (£12) occurs when Cut and Dry sells 3 haircuts for £14 each. If it sells 2 haircuts for £16 each or 4 haircuts for £12 each, Cut and Dry's economic profit will be only £8.

Marginal Revenue Equals Marginal Cost

You can see Cut and Dry's marginal revenue (*MR*) and marginal cost (*MC*) in Table 12.1 and Figure 12.4(b). When Cut and Dry increases output from 2 to 3 haircuts, *MR* is £10 and *MC* is £6. *MR* exceeds *MC* by £4 and Cut and Dry's profit increases by that amount. If Cut and Dry increases output yet further, from 3 to 4 haircuts, *MR* is £6 and *MC* is £10. In this case, *MC* exceeds *MR* by £4, so Cut and Dry's profit decreases by that amount.

When *MR* exceeds *MC*, profit increases if output increases. When *MC* exceeds *MR*, profit increases if output *decreases*. When *MC* equals *MR*, profit is maximized.

Figure 12.4(b) shows the maximum profit as price (on the demand curve *D*) minus average total cost (on the *ATC* curve) multiplied by the quantity produced – the blue rectangle.

Maximum Price the Market Will Bear

Unlike a firm in perfect competition, a monopoly influences the price of what it sells. But a monopoly doesn't set the price at the maximum *possible* price. At the maximum possible price, the firm would be able to sell only one unit of output, which in general is less than the profit-maximizing quantity. Rather, a monopoly

---

Table 12.1

A Monopoly's Output and Price Decision

Price (*P*) (pounds per haircut)	Quantity demanded (*Q*) (haircuts per hour)	Total revenue (*TR* = *P* × *Q*) (pounds)	Marginal revenue (*MR* = Δ*TR*/Δ*Q*) (pounds per haircut)	Total cost (*TC*) (pounds)	Marginal cost (*MC* = Δ*TC*/Δ*Q*) (pounds per haircut)	Profit (*TR* − *TC*) (pounds)
20	0	0		20		−20
			 18		 1	
18	1	18		21		−3
			 14		 3	
16	2	32		24		8
			 10		 6	
14	3	42		30		+12
			 6		 10	
12	4	48		40		+8
			 2		 15	
10	5	50		55		−5

Total revenue (*TR*) equals price (*P*) multiplied by the quantity sold (*Q*). Profit equals total revenue minus total cost (*TC*). Profit is maximized when the price is £14 a haircut and 3 haircuts are sold. Total revenue is £42 an hour, total cost is £30 an hour and economic profit is £12 an hour.

Figure 12.4   A Monopoly's Output and Price

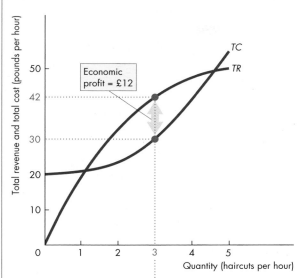

(a) Total revenue and total cost curves

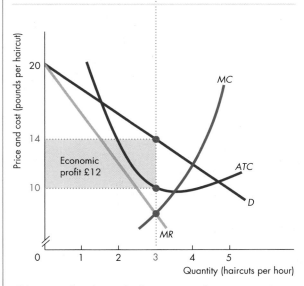

(b) Demand and marginal revenue and cost curves

In part (a), economic profit is the vertical distance equal to total revenue (*TR*) minus total cost (*TC*) and it is maximized at 3 haircuts an hour.

In part (b), economic profit is maximized when marginal cost (*MC*) equals marginal revenue (*MR*). The profit-maximizing output is 3 haircuts an hour. The price is determined by the demand curve (*D*) and is £14 a haircut. The average total cost is £10 a haircut, so economic profit, the blue rectangle, is £12, which equals the profit per haircut (£4) multiplied by 3 haircuts.

 Animation

produces the profit-maximizing quantity and sells that quantity for the highest price it can get.

All firms maximize profit by producing the output at which marginal revenue equals marginal cost. For a competitive firm, price equals marginal revenue, so price also equals marginal cost. For a monopoly, price exceeds marginal revenue, so price also exceeds marginal cost.

A monopoly charges a price that exceeds marginal cost, but does it always make an economic profit? In Figure 12.4(b), Cut and Dry produces 3 haircuts an hour. Its average total cost is £10 (read from the *ATC* curve) and its price is £14 (read from the *D* curve). It makes a profit of £4 a haircut (£14 minus £10). Cut and Dry's economic profit is shown by the blue rectangle, which equals the profit per haircut (£4) multiplied by the number of haircuts (3), for a total of £12 an hour.

If firms in a perfectly competitive market make a positive economic profit, new firms enter. That does *not* happen in monopoly. Barriers to entry prevent new firms from entering a market in which there is a monopoly. So a monopoly can make a positive economic profit and might continue to do so indefinitely. Sometimes that profit is large, as in the international diamond business.

Cut and Dry makes a positive economic profit. But suppose that the owner of the shop that Gina rents increases Cut and Dry's rent. If Cut and Dry pays an additional £12 an hour, its fixed cost increases by £12 an hour. Its marginal cost and marginal revenue don't change, so its profit-maximizing output remains at 3 haircuts an hour. Economic profit decreases by £12 an hour to zero. If Cut and Dry pays more than an additional £12 an hour for its shop rent, it incurs an economic loss. If this situation were permanent, Cut and Dry would go out of business.

Review Quiz

1   What is the relationship between marginal cost and marginal revenue when a single-price monopoly maximizes profit?
2   How does a single-price monopoly determine the price it will charge its customers?
3   What is the relationship between price, marginal revenue and marginal cost when a single-price monopoly is maximizing profit?
4   Why can a monopoly make a positive economic profit even in the long run?

You can work these questions in Study Plan 12.2 and get instant feedback.   myeconlab

Single-price Monopoly and Competition Compared

Imagine a market that is made up of many small firms operating in perfect competition. Then imagine that a single firm buys out all these small firms and creates a monopoly.

What will happen in this market? Will the price rise or fall? Will the quantity produced increase or decrease? Will economic profit increase or decrease? Will either the original competitive situation or the new monopoly situation be efficient?

These are the questions we're now going to answer. First, we look at the effects of monopoly on the price and quantity produced. Then we turn to the questions about efficiency.

Comparing Price and Output

Figure 12.5 shows the market we'll study. The market demand curve is D. The demand curve is the same regardless of how the market is organized. But the supply side and the equilibrium are different in monopoly and competition. First, let's look at the case of perfect competition.

Perfect Competition

Initially, with many small, perfectly competitive firms in the market, the market supply curve is S. This supply curve is obtained by summing the supply curves of all the individual firms in the market.

In perfect competition, equilibrium occurs where the market supply curve and market demand curve intersect. The quantity produced is Q_C and the price is P_C. Each firm takes the price P_C and maximizes its profit by producing the output at which its own marginal cost equals the price. Because each firm is a small part of the total market, there is no incentive for any firm to try to manipulate the price by varying its output.

Monopoly

Now suppose that this market is taken over by a single firm. Consumers do not change, so the market demand curve remains the same as in the case of perfect competition. But now the monopoly recognizes this demand curve as a constraint on the price at which it can sell its output. The monopoly's marginal revenue curve is MR.

The monopoly maximizes profit by producing the quantity at which marginal revenue equals marginal cost. To find the monopoly's marginal cost curve, first recall that in perfect competition the market supply curve is the sum of the supply curves of the firms in the market. Also recall that each firm's supply curve is its marginal cost curve (see Chapter 11, p. 255). So when the market is taken over by a single firm, the competitive market's supply curve becomes the monopoly's marginal cost curve. To remind you of this fact, the supply curve is also labelled MC.

The output at which marginal revenue equals marginal cost is Q_M. This output is smaller than the competitive output Q_C. And the monopoly charges the price P_M, which is higher than P_C. We have established that:

> **Compared with a perfectly competitive market, a single-price monopoly produces a smaller output and charges a higher price.**

We've seen how the output and price of a monopoly compare with those in a competitive market. Let's now compare the efficiency of the two types of market.

Figure 12.5 Monopoly's Smaller Output and Higher Price

A competitive market produces the quantity Q_C at price P_C. A single-price monopoly produces the quantity Q_M at which marginal revenue equals marginal cost and sells that quantity for the price P_M. Compared with perfect competition, a single-price monopoly produces a smaller output and charges a higher price.

myeconlab Animation

Efficiency Comparison

You saw in Chapter 11 (pp. 266–267) that perfect competition (with no external costs and benefits) is efficient. Figure 12.6(a) illustrates the efficiency of perfect competition and serves as a benchmark against which to measure the inefficiency of monopoly.

Along the demand curve and marginal social benefit curve ($D = MSB$), consumers are efficient. Along the supply curve and marginal social cost curve ($S = MSC$), producers are efficient. In competitive equilibrium, the price is P_C, the quantity is Q_C and marginal social benefit equals marginal social cost.

Consumer surplus is the green triangle under the demand curve and above the equilibrium price (see Chapter 5, p. 109). *Producer surplus* is the blue area above the supply curve and below the equilibrium price (see Chapter 5, p. 111). Total surplus (the sum of the consumer surplus and producer surplus) is maximized.

Also, in long-run competitive equilibrium, entry and exit ensure that each firm produces its output at the minimum possible long-run average cost.

To summarize: at the competitive equilibrium, marginal social benefit equals marginal social cost; total surplus is maximized; firms produce at the lowest possible long-run average cost; and resource use is efficient.

Figure 12.6(b) illustrates the inefficiency of monopoly and the sources of that inefficiency. A monopoly produces Q_M and charges P_M. The smaller output and higher price drive a wedge between marginal social benefit and marginal social cost and create a *deadweight loss*. The grey area shows the deadweight loss and its magnitude is a measure of the inefficiency of monopoly.

Consumer surplus shrinks for two reasons. First, consumers lose by having to pay more for the good. This loss to consumers is a gain for the producer and increases the producer surplus. Second, consumers lose by getting less of the good, and this loss is part of the deadweight loss.

Although the monopoly gains from a higher price, it loses some of the original producer surplus because it produces a smaller output. That loss is another part of the deadweight loss.

Because a monopoly restricts output below the market quantity of perfect competition and faces no competitive threat, it does not produce at the lowest possible long-run average cost. As a result, monopoly damages the consumer interest in three ways: it produces less, it increases the cost of production, and it raises the price to above the increased cost of production.

Figure 12.6 Inefficiency of Monopoly

(a) Perfect competition

(b) Monopoly

In perfect competition in part (a), output is Q_C and the price is P_C. Marginal social benefit (*MSB*) equals marginal social cost (*MSC*); total surplus, the sum of consumer surplus (the green triangle) and producer surplus (the blue area), is maximized; and in the long run, firms produce at the lowest possible average cost.

A monopoly in part (b) restricts output to Q_M and raises the price to P_M. Consumer surplus shrinks, the monopoly gains and a deadweight loss (the grey area) arises.

myeconlab Animation

Redistribution of Surpluses

You've seen that monopoly is inefficient because marginal social benefit exceeds marginal social cost and there is deadweight loss – a social loss. But monopoly also brings a *redistribution* of surpluses.

Some of the lost consumer surplus goes to the monopoly. In Figure 12.6(b), the monopoly gets the difference between the higher price, P_M, and the competitive price, P_C, on the quantity sold, Q_M. So the monopoly takes part of the consumer surplus. This portion of the loss of consumer surplus is not a loss to society. It is a redistribution from consumers to the monopoly producer.

Rent Seeking

You've seen that monopoly creates a deadweight loss and is inefficient. But the social cost of monopoly can exceed the deadweight loss because of an activity called rent seeking. Any surplus – consumer surplus, producer surplus or economic profit – is called **economic rent**. And **rent seeking** is the pursuit of wealth by capturing economic rent.

You've seen that a monopoly makes its economic profit by diverting part of consumer surplus to itself – by converting consumer surplus into economic profit. So the pursuit of economic profit by a monopoly is rent seeking. It is the attempt to capture consumer surplus.

Rent seekers pursue their goals in two main ways. They might:

◆ Buy a monopoly
◆ Create a monopoly

Buy a Monopoly

To rent seek by buying a monopoly, a person searches for a monopoly that is for sale at a lower price than the monopoly's economic profit. Trading of taxi licences is an example of this type of rent seeking. In some cities, taxis are regulated. The city restricts both the fares and the number of taxis that can operate so that operating a taxi results in economic profit or rent. A person who wants to operate a taxi must buy a licence from someone who already has one. People rationally devote time and effort to seeking out profitable monopoly businesses to buy. In the process, they use up scarce resources that could otherwise have been used to produce goods and services. The value of this lost production is part of the social cost of monopoly. The amount paid for a monopoly is not a social cost because the payment is just a transfer of an existing producer surplus from the buyer to the seller.

Create a Monopoly

Rent seeking by creating a monopoly is mainly a political activity. It takes the form of lobbying and seeking to influence the political process. Such influence is sometimes sought by making political contributions in exchange for legislative support or by indirectly seeking to influence political outcomes through publicity in the media or via more direct contacts with politicians and bureaucrats. An example of this type of rent seeking would be the donations that alcohol and tobacco companies make to political parties in an attempt to avoid a tightening of legislation on activities such as advertising and licensing, which might affect their profits.

This type of rent seeking is a costly activity that uses up scarce resources. In aggregate, firms spend millions of pounds lobbying Parliament in the pursuit of licences and laws that create barriers to entry and establish a monopoly. Everyone has an incentive to rent seek, and because there are no barriers to entry into rent seeking, there is a great deal of competition in this activity. The winners of the competition become monopolies.

Rent-seeking Equilibrium

How much will a person be willing to give up to acquire a monopoly right? The answer is the entire value of a monopoly's economic profit. Barriers to entry create monopoly. But there is no barrier to entry into rent seeking. Rent seeking is like perfect competition. If an economic profit is available, a new rent seeker will try to get some of it. And competition among rent seekers pushes up the price that must be paid for a monopoly to the point at which the rent seeker makes zero economic profit by operating the monopoly.

Figure 12.7 shows a rent-seeking equilibrium. The cost of rent seeking is a fixed cost that must be added to a monopoly's other costs. Rent seeking and rent-seeking costs increase to the point at which no economic profit is made. The average total cost curve, which includes the fixed cost of rent seeking, shifts upward until it just touches the demand curve. Economic profit is zero. It has been lost in rent seeking.

Consumer surplus is unaffected. But the deadweight loss of monopoly now includes the original deadweight loss plus the lost producer surplus, shown by the enlarged grey area in Figure 12.7.

Figure 12.7 Rent-seeking Equilibrium

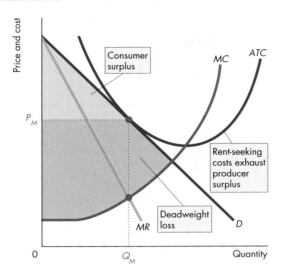

With competitive rent seeking, a monopoly uses all its economic profit to prevent another firm from taking its economic rent. The firm's rent-seeking costs are fixed costs. They add to total fixed cost and to average total cost and the *ATC* curve shifts upward. Rent seeking will continue until the *ATC* curve has shifted up by so much that at the profit-maximizing price, the firm breaks even. The grey area shows the deadweight loss.

 Animation

Review Quiz

1 Why does a single-price monopoly produce a smaller output and charge a higher price than what would prevail if the market were perfectly competitive?
2 How does a monopoly transfer consumer surplus to itself?
3 Why is a single-price monopoly inefficient?
4 What is rent seeking and how does it influence the inefficiency of monopoly?

You can work these questions in Study Plan 12.3 and get instant feedback.   myeconlab

---

So far, we've considered only a single-price monopoly. But many monopolies do not operate with a single price. Instead, they price discriminate. Let's now see how price-discriminating monopoly works.

Price Discrimination

You encounter *price discrimination* – selling a good or service at a number of different prices – when you travel, go to the cinema, go shopping or go out to eat. Many firms that price discriminate are not monopolies, but monopolies price discriminate when they can do so.

To be able to price discriminate, a monopoly must be able to identify and separate different buyer types and sell a product that cannot be resold.

Not all price *differences* are price *discrimination*. Some goods that are similar but not identical have different prices because they have different production costs. For example, the cost of producing electricity depends on the time of day. If an electric power company charges a higher price during the peak consumption periods from 7:00 to 9:00 in the morning and from 4:00 to 7:00 in the evening than it does at other times of the day, it is not price discriminating.

At first sight, price discrimination appears to be inconsistent with profit maximization. Why would a railway company give a student discount? Why would a hairdresser charge students and senior citizens less? Aren't these firms losing profit by being so generous to their customers?

Capturing Consumer Surplus

Price discrimination captures consumer surplus and converts it into economic profit. It does so by getting buyers to pay a price as close as possible to the maximum willingness to pay.

Firms price discriminate in two broad ways:

◆ Among groups of buyers
◆ Among units of a good

Discriminating Among Groups of Buyers

People differ in the value they place on a good – their marginal benefit and willingness to pay. Some of these differences are correlated with features such as age, employment status, and other easily distinguished characteristics. When such a correlation is present, firms can profit by price discriminating among the different groups of buyers.

For example, a face-to-face sales meeting with a customer might bring a large and profitable order. So for salespeople and other business travellers, the marginal benefit from a trip is large and the price that such a traveller is willing to pay for a trip is high. In contrast, for a holiday traveller, any of several different trips and even no holiday trip are options. So for holiday travellers, the marginal benefit of a trip is small and the price that such a traveller is willing to pay for a trip is low. Because business travellers are willing to pay more than holiday travellers are, it is possible for an airline to profit by price discriminating between these two groups.

Discriminating Among Units of a Good

Everyone experiences diminishing marginal benefit and has a downward-sloping demand curve. For this reason, if all the units of the good are sold for a single price, buyers end up with a consumer surplus equal to the value they get from each unit of the good minus the price paid for it.

A firm that price discriminates by charging a buyer one price for a single item and a lower price for a second or third item can capture some of the consumer surplus. Buy one pizza and get a second one free (or for a low price) is an example of this type of price discrimination.

(Note that some discounts for bulk arise from lower costs of production for greater bulk. In these cases, such discounts are not price discrimination.)

Let's see how price discriminating increases economic profit.

Profiting by Price Discriminating

Global Air has a monopoly on an exotic route. Figure 12.8 shows the demand curve (*D*) and the marginal revenue curve (*MR*) for travel on this route. It also shows Global Air's marginal cost curve (*MC*) and average total cost curve (*ATC*).

Initially, Global is a single-price monopoly and maximizes its profit by producing 8,000 trips a year (the quantity at which *MR* equals *MC*). The price is €1,200 per trip. The average total cost of producing a trip is €600, so economic profit is €600 a trip. On 8,000 trips, Global's economic profit is €4.8 million a year, shown by the blue rectangle. Global's customers enjoy a consumer surplus shown by the green triangle.

Global is struck by the fact that many of its customers are business travellers and it suspects they are willing to pay more than €1,200 a trip. So Global does some market research, which reveals that some business travellers are willing to pay as much as €1,800 a trip. Also, these customers frequently change their travel plans at the last moment. Another group of business travellers is willing to pay €1,600. These customers

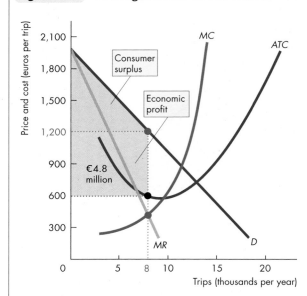

Figure 12.8 A Single Price of Air Travel

Global Air has a monopoly on an air route. The market demand curve is *D* and marginal revenue curve is *MR*. Global Air's marginal cost curve is *MC* and its average total cost curve is *ATC*. As a single-price monopoly, Global maximizes profit by selling 8,000 trips a year at €1,200 a trip. Its profit is €4.8 million a year – the blue rectangle. Global's customers enjoy a consumer surplus – the green triangle.

myeconlab Animation

know a week ahead when they will travel and they never want to stay over a weekend. Yet another group would pay up to €1,400. These travellers know two weeks ahead when they will travel and also don't want to stay over a weekend.

So Global announces a new fare schedule:

No restrictions, €1,800

7-day advance purchase, non-refundable, €1,600

14-day advance purchase, non-refundable, €1,400

14-day advance purchase, must stay over a weekend, €1,200.

Figure 12.9 shows the outcome with this new fare structure and also shows why Global is pleased with its new fares. Global sells 2,000 seats at each of its four prices. Global's economic profit increases by the dark blue steps in Figure 12.9. Its economic profit is now its original €4.8 million a year plus an additional €2.4 million from its new higher fares. Consumer surplus has shrunk to the total of the four green triangles.

Figure 12.9 Price Discrimination

Global revises its fare structure: no restrictions at €1,800, 7-day advance purchase at €1,600, 14-day advance purchase at €1,400, and must stay over a weekend at €1,200. Global sells 2,000 trips at each of its four new fares. Its economic profit increases by €2.4 million a year to €7.2 million a year, which is shown by the original blue rectangle plus the blue steps. Global's customers' consumer surplus (total green area) shrinks.

myeconlab Animation ——————————◆

Perfect Price Discrimination

Perfect price discrimination occurs if a firm is able to sell each unit of output for the highest price anyone is willing to pay for it. In such a case, the entire consumer surplus is eliminated and captured by the producer. To practise perfect price discrimination, a firm must be creative and come up with a host of prices and special conditions, each one of which appeals to a tiny segment of the market.

With perfect price discrimination, something special happens to marginal revenue. For the perfect price discriminator, the market demand curve becomes the firm's marginal revenue curve. The reason is that when the price is cut to sell a larger quantity, the firm sells only the marginal unit at the lower price. All the other units continue to be sold for the highest price that each buyer is willing to pay. So for the perfect price discriminator, marginal revenue *equals* price and the demand curve becomes the firm's marginal revenue curve.

With marginal revenue equal to price, Global can obtain even greater profit by increasing output up to the point at which price (and marginal revenue) is equal to marginal cost.

So Global now seeks additional travellers who will not pay as much as €1,200 a trip but who will pay more than marginal cost. Global offers a variety of holiday specials at different low fares that appeal only to new travellers. Existing customers continue to pay the higher fares. With all these fares and specials, Global increases sales, extracts the entire consumer surplus and maximizes economic profit.

Figure 12.10 shows the outcome with perfect price discrimination. The fares paid by the original 8,000 travellers extract the entire consumer surplus from this group. The new fares between €900 and €1,200 have attracted 3,000 additional travellers and taken their entire consumer surplus also. Global now makes an economic profit of more than €9 million.

Figure 12.10 Perfect Price Discrimination

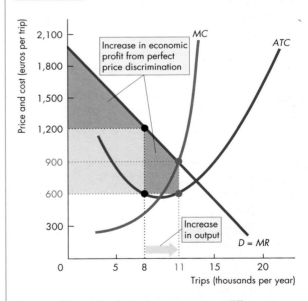

Dozens of fares discriminate among many different types of business travellers and many new low fares with restrictions appeal to holiday travellers. With perfect price discrimination, the market demand curve becomes Global's marginal revenue curve. Economic profit is maximized when the lowest price equals marginal cost. Here, Global sells 11,000 trips and makes an economic profit of more than €9 million a year.

myeconlab Animation ——————————◆

Efficiency and Rent Seeking with Price Discrimination

With perfect price discrimination, output increases to the point at which price equals marginal cost – where the marginal cost curve intersects the market demand curve. This output is identical to that of perfect competition. Perfect price discrimination pushes consumer surplus to zero but increases producer surplus to equal the sum of consumer surplus and producer surplus in perfect competition. Deadweight loss with perfect price discrimination is zero. So perfect price discrimination achieves efficiency.

> **The more perfectly the monopoly can discriminate, the closer its output gets to the competitive output and the more efficient is the outcome.**

But there are two differences between perfect competition and perfect price discrimination. First, the distribution of the total surplus is different. It is shared by consumers and producers in perfect competition, whereas the producer gets it all with perfect price discrimination. Second, because the producer grabs the entire total surplus, rent seeking becomes profitable.

People use resources in pursuit of economic rent, and the bigger the rents, the more resources get used in pursuing them. With free entry into rent seeking, the long-run equilibrium outcome is that rent seekers use up the entire producer surplus.

Real-world airlines are just as creative as Global, as you can see in the cartoon!

Would it bother you to hear how little I paid for this flight?

From William Hamilton, *Voodoo Economics*, 1992, Chronicle Books, p. 3. Reprinted with permission from William Hamilton.

Attempting Perfect Price Discrimination

If you want to spend a day at Disney World Paris (2 parks), it will cost you £61. The figure shows the prices for a second, third, fourth, and fifth day. The Disney Corporation hopes that it has read your willingness to pay correctly and not left you with too much consumer surplus. But notice that the fourth day costs more than the third. It seems that Disney has forgotten that your marginal benefit diminishes!

High price for up to 3 days extracts consumer surplus

Figure 1   Ticket Prices at Disney World Paris

Review Quiz

1   What is price discrimination and how is it used to increase a monopoly's profit?
2   Explain how consumer surplus changes when a monopoly price discriminates.
3   Explain how consumer surplus, economic profit and output change when a monopoly perfectly price discriminates.
4   What are some of the ways that real-world airlines use to price discriminate?

You can work these questions in Study Plan 12.4 and get instant feedback.

You've seen that monopoly is profitable, but costly for consumers. Monopoly results in inefficiency. Because of these features of monopoly, it is subject to policy debate and regulation. We'll now study key monopoly policy issues.

Monopoly Regulation

Natural monopoly presents a dilemma. With economies of scale, it produces at the lowest possible cost. But with market power, it has an incentive to raise the price above the competitive price and produce too little – to operate in the self-interest of the monopoly and not in the social interest.

Regulation – rules administered by a government agency to influence prices, quantities, entry, and other aspects of economic activity in a firm or industry – is a possible solution to this dilemma.

To implement regulation, the government establishes agencies to oversee and enforce the rules. For example, in the UK, OFGEN regulates prices for electricity and gas supply, and OFWAT regulates water prices. By the 1970s, almost a quarter of the nation's output was produced by regulated industries (far more than just natural monopolies) and a process of deregulation began.

Deregulation is the process of removing regulation of prices, quantities, entry and other aspects of economic activity in a firm or industry. During the past 30 years, deregulation has occurred in UK domestic airlines, telephone service, electricity, water and gas supply, national rail services, and banking and financial services among other things. While deregulation is progressing in other EU countries, it is not as widespread as in the UK.

Regulation is a possible solution to the dilemma presented by natural monopoly but not a guaranteed solution. There are two theories about how regulation actually works:

1 Social interest theory
2 Capture theory

The **social interest theory** is that the political and regulatory process relentlessly seeks out inefficiency and introduces regulation that eliminates deadweight loss and allocates resources efficiently.

The **capture theory** is that regulation serves the self-interest of the producer, who captures the regulator and maximizes economic profit. Regulation that benefits the producer but creates a deadweight loss gets adopted because the producer's gain is large and visible while each individual consumer's loss is small and invisible. No individual consumer has an incentive to oppose the regulation but the producer has a big incentive to lobby for it.

We're going to examine efficient regulation that serves the social interest and see why it is not a simple matter to design and implement such regulation.

Efficient Regulation of a Natural Monopoly

A gas distribution company is a natural monopoly – it can supply the entire market at a lower price than two or more competing firms can. Centrica is the current name for a private gas supplier that was a UK government monopoly called British Gas. The firm has invested heavily in household meters, pipes, regional storage facilities and other equipment. These fixed costs are part of the firm's average total cost. Its average total cost decreases as the number of customers supplied increases because the fixed cost is spread over a larger number of households.

Unregulated and acting as a monopoly after privatization, Centrica produces the quantity that maximizes profit. Like all single-price monopolies, the profit-maximizing quantity is less than the efficient quantity, and underproduction results in a deadweight loss.

How can Centrica be regulated to produce the efficient quantity of gas? The answer is by being regulated to set its price equal to marginal cost, known as the **marginal cost pricing rule**. The quantity demanded at a price equal to marginal cost is the efficient quantity – the quantity at which marginal social benefit equals marginal social cost.

Figure 12.11 illustrates the marginal cost pricing rule. The demand curve for gas is D. Centrica's marginal cost curve is MC, which is assumed to be constant at 10 pence per cubic metre. That is, the cost of supplying each additional household with gas is 10 pence per cubic metre. The efficient outcome occurs if the price is regulated at 10 pence per cubic metre with 4 million cubic metres a day produced.

But there is a problem: at the efficient output, because price equals marginal cost, the price is below average total cost. Average total cost minus the price is the loss per unit produced. It's pretty obvious that if Centrica is required to use a marginal cost pricing rule it will not stay in business for long. How can a company cover its costs and, at the same time, obey a marginal cost pricing rule?

There are two possible ways of enabling the firm to cover its costs: price discrimination and a two-part price (called a *two-part tariff*). For example, a mobile phone company offers plans at a fixed monthly price that give access to the phone network and unlimited free calls. The price of a call (zero) equals the marginal cost of a call. Similarly, a gas supplier can charge a one-time connection fee that covers its fixed cost and then charge a monthly fee equal to marginal cost.

Figure 12.11 Regulating a Natural Monopoly

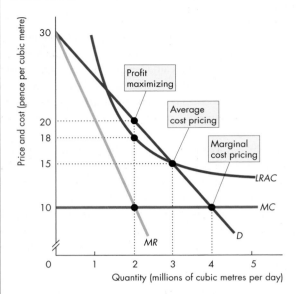

A natural monopoly gas producer faces the market demand curve *D*. The firm's marginal cost is constant at 10 pence per cubic metre, as shown by the curve labelled *MC*. The long-run average cost curve is *LRAC*.

Unregulated, as a profit-maximizer, the firm produces 2 million cubic metres a day and charges a price of 20 pence per cubic metre. An efficient marginal cost pricing rule sets the price at 10 pence per cubic metre. The monopoly produces 4 million cubic metres per day and incurs an economic loss. A second-best average cost pricing rule sets the price at 15 pence per cubic metre. The monopoly produces 3 million cubic metres per day and makes zero economic profit.

Second-best Regulation of a Natural Monopoly

A natural monopoly cannot always be regulated to achieve an efficient outcome. Two possible ways of enabling a regulated monopoly to avoid an economic loss are:

◆ Average cost pricing
◆ Government subsidy

Average Cost Pricing

An **average cost pricing rule** sets the price equal to average total cost. With this rule the firm produces the quantity at which the long-run average cost curve cuts the demand curve. This rule results in the firm making

zero economic profit – breaking even. But because for a natural monopoly average cost exceeds marginal cost, the quantity produced is less than the efficient quantity and a deadweight loss arises.

Figure 12.11 illustrates the average cost pricing rule. The price is 15 pence a cubic metre and 3 million cubic metres a day are produced.

Government Subsidy

A government subsidy is a direct payment to the firm equal to its economic loss. To pay a subsidy, the government must raise the revenue by taxing some other activity. You saw in Chapter 6 that taxes themselves generate deadweight loss.

And the Second-Best Is . . .

Which is the better option, average cost pricing or marginal cost pricing with a government subsidy? The answer depends on the relative magnitudes of the two deadweight losses. Average cost pricing generates a deadweight loss in the market served by the natural monopoly. A subsidy generates deadweight losses in the markets for the items that are taxed to pay for the subsidy. The smaller deadweight loss is the second-best solution to regulating a natural monopoly. Making this calculation in practice is too difficult and average cost pricing is generally preferred to a subsidy.

Implementing average cost pricing presents the regulator with a challenge because it is not possible to be sure what a firm's costs are. So regulators use one of two practical rules:

◆ Rate of return regulation
◆ Price cap regulation

Rate of Return Regulation

Under **rate of return regulation**, a firm must justify its price by showing that its return on capital doesn't exceed a specified target rate. This type of regulation can end up serving the self-interest of the firm rather than the social interest. The firm's managers have an incentive to inflate costs by spending on items such as private jets, free football tickets (disguised as public relations expenses), and lavish entertainment. Managers also have an incentive to use more capital than the efficient amount. The rate of return on capital is regulated but not the total return on capital, and the greater the amount of capital, the greater is the total return.

Price Cap Regulation

For the reason that we've just examined, rate of return regulation is increasingly being replaced by price cap regulation. **Price cap regulation** is a price ceiling – a rule that specifies the highest price the firm is permitted to set. This type of regulation gives a firm an incentive to operate efficiently and keep costs under control. Price cap regulation has become common for the electricity and telecommunications industries and is replacing rate of return regulation.

To see how a price cap works, let's suppose that the gas distribution company is subject to this type of regulation. Figure 12.12 shows that without regulation, the firm maximizes profit by producing 2 million cubic metres a day and charging a price of 20 pence a cubic metre. If a price cap is set at 15 pence a cubic metre, the

firm is permitted to sell any quantity it chooses at that price or at a lower price.

At 2 million cubic metres a day, the firm now incurs an economic loss. It can decrease the loss by increasing output to 3 million cubic metres a day. To increase output above 3 million cubic metres a day, the firm would have to lower the price and again it would incur an economic loss. So the profit-maximizing quantity is 3 million cubic metres a day – the same as with average cost pricing.

Notice that a price cap lowers the price and increases output. This outcome is in sharp contrast to the effect of a price ceiling in a competitive market that you studied in Chapter 6 (pp. 128–130). The reason is that in a monopoly, the unregulated equilibrium output is less than the competitive equilibrium output, and the price cap regulation replicates the conditions of a competitive market.

In Figure 12.12, the price cap delivers average cost pricing. In practice, the regulator might set the cap too high. For this reason, price cap regulation is often combined with *earnings sharing regulation* – a regulation that requires firms to make refunds to customers when profits rise above a target level.

Figure 12.12 Price Cap Regulation

A natural monopoly gas producer faces the market demand curve *D*. The firm's marginal cost is constant at 10 pence per cubic metre – shown by the curve labelled *MC*. The long-run average total cost curve is *LRAC*. Unregulated, the firm produces 2 million cubic metres a day and charges a price of 20 pence per cubic metre.

A price cap is set at 15 pence a cubic metre. The maximum price that the firm can charge is 15 pence a cubic metre, so the firm has an incentive to minimize cost and produce the quantity demanded at the price cap. The price cap regulation lowers the price to 15 pence a cubic metre and the firm increases the quantity to 3 million cubic metres a day.

 Animation ————————◆

You've now completed your study of monopoly. *Reading Between the Lines* on pp. 292–293 looks at Google's dominant position in the market for Internet search advertising.

In the next chapter, we study markets that lie between the extremes of perfect competition and monopoly and that blend elements of the two.

Reading Between the Lines

Google Accused of Anti-competitive Practice

The Telegraph, 24 February 2010

Google under Investigation for Alleged Breach of EU Competition Rule

The European Commission has launched an antitrust investigation against Google. . . . The investigation comes under the Lisbon Treaty's 'abuse of dominant position' powers and is the first time that Google has been targeted by the European Union. . . .

The Commission has written to Google with a series of questions over how its search functions operate and also questioned the way it sells advertising. It acted after complaints from the UK search site Foundem, a price comparison site, Ciao, an online shopping site owned by Microsoft, and ejustice.fr, a French site which details legal cases and solicitor services.

Foundem claims that Google, which has a 90pc share of the search market in the UK, has penalized the site with a 'search penalty' on its business. . . . Foundem said: "Google has always used various penalty filters to remove certain sites entirely from its search results or place them so far down the rankings that they will never be found."

Google has dismissed the claims, saying that its search algorithms are aimed at pointing people to the best sites and that it does not pick and choose favourites. Google said: "We've always worked hard to ensure that our success is earned the right way, through technological innovation and great products, rather than by locking in our users or advertisers or creating artificial barriers to entry."

© Telegraph Media Group Limited 2010.

The Essence of the Story

- The EU has started an investigation into claims that Google abuses its market position.

- Some companies claim Google uses advertising and penalty filters in its search function to limit access to competitors.

- Google has a 90 per cent share of the UK search market.

- Google dismisses the claims saying it did not have favourites or create barriers to entry and its success arises from innovation and good products which get people to the best sites.

Economic Analysis

◆ Google gained its dominant position in the search market by selling advertisements associated with search keywords within its innovative search engine.

◆ Google sells keywords based on a combination of willingness-to-pay and the number of clicks an advertisement receives.

◆ Google has steadily improved its search engine and its interface with both searchers and advertisers to make searches more powerful and advertising more effective.

◆ Figure 1 shows Google's extraordinary success in terms of its revenue, cost and profit.

◆ Google could have provided a basic search engine without innovation.

◆ If Google had followed this strategy, people would use competitor search engines and advertisers would have been willing to pay low prices for Google ads.

◆ Google would have faced the market described in Figure 2 and made a small economic profit.

◆ Instead, Google improved its search engine and the effectiveness of advertising. The demand for Google search and ads increased.

◆ Google's innovation is not a barrier to entry but by selling keywords to the highest bidder it achieves perfect price discrimination.

◆ Figure 3 shows how, with perfect price discrimination, Google's producer surplus is maximized. Google produces the efficient quantity of search and advertising by accepting ads as long as price exceeds marginal cost.

◆ Google has a dominant position but doesn't appear to be acting against the EU social interest: there is no anti-competition case to answer.

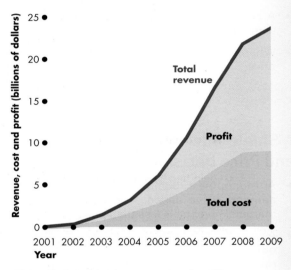

Figure 1 Google's revenue, cost and profit

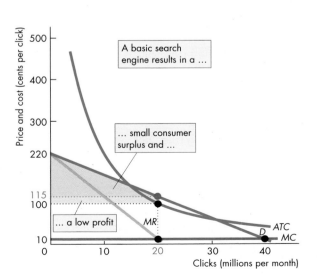

Figure 2 Basic search engine

Figure 3 Google with keywords and other features

SUMMARY

Key Points

Monopoly and How It Arises
(pp. 276–277)

◆ A monopoly is a market with a single supplier of a good or service that has no close substitutes and in which barriers to entry prevent competition.

◆ Barriers to entry may be legal (monopoly franchise, licence, patent or copyright), ownership of a resource, or natural (created by economies of scale).

◆ A monopoly might be able to price discriminate when there is no resale possibility.

◆ Where resale is possible, a firm charges one price.

Working Problems 1 to 4 will give you a better understanding of monopoly and how it arises.

A Single-price Monopoly's Output and Price Decision (pp. 278–281)

◆ A monopoly's demand curve is the market demand curve and a single-price monopoly's marginal revenue is less than price.

◆ A monopoly maximizes profit by producing the output at which marginal revenue equals marginal cost and by charging the maximum price that consumers are willing to pay for that output.

Working Problems 5 to 9 will give you a better understanding of a single-price monopoly's output and price.

Single-price Monopoly and Competition Compared (pp. 282–285)

◆ A single-price monopoly charges a higher price and produces a smaller quantity than a perfectly competitive market.

◆ A single-price monopoly restricts output and creates a deadweight loss.

◆ The total loss that arises from monopoly equals the deadweight loss plus the cost of the resources devoted to rent seeking.

Working Problems 10 to 12 will give you a better understanding of the comparison of single-price monopoly and perfect competition.

Price Discrimination (pp. 285–288)

◆ Price discrimination is an attempt by the monopoly to convert consumer surplus into economic profit.

◆ Perfect price discrimination extracts the entire consumer surplus; each unit is sold for the maximum price that each customer is willing to pay; the quantity produced is efficient.

◆ Rent seeking with perfect price discrimination might eliminate the entire consumer surplus and producer surplus.

Working Problems 13 to 16 will give you a better understanding of price discrimination.

Monopoly Regulation (pp. 289–291)

◆ Monopoly regulation might serve the social interest or the interest of the monopoly (monopoly captures the regulator).

◆ Price equal to marginal cost achieves efficiency but results in economic loss.

◆ Price equal to average cost enables the firm to cover its costs but is inefficient.

◆ Rate of return regulation creates incentives for inefficient production and inflated cost.

◆ Price cap regulation with earnings sharing regulation can achieve a more efficient outcome than rate of return regulation.

Working Problems 17 to 19 will give you a better understanding of monopoly regulation.

Key Terms

STUDY PLAN PROBLEMS AND APPLICATIONS

 You can work Problems 1 to 19 in MyEconLab Chapter 12 Study Plan and get instant feedback.

Monopoly and How It Arises
(Study Plan 12.1)

Use the following information to work Problems 1 to 3.

The Post Office has a monopoly on first class mail and the exclusive right to put mail in private mailboxes. Pfizer Inc. makes LIPITOR, a prescription drug that lowers cholesterol. Yorkshire Water is the sole supplier of drinking water in parts of northern England.

1 **a** What are the substitutes, if any, for the goods and services described above?

   b What are the barriers to entry, if any, that protect these three firms from competition?

2 Which of these three firms, if any, is a natural monopoly? Explain your answer and illustrate it by drawing an appropriate figure.

3 **a** Which of these three firms, if any, is a legal monopoly? Explain your answer.

   b Which of these three firms is most likely to be able to profit from price discrimination and which is most likely to sell its good or service for a single price?

4 **Barbie's Revenge: Brawl over Doll Is Heading to Trial**

   Four years ago, Mattel Inc. exhorted its executives to help save Barbie from a new doll clique called the Bratz. With its market share dropping at a 'chilling rate,' Barbie needed to be more 'aggressive, revolutionary, and ruthless.' Mattel has gone to court and is trying to seize ownership of the Bratz line, which Mattel accuses of stealing the idea for the pouty-lipped dolls with the big heads.

   Source: *The Wall Street Journal*, 23 May 2008

   a Before Bratz entered the market, what type of monopoly did Mattel Inc. possess in the market for 'the pouty-lipped dolls with the big heads'?

   b What is the barrier to entry that Mattel might argue should protect it from competition in the market for Barbie dolls?

   c Explain how the entry of Bratz dolls might be expected to change the demand for Barbie dolls.

A Single-price Monopoly's Output and Price Decision (Study Plan 12.2)

Use the following table to work Problems 5 to 8.

Minnie's Mineral Springs, a single-price monopoly, faces the market demand schedule:

Price (euros per bottle)	Quantity demanded (bottles)
10	0
8	1
6	2
4	3
2	4
0	5

5 **a** Calculate the total revenue schedule for Minnie's Mineral Springs.

   b Calculate the marginal revenue schedule.

6 **a** Draw a graph of the market demand curve and Minnie's marginal revenue curve.

   b Why is Minnie's marginal revenue less than the price?

7 **a** At what price is Minnie's total revenue maximized?

   b Over what range of prices is the demand for water from Minnie's Mineral Springs elastic?

8 Why will Minnie not produce a quantity at which the market demand for water is inelastic?

9 Minnie's Mineral Springs faces the demand schedule in Problem 5 and has the following total cost schedule:

Quantity produced (bottles)	Total cost (euros)
0	1
1	3
2	7
3	13
4	21
5	31

   a Calculate Minnie's profit-maximizing output and price.

   b Calculate economic profit.

Single-price Monopoly and Competition Compared (Study Plan 12.3)

Use the following news clip to work Problems 10 to 12.

Zoloft Faces Patent Expiration

Pfizer's antidepressant Zoloft, with $3.3 billion in 2005 sales, loses patent protection on June 30. When a brand name drug loses its patent, both the price of the drug and the dollar value of its sales each tend to drop 80 per cent over the next year, as competition opens to a host of generic drugmakers. The real winners are the patients and the insurers, who pay much lower prices. The Food and Drug Administration insists that generics work identically to brand-names.

Source: CNN, 15 June 2006

10 a Assume that Pfizer has a monopoly in the antidepressant market and that Pfizer cannot price discriminate. Use a graph to illustrate the market price and quantity of Zoloft sold.

b On your graph, identify consumer surplus, producer surplus, and deadweight loss.

11 How might you justify protecting Pfizer from competition with a legal barrier to entry?

12 a Explain how the market for an antidepressant drug changes when a patent expires.

b Draw a graph to illustrate how the expiration of the Zoloft patent will change the price and quantity in the market for antidepressants.

c Explain how consumer surplus, producer surplus, and deadweight loss change with the expiration of the Zoloft patent.

Price Discrimination (Study Plan 12.4)

Use the following news clip to work Problems 13 and 14.

The Saturday-Night Stay Requirement Is on Its Final Approach

The Saturday-night stay – the requirement that airlines instituted to ensure that business travellers pay an outrageous airfare if he or she wants to go home for the weekend – has gone the way of the dodo bird. Experts agree that low-fare carriers, such as Southwest, are the primary reason major airlines are adopting more consumer-friendly fare structures, which include the elimination of the Saturday-night stay, the introduction of one-way and walk-up fares, and the general restructuring of fares.

Source: *Los Angeles Times*, 15 August 2004

13 Explain why the opportunity for price discrimination exists for air travel. How does an airline profit from price discrimination?

14 Describe the change in price discrimination in the market for air travel when discount airlines entered the market and explain the effect of discount airlines on the price and the quantity of air travel.

Use the following information to work Problems 15 and 16.

La Bella Pizza can produce a pizza for a marginal cost of €2. Its standard price is €15 per pizza. It offers a second pizza for €5. It also distributes coupons that give a €5 rebate on a standard price pizza.

15 How can La Bella Pizza make a larger economic profit with this range of prices than it could if it sold every pizza for €14.99? Draw a figure that illustrates your answer.

16 How might La Bella Pizza make even more economic profit? Would La Bella Pizza then be more efficient than if it charged €15 for each pizza?

Monopoly Regulation (Study Plan 12.5)

Use the following information to work Problems 17 to 19.

The figure shows a situation similar to that facing Milford Haven pipelines owned by National Grid, a firm that operates a natural gas distribution system in the UK. The gas distributor is a natural monopoly that cannot price discriminate.

What quantity will the gas distributor produce, what price will it charge, what is total surplus and what is the deadweight loss if it is:

17 An unregulated profit-maximizing firm?

18 Regulated to make zero economic profit?

19 Regulated to be efficient?

ADDITIONAL PROBLEMS AND APPLICATIONS

 myeconlab You can work these problems in MyEconLab if assigned by your lecturer.

Monopoly and How It Arises

Use the following list, which gives some information about seven firms, to answer Problems 20 and 21.

- ◆ Coca-Cola cuts its price below that of Pepsi-Cola in an attempt to increase its market share.
- ◆ A single firm, protected by a barrier to entry, produces a personal service that has no close substitutes.
- ◆ A barrier to entry exists, but the good has some close substitutes.
- ◆ A firm offers discounts to students and seniors.
- ◆ A firm can sell any quantity it chooses at the going price.
- ◆ The government issues Nike an exclusive licence to produce footballs.
- ◆ A firm experiences economies of scale even when it produces the quantity that meets the entire market demand.

20 In which of the seven cases might monopoly arise?

21 Which of the seven cases are natural monopolies and which are legal monopolies? Which can price discriminate, which cannot, and why?

A Single-price Monopoly's Output and Price Decision

Use the following information to work Problems 22 to 26.

Hot Air Balloon Rides is a single-price monopoly. Columns 1 and 2 of the table set out the market demand schedule and columns 2 and 3 set out the total cost schedule:

Price (pounds per ride)	Quantity demanded (rides per month)	Total cost (pounds per month)
220	0	80
200	1	160
180	2	260
160	3	380
140	4	520
120	5	680

22 Construct Hot Air's total revenue and marginal revenue schedules.

23 Draw a graph of the market demand curve and Hot Air's marginal revenue curve.

24 Find Hot Air's profit-maximizing output and price and calculate the firm's economic profit.

25 If the government imposes a tax on Hot Air's profit, how do its output and price change?

26 If instead of taxing Hot Air's profit, the government imposes a sales tax on balloon rides of £30 a ride, what are the new profit-maximizing quantity, price and economic profit?

27 The figure illustrates the situation facing the publisher of the only newspaper containing local news in an isolated community.

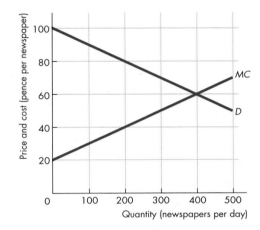

a On the graph, mark the profit-maximizing quantity and price.

b What is the publisher's daily total revenue?

Single-price Monopoly and Competition Compared

28 Show on the graph in Problem 27 the consumer surplus and the deadweight loss created by the monopoly. Explain why this market might encourage rent seeking.

29 If the newspaper market in Problem 27 were perfectly competitive, what would be the quantity, price, consumer surplus and producer surplus? Mark each on the graph.

30 **Telecoms Look to Grow by Acquisition**

Multibillion-dollar telecommunications mergers show how global cellular powerhouses are scouting for growth in emerging economies while consolidating in their own, crowded backyards. France Télécom offered to buy TeliaSonera, a Swedish–Finnish telecommunications operator, but within hours, TeliaSonera rejected the offer as too low. Analysts said higher bids – either from France Télécom or others – could persuade TeliaSonera to accept a deal. In the United States, Verizon Wireless agreed to buy Alltel for $28.1 billion – a deal that would make the company the biggest mobile phone operator in the United States. A combination of France Télécom and TeliaSonera would create the world's fourth-largest mobile operator, smaller only than China Mobile, Vodafone and Telefónica of Spain.

Source: *International Herald Tribune*, 5 June 2008

a Explain the rent-seeking behaviour of global telecommunications companies.

b Explain how mergers may affect the efficiency of the telecommunications market.

Price Discrimination

31 AT&T Moves Away from Unlimited-Data Pricing

AT&T said it will eliminate its $30 unlimited data plan as the crush of data use from the iPhone has hurt call quality. AT&T is introducing new plans costing $15 a month for 200 megabytes of data traffic or $25 a month for 2 gigabytes. AT&T says those who exceed 2 gigabytes of usage will pay $10 a month for each additional gigabyte. AT&T hopes that these plans will attract more customers.

Source: *The Wall Street Journal*, 2 June 2010

a Explain why AT&T's new plans might be price discrimination.

b Draw a graph to illustrate the original plan and the new plans.

Monopoly Regulation

32 Sky High Prices

Ofcom may force Sky to put a cap on its wholesale prices to rivals like BT Vision. Ofcom said that a cap on the prices Sky charged rivals to show sports and film channels was the 'most appropriate way to ensure fair and effective competition'. BT is ready to undercut Sky's prices for sports channels if prices are capped.

Source: BBC News, 30 March 2010

a What is the effect of Sky's monopoly of UK satellite television provision on the prices charged to access the satellite network?

b Explain why Ofcom thinks a price cap is the 'most appropriate way to ensure fair and effective competition'.

Use the following news clip to work Problems 33 and 34.

Google vs eBay

Google is the most popular search engine and 75 per cent of referrals to websites originate from its searches. Some bankers estimate Google's value at $15 billion or more. It is almost impossible for Google to stay permanently ahead of other search-engine technologies because it takes only a bright idea by another set of programmers to lose its lead. Google does not have the natural-monopoly advantages that have made eBay dominant – network effect of buyers and sellers knowing they do best by all trading in one place.

Source: *The Economist*, 30 October 2002

33 a Why is eBay a monopoly but Google not a monopoly?

b Under what circumstances would eBay's monopoly be illegal? Explain why.

34 a How would you regulate the Internet auction business to ensure that resources are used efficiently?

b 'Anyone is free to buy shares in eBay, so everyone could benefit from eBay's economic profit, and the bigger that economic profit, the better for all.' Evaluate this statement.

Economics in the News

35 After you have studied *Reading Between the Lines* on pp. 292–293 answer the following questions.

a Why do the companies that complained about Google say that it needs to be investigated? Do you agree? Explain why or why not.

b Explain why it would be inefficient to regulate Google to make it charge the same price per keyword click to all advertisers.

c Explain why selling keywords to the highest bidder can lead to an efficient allocation of advertising resources.

CHAPTER 13

Monopolistic Competition

After studying this chapter you will be able to:

◆ Define and identify monopolistic competition

◆ Explain how price and output are determined in a monopolistically competitive industry

◆ Explain why advertising and branding costs are high in monopolistic competition

Every day, Europeans enjoy the huge variety of choice created by the globalized trade in brand name products. Adidas, Puma, Umbro, Reebok and Nike are just a few of the makers of football gear. The iPhone is different from a Blackberry, but the brands are in competition. Many of the products you buy are like this. Do the firms in these markets operate like those in perfect competition or do they restrict output to increase profit like a monopoly? Find out in this chapter. And in *Reading Between the Lines* at the end of the chapter, see how Apple hopes its iPad will fight off the new wave of competition in the tablet computer market.

What Is Monopolistic Competition?

You have studied perfect competition in which a large number of firms produce at the lowest possible cost, make zero economic profit and are efficient. You've also studied monopoly, in which a single firm restricts output, produces at a higher cost and price than in perfect competition and is inefficient.

Most real-world markets are competitive but not perfectly competitive because firms in these markets have some power to set their prices as monopolies do. We call this type of market *monopolistic competition*.

Monopolistic competition is a market structure in which:

◆ A large number of firms compete.
◆ Each firm produces a differentiated product.
◆ Firms compete on product quality, price and marketing.
◆ Firms are free to enter and exit.

Large Number of Firms

In monopolistic competition, as in perfect competition, the industry consists of a large number of firms. The presence of a large number of firms has three implications for the firms in the industry.

Small Market Share

In monopolistic competition, each firm supplies a small part of the total industry output. Consequently, each firm has only limited market power to influence the price of its product. Each firm's price can deviate from the average market price by a relatively small amount.

Ignore Other Firms

A firm in monopolistic competition must be sensitive to the average market price of the product, but each firm does not pay attention to any one individual competitor. Because all the firms are relatively small and each firm has only a small share of the total market, no one firm can dictate market conditions. So no one firm's actions directly affect the actions of the other firms.

Collusion Impossible

Firms in monopolistic competition would like to be able to conspire to fix a higher price – called collusion.

But because there are many firms, collusion is not possible.

Product Differentiation

A firm practises **product differentiation** if it makes a product that is slightly different from the products of competing firms. A differentiated product is one that is a close substitute but not a perfect substitute for the products of the other firms. Some people are willing to pay more for one variety of the product, so when its price rises, the quantity demanded decreases but it does not (necessarily) fall to zero. For example, Adidas, Asics, Diadora, Etonic, Fila, New Balance, Nike, Puma and Reebok all make differentiated running shoes. Other things remaining the same, if the price of Adidas running shoes rises and the prices of the other shoes remain constant, Adidas sells fewer shoes and the other producers sell more. But Adidas shoes don't disappear unless the price rises by a large enough amount.

Competing on Quality, Price and Marketing

Product differentiation enables a firm to compete with other firms in three areas: product quality, price and marketing.

Quality

The quality of a product is the physical attributes that make it different from the products of other firms. Quality includes design, reliability, the service provided to the buyer and the buyer's ease of access to the product. Quality lies on a spectrum that runs from high to low. Some firms – such as Dell Computer Corp. – offer high-quality products. They are well designed and reliable, and the customer receives quick and efficient service. Other firms offer a lower-quality product that is less well designed, that might not work perfectly and that the buyer must travel some distance to obtain.

Price

Because of product differentiation, a firm in monopolistic competition faces a downward-sloping demand curve. So, like a monopoly, the firm can set both its price and its output. But there is a trade-off between the product's quality and price. A firm that makes a high-quality product can charge a higher price than a firm that makes a low-quality product.

Marketing

Because of product differentiation, a firm in monopolistic competition must market its product. Marketing takes two main forms: advertising and packaging. A firm that produces a high-quality product wants to sell it for a suitably high price. To be able to sell a high-quality product for a high price, a firm must advertise and package its product in a way that convinces buyers that they are getting the higher quality for which they are paying. For example, pharmaceutical companies advertise and package their brand-name drugs to persuade buyers that these items are superior to lower-priced generic alternatives. Similarly, a low-quality producer uses advertising and packaging to persuade buyers that although the quality is low, the low price more than compensates for this fact.

Entry and Exit

In monopolistic competition, there is free entry and free exit. Consequently, a firm cannot make an economic profit in the long run. When existing firms make economic profits, new firms enter the industry. This entry lowers prices and eventually eliminates economic profit. When firms incur economic losses, some firms leave the industry. This exit increases prices and eventually eliminates economic loss. In long-run equilibrium, firms neither enter nor leave the industry and the firms in the industry make zero economic profit.

Examples of Monopolistic Competition

Figure 1 in *Economics in Action* shows 10 examples of industries in the UK which are monopolistically competitive. These industries have a large number of firms, they produce differentiated products and they compete on quality, price and marketing. In the most concentrated of these industries, dairy products, the largest 5 firms produce 32 per cent of industry output and the largest 15 firms produce 57 per cent of industry output. In the least concentrated of these industries, furniture, the largest 5 firms produce only 5 per cent of industry output and the largest 15 firms produce 13 per cent of industry output.

Review Quiz

1   What are the distinguishing characteristics of monopolistic competition?
2   How do firms in monopolistic competition compete?
3   Provide some examples of industries near your university that operate in monopolistic competition (excluding those in the figure below).

You can work these questions in Study Plan 13.1 and get instant feedback.

ECONOMICS IN ACTION

Monopolistic Competition Today

These 10 industries operate in monopolistic competition. The red bar shows the percentage of industry output produced by the 5 largest firms and the blue bar shows the percentage of industry output produced by the next 10 largest firms. So the entire length of the bar shows the percentage of industry output produced by the largest 15 firms.

The industries shown have many firms that produce differentiated products and compete on quality, price and marketing.

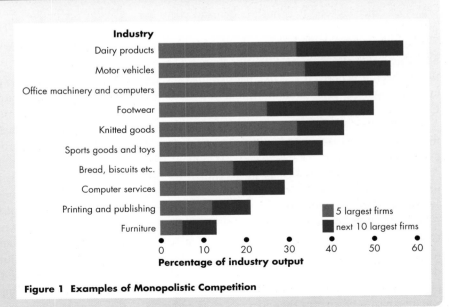

Figure 1 Examples of Monopolistic Competition

Price and Output in Monopolistic Competition

Suppose you've been employed by French Connection to manage the production and marketing of jackets. Think about the decisions that you must make at French Connection. First, you must decide on the design and quality of jackets and on your marketing plan. Second, you must decide on the quantity of jackets to produce and the price at which to sell them.

We'll suppose that French Connection has already made its decisions about design, quality and marketing, and now we'll concentrate on the output and pricing decision. We'll study quality and marketing decisions in the next section.

For a given quality of jackets and marketing activity, French Connection faces given costs and market conditions. How, given its costs and the demand for its jackets, does French Connection decide the quantity of jackets to produce and the price at which to sell them?

The Firm's Short-run Output and Price Decision

In the short run, a firm in monopolistic competition makes its output and price decision just like a monopoly firm does. Figure 13.1 illustrates this decision for French Connection jackets.

The demand curve for French Connection jackets is *D*. This demand curve tells us the quantity of French Connection jackets demanded at each price, given the prices of other jackets. It is not the demand curve for jackets in general.

The *MR* curve shows the marginal revenue curve associated with the demand curve for French Connection jackets. It is derived just like the marginal revenue curve of a single-price monopoly that you studied in Chapter 12.

The *ATC* curve and the *MC* curve show the average total cost and the marginal cost of producing French Connection jackets.

French Connection's goal is to maximize its economic profit. To do so, it will produce the output at which marginal revenue equals marginal cost. In Figure 13.1, this output is 125 jackets a day. French Connection charges the price that buyers are willing to pay for this quantity, which is determined by the demand curve. This price is £75 per jacket. When it produces 125 jackets a day, French Connection's average total cost is £25 per jacket and it makes an economic

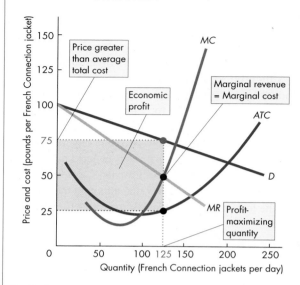

Figure 13.1 Economic Profit in the Short Run

Profit is maximized where marginal revenue equals marginal cost. The profit-maximizing quantity is 125 jackets a day. The price of £75 a jacket exceeds the average total cost of £25 a jacket, so the firm makes an economic profit of £50 a jacket. The blue rectangle illustrates economic profit, which equals £6,250 a day (£50 a jacket multiplied by 125 jackets a day).

 Animation

profit of £6,250 a day (£50 per jacket multiplied by 125 jackets a day). The blue rectangle shows French Connection's economic profit.

Profit Maximizing Might Be Loss Minimizing

Figure 13.1 shows that French Connection is making a healthy economic profit. But such an outcome is not inevitable. A firm might face a level of demand for its product that is too low for it to make an economic profit.

Excite@Home was such a firm. Offering high-speed Internet service, Excite@Home hoped to capture a large share of the Internet portal market in competition with AOL, MSN, Yahoo! and a host of other providers.

Figure 13.2 illustrates the situation facing Excite@Home in 2001. The demand curve for its portal service is *D*, the marginal revenue curve is *MR*, the average total cost curve is *ATC* and the marginal

Figure 13.2 Economic Loss in the Short Run

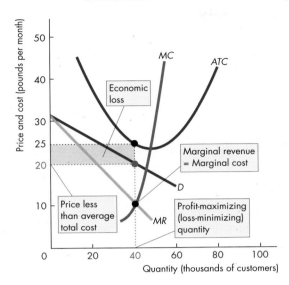

Profit is maximized where marginal revenue equals marginal cost. The loss-minimizing quantity is 40,000 customers. The price of £20 a month is less than the average total cost of £25 a month, so the firm incurs an economic loss of £5 a customer. The red rectangle illustrates economic loss, which equals £200,000 a month (£5 a customer multiplied by 40,000 customers).

myeconlab Animation

cost curve is *MC*. Excite@Home maximized profit – equivalently, it minimized its loss – by producing the output at which marginal revenue equals marginal cost. In Figure 13.2, this output is 40,000 customers.

Excite@Home charged the price that buyers were willing to pay for this quantity, which was determined by the demand curve and which was £20 a month. With 40,000 customers, Excite@Home's average total cost was £25 per customer, so it incurred an economic loss of £200,000 a month (£5 a customer multiplied by 40,000 customers). The red rectangle shows Excite@Home's economic loss.

So far, the firm in monopolistic competition looks like a single-price monopoly. It produces the quantity at which marginal revenue equals marginal cost and then charges the price that buyers are willing to pay for that quantity, determined by the demand curve. The key difference between monopoly and monopolistic competition lies in what happens next when firms either make an economic profit or incur an economic loss.

Long Run: Zero Economic Profit

A firm like Excite@Home is not going to incur an economic loss for long. Eventually, it goes out of business. Also, there is no restriction on entry in monopolistic competition, so if firms in an industry are making an economic profit, other firms have an incentive to enter that industry.

As Burberry, Gap and other firms start to make jackets similar to those made by French Connection, the demand for French Connection jackets decreases. The demand curve for French Connection jackets and the marginal revenue curve shift leftward. And as these curves shift leftward, the profit-maximizing quantity and price fall.

Figure 13.3 shows the long-run equilibrium. The demand curve for French Connection jackets and the marginal revenue curve have shifted leftward. The firm produces 75 jackets a day and sells them for £50 each. At this output level, average total cost is also £50 per jacket.

Figure 13.3 Output and Price in the Long Run

Economic profit encourages entry, which decreases the demand for each firm's product. When the demand curve touches the *ATC* curve at the quantity at which *MR* equals *MC*, the market is in long-run equilibrium. The output that maximizes profit is 75 jackets a day and the price is £50 per jacket. Average total cost is also £50 per jacket, so economic profit is zero.

myeconlab Animation

So French Connection is making zero economic profit on its jackets. When all the firms in the industry are making zero economic profit, there is no incentive for new firms to enter.

If demand is so low relative to costs that firms incur economic losses, exit will occur. As firms leave an industry, the demand for the products of the remaining firms increases and their demand curves shift rightward. The exit process ends when all the firms in the industry are making zero economic profit.

Monopolistic Competition and Perfect Competition

Figure 13.4 compares monopolistic competition and perfect competition and highlights two key differences between them:

◆ Excess capacity
◆ Markup

Excess Capacity

A firm has **excess capacity** if it produces below its **efficient scale**, which is the quantity at which average total cost is a minimum – the quantity at the bottom of the U-shaped *ATC* curve. In Figure 13.4, the efficient scale is 100 jackets a day. French Connection in part (a) produces 75 French Connection jackets a day and has *excess capacity* of 25 jackets a day. But if all jackets are alike and are produced by firms in perfect competition, each firm in part (b) produces 100 jackets a day, which is the efficient scale. Average total cost is the lowest possible only in *perfect* competition.

You can see the excess capacity in monopolistic competition all around you. Family restaurants (except for the truly outstanding ones) almost always have some empty tables. It is rare that every pump at a petrol station is in use with customers queuing up to be served. There is always an abundance of estate agents ready to help find or sell a home. These industries are examples

Figure 13.4 Excess Capacity and Markup

(a) Monopolistic competition

(b) Perfect competition

The efficient scale is 100 jackets a day. In monopolistic competition in the long run, because the demand curve for the firm's product is downward sloping, the quantity produced is less than the efficient scale and the firm has excess capacity. Price exceeds marginal cost and this gap is the firm's markup.

In contrast, because in perfect competition the demand for each firm's product is perfectly elastic, the quantity produced in the long run equals the efficient scale and price equals marginal cost. The perfectly competitive firm produces at the least possible cost and there is no markup.

of monopolistic competition. The firms have excess capacity. They could sell more by cutting their prices, but they would then incur economic losses.

Markup

A firm's **markup** is the amount by which the price exceeds marginal cost. Figure 13.4(a) shows French Connection's markup. In perfect competition, price always equals marginal cost and there is no markup. Figure 13.4(b) shows this case. In monopolistic competition, buyers pay a higher price than in perfect competition and also pay more than marginal cost.

Is Monopolistic Competition Efficient?

Resources are used efficiently when marginal social benefit equals marginal social cost. Price measures marginal social benefit and the firm's marginal cost equals marginal social cost (assuming there are no external benefits or costs). So if the price of a French Connection jacket exceeds the marginal cost of producing it, the quantity of French Connection jackets produced is less than the efficient quantity. And you've just seen that in long-run equilibrium in monopolistic competition, price *does* exceed marginal cost. So is the quantity produced in monopolistic competition less than the efficient quantity?

Making the Relevant Comparison

Two economists meet in the street, and one asks the other how her husband is. 'Compared to what?' is the quick reply. This bit of economic wit illustrates a key point: before we can conclude that something needs fixing, we must check out the available alternatives.

The markup that drives a gap between price and marginal cost in monopolistic competition arises from product differentiation. It is because French Connection jackets are not quite the same as jackets from Banana Republic, Diesel, DKNY, Earl Jackets, Gap or any of the other dozens of producers of jackets that the demand for French Connection jackets is not perfectly elastic. The only way in which the demand for jackets from French Connection might be perfectly elastic is if there is only one kind of jacket and all firms make it. In this situation, French Connection jackets are indistinguishable from all other jackets. They don't even have labels.

If there was only one kind of jacket, the total benefit from jackets would almost certainly be less than it is

with variety. People value variety – not only because it enables each person to select what he or she likes best but also because it provides an external benefit. Most of us enjoy seeing variety in the choices of others. Contrast a scene from the China of the 1960s, when everyone wore a Mao tunic, with the China of today, where everyone wears the clothes of their own choosing. Or contrast a scene from the Germany of the 1930s, when almost everyone who could afford a car owned a first-generation Volkswagen Beetle, with the world of today with its enormous variety of styles and types of cars.

If people value variety, why don't we see infinite variety? The answer is that variety is costly. Each different variety of any product must be designed, and then customers must be informed about it. These initial costs of design and marketing – called setup costs – mean that some varieties that are too close to others already available are just not worth creating.

The Bottom Line

Product variety is both valued and costly. The efficient degree of product variety is the one for which the marginal social benefit from product variety equals its marginal social cost. The loss that arises because the quantity produced is less than the efficient quantity is offset by a gain that arises from having a greater degree of product variety. So compared to the alternative – complete product uniformity – monopolistic competition is probably efficient.

Review Quiz

1 How does a firm in monopolistic competition decide how much to produce and at what price to offer its product for sale?
2 Why can a firm in monopolistic competition make an economic profit only in the short run?
3 Why do firms in monopolistic competition operate with excess capacity?
4 Why is there a price markup over marginal cost in monopolistic competition?
5 Is monopolistic competition efficient?

You can work these questions in Study Plan 13.2 and get instant feedback.

You've seen how the firm in monopolistic competition determines its output and price when it produces a given product and undertakes a *given* marketing effort. But how does the firm choose its product quality and marketing effort? We'll now study these decisions.

Product Development and Marketing

When we studied French Connection's price and output decision, we assumed that it had already made its product quality and marketing decisions. We're now going to study these decisions and the impact they have on the firm's output, price and economic profit.

Innovation and Product Development

The prospect of new firms entering the industry keeps firms in monopolistic competition on their toes!

To enjoy economic profits, firms in monopolistic competition must be continually seeking ways of keeping one step ahead of imitators – other firms that imitate the success of the economically profitable firms.

One major way of trying to maintain economic profit is for a firm to seek out new products that will provide it with a competitive edge, even if only temporarily. A firm that introduces a new and differentiated product faces a less elastic demand for its product and so the firm is able to increase its price and make an economic profit. But economic profit is an incentive for new firms to enter the market. So eventually imitators will enter the market and make close substitutes for the innovative product and compete away the economic profit arising from an initial advantage. So to restore economic profit, the firm must again innovate.

Profit-maximizing Product Innovation

The decision to innovate and develop a new or improved product is based on the same type of profit-maximizing calculation that you've already studied.

Innovation and product development are costly activities, but they also bring in additional revenues. The firm must balance the marginal cost and marginal revenue. The marginal pound spent on developing a new or improved product is the marginal cost of product development. The marginal pound that the new or improved product earns for the firm is the marginal revenue of product development.

At a low level of product development, the marginal revenue from a better product exceeds the marginal cost. At a high level of product development, the marginal cost of a better product exceeds the marginal revenue. When the marginal cost and the marginal revenue of product development are equal, the firm is

undertaking the profit-maximizing amount of product development.

Efficiency and Product Innovation

Is the profit-maximizing amount of product innovation also the efficient amount? Efficiency is achieved if the marginal social benefit from a new and improved product equals its marginal social cost.

The marginal social benefit from an innovation is the increase in the price that consumers are willing to pay for it. The marginal social cost is the amount that the firm must pay to make the innovation. Profit is maximized when marginal *revenue* equals marginal cost. But in monopolistic competition, marginal revenue is less than the price, so product innovation is probably not pushed to its efficient level.

Monopolistic competition brings many product innovations that cost little to implement and are purely cosmetic, such as new and improved packaging or a new scent in laundry powder. And even when there is a genuine improved product, the innovation is never as good as what the consumer would like. For example, 'The Legend of Zelda: Twilight Princess' is regarded as an almost perfect, and an incredibly cool video game, but reviewers complain that it isn't quite perfect. It is a game with features whose marginal revenue equals the marginal cost of creating them.

Advertising

A firm with a differentiated product needs to ensure that its customers know how its product is different from the competition. A firm also might attempt to create a consumer perception that its product is different from its competitors, even when that difference is small. Firms use advertising and packaging to achieve this goal.

Advertising Expenditures

Firms in monopolistic competition incur huge costs to ensure that buyers appreciate and value the differences between their own products and those of their competitors. So a large proportion of the price that we pay for a good covers the cost of selling it. Advertising in newspapers and magazines and on radio, television and the Internet is the main selling cost. But it is not the only one. Selling costs include the cost of shopping centres, glossy catalogues and brochures and the salaries, airfares and hotel bills of sales staff.

Advertising costs are only a part and often a small part of the total selling costs. The biggest part of the selling costs is the retailing services. The retailer's selling costs (and economic profit) are often as much as 50 per cent of the price you pay.

Advertising expenditures and other selling costs affect the profits of firms in two ways: they increase costs and they change demand. Let's look at these effects.

ECONOMICS IN ACTION

Advertising Expenditures

The total scale of advertising costs is hard to estimate, but, on average, probably 15 per cent of the price of an item is spent on advertising. The figure shows estimated UK advertising expenditure in different media.

Most UK advertising expenditure occurs on television and in the press, newspapers and magazines. The Internet has recently overtaken direct mail as the third most important medium for advertising.

Of the price that customers pay for a good, the cost of selling it is a large and rising component. Real advertising expenditure in the UK increased by 36 per cent between 1995 and 2005 and by 57 per cent between 1990 and 2005. With the downturn it fell by 2.5 per cent in 2008 and 13 per cent in 2009 to £14.5 billion. It is expected to rise by 3.4 per cent in 2010.

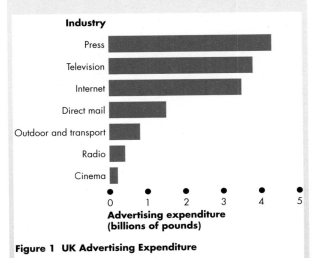

Figure 1 UK Advertising Expenditure

Source of data: Advertising Association,
http://www.adassoc.org.uk.

Selling Costs and Total Costs

Selling costs are fixed costs and they increase the firm's total cost. So, just like fixed production costs, advertising costs per unit decrease as production increases.

Figure 13.5 shows how selling costs change a firm's average total cost. The blue curve shows the average total cost of production. The red curve shows the firm's average total cost of production with advertising. The height of the shaded area between the two curves shows the average fixed cost of advertising. The *total* cost of advertising is fixed. But the *average* cost of advertising decreases as output increases.

Figure 13.5 shows that if advertising increases the quantity sold by a large enough amount, it can lower average total cost. For example, if the quantity sold increases from 25 jackets a day with no advertising to 100 jackets a day with advertising, average total cost falls from £60 to £40 a jacket. The reason is that although the *total* fixed cost has increased, the greater fixed cost is spread over a greater output, so average total cost decreases.

Figure 13.5 Selling Costs and Total Cost

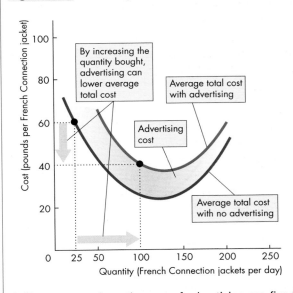

Selling costs such as the cost of advertising are fixed costs. When added to the average total cost of production, selling costs increase average total cost by a greater amount at small outputs than at large outputs. If advertising enables sales to increase from 25 jackets a day to 100 jackets a day, average total cost falls from £60 to £40 a jacket.

Selling Costs and Demand

Advertising and other selling efforts change the demand for a firm's product. But how? Does demand increase or does it decrease? The most natural answer is that advertising increases demand. By informing people about the quality of its products or by persuading people to switch from the products of other firms, a firm might expect to increase the demand for its own products.

But all firms in monopolistic competition advertise. And all seek to persuade customers that they have the best deal. If advertising enables a firm to survive, it might increase the number of firms in the market. And to the extent that the number of firms does increase, advertising *decreases* the demand faced by any one firm. Advertising by all the firms might also make the demand for any one firm's product more elastic. In this case, advertising ends up not only lowering average total cost but also lowering the markup and the price.

Figure 13.6 illustrates this possible effect of advertising. In part (a), with no advertising, the demand for French Connection jackets is not very elastic. Profit is

maximized at 75 jackets per day and the markup is large. In part (b), advertising, which is a fixed cost, increases average total cost from ATC_0 to ATC_1 but leaves marginal cost unchanged at MC. Demand for the firm's product becomes much more elastic, the profit-maximizing quantity increases and the markup shrinks.

Using Advertising to Signal Quality

Some advertising, like the David Beckham Gillette ads on television and in glossy magazines or the huge amounts that Coke and Pepsi spend, seems hard to understand. There doesn't seem to be any concrete information about a shaver in the smiling face of a footballer. And surely everyone knows about Coke and Pepsi. What is the gain from pouring millions of pounds a month into advertising these well-known colas?

One answer is that advertising is a signal to the consumer of a high-quality product. A **signal** is an action taken by an informed person (or firm) to send a message to uninformed people. Think about two shavers: Gillette

---

Figure 13.6   Advertising and the Markup

(a) No firms advertise

With no firms advertising, demand is low and not very elastic. The profit-maximizing output is small, the markup is large and the price is high.

(b) All firms advertise

Advertising increases average total cost and shifts the *ATC* curve upward from ATC_0 to ATC_1. With all firms advertising, the demand for each firm's product becomes more elastic. Output increases, the markup shrinks and the price falls.

Fusion and Bland. Bland knows that its blades are poor and of variable quality that depends on which cheap batch of unsold blades it happens to buy each week. So Bland knows that while it could get a lot of people to try Bland by advertising, they would all quickly discover what a poor product it is and switch back to the shaver they bought before. Gillette, in contrast, knows that its blade gives a high-quality consistent shave and that once consumers have tried it, there is a good chance they'll never use anything else. On the basis of this reasoning, Bland doesn't advertise but Gillette does.

And Gillette spends a lot of money to make a big splash. Fusion users who know that Gillette has done a $10 million deal with Beckham know that the firm would not spend so much money advertising if its product were not truly good. So consumers reason that a Gillette shaver is indeed a really good product. The flashy expensive ad has signalled that a Fusion shaver is really good without saying anything about the shaver.

Notice that if advertising is a signal, it doesn't need any specific product information. It just needs to be expensive and hard to miss. That's what a lot of advertising looks like. So the signalling theory of advertising predicts much of the advertising that we see.

Brand Names

Many firms create and spend a lot of money promoting a brand name. Why? What benefit does a brand name bring to justify the sometimes high cost of establishing it?

The basic answer is that a brand name provides information about the quality of a product to consumers and an incentive to the producer to achieve a high and consistent quality standard.

To see how a brand name helps the consumer, think about how you use brand names to get information about quality. You've decided to take a holiday in the sun and you're trying to decide where to go. You see advertisements for Club Med and Sheraton Resorts and for Joe's Beachside Shack and Annie's Dive. You know about Club Med and Sheraton Resorts because you've stayed in them before. You've also seen their advertisements and know what to expect from them.

You have no information at all about Joe's and Annie's. They might be better than the places you do know about, but without that knowledge, you're not going to chance them. You use the brand name as information and choose Club Med.

This same story explains why a brand name provides an incentive to achieve high and consistent quality.

Because no one would know whether Joe's and Annie's were offering a high standard of service, they have no incentive to do so. But equally, because everyone expects a given standard of service from Club Med, a failure to meet a customer's expectation would almost certainly lose that customer to a competitor. So Club Med has a strong incentive to deliver what it promises in the advertising that creates its brand name.

Efficiency of Advertising and Brand Names

To the extent that advertising and brand names provide consumers with information about the precise nature of product differences and product quality, they benefit the consumer and enable a better product choice to be made. But the opportunity cost of the additional information must be weighed against the gain to the consumer.

The final verdict on the efficiency of monopolistic competition is ambiguous. In some cases, the gains from extra product variety unquestionably offset the selling costs and the extra cost arising from excess capacity. The tremendous varieties of books and magazines, clothing, food and drinks are examples of such gains. It is less easy to see the gains from being able to buy a brand-name drug that has a chemical composition identical to that of a generic alternative. But many people do willingly pay more for the brand-name alternative.

Review Quiz

1 How, other than by adjusting price, do firms in monopolistic competition compete?
2 Why might product innovation and development be efficient and why might it be inefficient?
3 How do selling costs influence a firm's cost curves and its average total cost?
4 How does a firm's advertising influence demand?
5 Are advertising and brand names efficient?

You can work these questions in Study Plan 13.3 and get instant feedback.

Monopolistic competition is one of the most common market structures that you encounter in your daily life. *Reading Between the Lines* on pp. 310–311 applies the model of monopolistic competition to the market for tablet computers and shows why you can expect continual innovation and the introduction of new products from Apple and other producers of computer products.

Reading Between the Lines

Product Differentiation in the Tablet Computer Market

The Telegraph online, 21 October 2010

The Tablet Computer Has Gone Mainstream

Claudine Beaumont, Technology Editor

Apple's Steve Jobs believes his company is in an almost unassailable position and has the 'tiger by the tail' in this new market. But that isn't stopping everyone from BlackBerry to Next trying to emulate the iPad's success.

There's an avalanche of tablet computers, with some proving more successful than others.

Apple is bullish about the iPad's sales figures. . . . In the past three months, the company has recorded $20 billion (£12.6 billion) in sales, representing a tidy profit of $4.31 billion (£2.71 billion) over that period. Much of that success has been down to its latest gadget, the iPad . . . with around eight million sold to date. . . .

But, once again, Apple has managed to exploit the latent potential in a new segment of the market – just as it did with MP3 players and smartphones. . . .

Dozens of consumer electronics companies are now building their own tablet computers, with mixed results. Google's Android operating system . . . is proving particularly popular with manufacturers. Samsung's . . . Galaxy Tab . . . has earned rave reviews. . . . Research in Motion, the company behind the popular BlackBerry smartphone range, is also launching its own tablet.

In the six months since Apple's iPad went on sale, tablet computers have gone from niche products to mass-market devices. Even high street retailer Next has started selling one, at the almost pocket money price of £180. . . . Expect the avalanche of tablets to snowball in the next few months, with devices from HP, Microsoft and Asus set to hit the shelves.

These devices will have to be faultless . . . and . . . cost substantially less than Apple's £429 . . . to turn shoppers' heads.

The Essence of the Story

- Six months after launching the iPad, Apple says it has an unassailable position in the tablet computer market.

- Apple has sold 8 million iPads since the launch and earned $4.31 billion in profits over the last three months.

- Google, Samsung and other new competitors have flooded into the market. Next offers a tablet at only £180.

- Other makers, such as HP and Microsoft, are close behind but will have to price competitively and match Apple's quality.

Economic Analysis

- By creating a substantially differentiated product with its iPad, Apple attracted many new customers and sold 8 million units worldwide in the first six months.

- But within three months of the launch, many competing but differentiated tablet computers came onto the market.

- The monopolistic competition model explains what is happening in the tablet computer market.

- Figure 1 shows the market for Apple's iPad in its first three months, before competitors entered the market.

- Because the Apple iPad is different from other handheld devices and has features that users value, the demand curve, D, and marginal revenue curve, MR, create a large short-run profit opportunity.

- The marginal cost curve is MC and the average total cost curve is ATC. Apple maximizes its economic profit by producing the quantity at which MR equals MC, which is 4 million iPads per quarter.

- This quantity of iPads can be sold for the equivalent of £429 each.

- The blue rectangle shows Apple's economic profit.

- Apple thinks it will maintain its profit from the iPad but this is unlikely because this market is profitable and new firms will enter.

- Within three months of the iPad launch, many competitors had entered the market.

- Figure 2 shows how entry will affect Apple in the long run.

- The demand for the iPad will decrease as the market is shared with the new entrants.

- Apple's profit-maximizing price for the iPad will decrease as more firms enter the market for tablet computers.

Figure 1 Before entry

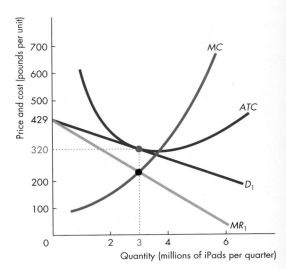

Figure 2 After entry

- Apple's profit-maximizing price will decrease and in the long run its economic profit will be eliminated.

- With zero economic profit, Apple will have an incentive to develop another new differentiated product and again start the cycle of innovation and short-run profit described here.

SUMMARY

Key Points

What Is Monopolistic Competition?
(pp. 300–301)

◆ In monopolistic competition, a large number of firms compete on product quality, price and marketing.

Working Problems 1 and 2 will give you a better understanding of what monopolistic competition is.

Price and Output in Monopolistic Competition (pp. 302–305)

◆ Each firm in monopolistic competition faces a downward-sloping demand curve and produces the profit-maximizing quantity.

◆ Entry and exit result in zero economic profit and excess capacity in long-run equilibrium.

Working Problems 3 to 12 will give you a better understanding of price and output in monopolistic competition.

Product Development and Marketing
(pp. 306–309)

◆ Firms innovate and develop new products.

◆ Advertising expenditures increase total cost, but average total cost might fall if the quantity sold increases by enough.

◆ Advertising expenditures might increase or decrease the demand for a firm's product.

◆ Whether monopolistic competition is inefficient depends on the value we place on product variety.

Working Problems 13 to 18 will give you a better understanding of product development and marketing.

Key Terms

Efficient scale, 304
Excess capacity, 304
Markup, 305
Monopolistic competition, 300
Product differentiation, 300
Signal, 308

STUDY PLAN PROBLEMS AND APPLICATIONS

  You can work Problems 1 to 19 in MyEconLab Chapter 13 Study Plan and get instant feedback.

What Is Monopolistic Competition?
(Study Plan 13.1)

1 Which of the following items are sold by firms in mono-polistic competition? Explain your selections.

  ◆ Satellite television service
  ◆ Wheat
  ◆ Athletic shoes
  ◆ Fizzy drinks
  ◆ Toothbrushes
  ◆ Ready-mix concrete

2 The five-firm concentration ratio for audio equipment makers is 30 and for electric lamp makers it is 89. Which of these markets is an example of monopolistic competition?

Price and Output in Monopolistic Competition (Study Plan 13.2)

Use the following information to work Problems 3 and 4.

Sara is a dot.com entrepreneur who has established a website at which people can design and buy sweatshirts. Sara pays £1,000 a week for her Web server and Internet connection. The sweatshirts that her customers design are made to order by another firm, and Sara pays this firm £20 a sweatshirt. Sara has no other costs. The table sets out the demand schedule for Sara's sweatshirts.

Price (pounds per sweatshirt)	Quantity demanded (sweatshirts per week)
0	100
20	80
40	60
60	40
80	20
100	0

3 Calculate Sara's profit-maximizing output, price and economic profit.

4 a Do you expect other firms to enter the Web sweatshirt business and compete with Sara?

  b What happens to the demand for Sara's sweatshirts in the long run? What happens to Sara's economic profit in the long run?

Use the following figure, which shows the situation facing a producer of running shoes, to work Problems 5 to 10.

5 What quantity does the firm produce, what price does it charge and what is its economic profit or economic loss?

6 In the long run, how does the number of firms producing running shoes change?

7 In the long run, how does the price of running shoes and the quantity the firm produces change? What happens to the market output?

8 Does the firm have excess capacity in the long run? If the firm has excess capacity in the long run, why doesn't it decrease its capacity?

9 In the long run, compare the price of a pair of running shoes and the marginal cost of producing the pair.

10 Is the market for running shoes efficient or inefficient in the long run?

11 Wake Up and Smell the Coffee

  Every change that Starbucks made over the past few years – automated espresso machines, pre-ground coffee, fewer soft chairs and less carpeting – was made for a reason: to smooth operations or boost sales. Those may have been the right choices at the time, but together they ultimately diluted the coffee-centric experience. By 2008, Starbucks experienced a drop in traffic as customers complained that in pursuing rapid growth, the company has strayed too far from its roots. Starbucks will once again grind beans in its stores for espresso coffee, give free espresso refills and provide two hours of wi-fi. The company will roll out its new sleek, low-rise espresso machine that makes the coffee server more visible.

  Source: *Time*, 7 April 2008

a Explain how Starbucks' past attempts to maximize profits ended up eroding product differentiation.

b Explain how Starbucks' new plan intends to increase economic profit.

12 The Shoe That Won't Quit

I finally decided to take the plunge and buy a pair of Uggs, but when I got around to shopping for my Uggs, the style that I wanted was sold out. The scarcity factor was not a glitch in the supply chain, but rather a carefully calibrated strategy by Ugg's parent Deckers Outdoor that is one of the big reasons behind the brand's success. Deckers tightly controls distribution to ensure that supply does not outstrip demand. If Deckers ever opened up the supply of Uggs to meet demand, sales would shoot up like a rocket, but they'd come back down just as fast.

Source: *Fortune*, 5 June 2008

a Explain why Deckers intentionally restricts the quantity of Uggs that the firm sells.

b Draw a graph to illustrate how Deckers maximizes the economic profit from Uggs.

Product Development and Marketing
(Study Plan 13.3)

Use the following information to work Problems 13 to 16.

Suppose that Tommy Hilfiger's marginal cost of a jacket is a constant £100 and the total fixed cost at one of its stores is £2,000 a day. This store sells 20 jackets a day, which is its profit-maximizing number of jackets. Then, the stores nearby start to advertise their jackets. The Tommy Hilfiger store now spends £2,000 a day advertising its jackets and its profit-maximizing number of jackets sold jumps to 50 a day.

13 a What is this store's average total cost of a jacket sold before the advertising begins?

b What is this store's average total cost of a jacket sold after the advertising begins?

14 a Can you say what happens to the price of a Tommy Hilfiger jacket? Why or why not?

b Can you say what happens to Tommy's markup? Why or why not?

c Can you say what happens to Tommy's economic profit? Why or why not?

15 How might Tommy Hilfiger use advertising as a signal? How is a signal sent and how does it work?

16 How does having a brand name help Tommy Hilfiger to increase its economic profit?

Use the following news clip to work Problems 17 and 18.

Food's Next Billion-dollar Brand?

While it's not the biggest brand in margarine, Smart Balance has an edge on its rivals in that it's made with a patented blend of vegetable and fruit oils that has been shown to help improve consumers' cholesterol levels. Smart Balance sales have skyrocketed while overall sales for margarine have stagnated. It remains to be seen if Smart Balance's healthy message and high price will resound with consumers.

Source: *Fortune*, 4 June 2008

17 How do you expect advertising and the Smart Balance brand name will affect Smart Balance's ability to make a positive economic profit?

18 Are long-run economic profits a possibility for Smart Balance? In long-run equilibrium, will Smart Balance have excess capacity or a markup?

Economics in the News
(Study Plan 13.N)

19 Computer Makers Prepare to Stake Bigger Claim in Phones

Emboldened by Apple's success with its iPhone, many PC makers and chip companies are charging into the mobile phone business, promising new devices that can pack the horsepower of standard computers into palm-size packages – devices that handle the full glory of the Internet, power two-way video conferences and stream high-definition movies to your TV. It is a development that spells serious competition for established mobile phone makers and phone companies.

Source: *The New York Times*, 15 March 2009

a Draw a graph of the cost curves and revenue curves of a mobile phone company that makes a positive economic profit in the short run.

b If mobile phone companies start to include the popular features introduced by PC makers, explain how this decision will affect their profit in the short run.

c What do you expect to happen to the mobile phone company's economic profit in the long run, given the information in the news clip?

d Draw a graph to illustrate your answer to part (c).

ADDITIONAL PROBLEMS AND APPLICATIONS

Myeconlab You can work these problems in MyEconLab if assigned by your lecturer.

What Is Monopolistic Competition?

20 Which of the following items are sold by firms in monopolistic competition? Explain your selections.

◆ Orange juice

◆ Canned soup

◆ PCs

◆ Chewing gum

◆ Breakfast cereals

◆ Corn

21 The five-firm concentration ratio for man-made fibre makers is 79 and for knitted goods makers it is 45. Which of these markets is an example of monopolistic competition?

Price and Output in Monopolistic Competition

Use the following information to work Problems 22 and 23.

Lorie teaches singing. Her fixed costs are £1,000 a month and it costs her £50 of labour to give one class. The table shows the demand schedule for Lorie's singing lessons.

Price (pounds per lesson)	Quantity demanded (lessons per week)
0	250
50	200
100	150
150	100
200	50
250	0

22 Calculate Lorie's profit-maximizing output, price and economic profit.

23 a Do you expect other firms to enter the singing lesson business and compete with Lorie?

 b What happens to the demand for Lorie's lessons in the long run? What happens to Lorie's economic profit in the long run?

Use the figure in the next column, which shows the situation facing Mike's Bikes, a producer of mountain bikes, to work Problems 24 to 28. The demand and costs of other bike producers are similar to those of Mike's Bikes.

24 What quantity does the firm produce and what price does it charge? Calculate the firm's economic profit or economic loss.

25 What will happen to the number of firms producing mountain bikes in the long run?

26 How will the price of a mountain bike and the number of bikes produced by Mike's Bikes change in the long run?

27 Is there any way for Mike's Bikes to avoid having excess capacity in the long run?

28 Is the market for mountain bikes efficient or inefficient in the long run? Explain your answer.

Use the following news clip to work Problems 29 and 30.

Groceries for the Gourmet Palate

No food, it seems, is safe from being repackaged to look like an upscale product. Samuel Adams' $120 Utopias, in a ridiculous copper-covered 24-oz. bottle meant to resemble an old-fashioned brew kettle, is barely beer. It's not carbonated like most beers, but aged in oak barrels like scotch. It has a vintage year, like a Bordeaux, is light, complex and free of any alcohol sting, despite having six times as much alcohol content as a regular can of brew.

Source: *Time*, 14 April 2008

29 a Explain how Samuel Adams has differentiated its Utopias to compete with other beer brands in terms of quality, price and marketing.

 b Predict whether Samuel Adams produces at, above or below the efficient scale in the short run.

30 a Predict whether the $120 price tag on the Utopias is at, above or below marginal cost:

(i) In the short run.

(ii) In the long run.

b Do you think that Samuel Adams Utopias makes the market for beer inefficient?

Use the following news clip to work Problems 31 and 32.

Swinging for Female Golfers

One of the hottest areas of innovation is in clubs for women, who now make up nearly a quarter of the 24 million golfers in the US. Callaway and Nike, two of the leading golf-equipment manufacturers, recently released new clubs designed specifically for women.

Source: *Time*, 21 April 2008

31 a How are Callaway and Nike attempting to maintain economic profit?

b Draw a graph to illustrate the cost curves and revenue curves of Callaway or Nike in the market for golf clubs for women.

c Show on your graph in part (b) the short-run economic profit.

32 a Explain why the economic profit that Callaway and Nike make on golf clubs for women is likely to be temporary.

b Draw a graph to illustrate the cost curves and revenue curves of Callaway or Nike in the market for golf clubs for women in the long run. Mark the firm's excess capacity.

Product Development and Marketing

Use the following information to work Problems 33 to 35.

Bianca bakes delicious cookies. Her total fixed cost is £40 a day and her average variable cost is £1 a bag. Few people know about Bianca's Cookies and she is maximizing her profit by selling 10 bags a day for £5 a bag. Bianca thinks that if she spends £50 a day on advertising, she can increase her market share and sell 25 bags a day for £5 a bag.

33 If Bianca's advertising works as she expects, can she increase her economic profit by advertising?

34 If Bianca advertises, will her average total cost increase or decrease at the quantity produced?

35 If Bianca advertises, will she continue to sell her cookies for £5 a bag or will she change her price?

Use the following news clip to work Problems 36 and 37.

A Thirst for More Champagne

Champagne exports have tripled in the past 20 years. That poses a problem for northern France, where the bubbly hails from – not enough grapes. So French authorities have unveiled a plan to extend the official Champagne grape-growing zone to cover 40 new villages. This revision has provoked debate. The change will take several years to become effective. In the meantime the vineyard owners whose land values will jump markedly if the changes are finalized certainly have reason to raise a glass.

Source: *Fortune*, 12 May 2008

36 a Why is France so strict about designating the vineyards that can use the Champagne label?

b Explain who most likely opposes this plan.

37 Assuming that vineyards in these 40 villages are producing the same quality of grapes with or without this plan, why will their land values 'jump markedly' if this plan is approved?

38 **Under Armour's Big Step Up**

Under Armour, the red-hot brand of athletic apparel, has joined Nike, Adidas and New Balance as a major player in the market for athletic footwear. Under Armour plans to revive the long-dead cross-training category. But will young athletes really spend $100 for a cross-training shoe to lift weights in?

Source: *Time*, 26 May 2008

What factors influence Under Armour's ability to make an economic profit in the cross-training shoe market?

Economics in the News

39 After you have studied *Reading Between the Lines* on pp. 310–311 answer the following questions.

a Describe the cost curves (*MC* and *ATC*) and the marginal revenue and demand curves for the iPad when Apple first introduced it.

b How do you think the creation of the iPad influenced the demand for laptop computers?

c Explain the effects of the introduction of the iPad on other firms in the market for hand-held computers.

d Draw a graph to illustrate your answer to part (c).

e Explain the effect on Apple of the decisions by HP and Samsung to bring their own tablet computers to market.

f Draw a graph to illustrate your answer to part (e).

g Do you think the tablet computer market is efficient? Explain your answer.

Oligopoly

After studying this chapter you will be able to:

◆ Define and identify oligopoly
◆ Use game theory to explain how price and output are determined in oligopoly
◆ Use game theory to explain other strategic decisions
◆ Describe the antitrust law that regulates oligopoly

In the markets for computer chips, batteries, and big aeroplanes, only two producers compete for market share in the pursuit of profit. In other markets such as airline cargo and soft drinks just a few companies compete. How does a market work when only a handful of firms compete? Is the market efficient and operating in the social interest? Or is the market inefficient like monopoly with the firms restricting output to increase profit? We answer these questions in this chapter with models of oligopoly that use game theory. And in *Reading Between the Lines* at the end of the chapter, you'll see how 11 air cargo companies formed a cartel to limit competition.

What Is Oligopoly?

Oligopoly, like monopolistic competition, lies between perfect competition and monopoly. The firms in oligopoly might produce an identical product and compete only on price, or they might produce a differentiated product and compete on price, product quality and marketing. **Oligopoly** is a market structure in which:

◆ Natural or legal barriers prevent the entry of new firms

◆ A small number of firms compete

Barriers to Entry

Either natural or legal barriers to entry can create oligopoly. You saw in Chapter 12 how economies of scale and demand form a natural barrier to entry that can create a *natural monopoly*. These same factors can create a *natural oligopoly*.

Figure 14.1 illustrates two natural oligopolies. The demand curve, *D* (in both parts of the figure), shows the market demand for taxi rides in a town. If the average total cost curve of a taxi company is ATC_1 in part (a), the market is a natural **duopoly** – an oligopoly with two firms. You can probably see some examples of duopoly where you live. Some cities have only two suppliers of milk, two local newspapers, two taxi companies, two car rental firms, two copy centres or two bookshops.

The lowest price at which the firm would remain in business is £10 a ride. At that price, the quantity of rides demanded is 60 a day, the quantity that can be provided by just two firms. There is no room in this market for three firms. But if there were only one firm, it would make an economic profit and a second firm would enter to take some of the business and economic profit.

If the average total cost curve of a taxi company is ATC_2 in part (b), the efficient scale of one firm is 20 rides a day. This market is large enough for three firms.

A legal oligopoly arises when a legal barrier to entry protects the small number of firms in a market. A city might license two taxi firms or two bus companies, for example, even though the combination of market demand and economies of scale leaves room for more than two firms.

Figure 14.1 Natural Oligoply

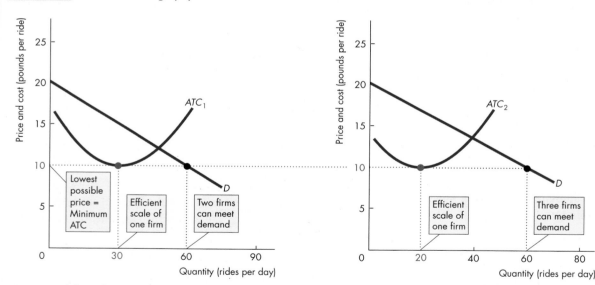

(a) Natural duopoly

The lowest possible price is £10 a ride, which is the minimum average total cost. When a firm produces 30 rides a day, the efficient scale, two firms can satisfy the market demand. This natural oligopoly has two firms – a natural duopoly.

(b) Natural oligopoly with three firms

When the efficient scale of one firm is 20 rides per day, three firms can satisfy the market demand at the lowest possible price. This natural oligopoly has three firms.

 Animation

Small Number of Firms

Because barriers to entry exist, oligopoly consists of a small number of firms, each of which has a large share of the market. Such firms are interdependent and they face a temptation to cooperate to increase their joint economic profit.

Interdependence

With a small number of firms in a market, each firm's actions influence the profits of all the other firms. When Starbucks opened in Meadowhall Shopping Centre all the other coffee shops took a hit. Within days, Café Moda began to attract Starbucks' customers with enticing offers and lower prices. Eventually, Café Moda survived but others went out of business. The coffee shops in Meadowhall are interdependent.

Temptation to Cooperate

When a small number of firms share a market, they can increase their profits by forming a cartel and acting like a monopoly. A **cartel** is a group of firms acting together – colluding – to limit output, raise price and increase economic profit. Cartels are illegal, but they do operate in some markets. But for reasons you'll discover in this chapter, cartels tend to break down.

Examples of Oligopoly

The *Economics in Action* shows some examples of oligopoly. The dividing line between oligopoly and monopolistic competition is hard to pin down. As a practical matter, we try to identify oligopoly by looking at the five-firm concentration ratio qualified with other information about the geographical scope of the market and barriers to entry. A concentration ratio that divides oligopoly from monopolistic competition is generally taken to be 60 per cent. A market in which the concentration ratio exceeds 60 per cent is usually an example of oligopoly and a market in which the concentration ratio is below 60 per cent is monopolistic competition.

Review Quiz

1 What are the two distinguishing characteristics of oligopoly?
2 Why are firms in oligopoly interdependent?
3 Why do firms in oligopoly face the temptation to collude?
4 Give some examples of oligopolies that you buy from.

You can work these questions in Study Plan 14.1 and get instant feedback.

ECONOMICS IN ACTION

Oligopoly in the UK

These 10 markets are oligopolies. The red bar shows the percentage of industry output produced by the five largest firms and the blue bar shows the percentage of industry output produced by the next 10 largest firms. So the entire length of the bar shows the percentage of industry output produced by the largest 15 firms.

  These UK markets have a few interdependent firms and the most concentrated are those with a five-firm concentration ratio above 60 per cent.

Source of data: UK Census of Production 2005.

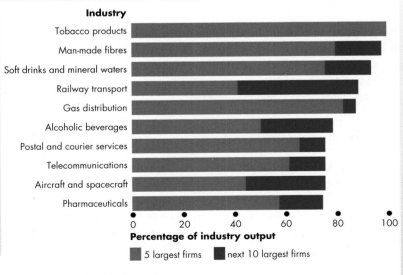

Figure 1 Examples of Oligopoly

◈ Oligopoly Games

Economists think about oligopoly as a game and to study oligopoly markets they use a set of tools called game theory. **Game theory** is a set of tools for studying *strategic behaviour* – behaviour that takes into account the expected behaviour of others and the recognition of mutual interdependence. Game theory was invented by John von Neumann in 1937 and extended by von Neumann and Oskar Morgenstern in 1944. Today, it is one of the major research fields in economics.

Game theory seeks to understand oligopoly as well as all other forms of economic, political, social and even biological rivalries, by using a method of analysis specifically designed to understand games of all types, including the familiar games of everyday life. We will begin our study of game theory and its application to the behaviour of firms by thinking about familiar games.

What Is a Game?

What is a game? At first thought, the question seems silly. After all, there are many different games – ball games and parlour games, games of chance and games of skill. But what is it about all these different activities that make them games? What do they have in common? All games share four features:

◆ Rules
◆ Strategies
◆ Payoffs
◆ Outcome

We're going to look at these features of a game by playing 'the prisoners' dilemma' game. This game captures some of the essential features of many games, including oligopoly, and it gives a good illustration of how game theory works. and generates predictions.

The Prisoners' Dilemma

Art and Bob have been caught red-handed, stealing a car. Facing airtight cases, they will receive a 2-year sentence each for their crime. During his interviews with the two prisoners, the police sergeant begins to suspect that he has stumbled on the two people who were responsible for a multimillion-pound bank robbery some months earlier. But this is just a suspicion. The police sergeant has no evidence on which he can convict them of the greater crime unless he can get them to

confess. But how can he extract a confession? He makes the prisoners play a game, which we now describe.

Rules

Each prisoner (player) is placed in a separate room and cannot communicate with the other prisoner. Each is told that he is suspected of having carried out the bank robbery and that:

> **If both of them confess to the larger crime, each will receive a sentence of 3 years for both crimes.**

> **If he alone confesses and his accomplice does not, he will receive an even shorter sentence of 1-year whereas his accomplice will receive a 10-year sentence.**

Strategies

In game theory, **strategies** are all the possible actions of each player. Art and Bob each have two possible actions:

1   Confess to the bank robbery
2   Deny having committed the bank robbery

Because there are two players, each with two strategies, there are four possible outcomes:

1   Both confess
2   Both deny
3   Art confesses and Bob denies
4   Bob confesses and Art denies

Payoffs

Each prisoner can work out his *payoff* in each of these four situations. We can tabulate the four possible payoffs for each of the prisoners in what is called a payoff matrix for the game. A **payoff matrix** is a table that shows the payoffs for every possible action by each player for every possible action by each other player.

Table 14.1 shows a payoff matrix for Art and Bob. The squares show the payoffs for each prisoner – the red triangle in each square shows Art's and the blue triangle shows Bob's. If both confess (top left), each gets a 3-year sentence. If Bob confesses but Art denies (top right), Art gets a 10-year sentence and Bob gets a 1-year sentence. If Art confesses and Bob denies (bottom left), Art gets a 1-year sentence and Bob gets a 10-year sentence. Finally, if both of them deny (bottom right), neither can be convicted of the bank robbery charge but both are sentenced for the car theft – a 2-year sentence.

Outcome

The choices of both players determine the outcome of the game. To predict that outcome, we use an equilibrium idea proposed by John Nash of Princeton University (who received the Nobel Prize for Economic Science in 1994 and was the subject of the 2001 film *A Beautiful Mind*). In a **Nash equilibrium**, player A takes the best possible action given the action of player B and player B takes the best possible action given the action of player A.

In the case of the prisoners' dilemma, the Nash equilibrium occurs when Art makes his best choice given Bob's choice and when Bob makes his best choice given Art's choice.

To find the Nash equilibrium, we compare all the possible outcomes associated with each choice and eliminate those that are dominated – that are not as good as some other choice. Let's find the Nash equilibrium for the prisoners' dilemma game.

Finding the Nash Equilibrium

Look at the situation from Art's point of view. If Bob confesses, Art's best action is to confess because in that case, he is sentenced to 3 years rather than 10 years. If Bob does not confess, Art's best action is still to confess because in that case he receives 1 year rather than 2 years. So Art's best action is to confess.

Now look at the situation from Bob's point of view. If Art confesses, Bob's best action is to confess because in that case, he is sentenced to 3 years rather than 10 years. If Art does not confess, Bob's best action is still to confess because in that case, he receives 1 year rather than 2 years. So Bob's best action is to confess.

Because each player's best action is to confess, each does confess, each gets a 3-year prison term, and the police sergeant has solved the bank robbery. This is the Nash equilibrium of the game.

The Nash equilibrium for the prisoners' dilemma is called a **dominant-strategy equilibrium**, which is an equilibrium in which the best strategy for each player is to confess *regardless of the strategy of the other player*.

The Dilemma

The dilemma arises as each prisoner contemplates the consequences of denying. Each prisoner knows that if both of them deny, they will receive only a 2-year sentence for stealing the car. But neither has any way of knowing that his accomplice will deny. But each also knows that if he denies it is in the best interest of the

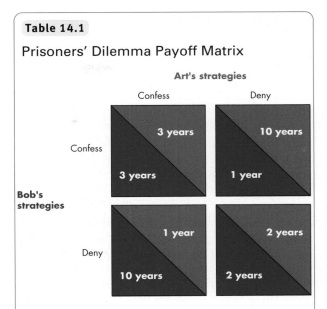

Table 14.1

Prisoners' Dilemma Payoff Matrix

Each square shows the payoffs for the two players, Art and Bob, for each possible pair of actions. In each square, the red triangle shows Art's payoff and the blue triangle shows Bob's. For example, if both confess, the payoffs are in the top left square. The equilibrium of the game is for both players to confess and each gets a 3-year sentence.

other to confess. So each considers whether to deny and rely on his accomplice to deny or to confess hoping that his accomplice denies but expecting him to confess. The dilemma leads to the equilibrium of the game.

A Bad Outcome

For the prisoners, the equilibrium of the game, with each confessing, is not the best outcome. If neither of them confesses, each gets only 2 years for the lesser crime. Isn't there some way in which this better outcome can be achieved? It seems that there is not, because the players cannot communicate with each other. Each player can put himself in the other player's place, and so each player can figure out that there is a best strategy for each of them. The prisoners are indeed in a dilemma. Each knows that he can serve 2 years *only* if he can trust the other to deny. But each prisoner also knows that it is *not* in the best interest of the other to deny. So each prisoner knows that he must confess, thereby delivering a bad outcome for both.

The firms in an oligopoly are in a similar situation to Art and Bob in the prisoners' dilemma game. Let's see how we can use this game to understand oligopoly.

An Oligopoly Price-fixing Game

We can use game theory and a game like the prisoners' dilemma to understand price fixing, price wars and other aspects of the behaviour of firms in oligopoly.

We'll begin with a price-fixing game. To understand price fixing, we're going to study the special case of duopoly – an oligopoly with two firms. Duopoly is easier to study than oligopoly with three or more firms, and it captures the essence of all oligopoly situations. Somehow, the two firms must share the market. And how they share it depends on the actions of each. We're going to describe the costs of the two firms and the market demand for the item they produce. We're then going to see how game theory helps us to predict the prices charged and the quantities produced by the two firms in a duopoly.

Cost and Demand Conditions

Two firms, Trick and Gear, produce switchgears. They have identical costs. Figure 14.2(a) shows their average total cost curve (*ATC*) and marginal cost curve (*MC*). Figure 14.2(b) shows the market demand curve for switchgears (*D*).

The two firms produce identical switchgears, so one firm's switchgear is a perfect substitute for the other's. So the market price of each firm's product is identical. The quantity demanded depends on that price – the higher the price, the smaller is the quantity demanded.

This industry is a natural duopoly. Two firms can produce this good at a lower cost than either one firm or three firms can. For each firm, average total cost is at its minimum when production is 3,000 units a week. And when price equals minimum average total cost, the total quantity demanded is 6,000 units a week. So two firms can just produce that quantity.

Collusion

We'll suppose that Trick and Gear enter into a collusive agreement. A **collusive agreement** is an agreement between two (or more) producers to form a cartel to restrict output, raise the price and increase profits. Because such an agreement is illegal in the European Union, it is undertaken in secret. The strategies that firms in a cartel can pursue are to:

1 Comply
2 Cheat

A firm that complies carries out the agreement. A firm that cheats breaks the agreement to its own benefit and to the cost of the other firm.

Because each firm has two strategies, there are four possible combinations of actions for the firms:

1 Both firms comply
2 Both firms cheat
3 Trick complies and Gear cheats
4 Gear complies and Trick cheats

Figure 14.2   Costs and Demand

(a) Individual firm

(b) Industry

The average total cost curve for each firm is *ATC* and the marginal cost curve is *MC* in part (a). Minimum average total cost is £6,000 a unit, and it occurs at a production of 3,000 units a week.

Part (b) shows the market demand curve. At a price of £6,000, the quantity demanded is 6,000 units per week. The two firms can produce this output at the lowest possible average cost. If the market had one firm, it would be profitable for another to enter. If the market had three firms, one would exit. There is room for only two firms in this industry. It is a natural duopoly.

Colluding to Maximize Profits

Let's work out the payoffs to the two firms if they collude to make the maximum profit for the cartel by acting like a monopoly. The calculations that the two firms perform are the same calculations that a monopoly performs. (You can refresh your memory of these calculations by looking at Chapter 12, pp. 280–281.)

The only thing that the duopolists must do beyond what a monopolist does is to agree on how much of the total output each of them will produce.

Figure 14.3 shows the price and quantity that maximize industry profit for the duopolists. Part (a) shows the situation for each firm and part (b) shows the situation for the industry as a whole. The curve labelled MR is the industry marginal revenue curve. This marginal revenue curve is like that of a single price monopoly (Chapter 12, p. 278). The curve labelled MC_I is the industry marginal cost curve if each firm produces the same level of output. That curve is constructed by adding together the outputs of the two firms at each level of marginal cost. That is, at each level of marginal cost, industry output is twice the output of each individual firm. So the curve MC_I in part (b) is twice as far to the right as the curve MC in part (a).

To maximize industry profit, the duopolists agree to restrict output to the rate that makes the industry marginal cost and marginal revenue equal. That output rate, as shown in part (b), is 4,000 units a week. The demand curve shows that the highest price for which the 4,000 switchgears can be sold is £9,000 each. Trick and Gear agree to charge this price.

To hold the price at £9,000 a unit, production must not exceed 4,000 units a week. So Trick and Gear must agree on production levels for each of them that total 4,000 units a week. Let's suppose that they agree to split the market equally so that each firm produces 2,000 switchgears a week. Because the firms are identical, this division is the most likely.

The average total cost of producing 2,000 switchgears a week is £8,000, so the profit per unit is £1,000 and economic profit is £2 million (2,000 units × £1,000 per unit). The economic profit of each firm is represented by the blue rectangle in Figure 14.3(a).

We have just described one possible outcome for a duopoly game: the two firms collude to produce the monopoly profit-maximizing output and divide that output equally between them. From the industry point of view, this solution is identical to a monopoly. A duopoly that operates in this way is indistinguishable from a monopoly. The economic profit that is made by a monopoly is the maximum total profit that can be made by the duopoly when the firms collude.

But with price greater than marginal cost, either firm might think of trying to increase its profit by cheating on the agreement and producing more than the agreed amount. Let's see what happens if one of the firms does cheat in this way.

Figure 14.3   Colluding to Make Monopoly Profits

(a) Individual firm

(b) Industry

The industry marginal cost curve, MC_I in part (b), is the horizontal sum of the two firms' marginal cost curves, MC in part (a). The industry marginal revenue curve is MR. To maximize profit, the firms produce 4,000 units a week (the quantity at which marginal revenue equals marginal cost). They sell that output for £9,000 a unit. Each firm produces 2,000 units a week. Average total cost is £8,000 a unit, so each firm makes an economic profit of £2 million (blue rectangle) – 2,000 units multiplied by £1,000 profit a unit.

myeconlab Animation

One Firm Cheats on a Collusive Agreement

To set the stage for cheating on their agreement, Trick convinces Gear that demand has decreased and that it cannot sell 2,000 units a week. Trick tells Gear that it plans to cut its price in order to sell the agreed 2,000 units each week. Because the two firms produce an identical product, Gear matches Trick's price cut but still produces only 2,000 units a week.

In fact, there has been no decrease in demand. Trick plans to increase output, which it knows will lower the price, and Trick wants to ensure that Gear's output remains at the agreed level.

Figure 14.4 illustrates the consequences of Trick's cheating. Part (a) shows Gear (the complier); part (b) shows Trick (the cheat); and part (c) shows the industry as a whole. Suppose that Trick increases output to 3,000 units a week. If Gear sticks to the agreement to produce only 2,000 units a week, total output is 5,000 a week, and given demand in part (c), the price falls to £7,500 a unit.

Gear continues to produce 2,000 units a week at a cost of £8,000 a unit and incurs a loss of £500 a unit, or £1 million a week. This economic loss is represented by the shaded rectangle in part (a). Trick produces 3,000 units a week at a cost of £6,000 a unit.

With a price of £7,500, Trick makes a profit of £1,500 a unit and therefore an economic profit of £4.5 million. This economic profit is the blue rectangle in part (b).

We've now described a second possible outcome for the duopoly game: one of the firms cheats on the collusive agreement. In this case, the industry output is larger than the monopoly output and the industry price is lower than the monopoly price. The total economic profit made by the industry is also smaller than the monopoly's economic profit. Trick (the cheat) makes an economic profit of £4.5 million and Gear (the complier) incurs an economic loss of £1 million. The industry makes an economic profit of £3.5 million. The industry profit is £0.5 million less than the economic profit a monopoly would make, but the profit is distributed unevenly. Trick makes a bigger economic profit than it would under the collusive agreement, while Gear incurs an economic loss.

A similar outcome would arise if Gear cheated and Trick complied with the agreement. The industry profit and price would be the same, but in this case, Gear (the cheat) would make an economic profit of £4.5 million and Trick (the complier) would incur an economic loss of £1 million.

Let's next see what happens if both firms cheat.

Figure 14.4   One Firm Cheats

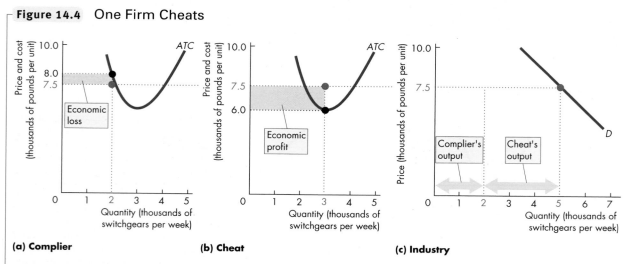

(a) Complier   **(b) Cheat**   **(c) Industry**

One firm, shown in part (a), complies with the agreement and produces 2,000 units. The other firm, shown in part (b), cheats on the agreement and increases its output to 3,000 units. Given the market demand curve in part (c) and with a total production of 5,000 units a week, the price

falls to £7,500. At this price, the complier in part (a) incurs an economic loss of £1 million (£500 per unit × 2,000 units), shown by the shaded rectangle. In part (b), the cheat makes an economic profit of £4.5 million (£1,500 per unit × 3,000 units), shown by the blue rectangle.

Both Firms Cheat

Suppose that both firms cheat and that each firm behaves like the cheating firm that we have just analysed. Each tells the other that it is unable to sell its output at the going price and that it plans to cut its price. But because both firms cheat, each will propose a successively lower price. As long as price exceeds marginal cost, each firm has an incentive to increase its production – to cheat. Only when price equals marginal cost is there no further incentive to cheat. This situation arises when the price has reached £6,000. At this price, marginal cost equals price. Also, price equals minimum average total cost. At a price less than £6,000, each firm incurs an economic loss. At a price of £6,000, each firm covers all its costs and makes zero economic profit (makes normal profit). Also, at a price of £6,000, each firm wants to produce 3,000 units a week, so the industry output is 6,000 units a week. Given the demand conditions, 6,000 units can be sold at a price of £6,000 each.

Figure 14.5 illustrates the situation just described. Each firm, in part (a), produces 3,000 units a week, and its average total cost is a minimum (£6,000 per unit). The market as a whole, in part (b), operates at the point at which the market demand curve (D) intersects the industry marginal cost curve (MC_I). Each firm has lowered its price and increased its output to try to gain an advantage over the other firm. Each has pushed this process as far as it can without incurring an economic loss.

We have now described a third possible outcome of this duopoly game: both firms cheat. If both firms cheat

on the collusive agreement, the output of each firm is 3,000 units a week and the price is £6,000. Each firm makes zero economic profit.

The Payoff Matrix

Now that we have described the strategies and payoffs in the duopoly game, we can summarize the strategies and the payoffs in the form of the game's payoff matrix. Then we can find the Nash equilibrium.

Table 14.2 sets out the payoff matrix for this game. It is constructed in the same way as the payoff matrix for the prisoners' dilemma in Table 14.1. The squares show the payoffs for the two firms – Gear and Trick. In this case, the payoffs are profits. (For the prisoners' dilemma, the payoffs were losses.)

The table shows that if both firms cheat (top left), they achieve the perfectly competitive outcome – each firm makes zero economic profit. If both firms comply (bottom right), the industry makes the monopoly profit and each firm makes an economic profit of £2 million. The top right and bottom left squares show what happens if one firm cheats while the other complies. The firm that cheats makes an economic profit of £4.5 million, and the one that complies incurs a loss of £1 million.

Nash Equilibrium in the Duopolists' Dilemma

The duopolists have a dilemma like the prisoners' dilemma. Do they comply or cheat? To answer this question, we must find the Nash equilibrium.

Figure 14.5 Both Firms Cheat

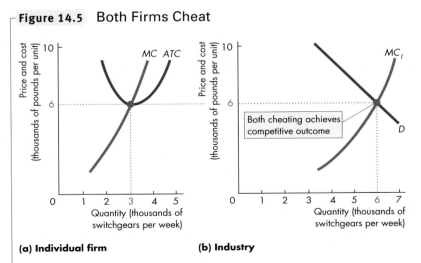

(a) Individual firm **(b) Industry**

If both firms cheat by increasing production, the collusive agreement collapses. The limit to the collapse is the competitive equilibrium. Neither firm will cut the price below £6,000 (minimum average total cost) because to do so will result in losses.

In part (a), each firm produces 3,000 units a week at an average total cost of £6,000. In part (b), with a total production of 6,000 units, the price falls to £6,000. Each firm now makes zero economic profit. This output and price are the ones that would prevail in a competitive industry.

Table 14.2

Duopoly Payoff Matrix

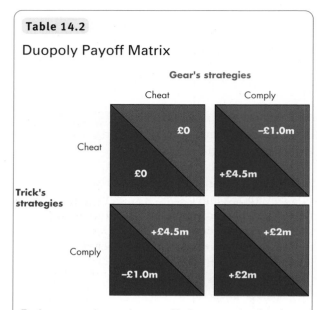

Each square shows the payoffs from a pair of actions. For example, if both firms comply with the collusive agreement, the payoffs are recorded in the bottom right square. The red triangle shows Gear's payoff, and the blue triangle shows Trick's. In the Nash equilibrium, both firms cheat.

Look at things from Gear's point of view. Gear reasons as follows. Suppose that Trick cheats. If I comply, I will incur an economic loss of £1 million. If I also cheat, I will make zero economic profit. Zero is better than *minus* £1 million, so I'm better off if I cheat. Now suppose Trick complies. If I cheat, I will make an economic profit of £4.5 million, and if I comply, I will make an economic profit of £2 million. A £4.5 million profit is better than a £2 million profit, so I'm better off if I cheat.

So regardless of whether Trick cheats or complies, it pays Gear to cheat. Cheating is Gear's best strategy.

Trick comes to the same conclusion as Gear because the two firms face an identical situation. So both firms cheat. The Nash equilibrium of the duopoly game is that both firms cheat. And, although the industry has only two firms, they charge the same price and produce the same quantity as those in a competitive industry. Also, as in perfect competition, each firm makes zero economic profit.

This conclusion is not general and will not always arise. We'll see why not first by looking at some other games that are like the prisoners' dilemma. Then we'll broaden the types of games we consider.

Other Oligopoly Games

Firms in oligopoly must decide whether to mount expensive advertising campaigns; whether to modify their product; whether to make their product more reliable and more durable; whether to price discriminate and, if so, among which groups of customers and to what degree; whether to undertake a large research and development (R&D) effort aimed at lowering production costs; and whether to enter or leave an industry.

All of these choices can be analysed as games that are similar to the one that we've just studied. Let's look at one example: an R&D game.

For example, in a duopoly R&D game, the success of the firm depends on its ability to create a product that people value highly relative to the cost of producing it. The firm that creates the most highly valued product at least-cost can undercut the rest of the market, increase its market share and increase its profit. But the R&D that achieves product improvements and cost reductions is costly. So the cost of R&D must be deducted from the profit resulting from the increased market share. If neither firm undertakes R&D, both firms might be better off, but if one firm does R&D, the other must follow.

Another game is the retail strategic game that is playing out in the UK supermarket sector. This industry is dominated by three companies – Tesco, Asda and Sainsbury's – that share 63 per cent of the market. Morrisons has the next largest share at 11 per cent and the remainder is taken by small independent chains. In 1997, Sainsbury's was the market leader and Tesco was in second position. In 2006, Tesco was market leader and Sainsbury's was in third position behind Asda. *Economics in Action* looks at this retail strategic game.

The Disappearing Invisible Hand

All the games that we've studied are versions of the prisoners' dilemma. The essence of that game lies in the structure of its payoffs. The worst possible outcome for each player arises from cooperating when the other player cheats. The best possible outcome, for each player to cooperate, is not a Nash equilibrium because it is in neither player's *self-interest* to cooperate if the other one cooperates. It is this failure to achieve the best outcome for both players – the best social outcome if the two players are the entire economy – that led John Nash to claim (as he was portrayed as doing in the film *A Beautiful Mind*) that he had challenged Adam Smith's idea that we are always guided, as if by an invisible hand, to promote the social interest when we are pursuing our self-interest.

ECONOMICS IN ACTION

A Prisoners' Dilemma in Supermarket Strategy

Tesco and Asda have expanded rapidly and Sainsbury's has stagnated. Table 1 shows sales data and Figure 1 shows market shares in recent years.

The battle for market share was fought and won on strategic marketing decisions. Three main strategies were used: loyalty cards to encourage repeat buying, expanding non-food retailing, and overseas expansion to capture new markets and economies of scale.

Tesco introduced its customer loyalty card in 1997 but Sainsbury's did not follow immediately. Tesco increased floor space and expanded into non-food retailing in 2000. Asda followed Tesco, but Sainsbury's did not. Tesco expanded overseas trading and floor space for computers in 2006, but Sainsbury's did not follow.

Tesco's marketing strategies were designed to increase sales and market share at the expense of its competitors, and they worked. With each strategy, Tesco increased market share and annual revenue.

The Game the Supermarkets Play

Table 2 represents the competition between Tesco and Sainsbury's as a strategic game. The payoffs in the table are changes in profit. If neither supermarket expands the floor space for computer retailing, both save marketing and development costs, market shares are similar and profits increase for both companies by 8 per cent (bottom right). Marketing and product development costs will cut profits, so if both companies expand computer retailing, market shares are similar and economic profits rise by only 4 per cent (top left).

The Nash equilibrium is for both firms to expand computer retailing. But Sainsbury's did not play its Nash equilibrium strategy. Profit increased by 16 per cent for Tesco and fell by 3 per cent for Sainsbury's (bottom left of table).

Sainsbury's paid a high price for not following Tesco's marketing lead in 1997, 2000 and 2006. It slipped to third place in market share behind the fast-growing Asda.

Today, Tesco and Asda are locked in a similar strategic game to that played previously by Tesco and Sainsbury's. So far, Tesco and Asda have matched each others' moves, but Tesco has the first mover advantage and will be hard to catch.

Table 1

UK Supermarket Sales

Supermarket	Annual revenue (billions of pounds)			
	2000	**2005**	**2006**	**2009**
Tesco	18.5	33.9	39.5	54.3
Sainsbury's	16.2	16.6	16.1	20.0
Asda	8.9	14.7	15.2	18.6

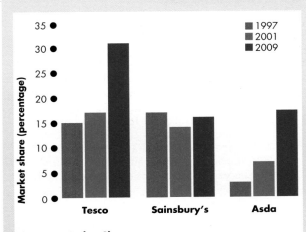

Figure 1 Market Share

Source of data: TNS (www.tns-global.com) Worldpanel grocery market press reports.

Table 2 A Strategic Game

A Game of Chicken

The Nash equilibrium for the prisoners' dilemma is unique: both players cheat (confess). Not all games have a unique equilibrium, and one that doesn't is a game called 'chicken'.

An Example of a Game of Chicken

A graphic, if disturbing, version of 'chicken' has two cars racing towards each other. The first driver to swerve and avoid a crash is the 'chicken'. The payoffs are a big loss for both if no one 'chickens out', zero for both if both 'chicken out', and a gain for the player who stays the course. If player 1 swerves, player 2's best strategy is to stay the course. And if player 1 stays the course, player 2's best strategy is to swerve.

An Economic Example of Chicken

An economic game of chicken can arise when R&D creates a new technology that cannot be kept secret or patented, so both firms benefit from the R&D of either firm. The chicken in this case is the firm that does the R&D.

Suppose, for example, that either Apple or Nokia spends £9 million developing a new touch-screen technology that both would end up being able to use regardless of which of them developed it.

Table 14.3 illustrates a payoff matrix for the game that Apple and Nokia play. Each firm has two strategies: do the R&D ('chicken out') or do not do the R&D. Each entry shows the additional profit (the profit from the new technology minus the cost of the research), given the strategies adopted.

If neither firm does the R&D, each makes zero additional profit. If both firms conduct the R&D, each firm makes an additional £5 million. If one of the firms does the R&D ('chickens out'), it makes £1 million and the other firm makes £10 million. Confronted with these payoffs the two firms calculate their best strategies. Nokia is better off doing R&D if Apple does no R&D. Apple is better off doing R&D if Nokia does no R&D. There are two Nash equilibrium outcomes: only one of them does the R&D, but we can't predict which one.

You can see that an outcome with no firm doing R&D isn't a Nash equilibrium because one firm would be better off doing it. Also both firms doing R&D isn't a Nash equilibrium because one firm would be better off not doing it. To decide which firm does the R&D, the firms might toss a coin, called a mixed strategy.

Table 14.3

An R&D Game of Chicken

Apple's strategies

	R&D	No R&D
R&D	£5m / £5m	£10m / £1m
No R&D	£1m / £10m	£0 / £0

Nokia's strategies

If neither firm does the R&D, their payoffs are in the bottom right square. When one firm 'chickens out' and does the R&D while the other does no R&D, their payoffs are in the top right and bottom left squares. When both 'chicken out' and do the R&D, the payoffs are in the top left square. The red triangle shows Apple's payoff, and the blue triangle shows Nokia's. The equilibrium for this R&D game of chicken is for only one firm to undertake the R&D. We cannot tell which firm will do the R&D and which will not.

Review Quiz

1   What are the common features of all games?
2   Describe the prisoners' dilemma game and explain why the Nash equilibrium delivers a bad outcome for both players.
3   Why does a collusive agreement to restrict output and raise price create a game like the prisoners' dilemma?
4   What creates an incentive for firms in a collusive agreement to cheat and increase production?
5   What is the equilibrium strategy for each firm in a duopolists' dilemma and why do the firms not succeed in colluding to raise the price and profits?
6   Describe two structures of payoffs for an R&D game and contrast the prisoners' dilemma and chicken game.

You can work these questions in Study Plan 14.2 and get instant feedback.

Repeated Games and Sequential Games

The games that we've studied are played just once. In contrast, many real-world games are played repeatedly. This feature of games turns out to enable real-world duopolists to cooperate, collude and make a monopoly profit.

Another feature of the game that we've studied is that the players move simultaneously. But in many real-world situations, one player moves first and then the other moves – the play is sequential rather than simultaneous. This feature of real-world games creates a large number of possible outcomes.

We're now going to examine these two aspects of strategic decision making.

A Repeated Duopoly Game

If two firms play a game repeatedly, one firm has the opportunity to penalize the other for previous 'bad' behaviour. If Gear cheats this week, perhaps Trick will cheat next week. Before Gear cheats this week, won't it consider the possibility that Trick will cheat next week? What is the equilibrium of this game?

Actually, there is more than one possibility. One is the Nash equilibrium that we have just analysed. Both players cheat, and each makes zero economic profit forever. In such a situation, it will never pay one of the players to start complying unilaterally because to do so would result in a loss for that player and a profit for the other. But a **cooperative equilibrium** in which the players make and share the monopoly profit is possible.

A cooperative equilibrium might occur if cheating is punished. There are two extremes of punishment. The smallest penalty is called 'tit for tat'. A *tit-for-tat strategy* is one in which a player cooperates in the current period if the other player cooperated in the previous period but cheats in the current period if the other player cheated in the previous period. The most severe form of punishment is called a trigger strategy. A *trigger strategy* is one in which a player cooperates if the other player cooperates but plays the Nash equilibrium strategy forever thereafter if the other player cheats.

In the duopoly game between Gear and Trick, a tit-for-tat strategy keeps both players cooperating and making monopoly profits. Let's see why with an example.

Table 14.4 shows the economic profit that Trick and Gear will make over a number of periods under two alternative sequences of events: colluding and cheating with a tit-for-tat response by the other firm.

If both firms stick to the collusive agreement in period 1, each makes an economic profit of £2 million. Suppose that Trick contemplates cheating in period 1. The cheating produces a quick £4.5 million economic profit and inflicts a £1 million economic loss on Gear.

But a cheat by Trick in period 1 produces a response from Gear in period 2. If Trick wants to get back into a profit-making situation, it must return to the agreement in period 2 even though it knows that Gear will punish it for cheating in period 1. So in period 2, Gear punishes Trick and Trick cooperates. Gear now makes an economic profit of £4.5 million, and Trick incurs an economic loss of £1 million.

Adding up the profits over two periods of play, Trick would have made more profit by cooperating – £4 million compared with £3.5 million.

What is true for Trick is also true for Gear. Because each firm makes a larger profit by sticking with the collusive agreement, both firms do so and the monopoly price, quantity and profit prevail.

In reality, whether a cartel works like a one-play game or a repeated game depends primarily on the number of players and the ease of detecting and punishing

---

Table 14.4

Cheating with Punishment

Period of play	Collude		Cheat with tit-for-tat	
	Trick's profit	Gear's profit	Trick's profit	Gear's profit
	(millions of pounds)		(millions of pounds)	
1	2	2	4.5	–1.0
2	2	2	–1.0	4.5
3	2	2	2.0	2.0
4	·	·	·	·

If duopolists repeatedly collude, each makes an economic profit of £2 million per period of play. If one player cheats in period 1, the other player plays a tit-for-tat strategy and cheats in period 2. The profit from cheating can be made for only one period and must be paid for in the next period by incurring a loss. Over two periods of play, the best that a duopolist can achieve by cheating is an economic profit of £3.5 million, compared to an economic profit of £4 million by colluding.

cheating. The larger the number of players, the harder it is to maintain a cartel.

Games and Price Wars

A repeated duopoly game can help us understand real-world behaviour and, in particular, price wars. Some price wars can be interpreted as the implementation of a tit-for-tat strategy. But the game is a bit more complicated than the one we've looked at because the players are uncertain about the demand for the product.

Playing a tit-for-tat strategy, firms have an incentive to stick to the monopoly price. But fluctuations in demand lead to fluctuations in the monopoly price, and sometimes, when the price changes, it might seem to one of the firms that the price has fallen because the other has cheated. In this case, a price war will break out. The price war will end only when each firm is satisfied that the other is ready to cooperate again. There will be cycles of price wars and the restoration of collusive agreements. Fluctuations in the world price of oil might be interpreted in this way.

Some price wars arise from the entry of a small number of firms into an industry that had previously been a monopoly. Although the industry has a small number of firms, the firms are in a prisoners' dilemma and they cannot impose effective penalties for price cutting.

A Computer Chip Price War

The prices of computer chips during 1995 and 1996 can be explained by the game you've just examined. Until 1995, the market for chips for IBM-compatible computers was dominated by Intel Corporation. Intel was able to make maximum economic profit by producing the quantity of chips at which marginal cost equalled marginal revenue. The price of Intel's chips was set to ensure that the quantity demanded equalled the quantity produced. Then in 1995 and 1996, with the entry of a small number of new firms, the industry became an oligopoly. If the firms had maintained Intel's price and shared the market, together they could have made economic profits equal to Intel's profit. But the firms were in a prisoners' dilemma, so prices fell towards the competitive level.

Let's now study a sequential game. There are many such games, and the one we'll examine is among the simplest. It has an interesting implication and it will give you the flavour of this type of game. We'll study an entry game in a contestable market.

A Sequential Entry Game in a Contestable Market

If two firms play a sequential game, one firm makes a decision at the first stage of the game and the other makes a decision at the second stage.

We're going to study a sequential game in a **contestable market** – a market in which firms can enter and leave so easily that firms in the market face competition from *potential* entrants. Examples of contestable markets are routes served by airlines and by barge companies that operate on Europe's major waterways. These markets are contestable because firms could enter if an opportunity for economic profit arose and could exit with no penalty if the opportunity for economic profit disappeared.

If the five-firm concentration ratio (see Chapter 9, p. 208) is used to determine the degree of competition, a contestable market appears to be uncompetitive. But a contestable market can behave as if it were perfectly competitive. To see why, let's look at an entry game for a contestable air route.

A Contestable Air Route

Agile Air is the only firm operating on a particular route. Demand and cost conditions are such that there is room for only one airline to operate. Wanabe plc is another airline that could offer services on the route.

We describe the structure of a sequential game by using a *game tree* like that in Figure 14.6. At the first stage, Agile Air must set a price. Once the price is set and advertised, Agile can't change it. That is, once set, Agile's price is fixed and Agile can't react to Wanabe's entry decision. Agile can set its price at either the monopoly level or the competitive level.

At the second stage, Wanabe must decide whether to enter or to stay out. Customers have no loyalty (there are no frequent flyer programmes) and they buy from the lowest-price firm. So if Wanabe enters, it sets a price just below Agile's and takes all the business.

Figure 14.6 shows the payoffs from the various decisions (Agile's in the red triangles and Wanabe's in the blue triangles).

To decide on its price, Agile's CEO reasons as follows. Suppose that Agile sets the monopoly price. If Wanabe enters, it earns 90 (think of all payoff numbers as thousands of pounds). If Wanabe stays out, it earns nothing. So Wanabe will enter. In this case Agile will lose 50.

Figure 14.6   Agile versus Wanabe: A Sequential Entry Game in a Contestable Market

If Agile sets the monopoly price, Wanabe makes 90 (thousand pounds) by entering and earns nothing by staying out. So if Agile sets the monopoly price, Wanabe enters.

If Agile sets the competitive price, Wanabe earns nothing if it stays out and incurs a loss if it enters. So if Agile sets the competitive price, Wanabe stays out.

myeconlab Animation

Now suppose that Agile sets the competitive price. If Wanabe stays out, it earns nothing and if it enters, it loses 10, so Wanabe will stay out. In this case, Agile will make zero economic profit.

Agile's best strategy is to set its price at the competitive level and make zero economic profit. The option of earning 100 by setting the monopoly price with Wanabe staying out is not available to Agile. If Agile sets the monopoly price, Wanabe enters, undercuts Agile, and takes all the business.

In this example, Agile sets its price at the competitive level and makes zero economic profit. A less costly strategy, called **limit pricing**, sets the price at the highest level that inflicts a loss on the entrant. Any loss is big enough to deter entry, so it is not always necessary to set the price as low as the competitive price. In the example of Agile and Wanabe, at the competitive price, Wanabe incurs a loss of 10 if it enters. A smaller loss would still keep Wanabe out.

This game is interesting because it points to the possibility of a monopoly behaving like a competitive industry and serving the consumer interest without regulation. But the result is not general and depends on one crucial feature of the setup of the game: at the second stage, Agile is locked into the price set at the first stage.

If Agile could change its price in the second stage, it would want to set the monopoly price if Wanabe stayed out – 100 with the monopoly price exceeds zero with the competitive price. But Wanabe can figure out what

Agile would do, so the price set at the first stage has no effect on Wanabe. Agile sets the monopoly price and Wanabe might either stay out or enter.

We've looked at two of the many possible repeated and sequential games, and you've seen how these types of game can provide insights into the complex forces that determine prices and profits.

Review Quiz

1   If a prisoners' dilemma game is played repeatedly, what punishment strategies might the players employ and how does playing the game repeatedly change the equilibrium?
2   If a market is contestable, how does the equilibrium differ from that of a monopoly?

You can work these questions in Study Plan 14.3 and get instant feedback.

So far, we've studied oligopoly with unregulated market power. Firms like Trick and Gear are free to collude to maximize their profit with no concern for the consumer or the law.

But when firms collude to achieve the monopoly outcome, they also have the same effects on efficiency and the social interest as monopoly. Profit is made at the expense of consumer surplus and a deadweight loss arises. We now look at how UK and EU competition and anti-monopoly law limits market power.

Antitrust Law

Antitrust law is any law that regulates oligopolies and prevents them from becoming monopolies or behaving like monopolies. The term 'antitrust law' is American, but is now widely used in Europe to describe what was previously called 'competition and monopoly law'.

UK and EU Antitrust Laws

In the UK, the two main sources of antitrust law are:

1 UK competition and monopoly laws

2 EU competition and monopoly laws

Antitrust law in the UK began in 1948 when the Monopolies and Restrictive Practices Act created a regulatory agency called the Monopolies and Mergers Commission to monitor and control monopolies that act against the social interest, as defined by the political leadership.

Several subsequent Acts have adapted and developed UK law, which is now defined under the Competition Act of 1998 and the Enterprise Act of 2002. The UK regulatory agency was renamed the Competition Commission under the 1988 Act because the focus of regulation switched from monopoly to anti-competitive practice. Under UK law, the Office of Fair Trading can investigate abuse of dominant market power (an entity having more than a 25 per cent share of the market) and a variety of anti-competitive practices and refer companies to the Competition Commission.

Table 14.5 summarizes the main focus of the two main UK antitrust laws. Both laws prohibit anti-competitive agreements between companies, in particular, any agreements that fix prices, directly or indirectly, that cut production or supply to raise prices, or that share market customers or rig bids for contracts. Examples of indirect price-fixing include agreements about relative price levels, rebates, discounts, transport charges and quotas.

EU law has focused on anti-competitive behaviour from the outset when the Treaty of Rome was signed in 1957. Since then, several new Treaties and Regulations have updated the law as the EU was formed and expanded. Table 14.6 sets out the main regulations. Since May 2004, all national competition authorities are empowered to apply EU law as well as national law. The European Commission has diverse powers to impose stringent fines, break up cartels, and impose legally binding requirements on firms. It can also reduce or eliminate fines under leniency rules for companies that confess.

Table 14.5	
UK Antitrust Laws	
Law	**Main Regulation**
Competition Act 1988	Prohibits agreements which restrict competition by: ◆ Fixing prices or trade terms ◆ Limiting production ◆ Sharing markets Prohibits abuse of dominant market position
Enterprise Act 2002	Prohibits cartels and merger agreements that: ◆ Fix prices ◆ Limit production or supply ◆ Share markets ◆ Engage in bid rigging Prohibits agreements whether carried out or not

The driving force of EU regulation is the criterion of abuse of a dominant position. Since Regulation 130 in 2004, this criterion applies to duopolies and oligopolies and all anti-competitive effects of mergers on oligopolistic markets. The European Commission can investigate any agreements which distort competition and any alleged cartel, duopoly or oligopoly or merger which might lead to a dominant position where the companies concerned have a Community dimension. The Community dimension is determined by a threshold of turnover worldwide and within the EU borders.

Price Fixing Always Illegal

Colluding with competitors to fix the price is always a violation of UK and EU antitrust law. If the Competition agency can prove the existence of a price fixing cartel, also called a horizontal price fixing agreement, defendants can offer no acceptable excuse.

The predictions of the effects of price fixing that you saw in the previous sections of this chapter provide the reasons for the unqualified attitude towards price fixing. A duopoly cartel can maximize profit and behave like a monopoly. To achieve the monopoly outcome, the cartel restricts production and fixes the price at the monopoly level. The consumer suffers because consumer surplus shrinks, and the outcome is inefficient because a deadweight loss arises.

Table 14.6

EU Antitrust Laws

Law	Main Regulation
Treaty of Rome 1957; Article 81, now Article 101 of the Treaty on the Functioning of the EU	Prohibits cartels Prohibits agreements between firms that distort competition within the Single Market including any form of price fixing, tying agreements, or limitations on supply in contracts.
Treaty of Rome 1957, Article 82, now Article 102 of the Treaty on the Functioning of the EU	Prohibits the abuse of a dominant market position, for example in the form of predatory pricing to eliminate competitors or actions to raise barriers to entry
European Union Merger Regulation 1989 (updated in Council Regulation 13/9/2004)	Identifies the 'dominant position' principal for examining mergers where a merger creates the economic power to influence the terms of competition, prices, production, product quality, marketing and innovation, and restricts competition appreciably.

It is for these reasons that the law declares that all price fixing is illegal. No excuse can justify the practice.

Other antitrust practices are more controversial and generate debate among lawyers and economists. We'll examine three of these practices.

Three Antitrust Policy Debates

The three practices that we'll examine are:

◆ Resale price maintenance
◆ Tying arrangements
◆ Predatory pricing

Resale Price Maintenance

Resale price maintenance is a distributor's agreement with a manufacturer to resell a product *at or above a specified minimum price*.

The Restrictive Trade Practices Act of 1956 and the Resale Prices Act of 1965 made resale price maintenance agreements in the UK illegal, unless proved otherwise under EU law. However, setting a minimum retail price is not illegal in the UK unless proved so on a case by case basis.

The UK Net Book Agreement was an allowed agreement on the minimum price books would be sold to the public. It was allowed because it helped publishers to produce less widely read, but socially valuable books. However, the Net Book Agreement ended in 1997 after a second legal review found it illegal. Since 1997, book prices have fallen as supermarkets and international book sellers have entered the popular book market and many small specialist bookshops have closed.

Does resale price maintenance create an inefficient or efficient use of resources? Economists can be found on both sides of this question.

Inefficient Resale Price Maintenance

Resale price maintenance is inefficient if it enables dealers to charge the monopoly price. By setting and enforcing the resale price, the manufacturer might be able to achieve the monopoly price.

Efficient Resale Price Maintenance

Resale price maintenance might be efficient if it enables a manufacturer to induce dealers to provide the efficient standard of service. Suppose that SilkySkin wants shops to demonstrate the use of its new unbelievable moisturizing cream in an inviting space. With resale price maintenance, SilkySkin can offer all the retailers the same incentive and compensation. Without resale price maintenance, a cut-price supermarket might offer SilkySkin products at a low price. Buyers would then have an incentive to visit a high-price shop for a product demonstration and then buy from the low-price shop. The low-price shop would be a free rider (like the consumer of a public good in Chapter 15, p. 351), and an inefficient level of service would be provided.

SilkySkin could pay a fee to retailers that provide good service and leave the resale price to be determined by the competitive forces of supply and demand. But it might be too costly for SilkySkin to monitor shops and ensure that they provide the desired level of service.

Tying Arrangements

A **tying arrangement** is an agreement to sell one product only if the buyer agrees to buy another, different product. With tying, the only way the buyer can get the one product is to also buy the other product. Microsoft has been accused of tying Internet Explorer and Windows. Textbook publishers sometimes tie a website and a textbook and force students to buy both. (You can't buy the book you're now reading, new, without the website. But you can buy the website access without the book, so these products are not tied.)

Could textbook publishers make more money by tying a book and access to a website? The answer is sometimes but not always. Suppose that you and other students are willing to pay £50 for a book and £10 for access to a website. The publisher can sell these items separately for these prices or bundled for £60. The publisher does not gain from bundling.

But now suppose that you and only half of the students are willing to pay £50 for a book and £10 for a website and the other half of the students are willing to pay £50 for a website and £10 for a book. Now if the two items are sold separately, the publisher can charge £50 for the book and £50 for the website. Half the students buy the book but not the website, and the other half buy the website but not the book. But if the book and website are bundled for £60, everyone buys the bundle and the publisher makes an extra £10 per student. In this case, bundling has enabled the publisher to price discriminate.

There is no simple, clear-cut test of whether a firm is engaging in tying or whether, by doing so, it has increased its market power and profit and created inefficiency.

Predatory Pricing

Predatory pricing is setting a low price to drive competitors out of business with the intention of setting a

---

ECONOMICS IN ACTION

The EU versus Microsoft

In 1998, Sun Microsystems complained to the European Commission that Microsoft would not give it the information needed to run Microsoft's operating system. In 2001 after the release of Windows 2000, complaints were made that Microsoft had engaged in anti-competitive tying of its Windows Media Player with its Windows PC operating system. In 2008, the European Commission began to investigate Microsoft for abusing its dominant position in the market for client PC operating systems by tying its browser, Internet Explorer, to the Windows operating system.

The Case Against Microsoft

The claims against Microsoft were that it

◆ Possessed monopoly power

◆ Used predatory pricing and tying arrangements

◆ Used other anticompetitive practices

Microsoft had 80 per cent of the market for PC operating systems, a dominant position. This dominant position arose from two barriers to entry: economies of scale and network economies. Microsoft's average total cost falls as production increases (economies of scale) because the fixed cost of developing an operating system such as Windows is large while the marginal cost of producing one copy of Windows is small. Further, as the number of Windows users increases, the range of Windows applications expands (network economies), so a potential competitor would need to produce not only a competing operating system but also an entire range of supporting applications as well.

When Microsoft entered the Web browser market with its Internet Explorer and the media market with Media Player, it offered the software for a zero price. Microsoft integrated the software with Windows so that anyone using Windows would not need a competing media package or browser. Microsoft's competitors claimed that this practice was an illegal tying arrangement.

Microsoft's Response

Microsoft challenged all these claims. It said that Windows was vulnerable to competition from other operating systems such as Linux and Apple's Mac OS and that there was a permanent threat of competition from new entrants. Microsoft claimed that integrating software like Internet Explorer with Windows provided a single, unified product of greater consumer value.

The Outcome

The European Commission agreed in 2004 that Microsoft's refusal to supply information limited competition and ordered Microsoft to disclose the information. It also agreed that tying Media Player to the operating system harmed competition and ordered Microsoft to provide a version of Windows without Media Player. Finally, in 2009, the Commission did not identify abuse of power. Microsoft offered to provide a Choice Screen so that the 100 million EU users could choose a different browser. The Commission made this offer legally binding from March 2010.

monopoly price when the competition has gone. Predatory pricing is an attempt to create a monopoly and as such it is illegal under Article 102 of the European Treaty.

It is easy to see that predatory pricing is an idea, not a reality. Economists are skeptical that predatory pricing occurs. They point out that a firm that cuts its price below the profit-maximizing level loses during the low-price period. Even if it succeeds in driving its competitors out of business, new competitors will enter as soon as the price is increased, so any potential gain from a monopoly position is temporary. A high and certain loss is a poor exchange for a temporary and uncertain gain. No case of predatory pricing has been definitively found.

Mergers and Acquisitions

Mergers, which occur when two or more firms agree to combine to create one larger firm, and *acquisitions*, which occur when one firm buys another firm, are common events. Mergers occurred when Chrysler and the German auto producer Daimler-Benz combined to form DaimlerChrysler and when the Belgian beer producer InBev bought the US brewing giant Anheuser-Busch and created a new combined company, Anheuser-Busch InBev. An acquisition occurred when Rupert Murdoch's News Corp bought Myspace.

The mergers and acquisitions that occur don't usually create a monopoly. But two (or more) firms might be tempted to try to merge so that they can gain market power and operate like a monopoly. If such a situation arises, the UK Office of Fair Trading and the European Commission take an interest in the move and can block the merger.

Before taking action, the European Commission must establish a *Community dimension* to the takeover. To do this, the European Commission uses two turnover rules from Articles 1(2) and 1(3) of the Merger Regulation. These are a combined worldwide turnover:

1   Above €5 billion and at least two firms having an EU turnover of at least €50 million or

2   Of €2.5 billion and above €100 million in at least three member states; and in those states, the turnover of at least two firms is above €25 million and the EU-wide turnover of at least two firms exceeds €100 million, unless each firm has more than two-thirds of its EU turnover in one member state.

The EU rarely blocks mergers or acquisitions, but it will if a monopoly position is likely to result. You can see such an example in the *Economics in Action*.

ECONOMICS IN ACTION

The EU Blocks No Frills Takeover

In 2006, Ryanair made a €1.48-billion aggressive takeover bid for its Irish rival, Aer Lingus. The bid was investigated by the European Commission and blocked under the EU competition rules in 2007. Ryanair contested the Commission ruling and applied to the European General Court to overrule the block. The basis for determining a Community dimension was contested. The European General Court decided in July 2010 that the Commission was right to block the takeover because it would have created a near monopoly on 22 of 35 routes to and from Dublin, Cork and Shannon airports.

The case did not have a Community dimension under the first EU rule and parts of the second EU rule, but the Community dimension was contested. How is turnover measured in each EU member state? Is turnover allocated by country of customer origin or destination, or simply where the ticket sale occurred? The Commission measured both and found evidence that turnover met the rules for Community dimension.

Review Quiz

1   What are the main antitrust laws affecting the UK and when were they enacted?
2   What is the main focus of EU antitrust law?
3   What are resale price maintenance, tying arrangements, and predatory pricing?
4   Under what circumstances is an EU merger unlikely to be approved?

You can work these questions in Study Plan 14.4 and get instant feedback.

Oligopoly is a market structure that you encounter in your daily life. *Reading Between the Lines* on pp. 336–337 looks at one whose services you might have used: a cartel among 11 EU air cargo carriers.

Reading Between the Lines

Cartel in the Air: Price Fixing Air Freight

Europa, Brussels, 9 November 2010

Antitrust: Commission Fines 11 Air Cargo Carriers €799 million in Price Fixing Cartel

The European Commission has fined 11 air cargo carriers a total of €799,445,000 for operating a worldwide cartel which affected cargo services within the European Economic area (EEA). . . . The carriers coordinated their action on surcharges for fuel and security without discounts over a six year period. Lufthansa (and its subsidiary Swiss) received full immunity from fines under the Commission's leniency programme, as it was the first to provide information about the cartel.

"It is deplorable that so many major airlines coordinated their pricing to the detriment of European businesses and European consumers" said Vice President for Competition Joaquín Almunia adding: "with today's decision the Commission is sending a clear message that it will not tolerate cartel behaviour". . . .

The cartel members coordinated various elements of price for a period of over six years, from December 1999 to 14 February 2006. The cartel arrangements consisted of numerous contacts between airlines . . . covering flights from, to and within the EEA. . . .

The aim of these contacts was to ensure that these surcharges were introduced by all the carriers involved and that increases (or decreases) of the surcharge levels were applied in full without exception.

The Essence of the Story

- ◆ The European Competition Commission fined 11 airline cargo firms €799.4 million for operating a cartel.

- ◆ The 11 airlines colluded to set the surcharges for fuel and security on cargo shipments over a period of six years.

- ◆ These surcharges were passed on to European businesses and customers, which raised their costs.

- ◆ Lufthansa (and its subsidiary) paid no fines as part of the leniency rules because it provided the Commission with information about the cartel.

Economic Analysis

- A small number of large airlines compete for global shipping contracts – the world airline cargo market is an oligopoly.

- Between 1999 and 2006, high fuel prices and heightened security concerns increased the airlines' costs and 11 firms formed a cartel to set fuel and security surcharges, like a monopoly.

- Figure 1 illustrates the effects of this collusion assuming that all the airlines have similar cost curves.

- Part (a) shows the average total cost, ATC and marginal cost, MC, for one airline, shipping 18 million tonnes/kilometre per week at a price of €1,300 per tonne. (The price includes a fuel and security surcharge).

- Part (b) shows the market demand, D, and industry marginal cost MC_I.

- To meet market demand without collusion, the industry produces 198 million tonnes/kilometre per week at a price of €1,300 per tonne.

- With no cartel and with each firm shipping 18 million tonnes/kilometre per week, economic profit is zero.

- After forming a cartel, the profit-maximizing output (monopoly profit) is 132 million tonnes/kilometre, where MR equals MC in part (b).

- The cartel members agree to increase the fuel and security surcharge by €200 per tonne, raising the price to €1,500 and cutting industry shipments to the profit-maximizing quantity of 12 million tonnes/kilometre each.

- Collusion generates a positive economic profit shown in part (a) for all firms in the cartel as long as the agreement holds.

- Under the EU leniency rule, no fine is imposed on the first firm that confesses to being in a cartel, which creates an incentive to be the first to confess.

- When Lufthansa confessed first, the firm stopped receiving the monopoly profit but was not hit with a fine.

- The other firms also stopped receiving the monopoly profit but were hit with a fine.

- If no firm had confessed, all would have continue to receive the cartel economic profit.

- The cartel operated for six years and may have earned substantially more than the fines imposed.

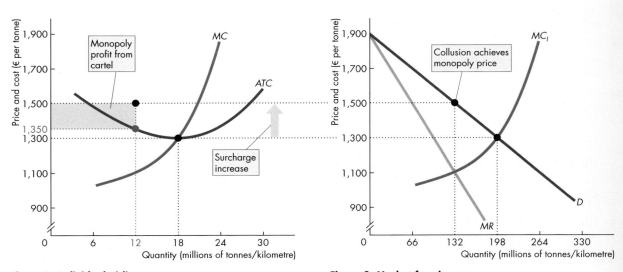

Figure 1 Individual airline

Figure 2 Market for air cargo

◢ SUMMARY

Key Points

What Is Oligopoly? (pp. 318–319)

◆ Oligopoly is a market in which a small number of firms compete.

Working Problems 1 to 3 will give you a better understanding of what oligopoly is.

Oligopoly Games (pp. 320–328)

◆ Oligopoly is studied by using game theory, which is a method of analysing strategic behaviour.

◆ In a prisoners' dilemma game, two prisoners acting in their own self-interest harm their joint interest.

◆ An oligopoly (duopoly) price-fixing game is a prisoners' dilemma in which the firms might collude or cheat.

◆ In Nash equilibrium, both firms cheat and output and price are the same as in perfect competition.

◆ Firms' decisions about advertising and R&D can be studied by using game theory.

Working Problems 4 to 7 will give you a better understanding of oligopoly games.

Repeated Games and Sequential Games (pp. 329–331)

◆ In a repeated game, a punishment strategy can produce a cooperative equilibrium in which price and output are the same as in monopoly.

◆ In a sequential contestable market game, a small number of firms can behave like firms in perfect competition.

Working Problem 8 will give you a better understanding of repeated games and sequential games.

Antitrust Law (pp. 332–335)

◆ The UK antitrust regulations are based on European Union Treaty rules and United Kingdom Acts of Parliament.

◆ All price-fixing agreements are violations of EU and UK laws.

◆ Resale price maintenance might be efficient if it enables a producer to ensure the efficient level of service by distributors.

◆ Tying arrangements can enable a monopoly to price discriminate and increase profit, but in many cases, tying would not increase profit.

◆ Predatory pricing is unlikely to occur because it brings losses and only temporary potential gains.

◆ The European Commission uses market turnover guidelines to determine whether there is a Community dimension on mergers to investigate and possibly block.

Working Problems 9 to 11 will give you a better understanding of antitrust law.

Key Terms

Antitrust law, 332
Cartel, 319
Collusive agreement, 322
Contestable market, 330
Cooperative equilibrium, 329
Dominant-strategy equilibrium, 321
Duopoly, 318
Game theory, 320
Limit pricing, 331
Nash equilibrium, 321
Oligopoly, 318
Payoff matrix, 320
Predatory pricing, 334
Resale price maintenance, 333
Strategies, 320
Tying arrangement, 333

STUDY PLAN PROBLEMS AND APPLICATIONS

myeconlab You can work Problems 1 to 12 in MyEconLab Chapter 14 Study Plan and get instant feedback.

What is Oligopoly? (Study Plan 14.1)

1 Two firms make most of the chips that power a PC: Intel and Advanced Micro Devices. What makes the market for PC chips a duopoly? Sketch the market demand curve and cost curves that describe the situation in this market and that prevent other firms from entering.

2 Sparks Fly for Energizer

Energizer is gaining market share against competitor Duracell and its profit is rising despite the sharp rise in the price of zinc, a key battery ingredient.

> Source: www.businessweek.com, August 2007

In what type of market are batteries sold? Explain your answer.

3 Oil City

In the late 1990s, Reliance spent $6 billion to build a world-class oil refinery at Jamnagar, India. Now Reliance is more than doubling the size of the facility, which will make it the world's biggest producer of petrol – 1.2 million gallons of petrol per day, or about 5% of global capacity. Reliance plans to sell the petrol in Europe and in the US where it's too expensive and politically difficult to build new refineries. The bulked-up Jamnagar will be able to move the market and Singapore traders expect a drop in fuel prices as soon as it's going at full steam.

> Source: *Fortune*, 28 April 2008

a Explain why the news clip claims that the global market for petrol is not perfectly competitive.

b What barriers to entry might limit competition in this market and give a firm like Reliance the power to influence the market price?

Oligopoly Games (Study Plan 14.2)

4 Consider a game with two players and in which each player is asked a question. The players can answer the question honestly or lie. If both answer honestly, each receives €100. If one answers honestly and the other lies, the liar receives €500 and the honest player gets nothing. If both lie, then each receives €50.

a Describe strategies and payoffs of this game.

b Construct the payoff matrix.

c What is the equilibrium of this game?

d Compare this game to the prisoners' dilemma. Are the two games similar or different? Explain your answer.

Use the following information to work Problems 5 and 6.

Two firms, Soapy plc and Suddsies plc, are the only producers of soap powder. They collude and agree to share the market equally. If neither firm cheats on the agreement, each makes €1 million economic profit. If either firm cheats, the cheat makes an economic profit of €1.5 million while the complier incurs an economic loss of €0.5 million. If both cheat, they break even. Neither firm can monitor the other's actions.

5 a What are the strategies in this game?

b Construct the payoff matrix.

6 a What is the equilibrium if the game is played only once?

b Is the equilibrium a dominant-strategy equilibrium? Explain.

7 The World's Largest Airline

On 3 May 2010, United Airlines and Continental Airlines announced a $3 billion merger that would create the world's biggest airline. The deal was completed in a remarkably short three weeks, and would give the airlines the muscle to fend off low-cost rivals at home and to take on foreign carriers abroad. For consumers, the merger could eventually result in higher prices although the new company does not intend to raise fares. One of the rationales for airline mergers is to cut capacity.

> Source: *The New York Times*, 7 June 2010

a Explain how this airline merger might increase US air travel prices.

b Explain how this airline merger might lower air travel production costs.

c Explain how cost savings arising from a cut in capacity might get passed on to travellers and might boost producers' profits. Which do you predict will happen from this airline merger and why?

Repeated Games and Sequential Games (Study Plan 14.3)

8 If Soapy plc and Suddies plc repeatedly play the duopoly game that has the payoffs described in Problem 5, on each round of play:

a What now are the strategies that each firm might adopt?

b Can the firms adopt a strategy that gives the game a cooperative equilibrium?

c Would one firm still be tempted to cheat in a cooperative equilibrium? Explain your answer.

Antitrust Law (Study Plan 14.4)

9 Intel Fined €1.06 billion for Abuse of Dominant Position

The European Commission has fined Intel €1.6 billion for abuse of a dominant market position (70 % share). It used anti-competitive practices to exclude competitors from the computer chip market. The Commission found Intel gave hidden rebates to computer manufacturers who bought their chip exclusively, and made payments to retailers who only stocked computers with their chips. Intel also paid manufacturers to limit production of computers with their chips. The European Commission forced Intel to stop these payments and said it had limited competition and innovation and harmed EU consumers. The European market has a 30% share of the €22 billion world market for computer chips.

Source: Europa Press Release, 13 May 2009

a How does Intel's actions reduce competition in the European computer chip market?

b Which aspects of EU antitrust laws have been breached?

10 Animal Feed Producers Fined for Price-fixing and Market-sharing.

The Commission fined producers of animal feed phosphates €175 million for creating a cartel operating for 30 years. The case began in 2003 when one firm applied for leniency. The cartel covered most of Europe and allocated market shares, sales quotas and shared customers as well as coordinated prices and sales conditions. It is a serious violation of Article 101 of the Treaty.

Source: Europa Press Release, 20 July 2010

a What types of anti-competitive practice did the cartel use?

b What is the purpose of the leniency rule?

11 Commission Agrees Acquisition of Arriva by Deutsche Bahn with Conditions

The European Commission has allowed the incumbent German rail and bus operator Deutsche Bahn to buy the UK rail and bus operator Arriva plc. Arriva operates services across Europe and is one of the few competitors for Deutsche Bahn in the German market. The Commission is concerned that the acquisition will increase existing barriers to entry in the German market and has said that Deutsche Bahn must sell Arriva's German operations for the acquisition to go ahead.

Source: Europa Press Release, 11 August 2010.

a Explain the guidelines for establishing a Community dimension for a merger or acquisition.

b Why has the Commission imposed a condition on the merger?

Economics in the News (Study Plan 14.N)

12 Commission Fines Wanadoo

The Commission fined Wanadoo Interactive, a subsidiary of France Télécom, €10.4 million for predatory pricing in the market for ADSL-based Internet access services. Up to 2002, Wanadoo's retail prices were below cost to restrict market entry by competitors. Wanadoo deliberately suffered losses to increase its market share from 46 to 72 per cent in 2002 to get the biggest share of the booming market. One competitor went out of business and all others saw their shares fall to 10 per cent or less.

Source: Europa Press Release, 16 July 2003

a Explain how Wanadoo violated EU antitrust laws.

b Explain why few firms use predatory pricing to permanently drive out competition.

c What is the crucial evidence that Wanadoo engaged in predatory pricing?

d Sketch a graph that shows the situation facing Wanadoo's competitor when it went out of business.

ADDITIONAL PROBLEMS AND APPLICATIONS

 You can work these problems in MyEconLab if assigned by your lecturer.

What is Oligopoly?

13 An Energy Drink with a Monster of a Stock

The $5.7 billion energy-drink category, in which Monster holds the No. 2 position behind industry leader Red Bull, has slowed down as copycat brands jostle for shelf space. Over the past five years Red Bull's market share in dollar terms has gone from 91 per cent to well under 50 per cent and much of that loss has been Monster's gain.

Source: *Fortune*, 25 December 2006

a Describe the structure of the energy-drink market. How has that structure changed over the past few years?

b If Monster and Red Bull formed a cartel, how would the price charged for energy drinks and the profits made change?

Oligopoly Games

Use the following information to work Problems 14 and 15.

Black and Green are the only two producers of aniseed beer, a New Age product designed to displace ginger beer. Black and Green are trying to figure out how much of this new beer to produce. They know the following:

(i) If they both limit production to 10,000 litres a day, they will make the maximum attainable joint profit of £200,000 a day – £100,000 a day each.

(ii) If either firm produces 20,000 litres a day while the other produces 10,000 a day, the one that produces 20,000 litres will make an economic profit of £150,000 and the other one will incur an economic loss of £50,000.

(iii) If both increase production to 20,000 litres a day, each firm will make zero economic profit.

14 Construct a payoff matrix for the game that Black and Green must play.

15 Find the Nash equilibrium of the game that Black and Green play.

16 Asian Rice Exporters to Discuss Cartel

The rice-exporting nations Thailand, Cambodia, Laos, and Myanmar planned to discuss a proposal by Thailand, the world's largest rice exporter, that they form a cartel. Ahead of the meeting, the countries said that the purpose

of the rice cartel would be to contribute to ensuring food stability, not just in an individual country but also to address food shortages in the region and the world. The cartel will not hoard rice and raise prices when there are shortages. The Philippines says that it is a bad idea. It will create an oligopoly, and the cartel could price the grain out of reach for millions of people.

Source: CNN, 6 May 2008

a Assuming the rice-exporting nations become a profit-maximizing colluding oligopoly, explain how they would influence the global market for rice and the world price of rice.

b Assuming the rice-exporting nations become a profit-maximizing colluding oligopoly, draw a graph to illustrate their influence on the global market for rice.

c Even in the absence of international antitrust laws, why might it be difficult for this cartel to successfully collude? Use the ideas of game theory to explain.

17 Suppose that Mozilla and Microsoft each develop their own versions of an amazing new Web browser that allows advertisers to target consumers with great precision. Also, the new browser is easier and more fun to use than existing browsers. Each firm is trying to decide whether to sell the browser or to give it away. What are the likely benefits from each action? Which action is likely to occur?

18 Why do Coca-Cola and PepsiCo spend huge amounts on advertising? Do they benefit? Does the consumer benefit? Explain your answer by constructing a game to illustrate the choices Coca-Cola and PepsiCo make.

Use the following information to work Problems 19 and 20.

Microsoft with Xbox 360, Nintendo with Wii, and Sony with PlayStation 3 are slugging it out in the market for the latest generation of video game consoles. Xbox 360 was the first to market; Wii has the lowest price; PS3 uses the most advanced technology and has the highest price.

19 a Thinking of the competition among these firms in the market for consoles as a game, describe the firms' strategies concerning design, marketing and price.

b What, based on the information provided, turned out to be the equilibrium of the game?

20 Can you think of reasons why the three consoles are so different?

Repeated Games and Sequential Games (Study Plan 14.3)

21 If Bud and Wise in Problem 15 play the game repeatedly, what is the equilibrium of the game?

22 Agile Airlines' profit on a route on which it has a monopoly is £10 million a year. Wanabe Airlines is considering entering the market and operating on this route. Agile warns Wanabe to stay out and threatens to cut the price so that if Wanabe enters it will make no profit. Wanabe determines that the payoff matrix for the game in which it is engaged with Agile is shown in the table.

Does Wanabe believe Agile's assertion? Does Wanabe enter or not? Explain.

23 Oil Trading Probe May Uncover Manipulation

Amid soaring oil prices the Commodity Futures Trade Commission (CFTC) is looking into manipulation of the oil market – withholding oil in an attempt to drive prices higher. The CFTC has found such evidence in the past and it's likely it will find evidence again. But it is unlikely that a single player acting alone would be able to run the price up from $90 to $135.

Source: CNN, 30 May 2008

What type of market does the news clip imply best describes the US oil market?

Antitrust Law

Use the following news clip to work Problems 24 and 25.

Commission Investigates IBM

The European Commission opened antitrust investigations against IBM Corporation for alleged breaches of EU antitrust rules related to the abuse of a dominant market position for mainframe computers. The mainframe market is worth €8.5 billion worldwide and €3 billion in Europe. Software developers complained that IBM ties mainframes to its operating system to limit competition by emulation software companies that could let users run critical applications on non-IBM hardware. The Commission also suspects IBM has engaged in discriminatory behaviour against mainframe maintenance companies, by limiting access to spare parts when IBM is the only source.

Source: Europa Press Release, 26 July 2010

24 a Describe the anti-competitive practice IBM is alleged to engage in.

    b Which parts of EU antitrust law might IBM infringe and why?

25 What is meant by abuse of a dominant market position?

Economics in the News

26 After you have studied *Reading Between the Lines* on pp. 336–337 answer the following questions.

    a What types of anti-competitive practice did the airline cargo cartel use and why did they not offer discounts to customers?

    b What effect did the rising cost of fuel and terrorist activity have on the cartel's decisions?

    c What is the likely impact of the cartel on businesses operating in the EU?

    d Why does the EU have a leniency rule and how was it applied in the airline cargo case?

    e Construct a payoff matrix for the game played by Lufthansa and the other airlines that led to Luftansa confessing.

    f Is there a unique equilibrium in this game? If not explain the possible outcomes.

    g What uncertainties faced each airline during the period that the cartel operated that might have influenced Lufthansa's decision to confess?

    h Draw a graph similar to Figure 2 on p. 337 and on it, illustrate the inefficiency that resulted from the cartel.

27 Boeing and Airbus Predict Asian Sales Surge

Airlines in the Asia-Pacific region are emerging as the biggest customers for aircraft makers Boeing and Airbus. The two firms predict that over the next 20 years, more than 8,000 planes worth up to $1.2 trillion will be sold there.

Source: BBC News, 3 February 2010

    a In what type of market are big airplanes sold?

    b Thinking of competition between Boeing and Airbus as a game, what are the strategies and the payoffs?

    c Set out a hypothetical payoff matrix for the game you've described in part (b). What is the equilibrium of the game?

    d Do you think the market for big airplanes is efficient? Explain and illustrate your answer.

Coping With Market Failure

Problems that Markets Alone Can't Solve

The chapters in this part deal with two economic problems that markets alone cannot solve:

◆ Providing the efficient quantity of public goods and

◆ Producing the efficient quantities of goods

We start in Chapter 15 by examining the 'free-rider' problem created by public goods and services. These are items that everyone can benefit from even if they don't pay their share of the cost of providing them. The 'free-rider' problem is that, because no one has an incentive to pay, we need government provision and compulsory payment through taxes to get the efficient quantities of these items. A similar problem arises with goods and services that bring substantial external benefits. These items, too, would be underprovided if left to unregulated markets. In Chapter 16 we study the problems of overproduction that brings pollution, climate change and the 'tragedy of the commons' – the over-exploitation of common resources.

Understanding Market Failure and Government Failure

To deal with the problems that we've just identified, societies need mechanisms that enable individuals to make *public choices*. Constitutions, government, laws and regulations are the devices that we use to provide such mechanisms. But as the drafters of all constitutions know, when governments get involved in the economic life, people try to steer the government's actions in directions that serve self-interest at the expense of the social interest.

The idea of creating a formal EU constitution was first put forward in 2001. It has taken nearly 10 years to get even close to that goal. The committee that drafted the new EU constitution struggled to craft a set of arrangements that would enable a large and growing number of national European governments to work together and achieve better economic outcomes for their people. Rejection of the new constitution by France and the Netherlands ended in a compromise – the Lisbon Treaty – just a revision of the former Treaty.

A constitution that makes despotic and tyrannical rule impossible is relatively easy to achieve. The constitutions of Australia, France, Germany, Japan, Switzerland and the United States are all examples of political arrangements based on sound economics. They are sophisticated systems of incentives – of carrots and sticks – designed to make the government responsive to public opinion and to limit the ability of individual self-interests to gain at the expense of the majority.

But no one has yet managed to design a constitution that effectively blocks the ability of special-interest groups to capture the consumer and producer surpluses that result from specialization and trade.

You will see in the chapters that follow some government mechanisms designed to overcome market failure and enable us to provide efficient quantities of national defence, law and order, education and healthcare, to regulate pollution and to conserve precious common natural resources.

But you will also see that government mechanisms don't bring a guarantee of success and discover that the pursuit of self-interest by politicians, bureaucrats, voters and entrepreneurs in a political marketplace can result in government failure – in the failure of government to deliver an efficient outcome and instead to be captured and diverted by the self-interest of individuals.

Ronald Coase (1910–), was born in England and educated at the London School of Economics, where he was deeply influenced by his teacher, Arnold Plant, and by the issues of his youth: communist central planning versus free markets.

Professor Coase has lived in the United States since 1951. He first visited America as a 20-year-old on a travelling scholarship during the depths of the Great Depression. It was on this visit, and before he had completed his bachelor's degree, that he conceived the ideas that 60 years later were to earn him the 1991 Nobel Prize for Economic Science.

Ronald Coase discovered and clarified the significance of transactions costs and property rights for the functioning of the economy. He has revolutionized the way we think about property rights and externalities and has opened up the growing field of law and economics.

'The question to be decided is: is the value of fish lost greater or less than the value of the product which contamination of the stream makes possible?'

RONALD H. COASE
The Problem of Social Cost

CHAPTER

15

Public Choices and Public Goods

After studying this chapter you will be able to:

◆ Explain why some choices are public choices and how these choices are made in the political marketplace

◆ Explain how the free-rider problem arises and how the quantity of public goods is determined

◆ Explain why mixed goods with external benefits lead to inefficient underproduction and how public production, subsidies and vouchers can achieve allocative efficiency

Flood rescue service, weather forecasting and university research and education: governments are involved in all these activities. But why? Why does the government provide some goods and services and not others? Why don't we leave it to private firms to provide these items? Will governments provide too much or too little of these items?

These are the questions that we study in this chapter. In *Reading Between the Lines* at the end of the chapter, we compare the provision of healthcare services in the UK and US and discover some surprising numbers.

Public Choices

All economic choices are made by individuals, but some choices are *private* and some are *public*. A *private choice* is a decision that has consequences for only the person making it. Decisions to buy (demand) or to sell (supply) goods and services in competitive markets are examples of private choices. At the market equilibrium price, these choices are consistent and one person's decision to buy or sell a little bit more or a little bit less has an imperceptible effect on the outcome.

A **public choice** is a decision that has consequences for many people and perhaps for an entire society. Decisions by political leaders and senior public servants about price and quantity regulations, taxes, international trade policy and government spending are examples of public choices.

You studied the consequences of some public choices in Chapter 6 where you saw how price ceilings and price floors prevent voluntary exchanges even though marginal social benefit exceeds marginal social cost; you also saw how taxes drive a wedge between marginal social benefit and marginal social cost. In Chapter 7, you saw how tariffs and import quotas restrict international trade. All of these public choices result in scarce resources being used inefficiently – they create deadweight loss.

Why do governments do things that create inefficiency? Aren't they supposed to make things better? If governments make things worse, why do they exist? Why aren't the successful societies those that have no government? The economic theory of government explains both why governments exist and why they do a less-than-perfect job.

Why Governments Exist

Governments exist for three major reasons. First, they establish and maintain property rights. Second, they provide non-market mechanisms for allocating scarce resources. Third, they implement arrangements that redistribute income and wealth.

Property rights are the fundamental foundation of the market economy. By establishing property rights and the legal system that enforces them, governments enable markets to function. In many situations, markets function well and allocate scarce resources efficiently. But sometimes the market results in inefficiency – market failure (see Chapter 5, pp. 113–114).

When market failure occurs, too many of some things and too few of some other things are produced. Choices made in the pursuit of self-interest have not served the social interest. By reallocating resources, it is possible to make some people better off while making no one worse off.

The market economy also delivers a distribution of income and wealth that most people regard as unfair. Equity requires some redistribution.

Replacing markets with government resource-allocation decisions is no simple matter. Just as there can be market failure, there can also be government failure. **Government failure** is a situation in which government actions lead to inefficiency – to either underprovision or overprovision.

Government failure can arise because government is made up of many individuals, each with their own economic objectives. Public choices are the outcome of the choices made by these individuals. To analyse these choices, economists have developed a public choice theory of the political marketplace.

Public Choice and the Political Marketplace

Four groups of decision makers, shown in Figure 15.1, interact in the political marketplace. They are:

◆ Voters

◆ Firms

◆ Politicians

◆ Bureaucrats

Voters

Voters evaluate politicians' policy proposals, benefit from public goods and services and pay some of the taxes. In the economic model of public choice, voters support the politicians whose policy proposals make them better off and express their demand for public goods and services by voting, helping in political campaigns, lobbying and making campaign contributions.

Firms

Firms also evaluate politicians' policy proposals, benefit from public goods and services and pay some of the taxes. Although firms don't vote, they do make campaign contributions and are a major source of funds for political parties. Firms also engage in lobbying to persuade politicians to propose policies that benefit them.

Politicians

Politicians are the elected persons in the EU, national and local governments – from the President of the EU parliament to your local council. Politicians at all levels

Figure 15.1   The Political Marketplace

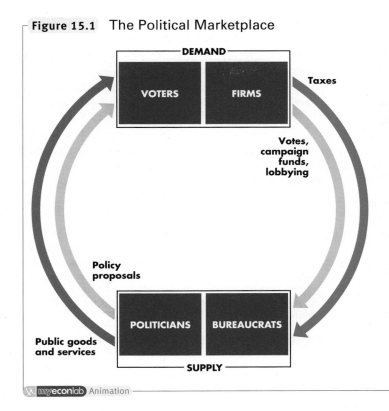

Voters express their demand for policies with their votes.

Voters and firms express their demand for policies with campaign contributions and by lobbying.

Politicians express their supply of policies with proposals that they hope will attract enough votes to get them elected and keep them in office. Politicians also set the taxes paid by voters and firms.

Bureaucrats provide public goods and services and try to get the largest possible budget for their departments.

A political equilibrium balances all these public choices.

myeconlab Animation

form coalitions – political parties – to develop policy proposals, which they present to voters in the hope of attracting majority support. Politicians also direct bureaucrats in the delivery of public goods and services and other policy actions. The goal of a politician is to get elected and to remain in office. Votes, to a politician, are like profit to a firm.

Bureaucrats

Bureaucrats are the public servants who work in government departments. They administer tax collection, the delivery of public goods and services and the administration of rules and regulations.

The self-interest of a bureaucrat is best served when the budget of her or his department is maximized. The bigger the budget of a department, the greater is the prestige of its chief and the greater are the opportunities for promotion for people further down the bureaucratic ladder. So all the members of a department have an interest in maximizing the department's budget. This economic assumption does not imply that bureaucrats do a poor job. Rather it implies that, in doing what they perceive to be a good job, they take care of their own self-interest too.

Political Equilibrium

Voters, firms, politicians and bureaucrats make their economic choices to achieve their own self-interest. Public choices, like private choices, are constrained by what is feasible. Each person's public choices are also constrained by the public choices of others.

The balance of forces in the political marketplace determines the outcome of all the public choices that people make. In a **political equilibrium** the choices of voters, firms, politicians and bureaucrats are all compatible and no group can see a way of improving its position by making a different choice.

Ideally, the political equilibrium will achieve allocative efficiency and serve the social interest, but such an outcome is not guaranteed, as you'll see later in this chapter.

We make public choices because some situations just don't permit private choices. The core of the reason we can't always make private choices is that some goods and services (and some factors of production) have a public nature – they are *public* goods and services.

Your next task is to see exactly what we mean by a *public* good or service.

What is a Public Good?

To see what makes a good a *public* good, we distinguish two features of all goods: the extent to which people can be *excluded* from consuming them and the extent to which one person's consumption *rivals* the consumption of others.

Excludable

A good is **excludable** if it is possible to prevent someone from enjoying its benefits. Brink's security services, Peterhead Seafood's fish and a U2 concert are examples. You must pay to benefit from them.

A good is **non-excludable** if everyone benefits from it regardless of whether they pay for it. The services of the London Metropolitan Police, fish in the North Sea and a concert on network television are examples. When police enforce the speed limit, everyone on the road benefits; anyone with a boat can fish in the ocean; and anyone with a TV can watch a network broadcast.

Rival

A good is **rival** if one person's use decreases the quantity available for someone else. A Brink's truck can't deliver cash to two banks at the same time. A fish can be consumed only once. And one seat at a concert can hold only one person at a time. These items are rival.

A good is **non-rival** if one person's use does not decrease the quantity available for someone else. The services of the police and a concert on network television are non-rival.

A Four-fold Classification

Figure 15.2 classifies goods, services and resources into four types.

Private Goods

A **private good** is both rival and excludable. A can of cola and a fish on Peterhead Seafood's farm are examples of private goods.

Public Goods

A **public good** is both non-rival and non-excludable. A public good simultaneously benefits everyone and no one can be excluded from enjoying its benefits. National defence is the best example of a public good.

Figure 15.2 Four-fold Classification of Goods

A private good is one that is rival and excludable. A public good is one that is non-rival and from which it is impossible to exclude a consumer. A common resource is one that is rival but non-excludable. And a good that is non-rival but excludable is produced by a natural monopoly.

myeconlab Animation

Common Resources

A **common resource** is rival and non-excludable. A unit of a common resource can be used only once, but no one can be prevented from using what is available. Ocean fish are a common resource. They are rival because a fish taken by one person isn't available for anyone else and they are non-excludable because it is difficult to prevent people from catching them.

Natural Monopoly Goods

A **natural monopoly good** is non-rival and excludable. When buyers can be excluded if they don't pay but the good is non-rival, marginal cost is zero. The fixed cost of producing such a good is usually high, so economies of scale exist over the entire range of output for which there is a demand (see Chapter 12, p. 276). An iTunes song and satellite television are examples.

Mixed Goods

Some goods don't fit neatly into the above four-fold classification. They are mixed goods. A **mixed good** is a private good the production or consumption of which creates an externality. An **externality** is a cost (external cost) or a benefit (external benefit) that arises from the production or consumption of a private good and that falls on someone other than its producer or consumer.

Is a Lighthouse a Public Good?

This lighthouse, built on Flamborough Head in 1806, protects ships from hitting the rocks off the North Yorkshire coast.

For two centuries, economists considered the lighthouse to be an example of a public good. No one can be prevented from seeing its warning light – *non-excludable* – and one person seeing its light doesn't prevent someone else from seeing it too – *non-rival*.

Ronald Coase, who won the 1991 Nobel Prize for ideas he first developed when he was an undergraduate at the London School of Economics, discovered that before the nineteenth century, lighthouses in England were built and operated by private companies that earned profits by charging tolls on ships docking at nearby ports. A ship that refused to pay the lighthouse toll was excluded from the port.

So the *benefit* arising from the services of a lighthouse *is* excludable. Because the services provided by a lighthouse are non-rival but *excludable*, a lighthouse is an example of a natural monopoly good and not a public good.

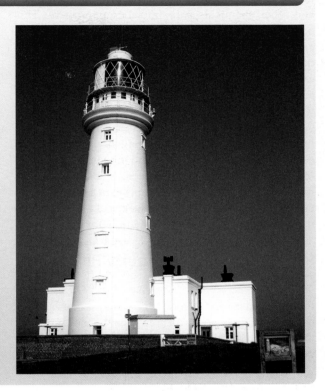

Mixed Goods with External Benefits

Two of the things that have the greatest impact on your welfare, your education and healthcare, are mixed goods with external benefits.

Think about a childhood measles vaccination. It is excludable because it would be possible to sell vaccinations and exclude those not willing to pay from benefiting from them. A measles vaccination is also rival because providing one person with a vaccination means one fewer available for everyone else. A vaccination is a private good, but it creates an externality.

If a parent decides to vaccinate a child, the child benefits from a lower risk of infection from a dangerous disease. But if the child does not get infected, other children who didn't get vaccinated have a better chance of avoiding measles too. A vaccination brings a benefit to others, so it is a mixed good with an external benefit.

The external benefit of a measles vaccination is like a public good. It is non-excludable because everyone with whom your child comes into contact can benefit. You can't selectively benefit only your friends! And it is non-rival – protecting one child from measles does not diminish the protection for others.

Education is another example of a mixed good with external benefits. If all education was organized by private schools and universities, those not willing or able to pay would be excluded, and one person's place in a class would rival another's. So education is a private good.

Your education brings benefits to others. It brings benefits to your friends who enjoy your sharp, educated wit and it brings benefits to the community in which you live because well-educated people with a strong sense of community and responsibility towards others make good neighbours. These external benefits are like a public good. You can't selectively decide who benefits from your good community spirit and one person's enjoyment of your good behaviour doesn't rival someone else's. So education is a mixed good with an external benefit.

Mixed Goods with External Costs

Mixed goods with external costs have become a huge political issue in recent years. The main ones are electricity and transport (road, rail and air) produced by burning hydrocarbon fuels – coal, oil and natural gas.

Electricity and transport are excludable and rival – they are private goods. But when you use electricity or travel by car, bus, train, or aeroplane, carbon dioxide and other chemicals pour into the atmosphere. This consequence of consuming a private good creates an external cost and is a public bad. (A 'bad' is the opposite of a good.) No one can be excluded from bearing the external cost and one person's discomfort doesn't rival another's. Electricity and transport are mixed goods with external costs.

Other private goods that generate external costs include logging and the clearing of forests, which destroy the habitat of wildlife and influence the amount of carbon dioxide in the atmosphere; smoking cigarettes in a confined space, which imposes a health risk on others; and driving under the influence of alcohol, which increases the risk of accident and injury for others.

Inefficiencies that Require Public Choices

Public goods, mixed goods, common resources and natural monopoly goods all create inefficiency problems that require public choices. Public choices must be made to:

◆ Provide public goods and mixed goods
◆ Conserve common resources
◆ Regulate natural monopoly

Provide Public Goods and Mixed Goods

Because no one can be excluded from enjoying the benefits of a public good, no one has an incentive to pay for their share of it. Even people with a social conscience have no incentive to pay because one person's enjoyment of a public good doesn't lower the enjoyment of others – it is non-rival.

If private firms tried to produce and sell public goods to consumers, they wouldn't remain in business for very long. The market economy would fail to deliver the efficient quantity of those goods. For example, there would be too little national defence, police services and law enforcement, courts and judges, storm-water and sewage disposal services.

Mixed goods pose a less extreme problem. The market economy would underprovide mixed goods with external benefits because their producers and consumers don't take the external benefits into account when they make their own choices. The market economy would overprovide mixed goods with external costs because

their producers and consumers don't take the external costs into account when they make their own choices.

Conserve Common Resources

Because no one can be excluded from enjoying the benefits of a common resource, no one has an incentive to pay for their share of it or to conserve the common resource for future enjoyment.

If boat owners are left to catch as much cod as they wish, the stock will deplete and eventually the species will vanish. The market economy would overproduce cod for sale while stocks lasted and then underproduce as stocks ran out.

This problem, called the tragedy of the commons, requires public choices to limit the overuse and eventual destruction of common resources.

Regulate Natural Monopoly

When people can be excluded from enjoying the benefits of a good if they don't pay for it, and when the good is non-rival, the marginal cost of producing it is zero. A natural monopoly can produce such a good at the lowest cost. But as Chapter 12 explains, when one firm serves a market, that firm maximizes profit by producing too little of the good.

You studied the regulation of natural monopoly in Chapter 12. This chapter and the next one study the other two public choices that must be made. In this chapter, we'll focus on the underprovision of public goods and mixed goods with external benefits. Chapter 16 studies mixed goods with external costs and conserving common resources.

Providing Public Goods

Why do governments provide flood rescue services? Why don't the people of Cornwall buy flood rescue services from a private firm – Flashflood – that competes for our pounds and euros in the marketplace in the same way that Costa Coffee does? The answer is that flood rescue is a public good. It is non-excludable and non-rival and it has a free-rider problem.

The Free-rider Problem

A free rider enjoys the benefits of a good or service without paying for it. Because a public good is provided for everyone to use and no one can be excluded from its benefits, no one has an incentive to pay his or her share of the cost. Everyone has an incentive to free ride. The **free-rider problem** is that the economy would provide an inefficiently small quantity of a public good. Marginal social benefit from the public good would exceed its marginal social cost and a deadweight loss would arise.

Let's look at the marginal social benefit and marginal social cost of a public good.

Marginal Social Benefit from a Public Good

Lisa and Max (the only people in a society) value flood rescue helicopters. Figure 15.3(a) and 15.3(b) graph their marginal benefits from the helicopters as MB_L for Lisa and MB_M for Max. The marginal benefit from a public good (like that from a private good) diminishes as the quantity of the good increases.

Figure 15.3(c) shows the marginal *social* benefit curve, *MSB*. Because everyone gets the same quantity of a public good, its marginal social benefit curve is the sum of the marginal benefits of all the individuals at each *quantity* – it is the *vertical* sum of the individual marginal benefit curves. So the curve *MSB* is the marginal social benefit curve for the economy made up of Lisa and Max. For each helicopter, Lisa's marginal benefit is added to Max's marginal benefit to calculate the marginal social benefit from that helicopter.

Contrast the *MSB* curve for a public good with that of a private good. To obtain the economy's *MSB* curve for a private good, we sum the *quantities demanded* by all the individuals in the economy at each price – we sum the individual marginal benefit curves *horizontally* (see Chapter 5, p. 108).

Figure 15.3 Benefits of a Public Good

(a) Lisa's marginal benefit

(b) Max's marginal benefit

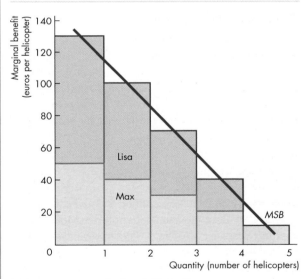

(c) Economy's marginal social benefit

The marginal social benefit at each quantity of the public good is the sum of the marginal benefits of all individuals in the economy. The marginal benefit curves are MB_L for Lisa and MB_M for Max. The economy's marginal social benefit curve is *MSB*.

 myeconlab Animation

Marginal Social Cost of a Public Good

The marginal social cost of a public good is determined in exactly the same way as that of a private good – see Chapter 5, p. 110. The principle of increasing marginal cost applies to the marginal cost of a public good, so the marginal social cost increases as the quantity of the public good increases.

Efficient Quantity of a Public Good

To determine the efficient quantity of a public good, we use the principles that you learned in Chapter 5. The efficient quantity is that at which marginal social benefit equals marginal social cost. Figure 15.4 shows the marginal social benefit curve, *MSB*, and the marginal social cost curve, *MSC*, for flood rescue helicopters. (We'll now think of society as consisting of Lisa and Max and the other 360 million Europeans.)

If marginal social benefit exceeds marginal social cost, as it does with 2 helicopters, resources can be used more efficiently by increasing the number of helicopters. The extra benefit exceeds the extra cost. If marginal social cost exceeds marginal social benefit, as it does with 4 helicopters, resources can be used more efficiently by decreasing the number of helicopters. The cost saving exceeds the loss of benefit.

If marginal social benefit equals marginal social cost, as it does with 3 helicopters, resources are allocated efficiently. Resources cannot be used more efficiently because to provide more than 3 helicopters increases cost by more than the extra benefit, and to provide fewer than 3 helicopters lowers the benefit by more than the cost saving.

Inefficient Private Provision

Could a private firm – Flashflood – deliver the efficient quantity of flood rescue helicopters? Most likely it couldn't, because no one would have an incentive to buy his or her share of the helicopters. Everyone would reason as follows: the number of helicopters provided by Flashflood is not affected by my decision to pay my share or not. But my own private consumption will be greater if I free ride and do not pay my share of the cost of the helicopters. If I don't pay, I enjoy the same level of flood rescue and I can buy more private goods. I will spend my money on private goods and free ride on flood rescue. Such reasoning is the free-rider problem. If everyone reasons the same way, Flashflood has no revenue and so provides no helicopters. Because the

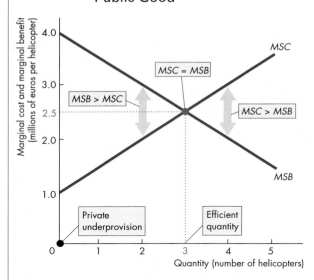

Figure 15.4 The Efficient Quantity of a Public Good

With fewer than 3 helicopters, marginal social benefit, *MSB*, exceeds marginal social cost, *MSC*. With more than 3 helicopters, *MSC* exceeds *MSB*. Only with 3 helicopters is *MSC* equal to *MSB* and the number of helicopters is efficient.

myeconlab Animation

efficient number of helicopters is 3, private provision is inefficient.

Efficient Public Provision

The outcome of the political process might be efficient or inefficient. We look first at an efficient outcome. There are two political parties: Fears and Hopes. They agree on all issues except the number of flood rescue helicopters: the Fears want 4, and the Hopes want 2. Both parties want to get elected, so they run a voter survey and discover the marginal social benefit curve of Figure 15.5. They also consult with helicopter producers to establish their marginal cost and the marginal social cost curve. The parties then do a 'what-if' analysis. If the Fears propose 4 helicopters and the Hopes propose 2, the voters will be equally unhappy with both parties. Compared to the efficient quantity, the Hopes want an underprovision of 1 helicopter and the Fears want an overprovision of 1 helicopter. The deadweight losses are equal and the election would be too close to call.

Contemplating this outcome, the Fears realize that they are too fearful to get elected. They figure that, if they scale back to 3 helicopters, they will win the election if the Hopes stick with 2. The Hopes reason in a similar way and figure that, if they increase the number of helicopters to 3, they can win the election if the Fears propose 4.

So they both propose 3 helicopters. The voters are indifferent between the parties, and each party receives 50 per cent of the vote. But regardless of which party wins the election, 3 helicopters are provided and this quantity is efficient. Competition in the political place results in the efficient provision of a public good.

The Principle of Minimum Differentiation

The **principle of minimum differentiation** is the tendency for competitors to make themselves similar to appeal to the maximum number of clients or voters. This principle not only describes the behaviour of political parties, but also explains why fast-food restaurants cluster in the same block. For example, if Dominoes opens a new pizza outlet, it is likely that Pizza Express will soon open nearby.

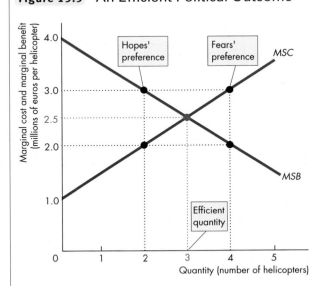

Figure 15.5   An Efficient Political Outcome

The Hopes would like to provide 2 helicopters and the Fears would like to provide 4 helicopters. The political outcome is 3 helicopters because unless each party proposes 3 helicopters, the other party will beat it in an election.

myeconlab Animation

Public Provision Without Public Production: Private Prison Services

Prisons are an example of a public good. Their benefits are enjoyed by all citizens (*non-excludable*) and one person's enjoyment of living in a safer society doesn't detract from the enjoyment of others (*non-rival*).

The cost of the UK prison system is large. In 2009, keeping a population of 85,000 people in prison cost £3.98 billion, or almost £47,000 per prisoner.

As a public good, the UK's prisons are provided by government and paid for with tax revenues. And traditionally, government ran the prisons. But while governments must *provide* and pay for prison services, they don't have to *produce* those services.

Today in the UK, many prisons are private. The first private prisons run by three firms, Kalyx, Serco and G45, opened in 1990.

Kalyx, Serco and G45 employ and train prison staff and produce prison services to maximize profit. And that is the benefit of private production. To maximize profit, these firms must produce prison services at the lowest possible cost.

If Kalyx tried to sell its services to each individual home, it wouldn't get enough revenue to remain in business. There would be a free-rider problem. The free-rider problem is avoided because the UK government buys the prison services from private producers – government is the *provider* of this public good and Kalyx and others are the *producers*.

For the political process to deliver the efficient outcome, voters must be well informed, evaluate the alternatives and vote in the election. Political parties must be well informed about voter preferences. As the next section shows, we can't expect to achieve this outcome.

Inefficient Public Overprovision

If competition between two political parties is to deliver the efficient quantity of a public good, bureaucrats must cooperate and help to achieve this outcome. But bureaucrats might have a different idea and end up frustrating rather than facilitating an efficient outcome. Their actions might bring government failure.

Objective of Bureaucrats

Bureaucrats want to maximize their department's budget because a bigger budget brings greater status and more power. So the Emergency Services Department's objective is to maximize the budget for flood rescue helicopters. Figure 15.6 shows the outcome if the bureaucrats are successful in the pursuit of their goal. They might try to persuade the politicians that 3 helicopters cost more than the originally budgeted amount; or they might press their position more strongly and argue for more than 3 helicopters.

In Figure 15.6, the Emergency Services Department persuades the politicians to provide 4 helicopters. Why don't the politicians block the bureaucrats? Won't overprovision of helicopters cost future votes? It will if voters are well informed and know what is best for them. But voters might not be well informed, and well-informed interest groups might enable the bureaucrats to achieve their objective and overcome the objections of the politicians.

Rational Ignorance

A principle of the economic analysis of public choices is that it is rational for a voter to be ignorant about an issue unless that issue has a perceptible effect on the voter's economic welfare. Each voter knows that he or she can make virtually no difference to the flood rescue policy of the UK government and that it would take an enormous amount of time and effort to become even moderately well informed about alternative flood rescue technologies. Rationally uninformed voters enable bureaucrats and special interest groups to overprovide public goods.

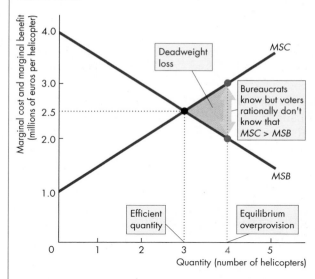

Figure 15.6 Bureaucratic Overprovision

Well-informed bureaucrats want to maximize their budget and rationally ignorant voters enable the bureaucrats to go some way towards achieving their goal. A public good might be inefficiently overprovided with a deadweight loss.

 Animation

Review Quiz

1 What is the free-rider problem? Why do free riders make the private provision of a public good inefficient?
2 Under what conditions will competition among politicians for votes result in an efficient quantity of a public good?
3 How do rationally ignorant voters and budget-maximizing bureaucrats prevent competition in the political marketplace from delivering the efficient quantity of a public good?
4 Explain why public choices might lead to the overprovision rather than the underprovision of a public good.

You can work these questions in Study Plan 15.2 and get instant feedback. 　myeconlab

You've seen how the political marketplace provides public goods and why it might overprovide them. Your next task is to see how the political marketplace provides mixed goods that bring external benefits.

Providing Mixed Goods with External Benefits

Most of the goods and services provided by governments are *mixed* goods, not *public* goods. Two of the largest mixed goods with external benefits are education and healthcare. We're going to look at how governments operate in such markets. We're also going to look at possible improvements on the current arrangements in these markets.

To keep our explanation clear, we'll focus first on the market for university education. We'll then apply the lessons we learn to the market for healthcare.

We begin our study of the provision of mixed goods by distinguishing between private benefits and social benefits.

Private Benefits and Social Benefits

A *private benefit* is a benefit that the consumer of a good or service receives. For example, expanded job opportunities and a higher income are private benefits of a university education.

Marginal benefit is the benefit from an additional unit of a good or service. So **marginal private benefit** (*MB*) is the benefit that the consumer of a good or service receives from an additional unit of it. When one additional student attends university, the benefit that student receives is the marginal private benefit from university education.

The *external benefit* from a good or service is the benefit that someone other than the consumer of the good or service receives. University graduates generate many external benefits. On average, they are better citizens, have lower crime rates and are more tolerant of the views of others. They enable the success of high quality newspapers and television channels, music, theatre and other organized social activities that bring benefits to many other people.

A **marginal external benefit** is the benefit from an additional unit of a good or service that people *other than its consumer* enjoy. The benefit that your friends and neighbours get from your university education is the marginal external benefit of your university education.

Marginal social benefit (*MSB*) is the marginal benefit enjoyed by society – by the consumer of a good or service (marginal private benefit) and by others (the marginal external benefit). That is,

$$MSB = MB + \text{Marginal external benefit}$$

Figure 15.7 shows an example of the relationship between marginal private benefit, marginal external benefit and marginal social benefit. The marginal benefit curve, *MB*, describes the marginal private benefit enjoyed by the people who receive a university education. Marginal private benefit decreases as the number of students attending university increases.

In the example in Figure 15.7, when 15 million students attend university, the marginal external benefit is €15,000 per student per year. The marginal social benefit curve, *MSB*, is the sum of marginal private benefit and marginal external benefit at each number of students. For example, when 15 million students a year attend university, the marginal private benefit is €10,000 per student and the marginal external benefit is €15,000 per student, so the marginal social benefit is €25,000 per student.

When people make schooling decisions, they ignore its external benefits and consider only its private benefits. So if education were provided by private

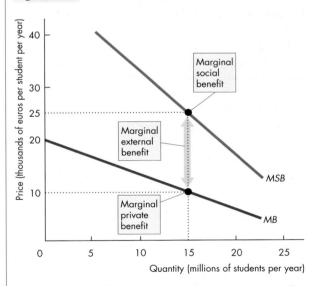

Figure 15.7   An External Benefit

The *MB* curve shows the marginal private benefit enjoyed by the people who receive a university education. The *MSB* curve shows the sum of marginal private benefit and marginal external benefit. When 15 million students attend university, the marginal private benefit is €10,000 per student, the marginal external benefit is €15,000 per student and the marginal social benefit is €25,000 per student.

myeconlab Animation

profit-maximizing firms that charged full-cost tuition, there would be too few university graduates.

Figure 15.8 illustrates this private underprovision. The supply curve is the marginal social cost curve, $S = MSC$. The demand curve is the marginal private benefit curve, $D = MB$. Market equilibrium occurs at a tuition of €15,000 per student per year and 7.5 million students per year. At this equilibrium, the marginal social benefit of €38,000 per student exceeds the marginal social cost by €23,000 per student. Too few students attend university. The efficient number of students is 15 million per year, where marginal social benefit equals marginal social cost. The grey triangle shows the deadweight loss created.

To get closer to producing the efficient quantity of a mixed good with an external benefit, we make public choices, through governments, to modify the market outcome.

Government Actions in the Market for a Mixed Good with External Benefits

To encourage more students to attend university – to achieve an efficient quantity of university education – students must be confronted with a lower price and taxpayers must somehow pay for the costs not covered by what the student pays.

Figure 15.9 illustrates an efficient outcome. With the marginal social cost curve MSC and the marginal social benefit curve MSB, the efficient number of university students is 15 million per year. The marginal *private* benefit curve MB tells us that 15 million students will attend university only if the price is €10,000 per year. But the marginal social cost of 15 million students is €25,000 per year. To enable the marginal social cost to be paid, taxpayers must pay the balance of €15,000 per student per year.

Figure 15.8   Inefficiency with an External Benefit

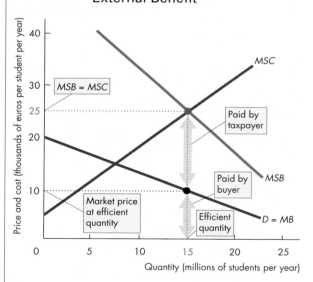

The market demand curve is the marginal private benefit curve, $D = MB$. The supply curve is the marginal social cost curve, $S = MSC$. Market equilibrium at a price of €15,000 a year and 7.5 million students is inefficient because marginal social benefit exceeds marginal social cost. The efficient quantity is 15 million students. A deadweight loss arises (grey triangle) because too few students attend university.

Figure 15.9   An Efficient Outcome with an External Benefit

The efficient number of university students is 15 million per year, where marginal social benefit equals marginal social cost. With the demand and marginal private benefit curve, $D = MB$, the price at which the efficient number will attend is €10,000 per year. If students pay this price, the taxpayer must somehow pay the rest, which equals the marginal external cost at the efficient quantity – €15,000 per student per year.

Three devices that governments can use to achieve a more efficient allocation of resources in the presence of external benefits are:

◆ Public production
◆ Private subsidies
◆ Vouchers

Public Production

With **public production**, a good or service is produced by a public authority that receives its revenue from the government. The education services produced by state universities and state schools are examples of public production.

In the example in Figure 15.9, efficient public production occurs if state universities receive funds from government equal to €15,000 per student per year, charge €10,000 per student per year, and 15 million students attend university.

Private Subsidies

A **subsidy** is a payment that the government makes to private producers. By making the subsidy depend on the level of output, the government can induce private decision-makers to consider external benefits when they make their choices.

In the example in Figure 15.9, efficient private provision would occur if private universities received a government subsidy of €15,000 per student per year. This subsidy reduces the universities' costs and would make their marginal cost equal to €10,000 per student at the efficient quantity. A price of €10,000 per year would cover this cost and the subsidy of €15,000 per student would cover the balance of the cost.

Vouchers

A **voucher** is a token that the government provides to households, which they can use to buy specified goods or services. Food stamps are examples of vouchers. The vouchers (food stamps) can be spent only on food and are designed to improve the diet and health of extremely poor families.

School vouchers are used in Sweden and have been advocated as a means of improving the quality of the UK secondary school system. A school voucher allows parents to choose the school their children will attend and use the voucher to pay part of the cost. The school cashes the vouchers to pay its bills. A voucher could be provided to a university student in a similar way, and although technically not a voucher, UK local authority fee payments for university students have a similar effect.

Because vouchers can be spent only on a specified item, they increase the willingness to pay for that item and so increase the demand for it.

Efficient provision of university education occurs if the government provides a voucher to each student with a value equal to the marginal external benefit at the efficient number of students. In the example in Figure 15.9, the efficient number of students is 15 million per year and the voucher is valued at €15,000 per student. Each student pays €10,000 and gives the university a €15,000 voucher. The universities receive €25,000 per student, which equals their marginal cost.

Bureaucratic Inefficiency and Government Failure

You've seen three government actions that achieve an efficient provision of a mixed good with an external benefit. In each case, if the government estimates the marginal external benefit correctly and makes marginal social benefit equal to marginal social cost, the outcome is efficient.

Does the comparison that we've just made mean that public provision, subsidized private provision and vouchers are equivalent? It does not. The reason lies in something that you've already encountered in your study of public goods earlier in this chapter – the behaviour of bureaucrats combined with rational ignorance that leads to government failure.

The Problem with Public Production

State universities (and schools) are operated by a bureaucracy and are subject to the same problems as the provision of public goods. If bureaucrats seek to maximize their budgets, the outcome might be inefficient. But *overprovision* of universities (and schools) doesn't seem to be a problem. Just the opposite: people complain about *underprovision* – about inadequate state university places and schools. One reason is that there is another type of bureaucratic budget maximization: budget padding and waste.

Bureaucrats often incur costs that exceed the minimum efficient cost. They might hire more assistants than the number needed to do their work efficiently; give themselves sumptuous offices; get generous expense allowances; build schools in the wrong places where land costs are too high.

Economists have studied the possibility that bureaucrats pad their budgets by comparing the production costs of private and state universities and schools. They have found that the costs per student of US state schools are of the order of *three times* the costs of comparable private schools.

Problems with Private Subsidies

Subsidizing private producers might overcome some of the problems created by public production. A private producer has an incentive to produce at minimum cost and avoid the budget padding of a bureaucratic producer. But two problems arise with private subsidies.

First, the subsidy budget must be allocated by a bureau. A national, state, or local department of education must lobby for its own budget and allocate it between school subsidies and its own administration costs. To the extent that bureaucrats succeed in maximizing their own administration budget, they siphon off resources from schools and a problem similar to that of public production arises.

Second, it is in the self-interest of subsidized producers to maximize their subsidy. These producers might spend some of the subsidy they receive lobbying for an even bigger one.

So neither public production nor subsidized private provision is likely to achieve an efficient allocation of resources in the face of external benefits.

Are Education Vouchers the Solution?

Education vouchers have four advantages over the other two approaches:

1 Vouchers can be used with public production, private provision or competition between the two.

2 Governments can set the value of vouchers and the total voucher budget to overcome bureaucratic overprovision and budget padding.

3 Vouchers spread the public contribution thinly across millions of consumers, so no one consumer has an interest in wasting part of the value received in lobbying for overprovision.

4 By giving the buying power to the final consumer, producers must compete for business and provide a high standard of service at the lowest attainable cost.

For these four reasons, vouchers are popular with economists, but they are controversial and opposed by most education administrators and teachers. Vouchers have been used in the UK for nursery education and currently there is debate about introducing vouchers for secondary education. Vouchers have also been used in a limited way to provide glasses in the UK (see *Economics in Action* below).

Healthcare Services

Healthcare is another example of a mixed good with external benefits. The external benefits from healthcare include avoiding infectious diseases and living and working with healthy neighbours. Another external benefit for most people is the pleasure they get from knowing that they live in a society that cares for the sick and the poor and provides them with access to affordable healthcare.

Because of the external benefits that healthcare brings, no country leaves its delivery entirely to the private market economy. Most countries have both private and public healthcare providers.

The private healthcare sector consists of two sets of markets: a market for health insurance and a market for healthcare services. People (or often employers) buy health insurance from private insurance companies and buy healthcare services from private doctors, nurses and hospitals. They pay for these services and get some reimbursement from their health insurance company.

ECONOMICS IN ACTION

Vouchers for Glasses

When the UK National Health Service (NHS) began in 1948 it provided (among other things) free eye testing and glasses. But NHS glasses were not the latest fashion statement and they became a mark of low income.

To resolve this problem, vouchers for glasses were introduced. Children, pensioners and low-income adults receive vouchers for glasses with a free eye test. In 2009, 21 per cent of adults were eligible for vouchers ranging in value from £36 to £182.

The voucher system removed the stigma associated with NHS glasses and allowed the growth of competitive low-cost optician services. In 2009 consumers spent £2.65 billion on optical services. Private opticians accounted for 41 per cent of the market and vouchers paid for 31 per cent of all glasses dispensed.

Source of data: Optical Goods and Eye Care 2010, Mintel.

Healthcare in Europe: Is Public or Private Provision More Efficient?

The mix of public and private healthcare varies across the countries of Europe. The percentage of total income spent on healthcare varies too. How does the mix of public and private healthcare influence total expenditure and the efficiency and quality of healthcare? The figures and the table provide some clues to the answer.

Germany has the smallest public component (Figure 1) and spends the largest percentage of income on healthcare (Figure 2). But as the numbers in Table 1 show, Germany ranks only fourth overall and fifth on efficiency and quality of care.

The Netherlands and UK, which have a larger public component and smaller spending, rank 1 and 2 overall and rank highly on efficiency and quality too.

Table 1

Health System Performance Ranking

	Germany	Netherlands	UK
Overall	4	1	2
Efficiency	5	3	1
Quality of care	5	2	3

While many factors contribute to the efficiency and quality of healthcare, and these factors may differ across the countries, it is striking that the high-spending, low-public component in Germany's healthcare system doesn't put that country at the top of the efficiency and quality league table.

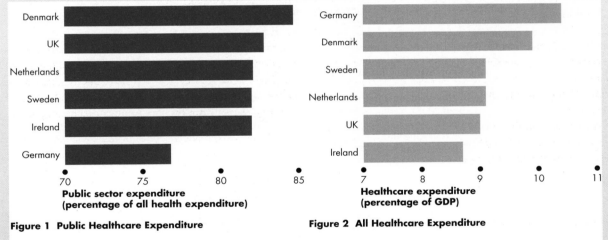

Figure 1 Public Healthcare Expenditure

Figure 2 All Healthcare Expenditure

Source of data: Mirror Mirror on the Wall Report, Commonwealth Fund, 2010.

In the public healthcare sector, services are provided at a zero price and doctors, nurses and hospitals receive their incomes from government.

Which is more efficient and which provides the best quality of care: public or private? And does spending more guarantee improved quality?

Economics in Action (above) suggests that public healthcare can be both efficient and of high quality. And *Reading Between the Lines* on pp. 360–361 reinforces this conclusion.

Aside from their limited use in providing glasses in the UK, healthcare vouchers have attracted little attention. But their advantages in education apply with equal force to healthcare and deserve closer consideration.

Reading Between the Lines on pp. 360–361

Review Quiz

1 What is special about education and healthcare that makes them mixed goods with external benefits?
2 Why would the market economy produce too little education and healthcare?
3 How might public production, private subsidies and vouchers achieve an efficient provision of a mixed good with external benefits?
4 What are the key differences among public production, private subsidies and vouchers?

You can work these questions in Study Plan 15.3 and get instant feedback.

Reading Between the Lines

Healthcare in the UK and US

Telegraph, 30 June 2010

US Government Spends More on Health than the NHS

It may surprise you that . . . the US Government now spends more on provision of healthcare than does Britain's. . . . The costs of running various US health programmes – Medicare and Medicaid most significantly – is, at 7.4 per cent of gross domestic product, greater than the 7.2 per cent of GDP the UK Government spends on the NHS. . . . The US must just have overtaken Britain this year on this basis (the latest figures date from 2008), having risen worryingly fast in recent years.

Obviously the first striking thing is just how much the US spends as a whole – at 16 per cent of GDP it is almost double Britain's 8.7 per cent.

Is this disproportionate amount of healthcare spending justified? . . . Based on two key measures of healthcare effectiveness – infant mortality and life expectancy, the US actually has worse outcomes than Britain.

However, an area which is rather less flattering for the UK is on the equipment provided by hospitals. . . . Britain has fewer CT scanners per head than Turkey or Poland, and fewer MRI units than the Slovak Republic. And yet despite these third-world levels of investment, the NHS still manages to provide a service of true developed world standards. . . .

The Essence of the Story

◆ The US government spends more on healthcare as a percentage of income than the UK government does on the National Health Service (NHS).

◆ Including public and private healthcare, the US spends nearly double what the UK spends.

◆ Despite higher expenditure, two major measures of health outcomes are worse in the US than in the UK: infant mortality and life expectancy.

◆ The UK has poor levels of specialist equipment per person when compared to other developed economies.

Economic Analysis

◆ Healthcare expenditure per person is vastly greater in the US than in the UK and other European countries.

◆ But US health outcomes are not much different from those in the UK and the rest of Europe.

◆ A possible reason is that much of the US expenditure is wasted – deadweight loss.

◆ The figures illustrate this possibility by comparing the US (Figure 1), the UK (Figure 2) and an efficient outcome (Figure 3).

◆ The three figures illustrate three healthcare systems. The numbers are purely illustrative and other things remain the same. In each case, marginal social cost is *MSC*, marginal private benefit is *MB*, and marginal social benefit is *MSB*.

◆ Figure 1 illustrates the US system. For most people, private healthcare is the only option and the *MB* curve is MB_1. In a year, 8 million of these people pay $18,000 per patient.

◆ Public healthcare is provided to the aged and the poor at a zero price and a further 12 million people ($8 + 12 = 20$ million total) receive healthcare services that cost $30,000 per patient per year to deliver. Large overprovision creates a deadweight loss.

◆ Figure 2 illustrates the UK system. Because everyone has access to the NHS, the willingness-to-pay is lower and the *MB* curve (MB_2) is below that in the US.

◆ In the UK, 3 million patients buy private healthcare for £13,000 per year. The NHS provides a capacity to treat 5 million patients a year and waiting times allocate the scarce resources. A deadweight loss arises from underprovision.

◆ Figure 3 illustrates an efficient heathcare system that uses healthcare vouchers. Such a scheme has been suggested for the US by economist Lawrence Kotlikoff of Boston University.

Figure 1 US overprovision

Figure 2 UK underprovision

Figure 3 Efficient provision

◆ Each patient receives a £10,000 voucher each year and pays a further £10,000 for healthcare services. (Kotlikoff's scheme has bigger vouchers for those with more serious health problems and in principle the value of the vouchers could depend on the health condition.)

SUMMARY

Key Points

Public Choices (pp. 346–350)

◆ Governments establish and maintain property rights, provide non-market mechanisms for allocating scarce resources and redistribute income and wealth.

◆ Public choice theory explains how voters, firms, politicians and bureaucrats interact in the political marketplace and why government failure might occur.

◆ A private good is a good or service that is rival and excludable.

◆ A public good is a good or service that is non-rival and non-excludable.

◆ A mixed good is a private good that creates an external benefit or external cost.

Working Problems 1 to 6 will give you a better understanding of public choices.

Providing Public Goods (pp. 351–354)

◆ Because a public good is a good or service that is *non-rival* and *non-excludable*, it creates a *free-rider* problem: no one has an incentive to pay their share of the cost of providing a public good.

◆ The efficient level of provision of a public good is that at which marginal social benefit equals marginal social cost.

◆ Competition between political parties can lead to the efficient scale of provision of a public good.

◆ Bureaucrats who maximize their budgets and voters who are rationally ignorant can lead to the inefficient overprovision of a public good – government failure.

Working Problems 7 to 15 will give you a better understanding of providing public goods.

Providing Mixed Goods with External Benefits (pp. 355–359)

◆ Mixed goods provide external benefits – benefits that are received by people other than the consumer of a good or service.

◆ Marginal social benefit equals marginal private benefit plus marginal external benefit.

◆ External benefits arise from education and healthcare.

◆ Vouchers provided to households can achieve a more efficient provision of education and healthcare than public production or subsidies to private producers.

Working Problems 16 to 20 will give you a better understanding of providing mixed goods with external benefits.

Key Terms

Common resource, 348
Excludable, 348
Externality, 348
Free-rider problem, 351
Government failure, 346
Marginal external benefit, 355
Marginal private benefit, 355
Marginal social benefit, 355
Mixed good, 348
Natural monopoly good, 348
Non-excludable, 348
Non-rival, 348
Political equilibrium, 347
Principle of minimum differentiation, 353
Private good, 348
Public choice, 346
Public good, 348
Public production, 357
Rival, 348
Subsidy, 357
Voucher, 357

STUDY PLAN PROBLEMS AND APPLICATIONS

 You can work Problems 1 to 20 in MyEconLab Chapter 15 Study Plan and get instant feedback.

Public Choices (Study Plan 15.1)

1 Classify each of the following items as excludable, non-excludable, rival or non-rival.

- A Big Mac
- The Humber Bridge
- A view of the Eiffel Tower

2 Classify each of the following items as a public good, a private good, a natural monopoly good or a common resource.

- Police patrol service
- City pavements
- Royal Mail
- FedEx courier service

3 Classify the following services for computer owners with an Internet connection as rival, non-rival, excludable or non-excludable:

- eBay
- A mouse
- A Twitter page
- MyEconLab website

4 Classify each of the following items as a public good, a private good, a mixed good or a common resource:

- Fire fighting service
- A courtside seat at the Wimbledon (tennis) Club
- A well-stocked buffet that promises all you can eat for £10
- The Danube River

5 Explain which of the following events creates an external benefit or an external cost:

- A huge noisy crowd gathers outside the lecture room
- Your neighbour grows beautiful flowers on his apartment patio.
- A fire alarm goes off accidentally during a lecture.
- Your tutor offers a free tutorial after class.

6 Wind Farm Clears Hurdle

The nation's first offshore wind farm with 130 turbines will be built five miles off the coast. Wind turbines are noisy, stand 440 feet tall, can be seen from the coast and will produce power for 75 per cent of nearby homes.

Source: *The New York Times*, 16 January 2009

List the externalities created by this wind farm.

Providing Public Goods (Study Plan 15.2)

7 For each of the following goods, explain whether there is a free-rider problem. If there is no such problem, how is it avoided?

- November 5th fireworks display
- M1 motorway in Britain
- Wireless Internet access in hotels
- The public library in your city

8 The table sets out the marginal benefits that Terri and Sue receive from police officers on duty on the university campus:

| Police officers on duty (number per night) | Marginal benefit | |
| | Terri | Sue |
	(pounds per police officer)	
1	18	22
2	14	18
3	10	14
4	6	10
5	2	6

a If the police officers are provided by the government, is the presence of the police on campus a private good or a public good?

b Suppose that Terri and Sue are the only students on the campus at night. Draw a graph to show the marginal social benefit from on-campus police officers on duty at night.

9 For each of the following goods and services, explain whether there is a free-rider problem. If there is no such problem, how is it avoided?

- National gale warning system
- Ambulance service
- Road safety signs
- A national coastguard

10 Vaccination Dodgers

Doctors struggle to eradicate polio worldwide, but one of the biggest problems is persuading parents to vaccinate their children. Since the discovery of the vaccine, polio has been eliminated from Europe and the law requires everyone to be vaccinated. People who refuse to be vaccinated are 'free riders'.

Source: *USA Today*, 12 March 2008

Explain why someone who has not opted out on medical or religious grounds and refuses to be vaccinated is a 'free rider'.

Use the following figure to work Problems 11 to 13.

The figure provides information about a waste disposal system that a city of 1 million people is considering installing.

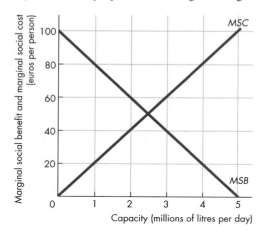

11 What is the efficient capacity of the waste disposal system? How much will each person have to pay in taxes for the city to install the efficient capacity?

12 What is the political equilibrium if voters are well informed?

13 What is the political equilibrium if voters are rationally ignorant and bureaucrats achieve the highest attainable budget?

Use the data on a mosquito control programme in the following table to work Problems 14 and 15.

Quantity (square miles sprayed per day)	Marginal social cost	Marginal social benefit
	(thousands of pounds per day)	
1	2	10
2	4	8
3	6	6
4	8	4
5	10	2

14 What quantity of spraying would a private mosquito control programme provide? What is the efficient quantity of spraying? In a single-issue election on the quantity of spraying, what quantity would the winner of the election provide?

15 If the government sets up a Department of Mosquito Control and appoints a bureaucrat to run it, would mosquito spraying most likely be underprovided, overprovided, or provided at the efficient quantity?

Providing Mixed Goods with External Benefits (Study Plan 15.3)

Use the following figure, which shows the marginal private benefit from university education, for Problems 16 to 19.

The marginal cost of a university education is a constant €6,000 per student per year. The marginal external benefit from a university education is a constant €4,000 per student per year.

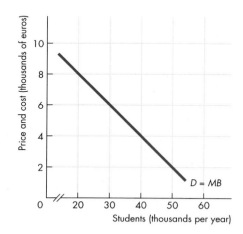

16 What is the efficient number of students? If all universities are private, how many people enrol in university and what is the tuition?

17 If the government provides public universities, what tuition will these universities charge to achieve the efficient enrolment? How much will taxpayers have to pay?

18 If the government subsidizes private universities, what subsidy will achieve the efficient enrolment?

19 If the government offers vouchers and no subsidy to those who attend university, what is the value of the voucher that will achieve the efficient enrolment?

20 **University Fees Rise as Support Cut**

Teaching subsidies to universities will be cut for the first time by £315 million this year. Some universities want tuition fees to rise from £3,225 to £7,000 a year alongside cuts in subsidies for student loans and grants.

Source: *The Times online*, 28 January 2010

If government cuts the subsidy to universities, why will tuition fees rise and the number of enrolled students decrease? Why might it be a better policy for government to maintain the subsidy to universities?

ADDITIONAL PROBLEMS AND APPLICATIONS

myeconlab You can work these problems in MyEconLab if assigned by your lecturer.

Public Choices

21 Classify each of the following items as excludable, non-excludable, rival or non-rival.

- ◆ Firefighting service
- ◆ A Starbucks coffee
- ◆ A view of Big Ben
- ◆ The Pennine Way
- ◆ Lake Windermere

22 Classify each of the following items as a public good, a private good, a natural monopoly good, a common resource or a mixed good.

- ◆ Measles vaccination
- ◆ Tuna in the Mediterranean Sea
- ◆ Air service in the UK
- ◆ Local flood-water protection system

23 Consider each of the following activities or events and say for each one whether it creates an externality. If so, say whether it creates an external benefit or external cost and whether the externality arises from production or consumption.

- ◆ Aeroplanes taking off from Heathrow during the tennis tournament taking place at nearby Wimbledon
- ◆ A sunset over the Mediterranean Sea
- ◆ An increase in the number of people who are studying for graduate degrees
- ◆ A person wears strong perfume in your tutorial class

24 Classify each of the following items as a public good, a private good or a mixed good and say whether it creates an external benefit, external cost or neither.

- ◆ Chewing gum
- ◆ The London M25 circular motorway at peak travel time
- ◆ The London Underground
- ◆ A skateboard
- ◆ A beach in the South of France

Providing Public Goods

Use the following news clip to work Problems 25 and 26.

Private versus State Education

UK parents must choose between moderate quality state secondary schools financed entirely by taxes or high-quality private schools financed entirely by fees. If quality is related to cost, a private school that was just a bit better than a state school would get no students, so only high quality private schools exist. Most parents choose state schools because they can't afford high quality. Most would prefer to contribute to the cost to raise the quality at state schools, but they are not allowed to. Instead people spend money on moving house or buying educational toys, which is inefficient.

Source: *The Independent*, 14 January 2010

25 Explain why government state education services can create a free-rider problem.

26 Explain why the allocation of funds between UK state schools and private schools is inefficient. How might a school voucher system achieve efficiency?

27 The table sets out the marginal benefits that Sam and Nick receive from the town's street lighting:

Number of street lights	Marginal benefit	
	Sam	Nick
	(pounds per street light)	
1	10	12
2	8	9
3	6	6
4	4	3
5	2	0

a Is the town's street lighting a private good or a public good?

b Suppose that Sam and Nick are the only residents of the town. Draw a graph to show the marginal social benefit from the town's street lighting.

28 What is the principle of diminishing marginal benefit? In Problem 27, does Sam's, Nick's or the society's marginal benefit diminish faster?

Use the following news clip for Problems 29 and 30.

A Bridge Too Far Gone

Petrol taxes paid for much of America's post-war motorway system. Now motorists pay about one-third in petrol taxes to drive a mile as they did in the 1960s. Yet raising such taxes is politically tricky. This would matter less if private cash was flooding into infrastructure or new ways were being found to control demand. Neither is happening, and private companies building toll roads brings howls of outrage.

Source: *The Economist*, 9 August 2007

29 Why is it 'politically tricky' to raise petrol taxes to finance infrastructure?

30 What in this news clip points to a distinction between public *production* of a public good and public *provision*? Give examples of three public goods that are produced by private firms but provided by government and paid for with taxes.

Providing Mixed Goods with External Benefits

Use the following information and figure to work Problems 31 to 34.

The marginal cost of educating a student is a constant £4,000 a year and the figure shows the students' marginal benefit curve. Suppose that university education creates an external benefit of a constant £2,000 per student per year.

31 If all universities are private and the market for education is competitive, how many students enrol, what is the tuition fee and what is the deadweight loss created?

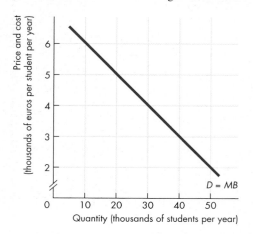

32 If the government decides to provide public universities, what tuition fees will these universities charge to achieve the efficient number of students? How much will taxpayers have to pay?

33 If the government decides to subsidize private universities, what subsidy will achieve the efficient number of university students?

34 If the government offers vouchers to those who enrol at a university and no subsidy, what is the value of the voucher that will achieve the efficient number of students?

35 My Child, My Choice

Fully vaccinating all US children born in a given year saves 33,000 lives, prevents 14 million infections and saves $10 billion in medical costs. Part of the reason is that vaccinations protect not only the kids that receive the shots but also those who can't receive them – such as newborns and cancer patients with suppressed immune systems.

Source: *Time*, 2 June 2008

a Describe the private benefits and external benefits of vaccinations and explain why a private market for vaccinations would produce an inefficient outcome.

b Draw a graph to illustrate a private market for vaccinations and show the deadweight loss.

c Explain how government intervention could achieve an efficient quantity of vaccinations and draw a graph to illustrate this outcome.

Economics in the News

36 After you have studied *Reading Between the Lines* on pp. 360–361 answer the following questions.

a What are the main differences in healthcare expenditures and health outcomes in the UK and US?

b Compare the main features of the UK public health system with the US public health system.

c Which of the two systems achieves the more efficient outcome and why?

d How does the UK public healthcare system limit over-provision?

e How could healthcare vouchers improve the UK and US healthcare systems?

37 Who's Hiding under Our Umbrella?

Students of the Cold War learn that, to deter possible Soviet aggression, the US placed a 'strategic umbrella' over NATO Europe and Japan, with the US providing most of their national security. Under President Ronald Reagan, the US spent 6 per cent of GDP on defence, whereas the Europeans spent only 2 to 3 per cent and the Japanese spent only 1 per cent, although all faced a common enemy. Thus the US taxpayer paid a disproportionate share of the overall defence spending, whereas NATO Europe and Japan spent more on consumer goods or saved.

Source: *International Herald Tribune*, 30 January 2008

a Explain the free-rider problem described in this news clip.

b Does the free-rider problem in international defence mean that the world has too little defence against aggression?

c How do nations try to overcome the free-rider problem among nations?

CHAPTER 16

Economics of the Environment

After studying this chapter you will be able to:

◆ Explain why external costs bring market failure and too much pollution, and how property rights, pollution taxes, emission charges and marketable permits might achieve an efficient outcome

◆ Explain the tragedy of the commons and its possible solutions

Environmental issues such as global warming and pollution are simultaneously everyone's problem and nobody's problem. Can government policy help us to take account of the damage that we cause others every time we turn on our heating or drive our cars? The wild fish stocks of the world are common resources. No one owns them and many are dangerously depleted. Can government policy stop overfishing and help conserve fish stocks? You can find out in this chapter.

In *Reading Between the Lines* at the end of the chapter, we look at the EU market for trading carbon emissions as a way of addressing global warming and climate change.

Negative Externality: Pollution

Can each individual be relied upon to make decisions that influence the Earth's carbon dioxide concentration in the social interest? Must governments change the incentives we face so that our self-interested choices are also in the social interest? How can governments change incentives? These questions about climate change that we posed in Chapter 1 (see p. 8) involve external costs and this chapter answers them.

This chapter also studies another environmental problem that requires public choices: the overuse and sometimes the depletion of renewable natural resources.

We first study the external costs of pollution and begin with a quick review of the production activities that pollute our environment.

Sources of Pollution

Economic activity pollutes air, water and land and these individual areas of pollution interact through the ecosystem. The three biggest sources of pollution are road transportation, electricity generation and industrial processes.

A common belief is that our advanced industrial economy is creating ever more pollution. But for many pollutants, in the rich countries that include the UK, pollution is less serious today than it was in earlier years (see *Economics in Action* below for a description of the trends in air pollution).

Effects of Pollution

While the facts about the sources and trends in air pollution are not in doubt, there is disagreement about the effects of air pollution. The least controversial is the acid rain caused by sulphur dioxide and nitrogen oxide emissions from coal- and oil-fired generators of power stations. Acid rain begins with air pollution, and it leads to water pollution and damages vegetation.

More than 180 other airborne substances (suspended particulates) such as lead from leaded petrol have been identified, which in sufficiently large concentrations, are believed to cause cancer and other life-threatening conditions.

Many scientists believe that carbon dioxide emissions are a major cause of global warming and climate change.

The effects of pollution mean that production and consumption decisions impose costs that are not taken fully into account when decisions are made. You are now going to see how economists analyse these decisions and solve the pollution problem.

> ECONOMICS IN ACTION

UK Air Pollution Trends

UK environmental laws and stringent EU regulations have driven down air pollution in the UK despite an increase in economic activity.

The figure shows the concentrations of five air pollutants in the UK as percentages of their 1990 levels. Lead has been almost eliminated from our air. Sulphur dioxide and particulates have been reduced to less than half of their 1990 levels. Even the more stubborn nitrogen dioxide has been nearly halved. And the concentration of carbon dioxide, the main greenhouse gas, has been cut, if only very slightly.

These reductions in air pollution are more impressive when they are seen against the trends in economic activity. Between 1990 and 2008, total UK production increased by 50 per cent, vehicle miles travelled increased by 23 per cent, and the population increased by 8 per cent.

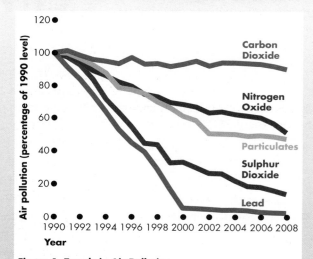

Figure 1 Trends in Air Pollution

Source of data: www.naei.org.uk

Private Cost and Social Cost of Pollution

To study the economics of the external costs that arise from pollution, we distinguish between the private cost and the social cost of production.

A *private cost* of production is a cost that is borne by the producer of a good or service. *Marginal cost* is the cost of producing an *additional unit* of a good or service. So **marginal private cost** (*MC*) is the cost of producing an additional unit of a good or service that is borne by its producer.

An *external cost* is a cost of producing a good or service that is *not* borne by the producer but borne by other people. A **marginal external cost** is the cost of producing an additional unit of a good or service that falls on people other than the producer.

Marginal social cost (*MSC*) is the marginal cost incurred by the producer and by everyone else on whom the cost falls – by society. It is the sum of marginal private cost and marginal external cost. That is,

$$MSC = MC + \text{Marginal external cost}$$

We express costs in pounds, but we must always remember that the cost of a good or service is its opportunity cost – something real, such as clean air or a clean river, that is given up to get it.

Valuing an External Cost

Economists use market prices to put a pound value on the cost of pollution. For example, suppose that there are two similar rivers, one polluted and the other clean. Five hundred identical homes are built along the side of each river. The homes on the clean river rent for £2,500 a month, and those on the polluted river rent for £1,500 a month. If the pollution is the only detectable difference between the two rivers and the two locations, the rent decrease of £1,000 per month is the cost of the pollution. With 500 homes on the polluted river, the external cost of pollution is £500,000 a month.

External Cost and Output

Figure 16.1 shows an example of the relationship between output and cost in a chemical industry that pollutes. The marginal cost curve, *MC*, describes the marginal private cost borne by the firms that produce the chemical. Marginal cost increases as the quantity of chemical produced increases.

If the firms dump waste into a river, they impose an external cost on other users of the river. We will assume that when the quantity of chemical produced increases, the amount of pollution increases and the external cost of pollution increases.

The marginal social cost curve, *MSC*, is found by adding the marginal external cost to the marginal private cost. So a point on the *MSC* curve shows the sum of the marginal cost of producing a given quantity of output and the marginal external cost created. For example, when output is 4,000 tonnes of chemical per month, marginal private cost of producing the chemical is £100 a tonne, marginal external cost created is £125 a tonne and marginal social cost is £225 a tonne.

Figure 16.1 shows the relationship between the quantity of chemical produced and the cost of the pollution it creates, but it doesn't tell us how much pollution the chemical industry produces. That quantity depends on the quantity of chemical produced, which depends on supply and demand in the market for the chemical. We now look at that market.

Figure 16.1 An External Cost

The *MC* curve shows the marginal private cost borne by the factories that produce a chemical. The *MSC* curve shows the sum of marginal private cost and marginal external cost. When output of the chemical is 4,000 tonnes a month, marginal private cost is £100 a tonne, marginal external cost is £125 a tonne and marginal social cost is £225 a tonne.

myeconlab Animation

Production and Pollution: How Much?

When an industry is unregulated, the amount of pollution it creates depends on the market equilibrium price and quantity of the good produced. In Figure 16.2, the demand curve for a pollution-creating chemical is *D*. This curve also measures the marginal social benefit, *MSB*, of the chemical. The supply curve is *S*. This curve also measures the marginal private cost, *MC*. The supply curve is the marginal private cost curve because when firms make their production and supply decisions, they consider only the costs that they will bear. Market equilibrium occurs at a price of £100 a tonne and a quantity of 4,000 tonnes of chemical a month.

This equilibrium is inefficient. You learned in Chapter 5 that the allocation of resources is efficient when marginal social benefit equals marginal social cost. But we must count *all* the costs – private and external – when we compare marginal social benefit and marginal social cost. So with an external cost, the allocation is efficient when marginal social benefit equals marginal *social* cost. This outcome occurs when the quantity of chemical produced is 2,000 tonnes a month. The market equilibrium overproduces by 2,000 tonnes a month and creates a deadweight loss shown by the grey triangle.

How can the people who live by the polluted river get the chemical factories to decrease their output of chemicals and create less pollution? If some method can be found to achieve this outcome, everyone – the owners of the chemical factories and the residents of the riverside homes – can gain. Let's explore some solutions.

Property Rights

Sometimes it is possible to reduce the inefficiency arising from an externality by establishing a property right where one does not currently exist. **Property rights** are legally established titles to the ownership, use and disposal of factors of production and goods and services that are enforceable in the courts.

Suppose that the chemical factories own the river and the 500 homes alongside it. The rent that people are willing to pay depends on the amount of pollution. Using the earlier example, people are willing to pay £2,500 a month to live alongside a pollution-free river but only £1,500 a month to live with the pollution created by 4,000 tonnes of chemical a month. If the factories produce this quantity, they lose £1,000 a month for each home – a total of £500,000 a month.

Figure 16.2 Inefficiency with an External Cost

The market supply curve is the marginal private cost curve, *S = MC*. The demand curve is the marginal social benefit curve, *D = MSB*. Market equilibrium occurs at a price of £100 a tonne and 4,000 tonnes of chemical a month. This market outcome is inefficient because the marginal social cost exceeds marginal social benefit. The efficient quantity of chemical is 2,000 tonnes a month. The grey triangle shows the deadweight loss created by the pollution.

myeconlab Animation

The chemical factories are now confronted with the cost of their pollution – forgone rent from the people who live by the river.

Figure 16.3 illustrates the outcome by using the same example as in Figure 16.2. With property rights in place, the *MC* curve no longer measures all the costs that the factories face in producing the chemical. It excludes the pollution costs that they must now bear. The *MSC* curve now becomes the marginal private cost curve *MC*. The factories bear *all* the costs, so the market supply curve is based on all the marginal costs and is the curve labelled *S = MC = MSC*.

Market equilibrium now occurs at a price of £150 a tonne of chemical and a quantity of 2,000 tonnes of chemical a month. This outcome is efficient. The factories still produce some pollution, but it is the efficient quantity.

Figure 16.3 Property Rights Achieve an Efficient Outcome

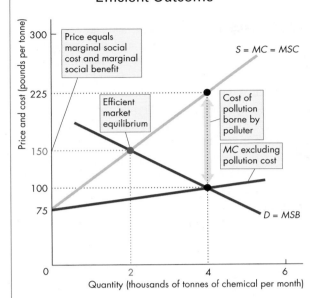

With property rights, the marginal cost curve that excludes pollution costs shows only part of the producers' marginal cost. The marginal cost of producing the chemical now includes the cost of pollution – the external cost. So the producers' supply curve is $S = MC = MSC$. Market equilibrium now occurs at a price of £150 a tonne and a quantity of 2,000 tonnes of chemical a month. This outcome is efficient because marginal social cost equals marginal social benefit. The pollution created is not zero, but it is the efficient quantity.

myeconlab Animation

The Coase Theorem

Does it matter how property rights are assigned? Does it matter whether the polluter or the victim of the pollution owns the resource that might be polluted? Until 1960, everyone – including economists who had thought long and hard about the problem – thought that it did matter. But in 1960, Ronald Coase had a remarkable insight, now called the Coase theorem.

The **Coase theorem** is the proposition that if property rights exist, if only a small number of parties are involved and if transactions costs are low, then private transactions are efficient. There are no externalities because the transacting parties take all the costs and benefits into account. Furthermore, it doesn't matter who has the property rights.

Application of the Coase Theorem

In the example that we've just studied, the factories own the river and the homes. Suppose that instead, the residents own their homes and the river. Now the factories must pay a fee to the homeowners for the right to dump their waste. The greater the quantity of waste dumped into the river, the more the factories must pay. So, again, the factories face the opportunity cost of the pollution they create. The quantity of chemical produced and the amount of waste dumped are the same whoever owns the homes and the river. If the factories own them, they bear the cost of pollution because they receive a lower income from home rents. And if the residents own the homes and the river, the factories bear the cost of pollution because they must pay a fee to the homeowners. In both cases, the factories bear the cost of their pollution and dump the efficient amount of waste into the river.

The Coase solution works only when transactions costs are low. **Transactions costs** are the opportunity costs of conducting a transaction. For example, when you buy a house, you incur a series of transactions costs. You might pay an estate agent to help you find the best place and a lawyer to run checks that assure you that the seller owns the property and that after you've paid for it, the ownership has been properly transferred to you.

In the example of the homes alongside a river, the transactions costs that are incurred by a small number of chemical factories and a few homeowners might be low enough to enable them to negotiate the deals that produce an efficient outcome. But in many situations, transactions costs are so high that it would be inefficient to incur them. In these situations, the Coase solution is not available.

Suppose, for example, that everyone owns the airspace above their homes up to, say, 10 miles. If someone pollutes your airspace, you can charge a fee. But to collect the fee, you must identify who is polluting your airspace and persuade them to pay you. Imagine the costs of negotiating and enforcing agreements with the more than 50 million people who live in the UK (and perhaps those that live in Europe) and the several thousand factories that emit sulphur dioxide and create acid rain that falls on your property! In this situation, we use public choices to cope with externalities. But the transactions costs that block a market solution are real costs, so attempts by the government to deal with externalities offer no easy solution. Let's look at some of these attempts.

Government Actions in the Face of External Costs

Three methods that governments use to cope with externalities are:

◆ Taxes
◆ Emission charges
◆ Cap-and-trade

Taxes

Governments can use taxes as an incentive for producers to cut back on pollution. Taxes used in this way are called **Pigovian taxes**, in honour of Arthur Cecil Pigou, the British economist who first worked out this method of dealing with externalities during the 1920s.

By setting the tax rate equal to the marginal external cost, firms can be made to behave in the same way as they would if they bore the cost of the externality directly. To see how government actions can change market outcomes in the face of externalities, let's return to the example of the chemical factories and the river.

Assume that the government has assessed the marginal external cost accurately and imposes a tax on the factories that exactly equals this marginal external cost. Figure 16.4 illustrates the effects of this tax.

The demand curve and marginal social benefit curve, $D = MSB$, and the firms' marginal private cost curve, MC, are the same as in Figure 16.2. The pollution tax equals the marginal external cost of the pollution. We add this tax to the marginal private cost to find the market supply curve. This curve is the one labelled $S = MC + tax = MSC$. This curve is the market supply curve because it tells us the quantity of chemical supplied at each price given the firms' marginal private cost and the tax they must pay.

The curve $S = MC + tax = MSC$ is also the marginal social cost curve because the pollution tax has been set equal to the marginal external cost.

◀ **ECONOMICS IN ACTION**

The Greatest Market Failure?

British economist Nicholas Stern reviewed the science and economics of global warming and climate change for the UK government and his report, the *Stern Review on the Economics of Climate Change,* attracted much attention. Stern calls climate change 'the greatest market failure the world has ever seen'.

As the figure shows, global temperature and carbon dioxide (CO_2) trends are starkly upwards. Stern says that to avoid the risk of catastrophic climate change, this upward trend must be stopped.

Scientists debate the contribution of human economic activity to these trends, but most say it is the major source. Although ice-core estimates show long swings in CO_2 concentration, the recent increase is the most rapid recorded.

The cost of achieving Stern's target is high, estimated at 1 per cent of the value of global production. If this cost is to be met by the people living in the rich countries, and realistically they are the only ones who can afford to pay, it will cost about $750 per person a year.

Some economists question Stern's assumptions and conclusions and argue that the cost of reducing emissions will be much lower if we go a bit more slowly and take advantage of future technological advances that will lower the cost of renewable energy sources – the sun, tide and wind.

All economists agree that solving the global warming problem will require changes in the incentives that people

Figure 1 Global Warming Trends

Source of data: Met Office Hadley Centre and Scripps Institution of Oceanography.

face. The cost of carbon-emitting activities must rise and the cost of the search for new energy technologies must fall. A carbon tax or tradeable carbon permits are two possible ways of addressing this problem.

Figure 16.4 A Pollution Tax

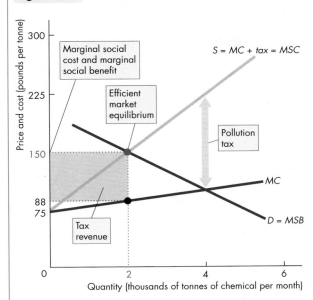

When the government imposes a pollution tax equal to the marginal external cost of pollution, the supply curve becomes the marginal private cost curve, *MC*, plus the tax – the curve *S = MC + tax*. Market equilibrium occurs at a price of £150 a tonne and a quantity of 2,000 tonnes of chemical a month. This equilibrium is efficient because marginal social cost equals marginal social benefit. The purple rectangle shows the government's tax revenue.

myeconlab Animation ─────────────◆

Demand and supply now determine the market equilibrium price at £150 a tonne and the equilibrium quantity at 2,000 tonnes of chemical a month. At this quantity of chemical production, the marginal social cost is £150 a tonne and the marginal social benefit is £150 a tonne, so the outcome is efficient. The firms incur a marginal private cost of £88 a tonne and pay a pollution tax of £62 a tonne. The government's tax revenue is £124,000 a month, as shown by the purple rectangle.

Emission Charges

Emission charges are an alternative to a tax for confronting a polluter with the external cost of pollution. The government sets a price per unit of pollution. The more pollution a firm creates, the more it pays in emission charges. This method of dealing with pollution externalities is common in Europe where, for example, France, Germany and the Netherlands make water polluters pay a waste disposal charge.

But to work out the emission charge that achieves efficiency, the government needs information about the polluting industry that, in practice, is rarely available.

Cap-and-trade

Instead of taxing or imposing emission charges on polluters, each potential polluter might be assigned a permitted pollution limit. Each firm knows its own costs and benefits of pollution, and making pollution limits marketable is a clever way of using this private information that is unknown to the government. The government issues each firm a permit to emit a certain amount of pollution, and firms can buy and sell these permits. Firms that have a low marginal cost of reducing pollution sell their permits, and firms that have a high marginal cost of reducing pollution buy permits. The market in permits determines the price at which firms trade permits. Each firm buys or sells permits until its marginal cost of pollution equals the market price.

This method of dealing with pollution provides an even stronger incentive than do emission charges to find lower-polluting technologies because the price of a pollution permit rises as the demand for permits increases.

Following the Kyoto Protocol on reducing carbon emissions, the EU set up a cap-and-trade system for carbon in 2005. The system covered a limited number of big producers in 2005 and failed to reduce carbon emissions. Since 2008, the scheme has been adapted and expanded to include many more producers and emission reductions are now expected.

Review Quiz

1. What is the distinction between private cost and social cost?
2. How do external costs prevent a competitive market from allocating resources efficiently?
3. How can external costs be eliminated by assigning property rights?
4. How do taxes help us to cope with external costs? At what level must a pollution tax be set to be efficient?
5. How do emission charges and marketable pollution permits work?

You can work these questions in Study Plan 16.1 and get instant feedback.

Your next task is to study common resources and government actions that can result in their efficient use.

The Tragedy of the Commons

Overgrazing the pastures around a village in Middle Ages England and overfishing the cod stocks of the North Sea and the North Atlantic Ocean during the recent past are tragedies of the commons. The **tragedy of the commons** is the overuse of a common resource that arises when its users have no incentive to conserve it and use it sustainably.

To study the tragedy of the commons and its possible remedies, we'll focus on the recent and current tragedy – overfishing and depleting the stock of Atlantic cod. We begin by thinking about the sustainable use of a renewable resource.

Sustainable Use of a Renewable Resource

A renewable natural resource is one that replenishes itself by the birth and growth of new members of the population. Fish, trees, and the fertile soil are all examples of this type of resource.

Focusing on fish, the sustainable catch is the quantity that can be caught year after year without depleting the stock. This quantity depends on the stock and in the interesting way illustrated in Figure 16.5. If the stock of

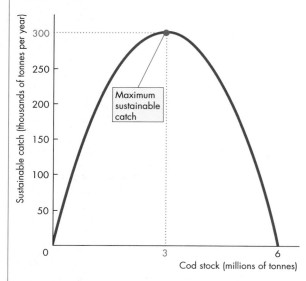

Figure 16.5 Sustainable Catch

Maximum sustainable catch

As the stock of fish (on the *x*-axis) increases, the sustainable catch (on the *y*-axis) increases to a maximum. Beyond that maximum catch, more fish must compete for food and the sustainable catch falls. If the catch exceeds the sustainable catch, the fish stock diminishes.

myeconlab Animation

ECONOMICS IN ACTION

The Original Tragedy of the Commons

The term 'tragedy of the commons' comes from fourteenth-century England where the commons – areas of rough grassland surrounding villages – were open to all and the villagers used the commons for grazing cows and sheep. Because the commons were open to all, no one had an incentive to ensure that the land was not overgrazed. The result was a severe overgrazing. Because the commons were overgrazed, the longer the overgrazing continued, the fewer the number of cows and sheep that the commons could feed.

During the sixteenth century, the price of wool increased and England became a wool exporter to the world. Sheep farming became profitable, and sheep owners wanted to gain more effective control of the land they used. So the commons were gradually privatized and enclosed. Overgrazing ended, and land use became more efficient.

One of Today's Tragedies of the Commons

Before 1970, Atlantic cod was abundant. It was fished for many centuries and was a major food source for the first European settlers in North America. During the sixteenth century, hundreds of European ships caught large quantities of cod in the north-west Atlantic off the coast of what is now New England and Newfoundland, Canada. By 1620, there were more than 1,000 fishing boats in the waters off Newfoundland, and in 1812 about 1,600 boats. During these years, cod were huge fish, typically weighing in at more than 220 pounds and measuring 3–6 feet in length.

Most of the fishing during these years was done using lines and productivity was low. But low productivity limited the catch and enabled cod to be caught sustainably over hundreds of years.

The situation changed dramatically during the 1960s with the introduction of high-efficiency nets (called trawls, seines and gill nets), sonar technology to find fish concentrations, and large ships with efficient processing and storage facilities. Figure 1 shows that these technological advances brought soaring cod harvests. In less than a decade, cod landings increased from less than 300,000 tonnes a year to 800,000 tonnes.

This volume of cod could not be taken without a serious collapse in the remaining stock and by the 1980s it became vital to regulate cod fishing. But regulation was of limited success and stocks continued to fall.

In 1992, a total ban on cod fishing in the North Atlantic stabilized the population but at a very low level. Two decades of ban have enabled the species to repopulate, and it is now hoped that one day cod fishing will return but at a low and sustainable rate.

By 2000, North Sea cod stocks were also on the brink of extinction at 30,000 tonnes, well below the sustainable minimum stock, reckoned to be 150,000 tonnes. The EU stopped all fishing of cod in nursery areas and agreed to recovery measures for a 10-year period. These measures fell short of a ban on cod fishing as member states could not agree. Instead, catch quotas were cut by 45 per cent. By 2009, North Sea cod stocks had recovered to 53,000 tonnes but were still short of the 150,000 tonnes needed for a sustainable stock.

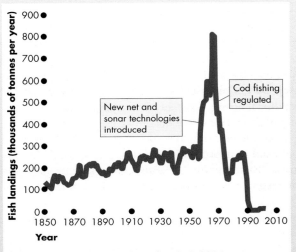

Figure 1 The Atlantic Cod Catch: 1850–2005

Source of data for graph: Millenium Ecosystem Assessment.

Source of information: Codfishes – Atlantic cod and its fishery, http://science.jrank.org/

---

fish is small, the quantity of new fish born is also small, so the sustainable catch is small.

If the fish stock is large, many fish are born, but they must compete with each other for food so only a small number survive to reproduce and to grow large enough to catch.

Between a small and a large stock is a quantity of fish stock that maximizes the sustainable catch. In Figure 16.5, this fish stock is 3 million tonnes and the sustainable catch is 300,000 tonnes a year. The maximum sustainable catch arises from a balancing of the birth of new fish from the stock and the availability of food to sustain the fish population.

If the quantity of fish caught is less than the sustainable catch, the fish stock grows; if the quantity caught exceeds the sustainable catch, the fish stock shrinks; and if the quantity caught equals the sustainable catch, the fish stock remains constant and is available for future generations of fishers in the same quantity that is available today.

If the fish stock exceeds the level that maximizes the sustainable catch, overfishing isn't a problem. But if the fish stock is less than the level that maximizes the sustainable catch, overfishing depletes the stock.

The Overuse of a Common Resource

Why might a fish stock be overused? Why might overfishing occur? The answer is that fishers face only their own private cost and don't face the cost they impose on others – external cost. The *social* cost of fishing combines the *private* cost and *external* cost. Let's examine the costs of catching fish to see how the presence of external cost brings overfishing.

Marginal Private Cost

You can think of the *marginal private cost* of catching fish as the additional cost incurred by keeping a boat and crew at sea for long enough to increase the catch by one tonne. Keeping a fishing boat at sea for an additional amount of time eventually runs into *diminishing marginal returns* (see Chapter 10, p. 244). As the crew gets tired, the storage facilities get overfull, and the boat's speed is cut to conserve fuel, the catch per hour decreases. The cost of keeping the boat at sea for an additional hour is constant so the marginal cost of catching fish increases as the quantity caught increases.

You've just seen that the *principle of increasing marginal cost* applies to catching fish just as it applies to other production activities: marginal private cost increases as the quantity of fish caught increases.

The marginal private cost of catching fish determines an individual fisher's supply of fish. A profit-maximizing fisher is willing to supply the quantity at which the market price of fish covers the marginal private cost. And the market supply is the sum of the quantities supplied by each individual fisher.

Marginal External Cost

The *marginal external cost* of catching fish is the cost per additional tonne that one fisher's catch imposes on all other fishers. This additional cost arises because one fisher's catch decreases the remaining stock, which in turn decreases the renewal rate of the stock and makes it harder for other fishers to find and catch fish.

Marginal external cost also increases as the quantity of fish caught increases. If the quantity of fish caught is so large that it drives the species to near extinction, the marginal external cost becomes infinitely large.

Marginal Social Cost

The *marginal social cost* of catching fish is the marginal private cost plus the marginal external cost. Because both of its components increase as the quantity caught increases, marginal social cost also increases with the quantity of fish caught.

Marginal Social Benefit and Demand

The marginal social benefit from fish is the price that consumers are willing to pay for an additional kilogram of fish. Marginal social benefit decreases as the quantity of fish consumed increases, so the demand curve (also the marginal social benefit curve) slopes downward.

Overfishing Equilibrium

Figure 16.6 illustrates overfishing and how it arises. The market demand curve for fish is the marginal social benefit curve, *MSB*. The market supply curve is the marginal private cost curve, *MC*. Market equilibrium occurs at the intersection point of these two curves. The

Figure 16.6   Why Overfishing Occurs

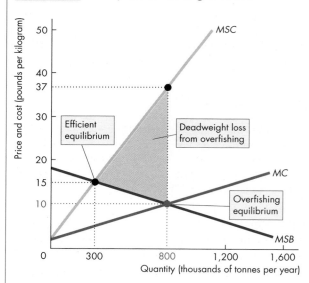

The supply curve is the marginal private cost curve, *MC*. The demand curve is the marginal social benefit curve *MSB*. Market equilibrium occurs at a quantity of 800,000 tonnes and a price of £10 per kilogram. The marginal social cost curve is *MSC* and at the market equilibrium there is overfishing – marginal social cost exceeds marginal social benefit. The quantity at which *MSC* equals *MSB* is the efficient quantity, 300,000 tonnes per year. The grey triangle shows the deadweight loss from overfishing.

equilibrium quantity is 800,000 tonnes per year and the equilibrium price is £10 per kilogram.

At this market equilibrium, overfishing is running down the fish stock. Figure 16.6 illustrates why overfishing occurs. At the market equilibrium quantity, marginal social benefit (and willingness to pay) is £10 per kilogram, but the marginal social cost exceeds this amount. The marginal external cost is the cost of running down the fish stock.

Efficient Equilibrium

The efficient use of a common resource is to use the quantity that makes the marginal social benefit from the resource equal to the marginal social cost. In Figure 16.6 the efficient quantity of fish is 300,000 tonnes per year – the quantity that makes marginal social cost (on the MSC curve) equal to marginal social benefit (on the MSB curve). At this quantity, the marginal catch of each individual fisher costs society what people are willing to pay for it.

Deadweight Loss from Overfishing

Deadweight loss measures the cost of overfishing. It is the marginal social cost minus the marginal social benefit from all the fish caught in excess of the efficient quantity – the area of the grey triangle in Figure 16.6.

Achieving an Efficient Outcome

Defining the conditions under which a common resource is used efficiently is easier than delivering those conditions. To use a common resource efficiently, it is necessary to design an incentive mechanism that confronts the users of the resource with the marginal social consequences of their actions. The same principles apply to common resources as those that you met earlier in this chapter when you studied the external cost of pollution. The three main methods that might be used to achieve the efficient use of a common resource are

◆ Property rights
◆ Production quotas
◆ Individual transferable quotas (ITQs)

Property Rights

A common resource that no one owns and that anyone is free to use contrasts with *private property*, which is a resource that someone owns and has an incentive to use

in the way that maximizes its value. One way of overcoming the tragedy of the commons is to convert a common resource to private property. By assigning private property rights to the resource, its owner faces the same conditions as society faces. It doesn't matter who owns the resource. The users of the resource will be confronted with the full cost of using it because they either own it or pay a fee to the owner for permission to use it.

When private property rights over a resource are established and enforced, the MSC curve becomes the marginal private cost curve, and the use of the resource is efficient.

Figure 16.7 illustrates an efficient outcome with property rights. The supply curve $S = MC = MSC$ and the demand curve $D = MSB$ determine the equilibrium price and quantity. The price equals both marginal social benefit and marginal social cost and the quantity is efficient.

Figure 16.7   Property Rights Achieve an Efficient Outcome

With private property rights, fishers pay the owner of the fish stock for permission to fish and face the full social cost of their actions. The marginal cost curve includes the external cost, so the supply curve is the marginal private cost curve and the marginal social cost curve, $S = MC = MSC$.

Market equilibrium occurs at £15 per kilogram and at that price, the quantity is 300,000 tonnes per year. At this quantity, marginal social cost equals marginal social benefit, and the catch is efficient. The property rights convert the fish stock from a common resource to a private resource and it is used efficiently.

myeconlab Animation

The private property solution to the tragedy of the commons is available in some cases. It was the solution to the original tragedy of the commons in England's Middle Ages. It is also a solution that has been used to prevent overuse of the airwaves that carry mobile-phone services. The right to use this space (called the frequency spectrum) has been auctioned by governments to the highest bidders. The owner of each part of the spectrum is the only one permitted to use it (or license someone else to use it).

But assigning private property rights is not always feasible. It would be difficult, for example, to assign private property rights to the oceans. It would not be impossible, but the cost of enforcing private property rights over thousands of square miles of ocean would be high. It would be even more difficult to assign and protect private property rights to the atmosphere.

In some cases, there is an emotional objection to assigning private property rights to a resource that is regarded as public. In the absence of property rights, some form of government intervention is used, one of which is a production quota.

Production Quotas

A *production quota* is an upper limit to the quantity of a good that may be produced in a specified period. The quota is allocated to individual producers, so each producer has its own quota.

You studied the effects of a production quota in Chapter 6 (pp. 139–140) and learned that a quota can drive a wedge between marginal social benefit and marginal social cost and create deadweight loss. In that earlier example, the market was efficient without a quota. But in the case of common resources, the market overuses the resource and produces an inefficient quantity. A production quota in this market brings a move towards a more efficient outcome.

Figure 16.8 shows a quota that achieves an efficient outcome. The quota limits the catch (production) to 300,000 tonnes, the efficient quantity at which marginal social benefit, *MSB*, equals marginal social cost, *MSC*. If everyone sticks to their own quota, the outcome is efficient. But implementing a production quota has two problems.

First, it is in every fisher's self-interest to catch more fish than the quantity permitted under the quota. The reason is that price exceeds marginal private cost, so by catching more fish, a fisher gets a higher income. If enough fishers break the quota, overfishing and the tragedy of the commons remain.

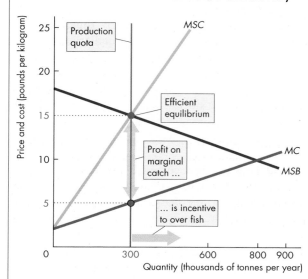

Figure 16.8 A Production Quota to Use a Common Resource Efficiently

A quota of 300,000 tonnes limits production to this quantity, raises the price to £15 per kilogram and lowers marginal cost to £5 per kilogram. A fisher who cheats and produces more than the allotted quota increases his profit by £10 per kilogram. If all (or most) fishers cheat, production exceeds the quota and there is a return to overfishing.

myeconlab Animation

Second, marginal cost is not, in general, the same for all producers – as we're assuming here. Efficiency requires that the quota be allocated to the producers with the lowest marginal cost. But bureaucrats who allocate quotas do not have information about the marginal cost of individual producers. Even if they tried to get this information, producers would have an incentive to lie about their costs so as to get a bigger quota.

So where producers are difficult, or very costly, to monitor or where marginal cost varies across producers, a production quota cannot achieve an efficient outcome.

Individual Transferable Quotas

Where producers are difficult to monitor or where marginal cost varies across producers, a more sophisticated quota system can be effective. It is an **individual transferable quota (ITQ)**, which is a production limit that is assigned to an individual who is then free to transfer (sell) the quota to someone else. A market in ITQs emerges and ITQs are traded at their market price.

The market price of an ITQ is the highest price that someone is willing to pay for one. That price is marginal social benefit minus marginal cost. The price of an ITQ will rise to this level because fishers who don't have a quota would be willing to pay this amount to get one.

A fisher with an ITQ could sell it for the market price, so by not selling the ITQ the fisher incurs an opportunity cost. The marginal cost of fishing, which now includes the opportunity cost of the ITQ, equals the marginal social benefit from the efficient quantity.

Figure 16.9 illustrates how ITQs work. Each fisher receives an allocation of ITQs such that the total catch permitted by the ITQs is 300,000 tonnes per year. Fishers trade ITQs: those with low marginal cost buy ITQs from those with high marginal cost and the market price of an ITQ settles at £10 per kilogram of fish. The marginal private cost is now equal to the marginal private cost, MC, plus the price of the ITQ. The marginal private cost curve shifts upwards to become MC + price of ITQ and each fisher is confronted with the marginal social cost of fishing. No one has an incentive to exceed the quota and the outcome is efficient.

Figure 16.9   ITQs to Use a Common Resource Efficiently

ITQs are issued to keep the total catch at the efficient level. The market price of an ITQ equals the marginal social benefit minus marginal cost. Because each fisher faces the opportunity cost of using the resource, self-interest achieves the social interest.

 Animation

Reading Between the Lines on pp. 380–381 looks at the the EU cap-and-trade system to lower carbon emissions.

The next two chapters examine the third big question of economics: for whom are goods and services produced? We examine the markets for factors of production and discover how factor incomes and the distribution of income are determined.

Reading Between the Lines

Cap-and-trade in the EU

The Telegraph, 7 December 2009

Copenhagen Climate Summit Issues: Carbon Trading

Rowena Mason

Countries have begun to look more favourably at the idea of emissions trading within individual nations, while complying with international standards. Europe has already been trading permits to emit carbon dioxide since 2005. . . .

The European Emissions Trading System is simple, but . . . fraught with problems. . . . Policy makers distribute permits to emit carbon to utility companies and heavy industrial polluters. At first these were given out free, but now a small proportion are auctioned off. . . . Any allowances not used . . . may be traded on the open market. . . .

Industrial players, . . . proved so effective at lobbying that they were showered with extra permits that they did not need . . . The recession has only exacerbated the glut as industrial emissions fall, pushing down the price of carbon credit to approximately 13 euros [per tonne]. This means there is not enough incentive for utility companies to switch from burning coal or gas. . . .

One key issue at Copenhagen will be whether countries ought to impose a lower limit – a 'floor price' – possibly up to 40 euros per tonne, to keep the cost of carbon high. . . .

The European system has so far failed in its fundamental aim to reduce emissions, meaning its only effect is to redistribute wealth among companies and traders.

© Telegraph Media Group Limited 2009.

 ## The Essence of the Story

- European countries started trading permits to emit carbon dioxide in 2005 but the system has not reduced emissions.

- Polluters receive permits to emit carbon, some free and some bought at auction, and trade unused permits.

- Polluters lobbied hard and got extra permits that they sold, which lowered the price of permits and killed the incentive to stop burning coal.

- A key issue is whether to set a price floor to keep the cost of carbon high.

Economic Analysis

◆ Generating electricity using coal increases the amount of carbon dioxide in the atmosphere, which brings global warming.

◆ To provide electric power utilities with an incentive to use cleaner technologies, the EU introduced a carbon trading scheme.

◆ The EU scheme is not having the desired effect.

◆ Figure 1 shows the UK market for electricity. The demand curve and marginal social benefit curve is $D = MSB$. The supply curve and private marginal cost curve is $S = MC$.

◆ Power stations produce 400 million MwH of electricity a year at a price of 8 pence per kWh where $MC = MSB$.

◆ Electricity production creates an external cost, which is part of the marginal social cost. The marginal social cost curve is MSC. The efficient outcome is where $MSB = MSC$. With no regulation, a deadweight loss (the grey area) arises.

◆ To achieve the efficient outcome, electric utilities must incur the marginal external cost. To confront them with this cost, the government issues tradeable pollution permits.

◆ Using the numbers assumed here, the efficient outcome would be achieved by issuing permits to create the amount of pollution that comes from generating 300 million MwH per year and allowing the permits to be traded.

◆ Figure 2 shows the UK market for carbon permits. The demand curve for permits is D. If the efficient quantity of permits is issued, the price of a permit is equivalent to 3 pence per kWh. Confronted with this price, utilities would scale back production and produce the efficient quantity shown in Figure 1.

◆ But the polluters' lobby has persuaded the government to issue too many permits.

◆ With demand curve D, the price falls to the equivalent of 1 pence per kWh, which isn't

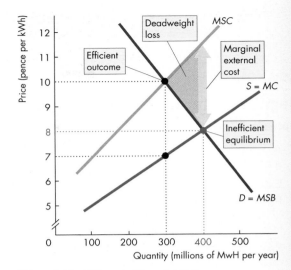

Figure 1 The UK market for electricity

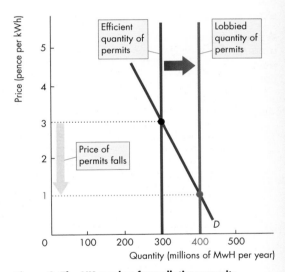

Figure 2 The UK market for pollution permits

high enough to induce the utilities to become efficient.

◆ Because most of the permits are provided free to the power companies, those with spare permits for sale end up profiting from the scheme.

◆ Setting a price floor for permits (using our numbers at the equivalent of 3 pence per kWh) would achieve the efficient outcome only if all producers have the same marginal cost and create the same marginal external cost.

◆ The benefit of cap-and-trade would be lost.

> SUMMARY

Key Points

Negative Externality: Pollution
(pp. 368–373)

◆ A competitive market would produce too much of a good that has external production costs.

◆ External costs are costs of production that fall on people other than the producer of a good or service. Marginal social cost equals marginal private cost plus marginal external cost.

◆ Producers take account only of marginal private cost and produce more than the efficient quantity when there is a marginal external cost.

◆ Sometimes it is possible to overcome a negative externality by assigning a property right.

◆ When property rights cannot be assigned, governments might overcome externalities by using taxes, emission charges or marketable permits.

Working Problems 1 to 12 will give you a better understanding of the external costs of pollution.

The Tragedy of the Commons
(pp. 374–379)

◆ Common resources create a problem that is called the tragedy of the commons – no one has a private incentive to conserve the resources and use them at an efficient rate.

◆ A common resource is used to the point at which the marginal social benefit equals the marginal private cost.

◆ A common resource might be used efficiently by creating a private property right, setting a quota, or issuing individual transferable quotas.

Working Problems 13 to 19 will give you a better understanding of the tragedy of the commons.

Key Terms

Coase theorem, 371
Individual transferable quota (ITQ), 378
Marginal external cost, 369
Marginal private cost, 369
Marginal social cost, 369
Pigovian taxes, 372
Property rights, 370
Tragedy of the commons, 374
Transactions costs, 371

STUDY PLAN PROBLEMS AND APPLICATIONS

myeconlab You can work Problems 1 to 19 in MyEconLab Chapter 16 Study Plan and get instant feedback.

Negative Externality: Pollution

(Study Plan 16.1)

Use the following figure to work Problems 1 to 5.

The figure illustrates the market for European cotton. Consider a small town surrounded by a large cotton farm. Suppose that the cotton grower sprays the plants with chemicals to control insects and the chemical waste flows into the river passing through the town. The marginal external cost of the chemical waste is equal to the marginal private cost of producing the cotton (that is, the marginal social cost of producing the cotton is double the marginal private cost).

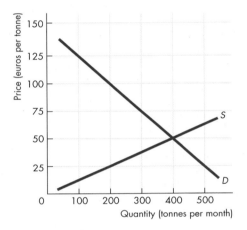

1   If no one owns the river and the town takes no action to control the waste, what is the quantity of cotton, and the deadweight loss created?

2   **a** Suppose that the town owns the river and makes the cotton grower pay the cost of pollution. How much cotton is produced and what does the grower pay the town per tonne of cotton produced?

   b Suppose that the cotton grower owns the river and rents it to the town. How much cotton is produced and how is the rent paid by the town to the grower (per tonne of cotton produced) influenced by cotton growing?

   c Compare the quantities of cotton produced in parts (a) and (b) and explain the relationship between these quantities.

3   Suppose that no one owns the river and that the city introduces a pollution tax. What is the tax per tonne of cotton produced that achieves an efficient outcome?

4   Compare the outcomes when property rights exist and when the pollution tax achieves the efficient amount of waste.

5   Suppose that no one owns the river and that the government issues two marketable pollution permits: one to the cotton grower and one to the city. Each permit allows the same amount of pollution of the river, and the total pollution created is the efficient amount.

   What is the quantity of cotton produced and what is the market price of a pollution permit? Who buys and who sells a permit?

Use the following news clip to work Problems 6 to 8.

Bag Revolution

Thin plastic carrier bags aren't biodegradable and often end up in the ocean or in the environment. In the UK we use about 10 billion bags a year, many from supermarkets. Supermarkets have agreed to take action to reduce carrier bag use to avoid governments forcing them to charge for bags.

Source: *The Independent*, 26 August 2010

6   **a** Describe the externality that arises from plastic bags.

   b Draw a graph to illustrate how plastic bags create deadweight loss.

7   **a** With the majority of plastic bags coming from supermarkets and grocery stores, the Irish government introduced a tax of 12p a bag in 2002, which has cut carrier bag use by 90 per cent. Explain the effects of the Irish policy on the use of plastic bags.

   b Draw a graph to illustrate the Irish policy and show the change in the deadweight loss that arises from this policy.

8   The Italian government has banned the use of non-biodegradable carrier bags from 2011. Explain why a complete ban on plastic bags might be inefficient.

Use the following news clip to work Problems 9 to 11.

The Year in Medicine: Mobile Phones

Talking on a hands-free mobile phone while driving might seem safe, but think again. People who used hands-free mobile phones in simulation trials exhibited slower reaction times and took longer to hit the brakes than drivers who weren't otherwise distracted. Data from real-life driving tests show that mobile-phone use rivals drowsy driving as a major cause of accidents.

Source: *Time*, 4 December 2006

9 a Explain the external costs that arise from using a mobile phone while driving.

  b Explain why the market for mobile phone service creates a deadweight loss.

10 Draw a graph to illustrate how a deadweight loss arises from the use of mobile phones.

11 Explain how government intervention might improve the efficiency of mobile phone use.

12 Pollution Rules Squeeze Strawberry Crop

Last year, Ventura County farmers harvested nearly 12,000 acres of strawberries valued at more than $323 million. To comply with the federal Clean Air Act, growers must use 50 per cent less pesticide. It is estimated that strawberry output will fall by 60 per cent.

Source: *USA Today*, 29 February 2008

Explain how a limit on pesticide will change the efficiency of the strawberry industry. Would a cap-and-trade scheme be more efficient?

The Tragedy of the Commons
(Study Plan 16.2)

Use the following figure to work Problems 13 to 15.

The figure shows the market for North Atlantic tuna.

13 a What is the quantity of tuna that fishing boats catch and the price of tuna? Is the tuna stock being used efficiently? Explain why or why not.

  b What would be the price of tuna if the stock of tuna is used efficiently?

14 a With a quota of 40 tonnes a month for the tuna fishing industry, what is the equilibrium price of tuna and the quantity of tuna that fishers catch?

  b Is the equilibrium an overfishing equilibrium?

15 If the government issues ITQs to individual fishing boats that limit the total catch to the efficient quantity, what is the market price of an ITQ?

16 Whaling 'Hurts Tourist Industry'

Leah Garces, the director of programmes at the World Society for the Protection of Animals, reported that whale watching is more economically significant and sustainable to people and communities than whaling. The global whale watching industry is estimated to be a $1.25 billion business enjoyed by over 10 million people in more than 90 countries each year.

Source: BBC, 2 June 2009

Describe the trade-off facing communities that live near whaling areas. How might a thriving whale watching industry avoid the tragedy of the commons?

Use the following information to work Problems 17 to 19.

A natural spring runs under land owned by 10 people. Each person has the right to sink a well and can take water from the spring at a constant marginal cost of £0.05 a litre. The table sets out the external cost and the social benefit of water.

Quantity of water (litres per day)	Marginal external cost	Marginal social benefit
	(pence per litre)	
10	1	10
20	2	9
30	3	8
40	4	7
50	5	6
60	6	5
70	7	4

17 Draw a graph to illustrate the market equilibrium. On your graph, show the efficient quantity of water taken.

18 If the government sets a quota on the total amount of water such that the spring is used efficiently, what would that quota be?

19 If the government issues ITQs to landowners that limit the total amount of water taken to the efficient quantity, what is the market price of an ITQ?

ADDITIONAL PROBLEMS AND APPLICATIONS

myeconlab You can work these problems in MyEconLab if assigned by your instructor.

Negative Externality: Pollution

20 Betty and Anna work at the same office in Brussels. They both must attend a meeting in Paris, so they decide to drive to the meeting together. Betty is a cigarette smoker and her marginal benefit from smoking a package of cigarettes a day is €40. Cigarettes are €6 a packet. Anna dislikes cigarette smoke, and her marginal benefit from a smoke-free environment is €50 a day. What is the outcome if:

  a Betty drives her car with Anna as a passenger?

  b Anna drives her car with Betty as a passenger?

Use the following information and the figure, which illustrates the market for a pesticide with no government intervention, to work Problems 21 to 24.

When factories produce pesticide, they also create waste, which they dump into a lake on the outskirts of the town. The marginal external cost of the waste is equal to the marginal private cost of producing the pesticide (that is, the marginal social cost of producing the pesticide is double the marginal private cost).

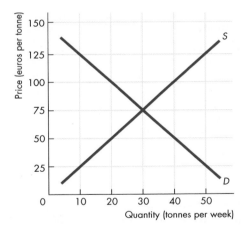

21 What is the quantity of pesticide produced if no one owns the lake and what is the efficient quantity of pesticide?

22 If the residents of the town own the lake, what is the quantity of pesticide produced and how much do residents of the town charge the factories to dump waste?

23 If the pesticide factories own the lake, how much pesticide is produced?

24 If no one owns the lake and the government levies a pollution tax, what is the tax that achieves the efficient outcome?

Use the following table to work Problems 25 to 27.

The first two columns of the table show the demand schedule for electricity from a European coal burning utility; the second and third columns show the utility's cost of producing electricity. The marginal external cost of the pollution created is equal to the marginal cost.

Price (cents per kilowatt)	Quantity (kilowatts per day)	Marginal cost (cents per kilowatt)
4	500	10
8	400	8
12	300	6
16	200	4
20	100	2

25 With no government action to control pollution, what is the quantity of electricity produced, the price of electricity, and the marginal external cost of the pollution generated?

26 With no government action to control pollution, what is the marginal social cost of the electricity generated and the deadweight loss created?

27 Suppose that the government levies a pollution tax, such that the utility produces the efficient quantity. What is the price of electricity? What is the tax levied, and the government's tax revenue per day?

28 **EPA Pushes to have Companies Track Greenhouse Gases**

The US government plans to make large polluters, such as oil refiners and automobile manufacturers, and makers of cement, aluminium, glass and paper, start tracking their emissions next year. The EPA's climate change division noted that this is an important step. A cap-and-trade scheme will be introduced for factories that emit 90 per cent of US greenhouse gases.

Source: *USA Today*, 11 March 2009

The monitoring cost of the scheme is expected to be about $127 million a year. Who will benefit from the scheme? Who will bear the burden of this scheme?

The Tragedy of the Commons

29 If hikers and other visitors were required to pay a fee to use the Pennine Trail,

  a Would the use of this common resource be more efficient?

  b Would it be even more efficient if the most popular spots along the trail had the highest prices?

  c Why do you think we don't see more market solutions to the tragedy of the commons?

Use the following figure for Problems 30 to 32.

A spring runs under a village. Everyone can sink a well on their own land and take water from the spring. The figure shows the marginal social benefit from and the marginal cost of taking water.

30 What is the quantity of water taken and what is the private cost of the water taken?

31 What is the efficient quantity of water taken and the marginal social cost at the efficient quantity?

32 If the village council sets a quota on the total amount of water such that the spring is used efficiently, what would be the quota and the market value of the water taken per day?

33 **Polar Ice Cap Shrinks Further and Thins**

With the warming of the planet, the polar ice cap is shrinking and the Arctic Sea is expanding. As the ice cap shrinks further, more and more underwater mineral resources will become accessible. Many countries are staking out territorial claims to parts of the polar region.

Source: *The Wall Street Journal*, 7 April 2009

Explain how ownership of these mineral resources will influence the amount of damage done to the Arctic Sea and its wildlife.

Economics in the News

34 After you have studied *Reading Between the Lines* on pp. 380–381 answer the following questions.

  a Why do carbon dioxide emissions make the marginal social cost of electricity production exceed the marginal private cost?

  b Why is a carbon cap-and-trade system superior to either a carbon tax or a fixed pollution quota as a way of reducing carbon dioxide emissions?

  c What is the main problem with the EU cap-and-trade system for pollution permits and how can auctions of new permits improve the efficiency of the market for pollution permits?

Use the following information to work Problems 35 and 36.

Where the Tuna Roam

To the first settlers, the Great Plains of North America posed the same problem as the oceans today: a vast, open area where there seemed to be no way to protect animals. But animals thrived once the settlers divvied up the land and devised ways to protect their livestock. Today, the oceans are much like an open range. Fishermen catch as much as they can this year, even if they are overfishing. They figure any fish they don't take for themselves will just be taken by someone else.

Source: *The New York Times*, 4 November 2006

35 **a** What are the similarities between the problems faced by the earliest American settlers and today's fishers?

  b Can the tragedy of the commons in the oceans be eliminated in the same manner used by the early settlers on the plains?

36 How can ITQs change the short-term outlook of fishers to a long-term outlook?

37 **Commuting More than Pain at Pump**

Half of the respondents polled in 10 cities said that traffic congestion increased their stress levels and cut their productivity. IBM has been devising ways for cities to cut traffic congestion, such as automated tolling, congestion pricing plans and real-time traffic modelling. Commuters want more options to work from home and improved public transit.

Source: CNN, 30 May 2008

  a Explain the problem of congested city streets that results in inefficient usage. Draw a graph to illustrate the inefficient equilibrium.

  b How could government policies be used to achieve an efficient use of city streets?

PART 5

Factor Markets, Inequality and Uncertainty

For Whom?

During the past 40 years, some dramatic changes have occurred in the levels and distribution of income. In almost every country, rich or poor, the rich have been getting richer at a faster rate than the poor and inequality has been increasing. But incomes have increased faster in the poorest countries than in the richest countries, so international inequality has decreased. In China and India, millions have been lifted from poverty and moved into the middle class.

The forces that generate these trends are demand and supply in factor markets, which determine wage rates, interest rates, rents and the prices of natural resources.

The first two chapters in this part study the forces at play in factor markets and explain how they have led to changes in the distribution of income. Chapter 19 is different from the other two: it looks at the problems of uncertainty and private information and shows how markets handle these problems.

Understanding Factor Markets, Inequality and Uncertainty

In Europe and America, human capital and entrepreneurship are the most prized factors of production and their incomes have grown most rapidly. In Asia, labour has seen its wage rates transformed. And in all regions rich in oil, coal and natural gas, incomes have risen rapidly on the back of high and fast-rising energy prices.

Rapid and sustained growth of income requires rapid and sustained productivity growth. Can we count on that happening?

Thomas Robert Malthus thought that we could not. He believed that population, unchecked, would grow at a geometric rate – 1, 2, 4, 8, 16, . . . – while food supply would grow at an arithmetic rate – 1, 2, 3, 4, 5, ... To prevent the population from outstripping the available food supply, there would be periodic wars, famines and plagues. Only what Malthus called 'moral restraint' could prevent such periodic disasters.

As industrialization proceeded through the nineteenth century, Malthus's idea came to be applied to all natural resources, especially those that are non-renewable.

Modern day Malthusians believe that his idea is correct and that if we continue to increase our use of energy we will eventually run out of resources and be doomed to a return of subsistence and poverty.

In 1931, in the depths of an economic depression, Harold Hotelling, an American economist, developed a theory of non-renewable natural resource prices with a starkly different implication than that of Malthus. The Hotelling Principle is that the prices of non-renewable natural resources will rise steadily and bring a slowing of the increase in the quantity demanded and used. Eventually the prices of these resources will rise to the point that an alternative will be discovered and used in their place. The oil age will end not because we run out of oil but because we switch to a lower-cost alternative source of energy.

Some economists argue that both Malthus and Hotelling are wrong and that human creativity and ingenuity is the ultimate natural resource. They believe that increasing population lessens the pressure on other natural resources and their prices will fall!

Thomas Robert Malthus (1766–1834), an English clergyman and economist, was an extremely influential social scientist. In his best-selling *An Essay on the Principle of Population*, published in 1798, he predicted that population growth would outstrip food production and said that wars, famine and disease were inevitable unless population growth was held in check by marrying at a late age and living a celibate life. (He married at 38 a wife of 27, marriage ages that he recommended for others.)

Malthus had a profound influence on Charles Darwin, who got the key idea that led him to the theory of natural selection from the *Essay on the Principle of Population*. But it was also Malthus's gloomy predictions that made economics the 'dismal science'.

'The passion between the sexes has appeared in every age to be so nearly the same, that it may always be considered, in algebraic language, as a given quantity.'

THOMAS ROBERT MALTHUS
An Essay on the Principle of Population

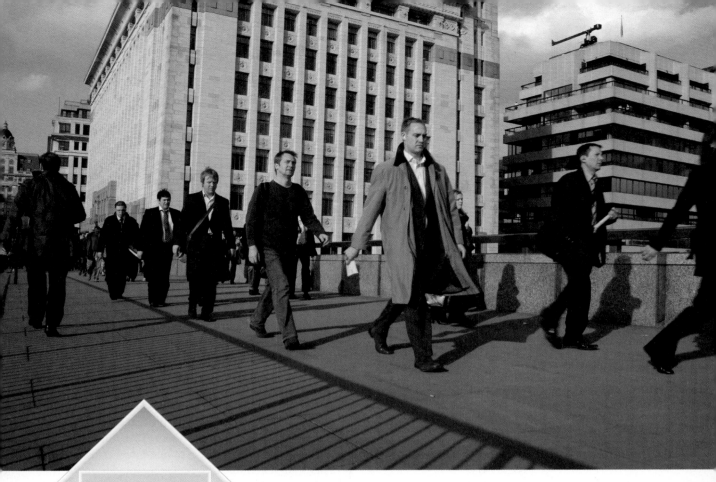

The Markets for Factors of Production

After studying this chapter you will be able to:

◆ Describe the anatomy of factor markets

◆ Explain how the value of marginal product determines the demand for a factor of production

◆ Explain how wage rates and employment are determined and how trades unions influence labour markets

◆ Explain how capital and land rental rates and natural resource prices are determined

Wages vary a lot. Julie Adams does vital work as a nurse and is paid £16,000 a year; Leo Messi, Europe's highest paid footballer, earns £29.6 million a year. Why are some jobs so well paid and others not? Why does a nurse who saves people's lives earn so much less than a footballer?

In this chapter we study labour markets as well as the markets for capital and natural resources. You will learn how the prices and quantities of factors of production are determined. In *Reading Between the Lines* at the end of the chapter, we look at what happened in the market for skilled financial workers in the City of London as it rebounded from a financial crisis.

The Anatomy of Factor Markets

The four factors of production are:

◆ Labour

◆ Capital

◆ Land (natural resources)

◆ Entrepreneurship

Let's take a brief look at the anatomy of the markets in which these factors of production are traded.

Markets for Labour Services

Labour services are the physical and mental work effort that people supply to produce goods and services. A labour market is a collection of people and firms who trade labour services. The price of labour services is the wage rate.

Some labour services are traded day by day. These services are called *casual labour*. People who pick fruit and vegetables often just show up at a farm and take whatever work is available that day. But most labour services are traded on a contract, called a **job**.

Most labour markets have many buyers and many sellers and are competitive. In these labour markets, the wage rate is determined by supply and demand, just as the price is determined in any other competitive market.

In some labour markets, a trades union organizes labour, which introduces an element of monopoly on the supply-side of the labour market. In this type of labour market, a bargaining process between the trades union and the employer determines the wage rate.

We'll study both competitive labour markets and trades unions in this chapter.

Markets for Capital Services

Capital consists of the tools, instruments, machines, buildings and other constructions that have been produced in the past and that businesses now use to produce goods and services. These physical objects are themselves goods – capital goods. Capital goods are traded in goods markets, just as bottled water and toothpaste are. The price of a dump truck, a capital good, is determined by supply and demand in the market for dump trucks. This market is not a market for capital services.

A market for *capital services* is a rental market – a market in which the services of capital are hired.

An example of a market for capital services is the vehicle rental market in which Avis, Budget, Hertz, U-Haul, and many other firms offer automobiles and trucks for hire. The price in a capital services market is a *rental rate*.

Most capital services are not traded in a market. Instead, a firm buys capital and uses it itself. The services of the capital that a firm owns and operates have an implicit price that arises from depreciation and interest costs (see Chapter 9, pp. 198–199). You can think of this price as the implicit rental rate of capital. Firms that buy capital and use it themselves are *implicitly* renting the capital to themselves.

Markets for Land Services and Natural Resources

Land consists of all the gifts of nature – natural resources. The market for land as a factor of production is the market for the services of land – the use of land. The price of the services of land is a rental rate.

Most natural resources, such as farmland, can be used repeatedly. But a few natural resources are non-renewable. **Non-renewable natural resources** are resources that can be used only once. Examples are oil, natural gas and coal. The prices of non-renewable natural resources are determined in global commodity markets and are called *commodity prices*.

Entrepreneurship

Entrepreneurial services are not traded in markets. Entrepreneurs receive the profit or bear the loss that results from their business decisions.

 Review Quiz

1 What are the factors of production and their prices?
2 What is the distinction between capital and the services of capital?
3 What is the distinction between the price of capital equipment and the rental rate of capital?

You can work these questions in Study Plan 17.1 and get instant feedback.

In the rest of this chapter, we explore the influences on the demand for and supply of factors of production. We begin by studying the demand for a factor of production.

The Demand for a Factor of Production

The demand for a factor of production is a **derived demand** – it is derived from the demand for the goods and services that the labour produces. You've seen, in Chapters 9 to 14, how a firm determines its profit-maximizing output. The quantities of factors of production demanded are a consequence of the firm's output decision. A firm hires the quantities of factors of production that produce the firm's profit-maximizing output.

To decide the quantity of a factor of production to hire, a firm compares the cost of hiring an additional unit of the factor with its value to the firm. The cost of hiring an additional unit of a factor of production is the factor price. The value to the firm of hiring one more unit of a factor of production is called the factor's **value of marginal product**. We calculate the value of marginal product as the price of a unit of output multiplied by the marginal product of the factor of production.

To study the demand for a factor of production, we'll use labour as the example. But what you learn here about the demand for labour applies to the demand for all factors of production.

Value of Marginal Product

Table 17.1 shows you how to calculate the value of marginal product of labour at Angelo's Bakery. The first two columns show Angelo's total product schedule – the number of loaves per hour that each quantity of labour can produce. The third column shows the marginal product of labour – the change in total product that results from a one-unit increase in the quantity of labour employed. (See Chapter 10, pp. 223–226 for a refresher on product schedules.)

Angelo can sell bread at the going market price of £2 a loaf. Given this information, we can calculate the value of marginal product (fourth column). It equals price multiplied by marginal product. For example, the marginal product of the second worker is 6 loaves. Each loaf sold brings in £2, so the value of marginal product of the second worker is £12 (6 loaves at £2 each).

A Firm's Demand for Labour

The value of marginal product of labour tells us what an additional worker is worth to a firm. It tells us the revenue that the firm makes by hiring one more worker. The wage rate tells us what an additional worker costs a firm.

The value of marginal product of labour and the wage rate together determine the quantity of labour demanded by a firm. Because the value of marginal product decreases as the quantity of labour employed increases, there is a simple rule for maximizing profit: hire the quantity of labour at which the value of marginal product equals the wage rate.

If the value of marginal product of labour exceeds the wage rate, a firm can increase its profit by hiring one more worker. If the wage rate exceeds the value of

---

Table 17.1

Value of Marginal Product at Angelo's Bakery

	Quantity of labour (L) (workers)	Total product (TP) (loaves per hour)	Marginal product ($MP = \Delta TP/\Delta L$) (loaves per worker)	Value of marginal product ($VMP = MP \times P$) (pounds per worker)
A	0	0		
			7	14
B	1	7		
			6	**12**
C	**2**	13		
			5	10
D	3	18		
			4	8
E	4	22		
			3	6
F	5	25		

The value of marginal product of labour equals the price of the product produced multiplied by marginal product of labour. If Angelo's hires 2 workers, the marginal product of the second worker is 6 loaves (in the third column). The price of a loaf is £2, so the value of marginal product of the second worker is £2 a loaf multiplied by 6 loaves, which is £12 (in the fourth column).

marginal product of labour, a firm can increase its profit by firing one worker. But if the wage rate equals the value of marginal product of labour, the firm cannot increase its profit by changing the number of workers it employs. The firm is making the maximum possible profit. So

> **The quantity of labour demanded by a firm is the quantity at which the value of marginal product of labour equals the wage rate.**

A Firm's Demand for Labour Curve

A firm's demand for labour curve is derived from its value of marginal product curve. Figure 17.1 shows these two curves. Figure 17.1(a) shows the value of marginal product curve at Angelo's Bakery. The blue bars graph the numbers in Table 17.1. The curve labelled *VMP* is Angelo's value of marginal product curve.

If the wage rate falls and other things remain the same, a firm hires more workers. Figure 17.1(b) shows Angelo's demand for labour curve.

Suppose the wage rate is £10 an hour. You can see in Figure 17.1(a) that if Angelo hires 2 workers, the value of marginal product of labour is £12 an hour. At a wage rate of £10 an hour, Angelo makes a profit of £2 an hour on the second worker. If Angelo hires a third worker, the value of marginal product of that worker is £10 an hour. So on this third worker, Angelo breaks even.

If Angelo hired 4 workers, his profit would fall. The fourth worker generates a value of marginal product of only £8 an hour but costs £10 an hour, so Angelo does not hire the fourth worker. When the wage rate is £10 an hour, the quantity of labour demanded by Angelo is 3 workers.

Figure 17.1(b) shows Angelo's demand for labour curve, *D*. At £10 an hour, the quantity of labour demanded by Angelo is 3 workers. If the wage rate increased to £12 an hour, Angelo would decrease the quantity of labour demanded to 2 workers. If the wage rate decreased to £8 an hour, Angelo would increase the quantity of labour demanded to 4 workers.

A change in the wage rate brings a change in the quantity of labour demanded and a movement along the demand for labour curve.

A change in any other influence on a firm's labour hiring plans changes the demand for labour and shifts the demand for labour curve.

Figure 17.1 The Demand for Labour at Angelo's Bakery

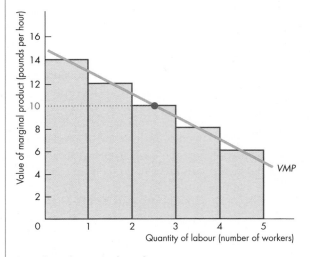

(a) Value of marginal product

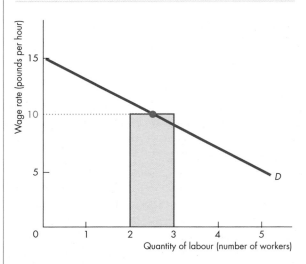

(b) Demand for labour

Angelo's Bakery can sell any quantity of bread at £2 a loaf. The blue bars in part (a) represent the firm's value of marginal product of labour (based on Table 17.1). The line labelled *VMP* is the firm's value of marginal product curve. Part (b) shows Angelo's demand for labour curve. Angelo hires the quantity of labour that makes the value of marginal product equal to the wage rate. The demand for labour curve slopes downward because the value of marginal product diminishes as the quantity of labour employed increases.

Changes in the Demand for Labour

A firm's demand for labour depends on:

◆ The price of the firm's output
◆ Other factor prices
◆ Technology

The Price of the Firm's Output

The higher the price of a firm's output, the greater is the firm's demand for labour. The price of output affects the demand for labour through its influence on the value of marginal product of labour. A higher price for the firm's output increases the value of marginal product of labour. A change in the price of a firm's output leads to a shift in the firm's demand for labour curve. If the price of the firm's output increases, the demand for labour curve shifts rightward.

For example, if the price of bread increased to £3 a loaf, the value of marginal product of Angelo's fourth worker would increase from £8 an hour to £12 an hour. At a wage rate of £10 an hour, Angelo would now hire 4 workers instead of 3.

Other Factor Prices

If the price of using capital decreases relative to the wage rate, a firm substitutes capital for labour and increases the quantity of capital it uses. Usually, the demand for labour will decrease when the price of using capital falls. For example, if the price of a breadmaking machine falls, Angelo might decide to install one machine and lay off a worker. But the demand for labour could increase if the lower price of capital led to a sufficiently large increase in the scale of production.

For example, with cheaper machines available, Angelo might install a machine and hire more labour to operate it. This type of factor substitution occurs in the long run when the firm can change the size of its plant.

Technology

New technologies decrease the demand for some types of labour and increase the demand for other types. For example, if a new automated breadmaking machine becomes available, Angelo might install one of these machines and fire most of his workforce – a decrease in the demand for bakery workers. But the firms that manufacture and service automated breadmaking machines hire more labour, so there is an increase in the demand

for this type of labour. An event similar to this one occurred during the 1990s when the introduction of electronic telephone exchanges decreased the demand for telephone operators and increased the demand for computer programmers and electronics engineers.

Table 17.2 summarizes the influences on a firm's demand for labour.

Table 17.2

A Firm's Demand for Labour

The Law of Demand

(Movements along the demand for labour curve)

The quantity of labour demanded by a firm

Decreases if:	*Increases if:*
◆ The wage rate increases	◆ The wage rate decreases

Changes in Demand

(Shifts in the demand for labour curve)

A firm's demand for labour

Decreases if:	*Increases if:*
◆ The price of the firm's output decreases	◆ The price of the firm's output increases
◆ The price of a substitute for labour falls	◆ The price of a substitute for labour rises
◆ The price of a complement of labour rises	◆ The price of a complement of labour falls
◆ A new technology decreases the marginal product of labour	◆ A new technology increases the marginal product of labour

---

Review Quiz

1 What is the value of marginal product of labour?
2 What is the relationship between the value of marginal product of labour and the marginal product of labour?
3 How is the demand for labour derived from the value of marginal product of labour?
4 What are the influences on the demand for labour?

You can work these questions in Study Plan 17.2 and get instant feedback.

Labour Markets

Labour services are traded in many different labour markets. Examples are markets for bakery workers, van drivers, train drivers, computer support specialists, air traffic controllers, dentists and economists. Some of these markets, such as the market for bakery workers, are local. They operate in a given urban area. Some labour markets, such as the market for air traffic controllers, are national. Firms and workers search across the nation for the right match of worker and job. And some labour markets are global, such as the market for superstar footballers and basketball players.

We'll look at a local market for bakery workers as an example. First, we'll look at a competitive labour market. Then, we'll see how monopoly elements can influence a labour market.

A Competitive Labour Market

A competitive labour market is one in which many firms demand labour and many households supply labour.

Market Demand for Labour

Earlier in the chapter, you saw how an individual firm decides how much labour to hire. The market demand for labour is derived from the demand for labour by individual firms. We determine the market demand for labour by adding together the quantities of labour demanded by all the firms in the market at each wage rate. (The market demand for a good or service is derived in a similar way – see Chapter 5, p. 108.)

Because each firm's demand for labour curve slopes downward, the market demand for labour curve also slopes downward.

The Market Supply of Labour

The market supply of labour is derived from the supply of labour decisions made by individual households.

Individual's Labour Supply Decision

People can allocate their time to two broad activities: labour supply and leisure. (Leisure is a catch-all term. It includes all activities other than supplying labour.) For most people, leisure is more fun than work so to induce them to work they must be offered a wage. Think about the labour supply decision of Jill, one of the workers at Angelo's Bakery. Let's see how the wage rate influences the quantity of labour she is willing to supply.

Reservation Wage Rate

Jill enjoys her leisure time, and she would be pleased if she didn't have to spend her time working at Angelo's Bakery. But Jill wants to earn an income, and as long as she can earn a wage rate of at least £5 an hour, she's willing to work. This wage is called her reservation wage. At any wage rate above her reservation wage, Jill supplies some labour.

The wage rate at Angelo's is £10 an hour, and at that wage rate, Jill chooses to work 30 hours a week. At a wage rate of £10 an hour, Jill regards this use of her time as the best available. Figure 17.2 illustrates.

Backward-bending Labour Supply Curve

If Jill were offered a wage rate between £5 and £10 an hour, she would want to work fewer hours. If she were offered a wage rate above £10 an hour, she would want to work more hours, but only up to a point. If Jill could earn £25 an hour, she would be willing to work 40 hours a week (and earn £1,000 a week). But at a wage rate above £25 an hour, with the goods and services that Jill

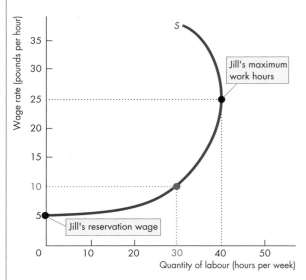

Figure 17.2 Jill's Labour Supply Curve

Jill's labour supply curve is *S*. Jill supplies no labour at wage rates below her reservation wage of £5 an hour. As the wage rate rises above £5 an hour, the quantity of labour that Jill supplies increases to a maximum of 40 hours a week at a wage rate of £25 an hour. As the wage rate rises above £25 an hour, Jill supplies a decreasing quantity of labour: her labour supply curve bends backward. The income effect on the demand for leisure dominates the substitution effect.

myeconlab Animation

can buy for £1,000, her priority would be a bit more leisure time. So if the wage rate increased above £25 an hour, Jill would cut back on her work hours and take more leisure. Jill's labour supply curve eventually bends backward.

Jill's labour supply decisions are influenced by a substitution effect and an income effect.

Substitution Effect

Other things remaining the same, the higher the wage rate Jill is offered, at least over a range, the greater is the quantity of labour that she supplies. The reason is that Jill's wage rate is her *opportunity cost of leisure*. If she takes an hour off work to go shopping, the cost of that extra hour of leisure is the wage forgone. The higher the wage rate, the less willing is Jill to forgo the income and take the extra leisure time. This tendency for a higher wage rate to induce Jill to work longer hours is a *substitution effect*.

But there is also an *income effect* that works in the opposite direction to the substitution effect.

Income Effect

The higher Jill's wage rate, the higher is her income. A higher income, other things remaining the same, induces Jill to increase her demand for most goods. Leisure is one of these goods. Because an increase in income creates an increase in the demand for leisure, it also creates a decrease in the quantity of labour supplied.

Market Supply Curve

Jill's supply curve shows the quantity of labour supplied by Jill as her wage rate varies. Most people behave like Jill and have a backward-bending labour supply curve, but their reservation wage rates and wage rates at which their labour supply curves bend backward are different.

A market supply curve shows the quantity of labour supplied by all households in a given job market. It is found by adding together the quantities of labour supplied by all households to that market at each wage rate.

Also, along a supply curve in a particular job market the wage rates available in other job markets remain the same. For example, along the supply curve of bakery workers, the wage rates of chefs, van drivers and all other labour are constant.

Despite the fact that an individual's labour supply curve eventually bends backward, the market supply curve of labour slopes upward. The higher the wage rate for bakery workers, the greater is the quantity of labour supplied in that labour market.

Let's now look at labour market equilibrium.

Competitive Labour Market Equilibrium

Labour market equilibrium determines the wage rate and employment. In Figure 17.3, the market demand curve for bakery workers is *D* and the market supply curve of bakery workers is *S*. The equilibrium wage rate is £10 an hour, and the equilibrium quantity is 300 bakery workers.

At a wage rate above £10 an hour, there is a surplus of bakery workers. More people are looking for jobs in bakeries than firms are willing to hire. In such a situation, the wage rate will fall because firms find it easy to hire people at a lower wage rate. At a wage rate below £10 an hour, there is a shortage of bakery workers. Firms are not able to fill all the positions they have available. In this situation, the wage rate will rise because firms find it necessary to offer a higher wage rate to attract labour. Only at a wage rate of £10 an hour are there no forces operating to change the wage rate.

Figure 17.3   The Market for Bakery Workers

A competitive labour market coordinates firms' and households' plans. The market is in equilibrium – the quantity of labour demanded equals the quantity supplied at a wage rate of £10 an hour when 300 workers are employed.

At a wage rate above £10 an hour, the quantity of labour supplied exceeds the quantity demanded and the wage rate will fall.

At a wage rate below £10 an hour, the quantity of labour demanded exceeds the quantity supplied and the wage rate will rise.

 Animation

A Labour Market with a Union

A **trades union** is an organized group of workers that aims to increase the wage rate and influence other job conditions. Let's see what happens when a union enters a competitive labour market.

Influences on Labour Supply

One way of raising the wage rate is to decrease the supply of labour. In some labour markets, a union can restrict supply by controlling entry into apprenticeship programmes or by influencing job qualification standards. Markets for skilled workers, doctors, dentists and lawyers are the easiest ones to control in this way.

If there is an abundant supply of non-union labour, a union can't decrease supply. For example, in the market for farm labour in south-east England, the flow of non-union labour from the EU makes it difficult for a union to control the supply. On the demand side of the labour market, the union faces a tradeoff: the demand for labour curve slopes downward, so restricting supply to raise the wage rate costs jobs. For this reason, unions also try to influence the demand for union labour.

Influences on Labour Demand

A union tries to increase the demand for the labour of its members in four main ways:

1   Increasing the value of marginal product of its members by organizing and sponsoring training schemes and apprenticeship programmes, and by professional certification.

2   Lobbying for import restrictions and encouraging people to buy goods made by unionized workers.

3   Supporting minimum wage laws, which increase the cost of employing low-skilled labour and lead firms to substitute high-skilled union labour for low-skilled non-union labour.

4   Lobbying for restrictive immigration laws to decrease the supply of foreign workers.

Labour Market Equilibrium with a Union

Figure 17.4 illustrates what happens to the wage rate and employment when a union successfully enters a competitive labour market. With no union, the demand curve is D_C, the supply curve is S_C, the wage rate is £10 an hour, and 300 workers have jobs. Now a union enters

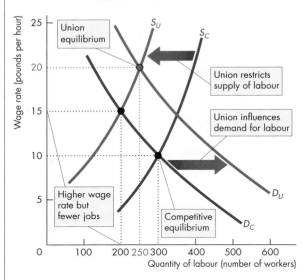

Figure 17.4   A Union Enters a Competitive Labour Market

In a competitive labour market, the demand curve is D_C and the supply curve is S_C. Competitive equilibrium occurs at a wage rate of £10 an hour and 300 workers are employed. If a union decreases the supply of labour and the supply of labour curve shifts to S_U, the wage rate rises to £15 an hour and employment decreases to 200 workers. If the union can also increase the demand for labour and shift the demand for labour curve to D_U, the wage rate rises to £20 an hour and 250 workers are employed.

myeconlab Animation ◆

this labour market. First, look at what happens if the union has sufficient control over the supply of labour to be able to restrict supply below its competitive level – to S_U. If that is all the union is able to do, employment falls to 200 workers and the wage rate rises to £15 an hour.

Suppose now that the union is also able to increase the demand for labour to D_U. The union can get an even bigger increase in the wage rate and with a smaller fall in employment. By maintaining the restricted labour supply at S_U, the union increases the wage rate to £20 an hour and achieves an employment level of 250 workers.

Because a union restricts the supply of labour in the market in which it operates, the union's actions spill over into non-union markets. Workers who can't get union jobs must look elsewhere for work. This action increases the supply of labour in non-union markets and lowers the wage rate in those markets. This spillover effect further widens the gap between union and non-union wages.

Monopsony in the Labour Market

Not all labour markets in which unions operate are competitive. Rather, some are labour markets in which the employer possesses market power and the union enters to try to counteract that power.

A market in which there is a single buyer is called a **monopsony**. A monopsony labour market has one employer. With the growth of large-scale production over the last century, large manufacturing plants such as coal mines, steel and textile mills and car production plants became the major employer in some regions, and in some places a single firm employed almost all the labour. Today, in some regions, managed healthcare organizations are the major employer of healthcare professionals. These firms have market power.

A monopsony acts on the buying side of a market in a similar way to a monopoly on the selling side. The firm maximizes profit by hiring the quantity of labour that makes the marginal cost of labour equal to the value of marginal product of labour and by paying the lowest wage rate at which it can attract this quantity of labour.

Figure 17.5 illustrates a monopsony labour market. Like all firms, a monopsony faces a downward-sloping value of marginal product curve, *VMP*, which is its demand for labour curve, *D* – the curve labelled *VMP = D* in the figure.

What is special about monopsony is the marginal cost of labour. For a firm in a competitive labour market, the marginal cost of labour is the wage rate. For a monopsony, the marginal cost of labour exceeds the wage rate. The reason is that being the only buyer in the market, the firm faces an upward-sloping supply of labour curve – the curve *S* in the figure.

To attract one more worker, the monopsony must offer a higher wage rate. But it must pay this higher wage rate to all its workers, so the marginal cost of a worker is the wage rate plus the increased wage bill that arises from paying all the workers the higher wage rate.

The supply curve is now the average cost of labour curve and the relationship between the supply curve and the marginal cost of labour curve, *MCL*, is similar to that between a monopoly's demand curve and marginal revenue curve (see Chapter 12, p. 278). The relationship between the supply curve and the *MCL* curve is also similar to that between a firm's average total cost curve and marginal cost curve (see Chapter 10, pp. 228–229).

To find the profit-maximizing quantity of labour, the monopsony sets the marginal cost of labour equal to the value of marginal product of labour. In Figure 17.5, this outcome occurs when the firm employs 100 workers.

To hire 100 workers, the firm must pay £10 an hour (on the supply of labour curve). Each worker is paid £10 an hour, but the value of marginal product of labour is £20 an hour, so the firm makes an economic profit of £10 an hour on the marginal worker.

If the labour market in Figure 17.5 were competitive, the equilibrium wage rate and employment would be determined by the demand and supply curves. The wage rate would be £15 an hour, and 150 workers would be employed. So compared with a competitive labour market, a monopsony pays a lower wage rate and employs fewer workers.

A Union and a Monopsony

A union is like a monopoly. If the union (monopoly seller) faces a monopsony buyer, the situation is called **bilateral monopoly**. An example of bilateral monopoly is the Writers Guild of America that represents film, television, and radio writers, and an employers'

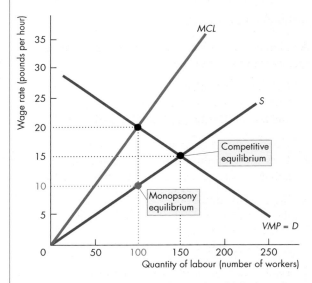

Figure 17.5 A Monopsony Labour Market

A monopsony is a market structure in which there is a single buyer. A monopsony in the labour market has a value of marginal product curve *VMP* and faces a labour supply curve *S*. The marginal cost of labour curve is *MCL*. The monopsony maximizes profit by making the marginal cost of labour equal to the value of marginal product. The monopsony employs 100 workers and pays the lowest wage for which that quantity of labour will work, which is £10 an hour.

myeconlab Animation

alliance that represents firms. Every three years, the Writers Guild and the employers' alliance negotiate a pay deal.

In bilateral monopoly, the outcome is determined by bargaining, which depends on the costs that each party can inflict on the other. The firm can shut down temporarily and lock out its workers, and the workers can shut down the firm by striking. Each party estimates the other's strength and what it will lose if it does not agree to the other's demands.

Usually, an agreement is reached without a strike or a lockout. The threat is usually enough to bring the bargaining parties to an agreement. When a strike or lockout does occur, it is because one party has misjudged the costs each party can inflict on the other. Such an event occurred in November 2007 when the writers and entertainment producers failed to agree on a compensation deal. A 100-day strike followed that ended up costing the entertainment industry an estimated £2 billion.

In the example in Figure 17.5, if the union and employer are equally strong, and each party knows the strength of the other, they will agree to split the gap between £10 (the wage rate on the supply curve) and £20 (the wage rate on the demand curve) and agree to a wage rate of £15 an hour.

You've now seen that in a monopsony, a union can bargain for a higher wage rate without sacrificing jobs. A similar outcome can arise in a monopsony labour market when a minimum wage law is enforced. Let's look at the effect of a minimum wage.

Monopsony and the Minimum Wage

In a competitive labour market, a minimum wage that exceeds the equilibrium wage decreases employment (see Chapter 6, pp. 131–132). But this outcome does not occur in all types of labour markets. In particular, it does not occur in monopsony. In a monopsony labour market, a minimum wage can end up increasing both the wage rate and employment. Let's see how.

Figure 17.6 shows a monopsony labour market in which the wage rate is £10 an hour and 100 workers are employed.

A minimum wage law is passed that requires employers to pay at least £15 an hour. The monopsony now faces a perfectly elastic supply of labour at £15 an hour up to 150 workers. To hire more than 150 workers, a wage rate above £15 an hour must be paid (along the supply of labour curve). Because the wage rate is £15 an hour up to 150 workers, so is the marginal cost of labour £15 up to 150 workers. To maximize profit, the monopsony

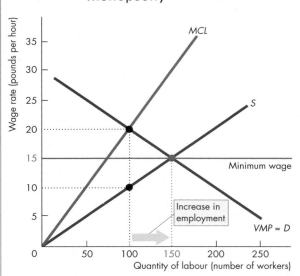

Figure 17.6 Minimum Wage Law in Monopsony

In a monopsony labour market, the wage rate is £10 an hour and 100 workers are hired. If a minimum wage law increases the wage rate to £15 an hour, the wage rate rises to this level and employment increases to 150 workers.

myeconlab Animation

sets the marginal cost of labour equal to the value of marginal product of labour (on the demand curve). The monopsony employs 150 workers at £15 an hour. The minimum wage law has succeeded in raising the wage rate by £5 an hour and increasing the number of workers employed.

Scale of Union–Non-union Wage Gap

You've seen how a union can influence the wage rate, but how much of a difference to wage rates do unions actually make? This question is difficult to answer. To measure the difference in wages attributable to unions, economists have looked at the wages of unionized and non-unionized workers who do similar work and have similar skills.

The evidence based on these comparisons is that the union–non-union wage gap lies between 10 and 25 per cent of the wage. For example, unionized airline pilots earn about 25 per cent more than non-union pilots with the same level of skill. In markets that have only a union wage rate, we might presume that the wage rate is 10 to 25 per cent higher than it would be in the absence of a union.

The Diversity of UK Wage Rates

The figure shows the averge hourly wage rate for 20 jobs selected from the 430 jobs in the Government's New Earnings Survey.

The lowest paid workers, a group that includes bar workers, hairdressers and barbers, earned less than £7 an hour – less than half the average wage rate. At the other extreme, company chief executives and corporate managers earned between £37 and £49 an hour. Remember these numbers are averages. Some earn a lot more than the average and some earn less.

Many more occupations earn a wage rate below the national average than above it. Most of the occupations that earn more than the national average require a university degree and postgraduate training.

Earning differences are explained by differences in the value of marginal product of the skills in the various occupations and by differences in market power.

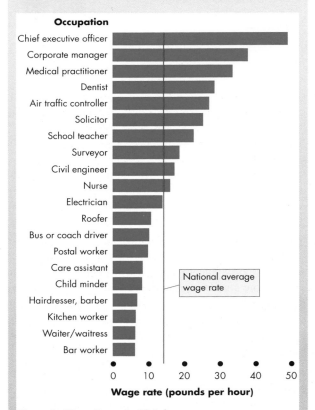

Figure 1 Wage Rates in 20 Jobs

Source of data: Office for National Statistics, *New Earnings Survey 2010*.

Trends and Differences in Wage Rates

You can use what you've learned about labour markets to explain the trend in wage rates and differences between wage rates.

Wage rates increase over time – trend upward. The reason is that the value of marginal product of labour trends upward. Technological change and the new types of capital that it brings make workers more productive. With greater labour productivity, the demand for labour increases and so does the average wage rate. Even for jobs in which productivity doesn't increase, experience can increase the *value* of marginal product. Childcare is an example. A childcare worker can't care for an increasing number of children, but an increasing number of parents who earn high wage rates are willing to hire childcare workers. The *value* of marginal product of these workers increases.

Wage rates are unequal, and in recent years they have become increasingly unequal. High wage rates have increased rapidly while low wage rates have stagnated or even fallen. The reasons are complex and not fully understood.

One reason is that the new technologies of the 1990s and 2000s made skilled workers more productive and destroyed some low-skilled jobs. An example is the ATM, which took the jobs of bank tellers and lowered their wage rate and at the same time created the jobs of computer programmers and electronic engineers and increased their wage rate. Another reason is that globalization has brought increased competition for domestic low-skilled workers from workers in other countries and has opened global markets for high-skilled workers.

1 What determines the amount of labour that households plan to supply?
2 How is the wage rate and employment determined in a competitive labour market?
3 How do unions influence wage rates?
4 What is a monopsony and why is a monopsony able to pay a lower wage rate than a firm in a competitive labour market?
5 How is the wage rate determined when a union faces a monopsony?
6 What is the effect of a minimum wage law in a monopsony labour market?

You can work these questions in Study Plan 17.3 and get instant feedback.

Capital and Natural Resource Markets

The markets for capital and land can be understood by using the same basic ideas that you've seen when studying a competitive labour market. But markets for non-renewable natural resources are different. We'll now examine three groups of factor markets:

◆ Capital rental markets

◆ Land rental markets

◆ Non-renewable natural resource markets

Capital Rental Markets

The demand for capital is derived from the *value of marginal product of capital*. Profit-maximizing firms hire the quantity of capital services that makes the value of marginal product of capital equal to the *rental rate of capital*. The *lower* the rental rate of capital, other things remaining the same, the *greater* is the quantity of capital demanded. The supply of capital responds in the opposite way to the rental rate. The *higher* the rental rate, other things remaining the same, the *greater* is the quantity of capital supplied. The equilibrium rental rate makes the quantity of capital demanded equal to the quantity supplied.

Figure 17.7 illustrates the rental market for tower cranes – capital used to construct high-rise buildings. The value of marginal product and the demand curve is *VMP = D*. The supply curve is *S*. The equilibrium rental rate is £1,000 per day and 100 tower cranes are rented.

Rent-versus-Buy Decision

Some capital services are obtained in a rental market like the market for tower cranes. And like tower cranes, many of the world's large airlines rent their aeroplanes. But not all capital services are obtained in a rental market. Instead, firms buy the capital equipment that they use. You saw in Chapter 9 (pp. 198–199) that the cost of the services from the capital that a firm owns and operates is an implicit rental rate that arises from depreciation and interest costs. Firms that buy capital *implicitly* rent the capital to themselves.

The decision to obtain capital services in a rental market rather than buy capital and rent it implicitly is made to minimize cost. The firm compares the cost of explicitly renting the capital and the cost of buying and implicitly renting it. This decision is the same as the one

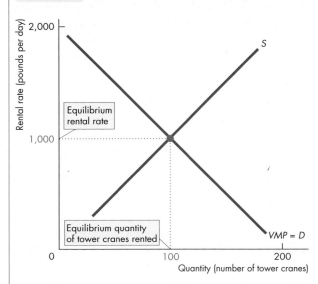

Figure 17.7 A Rental Market for Capital

The value of marginal product of tower cranes, *VMP*, determines the demand, *D*, for tower cranes. With the supply curve, *S*, the equilibrium rental rate is £1,000 a day and 100 cranes are rented.

 myeconlab Animation

that a household makes in deciding whether to rent or buy a home.

To make a rent-versus-buy decision, a firm must compare a cost incurred in the *present* with a stream of rental costs incurred over some *future* period. The Mathematical Note (pp. 406–407) explains how to make this comparison by calculating the *present value* of a future amount of money. If the *present value* of the future rental payments of an item of capital equipment exceeds the cost of buying the capital, the firm will buy the equipment. If the *present value* of the future rental payments of an item of capital equipment is less than the cost of buying the capital, the firm will rent (or lease) the equipment.

Land Rental Markets

The demand for land is based on the same factors as the demand for labour and the demand for capital – the *value of marginal product of land*. Profit-maximizing firms rent the quantity of land at which the value of marginal product of land is equal to the *rental rate of land*. The *lower* the rental rate, other things remaining the same, the *greater* is the quantity of land demanded.

But the supply of land is special: its quantity is fixed, so the quantity supplied cannot be changed by people's decisions. The supply of each particular block of land is perfectly inelastic.

The equilibrium rental rate makes the quantity of land demanded equal to the quantity available. Figure 17.8 illustrates the market for a plot of 10 hectares of land in Chelsea, London. The quantity supplied is fixed and the supply of land curve is *S*. The value of marginal product and the demand for land curve is *VMP = D*. The equilibrium rental rate is £1,000 a hectare per day.

The rental rate of land is high in Chelsea, London because the willingness to pay for the services produced by that land is high, which in turn makes the *VMP* of land high. A hair cut costs more at a salon in Chelsea than in Liverpool but not because the rental rate of land is higher in Chelsea.

The rental rate of land is higher in Chelsea because of the greater willingness to pay for a haircut (and other goods and services) in Chelsea than in Liverpool.

Figure 17.8 A Rental Market for Land

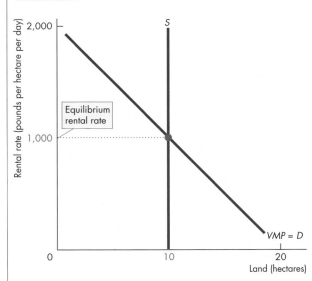

The value of marginal product of a 10-hectare block of land, *VMP*, determines the rental demand, *D*, for this land. With the supply curve, *S*, this block rents for £10,000 a day.

 myeconlab Animation

Non-renewable Natural Resource Markets

The non-renewable natural resources are oil, gas, and coal. Burning one of these fuels converts it to energy and other by-products, and the used resource cannot be re-used. The natural resources that we use to make metals are also non-renewable, but they can be used again, at some cost, by recycling them.

Oil, gas, and coal are traded in global commodity markets. The price of a given grade of crude oil is the same in New York, London and Singapore. Traders, linked by telephone and the Internet, operate these markets around the clock every day of the year.

Demand and supply determine the prices and the quantities traded in these commodity markets. We'll look at the influences on demand and supply by considering the global market for crude oil.

The Demand for Oil

The two key influences on the demand for oil are:

1 The value of marginal product of oil
2 The expected future price of oil

The value of marginal product of oil is the *fundamental* influence on demand. It works in exactly the same way for a non-renewable resource as it does for any other factor of production. The greater the quantity of oil used, the smaller is the value of marginal product of oil. Diminishing value of marginal product makes the demand curve for oil slope downward. The lower the price, the greater is the quantity of oil demanded.

The higher the expected future price of oil, the greater is the present demand for oil. The expected future price is a *speculative* influence on demand. Oil in the ground and oil in storage tanks are inventories that can be held or sold. A trader might plan to buy oil to hold now and to sell it later for a profit. Instead of buying oil to hold and sell later, the trader could buy a bond and earn interest. The *interest forgone* is the opportunity cost of holding the oil. If the price of oil is expected to rise by a bigger percentage than the interest rate, a trader will hold oil and incur the opportunity cost – the return from holding oil exceeds the return from holding bonds.

The Supply of Oil

The three key influences on the supply of oil are:

1 The known oil reserves
2 The scale of current oil production facilities
3 The expected future price of oil

Known oil reserves are the oil that has been discovered and can be extracted with today's technology. This quantity increases over time because advances in technology enable ever-less accessible sources to be discovered. The greater the size of known reserves, the greater is the supply of oil. But this influence on supply is small and indirect. It operates by changing the expected distant future price of oil. Even a major new discovery of oil would have a negligible effect on the current supply of oil.

The scale of current oil production facilities is the *fundamental* influence on the supply of oil. Producing oil is like any production activity: it is subject to increasing marginal cost. The increasing marginal cost of extracting oil means that the supply curve of oil slopes upward. The higher the price of oil, the greater is the quantity of oil supplied. When new oil wells are sunk or when new faster pumps are installed, the supply of oil increases and the supply of oil curve shifts rightward. When existing wells run dry, the supply of oil decreases and the supply of oil curve shifts leftward. Over time, the factors that increase supply are more powerful than those that decrease supply, so changes in the fundamental influence on the supply of oil increase it.

Speculative forces based on expectations about the future price also influence the supply of oil. The *higher* the expected future price of oil, the *smaller* is the present supply of oil. A trader with an oil inventory might plan to sell now or to hold and sell later. You've seen that interest forgone is the opportunity cost of holding the oil. If the price of oil is expected to rise by a bigger percentage than the interest rate, it is profitable to incur the opportunity cost of holding oil rather than selling it immediately.

The Equilibrium Price of Oil

The demand for oil and the supply of oil determine the equilibrium price and quantity of oil traded. Figure 17.9 illustrates the market equilibrium.

The value of marginal product of oil, *VMP*, is the fundamental determinant of the demand for oil, and the marginal cost of extraction, *MC*, is the fundamental determinant of the supply of oil. Together, they determine the market fundamentals price.

If expectations about the future price are also based on fundamentals, the equilibrium price is the market fundamentals price. But if expectations about the future price of oil depart from what the market fundamentals imply, speculation can drive a wedge between the equilibrium price and the market fundamentals price.

Figure 17.9   A Non-renewable Natural Resource Market

The value of marginal product of a non-renewable natural resource, *VMP*, and the marginal cost of extraction, *MC*, determine the market fundamentals price. Demand, *D*, and supply, *S*, which determine the equilibrium price, are influenced by the expected future price. Speculation can bring a gap between the market fundamentals price and the equilibrium price.

The Hotelling Principle

Harold Hotelling, an economist at Columbia University, had an incredible idea: traders expect the price of a non-renewable natural resource to rise at a rate equal to the interest rate. We call this idea the **Hotelling Principle**. Let's see why it is correct.

You've seen that the interest rate is the opportunity cost of holding an oil inventory. If the price of oil is expected to rise at a rate that exceeds the interest rate, it is profitable to hold a bigger inventory. Demand increases, supply decreases and the price rises. If the interest rate exceeds the rate at which the price of oil is expected to rise, it is not profitable to hold an oil inventory. Demand decreases, supply increases and the price falls. But if the price of oil is expected to rise at a rate equal to the interest rate, holding an inventory of oil is just as good as holding bonds. Demand and supply don't change and the price does not change. Only when the price of oil is expected to rise at a rate equal to the interest rate is the price at its equilibrium.

The World and EU Markets for Oil

The world produced about 31 billion barrels of oil in 2008 and the price shot upward from $85 a barrel in January to $135 a barrel in June. The high price and foreign dependence became major political issues.

Although the EU imports most of its oil from other countries, much of it comes from close to home. Figure 1 provides the details: only 15 per cent of the EU oil supply comes from the Middle East, 3 per cent comes from the US, 40 per cent comes from Russia and 20 per cent comes from Africa.

Even if the EU produced all its own oil, it would still face a fluctuating global price. EU producers, such as Norway, would not willingly sell to EU buyers for a price below the world price. So energy independence doesn't mean an independent oil price.

The Hotelling Principle tells us that we must expect the price of oil to rise at a rate equal to the interest rate. But expecting the price to rise at a rate equal to the interest rate doesn't mean that the price will rise at this rate. As you can see in Figure 2, the price of oil over the past 50 or so years has not followed the path predicted by the Hotelling Principle.

The forces that influence expectations are not well understood. The expected future price of oil depends on its expected future rate of use and the rate of discovery of new sources of supply. One person's expectation about a future price also depends on guesses about other people's expectations. These guesses can change abruptly and become self-reinforcing. When the expected future price of oil changes for whatever reason, demand and supply change, and so does the price. Prices in speculative markets are always volatile.

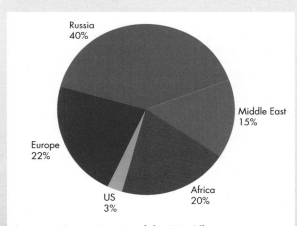

Figure 1 Diverse Sources of the EU's Oil

Source of data: http://ec.europa.eu/energy/observatory/oil/.

Figure 2 The Price of Oil and Its Hotelling Path

Source of data: Energy Information Administration.

Reading Between the Lines on pp. 404–405 focuses on the rising wages of financial sector workers and the increase in the number of people with high skills looking for financial sector work.

The next chapter looks at how the market economy distributes income and how government policy is used to redistribute income and modify the market outcome.

Review Quiz

1   What determines demand and supply in rental markets for capital and land?
2   What determines the demand for a non-renewable natural resource?
3   What determines the supply of a non-renewable natural resource?
4   What is the market fundamentals price and how might it differ from the equilibrium price?
5   Explain the Hotelling Principle.

You can work these questions in Study Plan 17.4 and get instant feedback.

Reading Between the Lines

A Job Market in Action

The Telegraph, 16 June 2010

City Job Vacancies Rocket as Financial Services Sector Recovers

Louisa Peacock

The number of City job vacancies has soared by 82pc year-on-year . . . There were 5,733 financial services vacancies in London in May 2010 . . . the survey by Morgan McKinley revealed.

The number of professionals looking for jobs also rose by 41pc compared to a year ago, up from 8,320 to 11,730 last month, as individuals took advantage of the early signs of economic recovery. . . .

The survey also found average salary for those placed in jobs in the City in May was also up 12pc to £55,353, compared to the same period last year.

Andrew Evans of Morgan McKinley . . . said: 'For the first time this year, salary rises clearly reflect the recent increasing competition for top talent across a number of job roles and functions in financial services. There has been particularly strong demand in change management, risk, compliance and finance roles as financial institutions address their changing operational and resource requirements following the cutbacks during the downturn. It now remains to be seen whether this level of hiring and consequent rise in salaries will continue into the second half of the year.' . . .

The Essence of the Story

◆ Three big changes occured in the market for skilled financial workers in the City of London during the year to May 2010.

◆ The number of unfilled jobs increased by 82 per cent to 5,733.

◆ The number of professionals looking for jobs increased by 41 per cent to 11,730.

◆ The average salary increased by 12 per cent to £55,353.

◆ Andrew Evans of Morgan McKinley said there was strong demand for some types of specialist workers.

◆ The change occurred as people responded to the early signs of recovery from a financial crisis in 2008.

Economic Analysis

◆ Skilled financial workers are a factor of production and their services are traded in a competitive market.

◆ The demand for skilled financial workers is derived from the value of marginal product (*VMP*) of their labour.

◆ If the annual wage increased by 12 per cent to £55,353, and other things remained the same, firms would cut employment to the level at which the *VMP* equalled £55,353.

◆ But in 2010, vacancies increased and the number of skilled financial workers seeking jobs increased, so the *VMP* and demand for skilled workers must have increased.

◆ The *VMP* and demand for skilled financial workers increased because the recovery from recession increased the global demand for London's financial services and the price of those services.

◆ Figure 1 illustrates the market for skilled financial workers in London in 2009 and 2010. In 2009, the demand curve was D_{09} and the supply curve was S_{09}. The equilibrium wage rate was £49,422 a year and the equilibrium number of workers was 300,000.

◆ In 2010, the demand for skilled financial workers increased to D_{10}. At the 2009 wage rate, there was a shortage of 5,733 workers. The shortage made the wage rate rise to £55,353 a year and an *increase in the quantity of workers supplied* increases employment to 303,000.

◆ In the summer and autumn of 2010, new graduates with the right qualifications and foreign workers who see better long-term job prospects in London's financial sector enter the market. These new entrants increase the supply of skilled financial workers.

◆ Figure 2 illustrates the effect of this increase in supply. Supply increases from S_{09} to S_{10} but demand remains at D_{10}. The wage rate falls and the number of workers employed increases.

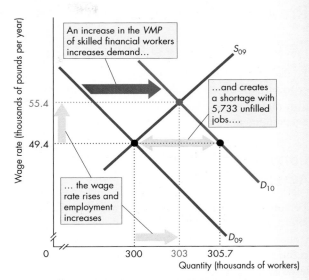

Figure 1 An increase in demand for skilled financial service workers

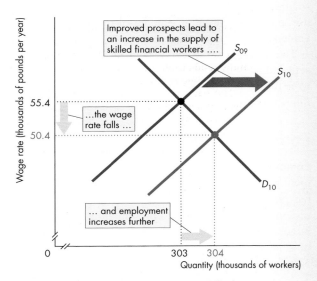

Figure 2 An increase in the supply of skilled financial workers

◆ MATHEMATICAL NOTE

Present Value and Discounting

Rent-versus-buy Decision

To decide whether to rent an item of capital equipment or to buy the capital equipment and implicitly rent it, a firm must compare the present expenditure on the capital equipment with its future rental cost.

Comparing Current and Future Amounts of Money

To compare a present expenditure with a future expenditure, we convert the future expenditure to its 'present value'. The **present value** of a future amount of money is the amount that, if invested today, will grow to be as large as that future amount when the interest it will earn is taken into account.

So the present value of a future amount of money is smaller than the future amount. The calculation that we use to convert the future amount of money to a present value is called **discounting**.

The easiest way to understand discounting and present value is to consider how a present value grows to a future amount of money because of *compound interest*.

Compound Interest

Compound interest is the interest on an initial investment plus the interest on the interest that the investment has previously earned. Because of compound interest, a present amount of money (a present value) grows into a larger future amount. The future amount is equal to the present amount (present value) plus the interest it will earn in the future. That is:

Future amount = Present value + Interest income

The interest income in the first year is equal to the present value multiplied by the interest rate, r, so:

Amount after 1 year = Present value + ($r \times$ Present value)

Amount after 1 year = Present value $\times (1 + r)$

If you invest £100 today and the interest rate is 10 per cent a year ($r = 0.1$), one year from today you will have £110 – the original £100 plus £10 interest. Check that the above formula delivers that answer:

$$£100 \times 1.1 = £110$$

If you leave this £110 invested to earn 10 per cent during a second year, at the end of that year, you will have

$$\text{Amount after 2 years} = \text{Present value} \times (1 + r)^2$$

With the numbers of the previous example, you invest £100 today at an interest rate of 10 per cent a year ($r = 0.1$). After one year you have £110 – the original £100 plus £10 interest. And after the second year, you have £121. In the second year, you earned £10 on your initial £100 plus £1 on the £10 interest that you earned in the first year.

Check that the above formula delivers that answer:

$$£100 \times (1.1)^2 = £100 \times 1.21 = £121$$

If you have £100 invested for n years, it will grow to:

$$\text{Amount after } n \text{ years} = \text{Present value} \times (1 + r)^n$$

With an interest rate of 10 per cent a year, your £100 will be £195 after 7 years ($n = 7$) – almost double the present value of £100.

Discounting a Future Amount

We have just calculated future values one year, two years and n years in the future, knowing the present amount and the interest rate. To calculate the present value of these future amounts, one year, two years and n years in the future, we just work backwards.

To find the present value of an amount one year in the future, we divide the future amount by $(1 + r)$.

That is:

$$\text{Present value} = \frac{\text{Amount of money 1 year in the future}}{(1 + r)}$$

Let's check that we can use the present value formula by calculating the present value of £110 one year from now when the interest rate is 10 per cent a year. You'll be able to guess that the answer is £100 because we just calculated that £100 invested today at 10 per cent a year becomes £110 in one year. So the present value of £110 one year from today is £100. But let's use the formula. Putting the numbers into the above formula, we have:

$$\text{Present value} = \frac{£110}{(1 + 0.1)}$$

$$= \frac{£110}{1.1} = £100$$

To calculate the present value of an amount of money two years in the future, we use the formula:

$$\text{Present value} = \frac{\text{Amount of money 2 years in future}}{(1 + r)^2}$$

Use this formula to calculate the present value of £121 two years from now at an interest rate of 10 per cent a year. With these numbers the formula gives:

$$\text{Present value} = \frac{£121}{(1 + 0.1)^2}$$

$$= \frac{£121}{(1.1)^2}$$

$$= \frac{£121}{1.21} = £100$$

We can calculate the present value of an amount of money n years in the future by using the general formula:

$$\text{Present value} = \frac{\text{Amount of money } n \text{ years in future}}{(1 + r)^n}$$

For example, if the interest rate is 10 per cent a year, £100 to be received 10 years from now has a present value of £38.55. That is, if £38.55 is invested today at an interest rate of 10 per cent a year, it will accumulate to £100 in 10 years.

Present Value of a Sequence of Future Amounts

You've seen how to calculate the present value of an amount of money one year, two years and n years in the future. Most practical applications of present value calculate the present value of a sequence of future amounts of money that spread over several years. An airline's rent for lease of aeroplanes is an example.

To calculate the present value of a sequence of amounts over several years, we use the formula you have learned and apply it to each year. We then sum the present values for each year to find the present value of the sequence of amounts.

For example, suppose that a firm expects to pay £100 a year for each of the next five years. And suppose that the interest rate is 10 per cent per year ($r = 0.1$). The present value of these five payments of £100 each is calculated by using the following formula:

$$PV = \frac{£100}{1.1} + \frac{£100}{1.1^2} + \frac{£100}{1.1^3} + \frac{£100}{1.1^4} + \frac{£100}{1.1^5}$$

which equals:

$$PV = £90.91 + £82.64 + £75.13 + £68.30 + £62.09$$

$$= £379.07$$

You can see that the firm pays £500 over five years. But because the money is paid in the future, it is not worth £500 today. Its present value is only £379.07. And the further in the future it is paid, the smaller is its present value. The £100 paid one year in the future is worth £90.91 today. And the £100 paid five years in the future is worth only £62.09 today.

The Decision

If this firm could lease a machine for five years at £100 a year or buy the machine for £500, it would jump at leasing. Only if the firm could buy the machine for less than £379.07 would it want to buy.

Many personal and business decisions turn on calculations like the one we've just made. A decision to rent or buy a flat, to lease or buy a car, to pay off a student loan or let the loan run another year can all be made using the above calculations.

SUMMARY

Key Points

The Anatomy of Factor Markets
(p. 390)

◆ The factor markets are: job markets for labour; rental markets (often implicit rental markets) for capital and land; and global commodity markets for non-renewable natural resources.

◆ The services of entrepreneurs are not traded in a factor market.

Working Problem 1 will give you a better understanding of the anatomy of factor markets.

The Demand for a Factor of Production (pp. 391–393)

◆ The value of marginal product determines the demand for a factor of production.

◆ The value of marginal product decreases as the quantity of the factor employed increases.

◆ The firm employs the quantity of each factor of production that makes the value of marginal product equal to the factor price.

Working Problems 2 to 8 will give you a better understanding of the demand for a factor of production.

Labour Markets (pp. 394–399)

◆ The value of marginal product of labour determines the demand for labour. A rise in the wage rate brings a decrease in the quantity demanded.

◆ The quantity of labour supplied depends on the wage rate. At low wage rates, a rise in the wage rate increases the quantity supplied. Beyond a high enough wage rate, a rise in the wage rate decreases the quantity supplied – the supply curve eventually bends backward.

◆ Demand and supply determine the wage rate in a competitive labour market.

◆ A trades union can raise the wage rate by restricting the supply or increasing the demand for labour.

◆ A monopsony can lower the wage rate below the competitive level.

◆ A union or a minimum wage in a monopsony labour market can raise the wage rate without a fall in employment.

Working Problems 9 to 11 will give you a better understanding of labour markets.

Capital and Natural Resource Markets
(pp. 400–403)

◆ The value of marginal product of capital (and land) determines the demand for capital (and land).

◆ Firms make a rent-versus-buy decision by choosing the option that minimizes cost.

◆ The supply of land is inelastic and the demand for land determines the rental rate.

◆ The demand for a non-renewable natural resource depends on the value of marginal product and on the expected future price.

◆ The supply of a non-renewable natural resource depends on the known reserves, the cost of extraction and the expected future price.

◆ The price of a non-renewable natural resource can differ from the market fundamentals price because of speculation based on expectations about the future price.

◆ The price of a non-renewable natural resource is expected to rise at a rate equal to the interest rate.

Working Problems 12 to 17 will give you a better understanding of capital and natural resource markets.

Key Terms

Bilateral monopoly, 397
Compound interest, 406
Derived demand, 391
Discounting, 406
Hotelling Principle, 402
Job, 390
Monopsony, 397
Non-renewable natural resources, 390
Present value, 406
Trades union, 396
Value of marginal product, 391

STUDY PLAN PROBLEMS AND APPLICATIONS

myeconlab You can work Problems 1 to 19 in MyEconLab Chapter 17 Study Plan and get instant feedback.

The Anatomy of Factor Markets
(Study Plan 17.1)

1 Tim is opening a new online store from Berlin. He plans to hire two people to key in the data at €10 an hour. Tim is also considering buying or leasing some new computers. The purchase price of a computer is €900 and after three years it is worthless. The annual cost of leasing a computer is €450.

   a In which factor markets does Tim operate?

   b What is the price of the capital equipment and the rental rate of capital?

The Demand for a Factor of Production (Study Plan 17.2)

Use the following data to work Problems 2 to 7.

Wanda owns a fish shop in Barcelona. She employs students to sort and pack the fish. Students can pack the following amounts of fish in an hour:

Number of students	Quantity of fish (kilograms)
1	20
2	50
3	90
4	120
5	145
6	165
7	180
8	190

The fish market is competitive and the market price of fish is 50¢ a kilogram and the wage rate of packers is €7.50 an hour.

2 Calculate the marginal product of the students and draw the marginal product curve.

3 Calculate the value of marginal product of labour and draw the value of marginal product curve.

4 **a** Find Wanda's demand for labour curve.

   b How many students does Wanda employ?

Use the following additional information to work Problems 5 and 6.

The market price of fish falls to 33¢ a kilogram, but the packers' wage rate remains at €7.50 an hour.

5 **a** How does the students' marginal product change?

   b How does the value of marginal product of labour change?

6 **a** How does Wanda's demand for labour change?

   b What happens to the number of students that Wanda employs?

7 At Wanda's fish shop, packers' wages increase to €10 an hour, but the price of fish remains at 50¢ a kilogram.

   a What happens to the value of marginal product of labour?

   b What happens to Wanda's demand for labour curve?

   c How many students does Wanda employ?

8 **British Construction Activity Falls**

   Construction activity in Britain declined in June at the fastest rate in 11 years. A major home builder was unable to raise more capital – both signs of worsening conditions in the battered housing industry. Employment of construction labour declined in June after 23 months of growth. Average house prices fell 0.9 per cent in June, the eighth consecutive month of decline, leaving the average 6.3 per cent below June 2007.

   Source: *Forbes*, 2 July 2008

   a Explain how a fall in house prices influences the market for construction labour.

   b On a graph illustrate the effect of falling house prices in the market for construction labour.

Labour Markets (Study Plan 17.3)

Use the following news clip to work Problems 9 to 11.

In Modern Rarity, Workers Form Union at Small Chain

In New York's low-income areas, trades unions have virtually no presence. But after a year-long struggle, 95 workers at a chain of 10 sports shoe stores have formed a union. After months of negotiations, the two sides signed a three-year contract that sets the wage rate at $7.25 an hour.

   Source: *The New York Times*, 5 February 2006

9 Why are trades unions scarce in New York's low-income areas?

10 Who wins from this union contract? Who loses?

11 How can this union try to change the demand for labour?

Capital and Natural Resource Markets
(Study Plan 17.4)

12 Classify the following items as a non-renewable natural resource, a renewable natural resource, or not a natural resource. Explain your answers.

a Canary Wharf

b Lake Garda

c Coal in a Polish coal mine

d The Internet

e The Lake District

f Power generated by wind turbines

13 **Most Expensive Property in the World**

Property developers are turning a 1930s building in St. James Square, London into 6 exclusive flats in the centre of the financial sector. One flat will cost £115 million and is now the most expensive flat in the world. The building is situated close to Buckingham Palace and Downing Street. Top market property prices have continued to rise despite the recession.

Source: The Times online, 16 March 2008

a Why has the price of land in St. James Square continued to increase despite the recession? In your answer include a discussion of the demand for and supply of land.

b Use a graph to show why the price of land in St. James Square increased over the past few years.

c Is the supply of land in St. James's Square perfectly inelastic?

14 In the news clip in Problem 8,

a Explain how a fall in house prices influences the market for construction equipment leases.

b Draw a graph to illustrate the effect of a fall in house prices in the market for construction equipment leases.

Use the following news clip to work Problems 15 and 16.

Fixing Farming

Solutions to the global food crisis will come from genetically engineered crops and large-scale farms. Demand for farm products will keep growing as the population grows. But the supply of farmland is limited and farms already use 55 per cent of the habitable land. The solution is for farmers to become more productive – generating more output from fewer inputs.

Source: Fortune, 22 May 2008

15 a Is farmland a renewable or non-renewable resource?

b Explain how the growing demand for farm products will affect the market for land and draw a graph to illustrate your answer.

16 How might farmers meet the growing demand for farm products without having to use a greater quantity of farmland?

17 **Copter Crisis**

Helicopters are in short supply these days. You could blame a rise in military spending, a jump in disaster relief, even crowded airports pushing executives into private travel. But the fastest growth is coming from the offshore oil-and-gas industry, where helicopters are the only way to ferry crews to and from rigs and platforms. Hundred-dollar oil has pushed producers to work existing fields harder and to open new deep-sea wells in Brazil, India and Alaska. The number of rigs and platforms has grown by 13 per cent over the past decade. Oil companies are facing a two-year backlog in orders for the Sikorsky S92, a favourite of the oil industry, and a 40 per cent rise in prices for used models.

Source: Fortune, 12 May 2008

a Explain how high oil prices influence the market for helicopter leases and services (such as the Sikorsky S92).

b What happens to the value of marginal product of a helicopter as a firm leases or buys additional helicopters?

Mathematical Note (Study Plan 17.MN)

18 Keshia is opening a new bookkeeping service in Brussels. She is considering buying or leasing some new laptop computers. The purchase price of a laptop is €1,500 and after three years it is worthless. The annual lease rate is €550 per laptop. The value of marginal product of one laptop is €700 a year. The value of marginal product of a second laptop is €625 a year. The value of marginal product of a third laptop is €575 a year. And the value of marginal product of a fourth laptop is €500 a year.

a How many laptops will Keshia lease or buy?

b If the interest rate is 4 per cent a year, will Keshia lease or buy her laptops?

c If the interest rate is 6 per cent a year, will Keshia lease or buy her laptops?

Economics in the News

19 **Baronet to the Rescue of Parkland under Threat**

Residents in Salford who are campaigning to block a proposed housing development discovered that the plot was once a farm owned by the ancestors of Sir Peter Heywood, the 6th Baronet of Claremont, and that they had sold it to the council in 1902 on the condition that it be used only for recreation. Council officials had claimed that there was little chance of tracking down descendants but now the council may be forced to rethink its plan to sell the land for £1.5 million.

Source: The Times, 4 April 2007

Explain why the plot of land in Salford would be worth £1.5 million.

ADDITIONAL PROBLEMS AND APPLICATIONS

 You can work these problems in MyEconLab if assigned by your lecturer.

The Anatomy of Factor Markets

20 Venus is opening a tennis school in France. She plans to hire a marketing graduate to promote the school and an administrator at €20 an hour. Venus is also considering buying or leasing a new tennis ball machine. The purchase price of the machine is €1,000 and after three years it is worthless. The annual cost of leasing the machine is €500.

a In which factor markets does Venus operate?

b What is the price of the capital equipment and the rental rate of capital?

The Demand for a Factor of Production

Use the following data to work Problems 21 to 24.

Kaiser's Smoothie Bar in Bonn hires workers to produce smoothies. The market for smoothies is perfectly competitive, and the price of a smoothie is €4. The labour market is competitive, and the wage rate is €40 a day. The table shows the workers' total product schedule:

Number of workers	Quantity produced (smoothies per day)
1	7
2	21
3	33
4	43
5	51
6	55

21 Calculate the marginal product of hiring the fourth worker and the fourth worker's value of marginal product.

22 How many workers will Kaiser's hire to maximize its profit and how many smoothies a day will Kaiser's produce?

23 If the price rises to €5 a smoothie, how many workers will Kaiser's hire?

24 Kaiser's installs a new machine that increases the productivity of workers by 50 per cent. If the price of a smoothie remains at €4 and the wage rate rises to €48 a day, how many workers does Kaiser's hire?

25 Detroit Oil Refinery Expansion Approved

Marathon Oil Saturday started work on a $1.9 billion expansion of its petrol refinery in Detroit. Marathon will employ 800 construction workers and add 135 permanent jobs to the existing 480 workers at the refinery.

Source: *United Press International*, 21 June 2008

a Explain how rising petrol prices influence the market for refinery labour.

b Draw a graph to illustrate the effects of rising petrol prices on the market for refinery labour.

Labour Markets

26 You May be Paid More (or Less) than You Think

It's hard to put a price on happiness, but if you've ever had to choose between a job you like and a better-paying one that you like less, you'd like to know what job satisfaction is worth.

John Helliwell and Haifang Huang (economists at the University of British Columbia) have estimated four key factors influencing job satisfaction: trust in management is like a 36 per cent pay raise; a job with lots of variety is like a 21 per cent pay raise; a job that requires a high level of skill is like a 19 per cent pay raise; and a job with enough time to finish your work is like an 11 per cent pay raise.

Source: CNN, 29 March 2006

a How might the job characteristics described here affect the supply of labour for different types of jobs?

b How might this influence on supply result in different wage rates that reflect the attractiveness of a job's characteristics?

Use the following news clip to work Problems 27 to 30.

The New War over Wal-Mart

Today, Wal-Mart employs more people – 1.7 million – than any other private employer in the world. With size comes power: Wal-Mart's prices are lower and United Food and Commercial Workers International Union argues that Wal-Mart's wages are also lower than its competitors. Last year, the workers at a Canadian outlet joined the union and Wal-Mart immediately closed the outlet. But does Wal-Mart behave any worse than its competitors? When it comes to payroll, Wal-Mart's median hourly wage tracks the national median wage for general merchandise retail jobs.

Source: *The Atlantic*, June 2006

27 a Assuming that Wal-Mart has market power in a labour market, explain how the firm could use that market power in setting wages.

b Draw a graph to illustrate how Wal-Mart might use labour market power to set wages.

28 a Explain how a union of Wal-Mart's employees would attempt to counteract Wal-Mart's wage offers (a bilateral monopoly).

b Explain the response by the Canadian Wal-Mart to the unionization of employees.

29 Based upon evidence presented in this article, does Wal-Mart function as a monopsony in labour markets, or is the market for retail labour more competitive? Explain.

30 If the market for retail labour is competitive, explain the potential effect of a union on the wage rates. Draw a graph to illustrate your answer.

Capital and Natural Resource Markets

Use the following news clip to work Problems 31 and 32.

Natural Gas Prices Create Land Rush

There is a land rush going on across Pennsylvania, but buyers aren't interested in the land itself. Buyers are interested in what lies beneath the earth's surface – mineral rights to natural gas deposits. Record high natural gas prices have already pushed up drilling activity across the state, but drilling companies have discovered a new technology that will enable deep gas-bearing shale to be exploited. Development companies, drilling companies and speculators have been crisscrossing the state, trying to lease mineral rights from landowners. The new drilling techniques might recover about 10 per cent of those reserves, and that would ring up at a value of $1 trillion.

Source: *Erie Times-News*, 15 June 2008

31 a Is natural gas a renewable or non-renewable resource? Explain.

b Explain why the demand for land in Pennsylvania has increased.

32 a If companies are responding to the higher prices for natural gas by drilling right now wherever they can, what does that imply about their assumptions about the future price of natural gas in relation to current interest rates?

b What could cause the price of natural gas to fall in the future?

33 New technology has allowed oil to be pumped from much deeper offshore oil fields than before. For example, 28 deep ocean rigs operate in the deep waters of the Gulf of Mexico.

a What effect do you think deep ocean sources have had on the world oil price?

b Who will benefit from drilling for oil in the Gulf of Mexico? Explain your answer.

34 Water is a natural resource that is plentiful in Yorkshire but not plentiful in London or the South East of England.

a If Yorkshire Water started to export bulk water to London and the South East, what do you predict will be the effect on the price of bulk water?

b Will Yorkshire eventually run out of water?

c Do you think the Hotelling Principle applies to Yorkshire's water? Explain why or why not.

Mathematical Note

35 Terry is opening a new online book shop in Leeds. He is considering buying or leasing some computers. The purchase price of a computer is £1,600 and after three years a computer is worthless. The annual lease is £550 per computer. The value of marginal product of one computer is £700 a year. The value of marginal product of a second computer is £650 a year. The value of marginal product of a third computer is £500 a year. And the value of marginal product of a fourth computer is £300 a year.

a How many computers will Terry lease or buy?

b If the interest rate is 4 per cent a year, will Terry lease or buy his computers?

c If the interest rate is 6 per cent a year, will Terry lease or buy his computers?

Economics in the News

36 After you have studied *Reading Between the Lines* on pp. 404–405 answer the following questions.

a Name some jobs for which you think future employment will expand and some for which it will shrink.

b What are the influences on the demand for labour that bring an increase in demand and what are the influences that bring a decrease in demand?

c In the past, computerization and satellite communications have had a major impact on global financial sector trading. How has technology affected the demand for skilled financial sector workers?

d Why might an increase in the demand for skilled financial service workers increase the supply of skilled financial service workers and what would be the effect on wages?

e Changes in technology are likely to reduce the demand for low-skilled factory workers over the next 10 years. Draw a graph of the market for factory workers in 2011 and 2021. Show the effects of a decrease in the demand for factory workers with no change in the supply on the employment and wage rate of factory workers.

f If the outcome you've shown in part (d) occurred, explain how the incentives faced by young workers just entering the labour force would be affected.

CHAPTER
18

Economic Inequality and Redistribution

After studying this chapter you will be able to:

◆ Describe the inequality in income and wealth in the UK and the trends in inequality

◆ Describe the distribution of income and the trends in inequality in selected countries and the world

◆ Explain the sources of economic inequality and its trends

◆ Describe the scale of government income redistribution in the UK

J.K. Rowling earned more than £45 million in 2010 and is Britain's highest-earning woman. But before she had the inspiration to write the Harry Potter stories, she was a typical single mother. Many single mothers earn almost nothing and rely on government benefits for their survival. Why are some people incredibly rich while others are abjectly poor? What contribution do government redistribution policies make to economic inequality and poverty? You will find some answers in this chapter. And *Reading Between the Lines* at the end of this chapter takes a close look at the problem of increasing inequality of wealth in the UK.

Economic Inequality in the UK

The most commonly used measure of economic inequality is the distribution of annual disposable income. **Disposable income** is defined as *original income* plus cash benefits from government minus income taxes. **Original income** is wages, interest, rent and profit earned in factor markets, *before* paying income taxes. Original income plus government cash benefits is called *gross income*. Individual incomes are estimated from household income survey data.

The Distribution of Income

Figure 18.1 shows the distribution of *disposable income* across the 63 million individuals in the UK in 2008. Note that the *x*-axis measures individual income and the *y*-axis is percentage of individuals.

The most common income in 2008, called the *mode income*, was received by the 10.5 per cent of the population whose incomes fell between £250 and £300 a week. The value of £275 marked on Figure 18.1 is the middle of that range.

The middle level of income in 2008, called the *median income*, was £393 a week. One half of the UK population had incomes greater than this amount, and the other half had incomes less than this amount.

The average weekly income in 2008, called the *mean income*, was £487 a week.

You can see in Figure 18.1 that the mode income is less than the median income and the median income is less than the mean income. This feature of the distribution of income tells us that there are more individuals with low incomes than with high incomes. But some individuals have high incomes that are off the scale, over £1,000 a week.

The income distribution in Figure 18.1 is called a *positively skewed* distribution, which means that it has a long tail of high values. This distribution contrasts with a bell-shaped distribution such as the distribution of people's heights. In a bell-shaped distribution, the mean, median and mode are all equal.

Another way of looking at the distribution of income is to measure the percentage of total income received by each given percentage of households. Data are reported for five groups – called quintiles or fifth shares – each consisting of 20 per cent of households.

Figure 18.2 shows the distribution based on these shares in 2009. The 20 per cent of households with the

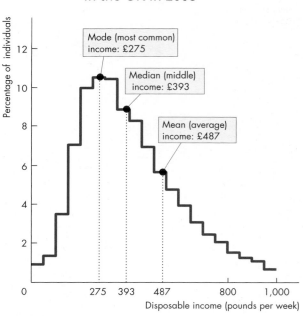

Figure 18.1 The Distribution of Income in the UK in 2008

The distribution of disposable income is positively skewed. The mode (most common) income is less than the median (middle) income, which in turn is less than the mean (average) income. The percentage of individuals with an income above £1,000 a week (not shown) falls off slowly and the highest incomes are more than £100,000 a week.

Source of data: Office for National Statistics.

myeconlab Animation

lowest incomes received 7 per cent of total income; the second 20 per cent received 11 per cent of total income; the middle 20 per cent received 15 per cent of total income; the next highest 20 per cent received 19 per cent of total income; and the highest 20 per cent received 48 per cent of total income.

The distribution of income in Figure 18.1 and the quintile shares in Figure 18.2 tell us that disposable income is distributed unequally. But we need a way of comparing the distribution of income in different periods and using different measures. A neat graphical tool called the *Lorenz curve* enables us to make such comparisons.

Figure 18.2   UK Quintile Shares in 2009

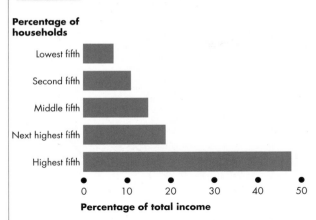

Percentage of households

Households (percentage)	Income (percentage of total income)
Lowest 20	7
Second 20	11
Middle 20	15
Next highest 20	19
Highest 20	48

In 2009, the 20 per cent of households with the lowest incomes received 7 per cent of total income; the second 20 per cent received 11 per cent of total income; the middle 20 per cent received 15 per cent; the next highest 20 per cent received 19 per cent; and the highest 20 per cent received 48 per cent.

Source of data: Office for National Statistics.

 Animation

The Income Lorenz Curve

The income **Lorenz curve** graphs the cumulative percentage of income against the cumulative percentage of households. Figure 18.3 shows the income Lorenz curve using the quintile shares from Figure 18.2. The table shows the percentage of disposable income of each quintile group. For example, row *A* tells us that the lowest quintile of households receives 7 per cent of total income. The table also shows the cumulative percentages of households and income. For example, row *B* tells us that the lowest two quintiles (lowest 40 per cent) of households receive 18 per cent of total income – 7 per cent for the lowest quintile and 11 per cent for the next lowest.

Figure 18.3   The Income Lorenz Curve in 2009

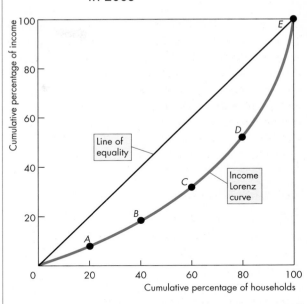

	Households		Income	
	Percentage	Cumulative percentage	Percentage	Cumulative percentage
A Lowest 20	20	7	7
B Second 20	40	11	18
C Middle 20	60	15	33
D Next highest 20	80	19	52
E Highest 20	100	48	100

The cumulative percentage of income is graphed against the cumulative percentage of households. Points *A* to *E* on the Lorenz curve correspond to the rows of the table.

If incomes were distributed equally, each 20 per cent of households would receive 20 per cent of total income and the Lorenz curve would fall along the line of equality. The Lorenz curve shows that income is unequally distributed.

Source of data: Office for National Statistics.

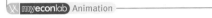 Animation

The Lorenz curve provides a direct visual clue about the degree of income inequality by comparing it with the line of equality. This line, identified in Figure 18.3, shows what the Lorenz curve would be if everyone had the same level of income.

If income were distributed equally across all the households, each quintile would receive 20 per cent of total income and the cumulative percentages of income received by the cumulative percentages of households would fall along the straight line labelled 'Line of equality'.

The actual distribution of income is shown by the curve labelled 'Income Lorenz curve'. The closer the Lorenz curve is to the line of equality, the more equal is the distribution.

The Distribution of Wealth

The distribution of wealth provides another way of measuring economic inequality. A household's **wealth** is the value of the things that it owns at a *point in time*. In contrast, income is the amount that the household receives over a given *period of time*.

Figure 18.4 shows the Lorenz curve for wealth in the UK in 2006–2008. During this period, average household wealth was £367,500. But the variation around this value is enormous. Wealth is extremely unequally distributed, and for this reason, the data are grouped by five unequal groups of households. The poorest 50 per cent of households own only 10 per cent of total wealth (row A' in the table in Figure 18.4). The next 25 per cent of households own 21 per cent of total wealth (row B' in the table). So the poorest 75 per cent of households own only 31 per cent of total wealth and the richest 25 per cent of households own 69 per cent of total wealth. Because this group owns such a large percentage of total wealth, we break it into smaller bits in rows C' to E'. The richest 1 per cent of households own 11 per cent of total wealth (row E').

Figure 18.4 shows the income Lorenz curve (from Figure 18.3) alongside the wealth Lorenz curve. You can see that the Lorenz curve for wealth is much farther away from the line of equality than is the Lorenz curve for income, which means that the distribution of wealth is much more unequal than the distribution of income.

Wealth or Income?

We've seen that wealth is much more unequally distributed than income. Which distribution provides the better description of the degree of inequality? To answer this question, we need to think about the connection between wealth and income.

Wealth is a stock of assets and *income* is the flow of earnings that results from the stock of wealth. Suppose

Figure 18.4 Lorenz Curves for Income and Wealth

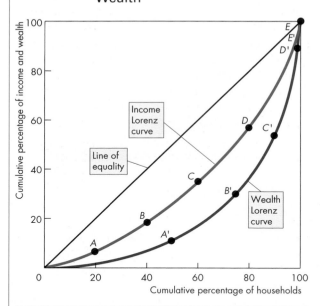

	Households		Wealth	
	Percentage	Cumulative percentage	Percentage	Cumulative percentage
A' Lowest 50	50	10	10
B' Next 25	75	21	31
C' Next 15	90	25	56
D' Next 9	99	33	89
E' Highest 1	100	11	100

The cumulative percentage of wealth is graphed against the cumulative percentage of households. Points A' to E' on the Lorenz curve for wealth correspond to the rows of the table. By comparing the Lorenz curves for income and wealth, we can see that wealth is distributed much more unequally than income.

Source of data: Office for National Statistics.

myeconlab Animation

that a person owns assets worth £1 million – has a wealth of £1 million. If the rate of return on assets is 5 per cent a year, then this person receives an income of £50,000 a year from those assets. We can describe this person's economic condition by using either the wealth of £1 million or the income of £50,000. When the rate of return is 5 per cent a year, £1 million of wealth equals

£50,000 of income in perpetuity. Wealth and income are just different ways of looking at the same thing.

But in Figure 18.4, the distribution of wealth is more unequal than the distribution of income. Why? It is because the wealth data do not include the value of human capital, while the income data measure income from all wealth, including human capital.

Think about Lee and Peter, two people with equal income and equal wealth. Lee's wealth is human capital and his entire income is from employment. Peter's wealth is in the form of investments in stocks and bonds and his entire income is from these investments.

When Lee and Peter are surveyed by the Office for National Statistics in a national wealth and income survey, their incomes are recorded being equal, but Lee's wealth is recorded as being zero, while Peter's wealth is recorded as the value of his investments. Peter looks vastly more wealthy than Lee in the survey data.

Because the national survey of wealth excludes human capital, the income distribution is a more accurate measure of economic inequality than the wealth distribution.

Annual or Lifetime Income and Wealth?

A typical household's income changes over its life cycle. Income starts out low, grows to a peak when the household's workers reach retirement age and then falls after retirement. Also, a typical household's wealth changes over time. Like income, wealth starts out low, grows to a peak at the point of retirement and then falls.

Suppose we look at three households that have identical lifetime incomes: one household is young, one is middle-aged and one is retired. The middle-aged household has the highest income and wealth, the retired household has the lowest and the young household falls in the middle. The distributions of annual income and wealth in a given year are unequal, but the distributions of lifetime income and wealth are equal.

Although some of the inequality in annual income arises because different households are at different stages in the life cycle, after allowing for this factor, a substantial amount of inequality remains.

So far, we have examined the extent of inequality in income and wealth in a few recent years. What are the trends in inequality? Is the distribution of income becoming less equal or more equal? We can see trends in the income distribution by looking at a number of years.

Trends in Inequality

To see trends in the income distribution, we need a measure that enables us to rank distributions on the scale of more equal and less equal. No perfect scale exists, but one that is much used is called the Gini coefficient.

The **Gini coefficient** is based on the Lorenz curve and equals the area between the line of equality and the Lorenz curve as a percentage of the entire area beneath the line of equality. The larger the Gini coefficient, the greater is the degree of income inequality. If income is equally distributed, the Lorenz curve is the same as the line of equality, so the Gini coefficient is zero. If one person has all the income and everyone else has none, the Gini coefficient is 100 per cent.

Figure 18.5 shows the UK Gini coefficient of disposable income from 1983 to 2008. The Gini coefficient has increased over the period, which means that on this measure, incomes have become more unequal.

The major increase in inequality occurred during the 1980s. Since 1990, the Gini coefficient has fluctuated around a very slightly falling trend. No one knows for

Figure 18.5   The UK Gini Coefficient: 1983–2008

Measured by the Gini coefficient, the distribution of income in the UK became more unequal between 1983 and 1990. Since 1990, the Gini coefficient has fluctuated around a very slightly falling trend.

Source of data: Office for National Statistics.

myeconlab Animation

sure why inequality increased during the 1980s, but a possibility that we'll explore later in this chapter is that it was the result of technological change in the information-age economy.

Who Are the Rich and the Poor?

The lowest-income household in the UK today is likely to be a person over 75 years of age, living alone in council rented accommodation, somewhere in Scotland. Among the employed, the lowest incomes are earned by people under 30 doing routine jobs that require only low skills. The highest-income household is likely to be one with two professionals aged between 30 and 49 with one child, living together in a house that they own, somewhere in England.

These snapshot profiles are the extremes of the characteristics shown in Figure 18.6. The figure illustrates the role of job type, economic status, household size and type, age of the householder, whether living in rented or owned housing and major region of residence.

All of these factors influence the likelihood that a household is poor and living on an income well below the average, or well off and living on an income well above the average. Job type, economic status and age are the three biggest contributors to economic well-being.

Poverty

The poorest households are considered to be living in **poverty**, a state in which a household's income is too low for it to be able to buy the quantities of food, shelter and clothing that are deemed necessary. Poverty is a relative concept, not an absolute one. The *poverty line* is a benchmark defined as 60 per cent of the median income.

Figure 18.6 The Distribution of Income by Selected Household Characteristics in 2008

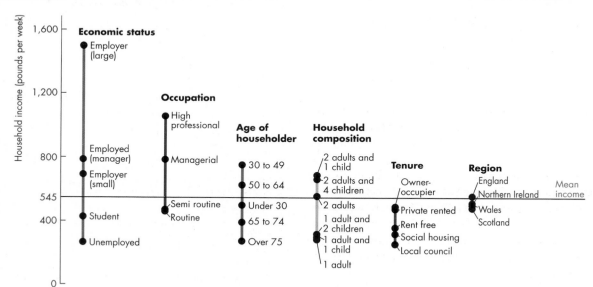

Single adults, single parents, those who are unemployed and those aged over 75 are likely to be among the poorest households in the UK.

Other poor households are those in which the main earner is employed as a manual worker and those who live in local council accommodation. Households who live in Scotland and Wales are, on average, poorer than those who live in England and Northern Ireland.

Source of data: Office for National Statistics, *Family Spending 2009: A Report on Living Costs and Food Survey* 2008.

ECONOMICS IN ACTION

Poverty in the EU

Defining the *poverty line* as 60 per cent of median EU income, poverty rates vary throughout the EU. The *poverty rate* is the percentage of people who fall below the *poverty line*.

Figure 1 shows that five of the early members, including the UK, have poverty rates that exceed the 2009 EU average. The accession of new low-income member states such as Bulgaria and Latvia in 2006 lowered EU median income and increased the number of member states with relatively high poverty rates.

Despite a lower median income in the 27 countries of the EU, the UK has a high poverty rate on the EU definition. Even if we define the poverty line as 60 per cent of median UK income, 17 per cent of UK households lived in poverty in 2009. Using this UK-based measure, UK poverty rates were at their highest in 1991 at 22 per cent and lowest in 1977 when just 10 per cent of UK households lived in poverty.

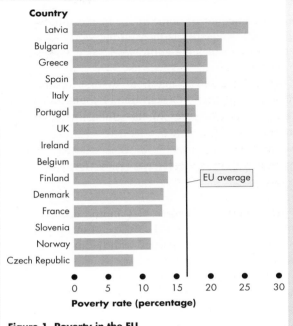

Figure 1 Poverty in the EU

Sources of data: Eurostat, *At Risk of Poverty* tables.

A person with an income below the poverty line is defined to be living in poverty. The *poverty rate* is the percentage of people who are living below the poverty line.

Economics in Action above gives some numbers on poverty rates in the EU and the UK. You can see that this measure of poverty crucially depends on the population being considered. The graph in *Economics in Action* uses the EU population and the poverty rate is more a measure of average income per person than of true poverty.

Because measures of poverty are relative, they don't provide information about the *absolute* level of poverty and how it is changing. People who are living in poverty in the UK would be considered well off in the black townships of South Africa. And people living in poverty in Ireland today would have been considered reasonably well off compared to the people of rural Ireland 40 years ago.

Review Quiz

1   Which is distributed more unequally: income or wealth? Why? Which is the better measure of inequality?
2   What does a Lorenz curve show and how do we use it to gauge the degree of inequality?
3   What is the Gini coefficient and how is it used to measure inequality?
4   Has the distribution of income in the UK become more unequal or less unequal? When did the largest changes occur?
5   What are the main characteristics of low-income households?
6   What is the poverty line and explain how it is used.

You can work these questions in Study Plan 18.1 and get instant feedback.

Inequality in the World Economy

Which countries have the greatest economic inequality and which have the least and the greatest equality? Where does the UK rank? Is it one of the most equal or most unequal or somewhere in the middle? And how much inequality is there in the world as a whole when we consider the entire world as a single global economy?

We'll answer these questions by first looking at the income distribution in a selection of countries and then by examining features of the global distribution of income.

Income Distributions in Selected Countries

By inspecting the income distribution data for every country, we can compare the degree of income inequality and identify the countries with the most inequality and those with the least inequality.

Figure 18.7 summarizes some extremes and compares them with the largest economy, the US, that falls between the extremes.

Look first at the numbers in the table. They tell us that in Brazil and South Africa, the poorest 20 per cent of households receive only 2 per cent of total income while the highest 20 per cent receive 65 per cent of total income. An average person in the highest quintile receives 32.5 times the income of an average person in the lowest quintile.

Contrast these numbers with those for Finland and Sweden. In these countries, the poorest 20 per cent receive 8 per cent of total income and the highest 20 per cent receive 35 per cent. So an average person in the highest quintile receives 4.4 times the income of an average person in the lowest quintile.

The numbers for the US lie between these extremes with an average person in the highest quintile receiving just under 10 times the amount received by an average person in the lowest quintile.

Brazil and South Africa are extremes not matched in any other major country or region. Inequality is large in these countries because they have a relatively small but rich European population and a large and relatively poor indigenous population.

Finland and Sweden are extremes, but they are not unusual. Income distributions similar to these are found in many European countries in which governments pursue aggressive income redistribution policies.

We look next at the global income distribution.

Figure 18.7 Lorenz Curves Compared

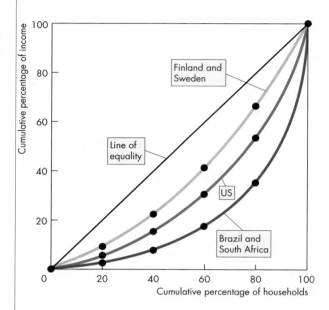

	Percentage of total income		
Households	**Brazil and South Africa**	**US**	**Finland and Sweden**
Lowest 20 per cent	2	5	8
Second 20 per cent	5	10	14
Middle 20 per cent	10	16	20
Next highest 20 per cent	18	22	23
Highest 20 per cent	65	47	35

The table shows the percentages of total income received by each quintile. The figure shows the cumulative percentage of income graphed against the cumulative percentage of households. The data and the Lorenz curves show that income is distributed most unequally in Brazil and South Africa and least unequally in Finland and Sweden. The degree of income inequality in the US lies between these extremes.

Sources of data: Brazil, South Africa, Finland and Sweden: Klaus W. Deininger and Lyn Squire, Measuring Income Inequality Database, World Bank, http://go.worldbank.org/. UK: National Office for Statistics.

 myeconlab Animation

Global Inequality and Its Trends

The global distribution of income is much more unequal than the distribution within any one country. The reason is that many countries, especially in Africa and Asia, are in a pre-industrial stage of economic development and are poor, while industrial countries such as the US and the UK are rich. When we look at the distribution of income across the entire world – from the low income of the poorest African to the high income of the richest European – we see a very large degree of inequality.

To put some raw numbers on this inequality, start with the poorest. Measured in the value of the US dollar in 2005, a total of 3 billion people or 50 per cent of the world population live on $2.50 a day or less. Another 2 billion people or 30 per cent of the world population live on more than $2.50 but less than $10 a day. So 5 billion people or 80 per cent of the world's population live on $10 a day or less.

In contrast, in the rich world of the US, the *average* person has an income of $115 per day and an average person in the highest income quintile has an income of $460 a day. So the average American earns 46 times ($115/$2.50) the income of one of the world's 3 billion poorest people and more than 11.5 times ($115/$10) the income of 80 per cent of the people who live in developing economies. An American with an average income in the highest quintile earns about 180 times that of the world's poorest people but only 15 times that of an average American in the lowest quintile.

World Gini Coefficient

We can compare world inequality with UK inequality by comparing Gini coefficients. The world Gini coefficient is about 64 per cent. The UK Gini coefficient for original income – before government benefits and taxes – was 52.1 per cent in 2009. Recalling the interpretation of the Gini coefficient in terms of the Lorenz curve, the world Lorenz curve lies much farther from the line of equality than the UK Lorenz curve.

World Trend

You saw (in Figure 18.5) that incomes became more unequal in the UK during the 1980s – the Gini coefficient increased. Similar changes are found in most economies. Increased income inequality is a big issue in two of the world's largest and poorer nations, China and India. In these two economies, urban middle classes are getting richer at a faster pace than the rural farmers.

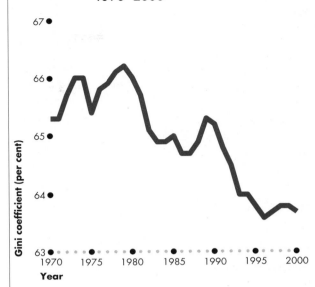

Figure 18.8 The World Gini Coefficient: 1970–2000

Measured by the Gini coefficient, the distribution of income in the entire world became more equal between 1970 and 2000.

Source of data: From 'The World Distribution of Income: Falling Poverty and . . . Convergence, Period' by Xavier Sala-i-Martin, *Quarterly Journal of Economics*, Vol. 121, No. 2, pp. 351–397, May 2006. MIT Press Journals.

myeconlab Animation

Despite greater inequality within countries, the world is becoming less unequal. Figure 18.8 shows the world Gini coefficient over time. How can the world income distribution become less unequal while individual countries become more unequal? The answer is that average incomes in poorer countries are rising much faster than average incomes in rich countries. While the gap between rich and poor is widening within countries, it is narrowing across countries.

Review Quiz

1 In which countries are incomes distributed most unequally and least unequally?
2 Which income distribution is more unequal and why: the income distribution in the US or in the entire world?
3 How can incomes become more unequally distributed within countries and less unequally distributed across countries?

You can work these questions in Study Plan 18.2 and get instant feedback.

The Sources of Economic Inequality

We've described economic inequality in the UK. Our task now is to explain it. We began this task in Chapter 17 by learning about the forces that influence demand and supply in the markets for labour, capital and land. We're now going to deepen our understanding of these forces.

Economic inequality arises from unequal labour market outcomes and from unequal ownership of capital. We'll begin by looking at labour markets and three features of them that contribute to differences in income:

◆ Human capital

◆ Discrimination

◆ Contests among superstars

Human Capital

A clerk in a legal firm earns less than a tenth of the amount earned by the barrister he assists. An operating room nurse earns less than a tenth of the amount earned by the surgeon with whom she works. A bank teller earns less than a tenth of the amount earned by the bank's CEO. Some of the differences in these earnings arise from differences in human capital.

To see the influence of human capital on labour incomes, consider the example of a legal clerk and the barrister he assists. (The same reasoning can be applied to an operating room nurse and surgeon, or a bank teller and bank CEO.)

Demand, Supply and Wage Rates

A barrister performs many tasks that a legal clerk cannot perform. Imagine an untrained legal clerk cross-examining a witness in a complicated trial. The tasks that the barrister performs are valued highly by her clients who willingly pay for her services. Using a term that you learned in Chapter 17, a barrister has a high value of marginal product, and a higher value of marginal product than her legal clerk. But you also learned in Chapter 17 that the value of marginal product of labour determines (is the same as) the demand for labour. So, because a barrister has a high value of marginal product, the demand for her services is also high.

To become a barrister, a person must acquire human capital. But human capital is costly to acquire. This cost – an opportunity cost – includes expenditures on tuition and textbooks. It also includes forgone earnings during the years spent in university and law school. It might also include low earnings doing on-the-job training in a law office during the summer.

Because the human capital needed to supply barrister services is costly to acquire, a person's willingness to supply these services reflects this cost. The supply of barrister services is smaller than the supply of legal-clerk services.

The demand for and supply of each type of labour determine the wage rate that each type of labour earns. Barristers earn a higher wage rate than legal clerks because the demand for barristers is greater and the supply of barristers is smaller. The gap between the wage rates reflects the higher value of marginal product of a barrister (demand) and the cost of acquiring human capital (supply).

Do Education and Training Pay?

You know that a barrister earns much more than a legal clerk, but does human capital add more to earning power generally and on average? The answer is that it does. Rates of return on university education have been estimated to be 35 per cent for women and 17.5 per cent for men, which suggests that a university degree is a better investment than almost any other that a person can undertake.

Human capital differences help to explain much of the inequality that we observe. High-income households tend to be better educated, professional, middle-aged couples (see Figure 18.6). Human capital differences are correlated with these household characteristics. Education contributes directly to human capital. Age contributes indirectly to human capital because older workers have more experience than younger workers. Human capital differences can also explain a small part of the inequality associated with sex and race. A larger proportion of men than women have a university degree and also a larger proportion of whites than blacks have a bachelor degree or higher. These differences in education levels among the sexes and the races are becoming smaller, but they have not been eliminated.

Career interruptions can decrease human capital. A person (most often a woman) who interrupts a career to raise young children usually returns to the labour force with a lower earning capacity than a similar person who has kept working. Likewise, a person who has suffered a spell of unemployment often finds a new job at a lower wage rate than that of a similar person who has not been unemployed.

Trends in Inequality Explained by Technological Change and Globalization

You've seen that high income households have earned an increasing share of total income while low-income households have earned a decreasing share: the distribution of income in the UK has become more unequal. Technological change and globalization are two possible sources of this increased inequality.

Technological Change

Information technologies such as computers and laser scanners are *substitutes* for low-skilled labour: they perform tasks that previously were performed by low-skilled labour. The introduction of these technologies has lowered the marginal product and the demand for low-skilled labour. These same technologies require high-skilled labour to design, program and run them. High-skilled labour and the information technologies are *complements*. So the introduction of these technologies has increased the marginal product, increased the value of marginal product of labour and increased the demand for high-skilled labour.

Figure 18.9 illustrates the effects on wages and employment. The supply curve of low-skilled labour in part (a) and that of high-skilled labour in part (b) are S, and initially, the demand curve in each market is D_0. The low-skill wage rate is £5 an hour, and the high-skill wage rate is £10 an hour. The demand for low-skilled labour decreases to D_1 in part (a) and the demand for high-skilled labour increases to D_1 in part (b). The low-skill wage rate falls to £4 an hour and the high-skill wage rate rises to £15 an hour.

Globalization

The entry of China and other developing countries into the global economy has lowered the prices of many manufactured goods. Lower prices for the firm's output lowers the value of marginal product of the firm's workers and decreases the demand for their labour. A situation like that in Figure 18.9(a) occurs. The wage rate falls and employment shrinks.

At the same time, the growing global economy increases the demand for services that employ high-skilled workers, and the value of marginal product and the demand for high-skilled labour increases. A situation like that in Figure 18.9(b) occurs. The wage rate rises, and employment opportunities for high-skilled workers expand.

Figure 18.9 Explaining the Trend in Income Distribution

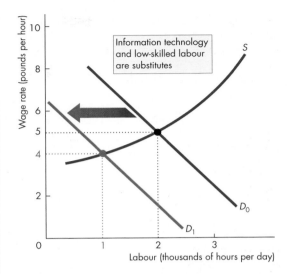

(a) A decrease in demand for low-skilled labour

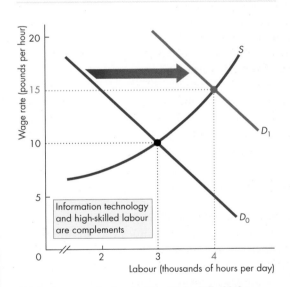

(b) An increase in demand for high-skilled labour

Low-skilled labour in part (a) and information technologies are substitutes. When these technologies were introduced, the demand for low-skilled labour decreased and the quantity of this type of labour employed and its wage rate decreased. High-skilled labour in part (b) and information technologies are complements. When these technologies were introduced, the demand for high-skilled labour increased and the quantity of this type of labour employed and its wage rate increased.

myeconlab Animation

Discrimination

Human capital differences can explain some of the economic inequality that we observe. But it can't explain all of it. Discrimination is another possible source of inequality.

An Example of Discrimination

Suppose that women and men have identical abilities as investment advisers. Figure 18.10 shows the supply curves of women, S_W in part (a), and of men, S_M in part (b). The value of marginal product of investment advisers shown by the two curves labelled *VMP* is the same for both groups.

If everyone is free of sex prejudice, the market determines a wage rate of £40,000 a year for investment advisers. But if the customers are prejudiced against women, this prejudice is reflected in the wage rate and employment. Suppose that the perceived value of marginal product of the women, when discriminated against, is VMP_{DA}. Suppose that the perceived value of marginal product of men, the group discriminated in favour of, is VMP_{DF}. With these *VMP* curves, women earn £20,000 a year and only 1,000 women work as investment advisers. Men earn £60,000 a year, and 3,000 of them work as investment advisers.

Counteracting Forces

Economists disagree about whether prejudice actually causes wage differentials and one line of reasoning implies that it does not. In the example you've just studied, customers who buy from men pay a higher service charge for investment advice than do the customers who buy from women. This price difference acts as an incentive to encourage people who are prejudiced to buy from the people against whom they are prejudiced.

This force could be strong enough to eliminate the effects of discrimination altogether. Suppose, as is true in manufacturing, that a firm's customers never meet its workers. If such a firm discriminates against women, it can't compete with firms that hire women because its costs are higher than those of the non-prejudiced firms. Only firms that do not discriminate survive in a competitive industry.

Whether because of discrimination or from some other source, women do earn lower incomes than men. Another possible source of lower wage rates of women arises from differences in the relative degree of specialization of women and men.

Figure 18.10 Discrimination

(a) Females

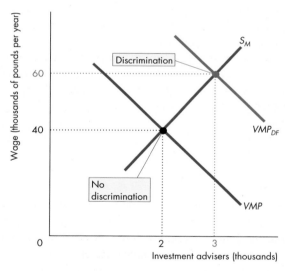

(b) Males

With no discrimination, the wage rate is £40,000 a year and 2,000 of each group are employed. With discrimination against women, the value of marginal product curve in part (a) is VMP_{DA}.

With discrimination in favour of men, the value of marginal product curve in part (b) is VMP_{DF}. The wage rate for women falls to £20,000 a year, and only 1,000 are employed. The wage rate for men rises to £60,000 a year, and 3,000 are employed.

 Animation

Differences in the Degree of Specialization

Couples must choose how to allocate their time between working for a wage and doing jobs in the home, such as cooking, cleaning, shopping, organizing holidays and, most important, bearing and rearing children. Let's look at the choices of Bob and Sue.

Bob might specialize in earning an income and Sue in taking care of the home. Or Sue might specialize in earning an income and Bob in taking care of the home. Or both of them might earn an income and share home production jobs.

The allocation they choose depends on their preferences and on the earning potential of each of them. The choice of an increasing number of households is for each person to diversify between earning an income and doing some home chores. But in most households, Bob will specialize in earning an income and Sue will both earn an income and bear a larger share of the task of running the home. With this allocation, Bob will probably earn more than Sue. If Sue devotes time and effort to ensuring Bob's mental and physical well-being, the quality of Bob's market labour will be higher than it would be if he were diversified. If the roles were reversed, Sue would be able to supply market labour that earns more than Bob.

To test whether the degree of specialization accounts for earnings differences between the sexes, economists have compared the incomes of never-married men and women. They have found that, on average, with equal amounts of human capital, the wages of these two groups are the same.

Contests Among Superstars

The differences in income that arise from differences in human capital affect a large proportion of the population, but human capital differences can't account for some of the really large income differences.

The super rich – those in the top one per cent of the income distribution whose income share has been rising – earn vastly more than can be explained by human capital differences. What makes a person super rich?

A clue to the answer is provided by thinking about the super rich in tennis and golf. What makes tennis players and golfers special is that their earnings depend on where they finish in a tournament. When Serena Williams won the Wimbledon Championship in 2010, she received £1,000,000. The runner-up in this event, Russian Vera Zvonareva, received £500,000. So Serena earned double the amount earned by Vera. And she earned 88 times the amount received by the players who lost in the first round of the tournament.

It is true that Serena Williams has a lot of human capital. She practises hard and long and is a remarkable athlete. But anyone who is good enough to get into a tennis Grand Slam tournament is similarly well equipped with human capital and has spent a similar number of long hours in training and practice. It isn't human capital that explains the differences in earnings. It is the tournament and the prize differences that accounts for the large differences in earnings.

But three questions jump out. First, why do we reward superstar tennis players (and golfers) with prizes for winning a contest? Second, why are the prizes so different? And third, do the principles that apply on the tennis court (and golf course) apply more generally?

Why Prizes for a Contest?

The answer to this question (which was noted in Chapter 5, see p. 106) is that contests with prizes do a good job of allocating scarce resources efficiently when the efforts of the participants are hard to monitor and reward directly. There is only one winner, but many people work hard in an attempt to be that person. So a great deal of diligent effort is induced by a contest.

Why Are Prizes So Different?

The prizes need to be substantially different to induce enough effort. If the winner received 10 per cent more than the runner up, the gain from being the winner would be insufficient to encourage anyone to work hard enough. Someone would win but no one would put in much effort. Tennis matches would be boring, golf scores would be high, and no one would be willing to pay to see these sports. Big differences are necessary to induce a big enough effort to generate the quality of performance that people are willing to pay to see.

Does the Principle Apply More Generally?

Winner-takes-all isn't confined to tennis and golf. Film stars, football superstars and top corporate executives can all be viewed as participants in contests that decide the winners. The winner's prize is an income at least double that of the runner up and many multiples of the incomes of those who drop out earlier in the tournament.

Do Contests Among Superstars Explain the Trend?

Contests among superstars can explain large differences in incomes. But can contests explain the trend toward greater inequality with an increasing share of total income going to the super rich?

An idea first suggested by University of Chicago economist Sherwin Rosen suggests that a winner-takes-all contest can explain the trend. The key is that globalization has increased the market reach of the winner and increased the spread between the winner and the runners-up.

Global television audiences now watch all the world's major sporting events and the total revenue generated by advertising spots during these events has increased. Competition among terrestrial and cable and satellite television distributors has increased the fees that event organizers receive. To attract the top star performers, prize money has increased and the winner gets the biggest share of the prize pot.

So the prizes in sports have become bigger and the share of income going to the 'winner' has increased.

A similar story can be told about superstars and the super rich in business. As the cost of doing business on a global scale has fallen, more and more businesses have become global in their reach. Not only are large multi-national corporations sourcing their inputs from far afield and selling in every country, they are also recruiting their top executives from a global talent pool. With a larger source of talent, and greater total revenue, firms must make the 'prize' – the reward for the top job – more attractive to compete for the best managers.

We've examined some sources of inequality in the labour market. Let's now look at the way inequality arises from unequal ownership of capital.

Unequal Wealth

You've seen that inequality in wealth (excluding human capital) is much greater than inequality in income. This inequality arises from saving and transfers of wealth from one generation to the next.

The higher a household's income, the more that household tends to save and pass on to the next generation. Saving is not always a source of increased inequality. If a household's saving redistributes an uneven income over the household's life, consumption will fluctuate less than its income and saving decreases inequality. If a lucky generation that has a high income saves a large part of that income and leaves capital to a

succeeding generation that is unlucky, this act of saving also decreases the degree of inequality. But two features of intergenerational transfers of wealth lead to increased inequality: people can't inherit debts, and marriage tends to concentrate wealth.

Intergenerational Transfers

Some households inherit wealth from the previous generation. Some save more than enough on which to live during retirement and transfer wealth to the next generation. But these intergenerational transfers of wealth do not always increase wealth inequality. If a generation that has a high income saves a large part of that income and leaves wealth to a succeeding generation that has a lower income, this transfer decreases the degree of inequality. But one feature of intergenerational transfers of wealth leads to increased inequality: wealth concentration through marriage.

Marriage and Wealth Concentration

People tend to marry within their own socioeconomic class – a phenomenon called *assortative mating*. In everyday language, 'like attracts like'. Although there is a good deal of folklore that 'opposites attract', perhaps such Cinderella tales appeal to us because they are so rare in reality. Wealthy people seek wealthy partners.

Because of assortative mating, wealth becomes more concentrated in a small number of families and the distribution of wealth becomes more unequal.

Review Quiz

1. What role does human capital play in accounting for income inequality?
2. What role might discrimination play in accounting for income inequality?
3. What role might contests among superstars play in accounting for income inequality?
4. How might technological change and globalization explain trends in the distribution of income?
5. Does inherited wealth make the distribution of income less equal or more equal?

You can work these questions in Study Plan 18.3 and get instant feedback.

Next we're going to see how taxes and government policies redistribute income and wealth and decrease the degree of economic inequality.

Income Redistribution

Governments use three main types of policies to redistribute income. They are:

◆ Income taxes
◆ Benefit payments
◆ Subsidized welfare services

Income Taxes

Income taxes may be progressive, regressive or proportional. A **progressive income tax** is one that taxes income at an average rate that increases as income increases. A **regressive income tax** is one that taxes income at an average rate that decreases as income increases. A **proportional income tax** (also called a *flat-rate income tax*) is one that taxes income at a constant average rate regardless of the level of income.

Income taxes are progressive in all EU member states. For example, in 2009–2010 in the UK, people who earned £6,475 a year or less paid no income tax. A tax of 20 per cent was paid on the first £37,400 above £6,475. Any income above this amount was taxed at 40 per cent. From 2010/11, an additional tax band of 50 per cent will be imposed on incomes over £150,000.

Benefit Payments

Benefit payments redistribute income by making direct payments to people with low incomes. In 2008/09, the UK government paid £152 billion in benefit payments. The main types of benefit payments are:

◆ Income support payments
◆ Tax credits
◆ State pensions

Income Support Payments

Governments use a wide range of payments to raise household incomes and reduce poverty, including income support, unemployment and incapacity payments and child benefit. For example, in the UK, the Job Seekers' Allowance is paid for a limited period to individuals who have lost their jobs involuntarily and have no other main source of income. This allowance was £65.45 a week for people over 25 years of age in 2009/10 compared to the incapacity benefit which was £91.40 a week.

Tax Credits

Tax credits are a method of helping low-income employed households. A tax credit increases a household's disposable income by reducing their tax bill. In 2009/10, the Working Tax Credit for a single person caring for one child was a maximum of £175 a week. An additional child tax credit was also available to couples who have joint incomes of up to £60,000.

State Pensions

State pensions for the elderly are the main component of government benefit payments in all EU member states. These pensions are paid out of current taxes, so they result in redistribution from people currently working to those retired. In the UK in 2009/10, more than 7 million people received a state pension of up to £132.60 a week for a single person (more for a couple).

Subsidized Welfare Services

A great deal of redistribution takes place in most European countries through the subsidized provision of welfare goods and services. These are the goods and services provided by the government at prices below marginal cost. Taxpayers who consume these goods and services receive a transfer in kind from taxpayers who do not consume them. The two main areas in which this form of redistribution takes place are education – from nursery care through to university – and healthcare.

In the UK, 50 per cent of government expenditure is on benefits in kind: 24 per cent on the National Health Service, 21 per cent on education and the remainder on other services. The National Health Service provides almost all healthcare services free at the point of demand. Primary and secondary education is provided free for all children in the UK.

In the EU, the extent and method of subsidizing education and healthcare services varies greatly across member states. For example, in some countries healthcare is free at the point of demand, and in other countries healthcare is privately provided and the government reimburses patients' costs. In some countries, people are required to pay into compulsory health insurance systems.

Whatever the method, subsidized provision of services improves access to good-quality healthcare and education and reduces inequality in health status and basic human capital.

> ## ECONOMICS IN ACTION

Redistribution in the EU

EU governments use both progressive income taxes and benefit payments to redistribute income.

The role of income tax varies a great deal. Income taxes constitute just 14 per cent of all tax revenue in the UK and Ireland, 19 per cent in Spain and Portugal, 25 per cent in Finland and the Netherlands and more than 30 per cent in Sweden and Denmark.

Benefit payments also vary. Figure 1 compares EU member state spending on benefit payments as a percentage of total income in 2006.

EU benefit spending as a percentage of income is much higher in the rich northern countries than in the poorer southern countries and the new member states from central Europe. EU poverty rates shown in *Economics in Action* on p. 419 are affected by the level of benefits and the level of taxes.

Figure 2 shows the combined impact of taxes and benefits in the UK in 2009 for the five quintile income groups, from lowest fifth to highest fifth.

On average, the fifth with the lowest incomes received £6,431 in cash benefits each year, whereas the fifth with the highest incomes received only £1,805. (The group with the highest incomes receives benefits because some benefits, such as pensions, are universally available.) The effect of cash benefits and tax credits is limited because many who are entitled to benefits fail to claim them.

Benefits in kind – mainly health benefits provided by the National Health Service and free or heavily subsidized education – are strongly progressive and represent 50 per cent of post-tax income for the fifth with the lowest incomes but only 6 per cent for the fifth with the highest incomes.

Income taxes have a strong effect on the distribution of income. The fifth with the highest incomes pay £18,255 in income taxes each year and the fifth with the lowest incomes pay £1,270 each year.

Expenditure taxes such as VAT have a smaller effect because the groups with low incomes spend a larger percentage of income on goods and services.

Overall, the net impact of UK taxes and benefits is a redistribution of income from the 40 per cent of households with the highest incomes to the 40 per cent with the lowest incomes, with a small net gain to the middle 20 per cent of households.

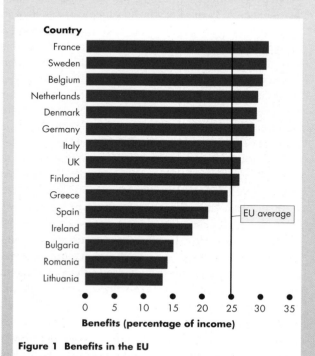

Figure 1 Benefits in the EU

Source of data: Eurostat Yearbook 2010, Table 6.3.

Figure 2 The Effects of Benefits and Taxes on the Distribution of Income

Source of data: Office for National Statistics, *Social Trends*, 2010.

The Big Trade-off

All income redistribution creates what has been called the **big trade-off**, a trade-off between equity and efficiency – see Chapter 5, p. 117. To achieve greater equity, we redistribute from the rich to the poor by imposing taxes on the rich and paying benefits to the poor. The big trade-off arises because redistribution uses scarce resources and weakens incentives. Both taxes and benefits bring inefficiency, which is the cost that must be borne to achieve greater equity.

Inefficient Taxes

Taxes are inefficient because they drive a wedge between marginal social cost and marginal social benefit and create deadweight loss. (Pigovian taxes that correct an externality are an exception – see Chapter 16, p. 372.) When a 40 per cent income tax is imposed on a high-income person, the marginal product of that person is 40 per cent greater than the marginal cost to that person of working. A potentially large deadweight loss arises. The taxes on the rich reduce their incentive to work and save. And the weaker incentive to save spills over to the poor because it means less capital is accumulated and fewer jobs are created.

Inefficient Benefits

Benefits for the poor are also inefficient. They lower the incentive of low-skilled people to work. More seriously, benefits lower the incentive to acquire human capital and move into a higher income group.

The inefficiencies arising from taxes and benefits result in less output and consumption for everybody – rich and poor. The disincentive effect of the benefits system is so severe that it gives rise to what is called a *benefit trap*.

The Benefit Trap

A *benefit trap* arises if a person who receives benefits takes a job or works longer hours and the loss of benefits exceeds the income earned. If a person loses £1 of benefit for every extra £1 earned – a *withdrawal rate* of 100 per cent – there is no gain from working. The person in effect faces a tax rate of 100 per cent!

There are two main types of benefit trap – the unemployment trap and the poverty trap. In the unemployment trap, people make decisions based on the expected wage they might earn compared to the benefit payments they will lose if they take a job. If the expected wage is only slightly higher than the unemployment benefit, the rational choice is to remain unemployed.

In the poverty trap, people are in low-paid work but are receiving benefit payments. They may want to work longer hours to earn an extra £10, but they may pay tax on the extra £10 and lose up to £10 of benefit payments. Again, the rational choice is not to work more hours.

Benefit Reform

In 2010, the UK government announced a radical simplification of the welfare benefit system with changes aimed at reducing poverty and unemployment traps. The government will merge five of the main income support benefits into one universal credit in 2013 and withdraw the benefits more slowly for part-time workers who earn more. Under the current system, some people in part-time work keep just 4 pence of every extra pound they earn as benefits are withdrawn and extra tax is paid. Under the new system, taxpayers will keep 24 pence of every extra pound earned and non-taxpayers will keep 35 pence.

The changes to the UK benefit system are not cost free. They will cost £2 billion before 2013 which must come from higher taxes on the rich. The inefficiency created by redistribution in a tax and benefit system results in less output and consumption for everybody – rich and poor – but this must be weighed against increased equality.

Review Quiz

1. How do EU governments redistribute income?
2. Describe the scale of redistribution in the UK.
3. What is the benefit trap and how does the UK government plan to tackle it?

You can work these questions in Study Plan 18.4 and get instant feedback.

We've examined economic inequality in the UK, and we've seen how inequality arises. We've also seen that inequality increased during the 1980s. *Reading Between the Lines* on pp. 430–431 looks at the stubborn persistence of the inequality of wealth in the UK.

The next chapter studies some problems for the market economy that arise from uncertainty and incomplete information. But unlike the cases we studied in Chapters 15 and 16, the market does a good job of coping with the problems.

Reading Between the Lines

Wealth: Rising Inequality in the UK

The Guardian, 27 January 2010

Unequal Britain: Richest 10% are now 100 times Better off than the Poorest

Amelia Gentelman and Helene Mulholland

A detailed and startling analysis of how unequal Britain has become offers a snapshot of an increasingly divided nation. . . . The report, *An Anatomy of Economic Inequality in the UK*, scrutinises the degree to which the country has become more unequal over the past 30 years. . . .

The household wealth of the top 10% of the population stands at £853,000 and more – over 100 times higher than the wealth of the poorest 10%, which is £8,800 or below. . . . When the highest-paid workers, such as bankers and chief executives, are put into the equation, the division in wealth is even more stark, with individuals in the top 1% of

the population each possessing total household wealth of £2.6m or more.

It concludes that the government has failed to plug the gulf that existed between the poorest and richest in society in the 1980s. . . .

These inequalities accumulate over the life cycle, the report concludes. . . . Researchers analysed the total wealth accrued by households over a lifetime. The top 10%, led by higher professionals, had amassed wealth of £2.2m, including property and pension assets, by the time they drew close to retirement (aged 55–64), while the bottom 10% of households, led by routine manual workers, had amassed less than £8,000.

The Essence of the Story

- A recent UK report shows the richest 10 per cent of the population have 100 times the wealth of the poorest 10 per cent.

- Inequality of wealth has increased since the 1980s.

- Government has failed to lessen the degree of wealth inequality.

- The richest 10 per cent are professional workers who acquire £2.2 million of wealth at retirement age compared to the poorest 10 per cent who are routine workers with only £8,800 at retirement.

Economic Analysis

◆ The news article reports data on the UK distribution of wealth and implies that wealth is too unequally distributed and government has failed to lessen this inequality.

◆ The wealth data used in the survey are *private wealth*, not *total wealth*: they ignore wealth arising from government redistribution.

◆ The survey accurately reports that the private wealth of the richest 10 per cent is 100 times that of the poorest 10 per cent.

◆ Also, private wealth has become more unequal as Figure 1 shows. The Gini coefficient for wealth increased during the 1990s.

◆ An increase in the Gini coefficient means that the distribution of wealth has become more unequal. The Lorenz curve for wealth has shifted further away from the line of equality.

◆ Figure 2 provides some details on who is wealthy and who is poor.

◆ The figure shows the median wealth for people in different job types in 2006–2008 by the time they reach retirement age.

◆ The median level of wealth for higher managerial and professional workers at retirement age was over £900,000. Some of these workers are among the richest 10 per cent who have amassed over £2.2 million of wealth by retirement.

◆ By comparison, routine and semi-routine workers typically amass around £200,000 by retirement.

◆ The report suggests that government redistribution policies, mostly aimed at redistributing income, have failed to stop the inequality of wealth rising.

◆ In fact, the report ignores the effect of government actions on wealth distribution.

◆ UK residents, poor and rich, are entitled to receive a state pension. At current levels of state pension and life expectancy, the state pension translates into wealth at age 65 of

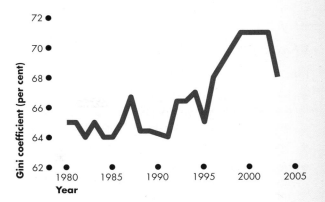

Figure 1 Gini coefficient for wealth

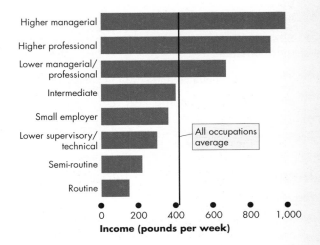

Figure 2 Distribution of wealth age 55 to 64

£86,000. (That number is the present value of the 2011 pension rate over the expected retirement years.)

◆ Adding £86,000 to the averages in the news article, the richest 10 per cent have wealth of £939,000 and the poorest 10 per cent have £94,800 at retirement.

◆ After taking government actions into account, the richest 10 per cent are 10 times, not 100 times, wealthier than the poorest 10 per cent.

SUMMARY

Key Points

Economic Inequality in the UK
(pp. 414–419)

◆ In 2008, the mode disposable income was £275 a week, the median disposable income was £393, and the mean disposable income was £487.

◆ The income distribution is positively skewed.

◆ In 2009, the 20 per cent of households with the lowest incomes received 7 per cent of total income and the 20 per cent with the highest incomes received 43 per cent of total income.

◆ Wealth is distributed more unequally than income because the wealth data exclude the value of human capital.

◆ Since 1983, the distribution of income has become more unequal.

◆ Occupation, economic status, type and region of household, age of householder and tenure all affect household income.

Working Problems 1 to 7 will give you a better understanding of economic inequality in the UK.

Inequality in the World Economy
(pp. 420–421)

◆ Incomes are distributed most unequally in Brazil and South Africa and least unequally in Finland, Sweden, and some other European economies.

◆ The US income distribution lies between the extremes.

◆ The distribution of income across individuals in the global economy is more unequal than in the US.

◆ The global income distribution has been getting less unequal as rapid income growth in China and India has lifted millions from poverty.

Working Problems 8 to 11 will give you a better understanding of inequality in the world.

The Sources of Economic Inequality
(pp. 422–426)

◆ Inequality arises from differences in human capital and from contests among superstars.

◆ Trends in the distribution of human capital and the rewards to superstars that arise from technological change and globalization can explain some of the increased trend in inequality.

◆ Inequality might arise from discrimination.

◆ Inequality between men and women might arise from differences in the degree of specialization.

◆ Intergenerational transfers of wealth lead to increased inequality because people can't inherit debts and assortative mating tends to concentrate wealth.

Working Problems 12 to 15 will give you a better understanding of the sources of economic inequality.

Income Redistribution (pp. 427–429)

◆ Governments redistribute income through progressive income taxes and the payment of cash benefits and benefits in kind.

◆ Redistribution in the UK transfers income from the richest 40 per cent of households to the poorest 40 per cent and has little effect on the middle 20 per cent.

◆ Because the redistribution of income weakens incentives, it creates a trade-off between equity and efficiency.

◆ Major UK benefit reform aims to lessen the severity of the benefit trap.

Working Problems 16 and 17 will give you a better understanding of income redistribution.

Key Terms

Big trade-off, 429
Disposable income, 414
Gini coefficient, 417
Lorenz curve, 415
Original income, 414
Poverty, 418
Progressive income tax, 427
Proportional income tax, 427
Regressive income tax, 427
Wealth, 416

STUDY PLAN PROBLEMS AND APPLICATIONS

 You can work Problems 1 to 17 in MyEconLab Chapter 18 Study Plan and get instant feedback.

Economic Inequality in the UK
(Study Plan 18.1)

1 What is disposable income? Describe the distribution of disposable income in the UK in 2008.

2 The table shows shares of US income in 1967 and 2007.

	Gross income	
	1967	2007
Households	(percentage of total)	
Lowest 20 per cent	4.0	3.4
Second 20 per cent	10.8	8.6
Middle 20 per cent	17.3	14.6
Next highest 20 per cent	24.2	23.2
Highest 20 per cent	43.7	50.2

 a Draw the US Lorenz curve for the gross income in 1967 and compare it with the Lorenz curve in 2007.

 b Was US gross income distributed more equally or less equally in 2007 than it was in 1967?

Use the following news clip for Problems 3 to 6.

Only Work Ends Poverty

According to Jim Murphy, the employment and welfare minister, work is the only route out of poverty. The welfare state will never pay enough in benefits to lift people out of poverty. His remarks were greeted with consternation by anti-poverty campaigners. 'The more successful they are in getting people off benefit and into work, the more important it is that those who are left behind, and who cannot work, still have a decent standard of living.'

Source: FT.com, 26 March 2007

3 How is poverty measured? Explain the difference between a relative measure of poverty based on income and an absolute level of poverty.

4 What does the minister mean when he says that the welfare state will never pay enough in benefits to lift people out of poverty?

5 Why are the anti-poverty campaigners aghast? Explain your answer.

6 How will the minister's suggestion help those who cannot work to have a decent standard of living?

7 **Census: Income Fell Sharply Last Year**

The US Census Bureau reported that in 2008 the median household income fell 3.6%. The share of people living in poverty rose to 13.2% in 2008 from 12.5% in 2007. Only households led by people aged 65 or older enjoyed income gains – a 1.2% increase.

Source: *USA Today*, 11 September 2009

 a What does the information in this news report tell you about changes in the distribution of US income in 2008?

 b What additional information would you need to describe how the US Lorenz curve changed?

Inequality in the World Economy
(Study Plan 18.2)

8 Incomes in China and India are a small fraction of incomes in the US. But incomes in China and India are growing at more than twice the rate of those in the US.

 a Explain how economic inequality in China and India is changing relative to that in the US.

 b How is the world Lorenz curve and world Gini coefficient changing?

Use the following table for Problems 9 to 11.

The table shows shares of disposable income in Canada and the UK.

	Canadian income	UK income
Households	(percentage of total)	
Lowest 20 per cent	5	7
Second 20 per cent	11	11
Middle 20 per cent	16	15
Next highest 20 per cent	24	19
Highest 20 per cent	44	48

9 Create a table that shows the cumulative distribution of Canadian and UK incomes. Is the distribution of income more unequal in Canada or in the UK?

10 Draw a Lorenz curve for Canada and compare it with the Lorenz curve for the US in 2007. (Use the US data in Problem 2.) In which country is income less equally distributed?

11 Draw a Lorenz curve for the UK and compare it with the Lorenz curve for the US in 2007. (Use the US data in Problem 2.) In which country is income less equally distributed?

The Sources of Economic Inequality
(Study Plan 18.3)

12 The following figure shows the market for low-skilled labour in Europe.

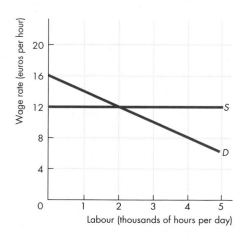

The value of marginal product of high-skilled workers is €16 an hour greater than that of low-skilled workers at each quantity of labour. The cost of acquiring human capital adds €12 an hour to the wage that must be offered to attract high-skilled labour.

Compare the equilibrium wage rates of low-skilled labour and high-skilled labour. Explain why the difference between these wage rates equals the cost of acquiring human capital.

Use the following information to work Problems 13 and 14.

In 2000, 30 million Americans had full-time professional jobs that paid about $800 a week while 10 million Americans had full-time sales jobs that paid about $530 a week.

13 Explain why US professionals are paid more than salespeople and why, despite the higher weekly wage, more people are employed as professionals than as salespeople.

14 If the online shopping trend continues, how do you think the market for salespeople will change in coming years?

15 The figure shows the European market for a group of workers who are discriminated against. Suppose that other workers in the same industry are not discriminated against and their value of marginal product is perceived to be twice that of the workers who are discriminated against. Suppose also that the supply of these other workers is 2,000 hours per day less at each wage rate.

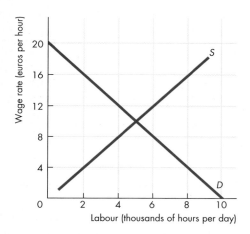

a What is the wage rate of the workers who are discriminated against?

b What is the quantity of workers employed who are discriminated against?

c What is the wage rate of the workers who do not face discrimination?

d What is the quantity of workers employed who do not face discrimination?

Income Redistribution (Study Plan 18.4)

Use the following table for Problems 16 and 17.

The table shows three European redistribution schemes.

Before-tax income (euros)	Plan A tax (euros)	Plan B tax (euros)	Plan C tax (euros)
10,000	1,000	1,000	2,000
20,000	2,000	4,000	2,000
30,000	3,000	9,000	2,000

16 Which scheme has a proportional tax? Which scheme has a regressive tax? Which scheme has a progressive tax?

17 Which scheme will increase economic inequality? Which scheme will reduce economic inequality? Which scheme will have no effect on economic inequality?

ADDITIONAL PROBLEMS AND APPLICATIONS

myeconlab You can work these problems in MyEconLab if assigned by your lecturer.

Economic Inequality in the UK

Use the following table to work Problems 18 and 19.

The table shows distribution of US original income in 2007.

Households	Original income (percentage of total)
Lowest 20 per cent	1.1
Second 20 per cent	7.1
Middle 20 per cent	13.9
Next highest 20 per cent	22.8
Highest 20 per cent	55.1

18 **a** What is the definition of original income?

    b Draw the Lorenz curve for the distribution of original income.

19 Compare the distribution of original income in 2007 with the distribution of gross income in 2007 shown in Problem 2. Which distribution is more unequal and why?

Inequality in the World Economy

Use the following table to work Problems 20 to 22.

The table shows shares of income in Australia.

Households	Income share (percentage of total)
Lowest 20 per cent	7
Second 20 per cent	13
Middle 20 per cent	18
Next highest 20 per cent	25
Highest 20 per cent	37

20 Draw the Lorenz curve for the income distribution in Australia and in Brazil and South Africa (use the data in Figure 18.7 on p. 420). Is income distributed more equally or less equally in Brazil and South Africa than in Australia?

21 Is the Gini coefficient for Australia larger or smaller than that for Brazil and South Africa? Explain your answer.

22 What are some reasons for the differences in the distribution of income in Australia and in Brazil and South Africa?

The Sources of Economic Inequality

Use the following news clip to work Problems 23 to 26.

Bernanke Links Education and Equality

Ben Bernanke, the chairman of the US central bank, said that increased education opportunities would help reduce the increased economic inequality that has occurred over the last 30 years. He also said that globalization and the advent of new technologies, the two main causes of income inequality, will lead to economic growth, but inhibiting them will do far more harm than good in the long run. Instead, Bernanke said that the best method to improve economic opportunities is to focus on raising the level of and access to education. Workers will become more skilful, and firms will undertake more innovation. It is time to recognize that education should be lifelong and can come in many forms: early childhood education, community colleges, vocational schools, on-the-job training, online courses, adult education. With increased skills, lifetime earning power will increase.

Source: *International Herald Tribune*, 5 June 2008

23 Explain how the two main causes of increased income inequality in the US identified by Mr Bernanke work.

24 Draw a graph to illustrate how the two main causes of increased income inequality generate this outcome.

25 What are the short-term costs and long-term benefits associated with these two causes of inequality?

26 Explain Bernanke's solutions to help address growing income inequality.

27 **Where Women's Pay Trumps Men's**

Men work more than women on the job, at least in terms of overall hours. That's just one reason why in most fields, men's earnings exceed women's earnings. But Warren Farrell found 39 occupations in which women's median earnings exceeded men's earnings by at least 5 per cent and in some cases by as much as 43 per cent. In fields like engineering, a company may get one woman and seven men applying for a job. If the company wants to hire the woman, it might have to pay a premium to get her. Also, where women can combine technical expertise with people skills – such as those required in sales and where customers prefer dealing with a woman – that's likely to contribute to a premium in pay.

Source: CNN, 2 March 2006

a Draw a graph to illustrate why discrimination could result in female workers getting paid more than male workers for some jobs.

b Explain how market competition could potentially eliminate this wage differential.

c If customers 'prefer dealing with a woman' in some markets, how might that lead to a persistent wage differential between men and women?

Income Redistribution

28 Use the information provided in Figure 18.2 on p. 415 and the following table.

Households (percentage)	Original income (percentage of total income)
Lowest 20	4
Second 20	8
Middle 20	14
Next highest 20	22
Highest 20	52

a What is the percentage of total income that is redistributed from the highest income group?

b What percentages of total income are redistributed to the lower income groups?

29 Describe the effects of increasing the amount of income redistribution in the UK to the point at which the lowest income group receives 15 per cent of total income and the highest income group receives 30 per cent of total income.

Use the following news clip to work Problems 30 and 31.

The Tax Debate Americans Should be Having

A shrinking number of Americans are bearing an even bigger share of the nation's income tax burden. In 2005, the bottom 40 per cent of Americans by income had, in the aggregate, an effective tax rate that's negative: Their households received more money through the income tax system, largely from the earned income tax credit, than they paid. The top 50% of taxpayers pay 97% of total income tax and the top 10% of taxpayers pay 70%. The top 1% paid almost 40% of all income tax, a proportion that has jumped dramatically since 1986. Given the US tax system, any tax cut must benefit the rich, but in terms of the change in effective tax rates: the bottom 50% got a much bigger tax cut under the Bush tax cut than the top 1%. Did the dollar value of Bush's tax cuts go mostly to the wealthy? Absolutely.

Source: *Fortune*, 14 April 2008

30 Explain why tax cuts in a progressive income tax system are consistently criticized for favouring the wealthy.

31 How might the benefits of tax cuts 'trickle down' to others whose taxes are not cut?

Economics in the News

32 After you have studied *Reading Between the Lines* on pp. 430–431 answer the following questions.

a What are the broad facts reported in the news article about the inequality of wealth in the UK?

b What types of jobs do the richest and the poorest people in the UK do?

c What is the distinction between private wealth and total wealth?

d Can you think of other respects in which the survey reported in the news article omits the effects of UK government actions on economic inequality?

33 **The Best and Worst Degrees by Salary**

Business is always a strong contender for honours degrees at the most popular universities. This is no surprise since students think business is the way to make big salaries. But is business really as lucrative as students and their parents believe? No. In a new survey by PayScale, Inc. of salaries by degree type, business didn't even break into the list of the top 10 or 20 most lucrative degrees. A variety of engineering degrees claim eight of the top 10 salary spots with chemical engineering ($65,700) winning best for starting salaries. Out of 75 undergraduate degrees, business ($42,900) came in 35th, behind such degrees as occupational therapy ($61,300), information technology ($49,400), and economics ($48,800).

Source: moneywatch.com, 21 July 2009

a Why do university graduates with different degrees have drastically different starting salaries?

b Draw a graph of the labour markets for economics degrees and business degrees to illustrate your explanation of the differences in the starting salaries of these two groups.

Uncertainty and Information

After studying this chapter you will be able to:

◆ Explain how people make decisions when they are uncertain about the consequences

◆ Explain how markets enable people to buy and sell risk

◆ Explain how markets cope with private information

◆ Explain how uncertainty and incomplete information influences efficiency

Life is like a lottery. You work hard at university but what will the payoff be? Will you get a good job or a miserable one?

Buying a used car can be fun, but it can also be scary. You might be stuck with a lemon. How do car dealers induce us to buy cars that might turn out to be defective?

Although markets do a good job in helping people to use scarce resources efficiently, there are impediments to efficiency. Can markets lead to an efficient outcome when there is uncertainty and incomplete information?

In *Reading Between the Lines* at the end of the chapter, find out why you don't want to be in a course where everyone gets an A!

Decisions in the Face of Uncertainty

Tania, a student, is trying to decide which of two summer jobs to take. She can work as a house painter and earn enough for her to save £2,000 by the end of the summer. There is no uncertainty about the income from this job. If Tania takes it, she will definitely have £2,000 in her bank account at the end of the summer.

The other job, working as a telemarketer selling subscriptions to a magazine, is risky. If Tania takes this job, her bank balance at the end of the summer will depend on her success at selling. She will earn enough to save £5,000 if she is successful but only £1,000 if she turns out to be a poor salesperson. Tania has never tried selling, so she doesn't know how successful she'll be. But some of her friends have done this job, and 50 per cent of them do well and 50 per cent do poorly. Basing her expectations on this experience, Tania thinks there is a 50 per cent chance that she will earn £5,000 and a 50 per cent chance that she will earn £1,000.

Tania is equally as happy to paint as she is to make phone calls. She cares only about the money. Which job does she prefer: the one that provides her with £2,000 for sure or the one that offers her a 50 per cent chance of making only £1,000?

To answer this question, we need a way of comparing the two outcomes. One comparison is the expected wealth that each job creates.

Expected Wealth

Expected wealth is the money value of what a person expects to own at a given point in time. An expectation is an average calculated by using a formula that weights each possible outcome with the probability (chance) that it will occur.

For Tania, the probability that she will have £5,000 is 0.5 (a 50 per cent chance) and the probability that she will have £1,000 is also 0.5. Notice that the probabilities sum to 1. Using these numbers, we calculate Tania's expected wealth, *EW*, as:

$$EW = (£5,000 \times 0.5) + (£1,000 \times 0.5) = £3,000$$

Notice that expected wealth decreases if the risk of a poor outcome increases. For example, if Tania has a 20 per cent chance of success (and 80 per cent chance of failure), her expected wealth falls to:

$$EW = (£5,000 \times 0.2) + (£1,000 \times 0.8) = £1,800$$

Tania can now compare the expected wealth from each job – £3,000 for the risky job and £2,000 for the non-risky job.

So does Tania prefer the risky job because it gives her a greater expected wealth? The answer is we don't know because we don't know how much Tania dislikes risk.

Risk Aversion

Risk aversion is the dislike of risk. Almost everyone is risk averse but some more than others. In rugby, running is less risky than passing. In international rugby, a team coach who favours a cautious running game is risk averse. A team coach who favours a risky passing game is less risk averse. But almost everyone is risk averse to some degree.

We can measure the degree of risk aversion by the compensation needed to make a given amount of risk acceptable. Returning to Tania: if she needs to be paid more than £1,000 to take on the risk arising from the telemarketing job, she will choose the safe painting job and take the £2,000 non-risky income.

But if she thinks that the extra £1,000 of expected income is enough to compensate her for the risk, she will take the risky job.

To make this idea concrete, we need a way of thinking about how a person values different levels of wealth. The concept that we use is *utility*. We apply the same idea that explains how people make expenditure decisions to explain risk aversion and decisions in the face of risk.

Utility of Wealth

Wealth (money in the bank and other assets of value) is like all good things. It yields utility. The more wealth a person has, the greater is that person's *total utility*. But each additional dollar of wealth brings a diminishing increment in total utility – the *marginal utility* of wealth diminishes as wealth increases.

Diminishing marginal utility of wealth means that the gain in utility from an increase in wealth is smaller than the loss in utility from an equal decrease in wealth. Stated differently, *the pain from a loss is greater than the pleasure from a gain of equal size.*

Figure 19.1 illustrates Tania's utility of wealth. Each point *A* to *F* on Tania's utility of wealth curve corresponds to the value identified by the same letter in the table. For example, at point *C*, Tania's wealth is £2,000, and her total utility is 70 units. As Tania's wealth increases, her total utility increases and her marginal utility decreases. Her marginal utility is 25 units when wealth increases from £1,000 to £2,000, but only 13 units when wealth increases from £2,000 to £3,000.

We can use a person's utility of wealth curve to calculate expected utility and the cost of risk.

Expected Utility

Expected utility is the utility value of what a person expects to own at a given point in time. Like expected wealth, it is calculated by using a formula that weights each possible outcome with the probability that it will occur. But it is the utility outcome, not the money outcome, that is used to calculate expected utility.

Figure 19.2 illustrates the calculation for Tania. Wealth of £5,000 gives 95 units of utility and wealth of £1,000 gives 45 units of utility. Each outcome has a probability of 0.5 (a 50 per cent chance). Using these numbers, we can calculate Tania's expected utility, EU, which is:

$$EU = (95 \times 0.5) + (45 \times 0.5) = 70$$

Figure 19.1 The Utility of Wealth

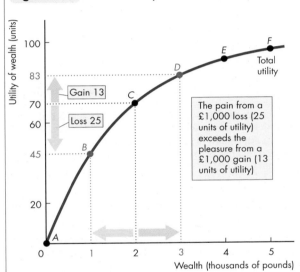

	Wealth (pounds)	Total utility (units)	Marginal utility (units)
A	0	0	
			45
B	1,000	45	
			25
C	2,000	70	
			13
D	3,000	83	
			8
E	4,000	91	
			4
F	5,000	95	

The table shows Tania's utility of wealth schedule, and the figure shows her utility of wealth curve. Utility increases as wealth increases, but the marginal utility of wealth diminishes.

Figure 19.2 Expected Utility

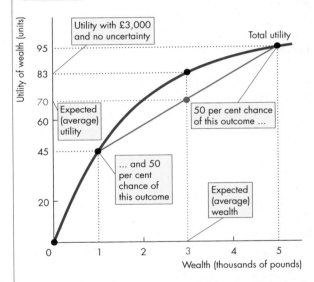

Tania has a 50 per cent chance of having £5,000 of wealth and a total utility of 95 units. She also has a 50 per cent chance of having £1,000 of wealth and a total utility of 45 units.

Tania's expected wealth is £3,000 (the average of £5,000 and £1,000) and her expected utility is 70 units (the average of 95 and 45).

With a wealth of £3,000 and no uncertainty, Tania's total utility is 83 units. For a given expected wealth, the greater the range of uncertainty, the smaller is expected utility.

Expected utility decreases if the risk of a poor outcome increases. For example, if Tania has a 20 per cent chance of success (and an 80 per cent chance of failure), her expected utility is 55 units:

$$(95 \times 0.2) + (45 \times 0.8) = 55$$

Notice how the range of uncertainty affects expected utility. Figure 19.2 shows that with £3,000 of wealth and no uncertainty, total utility is 83 units. But with the same expected wealth and Tania's uncertainty – a 50 per cent chance of having £5,000 and a 50 per cent chance of having £1,000 – expected utility is only 70 units. Tania's uncertainty lowers her expected utility by 13 units.

Expected utility combines expected wealth and risk into a single index.

Making a Choice with Uncertainty

Faced with uncertainty, a person chooses the action that maximizes expected utility. To select the job that gives her the maximum expected utility, Tania must:

1   Calculate the expected utility from the risky telemarketing job

2   Calculate the expected utility from the safe painting job

3   Compare the two expected utilities

Figure 19.3 illustrates the calculations. You've just seen that the risky telemarketing job gives Tania an expected utility of 70 units. The safe painting job also gives Tania a utility of 70. That is, the total utility of £2,000 with no risk is 70 units. So with either job, Tania has an expected utility of 70 units. She is indifferent between these two jobs.

If Tania had only a 20 per cent chance of success and an 80 per cent chance of failure in the telemarketing job, her expected utility would be 55 (calculated above). In this case, she would take the painting job and get 70 units of utility. But if the probabilities were reversed and she had an 80 per cent chance of success and only a 20 per cent chance of failure in the telemarketing job, her expected utility would be 85 units:

$$(95 \times 0.8) + (45 \times 0.2) = 85$$

In this case, Tania would take the risky telemarketing job. We can calculate the cost of risk by comparing the expected wealth in a given risky situation with the wealth that gives the same total utility but no risk.

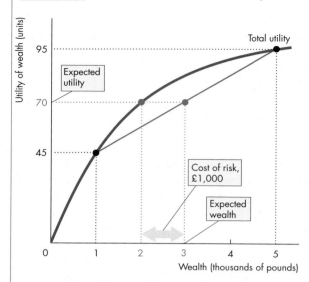

Figure 19.3   Choice under Uncertainty

With a 50 per cent chance of having £5,000 of wealth and a 50 per cent chance of having £1,000 of wealth, Tania's expected wealth is £3,000 and her expected utility is 70 units. Tania would have the same 70 units of total utility with wealth of £2,000 and no risk, so Tania's cost of bearing this risk is £1,000. Tania is indifferent between the job that pays £2,000 with no risk and the job that offers an equal chance of £5,000 and £1,000.

myeconlab Animation

Using this principle, we can find Tania's cost of bearing the risk that arises from the telemarketing job. That cost, highlighted in Figure 19.3, is £1,000.

Review Quiz

1   What is the distinction between expected wealth and expected utility?

2   How does the concept of the utility of wealth capture the idea that pain of loss exceeds the pleasure of gain?

3   What do people try to achieve when they make a decision under uncertainty?

4   How is the cost of risk calculated when making a decision under uncertainty?

You can work these questions in Study Plan 19.1 and get instant feedback.

You've now seen how a person makes a risky decision. In the next section, we'll see how markets enable people to reduce the risks they face.

Buying and Selling Risk

You've seen at many points in your study of markets how both buyers and sellers gain from trade. Buyers gain because they value what they buy more highly than the price they must pay – they receive a *consumer surplus*. And sellers gain because they face costs that are less than the price at which they can sell – they receive a *producer surplus*.

Just as buyers and sellers gain from trading goods and services, so they can also gain by trading risk. But risk is a bad, not a good. The good that is traded is risk avoidance. A buyer of risk avoidance can gain because the value of avoiding risk is greater than the price that must be paid to someone else to get them to bear the risk. The seller of risk avoidance faces a lower cost of risk than the price that people are willing to pay to avoid the risk.

We're going to put some flesh on the bare bones of this brief account of how people can gain from trading risk by looking at insurance markets.

Insurance Markets

Insurance plays a huge role in our economic lives. We'll explain:

◆ How insurance reduces risk
◆ Why people buy insurance
◆ How insurance companies earn a profit

How Insurance Reduces Risk

Insurance reduces the risk that people face by sharing or pooling the risks. When people buy insurance against the risk of an unwanted event, they pay an insurance company a *premium*. If the unwanted event occurs, the insurance company pays out the amount of the insured loss.

Think about car collision insurance. The probability that any one person will have a serious car accident is small. But a person who does have a car accident incurs a large loss. For a large population, the probability of one person having an accident is the proportion of the population that has an accident. But this proportion is known, so the probability of an accident occurring and the total cost of accidents can be predicted. An insurance company can pool the risks of a large population and enable everyone to share the costs. It does so by collecting premiums from everyone and paying out benefits to those who suffer a loss. An insurance com-

pany that remains in business collects at least as much in premiums as it pays out in benefits.

Why People Buy Insurance

People buy insurance and insurance companies earn a profit by selling insurance because people are risk averse. To see why people buy insurance and why it is profitable, let's consider an example. Dan owns a car worth £10,000, and that is his only wealth. There is a 10 per cent chance that Dan will have a serious accident that makes his car worth nothing. So there is a 90 per cent chance that Dan's wealth will remain at £10,000 and a 10 per cent chance that his wealth will be zero.

Dan's expected wealth is £9,000:

$$(£10,000 \times 0.9) + (£0 \times 0.1)$$

Dan is risk averse (just like Tania in the previous example). Because Dan is risk averse, he will be better off by buying insurance to avoid the risk that he faces, if the insurance premium isn't too high.

Without knowing some details about just how risk averse Dan is, we don't know the most that he would be willing to pay to avoid this risk. But we do know that he would pay more than £1,000. If Dan did pay £1,000 to avoid the risk, he would have £9,000 of wealth and face no uncertainty about his wealth. If he does not have an accident, his wealth is the £10,000 value of his car minus the £1,000 he pays the insurance company. If he does lose his car, the insurance company pays him £10,000, so he still has £9,000. Being risk averse, Dan's expected utility from £9,000 with no risk is greater than his expected utility from an expected £9,000 with risk. So Dan would be willing to pay more than £1,000 to avoid this risk.

How Insurance Companies Earn a Profit

For the insurance company, £1,000 is the minimum amount at which it would be willing to insure Dan and other people like him. With say 50,000 customers all like Dan, 5,000 customers (50,000 × 0.1) lose their cars and 45,000 don't. Premiums of £1,000 give the insurance company a total revenue of £50,000,000. With 5,000 claims of £10,000, the insurance company pays out £50,000,000. So a premium of £1,000 enables the insurance company to break even (make zero economic profit) on this business.

But Dan (and everyone else) is willing to pay more than £1,000, so insurance is a profitable business and there is a gain from trading risk.

The gain from trading risk is shared by Dan (and the other people who buy insurance) and the insurance company. The exact share of the gain depends on the state of competition in the market for insurance.

If the insurance market is a monopoly, the insurance company can take all the gains from trading risk. But if the insurance market is competitive, economic profit will induce entry and profits will be competed away. In this case, Dan (and the other buyers of insurance) get the gain.

A Graphical Analysis of Insurance

We can illustrate the gains from insurance by using a graph of Dan's utility of wealth curve. We begin, in Figure 19.4, with the situation if Dan doesn't buy insurance and decides to bear the risk he faces.

Risk-taking Without Insurance

With no accident, Dan's wealth is £10,000 and his total utility is 100 units. If Dan has an accident, his car is worthless, he has no wealth and no utility. Because the chance of an accident is 10 per cent (or 0.1), the chance of not having an accident is 90 per cent (or 0.9). Dan's expected wealth is £9,000: (£10,000 × 0.9) + (£0 × 0.1). And his expected utility is 90 units: (100 × 0.9) + (0 × 0.1).

You've just seen that without insurance, Dan gets 90 units of utility. But Dan also gets 90 units of utility if he faces no uncertainty with a smaller amount of wealth.

We're now going to see how much Dan will pay to avoid uncertainty.

The Value and Cost of Insurance

Figure 19.5 shows the situation when Dan buys insurance. You can see that for Dan, having £7,000 with no risk is just as good as facing a 90 per cent chance of having £10,000 and a 10 per cent chance of having no wealth. So if Dan pays £3,000 for insurance, he has £7,000 of wealth, faces no uncertainty, and gets 90 units of utility. The amount of £3,000 is the maximum that Dan is willing to pay for insurance. It is the value of insurance to Dan.

Figure 19.5 also shows the cost of insurance. With a large number of customers each of whom has a 10 per cent chance of making a £10,000 claim for the loss of a vehicle, the insurance company can provide insurance at a cost of £1,000 (10 per cent of £10,000). If Dan pays

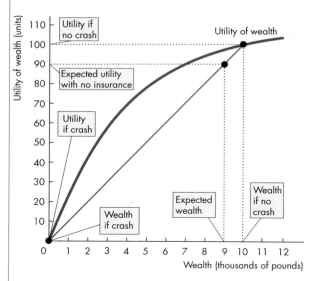

Figure 19.4   Taking a Risk without Insurance

Dan's wealth (the value of his car) is £10,000, which gives him 100 units of utility.

With no insurance, if Dan has a crash, he has no wealth and no utility.

With a 10 per cent chance of a crash, Dan's expected wealth is £9,000 and his expected utility is 90 units.

myeconlab Animation

only £1,000 for insurance, his wealth is £9,000 (the £10,000 value of his car minus the £1,000 he pays for insurance), and his utility from £9,000 of wealth with no uncertainty is about 98 units.

Gains from Trade

Because Dan is willing to pay up to £3,000 for insurance that costs the insurance company £1,000, there is a gain from trading risk of £2,000 per insured person. How the gains are shared depends on the nature of the market.

If the insurance market is competitive, entry will increase supply of insurance and lower the price to £1,000 (plus zero economic profit and operating costs). Dan (and the other buyers of insurance) enjoy a consumer surplus. If the insurance market is a monopoly, the insurance company takes the £2,000 per insured person as economic profit.

Figure 19.5   The Gains from Insurance

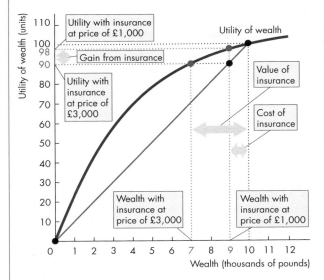

If Dan pays £3,000 for insurance, his wealth is £7,000 and his utility is 90 units – the same utility as with no insurance – so £3,000 is the value of insurance for Dan.

If Dan pays £1,000 for insurance, which is the insurance company's cost of providing insurance, his wealth is £9,000 and his utility is about 98 units.

Dan and the insurance company share the gain from insurance.

myeconlab Animation

Risk That Can't Be Insured

The gains from car collision insurance that we've studied here apply to all types of insurance. Examples are property and casualty insurance, life insurance and healthcare insurance. One person's risks associated with driving, life and health are independent of other persons. That's why insurance is possible. The risks are spread across a population.

But not all risks can be insured. To be insurable, risks must be independent. If an event causes everyone to be a loser, it isn't possible to spread and pool the risks. For example, flood insurance is often not available for people who live on a floodplain because if one person incurs a loss, most likely all do.

Also, to be insurable, a risky event must be observable to both the buyer and seller of insurance. But much of the uncertainty that we face arises because we know less (or more) than others with whom we do business. In the next section, we look at the way markets cope when buyers and sellers have different information.

Insurance in the UK

We spend close to 12 per cent of our income on private insurance. That's as much as we spend on housing and more than we spend on cars and food. In addition, we buy insurance through our taxes in the form of National Insurance and unemployment insurance. Figure 1 shows the relative size of the three main types of private insurance along with all others in the UK. More than 75 per cent of UK households have home contents and motor insurance, but only 35 per cent have life insurance. Only 15 per cent have private pension coverage and just 10 per cent have private medical insurance.

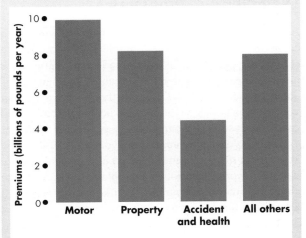

Figure 1 The UK Insurance Industry

Source of data: Association of British Insurers. UK Insurance: Key Facts, September 2010.

Review Quiz

1 How does insurance reduce risk?
2 How do we determine the value (willingness to pay) of insurance?
3 How can an insurance company offer people a deal worth taking? Why do both the buyers and sellers of insurance gain?
4 What kinds of risks can't be insured?

You can work these questions in Study Plan 19.2 and get instant feedback.   myeconlab

Private Information

In all the markets that you've studied so far, the buyers and the sellers are well informed about the good, service or factor of production being traded. But in some markets, either the buyers or the sellers – usually the sellers – are better informed about the value of the item being traded than the person on the other side of the market. Information about the value of the item being traded that is possessed by only buyers or sellers is called **private information**. And a market in which the buyers or sellers have private information has **asymmetric information**.

Asymmetric Information: Examples and Problems

Asymmetric information affects many of your own economic transactions. One example is your knowledge about your driving skills and temperament. You know much more than your car insurance company does about how carefully and defensively you drive – about your personal risk of having an accident that would cause the insurance company to pay a claim. Another example is your knowledge about your work effort. You know more than your employer about how hard you are willing to work. Yet another example is your knowledge about the quality of your car. You know whether it's a lemon, but the person to whom you are about to sell it does not know and can't find out until after he or she has bought it.

Asymmetric information creates two problems:

◆ Adverse selection
◆ Moral hazard

Adverse Selection

Adverse selection is the tendency for people to *enter into agreements* in which they can use their private information to their own advantage and to the disadvantage of the less informed party.

For example, if Jackie offers salespeople a fixed wage, she will attract lazy salespeople. Hardworking salespeople will prefer not to work for Jackie because they can earn more by working for someone who pays by results. The fixed-wage contract adversely selects those with private information (knowledge about their work habits) who can use that knowledge to their own advantage and to the disadvantage of the other party.

Moral Hazard

Moral hazard is the tendency for people with private information, after entering into an agreement, to use that information for their own benefit and at the cost of the less-informed party.

For example, Jackie hires Mitch as a salesperson and pays him a fixed wage regardless of his sales. Mitch faces a moral hazard. He has an incentive to put in the least possible effort, benefiting himself and lowering Jackie's profits. For this reason, salespeople are usually paid by a formula that makes their income higher the greater is the volume (or value) of their sales.

A variety of devices have evolved that enable markets to function in the face of adverse selection and moral hazard. We've just seen one, the use of incentive payments for salespeople. We're going to look at how three markets cope with adverse selection and moral hazard. They are:

◆ The market for used cars
◆ The market for loans
◆ The market for insurance

The Market for Used Cars

When a person buys a car, it might turn out to be a lemon. If the car is a lemon, it is worth less to the buyer and to everyone else than if it has no defects. Does the used car market have two prices reflecting these two values – a low price for lemons and a higher price for cars without defects? It turns out that it does. But it needs some help to do so and to overcome what is called the **lemon problem** – the problem that in a market in which it is not possible to distinguish reliable products from lemons, there are too many lemons and too few reliable products traded.

To see how the used car market overcomes the lemon problem, we'll first look at a used car market that has a lemon problem.

The Lemon Problem in a Used Car Market

To explain the lemon problem as clearly as possible, we'll assume that there are only two kinds of cars: defective cars – lemons – and cars without defects that we'll call good cars. Whether or not a car is a lemon is private information that is available only to the current owner. The buyer of a used car can't tell whether he is buying a lemon until after he has bought the car and learned as much about it as its current owner knows.

Some people with low incomes and the time and ability to fix cars are willing to buy lemons as long as they know what they're buying and pay an appropriately low price. Suppose that a lemon is worth £5,000 to a buyer. More people want to buy a good car and we'll assume that a good car is worth £25,000 to a buyer.

But the buyer can't tell the difference between a lemon and a good car. Only the seller has this information. And telling the buyer that a car is not a lemon does not help. The seller has no incentive to tell the truth.

So the most that the buyer knows is the probability of buying a lemon. If half of the used cars sold turn out to be lemons, the buyer knows that he has a 50 per cent chance of getting a good car and a 50 per cent chance of getting a lemon.

The price that a buyer is willing to pay for a car of unknown quality is more than the value of a lemon because the car might be a good one. But the price is less than the value of a good car because it might turn out to be a lemon.

Now think about the sellers of used cars, who know the quality of their cars. Someone who owns a good car is going to be offered a price that is less than the value of that car to the buyer. Many owners will be reluctant to sell for such a low price. So the quantity of good used

cars supplied will not be as large as it would be if people paid the price they are worth.

In contrast, someone who owns a lemon is going to be offered a price that is greater than the value of that car to the buyer. So owners of lemons will be eager to sell and the quantity of lemons supplied will be greater than it would be if people paid the price that a lemon is worth.

Figure 19.6 illustrates the used car market that we've just described. Part (a) shows the demand for used cars, D, and the supply of used cars, S. Equilibrium occurs at a price of £10,000 per car with 400 cars traded each month.

Some cars are good ones and some are lemons, but buyers can't tell the difference until it is too late to influence their decision to buy. But buyers do know what a good car and a lemon are worth to them, and sellers know the quality of the cars they are offering for sale. Figure 19.6(b) shows the demand curve for good cars, D_G and the supply curve of good cars, S_G. Figure 19.6(c) shows the demand curve for lemons, D_L, and the supply curve of lemons, S_L.

At the market price of £10,000, owners of good cars, in Figure 19.6(b), supply 200 cars a month for sale. Owners of lemons, in Figure 19.6(c), supply 200 cars a month for sale. The used car market is inefficient

Figure 19.6   The Lemon Problem

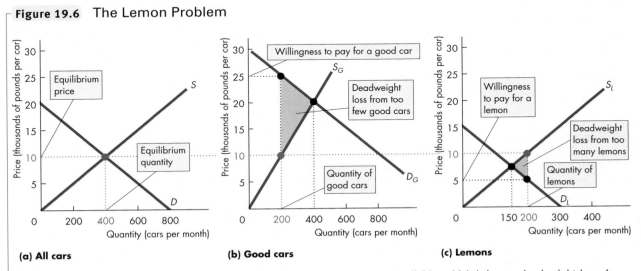

(a) All cars   **(b) Good cars**   **(c) Lemons**

Buyers can't tell a good used car from a lemon. Demand and supply determine the price and quantity of used cars traded in part (a). In part (b), D_G is the demand curve for good used cars and S_G is the supply curve. At the market price, too few good cars are available, which brings a deadweight loss. In part (c), D_L is the demand curve for lemons and S_L is the supply curve. At the market price, too many lemons are available, which brings a deadweight loss.

myeconlab Animation

because there are too many lemons and not enough good cars for sale. Figure 19.6 makes this inefficiency clear by using the concept of deadweight loss (see Chapter 5, pp. 113–114).

At the quantity of good cars supplied, buyers are willing to pay £25,000 for a good car. They are willing to pay more than a good car is worth to its current owner for all good cars up to 400 cars a month. The grey triangle shows the deadweight loss that results from there being too few good used cars.

At the quantity of lemons supplied, buyers are willing to pay £5,000 for a lemon. They are willing to pay less than a lemon is worth to its current owner for all lemons above 150 cars a month. The grey triangle shows the deadweight loss that results from there being too many lemons.

You can see *adverse selection* in this used car market because there is a greater incentive to offer a lemon for sale. You can also see *moral hazard* because the owner of a lemon has little incentive to take good care of the car, so it is likely to become an even worse lemon. The market for used cars is not working well. Too many lemons and too few good used cars are traded.

A Used Car Market with Dealers' Warranties

How can used car dealers convince buyers that a car isn't a lemon? The answer is by giving a guarantee in the form of a warranty. By providing warranties only on good cars, dealers signal which cars are good ones and which are lemons.

Signalling occurs when an informed person takes actions that send information to uninformed persons. The grades and degrees that a university awards students are signals. They inform potential (uninformed) employers about the ability of the people they are considering hiring.

In the market for used cars, dealers send signals by giving warranties on the used cars they offer for sale. The message in the signal is that the dealer agrees to pay the costs of repairing the car if it turns out to have a defect.

Buyers believe the signal because the cost of sending a false signal is high. A dealer who gives a warranty on a lemon ends up bearing a high cost of repairs – and gains a bad reputation. A dealer who gives a warranty only on good cars has no repair costs and a reputation

---

Figure 19.7   Warranties Make the Used Car Market Efficient

(a) Good cars

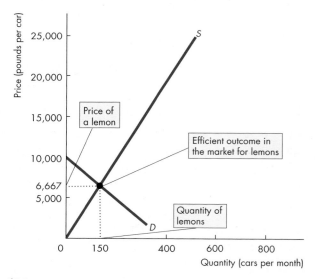

(b) Lemons

With dealers' warranties as signals, the equilibrium price of a good used car is £20,000 and 400 cars are traded. The market for good used cars is efficient. Because the signal

enables buyers to spot a lemon, the price of a lemon is £6,667 and 150 lemons are traded. The market for lemons is efficient.

that gets better and better. It pays dealers to send an accurate signal, and it is rational for buyers to believe the signal.

So a car with a warranty is a good car; a car without a warranty is a lemon. Warranties solve the lemon problem and enable the used car market to function efficiently with two prices: one for lemons and one for good cars.

Figure 19.7 illustrates this outcome. In part (a) the demand for and supply of good cars determine the price of a good car. In part (b), the demand for and supply of lemons determine the price of a lemon. Both markets are efficient.

Pooling Equilibrium and Separating Equilibrium

You've seen two outcomes in the market for used cars. Without warranties, there is only one message visible to the buyer: All cars look the same. So there is one price regardless of whether the car is a good car or a lemon. We call the equilibrium in a market when only one message is available and an uninformed person cannot determine quality a **pooling equilibrium**.

But in a used car market with warranties, there are two messages. Good cars have warranties and lemons don't. So there are two car prices for the two types of cars. We call the equilibrium in a market when signalling provides full information to a previously uninformed person a **separating equilibrium**.

The Market for Loans

When you buy a tank of petrol and swipe your credit card, you are taking a loan from the bank that issued your card. You demand and your bank supplies a loan. Have you noticed the interest rate on an unpaid credit card balance? It ranges between 12 per cent a year and 20 per cent a year. Why are these interest rates so high? And why is there such a huge range?

The answer is that when banks make loans, they face the risk that the loan will not be repaid. The risk that a borrower, also known as a creditor, might not repay a loan is called **credit risk** or **default risk**. For credit card borrowing, the credit risk is high and it varies among borrowers. The borrowers with the highest risk for default pay the highest interest rate.

Interest rates and the price of credit risk are determined in the market for loans. The lower the interest rate, the greater is the quantity of loans demanded and for a given level of credit risk, the higher the interest rate, the greater is the quantity of loans supplied.

Demand and supply determine the interest rate and the price of credit risk.

If lenders were unable to charge different interest rates to reflect different degrees of credit risk, there would be a pooling equilibrium and an inefficient loans market.

Inefficient Pooling Equilibrium

To see why a pooling equilibrium would be inefficient, suppose that banks can't identify the individual credit risk of their borrowers: they have no way of knowing how likely it is that a given loan will be repaid. In this situation, every borrower pays the same interest rate and the market is in a pooling equilibrium.

If all borrowers pay the same interest rate, the market for loans has the same problem as the used car market. Low-risk customers borrow less than they would if they were offered the low interest rate appropriate for their low credit risk. High-risk customers borrow more than they would if they faced the high interest rate appropriate for their high credit risk. So banks face an *adverse selection* problem. Too many borrowers are high risk and too few are low risk.

Signalling and Screening in the Market for Loans

Lenders don't know how likely it is that a given loan will be repaid, but the borrower does know. Low-risk borrowers have an incentive to signal their risk by providing lenders with relevant information. Signals might include information about the length of time a person has been in the current job or has lived at the current address, home ownership, marital status, age and business records.

High-risk borrowers might be identified simply as those who have failed to signal low risk. These borrowers have an incentive to mislead lenders; and lenders have an incentive to induce high-risk borrowers to reveal their risk level. Inducing an informed party to reveal private information is called **screening**.

By not lending to people who refuse to reveal relevant information, banks are able to screen as well as receive signals that help them to separate their borrowers into a number of credit-risk categories. If lenders succeed, the market for loans comes to a separating equilibrium with a high interest rate for high-risk borrowers and a low interest rate for low-risk borrowers. Signalling and screening work like warranties in the used car market and avoid the deadweight loss of a pooling equilibrium.

The Sub-prime Credit Crisis

A sub-prime mortgage is a loan to a homebuyer who has a high risk of default. Figure 1 shows that between 2001 and 2005, the price of risk was low. Figure 2 shows why: the supply of credit, S_0, was large and so was the amount of risk taking. In 2007, the supply of credit decreased to S_1. The price of risk jumped and, faced with a higher interest rate, many sub-prime borrowers defaulted. Defaults in the sub-prime mortgage market spread to other markets that supplied the funds that financed mortgages.

Figure 1 The Price of Commercial Credit Risk

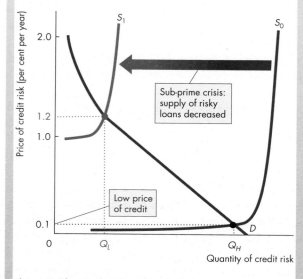

Figure 2 The Market for Risky Loans

The Market for Insurance

People who buy insurance face moral hazard, and insurance companies face adverse selection. Moral hazard arises because a person with insurance against a loss has less incentive than an uninsured person to avoid the loss. For example, a business with fire insurance has less incentive to install a fire alarm or sprinkler system than a business with no fire insurance does. Adverse selection arises because people who create greater risks are more likely to buy insurance. For example, a person with a family history of serious illness is more likely to buy health insurance than is a person with a family history of good health.

Insurance companies have an incentive to find ways around the moral hazard and adverse selection problems. By doing so, they can lower premiums for low-risk people and raise premiums for high-risk people.

One device that car insurance companies use is the *no-claim bonus*. A driver accumulates a no-claim bonus by driving safely and avoiding accidents and claims. The greater the bonus, the greater is the incentive to drive carefully.

Car insurance companies also use a deductible as a signal. A *deductible* is the amount of a loss that the insured person agrees to bear. The premium is smaller the greater is the deductible, and the decrease in the premium is more than proportionate to the increase in the deductible. By offering insurance with full coverage – no deductible – on terms that are attractive only to the highest-risk people and by offering coverage with a deductible on more favourable terms that are attractive to other people, insurance companies can do profitable business with everyone. High-risk people choose policies with low deductibles and high premiums; low-risk people choose policies with high deductibles and low premiums.

1 How does private information create moral hazard and adverse selection?
2 How do markets for cars use warranties to cope with private information?
3 How do markets for loans use signalling and screening to cope with private information?
4 How do markets for insurance use no-claim bonuses to cope with private information?

You can work these questions in Study Plan 19.3 and get instant feedback.

Uncertainty, Information and the Invisible Hand

A recurring theme throughout microeconomics is the big question: When do choices made in the pursuit of self-interest also promote the social interest? When does the invisible hand work well and when does it fail us? You've learned about the concept of efficiency, a major component of what we mean by the social interest. And you've seen that while competitive markets generally do a good job in helping to achieve efficiency, impediments such as monopoly and the absence of well-defined property rights can prevent the attainment of an efficient use of resources.

How do uncertainty and incomplete information affect the ability of self-interested choices to lead to a social interest outcome? Are these features of economic life another reason why markets fail and why some type of government intervention is required to achieve efficiency?

These are hard questions, and there are no definitive answers. But there are some useful things that we can say about the effects of uncertainty and a lack of complete information on the efficiency of resource use. We'll begin our brief review of this issue by thinking about information as just another good.

Information as a Good

More information is generally useful. And less uncertainty about the future is generally useful. Think about information as one of the goods of which we always want more.

The most basic lesson about efficiency that you learned in Chapter 2 can be applied to information. Along our production possibilities frontier, we face a trade-off between information and all other goods and services. Information, like everything else, can be produced at an increasing opportunity cost – an increasing marginal cost. For example, we could get more accurate weather forecasts, but only at increasing marginal cost, as we increased the amount of information that we gather from the atmosphere and the amount of money that we spend on super-computers to process the data.

The principle of decreasing marginal benefit also applies to information. More information is valuable, but the more you know, the less you value another increment in information. For example, knowing that it will rain tomorrow is valuable information. Knowing

the amount of rain to within an inch is even more useful. But knowing the amount of rain to within a couple of millimetres probably isn't worth much more.

Because the marginal cost of information is increasing and the marginal benefit is decreasing, there is an efficient amount of information. It would be inefficient to be overinformed.

In principle, competitive markets in information might deliver this efficient quantity. Whether they actually do so is hard to determine.

Monopoly in Markets That Cope with Uncertainty

There are probably large economies of scale in providing services that cope with uncertainty and incomplete information. The banking and insurance industries, for example, are highly concentrated and have very large economies of scale. Where monopoly elements exist, exactly the same inefficiency issues arise as they do in markets where uncertainty and incomplete information are not big issues. So it is likely that in some information markets, including the markets for loans and insurance, there is underproduction arising from the attempt to maximize monopoly profit.

Review Quiz

1 Thinking about information as a good, what determines the information that people are willing to pay for?
2 Why is it inefficient to be over-informed?
3 Why are some of the markets that provide information likely to be dominated by monopolies?

You can work these questions in Study Plan 19.4 and get instant feedback.

You've seen how people make decisions when faced with uncertainty and how markets work when there is asymmetric information. *Reading Between the Lines* on pages 450–451 looks at the way markets in human capital and labour use university grades as signals that sort students by ability so that employers can hire the type of labour they seek. You'll discover that grade deflation can be efficient and grade inflation is inefficient. Discriminating grades are in the social interest and in the self-interest of universities and students.

Reading Between the Lines

Grades as Signals

The Telegraph, 1 January 2011

Dumbing Down of University Grades Revealed

David Barrett

Degree results . . . show six out of 10 students were handed either a first or an upper second in 2010, compared with just one in three graduates in 1970. . . . Traditionally, first class honours have been awarded sparingly to students who show exceptional depth of knowledge and originality. . . .

The universities awarding the highest proportion of firsts or 2:1s last year were Exeter, where 82 per cent of graduates received the top degrees compared with just 29 per cent in 1970, and St Andrews . . . where the figure was also 82 per cent compared with just 25 per cent in 1970.

Imperial College London and Warwick both granted 80 per cent firsts or 2:1s last year, compared with 49 per cent and 39 per cent respectively in 1970. At Bath University the figure was 76 per cent last year compared with just 35 per cent in 1970. . . .

Prof Alan Smithers, director of Buckingham University's centre for education and employment research, . . . said: 'There has been the most extraordinary grade inflation'. . . .

Professor Smithers said universities had been awarding more firsts and upper seconds because of competition for research grants, places for which are only awarded to students with higher grades. He said: 'There has been compromise across the system and employers no longer fully trust degree results, and tend to look back to A-level results as a more reliable indicator'. . . .

The Essence of the Story

◆ Sixty per cent of British university honours students were awarded a first or upper second class degree in 2010, compared with just 33 per cent in 1970.

◆ The trend is similar across many of the UK's top universities.

◆ Universities have been accused of grade inflation brought about by the pressure to gain research grants.

◆ Grade inflation may mean that employers no longer trust degree results and rely more on A-level results.

Economic Analysis

- Accurate grades provide valuable information to students and potential employers about a student's ability.

- Universities try to provide accurate grades but face pressures to grade more softly to attract more research income.

- Figure 1 shows a labour market for university graduates when there is grade inflation.

- Students with high ability are not distinguished from other students, and the supply curve represents the supply of students of all ability levels.

- The demand curve shows the employers' willingness to hire new workers without knowledge of their ability.

- All graduates get jobs at the same low wage rate.

- Figures 2 and 3 show the outcome with accurate grading. In Figure 2, students with high grades get high-wage jobs and in Figure 3, students with low grades get low-wage jobs.

- Even with grade inflation, employers discover ability from on-the-job performance and eventually, even with grade inflation, earnings reflect ability.

- But accurate grades are valuable because they enable employers and graduates to avoid the costly process of discovering and revealing true ability on the job and to get people into the right jobs at the time of graduation.

- Continued grade inflation leads employers to distrust the degree result as a signal of student ability.

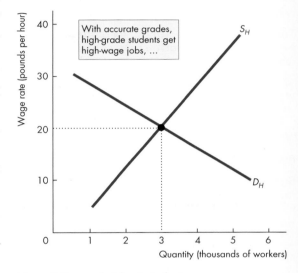

Figure 2 The market for A students

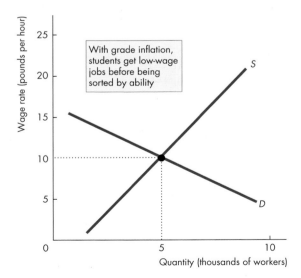

Figure 1 Market with grade inflation

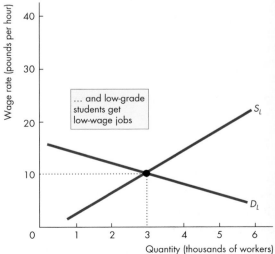

Figure 3 The market for D students

SUMMARY

Key Points

Decisions in the Face of Uncertainty
(pp. 438–440)

◆ To make a rational choice under uncertainty, people choose the action that maximizes the expected utility of wealth.

◆ A decreasing marginal utility of wealth makes people risk averse. A sure outcome with a given expected wealth is preferred to a risky outcome with the same expected wealth – risk is costly.

◆ The cost of risk is found by comparing the expected wealth in a given risky situation with the wealth that gives the same utility but with no risk.

Working Problems 1 to 3 will give you a better understanding of decisions in the face of uncertainty.

Buying and Selling Risk (pp. 441–443)

◆ People trade risk in markets for insurance.

◆ By pooling risks, insurance companies can reduce the risks people face (from insured activities) at a lower cost than the value placed on the lower risk.

Working Problems 4 to 6 will give you a better understanding of buying and selling risk.

Private Information (pp. 444–448)

◆ Asymmetric information creates adverse selection and moral hazard problems.

◆ When it is not possible to distinguish good-quality products from lemons, too many lemons and too few good-quality products are traded in a pooling equilibrium.

◆ Signalling can overcome the lemon problem.

◆ In the market for used cars, warranties signal good cars and enable an efficient separating equilibrium.

◆ Private information about credit risk is overcome by using signals and screening based on personal characteristics.

◆ Private information about risk in insurance markets is overcome by using the no-claim bonus and deductibles.

Working Problems 7 to 11 will give you a better understanding of private information.

Uncertainty, Information and the Invisible Hand (p. 449)

◆ Less uncertainty and more information can be viewed as a good that has increasing marginal cost and decreasing marginal benefit.

◆ Competitive information markets might be efficient, but economies of scale might bring inefficient underproduction of information and insurance.

Working Problems 12 and 13 will give you a better understanding of uncertainty, information and the invisible hand.

Key Terms

Adverse selection, 444
Asymmetric information, 444
Credit risk or default risk, 447
Expected utility, 439
Expected wealth, 438
Lemon problem, 444
Moral hazard, 444
Pooling equilibrium, 447
Private information, 444
Risk aversion, 438
Screening, 447
Separating equilibrium, 447
Signalling, 446

STUDY PLAN PROBLEMS AND APPLICATIONS

 myeconlab You can work Problems 1 to 15 in MyEconLab Chapter 19 Study Plan and get instant feedback.

Decisions in the Face of Uncertainty
(Study Plan 19.1)

1 The figure shows Lee's utility of wealth curve.

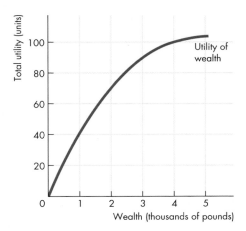

Lee is offered a job as a salesperson in which there is a 50 per cent chance that she will make £4,000 a month and a 50 per cent chance that she will make nothing.

a What is Lee's expected income from taking this job?

b What is Lee's expected utility from taking this job?

c How much would another firm have to offer Lee with certainty to persuade her not to take the risky sales job?

d What is Lee's cost of risk?

Use the following news clip to work Problems 2 and 3.

Larry Page on How to Change the World

As president of Google, Larry Page said that the risks that Google has taken have led to hot new applications like Gmail and Google Maps. In 2004, Page set out Google's risk strategy: Google would do some things that would have only a 10 per cent chance of making $1 billion over the long term, but not many people will work on those things; 90 per cent work on everything else. So that's not a big risk. Many of Google's new features come from the riskier investments. Before we began, we thought that Google might fail and we almost didn't do it. The reason we started Google was probably Stanford's decision that we could go back and finish our Ph.D.s if we didn't succeed.

Source: *Fortune*, 12 May 2008

2 If much of Google's success has come from 'riskier investments', explain why Google doesn't dedicate all of their resources towards these riskier innovations.

3 In spite of the many risks that Larry Page has taken with Google, what evidence does this news clip provide that he is risk averse?

Buying and Selling Risk (Study Plan 19.2)

4 Lee in Problem 1 has built a small weekend shack on a steep, unstable hillside. She spent all her wealth, which is £5,000, on this project. There is a 75 per cent chance that the house will be washed down the hill and be worthless. How much is Lee willing to pay for an insurance policy that pays her £5,000 if the house is washed away?

Use the following information to work Problems 5 and 6.

Larry lives in a neighbourhood in which 20 per cent of the cars are stolen every year. Larry's only wealth is his car, which he parks on the street overnight. His car is worth £20,000. The table shows Larry's utility of wealth schedule.

Wealth (pounds)	Utility (units)
20,000	400
16,000	350
12,000	280
8,000	200
4,000	110
0	0

5 If Larry cannot buy car theft insurance, what is his expected wealth and his expected utility?

6 High-Crime Car Theft, an insurance company, offers to sell Larry insurance at £8,000 a year and promises to provide Larry with a replacement car worth £20,000 if his car is stolen. Is Larry willing to buy this insurance? If not, is he willing to pay £4,000 a year for such insurance?

Private Information (Study Plan 19.3)

Use the following information to work Problems 7 and 8.

Zaneb is a high-school teacher and is well known in her community for her honesty and integrity. She is shopping for a new car and plans to borrow the money to pay for it from her local bank.

7 **a** Does Zaneb create any moral hazard or adverse selection problems either for the bank or the car dealer? Explain your answer.

b Do the bank or the car dealer create any moral hazard or adverse selection problems for Zaneb? Explain your answer.

8 What arrangements is Zaneb likely to encounter that are designed to help cope with the moral hazard and adverse selection problems she encounters in her car buying and bank loan transactions?

9 Suppose that there are three national football leagues: the Time League, the Goal Difference League and the Bonus for Win League. The leagues are of equal quality, but the players in each league are paid differently. In the Time League, they are paid by the hour for time spent practising and time spent playing. In the Goal Difference league, they are paid an amount that depends on the number of points that the team scores minus the number of points scored against it. In the Bonus for Win League, the players are paid one wage for a loss, a higher wage for a tie and the highest wage of all for a win.

a Briefly describe the predicted differences in the quality of the games played by each of these leagues.

b Which league will be the most attractive to players?

c Which league will generate the largest profits?

10 **We All Pay for the Uninsured**

When buying private healthcare, most of us don't behave like regular consumers: 70 per cent of what we spend is somebody else's money, and we don't have very good information about doctors or hospitals. You can go online and find out your treatment fees before you make an appointment. That's helpful for a routine service, but when you have a serious condition, you really want to know about the quality of care. Now, with the collaboration of doctors, to agree on quality standards and all health plans willing to pool their data, consumers can look at a set of performance indicators and be able to judge the quality of their healthcare.

Source: *Fortune*, 12 May 2008

a Explain how the adverse selection problem applies to private healthcare.

b How does the moral hazard problem apply to healthcare insurance?

11 You can't buy insurance against the risk of being sold a lemon. Why isn't there a market in insurance against being sold a lemon? How does the market provide a buyer with some protection against being sold a lemon? What are the main ways in which markets overcome the lemon problem?

Uncertainty, Information and the Invisible Hand (Study Plan 19.4)

12 In Problem 10, what role can better information play in the healthcare market? Is it possible for there to be too much information in this market?

13 **Show Us Our Money**

I have no clue what my colleagues make and I consider my salary my own business. It turns out that could be a huge mistake. What if employers made all employee salaries known? If you think about it, who is served by all the secrecy? Knowing what other workers make might be more ammunition to gun for a raise.

Source: *Time Magazine*, 12 May 2008

Explain why a worker might be willing to pay for the salary information of other workers.

Economics in the News (Study Plan 19.N)

14 **Making the Grade**

Grade inflation is unfair to students who truly deserve exceptional marks. It also is unfair to graduate applicants who come from universities that don't inflate grades.

Source: NJ.com, 25 September 2007

a What economic role do accurate grades play?

b Who benefits from grade inflation: students, professors, universities or future employers?

c Who bears the cost of grade inflation? How do you think grade inflation might be controlled?

d Is grade inflation efficient?

15 **Manchester United Star Wayne Rooney has £30m 'Break Clause' in New Contract**

Wayne Rooney has signed a new five-year contract with Manchester United that will pay him about £160,000 a week. It is believed that his contract includes a 'break clause' which would allow Rooney to leave for £30 million if yearly targets set for the club are not met.

Source: goal.com, 24 October 2010

a Provide some examples of private information that Wayne Rooney possesses.

b Does a football player present a moral hazard to his team?

c Does a football player present adverse selection problems to his team?

d How does Manchester United get the best possible performance out of Wayne Rooney?

ADDITIONAL PROBLEMS AND APPLICATIONS

 myeconlab You can work these problems in MyEconLab if assigned by your lecturer.

Decisions in the Face of Uncertainty

Use the following table to work Problems 16 to 18.

The table sets out Jimmy's and Zenda's utility of wealth schedules:

Wealth	Jimmy's utility	Zenda's utility
0	0	0
100	200	512
200	300	640
300	350	672
400	375	678
500	387	681
600	393	683
700	396	684

16 What are Jimmy's and Zenda's expected utilities from a bet that gives them a 50 per cent chance of having a wealth of £600 and a 50 per cent chance of having nothing?

17 a Calculate Jimmy's and Zenda's marginal utility of wealth schedules.

    b Who is more risk averse, Jimmy or Zenda? How do you know?

18 Suppose that Jimmy and Zenda have £400 each and that each sees a business project that involves committing the entire £400 to the project. They reckon that the project could return £600 (a profit of £200) with a probability of 0.85 or £200 (a loss of £200) with a probability of 0.15. Who goes for the project and who hangs onto the initial £400?

Use the following information to work Problems 19 to 21.

Two students, Jim and Kim, are offered summer jobs managing a student house-painting business. There is a 50 per cent chance that either of them will be successful and end up with £21,000 of wealth to get them through the next school year. But there is also a 50 per cent chance that either will end up with only £3,000 of wealth. Each could take a completely safe but back-breaking job picking fruit that would leave them with a guaranteed £9,000 at the end of the summer. The table in the next column shows Jim's and Kim's utility of wealth schedules.

Wealth	Jim's utility	Kim's utility
0	0	0
3,000	100	200
6,000	200	350
9,000	298	475
12,000	391	560
15,000	491	620
18,000	586	660
21,000	680	680

19 Does anyone take the painting job? If so, who takes it and why? Does anyone take the fruit-picking job? If so, who takes it and why?

20 What is each student's maximized expected utility? Who has the larger expected wealth? Who ends up with the larger wealth at the end of the summer?

21 If one of the students takes the risky job, how much more would the fruit-picking job have needed to pay to attract that student?

Buying and Selling Risk

Use the following table, which shows Chris's utility of wealth schedule, for Problems 22 and 23.

Chris's wealth is £5,000 and it consists entirely of her share in a risky ice cream business. If the summer is cold, the business will fail, and she will have no wealth. Where Chris lives there is a 50 per cent chance each year that the summer will be cold.

Wealth (pounds)	Utility (units)
5,000	150
4,000	140
3,000	120
2,000	90
1,000	50
0	0

22 If Chris cannot buy cold summer insurance, what is her expected wealth and what is her expected utility?

23 Business Loss Recovery, an insurance company, is willing to sell Chris cold summer insurance at a price of £3,000 a year and promises to pay her £5,000 if the summer is cold and the business fails. Is Chris willing to buy this loss insurance? If she is, is she willing to pay £4,000 a year for it?

Private Information

Use the following information for Problems 24 to 26.

Larry has a good car that he wants to sell; Harry has a lemon that he wants to sell. Each knows what type of car he is selling. You are looking at used cars and plan to buy one.

24 If both Larry and Harry are offering their cars for sale at the same price, from whom would you most want to buy, Larry or Harry, and why?

25 If you made an offer of the same price to Larry and Harry, who would sell to you and why? Describe the adverse selection problem that arises if you offer the same price to Larry and Harry.

26 How can Larry signal that he is selling a good car so that you are willing to pay Larry the price that he knows his car is worth, and a higher price than what you are willing to offer Harry?

27 Pam is a safe driver and Fran is a reckless driver. Each knows what type of driver she is, but no one else knows. What might a car insurance company do to get Pam to signal that she is a safe driver so that it can offer her insurance at a lower premium than it offers to Fran?

28 Why do you think it is not possible to buy insurance against having to put up with a low-paying, miserable job? Explain why a market in insurance of this type would be valuable to workers but unprofitable for an insurance provider and so would not work.

Uncertainty, Information and the Invisible Hand

Use the following news clip for Problems 29 and 30.

Why We Worry About the Things We Shouldn't . . . and Ignore the Things We Should

We pride ourselves on being the only species that understands the concept of risk, yet we have a confounding habit of worrying about mere possibilities while ignoring probabilities, building barricades against perceived dangers while leaving ourselves exposed to real ones: 20 per cent of all adults still smoke; nearly 20 per cent of drivers and more than 30 per cent of backseat passengers don't use seat belts; two-thirds of us are overweight or obese. We dash across the street against the light and build our homes in flood prone areas – and when they're demolished by a storm, we rebuild in the same spot.

Source: *Time Magazine*, 4 December 2006

29 Explain how 'worrying about mere possibilities while ignoring probabilities' can result in people making decisions that not only fail to satisfy social interest, but also fail to satisfy self-interest.

30 How can information be used to improve people's decision making?

Economics in the News

31 After you have studied *Reading Between the Lines* on pp. 450–451, answer the following questions:

a What information do accurate grades provide that grade inflation hides?

b If grade inflation became widespread in secondary schools and universities, what new arrangements do you predict would emerge to provide better information about student ability?

c Do you think grade inflation is in anyone's self-interest? Explain who benefits and how they benefit from grade inflation.

d How do you think grade inflation might be controlled?

32 **Are You Paid What You're Worth?**

How do you know if your pay adequately reflects your contributions to your employer's profits? In many instances, you don't. Your employer has more and better information than you do about how your salary and bonus compare to others in your field, to others in your office, and relative to the company's profits in any given year. You can narrow the information gap a bit if you're willing to buy salary reports from compensation sources. For example, at $200, a quick-call salary report from the US Economic Research Institute will offer you compensation data for your position based on your years of experience, your industry and the place where your company is located.

Source: CNN, 3 April 2006

a Explain the role that asymmetric information can play in worker wages.

b What adverse selection problem exists if a firm offers lower wages to existing workers?

c What will determine how much a worker should actually pay for a detailed salary report?

Monitoring Macroeconomic Performance

The Big Picture

Macroeconomics is a large and controversial subject that is interlaced with political ideological disputes. And it is a field in which charlatans as well as serious thinkers have much to say.

The subject seeks to understand the causes of economic growth, business cycles (booms and busts), unemployment, inflation, exchange rate and interest rate fluctuations, government budget surpluses and deficits, and international payments surpluses and deficits.

Macroeconomics is data-driven. In governments and international organizations, economic statisticians measure and record the performance of the economy.

The two chapters in this part (20 and 21) explain how two main macroeconomic variables, GDP and unemployment, are monitored and measured. You will learn how we use GDP to assess the standard of living and how we use the unemployment rate to assess the overall state of health of the economy.

Understanding Macroeconomic Performance

The first step towards the scientific study of macroeconomics was a reaction against a popular belief, known as *Mercantilism*, that a nation's wealth depends on the amount of gold (or more generally money) that it possesses. Mercantilists said that by imposing tariffs to discourage imports and by increasing its exports, a nation could earn more than it spends and become more wealthy.

Writing in the early 1740s, David Hume (who can lay claim to being the first macroeconomist though the term wasn't coined until well into the twentieth century) explained why the quantity of money (gold in his day) has no effect on a nation's wealth and only affects the general level of prices and the value of money. You will learn about Hume's 'quantity theory of money' later in this book.

In the 1740s, data were scarce and Hume was not able to confirm his theories by checking them against facts. Instead, he conducted thought experiments. He imagined how things would change as the quantity of money increased. Today, macroeconomics is a ruthlessly empirical discipline. It uses data, both historical and current, to probe the causes of economic growth and its fluctuations, and inflation and deflation.

The very idea of making a graph of time-series data arose in a macroeconomic context. In 1776, coincidentally the year in which David Hume died and Adam Smith published his *Wealth of Nations*, yet another Scot, William Playfair, created the first time-series graph. His graph showed the exports, imports and balance of trade between England and a number of other countries. Graphs that you can make with a click of a mouse took hours of painstaking pen and ink drawing at that time and the data on which they were based were extremely scarce.

Today the Office of National Statistics, the OECD, the International Monetary Fund and the statistical departments of every major government and central bank pump out macroeconomic data every day.

It is a good idea to get into the habit of doing your own macroeconomic monitoring. Make a start by visiting www.statistics.gov.uk and dig around.

David Hume, a Scot who lived from 1711 to 1776, did not call himself an economist. 'Philosophy and general learning' is how he described the subject of his life's work. Hume was an extraordinary thinker and writer. Published in 1742, his *Essays, Moral and Political*, range across economics, political science, moral philosophy, history, literature, ethics and religion, and explore such topics as love, marriage, divorce, suicide, death and the immortality of the soul!

His economic essays provide astonishing insights into the forces that cause inflation, business cycle fluctuations, balance of payments deficits and interest rate fluctuations; and they explain the effects of taxes and government deficits and debts.

Data were scarce in Hume's day, so he was not able to draw on detailed evidence to support his analysis. But he was empirical. He repeatedly appealed to experience and evidence as the ultimate judge of the validity of an argument. Hume's fundamentally empirical approach dominates macroeconomics today.

'. . . in every kingdom into which money begins to flow in greater abundance than formerly, everything takes a new face: labour and industry gain life; the merchant becomes more enterprising, the manufacturer more diligent and skilful, and even the farmer follows his plough with greater alacrity and attention.'

DAVID HUME
Essays, Moral and Political

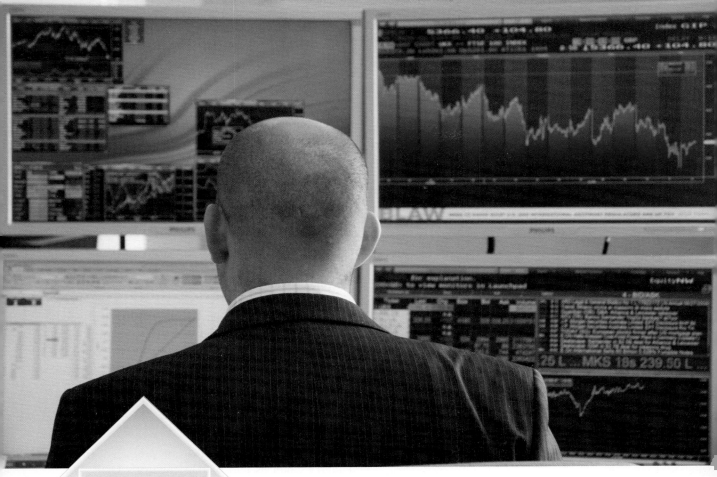

CHAPTER 20

Measuring GDP and Economic Growth

After studying this chapter you will be able to:

◆ Define GDP and explain why it equals aggregate expenditure and aggregate income

◆ Explain how the Office for National Statistics measures UK GDP

◆ Describe how GDP is used and explain its limitations

The recent recession in the UK has been described as the worst since the 1930s. To assess the state of the economy, economists, commentators and politicians turn to the measure of GDP and the growth of GDP. What exactly is GDP and what does it tell us about the state of the economy? And how can we compare economic growth in the 2000s with that in the 1930s?

This chapter explains how the economic statisticians at the Office for National Statistics measure GDP. *Reading Between the Lines* at the end of the chapter, looks at the recession of 2008–2009 and compares it with the recession during the 1930s.

Gross Domestic Product

What exactly is GDP, how is it calculated, what does it mean and why do we care about it? You are going to discover the answers to these questions in this chapter. First, what is GDP?

GDP Defined

GDP or **gross domestic product** is the market value of all the final goods and services produced within a country in a given time period – usually a year. This definition has four parts:

◆ Market value
◆ Final goods and services
◆ Produced within a country
◆ In a given time period

We examine each in turn.

Market Value

To measure total production, we must add together the production of apples and oranges, computers and popcorn. Just counting the items doesn't get us very far. For example, which is the greater total production: 100 apples and 50 oranges, or 50 apples and 100 oranges?

GDP answers this question by valuing items at their *market values* – the prices at which items are traded in markets. If the price of an apple is 10 pence, the market value of 50 apples is £5. If the price of an orange is 20 pence, the market value of 100 oranges is £20. By valuing production at market prices, we can add the apples and oranges together. The market value of 50 apples and 100 oranges is £5 plus £20, or £25.

Final Goods and Services

To calculate GDP, we value the *final goods and services* produced. A **final good** (or service) is an item that is bought by its final user during a specified time period. It contrasts with an **intermediate good** (or service), which is an item that is produced by one firm, bought by another firm and used as a component of a final good or service.

For example, a Ford Focus is a final good, but a tyre on the Ford Focus is an intermediate good. A Dell computer is a final good, but an Intel Pentium chip inside it is an intermediate good.

If we were to add the value of intermediate goods and services produced to the value of final goods and services, we would count the same thing many times – a problem called *double counting*. The value of a Ford Focus already includes the value of the tyres, and the value of a Dell PC already includes the value of the Pentium chip inside it.

Some goods can be an intermediate good in some situations and a final good in other situations. For example, the ice cream that you buy on a hot summer day is a final good, but the ice cream that a café buys and uses to make sundaes is an intermediate good. The sundae is the final good. So whether a good is an intermediate good or a final good depends on what it is used for, not on what it is.

Some items that people buy are neither final goods nor intermediate goods and they are not part of GDP. Examples of such items include financial assets – stocks and bonds – and secondhand goods – used cars or existing homes. A secondhand good was part of GDP in the year in which it was produced, but not in GDP this year.

Produced Within a Country

Only goods and services that are produced *within a country* count as part of that country's GDP. When James Dyson, a British entrepreneur who makes vacuum cleaners, produces them in Malaysia, the market value of those cleaners is part of Malaysia's GDP, not part of the UK's GDP. Toyota, a Japanese firm, produces cars in Deeside, Wales, and the value of this production is part of UK GDP, not part of Japan's GDP.

In a Given Time Period

GDP measures the value of production *in a given time period* – normally either a quarter of a year (called the quarterly GDP data) or a year (called the annual GDP data).

GDP measures not only the value of total production but also total income and total expenditure. The equality between the value of total production and total income is important because it shows the direct link between productivity and living standards. Our standard of living rises when our incomes rise and we can afford to buy more goods and services. But we must produce more goods and services if we are to be able to buy more goods and services.

Rising incomes and a rising value of production go together. They are two aspects of the same phenomenon: increasing production. To see why, we study the circular flow of expenditure and income.

GDP and the Circular Flow of Expenditure and Income

Figure 20.1 illustrates the circular flow of expenditure and income. The economy consists of households, firms, governments and the rest of the world (the rectangles), which trade in factor markets and goods (and services) markets. Let's focus first on households and firms.

Households and Firms

Households sell and firms buy the services of labour, capital and land in factor markets. For these factor services, firms pay income to households: wages for labour services, interest for the use of capital and rent for the use of land. A fourth factor of production, entrepreneurship, receives profit.

Firms' retained earnings – profits that are not distributed to households – are also part of the household sector's income. You can think of retained earnings as being income that households save and lend back to firms. Figure 20.1 shows the *aggregate income* received by all households, including retained earnings, as the blue flow labelled Y.

Households buy and firms sell consumption goods and services – such as beer, pizzas and dry cleaning services – in goods markets. Total payment for these goods and services is **consumption expenditure**, shown by the red flow labelled C.

Firms buy and sell new capital equipment – such as computer systems, aeroplanes, trucks, trains and assembly line equipment – in goods markets.

Some of what firms produce is not sold but is added to their stocks (or inventories). For example, if Ford produces 1,000 cars and sells 950 of them, the other 50 cars remain unsold and the firm's stock of cars increases by 50. When a firm adds unsold output to its stocks, we can think of the firm as buying goods from itself. The purchase of new plant, equipment and buildings, and the additions to stocks, are **investment**, shown by the red flow labelled I.

Figure 20.1 The Circular Flow of Expenditure and Income

Households make consumption expenditures (*C*); firms make investments (*I*); the government purchases goods and services (*G*); the rest of the world buys net exports (*X – M*). Firms pay incomes (*Y*) to households.

Aggregate income (blue flow) equals aggregate expenditure (red flows).

Billions of pounds in 2010

C =	948
I =	208
G =	338
X – M =	–46
Y =	1,448

Governments

Governments buy goods and services from firms and their expenditure on goods and services is called **government expenditure**. In Figure 20.1, government expenditure on goods and services is shown as the red flow G.

Governments finance their expenditure with taxes, but taxes are not part of the circular flow of expenditure and income. Governments also make financial transfers to households, such as unemployment benefits and subsidies to firms. These financial transfers, like taxes, are not part of the circular flow of expenditure and income. Financial transfers and taxes are neither expenditures on goods and services nor income from the services of factors of production.

Rest of World

Firms in the UK sell goods and services to the rest of the world, **exports**, and buy goods and services from the rest of the world, **imports**. The value of exports (X) minus the value of imports (M) is called **net exports**. Figure 20.1 shows net exports by the red flow $X - M$.

If net exports are positive, the net flow of goods and services is from the rest of the world to UK firms. If net exports are negative, the net flow of goods and services is from UK firms to the rest of the world.

GDP Equals Expenditure Equals Income

GDP can be measured in two ways: by the total expenditure on goods and services (called the expenditure approach) or by the total income earned by producing goods and services (called the income approach).

The total expenditure – *aggregate expenditure* – is the sum of the red flows in Figure 20.1. Aggregate expenditure equals consumption expenditure plus investment plus government expenditure plus net exports.

Aggregate income earned by producing goods and services is equal to the total amount paid for the factors used – wages, interest, rent and profit. The blue flow in Figure 20.1 shows aggregate income. Because firms pay out as incomes (including retained profits) everything they receive from the sale of their output, aggregate income (the blue flow) equals aggregate expenditure (the sum of the red flows). That is:

$$Y = C + I + G + X - M$$

The table in Figure 20.1 shows the UK numbers for 2010. You can see that the sum of the expenditures is £1,448 billion, which also equals aggregate income.

Because aggregate expenditure equals aggregate income, these two methods of valuing GDP give the same answer. So:

> **GDP equals aggregate expenditure and equals aggregate income.**

The circular flow model is the foundation on which the national economic accounts are built.

Why Is Domestic Product 'Gross'?

What does the 'gross' in GDP mean? *Gross* means before deducting the depreciation of capital. The opposite of 'gross' is net, which means after deducting the depreciation of capital.

Depreciation is the decrease in the value of a firm's capital that results from wear and tear and obsolescence. The total amount spent on purchases of new capital and on replacing depreciated capital is called **gross investment**. The amount by which the value of the firm's capital increases is called **net investment**.

> Net investment = Gross investment – Depreciation

For example, if easyJet buys 5 new aeroplanes and retires 2 old aeroplanes from service, its gross investment is the value of the 5 new aeroplanes, depreciation is the value of the 2 old aeroplanes retired, and net investment is the value of 3 new aeroplanes.

Gross investment is one of the expenditures included in the expenditure approach to measuring GDP. So the resulting value of total product is a gross measure.

Gross profit, which is a firm's profit before subtracting depreciation, is one of the incomes included in the income approach to measuring GDP. So again, the resulting value of total product is a gross measure.

Review Quiz

1. Define GDP and distinguish between a final good and an intermediate good. Provide examples.
2. Why does GDP equal aggregate income and also equal aggregate expenditure?
3. What is the distinction between gross and net?

You can work these questions in Study Plan 20.1 and get instant feedback.

Let's now see how the ideas that you have just studied can be used in practice. We'll see how GDP and its components are measured in the UK today.

Measuring UK GDP

The Office for National Statistics uses the concepts that you met in the circular flow model to measure GDP and its components, which it publishes in the *United Kingdom National Accounts – The Blue Book*.

Because the value of aggregate output equals aggregate expenditure and aggregate income, there are two approaches available for measuring GDP, and both are used. They are:

◆ The expenditure approach

◆ The income approach

The Expenditure Approach

The *expenditure approach* measures GDP as the sum of consumption expenditure (*C*), investment (*I*), government expenditure on goods and services (*G*) and net exports of goods and services (*X – M*), corresponding to the red flows in the circular flow model in Figure 20.2. Table 20.1 shows the results of this approach for 2010. The table also shows the terms used in the *United Kingdom National Accounts – The Blue Book*.

Consumption expenditure is the expenditure by households on goods and services produced in the UK and the rest of the world. It includes goods such as beer, CDs, books and magazines; and services such as insurance, banking and legal advice. It includes the purchases of consumer durable goods such as cars and washing

Table 20.1

GDP: The Expenditure Approach

Item	Symbol	Amount in 2010 (billions of pounds)	Percentage of GDP
Consumption expenditure (Final consumption expenditure: personal)	*C*	948	65.5
Investment (Gross capital formation)	*I*	208	14.4
Government expenditure (Final consumption expenditure: governments)	*G*	338	23.3
Net exports (External balance of goods and services)	*X – M*	– 46	–3.2
Gross domestic product	*Y*	1,448	100.0

The expenditure approach measures GDP as the sum of consumption expenditure (*C*), investment (*I*) government expenditure (*G*) and net exports (*X – M*). In 2010, GDP as measured by the expenditure approach was £1,448 billion. Almost two-thirds of aggregate expenditure is consump-tion expenditure.

Source of data: Office for National Statistics, *Statistical Bulletin*, 28 September 2010.

machines, but it does *not* include the purchase of new houses, which is counted as part of investment.

Investment is expenditure on capital equipment and buildings by firms and expenditure on new residential houses by households. It also includes the change in firms' stocks or inventories.

Government expenditure is the expenditure on goods and services by all levels of government – from Westminster to the local town hall. This item includes expenditure on national defence, law and order, street lighting and refuse collection. It does *not* include unemployment benefits because they are not purchases of goods and services.

Net exports are the value of UK exports minus the value of UK imports. When a UK company sells a car to a buyer in the US, the value of that car is part of UK exports. When your local Skoda dealer stocks up on the latest model, its expenditure is part of UK imports.

Table 20.1 shows the relative magnitudes of the four items of aggregate expenditure.

Figure 20.2 Aggregate Expenditure

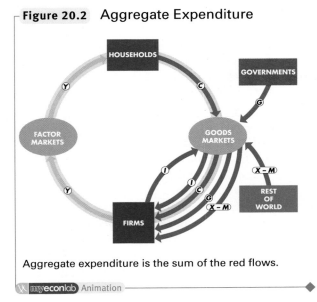

Aggregate expenditure is the sum of the red flows.

myeconlab Animation

The Income Approach

The *income approach* measures GDP by summing the incomes paid by firms to households for the services of the factors of production they hire – wages for labour, interest for capital, rent for land and profit for entrepreneurship. Let's see how the income approach works.

In the *United Kingdom National Accounts – The Blue Book*, incomes are grouped into three components:

1   Compensation of employees
2   Gross operating surplus
3   Mixed income

Compensation of employees is the total payments by firms for labour services. This item includes gross wages and benefits, such as pension contributions and is shown by the blue flow *W* in Figure 20.3.

Gross operating surplus is the total profit made by companies and the surpluses generated by publicly owned enterprises. Some of the profits are paid to households in the form of dividends, and some are retained by companies as undistributed profits. The surpluses from publicly owned enterprises are either retained by the enterprises or paid to the government as part of its general revenue. They are all income and are shown by the blue flow *P* in Figure 20.3.

Mixed income is a combination of rental income and income from self-employment. Rental income is the payment for the use of land and other rented inputs. It includes payments for rented housing and imputed rent for owner-occupied housing. (Imputed rent is an

---

Table 20.2

GDP: The Income Approach

Item	Amount in 2010 (billions of pounds)	Percentage of GDP
Compensation of employees	788	54.4
Gross operating surplus	308	21.3
Mixed income	170	11.7
Gross domestic income at factor cost	1,266	87.4
Indirect taxes less subsidies	182	12.6
Gross domestic product	1,448	100.0

The sum of all factor incomes equals gross domestic income at factor cost. GDP equals net domestic income at factor cost plus indirect taxes less subsidies. In 2010, GDP measured by the factor incomes approach was £1,448 billion. Compensation of employees was by far the largest part of total factor income.

Source of data: Office for National Statistics, *Statistical Bulletin*, 28 September 2010.

---

estimate of what homeowners would pay to rent the housing they own and use themselves. By including this item in the national accounts, we measure the total value of housing services, whether they are owned or rented.) Income from self-employment is a mixture of the factor incomes that we have just reviewed. The proprietor of an owner-operated business supplies labour, capital and perhaps land and buildings to the business.

Table 20.2 shows these three components of aggregate income and their relative magnitudes.

The sum of the incomes is called *gross domestic income at factor cost*. The term *factor cost* is used because it is the cost of the *factors of production* used to produce final goods and services. When we sum all the expenditures on final goods and services, we arrive at a total called *domestic product at market prices*. Market prices and factor cost would be the same except for indirect taxes and subsidies.

An *indirect tax* is a tax paid by consumers when they buy goods and services, such as VAT. An indirect tax makes the market price exceed the factor cost. A *subsidy* is a payment by the government to a producer. With a subsidy, the factor cost exceeds the market price. To get from factor cost to market price, we add indirect taxes and subtract subsidies.

Figure 20.3   Aggregate Income

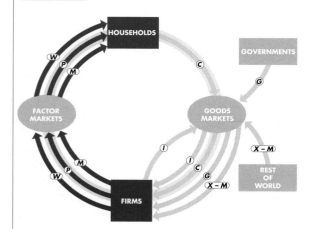

Aggregate income is the sum of the components of the blue flows.

Nominal GDP and Real GDP

Often, we want to compare GDP in two periods, say 2000 and 2010. In 2000, GDP was £977 billion and in 2010 it was £1,448 billion – 48 per cent higher than in 2000. This increase in GDP is a combination of an increase in production and a rise in prices. To isolate the increase in production from the rise in prices, we distinguish between *real* GDP and *nominal* GDP.

Real GDP is the value of final goods and services produced in a given year when valued at the *prices of a reference base year*. By comparing the value of production in the two years at the same prices, we reveal the change in production.

Currently, the reference base year is 2006 and we describe real GDP as measured in 2006 pounds – in terms of what the pound would buy in 2006.

Nominal GDP is the value of final goods and services produced in a given year when valued at the prices of that year. Nominal GDP is just a more precise name for GDP.

Economic statisticians at the Office for National Statistics calculate real GDP using the method described in the Mathematical Note on pp. 476–477. Here, we'll explain the basic idea but not the technical details.

Calculating Real GDP

We'll calculate real GDP for an economy that produces one consumption good, one capital good and one government service. Net exports are zero.

Table 20.3 shows the quantities produced and the prices in 2006 (the base year) and in 2010. In part (a), we calculate nominal GDP in 2006. For each item, we multiply the quantity produced in 2006 by its price in 2006 to find the total expenditure on the item. We sum the expenditures to find nominal GDP, which in 2006 is £100 million. Because 2006 is the base year, both real GDP and nominal GDP equal £100 million.

In Table 20.3(b), we calculate nominal GDP in 2010, which is £300 million. Nominal GDP in 2010 is three times its value in 2006. But by how much has production increased? Real GDP will tell us.

In Table 20.3(c), we calculate real GDP in 2010. The quantities of the goods and services produced are those of 2010, as in part (b). The prices are those in the reference base year – 2006, as in part (a).

For each item, we multiply the quantity produced in 2010 by its price in 2006. We then sum these expenditures to find real GDP in 2010, which is £160 million. This number is what total expenditure would have been

in 2010 if prices had remained the same as they were in 2006.

Nominal GDP in 2010 is three times its value in 2006, but real GDP in 2010 is only 1.6 times its 2006 value – a 60 per cent increase in production.

Table 20.3

Calculating Nominal GDP and Real GDP

Item	Quantity (millions)	Price (pounds)	Expenditure (millions of pounds)
(a) In 2006			
C Shirts	10	5	50
I Computer chips	3	10	30
G Security services	1	20	20
Y Real and Nominal GDP in 2006			100
(b) In 2010			
C Shirts	4	5	20
I Computer chips	2	20	40
G Security services	6	40	240
Y Nominal GDP in 2010			300
(c) Quantities of 2010 valued at prices of 2006			
C Shirts	4	5	20
I Computer chips	2	10	20
G Security services	6	20	120
Y Real GDP in 2010			160

In 2006, the reference base year, real GDP equals nominal GDP and was £100 million. In 2010, nominal GDP increased to £300 million. But real GDP in 2010 in part (c), which is calculated by using the quantities of 2010 in part (b) and the prices of 2006 in part (a), was only £160 million – a 60 per cent increase from 2006.

Review Quiz

1 What is the expenditure approach to measuring GDP?
2 What is the income approach to measuring GDP?
3 What adjustment must be made to total income to make it equal to GDP?
4 What is the distinction between nominal GDP and real GDP?
5 How is real GDP calculated?

You can work these questions in Study Plan 20.2 and get instant feedback.

The Uses and Limitations of Real GDP

We use estimates of real GDP for two main purposes. They are:

◆ To compare the standard of living over time
◆ To compare the standard of living across countries

The Standard of Living Over Time

One method of comparing the standard of living over time is to calculate real GDP per person in different years. **Real GDP per person** is real GDP divided by the population. Real GDP per person tells us the value of goods and services that the average person can enjoy. By using *real* GDP, we remove any influence that rising prices and a rising cost of living might have had on our comparison.

We're interested in both the long-term trends and the shorter-term cycles in the standard of living.

Long-term Trend

A handy way of comparing real GDP per person over time is to express it as a ratio of some reference year. For example, in 1960 real GDP per person was £8,070 and in 2010 it was £21,216. So real GDP per person in 2010 was 2.6 times its 1960 level – that is, £21,216 divided by £8,070. To the extent that real GDP per person measures the standard of living, people were 2.6 times as well off in 2010 as their grandparents had been in 1960.

Figure 20.4 shows the path of UK real GDP per person for the 50 years from 1960 to 2010 and highlights two features of our expanding living standard:

◆ The growth of potential GDP per person
◆ Fluctuations of real GDP per person

The Growth of Potential GDP
Potential GDP is the value of production when all the economy's labour, capital, land and entrepreneurial ability are fully employed. Potential GDP per person, the smoother black line in Figure 20.4, grows at a steady pace because the quantities of the factors of production and their productivities grow at a steady pace.

But potential GDP per person doesn't grow at a constant pace. During the 1960s, it grew at 2.8 per cent per year but slowed to only 2.1 per cent per year during the

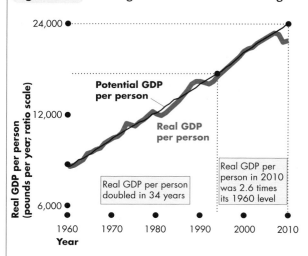

Figure 20.4 Rising UK Standard of Living

Real GDP per person in the UK doubled between 1960 and 1994. In 2010, real GDP per person was 2.6 times its 1960 level. Real GDP per person, the red line, fluctuates around potential GDP per person, the black line. (The y-axis is a ratio scale – see the Appendix, pp. 474–475.)

Source of data: Office for National Statistics, *Statistical Bulletin*. 28 September 2010.

 Animation

1970s. This slowdown might seem small, but it had big consequences, as you'll soon see.

Fluctuations of Real GDP
You can see that real GDP per person, shown by the red line in Figure 20.4, fluctuates around potential GDP per person, and sometimes real GDP per person shrinks.

Let's take a closer look at the two features of our expanding living standard that we've just outlined.

Productivity Growth Slowdown

How costly was the slowdown in productivity growth after 1970? The answer is provided by the *Lucas wedge*, which is the pound value of the accumulated gap between what real GDP per person would have been if the 1960s growth rate had persisted and what real GDP per person turned out to be. (Nobel Laureate Robert E. Lucas Jr. drew attention to this gap.)

Figure 20.5 illustrates the Lucas wedge. The wedge started out small during the 1970s, but by 2010 real GDP per person was £5,962 per year lower than it would have been with no growth slowdown and the accumulated gap was £88,000 per person.

Figure 20.5   The Cost of Slower Growth

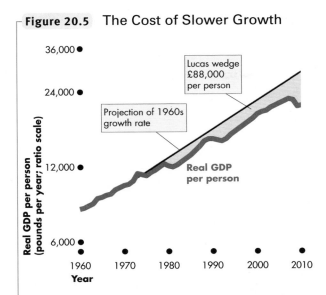

The black line projects the 1960s growth rate of real GDP per person to 2010. The Lucas wedge arises from the slowdown of productivity growth that began during the 1970s. The cost of the slowdown is £88,000 per person.

Source of data: Office for National Statistics, *Statistical Bulletin*. 28 September 2010.

myeconlab Animation

Real GDP Fluctuations – The Business Cycle

We call the fluctuations in the pace of expansion of real GDP the business cycle. The **business cycle** is a periodic but irregular up-and-down movement of total production and other measures of economic activity. The business cycle isn't a regular predictable cycle like the phases of the moon, but every cycle has two phases:

1   Expansion

2   Recession

and two turning points:

1   Peak

2   Trough

Figure 20.6 shows these features of the most recent UK business cycle.

An **expansion** is a period during which real GDP increases. In the early stage of an expansion real GDP returns to potential GDP and as the expansion progresses, potential GDP grows and real GDP eventually exceeds potential GDP.

A common definition of **recession** is a period during which real GDP decreases – its growth rate is negative – for at least two successive quarters. The definition used by the National Bureau of Economic Research, which dates the US business cycle phases and turning points, is 'a period of significant decline in total output, income, employment and trade, usually lasting from six months to a year, and marked by contractions in many sectors of the economy'.

An expansion ends and a recession begins at a business cycle peak, which is the highest level that real GDP has attained up to that time. A recession ends at a trough, when real GDP reaches a temporary low point and from which the next expansion begins.

In the second quarter of 2008 the UK economy went into recession. From a long way below potential GDP, a recovery began at the end of 2009. The recovery looked strong in the first half of 2010, but doubts are beginning to emerge about whether the pace of the recovery will be sustained. *Reading Between the Lines* on pp. 472–473 discusses why.

Figure 20.6   The Most Recent UK Business Cycle

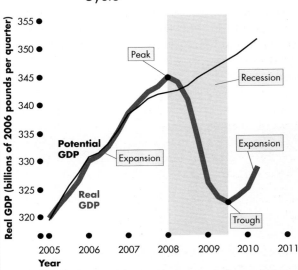

A business cycle expansion, which began in the fourth quarter of 2001, ended at a peak in the second quarter of 2008. A deep and long recession followed the 2008 peak and ended in a trough at the end of 2009 when an expansion began.

Source of data: Office for National Statistics, *Statistical Bulletin*. 28 September 2010.

myeconlab Animation

The Standard of Living Across Countries

Two problems arise in using real GDP to compare living standards across countries. First, the real GDP of one country must be converted into the same currency units as the real GDP of the other country. Second, the goods and services in both countries must be valued at the same prices. Comparing the US and China provides a striking example of these two problems.

China and the US in US Dollars

In 2010, real GDP per person in the US was $42,800 and in China it was 23,400 yuan. The yuan is the currency of China and the price at which the dollar and the yuan exchanged, the market exchange rate, was 8.2 yuan per US$1. Using this exchange rate, 23,400 yuan converts to $2,850. These numbers tell us that real GDP per person in the US was 15 times that in China.

The red line in Figure 20.7 shows real GDP per person in China from 1980 to 2010 when the market exchange rate is used to convert yuan to US dollars.

China and the US at PPP

Figure 20.7 shows a second estimate of China's real GDP per person that values China's production on the same terms as US production. It uses *purchasing power parity* or *PPP* prices, which are the *same prices* for both countries.

Figure 20.7 Two Views of Real GDP in China

Real GDP per person in China has grown rapidly. But how rapidly it has grown and to what level depends on how real GDP is valued. When GDP in 2010 is valued at the market exchange rate, US income per person is 15 times that in China. China looks like a poor developing country. But the comparison is misleading. When GDP is valued at purchasing power parity prices, US income per person is only 6.5 times that in China.

Source of data: International Monetary Fund, World Economic Outlook database, April 2010.

myeconlab Animation

The price of a Big Mac is $3.75 in Chicago and 13.25 yuan or $1.62 in Shanghai. To compare real GDP in China and the US, we must value China's Big Macs at the $3.75 US price – the PPP price.

The prices of some goods are higher in the US than in China, so these items get a smaller weight in China's real GDP than they get in US real GDP. An example is a Big Mac that costs $3.75 in Chicago. In Shanghai, a Big Mac costs 13.25 yuan which is the equivalent of $1.62. So in China's real GDP, a Big Mac gets less than half the weight that it gets in US real GDP.

Some prices in China are higher than in the US but more prices are lower, so Chinese prices put a lower value on China's production than do US prices.

According to the PPP comparisons, real GDP per person in the US in 2010 was 6.5 times that of China, not 15 times.

You've seen how real GDP is used to make standard of living comparisons over time and across countries. But real GDP isn't a perfect measure of the standard of living and we'll now examine its limitations.

Limitations of Real GDP

Real GDP measures the value of goods and services that are bought in markets. Some of the factors that influence the standard of living and that are not part of GDP are:

◆ Household production
◆ Underground economic activity
◆ Health and life expectancy
◆ Leisure time
◆ Environmental quality
◆ Political freedom and social justice

Household Production

An enormous amount of production takes place every day in our homes. Changing a light bulb, cutting the grass, washing the car and growing vegetables are all examples of household production. Because these productive activities are not traded in markets, they are not included in GDP.

The omission of household production from GDP means that GDP *underestimates* total production. But it also means that the growth rate of GDP *overestimates* the growth rate of total production. The reason is that some of the growth rate of market production (included in GDP) is a replacement for home production. So part of the increase in GDP arises from a decrease in home production.

Two trends point in this direction. One is the trend in the number of women who have jobs, which increased from 52.7 per cent of the female population of working age in 1971 to 56.7 per cent in 2010. The other is the trend in the purchase of traditionally home-produced goods and services in the market. For example, more households now buy takeaways, eat in restaurants and use childcare services. This trend means that increasing proportions of food preparation and childcare that used to be part of household production are now measured as part of GDP. So real GDP grows more rapidly than does real GDP plus home production.

Underground Economic Activity

The *underground economy* is the part of the economy purposely hidden from view by the people operating in it to avoid taxes and regulations or because the goods and services they are producing are illegal. Because underground economic activity is unreported, it is omitted from GDP.

The underground economy is easy to describe, even if it is hard to measure. It includes the production and distribution of illegal drugs, prostitution, production that uses illegal labour that is paid less than the minimum wage, and jobs done for cash to avoid paying income taxes. This last category might be quite large and includes tips earned by taxi drivers, hairdressers and hotel and restaurant workers.

Estimates of the scale of the underground economy range between 3.5 and 13.5 per cent of GDP (£51 billion to £195 billion) in the UK and much more in some countries, particularly in Eastern European countries that are making the transition from centrally planned economies to market economies.

If the underground economy is a constant proportion of the total economy, the growth rate of real GDP provides a useful estimate of *changes* in economic welfare and the standard of living. But sometimes production shifts from the underground economy to the rest of the economy, and sometimes it shifts the other way. The underground economy expands relative to the rest of the economy if taxes rise sharply or if regulations become especially restrictive. And the underground economy shrinks relative to the rest of the economy if the burdens of taxes and regulations ease.

Whose production is more valuable: the chef's whose work gets counted in GDP . . .

. . . or the busy mother's whose dinner preparations and child minding don't get counted?

During the 1980s, when tax rates were cut, there was an increase in the reporting of previously hidden income and tax revenues increased. So some part (but probably a very small part) of the expansion of real GDP during the 1980s represented a shift from the underground economy rather than an increase in production.

Health and Life Expectancy

Good health and a long life – the hopes of everyone – do not show up in real GDP, at least not directly. A higher real GDP does enable us to spend more on medical research, healthcare, healthy food and exercise equipment. As real GDP has increased, our life expectancy has lengthened – from 70 years at the end of the Second World War to approaching 80 years today.

But we face new health and life expectancy problems every year. AIDS, drug abuse, suicide and murder are taking young lives at a rate that causes serious concern. When we take these negative influences into account, we see that real GDP growth overstates the improvements in the standard of living.

Leisure Time

Leisure time is an economic good that adds to our standard of living. Other things remaining the same, the more leisure we have, the better off we are. Our time spent working is valued as part of GDP, but our leisure time is not. Yet that leisure time must be at least as valuable to us as the wage that we earn for the last hour worked. If it were not, we would work instead of taking the leisure. Over the years, leisure time has steadily increased. The working week has become shorter and the number and length of holidays have increased. These improvements in economic well-being are not reflected in GDP.

Environmental Quality

Economic activity directly influences the quality of the environment. The burning of hydrocarbon fuels is the most visible activity that damages our environment. But it is not the only example. The depletion of non-renewable resources, the mass clearing of forests, and the pollution of lakes and rivers are other major environmental consequences of industrial production.

Resources used to protect the environment are valued as part of GDP. For example, the value of catalytic converters that help to protect the atmosphere from vehicle emissions is part of GDP. But if we did not use such pieces of equipment and instead polluted the atmosphere, we would not count the deteriorating air that we were breathing as a negative part of GDP.

An industrial society possibly produces more atmospheric pollution than does an agricultural society. But pollution does not always increase as we become wealthier. Wealthy people value a clean environment and are willing to pay for one. Compare the pollution in China today with pollution in the UK. China, a poor country, pollutes its rivers, lakes and atmosphere in a way that is unimaginable in the UK.

Political Freedom and Social Justice

Most people value political freedoms such as those provided by the western democracies. They also value social justice or fairness – equality of opportunity and of access to social security safety nets that protect people from the extremes of misfortune.

A country might have a very large real GDP per person but have limited political freedom and equity. For example, a small elite might enjoy political liberty and extreme wealth, while the vast majority are effectively enslaved and live in abject poverty. Such an economy would generally be regarded as having less economic welfare than one that had the same amount of real GDP but in which political freedoms were enjoyed by everyone. Today, China is the world's fastest-growing economy but the Chinese people have limited political freedoms. India's economy is growing less quickly than China's but the people of India enjoy a democratic political system. Economists have no easy way to determine which of these two countries is better off.

The Bottom Line

Do we get the wrong message about the growth in economic welfare by looking at the growth of real GDP? The influences that are omitted from real GDP are probably important and could be large.

Developing countries have more household production and a larger underground economy than do developed countries, so the gap between their living standards is exaggerated. Also, as real GDP grows, part of the measured growth might reflect a switch from home production to market production and from underground to regular production. This measurement error overstates the growth in economic well-being and the improvement in the standard of living.

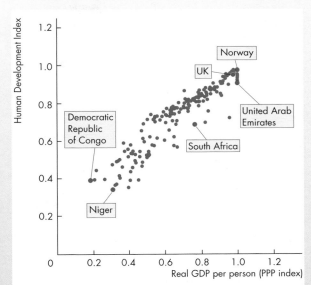

A Broader Indicator of Economic Well-being

The limitations of real GDP reviewed in this chapter affect the standard of living and general well-being of every country. So to make international comparisons of the general state of economic well-being, we must look at real GDP and other indicators.

The United Nations has constructed a broader measure called the Human Development Index (HDI), which combines real GDP, life expectancy and health and education. Real GDP per person (measured on the PPP basis) is a major component of the HDI.

The dots in the figure show the relationship between real GDP per person and the HDI. The United Arab Emirates (UAE) has one of the highest real GDP per person, but it ranks 35th on the HDI. Norway has the highest HDI, and the UK, Australia and Japan have a higher HDI than the UAE. The HDI of the UAE is lower than that of 34 other countries because the people of those countries live longer and have better access to healthcare and education than do citizens of the UAE.

African nations have the lowest levels of economic well-being. The Democratic Republic of Congo has the lowest real GDP per person and Niger has the lowest HDI. But real

Figure 1   The Human Development Index

Source of data: United Nations, hdr.undp.org/en/statistics/data

GDP per person in South Africa is in the middle of the range and its HDI is also in the middle of the range.

Other influences on the standard of living include the amount of leisure time available, the quality of the environment, the security of jobs and homes and the safety of city streets.

It is possible to construct broader measures that combine the many influences that contribute to human happiness. Real GDP will be one element in those broader measures, but it will by no means be the whole of those measures. The United Nation's Human Development Index (HDI) is one example of attempts to provide broader measures of economic well-being and the standard of living. This measure places a good deal of weight on real GDP. Dozens of other measures have been proposed. One includes resource depletion and emissions in a Green GDP measure. Another emphasizes the enjoyment of life rather than the production of goods in a 'genuine progress index' or GPI.

Despite all the alternatives, real GDP per person remains the most widely used indicator of economic well-being and the standard of living.

Review Quiz

1   Distinguish between real GDP and potential GDP and describe how each grows over time.
2   How does the growth rate of real GDP contribute to an improved standard of living?
3   What is a business cycle and what are its phases and turning points?
4   What is PPP and how does it help us to make valid international comparisons of real GDP?
5   Explain why real GDP might be an unreliable indicator of the standard of living.

You can work these questions in Study Plan 20.3 and get instant feedback.

You now know how economists measure GDP and what the GDP data tell us. In *Reading Between the Lines* on pp. 472–473, we examine the path of GDP as we emerge from recession during 2010. Your task in the next chapter is to learn how we monitor employment and unemployment and retail prices.

Reading Between the Lines

The Fragile UK Recovery

The Financial Times, 6 October 2010

Employers Fear Recovery is in Peril from Spending Cuts

Daniel Pimlotte

The economy grew at a reasonable pace in the third quarter but businesses are increasingly alarmed about the prospects for another recession or much weaker growth, according to a closely watched survey. Growth between July and September looks likely to have been 0.4 to 0.5 per cent, according to polling company Markit, an estimate based on its surveys of purchasing managers in the service, manufacturing and building sectors.

That is not far from the 0.6 per cent long-run average pace at which the UK has grown but much slower than the 1.2 per cent growth in the second quarter. Markit warned that many companies were worried about spending cuts, with greater detail on the austerity measures due this month in the government's spending review.

'Orders are not coming through at anything like the pace before the public sector contracts are being cut. Businesses believe these cuts are arriving at the wrong time.'

The evidence of business fears came as Markit published its combined index of activity in services, manufacturing and construction.

Services sector data published on Tuesday showed weak business confidence and new orders rising at the slowest pace in 15 months.

The Essence of the Story

- A poll of purchasing managers suggest that growth in the third quarter of 2010 could be between 0.4 and 0.5 per cent.

- This quarterly growth rate translates into an annual growth rate of 2 per cent, which is not far from the UK long-term growth rate of 2.4 to 2.5 per cent a year.

- Many businesses are worried about cuts in government spending that might depress demand and stall the recovery.

- The fragility of demand and the growth of GDP have raised the prospect that the economy may recover very slowly or even turn down into a double-dip recession.

Economic Analysis

◆ The 2008–2009 recession was an unusually deep one and although the second quarter of 2010 showed a strong recovery, predictions for subsequent quarters were for weak growth.

◆ Figure 1 illustrates the severity of the 2008–2009 recession using the concepts of potential GDP and real GDP that you learned about in this chapter.

◆ At the trough in the third quarter of 2009, real GDP was about £25 billion below potential GDP or 7 per cent of potential GDP.

◆ To put the magnitude of the gap between potential GDP and real GDP into perspective, each person's share (your share) of the lost production for the whole of 2009 was about £1,667.

◆ The prediction from the Markit survey is that the economy will grow by only 0.5 per cent in the third quarter of 2010, which shows the fragility of the recovery and possibly a second downturn.

◆ However, a slowdown in the growth rate does not necessarily mean that the economy will slip back into recession.

◆ The 2008–2009 recession has been described as the worst recession since the 1930s. Figure 2 shows the quarterly profile of the 1930s recession plotted alongside the 2008–2009 recession.

◆ The similarity of the downturn and the recovery between the two periods is striking. It is also the case that just when the economy came out of deep recession in 1931 the economy slipped back into recession in 1932.

◆ While the recession and recovery during the 1930s looks similar to the quarterly profile of 2008–2009 there are many differences in policy that do not make it obvious that the economy will turn downwards in 2011, as it did in 1932.

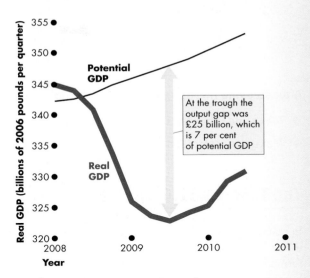

Figure 1 The deep 2008–2009 recession

Figure 2 The 1930s versus 2008–2009

◆ *The Economist* magazine publishes the results of a weekly poll of forecasters and on 9 October 2010 the range of forecasts for UK GDP growth in 2011 was from a low of 0.6 per cent a year to a high of 2.4 per cent a year.

Chapter 20 Appendix

Graphs in Macroeconomics

After studying this appendix, you will be able to:

◆ Make and interpret a time-series graph

◆ Make and interpret a graph that uses a ratio scale

The Time-series Graph

In macroeconomics we study the fluctuations and trends in the key variables that describe macroeconomic performance and policy. These variables include GDP and its expenditure and income components that you've learned about in this chapter. They also include variables that describe the labour market and consumer prices that you study in Chapter 22.

Regardless of the variable of interest, we want to be able to compare its value today with that in the past; and we want to describe how the variable has changed over time. The most effective way to do these things is to make a time-series graph.

Making a Time-series Graph

A **time-series graph** measures time (for example, years, quarters or months) on the *x*-axis and the variable or variables in which we are interested on the *y*-axis. Figure A20.1 is an example of a time-series graph. It provides some information about unemployment in the UK since 1980. In this figure, we measure time in years starting in 1980. We measure the unemployment rate (the variable that we are interested in) on the *y*-axis.

A time-series graph enables us to visualize how a variable has changed over time and how its value in one period relates to its value in another period. It conveys an enormous amount of information quickly and easily.

Let's see how to 'read' a time-series graph.

Reading a Time-series Graph

To practise reading a time-series graph, take a close look at Figure A20.1. The graph shows the level, change and speed of change of the variable.

Figure A20.1   A Time-series Graph

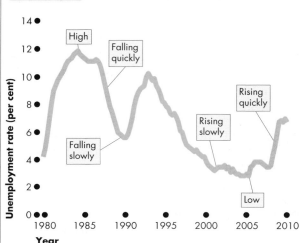

A time-series graph plots the level of a variable on the *y*-axis against time (here measured in years) on the *x*-axis. This graph shows the unemployment rate each year from 1980 to 2010. It shows when unemployment was high, when it was low, when it increased, when it decreased and when it changed quickly and changed slowly.

myeconlab Animation

◆ The *level* of the variable: it tells us when unemployment is high and low. When the line is a long distance above the *x*-axis, the unemployment rate is high, as it was, for example, in 1983 and again in 2009. When the line is close to the *x*-axis, the unemployment rate is low, as it was, for example, in 2001.

◆ The *change* in the variable: it tells us how unemployment changes – whether it increases or decreases. When the line slopes upward, as it did in 2008 and 2009, the unemployment rate is rising. When the line slopes downward, as it did in 1984 and 1997, the unemployment rate is falling.

◆ The *speed* of change in the variable: it tells us whether the unemployment rate is rising or falling quickly or slowly. If the line is very steep, then the unemployment rate increases or decreases quickly. If the line is not steep, the unemployment rate increases or decreases slowly. For example, the unemployment rate rose quickly in 2008 and slowly in 2003 and it fell quickly in 1987 and slowly in 1989.

Ratio Scale Reveals Trend

A time-series graph also reveals whether a variable has a **cycle**, which is a tendency for a variable to alternate between upward and downward movements, or a **trend**, which is a tendency for a variable to move in one general direction.

The unemployment rate in Figure A20.1 has a cycle but no strongly visible trend. When a trend is present, a special kind of time-series graph, one that uses a ratio scale on the *y*-axis, reveals the trend.

A Time-series with a Trend

Many macroeconomics variables, among them GDP and the average level of prices, have an upward trend. Figure A20.2 shows an example of such a variable: the average prices paid by consumers.

In Figure A20.2(a), consumer prices since 1970 are graphed on a normal scale. In 1970 the level is 100. In other years, the average level of prices is measured as a percentage of the 1970 level.

The graph clearly shows the upward trend of prices. But it doesn't tell us when prices were rising fastest or whether there was any change in the trend. Just looking at the upward-sloping line in Figure A20.2(a) gives the impression that the pace of growth of consumer prices was constant.

Using a Ratio Scale

On a graph axis with a normal scale, the gap between 1 and 2 is the same as that between 3 and 4. On a graph axis with a ratio scale, the gap between 1 and 2 is the same as that between 2 and 4. The ratio 2 to 1 equals the ratio 4 to 2. By using a ratio scale, we can 'see' when the growth rate (the percentage change per unit of time) changes.

Figure A20.2(b) shows an example of a ratio scale. Notice that the values on the *y*-axis get closer together but the gap between 400 and 200 equals the gap between 200 and 100. The ratio gaps are equal.

Graphing the data on a ratio scale reveals the trends. In the case of consumer prices, the trend is much steeper during the 1970s and early 1980s than in the later years. The steeper the line in the ratio-scale graph in part (b), the faster are prices rising. Prices rose rapidly during the 1970s and early 1980s and more slowly in the later 1980s and 1990s. The ratio-scale graph reveals this fact. We use ratio-scale graphs extensively in macroeconomics.

Figure A20.2   Ratio Scale Reveals Trend

(a) Normal scale

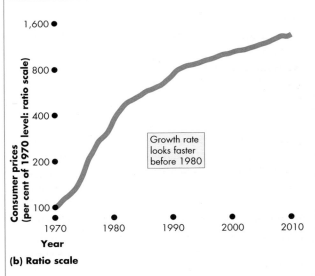

(b) Ratio scale

The graph shows the average of consumer prices from 1970 to 2010. The level is 100 in 1970 and the value in other years is a percentage of the 1970 level. Consumer prices normally rise each year so the line slopes upward. In part (a), where the *y*-axis scale is normal, the rate of increase appears to be constant.

In part (b), where the *y*-axis is a ratio scale (the ratio of 400 to 200 equals the ratio 200 to 100), prices rose faster in the 1970s and early 1980s and slower in the later years. The ratio scale reveals this trend.

MATHEMATICAL NOTE

Chain Volume Measure of Real GDP

In the real GDP calculation on p. 465, real GDP in 2010 is 1.6 times its value in 2006. But suppose that we use 2010 as the reference base year and value real GDP in 2006 at 2010 prices. If you do the mathematics, you will see that real GDP in 2006 is £150 million at 2010 prices. GDP in 2010 is £300 million (in 2010 prices), so now the numbers say that real GDP has doubled. Which is correct? Did real GDP increase 1.6 times or double? Should we use the prices of 2006 or 2010? The answer is that we need to use both sets of prices.

The Office for National Statistics uses a measure of real GDP called the **chain volume measure** of real GDP. Three steps are needed to calculate this measure:

◆ Value production in the prices of adjacent years
◆ Find the average of two percentage changes
◆ Link (chain) back to the reference base year

Value Production in Prices of Adjacent Years

The first step is to value production in adjacent years at the prices of both years. We'll make these calculations for 2010 and its preceding year, 2009.

Table 1 shows the quantities produced and prices in the two years. Part (a) shows the nominal GDP calculation for 2009 – the quantities produced in 2009 valued at the prices of 2009. Nominal GDP in 2009 is £145 million. Part (b) shows the nominal GDP calculation for 2010 – the quantities produced in 2010 valued at the prices of 2010. Nominal GDP in 2010 is £300 million. Part (c) shows the value of the quantities produced in 2010 at the prices of 2009 – a total of £160 million. And part (d) shows the value of the quantities produced in 2009 at the prices of 2010 – a total of £275 million.

Find the Average of Two Percentage Changes

The second step is to find the percentage change in the value of production based on the prices in the two adjacent years. Table 2 summarizes these calculations.

Part (a) shows that, valued at the prices of 2009, production increased from £145 million in 2009 to £160 million in 2010, an increase of 10.3 per cent.

Table 1

Real GDP Calculation Step 1: Value Production in Adjacent Years at Prices in Both Years

Item	Quantity (millions)	Price (pounds)	Expenditure (millions of pounds)
(a) In 2009			
C Shirts	3	5	15
I Computer chips	3	10	30
G Security services	5	20	100
Y Real and Nominal GDP in 2009			**145**
(b) In 2010			
C Shirts	4	5	20
I Computer chips	2	20	40
G Security services	6	40	240
Y Nominal GDP in 2010			**300**
(c) Quantities of 2010 valued at prices of 2009			
C Shirts	4	5	20
I Computer chips	2	10	20
G Security services	6	20	120
Y 2010 production at 2009 prices			**160**
(d) Quantities of 2009 valued at prices of 2010			
C Shirts	3	5	15
I Computer chips	3	20	60
G Security services	5	40	200
Y 2009 production at 2010 prices			**275**

Step 1 is to value the production of adjacent years at the prices of both years. Here, we value the production of 2009 and 2010 at the prices of both 2009 and 2010. The value of 2009 production at 2009 prices, in part (a), is nominal GDP in 2009. The value of 2010 production at 2010 prices, in part (b), is nominal GDP in 2010. Part (c) calculates the value of 2010 production at 2009 prices, and part (d) calculates the value of 2009 production at 2010 prices. We use these numbers in Step 2.

Part (b) shows that, valued at the prices of 2010, production increased from £275 million in 2009 to £300 million in 2010, an increase of 9.1 per cent. Part (c) shows that the average of these two percentage changes in the value of production is 9.7. That is, $(10.3 + 9.1) \div 2 = 9.7$.

By applying this average percentage change to real GDP, we can find the value of real GDP in 2010. Real GDP in 2009 is £145 million, so a 9.7 per cent increase

Table 2

**Real GDP Calculation Step 2:
Find Average of Two Percentage Changes**

Value of Production	Millions of pounds
(a) At 2009 prices	
Nominal GDP in 2009	145
2010 production at 2009 prices	160
Percentage change in production at 2009 prices	**10.3**
(b) At 2010 prices	
2009 production at 2010 prices	275
Nominal GDP in 2010	300
Percentage change in production at 2010 prices	**9.1**
(c) Average percentage change in 2010	**9.7**

Using the numbers in Step 1, the percentage change in production from 2009 to 2010 valued at 2009 prices is 10.3 per cent, in part (a). The percentage change in production from 2009 to 2010 valued at 2010 prices is 9.1 per cent, in part (b). The average of these two percentage changes is 9.7 per cent, in part (c).

Table 3

**Real GDP Calculation Step 3:
Repeat Growth Rate Calculations**

Year	2006	2007	2008	2009	2010
Growth rate	8.0	6.0	7.0	8.0	**9.7**

is £14 million. Then real GDP in 2010 is £145 million plus £14 million, which equals £159 million. Because real GDP in 2009 is in 2009 pounds, real GDP in 2010 is also in 2009 pounds.

Although the real GDP of £159 million is expressed in 2009 pounds, the calculation uses the average of the prices of the final goods and services that make up GDP in 2009 and 2010.

Link (Chain) Back to the Base Year

The third step is to express GDP in the prices of the reference base year. To do this, the Office for National Statistics performs calculations like the ones that you've just worked through to find the percentage change in real GDP in each pair of years. It then selects a base year (currently 2006) in which, by definition, real GDP equals nominal GDP. Finally, it uses the percentage changes to calculate real GDP in 2006 prices starting from real GDP in 2006.

To illustrate this third step, we'll assume that the Office for National Statistics has calculated the growth rates since 2006 shown in Table 3. The 2010 growth rate that we've just calculated is highlighted in the table. The other (assumed) growth rates are calculated in exactly the same way as that for 2010.

Figure 1 illustrates the chain link calculations. In the reference base year, 2006, real GDP equals nominal GDP, which we'll assume is £135 million. Table 3 tells us that the growth rate in 2006 was 8 per cent, so real GDP in 2006 is 8 per cent higher than it was in 2005, which means that real GDP in 2005 is £125 million ($125 \times 1.08 = 135$).

Table 3 also tells us that the growth rate in 2007 was 6 per cent, so real GDP in 2007 is 6 per cent higher than it was in 2006, which means that real GDP in 2007 is £143 million ($135 \times 1.06 = 143$).

By repeating these calculations for each year, we obtain the chain volume measure of real GDP in 2006 pounds for each year. In 2009, chain volume measure of real GDP in 2006 pounds is £165 million. So the 9.7 per cent growth rate in 2010 that we calculated in Table 2 means that real GDP in 2010 is £181 million.

Notice that the growth rates are independent of the reference base year, so changing the reference base year does not change the growth rates.

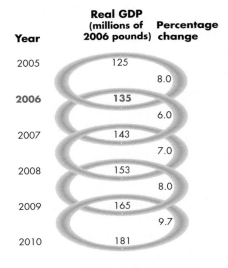

**Figure 1 Real GDP calculation step 3:
link (chain) back to base year**

SUMMARY

Key Points

Gross Domestic Product (pp. 460–462)

◆ GDP, or gross domestic product, is the market value of all the final goods and services produced in a country during a given period.

◆ A final good is an item that is bought by its final user and it contrasts with an intermediate good, which is a component of a final good.

◆ GDP is calculated by using the expenditure or income totals in the circular flow model of expenditure and income.

◆ Aggregate expenditure on goods and services equals aggregate income and GDP.

Working Problems 1 to 7 will give you a better understanding of gross domestic product.

Measuring UK GDP (pp. 463–465)

◆ Because aggregate expenditure, aggregate income and the value of aggregate output are equal, we can measure GDP by either the expenditure approach or the income approach.

◆ The expenditure approach adds together consumption expenditure, investment, government expenditure on goods and services and net exports.

◆ The income approach adds together the incomes paid to the factors of production – wages, interest, rent and profit – and indirect taxes less subsidies.

◆ Real GDP is measured using a common set of prices to remove the effects of inflation from GDP.

Working Problems 8 to 15 will give you a better understanding of measuring UK GDP.

The Uses and Limitations of Real GDP (pp. 466–471)

◆ Real GDP is used to compare the standard of living over time and across countries.

◆ Real GDP per person grows and fluctuates around the more smoothly growing potential GDP.

◆ A slowing of the growth rate of real GDP per person during the 1970s has lowered incomes by a large amount.

◆ International real GDP comparisons use PPP prices.

◆ Real GDP is not a perfect measure of economic welfare because it excludes household production, the underground economy, health and life expectancy, leisure time, environmental quality and political freedom and social justice.

Working Problem 16 will give you a better understanding of the uses and limitations of real GDP.

Key Terms

Business cycle, 467
Chain volume measure, 476
Consumption expenditure, 461
Cycle, 475
Depreciation, 462
Expansion, 467
Exports, 462
Final good, 460
Government expenditure, 462
Gross domestic product (GDP), 460
Gross investment, 462
Imports, 462
Intermediate good, 460
Investment, 461
Net exports, 462
Net investment, 462
Nominal GDP, 465
Potential GDP, 466
Real GDP, 465
Real GDP per person, 466
Recession, 467
Time-series graph, 474
Trend, 475

STUDY PLAN PROBLEMS AND APPLICATIONS

 You can work Problems 1 to 17 in MyEconLab Chapter 20 Study Plan and get instant feedback.

Gross Domestic Product (Study Plan 20.1)

1 Classify each of the following items as a final good or service or an intermediate good or service and identify which is a component of consumption expenditure, investment, or government expenditure on goods and services:

◆ Banking services bought by a student.

◆ New cars bought by Hertz, the car rental firm.

◆ Newsprint bought by *The Times* newspaper.

◆ The purchase of a new limo for the prime minister.

◆ New house bought by Wayne Rooney.

2 The firm that printed this textbook bought the paper from XYZ Paper Mills. Was this purchase of paper part of GDP? If not, how does the value of the paper get counted in GDP?

Use the following figure, which illustrates the circular flow model, to work Problems 3 and 4.

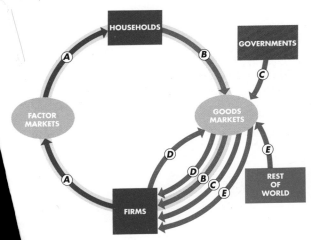

During 2008, in an economy:

◆ Flow *B* was £90 billion.

◆ Flow *C* was £20 billion.

◆ Flow *D* was £30 billion.

◆ Flow *E* was –£7 billion.

~~me~~ the flows and calculate the value of:

~~~~ggregate income.

~~~~DP.

4 During 2009, flow A was £130 billion, flow B was £91 billion, flow D was £33 billion, and flow E was –£8 billion.

Calculate the 2009 values of

a GDP.

b Government expenditure.

5 Use the following data to calculate aggregate expenditure and imports of goods and services.

◆ Government expenditure: £20 billion.

◆ Aggregate income: £100 billion.

◆ Consumption expenditure: £67 billion.

◆ Investment: £21 billion.

◆ Exports of goods and services: £30 billion.

6 US Economy Shrinks Modestly

GDP fell 1 per cent as businesses cut investment by 8.9 per cent, consumers cut spending by 1.2 per cent, purchases of new houses fell 38 per cent, and exports fell 29.9 per cent.

Source: Reuters, 31 July 2009

Use the letters on the figure in Problem 3 to indicate the flow in which each item in the news clip occurs. How can GDP have fallen by only 1.0 per cent with the big expenditure cuts reported?

7 A market research firm deconstructed an Apple iPod and studied the manufacturers' costs and profits of each of the parts and components. The final results are:

◆ An Apple iPod sells in the US for $299.

◆ A Japanese firm, Toshiba, makes the hard disk and display screen, which cost $93.

◆ Other components produced in South Korea cost $25.

◆ Other components produced in the US cost $21.

◆ The iPod is assembled in China at a cost of $5.

◆ The costs and profits of retailers, advertisers and transportation firms in the US are $75.

a What is Apple's profit?

b Where in the national accounts of the US, Japan, South Korea and China are these transactions recorded.

c What contribution does one iPod make to world GDP?

Measuring UK GDP (Study Plan 20.2)

Use the following table, which lists some macroeconomic data for the UK, to work Problems 8 and 9.

Item	Billions of pounds
Compensation of employees	750
Consumption expenditure	900
Gross operating surplus	300
Investment	250
Government expenditure	300
Net exports	−40
Mixed income	150

8 Calculate UK GDP.

9 Given the data supplied, which approach (expenditure or income) to measuring GDP can you use to calculate UK GDP? Explain your answer.

Use the following data to work Problems 10 and 11.

The national accounts of Parchment Paradise are kept on (you guessed it) parchment. A fire destroys the statistics office. The accounts are now incomplete but they contain the following data:

◆ Consumption expenditure: £2,000.

◆ Indirect taxes less subsidies: £100.

◆ Gross operating surplus: £500.

◆ Investment: £800.

◆ Government expenditure: £400.

◆ Compensation of employees: £2,000.

◆ Net exports: −£200.

10 Calculate GDP.

11 Calculate gross domestic income at factor cost.

Use the following data to work Problems 12 and 13.

Tropical Republic produces only bananas and coconuts. The base year is 2009. The table gives the quantities produced and the prices.

Quantities	2009	2010
Bananas	800 kilograms	900 kilograms
Coconuts	400	500

Prices	2008	2009
Bananas	£2 per kilogram	£4 per kilogram
Coconuts	£10 each	£5 each

12 Calculate nominal GDP in 2009 and 2010.

13 Calculate real GDP in 2010 expressed in base-year prices.

Use the following news clip to work Problems 14 and 15.

Toyota to Shift US Manufacturing Efforts

Toyota plans to adjust its US manufacturing operations to meet customer demands for smaller, more fuel-efficient vehicles. In 2008, Toyota started building a plant to produce the 2010 Prius for the US market in Blue Springs, Mississippi. Earlier models of the Prius were produced in Asia.

Source: CNN, 10 July 2008

14 Explain how this change by Toyota will influence US GDP and the components of aggregate expenditure.

15 Explain how this change by Toyota will influence the factor incomes that make up US GDP.

The Uses and Limitations of Real GDP (Study Plan 20.3)

16 Based on the following data in which year did the US standard of living (i) increase and (ii) decrease. Explain your answer.

Year	Real GDP	Population
2006	$13.0 trillion	300 million
2007	$13.2 trillion	302 million
2008	$13.2 trillion	304 million
2009	$12.8 trillion	307 million

Mathematical Note (Study Plan 20.MN)

17 The table provides data on the economy of Mari Republic that produces only fish and crabs.

Quantities	2009	2
Fish	1,000 tonnes	1,1
Crabs	500 tonnes	5

Prices	2009
Fish	£20 per tonne
Crabs	£10 per tonne

a Calculate Maritime Republic's and 2010.

b Calculate Maritime Republic of real GDP in 2010 expres

Data Graphing

Use the Data Grapher in M and 19.

18 In which country i GDP per person hi

19 In which countr GDP per perso

ADDITIONAL PROBLEMS AND APPLICATIONS

 myeconlab You can work these problems in MyEconLab if assigned by your lecturer.

Gross Domestic Product

20 Classify each of the following items as a final good or service or an intermediate good or service and identify which is a component of consumption expenditure, investment, or government expenditure on goods and services:

◆ Banking services bought Google.

◆ Security system bought by Barclays.

◆ Coffee beans bought by Starbucks.

◆ New coffee grinders bought by Starbucks.

◆ Starbuck's grande mocha frappuccino bought by a student.

◆ An aircraft carrier bought by the Royal Navy.

Use the figure in Problem 3 on p. 479 to work Problems 21 and 22.

21 In 2009, flow *A* was £1,000 billion, flow *C* was £250 billion, flow *B* was £650 billion, and flow *E* was £50 billion. Calculate investment.

22 In 2010, flow *D* was £2 trillion, flow *E* was –£1 trillion, flow *A* was £10 trillion, and flow *C* was £4 trillion. Calculate consumption expenditure.

Use the following information to work Problems 23 and 24.

Mitsubishi Heavy Industries makes the wings of the new Boeing 787 Dreamliner in Japan. Toyota assembles cars for the US market in Kentucky.

23 Explain where these activities appear in the US national accounts.

24 Explain where these activities appear in Japan's national accounts.

Use the following news clip to work Problems 25 and 26, and use the circular flow model to illustrate your answers.

Boeing Bets the House

Boeing is producing some components of its new 787 Dreamliner in Japan and is assembling it in the US. Much of the first year's production will be sold to ANA (All Nippon Airways), a Japanese airline.

Source: *The New York Times*, 7 May 2006

25 Explain how Boeing's activities and its transactions affect US and Japanese GDP.

26 Explain how ANA's activities and its transactions affect US and Japanese GDP.

Measuring UK GDP

Use the following data to work Problems 27 and 28.

The table lists some macroeconomic data for the UK.

Item	Billions of pounds
Compensation of employees	770
Consumption expenditure	900
Gross operating surplus	300
Investment	200
Government expenditure	2,900
Net exports	–30

27 Calculate UK GDP.

28 Given the data supplied, which approach (expenditure or income) to measuring GDP can you use to calculate UK GDP? Explain your answer.

Use the following data to work Problems 29 to 31.

An economy produces only apples and oranges. The base year is 2009, and the table gives the quantities produced and the prices.

Quantities	2009	2010
Apples	60	160
Oranges	80	220

Prices	2009	2010
Apples	£0.50 each	£1 each
Oranges	£0.25 each	£2 each

29 Calculate nominal GDP in 2009 and 2010.

30 Calculate real GDP in 2009 and 2010 expressed in base-year prices.

31 **GDP Expands 11.4 per cent, Fastest in 13 Years**

China's gross domestic product grew 11.4 per cent last year and marked a fifth year of double-digit growth. The increase was especially remarkable given that the US is experiencing a slowdown due to the sub-prime crisis and housing slump. Citigroup estimates that each 1 per cent drop in the US economy will shave 1.3 per cent off China's growth, because Americans are heavy users of Chinese products. In spite of the uncertainties, China is expected to post its sixth year of double-digit growth next year.

Source: *The China Daily*, 24 January 2008

Use the expenditure approach for measuring China's GDP to explain why 'each 1 per cent drop in the US economy will shave 1.3 per cent off China's growth'.

The Uses and Limitations of Real GDP

32 The United Nations' Human Development Index (HDI) is based on real GDP per person, life expectancy at birth, and indicators of the quality and quantity of education.

  a Explain why the HDI might be better than real GDP as a measure of economic welfare.

  b Which items in the HDI are part of real GDP and which items are not in real GDP?

  c Do you think the HDI should be expanded to include items such as pollution, resource depletion, and political freedom? Explain.

  d What other influences on economic welfare should be included in a comprehensive measure?

33 **UK Living Standards Outstrip US**

Oxford analysts report that living standards in Britain are set to rise above those in America for the first time since the nineteenth century. Real GDP per person in Britain will be £23,500 this year, compared with £23,250 in America, reflecting not only the strength of the pound against the dollar but also the UK economy's record run of growth since 2001. But the Oxford analysts also point out that Americans benefit from lower prices than those in Britain.

                Source: *The Sunday Times*, 6 January 2008

If real GDP per person is more in the UK than in the US but Americans benefit from lower prices, does this comparison of real GDP per person really tell us which country has the higher standard of living?

34 Use the news clip in Problem 31.

  a Why might China's recent GDP growth rates overstate the actual increase in the level of production taking place in China?

  b Explain the complications involved with attempting to compare economic welfare in China and the US by using the GDP for each country.

35 **Poor India Makes Millionaires at Fastest Pace**

India, with the world's largest population of poor people created millionaires at the fastest pace in the world in 2007. India added another 23,000 more millionaires in 2007 to its 2006 tally of 100,000 millionaires measured in euros. That is 1 millionaire for about 7,000 people living on less than €2 a day.

                Source: *The Times of India*, 25 June 2008

  a Why might real GDP per person misrepresent the standard of living of the average Indian?

  b Why might €2 a day underestimate the standard of living of the poorest Indians?

Economics in the News

36 After you have studied *Reading Between the Lines* on pp. 472–473 answer the following questions.

  a Which measure of GDP would you use to describe the shape of the recovery from recession: real GDP or nominal GDP? Explain your answer.

  b Which measure of GDP would you use to describe the rate of growth of the standard of living: real GDP or nominal GDP? Explain your answer.

  c If the growth rate of potential GDP is 2.5 per cent a year, how fast must the UK economy grow to close the gap between actual GDP and potential GDP: less than 2.5 per cent a year, more than 2.5 per cent a year or 2.5 per cent a year?

  d Why might the news article be wrong about the economy sliding into a double-dip recession?

37 **Totally Gross**

GDP has proved useful in tracking both short-term fluctuations and long-run growth. Which isn't to say GDP doesn't miss some things. Amartya Sen, at Harvard, helped create the UN Human Development Index, which combines health and education data with per capita GDP to give a better measure of the wealth of nations. Joseph Stiglitz, at Columbia, advocates a 'green net national product' that takes into account the depletion of natural resources. Others want to include happiness in the measure. These alternative benchmarks have merit but can they be measured with anything like the frequency, reliability and impartiality of GDP?

                Source: *Time*, 21 April 2008

  a Explain the factors that the news clip identifies as limiting the usefulness of GDP as a measure of economic welfare.

  b What are the challenges involved in trying to incorporate measurements of those factors in an effort to better measure economic welfare?

  c What does the ranking of the UK in the Human Development Index imply about the levels of health and education relative to other nations?

Mathematical Note

38 Use the information in Problem 29 to calculate the chain volume measure of real GDP in 2010 expressed in 2009 pounds.

Data Graphing

Use the Data Grapher in MyEconLab to work Problems 39 and 40.

39 In which country in 2009 was the growth rate of real GDP per person highest: UK, Japan or France?

40 In which country in 2009 was the growth rate of real GDP per person lowest: China, the US or Australia?

Monitoring Jobs and Inflation

After studying this chapter you will be able to:

◆ Explain why unemployment is a problem and describe the trends and cycles in labour market indicators

◆ Explain why unemployment is an imperfect measure of underutilized labour and why it is present even at full employment

◆ Explain why inflation is a problem, how we measure it and why the official measures might be biased

Each month, we track the course of employment and unemployment as measures of economic health. How do we measure the unemployment rate? Is it a reliable vital sign for the economy?

Having a good job that pays a decent wage is only one half of the equation that translates into a good standard of living. The other half is the cost of living. We track the cost of the items we buy with two other numbers that are published every month: the CPI and RPI. How are these numbers calculated and do they provide a good guide to the changes in our cost of living?

These are the questions we study in this chapter. In *Reading Between the Lines* at the end of the chapter, we put the spotlight on the CPI and RPI.

Employment and Unemployment

The state of the labour market has a big impact on our incomes and our lives. In a few years you will be entering the labour market. What kind of market will you enter? Will there be plenty of good jobs to choose among, or will jobs be so hard to find that you end up taking one that doesn't use your education and pays a low wage? The answer depends, to a large degree, on the total number of jobs available and on the number of people competing for them.

Those leaving university in 2010 had an unusually tough time in the jobs market. As recession deepened, the number of unemployed steadily increased until, in May 2009, it passed the 2.4 million mark. Unemployment remained above that level for the rest of 2009 and the whole of 2010. In a normal year, unemployment is less than half that level. And in normal times, the UK economy is an incredible job-creating machine. Even in 2009, 26 million people had jobs. But in recent years, population growth has outstripped jobs growth, so unemployment has become a major problem.

Why Unemployment is a Problem

Unemployment is a serious personal, social and economic problem for two main reasons. It results in:

◆ Lost incomes and production
◆ Lost human capital

Lost Incomes and Production

The loss of a job brings with it a loss of income and lost production. These losses are devastating for the people who have to bear them. Unemployment benefits create a safety net and cushion the blow of loss of earnings, but they do not replace lost earnings.

Lost production means lower income and lower consumption. It also means lower investment in capital, which lowers the standard of living both in the present and the future.

Lost Human Capital

Prolonged unemployment permanently damages a person's job prospects by destroying human capital.

◆ ECONOMICS IN ACTION

What Kept John Maynard Keynes Awake at Night

In 1921, the UK unemployment rate shot up to 15 per cent. It remained between 10 and 15 per cent until the early 1930s when it jumped yet higher to almost 25 per cent. Unemployment wouldn't return to below 5 per cent until the first years of World War II in the 1940s.

Puzzled by persistently high unemployment, economist John Maynard Keynes set to work trying to understand how it could happen and what might be done about it. He published his answers in 1936 in the *General Theory of Employment, Interest, and Money*, a book that created what we now call macroeconomics.

Many economists have studied this period of economic history and a shorter yet equally severe Great Depression that occurred in the US and many other economies. Among them are the current chairman of the US Federal Reserve System, Ben Bernanke.

A key reason why the Federal Reserve and the Bank of England were so aggressive in cutting interest rates and injecting money to save banks like Bear Stearns in the US and Northern Rock and the Royal Bank of Scotland in the

UK during the recent recession is that economists today are keenly aware of the horrors of total economic collapse. Both the Federal Reserve and the Bank of England were determined to avoid what they see as the mistakes of the 1920s and 1930s that brought Britain's interwar depression and the Great Depression in the US.

Think about a manager who loses his job when his employer downsizes. He takes work as a taxi driver. After a year he finds out that he can't compete with fresh graduates. Eventually he gets a management job but in a small firm at a lower salary than he was earning before. He has lost some of his human capital.

The cost of unemployment is spread unequally and is one of the most important causes of poverty and social deprivation.

Governments try to measure unemployment accurately and adopt policies to ease its pain. Let's see how the UK government measures unemployment.

Labour Force Survey

Every working day, interviewers of the Social and Vital Statistics Division of the Office for National Statistics (the ONS) contact close to 1,000 households (60,000 in a three-month period) and ask them questions about the age and labour market status of the household's members. This survey is called the Labour Force Survey (or LFS). The ONS uses the information obtained to describe the changing anatomy of the labour market.

Figure 21.1 shows the population categories used by the ONS and the relationships among them. The population divides into two groups: the working-age population and others. The **working-age population** is the total number of men aged 16 to 64 and women aged 16 to 59 who are not in prison, hospital or some other form of institutional care.

Members of the working-age population are either economically active or economically inactive. The **economically active** – also called the **workforce** – are people who have a job or are willing and able to take a job. The **economically inactive** are people who don't want a job. Most of the economically inactive are in full-time education or have retired.

The economically active are either employed or unemployed. To be counted as employed, a person must have either a full-time job or a part-time job. A student who does part-time work is counted as employed. To be counted as *un*employed, people must be available for work within the two weeks following their interview and must be in one of three categories:

1 Without work, but having made specific efforts to find a job within the previous four weeks.

2 Waiting to be called back to a job from which they have been laid off.

3 Waiting to start a new job within 30 days.

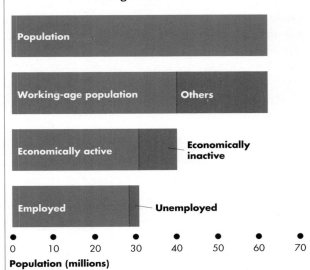

Figure 21.1   Population Workforce Categories

Population (millions)

The population is divided into the working-age population and others (the young, the retired and institutionalized). The working-age population is divided into those who are economically active (in the workforce) and those who are economically inactive. The economically active are either employed or unemployed.

Source of data: Office for National Statistics.

myeconlab Animation

People in the working-age population who are neither employed nor unemployed are classified as economically inactive.

In 2010, the population of the UK was 62.1 million. There were 22.1 million below or above working age or living in institutions. So the working-age population in 2010 was 40 million. Of this number, 9.3 million were economically inactive (not in the workforce). The remaining 30.7 million were economically active. Of the economically active, 28.3 million were employed and 2.4 million were unemployed.

Three Labour Market Indicators

The Office for National Statistics calculates three indicators of the state of the labour market. They are:

◆ The unemployment rate

◆ The employment rate

◆ The economic activity rate

The Unemployment Rate

The amount of unemployment is an indicator of the extent to which people who want jobs can't find them. The **unemployment rate** is the percentage of economically active people who are unemployed.

$$\text{Unemployment rate} = \frac{\text{Number of people unemployed}}{\text{Workforce}} \times 100$$

and

$$\text{Workforce} = \text{Number employed} + \text{Number unemployed}$$

In the UK in 2010, the number of people employed was 28.3 million and the number unemployed was 2.4 million. By using the above equations, the workforce was 30.7 million (28.3 million plus 2.4 million) and the unemployment rate was 7.8 per cent (2.4 million divided by 30.7 million, multiplied by 100).

Figure 21.2 shows the unemployment rate between 1980 and 2010. The average unemployment rate was 10 per cent during the decade of the 1980s and 8.3 per cent during the 1990s, but during the 2000s it was 5.5 per cent. The unemployment rate fluctuates and reached peak values at the end of recessions in 1980–1982 and 1990–1992. In 2010, it was not possible to say if the unemployment rate had reached a peak.

The Employment Rate

The number of people of working age who have jobs is an indicator of the availability of jobs and the degree of match between people's skills and jobs. The **employment rate** is the percentage of the people of working age who have jobs. That is:

$$\text{Employment rate} = \frac{\text{Number of people employed}}{\text{Working-age population}} \times 100$$

In 2010, the number of people employed in the UK was 28.3 million and the working-age population was 40 million. By using the above equation, you can calculate the employment rate. It was 70.8 per cent (28.3 million divided by 40 million, multiplied by 100).

Figure 21.3 shows the UK employment rate. It has followed a gently rising trend through the period since 1980. This upward trend means that the economy has created jobs at a faster rate than the working-age population has grown.

Figure 21.2 The Unemployment Rate: 1980–2010

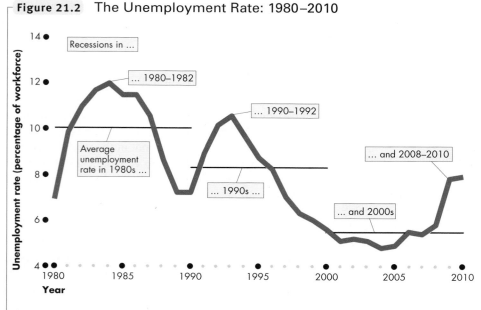

The average unemployment rate was 10 per cent during the 1980s, 8.3 per cent during the 1990s and 5.5 per cent during the 2000s.

The unemployment rate increases in recessions and decreases in expansions.

In 2010, it was unclear whether the unemployment rate had peaked.

Source of data: Office for National Statistics.

Figure 21.3   Economic Activity Rate and Employment Rate: 1980–2010

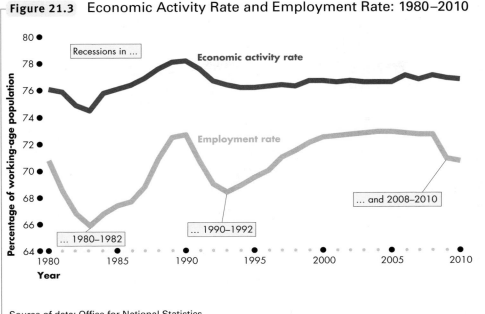

The employment rate decreases in recessions and increases in expansions. It has a slight upward trend. The economic activity rate has no trend The employment rate fluctuates more than the economic activity rate and reflects cyclical fluctuations in the unemployment rate. Fluctuations in the economic activity rate arise from fluctuations in the number of workers who want a job.

Source of data: Office for National Statistics.

myeconlab Animation

This labour market indicator also fluctuates over the business cycle. It reached a trough of 65.9 per cent in 1983, and its fluctuations coincide with, but are opposite to, those in the unemployment rate.

The Economic Activity Rate

The number of people in the workforce is an indicator of the willingness of the people of working age to take jobs. The **economic activity rate** is the percentage of the working-age population who are economically active. They are the members of the workforce.

$$\frac{\text{Economic}}{\text{activity rate}} = \frac{\text{Workforce}}{\text{Working-age population}} \times 100$$

In 2010, the workforce was 30.7 million and the working-age population was 40 million. By using the above equation, you can calculate the economic activity rate. It was 76.8 per cent (30.7 million divided by 40 million, multiplied by 100).

Figure 21.3 shows the economic activity rate. It rose slightly from 76.1 per cent in 1980 to 76.8 per cent in 2010. It also had some mild fluctuations, which result from unsuccessful job seekers leaving the workforce during a recession and re-entering during an expansion.

Other Definitions of Economic Inactivity and Unemployment

Do fluctuations in the economic activity rate over the business cycle mean that people who leave the workforce during a recession should be counted as unemployed? Or are they correctly counted as economically inactive?

The ONS believes that the official unemployment definition gives the correct measure of the unemployment rate. But the ONS provides data on the reasons for economic inactivity. These data provide information on two relevant groups of people:

◆ Discouraged workers

◆ Others who want a job

Discouraged Workers

A **discouraged worker** is someone who is available and willing to work but who has stopped actively looking for a job because he or she believes that no jobs are available. These workers often temporarily leave the workforce during a recession and re-enter during an expansion.

The distinction between an unemployed person and a discouraged worker turns on whether there has been recent job search activity. Both are available for work and want work but the unemployed person has looked for a job while the discouraged worker has given up looking.

Figure 21.4 shows the percentage of economically inactive people who are discouraged workers from 1993 (when the ONS started measuring this number) to 2010.

You can see that discouraged workers are a tiny percentage of the economically inactive and have become less important during the 2000s. The number did, though, increase during the recent recession.

Others Who Want a Job

Others who want a job are people who are economically inactive and are willing to work but who have stopped actively looking for a job and who are not available to start a job in the next two weeks.

Like the discouraged workers, many of these people temporarily leave the workforce during a recession and re-enter during an expansion.

Figure 21.4 shows the percentage of economically inactive people who say they want a job (excluding discouraged workers) from 1993 to 2010.

You can see that this category of people is large. On average, about 25 per cent of the economically inactive say they want a job. This percentage fluctuates between a low of 22 per cent and a high of more than 27 per cent. The correlation between these fluctuations and the business cycle is not strong.

The official unemployment measure excludes economically inactive people because they haven't made specific efforts to find a job within the past four weeks and they are not available for work in the next two weeks. In other respects, they are unemployed.

Most Costly Unemployment

All unemployment is costly, but the most costly is long-term unemployment that results from job loss. People who are unemployed for a few weeks and then find another job bear some costs of unemployment. But these costs are low compared to the costs borne by people who remain unemployed for many weeks.

Also, people who are unemployed because they voluntarily leave their jobs to find better ones or because they have just entered or re-entered the labour market bear some costs of unemployment. But these costs are lower than those borne by people who lose their job and are forced back into the job market.

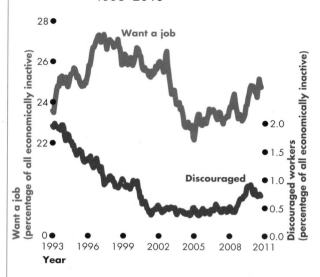

Figure 21.4 Discouraged Workers and Others Who Want a Job: 1993–2010

Discouraged workers make up a very small percentage of the economically inactive. They fell from 2 per cent in 1993 to about 0.5 per cent during most of the 2000s. In the 2009 recession, they increased to almost 1 per cent. Others who want a job average about 25 per cent of the economically inactive and this percentage fluctuates but does not correlate closely with the business cycle.

Source of data: Office for National Statistics.

 Animation

You've now seen how we measure employment and unemployment. Your next task is to see what we mean by full employment and how unemployment and real GDP fluctuate over the business cycle.

Unemployment and Full Employment

There is always someone without a job who is searching for one, so there is always some unemployment. The key reason is that the economy is a complex mechanism that is always changing – it experiences frictions, structural change and cycles.

Frictional Unemployment

There is an unending flow of people into and out of the workforce as people move through the stages of life – from being in school to finding a job, to working, perhaps to becoming unhappy with a job and looking for a new one and, finally, to retiring from full-time work.

There is also an unending process of job creation and job destruction as new firms are born, firms expand or contract and some firms fail and go out of business.

The flows into and out of the workforce and the processes of job creation and job destruction create the need for people to search for jobs and for businesses to search for workers. Businesses don't usually hire the first person who applies for a job, and unemployed people don't usually take the first job that comes their way. Instead, both firms and workers spend time searching for what they believe will be the best available match. By this process of search, people can match their own skills and interests with the available jobs and find a satisfying job and a good income.

The unemployment that arises from the normal labour turnover we've just described – from people entering and leaving the workforce and from the ongoing creation and destruction of jobs – is called **frictional unemployment**. Frictional unemployment is a permanent and healthy phenomenon in a dynamic growing economy.

Structural Unemployment

The unemployment that arises when changes in technology or international competition change the skills needed to perform jobs or change the location of jobs is called **structural unemployment**. Structural unemployment usually lasts longer than frictional unemployment because workers must usually retrain and possibly relocate to find a job. For example, on the day the shipyards in the Upper Clyde announced the loss of 600 jobs, a computer chip company in Gwent announced the creation of 750 new jobs. The unemployed former shipyard workers remained unemployed for several months until

they moved home, retrained and got one of the new jobs created in other parts of the country.

Structural unemployment is painful, especially for older workers for whom the best available option might be to retire early or to take a lower-skilled, lower-paid job.

Cyclical Unemployment

The higher than normal unemployment at a business cycle trough and the lower than normal unemployment at a business cycle peak is called **cyclical unemployment**. A worker who is laid off because the economy is in a recession and who gets rehired some months later when the expansion begins has experienced cyclical unemployment.

'Natural' Unemployment

Natural unemployment is the unemployment that arises from frictions and structural change when there is no cyclical unemployment – when all the unemployment is frictional and structural. Natural unemployment as a percentage of the workforce is called the **natural unemployment rate**.

Full employment is defined as a situation in which the unemployment rate equals the natural unemployment rate.

What determines the natural unemployment rate? Is it constant or does it change over time?

The natural unemployment rate is influenced by many factors but the most important ones are:

◆ The age distribution of the population
◆ The scale of structural change
◆ The real wage rate
◆ Unemployment benefits

The Age Distribution of the Population

An economy with a young population has a large number of new job seekers every year and has a high level of frictional unemployment. An economy with an ageing population has fewer new job seekers and a low level of frictional unemployment.

The Scale of Structural Change

The scale of structural change is sometimes small. The same jobs using the same machines remain in place for many years. But sometimes there is a technological upheaval. The old ways are swept aside: millions of jobs are lost and the skill to perform them loses value. The amount of structural unemployment fluctuates with the pace and volume of technological change and the change driven by fierce international competition, especially from fast-changing Asian economies. A high level of structural unemployment is present in many parts of the UK today.

The Real Wage Rate

The natural unemployment rate is influenced by the level of the real wage rate. Real wage rates that bring unemployment are a minimum wage and an efficiency wage. Chapter 6 (see pp. 131–132) explains how the minimum wage creates unemployment. An *efficiency wage* is a wage set above the going market wage to enable firms to attract the most productive workers, get them to work hard and discourage them from leaving.

Unemployment Benefits

Unemployment benefits increase the natural unemployment rate by lowering the opportunity cost of job search. European countries have more generous unemployment benefits and higher natural unemployment rates than the US. Extending unemployment benefits increases the natural unemployment rate.

There is no controversy about the existence of a natural unemployment rate. Nor is there disagreement that the natural unemployment rate changes. But economists don't know its exact size or the extent to which it fluctuates.

There is no official estimate of the natural unemployment rate for the UK. The one in Figure 21.5 is our own estimate. In 2010 our estimate of the natural unemployment rate was 4.8 per cent – about a half of the unemployment in that year.

Real GDP and Unemployment Over the Business Cycle

The quantity of real GDP at full employment is potential GDP (p. 466). Over the business cycle, real GDP fluctuates around potential GDP. The gap between real GDP and potential GDP is called the **output gap**. As the output gap fluctuates over the business cycle, the unemployment rate fluctuates around the natural unemployment rate.

Figure 21.5 The Output Gap and the Unemployment Rate

(a) Output gap

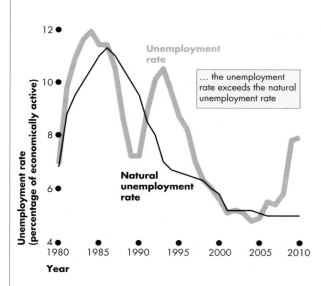

(b) Unemployment rate

As real GDP fluctuates around potential GDP in part (a), the unemployment rate fluctuates around the natural unemployment rate in part (b). During the recession in the early 1990s, the output gap became negative and the unemployment rate increased to 10 per cent. During the 1980s the natural unemployment rate fell. The graph shows our estimate of how far it fell.

Sources of data: Office for National Statistics; and authors' assumptions and calculations.

myeconlab Animation

ECONOMICS IN ACTION

Jobs in Recession and Recovery

You've seen in Figure 21.5 how fluctuations in the output gap line up with fluctuations in the unemployment rate around the natural unemployment rate.

Here, we are looking at the relationship between real GDP and employment. When real GDP falls during a recession, employment falls too; when real GDP rises in an expansion, employment rises. But there is a delay in the response of employment that is visible in high frequency quarterly data.

The figure shows the changes in real GDP and employment during the recession and expansion during 2008 to 2010. Real GDP shrank until the third quarter of 2009 and then started to expand. Total employment shrank with real GDP, but kept on shrinking until the first quarter of 2010. Only in the second quarter of 2010 did total employment begin to increase.

There is an interesting difference in the way that part-time and full-time employment change during recession and expansion. Part-time employment increases right through the recession. Full-time employment falls until the expansion has been running for six months.

In a recession firms are reluctant to take on new full-time workers. Hiring part-time workers gives them greater flexibility to respond in either direction to changes in production.

Figure 1   Real GDP and Employment in Recession and Recovery

Source of data: Office for National Statistics.

Figure 21.5 illustrates these fluctuations in the UK between 1980 and 2010 – the output gap in part (a) and the unemployment rate and natural unemployment rate in part (b).

When the economy is at full employment, the unemployment rate equals the natural unemployment rate and real GDP equals potential GDP so the output gap is zero. When the unemployment rate is less than the natural unemployment rate, real GDP is greater than potential GDP and the output gap is positive. And when the unemployment rate is greater than the natural unemployment rate, real GDP is less than potential GDP and the output gap is negative.

Figure 22.5(b) shows an estimate of the natural unemployment rate that is consistent with the estimate of the output gap in part (a). While we have a good estimate of real GDP and unemployment, we must use assumptions to estimate potential GDP, the output gap and the natural unemployment rate. So the picture presented in the figure is just one estimate. In the figure, the natural unemployment rate is high during the 1980s but falls steadily through the 1980s and 1990s to 5 per cent by

2006. This estimate of the natural unemployment rate in the UK is one that many, but not all, economists would accept.

Review Quiz

1   Define frictional, structural and cyclical unemployment and provide an example of each type of unemployment.
2   What is the natural unemployment rate?
3   What factors might make the natural unemployment rate change?
4   How does the unemployment rate fluctuate over the business cycle?

You can work these questions in Study Plan 21.2 and get instant feedback.

Your final task in this chapter is to learn about another vital sign that gets monitored every month, the Retail Prices Index (RPI) and the Consumer Prices Index (CPI). What are the RPI and CPI, how do we measure them and what do they mean?

The Price Level, Inflation and Deflation

What will it *really* cost you to pay off your student loan? What will your parents' life savings buy when they retire? The answers depend on what happens to the **price level**, the average level of prices and the value of money. A persistently rising price level is called **inflation**; a persistently falling price level is called **deflation**.

We are interested in the price level, inflation and deflation for two main reasons. First, we want to measure the price level and the inflation rate or deflation rate. Second, we want to distinguish between the money values and real values of economic variables such as your student loan and your parent's savings.

We begin by explaining why inflation and deflation are problems, then we look at how we measure the price level and the inflation rate and finally, we return to the task of distinguishing real values from money values.

Why Inflation and Deflation are Problems

Low, steady and anticipated inflation or deflation isn't a problem, but an unexpected burst of inflation or period of deflation brings four big problems and costs:

◆ Redistributes income
◆ Redistributes wealth
◆ Lowers real GDP and employment
◆ Diverts resources from production

Redistributes Income

Workers and employers sign wage contracts that last for a year or more. An unexpected burst of inflation raises prices but doesn't immediately raise wages. Workers are worse off because their wages buy less than they bargained for and employers are better off because their profits rise.

An unexpected deflation has the opposite effect. With a fall in prices, workers are better off because their fixed wages buy more than they bargained for and employers are worse off with lower profits.

Redistributes Wealth

People enter into loan contracts that are fixed in money terms and that pay an interest rate agreed as a percentage of the money borrowed and lent. With an unexpected

burst of inflation, the money that the borrower repays to the lender buys less than the money originally loaned. The borrower wins and the lender loses. The interest paid on the loan doesn't compensate the lender for the loss in the value of the money loaned. With an unexpected deflation, the money that the borrower repays to the lender buys more than the money originally loaned. The borrower loses and the lender wins.

Lowers Real GDP and Employment

Unexpected inflation that raises firms' profits brings a rise in investment and a boom in production and employment. Real GDP rises above potential GDP and the unemployment rate falls below the natural rate. But this situation is temporary. Profitable investment dries up, spending falls, real GDP falls below potential GDP and the unemployment rate rises. Avoiding these swings in production and jobs means avoiding unexpected swings in the inflation rate.

An unexpected deflation has even greater consequences for real GDP and jobs. Businesses and households that are in debt (borrowers) are worse off and they cut their spending. A fall in total spending brings a recession and rising unemployment.

Diverts Resources from Production

Unpredictable inflation or deflation turns the economy into a casino and diverts resources from productive activities to forecasting inflation. It can become more profitable to forecast the inflation rate or deflation rate correctly than to invent a new product. Doctors, lawyers, accountants, farmers – just about everyone – can make themselves better off, not by specializing in the profession for which they have been trained but by spending more of their time dabbling as amateur economists and inflation forecasters and managing their investments.

From a social perspective, the diversion of talent that results from unpredictable inflation is like throwing scarce resources into a landfill. This waste of resources is a cost of inflation.

At its worst, inflation becomes **hyperinflation** – an inflation rate of 50 per cent a month or higher that grinds the economy to a halt and society to a collapse. Hyperinflation is rare, but Zimbabwe has experienced it in recent years.

The ONS monitors the price level every month and devotes considerable resources to measuring it accurately. You're now going to see how the ONS does this.

The Price Indexes

The ONS calculates two price indexes every month. They are the **Retail Prices Index (RPI)** and the **Consumer Prices Index (CPI)** and both measure an average of the prices paid by consumers for a fixed 'basket' of goods and services. What you learn in this section will help you to interpret the RPI and the CPI and see how they tell you what has happened to the value of your money.

Reading the RPI and CPI

The RPI is defined to equal 100 for a period called the **reference base period**. Currently, the reference base period is January 1987. That is, for January 1987, the RPI equals 100. In January 2010, the RPI was 217.9. This number tells us that the average of the prices paid by households for a particular basket of consumer goods and services was 117.9 per cent higher in January 2010 than it was in January 1987.

The reference base period for the CPI is June 2005 and in June 2010, the CPI was 114.6. We read the CPI and calculate the percentage change since the base period in the same way as you've just seen for the RPI. The CPI in June 2010 was 14.6 per cent higher than in June 2005.

Constructing the RPI and CPI

Constructing the RPI and the CPI is a huge operation that costs millions of pounds and involves three stages:

◆ Selecting the basket
◆ Conducting a monthly price survey
◆ Calculating the price index

Selecting the Basket

The first stage in constructing a price index is to select the 'basket' of goods and services that the index will cover. The RPI basket contains the goods and services bought by an average household in the UK. The idea is to make the relative importance of the items in the RPI basket the same as that in the budget of an average household. For example, because people spend more on housing than on bus rides, the RPI places more weight on the price of housing than on the price of a bus ride.

The CPI basket is a bit different from the RPI basket and covers *all* expenditure on consumer goods and services made in the UK by private households, residents of institutions and tourists.

To determine the spending patterns of households and to select the RPI and CPI baskets, the ONS conducts periodic expenditure surveys. These surveys are costly and so are undertaken infrequently. Figure 21.6 shows the RPI and CPI baskets in 2010.

Figure 21.6   The RPI and CPI Baskets

(a) The RPI basket

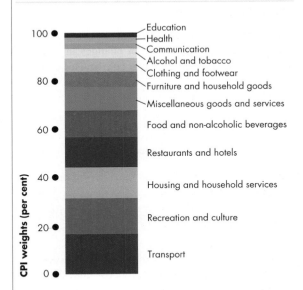

(b) The CPI basket

The RPI basket contains items that a typical household buys. The CPI basket is broader and contains all the goods and services bought by households in the UK.

Source of data: Office for National Statistics.

myeconlab Animation

For the RPI, there are five major categories of which by far the largest is housing and household expenditure. Travel and leisure comes next and is larger than food, alcoholic drinks and tobacco combined.

The ONS breaks down each of these categories into ever smaller ones, right down to distinguishing between packaged and loose new potatoes!

The CPI basket contains 12 major categories of which transport and recreation and culture are the largest.

As you look at the relative importance of the items in the RPI and CPI baskets, remember that they apply to an *average* household. *Individual* households are spread around the average. Think about your own expenditure and compare the basket of goods and services you buy with the RPI and CPI baskets.

Conducting a Monthly Price Survey

Each month, ONS employees check 110,000 prices of more than 550 types of goods and services. They visit shops in about 150 places throughout the UK to see the goods and the prices to ensure accuracy. Because the RPI and CPI aim to measure price *changes*, it is important that the prices recorded each month refer to exactly the same item. For example, suppose the price of a packet of biscuits has decreased but a packet now contains fewer biscuits. Has the price of biscuits decreased, remained the same or increased? The ONS price checker must record the details of changes in quality or packaging so that price changes can be isolated from other changes.

Calculating the Price Index

The RPI and CPI calculations have three steps:

1 Find the cost of the basket at base-period prices.

2 Find the cost of the basket at current-period prices.

3 Calculate the index for the base period and the current period.

We'll work through these three steps for a simple example of an RPI calculation. Suppose the RPI basket contains only two goods and services: oranges and haircuts. We'll construct an annual price index rather than a monthly index with the reference base period 2010 and the current period 2011.

Table 21.1 shows the quantities in the RPI basket and the prices in the base period and current period. Part (a) contains the data for the base period. In that period, consumers bought 10 oranges at £1 each and 5 haircuts at

---

Table 21.1

The RPI: A Simplified Calculation

(a) The cost of the RPI basket at base-period prices: 2010

RPI basket

Item	Quantity	Price	Cost of basket
Oranges	10	£1	£10
Haircuts	5	£8	£40
Cost of the RPI basket at base-period prices			£50

(b) The cost of the RPI basket at current-period prices: 2011

RPI basket

Item	Quantity	Price	Cost of basket
Oranges	10	£2	£20
Haircuts	5	£10	£50
Cost of the RPI basket at current-period prices			£70

£8 each. To find the cost of the RPI basket in the base-period prices, multiply the quantities in the basket by the base-period prices. The cost of oranges is £10 (10 at £1 each), and the cost of haircuts is £40 (5 at £8 each). So total cost of the RPI basket in the base period is £50 (£10 + £40).

Part (b) contains the price data for the current period. The price of an orange increased from £1 to £2, which is a 100 per cent increase (£1 ÷ £1 × 100 = 100). The price of a haircut increased from £8 to £10, which is a 25 per cent increase (£2 ÷ £8 × 100 = 25).

A price index provides a way of averaging these price increases by comparing the cost of the basket rather than the price of each item. To find the cost of the RPI basket in the current period, 2011, multiply the quantities in the basket by their 2011 prices. The cost of oranges is £20 (10 at £2 each) and the cost of haircuts is £50 (5 at £10 each). So total cost of the basket at current-period prices is £70 (£20 + £50).

You've now taken the first two steps towards calculating a RPI: calculating the cost of the RPI basket in the base period and the current period. The third step uses the numbers you've just calculated to find the value of the RPI in 2010 and 2011.

To calculate the RPI, we use the formula:

$$RPI = \frac{\text{Cost of basket at current-period prices}}{\text{Cost of basket at base-period prices}} \times 100$$

In Table 21.1 you have established that in 2010 the cost of the RPI basket was £50 and in 2011 it was £70. You also know that the base period is 2010. So the cost of the RPI basket at base-period prices is £50. If we use these numbers in the formula above, we can find the RPI for 2010 and 2011. For 2010:

$$\text{RPI in } 2010 = \frac{£50}{£50} \times 100 = 100$$

For 2011:

$$\text{RPI in } 2011 = \frac{£70}{£50} \times 100 = 140$$

The principles that you've applied in this simplified RPI calculation apply to the more complex calculations performed every month by the ONS.

Measuring the Inflation Rate

A major purpose of the RPI is to measure *changes* in the cost of living and in the value of money. To measure these changes, we calculate the **inflation rate**, which is the percentage change in the price level from one year to the next. To calculate the inflation rate, we use the formula:

$$\text{Inflation rate} = \frac{(\text{RPI this year} - \text{RPI last year})}{\text{RPI last year}} \times 100$$

We can use this formula to calculate the inflation rate in 2010. The RPI in September 2009 was 215.3, and the RPI in September 2010 was 225.3. So the inflation rate during the year ended September 2010 was:

$$\text{Inflation rate} = \frac{(225.3 - 215.3)}{215.3} \times 100$$

$$= 4.6 \text{ per cent}$$

Distinguishing High Inflation from a High Price Level

Figure 21.7 shows the RPI and the inflation rate from 1970 to 2010. The two parts of the figure are related and emphasize the distinction between high inflation and high prices.

Figure 21.7   The RPI and the Inflation Rate

(a) RPI

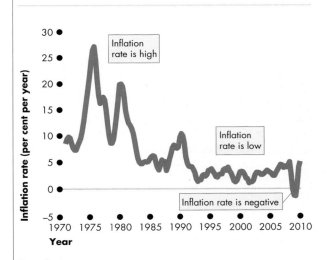

(b) Inflation rate

During the 1970s and early 1980s, the price level in part (a) increased rapidly and the inflation rate in part (b) was high. After 1985, the price level increased more slowly and the inflation rate was lower. In 2009, the price level fell and inflation was negative – there was deflation.

Source of data: Office for National Statistics.

myeconlab Animation

When the price *level* in part (a) *rises rapidly*, the inflation rate in part (b) is *high*. When the price level in part (a) *rises slowly*, the inflation rate in part (b) is *low*.

A high inflation rate means that the price level is rising rapidly, while a high price level means that there has been a sustained period of inflation.

When the price level in part (a) falls, as it did in 2009, the inflation rate in part (b) is negative – *deflation*.

The RPI is not a perfect measure of the price level, and changes in the RPI can overstate the inflation rate. Let's look at the sources of bias in price indexes such as the RPI and CPI against which the ONS must guard.

Biased Price Indexes

The main sources of bias in a price index are:

◆ New goods bias
◆ Quality change bias
◆ Substitution bias

New Goods Bias

New goods keep replacing old goods. For example, CDs have replaced LP records and PCs have replaced typewriters. If you want to compare the price level in 2005 with that in 1975, you somehow have to compare the price of a CD and a computer today with that of an LP and typewriter in 1975. Because CDs and PCs are more expensive today than LPs and typewriters, the arrival of these new goods puts an upward bias into the estimate of the price level.

Quality Change Bias

Most goods undergo constant quality improvement. Cars, computers, CD players and even textbooks get better year after year. Quality improvements often increase the price, but such price increases are not inflation. For example, suppose that a 1999 car is 5 per cent better and costs 5 per cent more than a 1995 car. Adjusted for the quality change, the price of the car has not changed. But in calculating the RPI, the price of the car will have increased by 5 per cent.

Estimates have been made of the quality change bias, especially for obvious changes such as those in cars and computers. Allowing for quality improvements changes the inflation picture by 1 percentage point a year, on average, according to some economists. That is, correctly measured, the inflation rate might be as much as 1 percentage point a year less than the published numbers.

Substitution Bias

A change in the price index measures the percentage change in the price of a *fixed* basket of goods and services. But changes in relative prices lead consumers to seek less costly items. For example, by shopping more frequently at discount shops and less frequently at corner shops, consumers can cut the prices they pay. By using discount fares on airlines, they can cut the cost of travel. This kind of substitution of cheaper items for more costly items is not picked up by the price index. Because consumers make such substitutions, a price index based on a fixed basket overstates the effects of a given price change on the inflation rate.

Some Consequences of Bias in the RPI and CPI

The RPI is also used to calculate increases in pensions and other government outlays. So a bias in the RPI could end up swelling government expenditure (and taxes). The CPI is used by the Bank of England to determine whether the interest rate needs to be raised or lowered. So a bias in the CPI could lead to an inappropriate policy decision.

Mindful of these potentially harmful effects, our price indexes are constructed with the greatest possible care to minimize the biases we've just examined.

An Alternative Price Index: The GDP Deflator

The RPI and the CPI are just two of many alternative price level index numbers. Because of the bias in the price indexes, other measures are used for some purposes. One of these alternative price indexes is the **GDP deflator**, which is an index of the prices of all the items in GDP. These items are consumption expenditure, investment, government expenditure and net exports.

The RPI and CPI measure only the prices of consumption goods and services, so they cover a narrower range of items than does the GDP deflator.

The GDP deflator is calculated using two numbers that you have already met: GDP and real GDP and the formula for the GDP deflator is:

GDP deflator = (Nominal GDP ÷ Real GDP) × 100

This broader price index is appropriate for macroeconomics because it is a comprehensive measure of the cost of the real GDP basket of goods and services.

Another difference between the GDP deflator and the other two indexes is the dating of the expenditure basket. Because real GDP is a *chained volume measure* (see pp. 476–477), it is based on expenditures in the two adjacent years that are being compared and then 'chained' back to the reference base year. This procedure means that the weights in the GDP deflator are current weights so they avoid some of the sources of bias that we described above.

The main disadvantage of the GDP deflator is that it is calculated only every quarter and with a time lag and is subject to ongoing revisions. These features make it unsuitable for timely and firm estimation of the inflation rate. But it is a good measure for macroeconomic analysis and our efforts to understand economic performance.

The Alternatives Compared

No matter whether we calculate the inflation rate using the RPI, the CPI or the GDP deflator, the number bounces around a good deal from quarter to quarter. How do the alternative measures compare? How different are the inflation stories they tell?

The three measures give different average inflation rates and different inflation fluctuations. Since 2000, the RPI has increased at an average rate of 2.7 per cent per year, the CPI at an average rate of 1.9 per cent per year and the GDP deflator at 2.5 per cent per year.

Figure 21.8 shows the path of each measure of inflation since 2000. You can see that the RPI is much more variable than the other two measures and it is the only one to show deflation in 2009. The CPI has a mild upward trend and the GDP deflator has no trend.

The key conclusion is that there is no unique measure of inflation and we must carefully determine which measure is most useful for the purpose at hand.

Real Variables in Macroeconomics

One major purpose of price index numbers is to measure and distinguish nominal variables and real variables. You saw in Chapter 20 how we measure real GDP. And you've seen in this chapter how we can use nominal GDP and real GDP to calculate the GDP deflator measure of the price level.

Viewing real GDP as nominal GDP deflated, opens up the idea of other real variables. By using the GDP deflator, we can deflate other nominal variables such as the nominal wage rate to find their real values.

There is one variable that is a bit different – an interest rate. A real interest rate is not a nominal interest rate divided by the price level. You'll learn how to adjust the nominal interest rate for inflation to find the real interest rate in Chapter 23. But all the other real variables of macroeconomics are calculated by dividing a nominal variable by the price level.

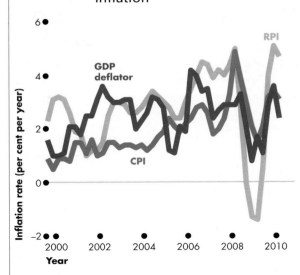

Figure 21.8 Comparing Three Measures of Inflation

The three measures of the inflation rate give different average rates and different fluctuations. The RPI and CPI measures tend to increase and decrease together, but the RPI measure fluctuates more. The GDP deflator measure is the least volatile.

Source of data: Office for National Statistics.

 Animation

Review Quiz

1   What is the price level?
2   What are the RPI and CPI and how are they calculated?
3   How do we calculate the inflation rate and what is the relationship between the price index and the inflation rate?
4   How might a price index be biased?
5   What problems arise from the biased RPI and CPI?
6   What is the GDP deflator and what are its advantages and disadvantages?

You can work these questions in Study Plan 21.3 and get instant feedback.   myeconlab

You've now completed your study of the measurement of macroeconomic performance. Your task in the following chapters is to learn what determines that performance. But first, take a look at the differences in the CPI and the RPI in the period 2008 to 2010 in *Reading Between the Lines* on pp. 498–499.

Reading Between the Lines

Measuring Inflation

The Financial Times, 14 September 2010

Measuring up with a Tale of Two Indices

FT

Chris Giles

What measure of inflation should trade unionists, meeting in Manchester this week, use for pay bargaining this autumn? The answer is likely to lead to much dispute.

Inflation, according to the retail prices index, was 4.6 per cent in August, while it was 3.1 per cent if measured by the newer consumer price index.

These debates are both unfortunate and bogus, argues Stephen Nickell, Warden of Nuffield College, Oxford, and a former member of the monetary policy committee.

The average British household faces only one inflation rate, and . . . [w]hat matters is that there is a reliable, single inflation statistic that measures the changing cost of consumption.

Some of the differences between the RPI and CPI are well known, such as the historic inclusion of mortgage interest payments in the RPI and the exclusion of owner-occupied housing costs in the CPI. . . . In August these housing differences contributed 0.72 per-

centage points of the difference between the indices. . . .

Much less well-known, however, is that another important discrepancy between the two inflation measures has emerged this year. . . . This relates to different techniques for averaging prices in shops.

In August, clothing and footwear inflation measured by the RPI stood at 6.3 per cent, while the CPI inflation for the same goods was –1.7 per cent – a total difference of 8 percentage points. . . .

The upshot for union wage bargainers is that, unless they are sure their members need to wear Nicole Farhi, the RPI is probably overstating the inflation rate they experience. 'Put simply, the CPI is the better guide,' says Allan Monks of JP Morgan.

The measure of inflation most used for wage settlements is the Retail Price Index, . . . which . . . climbed in the 12 months to November by 3.9 per cent, . . . the highest reading since May 1998.

© The Financial Times Ltd.

The Essence of the Story

◆ In August 2010, the annual inflation rate was 4.6 per cent according to the RPI and 3.1 per cent according to the CPI.

◆ Among many differences in coverage of the two indexes, the RPI includes mortgage interest payments but the CPI excludes them.

◆ The two indexes use different price sampling methods.

◆ A consequence of these differences is that the RPI said clothing and footwear prices increased 6.3 per cent in August while the CPI said they *decreased* 1.7 per cent.

Economic Analysis

- The CPI and the RPI give conflicting accounts of UK inflation.

- Figure 1 shows the CPI inflation rate minus the RPI inflation rate for each month from January 2009 to September 2010. The CPI inflation rate was higher in 2009 and the RPI inflation rate was higher in 2010.

- The actual items included in the baskets of the two price indexes are different even when the category has the same name.

- For example, clothing and footwear, noted in the news article, includes different items in the two baskets.

- Even for goods that are common, such as alcohol and tobacco, the two inflation measures differ.

- Figure 2 shows the inflation rate of alcohol and tobacco measured by the CPI and the RPI. Sampling bias makes the CPI alcohol and tobacco inflation rate higher than the RPI inflation rate.

- Trades unions may want to use the RPI rate of inflation as the basis for wage bargaining because the RPI measure of inflation is higher than the CPI measure. But Figure 3 shows that earnings growth has followed neither measure of inflation.

- Real wage rates are determined in the market for labour. To translate real wage rates into money wage rates, unions and employers need a good measure of inflation.

- While the ONS tries to measure inflation so that there is a minimum of bias, both the CPI and the RPI remain imperfect measures of inflation.

- Unions and employers find it necessary to look at both measures of inflation in seeking what Stephen Nickell calls a 'reliable, single inflation statistic that measures the changing cost of consumption'.

Figure 1 The difference between the CPI and RPI inflation rates

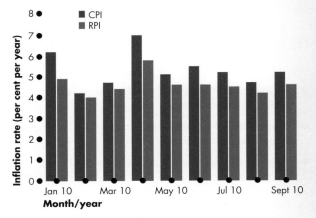

Figure 2 Inflation rates of alcohol and tobacco in two indexes

Figure 3 Inflation and wage rate

SUMMARY

Key Points

Employment and Unemployment
(pp. 484–488)

◆ Unemployment is a serious personal, social and economic problem because it results in lost output and income and human capital.

◆ The unemployment rate averaged 10 per cent during the 1980s, 8.3 per cent during the 1990s and 5.5 per cent during the 2000s.

◆ The unemployment rate, the economic activity rate and the employment rate fluctuate with the business cycle.

Working Problems 1 to 7 will give you a better understanding of employment and unemployment.

Unemployment and Full Employment
(pp. 489–491)

◆ People are constantly entering and leaving the state of unemployment.

◆ Three types of unemployment are frictional, structural and cyclical.

◆ When all the unemployment is frictional and structural, the unemployment rate equals the natural unemployment rate, the economy is at full employment and real GDP equals potential GDP.

◆ Over the business cycle, real GDP fluctuates around potential GDP and the unemployment rate fluctuates around the natural unemployment rate.

Working Problems 8 to 13 will give you a better understanding of unemployment and full employment.

The Price Level, Inflation and Deflation (pp. 492–497)

◆ Inflation and deflation that are unexpected redistribute income and wealth and divert resources from production.

◆ The Retail Prices Index (RPI) and the Consumer Prices Index (CPI) measure the average prices paid by consumers for a specified basket of goods and services.

◆ The inflation rate is the percentage change in the RPI (or CPI) from one year to the next.

◆ The RPI and CPI probably overstate the inflation rate because of the bias that arises from new goods, quality changes and substitutions between goods and services.

◆ The RPI bias increases government outlays and the CPI bias might lead to inappropriate interest rate policy.

Working Problems 14 to 27 will give you a better understanding of the price level, inflation and deflation.

Key Terms

Consumer Prices Index (CPI), 493
Cyclical unemployment, 489
Deflation, 492
Discouraged worker, 487
Economic activity rate, 487
Economically active, 485
Economically inactive, 485
Employment rate, 486
Frictional unemployment, 489
Full employment, 489
GDP deflator, 496
Hyperinflation, 492
Inflation, 492
Inflation rate, 495
Natural unemployment rate, 489
Output gap, 490
Price level, 492
Reference base period, 493
Retail Prices Index (RPI), 493
Structural unemployment, 489
Unemployment rate, 486
Workforce, 485
Working-age population, 485

STUDY PLAN PROBLEMS AND APPLICATIONS

myeconlab   You can work Problems 1 to 27 in MyEconLab Chapter 21 Study Plan and get instant feedback.

Employment and Unemployment

(Study Plan 21.1)

1 In 2008, the Labour Force Survey measured the economically active at 30,512,000, employment at 28,771,000 and the working-age population at 39,575,000. Calculate for 2008:

  a The unemployment rate.

  b The economic activity rate.

  c The employment rate.

2 During 2009, the working-age population increased by 230,000, employment fell by 549,000 and the number of economically active people increased by 98,000. Use this information along with the data in Problem 1 to calculate the change in unemployment during 2009.

Use the following information to work Problems 3 and 4.

In July 2009, in the economy of Sandy Island, 10,000 people were employed, 1,000 were unemployed and 5,000 were economically inactive.

3 Calculate the unemployment rate and the employment rate in July 2009.

4 During August 2009, 80 people lost their jobs and didn't look for new ones, 20 people quit their jobs and retired, 150 unemployed people were hired, 50 people quit the workforce and became economically inactive and 40 people entered the workforce to look for work.

  Calculate the number of people unemployed, the number of people employed and the unemployment rate at the end of August 2009.

Use the following information to work Problems 5 and 6.

The UK unemployment rate was 6.9 per cent in January 2009 and 8.1 per cent in January 2010.

5 Predict what happened to unemployment between January 2009 and January 2010 if the economically active population remained the same.

6 Predict what happened to the economically active population if the number of people unemployed remained the same.

7 **Shrinking US Workforce Keeps Unemployment Rate From Rising**

  An exodus of discouraged workers from the US job market has kept the unemployment rate from climbing to 10 per cent. Had the workforce not decreased by 661,000, the unemployment rate would have been 10.4 per cent. The number of discouraged workers rose to 929,000 last month.

  Source: Bloomberg, 9 January 2010

  What is a discouraged worker? Explain how an increase in discouraged workers influences the official unemployment rate.

Unemployment and Full Employment

(Study Plan 21.2)

Use the following news clip to work Problems 8 to 10.

Jobs Market is on the 'Road to Recovery'

A new study suggests the job market is on the 'road to recovery', despite 2.5 million people unemployed. With a strong rise in demand for permanent staff in the past four months and with the rise in demand for temporary staff in December the biggest in six months, the recovery looks strong. But KPMG warns the future of the recovery is uncertain, as the government's austerity measures take effect.

Source: BBC News, 12 January 2011

8 With the demand for permanent and temporary workers rising strongly, explain which type of unemployment is most likely to fall if the recovery continues.

9 As the government's austerity measures take effect, explain which type of unemployment might increase.

10 Why might the government's cutbacks in the public service (part of the austerity measures) change the natural unemployment rate in the UK?

Use the following news clip to work Problems 11 to 13.

US Economic Pain Deepens

A spike in the unemployment rate – the biggest in more than two decades – raised new concerns that the US economy is heading into a recession. The unemployment rate soared to 5.5 per cent in May from 5 per cent in April – much higher than forecasted. The surge marked the biggest one-month jump in unemployment since February 1986, and the 5.5 per cent rate is the highest seen since October 2004.

Source: CNN, 6 June 2008

11 Based on information in the news clip, how does the US unemployment rate in May 2008 compare to that in earlier recessions?

12 Why might the unemployment rate tend to actually underestimate the unemployment problem, especially during a recession?

13 Given the information in the news clip, does the jump in the US unemployment rate in May 2008 look like an increase in the natural unemployment rate or an increase in the cyclical unemployment rate? What information would you need on the output gap to confirm your answer?

The Price Level, Inflation and Deflation (Study Plan 21.3)

Use the following information to work Problems 14 and 15.

The people on Coral Island buy only juice and cloth. The RPI basket contains the quantities bought in 2009. The average household spent €60 on juice and €30 on cloth in 2009 when the price of juice was €2 a bottle and the price of cloth was €5 a metre. In the current year, 2010, juice is €4 a bottle and cloth is €6 a metre.

14 Calculate the RPI basket and the percentage of the household's budget spent on juice in 2009.

15 Calculate the RPI and the inflation rate in 2010.

Use the following data to work Problems 16 to 18.

The Office for National Statistics reported the following RPI data:

    June 2008: 216.8

    June 2009: 213.4

    June 2010: 221.1

16 Calculate the inflation rates for the years ended June 2009 and June 2010. How did the inflation rate change in 2010?

17 Why might these RPI numbers be biased?

18 Does the GDP deflator help to avoid some of the bias in the RPI numbers?

19 **Inflation Can Act as a Safety Valve**

Workers will more readily accept a real wage cut that arises from an increase in the price level than a cut in their nominal wage rate.

                    Source: FT.com, 28 May 2009

How does inflation influence the real wage rate?

20 The IMF *World Economic Outlook* reports the following price level data (2000 = 100):

Region	2006	2007	2008
US	117.1	120.4	124.0
Eurozone	113.6	117.1	119.6
Japan	98.1	98.1	98.8

a In which region was inflation the highest in 2007 and 2008?

b Describe the path of the price level in Japan.

21 **We are Heading Back to Massive Inflation**

Inflation is an arbitrary tax that falls hardest on those who have done the right thing: it penalises thrift, disadvantages businesses and weakens competitiveness.

                  Source: *The Telegraph*, 13 January 2011

a Explain why unexpected inflation 'penalizes thrift'.

b Explain why unexpected inflation 'disadvantages businesses'.

c Explain why unexpected inflation 'weakens competitiveness'.

Use the following data to work Problems 22 to 24.

The Office for National Statistics reported that the annual CPI inflation rate in November 2010 was 3.3 per cent and the annual RPI inflation rate was 4.7 per cent.

Food and non-alcoholic drink prices rose by 1.6 per cent, compared to a 0.6 per cent rise a year earlier. Bread and cereal prices rose by 1.9 per cent and meat prices rose by 1.0 per cent.

Clothing and footwear prices rose by 2.0 per cent, compared with 0.6 per cent a year earlier, while furniture and household equipment rose 1.6 per cent.

Air transport fares fell by 6.4 per cent, compared with a fall of 2.6 per cent a year earlier. Fuel and lubricant prices rose by 1.6 per cent, compared with 2.8 per cent a year earlier. Recreation and culture prices fell by 0.2 per cent this year but rose by 0.2 per cent a year earlier.

22 Which components of the CPI basket experienced price increases (i) faster than the average and (ii) slower than the average?

23 The change in which price contributed most to the 3.3 per cent increase in the CPI?

24 Distinguish between the CPI and RPI. Why might the RPI inflation rate be higher than the CPI inflation rate?

25 What is the GDP deflator and what are the main differences between it and the RPI and CPI?

26 Why might the GDP deflator provide a more reliable indicator of the inflation rate than the CPI and RPI?

27 If the GDP deflator does provide a more reliable indicator of the inflation rate than the CPI and RPI, why might we nevertheless use the CPI and RPI?

ADDITIONAL PROBLEMS AND APPLICATIONS

myeconlab You can work these problems in MyEconLab if assigned by your lecturer.

Employment and Unemployment

28 What is the unemployment rate supposed to measure and why is it an imperfect measure?

29 The Office for National Statistics reported the following data for 2010:

Economic activity rate: 76.6 per cent

Working-age population: 40.01 million

Employment rate: 70.7 per cent

Calculate the

a Workforce.

b The number of people employed

c Unemployment rate.

30 In 2009, the Labour Force Survey measured the economically active at 30.6 million, employment at 28.2 million and the working-age population at 39.8 million. Calculate for 2009:

a The unemployment rate.

b The economic activity rate.

c The employment rate.

31 The ONS reported the following reasons for economic inactivity in August to October 2010 (the numbers are thousands):

Students	2,209
Looking after family at home	2,265
Temporarily sick	175
Long-term sick	2,216
Discouraged workers	67
Retired	1,530
Other	823
Do not want a job	6,969
Want a job	2,367

a Which of the above categories were counted in the official unemployment rate? Explain your answer.

b Which of the above categories of reasons for economic inactivity would you expect to fluctuate with real GDP over the business cycle?

c What are the implications of your answer to part (b) for the mismeasurement of the unemployment rate?

32 A high unemployment rate tells us that a large percentage of the workforce is unemployed, but it doesn't tell us why the unemployment rate is high. What other information would be useful to tell us why the unemployment rate is high?

33 Why might the official unemployment rate underestimate the underutilization of labour resources?

34 **Some Firms Struggle to Hire Despite High Unemployment**

With about 15 million Americans looking for work, some employers are swamped with job applicants, but many employers can't hire enough workers. During the recession, millions of middle-skill, middle-wage jobs disappeared. Now with the recovery, these people can't find the skilled jobs that they seek and have a hard time adjusting to lower-skilled work with less pay.

Source: *The Wall Street Journal*, 9 August 2010

a What has changed in the jobs market?

b If the government decided to extend the period over which a worker can claim unemployment benefits, how will the cost of unemployment change?

Unemployment and Full Employment

Use the following data to work Problems 35 to 37.

The IMF *World Economic Outlook* reports the following unemployment rates:

Region	2007	2008
US	4.6	5.4
Eurozone	7.4	7.3
Japan	3.9	3.9

35 What do these numbers tell you about the phase of the business cycle in the three regions in 2008?

36 What do these numbers tell us about the relative size of the natural unemployment rates in the three regions?

37 Do these numbers tell us anything about the relative size of the economic activity rate and the employment rate in the three regions?

38 **A Half-Year of Job Losses**

Employers trimmed jobs in June for the sixth straight month, with the total for the first six months at 438,000 jobs lost by the US economy.

The job losses in June were concentrated in manufacturing and construction, two sectors that have been badly battered in the recession.

Source: CNN, 3 July 2008

a Based on the news clip, what might be the main source of increased unemployment?

b Based on the news clip, what might be the main type of unemployment that increased?

The Price Level, Inflation and Deflation

39 A typical family on Sandy Island consumes only juice and cloth. Last year, which was the reference base year, the family spent €40 on juice and €25 on cloth. Last year, juice was €4 a bottle and cloth was €5 a metre. This year, juice is €4 a bottle and cloth is €6 a metre. Calculate:

   a The RPI basket.

   b The RPI in the current year.

   c The inflation rate in the current year.

40 Amazon.com agreed to pay its workers $20 an hour in 1999 and $22 an hour in 2001. The price level for these years was 166 in 1999 and 180 in 2001. Calculate the real wage rate in each year. Did these workers really get a pay raise between 1999 and 2001?

41 In the third quarter of 2010, UK real GDP was £331.2 billion and nominal GDP was £365.9 billion. In the third quarter of 2009, real GDP was £322.7 billion and nominal GDP was £348.1 billion. Calculate the GDP deflator in these two quarters and the inflation rate over the year.

Economics in the News

42 After you have studied *Reading Between the Lines* on pp. 498–499 answer the following questions.

   a What was the inflation rate as measured by the CPI and the RPI in August 2010?

   b Explain why the two measures of inflation deliver different inflation rates.

   c If you were the wage negotiator for your local union, explain which of these two measures of inflation you would use as your basis of negotiation.

   d If you were an entrepreneur and your workers asked for an increase in their wage to keep their real wage constant, which measure of inflation would you use to calculate the increase in the real wage? Explain.

43 **Out of a Job and Out of Luck at 54**

Too young to retire, too old to get a new job. That's how many older workers feel after getting the sack and spending time on the unemployment line. Many lack the skills to craft resumes and search online, experts say. Older workers took an average of 21.1 weeks to get a new job in 2007, about 5 weeks longer than younger people. 'Older workers will be more adversely affected because of the time it takes to transition into another job', said Deborah Russell, AARP's director of workforce issues.

Source: CNN, 21 May 2008

   a What type of unemployment might older workers be more prone to experience?

   b Explain how the unemployment rate of older workers is influenced by the business cycle.

   c Why might older unemployed workers become discouraged workers during a recession?

44 **Land Rover Jaguar Job Applications 'Overwhelm' Halewood**

More than 14,000 people applied for 1,500 new jobs at a new Jaguar Land Rover car plant at Halewood on Merseyside. The jobs have been created by the decision to produce a new Range Rover at this plant.

Source: BBC, 15 January 2010

   a What does this news clip suggest about unemployment on Merseyside?

   b How will this new car plant change the economic activity rate, the employment rate and the working age population on Merseyside?

   c How will this new car plant change the natural unemployment rate and the cyclical unemployment rate on Merseyside?

Data Graphing

Use the Data Grapher in MyEconLab to work Problems 45 to 47.

45 In which country in 2009 was the unemployment rate highest and in which was it lowest: Canada, Japan, France or the UK?

46 In which country in 2009 was the inflation rate highest and in which was it lowest: Australia, the UK, France or the US?

47 Make a scatter diagram of UK inflation and unemployment. Describe the relationship.

PART 7

Macroeconomic Trends

Expanding the Frontier

Economic growth maintained at a steady pace over a number of decades is the single most powerful influence on any society. It brings a transformation that continues to amaze thoughtful people. Maintained at a rapid rate, economic growth transforms a society in years, not decades. Such transformations are taking place right now in many Asian countries. These transformations are economic miracles.

The first two chapters in this part deal with the standard of living and the miracle of rapid economic growth. Chapter 22 explains how potential GDP and full employment are determined and what makes potential

GDP grow. The key to economic growth is labour productivity growth and the chapter explains the sources of this growth. Chapter 23 looks at the financial markets that channel the funds that enable businesses and governments to invest in capital.

Money that makes possible specialization and exchange in markets is a huge contributor to economic growth. But too much money brings a rising cost of living with no improvement in the standard of living. Chapters 24 and 25 explain what money is and how central banks regulate its quantity to determine inflation and exchange rate movements.

Understanding Macroeconomic Trends

Economics is about how we cope with scarcity. We cope as individuals by making choices that balance marginal benefits and marginal costs so that we use our scarce resources efficiently. We cope as societies by creating incentive systems and social institutions that encourage specialization and exchange.

These choices and the incentive systems that guide them determine what we specialize in; how much work we do; how hard we work at school to learn the mental skills that form our human capital and that determine the kinds of jobs we get and the incomes we earn; how much we save for future big-ticket expenditures; how much businesses and governments spend on new capital – on satellites, car assembly lines, computers and fibre cables, shopping malls, roads, bridges and tunnels and the problems that scientists, engineers and other inventors work on to develop new technologies.

Rapid and sustained growth of incomes require rapid and sustained productivity growth. Can we count on that happening? Thomas Robert Malthus thought that we could not. He believed that population, unchecked, would grow at a geometric rate – 1, 2, 4, 8, 16, . . . – while food supply would grow at an arithmetic rate – 1, 2, 3, 4, 5, ... To prevent the population from outstripping the available food supply, there would be periodic wars, famines and plagues. As industrialization proceeded through the nineteenth century, Malthus's idea came to be applied not only to food but also to all natural resources, especially those that are non-renewable. Modern day Malthusians believe that his idea is correct and that if we continue to increase our use of energy we will eventually run out of resources and be doomed to a return of subsistence and poverty.

Some economists argue that Malthus was wrong and that human creativity and ingenuity is the ultimate natural resource. They believe that increasing population lessens the pressure on other natural resources as more creative thinkers find more efficient ways of using our resources. Joseph Schumpeter was the unwitting founder of this modern growth theory. But he didn't see the process as plain sailing through tranquil waters.

Joseph Schumpeter (1883–1950), the son of a textile factory owner, was born in Austria. He moved to Germany during the tumultuous 1920s when both countries experienced hyperinflation. In 1932, in the depths of the Great Depression, he went to the US and became a professor of economics at Harvard University.

This creative economic thinker wrote about economic growth and development, business cycles, political systems and economic biography. He was a person of strong opinions who expressed them forcefully and delighted in verbal battles.

Schumpeter saw the development and diffusion of new technologies by profit-seeking entrepreneurs as the source of economic progress. But he saw economic progress as a process of creative destruction – the creation of new profit opportunities and the destruction of currently profitable businesses. For Schumpeter, economic growth and the business cycle were a single phenomenon.

'Economic progress, in capitalist society, means turmoil.'

JOSEPH SCHUMPETER
Capitalism, Socialism, and Democracy

22

Economic Growth

After studying this chapter you will be able to:

◆ Define economic growth and explain the implications of sustained growth

◆ Describe the economic growth trends in the UK and other countries and regions

◆ Explain how population growth and labour productivity growth make potential GDP grow

◆ Explain the sources of labour productivity growth

◆ Explain the theories of economic growth, the empirical evidence on its causes and policies to increase its rate

In China, India and some other Asian economies, real GDP doubles in seven years. In the UK, it doubles every 25 years or so. In many African economies, real GDP barely changes from one year to the next. Why?

What makes an economic miracle like the ones we see in East Asia today? Can China and India continue to expand at the current dizzying rate? Or will this growth come to an end? And if so, what kind of end: abrupt or gradual? And why do some countries stagnate?

You'll find some answers in this chapter. And in *Reading Between the Lines* at the end of the chapter, we'll speculate about the future economic growth rates of China and its Asian neighbours.

The Basics of Economic Growth

Economic growth is a sustained expansion of production possibilities measured as the increase in real GDP over a given period.

Even slow economic growth maintained over many centuries brings great wealth. That is the story of human economic growth up to the Industrial Revolution that began around 1760.

Rapid economic growth maintained over only a small number of years can transform a poor nation into a rich one. That has been the story of Hong Kong, South Korea and Taiwan, and it is the story of China, India and some other Asian economies today.

The absence of growth can condemn a nation to devastating poverty. Such has been the fate of Sierra Leone, Somalia, Zambia and much of the rest of Africa.

The goal of this chapter is to help you to understand why some economies expand rapidly and others stagnate. We'll begin by learning how to calculate the economic growth rate and by discovering the magic of sustained growth.

Calculating Growth Rates

We express the **economic growth rate** as the annual percentage change of real GDP. To calculate this growth rate, we use the formula:

$$\text{Real GDP growth rate} = \frac{\text{Real GDP in current year} - \text{Real GDP in previous year}}{\text{Real GDP in previous year}} \times 100$$

For example, if real GDP in the current year is £1,320 billion and if real GDP in the previous year was £1,200 billion, then the economic growth rate is 10 per cent.

The growth rate of real GDP tells us how rapidly the *total* economy is expanding. This measure is useful for telling us about potential changes in the balance of economic power among nations. But it does not tell us about changes in the standard of living.

The standard of living depends on **real GDP per person** (also called *per capita* real GDP), which is real GDP divided by the population. So the contribution of real GDP growth to the change in the standard of living depends on the growth rate of real GDP per person. We use the above formula to calculate this growth rate, replacing real GDP with real GDP per person.

Suppose, for example, that in the current year, when real GDP is £1,320 billion, the population is 60.6 million. Then real GDP per person is £1,320 billion divided by 60.6 million, which equals £21,782. And suppose that in the previous year, when real GDP was £1,200 billion, the population was 60 million. Then real GDP per person in that year was £1,200 billion divided by 60 million, which equals £20,000. Use these two real GDP per person values with the growth formula above to calculate the growth rate of real GDP per person. That is,

$$\text{Real GDP per person growth rate} = \frac{£21,782 - £20,000}{£20,000} \times 100 = 8.9 \text{ per cent}$$

The growth rate of real GDP per person can also be calculated (approximately) by subtracting the population growth rate from the real GDP growth rate. In the example you've just worked through, the growth rate of real GDP is 10 per cent. The population changes from 60 million to 60.6 million, so the population growth rate is 1 per cent. The growth rate of real GDP per person is approximately equal to 10 per cent minus 1 per cent, which equals 9 per cent.

Real GDP per person grows only if real GDP grows faster than the population grows. If the growth rate of the population exceeds the growth of real GDP, real GDP per person falls.

The Magic of Sustained Growth

Sustained growth of real GDP per person can transform a poor society into a wealthy one. The reason is that economic growth is like compound interest.

Compound Interest

Suppose that you put £100 in the bank and earn 5 per cent a year interest on it. After one year, you have £105. If you leave that £105 in the bank for another year, you earn 5 per cent interest on the original £100 and on the £5 interest that you earned last year. You are now earning interest on interest! The next year, things get even better. Then you earn 5 per cent on the original £100 and on the interest earned in the first year and the second year. You are even earning interest on the interest that you earned on the interest of the first year.

Your money in the bank is growing at a rate of 5 per cent a year. Before too many years have passed, your initial deposit of £100 will have grown to £200. But after how many years?

The answer is provided by a formula called the **Rule of 70**, which states that the number of years it takes for

Figure 22.1   The Rule of 70

Growth rate (per cent per year)	Years for level to double
1	70.0
2	35.0
3	23.3
4	17.5
5	14.0
6	11.7
7	10.0
8	8.8
9	7.8
10	7.0
11	6.4
12	5.8

The number of years it takes for the level of a variable to double is approximately 70 divided by the annual percentage growth rate.

myeconlab Animation

the level of any variable to double is approximately 70 divided by the annual percentage growth rate of the variable. Using the Rule of 70, you can now calculate how many years it takes your £100 to become £200. It is 70 divided by 5, which is 14 years.

Applying the Rule of 70

The Rule of 70 applies to any variable, so it applies to real GDP per person. Figure 22.1 shows the doubling time for growth rates of 1 per cent per year to 12 per cent per year.

You can see that real GDP per person doubles in 70 years (70 divided by 1) – an average human life span – if the growth rate is 1 per cent a year. It doubles in 35 years if the growth rate is 2 per cent a year and in just 10 years if the growth rate is 7 per cent a year.

We can use the Rule of 70 to answer other questions about economic growth. For example, in 2000, US real GDP per person was approximately 8 times that of China. China's recent growth rate of real GDP per person was 7 per cent a year. If this growth rate were maintained, how long would it take China's real GDP per person to reach that of the US in 2000?

The answer, provided by the Rule of 70, is 30 years. China's real GDP per person doubles in 10 (70 divided

by 7) years. It doubles again to 4 times its current level in another 10 years. And it doubles yet again to 8 times its current level in another 10 years. So after 30 years of growth at 7 per cent a year, China's real GDP per person will be 8 times its current level and equal that of the US in 2000. Of course, after 30 years, US real GDP per person would have increased, so China would still not have caught up to the US.

Review Quiz

1   What is economic growth and how do we calculate its rate?
2   What is the relationship between the growth rate of real GDP and the growth rate of real GDP per person?
3   Use the Rule of 70 to calculate the growth rate that leads to a doubling of real GDP per person in 20 years.

You can work these questions in Study Plan 22.1 and get instant feedback.

You now know the basics of economic growth. Let's next review the trends in economic growth in the UK and around the world.

Economic Growth Trends

You've seen the power of economic growth to increase incomes. At a 1 per cent growth rate, it takes a human life span to double the standard of living. But at a 7 per cent growth rate, the standard of living doubles every decade. How fast is our economy growing? How fast are other economies growing? Are poor countries catching up to rich ones, or do the gaps between the rich and poor persist or even widen? Let's answer these questions.

Growth in the UK Economy

Figure 22.2 shows real GDP per person in the UK for the 100 years from 1910 to 2010. The red line is the path of real GDP and the black line is potential GDP. The trend in potential GDP per person tells us about economic growth. Fluctuations around potential GDP tell us about the business cycle.

Some extraordinary events dominate the first 50 years in this graph: two World Wars and two periods, the 1920s and the 1930s, of extreme recession and depression. The recession of 2008–2009 is clearly visible in the graph as a serious event but it is not on the scale of severity of those interwar depressions.

For the century as a whole, the average growth rate was 1.6 per cent a year, which represents a doubling of real GDP per person every 44 years.

But the economic growth rate has varied. During the years to 1950, it was 1.2 per cent per year – too slow to double real GDP per person in the 50-year period. In the 50 years to 2010, the growth rate was 2.1 per cent per year – doubling the level in 33 years.

Growth was most rapid during the 1960s at 2.2 per cent per year and the 1980s at 2.8 per cent per year.

A major goal of this chapter is to explain why our economy grows and why the long-term growth rate varies. Another goal is to explain variations in the economic growth rate across countries. Let's look at some facts about other countries' growth rates.

Figure 22.2 One Hundred Years of Economic Growth in the UK

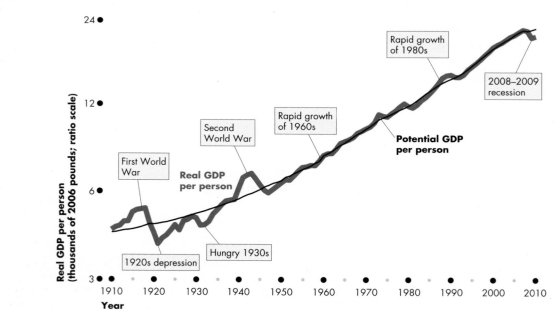

During the 100 years from 1910 to 2010, real GDP per person in the UK grew by 1.6 per cent a year, on average. The growth rate was slower during the first 50 years, at 1.2 per cent (58 years to double) than in the second 50 years at 2.1 per cent (33 years to double). Growth was fastest during the 1960s and the 1980s.

Sources of data: Charles Feinstein, *National Income Expenditure and Output of the United Kingdom 1855–1965*, Cambridge, Cambridge University Press, 1972; Office for National Statistics.

myeconlab Animation

Real GDP Growth in the World Economy

Figure 22.3 shows real GDP per person in the US and in other countries between 1960 and 2010. Part (a) looks at the seven richest countries – known as the G7 nations. Among these nations, the US has the highest real GDP per person. In 2010, Canada had the second-highest real GDP per person, ahead of Japan and France, Germany, Italy and the UK (collectively the Europe Big 4).

During the 50 years shown here, the gaps between the US, Canada and the Europe Big 4 have been almost constant. But starting from a long way below, Japan grew fastest. It caught up to Europe in 1982 and to Canada in 1990. But during the 1990s, Japan's economy stagnated.

Many other countries are growing more slowly than, and falling farther behind, the US. Figure 22.3(b) looks at some of these countries.

In Central and South America, real GDP per person was 28 per cent of the US level in 1960 and reached 30 per cent of the US level by 1980, but then growth slowed and by 2010, real GDP per person in these countries was 23 per cent of the US level.

In Eastern Europe, real GDP per person has grown more slowly than anywhere except Africa, and fell from 32 per cent of the US level in 1980 to 19 per cent in 2003 and then increased again to 22 per cent in 2010.

Real GDP per person in Africa, the world's poorest continent, fell from 10 per cent of the US level in 1960 to 5 per cent in 2007 and then increased slightly to 6 per cent in 2010.

Figure 22.3 Economic Growth Around the World: Catch-up or Not?

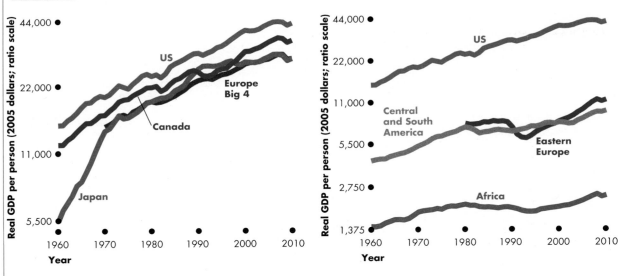

(a) Catch-up?

Real GDP per person has grown throughout the world. Among the rich industrial countries in part (a), real GDP per person has grown slightly faster in the US than in Canada and the four big countries of Europe (France, Germany, Italy, and the UK). Japan had the fastest growth rate before 1973 but then growth slowed and Japan's economy stagnated during the 1990s.

(b) No catch-up?

Among a wider range of countries shown in part (b), growth rates have been lower than that of the US. The gaps between the real GDP per person in the US and in these countries have widened. The gaps between the real GDP per person in the US and Africa and in the US and Eastern Europe have widened.

Sources of data: (1960–2007) Alan Heston, Robert Summers and Bettina Aten, Penn World Table Version 6.3, Center for International Comparisons at the University of Pennsylvania (CICUP), August 2009; and (2008–2010) International Monetary Fund, World Economic Outlook, April 2010.

ECONOMICS IN ACTION

Fast Trains on the Same Track

Four Asian economies, Hong Kong, Korea, Singapore and China, have experienced spectacular growth, which you can see in Figure 1. During the 1960s, real GDP per person in these economies ranged from 3 to 28 per cent of that in the US. But by 2010, real GDP per person in Singapore and Hong Kong had surpassed that of the US.

The figure also shows that China is catching up rapidly but from a long way behind. China's real GDP per person increased from 3 per cent of the US level in 1960 to 26 per cent in 2010.

The Asian economies shown here are like fast trains running on the same track at similar speeds and with a roughly constant gap between them. Singapore and Hong Kong are hooked together as the lead train, which runs about 20 years in front of Korea and about 34 years in front of China.

Real GDP per person in Korea in 2010 was similar to that in Hong Kong in 1988, and real GDP in China in 2010 was similar to that of Hong Kong in 1976. Between 1976 and 2010, Hong Kong transformed itself from a poor developing economy into one of the richest economies in the world.

The rest of China is now doing what Hong Kong has done. China has a population 200 times that of Hong Kong and more than 4 times that of the US. So if China continues its rapid growth, the world economy will change dramatically.

As these fast-growing Asian economies catch up with the US, we can expect their growth rates to slow. But it will be surprising if China's growth rate slows much before it has closed the gap on the US.

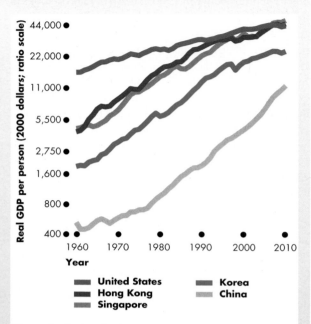

Figure 1 Closing the Gap

Sources of data: (1960–2007) Alan Heston, Robert Summers, and Bettina Aten, Penn World Table Version 6.3, Center for International Comparisons at the University of Pennsylvania (CICUP), August 2009; and (2008–2010) International Monetary Fund, *World Economic Outlook*, April 2010.

Even modest differences in economic growth rates sustained over a number of years bring enormous differences in the standard of living. So the facts about economic growth in the UK and around the world raise some big questions.

What are the preconditions for economic growth and what sustains it? How can we identify the sources of economic growth and measure the contribution that each source makes? What can we do to increase the sustainable rate of economic growth?

We're now going to address these questions. We start by seeing how potential GDP is determined and what makes it grow. You will see that labour productivity growth is the key to rising living standards and go on to explore the sources of this growth.

Review Quiz

1 What has been the average growth rate in the UK over the past 100 years? In which period was growth most rapid and in which was it slowest?

2 Describe the gaps between the levels of real GDP per person in the US and other countries. For which countries are the gaps narrowing? For which countries are the gaps widening? For which countries are the gaps remaining unchanged?

3 Compare the growth rates and levels of real GDP per person in Hong Kong, Singapore, South Korea, China and the US. How far is China behind the other Asian economies?

You can work these questions in Study Plan 22.2 and get instant feedback.

How Potential GDP Grows

Economic growth occurs when real GDP increases. But a one-shot rise in real GDP or a recovery from recession isn't economic growth. Economic growth is a sustained, year-after-year increase in potential GDP.

So what determines potential GDP and what are the forces that make it grow?

What Determines Potential GDP?

Labour, capital, land and entrepreneurship produce real GDP, and the productivity of the factors of production determines the quantity of real GDP that can be produced.

The quantity of land is fixed and on any given day, the quantities of entrepreneurial ability and capital are also fixed and their productivities are given. The quantity of labour employed is the only variable factor of production. Potential GDP is the level of real GDP when the quantity of labour employed is the full-employment quantity.

To determine potential GDP, we use a model with two components:

◆ An aggregate production function
◆ An aggregate labour market

Aggregate Production Function

When you studied the limits to production in Chapter 2 (see p. 32), you learned that the production possibilities frontier is the boundary between the combinations of goods and services that can be produced and those that cannot. We're now going to think about the production possibilities frontier for two special 'goods': real GDP and the quantity of leisure time.

Think of real GDP as a number of big shopping carts. Each cart contains some of each kind of different goods and services produced, and one cartload of items costs £1 billion. To say that real GDP is £1.3 trillion (or £1,300 billion) means that it is 1,300 very big shopping carts of goods and services.

The quantity of leisure time is the number of hours spent not working. Each leisure hour could be spent working. If we spent all our time taking leisure, we would do no work and produce nothing. Real GDP would be zero. The more leisure we forgo, the greater is the quantity of labour we supply and the greater is the quantity of real GDP produced.

But labour hours are not all equally productive. We use our most productive hours first and as more hours are worked, less and less productive hours are used. So for each additional hour of leisure forgone (each additional hour of labour), real GDP increases by successively smaller amounts.

The **aggregate production function** is the relationship that tells us how real GDP changes as the quantity of labour changes when all other influences on production remain the same. Figure 22.4 shows this relationship – the curve labelled *PF*. An increase in the quantity of labour (and a corresponding decrease in leisure hours) brings a movement along the production function and an increase in real GDP.

Aggregate Labour Market

In macroeconomics, we pretend that there is one large labour market that determines the quantity of labour employed and the quantity of real GDP produced. To see how this aggregate labour market works, we study the demand for labour, the supply of labour and labour market equilibrium.

The Demand for Labour
The demand for labour is the relationship between the quantity of labour demanded and the real wage rate. The

Figure 22.4 The Aggregate Production Function

At point A on the aggregate production function *PF*, 50 billion hours of labour produce £1.3 trillion of real GDP.

myeconlab Animation

quantity of labour demanded is the number of labour hours hired by all the firms in the economy during a given period. This quantity depends on the price of labour, which is the real wage rate.

The **real wage rate** is the quantity of goods and services that an hour of labour earns. It contrasts with the money wage rate, which is the number of pounds that an hour of labour earns. The real wage rate is calculated by dividing the money wage rate by the price level.

The *real* wage rate influences the quantity of labour demanded because what matters to firms is not the number of pounds they pay (money wage rate) but how much output they must sell to earn those pounds.

The quantity of labour demanded *increases* as the real wage rate *decreases* – the demand for labour curve slopes downward. Why? The answer lies in the shape of the production function.

You've seen that along the production function, each additional hour of labour increases real GDP by successively smaller amounts. This tendency has a name: *the law of diminishing returns*. Because of diminishing returns, firms will hire more labour only if the real wage rate falls to match the fall in the extra output produced by that labour.

The Supply of Labour

The *supply of labour* is the relationship between the quantity of labour supplied and the real wage rate. The quantity of labour supplied is the number of labour hours that all the households in the economy plan to work during a given period. This quantity depends on the real wage rate.

The *real* wage rate influences the quantity of labour supplied because what matters to households is not the number of pounds they earn (money wage rate) but what they can buy with those pounds.

The quantity of labour supplied *increases* as the real wage rate *increases* – the supply of labour curve slopes upward. At a higher real wage rate, more people choose to work and more people choose to work longer hours if they can earn more per hour.

Labour Market Equilibrium

The price of labour is the real wage rate. The forces of supply and demand operate in labour markets to eliminate a shortage or a surplus but a shortage or a surplus of labour brings only a gradual change in the real wage rate. If there is a shortage of labour, the real wage rate rises to eliminate it; and if there is a surplus of labour, the real wage rate eventually falls to eliminate it. When there is neither a shortage nor a surplus, the

labour market is in equilibrium – a full-employment equilibrium.

Figure 22.5 illustrates labour market equilibrium. The demand for labour curve is *LD* and the supply of labour curve is *LS*. This labour market is in equilibrium at a real wage rate of £15 an hour and 50 billion hours a year are employed.

If the real wage rate exceeds £15 an hour, the quantity of labour supplied exceeds the quantity demanded and there is a surplus of labour. When there is a surplus of labour, the real wage rate falls towards the equilibrium real wage rate where the surplus is eliminated.

If the real wage rate is less than £15 an hour, the quantity of labour demanded exceeds the quantity supplied and there is a shortage of labour. When there is a shortage of labour, the real wage rate rises towards the equilibrium real wage rate where the shortage is eliminated.

If the real wage rate is £15 an hour, the quantity of labour demanded equals the quantity supplied and there is neither a shortage nor a surplus of labour. In this

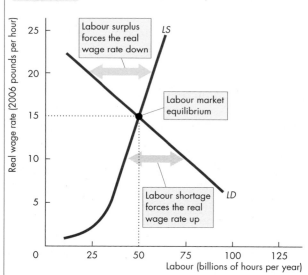

Figure 22.5 Labour Market Equilibrium

Labour market equilibrium occurs when the quantity of labour demanded equals the quantity of labour supplied. The equilibrium real wage rate is £15 per hour and equilibrium employment is 50 billion hours per year.

At a wage rate above £15 an hour, there is a surplus of labour and the real wage rate falls to eliminate the surplus. At a wage rate below £15 an hour, there is a shortage of labour and the real wage rate rises to eliminate the shortage.

situation, there is no pressure in either direction on the real wage rate. So the real wage rate remains constant and the market is in equilibrium. At this equilibrium real wage rate and level of employment, the economy is at full employment.

Potential GDP

You've seen that the production function tells us the quantity of real GDP that a given amount of labour can produce – see Figure 22.4. The quantity of real GDP produced increases as the quantity of labour increases. At the equilibrium quantity of labour, the economy is at full employment and the quantity of real GDP at full employment is potential GDP. So the full-employment quantity of labour produces potential GDP.

Figure 22.6 illustrates the determination of potential GDP. Part (a) shows the labour market. At the equilibrium real wage rate, equilibrium employment is 50 billion hours. Part(b) shows the production function. With 50 billion hours of labour, the economy can produce a real GDP of £1.3 trillion. This amount is potential GDP.

What Makes Potential GDP Grow?

We can divide all the forces that make potential GDP grow into two categories:

◆ Growth of the supply of labour
◆ Growth of labour productivity

Growth of the Supply of Labour

When the supply of labour grows, the supply of labour curve shifts rightward. The quantity of labour at a given real wage rate increases.

The quantity of labour is the number of workers employed multiplied by average hours per worker; and the number employed equals the employment rate multiplied by the working-age population (see Chapter 21, pp. 486–487). So the quantity of labour changes as a result of changes in

1 Average hours per worker
2 The employment rate
3 The working-age population

Average hours per worker have decreased as the workweek has become shorter and the employment rate has increased as more women have entered the labour force. The combined effects of these factors have kept average hours per working-age person (approximately) constant.

Figure 22.6 The Labour Market and Potential GDP

(a) The labour market

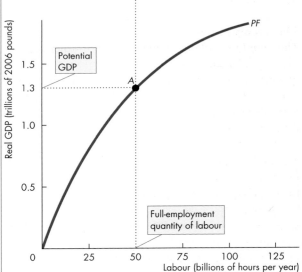

(b) Potential GDP

The economy is at full employment when the quantity of labour demanded equals the quantity of labour supplied, in part (a). The real wage rate is £15 an hour and employment is 50 billion hours per year. In part (b), potential GDP is determined by the production function and the full-employment quantity of labour.

myeconlab Animation

Growth in the supply of labour has come from growth in the working-age population. In the long run, the working-age population grows at the same rate as the total population.

The Effects of Population Growth

Population growth brings growth in the supply of labour, but it does not change the demand for labour or the production function. The economy can produce more output by using more labour, but there is no change in the quantity of real GDP that a given quantity of labour can produce.

With an increase in the supply of labour and no change in the demand for labour, the real wage rate falls and the equilibrium quantity of labour increases. The increased quantity of labour produces more output and potential GDP increases.

Illustrating the Effects of Population Growth

Figure 22.7 illustrates the effects of an increase in the population. In Figure 22.7(a), the demand for labour curve is LD and initially the supply of labour curve is LS_0. The equilibrium real wage rate is £15 an hour and the quantity of labour is 50 billion hours a year. In Figure 22.7(b), the production function, PF, shows that with 50 billion hours of labour employed, potential GDP is £1.3 trillion at point A.

An increase in the population increases the supply of labour and the supply of labour curve shifts rightward to LS_1. At a real wage rate of £15 an hour, there is now a surplus of labour. So the real wage rate falls. In this example, the real wage rate will fall until it reaches £10 an hour. At £10 an hour, the quantity of labour demanded equals the quantity of labour supplied. The equilibrium quantity of labour increases to 75 billion hours a year.

Figure 22.7(b) shows the effect on real GDP. As the equilibrium quantity of labour increases from 50 billion to 75 billion hours, potential GDP increases along the production function from £1.3 trillion to £1.6 trillion at point B.

So an increase in the population increases the full-employment quantity of labour, increases potential GDP and lowers the real wage rate. But the population increase decreases potential GDP per hour of labour. Initially, it was £26 (£1.3 trillion divided by 50 billion). With the population increase, potential GDP per hour of labour is £21.33 (£1.6 trillion divided by 75 billion).

Diminishing returns are the source of the decrease in potential GDP per hour of labour.

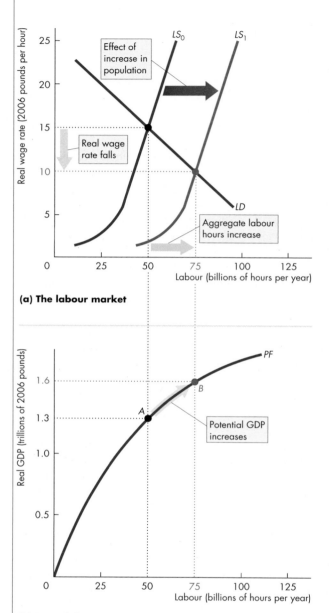

Figure 22.7 The Effects of an Increase in Population

(a) The labour market

(b) Potential GDP

In part (a) an increase in the population increases the supply of labour and shifts the supply of labour curve rightward. The real wage rate falls and the full-employment quantity of labour increases. In part (b), the increase in aggregate labour hours brings an increase in potential GDP. But diminishing returns bring a decrease in potential GDP per hour of labour.

myeconlab Animation

Growth of Labour Productivity

Labour productivity is the quantity of real GDP produced by an hour of labour. It is calculated by dividing real GDP by aggregate labour hours. For example, if real GDP is £1.3 trillion and aggregate hours are 50 billion, labour productivity is £26 per hour.

When labour productivity grows, real GDP per person grows and brings a rising standard of living. Let's see how an increase in labour productivity changes potential GDP.

Effects of an Increase in Labour Productivity

If labour productivity increases, production possibilities expand. The quantity of real GDP that any given quantity of labour can produce increases. If labour is more productive, firms are willing to pay more for a given number of hours of labour so the demand for labour also increases.

With an increase in the demand for labour and *no change in the supply of labour*, the real wage rate rises and the quantity of labour supplied increases. The equilibrium quantity of labour also increases.

So an increase in labour productivity increases potential GDP for two reasons: labour is more productive and more labour is employed.

Illustrating the Effects of an Increase in Labour Productivity

Figure 22.8 illustrates an increase in labour productivity. In part (a), the production function initially is PF_0. With 50 billion hours of labour employed, potential GDP is £1.3 trillion at point *A*. In part (b), the demand for labour curve is LD_0 and the supply of labour curve is *LS*. The real wage rate is £15 an hour and the equilibrium quantity of labour is 50 billion hours a year.

Now labour productivity increases. In Figure 22.8(a), the increase in labour productivity shifts the production function upward to PF_1. At each quantity of labour, more real GDP can be produced. For example, at 50 billion hours, the economy can now produce £1.8 trillion of real GDP at point *B*.

In Figure 22.8(b), the increase in labour productivity increases the demand for labour and the demand for labour curve shifts rightward to LD_1. At the initial real wage rate of £15 an hour, there is now a shortage of labour. The real wage rate rises. In this example, the real wage rate will rise until it reaches £20 an hour. At £20 an hour, the quantity of labour demanded equals the quantity of labour supplied and the equilibrium quantity of labour is 55 billion hours a year.

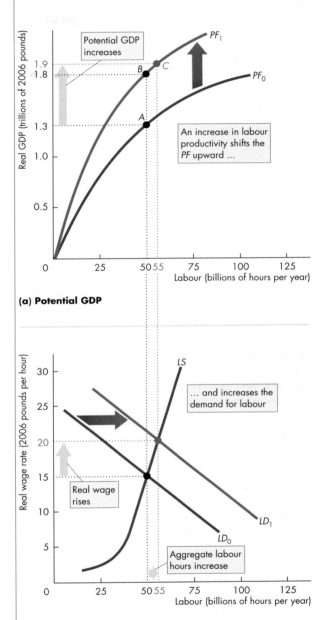

Figure 22.8 The Effects of an Increase in Labour Productivity

(a) Potential GDP

(b) The labour market

An increase in labour productivity shifts the production function upward from PF_0 to PF_1 in part (a) and shifts the demand for labour curve rightward from LD_0 to LD_1 in part (b). The real wage rate rises to £20 an hour, and aggregate labour hours increase from 50 billion to 55 billion. Potential GDP increases from £1.3 trillion to £1.9 trillion.

 Animation

Figure 22.8(a) shows the effects of the increase in labour productivity on potential GDP. There are two effects. At the initial quantity of labour, real GDP increases to point *B* on the new production function. But as the equilibrium quantity of labour increases from 50 billion to 55 billion hours, potential GDP increases to £1.9 trillion at point *C*.

Potential GDP per hour of labour also increases. Initially, it was £26 (£1.3 trillion divided by 50 billion). With the increase in labour productivity, potential GDP per hour of labour is £34.55 (£1.9 trillion divided by 55 billion).

The increase in aggregate labour hours that you have just seen is a consequence of an increase in labour productivity. This increase in aggregate labour hours and labour productivity is an example of the interaction effects that economists seek to identify in their search for the ultimate causes of economic growth.

In the case that we've just studied, aggregate labour hours increase but that increase is a *consequence*, not a *cause*, of the growth of potential GDP. The source of the increase in potential GDP is an increase in labour productivity.

Labour productivity is the key to increasing output per hour of labour and rising living standards. But what brings an increase in labour productivity? The next section answers this question.

Why Labour Productivity Grows

You've seen that labour productivity growth makes potential GDP grow; and you've seen that labour productivity growth is essential if real GDP per person and the standard of living are to grow. But why does labour productivity grow? What are the preconditions that make labour productivity growth possible and what are the forces that make it grow? Why does labour productivity grow faster at some times and in some places than others?

Preconditions for Labour Productivity Growth

The fundamental precondition for labour productivity growth is the *incentive* system created by firms, markets, property rights and money. These four social institutions are the same as those described in Chapter 2 (see pp. 43–44) that enable people to gain by specializing and trading.

ECONOMICS IN ACTION

Intellectual Property Rights Propel Economic Growth

In 1760, when the states that 16 years later would become the United States of America were developing agricultural economies, England was on the cusp of an economic revolution, the Industrial Revolution.

For 70 dazzling years, technological advances in the use of steam power, the manufacture of cotton, wool, iron and steel, and in transport, accompanied by massive capital investment associated with these technologies, transformed the economy of England. Incomes rose and brought an explosion in an increasingly urbanized population.

By 1825, advances in steam technology had reached a level of sophistication that enabled Robert Stephenson to build the world's first steam-powered rail engine (the Rocket pictured here) and the birth of the world's first railroad.

Why did the Industrial Revolution happen? Why did it start in 1760? And why in England?

Economic historians say that intellectual property rights – England's patent system – provides the answer.

England's patent system began with the Statute of Monopolies of 1624, which gave inventors a monopoly to use their idea for a term of 14 years. For about 100 years,

It was the presence of secure property rights in Britain in the middle 1700s that got the Industrial Revolution going (see Economics in Action below). And it is their absence in some parts of Africa today that is keeping labour productivity stagnant.

With the preconditions for labour productivity growth in place, three things influence its pace:

◆ Physical capital growth
◆ Human capital growth
◆ Technological advances

Physical Capital Growth

As the amount of capital per worker increases, labour productivity also increases. Production processes that use hand tools can create beautiful objects, but production methods that use large amounts of capital per worker are much more productive. The accumulation of capital on farms, in textile factories, in iron foundries and steel mills, in coal mines, on building sites, in chem-

the system was used to reward friends of the royal court rather than true inventors. But from around 1720 onward, the system started to work well. To be granted a 14-year monopoly, an inventor only had to pay the required £100 fee (about £14,000 in today's money) and register his or her invention. The inventor was not required to describe the invention in too much detail, so registering and getting a patent didn't mean sharing the invention with competitors.

This patent system, which is in all essentials the same as today's, aligned the self-interest of entrepreneurial inventors with the social interest and unleashed a flood of inventions, the most transformative of which was steam power and, by 1825, the steam locomotive.

ical plants, in car plants, in banks and insurance companies and in shopping malls has added incredibly to our labour productivity.

Human Capital Growth

Human capital – the accumulated skill and knowledge of human beings – is the fundamental source of labour productivity growth. Human capital grows when a new discovery is made and it grows as more and more people learn how to use past discoveries.

The development of one of the most basic human skills – writing – was the source of some of the earliest major gains in productivity. The ability to keep written records made it possible to reap ever-larger gains from specialization and trade.

Later, the development of mathematics laid the foundation for the eventual extension of knowledge about physical forces and chemical and biological processes. This base of scientific knowledge was the foundation for the technological advances of the Industrial Revolution and of today's information revolution.

But a lot of human capital that is extremely productive is much more humble. It takes the form of millions of individuals learning and becoming remarkably more productive by repetitively doing simple production tasks. One much-studied example of this type of human capital growth occurred in the Second World War. With no change in physical capital, thousands of workers and managers in US shipyards learned from experience and accumulated human capital that more than doubled their productivity in less than two years.

Technological Advances

The accumulation of physical capital and human capital have made a large contribution to labour productivity growth. But technological change – the discovery and the application of new technologies – has made an even greater contribution.

Labour is many times more productive today than it was a hundred years ago but not because we have more steam engines and more horse-drawn carriages per person. Rather, it is because we have transport equipment that uses technologies that were unknown a hundred years ago and that are more productive than the old technologies were.

To reap the benefits of technological change, capital must increase. Some of the most powerful and far-reaching fundamental technologies are embodied in human capital – for example, language, writing and mathematics. But most technologies are embodied in physical capital. For example, to reap the benefits of the internal combustion engine, millions of horse-drawn carriages had to be replaced with cars; and to reap the benefits of digital music, millions of Discmans had to be replaced by iPods and giant server farms had to be built to operate iTunes and other online shops.

A Crucial Distinction

Although all three influences on labour productivity – physical capital, human capital and technological change – contribute to productivity growth, there is a crucial distinction between their contributions: physical capital is subject to diminishing returns while the other two are not.

The *law of diminishing returns* states that as the quantity of one factor of production increases with the quantities of all other factors remaining the same, output increases but by ever smaller increments.

You've seen how the law of diminishing returns applies to labour (p. 514). With a given amount of capital, each additional hour of labour produces less additional output than the previous hour. Sharing one computer, two typists produce fewer than twice as many pages per day as one typist produces.

The law of diminishing returns also applies to physical capital. If a given number of hours of labour use more capital (with the same human capital and technology), the additional output that results from the additional capital gets smaller as the amount of capital increases. A typist working with two computers can't produce twice as much as a typist working with one computer. The second computer increases productivity much less than the first computer does.

We can illustrate the diminishing marginal product of physical capital with a **productivity curve**, which is a relationship between labour productivity and physical capital per hour of labour when the amount of human capital and the state of technology are fixed.

Figure 22.9 shows the productivity curve. Its shape reflects the law of diminishing returns. On productivity curve PC_0, one hour of labour working with £40 of capital can't produce twice as much as one hour of labour working with £20 of capital.

An increase in human capital or an advance in technology increases the real GDP per hour of labour that can be produced by a given amount of capital per hour of labour and shifts the productivity curve upward. For example, if capital per hour of labour is £20 and a technological change increases labour productivity from £7

Figure 22.9   How Labour Productivity Grows

The productivity curve, *PC*, shows the effects of an increase in capital per hour of labour on productivity. Here, when capital per hour of labour increases from £20 to £40, labour productivity increases from £7 to £10 along the productivity curve PC_0.

Technological advance shifts the productivity curve upward. Here, the advance in technology shifts the productivity curve from PC_0 to PC_1. When capital per hour of labour is £40, the advance in technology increases labour productivity from £10 to £14.

myeconlab Animation

to £10, the productivity curve shifts upward from PC_0 to PC_1.

The productivity curve illustrates a fundamental fact about productivity growth; growth of physical capital alone brings a slowing rate of productivity growth. To sustain a high growth rate, it is vital to accumulate human capital and make technology advance.

Review Quiz

1   What are the preconditions for labour productivity growth?
2   What are the three influences on the pace of labour productivity growth?
3   What is the crucial distinction between the influences on labour productivity growth?
4   What is the productivity curve and how does it illustrate the crucial distinction between the influences on labour productivity growth?

You can work these questions in Study Plan 22.4 and get instant feedback.

Growth Theories, Evidence and Policies

You've seen how the growth of population and labour productivity make potential GDP grow. You've also seen that the growth of physical capital and human capital and technological advances make labour productivity grow. How do these factors interact? What is cause and what is effect? Growth theories address these questions.

Alternative theories of economic growth provide insights into the process of economic growth, but none provides a complete and definite answer to the basic questions: What causes economic growth and why do growth rates vary? Economics has some way to go before it can provide definite answers to these questions. We look at the current state of the empirical evidence. Finally, we'll look at the policies that might achieve faster growth.

Let's start by studying the three main theories of economic growth:

◆ Classical growth theory
◆ Neoclassical growth theory
◆ New growth theory

Classical Growth Theory

Classical growth theory is the view that the growth of real GDP per person is temporary and that when it rises above the subsistence level, a population explosion eventually brings it back to the subsistence level. Adam Smith, Thomas Robert Malthus and David Ricardo – the leading economists of the late eighteenth century and early nineteenth century – proposed this theory, but the view is most closely associated with the name of Malthus and is sometimes called the *Malthusian theory*. Charles Darwin's ideas about evolution by natural selection were inspired by the insights of Malthus.

Modern-day Malthusians

Many people today are Malthusians. They say that if today's global population of 6.9 billion explodes to 11 billion by 2050 and perhaps 35 billion by 2300, we will run out of resources, real GDP per person will decline and we will return to a primitive standard of living. We must, say Malthusians, contain population growth.

Modern-day Malthusians also point to global warming and climate change as reasons to believe that eventually, real GDP per person will decrease.

Neoclassical Growth Theory

Neoclassical growth theory is the proposition that real GDP per person grows because technological change induces saving and investment that make physical capital grow. Diminishing returns end growth if technological change stops. Robert Solow of MIT suggested the most popular version of this growth theory in the 1950s.

Neoclassical growth theory's big break with its classical predecessor is its view about population growth.

The Neoclassical Theory of Population Growth

The population explosion of eighteenth century Europe that created the classical theory of population eventually ended. The birth rate fell, and while the population continued to increase, its rate of increase moderated.

The opportunity cost of a woman's time is the key influence that slowed the population growth rate. As women's wage rates increase and their job opportunities expand, the opportunity cost of having children increases. Faced with a higher opportunity cost, families choose to have fewer children and the birth rate falls.

Technological advances that bring higher incomes also bring advances in healthcare that extends lives. So as incomes increase, both the birth rate and the death rate decrease. These opposing forces offset each other and result in a slowly rising population.

This modern view of population growth and the historical trends that support it contradict the views of the classical economists. They also call into question the modern doomsday view that the planet will be swamped with more people than it can support.

Technological Change and Diminishing Returns

In neoclassical growth theory, the pace of technological change influences the economic growth rate but economic growth does not influence the pace of technological change. It is assumed that technological change results from chance. When we're lucky, we have rapid technological change, and when bad luck strikes, the pace of technological advance slows.

To understand neoclassical growth theory, imagine the world of the mid-1950s, when Robert Solow is explaining his idea. Income per person is around $12,000 a year in today's money. The population is growing at about 1 per cent a year. Saving and investment are about 20 per cent of GDP, enough to keep the quantity of capital per hour of labour constant. Income per person is growing but not very fast.

Then technology begins to advance at a more rapid pace across a range of activities. The transistor revolutionizes an emerging electronics industry. New plastics revolutionize the manufacture of household appliances. The interstate highway system revolutionizes road transportation. Jet airliners start to replace piston-engine airplanes and speed air transportation.

These technological advances bring new profit opportunities. Businesses expand, and new businesses are created to exploit the newly available profitable technologies. Investment and saving increase. The economy enjoys new levels of prosperity and growth. But will the prosperity last? And will the growth last? Neoclassical growth theory says that the prosperity will last but the growth will not last unless technology keeps advancing.

According to neoclassical growth theory, the prosperity will persist because there is no classical population growth to induce the wage rate to fall. So the gains in income per person are permanent.

Growth Stops Without Technological Change

Growth will eventually stop if technology stops advancing because of diminishing returns to capital. The high profit rates that result from technological change bring increased saving and capital accumulation. But as more capital is accumulated, more and more projects are undertaken that have lower rates of return – diminishing returns. As the return on capital falls, the incentive to invest weakens. With weaker incentives to save and invest, saving decreases and the rate of capital accumulation slows. Eventually, the pace of capital accumulation slows so that it is only keeping up with population growth. Capital per worker remains constant.

A Problem with Neoclassical Growth Theory

All economies have access to the same technologies and capital is free to roam the globe, seeking the highest available real interest rate. Capital will flow until rates of return are equal, and rates of return will be equal when capital per hour of labour are equal. Real GDP growth rates and income levels per person around the world will converge. Figure 22.3 on p. 511 shows that while there is some sign of convergence among the rich countries in part (a), convergence is slow, and part (b) shows that it does not appear to be imminent for all countries. New growth theory overcomes this shortcoming of neoclassical growth theory. It also explains what determines the pace of technological change.

New Growth Theory

New growth theory holds that real GDP per person grows because of the choices people make in the pursuit of profit and that growth will persist indefinitely. Paul Romer of Stanford University developed this theory during the 1980s, based on ideas of Joseph Schumpeter during the 1930s and 1940s.

According to the new growth theory, the pace at which new discoveries are made – and at which technology advances – is not determined by chance. It depends on how many people are looking for a new technology and how intensively they are looking. The search for new technologies is driven by incentives.

Profit is the spur to technological change. The forces of competition squeeze profits, so to increase profit, people constantly seek either lower-cost methods of production or new and better products for which people are willing to pay a higher price. Inventors can maintain a profit for several years by taking out a patent or a copyright, but eventually, a new discovery is copied and profits disappear. So more research and development is undertaken in the hope of creating a new burst of profitable investment and growth.

A Public Good and No Diminishing Returns

Two facts about discoveries and technological knowledge play a key role in the new growth theory: discoveries are (at least eventually) a public capital good; and knowledge is capital that is not subject to diminishing returns.

Economists call a good a public good when no one can be excluded from using it and when one person's use does not prevent others from using it. National defence is the classic example of a public good. The programming language used to write apps for the iPhone is another.

Because knowledge is a *public good*, as the benefits of a new discovery spread, free resources become available. Nothing is given up when they are used: they have a zero opportunity cost. When a student in York writes a new iPhone app, his use of the programming language doesn't prevent another student in Leeds from using it.

Knowledge is even more special because it is not subject to diminishing returns. But increasing the stock of knowledge makes both labour and machines more productive. Knowledge capital does not bring diminishing returns. Biotech knowledge illustrates this idea well. Biologists have spent a lot of time developing DNA sequencing technology. As more has been discovered, the productivity of this knowledge capital has relentlessly increased. In 1990, it cost about £50 to sequence one DNA base pair. That cost had fallen to £1 by 2000 and to 1/10,000th of a penny by 2010.

The implication of this simple and appealing observation is astonishing. Unlike the other two theories, new growth theory has no growth-stopping mechanism. As physical capital accumulates, the return to capital – the real interest rate – falls. But the incentive to innovate and earn a higher profit becomes stronger. So innovation occurs, capital becomes more productive, the demand for capital increases, and the real interest rate rises again.

Labour productivity grows indefinitely as people discover new technologies that yield a higher real interest rate. The growth rate depends only on people's incentives and ability to innovate.

A Perpetual Motion Economy

New growth theory sees the economy as a perpetual motion machine, which Figure 22.10 illustrates.

No matter how rich we become, our wants exceed our ability to satisfy them. We always want a higher standard of living. In the pursuit of a higher standard of living, human societies have developed incentive systems – markets, property rights and money – that enable people to profit from innovation. Innovation leads to the development of new and better techniques of production and new and better products. To take advantage of new techniques and to produce new products, new firms start up and old firms go out of business – firms are born and die. As old firms die and new firms are born, some jobs are destroyed and others are created. The new jobs created are better than the old ones and they pay higher real wage rates. Also, with higher wage rates and more productive techniques, leisure increases. New and better jobs and new and better products lead to more consumption goods and services and, combined with increased leisure, bring a higher standard of living.

But our insatiable wants are still there, so the process continues: wants and incentives create innovation, new and better products, and a yet higher standard of living.

Figure 22.10   A Perpetual Motion Machine

People want a higher standard of living and are spurred by profit incentives to make the innovations that lead to new and better techniques and new and better products, which in turn lead to the birth of new firms and the death of some old firms, new and better jobs, more leisure and more consumption of goods and services. The result is a higher standard of living. But people want a still higher standard of living and the growth process continues.

Source: Based on a similar figure in *These Are the Good Old Days: A Report on United States Living Standards*, Federal Reserve Bank of Dallas 1993 Annual Report.

myeconlab Animation

New Growth Theory versus Malthusian Theory

The contrast between the Malthusian theory and new growth theory couldn't be more sharp. Malthusians see the end of prosperity as we know it today and new growth theorists see unending plenty. The contrast becomes clearest by thinking about the differing views about population growth.

To a Malthusian, population growth is part of the problem. To a new growth theorist, population growth is part of the solution. People are the ultimate economic resource. A larger population brings forth more wants, but it also brings a greater amount of scientific discovery and technological advance. So rather than being the source of falling real GDP per person, population growth generates faster labour productivity growth and rising real GDP per person. Resources are limited, but the human imagination and ability to increase productivity are unlimited.

Sorting Out the Theories

Which theory is correct? None of them tells us the whole story, but each teaches us something of value.

Classical growth theory reminds us that our physical resources are limited and that without advances in technology, we must eventually hit diminishing returns.

Neoclassical growth theory reaches the same conclusion but not because of a population explosion. Instead, it emphasizes diminishing returns to capital and reminds us that we cannot keep growth going just by accumulating physical capital. We must also advance technology and accumulate human capital. We must become more creative in our use of scarce resources.

New growth theory emphasizes the capacity of human resources to innovate at a pace that offsets diminishing returns. New growth theory fits the facts of today's world more closely than do either of the other two theories, but that doesn't make it correct.

The Empirical Evidence on the Causes of Economic Growth

Economics makes progress by the interplay between theory and empirical evidence. A theory makes predictions about what we will observe if the theory is correct. Empirical evidence, the data generated by history and the natural experiments that it performs, provide the data for testing the theory.

Economists have done an enormous amount of research confronting theories of growth with the empirical evidence. The way in which this research has been conducted has changed over the years.

In 1776, when Adam Smith wrote about 'the nature and causes of the Wealth of Nations' in his celebrated book, empirical evidence took the form of carefully selected facts described in words and stories. Today, large databases, sophisticated statistical methods, and fast computers provide numerical measurements of the causes of economic growth.

Economists have looked at the growth rate data for more than 100 countries for the period since 1960 and explored the correlations between the growth rate and more than 60 possible influences on it. The conclusion of this data crunching is that most of these possible influences have variable and unpredictable effects, but a few of them have strong and clear effects. Table 22.1 summarizes these more robust influences. They are arranged in order of difficulty (or in the case of region, the impossibility) of changing. Political and economic systems are hard to change, but market distortions, investment and openness to international trade are features of a nation's economy that can be influenced by policy.

Let's now look at growth policies.

Policies for Achieving Faster Growth

Growth theory supported by empirical evidence tells us that to achieve faster economic growth, we must increase the growth rate of physical capital, the pace of technological advance, or the growth rate of human capital and openness to international trade.

The main suggestions for achieving these objectives are:

◆ Stimulate saving

◆ Stimulate research and development

◆ Improve the quality of education

◆ Provide international aid to developing nations

◆ Encourage international trade

Stimulate Saving

Saving finances investment, so stimulating saving increases economic growth. The East Asian economies have the highest growth rates and the highest saving rates. Some African economies have the lowest growth rates and the lowest saving rates.

Table 22.1

The Influences on Economic Growth

Influence	Good for Economic Growth	Bad for Economic Growth
Region	◆ Far from equator	◆ Sub-Sahara Africa
Politics	◆ Rule of law	◆ Revolutions
	◆ Civil liberties	◆ Military coups
		◆ Wars
Economic system	◆ Capitalist	
Market distortions		◆ Exchange rate distortions
		◆ Price controls and black markets
Investment	◆ Human capital	
	◆ Physical capital	
International trade	◆ Open to trade	

Source of information: Xavier Sala-i-Martin, 'I Just Ran Two Million Regressions', *The American Economic Review*, Vol. 87, No 2 (May 1997), pp. 178–183.

Tax incentives can increase saving. Economists claim that a tax on consumption rather than income provides the best saving incentive.

Stimulate Research and Development

Everyone can use the fruits of basic research and development efforts. For example, all biotechnology firms can use advances in gene-splicing technology. Because basic inventions can be copied, the inventor's profit is limited and the market allocates too few resources to this activity. Governments can direct public funds towards financing basic research, but this solution is not foolproof. It requires a mechanism for allocating the public funds to their highest-valued use.

Improve the Quality of Education

The free market produces too little education because it brings benefits beyond those valued by the people who receive the education. By funding basic education and by ensuring high standards in basic skills such as language, mathematics and science, governments can contribute to a nation's growth potential. Education can also be stimulated and improved by using tax incentives to encourage improved private provision.

Provide International Aid to Developing Nations

It seems obvious that if rich countries give financial aid to developing countries, investment and growth will increase in the recipient countries. Unfortunately, the obvious does not routinely happen. A large amount of data-driven research on the effects of aid on growth has turned up a zero and even negative effect. Aid often gets diverted and spent on consumption.

Encourage International Trade

Trade, not aid, stimulates economic growth. It works by extracting the available gains from specialization and trade. The fastest-growing nations are those most open to trade. If the rich nations truly want to aid economic development, they will lower their trade barriers against developing nations, especially in farm products. The World Trade Organization's efforts to achieve more open trade are being resisted by the richer nations.

Review Quiz

1   What is the central idea of classical growth theory that leads to the dismal outcome?
2   What, according to the neoclassical growth theory, is the fundamental cause of economic growth?
3   What is the key proposition of the new growth theory that makes growth persist?

You can work these questions in Study Plan 22.5 and get instant feedback.

To complete your study of economic growth, take a look at *Reading Between the Lines* on pp. 526–527 and see why China's spectacular economic growth might slow in the coming years.

Reading Between the Lines

China's Long-term Growth

The Financial Times, 28 September 2010

ADB Warns on China's Long-term Growth

FT

Kevin Brown

China's average annual rate of economic growth over the next two decades will fall to little more than half the current level as its ability to sustain huge investment declines, according to the Asian Development Bank. . . .

In its first official attempt to quantify China's long-term growth prospects, the ADB said on Tuesday that its baseline projection was just 5.5 per cent on average for the 20 years to 2030, compared with 9.4 per cent between 1981 and 2007 and a forecast 9.6 per cent this year.

Growth could average 6.6 per cent if China implemented reforms to reduce its dependence on investment and increase productivity through improvements in education, property rights and research and development, the ADB said.

Jong-Wha Lee, ADB chief economist, said many other countries in Asia would face the same growth problem because their rapid rates of economic growth over the past three decades had been underpinned by unsustainable levels of investment. . . .

The ADB report forecasts that South Korea's long-term economic growth will fall from an average of 6.3 per cent to a baseline projection of 3.9 per cent, Taiwan's from 6.1 per cent to 3.1 per cent, Indonesia's from 4.8 per cent to 4.4 per cent and India's from 5.5 per cent to 4.5 per cent. . . .

Countries that have invested less in the past three decades are forecast to increase average growth rates, with Pakistan moving from 5.1 per cent a year to a baseline 6.5 per cent and the Philippines from 3.4 per cent to 5.7 per cent.

The Essence of the Story

- The Asian Development Bank (ADB) predicts that China's real GDP growth rate will slow from 9.4 per cent per year during the past 16 years to 5.5 per cent per year.

- The ADB also predicts that the real GDP growth rates will slow in South Korea, Taiwan and Indonesia.

- The ADB says that China has had an excessive dependence on physical capital accumulation and it needs to invest more in human capital, property rights and technological change.

- Pakistan and the Philippines, countries that have accumulated a smaller amount of physical capital, will have higher future growth rates.

Economic Analysis

◆ Figure 1 shows the growth rates for six Asian economies for 1981–2007 and the ADB's projected growth rates for 2011–2030.

◆ The ADB says China, South Korea and Taiwan will grow at a slower rate while Pakistan and the Philippines will grow at a faster rate.

◆ Figure 2 illustrates the reasoning behind the ADB forecasts. In 1981, China had a small amount of capital per hour of labour and capital accumulation brought rapid real GDP growth.

◆ But 30 years of high investment has brought diminishing returns to capital and over the coming years will bring even stronger diminishing returns shown by the falling slope of the productivity curve.

◆ Figure 3 shows the ADB's decomposition of the sources of China's real GDP growth rate both in the past and the future.

◆ Capital growth will still contribute the most to overall growth in 2011–2030. The next most important contributor is education and technological change. The shift in the productivity curve from PC_0 to PC_1 in Figure 2 illustrates this influence on real GDP per hour of labour.

◆ Capital growth is projected to contribute less to real GDP in the future than it did in the past because of diminishing returns to capital.

◆ It is hard to predict what the contribution of technological advance will be in the future.

◆ China might be at the same stage of economic development as Japan was in the decade after the Second World War.

◆ By copying Western technology, Japan learned to innovate and experienced rapid technological change. The same could happen in China and its fast growth would be sustained despite diminishing returns to capital.

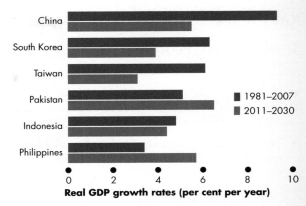

Figure 1 Real GDP growth in six Asian economies

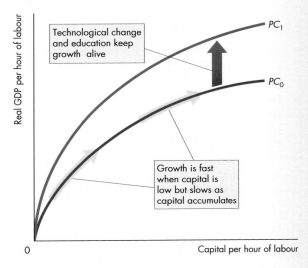

Figure 2 The sources of real GDP growth

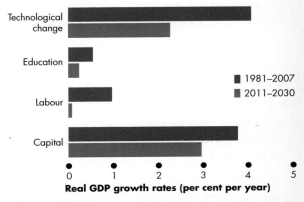

Figure 3 The changing sources of China's real GDP growth

SUMMARY

Key Points

The Basics of Economic Growth
(pp. 508–509)

◆ Economic growth is the sustained expansion of production possibilities and is measured as the annual percentage growth rate of real GDP.

◆ The Rule of 70 tells us the number of years in which real GDP doubles – 70 divided by the annual percentage growth rate.

Working Problems 1 to 5 will give you a better understanding of the basics of economic growth.

Economic Growth Trends (pp. 510–512)

◆ Real GDP per person in the UK has grown at an average rate of 1.6 per cent per year. Growth was more rapid during the 1960s and the 1980s.

◆ The gap in real GDP per person between the US and Central and South America has persisted. The gaps between the US and Hong Kong, Korea and China have narrowed. The gaps between the US and Africa and Central Europe have widened.

Working Problem 6 will give you a better understanding of economic growth trends.

How Potential GDP Grows (pp. 513–518)

◆ Potential GDP grows if the labour supply grows or if labour productivity grows.

◆ Only labour productivity growth makes real GDP per person and the standard of living grow.

Working Problems 7 to 14 will give you a better understanding of how potential GDP grows.

Why Labour Productivity Grows
(pp. 518–520)

◆ Labour productivity growth requires an incentive system created by firms, markets, property rights and money.

◆ The sources of labour productivity growth are growth of physical capital and human capital and advances in technology.

◆ Physical capital growth has diminishing returns but human capital growth and advances in technology don't have diminishing returns.

Working Problems 15 and 16 will give you a better understanding of why labour productivity grows.

Growth Theories, Evidence and Policies (pp. 521–525)

◆ In classical theory, real GDP per person keeps returning to the subsistence level.

◆ In neoclassical growth theory, diminishing returns to capital limit economic growth.

◆ In new growth theory, economic growth persists indefinitely at a rate determined by decisions that lead to innovation and technological change.

◆ Policies for achieving faster growth include stimulating saving and research and development, encouraging international trade and improving the quality of education.

Working Problems 17 and 18 will give you a better understanding of growth theories, evidence and policies.

Key Terms

Aggregate production function, 513
Classical growth theory, 521
Economic growth, 508
Economic growth rate, 508
Labour productivity, 517
Neoclassical growth theory, 521
New growth theory, 522
Productivity curve, 520
Real GDP per person, 508
Real wage rate, 514
Rule of 70, 508

STUDY PLAN PROBLEMS AND APPLICATIONS

myeconlab   You can work Problems 1 to 18 in MyEconLab Chapter 22 Study Plan and get instant feedback.

The Basics of Economic Growth
(Study Plan 22.1)

1 Brazil's real GDP was 1,360 trillion reais in 2009 and 1,434 trillion reais in 2010. Brazil's population was 191.5 million in 2009 and 193.3 million in 2010. Calculate:

  a The economic growth rate.

  b The growth rate of real GDP per person.

  c The approximate number of years it takes for real GDP per person in Brazil to double if the 2010 economic growth rate and population growth rate are maintained.

2 Japan's real GDP was 525 trillion yen in 2009 and 535 trillion yen in 2010. Japan's population was 127.6 million in 2009 and 127.5 million in 2010. Calculate:

  a The economic growth rate.

  b The growth rate of real GDP per person.

  c The approximate number of years it takes for real GDP per person in Japan to double if the real GDP economic growth rate returns to 3 per cent a year and the population growth rate is maintained.

Use the following data to work Problems 3 and 4.

China's real GDP per person was 9,280 yuan in 2009 and 10,110 yuan in 2010. India's real GDP per person was 30,880 rupees in 2009 and 32,160 rupees in 2010.

3 By maintaining their current growth rates, which country will double its 2010 standard of living first?

4 The population of China is growing at 1 per cent a year and the population of India is growing at 1.4 per cent a year. Calculate the growth rate of real GDP in each country.

5 **China's Economy Picks Up Speed**

China's trend growth rate of real GDP per person was 2.2 per cent a year before 1980 and 8.7 per cent a year after 1980. In the year to August 2009, China's output increased by 11.3 per cent.

      Source: World Economic Outlook and FT.com, 14 September 2009

  a Distinguish between a rise in China's economic growth rate and a temporary cyclical expansion.

  b How long, at the current growth rate, will it take for China to double its real GDP per person?

Economic Growth Trends (Study Plan 22.2)

6 China was the largest economy for centuries because everyone had the same type of economy – subsistence – and so the country with the most people would be economically biggest. Then the Industrial Revolution sent the West on a more prosperous path. Now the world is returning to a common economy, this time technology- and information-based, so once again population triumphs.

  a Why was China the world's largest economy until 1890?

  b Why did the US surpass China in 1890 to become the world's largest economy?

How Potential GDP Grows
(Study Plan 22.3)

Use the following information to work Problems 7 and 8.

Suppose that France cracks down on illegal immigrants and returns millions of workers to their home countries.

7 Explain what will happen to potential GDP, employment and the real wage rate in France.

8 Explain what will happen to potential GDP, employment and the real wage rate in the countries to which the immigrants return.

Use the following news clip to work Problems 9 to 11.

US Workers World's Most Productive

Americans work longer hours than those in other rich nations. Americans also produce more per person but only part of US productivity growth can be explained by the longer hours they work. Americans also create more wealth per hour of work. US employees worked an average of 1,804 hours in 2006, compared to 1,564.4 for the French, but far less than the 2,200 hours that Asians worked. But in Asian countries, average labour productivity is lower.

      Source: CBS News, 3 September 2007

9 What is the difference between productivity in this news clip and real GDP per person?

10 Identify and correct a confusion in the news clip between levels and growth rates of labour productivity.

11 If workers in developing Asian economies work more hours than Americans, why are they not the world's most productive?

Use the following tables to work Problems 12 to 14.

The tables describe an economy's labour market and its production function in 2010.

Real wage rate (euros per hour)	Labour hours supplied	Labour hours demanded
80	45	5
70	40	10
60	35	15
50	30	20
40	25	25
30	20	30
20	15	35

Labour (hours)	Real GDP (2005 euros)
5	425
10	800
15	1,125
20	1,400
25	1,625
30	1,800
35	1,925
40	2,000

12 What are the equilibrium real wage rate, the quantity of labour employed in 2010, labour productivity and potential GDP in 2010?

13 In 2011, the population increases and labour hours supplied increase by 10 at each real wage rate. What are the equilibrium real wage rate, labour productivity and potential GDP in 2011?

14 In 2011, the population increases and labour hours supplied increase by 10 at each real wage rate. Does the standard of living in this economy increase in 2011? Explain why or why not.

Why Labour Productivity Grows

(Study Plan 22.4)

15 **Labour Productivity on the Rise**

During the year ended June 2009, US non-farm sector output fell 5.5 per cent as labour productivity increased 1.9 per cent – the largest increase since 2003. But in the manufacturing sector, output fell 9.8 per cent as labour productivity increased by 4.9 per cent – the largest increase since the first quarter of 2005.

Source: bls.gov/news.release, 11 August 2009

In both sectors, output fell while labour productivity increased. Did the quantity of labour (aggregate hours) increase or decrease? In which sector was the change in the quantity of labour larger?

16 For three years, there was no technological change in Longland but capital per hour of labour increased from €10 to €20 to €30 and real GDP per hour of labour increased from €3.80 to €5.70 to €7.13. Then, in the fourth year, capital per hour of labour remained constant, but real GDP per hour of labour increased to €10. Does Longland experience diminishing returns? Explain why or why not.

Growth Theories, Evidence and Policies (Study Plan 22.5)

17 Explain the processes that will bring the growth of real GDP per person to a stop according to:

a Classical growth theory.

b Neoclassical growth theory.

c New growth theory.

18 In the economy of Cape Despair, the subsistence real wage rate is €15 an hour. Whenever real GDP per hour rises above €15, the population grows, and whenever real GDP per hour of labour falls below this level, the population falls. The table shows Cape Despair's production function:

Labour (billions of hours per year)	Real GDP (billions of 2005 euros)
0.5	8
1.0	15
1.5	21
2.0	26
2.5	30
3.0	33
3.5	35

Initially, the population of Cape Despair is constant and real GDP per hour of labour is at the subsistence level of €15. Then a technological advance shifts the production function upward by 50 per cent at each level of labour.

a What are the initial levels of real GDP and labour productivity?

b What happens to labour productivity immediately following the technological advance?

ADDITIONAL PROBLEMS AND APPLICATIONS

myeconlab   You can work these problems in MyEconLab if assigned by your lecturer.

The Basics of Economic Growth

19 If in 2012 China's real GDP is growing at 9 per cent a year, its population is growing at 1 per cent a year, and these growth rates continue, in what year will China's real GDP per person be twice what it is in 2012?

20 South Africa's real GDP was 1,782 billion rand in 2009 and 1,835 billion rand in 2010. South Africa's population was 49.3 million in 2009 and 49.9 million in 2010. Calculate:

a The economic growth rate.

b The growth rate of real GDP per person.

c The approximate number of years it takes for real GDP per person in South Africa to double if the 2010 economic growth rate and population growth rate are maintained.

21 Turkey's real GDP was 97.1 billion Turkish lira in 2009 and 104.7 billion Turkish lira in 2010. Turkey's population was 70.5 million in 2009 and 71.4 million in 2010. Calculate:

a The economic growth rate.

b The growth rate of real GDP per person.

c The approximate number of years it takes for real GDP per person in Turkey to double if economic growth returns to its average since 2009 of 3.6 per cent a year and is maintained.

Economic Growth Trends

22 The New World Order

While gross domestic product growth is cooling a bit in emerging market economies, the results are still tremendous compared with the US and much of Western Europe. The emerging market economies posted a 6.7 per cent jump in real GDP in 2008, down from 7.5 per cent in 2007. The advanced economies grew an estimated 1.6 per cent in 2008. The difference in growth rates represents the largest spread between emerging market economies and advanced economies in the 37-year history of the survey.

Source: *Fortune*, 14 July 2008

Do growth rates over the past few decades indicate that gaps in real GDP per person around the world are shrinking, growing or staying the same? Explain.

How Potential GDP Grows

23 If a large increase in investment increases labour productivity, explain what happens to:

a Potential GDP.

b Employment.

c The real wage rate.

24 If a severe drought decreases labour productivity, explain what happens to:

a Potential GDP.

b Employment.

c The real wage rate.

Use the following tables to work Problems 25 to 27.

The first table describes an economy's labour market and the second table describes its production function in 2010.

Real wage rate (euros per hour)	Labour hours supplied	Labour hours demanded
80	55	15
70	50	20
60	45	25
50	40	30
40	35	35
30	30	40
20	25	45

Labour (hours)	Real GDP (2005 euros)
15	1,425
20	1,800
25	2,125
30	2,400
35	2,625
40	2,800
45	2,925
50	3,000

25 What are the equilibrium real wage rate and the quantity of labour employed in 2010?

26 What are labour productivity and potential GDP in 2010?

27 Suppose that labour productivity increases in 2010. What effect does the increased labour productivity have on the demand for labour, the supply of labour, potential GDP and real GDP per person?

Why Labour Productivity Grows

28 India's Economy Hits the Wall

Just six months ago, India was looking good. Annual growth was 9 per cent, consumer demand was huge, and foreign investment was growing. But now most economic forecasts expect growth to slow to 7 per cent – a big drop for a country that needs to accelerate growth. India needs urgently to upgrade its infrastructure and education and healthcare facilities. Agriculture is unproductive and needs better technology. The legal system needs to be strengthened with more judges and courtrooms.

Source: *Business Week*, 1 July 2008

Explain five potential sources for faster economic growth in India suggested in this news clip.

Growth Theories, Evidence and Policies

29 The Productivity Watch

According to former Federal Reserve chairman Alan Greenspan, IT investments in the 1990s boosted productivity, which boosted corporate profits, which led to more IT investments, and so on, leading to a nirvana of high growth.

Source: *Fortune*, 4 September 2006

Which of the growth theories that you've studied in this chapter best corresponds to the explanation given by Mr Greenspan?

30 Is faster economic growth always a good thing? Argue the case for faster growth and the case for slower growth. Then reach a conclusion on whether growth should be increased or slowed.

31 Makani Power: A Mighty Wind

Makani Power aims to generate energy from what are known as high-altitude wind-extraction technologies. And that's about all its 34-year-old Aussie founder, Saul Griffith, wants to say about it. But Makani can't hide entirely, not when its marquee investor is Google.org, the tech company's philanthropic arm. Makani's plan is to capture that high-altitude wind with a very old tool: kites. Harnessing higher-altitude wind, at least in theory, has greater potential than the existing wind industry because at a thousand feet above the ground, the wind is stronger and more consistent.

Source: *Fortune*, 28 April 2008

Explain which growth theory best describes the news clip.

Economics in the News

32 After you have studied *Reading Between the Lines* on pp. 526–527 answer the following questions:

a What does the Asia Development Bank expect will happen to the economic growth rate of China over the next two decades?

b What is the reasoning behind the ADB's expectation?

c On which growth theory have the ADB economists based their forecast? Explain your answer.

d What policy does the ADB suggest will sustain China's high economic growth rate of the recent past? Explain your answer.

33 Make Way for India – The Next China

China grows at around 9 per cent a year, but its one-child policy will start to reduce the size of China's working population within the next 10 years. India, by contrast, will have an increasing working population for another generation at least.

Source: *The Independent*, 1 March 2006

a Given the expected population changes, do you think China or India will have the greater economic growth rate? Why?

b Would China's growth rate remain at 9 per cent a year without the restriction on its population growth rate?

c India's population growth rate is 1.6 per cent a year, and in 2005 its economic growth rate was 8 per cent a year. China's population growth rate is 0.6 per cent a year and in 2005 its economic growth rate was 9 per cent a year. In what year will real GDP per person double in each country?

Data Graphing

34 Use the Data Grapher to create a graph of the growth rate of real GDP per person in the US, Canada, Germany and the UK.

a Which country had the fastest growth of real GDP per person since 1980 and which had the slowest?

b In which country has real GDP per person fluctuated most?

Finance, Saving and Investment

After studying this chapter you will be able to:

◆ Describe the flows of funds through financial markets and institutions

◆ Explain how investment and saving along with borrowing and lending decisions are made and interact in the loanable funds market

◆ Explain how a government deficit (or surplus) influences the real interest rate, saving and investment

◆ Explain how international borrowing and lending influence the real interest rate, saving and investment

On 17 September 2007, long queues of depositors wanting to withdraw their funds formed outside the branches of the mortgage lender Northern Rock. On that same day in Detroit, Michigan, a distraught family loaded its pick-up truck, locked the door of its mortgaged home and drove away from its debt. How are these two events connected? They are connected through the global financial market that you study in this chapter. You will learn how financial markets work – mostly very well but sometimes badly.

In *Reading Between the Lines* at the end of the chapter, you will apply what you've learned to understand the influence on financial markets of large government budget deficits in the UK, Portugal, Ireland, Greece and Spain.

Financial Institutions and Financial Markets

The financial institutions and markets that we study in this chapter play a crucial role in the economy. They provide the channels through which saving flows to finance the investment in new capital that makes the economy grow. In studying the economics of financial institutions and markets, we distinguish between:

◆ Finance and money
◆ Physical capital and financial capital

Finance and Money

In economics, we use the term *finance* to describe the activity of borrowing and lending. Borrowing and lending provides the funds that finance expenditures on capital that make productivity grow.

The study of finance examines how households, firms and governments obtain and use financial resources and how they cope with the risks that arise in this activity.

We use the term *money* to describe the stuff that we use to make payments for goods and services, for factors of production including expenditures on new capital and to make financial transactions – to receive and repay loans.

The study of money looks at how households and firms use it, how much of it they hold, how banks create and manage it, and how its quantity influences the economy.

In the economic lives of individuals, businesses and governments, finance and money are closely interrelated. Money is what you get when you borrow from a bank. Money is what you use when you finance the purchase of a new car. And banks and other financial institutions provide both financial services and monetary services. Nevertheless, by distinguishing between *finance* and *money* and studying them separately, we will better understand our financial and monetary markets and institutions.

For the rest of this chapter, we study finance. Money is the topic of the next chapter.

Physical Capital and Financial Capital

Economists distinguish between physical capital and financial capital. *Physical capital* is the tools, instruments, machines, buildings and other items that have been produced in the past and that are used today to produce goods and services. Inventories of raw materials, semifinished goods, and components are part of physical capital. When economists use the term capital, they mean physical capital. The funds that firms use to buy physical capital are called **financial capital**.

Along the *aggregate production function* in Chapter 22 (see p. 513), the quantity of capital is fixed. An increase in the quantity of capital increases production possibilities and shifts the aggregate production function upward. You're going to see, in this chapter, how investment, saving, borrowing and lending decisions influence the quantity of capital and make it grow, and, as a consequence, make real GDP grow. We begin by describing the links between capital and investment and between wealth and saving.

Capital and Investment

The quantity of capital changes because of investment and depreciation. *Investment* increases the quantity of capital and *depreciation* decreases it (see Chapter 20, p. 462). The total amount spent on new capital is called **gross investment**. The change in the value of capital is called **net investment**. Net investment equals gross investment minus depreciation. Figure 23.1 illustrates these terms. On 1 January 2011, Ace Bottling Inc. had machines worth €30,000 – Ace's initial capital. During 2011, the market value of Ace's machines fell by 67 per cent – €20,000. After this depreciation, Ace's machines were valued at €10,000. During 2011, Ace spent €30,000 on new machines. This amount is Ace's gross investment. By 31 December 2011, Ace Bottling had capital valued at €40,000, so its capital had increased by €10,000. This amount is Ace's net investment. Ace's net investment equals its gross investment of €30,000 minus depreciation of its initial capital of €20,000.

Wealth and Saving

Wealth is the value of all the things that people own. What people own is related to what they earn, but it is not the same thing. People earn an income, which is the amount they receive during a given time period from supplying the services of the resources they own. **Saving** is the amount of income that is not paid in taxes or spent on consumption goods and services.

Saving increases wealth. Wealth also increases when the market value of assets rises – called capital gains – and decreases when the market value of assets falls – called capital losses.

Figure 23.1   Capital and Investment

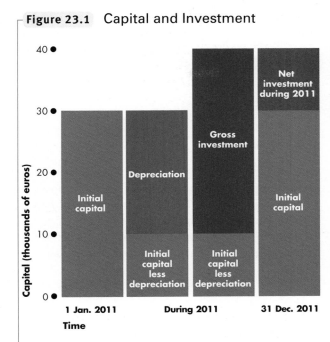

On 1 January 2011, Ace Bottling had capital worth €30,000. During the year, the value of Ace's capital fell by €20,000 – depreciation – and it spent €30,000 on new capital – gross investment. Ace's net investment was €10,000 (€30,000 gross investment minus €20,000 depreciation) so that at the end of 2011, Ace had capital worth €40,000.

myeconlab Animation ──────────────────◆

For example, at the end of term you have €250 in the bank and a coin collection worth €300, so your wealth is €550. During the summer, you earn €5,000 (net of taxes) and spend €1,000 on consumption goods and services, so your saving is €4,000. Your bank account increases to €4,250 and your wealth becomes €4,550. The €4,000 increase in wealth equals saving. If coins rise in value and your coin collection is now worth €500, you have a capital gain of €200, which is also added to your wealth.

National wealth and national saving work like this personal example. The wealth of a nation at the end of a year equals its wealth at the start of the year plus its saving during the year, which equals income minus consumption expenditure.

To make real GDP grow, saving and wealth must be transformed into investment and capital. This transformation takes place in the markets for financial capital and through the activities of financial institutions. We're now going to describe these markets and institutions.

Financial Capital Markets

Saving is the source of the funds that are used to finance investment, and these funds are supplied and demanded in three types of financial markets:

◆ Loan markets
◆ Bond markets
◆ Stock markets

Loan Markets

Businesses often want short-term finance to buy inventories or to extend credit to their customers. Sometimes they get this finance in the form of a loan from a bank. Households often want finance to purchase a high expenditure item, such as a car or household furnishings and appliances. They get this finance as bank loans, often in the form of outstanding credit card balances. Households also get finance to buy new homes. (Expenditure on new homes is counted as part of investment.) These funds are usually obtained as a loan that is secured by a **mortgage** – a legal contract that gives ownership of a home to the lender in the event that the borrower fails to meet the agreed loan payments (repayments and interest). Mortgage loans were at the centre of the sub-prime loans crisis of 2007–2008. All of these types of financing take place in loan markets.

Bond Markets

When Wal-Mart (the largest retailer in the world) expands its business into China, it gets the finance it needs by selling bonds. National and local governments also raise finance by issuing bonds.

A **bond** is a promise to make specified payments on specified dates. For example, you can buy a Wal-Mart bond that promises to pay $5.00 every year until 2024 and then to make a final payment of $100 in 2025.

The buyer of a bond from Wal-Mart makes a loan to the company and is entitled to the payments promised by the bond. When a person buys a newly issued bond, he or she may hold the bond until the borrower has repaid the amount borrowed or sell it to someone else. Bonds issued by firms and governments are traded in the **bond market**.

The term of a bond might be long (decades) or short (just a month or two). Firms often issue very short-term bonds as a way of getting paid for their sales before the buyer is able to pay. These short-term bonds are called commercial paper. For example, when Rolls Royce sells

£100 million of aero engines to Qantas, Rolls Royce wants to be paid when the items are shipped. But Qantas doesn't want to pay until the engines are installed and the engines are earning an income. In this situation, Qantas might promise to pay GM £101 million three months in the future. A bank would be willing to buy this promise for (say) £100 million. Rolls Royce gets £100 million immediately and the bank gets £101 million in three months when Qantas honours its promise. The UK Treasury issues promises of this type, called Treasury bills.

Another type of bond is a **mortgage-backed security**, which entitles its holder to the income from a package of mortgages. Mortgage lenders create mortgage-backed securities. They make mortgage loans to homebuyers and then create securities that they sell to obtain more funds to make more mortgage loans. The holder of a mortgage-backed security is entitled to receive payments that derive from the payments received by the mortgage lender from the homebuyer–borrower.

Mortgage-backed securities were at the centre of the storm in the financial markets in 2007–2008.

Stock Markets

When Boeing wants finance to expand its aeroplane building business, it issues stock. A **stock** is a certificate of ownership and claim to the firm's profits. Boeing has issued about 900 million shares of its stock. So if you owned 900 Boeing shares, you would own one millionth of Boeing and be entitled to receive one millionth of its profits. Unlike a stockholder, a bondholder does not own part of the firm that issued the bond.

A **stock market** is a financial market in which shares of stocks of corporations are traded. The London Stock Exchange, the Frankfurt Stock Exchange, the New York Stock Exchange and the Tokyo Stock Exchange are all examples of stock markets.

Financial Institutions

Financial markets are highly competitive because of the role played by financial institutions in those markets. A **financial institution** is a firm that operates on both sides of the markets for financial capital. The financial institution is a borrower in one market and a lender in another.

Financial institutions also stand ready to trade so that households with funds to lend and firms or households seeking funds can always find someone on the other side of the market with whom to trade.

The key financial institutions are:

◆ Commercial banks
◆ Mortgage companies (building societies)
◆ Pension funds
◆ Insurance companies

Commercial Banks

Commercial banks are financial institutions that accept deposits, provide payment services and make loans to firms and households. The bank that you use for your own banking services and that issues your debit card is a commercial bank. These institutions play a central role in the monetary system and we study them in detail in Chapter 24.

Mortgage Companies (Building Societies)

Mortgage companies are financial institutions that specialise in making loans for property purchases. In the UK these companies are called building societies. Traditionally building societies took deposits and made loans from the deposit funds they held. Since the 1990s, the building societies began to borrow funds from other financial institutions to make mortgage loans. Many building societies became banks so that they could fund their mortgage business by borrowing from the global interbank market.

In the US, two large financial institutions that specialize in mortgages, the Federal National Mortgage Association, or Fannie Mae, and the Federal Home Loan Mortgage Corporation, or Freddie Mac, were at the epicentre of the global financial crisis (see *Economics in Action* opposite). These financial institutions bought mortgages from banks, packaged them into mortgage-backed securities, and sold them to financial institutions all over the world.

In September 2008, Fannie and Freddie owned or guaranteed $6 trillion worth of mortgages (half of the US$12 trillion of mortgages) and were taken over by the US federal government.

Many former UK building societies followed the model of Fannie Mae and Freddie Mac. They borrowed funds in the global interbank loans market and loaned them to house buyers. They then packaged the mortgage loans into mortgage-backed securities and sold them to other financial institutions. Often the buyers of these securities would be the lenders of the funds that were used to make the loans to house buyers.

Pension Funds

Pension funds are financial institutions that use the pension contributions of firms and workers to buy bonds and stocks. The mortgage backed securities of Fannie Mae and Freddie Mac and specialized mortgage lenders in the UK are among the assets of pension funds. Some pension funds are very large and play an active role in the firms whose stock they hold.

Insurance Companies

Insurance companies enable households and firms to cope with risks such as accident, theft, fire, ill-health and a host of other misfortunes. They receive premiums from their customers and pay claims. Insurance companies use the funds they have received but not paid out as claims to buy bonds and stocks on which they earn interest income.

In normal times, insurance companies have a steady inflow of funds from premiums and interest and a steady, but smaller, outflow of funds paying claims. Their profit is the gap between the two flows.

In unusual times, when large and widespread losses are being incurred, insurance companies can run into difficulty in meeting their obligations.

Insolvency and Illiquidity

A financial institution's **net worth** is the market value of what it has lent minus the market value of what it has borrowed. If net worth is positive, the institution is solvent. But if net worth is negative, the institution is insolvent and must go out of business. The owners of an insolvent financial institution – usually its stockholders – bear the loss.

A financial institution both borrows and lends, so it is exposed to the risk that its net worth might become negative. To limit that risk, financial institutions are regulated and a minimum amount of their lending must be backed by their net worth.

Sometimes, a financial institution is solvent but illiquid. A firm is *illiquid* if it has made long-term loans with borrowed funds and is faced with a sudden demand to repay more of what it has borrowed than its available cash.

In normal times, a financial institution that is illiquid can borrow from another institution. But if all the financial institutions are short of cash, the market for loans among financial institutions dries up. In such a situation, the central bank can provide funds.

Insolvency and illiquidity were at the core of the financial meltdown of 2007–2008.

ECONOMICS IN ACTION

The 2008 Financial Crisis

Bear Stearns: absorbed by JPMorgan Chase with help from the US Federal Reserve. Lehman Brothers: gone. Fannie Mae and Freddie Mac: taken into government oversight. Merrill Lynch: absorbed by Bank of America. AIG: given an $85 billion lifeline by the Federal Reserve and sold off in parcels to financial institutions around the world. Wachovia: taken over by Wells Fargo. Washington Mutual: taken over by JPMorgan Chase. Morgan Stanley: 20 per cent bought by Mitsubishi, a large Japanese bank. These are some of the events in the financial crisis of 2008. What was going on?

Between 2002 and 2005, mortgage lending exploded and home prices rocketed. Mortgage lenders bundled their loans into mortgage-backed securities and sold them to eager buyers around the world. When interest rates began to rise in 2006 and asset prices fell, financial institutions took big losses. Some losses were too big to bear and big-name institutions failed.

Interest Rates and Asset Prices

Stocks, bonds, short-term securities and loans are collectively called financial assets. The interest rate on a financial asset is the interest received expressed as a percentage of the price of the asset.

Because the interest rate is a percentage of the price of an asset, if the asset price rises, other things remaining the same, the interest rate falls. Conversely, if the asset price falls, other things remaining the same, the interest rate rises.

To see this inverse relationship between an asset price and the interest rate, let's look at an example. We'll consider a bond that promises to pay its holder €5 a year forever. What is the rate of return – the interest rate – on this bond? The answer depends on the price of the bond. If you could buy this bond for €50, the interest rate would be 10 per cent per year:

Interest rate = (€5 ÷ €50) × 100 = 10 per cent.

But if the price of this bond increased to €200, its rate of return or interest rate would be only 2.5 per cent per year. That is,

Interest rate = (€5 ÷ €200) × 100 = 2.5 per cent.

This relationship means that the price of an asset and the interest rate on that asset are determined simultaneously – one implies the other.

This relationship also means that if the interest rate on the asset rises, the price of the asset falls, debts become harder to pay and the net worth of the financial institution falls. Insolvency can arise from a previously unexpected large rise in the interest rate. In the next part of this chapter, we learn how interest rates and asset prices are determined in the financial markets.

The Loanable Funds Market

In macroeconomics, we group all the financial markets that we described in the previous section into a single loanable funds market. The **loanable funds market** is the aggregate of all the individual financial markets.

The circular flow model of Chapter 20 (see p. 461) can be extended to include flows in the loanable funds market that finance investment.

Funds that Finance Investment

Figure 23.2 shows the flows of funds that finance investment. They come from three sources:

1 Household saving
2 Government budget surplus
3 Borrowing from the rest of the world

Households' income, Y, is spent on consumption goods and services, C, saved, S, or paid in net taxes, T. **Net taxes** are the taxes paid to governments minus the cash transfers received from governments (such as Social Security and unemployment benefits). So income is equal to the sum of consumption expenditure, saving and net taxes:

$$Y = C + S + T$$

You saw in Chapter 20 (p. 462) that Y also equals the sum of the items of aggregate expenditure: consumption expenditure, C, investment, I, government expenditure, G, and exports, X, minus imports, M. That is:

$$Y = C + I + G + X - M$$

By using these two equations, you can see that

$$I + G + X = M + S + T$$

Subtract G and X from both sides of the last equation to obtain

$$I = S + (T - G) + (M - X)$$

This equation tells us that investment, I, is financed by household saving, S, the government budget surplus, $(T - G)$, and borrowing from the rest of the world, $(M - X)$.

A government budget surplus ($T > G$) contributes funds to finance investment, but a government budget deficit ($T < G$), competes with investment for funds and decreases the amount available to invest.

Figure 23.2 Financial Flows and the Circular Flow of Expenditure and Income

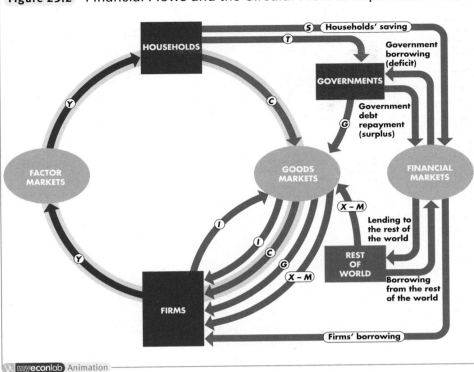

Households use their income for consumption expenditure (*C*), saving (*S*) and net taxes (*T*). Firms borrow to finance their investment expenditure.

Governments borrow to finance a budget deficit or repay debt if they have a budget surplus. The rest of the world borrows to finance its deficit or lends its surplus.

myeconlab Animation

If we export less than we import, we borrow ($M - X$) from the rest of the world to finance some of our investment. If we export more than we import, we lend ($X - M$) to the rest of the world and part of US saving finances investment in other countries.

The sum of private saving, *S*, and government saving, ($T - G$), is called **national saving**. National saving and foreign borrowing finance investment.

In 2010, total investment in the UK was £208 billion. The government (national and local combined) had a deficit of £144 billion. This total of £352 billion was financed by private saving of £306 billion and borrowing from the rest of the world (negative net exports) of £46 billion.

You're going to see how investment and saving and the flows of loanable funds – all measured in constant 2005 euros – are determined. The price in the loanable funds market that achieves equilibrium is an interest rate, which we also measure in real terms as the real interest rate. In the loanable funds market, there is just one interest rate, which is an average of the interest rates on all the different types of financial securities that we described earlier. Let's see what we mean by the real interest rate.

The Real Interest Rate

The **nominal interest rate** is the number of pounds or euros that a borrower pays and a lender receives in interest in a year expressed as a percentage of the number of pounds or euros borrowed and lent. For example, if the annual interest paid on a €500 loan is €25, the nominal interest rate is 5 per cent per year: €25 ÷ €500 × 100 or 5 per cent.

The **real interest rate** is the additional goods and services that the lender can buy with the interest received. It is the nominal interest rate adjusted to remove the effects of inflation on the buying power of money. The real interest rate is approximately equal to the nominal interest rate minus the inflation rate.

You can see why if you suppose that you have put €500 in a savings account that earns 5 per cent a year. At the end of a year, you have €525 in your savings account. Suppose that the inflation rate is 2 per cent per year – during the year, all prices increased by 2 per cent. Now, at the end of the year, it costs €510 to buy what €500 would have bought one year ago. Your money in the bank has really only increased by €15, from €510 to €525. That €15 is equivalent to a real interest rate of

3 per cent a year on your original €500. So the real interest rate is the 5 per cent nominal interest rate minus the 2 per cent inflation rate.[1]

The real interest rate is the opportunity cost of loanable funds. The real interest paid on borrowed funds is the opportunity cost of borrowing. And the real interest rate forgone when funds are used either to buy consumption goods and services or to invest in new capital goods is the opportunity cost of not saving or not lending those funds.

We're now going to see how the loanable funds market determines the real interest rate, the quantity of funds loaned, saving and investment. In the rest of this section, we will ignore the government and the rest of the world and focus on households and firms in the loanable funds market. We will study:

◆ The demand for loanable funds

◆ The supply of loanable funds

◆ Equilibrium in the loanable funds market

The Demand for Loanable Funds

The *quantity of loanable funds demanded* is the total quantity of funds demanded to finance investment, the government budget deficit and international investment or lending during a given period. Our focus here is on investment. We'll bring the other two items into the picture in later sections of this chapter.

What determines investment and the demand for loanable funds to finance it? Many details influence this decision, but we can summarize them in two factors:

1 The real interest rate

2 Expected profit

Firms invest in capital only if they expect to earn a profit and fewer projects are profitable at a high real interest rate than at a low real interest rate, so:

Other things remaining the same, the higher the real interest rate, the smaller is the quantity of loanable funds demanded; and the lower the real interest rate, the greater is the quantity of loanable funds demanded.

---

[1] The exact real interest rate formula, which allows for the change in the purchasing power of both the interest and the loan is:
Real interest rate = (Nominal interest rate − Inflation rate) ÷ (1 + Inflation rate/100). If the nominal interest rate is 5 per cent a year and the inflation rate is 2 per cent a year, the real interest rate is: $(5 - 2) \div (1 + 0.02) = 2.94$ per cent a year.

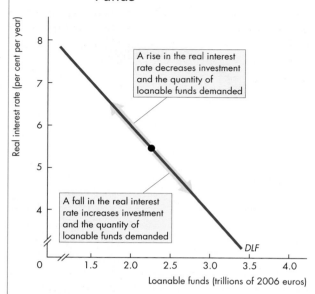

Figure 23.3 The Demand for Loanable Funds

A rise in the real interest rate decreases investment and the quantity of loanable funds demanded

A fall in the real interest rate increases investment and the quantity of loanable funds demanded

A change in the real interest rate changes the quantity of loanable funds demanded and brings a movement along the demand for loanable funds curve.

myeconlab Animation

Demand for Loanable Funds Curve

The **demand for loanable funds** is the relationship between the quantity of loanable funds demanded and the real interest rate, when all other influences on borrowing plans remain the same. The demand curve *DLF* in Figure 23.3 is a demand for loanable funds curve.

To understand the demand for loanable funds, think about Amazon.com's decision to borrow €100 million to build a new warehouse. If Amazon expects a return of €5 million a year from this investment before paying interest costs and the interest rate is less than 5 per cent a year, Amazon would make a profit, so it builds the warehouses. But if the interest rate is more than 5 per cent a year, Amazon would incur a loss, so it doesn't build the warehouses. The quantity of loanable funds demanded is greater the lower is the real interest rate.

Changes in the Demand for Loanable Funds

When the expected profit changes, the demand for loanable funds changes. Other things remaining the same, the greater the expected profit from new capital, the greater is the amount of investment and the greater the demand for loanable funds.

Expected profit rises during a business cycle expansion and falls during a recession; rises when technological change creates profitable new products; rises as a growing population brings increased demand for goods and services; and fluctuates with contagious swings of optimism and pessimism, called 'animal spirits' by Keynes and 'irrational exuberance' by Alan Greenspan.

When expected profit changes, the demand for loanable funds curve shifts.

The Supply of Loanable Funds

The *quantity of loanable funds supplied* is the total funds available from private saving, the government budget surplus and international borrowing during a given period. Our focus here is on saving. We'll bring the other two items into the picture later.

How do you decide how much of your income to save and supply in the loanable funds market? Your decision is influenced by many factors, but chief among them are:

1   The real interest rate
2   Disposable income
3   Expected future income
4   Wealth
5   Default risk

We begin by focusing on the real interest rate.

Other things remaining the same, the higher the real interest rate, the greater is the quantity of loanable funds supplied; and the lower the real interest rate, the smaller is the quantity of loanable funds supplied.

The Supply of Loanable Funds Curve

The **supply of loanable funds** is the relationship between the quantity of loanable funds supplied and the real interest rate when all other influences on lending plans remain the same. The curve *SLF* in Figure 23.4 is a supply of loanable funds curve.

Think about a student's decision to save some of what she earns from her summer job. With a real interest rate of 2 per cent a year, she decides that it is not worth saving much – better to spend the income and take a student loan if funds run out during the semester. But if the real interest rate jumped to 10 per cent a year, the payoff from saving would be high enough to encourage her to cut back on spending and increase the amount she saves.

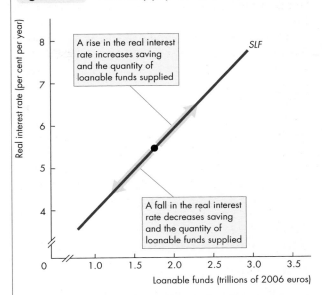

Figure 23.4   The Supply of Loanable Funds

A change in the real interest rate changes the quantity of loanable funds supplied and brings a movement along the supply of loanable funds curve.

myeconlab Animation

Changes in the Supply of Loanable Funds

The supply of loanable funds changes if disposable income, expected future income, wealth or default risk changes.

Disposable Income

A household's *disposable income* is the income minus net taxes. When disposable income increases, both saving and consumption expenditure increase. So the greater a household's disposable income, other things remaining the same, the greater is its saving.

Expected Future Income

The higher a household's expected future income, the smaller is its saving today.

Wealth

The higher a household's wealth, other things remaining the same, the smaller is its saving. If a person's wealth increases because of a capital gain, the person sees less need to save.

For example, during 2007 when house prices were still rising, wealth increased despite the fact that personal saving dropped close to zero.

Default Risk

Default risk is the risk that a loan will not be repaid. The greater that risk, the higher is the interest rate needed to induce a person to lend and the smaller is the supply of loanable funds.

Shifts of the Supply of Loanable Funds Curve

When any of the four influences on the supply of loanable funds changes, the supply of loanable funds changes and the supply curve shifts. An increase in disposable income, a decrease in expected future income, a decrease in wealth, or a fall in default risk increases saving and increases the supply of loanable funds.

Equilibrium in the Loanable Funds Market

You've seen that other things remaining the same, the higher the real interest rate, the greater is the quantity of loanable funds supplied and the smaller is the quantity of loanable funds demanded. There is one real interest rate at which the quantities of loanable funds demanded and supplied are equal, and that interest rate is the equilibrium real interest rate.

Figure 23.5 shows how the demand for and supply of loanable funds determine the real interest rate. The *DLF* curve is the demand curve and the *SLF* curve is the supply curve. If the real interest rate exceeds 6 per cent a year, the quantity of loanable funds supplied exceeds the quantity demanded – a surplus of funds. Borrowers find it easy to get funds, but lenders are unable to lend all their funds. The real interest rate falls until the quantity of funds supplied equals the quantity demanded.

If the real interest rate is less than 6 per cent a year, the quantity of loanable funds supplied is less than the quantity demanded – a shortage of funds. Borrowers can't get the funds they want, but lenders are able to lend all the funds they have available. So the real interest rate rises and continues to rise until the quantity of funds supplied equals the quantity demanded.

Regardless of whether there is a surplus or a shortage of loanable funds, the real interest rate changes and is pulled towards an equilibrium level. In Figure 23.5, the equilibrium real interest rate is 6 per cent a year. At this interest rate there is neither a surplus nor a shortage of loanable funds. Borrowers can get the funds they want, and lenders can lend all the funds they have available. The investment plans of borrowers and the saving plans of lenders are consistent with each other.

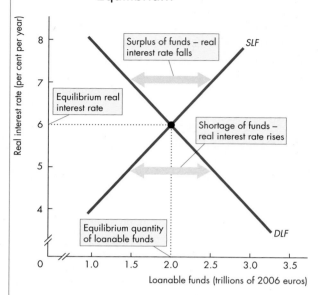

Figure 23.5 Loanable Funds Market Equilibrium

A surplus of funds lowers the real interest rate and a shortage of funds raises it. At an interest rate of 6 per cent a year, the quantity of funds demanded equals the quantity supplied and the market is in equilibrium.

myeconlab Animation

Changes in Demand and Supply

Financial markets are highly volatile in the short run but remarkably stable in the long run. Volatility in the market comes from fluctuations in either the demand for loanable funds or the supply of loanable funds. These fluctuations bring fluctuations in the real interest rate and in the equilibrium quantity of funds lent and borrowed. They also bring fluctuations in asset prices.

Here we'll illustrate the effects of increases in demand and supply in the loanable funds market.

An Increase in Demand

If the profits that firms expect to earn increase, they increase their planned investment and increase their demand for loanable funds to finance that investment. With an increase in the demand for loanable funds, but no change in the supply of loanable funds, there is a shortage of funds. As borrowers compete for funds, the interest rate rises and lenders increase the quantity of funds supplied.

Figure 23.6(a) illustrates these changes. An increase in the demand for loanable funds shifts the demand curve rightward from DLF_0 to DLF_1. With no change in

Figure 23.6 Changes in Demand and Supply

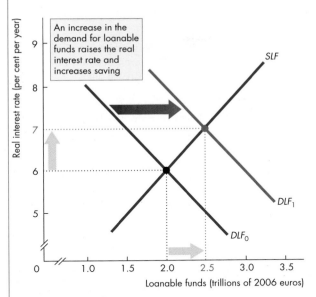

An increase in the demand for loanable funds raises the real interest rate and increases saving

(a) An increase in demand

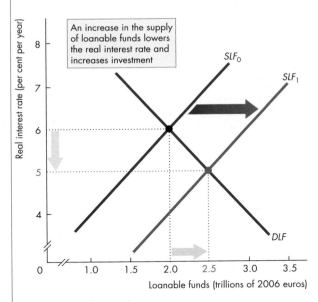

An increase in the supply of loanable funds lowers the real interest rate and increases investment

(b) An increase in supply

In part (a), the demand for loanable funds increases and supply doesn't change. The real interest rate rises (financial asset prices fall) and the quantity of funds increases.

In part (b), the supply of loanable funds increases and demand doesn't change. The real interest rate falls (financial asset prices rise) and the quantity of funds increases.

 Animation

the supply of loanable funds, there is a shortage of funds at a real interest rate of 6 per cent a year. The real interest rate rises until it is 7 per cent a year. Equilibrium is restored and the equilibrium quantity of funds has increased.

An Increase in Supply

If one of the influences on saving plans changes and increases saving, the supply of loanable funds increases. With no change in the demand for loanable funds, the market is flush with loanable funds. Borrowers find bargains and lenders find themselves accepting a lower interest rate. At the lower interest rate, borrowers find additional investment projects profitable and increase the quantity of loanable funds that they borrow.

Figure 23.6(b) illustrates these changes. An increase in supply shifts the supply curve rightward from SLF_0 to SLF_1. With no change in demand, there is a surplus of funds at a real interest rate of 6 per cent a year. The real interest rate falls until it is 5 per cent a year. Equilibrium is restored and the equilibrium quantity of funds has increased.

Long-run Growth of Demand and Supply

Over time, both demand and supply in the loanable funds market fluctuate and the real interest rate rises and falls. Both the supply of loanable funds and the demand for loanable funds tend to increase over time. On the average, they increase at a similar pace, so although demand and supply trend upward, the real interest rate has no trend. It fluctuates around a constant average level.

Review Quiz

1. What is the loanable funds market?
2. Why is the real interest rate the opportunity cost of loanable funds?
3. How do firms make investment decisions?
4. What determines the demand for loanable funds and what makes it change?
5. How do households make saving decisions?
6. What determines the supply of loanable funds and what makes it change?
7. How do changes in the demand for and supply of loanable funds change the real interest rate and quantity of loanable funds?

You can work these questions in Study Plan 23.2 and get instant feedback.

> ◆ ECONOMICS IN ACTION

Loanable Funds Fuel the US Home Price Bubble

The financial crisis that gripped the US and global economies in 2007 and cascaded through the financial markets in 2008 had its origins much earlier in events taking place in the loanable funds market.

Between 2001 and 2005, a massive injection of loanable funds occurred. Some funds came from the rest of the world, but that source of supply has been stable. The Federal Reserve (the US central bank) provided funds to keep interest rates low and that was a major source of the increase in the supply of funds. (The next chapter explains how a central bank does this.)

Figure 1 illustrates the loanable funds market starting in 2001. In that year, the demand for loanable funds was DLF_{01} and the supply of loanable funds was SLF_{01}. The equilibrium real interest rate was 4 per cent a year and the equilibrium quantity of loanable funds was $29 trillion (in 2005 dollars).

During the ensuing four years, a massive increase in the supply of loanable funds shifted the supply curve rightward to SLF_{05}. A smaller increase in demand shifted the demand for loanable funds curve to DLF_{05}. The real interest rate fell to 1 per cent a year and the quantity of loanable funds increased to $36 trillion – a 24 per cent increase in just four years.

With this large increase in available funds, much of it in the form of mortgage loans to home buyers, the demand for homes increased by more than the increase in the supply of homes. Home prices rose and the expectation of further increases fuelled the demand for loanable funds.

By 2006, the expectation of continued rapidly rising home prices brought a very large increase in the demand for loanable funds. At the same time, the Federal Reserve began to tighten credit. The result of the Fed's tighter credit policy was a slowdown in the pace of increase in the supply of loanable funds.

Figure 2 illustrates these events. In 2006, the demand for loanable funds increased from DLF_{05} to DLF_{06} and the supply of loanable funds increased by a smaller amount from SLF_{05} to SLF_{06}. The real interest rate increased to 3 per cent a year.

The rise in the real interest rate (and a much higher rise in the nominal interest rate) put many home owners in financial difficulty. Mortgage repayments increased and some borrowers stopped repaying their loans.

By August 2007, the damage from mortgage default and foreclosure was so large that the credit market began to dry up. A large decrease in both demand and supply kept interest rates roughly constant but decreased the quantity of new business.

The total quantity of loanable funds didn't decrease, but the rate of increase slowed to a snail's pace and financial institutions most exposed to the bad mortgage debts and the securities that they backed (described on p. 536) began to fail.

These events illustrate the crucial role played by the loanable funds market.

Figure 1 The Foundation of the Crisis: 2001–2005

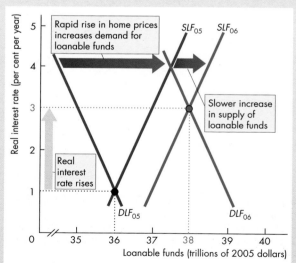

Figure 2 The Start of the Crisis: 2005–2006

Government in the Loanable Funds Market

Government enters the loanable funds market when it has a budget surplus or budget deficit. A government budget surplus increases the supply of loanable funds and contributes to financing investment; a government budget deficit increases the demand for loanable funds and competes with businesses for funds. Let's study the effects of government on the loanable funds market.

A Government Budget Surplus

A government budget surplus increases the supply of loanable funds. The real interest rate falls, which decreases household saving and decreases the quantity of private funds supplied. The lower real interest rate increases the quantity of loanable funds demanded and increases investment.

Figure 23.7 shows these effects of a government budget surplus. The private supply of loanable funds curve is *PSLF*. The supply of loanable funds curve, *SLF*,

shows the sum of private supply and the government budget surplus. Here, the government budget surplus is €1 trillion, so at each real interest rate the *SLF* curve lies €1 trillion to the right of the *PSLF* curve. That is, the horizontal distance between the *PSLF* curve and the *SLF* curve equals the government budget surplus.

With no government surplus, the real interest rate is 6 per cent a year, the quantity of loanable funds is €2 trillion a year and investment is €2 trillion a year. But with the government surplus of €1 trillion a year, the equilibrium real interest rate falls to 5 per cent a year and the equilibrium quantity of loanable funds increases to €2.5 trillion a year.

The fall in the interest rate decreases private saving to €1.5 trillion, but investment increases to €2.5 trillion, which is financed by private saving plus the government budget surplus (government saving).

Government budget surpluses are rare today. Most governments including the UK, US and most in the EU, have deficits and some of them very large ones.

Let's see how a government budget deficit influences the loanable funds market.

A Government Budget Deficit

A government budget deficit increases the demand for loanable funds. The real interest rate rises, which increases household saving and increases the quantity of private funds supplied. But the higher real interest rate decreases investment and the quantity of loanable funds demanded by firms to finance investment.

Figure 23.8 shows these effects of a government budget deficit. The private demand for loanable funds curve is *PDLF*. The demand for loanable funds curve, *DLF*, shows the sum of private demand and the government budget deficit. Here, the government budget deficit is €1 trillion, so at each real interest rate the *DLF* curve lies €1 trillion to the right of the *PDLF* curve. That is, the horizontal distance between the *PDLF* curve and the *DLF* curve equals the government budget deficit.

With no government deficit, the real interest rate is 6 per cent a year, the quantity of loanable funds is €2 trillion a year and investment is €2 trillion a year. But with the government budget deficit of €1 trillion a year, the equilibrium real interest rate rises to 7 per cent a year and the equilibrium quantity of loanable funds increases to €2.5 trillion a year.

The rise in the real interest rate increases private saving to €2.5 trillion, but investment decreases to €1.5 trillion because €1 trillion of private saving must finance the government budget deficit.

Figure 23.7   A Government Budget Surplus

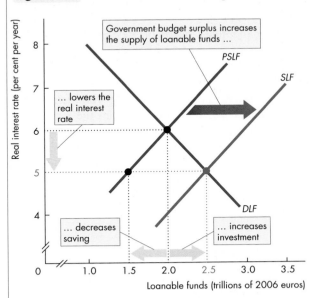

A government budget surplus of €1 trillion is added to private saving and the private supply of loanable funds (*PSLF*) to determine the supply of loanable funds, *SLF*. The real interest rate falls to 5 per cent a year, private saving decreases, but investment increases to €2.5 trillion.

myeconlab Animation

Figure 23.8 A Government Budget Deficit

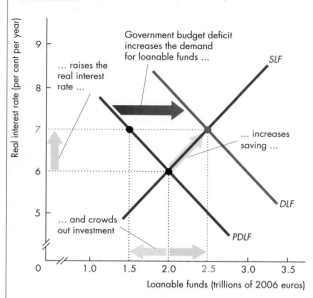

A government budget deficit adds to the private demand for loanable funds curve (*PDLF*) to determine the demand for loanable funds curve, *DLF*. The real interest rate rises, saving increases, but investment decreases – a crowding-out effect.

myeconlab Animation

Figure 23.9 The Ricardo–Barro Effect

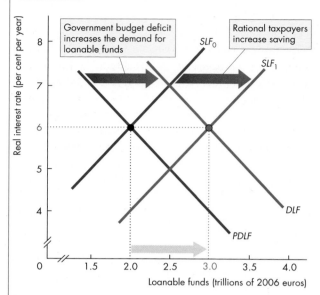

A budget deficit increases the demand for loanable funds. Rational taxpayers increase saving, which increases the supply of loanable funds curve from SLF_0 to SLF_1. Crowding out is avoided: increased saving finances the budget deficit.

myeconlab Animation

The Crowding-out Effect

The tendency for a government budget deficit to raise the real interest rate and decrease investment is called the **crowding-out effect**. The budget deficit crowds out investment by competing with businesses for scarce financial capital.

The crowding-out effect does not decrease investment by the full amount of the government budget deficit because the higher real interest rate induces an increase in private saving that partly contributes toward financing the deficit.

The Ricardo–Barro Effect

First suggested by the English economist David Ricardo in the eighteenth century and refined by Robert J. Barro of Harvard University, the Ricardo–Barro effect holds that both of the effects we've just shown are wrong and the government budget, whether in surplus or deficit, has no effect on either the real interest rate or investment.

Barro says that taxpayers are rational. They can see that a budget deficit today means that future taxes will

be higher and future disposable incomes will be smaller. With smaller expected future disposable incomes, saving increases today. Private saving and the private supply of loanable funds increase to match the quantity of loanable funds demanded by the government. So the budget deficit has no effect on either the real interest rate or investment. Figure 23.9 shows this outcome.

Most economists regard the Ricardo–Barro view as extreme. But there might be some change in private saving that goes in the direction suggested by the Ricardo–Barro effect that lessens the crowding-out effect.

Review Quiz

1 How does a government budget surplus or deficit influence the loanable funds market?
2 What is the crowding-out effect and how does it work?
3 What is the Ricardo–Barro effect and how does it modify the crowding-out effect?

You can work these questions in Study Plan 23.3 and get instant feedback.

The Global Loanable Funds Market

The loanable funds market is global, not national. Lenders on the supply side of the market want to earn the highest possible real interest rate and they will seek it by looking everywhere in the world. Borrowers on the demand side of the market want to pay the lowest possible real interest rate and they will seek it by looking everywhere in the world. Financial capital is mobile: it moves to the best advantage of lenders and borrowers.

International Capital Mobility

If a US supplier of loanable funds can earn a higher interest rate in Tokyo than in New York, funds supplied in Japan will increase and funds supplied in the US will decrease – funds will flow from the US to Japan.

If a US demander of loanable funds can pay a lower interest rate in Paris than in New York, the demand for funds in France will increase and the demand for funds in the US will decrease – funds will flow from France to the US.

Because lenders are free to seek the highest real interest rate and borrowers are free to seek the lowest real interest rate, the loanable funds market is a single, integrated, global market. Funds flow into the country in which the interest rate is highest and out of the country in which the interest rate is lowest.

When funds leave the country with the lowest interest rate, a shortage of funds raises the real interest rate. When funds move into the country with the highest interest rate, a surplus of funds lowers the real interest rate. The free international mobility of financial capital pulls real interest rates around the world toward equality.

Only when the real interest rates in New York, Tokyo and Paris are equal does the incentive to move funds from one country to another stop.

Equality of real interest rates does not mean that if you calculate the average real interest rate in New York, Tokyo and Paris, you'll get the same number. To compare real interest rates, we must compare financial assets of equal risk.

Lending is risky. A loan might not be repaid. Or the price of a stock or bond might fall. Interest rates include a risk premium – the riskier the loan, other things remaining the same, the higher is the interest rate. The interest rate on a risky loan minus that on a safe loan is called the *risk premium* and the gaps between interest rates are called *interest rate spreads*.

International capital mobility brings real interest rates in all parts of the world to equality except for differences that reflect differences in risk – differences in the risk premium.

International Borrowing and Lending

A country's loanable funds market connects with the global market through net exports. If a country's net exports are negative ($X < M$), the rest of the world supplies funds to that country and the quantity of loanable funds in that country is greater than national saving. If a country's net exports are positive ($X > M$), the country is a net supplier of funds to the rest of the world and the quantity of loanable funds in that country is less than national saving.

Demand and Supply in the Global and National Markets

The demand for and supply of funds in the global loanable funds market determines the world equilibrium real interest rate. This interest rate makes the quantity of loanable funds demanded equal the quantity supplied in the world economy. But it does not make the quantity of funds demanded and supplied equal in each national economy. The demand for and supply of funds in a national economy determine whether the country is a lender to or a borrower from the rest of the world.

The Global Loanable Funds Market

Figure 23.10(a) illustrates the global market. The demand for loanable funds curve, DLF_W is the sum of the demands in all countries. Similarly, the supply of loanable funds curve, SLF_W is the sum of the supplies in all countries. The world equilibrium real interest rate makes the quantity of funds supplied in the world as a whole equal to the quantity demanded. In this example, the equilibrium real interest rate is 5 per cent a year and the equilibrium quantity of funds is €10 trillion.

An International Borrower

Figure 23.10(b) shows the loanable funds market in a country that borrows from the rest of the world. The country's demand for loanable funds curve, DLF, is part of the world demand in Figure 23.10(a). The country's supply of loanable funds curve, SLF_D, is part of the world supply.

Figure 23.10 Borrowing and Lending in the Global Loanable Funds Market

(a) The global market

(b) An international borrower

(c) An international lender

In the global loanable funds market in part (a), the demand for loanable funds curve, DLF_W, and the supply of funds curve, SLF_W, determine the world real interest rate. Each country can get funds at the world real interest rate and faces the (horizontal) supply curve SLF in parts (b) and (c).

At the world real interest rate, borrowers in part (b)

want more funds than the quantity supplied by domestic lenders (SLF_D). The shortage is made up by international borrowing.

At the world real interest rate, domestic lenders in part (c) want to lend more than domestic borrowers demand. The excess quantity supplied goes to foreign borrowers.

If this country were isolated from the global market, the real interest rate would be 6 per cent a year (where the DLF and SLF_D curves intersect). But if the country is integrated into the global economy, with an interest rate of 6 per cent a year, funds would *flood into* it. With a real interest rate of 5 per cent a year in the rest of the world, suppliers of loanable funds would seek the higher return in this country. In effect, the country faces the supply of loanable funds curve SLF, which is horizontal at the world equilibrium real interest rate.

The country's demand for loanable funds and the world interest rate determine the equilibrium quantity of loanable funds – €2.5 billion in Figure 23.10(b).

An International Lender

Figure 23.10(c) shows the situation in a country that lends to the rest of the world. As before, the country's demand for loanable funds curve, DLF, is part of the world demand and the country's supply of loanable funds curve, SLF_D, is part of the world supply in Figure 23.10(a).

If this country were isolated from the global economy, the real interest rate would be 4 per cent a year (where the DLF and SLF_D curves intersect). But if this country is integrated into the global economy, with an interest rate of 4 per cent a year, funds would quickly

flow out of it. With a real interest rate of 5 per cent a year in the rest of the world, domestic suppliers of loanable funds would seek the higher return in other countries. Again, the country faces the supply of loanable funds curve SLF, which is horizontal at the world equilibrium real interest rate.

The country's demand for loanable funds and the world interest rate determine the equilibrium quantity of loanable funds – €1.5 billion in Figure 23.10(c).

Changes in Demand and Supply

A change in the demand or supply in the global loanable funds market changes the real interest rate in the way shown in Figure 23.6 (see p. 543). The effect of a change in demand or supply in a national market depends on the size of the country. A change in demand or supply in a small country has no significant effect on global demand or supply, so it leaves the world real interest rate unchanged and changes only the country's net exports and international borrowing or lending. A change in demand or supply in a large country has a significant effect on global demand or supply, so it changes the world real interest rate as well as the country's net exports and international borrowing or lending. Every country feels some of the effect of a large country's change in demand or supply.

ECONOMICS IN ACTION

Greenspan's Interest Rate Puzzle

The real interest rate paid by big corporations in the US fell from 5.5 per cent a year in 2001 to 2.5 per cent a year in 2005. Alan Greenspan, then the Chairman of the Federal Reserve, said he was puzzled that the real interest rate was falling at a time when the US government budget deficit was increasing.

Why did the real interest rate fall?

The answer lies in the global loanable funds market. Rapid economic growth in Asia and Europe brought a large increase in global saving, which in turn increased the global supply of loanable funds. The supply of loanable funds increased because Asian and European saving increased strongly.

The US government budget deficit increased the US and global demand for loanable funds. But this increase was very small compared to the increase in the global supply of loanable funds.

The result of a large increase in supply and a small increase in demand was a fall in the world equilibrium real interest rate and an increase in the equilibrium quantity of loanable funds.

Figure 1 illustrates these events. The supply of loanable funds increased from SLF_{01} in 2001 to SLF_{05} in 2005. (In the figure, we ignore the change in the global demand for loanable funds because it was small relative to the increase in supply.)

With the increase in supply, the real interest rate fell from 5.5 per cent to 2.5 per cent a year and the quantity of loanable funds increased.

In the US, borrowing from the rest of the world increased to finance the increased government budget deficit.

The interest rate puzzle illustrates the important fact that the loanable funds market is a global market, not a national market.

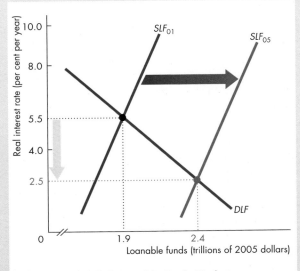

Figure 1 The Global Loanable Funds Market

Review Quiz

1 Why do loanable funds flow among countries?
2 What determines the demand for and supply of loanable funds in an individual economy?
3 What happens if a country has a shortage of loanable funds at the world real interest rate?
4 What happens if a country has a surplus of loanable funds at the world real interest rate?
5 How is a government budget deficit financed in an open economy?

You can work these questions in Study Plan 23.4 and get instant feedback.

To complete your study of financial markets, take a look at *Reading Between the Lines* on pp. 550–551 and see how you can use the model of the loanable funds market to understand the events in the EU financial market crisis of 2010.

Reading Between the Lines

Budget Deficits in Europe

The Financial Times, 25 October 2010

Eurozone Nations are Prepared to Slash Spending

Daniel Pimlott

The UK is far from alone within Europe in moving rapidly to curtail government borrowing. Greece, Ireland, Spain and Portugal are already committed to swinging the axe; all are still struggling to escape recession.

The coalition's deficit policies are almost as radical as those pursued by some of Britain's struggling neighbours in the EU, in spite of much more favourable borrowing conditions for the UK.

The Greek deficit was more than 15 per cent of GDP in 2009, in Spain it was 11.2 per cent and 9.4 per cent in Portugal. This year Ireland's is set to hit a staggering 32 per cent if the costs of its bank bail-out are factored in.

By comparison, Britain's deficit was 11 per cent of GDP in the last financial year.

If all goes to plan, Greece and Ireland should bring their deficits below the 3 per cent limit set in the Maastricht Treaty by 2014, Spain by 2013 and Portugal by 2012. Britain appears a relative laggard, dropping below the 3 per cent threshold only in 2014–15. . . .

Greece is cutting public sector salaries and pensions by 15 to 20 per cent, Portugal has warned of pay cuts of up to 10 per cent and Ireland and Spain have also pared back pay and reduced pension costs. Ireland and Portugal have both cut child benefits and other programmes.

In Britain, public sector pay freezes will last for two years, and there will be an average rise in pension contributions of about 3 percentage points; the benefits bill will be cut by about 10 per cent. . . .

The Essence of the Story

- Many governments are cutting spending to reduce their budget deficits.

- The UK is facing severe cuts in government spending although the government faces more favourable borrowing conditions than some other EU countries.

- Greece, Ireland, Spain and Portugal are projected to bring their budgets down to 3 per cent of GDP in the period 2012–2014.

- The UK is not expected to bring the budget deficit down to below 3 per cent of GDP until 2014–2015.

Economic Analysis

◆ A budget deficit increases the demand for loanable funds and, other things being equal, raises the real rate of interest, which raises the cost of government borrowing.

◆ Governments in some countries face a cost of borrowing that makes their budget unsustainable.

◆ A high cost of borrowing means that a government uses its budget to pay higher interest charges, which diverts resources from public services.

◆ A cut in public services can put political pressure on governments to default on their debt. When this happens, default risk rises, and this brings a decrease in the supply of loanable funds, which raises the real interest rate (and cost of borrowing) even further.

◆ Figure 1 illustrates this effect of a budget deficit. The deficit increases the demand for loanable funds and shifts the *DLF* curve rightward and the increase in default risk decreases the supply of loanable funds, which shifts the *SLF* curve leftward. The real interest rate rises.

◆ Figure 2 shows the sources of increased default risk: the government deficits and debts as percentages of GDP for the UK, Ireland, Spain, Portugal and Greece in 2009–2010.

◆ Figure 3 shows the interest rate spreads on the five governments' bonds relative to German government bond rate, which is considered to have a low (zero) risk of default.

◆ The global loanable funds market puts a high risk premium on Greece's debt.

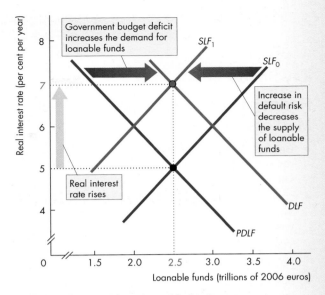

Figure 1 The market for loanable funds

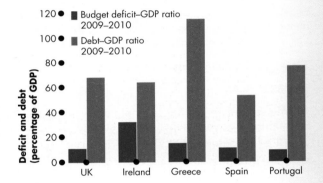

Figure 2 Budget deficits and debts

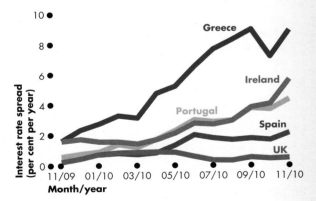

Figure 3 Bond interest rate spreads

SUMMARY

Key Points

Financial Institutions and Financial Markets (pp. 534–538)

◆ Capital (*physical capital*) is a real productive resource; financial capital is the funds used to buy capital.

◆ Gross investment increases the quantity of capital and depreciation decreases it. Saving increases wealth.

◆ The markets for financial capital are the markets for loans, bonds and stocks.

◆ Financial institutions ensure that borrowers and lenders can always find someone with whom to trade.

Working Study Plan Problems 1 to 5 will give you a better understanding of financial institutions and markets.

The Loanable Funds Market (pp. 538–544)

◆ Investment in capital is financed by household saving, a government budget surplus and funds from the rest of the world.

◆ The quantity of loanable funds demanded depends negatively on the real interest rate and the demand for loanable funds changes when profit expectations change.

◆ The quantity of loanable funds supplied depends positively on the real interest rate and the supply of loanable funds changes when disposable income, expected future income, wealth and default risk change.

◆ Equilibrium in the loanable funds market determines the real interest rate and quantity of funds.

Working Study Plan Problems 6 to 9 will give you a better understanding of the loanable funds market.

Government in the Loanable Funds Market (pp. 545–546)

◆ A government budget surplus increases the supply of loanable funds, lowers the real interest rate and increases investment and the equilibrium quantity of loanable funds.

◆ A government budget deficit increases the demand for loanable funds, raises the real interest rate and increases the equilibrium quantity of loanable funds, but decreases investment in a crowding-out effect.

◆ The Ricardo–Barro effect is the response of rational taxpayers to a budget deficit: private saving increases to finance the budget deficit. The real interest rate remains constant and the crowding-out effect is avoided.

Working Study Plan Problems 10 to 15 will give you a better understanding of government in the loanable funds market.

The Global Loanable Funds Market (pp. 547–549)

◆ The loanable funds market is a global market.

◆ The equilibrium real interest rate is determined in the global loanable funds market and national demand and supply determine the quantity of international borrowing or lending.

Working Study Plan Problems 16 to 18 will give you a better understanding of the global loanable funds market.

Key Terms

Bond, 535
Bond market, 535
Crowding-out effect, 546
Demand for loanable funds, 540
Financial capital, 534
Financial institution, 536
Gross investment, 534
Loanable funds market, 538
Mortgage, 535
Mortgage-backed security, 536
National saving, 539
Net investment, 534
Net taxes, 538
Net worth, 537
Nominal interest rate, 539
Real interest rate, 539
Saving, 534
Stock, 536
Stock market, 536
Supply of loanable funds, 541
Wealth, 534

STUDY PLAN PROBLEMS AND APPLICATIONS

myeconlab   You can work Problems 1 to 18 in MyEconLab Chapter 23 Study Plan and get instant feedback.

Financial Institutions and Financial Markets (Study Plan 23.1)

Use the following information to work Problems 1 and 2.

Michael is an Internet service provider. On 31 December 2009, he bought an existing business with servers and a building worth €400,000. During his first year of operation, his business grew and he bought new servers for €500,000. The market value of some of his older servers fell by €100,000.

1 What was Michael's gross investment, depreciation, and net investment during 2010?

2 What is the value of Michael's capital at the end of 2010?

3 Lori is a student who teaches golf on the weekend and in a year earns €20,000 after paying her taxes. At the beginning of 2010, Lori owned €1,000 worth of books, CDs, and golf clubs and she had €5,000 in a savings account at the bank. During 2010, the interest on her savings account was €300 and she spent a total of €15,300 on consumption goods and services. There was no change in the market values of her books, CDs and golf clubs.

    a How much did Lori save in 2010?

    b What was her wealth at the end of 2010?

4 In a speech at the CFA Society of Nebraska in February 2007, William Poole, former Chairman of the St Louis Federal Reserve Bank said:

Over most of the post–Second World War period, the personal saving rate averaged about 6 per cent, with some higher years from the mid-1970s to mid-1980s.

The negative trend in the saving rate started in the mid-1990s, about the same time the stock market boom started. Thus it is hard to dismiss the hypothesis that the decline in the measured saving rate in the late 1990s reflected the response of consumption to large capital gains from corporate equity stock.

Evidence from panel data of households also supports the conclusion that the decline in the personal saving rate since 1984 is largely a consequence of capital gains on corporate equities.

    a Is the purchase of corporate equities part of household consumption or saving? Explain your answer.

    b Equities reap a capital gain in the same way that houses reap a capital gain. Does this mean that the purchase of equities is investment? If not, explain why it is not.

5 **G-20 Leaders Look to Shake off Lingering Economic Troubles**

The G-20 aims to take stock of the economic recovery. One achievement of the G-20 in Pittsburgh could be a deal to require that financial institutions hold more capital.

Source: *USA Today*, 24 September 2009

What are the financial institutions that the G-20 might require to hold more capital? What exactly is the 'capital' referred to in the news clip? How might the requirement to hold more capital make financial institutions safer?

The Loanable Funds Markets (Study Plan 23.2)

Use the following information to work Problems 6 and 7.

First Call, plc, is a mobile phone company. It plans to build an assembly plant that costs £10 million if the real interest rate is 6 per cent a year. If the real interest rate is 5 per cent a year, First Call will build a larger plant that costs £12 million. And if the real interest rate is 7 per cent a year, First Call will build a smaller plant that costs £8 million.

6 Draw a graph of First Call's demand for loanable funds curve.

7 First Call expects its profit from the sale of mobile phones to double next year. If other things remain the same, explain how this increase in expected profit influences First Call's demand for loanable funds.

8 Draw a graph to illustrate how an increase in the supply of loanable funds and a decrease in the demand for loanable funds can lower the real interest rate and leave the equilibrium quantity of loanable funds unchanged.

9 Use the information in Problem 4.

    a US household income has grown considerably since 1984. Has US saving been on a downward trend because Americans feel wealthier?

    b Explain why households preferred to buy corporate equities rather than bonds.

Government in the Loanable Funds Market (Study Plan 23.3)

Use the following table to work Problems 10 to 12.

The table shows an economy's demand for loanable funds and the supply of loanable funds schedules, when the government's budget is balanced.

Real interest rate (per cent per year)	Loanable funds demanded	Loanable funds supplied
	(billions of 2006 euros)	
4	850	550
5	800	600
6	750	650
7	700	700
8	650	750
9	600	800
10	550	850

10 Suppose that the government has a budget surplus of €100 billion. What are the real interest rate, the quantity of investment, and the quantity of private saving? Is there any crowding out in this situation?

11 Suppose that the government has a budget deficit of €100 billion. What are the real interest rate, the quantity of investment, and the quantity of private saving? Is there any crowding out in this situation?

12 Suppose that the government has a budget deficit of €100 billion and the Ricardo–Barro effect occurs. What are the real interest rate and the quantity of investment?

Use the table in Problem 10 to work Problems 13 to 15.

Suppose that the quantity of loanable funds demanded increases by €100 billion at each real interest rate and the quantity of loanable funds supplied increases by €200 billion at each interest rate.

13 If the government budget is balanced, what are the real interest rate, the quantity of loanable funds, investment, and private saving? Does any crowding out occur?

14 If the government budget becomes a deficit of €100 billion, what are the real interest rate, the quantity of loanable funds, investment, and private saving? Does any crowding out occur?

15 If the government wants to stimulate investment and increase it to €900 billion, what must it do?

The Global Loanable Funds Market (Study Plan 23.4)

Use the following information to work Problems 16 and 17.

Global Saving Glut and US Current Account, remarks by Ben Bernanke (when a governor of the Federal Reserve) on 10 March 2005:

The US economy appears to be performing well: output growth has returned to healthy levels, the labor market is firming, and inflation appears to be under control. But, one aspect of US economic performance still evokes concern: the nation's large and growing current account deficit (negative net exports). Most forecasters expect the nation's current account imbalance to decline slowly at best, implying a continued need for foreign credit and a concomitant decline in the US net foreign asset position.

16 Why is the US, with the world's largest economy, borrowing heavily on international capital markets – rather than lending, as would seem more natural?

17 a What implications do the US current account deficit (negative net exports) and our reliance on foreign credit have for economic performance in the US?

b What policies, if any, should be used to address this situation?

18 IMF Says It Battled Crisis Well

The International Monetary Fund (IMF) reported that it acted effectively in combating the global recession. Since September 2008, the IMF made $163 billion available to developing countries. While the IMF urged developed countries and China to run deficits to stimulate their economies, the IMF required developing countries with large deficits to cut spending and not increase spending.

Source: *The Wall Street Journal*, 29 September 2009

a Explain how increased government budget deficits change the loanable funds market.

b Would the global recession have been less severe had the IMF made larger loans to developing countries?

ADDITIONAL PROBLEMS AND APPLICATIONS

myeconlab You can work these problems in MyEconLab if assigned by your lecturer.

Financial Institutions and Financial Markets

19 On 1 January 2009, Terry's Towing Service owned 4 tow trucks valued at €300,000. During 2009, Terry's bought 2 new trucks for a total of €180,000. At the end of 2009, the market value of all of the firm's trucks was €400,000. What was Terry's gross investment? Calculate Terry's depreciation and net investment.

Use the following information to work Problems 20 and 21.

The Office for National Statistics reported that the UK capital stock was £4689.2 billion at the end of 2007, £4816.8 billion at the end of 2008, and £4908.6 billion at the end of 2009. Depreciation in 2008 was £105 billion, and gross investment during 2009 was £197 billion (all in 2006 pounds).

20 Calculate UK net investment and gross investment during 2008.

21 Calculate UK depreciation and net investment during 2009.

22 Annie runs a fitness centre. On 31 December 2009, she bought an existing business with exercise equipment and a building worth €300,000. During 2010, business improved and she bought some new equipment for €50,000. At the end of 2010, her equipment and buildings were worth €325,000. Calculate Annie's gross investment, depreciation and net investment during 2010.

23 Karrie is a golf pro, and after she paid taxes, her income from golf and interest from financial assets was €1,500,000 in 2010. At the beginning of 2010, she owned €900,000 worth of financial assets. At the end of 2010, Karrie's financial assets were worth €1,900,000.

   a How much did Karrie save during 2010?

   b How much did she spend on consumption goods and services?

The Loanable Funds Markets

Use the following information to work Problems 24 and 25.

In 2010, the Lee family had disposable income of £80,000, wealth of £140,000, and an expected future income of £80,000 a year. At a real interest rate of 4 per cent a year, the Lee family saves £15,000 a year; at a real interest rate of 6 per cent a year, they save £20,000 a year; and at a real interest rate of 8 per cent a year, they save £25,000 a year.

24 Draw a graph of the Lee family's supply of loanable funds curve.

25 In 2011, suppose that the stock market crashes and the default risk increases. Explain how this increase in default risk influences the Lee family's supply of loanable funds curve.

26 Draw a graph to illustrate the effect of an increase in the demand for loanable funds and an even larger increase in the supply of loanable funds on the real interest rate and the equilibrium quantity of loanable funds.

27 **Greenspan's Conundrum Spells Confusion for Us All**

In January 2005, the interest rate on bonds was 4 per cent a year and it was expected to rise to 5 per cent a year by the end of 2005. As the rate rose to 4.3 per cent a year during February, most commentators focused, not on why the interest rate rose, but on why it was so low before. Explanations of this 'conundrum' included that unusual buying and expectations for an economic slowdown were keeping the interest rate low.

          Source: *Financial Times*, 26 February 2005

   a Explain how 'unusual buying' might lead to a low real interest rate.

   b Explain how investors' 'expectations for an economic slowdown' might lead to a lower real interest rate.

Government in the Loanable Funds Market

Use the following news clip to work Problems 28 and 29.

India's Economy Hits the Wall

At the start of 2008, India had an annual growth of 9 per cent, huge consumer demand, and increasing foreign investment. But by July 2008, India had 11.4 per cent a year inflation, large government deficits, and rising interest rates. Economic growth is expected to fall to 7 per cent a year by the end of 2008. A Goldman Sachs report suggests that India needs to lower the government's deficit, raise educational achievement, control inflation and liberalize its financial markets.

          Source: *Business Week*, 1 July 2008

28 If the Indian government reduces its deficit and returns to a balanced budget, how will the demand or supply of loanable funds in India change?

29 With economic growth forecasted to slow, future incomes are expected to fall. If other things remain the same, how will the demand or supply of loanable funds in India change?

30 Federal Deficit Surges to $1.38 trillion in August

US House Republican Leader John Boehner of Ohio asks: when will the White House tackle these jaw-dropping deficits that pile more and more debt on future generations while it massively increases federal spending?

Source: *USA Today*, 11 September 2009

Explain the effect of the federal deficit and the mounting debt on US economic growth.

The Global Loanable Funds Market

31 The Global Savings Glut and Its Consequences

Several developing countries are running large current account surpluses (representing an excess of savings over investment) and rapid growth has led to high saving rates as people save a large fraction of additional income. In India, the saving rate has risen from 23 per cent a decade ago to 33 per cent today. China's saving rate is 55 per cent. The glut of saving in Asia is being put into US bonds. When a poor country buys US bonds, it is in effect lending to the US.

Source: The Cato Institute, 8 June 2007

a Graphically illustrate and explain the impact of the 'glut of savings' on the real interest rate and the quantity of loanable funds.

b How do the high saving rates in Asia influence investment in the US?

Use the following information to work Problems 32 to 35.

Most economists agree that the problems we are witnessing today developed over a long period of time. For more than a decade, a massive amount of money flowed into the US from investors abroad because the US is an attractive and secure place to do business. This large influx of money to US financial institutions – along with low interest rates – made it easier for Americans to get credit. These developments allowed more families to borrow money for cars and homes and college tuition – some for the first time. They allowed more entrepreneurs to get loans to start new businesses and create jobs.

President George W. Bush, *Address to the Nation*, 24 September 2008

32 Explain why, for more than a decade, a massive amount of money flowed into the US. Compare and contrast your explanation with that of the President.

33 Provide a graphical analysis of the reasons why the interest rate was low.

34 Funds have been flowing into the US since the early 1980s. Why might they have created problems in 2008 but not earlier?

35 Could the US stop funds from flowing in from other countries? How?

Economics in the News

36 After you have studied *Reading Between the Lines* on pp. 550–551 answer the following questions.

a Why are governments in the Eurozone and the UK taking actions aimed at cutting their budget deficits?

b In what ways might it be argued that the UK has a less acute budget problem than Ireland, Greece, Spain and Portugal?

c Why are borrowing costs for Greece, Ireland, Spain and Portugal so high compared to those for the UK and Germany?

d Draw a graph of the loanable funds market for Greece to illustrate your answer to part (c).

CHAPTER 24

Money, the Price Level and Inflation

After studying this chapter you will be able to:

◆ Define money and describe its functions

◆ Explain what banks are and do

◆ Describe the functions of a central bank

◆ Explain how the banking system creates money

◆ Explain how the demand for and supply of money determine the nominal interest rate

◆ Explain how the quantity of money influences the price level and the inflation rate

When you want to buy something, you use coins, notes, write a cheque, or present a debit or credit card. Are all these things money? When you deposit some coins or notes in the bank, is it still money? What happens when the bank lends your money to someone else? How can you still get it back if it's been lent out? Why does the amount of money in the economy matter? How does it affect the interest rate? You can find the answers in this chapter. And in *Reading Between the Lines* at the end of the chapter, you can see how the quantity of money changed in the Eurozone in 2010.

What Is Money?

What do cowrie shells, wampum, whales' teeth, tobacco, cattle and pennies have in common? The answer is that all of them are (or have been) forms of money. **Money** is any commodity or token that is generally acceptable as a means of payment. A **means of payment** is a method of settling a debt. When a payment has been made there is no remaining obligation between the parties to a transaction. So what cowrie shells, wampum, whales' teeth, cattle and pennies have in common is that they have served (or still do serve) as the means of payment. But money has three other functions:

◆ A medium of exchange
◆ A unit of account
◆ A store of value

Medium of Exchange

A *medium of exchange* is an object that is generally accepted in exchange for goods and services. Money acts as such a medium. Without money, it would be necessary to exchange goods and services directly for other goods and services – an exchange called *barter*. Barter requires a double coincidence of wants, a situation that rarely occurs. For example, if you want a pizza, you might offer a CD in exchange for it. But you must find someone who is selling pizza and who wants your CD.

A medium of exchange overcomes the need for a double coincidence of wants. And money acts as a medium of exchange because people with something to sell will always accept money in exchange for it. But money isn't the only medium of exchange. You can buy with a credit card. But a credit card isn't money. It doesn't make a final payment and the debt it creates must eventually be settled by using money.

Unit of Account

A *unit of account* is an agreed measure for stating the prices of goods and services. To get the most out of your budget you have to work out, among other things, whether seeing one more film is worth the price you have to pay, not in pounds and pence, but in terms of the number of ice creams, beers or cups of tea that you have to give up. It's easy to do such calculations when all these goods have prices in terms of pounds and pence (see Table 24.1). If the price of a cinema ticket is £4 and

a pint of beer in the Students' Union costs £1, you know straight away that seeing one more film costs you 4 pints of beer. If the price of a cup of tea is 50 pence, one more cinema ticket costs 8 cups of tea. You need only one calculation to work out the opportunity cost of any pair of goods and services.

But imagine how troublesome it would be if your local cinema posted its price as 4 pints of beer; and if the Students' Union announced that the price of a pint of beer was 2 ice creams; and if the corner shop posted the price of an ice cream as 1 cup of tea; and if the café priced a cup of tea as 5 rolls of mints!

Now how much running around and calculating do you have to do to work out how much that film is going to cost you in terms of the beer, ice cream, tea or mints that you must give up to see it? You get the answer for beer from the sign posted at the cinema, but for all the other goods you're going to have to visit many different shops to establish the prices you need to work out the opportunity costs you face.

Cover up the column labelled 'price in money units' in Table 24.1 and see how hard it is to work out the number of local telephone calls it costs to see one film.

It is much simpler for everyone to express their prices in terms of pounds and pence.

Table 24.1

The Unit of Account Function of Money Simplifies Price Comparisons

Good	Price in money units	Price in units of another good
Cinema ticket	£4.00 each	4 pints of beer
Beer	£1.00 per pint	2 ice creams
Ice cream	£0.50 per cone	1 cup of tea
Tea	£0.50 per cup	5 rolls of mints
Mints	£0.10 per roll	1 local phone call

Money as a unit of account. The price of a cinema ticket is £4 and the price of a cup of tea is 50 pence, so a cinema ticket costs 8 cups of tea (£4.00/£0.50 = 8).

No unit of account. You go to a cinema and learn that the price of a ticket is 4 pints of beer. You go to a café and learn that a cup of tea costs 5 rolls of mints. But how many rolls of mints does it cost you to see a film? To answer that question, you go to the Students' Union bar and find that a pint of beer costs 2 ice creams. Now you head for the ice cream shop, where an ice cream costs 1 cup of tea. Now you get out your pocket calculator: 1 cinema ticket costs 4 pints of beer, or 8 ice creams, or 8 cups of tea, or 40 rolls of mints!

Sometimes we use a unit of account that is not money. An example is the European Currency Unit that preceded the euro. Also, the euro existed as a unit of account before it became money – a means of payment – on 1 January 2002.

Store of Value

Money is a *store of value* in the sense that it can be held and exchanged later for goods and services. If money were not a store of value, it could not serve as a means of payment.

Money is not alone in acting as a store of value. A physical object such as a house, a car, a work of art or a computer can act as a store of value. The most reliable and useful stores of value are items that have a stable value. The more stable the value of a commodity or token, the better it can act as a store of value and the more useful it is as money. No store of value has a completely stable value. The value of a house, a car or a work of art fluctuates over time. The value of the commodities and tokens that are used as money also fluctuate over time. And when there is inflation, their values persistently fall.

Because inflation brings a falling value of money, a low inflation rate is needed to make money as useful as possible as a store of value.

Money in the UK Today

In the UK today, money consists of:

◆ Currency
◆ Deposits at banks and building societies

Currency

The notes and coins held by individuals and businesses are known as **currency**. These notes and coins are money because the government declares them to be so. The Royal Mint maintains the inventory of coins in circulation and the Bank of England issues notes. (In Scotland and Northern Ireland, private banks also issue notes, but they must hold £1 of Bank of England notes for every £1 they issue.)

Deposits at Banks and Building Societies

Deposits at banks and building societies are also money. This type of money is an accounting entry in an electronic database in the banks' and building societies' computers. They are money because they can be converted instantly

into currency and because they are used directly to settle debts. In fact, deposits are the main means of settling debts in modern societies. The owner of a deposit transfers ownership to another person simply by writing a cheque – an instruction to a bank – that tells the bank to change its database, debiting the account of one depositor and crediting the account of another.

The Official UK Measure of Money

The official measure of money in the UK today is known as M4. **M4** consists of currency held by the public plus bank deposits and building society deposits. M4 does *not* include currency held by banks and building societies and it does *not* include currency or bank deposits owned by the UK government. Figure 24.1 shows the components that make up M4.

Figure 24.1 The Official UK Measure of Money

	£ billions in Nov 2010	
M4	2,173	
Large deposits	946	44%
Sight and time deposits	1,177	54%
Currency held by the public	50	2%

M4 is the official measure of money in the UK. It is the sum of currency held by the public, bank deposits and building society deposits. Currency represents only 2 per cent of the money in the UK economy.

Source of data: Bank of England.

Are All the Components of M4 Really Money?

Money is the means of payment. So the test of whether something is money is whether it serves as a means of payment. Currency passes the test.

Deposits are divided into two types: sight deposits and time deposits. A *sight deposit* (sometimes called a chequeable deposit) can be transferred from one person to another by writing a cheque or using a debit card. So a sight deposit is clearly money. A *time deposit* is a deposit that has a fixed term to maturity. Although not usually a chequeable deposit, technological advances in the banking industry have made it easy to switch funds from a time deposit to a sight deposit. Because of the ease with which funds in a time deposit can be switched into a sight deposit, time deposits are included in the definition of money.

Cheques, Debit Cards and Credit Cards Are Not Money

The funds you've got in the bank are your money. When you write a cheque, you are telling your bank to move some funds from your account to the account of the person to whom you've given the cheque. Writing a cheque doesn't create more money. The money existed before you wrote the cheque. When your cheque is paid, the money is still there but it moves from you to the person to whom you wrote the cheque.

Using a debit card is just like writing a cheque except that the transaction takes place in an instant. The funds are electronically transferred from your account to that of the person you are paying the moment your card is read.

A credit card is just an ID card, but one that lets you take a loan at the instant you buy something. When you sign a credit card sales slip, you are saying: "I agree to pay for these goods when the credit card company bills me." Once you get your statement from the credit card company, you must make the minimum payment due (or clear your balance). To make that payment you need money – currency or a bank deposit. So although you use a credit card when you buy something, the credit card is not the *means of payment* and it is not money. The currency or the bank deposit that you use is money.

We've seen that the main component of money is deposits at banks and building societies. These institutions play a crucial role in our economic life and we're now going to examine that role.

Money in the Eurozone

The official Eurozone measure of money is called M3, but the items included in the Eurozone M3 are very similar to those in M4 in the UK. Figure 1 shows the numbers. The most interesting feature of euro money is the large amount of currency held by the public, 8 per cent of the total, compared with 2 per cent in the UK. Think about the reasons for this huge difference!

	€ billions in Nov 2010	
M3	9,475	
Marketable instruments	1,070	11.3%
Time deposits	3,715	39.2%
Sight deposits	3,900	41.2%
Currency held by the public	790	8.3%

Figure 1 Official Eurozone Measure of Money

Source of data: European Central Bank.

Review Quiz

1   What makes something money? What functions does money perform? Why do you think Polo mints don't serve as money?
2   What are the largest components of money in the UK and in the Eurozone today?
3   Are all the components of M4 really money?
4   Why are cheques, debit cards and credit cards not money?

You can work these questions in Study Plan 24.1 and get instant feedback.

Monetary Financial Institutions

A **monetary financial institution** is a financial firm that takes deposits from households and firms. These deposits are components of M4. You will learn what these institutions are, what they do, the economic benefits they bring, how they are regulated and how they have innovated to create new financial products.

Types of Monetary Financial Institutions

The deposits of two types of financial firms make up the UK's money. They are

◆ Commercial banks
◆ Building Societies

Commercial Banks

A *commercial bank* is a private firm, licensed by the Bank of England under the Banking Act 1987 to take deposits and make loans.

UK commercial banks are very large and five firms dominate the banking markets: Barclays, HSBC, Lloyds Banking Group, Royal Bank of Scotland Group and Standard Chartered. The assets of the largest commercial banks exceed £2 trillion.

These very large firms offer a wide range of banking services and have extensive international operations. The deposits of commercial banks represent the bulk of the deposits in the M4 definition of money.

Building Societies

A *building society* is a private firm licensed under the Building Societies Act 1986 to accept deposits and make loans mostly to mortgage borrowers.

Building societies are much smaller than commercial banks and most of them serve their local communities. The largest, Nationwide, has assets of £150 billion. Size falls steeply with the assets of the next largest, Britannia, at £32 billion and the third largest, Yorkshire at £16 billion.

Unlike a bank, a building society is owned by its depositors, obtains its funds in the form of savings accounts and keeps its reserves not at the Bank of England but as a deposit in a commercial bank.

The combined deposits of the largest 50 Building Societies in November 2010 was £290 billion.

What Monetary Financial Institutions Do

Monetary financial institutions provide services such as cheque clearing, account management, credit cards and Internet banking, all of which provide an income from service fees. But they earn most of their income by using the funds they receive from depositors to make loans and to buy securities that earn a higher interest rate than that paid to depositors. In this activity, they must perform a balancing act, weighing return against risk. To see this balancing act, we'll focus on the commercial banks.

A commercial bank puts the funds it receives from depositors and other funds that it borrows into four types of assets:

1 A bank's **reserves** are notes and coins in the bank's vault or in a deposit account at the Bank of England. (We'll study the Bank of England later in this chapter.) These funds are used to meet depositors' currency withdrawals and to make payments to other banks. In normal times, a bank keeps about one per cent of deposits as reserves.

2 *Liquid assets* are overnight loans to other banks and institutions, UK government Treasury bills and commercial bills. These assets are the banks' first line of defence if they need reserves. Liquid assets can be sold and instantly converted into reserves with virtually no risk of loss. Because they have a low risk, they earn a low interest rate.

The interest rate on overnight loans is closely linked to the interest rate set by the Bank of England as its main policy interest rate (see p. 565).

3 *Investment securities* are UK government bonds and other bonds such as mortgage-backed securities. These assets can be sold and converted into reserves but at prices that fluctuate, so they are riskier than liquid assets and have a higher interest rate.

4 *Loans and advances* are funds committed for an agreed-upon period of time to corporations to finance investment and to households to finance the purchase of homes, cars and other durable goods. The outstanding balances on credit card accounts are also bank loans. Loans are a bank's riskiest and highest-earning assets: They can't be converted into reserves until they are due to be repaid, and some borrowers default and never repay.

Table 24.2 provides a snapshot of the sources and uses of funds of all the monetary financial institutions in the UK in November 2010.

Economic Benefits Provided by Monetary Financial Institutions

You've seen that a monetary financial institution earns part of its profit because it pays a lower interest rate on deposits than it earns on loans. What benefits do these institutions provide that make this outcome occur? Monetary financial institutions provide four benefits:

◆ Create liquidity
◆ Pool risk
◆ Lower the cost of borrowing
◆ Lower the cost of monitoring borrowers

Create Liquidity

Monetary financial institutions create liquidity by *borrowing short and lending long* – taking deposits and standing ready to repay them on short notice or on demand and making loan commitments that run for terms of many years.

Pool Risk

A loan might not be repaid – a default. If you lend to one person who defaults, you lose the entire amount loaned. If you lend to 1,000 people (through a bank) and one person defaults, you lose almost nothing. Monetary financial institutions pool risk.

Lower the Cost of Borrowing

Imagine there are no monetary financial institutions and a firm is looking for £1 million to buy a new factory. It hunts around for several dozen people from whom to borrow the funds. Monetary financial institutions lower the cost of this search. The firm gets its £1 million from a single institution that gets deposits from a large number of people but spreads the cost of this activity over many borrowers.

Lower the Cost of Monitoring Borrowers

By monitoring borrowers, a lender can encourage good decisions that prevent defaults. But this activity is costly. Imagine how costly it would be if each household that lent money to a firm incurred the costs of monitoring that firm directly. Monetary financial institutions can perform this task at a much lower cost.

How Monetary Financial Institutions Are Regulated

The collapse of a large bank would have damaging effects on the entire financial system and economy. Regulation seeks to lower the risk of collapse and lessen the damage if it occurs.

To lower the risk of bank failure, commercial banks are required to hold levels of reserves and owners' capital that equal or surpass ratios laid down by regulation.

The **required reserve ratio** is the minimum percentage of deposits that a bank is required to hold in reserves. This minimum is designed to ensure that a bank does not run out of cash. The *required capital ratio* is the minimum percentage of assets that must be financed by the bank's owners. This ratio is designed to ensure that a bank's assets will never be worth less than its deposits.

A new Banking Act of 2009 seeks to lessen the damage if failure occurs. It gives powers to the so-called *Tripartite Authorities* (HM Treasury, the Financial Services Authority and the Bank of England) to intervene in a distressed bank or building society to reduce the effects of failure on overall economic stability.

Table 24.2

Monetary Financial Institutions: Sources and Uses of Funds

	Funds (billions of pounds)	Percentage of deposits
Total funds	3,759	132
Sources		
Deposits	2,837	100
Borrowing	520	18
Own capital and other sources	402	14
Uses		
Reserves	158	6
Liquid assets	336	12
Investment securities*	669	24
Loans and advances	2,596	92

Commercial banks get most of their funds from depositors and use most of them to make loans and advances. In normal times banks hold about 1 per cent of deposits as reserves but in 2010 they held an unusually large 6 per cent as reserves.

Source of data: The Bank of England. The data are for November, 2010. *Investment securities includes other assets.

Northern Rock and the Sub-prime Loans Crisis

Northern Rock plc is a UK bank that was taken into public ownership at the height of the financial crisis caused by the problems created by US sub-prime loans.

Formerly a building society that converted to a bank in 1997, Northern Rock continued to specialize in mortgage lending. During the 2000s the bank expanded its deposits and borrowing from £22 billion in 2000 to £109 billion in 2007. Its profit rose from £149 million in 1997 to a peak of £557 million in 2006.

Northern Rock's business model was 'originate' and 'distribute'. The bank borrowed on the interbank loans market and used the funds to make mortgage loans to its customers (originate). By 2006, some of its lending was in the form of sub-prime (high-risk) mortgages. It then created mortgage-backed securities, which it sold on the global capital market (distribute).

The interest the bank received on its mortgage loans was paid to the holders of the mortgage-backed securities and the funds raised by selling these securities was used to pay back lenders in the interbank loans market.

This part of Northern Rock's business was kept separate from its normal banking business and no required capital ratio applied to it, so the bank was able to expand its borrowing and lending without having to use any of its own funds.

Figure 1 shows how the bank's balance sheet expanded and the bank's growing dependence on borrowing (the red bars) rather than on customers' deposits (the blue bars).

When the sub-prime loans crisis hit the world economy, Northern Rock was unable to raise funds in the interbank market, and as customers queued to withdraw their deposits, the bank faced a liquidity crisis. In February 2008 the bank was taken into public ownership.

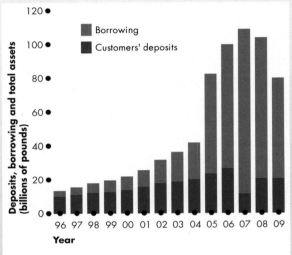

Figure 1 Northern Rock's Spectacular Rise and Fall

Source of data: Bureau van dijk Bankscope.

Financial Innovation

In the pursuit of larger profit, banks and building societies are constantly seeking ways to improve their products in a process called financial innovation. The major financial innovations included the introduction of credit cards, debit cards, automatic teller machines, interest-bearing sight deposits and automatic transfers between sight and time deposits. These innovations occurred because the development of computing power lowered the cost of calculations and record keeping.

During the 2000s, when interest rates were low and banks were flush with funds, sub-prime mortgages were developed in the US. To avoid the risk of carrying these mortgages, mortgage-backed securities were developed. The original lending institution sold these securities, lowered their own exposure to risk and obtained funds to make more loans. The model of originating mortgage loans and selling them as mortgage backed securities to other financial institutions was copied by a number of UK banks – the most notorious being Northern Rock.

Review Quiz

1 What is a monetary financial institution?
2 What are the main economic functions of a monetary financial institution?
3 What are the four types of assets held by banks?
4 How do monetary financial institutions create liquidity, pool risk, and lower borrowing costs?

You can work these questions in Study Plan 24.2 and get instant feedback.

You now know what money is. Your next task is to learn about central banking and the ways in which a central bank can influence the quantity of money.

Central Banking

A central bank is a public authority that provides banking services to governments and commercial banks, supervises and regulates financial institutions and markets and conducts monetary policy. *Monetary policy* is the attempt to control inflation, moderate the business cycle and provide the foundation for sustained economic growth by influencing the quantity of money, interest rates and the exchange rate. We study monetary policy in Chapter 30. Our aim in this chapter is to learn about the role of a central bank in the process of creating and influencing the quantity of money and the interest rate. We'll briefly describe two central banks:

◆ The European Central Bank
◆ The Bank of England

The European Central Bank

The **European Central Bank (ECB)** is the central bank of the Eurozone – the members of the European Union that use the euro as their currency. The ECB was established on 1 June 1998.

National central banks, the largest of which are the Banque de France, Deutsche Bundesbank and Banca d'Italia, provide banking services to their governments and commercial banks and supervise and regulate their national financial institutions and markets. The Executive Board of the ECB together with the Governors of the national central banks of the Eurozone constitute the Governing Council, which is the highest decision-making body in the ECB. Through this membership of the Governing Council, national central banks play a role in setting Eurozone monetary policy.

The Bank of England

The **Bank of England** is the central bank of the UK. It was established by Parliament in 1694 in a deal between a syndicate of wealthy individuals and the government of King William and Queen Mary. The syndicate lent the government £1.2 million in return for the right to issue bank notes. And so the Bank of England notes we use today were born.

The Bank of England was first formally recognized as the central bank with the passage of the Bank of England Act of 1946, which took the Bank into public ownership.

For the next 50 years, the Bank of England was under the firm day-to-day control of the Treasury (the government) and its role was simply to implement the government's decisions. But in 1997, a major change occurred and the Bank was given independence to determine monetary policy, subject to objectives set by the government. The centrepiece of the new arrangement, which remains in place today, was the creation of the Monetary Policy Committee.

Monetary Policy Committee

The Bank of England's **Monetary Policy Committee (MPC)** formulates the UK's monetary policy. Its members are the Governor and two Deputy Governors of the Bank, two members appointed by the Governor of the Bank after consultation with the Chancellor of the Exchequer and four members appointed by the Chancellor of the Exchequer. The persons appointed by the Chancellor must have 'knowledge or experience which is likely to be relevant to the Committee's functions' – which in practice means that they are academic economists.

To appreciate the monetary policy tools available to a central bank, we must first learn about its financial structure, summarized in its balance sheet. We'll focus here on the Bank of England but the principles apply to all central banks.

The Bank of England's Balance Sheet

The Bank of England influences the economy through the size and composition of it balance sheet – the assets that it owns and the liabilities that it owes.

The Bank's Assets

The Bank of England has two main assets:

1 UK government securities
2 Loans to monetary financial institutions

The Bank holds UK government securities – Treasury bills and longer term government bonds – that it buys in the bond market. When the Bank buys or sells bonds, it participates in the *loanable funds market* (see pp. 538–543).

The Bank makes loans to monetary financial institutions. These loans are made using *repurchase agreements*. Under a repurchase agreement – called a **repo** – a commercial bank sells a government bond to the Bank of England and simultaneously agrees to *repurchase* it (buy it back) usually two weeks later. In normal times, this item is small but during the global financial crisis, the Bank provided loans on an unprecedented scale.

The Bank's Liabilities

The Bank has two liabilities:

1 Notes in circulation
2 Deposits of commercial banks

Bank of England notes are the £5, £10, £20 and £50 notes that we use in our cash transactions. Some of these notes are part of *currency* – a component of the M4 definition of money (see p. 559). And some of them are in the tills and vaults of the commercial banks – part of the banks' reserves.

The Bank of England's other liability is the deposits of commercial banks, which are part of these institutions' reserves.

The Monetary Base

The Bank of England's liabilities plus the coins issued by the Royal Mint make up the **monetary base**. Coins are part of the monetary base but do not appear in the Bank of England balance sheet because the Royal Mint, which issues coins, is a branch of the government and not a part of the Bank of England.

The Bank's assets are the sources of the monetary base. They are also called the backing for the monetary base. The Bank's liabilities are the uses of the monetary base as currency held by the public and bank reserves (notes and coins in the bank's vault or in a deposit account at the Bank of England). Table 24.3 provides a snapshot of the sources and uses of the monetary base in December 2010.

We'll next look at the Bank's tool kit.

Table 24.3

The Sources and Uses of the Monetary Base

Sources (billions of pounds)		Uses (billions of pounds)	
Government bonds	14	Notes held by the public	53
Loans to banks	181	Bank reserves	142
Monetary base	**195**	**Monetary base**	**195**

Source of data: Bank of England. The data are for 15 December 2010.

The Bank of England's Policy Tools

The Bank of England has four policy tools to influence the quantity of money and the interest rate. They are:

◆ Bank Rate
◆ Open market operations
◆ Lender of last resort
◆ Required reserve ratio

Bank Rate

Bank Rate is the interest rate that the Bank of England charges on secured overnight loans to commercial banks. It is the official policy interest rate to which many other interest rates are linked. Among them are the interest rate that the Bank pays to commercial banks on their reserve deposits and the interest rates the commercial banks pay on deposits and charge on loans.

Open Market Operations

An **open market operation** is the purchase or sale of securities by the central bank in the *loanable funds market*. The term 'open market' refers to commercial banks and the general public but not the government. The Bank of England does not transact with the government.

When the Bank buys government bonds, it pays for them with newly created bank reserves. When the Bank sells government bonds, the Bank is paid with reserves held by the commercial banks. So open market operations directly influence the reserves of banks. By changing the quantity of bank reserves, the Bank of England changes the amount of bank lending, which influences the quantity of money and the economy more broadly.

An Open Market Purchase

To see how an open market operation changes bank reserves, suppose the Bank of England buys £100 million of government securities from HSBC. When the Bank of England makes this transaction, two things happen:

1 HSBC has £100 million less securities, and the Bank has £100 million more securities.
2 The Bank places £100 million in HSBC's deposit account at the Bank of England (bank reserves in Table 24.3) to pay for the securities.

Figure 24.2 shows the effects of these actions on the balance sheets of the Bank and HSBC. Ownership of the securities passes from HSBC to the Bank of England, so

Figure 24.2 The Bank of England Buys Securities in the Open Market

When the Bank of England buys securities in the open market, it increases bank reserves. The Bank of England's assets and liabilities increase and the selling bank's reserves increase and securities decrease.

myeconlab Animation ────────────────◆

HSBC's assets decrease by £100 million and the Bank's assets increase by £100 million, as shown by the blue arrow running from HSBC to the Bank. The Bank pays for the securities by placing £100 million in HSBC's reserve account at the Bank, as shown by the green arrow running from the Bank to HSBC. The Bank's assets and liabilities increase by £100 million. HSBC's total assets are unchanged: it sold securities to increase its reserves.

An Open Market Sale
If the Bank of England sells £100 million of government securities to HSBC in the open market:

1   HSBC has £100 million more securities, and the Bank has £100 million less securities.

2   HSBC pays for the securities by using £100 million of its reserve deposit at the Bank.

You can follow the effects of these actions by reversing the arrows and the plus and minus signs in Figure 24.2. Ownership of the securities passes from the Bank to HSBC, so the Bank's assets decrease by £100 million and HSBC's assets increase by £100 million. HSBC uses £100 million of its reserves to pay for the securities. Both the Bank's assets and liabilities decrease by £100 million. HSBC's total assets are unchanged: it has used reserves to buy securities.

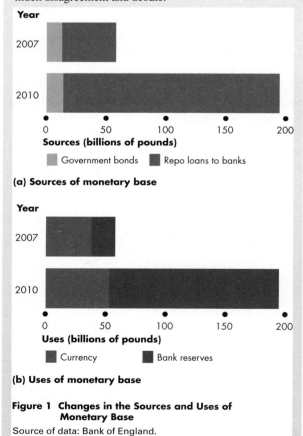

ECONOMICS IN ACTION

The Bank of England's Balance Sheet Explodes

The Bank of England's balance sheet underwent some remarkable changes during the financial crisis of 2007–2008 and the recession that the crisis triggered.

The figure shows the effects of these changes on the size and composition of the monetary base by comparing the situation in December 2010 with that before the financial crisis began in January 2007.

In 2007, a normal year, the monetary base was £58 billion and more than half of the base was currency. But between 2007 and 2010 the Bank made huge repo loans to commercial banks that more than tripled the monetary base to £194 billion. Almost all of this increase was composed of bank reserves, which increased from £20 billion in 2007 to a staggering £142 billion in 2010.

Left unchecked, this huge volume of reserves would eventually be loaned by the banks and create an explosion in the quantity of money.

When, and how quickly, to unwind the large increase in the monetary base and bank reserves is a source of much disagreement and debate.

(a) Sources of monetary base

(b) Uses of monetary base

Figure 1   Changes in the Sources and Uses of Monetary Base

Source of data: Bank of England.

Lender of Last Resort

The Bank of England is the **lender of last resort**, which means that if all the banks are short of reserves, they can borrow from the central bank. Normally, last-resort loans are made overnight and secured with a repurchase agreement (a *repo*).

In recent years the Bank of England has lent on repurchase agreements for longer periods and boosted the reserves of the commercial banks massively. This form of injection of reserves is called **quantitative easing**. The reserves made available by quantitative easing are indicated in Table 24.3 as 'Loans to banks'.

In September 2007 the Bank of England made a large last-resort loan facility available to the bank Northern Rock when it was unable to obtain funds from the wholesale interbank market.

Required Reserve Ratio

The *required reserve ratio* (the minimum percentage of deposits that a bank is required to hold as reserves) can be varied to make banks hold more reserves. The Bank of England doesn't vary this percentage very often. But some central banks (the People's Bank of China is one) frequently use this tool and it is available to the Bank of England if it should choose to use it.

Review Quiz

1 What is a central bank?
2 What are the central banks of the Eurozone and the UK and what functions do they perform?
3 What are the main items in the balance sheet of a central bank?
4 What is the monetary base and how does it relate to the items in the Bank of England's balance sheet?
5 What are a central bank's policy tools?
6 How does an open market operation change the monetary base?
7 What is quantitative easing and how does it change the monetary base?

You can work these questions in Study Plan 24.3 and get instant feedback.

Next, we're going to see how the banking system – the commercial banks and the Bank of England – creates money and how the quantity of money changes when the Bank of England changes the monetary base.

How Banks Create Money

Banks* create money. But this doesn't mean that they have smoke-filled back rooms in which counterfeiters are busily working. Remember that most money is in the form of deposits, not currency. What banks create is deposits and they do so by making loans.

Creating Deposits by Making Loans

The easiest way to see that banks create deposits is to think about what happens when Helen fills up her car with petrol at a BP service station and pays using her Visa credit card issued by Barclays. When Helen keys in her PIN, she takes a loan from Barclays and obligates herself to repay the loan at a later date. The electronic transfer of funds from Helen's Barclays Visa account to BP's bank is instantaneous. Barclays credits BP's bank account with the value of the sale (less the commission).

You can see that these transactions have created a bank deposit and a loan. Helen has increased the size of her loan (her credit card balance), and BP has increased the size of its bank deposit (minus the bank's commission). And because deposits are money, this transaction has created money.

If Helen and BP use the same bank, no further transactions take place. But the outcome is essentially the same when two banks are involved. If BP's bank is the Royal Bank of Scotland, then Barclays uses its reserves to pay the Royal Bank.

Barclays still has an increase in loans but now it has a decrease in its reserves at the Bank of England; the Royal Bank of Scotland has an increase in its reserves at the Bank of England and an increase in deposits.

The banking system as a whole has an increase in loans and deposits and no change in reserves.

You know that the interest rate that banks pay on deposits is much less than what they receive on loans. So creating deposits by making loans is a profitable business. What keeps this business in check?

The quantity of loans and deposits that the banking system can create is limited by three factors:

◆ The monetary base

◆ Desired reserves

◆ Desired currency holding

---

* In this section, we'll use the term banks to refer to commercial banks and building societies – the monetary financial institutions whose deposits are money.

The Monetary Base

You've seen that the *monetary base* is the sum of Bank of England notes and banks' deposits at the Bank of England – the Bank of England's liabilities – plus coins issued by the Royal Mint. The size of the monetary base limits the total quantity of money that the banking system can create because banks have a desired level of reserves, households and firms have a desired level of currency holding and both of these desired holdings of the monetary base depend on the quantity of deposits.

Desired Reserves

A bank's *desired reserves* – the reserves that it *plans* to hold – contrast with its *required reserves*, which is the minimum quantity of reserves that a bank must hold.

The quantity of desired reserves depends on the level of deposits and is determined by the **desired reserve ratio** – the ratio of reserves to deposits that the banks plan to hold. The desired reserve ratio exceeds the required reserve ratio by an amount that the banks determine to be prudent on the basis of their daily requirements and in the light of the current situation.

Desired Currency Holding

The ratio of money held as currency to money held as bank deposits depends on how households and firms choose to make payments: whether they plan to use currency or debit cards and cheques. These plans change slowly so the desired ratio of currency to deposits also changes slowly. If bank deposits increase, desired currency holding also increases. For this reason, when banks make loans that increase deposits, some currency leaves the banks – the banking system leaks reserves. We call the leakage of reserves into currency the *currency drain* and we call the ratio of currency to deposits the **currency drain ratio**.

We've sketched the way that a loan creates a deposit and described the three factors that limit the amount of loans and deposits that can be created. We're now going to examine the money creation process more closely and discover a money multiplier.

The Money Creation Process

The money creation process begins with an increase in the monetary base, which occurs if the Bank of England buys securities. The Bank pays for the securities it buys with newly created bank reserves.

When the Bank of England buys securities from a bank, the bank's reserves increase but its deposits don't change. So the bank has excess reserves. A bank's **excess reserves** are its actual reserves minus its desired reserves.

When a bank has excess reserves, it makes loans and creates deposits and money in a process like the one we described on the previous page when Helen buys petrol with her credit card.

When the entire banking system has excess reserves, total loans and deposits increase. One bank can make a loan and get rid of excess reserves. But the banking system as a whole can't get rid of excess reserves so easily. When the banks make loans and create deposits, the extra deposits lower excess reserves for two reasons:

1 The increase in deposits increases desired reserves.
2 A currency drain decreases total reserves.

But excess reserves don't completely disappear, so the banks lend some more and the process repeats.

As the process of making loans and increasing deposits repeats, desired reserves increase, total reserves decrease through the currency drain and eventually, enough new deposits have been created to use all the new monetary base.

Figure 24.3 summarizes one round in the process we've just described. The sequence, which repeats until excess reserves are eliminated, has the following eight steps:

1 Banks have excess reserves.
2 Banks lend excess reserves.
3 The quantity of money increases.
4 New money is used to make payments.
5 Some of the new money remains on deposit.
6 Some of the new money is a *currency drain*.
7 Desired reserves increase because deposits have increased.
8 Excess reserves decrease.

If the Bank of England sells securities, then banks have negative excess reserves – they are short of reserves. When the banks are short of reserves, loans and deposits decrease and the process we've described above works in a downward direction until desired reserves plus desired currency holdings have decreased by an amount equal to the decrease in monetary base.

A money multiplier determines the change in the quantity of money that results from a change in the monetary base.

Figure 24.3   How the Banking System Creates Money by Making Loans

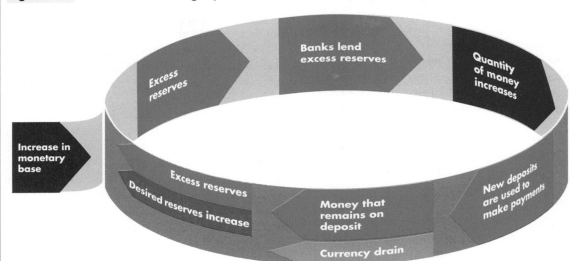

The Bank of England increases the monetary base, which increases bank reserves and creates excess reserves. Banks lend the excess reserves, new bank deposits are created and the quantity of money increases. New money is used to make payments. Some of the new money remains on deposit at banks and some leaves the banks in a currency drain. The increase in bank deposits increases banks' desired reserves. But the banks still have excess reserves, though less than before. The process repeats until excess reserves have been eliminated.

myeconlab Animation

The Money Multiplier

The **money multiplier** is the ratio of the change in the quantity of money to the change in monetary base. For example, if a £1 million increase in the monetary base increases the quantity of money by £2.5 million, then the money multiplier is 2.5.

The smaller the banks' desired reserve ratio and the smaller the currency drain ratio, the larger is the money multiplier. (See the Mathematical Note on pp. 578–579 for details on the money multiplier.)

Review Quiz

1   How do banks create money?
2   What factors limit the quantity of money that the banking system can create?
3   A bank manager tells you that she doesn't create money. She just lends the money that people deposit in the bank. Explain to her why she's wrong.

You can work these questions in Study Plan 24.4 and get instant feedback.   myeconlab

ECONOMICS IN ACTION

The Variable Money Multiplier

We can measure the money multiplier, other things remaining the same, as the ratio of the quantity of money to the monetary base.

In the UK in 2007, the monetary base (in round numbers) was £60 billion and M4 was £1,500 billion, so M4 was 25 times the monetary base. The money multiplier was 25: a £1 million change in the monetary base would bring a £25 million change in M4.

The situation in 2010 was very different from that in 2007. In 2010, the monetary base was £200 billion and M4 was £2,200 billion, so M4 was only 11 times the monetary base. The money multiplier was 11: a £1 million change in the monetary base would bring an £11 million change in M4.

What happened to make the money multiplier fall so much? The answer is a global financial crisis and a very large increase in the commercial banks' desired reserve ratio. The currency drain ratio actually increased slightly.

The Money Market

There is no limit to the amount of money we would like to *receive* in payment for our labour or as interest on our savings. But there is a limit to how big an inventory of money we would like to *hold* and neither spend nor use to buy assets that generate an income. The *quantity of money demanded* is the inventory of money that people plan to hold on any given day. It is the quantity of money in our wallets and in our deposit accounts at banks. The quantity of money held must equal the quantity supplied, and the forces that bring about this equality in the money market have powerful effects on the economy, as you will see in the rest of this chapter.

But first, we need to explain what determines the amount of money that people plan to hold.

The Influences on Money Holding

The quantity of money that people choose to hold depends on four main factors. They are:

◆ The price level
◆ The *nominal* interest rate
◆ Real GDP
◆ Financial innovation

Let's look at each of them.

The Price Level

The quantity of money measured in pounds is *nominal money*. The quantity of nominal money demanded is proportional to the price level, other things remaining the same: if the price level rises by 10 per cent, people hold 10 per cent more nominal money. If you hold £20 to buy your weekly movies and coffee, you will increase your money holding to £22 if the prices of movies and coffee – and your wage rate – increase by 10 per cent.

The quantity of money measured in constant pounds (for example, in 2006 pounds) is real money. *Real money* is equal to nominal money divided by the price level and is the quantity of money measured in terms of what it will buy.

In the above example, when the price level rises by 10 per cent and you increase your money holding by 10 per cent, your real money holding is constant. Your £22 at the new price level buys the same quantity of goods and is the same quantity of real money as your £20 at the original price level. *The quantity of real money demanded is independent of the price level.*

The *Nominal* Interest Rate

A fundamental principle of economics is that as the opportunity cost of something increases, people try to find substitutes for it. Money is no exception. The higher the opportunity cost of holding money, other things remaining the same, the smaller is the quantity of real money demanded.

The interest rate is the opportunity cost of holding money. To see why, recall that the opportunity cost of any activity is the value of the best alternative forgone. The alternative to holding money is holding a savings bond or a Treasury bill that earns interest. By holding money instead, you forgo the interest that you otherwise would have received. This forgone interest is the opportunity cost of holding money.

Money loses value because of inflation. Shouldn't the inflation rate be part of the cost of holding money? It is. Other things remaining the same, the higher the expected inflation rate, the higher is the interest rate and so the higher is the opportunity cost of holding money.

Real GDP

The quantity of money that households and firms plan to hold depends on the amount they spend, and the quantity of money demanded in the economy as a whole depends on aggregate expenditure – real GDP.

Again, suppose that you hold an average of £50 to finance your weekly purchases of goods. Now imagine that the prices of these goods and of all other goods remain constant, but that your income increases. As a consequence, you now spend more and you also keep a larger amount of money on hand to finance your higher volume of expenditure.

Financial Innovation

Technological change and the arrival of new financial products – called *financial innovation* – change the quantity of money held. The major financial innovations are the widespread use of:

1   Interest-bearing sight deposits
2   Automatic transfers between sight and time deposits
3   Automatic teller machines
4   Credit cards and debit cards

These innovations have occurred because of the development of computing power that has lowered the cost of calculations and record keeping.

The Demand for Money Curve

We summarize the effects of the influences on money holding by using the demand for money curve. The **demand for money** is the relationship between the quantity of real money demanded and the interest rate – the opportunity cost of holding money – all other influences on the amount of money that people wish to hold remaining the same.

Figure 24.4 shows a demand for money curve, *MD*. When the interest rate rises, everything else remaining the same, the opportunity cost of holding money rises and the quantity of money demanded decreases – there is a movement along the demand for money curve. Similarly, when the interest rate falls, the opportunity cost of holding money falls and the quantity of money demanded increases – there is a downward movement along the demand for money curve.

When any influence on the amount of money that people plan to hold changes, there is a change in the demand for money and the demand for money curve shifts. Let's look at these shifts.

Shifts in the Demand for Money Curve

A change in real GDP or a financial innovation changes the demand for money and shifts the demand for money curve.

Figure 24.5 illustrates the changes in the demand for money. A decrease in real GDP decreases the demand for money and shifts the demand for money curve leftward from MD_0 to MD_1. An increase in real GDP has the opposite effect: it increases the demand for money and shifts the demand for money curve rightward from MD_0 to MD_2.

The influence of financial innovation on the demand for money curve is more complicated. Financial innovation decreases the demand for currency and might increase the demand for some types of deposits and decrease the demand for others. But generally financial innovation decreases the demand for money.

Changes in real GDP and financial innovation have brought large shifts in the UK demand for money curve.

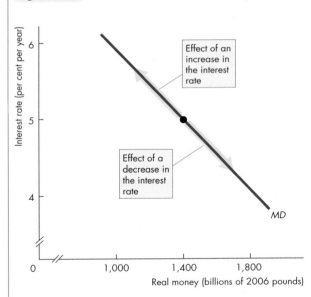

Figure 24.4 The Demand for Money

The demand for money curve, *MD*, shows the relationship between the quantity of real money that people plan to hold and the interest rate, other things remaining the same. The interest rate is the opportunity cost of holding money. A change in the interest rate leads to a movement along the demand for money curve.

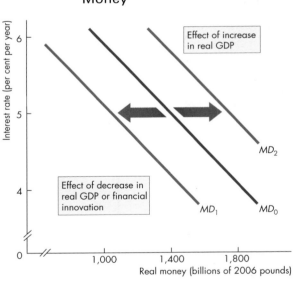

Figure 24.5 Changes in the Demand for Money

A decrease in real GDP decreases the demand for money and shifts the demand curve leftward from MD_0 to MD_1. An increase in real GDP increases the demand for money and shifts the demand curve rightward from MD_0 to MD_2. Financial innovation can either increase or decrease the demand for money depending on the specific innovation.

Money Market Equilibrium

You now know what determines the demand for money, and you've seen how the banking system creates money. Let's now see how the money market reaches equilibrium.

Money market equilibrium occurs when the quantity of money demanded equals the quantity of money supplied. The adjustments that occur to bring money market equilibrium are fundamentally different in the short run and the long run.

Short-run Equilibrium

The quantity of money supplied is determined by the actions of the banks and the Bank of England. A change in the quantity of money brings a change in the interest rate.

In Figure 24.6, the Bank uses open market operations to make the quantity of real money supplied £1,400 billion and the supply of money curve *MS*. With the demand for money curve *MD*, the equilibrium interest rate is 5 per cent a year.

Figure 24.6   Money Market Equilibrium

Money market equilibrium occurs when the quantity of money demanded equals the quantity supplied. In the short run, real GDP determines the demand for money curve, *MD*, and the Bank of England determines the quantity of real money supplied and the supply of money curve, *MS*. The interest rate adjusts to achieve equilibrium, here 5 per cent a year.

If the interest rate were 4 per cent a year, people would want to hold more money than is available. They would sell bonds, bid down their price and the interest rate would rise. If the interest rate were 6 per cent a year, people would want to hold less money than is available. They would buy bonds, bid up their price and the interest rate would fall.

The Short-run Effect of a Change in the Supply of Money

Starting from a short-run equilibrium, if the Bank of England increases the quantity of money, people find themselves holding more money than the quantity demanded. With a surplus of money holding, people enter the loanable funds market and buy bonds. The increase in demand for bonds raises the price of a bond and lowers the interest rate (refresh your memory by looking at p. 538).

If the Bank of England decreases the quantity of money, people find themselves holding less money than the quantity demanded. They enter the loanable funds market and sell bonds. The increase in the supply of bonds lowers the price of a bond and raises the interest rate.

Figure 24.7 illustrates the effects of the changes in the quantity of money that we've just described. When the supply of money curve shifts rightward from MS_0 to MS_1, the interest rate falls to 4 per cent a year; when the supply of money curve shifts leftward to MS_2, the interest rate rises to 6 per cent a year.

Long-run Equilibrium

You've just seen how the nominal interest rate is determined in the money market at the level that makes the quantity of money demanded equal the quantity supplied. You learned in Chapter 23 (on p. 542) that the real interest rate is determined in the loanable funds market at the level that makes the quantity of loanable funds demanded equal the quantity of loanable funds supplied. You also learned in Chapter 23 (on p. 539) that the real interest rate equals the nominal interest rate minus the inflation rate.

When the inflation rate equals the expected (or forecast) inflation rate and when real GDP equals potential GDP, the money market, the loanable funds market, the goods market and the labour market are in long-run equilibrium – the economy is in long-run equilibrium.

If in long-run equilibrium, the quantity of money increases, eventually a new long-run equilibrium is

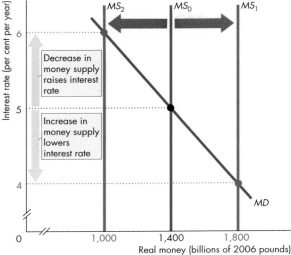

An increase in the supply of money shifts the supply of money curve from MS_0 to MS_1 and the interest rate falls. A decrease in the supply of money shifts the supply of money curve from MS_0 to MS_2 and the interest rate rises.

myeconlab Animation ◆

reached in which nothing real has changed. Real GDP, employment, the real quantity of money and the real interest rate all return to their original levels. But something does change: the price level. The price level rises by the same percentage as the rise in the quantity of money. Why does this outcome occur in the long run?

The reason is that real GDP and employment are determined by the demand for labour, the supply of labour and the production function – the real forces described in Chapter 22 (pp. 513–515); and the real interest rate is determined by the demand for and supply of (real) loanable funds – the real forces described in Chapter 23 (pp. 540–542). The only variable that is free to respond to a change in the supply of money in the long run is the price level. The price level adjusts to make the quantity of real money supplied equal to the quantity demanded.

So when the nominal quantity of money changes, in the long run the price level changes by a percentage equal to the percentage change in the quantity of nominal money. In the long run, the change in the price level is proportional to the change in the quantity of money.

The Transition from the Short Run to the Long Run

How does the economy move from the first short-run response to an increase in the quantity of money to the long-run response?

The adjustment process is lengthy and complex. Here, we'll only provide a sketch of the process. A more thorough account must wait until you get to Chapter 26.

We start out in long-run equilibrium and the Bank of England increases the quantity of money by 10 per cent. There is an excess demand for money and the nominal interest rate falls (just like you saw in Figure 24.6). The real interest rate falls too.

With a lower real interest rate, people want to borrow and spend more. Firms want to borrow to invest and households want to borrow to invest in bigger homes or to buy more consumer goods.

The increase in the demand for goods cannot be met by an increase in supply because the economy is already at full employment. So there is a general shortage of all kinds of goods and services, which makes the price level rise. As the price level rises, the real quantity of money decreases. The decrease in the quantity of real money raises the nominal interest rate and the real interest rate. As the interest rate rises, spending plans are cut back, and eventually, the original full-employment equilibrium is restored. At the new long-run equilibrium, the price level has risen by 10 per cent and nothing real has changed.

Review Quiz

1. What are the main influences on the quantity of real money that people and businesses plan to hold?
2. Show the effects of a change in the nominal interest rate and a change in real GDP using the demand for money curve.
3. How is money market equilibrium determined in the short run?
4. How does a change in the supply of money change the interest rate in the short run?
5. How does a change in the supply of money change the interest rate in the long run?

You can work these questions in Study Plan 24.5 and get instant feedback.

We explore the long-run link between money and the price level on the next two pages, where we study the quantity theory of money.

The Quantity Theory of Money

In the long run, the price level adjusts to make the quantity of real money demanded equal the quantity supplied. A special theory of the price level and inflation – the quantity theory of money – explains this long-run adjustment of the price level.

The **quantity theory of money** is the proposition that in the long run, an increase in the quantity of money brings an equal percentage increase in the price level. To explain the quantity theory of money, we first need to define the velocity of circulation.

The **velocity of circulation** is the average number of times a pound of money is used annually to buy the goods and services that make up GDP. But GDP equals the price level (P) multiplied by real GDP (Y). That is:

$$GDP = PY$$

Call the quantity of money M. The velocity of circulation, V, is determined by the equation:

$$V = PY/M$$

For example, if GDP is £1,000 billion ($PY = £1,000$ billion) and the quantity of money is £250 billion, then the velocity of circulation is 4.

From the definition of the velocity of circulation, the *equation of exchange* tells us how M, V, P and Y are connected. This equation is:

$$MV = PY$$

Given the definition of the velocity of circulation, the equation of exchange is always true – it is true by definition. It becomes the quantity theory of money if the quantity of money does not influence the velocity of circulation or real GDP. In this case, the equation of exchange tells us that the price level in the long run is determined by the quantity of money. That is:

$$P = M(V/Y)$$

where (V/Y) is independent of M. So a change in M brings a proportional change in P.

We can also express the equation of exchange in growth rates,[1] in which form it states that:

$$\text{Money growth rate} + \text{Rate of velocity change} = \text{Inflation rate} + \text{Real GDP growth rate}$$

Solving this equation for the inflation rate gives:

$$\text{Inflation rate} = \text{Money growth rate} + \text{Rate of velocity change} - \text{Real GDP growth rate}$$

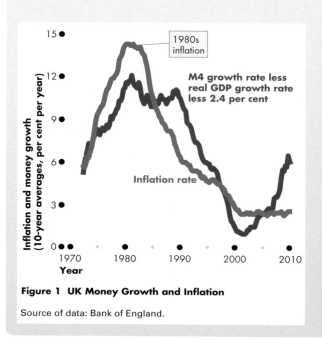

Does the Quantity Theory Work?

On average, as predicted by the quantity theory of money, the inflation rate fluctuates in line with fluctuations in the money growth rate plus the velocity growth rate minus the real GDP growth rate. Figure 1 shows the relationship between money growth (M4 definition) and inflation in the UK. You can see a clear relationship between the two variables.

Figure 1 UK Money Growth and Inflation

Source of data: Bank of England.

In the long run, the rate of velocity change is not influenced by the money growth rate. More strongly, in the long run, the rate of velocity change is approximately zero. With this assumption, the inflation rate in the long run is determined as

---

[1] To obtain this equation, begin with

$$MV = PY$$

and then changes in these variables are related by the equation

$$\Delta MV + M\Delta V = \Delta PY + P\Delta Y$$

Divide this equation by the equation of exchange to obtain

$$\Delta M/M + \Delta V/V = \Delta P/P + \Delta Y/Y$$

The term $\Delta M/M$ is the money growth rate, $\Delta V/V$ is the rate of velocity change, $\Delta P/P$ is the inflation rate and $\Delta Y/Y$ is the real GDP growth rate.

Over the period since 1973, velocity has steadily decreased at an average annual rate of 2.5 per cent and we have subtracted that constant from the growth rate of M4 minus the growth rate of real GDP. These data are 10-year averages to reflect the long-run nature of the quantity theory.

International data also support the quantity theory. Figure 2 shows a scatter diagram of the inflation rate and the money growth rate in 134 countries and Figure 3 shows the inflation rate and money growth rate in countries with inflation rates below 20 per cent a year. You can see

a general tendency for money growth and inflation to be correlated, but the quantity theory (the red line) does not predict inflation precisely.

The correlation between money growth and inflation isn't perfect, and the correlation does *not* tell us that money growth *causes* inflation.

Money growth might cause inflation; inflation might cause money growth; or some third variable might cause both inflation and money growth. Other evidence does confirm, though, that *causation runs from money growth to inflation.*

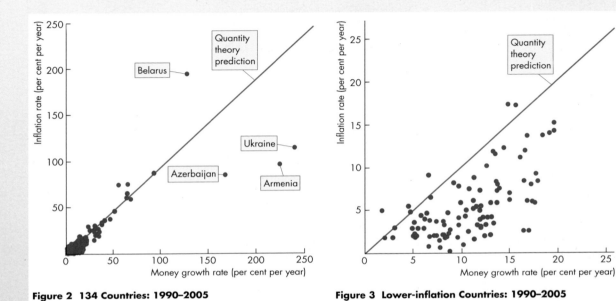

Figure 2 134 Countries: 1990–2005

Figure 3 Lower-inflation Countries: 1990–2005

Sources of data: International Financial Statistics Yearbook, 2008 and International Monetary Fund, World Economic Outlook, October, 2008.

$$\frac{\text{Inflation}}{\text{rate}} = \frac{\text{Money}}{\text{growth rate}} - \frac{\text{Real GDP}}{\text{growth rate}}$$

In the long run, fluctuations in the money growth rate minus the real GDP growth rate bring equal fluctuations in the inflation rate.

Also, in the long run, with the economy at full employment, real GDP equals potential GDP, so the real GDP growth rate equals the potential GDP growth rate. This growth rate might be influenced by inflation, but the influence is most likely small and the quantity theory assumes that it is zero. So the real GDP growth rate is given and doesn't change when the money growth rate changes – inflation is correlated with money growth.

Review Quiz

1 What is the quantity theory of money?
2 How is the velocity of circulation calculated?
3 What is the equation of exchange?
4 Does the quantity theory accurately predict the effects of money growth on inflation?

You can work these questions in Study Plan 24.6 and get instant feedback.

You now know what money is, how the banks create it and how the quantity of money influences the nominal interest rate in the short run and the price level in the long run. *Reading Between the Lines* on pp. 576–577 looks at the actions taken by the ECB to increase the quantity of money and lower interest rates.

Reading Between the Lines

ECB Conducts Expansionary Monetary Policy

The Financial Times, 8 November 2010

ECB Forced to Act as Crisis Fears Rise

FT

Ralph Atkins, David Oakley and Peter Wise

The European Central Bank has been forced to intervene in government bond markets for the first time in almost a month, as financial markets fret that the escalating Eurozone crisis is moving into a new and more dangerous phase.

The ECB said it spent €711m buying government debt last week, [but that] almost certainly understated significantly the scale of its actions. . . .

Bond yields in the so called Eurozone 'peripheral' economies rose to record levels on Monday. . . .

Irish 10-year bond yields rose to 7.75 per cent, the highest since the launch of the euro, while Portuguese yields increased to 6.67 per cent, close to a level the government has indicated as being the limit of what Lisbon can sustain.

Its latest intervention pointed to mounting ECB concern, but last week's bond purchases were still small in comparison with the €64bn spent since May. . . .

The ECB has so far refused to embark on asset purchases on the scale seen at the US Federal Reserve, which last week announced it was pumping $600bn into the financial system. Jean Claude Trichet, [ECB] president, has said the ECB programme was aimed simply at ensuring the correct functioning of markets.

Axel Weber, Germany's Bundesbank president, has voiced public opposition to even the current programme, which he fears is creating inflation risks. Last month, Mr Weber called for the programme to be phased out. . . .

 ## The Essence of the Story

- The ECB conducted a €711 million open market purchase of government bonds in the first week of November 2010.

- The move was prompted by a sharp rise in the interest rate on Ireland's and Portugal's government bonds arising from concerns that these countries might default on their debt.

- The ECB has injected €64 billion of monetary base during 2010 and the German central bank warned that the increase in the quantity of money brought the risk of a rise in the inflation rate.

- The ECB bond purchases are much smaller than those of the US Federal Reserve.

Economic Analysis

◆ The ECB conducted a €711million open market purchase of government bonds in the first week of November 2010.

◆ As Figure 1 shows, this purchase was tiny compared with the €65 billion accumulated purchases of bonds since May 2010.

◆ Bond purchases are open market operations that increase the monetary base. Bond sales decrease the monetary base.

◆ From May to November 2010, the Eurozone monetary base increased by €27 billion, an increase of 3.5 per cent.

◆ During the same seven months, the Eurozone quantity of M3 money increased by €146 billion, an increase of 1.6 per cent.

◆ Figure 2 shows the *changes* in the monetary base and M3 from May to November 2010. The €27 billion increase in the monetary base brought a €146 billion increase in M3 money: a money multiplier of 5.4.

◆ In 2010, the *level* of M3 was €9,452 billion and the *level* of the monetary base was €786 billion: a money multiplier of 12.

◆ The multiplier effect of a *change* in the monetary base was smaller than the ratio of the *level* of M3 to the monetary base because the banks desired reserve ratios increased.

◆ Figure 3 shows that the Eurozone M3 multiplier fell from 12.2 in April to less than 12 in November.

◆ Banks have a larger desired reserve ratio because the global financial crisis made them less willing to lend to each other.

◆ As long as the banks hold the additional monetary base as reserves, the inflation risk noted by the German central bank is small.

◆ If inflation does appear on the horizon, the ECB can sell bonds and decrease the monetary base to prevent the quantity of M3 from growing too quickly.

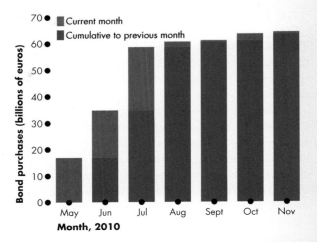

Figure 1 **ECB bond purchases in 2010: May to November**

Figure 2 **Changes in monetary base and M3: May to November 2010**

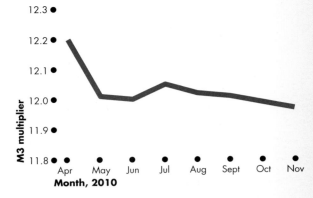

Figure 3 **The M3 money multiplier in 2010**

The Money Multiplier

This note explains the basic maths of the money multiplier and shows how the value of the multiplier depends on the banks' desired reserve ratio and the currency drain ratio.

To make the process of money creation concrete, we work through an example for a banking system in which each bank has a desired reserve ratio of 10 per cent of deposits and the currency drain ratio is 50 per cent of deposits. (Although these ratios are larger than the ones in the UK economy, they make the process end more quickly and enable you to see more clearly the principles at work.)

Figure 1 keeps track of the numbers. Before the process begins, all the banks have no excess reserves. Then the monetary base increases by £100,000 and one bank has excess reserves of this amount.

The bank lends the £100,000 of excess reserves. When this loan is made, new money increases by £100,000.

Some of the new money will be held as currency and some as deposits. With a currency drain ratio of 50 per cent of deposits, one-third of the new money will be held as currency and two-thirds will be held as deposits. That is, £33,333 drains out of the banks as currency and £66,667 remains in the banks as deposits. The increase in the quantity of money of £100,000 equals the increase in deposits plus the increase in currency holdings.

The increased bank deposits of £66,667 generate an increase in desired reserves of 10 per cent of that amount, which is £6,667. Actual reserves have increased by the same amount as the increase in deposits: £66,667. So the banks now have excess reserves of £60,000.

The process we've just described repeats but begins with excess reserves of £60,000. The figure shows the next two rounds. At the end of the process, the quantity of money has increased by a multiple of the increase in the monetary base. In this case, the increase is £250,000, which is 2.5 times the increase in the monetary base.

The sequence in the figure shows the first stages of the process that finally reaches the total shown in the final row of the 'money' column.

To calculate what happens at the later stages in the process and the final increase in the quantity of money,

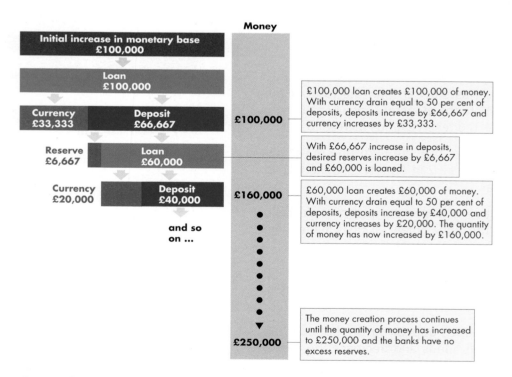

Figure 1 The money creation process

look closely at the numbers in the figure. The initial increase in reserves is £100,000 (call it A). At each stage, the loan is 60 per cent (0.6) of the previous loan and the quantity of money increases by 0.6 of the previous increase. Call that proportion L ($L = 0.6$). We can write down the complete sequence for the increase in the quantity of money as:

$$A + AL + AL^2 + AL^3 + AL^4 + AL^5 + \ldots$$

Remember, L is a fraction, so at each stage in this sequence, the amount of new loans and new money gets smaller. The total value of loans made and money created at the end of the process is the sum of the sequence,[1] which is:

$$A/(1 - L)$$

If we use the numbers from the example, the total increase in the quantity of money is:

£100,000 + 60,000 + 36,000 + . . .

$$= £100,000 \, (1 + 0.6 + 0.36 + \ldots)$$

$$= £100,000 \, (1 + 0.6 + 0.6^2 + \ldots)$$

$$= £100,000 \times 1/(1 - 0.6)$$

$$= £100,000 \times 1/(0.4)$$

$$= £100,000 \times 2.5$$

$$= £250,000$$

The magnitude of the money multiplier depends on the banks' desired reserve ratio and the currency drain ratio. Let's explore this relationship.

The money multiplier is the ratio of money to the monetary base. Call the money multiplier mm, the quantity of money M, and the monetary base MB. Then:

$$mm = M/MB$$

Next recall that money, M, is the sum of deposits and currency. Call deposits D and currency C. Then:

$$M = D + C$$

Finally, recall that the monetary base, MB, is the sum of banks' reserves and currency. Call banks' reserves R. Then:

$$MB = R + C$$

Use the equations for M and MB in the mm equation to give:

$$mm = M/MB = (D + C)/(R + C)$$

Now divide all the variables on the right-hand side of the equation by D to give:

$$mm = M/MB = (1 + C/D)/(R/D + C/D)$$

In this equation, C/D is the *currency drain ratio* and R/D is the banks' reserve ratio. If we use the values of the example on the previous page, $C/D = 0.5$ and $R/D = 0.1$, and:

$$mm = (1 + 0.5)/(0.1 + 0.5)$$

$$= 1.5/0.6 = 2.5$$

The UK Money Multiplier

The money multiplier in the UK can be found by using the formula above along with the values of C/D and R/D in the UK economy.

Using the M4 definition of money to measure deposits, D, the numbers for December 2010 are:

$$C = £50 \text{ billion}$$

$$R = £150 \text{ billion}$$

$$MB = £200 \text{ billion}$$

$$D = £2{,}150 \text{ billion}$$

$$C/D = 0.023$$

$$R/D = 0.070$$

So

$$mm = (1 + 0.023)/(0.023 + 0.070) = 11$$

---

[1] The sequence of values is called a convergent geometric series. To find the sum of a series such as this, begin by calling the sum S. Then write the sum as

$$S = A + AL + AL^2 + AL^3 + AL^4 + AL^5 + \ldots$$

Multiply by L to get

$$LS = AL + AL^2 + AL^3 + AL^4 + AL^5 + AL^6 + \ldots$$

and then subtract the second equation from the first to get

$$S(1 - L) = A$$

or

$$S = A/(1 - L)$$

SUMMARY

Key Points

What is Money? (pp. 558–560)

◆ Money is the means of payment and it functions as a medium of exchange, unit of account and store of value.

◆ M4 – currency held by the public and bank and building society deposits – is the main measure of money in the UK today.

Working Problems 1 to 4 will give you a better understanding of what money is.

Monetary Financial Institutions

(pp. 561–563)

◆ Commercial banks and building societies are monetary financial institutions: their liabilities are money.

◆ Monetary financial institutions create liquidity, minimize the cost of borrowing, minimize the cost of monitoring borrowers and pool risk.

Working Problems 5 and 6 will give you a better understanding of monetary financial institutions.

Central Banking (pp. 564–567)

◆ A central bank is a public authority that provides banking services to banks and governments and manages the nation's financial system.

◆ The liabilities of the central bank are bank notes and bank reserves. These items plus coins are the monetary base.

Working Problems 7 to 9 will give you a better understanding of central banks.

How Banks Create Money (pp. 567–569)

◆ Banks create money by making loans.

◆ The total quantity of money that can be created is limited by the monetary base, the banks' desired reserve ratio and the currency drain ratio.

Working Problems 10 to 14 will give you a better understanding of how banks create money.

The Money Market (pp. 570–573)

◆ The quantity of money demanded is the amount of money that people plan to hold.

◆ The quantity of real money equals the quantity of nominal money divided by the price level.

◆ The quantity of real money demanded depends on the nominal interest rate, real GDP and financial innovation.

◆ The nominal interest rate makes the quantity of money demanded equal the quantity supplied.

◆ When the quantity of money increases, the nominal interest rate falls (the short-run effect).

◆ In the long run, when the quantity of money increases, the price level rises and the nominal interest rate returns to its initial level.

Working Problems 15 and 16 will give you a better understanding of the money market.

The Quantity Theory of Money

(pp. 574–575)

◆ The quantity theory of money is the proposition that money growth and inflation move up and down together in the long run.

Working Problem 17 will give you a better understanding of the quantity theory of money.

Key Terms

Bank of England, 564
Bank Rate, 565
Currency, 559
Currency drain ratio, 568
Demand for money, 571
Desired reserve ratio, 568
European Central Bank (ECB), 564
Excess reserves, 568
Lender of last resort, 567
M4, 559
Means of payment, 558
Monetary base, 565
Monetary financial institution, 561
Monetary Policy Committee (MPC), 564
Money, 558
Money multiplier, 569
Open market operation, 565
Quantitative easing, 567
Quantity theory of money, 574
Repo, 564
Required reserve ratio, 562
Reserves, 561
Velocity of circulation, 574

STUDY PLAN PROBLEMS AND APPLICATIONS

myeconlab You can work Problems 1 to 19 in MyEconLab Chapter 24 Study Plan and get instant feedback.

What is Money? (Study Plan 24.1)

1 In the UK today, money includes which of the following items?

 a Bank of England bank notes in Barclay's cash machines

 b Your bank debit card

 c Coins inside a vending machine

 d A £10 bank note in your wallet

 e The cheque you've just written to pay for your rent

 f The loan you took out last August to pay for your university fees

2 Suppose that in June, currency held by individuals and businesses was £400 billion; sight deposits were £4,800 billion; time deposits were £2,000 billion; M4 was £9,000 billion. What is the other item that makes up M4 and what is its value?

3 Suppose that in July, the public held £1,500 billion in currency, £5,000 billion in bank deposits and £7,000 billion in building societies. Banks held £10,000 billion in currency and building societies held £2,000 billion in currency. Calculate M4.

4 **One More Thing Cell Phones Could Do: Replace Wallets**

Soon you'll be able to pull out your cell phone and wave it over a scanner to make a payment. The convenience of whipping out your phone as a payment mechanism is driving the transition.

Source: *USA Today*, 21 November 2007

If people can use their cell phones to make payments, will currency disappear? How will the components of M4 change?

Monetary Financial Institutions

(Study Plan 24.2)

Use the following news clip to work Problems 5 and 6.

Basel Committee Unveils Bank Capital Buffer Plan

Regulators want banks to hold a 'counter-cyclical capital buffer' – a required capital ratio that fluctuates with the state of the economy. The idea is to strengthen the global banking industry by putting the brakes on lending when a bubble emerges and provide a cushion to protect the banks from falling into financial difficulty.

Source: *Financial Times*, 17 July 2010

5 Explain a bank's 'balancing act' and how the required capital ratio makes bank failure less likely.

6 During the time of an emerging credit bubble, why might it be beneficial for the banks to be required to have a larger capital ratio?

Central Banking (Study Plan 24.3)

7 Suppose that at the end of December 2009, the monetary base was €700 billion, euro bank notes were €650 billion, and banks' reserves at the ECB were €20 billion. Calculate the quantity of coins.

8 **Fast Growth in 'Broad' Money**

The Bank of England's quantitative easing programme may be having an increasing effect. Holdings of M4 'broad' money were up from 6.2 per cent in the three months to April. The Bank of England pumped £200bn in newly created cash into the economy between February 2009 and early 2010.

Source: *Financial Times*, 30 June 2010

What are the Bank of England's policy tools and which policy tool did it use when it 'pumped £200bn in newly created cash into the economy'?

9 The Bank of England sells £20 million of securities to HSBC. Enter the transactions that take place to show the changes in the following balance sheets.

Bank of England

Assets (millions)	Liabilities (millions)

HSBC

Assets (millions)	Liabilities (millions)

How Banks Create Money (Study Plan 24.4)

10 The commercial banks in Zap have

Reserves €250 million

Loans €1,000 million

Deposits €2,000 million

Total assets €2,500 million

If the banks hold no excess reserves, calculate their desired reserve ratio.

Use the following information to work Problems 11 and 12.

In the economy of Nocoin, banks have deposits of €300 billion. Their reserves are €15 billion, two-thirds of which is in deposits with the central bank. Households and businesses hold €30 billion in bank notes. There are no coins!

11 Calculate the monetary base and the quantity of money.

12 Calculate the banks' desired reserve ratio and the currency drain ratio (as percentages).

Use the following news clip to work Problems 13 and 14.

Banks Drop on Higher Reserve Requirement

China's central bank will raise its reserve ratio requirement by a percentage point to a record 17.5 per cent, stepping up a battle to contain lending growth. Banks' ratio of excess reserves to deposits was 2 per cent. Every half-point increase in the required reserve ratio cuts banks' profits by 1.5 per cent.

Source: *People's Daily Online*, 11 June 2008

13 Explain how increasing the required reserve ratio influences the banks' money creation process.

14 Why might a higher required reserve ratio decrease bank profits?

The Money Market (Study Plan 24.5)

15 The spreadsheet provides information about the demand for and supply of money in Minland. Column A is the nominal interest rate, *r*. Columns B and C show the quantity of money demanded at two different levels of real GDP: Y_0 is £10 billion and Y_1 is £20 billion. The quantity

	A	B	C
	r	Y_0	Y_1
1	7	1.0	1.5
2	6	1.5	2.0
3	5	2.0	2.5
4	4	2.5	3.0
5	3	3.0	3.5
6	2	3.5	4.0
7	1	4.0	4.5

of money supplied is £3 billion. Initially, real GDP is £20 billion. What happens in Minland if the interest rate:

a Exceeds 4 per cent a year.

b Is less than 4 per cent a year.

16 The figure shows the demand for money curve.

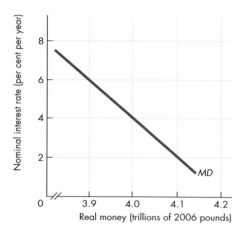

If the central bank decreases the quantity of real money supplied from £4 trillion to £3.9 trillion, explain how the price of a bond will change.

The Quantity Theory of Money
(Study Plan 24.6)

17 Quantecon is a country in which the quantity theory of money operates. In year 1, the economy is at full employment and real GDP is £400 million, the price level is 200, and the velocity of circulation is 20. In year 2, the quantity of money increases by 20 per cent. Calculate the quantity of money, the price level, real GDP, and the velocity of circulation in year 2.

Mathematical Note (Study Plan 24.MN)

18 In Problem 11, the banks have no excess reserves. Suppose that the Bank of Nocoin, the central bank, increases bank reserves by €0.5 billion.

a What happens to the quantity of money?

b Explain why the change in the quantity of money is not equal to the change in the monetary base.

c Calculate the money multiplier.

19 In Problem 11, the banks have no excess reserves. Suppose that the Bank of Nocoin, the central bank, decreases bank reserves by €0.5 billion.

a Calculate the money multiplier.

b What happens to the quantity of money, deposits and currency?

ADDITIONAL PROBLEMS AND APPLICATIONS

myeconlab You can work these problems in MyEconLab if assigned by your lecturer.

What is Money?

20   Sara withdraws £1,000 from her savings account at the Lucky Building Society, keeps £50 in cash, and deposits the balance in her chequing account at HSBC. What is the immediate change in currency and in M4?

21   Rapid inflation in Brazil in the early 1990s caused the cruzeiro to lose its ability to function as money. Which of the following commodities would most likely have taken the place of the cruzeiro in the Brazilian economy? Explain why.

  a   Tractor parts

  b   Packs of cigarettes

  c   Loaves of bread

  d   Impressionist paintings

22   **From Paper-Clip to House, in 14 Trades**

A 26-year-old Montreal man appears to have succeeded in his quest to barter a single, red paperclip all the way up to a house. It took almost a year and 14 trades.

Source: *CBC News*, 7 July 2006

Is barter a means of payment? Is it just as efficient as money when trading on e-Bay? Explain.

Monetary Financial Institutions

Use the following news clip to work Problems 23 and 24.

The War on Moral Hazard Begins at Home

Northern Rock was a narrow bank, with only retail customers, and Northern Rock failed; Lehman Brothers was a pure investment bank, but Lehman too failed. The issues in financial reform are to do with the behaviour of businesses, not the structure of their industry. Wrong. The point of structural reform of the banking system is not to prevent banks from failing. It is to allow them to fail without imposing large costs on taxpayers, their customers and the global economy.

Source: *Financial Times*, 26 January 2011

23   Explain why attempts by banks to maximize profits can sometimes lead to bank failures.

24   Explain the effects of higher required capital ratios, higher required reserve ratios and restrictions on the types of investments banks are permitted to make. What types of structural reforms might allow banks to fail without imposing large costs on taxpayers and bank customers?

Central Banking

25   Explain the distinction between a central bank and a commercial bank.

26   If the Bank of England makes an open market sale of £1 million of securities to a bank, what initial changes occur in the economy?

27   Set out the transactions that the Bank of England undertakes to increase the quantity of money.

28   Describe the Bank of England's assets and liabilities. What is the monetary base and how does it relate to the Bank of England's balance sheet?

29   **Eurozone Banks Reluctant to Return ECB's Funds**

The European Central Bank (ECB) injected €73.5 billion into the region's banks to combat the Irish debt crisis by buying government bonds. The banks are reluctant to return these funds and offered the ECB just over €60 billion. They want to keep the extra liquidity.

Source: *Financial Times*, 29 December 2010

What is the rationale behind the ECB injecting funds into the region's banks and why might the banks be reluctant to repay the funds?

How Banks Create Money

30   Banks in New Transylvania have a desired reserve ratio of 10 per cent and no excess reserves. The currency drain ratio is 50 per cent. Then the central bank increases the monetary base by €1,200 billion.

  a   How much do the banks lend in the first round of the money creation process?

  b   How much of the initial amount lent flows back to the banking system as new deposits?

  c   How much of the initial amount lent does not return to the banks but is held as currency?

  d   Why does a second round of lending occur?

The Money Market

31 Explain the change in the nominal interest rate in the short run if

  a Real GDP increases.

  b The money supply increases.

  c The price level rises.

32 In Minland in Problem 15, the interest rate is 4 per cent a year. Suppose that real GDP decreases to $10 billion and the quantity of money supplied remains unchanged. Do people buy bonds or sell bonds? Explain how the interest rate changes.

The Quantity Theory of Money

33 The table provides some data for the US in the first decade following the Civil War.

Item	1869	1879
Quantity of money	$1.3 billion	$1.7 billion
Real GDP (1929 dollars)	$7.4 billion	Z
Price level (1929 = 100)	X	54
Velocity of circulation	4.50	4.61

Source of data: Milton Friedman and Anna J. Schwartz, *A Monetary History of the United States 1867–1960*

  a Calculate the value of X in 1869.

  b Calculate the value of Z in 1879.

  c Are the data consistent with the quantity theory of money? Explain your answer.

Mathematical Note

34 In the UK, the currency drain ratio is 0.38 of deposits and the reserve ratio is 0.002. In Australia, the quantity of money is $150 billion, the currency drain ratio is 33 per cent of deposits, and the reserve ratio is 8 per cent.

  a Calculate the UK money multiplier.

  b Calculate the monetary base in Australia.

Economics in the News

35 After you have studied *Reading Between the Lines* on pp. 576–577 answer the following questions.

  a By how much did the monetary base of the Eurozone increase between May 2010 and November 2010?

  b How did the ECB increase the monetary base?

  c How did the increase in the monetary base increase M3?

  d Was the percentage increase in the money base the same as that predicted by the money multiplier?

  e Why did M3 not grow by a larger percentage than the monetary base?

  f If when the monetary base increased, the banks had not increased their excess reserves, what does the quantity theory predict would have happened to the inflation rate?

36 **US Federal Reserve at Odds with ECB over Value of Policy Tool**

Many central banks use monetary aggregates as a guide to policy decision, but Bernanke believes US reliance on monetary aggregates would be unwise because the empirical relationship between US money growth, inflation and output growth is unstable. Bernanke said that the Federal Reserve had 'philosophical' and economic differences with the European Central Bank and the Bank of England regarding the role of money and that debate between institutions is healthy. 'Unfortunately, forecast errors for money growth are often significant', reducing their effectiveness as a tool for policy, Bernanke said. 'There are differences between the US and Europe in terms of the stability of money demand', Bernanke said. Ultimately, the risk of bad policy arising from a devoted following of money growth led the Federal Reserve to downgrade the importance of money measures.

Source: *International Herald Tribune*,
10 November 2006

  a Explain how the debate surrounding the quantity theory of money could make monetary aggregates a less useful tool for policy makers.

  b What do Bernanke's statements reveal about his stance on the accuracy of the quantity theory of money?

International Finance

After studying this chapter you will be able to:

◆ Describe the foreign exchange market
◆ Explain the fluctuations in the exchange rate
◆ Describe the alternative exchange rate regimes
◆ Explain the benefits and costs of the euro
◆ Describe the balance of payments accounts and explain what causes international deficits and surpluses

The pound, the euro, the yen and the US dollar are the world's four most widely used currencies. The prices of these currencies fluctuate every day. Why? Why don't they have stable prices? What causes the value of currencies to rise and fall?

Many famous British companies have been bought by foreigners: Rover by BMW (German); MG by Nanjing Automobiles (China); Cadbury by Kraft (US). Why? What makes it possible for people to buy assets and businesses in other countries?

In *Reading Between the Lines* at the end of the chapter, you will see how some countries manipulate their currencies in an attempt to boost exports.

The Foreign Exchange Market

When Tesco imports DVD players from Japan, it pays for them using Japanese yen. And when China Airlines buys aircraft engines from Rolls Royce, it pays using pounds sterling. Whenever people buy things from another country, they use the currency of that country to make the transaction. It doesn't make any difference what the item is that is being traded internationally. It might be a DVD player, a jet engine, insurance or banking services, property, the stocks and bonds of a government or corporation, or even an entire business.

Foreign Currencies

Foreign money is just like money in the UK. It consists of notes and coins issued by a central bank and mint and deposits in banks and other monetary financial institutions. When we described UK and EU money in Chapter 24, we distinguished between currency (notes and coins) and deposits. But when we talk about foreign money, we refer to it as foreign currency. **Foreign currency** is the money of other countries regardless of whether that money is in the form of notes, coins, or bank deposits.

UK pounds are called *pounds sterling*. We buy foreign currencies in exchange for pounds sterling and foreigners buy pounds sterling in exchange for their own currencies in the foreign exchange market.

Trading Currencies

The currency of one country is exchanged for the currency of another in the **foreign exchange market**. The foreign exchange market consists of thousands of buyers and sellers. Some of these people are importers and exporters of goods and services; some are banks and other financial institutions; and some are specialist traders called *foreign exchange brokers*.

The foreign exchange market opens on Monday morning in Hong Kong. As the day advances, the foreign exchange markets in Singapore, Tokyo, Bahrain, Frankfurt, London, New York, Chicago and San Francisco open for trade. As the US West Coast markets close, Hong Kong is only an hour away from opening for the next day of business. The sun barely sets on the foreign exchange market. Dealers around the world are continually in contact by telephone and on a typical day in 2010, around $3 trillion (of all currencies) were traded in the foreign exchange market – or more than $600 trillion in a year.

Exchange Rates

An **exchange rate** is the price at which one currency exchanges for another currency in the foreign exchange market. For example, on 4 January 2011, £1 would buy 1.56 US dollars, 127 Japanese yen or 1.17 euros. So the exchange rate was 1.56 dollars per pound, or equivalently, 127 yen and 117 euro cents per pound.

The exchange rate fluctuates. Sometimes it rises and sometimes it falls. A rise in the exchange rate is called an *appreciation* of the pound, and a fall in the exchange rate is called a *depreciation* of the pound. For example, when the exchange rate rises from 1.60 dollars to 2.00 dollars per pound, the pound appreciates, and when the exchange rate falls from 2.00 dollars to 1.50 dollars per pound, the pound depreciates.

Economics in Action on the next page shows the fluctuations in the pound sterling against three currencies since 2000. Two important questions arise from an examination of the movements of the exchange rate. First, how is the exchange rate determined? Second, how do exchange rate fluctuations influence our international trade and international payments? We begin by learning how trading in the foreign exchange market determines the exchange rate.

An Exchange Rate is a Price

An exchange rate is a price and like all prices an exchange rate is determined in a market – the *foreign exchange market*.

The pound sterling trades in the foreign exchange market and is supplied and demanded by tens of thousands of traders every hour of every business day.

Because it has many traders and no restrictions on who may trade, the foreign exchange market is a *competitive market*.

In a competitive market, demand and supply determine the price. So to understand the forces that determine the exchange rate, we need to study the factors that influence demand and supply in the foreign exchange market. But there is a feature of the foreign exchange market that makes it special.

The Demand for One Money Is the Supply of Another Money

When people who are holding the money of some other country want to exchange it for pounds sterling, they demand pounds sterling and supply that other country's money. And when people who are holding pounds

The Pound Sterling Against the Euro, the Dollar and the Yen

The figure shows the pound sterling exchange rate against the three big currencies – the euro, the US dollar and the Japanese yen – since January 2000.

Against the euro, the pound has been on a one-way track – downward. In January 2000, you would have needed €1.60 to buy £1.00. In December 2010, €1.15 would buy £1.00. The fall has come in three stages: a drop of about 20 euro cents in 2003, a drop of another 20 euro cents in 2007 and the first quarter of 2008 and another drop of 10 euro cents in the last quarter of 2008.

Against the US dollar and the yen, the pound has moved in both directions. From January 2000 to 2007, the pound appreciated. It rose from $1.60 to more than $2.00 and from ¥180 to ¥240.

But through the global financial crisis and the following recession, the pound crashed against these two big currencies.

The fall was most spectacular against the yen – a *depreciation* of almost 50 per cent from ¥247 per pound to ¥130 per pound.

The fall against the US dollar was from $2.02 down to $1.56 per pound, a depreciation of 23 per cent – about the same as the appreciation from 2000 to 2007.

Notice that the exchange rates display high-frequency fluctuations (rapid brief up and down movements) around the broad trends that we've just described.

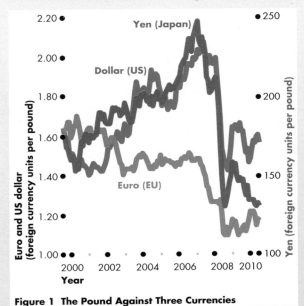

Figure 1 The Pound Against Three Currencies

sterling want to exchange them for the money of some other country, they supply pounds sterling and demand that other country's money.

So the factors that influence the demand for pounds sterling also influence the supply of US dollars, or EU euros, or Japanese yen. And the factors that influence the demand for that other country's money also influence the supply of pounds sterling.

We'll first look at the influences on the demand for pounds sterling in the foreign exchange market.

Demand in the Foreign Exchange Market

People buy pounds sterling in the foreign exchange market so that they can buy UK-produced goods and services – UK exports. They also buy pounds sterling so that they can buy UK assets such as bonds, stocks, businesses and property or so that they can keep part of their money holding in a UK bank account.

The quantity of pounds demanded in the foreign exchange market is the amount that traders plan to buy during a given time period at a given exchange rate. This quantity depends on many factors, but the main ones are:

1   The exchange rate

2   World demand for UK exports

3   Interest rates in the UK and other countries

4   The expected future exchange rate

We look first at the relationship between the quantity of pounds sterling demanded in the foreign exchange market and the exchange rate when the other three influences remain the same.

The Law of Demand for Foreign Exchange

The law of demand applies to pounds sterling just as it does to anything else that people value. Other things remaining the same, the higher the exchange rate, the smaller is the quantity of pounds demanded in the foreign exchange market. The exchange rate influences the quantity of pounds demanded for two reasons:

◆ Exports effect
◆ Expected profit effect

Exports Effect

The larger the value of UK exports, the larger is the quantity of pounds demanded in the foreign exchange market. But the value of UK exports depends on the prices of UK-produced goods and services *expressed in the currency of the foreign buyer.* And these prices depend on the exchange rate. The lower the exchange rate, other things remaining the same, the lower are the prices of UK-produced goods and services to foreigners and the greater is the volume of UK exports. So if the exchange rate falls (and other influences remain the same), the quantity of pounds demanded in the foreign exchange market increases.

To see the exports effect at work, think about orders for the Rolls Royce Ardour turbine engine by the US navy. If the price of an engine is £300,000 and the exchange rate is $2.00 per pound, the price of the engine to the US Navy is $600,000. The navy decides that this price is too high. But if the exchange rate falls to $1.50 per pound and other things remain the same, the price of an engine falls to $450,000. The US Navy now decides to buy the engine and buys pounds in the foreign exchange market to pay for it.

Expected Profit Effect

The larger the expected profit from holding pounds, the greater is the quantity of pounds demanded in the foreign exchange market. But expected profit depends on the exchange rate. For a given expected future exchange rate, the lower the exchange rate today, the larger is the expected profit from buying pounds today and holding them, so the greater is the quantity of pounds demanded in the foreign exchange market today. Let's look at an example. Suppose that the Bank of New York Mellon expects the exchange rate to be $1.50 per pound at the end of the year. If today's exchange rate is also $1.50 per pound, BNY Mellon expects no profit from buying

pounds sterling and holding them until the end of the year. But if today's exchange rate is $1.40 per pound and BNY Mellon buys pounds, it expects to sell those pounds at the end of the year for $1.50 per pound and make a profit of 10 cents per pound sterling.

The lower the exchange rate today, other things remaining the same, the greater is the expected profit from holding pounds and the greater is the quantity of pounds sterling demanded in the foreign exchange market today.

Demand Curve for Pounds Sterling

Figure 25.1 shows the demand curve for pounds sterling in the foreign exchange market. A change in the exchange rate, other things remaining the same, brings a change in the quantity of pounds demanded and a movement along the demand curve. The arrows show such movements.

We will look at the factors that change demand in the next section of this chapter. Before doing that, let's see what determines the supply of pounds.

Figure 25.1   The Demand for Pounds

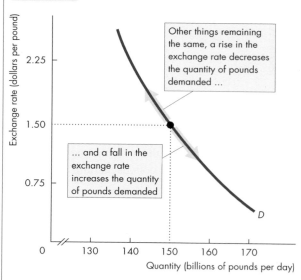

Other things remaining the same, a rise in the exchange rate decreases the quantity of pounds demanded ...

... and a fall in the exchange rate increases the quantity of pounds demanded

The quantity of pounds that people plan to buy depends on the exchange rate. Other things remaining the same, if the exchange rate rises, the quantity of pounds demanded decreases and there is a movement up along the demand curve for pounds. If the exchange rate falls, the quantity of pounds demanded increases and there is a movement down along the demand curve for pounds.

Supply in the Foreign Exchange Market

People sell pounds and buy other currencies so that they can buy foreign-produced goods and services – UK imports. People also sell pounds and buy foreign currencies so that they can buy foreign assets such as bonds, stocks, businesses and real estate or so that they can hold part of their money in bank deposits denominated in a foreign currency. The quantity of pounds supplied in the foreign exchange market is the amount that traders plan to sell during a given time period at a given exchange rate. This quantity depends on many factors, but the main ones are:

1 The exchange rate

2 UK demand for imports

3 Interest rates in the UK and other countries

4 The expected future exchange rate

Let's look at the law of supply in the foreign exchange market – the relationship between the quantity of pounds supplied in the foreign exchange market and the exchange rate when the other three influences remain the same.

The Law of Supply of Foreign Exchange

Other things remaining the same, the higher the exchange rate, the greater is the quantity of pounds sterling supplied in the foreign exchange market.

The exchange rate influences the quantity of dollars supplied for two reasons:

◆ Imports effect

◆ Expected profit effect

Imports Effect

The larger the value of UK imports, the larger is the quantity of pounds sterling supplied in the foreign exchange market. But the value of UK imports depends on the prices of foreign-produced goods and services *expressed in pounds*. These prices depend on the exchange rate.

The higher the exchange rate, other things remaining the same, the lower are the prices of foreign-produced goods and services to residents in the UK and the greater is the volume of imports. So if the exchange rate rises (and other influences remain the same), the

quantity of pounds supplied in the foreign exchange market increases.

Expected Profit Effect

This effect works just like that on the demand for pounds but in the opposite direction. For given expected future exchange rates, the higher the exchange rate of the pound today, other things remaining the same, the larger is the expected profit from selling pounds today and holding foreign currencies, so the greater is the quantity of pounds supplied.

Supply Curve of Pounds Sterling

Figure 25.2 shows the supply curve of pounds in the foreign exchange market. A change in the exchange rate, other things remaining the same, brings a change in the quantity of pounds supplied and a movement along the supply curve. The arrows show such movements.

Next we bring demand and supply together and determine equilibrium in the foreign exchange market.

Figure 25.2 The Supply of Pounds

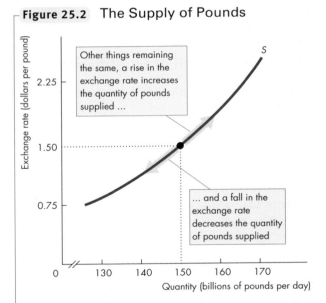

The quantity of pounds that people plan to sell depends on the exchange rate. Other things remaining the same, if the exchange rate rises, the quantity of pounds supplied increases and there is a movement up along the supply curve of pounds. If the exchange rate falls, the quantity of pounds supplied decreases and there is a movement down along the supply curve of pounds.

myeconlab Animation

Market Equilibrium

Equilibrium in the foreign exchange market depends on how the Bank of England, the ECB and other central banks operate. Here, we will study equilibrium when central banks keep out of this market. In a later section (on pp. 596–597), we examine the effects of alternative actions that the Bank of England or another central bank might take in the foreign exchange market.

Figure 25.3 shows the demand curve for pounds, D, from Figure 25.1 and the supply curve of pounds, S, from Figure 25.2, and the equilibrium exchange rate.

The exchange rate acts as a regulator of the quantities demanded and supplied. If the exchange rate is too high, there is a surplus – the quantity supplied exceeds the quantity demanded. For example, in Figure 25.3, if the exchange rate is $2.25 per pound, there is a surplus of pounds. If the exchange rate is too low, there is a shortage – the quantity supplied is less than the quantity demanded. For example, if the exchange rate is $0.75 per pound, there is a shortage of pounds.

At the equilibrium exchange rate, there is neither a shortage nor a surplus – the quantity supplied equals the quantity demanded. In Figure 25.3, the equilibrium exchange rate is $1.50 per pound. At this exchange rate, the quantity demanded and the quantity supplied are each £150 billion a day.

The Powerful Pull of Equilibrium

The foreign exchange market is constantly pulled to its equilibrium by the forces of supply and demand. Foreign exchange traders are constantly looking for the best price they can get. If they are selling, they want the highest price available. If they are buying, they want the lowest price available. Information flows from trader to trader through the worldwide computer network, and the price adjusts minute by minute to keep buying plans and selling plans in balance. That is, the price adjusts minute by minute to keep the exchange rate at its equilibrium. Figure 25.3 shows how the exchange rate between the pound sterling and the US dollar is determined. The exchange rates between the pound and all other currencies are determined in a similar way. So are the exchange rates among the other currencies. But the exchange rates are tied together so that no profit can be made by buying one currency, selling it for a second one, and then buying back the first one. If such a profit were available, traders would spot it, demand and supply would change, and the exchange rates would snap into alignment.

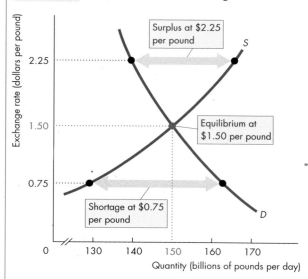

Figure 25.3 Equilibrium Exchange Rate

The demand curve for pounds is D and the supply curve is S. If the exchange rate is $2.25 per pound, there is a surplus of pounds and the exchange rate falls. If the exchange rate is $0.75 per pound, there is a shortage of pounds and the exchange rate rises. If the exchange rate is $1.50 per pound, there is neither a shortage nor a surplus of pounds and the exchange rate remains constant. The market is in equilibrium.

myeconlab Animation

Review Quiz

1 What are the influences on the demand for pounds in the foreign exchange market?
2 Provide an example of the exports effect on the demand for pounds.
3 What are the influences on the supply of pounds in the foreign exchange market?
4 Provide an example of the imports effect on the supply of pounds.
5 How is the equilibrium exchange rate determined?
6 What happens if there is a shortage or a surplus of pounds in the foreign exchange market?

You can work these questions in Study Plan 25.1 and get instant feedback.

Exchange Rate Fluctuations

You've seen (in *Economics in Action* on p. 587) that the pound fluctuates a lot against the euro, the dollar and the yen. Changes in the demand for pounds or the supply of pounds bring these exchange rate fluctuations. We'll now look at the factors that make demand and supply change, starting with the demand side of the market.

Changes in the Demand for Pounds

The demand for pounds in the foreign exchange market changes when there is a change in:

◆ World demand for UK exports

◆ UK interest rate relative to the foreign interest rate

◆ The expected future exchange rate

World Demand for UK Exports

An increase in world demand for UK exports increases the demand for pounds. To see this effect, think about the sale of commercial air engines by Rolls Royce. An increase in demand for air travel in Australia sends Qantas on a global shopping spree to buy the Rolls Royce Trent 900 to power its expanding fleet of Super Airbuses. The demand for pounds now increases.

UK Interest Rate Relative to the Foreign Interest Rate

People and businesses buy financial assets to make a return. The higher the interest rate that people can make on UK assets compared with foreign assets, the more UK assets they buy.

What matters is not the level of the UK interest rate but the UK rate minus the foreign rate – a gap that is called the **UK interest rate differential**. If the UK interest rate rises and the foreign interest rate remains constant, the UK interest rate differential increases. The larger the UK interest rate differential, the greater is the demand for UK assets and the greater is the demand for pounds in the foreign exchange market.

The Expected Future Exchange Rate

For a given current exchange rate, other things remaining the same, a rise in the expected future exchange rate increases the profit that people expect to make by holding pounds and the demand for pounds increases today.

Figure 25.4 summarizes the influences on the demand for pounds. An increase in the demand for UK exports, a rise in the UK interest rate differential, or a rise in the expected future exchange rate increases the demand for pounds today and shifts the demand curve rightward from D_0 to D_1. A decrease in the demand for UK exports, a fall in the UK interest rate differential, or a fall in the expected future exchange rate decreases the demand for pounds today and shifts the demand curve leftward from D_0 to D_2.

Figure 25.4 Changes in the Demand for Pounds

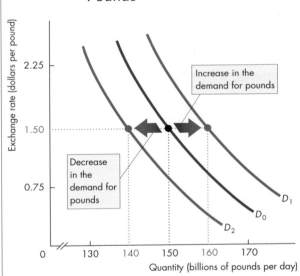

A change in any influence on the quantity of pounds that people plan to buy, other than the exchange rate, brings a change in the demand for pounds.

The demand for pounds

Increases if	*Decreases if*
◆ World demand for UK exports increases	◆ World demand for UK exports decreases
◆ The UK interest rate differential rises	◆ The UK interest rate differential falls
◆ The expected future exchange rate rises	◆ The expected future exchange rate falls

myeconlab Animation

Changes in the Supply of Pounds

The supply of pounds in the foreign exchange market changes when there is a change in:

◆ UK demand for imports
◆ UK interest rate differential
◆ The expected future exchange rate

UK Demand for Imports

An increase in the UK demand for imports increases the supply of pounds in the foreign exchange market. To see why, think about Tesco's purchase of DVD players. An increase in the demand for DVD players sends Tesco out on a global shopping spree. Tesco decides that Panasonic DVD players produced in Japan are the best buy, so it increases its purchases of these players. The supply of pounds now increases as Tesco goes to the foreign exchange market for Japanese yen to pay Panasonic.

UK Interest Rate Differential

The effect of the UK interest rate differential on the supply of pounds is the opposite of its effect on the demand for pounds. The larger the UK interest rate differential, the smaller is the supply of pounds in the foreign exchange market. With a higher UK interest rate differential, people decide to keep more of their funds in sterling assets and less in foreign currency assets. They buy a smaller quantity of foreign currency and sell a smaller quantity of pounds in the foreign exchange market. So, a rise in the UK interest rate, other things remaining the same, decreases the supply of pounds in the foreign exchange market.

The Expected Future Exchange Rate

For a given current exchange rate, other things remaining the same, a fall in the expected future exchange rate decreases the profit that can be made by holding pounds and decreases the quantity of pounds that people want to hold. To reduce their holdings of sterling assets, people must sell pounds. When they do so, the supply of pounds in the foreign exchange market increases.

Figure 25.5 summarizes the influences on the supply of pounds. If the supply of pounds decreases, the supply curve shifts leftward from S_0 to S_1. And if the supply of pounds increases, the supply curve shifts rightward from S_0 to S_2.

Figure 25.5   Changes in the Supply of Pounds

A change in any influence on the quantity of pounds that people plan to sell, other than the exchange rate, brings a change in the supply of pounds.

The supply of pounds

Increases if	*Decreases if*
◆ UK demand for imports increases	◆ UK demand for imports decreases
◆ The UK interest rate differential falls	◆ The UK interest rate differential rises
◆ The expected future exchange rate falls	◆ The expected future exchange rate rises

Changes in the Exchange Rate

If the demand for pounds increases and the supply does not change, the exchange rate rises. If the demand for pounds decreases and the supply does not change, the exchange rate falls. Similarly, if the supply of pounds decreases and the demand does not change, the exchange rate rises. If the supply of pounds increases and the demand does not change, the exchange rate falls.

These predictions are exactly the same as those for any other market. Two episodes in the life of the pound illustrate these predictions.

ECONOMICS IN ACTION

The Rise and Fall of the Pound

The foreign exchange market is a striking example of a competitive market. The expectations of thousands of traders around the world influence this market minute-by-minute throughout the 24-hour global trading day.

Demand and supply rarely stand still and their fluctuations bring a fluctuating exchange rate. Two episodes in the life of the pound and yen illustrate these fluctuations: 2001–2007, when the pound appreciated and 2007–2009, when the pound depreciated.

An Appreciating Pound: 2001–2007

Between January 2001 and July 2007, the pound appreciated against the yen: it rose from 172 to 247 yen per pound. Part (a) of the figure provides an explanation for this appreciation.

In 2001, the demand and supply curves were those labelled D_{01} and S_{01}. The exchange rate was 172 yen per pound. During this period the UK was a good place to invest money. Property prices were rising and banks in the UK increasingly borrowed from foreign banks, particularly Japanese banks, in the global market for mortgage-backed securities. The Bank of England raised the *bank rate* from 3.5 per cent in 2003 to 5.75 per cent in July 2007 but interest rates in Japan barely changed. With the rise in the UK interest rate differential, funds flowed into the UK. Also, currency traders, anticipating this increased flow of funds into the UK expected the pound to appreciate against

the yen. The demand for pounds increased, and the supply of pounds decreased.

In the figure, the demand curve shifted rightward from D_{01} to D_{07} and the supply curve shifted leftward from S_{01} to S_{07}. The exchange rate rose to 247 yen per pound. In the figure, the equilibrium quantity remained unchanged – an assumption.

A Depreciating Pound: 2007–2009

Between July 2007 and October 2009, the pound depreciated against the yen: it fell from 247 to 184 yen per pound. Part (b) of the figure provides a possible explanation for this depreciation. The demand and supply curves D_{07} and S_{07} are the same as in part (a).

From the third quarter of 2007 to the third quarter of 2009, the UK economy, along with the US and other developed economies, entered a severe financial crisis. Investment returns and property values fell sharply. The Bank of England cut the *bank rate*, but the Bank of Japan kept the interest rate in Japan unchanged. With a narrowing of the UK interest rate differential and a reversal of investment returns, funds flowed out of the UK. Also, currency traders expected the pound to depreciate against the yen. The demand for pounds decreased and the supply of pounds increased.

In part (b) of the figure, the demand curve shifted leftward from D_{07} to D_{09}, the supply curve shifted rightward from S_{07} to S_{09}, and the exchange rate fell to 184 yen per pound.

(a) 2001–2007

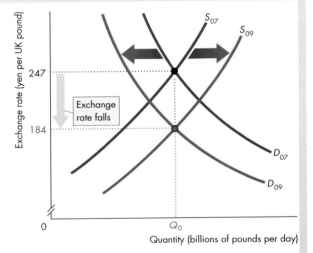

(b) 2007–2009

Figure 1 The Rising and Falling UK Pound

Fundamentals, Expectations and Arbitrage

Changes in the expected exchange rate change the actual exchange rate. But what makes the expected exchange rate change? The answer is new information about the *fundamental influences* on the exchange rate – the world demand for UK exports, UK demand for imports, and the UK interest rate relative to the foreign interest rate. Expectations about these variables change the exchange rate through their influence on the expected exchange rate, and the effect is instant.

To see why, suppose news breaks that the Bank of England will raise the interest rate next week. Traders now expect the demand for pounds to increase, the supply of pounds to decrease and the pound to appreciate. They expect to profit by buying pounds today and selling them next week for a higher price than they paid. The rise in the expected future value of the pound increases the demand for pounds today, decreases the supply of pounds today and raises the exchange rate. The exchange rate changes as soon as the news about a fundamental influence is received.

Profiting by trading in the foreign exchange market often involves arbitrage – the practice of buying in one market and selling for a higher price in another related market. Arbitrage ensures that the exchange rate is the same in New York, Tokyo, London and all other trading centres. It isn't possible to buy at a low price in London and sell for a higher price in New York. If it were possible, demand would increase in London and decrease in New York to make the prices equal.

Arbitrage also removes profit from borrowing in one currency and lending in another and buying goods in one currency and selling them in another. These arbitrage activities bring about:

◆ Interest rate parity
◆ Purchasing power parity

Interest Rate Parity

Suppose a bank deposit in pounds in London earns 5 per cent a year and a US dollar bank deposit in New York earns 3 per cent a year. In this situation, why does anyone deposit money in New York? Why doesn't all the money flow to London? The answer is because of exchange rate expectations. Suppose people expect the pound to depreciate by 2 per cent a year. This 2 per cent depreciation must be subtracted from the 5 per cent interest to obtain the net return of 3 per cent a year that

an American can earn by depositing funds in London. The two returns are equal. This situation is one of **interest rate parity**, which means *equal rates of return*.

Adjusted for risk, interest rate parity always prevails. Funds move to get the highest return available. If for a few seconds a higher return is available in London than in New York, the demand for pounds increases and the pound appreciates until interest rate parity is restored.

Purchasing Power Parity

Suppose the price of a pair of Levi's jeans is £20 in London and $30 in New York. If the exchange rate is $1.50 per pound, the two monies have the same value. You can buy the jeans in London or New York for either £20 or $30 and it costs you the same in the two currencies.

The situation we've just described is called **purchasing power parity**, which *means equal value of money*. If purchasing power parity does not prevail, powerful arbitrage forces go to work.

Arbitrage Forces

To see these forces, suppose that the price of Levi's jeans in London rises to £30, but in New York, they remain at $30. The exchange rate remains at $1.50 per pound. In this case, a pair of jeans in New York still costs $30 or £20, but in London it costs £30 or $45. Money buys more in the US than in the UK. Money is not of equal value in the two countries.

If all (or most) prices have increased in the UK and not increased in the US, then people will generally expect that the value of the pound in the foreign exchange market must fall. In this situation, the exchange rate is expected to fall. The demand for pounds decreases, and the supply of pounds increases. The exchange rate falls, as expected. If the exchange rate falls to $1.00 per pound and there are no further price changes, purchasing power parity is restored. A pair of jeans that costs £30 in London also costs the equivalent of £30 ($30) in New York.

If prices rise in the US and other countries but remain constant in the UK, then people will expect the pound to appreciate. The demand for pounds increases, and the supply of pounds decreases. The exchange rate rises, as expected.

So far we've been looking at the forces that determine the *nominal* exchange rate – the amount of one money that another money buys. We're now going to study the *real* exchange rate.

The Real Exchange Rate

The **real exchange rate** is the relative price of UK-produced goods and services to foreign-produced goods and services. It is a measure of the quantity of the real GDP of other countries that a unit of UK real GDP buys.

The real US dollar exchange rate, RER, is

$$RER = (E \times P)/P^*$$

where E is the exchange rate ($ per £), P is the UK price level, and P^* is the US price level.

To understand the real exchange rate, suppose that each country produces only one good and that the exchange rate E is $1.50 per pound. The UK produces only bagpipes priced at £300 each, so P equals £300 and $E \times P$ equals $450. The US produces only Stetson hats priced at $100, so P^* equals $100. Then the real pound exchange rate is

$$RER = (1.5 \times 300)/100 = 4.5 \text{ Stetson hats per bagpipe}$$

The Short Run

In the short run, if the nominal exchange rate changes, the real exchange rate also changes. The reason is that prices and the price levels in the UK and US don't change every time the exchange rate changes. Sticking with the bagpipes and Stetson hats example, if the pound appreciates to $2.00 per pound and prices don't change, the real exchange rate rises to 6 Stetson hats per bagpipe. The price of a Stetson hat in the UK falls to £50 ($100 ÷ $2.00 per pound = £50).

Changes in the real exchange rate bring short-run changes in the quantity of imports demanded and the quantity of exports supplied.

The Long Run

In the long run, the situation is radically different: the nominal exchange rate and the price level are determined together and the real exchange rate does not change when the nominal exchange rate changes.

In the long run, demand and supply in the markets for goods and services determine prices. In the bagpipes and Stetson hats example, the world markets for bagpipes (they make them in Pakistan, India and Canada as well!) and Stetson hats determine their relative price. In our example the relative price is 4.5 hats per bagpipe. The same forces determine all relative prices and so determine nations' relative price levels. The quantity of money determines the price level and the exchange rate.

The Quantity Theory of Money Again

In the long run, if the pound appreciates prices do change. To see why, recall the quantity theory of money that you met in Chapter 24 (pp. 574–575).

In the long run, the quantity of money determines the price level. But the quantity theory of money applies to all countries, so the US quantity of money determines the US price level and the UK quantity of money determines the UK price level.

For a given real exchange rate, a change in the quantity of money brings a change in the price level *and* a change in the exchange rate.

Suppose that the quantity of money in the US doubles. The pound appreciates (the dollar depreciates) from $1.50 per pound to $3.00 per pound and all US prices double, so the price of a Stetson hat rises from $100 to $200. At the new US price and the new exchange rate, a Stetson hat in the UK still costs £66.67 ($200 ÷ $3.00 per pound or £66.67); and the real exchange rate remains at 4.5 Stetson hats per bagpipe.

If the US and the UK produced identical goods (if GDP in both countries consisted only of bagpipes), the real exchange rate in the long run would equal 1.

In reality, although there is overlap in what each country produces, UK real GDP is a different bundle of goods and services from US real GDP. So the relative price of US and UK real GDP – the real exchange rate – is not 1, and it changes over time.

The forces of demand and supply in the markets for the millions of goods and services that make up real GDP determine the relative price of US and UK real GDP, and changes in these forces change the real exchange rate.

Review Quiz

1 Why does the demand for pounds change?
2 Why does the supply of pounds change?
3 What makes the pound exchange rate change?
4 What is interest parity and what happens when this condition does not hold?
5 What is purchasing power parity and what happens when this condition does not hold?
6 What determines the real exchange rate and the nominal exchange rate in the short run?
7 What determines the real exchange rate and the nominal exchange rate in the long run?

You can work these questions in Study Plan 25.2 and get instant feedback.

Exchange Rate Policy

Because the exchange rate is the price of a country's money in terms of another country's money, governments and central banks must have a policy towards the exchange rate. Three possible exchange rate policies are:

◆ Flexible exchange rate
◆ Fixed exchange rate
◆ Crawling peg

Flexible Exchange Rate

A **flexible exchange rate** is an exchange rate that is determined by demand and supply in the foreign exchange market with no direct intervention by the central bank.

Today, most countries, including the UK, operate a flexible exchange rate, and the foreign exchange market that we have studied so far in this chapter is an example of a flexible exchange rate regime.

But even a flexible exchange rate is influenced by central bank actions. If the Bank of England raises the UK interest rate and other countries keep their interest rates unchanged, the demand for pounds increases, the supply of pounds decreases, and the exchange rate rises. (Similarly, if the Bank of England lowers the UK interest rate, the demand for pounds decreases, the supply increases, and the exchange rate falls.)

In a flexible exchange rate regime, when the central bank changes the interest rate, its purpose is not usually to influence the exchange rate, but to achieve some other monetary policy objective. (We return to this topic at length in Chapter 31.)

Fixed Exchange Rate

A **fixed exchange rate** is an exchange rate that is determined by a decision of the government or the central bank and is achieved by central bank intervention in the foreign exchange market to block the unregulated forces of demand and supply.

The world economy operated a fixed exchange rate regime from the end of World War II to the early 1970s. China had a fixed exchange rate until recently. Hong Kong has had a fixed exchange rate for many years and continues with that policy today.

Active intervention in the foreign exchange market is required to achieve a fixed exchange rate. If the Bank of England wanted to fix the pound sterling exchange rate

against the US dollar, the Bank of England would have to sell pounds to prevent the exchange rate from rising above the target value and buy pounds to prevent the exchange rate from falling below the target value.

There is no limit to the quantity of pounds that the Bank of England can *sell*. The Bank of England creates pounds and can create any quantity it chooses. But there is a limit to the quantity of pounds the Bank of England can *buy*. That limit is set by the foreign currency reserves held at the Bank of England because to buy pounds the Bank of England must sell foreign currency. Intervention to buy pounds stops when the foreign currency reserves run out.

Let's look at the foreign exchange interventions that the Bank of England can make.

Suppose the Bank of England wants the exchange rate to be steady at $1.50. If the exchange rate rises above $1.50, the Bank of England sells pounds. If the exchange rate falls below $1.50, the Bank of England buys pounds. By these actions, the Bank of England keeps the exchange rate close to its target rate of $1.50 per pound.

Figure 25.6 shows the Bank of England's intervention in the foreign exchange market. The supply of pounds is S and initially the demand for pounds is D_0. The equilibrium exchange rate is $1.50 per pound. This exchange rate is also the Bank of England's target exchange rate, shown by the horizontal red line.

When the demand for pounds increases and the demand curve shifts rightward to D_1, the Bank of England sells £10 billion. This action prevents the exchange rate from rising. When the demand for pounds decreases and the demand curve shifts leftward to D_2, the Bank of England buys £10 billion. This action prevents the exchange rate from falling.

If the demand for pounds fluctuates between D_1 and D_2 and on average is D_0, the Bank of England can repeatedly intervene in the way we've just seen. Sometimes the Bank of England buys and sometimes it sells but, on average, it neither buys nor sells.

But suppose the demand for the pound *increases permanently* from D_0 to D_1. To maintain the exchange rate at $1.50, the Bank of England must sell pounds and buy dollars, so foreign currency reserves would be increasing. At some point, the Bank of England would abandon the exchange rate of $1.50 per pound and stop piling up foreign currency reserves.

Now suppose the demand for pounds *decreases permanently* from D_0 to D_2. In this situation, the Bank of England cannot maintain the exchange rate at $1.50 per pound indefinitely. To hold the exchange rate at $1.50,

Figure 25.6 Foreign Exchange Market
Intervention

Initially, the demand for pounds is D_0, the supply of
pounds is S, and the exchange rate is $1.50 per pound.
The Bank of England can intervene in the foreign
exchange market to keep the exchange rate close to
target ($1.50 per pound in this example). If the demand
for pounds increases and the demand curve shifts to D_1,
the Bank sells pounds. If the demand for pounds
decreases and the demand curve shifts to D_2, the Bank
buys pounds. Persistent intervention on one side of the
market cannot be sustained.

 Animation

the Bank of England must buy pounds. When the Bank
of England buys pounds in the foreign exchange market,
it uses its foreign currency reserves. So the Bank of
England's action decreases its foreign currency reserves.
Eventually, the Bank of England would run out of foreign currency and would then have to abandon the target
exchange rate of $1.50.

Crawling Peg

A **crawling peg** is an exchange rate that follows a path
determined by a decision of the government or the central bank and is achieved in a similar way to a fixed
exchange rate by central bank intervention in the foreign
exchange market. A crawling peg works like a fixed
exchange rate except that the target value might change
at fixed intervals or at random intervals. The peg seeks
only to prevent large swings in the expected future

exchange rate that change demand and supply and make
the exchange rate fluctuate too wildly.

A crawling peg departs from the ideal if, as often
happens with a fixed exchange rate, the target rate
departs from the equilibrium exchange rate for too long.
When this happens, the country either runs out of
reserves or piles up reserves.

Review Quiz

1   What is a flexible exchange rate and how does
    it work?
2   What is a fixed exchange rate and how is its
    value fixed?
3   What is a crawling peg and how does it work?

You can work these questions in Study
Plan 25.3 and get instant feedback.

European Monetary Union

The European Monetary Union (EMU), formed on 1 January 1999, now consists of 17 member states of the EU that use the euro as their national currency. The UK is the only major member state to have remained outside the euro area. What is the UK missing and what is it gaining? Let's review the benefits and costs of the euro.

The Benefits of the Euro

A single currency in Europe has three benefits. It:

◆ Improves transparency and competition
◆ Decreases transactions costs
◆ Eliminates foreign exchange risk

Improves Transparency and Competition

A single currency provides a single unit of account so that prices are easily compared across the entire Euro-zone. A country might gain a competitive advantage by becoming more efficient, but it cannot gain an advantage by artificially lowering the prices of its exports through a depreciation of its currency.

Decreases Transactions Costs

A single currency eliminates foreign exchange trans-actions costs – the costs of exchanging pesetas for francs at a bank or travel agent, such as commission charges or the margin between the buy and sell exchange rates we see posted in banks and currency exchanges. The removal of these costs benefits the consumer, who knows that a euro in France buys the same as a euro in Germany.

The total benefit from eliminating the transactions costs of currency exchange has been estimated at 0.3 to 0.4 per cent of EU GDP a year. For a country with an advanced banking system as in the UK, the EU Commission estimates that the benefits would be 0.1 per cent of GDP a year.

Eliminates Foreign Exchange Risk

With a single currency, exporters and importers no longer face foreign exchange risk. For example, Alpine Gardens, an Austrian garden company, has ordered a consignment of garden gnomes to be supplied by Britannia Gnomes Ltd, a Gloucester company, in three months' time. The contract and the price are set today, but payment will take place in three months' time.

Alpine Gardens has to pay £50,000 in three months' time. To protect itself against an adverse change in the exchange rate, it buys £50,000 today in the forward market at today's exchange rate.

The reduction in exchange rate risk improves trade between EU countries. Cacharel, the French clothing designer, can source its material from Rome or Paris. On a strict exchange rate comparison, the Italian product is cheaper. But in the pre-euro days, the exchange rate between the French franc and Italian lira fluctuated unpredictably. Cacharel would not have wanted to be tied into a contract with the Italian supplier if the price in francs fluctuated with the exchange rate. Cacharel would have sourced the material from the more expensive French supplier because the price was guaranteed, but Cacharel had to charge its customers a higher price. Now, with the euro, a single currency eliminates this exchange rate risk. Cacharel can source its material from Rome, pay a lower price and pass the benefits of the lower price on to its customers. The lower price increases the quantity demanded of Cacharel clothing, which in turn increases the orders from Rome.

The removal of exchange risk means that many large companies are able to reduce their administration and financial management costs. They also no longer need to diversify their operations across borders and can consolidate them in one location.

If the euro had only benefits, a nation's choice would be simple, but the euro has costs too.

The Economic Costs of the Euro

A single currency in Europe has two costs:

◆ Loss of sovereignty
◆ Inability to respond to national shocks

Loss of Sovereignty

The pursuit of national economic goals requires policy instruments under the control of a national government. The EMU places all the instruments of monetary policy beyond the reach of national governments and a Stability and Growth Pact places strict limits on the use of fiscal policy and regional policy.

Common regional policy enables transfers to be made from Germany and France to Italy and Spain. But a political consensus must be found to sustain such transfers. In effect, a single currency implies a political union. A loss of monetary sovereignty implies a loss of political sovereignty.

Inability to Respond to National Shocks

Many, perhaps most, economic shocks that call for a monetary policy response are country-specific shocks or shocks that affect different countries in different ways.

For example, the dismantling of the Berlin Wall had a major impact on the German economy but barely any effect on the economies of Ireland and Portugal. Also, the shock had different effects on the two parts of Germany. East German workers were less productive and earned lower wage rates than their West German counterparts. Productivity and earnings differences induced a massive reallocation and relocation of jobs and people. A common monetary policy might stimulate the economy in the East and bring inflation to the West or keep inflation in check in the West and bring prolonged recession in the East.

An oil price increase is an example of a common shock that has different effects on different economies. In Germany, an oil importer, the price rise imparts a negative aggregate supply shock and creates a current account deficit. In the UK, an oil exporter, the price rise imparts a positive supply shock and creates a current account surplus. A common monetary policy might stimulate economic activity in Germany and bring inflation to the UK or hold inflation in check in the UK and bring stagnation in Germany.

A common monetary policy is inadequate to deal with the results of country-specific shocks.

The Optimum Currency Area

When there are benefits and costs, they must be weighed against each other and an optimum outcome found. Imagine a world in which the Welsh leek and Scottish thistle exchange for each other and for the English pound at exchange rates that fluctuate every day. The UK is almost certainly better off using one currency rather than three. Is Europe better off using the euro than 17 national currencies? And why stop at Europe! Would the world be better off with one currency rather than its 200-plus currencies?

To answer these questions, we need the concept of an **optimal currency area**, a geographical area that is better served by a single currency than by several currencies. Robert Mundell, an economics professor at Columbia University in New York City, won the Nobel Prize in 1999 for his work on this topic. Mundell claimed that the key factor required for an optimal currency area is free labour mobility either across regions or between jobs.

On this criterion, Scotland, Wales and England are better off with a single currency than they would be with an English pound, a 'Welsh leek' and a 'Scottish thistle'. No cultural or language barriers hamper the movement of labour. If a factory closes down in Merseyside and another opens in Clwyd, workers from Merseyside can travel to Wales to seek employment.

Lack of regional mobility is not a problem if there is mobility between jobs. For example, if Volkswagen closes a Polo production plant in Pamplona, Spain, and opens a new plant in Wolfsburg, Germany, we would not expect former Spanish car workers to migrate to Germany – although by current EU labour laws there is nothing stopping them from doing just that. If jobless car workers in Pamplona can easily retrain and find a new job in Spain, the absence of regional labour mobility doesn't weaken the case for a single currency.

A second criterion for an optimal currency area is that regions within the area face common economic shocks. It is claimed by some economists that economies with similar industrial structures and extensive trade with each other satisfy this criterion. And it is further claimed that the Eurozone countries have sufficiently similar industrial structures and sufficiently extensive trade links to meet this criterion.

Unlike the country-specific shocks that we've just considered, common shocks can be dealt with by a common monetary policy run by a common central bank. For example, if a rise in the price of oil affected all the countries in a monetary union in the same way, the central bank could react in a way that is appropriate for all the countries in the union.

Even if a country does not share a similar industrial structure and have extensive trade links with its neighbours, some argue that a single currency area will bring convergence to a common industrial structure and stimulate trade flows. For example, each major Canadian city is closer to a major US city than to other Canadian cities. But there is significantly more trade among Canadian cities (using one currency) than between the closer Canadian and US cities (using two currencies).

Review Quiz

1 What is the EMU?
2 What are the benefits of a single currency for Europe?
3 What are the costs of a single currency for Europe?
4 What is an optimal currency area?

You can work these questions in Study Plan 25.4 and get instant feedback.

Financing International Trade

You now know how the exchange rate is determined, but what is the effect of the exchange rate? How does currency depreciation or currency appreciation influence our international trade and payments? We're going to lay the foundation for addressing these questions by looking at the scale of international trading, borrowing, and lending and at the way in which we keep our records of international transactions. These records are called the *balance of payments accounts*.

Balance of Payments Accounts

A country's **balance of payments accounts** record its international trading and its borrowing and lending. There are three balance of payments accounts:

◆ Current account
◆ Capital and financial account
◆ Change in reserve assets

Current Account

The **current account** records the receipts from the sale of goods and services to foreigners, the payments for goods and services bought from foreigners, income and other transfers (such as foreign aid payments) received from and paid to foreigners. The large items in the current account are the receipts from the sale of goods and services to foreigners (exports) and the payments made for goods and services bought from foreigners (imports). Net income is the earnings from foreign financial assets such as bonds and shares, and net earnings of UK workers abroad and foreign workers in the UK. Net transfers – gifts to foreigners minus gifts from foreigners – are relatively small items.

Capital and Financial Account

The **capital and financial account** records all UK investments abroad and foreigners' investments in the UK. This account balance equals the amount that a country borrows from the rest of the world minus the amount that it lends to it.

Change in Reserve Assets

The **change in reserve assets** shows the net increase or decrease in a country's holdings of foreign currency reserves that comes about from the official financing of the difference between the current account and the capital and financial account balances. In practice, the change in reserve assets is an item in the capital account. It is itemized separately here so that you can see how the financing of the gap between the current account and the capital and financial account adds to or subtracts from reserve assets.

The Data in 2010

Table 25.1 shows the UK balance of payments accounts in 2010. Items in the current and capital and financial accounts with a positive sign provide the UK with foreign currency and items that have a minus sign cost the UK foreign currency. The table shows that UK imports of goods and services exceeded UK exports of goods and services in 2010 and that the current account balance was –£32 billion. How do we pay for our current account deficit? We pay by borrowing from abroad. The capital and financial account tells us by how much. We borrowed £525 billion but made loans of £513 billion, so our net foreign borrowing was £12 billion.

Some capital and current account transactions do not get recorded. These transactions include unidentified capital flows and illegal international trade such as that in illegal drugs and smuggling to evade tariffs or taxes.

Table 25.1	
UK Balance of Payments Accounts in 2010	
	(billions of pounds)
Current account	
Exports of goods and services	+423
Imports of goods and services	−467
Net income	+29
Net transfers	−17
Current account balance	−32
Capital and financial account	
Foreign investment in the UK	+525
UK investment abroad	−513
Capital and financial account balance	12
Balancing item	14
Change in reserve assets	
Increase(+)/Decrease(−) in the UK's official foreign currency reserves	+6

Source of data: Office for National Statistics, *UK Balance of Payments: The Pink Book*, 2010. Based on first three quarters of 2010.

ECONOMICS IN ACTION

Persistent Current Account Deficits

Figure 1 The UK Balance of Payments

Source of data: Office for National Statistics.

The numbers in Table 25.1 give a snapshot of the balance of payments accounts in 2010. The figure here puts that snapshot into a longer perspective by showing the balances over the period 1990 to 2010.

The UK has had a current account deficit every year. In 1997, the current account deficit got close to zero but not quite.

The capital and financial account balance is almost a mirror image of the current account deficit.

We call the net total of all these items the balancing item, which in 2010 was £14 billion.

Net borrowing from abroad minus the current account deficit is the balance that is financed from official UK reserves – the government's holdings of foreign currency. In 2010, those reserves changed by £6 billion.

The sum of the balances on the three balance of payments accounts equals zero.

To see more clearly what the nation's balance of payments accounts mean, think about your own balance of payments accounts. They are similar to the nation's accounts.

Individual Balance of Payments Accounts

An individual's current account records the income from supplying the services of factors of production and the expenditure on goods and services. Consider, for example, Joanne. She earned an income in 2010 of £25,000. Joanne has £10,000 worth of investments that earned her an income of £1,000. Joanne's current account shows an income of £26,000. Joanne spent £18,000 buying goods and services for consumption.

She also bought a new studio apartment, which cost her £60,000. So Joanne's total expenditure was £78,000. The difference between her expenditure and income is £52,000 (£78,000 minus £26,000). This amount is Joanne's current account deficit.

To pay for expenditure of £52,000 in excess of her income, Joanne has either to use the money that she has in the bank or to take out a loan. In fact Joanne took a mortgage of £50,000 to help buy her house. This mortgage was the only borrowing that Joanne did, so her capital account surplus was £50,000. With a current account deficit of £52,000 and a capital account surplus of £50,000, Joanne was still £2,000 short. She got that £2,000 from her own bank account. Her cash holdings decreased by £2,000.

Joanne's income from her work and investments is analogous to a country's income from its exports. Her purchases of goods and services, including her purchase of a house, are analogous to a country's imports. Joanne's mortgage – borrowing from someone else – is analogous to a country's foreign borrowing. The change in her bank account is analogous to the change in the country's reserve assets.

Borrowers and Lenders, Debtors and Creditors

A country that is borrowing more from the rest of the world than it is lending to it is called a **net borrower**. Similarly, a **net lender** is a country that is lending more to the rest of the world than it is borrowing from it. A net borrower might be going deeper into debt or might simply be reducing its net assets held in the rest of the world. The total stock of foreign investment determines whether a country is a debtor or a creditor.

A **debtor nation** is a country that during its entire history has borrowed more from the rest of the world than it has lent to it. It has a stock of outstanding debt to the rest of the world that exceeds the stock of its own claims on the rest of the world. The UK is currently a debtor nation, but for a long time it was a creditor. A **creditor nation** is a country that has invested more in the rest of the world than other countries have invested in it. The largest creditor nation today is Japan.

Flows and Stocks

At the heart of the distinction between a net borrower and a debtor nation or a net lender and a creditor nation is the distinction between flows and stocks, which you have encountered many times in your study of macroeconomics.

Borrowing and lending are *flows* – amounts borrowed or lent per unit of time. Debts are *stocks* – amounts owed at a point in time. The flow of borrowing and lending changes the stock of debt. But the outstanding stock of debt depends mainly on past flows of borrowing and lending, not on the current period's flows. The current period's flows determine the change in the stock of debt outstanding.

During the 1960s and the 1970s, the UK current account periodically swung from surplus to deficit. When the current account was a surplus, the capital account was a deficit. On the whole the UK was a net lender to the rest of the world. It was not until the late 1980s that it became a significant net borrower.

The UK today is a small net debtor. But there are many countries that are debtor nations. The US is one. But the largest debtor nations are the capital-hungry developing countries. The international debt of these countries grew from less than one-third to more than one-half of their gross domestic product during the 1980s and created what was called the 'Third World debt crisis'.

Is Borrowing and Debt a Problem?

Does it matter if a country is a net borrower rather than a net lender? The answer to this question depends mainly on what the net borrower is doing with the borrowed money. If borrowed money is used to finance investment that in turn is generating economic growth and higher income, borrowing is not a problem. If the borrowed money is being used to finance consumption, then higher interest payments are being incurred and, as a consequence, consumption will eventually have to be reduced. In this case, the more the borrowing and the longer it goes on, the greater is the reduction in consumption that will eventually be necessary.

Current Account Balance

What determines the current account balance and the scale of a country's net foreign borrowing or lending? You've seen in Table 25.1 that the current account balance equals net exports plus two small items, net interest and net transfers. So net exports drives the current account balance. But what determines net exports?

To answer this question, we need to use the national income accounts. Table 25.2 will refresh your memory and summarize the necessary calculations for you. Part (a) lists the national income variables that are needed, with their symbols. Their values in the UK in 2010 are also shown.

Part (b) presents two key national income equations. First, equation (1) reminds us that GDP, Y, equals aggregate expenditure, which is the sum of consumption expenditure, C, investment, I, government expenditure on goods and services, G, and net exports (exports, X, minus imports, M). Equation (2) reminds us that aggregate income is used in three different ways. It can be consumed, saved or paid to the government in net taxes (taxes net of transfer payments). Equation (1) tells us how our expenditure generates our income. Equation (2) tells us how we dispose of that income.

Part (c) of the table looks at three balances – net exports, the government budget and the private sector. To get these balances, first subtract equation (2) from equation (1) in Table 25.2. The result is equation (3). By rearranging equation (3), we obtain a relationship for net exports that appears as equation (4) in the table.

Net exports, in equation (4), is made up of two components. The first is net taxes minus government expenditure and the second is saving minus investment. These items are the balances of the government and private

Table 25.2

Sector Balances in 2010

	Symbols and equations	Billions of pounds
(a) Variables		
Gross domestic product (GDP)	Y	1,448
Consumption expenditure	C	948
Investment	I	208
Government expenditure on goods and services	G	338
Exports	X	424
Imports	M	470
Saving	S	306
Net taxes	T	194
(b) Domestic Income and Expenditure		
Aggregate expenditure	(1) $Y = C + I + G + X - M$	
Uses of income	(2) $Y = C + S + T$	
(1) minus (2)	(3) $0 = I - S + G - T + X - M$	
(c) Surpluses and Deficits		
Net exports	(4) $X - M = (T - G) + (S - I)$	
	$= -144 + 98 = -46$	
Government budget	(5) $T - G = 194 - 338 = -144$	
Private sector	(6) $S - I = 306 - 208 = 98$	
(d) Financing Investment		
Investment is financed by the sum of:		
Private saving,	$S = 306$	
Net government saving and	$T - G = -144$	
Net foreign saving	$M - X = 46$	
That is:	(7) $I = S + (T - G) + (M - X)$	
	$= 208$	

Source of data: Office for National Statistics: Data are based on the first three quarters of 2010.

sectors. Net taxes minus government expenditure on goods and services is the *government's budget balance*. If that number is positive, the government's budget is a surplus and if the number is negative, it is a deficit.

The *private sector balance* is saving minus investment. If saving exceeds investment, the private sector has a surplus to lend to other sectors. If investment exceeds saving, the private sector has a deficit that has to be financed by borrowing from other sectors. As you can see from our calculations, the current account deficit

is equal to the sum of the government's budget deficit and the private sector surplus. In the UK in 2010, the private sector had a balance of £98 billion and the government sector had a balance of –£144 billion. The government sector balance plus the private sector balance equals net exports of –£46 billion.

Part (d) of Table 25.2 shows how investment is financed. To increase investment, either private saving or the government surplus must increase, or net exports must decrease.

Where Is the Exchange Rate?

We haven't mentioned the exchange rate while discussing the balance of payments. Doesn't it play a role? The answer is that in the short run it does but in the long run it doesn't.

In the short run, a fall in the pound lowers the real exchange rate, which makes imports into the UK more costly and UK exports more competitive. A higher price of imported consumption goods and services might induce a decrease in consumption expenditure and an increase in saving. A higher price of imported capital goods might induce a decrease in investment. Other things remaining the same, an increase in saving or a decrease in investment decreases the private sector deficit and decreases the current account deficit.

But in the long run, a change in the nominal exchange rate leaves the real exchange rate unchanged and plays no role in influencing the current account balance.

Review Quiz

1   What are the transactions that we record in the balance of payments accounts?
2   Is the UK a net borrower or a net lender? Is it a debtor nation or a creditor nation?
3   How are the current account balance, the government sector balance and the private sector balance related?

You can work these questions in Study Plan 25.5 and get instant feedback.

You have now completed your study of the foreign exchange market and the determination of the exchange rate and the balance of payments. You can round out this chapter in *Reading Between the Lines* on pp. 604–605, which looks at what Chile is doing in the foreign exchange market to try to boost its exports.

Reading Between the Lines

Intervention in the Foreign Exchange Market

The Financial Times, 4 January 2011

Chile Joins Currency War to Help Exporters

Daniel Schweimler

Chile is set to become the latest country to join the 'global currency wars' on Tuesday after the central bank said it would spend up to $12bn this year to curb the peso's strength and so help exporters from one of Latin America's most open and best managed economies.

The move, announced late on Monday after the peso rose to nearly a three-year high against the dollar, took markets by surprise as Chile's central bank is known for its hands-off approach to its free-floating exchange rate.

The peso weakened by about 4 per cent on Tuesday as the news sunk in that the central bank would spend $50m a day from today selling pesos. Equivalent, in total, to 6 per cent of gross domestic product, the programme is the biggest intervention in Chile's history and only its fourth since 1999.

Felipe Larrain, Chile's finance minister, said: 'We are supporting domestic producers, our exporters, in the farm as well as industrial sectors who depend on exchange rates. We think it is a well targeted step that is going to have an effect on the exchange rate.'

Mexico is now the only big Latin American economy not seeking to weaken its currency via intervention, or by putting in place controls on capital inflows such as Brazil's 6 per cent tax on bond inflows. . . .

Some analysts fear that the surprise move by Chile could open the way for further unorthodox policies in other emerging markets.

Chile is expected to grow 6 per cent this year, boosted by exports of copper, which hit a record high of $9,754 a tonne on Tuesday, . . .

The Essence of the Story

◆ The Chilean peso has appreciated and is now at a three-year high against the US dollar.

◆ Worried that an appreciating peso would hurt exports of other goods and services, Chile's central bank is selling pesos and buying US dollars at the rate of $50 million a day.

◆ The Chilean central bank says it will spend up to $12 billion in selling pesos (6 per cent of Chile's GDP) in trying to stop the peso from appreciating.

◆ Other Latin American central banks are also intervening in the foreign exchange market to slow the appreciation of their currencies.

Economic Analysis

◆ Copper is one of Chile's main exports and an increase in the global demand for copper has increased the demand for Chilean pesos and increased Chile's *real* exchange rate.

◆ The central bank of Chile is manipulating the *nominal* exchange rate, but it can't manipulate the real exchange rate in the long run.

◆ Figure 1 shows the steady appreciation[1] of the peso that worries the Chilean central bank. It shows the depreciation on 4 January 2011 when the central bank announced it would spend $50 million per day to stop the appreciation.

◆ Figure 2 shows the market for the peso. In mid-December 2010, the demand curve for pesos was D_0 and the supply curve of pesos was S_0. The exchange rate was $2.11 per 1,000 peso (or 474 pesos per dollar).

◆ The increase in copper exports increased the demand for pesos and the demand curve shifted rightward from D_0 to D_1. The peso appreciated to $2.15 per 1,000 pesos (465 pesos per dollar).

◆ To stop the peso from appreciating too much, the central bank of Chile sells pesos and buys $50 million per day. This action increases the supply of pesos on the foreign exchange market from S_0 to S_1 and lowers the exchange rate to $2.04 per 1,000 pesos (490 pesos per dollar).

◆ The effect of this intervention will be temporary. Chile has a large current account surplus that brings a sustained high demand for pesos in the foreign exchange market. Figure 3 shows this surplus in 2010, which totalled $15 billion.

◆ The cental bank's foreign exchange market intervention will eventually increase the quantity of money in Chile, which will increase the price level and the real exchange rate.

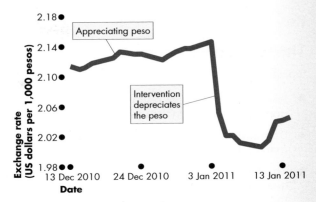

Figure 1 The Chilean peso exchange rate

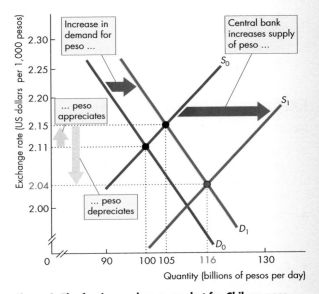

Figure 2 The foreign exchange market for Chilean peso

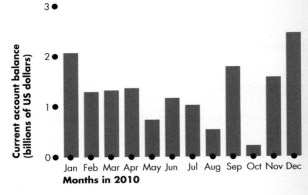

Figure 3 Chile's current account balance in 2010

---

[1] We express the price of the peso as US dollars per 1,000 pesos. For example, if 500 pesos buys US$1, the price of 1,000 pesos is $2.00.

◆ SUMMARY

Key Points

The Foreign Exchange Market
(pp. 586–590)

- Foreign currency is obtained in exchange for domestic currency in the foreign exchange market.

- Demand and supply in the foreign exchange market determine the exchange rate.

- The higher the exchange rate, the smaller is the quantity of pounds demanded and the greater is the quantity of pounds supplied.

- The equilibrium exchange rate makes the quantity of pounds demanded equal the quantity of pounds supplied.

Working Problems 1 to 6 will give you a better understanding of the foreign exchange market.

Exchange Rate Fluctuations
(pp. 591–595)

- Changes in the world demand for UK exports, the UK interest rate differential, and the expected future exchange rate change the demand for pounds.

- Changes in UK demand for imports, the UK interest rate differential, and the expected future exchange rate change the supply of pounds.

- Exchange rate expectations are influenced by purchasing power parity and interest rate parity.

- In the long run, the nominal exchange rate is a monetary phenomenon and the real exchange rate is independent of the nominal exchange rate.

Working Problems 7 to 15 will give you a better understanding of exchange rate fluctuations.

Exchange Rate Policy (pp. 596–597)

- An exchange rate can be flexible, fixed or on a crawling peg.

- To achieve a fixed or crawling exchange rate, a central bank must intervene in the foreign exchange market and either buy or sell foreign currency.

Working Problems 16 and 17 will give you a better understanding of exchange rate policy.

European Monetary Union (pp. 598–599)

- The EMU is a group of 17 EU member states that use the euro as their national currency.

- The benefits of a single currency are improved transparency and competition, lower transactions costs and the elimination of exchange risk.

- The costs of a single currency are the loss of the ability to respond to a national economic shock and the loss of sovereignty.

- An optimal currency area is one for which the benefits outweigh the costs.

Working Problems 18 and 19 will give you a better understanding of the European Monetary Union.

Financing International Trade
(pp. 600–603)

- International trade, borrowing and lending are financed using foreign currency.

- A country's balance of payments accounts record its international transactions.

- The current account balance is similar to net exports and is determined by the government sector balance and the private sector balance.

Working Problems 20 and 21 will give you a better understanding of financing international trade.

Key Terms

Balance of payments accounts, 600
Capital and financial account, 600
Change in reserve assets, 600
Crawling peg, 597
Creditor nation, 602
Current account, 600
Debtor nation, 602
Exchange rate, 586
Fixed exchange rate, 596
Flexible exchange rate, 596
Foreign currency, 586
Foreign exchange market, 586
Interest rate parity, 594
Net borrower, 602
Net lender, 602
Optimal currency area, 599
Purchasing power parity, 594
Real exchange rate, 595
UK interest rate differential, 591

STUDY PLAN PROBLEMS AND APPLICATIONS

 You can work Problems 1 to 21 in MyEconLab Chapter 25 Study Plan and get instant feedback.

The Foreign Exchange Market

(Study Plan 25.1)

Use the following data to work Problems 1 to 3.

The US dollar exchange rate decreased from 83.8 euro cents in January 2009 to 76.9 euro cents in January 2010, and it increased from $0.89 Canadian in June 2009 to $0.96 Canadian in June 2010.

1 Did the US dollar appreciate or depreciate against the euro? Did the US dollar appreciate or depreciate against the Canadian dollar?

2 What was the value of the Canadian dollar in terms of US dollars in June 2009 and June 2010? Did the Canadian dollar appreciate or depreciate against the US dollar over the year June 2009 to June 2010?

3 What was the value of one euro (100 euro cents) in terms of US dollars in January 2009 and January 2010? Did the euro appreciate or depreciate against the US dollar in 2009?

Use the following data to work Problems 4 to 6.

In January 2010, the exchange rate was 91 yen per US dollar. By September 2010, the exchange rate had fallen to 84 yen per US dollar.

4 Explain the exports effect of this change in the exchange rate.

5 Explain the imports effect of this change in the exchange rate.

6 Explain the expected profit effect of this change in the exchange rate.

Exchange Rate Fluctuations

(Study Plan 25.2)

7 On 3 August 2010, the US dollar was trading at 86 yen per US dollar on the foreign exchange market. On 13 September 2010, the US dollar was trading at 83 yen per US dollar.

  a What events in the foreign exchange market might have brought this fall in the value of the US dollar?

  b Did the events change the demand for US dollars, the supply of US dollars, or both demand and supply in the foreign exchange market?

8 Colombia is the world's biggest producer of roses. The global demand for roses increases and at the same time, the central bank in Colombia increases the interest rate. In the foreign exchange market for Columbian pesos, what happens to:

  a The demand for pesos?

  b The supply of pesos?

  c The quantity of pesos demanded?

  d The quantity of pesos supplied?

  e The exchange rate of the peso against the US dollar?

9 If a euro deposit in a bank in Paris, France, earns interest of 4 per cent a year and a yen deposit in Tokyo, Japan, earns 0.5 per cent a year, other things remaining the same and adjusted for risk, what is the exchange rate expectation of the Japanese yen?

10 The UK pound is trading at 1.54 US dollars per UK pound. There is purchasing power parity at this exchange rate. The interest rate in the US is 2 per cent a year and the interest rate in the UK is 4 per cent a year.

  a Calculate the UK interest rate differential.

  b What is the UK pound expected to be worth in terms of US dollars one year from now?

  c Which country more likely has the lower inflation rate? How can you tell?

11 Suppose that you can purchase a particular laptop from an online computer store for 827.12 euros or 477.25 pounds. The exchange rate is 1.4831 euros per pound. Does purchasing power parity prevail?

12 **When the Chips Are Down**

The *Economist* uses the price of a Big Mac to determine whether a currency is undervalued or overvalued. In July 2010, the price of a Big Mac was $3.73 in New York, 13.2 yuan in Beijing, and 6.50 Swiss francs in Geneva. The exchange rates were 6.78 yuan per US dollar and 1.05 Swiss francs per US dollar.

Source: *The Economist*, 22 July 2010

  a Was the yuan undervalued or overvalued relative to purchasing power parity?

  b Was the Swiss franc undervalued or overvalued relative to purchasing power parity?

  c Do you think the price of a Big Mac in different countries provides a valid test of purchasing power parity?

13 **The Lesson: Buy Ruffles in Myanmar**

A small bag of cheese-flavoured Ruffles potato chips is $1.69 in Japan and only 8 cents in Myanmar. One hour at an Internet cafe costs $0.62 in Vietnam, $1.48 in China and $3.40 in South Africa .

The Los Angeles Times, 23 April 2006

Do these prices indicate that purchasing power parity does not prevail? Why or why not?

14 The price level in the Eurozone is 112.4, the price level in the US is 109.1, and the nominal exchange rate was 80 euro cents per US dollar. What is the real exchange rate expressed as Eurozone real GDP per unit of US real GDP?

15 The US price level is 106.3, the Japanese price level is 95.4, and the real exchange rate is 103.6 Japanese real GDP per unit of US real GDP. What is the nominal exchange rate?

Exchange Rate Policy (Study Plan 25.3)

16 With the strengthening of the yen against the US dollar in 2010, Japan's central bank did not take any action. A leading Japanese politician has called on the central bank to take actions to weaken the yen, saying it will help exporters in the short run and have no long-run effects.

  a What is Japan's current exchange rate policy?

  b What does the politician want the exchange rate policy to be in the short run? Why would such a policy have no effect on the exchange rate in the long run?

17 **Double-talking the Dollar**

In the 1970s and 1980s, the US was constantly buying and selling foreign currencies to change the value of the dollar, but since 1995 it has made only a few transactions and since 2000 none at all. The foreign exchange market is so huge, trying to manipulate the dollar is largely futile. A currency's value reflects an economy's fundamentals: How well a country allocates resources, how productive its workers are, how it contains inflation, etc., but for years on end, currencies can move in directions that seem to have little to do with fundamentals. They overshoot their correct values, in part because nobody is ever sure exactly what those correct values are.

Source: *Time*, 5 May 2008

  a How has US exchange rate policy evolved since the early 1970s?

  b Explain why 'trying to manipulate the dollar is largely futile', especially in the long run.

  c Explain why a currency can experience short-run fluctuations 'that seem to have little to do with fundamentals'. Illustrate with a graph.

European Monetary Union (Study Plan 25.4)

18 In the coalition accord following the 2010 General Election, the Conservative and Liberal Democrat parties agreed that 'Britain will not join or prepare to join the euro in this parliament'.

What are the costs of membership of the EMU that the UK avoids by retaining the pound sterling as its national currency? What are the benefits of membership that the UK is missing?

19 What are the benefits and costs that would arise if Wales left the pound sterling and established the 'Welsh leek' as its currency? Why might the balance of costs and benefits go against such a move?

Financing International Trade
(Study Plan 25.5)

20 The table gives some information about the UK international transactions in 2006.

Item	Billions of pounds
Imports of goods and services	424
Foreign investment in the UK	680
Exports of goods and services	370
UK investment abroad	656
Net interest income	23
Net transfers	−12

  a Calculate the current account balance.

  b Calculate the capital and financial account balance.

  c Did UK reserves assets increase or decrease?

  d Was the UK a net borrower or a net lender in 2006? Explain your answer.

21 **The US Debtor Nation**

The US is a debtor nation, and for most of the past 30 years it has been piling up large trade deficits. The current account has now reached a deficit of 6 per cent of GDP and must be financed by capital inflows. Foreigners must purchase large amounts of US assets, or the current account deficit cannot be financed.

Source: *Asia Times*, 28 September 2006

  a Explain why a current account deficit 'must be financed by capital inflows'.

  b Under what circumstances should the debtor nation status of the US be a concern?

ADDITIONAL PROBLEMS AND APPLICATIONS

  You can work these problems in MyEconLab if assigned by your lecturer.

The Foreign Exchange Market

22 Suppose that yesterday, the euro was trading on the foreign exchange market at 0.75 euros per US dollar and today the euro is trading at 0.78 euros per US dollar. Which of the two currencies (the euro or the US dollar) appreciated and which depreciated today?

23 Suppose that the exchange rate fell from 1.20 euros per pound to 1.16 euros per pound. What is the effect of this change on the quantity of euros that people plan to buy in the foreign exchange market?

24 Suppose that the exchange rate rose from 71 yen per US dollar to 100 yen per US dollar. What is the effect of this change on the quantity of US dollars that people plan to sell in the foreign exchange market?

25 Today's exchange rate between the yuan and the US dollar is 6.78 yuan per dollar and the central bank of China is buying US dollars in the foreign exchange market. If the central bank of China did not purchase US dollars would there be excess demand or excess supply of US dollars in the foreign exchange market? Would the exchange rate remain at 6.78 yuan per US dollar? If not, which currency would appreciate?

Exchange Rate Fluctuations

26 Yesterday, the current exchange rate was 0.95 US dollars per Canadian dollar and traders expected the exchange rate to remain unchanged for the next month. Today, with new information, traders now expect the exchange rate next month to rise to 1 US dollar per Canadian dollar. Explain how the revised expected future exchange rate influences the demand for Canadian dollars, or the supply of Canadian dollars, or both in the foreign exchange market.

27 On 1 January 2010, the exchange rate was 91 yen per US dollar. Over the year, the supply of US dollars increased and by January 2011, the exchange rate fell to 84 yen per US dollar. What happened to the quantity of US dollars that people planned to buy in the foreign exchange market?

Use the following news clip to work Problems 28 and 29.

Top US Real Estate Markets for Investment

Rahul Reddy has been investing in Australian real estate for the last two years. Now, with the Australian dollar growing in strength and the American housing market strained, he's got his eye on real estate in Florida and California. Encouraged by a weak US dollar and a belief in the resiliency of the US economy, investors are seeking investment properties and development opportunities in the US. Reddy says that the US is good for speculative higher-risk investments from our perspective because the strong Australian dollar will enable us to gain hold of real estate at prices we will probably not see for a long time. The US is an economic powerhouse that will recover, and if the exchange rate goes back to what it was a few years ago, investors will benefit.

Source: *Forbes*, 10 July 2008

28 Explain why foreigners are 'seeking investment properties and development opportunities in the US'.

29 Explain what would happen if the speculation made by Reddy became widespread. Would expectations become self-fulfilling?

Use the following information to work Problems 30 and 31.

Brazil's Overvalued Real

The Brazilian real has appreciated 33 per cent against the US dollar and has pushed up the price of a Big Mac in Sao Paulo to $4.60, higher than the New York price of $3.99. Despite Brazil's interest rate being at 8.75 per cent a year compared to the US interest rate at near zero, foreign funds flowing into Brazil surged in October.

Source: Bloomberg News, 27 October 2009

30 Does purchasing power parity hold? If not, does PPP predict that the Brazilian real will appreciate or depreciate against the US dollar? Explain.

31 Does interest rate parity hold? If not, why not? Will the Brazilian real appreciate further or depreciate against the US dollar if the US central bank raises the interest rate while the Brazilian interest rate remains at 8.75 per cent a year?

Exchange Rate Policy (Study Plan 25.3)

Use the following news clip to work Problems 32 to 35.

US Declines to Cite China as Currency Manipulator

The US has declined to cite China for manipulating its currency to gain unfair trade advantages against the US. America's growing trade deficit with China, which last year hit an all-time high of $256.3 billion, is the largest deficit ever recorded with a single country. Chinese currency, the yuan, has risen in value by 18.4 per cent against the US dollar since the Chinese government loosened its currency system in July 2005. However, US manufacturers contend the yuan is still undervalued by as much as 40 per cent, making Chinese products more competitive in the US and US goods more expensive in China. China buys US dollar-denominated securities to maintain the value of the yuan in terms of the US dollar.

Source: MSN, 15 May 2008

32 What was the exchange rate policy adopted by China until July 2005? Explain how it worked. Draw a graph to illustrate your answer.

33 What was the exchange rate policy adopted by China after July 2005? Explain how it works.

34 Explain how fixed and crawling peg exchange rates can be used to manipulate trade balances in the short run, but not the long run.

35 Explain the long-run effect of China's current exchange rate policy.

36 Aussie Dollar Hit by Interest Rate Talk

The Australian dollar fell against the US dollar to its lowest value in the past two weeks. The CPI inflation rate was reported to be generally as expected but not high enough to justify previous expectations for an aggressive interest rate rise by Australia's central bank next week.

Source: Reuters, 28 October 2009

a What is Australia's exchange rate policy? Explain why expectations about the Australian interest rate lowered the value of the Australian dollar against the US dollar.

b To avoid the fall in the value of the Australian dollar against the US dollar, what action could the central bank of Australia have taken? Would such an action signal a change in Australia's exchange rate policy?

37 Japan's foreign exchange reserves have grown from $0.25 trillion in 2001 to $1.1 trillion in 2010. What has been Japan's exchange rate policy through these years?

European Monetary Union

38 The unemployment rate is much higher in Spain than in Germany. Does this fact mean that Spain would be better off leaving the euro and re-establishing the peseta as its national currency?

39 If the euro is a good idea, why isn't a single currency for the entire global economy an even better idea?

Financing International Trade

Use the following data to work Problems 40 to 42. The table gives some data about the UK economy in 2006.

Item	Billions of pounds
Consumption expenditure	827
Exports of goods and services	370
Government expenditure	288
Net taxes	278
Investment	229
Saving	185

40 Calculate the private sector balance.

41 Calculate the government sector balance.

42 Calculate net exports and show the relationship between the government sector balance and net exports.

Economics in the News

43 After you have studied *Reading Between the Lines* on pp. 604–605 answer the following questions.

a What does the Bank of Chile hope to achieve through its announced intervention in the foreign exchange market?

b What is the reason for the intervention?

c How will the announced intervention influence expectations?

d What will be the effects of the intervention in the short run and the long run?

44 Gulf Countries Must Opt for Basket of Currencies

Before 2008, the six countries of the Gulf Cooperation Council (GCC) had fixed exchange rates against the US dollar. Faced with a surge in inflation, they decided to establish the Gulf Monetary Union and common currency so that they could pursue a monetary policy independent of the US. The new currency would be pegged to a basket of currencies, comprising the US dollar, the Euro, the Japanese yen and the British pound. The exchange rate would be managed to tailor monetary policy to domestic conditions and withstand external shocks.

Source: *The Gulf Daily News*, 18 December 2008

a Explain why the GCC countries lacked independent monetary policy when their currencies were fixed to the US dollar.

b If the GCC countries had pursued an independent monetary policy and held their inflation steady, what would have happened to their exchange rates? Explain and illustrate.

c Why might a new common currency for the GCC countries linked to the US dollar, euro, yen and pound provide better insulation from US monetary policy?

d What would be the benefits arising from Gulf Monetary Union? What would be the costs of monetary union?

Macroeconomic Fluctuations

Boom and Bust

To cure a disease and restore a patient to good health, doctors must first understand how the disease responds to different treatments. It also helps to understand the mechansims that operate to cause the disease.

Curing the economic ills of boom and bust is similar to curing our medical ills. We need to understand how the economy responds to the treatments we might prescribe to restore it to good health. We also need to understand the mechanisms that operate to cause a succession of boom and bust. The goal of the three chapters in this part is to explain what economists understand about these mechanisms.

Chapter 26 studies the *AS–AD* model, a model that explains what determines real GDP and the price level in the short run. The *AS–AD* model also enables us to see the ideas of the different schools of macroeconomic thought on the sources of aggregate fluctuations.

Chapter 27 explains the Keynesian aggregate expenditure model. This model provides the details on fluctuations in aggregate demand.

Chapter 28 looks at all the alternative theories of inflation and the business cycle and the short-run trade-off between output and inflation (and between jobs and inflation).

Understanding Macroeconomic Fluctuations

During the Industrial Revolution, as technological change created new jobs and destroyed old ones, people began to wonder whether the economy could create enough jobs and sufficient demand to buy all the things that the new industrial economy could produce.

'No problem!' said John Baptiste Say. Writing in his 1803 book, *Traité d'économie politique* (*A Treatise on Political Economy*), he argues that production creates incomes that are sufficient to buy everything that is produced. This idea, put simply as 'supply creates its own demand', came to be known as *Say's Law*.

'A big problem!' said John Maynard Keynes. He turned Say's idea around and said it is demand that creates supply. Writing in his 1936 book, *The General Theory of Employment, Interest and Money*, he argued that aggregate production depends on what people are willing to buy. Production, said Keynes, depends on *effective* demand. Households, he noted, don't spend all their incomes on consumption. They save some of it. If businesses fail to spend on new capital (business investment) the amount that people save, aggregate demand will be less than aggregate supply and resources, particularly labour resources, will be unemployed and they could remain in that state indefinitely. According to Keynes, there are no automatic forces to restore full employment.

The aggregate supply–aggregate demand (*AS–AD*) model that you study in Chapter 26 combines the ideas of Say and Keynes. It is a model that translates Keynes' *General Theory* to explain how real GDP fluctuates around full employment. In this model, there is a mechanism that eventually restores full employment but it works slowly when resources are underemployed. At full employment, Say's Law operates and supply does create its own demand.

What you study in the next three chapters lays the foundation for the final part that investigates the role and power of fiscal policy and monetary policy to achieve inflation-free sustained growth of real GDP at full employment.

John Maynard Keynes, born in England in 1883, was one of the outstanding minds of the twentieth century. He represented Britain at the Versailles peace conference at the end of the First World War, was a master speculator on international financial markets (an activity he conducted from bed every morning and which made and lost him several fortunes) and played a prominent role in creating the International Monetary Fund.

He was a member of the Bloomsbury Group, a circle of outstanding artists and writers that included E. M. Forster, Bertrand Russell and Virginia Woolf.

Keynes was a controversial and quick-witted figure. A critic once complained that Keynes had changed his opinion on some matter, to which Keynes retorted: "When I discover I am wrong, I change my mind. What do you do?"

Keynes' book, *The General Theory of Employment, Interest and Money*, written during the Great Depression and published in 1936, revolutionized macroeconomics.

'The ideas of economists and political philosophers, both when they are right and when they are wrong, are more powerful than is commonly understood. Indeed the world is ruled by little else.'

JOHN MAYNARD KEYNES
The General Theory of Employment, Interest and Money

CHAPTER

26

Aggregate Supply and Aggregate Demand

After studying this chapter you will be able to:

◆ Explain what determines aggregate supply

◆ Explain what determines aggregate demand

◆ Explain how real GDP and the price level are determined and what brings economic growth, inflation and the business cycle

◆ Describe the main schools of thought in macroeconomics

The pace at which production grows and prices rise is uneven. Sometimes our economy is expanding and sometimes production and jobs shrink.

This chapter explains a model – the aggregate supply–aggregate demand model or *AS–AD* model – that represents the consensus view of macroeconomists about the forces that make our economy expand, that bring inflation and that cause business cycle fluctuations.

In *Reading Between the Lines* at the end of the chapter, we use the *AS–AD* model to interpret the course of real GDP and the price level in the German economy in 2010.

Aggregate Supply

The purpose of the aggregate supply–aggregate demand model that you study in this chapter is to explain how real GDP and the price level are determined and how they interact. The model uses similar ideas to those that you encountered in Chapter 3 when you learned how the quantity and price in a competitive market are determined. But the *aggregate* supply–*aggregate* demand model (*AS–AD* model) isn't just an application of the competitive market model. Some differences arise because the *AS–AD* model is a model of an imaginary market for the total of all the final goods and services. The quantity in this 'market' is real GDP and the price is the price level measured by the GDP deflator.

One thing that the *AS–AD* model shares with the competitive market model is that both distinguish between *supply* and the *quantity supplied*. We begin by explaining what we mean by the quantity of real GDP supplied.

Quantity Supplied and Supply

The *quantity of real GDP supplied* is the total quantity of goods and services, valued in constant base year (2006) pounds, that firms plan to produce during a given period. This quantity depends on the quantity of labour employed, the quantity of physical and human capital and the state of technology.

At any given time, the quantity of capital and the state of technology are fixed. They depend on decisions that were made in the past. The population is also fixed. But the quantity of labour is not fixed. It depends on decisions made by households and firms about the supply of and demand for labour.

The labour market can be in any one of three states: at full employment, above full employment, or below full employment. At full employment, the quantity of real GDP supplied is *potential GDP*, which depends on the full-employment quantity of labour (see Chapter 22, pp. 513–515). Over the business cycle, employment fluctuates around full employment and the quantity of real GDP supplied fluctuates around potential GDP.

Aggregate Supply Time Frames

Aggregate supply is the relationship between the quantity of real GDP supplied and the price level. This relationship is different in the long run than in the short run and to study aggregate supply, we distinguish between two time frames:

- ◆ Long-run aggregate supply
- ◆ Short-run aggregate supply

Long-run Aggregate Supply

Long-run aggregate supply is the relationship between the quantity of real GDP supplied and the price level when the money wage rate changes in step with the price level to maintain full employment. The quantity of real GDP supplied at full employment equals potential GDP and this quantity is the same regardless of the price level.

The *long-run aggregate supply curve* in Figure 26.1 illustrates long-run aggregate supply as the vertical line at potential GDP labelled *LAS*. Along the long-run aggregate supply curve, as the price level changes, the money wage rate also changes so the real wage rate remains at the full-employment equilibrium level and real GDP remains at potential GDP. The long-run aggregate supply curve is always vertical and is always located at potential GDP.

The long-run aggregate supply curve is vertical because potential GDP is independent of the price level. The reason for this independence is that a movement along the *LAS* curve is accompanied by a change in two sets of prices: the prices of goods and services – the price level – and the prices of the factors of production, most notably, the money wage rate. A 10 per cent increase in the prices of goods and services is matched by a 10 per cent increase in the money wage rate. Because the price level and the money wage rate change by the same percentage, the real wage rate remains unchanged at its full-employment equilibrium level. So when the price level changes and the real wage rate remains constant, employment remains constant and real GDP remains constant at potential GDP.

Production at a Pepsi Plant

You can see more clearly why real GDP is unchanged when all prices change by the same percentage by thinking about production decisions at a Pepsi bottling plant. How does the quantity of Pepsi supplied change if the price of Pepsi changes and the wage rate of the workers and prices of all the other resources used vary by the same percentage? The answer is that the quantity supplied doesn't change. The firm produces the quantity that maximizes profit. That quantity depends on the price of Pepsi relative to the cost of producing it. With no change in price relative to cost, production doesn't change.

Short-run Aggregate Supply

Short-run aggregate supply is the relationship between the quantity of real GDP supplied and the price level when the money wage rate, the prices of other resources and potential GDP remain constant. Figure 26.1 illustrates this relationship as the short-run aggregate supply curve *SAS* and the short-run aggregate supply schedule. Each point on the *SAS* curve corresponds to a row of the short-run aggregate supply schedule. For example, point *A* on the *SAS* curve and row *A* of the schedule tell us that if the price level is 100, the quantity of real GDP supplied is £1,200 billion. In the short run, a rise in the price level brings an increase in the quantity of real GDP supplied. The short-run aggregate supply curve slopes upward.

With a given money wage rate, there is one price level at which the real wage rate is at its full-employment equilibrium level. At this price level, the quantity of real GDP supplied equals potential GDP and the *SAS* curve intersects the *LAS* curve. In this example, that price level is 110. If the price level rises above 110, the quantity of real GDP supplied increases along the *SAS* curve and exceeds potential GDP; if the price level falls below 110, the quantity of real GDP supplied decreases along the *SAS* curve and is less than potential GDP.

Back at the Pepsi Plant

You can see why the short-run aggregate supply curve slopes upward by returning to the Pepsi bottling plant. If production increases, marginal cost rises and if production decreases, marginal cost falls (see Chapter 2, p. 35).

If the price of Pepsi rises with no change in the money wage rate and other costs, Pepsi can increase profit by increasing production. Pepsi is in business to maximize its profit, so it increases production.

Similarly, if the price of Pepsi falls while the money wage rate and other costs remain constant, Pepsi can avoid a loss by decreasing production. The lower price weakens the incentive to produce, so Pepsi decreases production.

And for the Economy

What's true for Pepsi bottlers is true for the producers of all goods and services. When all prices rise, the *price level* rises. If the price level rises and the money wage rate and other factor prices remain constant, all firms increase production and the quantity of real GDP supplied increases. A fall in the price level has the opposite effect and decreases the quantity of real GDP supplied.

Figure 26.1 Long-run and Short-run Aggregate Supply

	Price level (GDP deflator)	Real GDP (billions of 2006 pounds)
A	100	1,200
B	105	1,250
C	110	1,300
D	115	1,350
E	120	1,400

In the long run, the quantity of real GDP supplied is potential GDP and the *LAS* curve is vertical at potential GDP. In the short-run, the quantity of real GDP supplied increases if the price level rises, while all other influences on supply plans remain the same.

The short-run aggregate supply curve, *SAS*, slopes upward. The short-run aggregate supply curve is based on the aggregate supply schedule in the table. Each point *A* to *E* on the curve corresponds to the row in the table identified by the same letter.

When the price level is 110, real GDP equals potential GDP (£1,300 billion). If the price level is greater than 110, real GDP exceeds potential GDP; if the price level is below 110, real GDP is less than potential GDP.

myeconlab Animation

Changes in Aggregate Supply

A change in the price level brings a change in the quantity of real GDP supplied, which is illustrated by a movement along the short-run aggregate supply curve. It does not change aggregate supply. Aggregate supply changes when an influence on production plans other than the price level changes. These other influences are changes in potential GDP and changes in the money wage rate. Let's begin by looking at a change in potential GDP.

Changes in Potential GDP

An increase in potential GDP increases both long-run aggregate supply and short-run aggregate supply. Figure 26.2 shows these effects.

Initially, the long-run aggregate supply curve is LAS_0 and the short-run aggregate supply curve is SAS_0. If potential GDP increases to £1,400 billion, long-run aggregate supply increases and the long-run aggregate supply curve shifts rightward to LAS_1. Short-run aggregate supply also increases, and the short-run aggregate supply curve shifts rightward to SAS_1. The two supply curves shift by the same amount only if the full-employment price level remains constant, which we will assume to be the case.

Potential GDP can increase for any of three reasons:

◆ An increase in the full-employment quantity of labour

◆ An increase in the quantity of capital

◆ An advance in technology

Let's look at these influences on potential GDP and the aggregate supply curves.

An Increase in the Full-employment Quantity of Labour

A Pepsi bottling plant that employs 100 workers bottles more Pepsi than an otherwise identical plant that employs 10 workers. The same is true for the economy as a whole. The larger the quantity of labour employed, the greater is real GDP.

Over time, real GDP increases because the labour force increases. But (with constant capital and technology) *potential* GDP increases only if the full-employment quantity of labour increases. Fluctuations in employment over the business cycle bring fluctuations in real GDP. But these changes in real GDP are fluctuations around potential GDP and long-run aggregate supply.

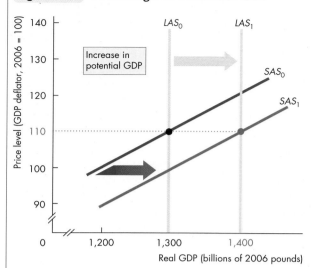

Figure 26.2   A Change in Potential GDP

An increase in potential GDP increases both long-run aggregate supply and short-run aggregate supply. The long-run aggregate supply curve shifts rightward from LAS_0 to LAS_1 and the short-run aggregate supply curve shifts from SAS_0 to SAS_1.

myeconlab Animation

An Increase in the Quantity of Capital

A Pepsi bottling plant that has two production lines has more capital and produces more output than an otherwise identical plant that has one production line. For the economy, the larger the quantity of capital, the more productive is the workforce and the greater is its potential GDP. Potential GDP per person in capital-rich EU economies is vastly greater than that in capital-poor China and Russia.

Capital includes *human capital*. One bottling plant is managed by an economics graduate with an MBA and has a workforce with an average of 10 years of experience. This plant produces a much larger output than an otherwise identical plant that is managed by someone with no business training or experience and that has a young workforce that is new to bottling. The first plant has a greater amount of human capital than the second. For the economy as a whole, the larger the quantity of *human capital* – the skills that people have acquired in school and through on-the-job-training – the greater is potential GDP.

An Advance in Technology

A Pepsi bottling plant that has pre-computer age machines produces less than one that uses the latest robot technology. Technological change enables firms to produce more from any given amount of inputs. So even with fixed quantities of labour and capital, improvements in technology increase potential GDP.

Technological advances are by far the most important source of increased production over the past two centuries. Because of technological advances, one farmer in the UK today can feed 100 people and one auto worker can produce almost 14 cars and lorries in a year.

Let's now look at the effects of changes in the money wage rate and other resource prices.

Changes in the Money Wage Rate and Other Resource Prices

When the money wage rate or the money prices of other resources (such as the price of oil) change, short-run aggregate supply changes but long-run aggregate supply does not change.

Figure 26.3 shows the effect on aggregate supply of an increase in the money wage rate. Initially, the short-run aggregate supply curve is SAS_0. A rise in the money wage rate *decreases* short-run aggregate supply and shifts the short-run aggregate supply curve leftward to SAS_2.

The money wage rate (and other resource prices) affect short-run aggregate supply because they influence firms' costs. The higher the money wage rate, the higher are firms' costs and the smaller is the quantity that firms are willing to supply at each price level. So an increase in the money wage rate decreases short-run aggregate supply.

A change in the money wage rate does not change long-run aggregate supply because on the *LAS* curve, a change in the money wage rate is accompanied by an equal percentage change in the price level. With no change in *relative* prices, firms have no incentive to change production and real GDP remains constant at potential GDP. With no change in potential GDP, the long-run aggregate supply curve remains at *LAS*.

What Makes the Money Wage Rate Change?

The money wage rate can change for two reasons: departures from full employment and expectations about inflation. Unemployment above the natural rate puts downward pressure on the money wage rate, and unemployment below the natural rate puts upward pressure on the money wage rate. An expected increase in

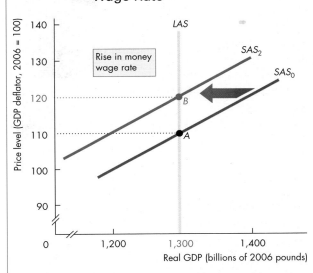

Figure 26.3   A Change in the Money Wage Rate

A rise in the money wage rate decreases short-run aggregate supply and shifts the short-run aggregate supply curve leftward from SAS_0 to SAS_2. A rise in the money wage rate does not change potential GDP, so the long-run aggregate supply curve does not shift.

myeconlab   Animation

the inflation rate makes the money wage rate rise faster, and an expected decrease in the inflation rate slows the rate at which the money wage rate rises.

Review Quiz

1   If the price level and the money wage rate rise by the same percentage, what happens to the quantity of real GDP supplied? Along which aggregate supply curve does the economy move?

2   If the price level rises and the money wage rate remains constant, what happens to the quantity of real GDP supplied? Along which aggregate supply curve does the economy move?

3   If potential GDP increases, what happens to aggregate supply? Is there a shift of or a movement along the *LAS* curve? Does the *SAS* curve shift or is there a movement along the *SAS* curve?

4   If the money wage rate rises and potential GDP remains the same, does the *LAS* curve or the *SAS* curve shift or is there a movement along the *LAS* curve or the *SAS* curve?

You can work these questions in Study Plan 26.1 and get instant feedback.

Aggregate Demand

The quantity of real GDP demanded is the sum of real consumption expenditure (C), investment (I), government expenditure (G) and exports (X) minus imports (M). That is:

$$Y = C + I + G + X - M$$

The *quantity of real GDP demanded* is the total amount of final goods and services produced in the UK that people, businesses, governments and foreigners plan to buy.

These buying plans depend on many factors. The four main ones are:

1 The price level
2 Expectations
3 Fiscal policy and monetary policy
4 The world economy

We first focus on the relationship between the quantity of real GDP demanded and the price level. To study this relationship, we keep all other influences on buying plans the same and ask: How does the quantity of real GDP demanded vary as the price level varies?

The Aggregate Demand Curve

Other things remaining the same, the higher the price level, the smaller is the quantity of real GDP demanded. This relationship between the quantity of real GDP demanded and the price level is called **aggregate demand**. Aggregate demand is described by an aggregate demand schedule and an aggregate demand curve.

Figure 26.4 shows an aggregate demand curve (*AD*) and an aggregate demand schedule. Each point on the *AD* curve corresponds to a row of the schedule. For example, point *C'* on the *AD* curve and row *C'* of the schedule tell us that if the price level is 110, the quantity of real GDP demanded is £1,300 billion.

The aggregate demand curve slopes downward for two reasons:

◆ Wealth effect
◆ Substitution effects

Wealth Effect

When the price level rises but other things remain the same, *real* wealth decreases. Real wealth is the amount

Figure 26.4 Aggregate Demand

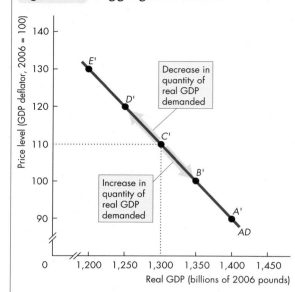

	Price level (GDP deflator)	Real GDP (billions of 2006 pounds)
A'	90	1,400
B'	100	1,350
C'	110	1,300
D'	120	1,250
E'	130	1,200

The aggregate demand curve (*AD*) shows the relationship between the quantity of real GDP demanded and the price level. The aggregate demand curve is based on the aggregate demand schedule in the table. Each point *A'* to *E'* on the curve corresponds to the row in the table identified by the same letter. For example, when the price level is 110, the quantity of real GDP demanded is £1,300 billion, shown by point *C'* in the figure.

A change in the price level with all other influences on aggregate buying plans remaining the same brings a change in the quantity of real GDP demanded and a movement along the *AD* curve.

of money in the bank, bonds, shares and other assets that people own, measured not in pounds but in terms of the goods and services that this money, bonds and shares will buy.

People save and hold money, bonds, shares and other assets for many reasons. One reason is to build up funds for education expenses. Another reason is to build up enough funds to meet possible medical or other big bills. But the biggest reason is to build up enough funds to provide a retirement income.

If the price level rises, real wealth decreases. People then try to restore their wealth. To do so, they must increase saving and, equivalently, decrease current consumption. Such a decrease in consumption is a decrease in aggregate demand.

Maria's Wealth Effect

You can see how the wealth effect works by thinking about Maria's buying plans. Maria lives in Moscow, Russia. She has worked hard all summer and saved 20,000 rubles (the ruble is the currency of Russia), which she plans to spend attending graduate school when she has finished her economics degree. So Maria's wealth is 20,000 rubles. Maria has a part-time job, and her income from this job pays her current expenses. The price level in Russia rises by 100 per cent, and now Maria needs 40,000 rubles to buy what 20,000 rubles once bought. To try to make up some of the fall in value of her savings, Maria saves even more and cuts her current spending to the bare minimum.

Substitution Effects

When the price level rises and other things remain the same, interest rates rise. The reason is related to the wealth effect that you've just studied. A rise in the price level decreases the real value of the money in people's pockets and bank accounts. With a smaller amount of real money around, banks can get a higher interest rate on loans. But faced with higher interest rates, people and businesses delay plans to buy new capital and consumer durable goods and cut back on spending.

This substitution effect involves changing the timing of capital consumer durable goods purchases and is called an *intertemporal* substitution effect – a substitution across time. Saving increases to increase future consumption.

To see this intertemporal substitution effect more clearly, think about your own plan to buy a new computer. At an interest rate of 5 per cent a year, you might borrow £1,000 and buy the new machine you've been researching. But at an interest rate of 10 per cent a year, you might decide that the payments would be too high. You don't abandon your plan to buy the computer, but you decide to delay your purchase.

A second substitution effect works through international prices. When the UK price level rises and other things remain the same, UK-made goods and services become more expensive relative to foreign-made goods and services. This change in *relative prices* encourages people to spend less on UK-made items and more on foreign-made items. For example, if the UK price level rises relative to the price level in France, fewer Vauxhall Vectras are sold in France and more Renaults are sold in the UK. Exports from the UK decrease, imports into the UK increase and the quantity of UK real GDP demanded decreases.

Maria's Substitution Effects

In Moscow, Maria makes some substitutions. She was planning to trade in her old motor scooter and get a new one. But with a higher price level and faced with higher interest rates, she decides to make her old scooter last one more year. Also, with the prices of Russian goods sharply increasing, Maria substitutes a low-cost dress made in Malaysia for the Russian-made dress she had originally planned to buy.

Changes in the Quantity of Real GDP Demanded

When the price level rises and other things remain the same, the quantity of real GDP demanded decreases – a movement up along the *AD* curve as shown by the arrow in Figure 26.4. When the price level falls and other things remain the same, the quantity of real GDP demanded increases – a movement down along the *AD* curve.

We've now seen how the quantity of real GDP demanded changes when the price level changes. How do other influences on buying plans affect aggregate demand?

Changes in Aggregate Demand

A change in any factor that influences buying plans other than the price level brings a change in aggregate demand. The main factors are:

◆ Expectations
◆ Fiscal policy and monetary policy
◆ The world economy

Expectations

An increase in expected future disposable income, other things remaining the same, increases the amount of consumption goods (especially items such as cars) that people plan to buy today and increases aggregate demand today.

An increase in the expected future inflation rate increases aggregate demand today because people decide to buy more goods and services at today's relatively lower prices. An increase in expected future profit increases the investment that firms plan to undertake today and increases aggregate demand today.

Fiscal Policy and Monetary Policy

The government's attempt to influence the economy by setting and changing taxes, making transfer payments and purchasing goods and services is called **fiscal policy**. A tax cut or an increase in transfer payments – for example, unemployment benefits or welfare payments – increases aggregate demand. Both of these influences operate by increasing households' *disposable* income. **Disposable income** is aggregate income minus taxes plus transfer payments. The greater the disposable income, the greater is the quantity of consumption goods and services that households plan to buy and the greater is aggregate demand.

Government expenditure on goods and services is one component of aggregate demand. So if the government spends more on hospitals, schools and motorways, aggregate demand increases.

Monetary policy consists of changes in interest rates and in the quantity of money in the economy. The quantity of money in the UK is determined by the Bank of England and the banks (in a process described in Chapter 24). An increase in the quantity of money increases aggregate demand.

To see why money affects aggregate demand, imagine that the Bank of England borrows the army's helicopters, loads them with millions of new £5 notes and sprinkles these notes like confetti across the nation. People gather the newly available money and plan to spend some of it. So the quantity of goods and services demanded increases. But people don't plan to spend all the new money. They save some of it and lend it to others through the banks. The interest rate falls, and with a lower interest rate, people plan to buy more consumer durables and firms plan to increase their investment.

The World Economy

Aggregate demand in each individual country is influenced by events in the world economy. The two main influences are changes in the foreign exchange rate and changes in world income. The *foreign exchange rate* is the amount of a foreign currency that you can

ECONOMICS IN ACTION

Fiscal Policy to Fight Recession

In 2008, as recession deepened, the world's two largest economies embarked on a massive fiscal stimulus. The US Congress cut taxes by $300 billion and increased government expenditure by $540 billion, totalling 6 per cent of US GDP. In China, government spending was increased by $200 billion or 5 per cent of GDP. The UK stimulus was 1.5 per cent of GDP.

The idea of these fiscal measures was to stimulate business investment and consumption expenditure and increase aggregate demand.

Monetary Policy to Fight Recession

In October 2008 and the months that followed, the central banks of the major Western economies, the US Federal Reserve, the European Central Bank, the Bank of Canada and the Bank of England, together cut their interest rates and took other measures to ease credit and encourage banks and other financial institutions to increase their lending.

Like the accompanying fiscal stimulus packages, the idea of these interest rate cuts and easier credit was to stimulate business investment and consumption expenditure and increase aggregate demand.

 0.20%
Ben Bernanke
Federal Reserve

 1.75%
Jean-Claude Trichet
ECB

 0.50%
Mervyn King
Bank of England

 0.25%
Mark Carney
Bank of Canada

buy with a unit of domestic currency. Other things remaining the same, a rise in a country's foreign exchange rate decreases aggregate demand.

To see how the UK's foreign exchange rate influences aggregate demand in the UK, suppose that £1 is worth €1.10. A pair of Gucci shoes made in Italy costs €220 and an equivalent pair of Church's shoes made in England costs £190. In pounds, the Gucci shoes cost £200, so people around the world buy the cheaper Church's shoes from the UK.

Now suppose the exchange rate rises to €1.40 per pound. The Gucci shoes now cost £157.14 and are cheaper than the Church's shoes. People switch from Church's to Gucci shoes. As they make this switch, UK exports decrease, UK imports increase and aggregate demand in the UK decreases.

An increase in foreign income increases UK exports and increases UK aggregate demand – the aggregate demand for UK-produced goods and services. For example, an increase in income in the US, Japan and Germany increases the American, Japanese and German consumers' and producers' planned expenditures on UK-produced consumption goods and capital goods.

Shifts of the Aggregate Demand Curve

When aggregate demand changes, the aggregate demand curve shifts. Figure 26.5 shows two changes in aggregate demand and summarizes the factors that bring about such changes.

Aggregate demand increases and the aggregate demand curve shifts rightward from AD_0 to AD_1 when expected future disposable income, inflation or profit increases; government expenditure on goods and services increases; taxes are cut; transfer payments increase; the quantity of money increases and interest rates fall; the foreign exchange rate falls; or foreign income increases.

Aggregate demand decreases and the aggregate demand curve shifts leftward from AD_0 to AD_2 when expected future disposable income, inflation or profit decreases; government expenditure on goods and services decreases; taxes increase; transfer payments decrease; the quantity of money decreases and interest rates rise; the foreign exchange rate rises; or foreign income decreases.

Figure 26.5 Changes in Aggregate Demand

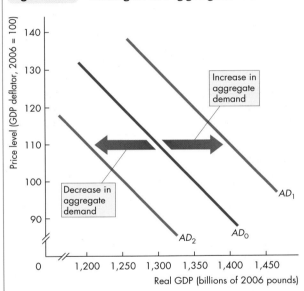

Aggregate demand

Decreases if:

◆ Expected future disposable income, inflation or profit decreases

◆ Fiscal policy decreases government expenditure on goods and services, increases taxes or decreases transfer payments

◆ Monetary policy increases interest rates and decreases the quantity of money

◆ The foreign exchange rate increases or foreign income decreases

Increases if:

◆ Expected future disposable income, inflation or profit increases

◆ Fiscal policy increases government expenditure on goods and services, decreases taxes or increases transfer payments

◆ Monetary policy decreases interest rates and increases the quantity of money

◆ The foreign exchange rate decreases or foreign income increases

myeconlab Animation ────────────── ◆

Review Quiz

1 What does the aggregate demand curve show? What factors change and what factors remain the same when there is a movement along the aggregate demand curve?
2 Why does the aggregate demand curve slope downward?
3 How do changes in expectations, fiscal policy, monetary policy and the world economy change aggregate demand and the aggregate demand curve?

You can work these questions in Study Plan 26.2 and get instant feedback.

Explaining Macroeconomic Trends and Fluctuations

The purpose of the *AS–AD* model is to explain changes in real GDP and the price level. The model's main purpose is to explain business cycle fluctuations in these variables. But the model also aids our understanding of economic growth and inflation trends. We begin by combining aggregate supply and aggregate demand to determine real GDP and the price level in equilibrium. Just as there are two time frames for aggregate supply, there are two time frames for macroeconomic equilibrium: a long-run equilibrium and a short-run equilibrium. We'll first look at short-run equilibrium.

Short-run Macroeconomic Equilibrium

The aggregate demand curve tells us the quantity of real GDP demanded at each price level, and the short-run aggregate supply curve tells us the quantity of real GDP supplied at each price level. **Short-run macroeconomic equilibrium** occurs when the quantity of real GDP demanded equals the short-run quantity of real GDP supplied at the point of intersection of the *AD* curve and the *SAS* curve. Figure 26.6 illustrates such an equilibrium at a price level of 110 and real GDP of £1,300 billion (point *C* and *C'*).

To see why this position is the equilibrium, think about what happens if the price level is something other than 110. Suppose, for example, that the price level is 120 and that real GDP is £1,400 billion (at point *E* on the *SAS* curve). The quantity of real GDP demanded is less than £1,400 billion, so firms are unable to sell all their output. Unwanted inventories (stocks) pile up, and firms cut both production and prices. Production and prices are cut until firms can sell all their output. This situation occurs only when real GDP is £1,300 billion and the price level is 110.

Now suppose that the price level is 100 and real GDP is £1,200 billion (at point *A* on the *SAS* curve). The quantity of real GDP demanded exceeds £1,200 billion, so firms are unable to meet demand for their output. Inventories (stocks of finished but unsold items) decrease and customers clamour for more goods and services than firms are producing. So firms increase production and raise prices. Production and prices increase until firms can meet demand. This situation occurs only when real GDP is £1,300 billion and the price level is 110.

Figure 26.6 Short-run Macroeconomic Equilibrium

Short-run macroeconomic equilibrium occurs when real GDP demanded equals real GDP supplied – at the intersection of the aggregate demand curve (*AD*) and the short-run aggregate supply curve (*SAS*).

 Animation

In short-run macroeconomic equilibrium, the money wage rate is fixed. It does not adjust to bring full employment. So in the short run, real GDP can be greater than or less than potential GDP. But in the long run, the money wage rate does adjust and real GDP moves towards potential GDP. Let's look at the long-run equilibrium and see how we get there.

Long-run Macroeconomic Equilibrium

Long-run macroeconomic equilibrium occurs when real GDP equals potential GDP – equivalently, when the economy is on its *LAS* curve.

When the economy is away from long-run equilibrium, the money wage rate adjusts. If the money wage rate is too high, short-run equilibrium is below potential GDP and the unemployment rate is above the natural rate. With an excess supply of labour, the money wage rate falls. If the money wage rate is too low, short-run equilibrium is above potential GDP and the unemployment rate is below the natural rate. With an excess demand for labour, the money wage rate rises.

Figure 26.7 shows the long-run equilibrium and how it comes about. If the short-run aggregate supply curve is SAS_1, the money wage rate is too high to achieve full employment. A fall in the money wage rate shifts the SAS curve to SAS* and brings full employment. If the short-run aggregate supply curve is SAS_2, the money wage rate is too low to achieve full employment. Now, a rise in the money wage rate shifts the SAS curve to SAS* and brings full employment.

In long-run equilibrium, potential GDP determines real GDP and potential GDP and aggregate demand together determine the price level. The money wage rate adjusts to put the SAS curve through the long-run equilibrium point.

Let's now see how the AS–AD model helps us to understand economic growth and inflation.

Economic Growth and Inflation in the *AS–AD* Model

Economic growth results from a growing labour force and increasing labour productivity, which together make potential GDP grow (Chapter 22, pp. 515–518). Inflation results from a growing quantity of money that outpaces the growth of potential GDP (Chapter 24, pp. 574–575).

The AS–AD model explains and illustrates economic growth and inflation. It explains economic growth as increasing long-run aggregate supply and it explains inflation as a persistent increase in aggregate demand at a faster pace than that of the increase in potential GDP.

ECONOMICS IN ACTION

UK Economic Growth and Inflation

The figure is a scatter diagram of UK real GDP and the price level. The graph has the same axes as those of the AS–AD model. Each dot represents a year between 1960 and 2010. The red dots are recession years. The pattern formed by the dots shows the combination of economic growth and inflation. Economic growth was fastest during the 1960s; inflation was fastest during the 1970s.

The AS–AD model interprets each dot as being at the intersection of the SAS and AD curves.

Figure 1 The Path of Real GDP and the Price Level

Source of data: Office for National Statistics

Figure 26.7 Long-run Macroeconomic Equilibrium

In long-run macroeconomic equilibrium, real GDP equals potential GDP. So long-run equilibrium occurs where the aggregate demand curve AD intersects the long-run aggregate supply curve LAS. In the long run, aggregate demand determines the price level and has no effect on real GDP. The money wage rate adjusts in the long run, so the SAS curve intersects the LAS curve at the long-run equilibrium price level.

myeconlab Animation

Figure 26.8 illustrates this explanation in terms of the shifting *LAS*, *SAS* and *AD* curves.

When the *LAS* curve shifts rightward from LAS_0 to LAS_1, potential GDP grows from £1,300 billion to £1,400 billion and in long-run equilibrium, real GDP also grows to £1,400 billion.

When the *AD* curve shifts rightward from AD_0 to AD_1, which is a growth of aggregate demand that outpaces the growth of potential GDP, the price level rises from 110 to 120.

If aggregate demand were to increase at the same pace as long-run aggregate supply, real GDP would grow with no inflation.

Our economy experiences periods of growth and inflation, like those shown in Figure 26.8, but it does not experience steady growth and steady inflation. Real GDP fluctuates around potential GDP in a business cycle. When we study the business cycle, we ignore economic growth and focus on the fluctuations around the trend. By doing so, we see the business cycle more clearly. Let's now see how the *AS–AD* model explains the business cycle.

The Business Cycle in the *AS–AD* Model

The business cycle occurs because aggregate demand and short-run aggregate supply fluctuate but the money wage rate does not adjust quickly enough to keep real GDP at potential GDP. Figure 26.9 shows three types of short-run equilibrium.

Figure 26.9(a) shows an above full-employment equilibrium. An **above full-employment equilibrium** is an equilibrium in which real GDP exceeds potential GDP. The gap between real GDP and potential GDP is the **output gap**. When real GDP exceeds potential GDP, the output gap is called an **inflationary gap**.

The above full-employment equilibrium shown in Figure 26.9(a) occurs where the aggregate demand curve AD_0 intersects the short-run aggregate supply

---

Figure 26.8 Economic Growth and Inflation

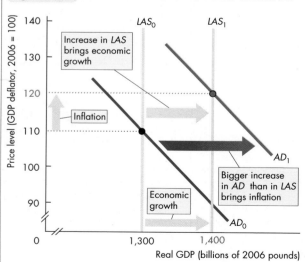

Economic growth is the persistent increase in potential GDP. Economic growth is shown as an ongoing rightward shift of the *LAS* curve. Inflation is the persistent rise in the price level. Inflation occurs when aggregate demand increases by more than the increase in long-run aggregate supply.

ECONOMICS IN ACTION

The UK Business Cycle

The UK economy had an inflationary gap in 2004 (at *A* in the figure), full employment in 2008 (at *B*) and a recessionary gap in 2009 (at *C*). The fluctuating output gap in the figure is the real-world version of Figure 26.9(d) and is generated by fluctuations in aggregate demand and short-run aggregate supply.

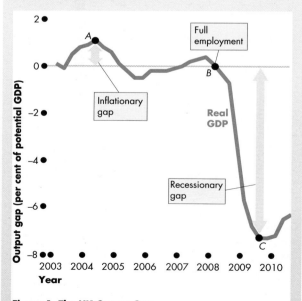

Figure 1 The UK Output Gap

Source of data: Office for National Statistics.

curve SAS_0 at a real GDP of £1,320 billion. There is an inflationary gap of £20 billion.

Figure 26.9(b) is an example of **full-employment equilibrium**, in which real GDP equals potential GDP. In this example, the equilibrium occurs where the aggregate demand curve AD_1 intersects the short-run aggregate supply curve SAS_1 at an actual and potential GDP of £1,300 billion.

In part (c), there is a below full-employment equilibrium. A **below full-employment equilibrium** is an equilibrium in which potential GDP exceeds real GDP. When potential GDP exceeds real GDP, the output gap is called a **recessionary gap**.

The below full-employment equilibrium shown in Figure 26.9(c) occurs where the aggregate demand curve AD_2 intersects the short-run aggregate supply curve SAS_2 at a real GDP of £1,280 billion with a recessionary gap of £20 billion.

The economy moves from one type of macroeconomic equilibrium to another as a result of fluctuations in aggregate demand and in short-run aggregate supply. These fluctuations produce fluctuations in real GDP. Figure 26.9(d) shows how real GDP fluctuates around potential GDP.

Let's now look at some of the sources of these fluctuations around potential GDP.

Figure 26.9   The Business Cycle

(a) Above full-employment equilibrium

(b) Full-employment equilibrium

(c) Below full-employment equilibrium

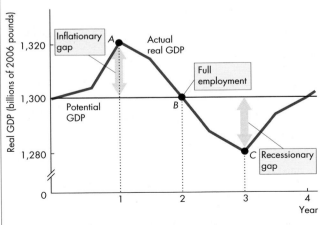

(d) Fluctuations in real GDP

Part (a) shows an above full-employment equilibrium in year 1, part (b) shows full-employment equilibrium in year 2 and part (c) shows a below full-employment equilibrium in year 3. Part (d) shows how real GDP fluctuates around potential GDP in a business cycle.

In year 1, an inflationary gap exists and the economy is at point A, in parts (a) and (d). In year 2, the economy is in full-employment equilibrium and the economy is at point B in parts (b) and (d). In year 3, a recessionary gap exists and the economy is at point C in parts (c) and (d).

Fluctuations in Aggregate Demand

One reason real GDP fluctuates around potential GDP is that aggregate demand fluctuates. Let's see what happens when aggregate demand increases.

Figure 26.10(a) shows an economy at full employment. The aggregate demand curve is AD_0, the short-run aggregate supply curve is SAS_0 and the long-run aggregate supply curve is LAS. Real GDP equals potential GDP at £1,300 billion and the price level is 110.

Now suppose that the world economy expands and that the demand for UK-made goods increases in Japan, Canada and the US. The increase in UK exports increases aggregate demand and the aggregate demand curve shifts rightward from AD_0 to AD_1 in Figure 26.10(a).

Faced with an increase in demand, firms increase production and raise prices. Real GDP increases to £1,350 billion and the price level rises to 115. The economy is now in an above full-employment equilibrium.

Real GDP exceeds potential GDP and there is an inflationary gap.

The increase in aggregate demand has increased the prices of all goods and services. Faced with higher prices, firms have increased their output rates. At this stage, prices of goods and services have increased but the money wage rate has not changed. (Recall that as we move along a short-run aggregate supply curve, the money wage rate is constant.)

Because the price level has increased and the money wage rate is unchanged, workers have experienced a fall in the buying power of their wages and firms' profits have increased. In these circumstances, workers demand higher wages and firms, anxious to maintain their employment and output levels, meet those demands. If firms do not raise the money wage rate, they will either lose workers or have to hire less productive ones.

As the money wage rate rises, the short-run aggregate supply curve begins to shift leftward. In Figure 26.10(b),

Figure 26.10   An Increase in Aggregate Demand

(a) Short-run effect

(b) Long-run effect

An increase in aggregate demand shifts the aggregate demand curve from AD_0 to AD_1. In the short run (part a), real GDP increases from £1,300 billion to £1,350 billion and the price level rises from 110 to 115. The economy has moved up along the SAS curve. In this situation, an inflationary gap exists.

In the long run (part b), with an inflationary gap, the money wage rate starts to rise. The short-run aggregate supply curve starts to shift leftward from SAS_0 to SAS_1. As the SAS curve shifts leftward, it intersects the aggregate demand curve AD_1 at higher price levels and real GDP decreases. Eventually, the price level rises to 125 and real GDP decreases to £1,300 billion – potential GDP.

the short-run aggregate supply curve shifts from SAS_0 towards SAS_1. The rise in the money wage rate and the shift in the SAS curve produce a sequence of new equilibrium positions. Along the adjustment path, real GDP decreases and the price level rises. The economy moves up along its aggregate demand curve as the arrow heads show.

Eventually, the money wage rate rises by the same percentage as the price level. At this time, the aggregate demand curve AD_1 intersects SAS_1 at a new long-run equilibrium. The price level has risen to 125, and real GDP is back where it started, at potential GDP.

A decrease in aggregate demand has similar but opposite effects to those of an increase in aggregate demand. That is, a decrease in aggregate demand shifts the aggregate demand curve leftward. Real GDP decreases to less than potential GDP and a recessionary gap emerges. Firms cut prices. The lower price level increases the purchasing power of wages and increases firms' costs relative to their output prices because the money wage rate remains unchanged. Eventually, the money wage rate falls and the short-run aggregate supply curve shifts rightward. But the money wage rate changes slowly, so real GDP slowly returns to potential GDP and the price level falls slowly.

Let's now work out how real GDP and the price level change when aggregate supply changes.

Fluctuations in Aggregate Supply

Fluctuations in short-run aggregate supply can bring fluctuations in real GDP around potential GDP. Suppose that initially, real GDP equals potential GDP. Then there is a large but temporary rise in the price of oil. What happens to real GDP and the price level?

Figure 26.11 answers this question. The aggregate demand curve is AD_0, the short-run aggregate supply curve is SAS_0 and the long-run aggregate supply curve is LAS. Equilibrium real GDP is £1,300 billion, which equals potential GDP, and the price level is 110. Then the price of oil rises. Faced with higher energy and transportation costs, firms decrease production. Short-run aggregate supply decreases and the short-run aggregate supply curve shifts leftward to SAS_1. The price level rises to 120 and real GDP decreases to £1,250 billion.

Because real GDP decreases, the economy experiences recession. Because the price level increases, the economy experiences inflation. A combination of recession and inflation, called **stagflation**, actually occurred in the UK in the mid-1970s.

Figure 26.11 A Decrease in Aggregate Supply

An oil price rise decreases short-run aggregate supply

An increase in the price of oil decreases short-run aggregate supply and shifts the short-run aggregate supply curve leftward from SAS_0 to SAS_1. Real GDP decreases from £1,300 billion to £1,250 billion, and the price level increases from 110 to 120. The economy experiences both recession and inflation – a situation known as stagflation.

 Animation

Review Quiz

1 Does economic growth result from increases in aggregate demand, short-run aggregate supply or long-run aggregate supply?
2 Does inflation result from increases in aggregate demand, short-run aggregate supply or long-run aggregate supply?
3 Describe the three types of short-run macro-economic equilibrium.
4 How do fluctuations in aggregate demand and short-run aggregate supply bring fluctuations in real GDP around potential GDP?

You can work these questions in Study Plan 26.3 and get instant feedback.   **myeconlab**

We can use the AS–AD model to explain and illustrate the views of the alternative schools of thought in macroeconomics. That is your next task.

Macroeconomic Schools of Thought

Macroeconomics is an active field of research and much remains to be learned about the forces that make our economy grow, bring inflation and generate business cycles. There is a greater degree of consensus and certainty about economic growth and inflation trends – the longer term changes in real GDP and the price level – than there is about the business cycle – the short-term fluctuations in these variables. Here, we'll look only at differences of view about short-term fluctuations.

The *AS–AD* model that you've studied in this chapter provides a good foundation for understanding the range of views that macroeconomists hold about this topic. But what you will learn here is just a first glimpse at the scientific controversy and debate. We'll return to these issues at various later points in the text and deepen your appreciation of the alternative views.

Classification usually requires simplification. And classifying macroeconomists is no exception to this general rule. The classification that we'll use here is simple, but it is not misleading. We identify three macroeconomic schools of thought and examine the views of each group in turn. We examine:

◆ The classical view
◆ The Keynesian view
◆ The monetarist view

The Classical View

A **classical** macroeconomist believes that the economy is self-regulating and that it is always at full employment. The term 'classical' derives from the name of the founding school of economics that includes Adam Smith, David Ricardo and John Stuart Mill.

A **new classical** view is that business cycle fluctuations are the efficient responses of a well-functioning market economy that is bombarded by shocks that arise from the uneven pace of technological change.

The classical view can be understood in terms of beliefs about aggregate demand and aggregate supply.

Aggregate Demand Fluctuations

In the classical view, technological change is the most significant influence on both aggregate demand and aggregate supply. For this reason, classical macroeconomists don't use the *AS–AD* framework. But their

views can be interpreted in this framework. A technological change that increases the productivity of capital brings an increase in aggregate demand because firms increase their expenditure on new plant and equipment. A technological change that lengthens the useful life of existing capital decreases the demand for new capital, which decreases aggregate demand.

Aggregate Supply Response

In the classical view, the money wage rate that lies behind the short-run aggregate supply curve is instantly and completely flexible. The money wage rate adjusts so quickly to maintain equilibrium in the labour market that real GDP always adjusts to equal potential GDP.

Potential GDP itself fluctuates for the same reasons that aggregate demand fluctuates: technological change. When the pace of technological change is rapid, potential GDP increases quickly and so does real GDP. When the pace of technological change slows, so does the growth rate of potential GDP.

Classical Policy

The classical view of policy emphasizes the potential for taxes to stunt incentives and create inefficiency. By minimizing the disincentive effects that taxes have, employment, investment and technological advance are at their efficient levels and the economy expands at an appropriate and rapid pace.

The Keynesian View

A **Keynesian** macroeconomist believes that left alone, the economy would rarely operate at full employment and that to achieve and maintain full employment, active help from fiscal policy and monetary policy is required. The term 'Keynesian' derives from the name of one of the twentieth century's most famous economists, John Maynard Keynes.

The Keynesian view is based on beliefs about the forces that determine aggregate demand and short-run aggregate supply.

Aggregate Demand Fluctuations

In the Keynesian view, *expectations* are the most significant influence on aggregate demand. And expectations are based on herd instinct or, what Keynes himself called 'animal spirits'. A wave of pessimism about future profit prospects can lead to a fall in aggregate demand and plunge the economy into recession.

Aggregate Supply Response

In the Keynesian view, the money wage rate that lies behind the short-run aggregate supply curve is extremely sticky downward. Basically, the money wage rate doesn't fall. So if there is a recessionary gap, there is no automatic mechanism for getting rid of it. If it were to happen, a fall in the money wage rate would increase short-run aggregate supply and restore full employment. But the money wage rate doesn't fall, so the economy remains stuck in recession.

A modern version of the Keynesian view known as the **new Keynesian** view holds that not only is the money wage rate sticky but that prices of goods and services are also sticky. With a sticky price level, the short-run aggregate supply curve is horizontal at a fixed price level.

Policy Response Needed

The Keynesian view calls for fiscal policy and monetary policy to actively offset the changes in aggregate demand that bring recession. By stimulating aggregate demand in a recession, full employment can be restored.

The Monetarist View

A **monetarist** is a macroeconomist who believes that the economy is self-regulating and that it will normally operate at full employment, provided that monetary policy is not erratic and that the pace of money growth is kept steady. The term 'monetarist' was coined by an outstanding twentieth century economist, Karl Brunner, to describe his own and Milton Friedman's views.

The monetarist view can be interpreted in terms of beliefs about the forces that determine aggregate demand and short-run aggregate supply.

Aggregate Demand Fluctuations

In the monetarist view, the *quantity of money* is the most significant influence on aggregate demand. And the quantity of money is determined by the Bank of England. If the Bank of England keeps money growing at a steady pace, aggregate demand fluctuations will be minimized and the economy will operate close to full employment. But if the Bank of England decreases the quantity of money or even just slows its growth rate too

abruptly, the economy will go into recession. In the monetarist view, all recessions result from inappropriate monetary policy.

Aggregate Supply Response

The monetarist view of short-run aggregate supply is the same as the Keynesian view – the money wage rate is sticky. If the economy is in recession, it will take an unnecessarily long time for it to return unaided to full employment.

Monetarist Policy

The monetarist view of policy is the same as the classical view on fiscal policy. Taxes should be kept low to avoid disincentive effects that decrease potential GDP. Provided that the quantity of money is kept on a steady growth path, no active stabilization is needed to offset changes in aggregate demand.

The Way Ahead

You will encounter classical, Keynesian and monetarist views in the chapters that follow. In the next chapter, we study the classical model. Then we study the Keynesian model. From there, we study money and inflation and lay the foundation for a deeper look at the sources of macroeconomic fluctuations and economic growth. We finish with a close look at the fiscal policy and monetary policy that try to achieve faster growth, stable prices and a smoother cycle.

Review Quiz

1 What are the defining features of classical macroeconomics and what policies do classical macroeconomists recommend?
2 What are the defining features of Keynesian macroeconomics and what policies do Keynesian macroeconomists recommend?
3 What are the defining features of monetarist macroeconomics and what policies do monetarist macroeconomists recommend?

You can work these questions in Study Plan 26.4 and get instant feedback.

To complete your study of the *AS–AD* model, take a look at the German economy in 2009–2010 through the eyes of this model in *Reading Between the Lines* on pp. 630–631.

Reading Between the Lines

Aggregate Supply and Aggregate Demand in Action

The Financial Times, 12 January 2011

Domestic Demand Spurs Growth in Germany

FT

Ralph Atkins and Quentin Peel

Germany last year experienced its most dramatic economic turn round since the country's reunification. Gross domestic product expanded 3.6 per cent compared with the previous year – at least partly reversing a 4.7 per cent contraction in 2009, the federal statistical office in Wiesbaden reported on Wednesday.

The improvement in Europe's largest economy, led by a rebound in investment spending after its worst recession since the Second World War, provided welcome news for Eurozone policymakers – and also strengthened Germans' convictions that their focus on fiscal discipline is justified.

A surge in imports and modest pick-up in consumer spending, as well as the investment splurge, were cited by economists as evidence that domestic demand was increasingly driving growth – boosting the prospects that Germany's revival will have a knock-on effect in the Eurozone.

But despite Berlin's proclaimed fiscal prudence, the full effects of tightening measures implemented by Berlin have yet to be felt. Government spending rose 2.2 per cent last year, while the public sector deficit rose to 3.5 per cent of GDP.

Germany was . . . better placed than most European economies to benefit last year from rapid growth in countries such as China. . . . Hopes that the export and investment-led growth of 2010 will spark a rebound in consumer spending this year are based on the unexpectedly strong improvement in Germany's labour market.

Nevertheless, the composition of growth in 2010 left some observers sceptical about the speed with which Germany's export dependency is waning. Held back by weak car sales, consumer spending rose just 0.5 per cent last year. The proportion of their disposable incomes that Germans saved also rose.

The Essence of the Story

- During 2010 real GDP in Germany grew by 3.6 per cent.

- The rapid growth of GDP was led by growth in investment and exports.

- Consumer spending increased by only 0.5 per cent as Germans saved more.

- Germany is heavily dependent on exports for growth in demand.

Economic Analysis

◆ The quantity of real GDP demanded is the sum of real consumption, C, investment, I, government expenditure, G, and net exports, $X - M$:

$$Y = C + I + G + X - M$$

◆ The large increase in Germany's real GDP in 2010 resulted from an increase in aggregate demand that came mainly from investment and exports.

◆ Figure 1 shows the growth rates of consumption, investment and exports from the third quarter of 2008 to the fourth quarter of 2010.

◆ Figure 1 shows that the fluctuations in investment and exports are much larger than those in consumption. (The growth rate of real GDP is not shown but it lies between the three curves in the figure.)

◆ The rapid growth in Germany's exports, particularly those of engineering goods, resulted from a large increase in demand from China and other rapidly expanding economies in East Asia.

◆ A depreciation of the euro against the Chinese yuan and the US dollar also helped to boost Germany's exports.

◆ Germany's rapid real GDP growth decreased its recessionary gap.

◆ We estimate Germany's recessionary gap at the end of 2010 at 1 per cent of potential GDP.

◆ Figure 2 shows Germany's aggregate demand and aggregate supply curves in 2009 and 2010.

◆ The long-run aggregate supply curve is *LAS* and the short-run aggregate supply curve is *SAS*.

◆ In 2009, the aggregate demand curve was AD_0. Real GDP was €2,170 billion (in 2000 prices) and the price level was 109.

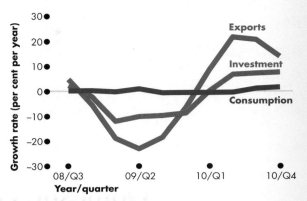

Figure 1 **Growth of Germany's consumption, investment and exports**

Figure 2 **Germany's aggregate demand and aggregate supply**

◆ In 2010, aggregate demand increased and the *AD* curve shifted rightward to AD_1. Real GDP increased to €2,250 billion and the recessionary gap closed to 1 per cent of potential GDP.

◆ The news article implies that Germany relies too much on exports and not enough on domestic consumption.

◆ That view is not correct. Germany has a comparative advantage in many engineering prodution activities, and Germany and its trading partners gain from international trade.

SUMMARY

Key Points

Aggregate Supply (pp. 614–617)

◆ In the long run, the quantity of real GDP supplied is potential GDP.

◆ In the short run, a rise in the price level increases the quantity of real GDP supplied.

◆ A change in potential GDP changes both long-run and short-run aggregate supply. A change in the money wage rate or other resource prices changes only short-run aggregate supply.

Working Problems 1 to 3 will give you a better understanding of aggregate supply.

Aggregate Demand (pp. 618–621)

◆ A rise in the price level decreases the quantity of real GDP demanded because of wealth and substitution effects.

◆ Changes in expectations, fiscal policy, monetary policy and the world economy change aggregate demand.

Working Problems 4 to 7 will give you a better understanding of aggregate demand.

Explaining Macroeconomic Trends and Fluctuations (pp. 622–627)

◆ Aggregate demand and short-run aggregate supply determine real GDP and the price level.

◆ In the long run, real GDP equals potential GDP and aggregate demand determines the price level.

◆ Economic growth occurs because potential GDP increases and inflation occurs because aggregate demand grows more quickly than potential GDP.

◆ Business cycles occur because aggregate demand and aggregate supply fluctuate.

Working Problems 8 to 16 will give you a better understanding of macroeconomic trends and fluctuations

Macroeconomic Schools of Thought
(pp. 628–629)

◆ Classical economists believe that the economy is self-regulating and always at full employment.

◆ Keynesian economists believe that full employment can be achieved only with active policy.

◆ Monetarist economists believe that recessions result from inappropriate monetary policy.

Working Problems 17 to 19 will give you a better understanding of macroeconomic schools of thought.

Key Terms

Above full-employment equilibrium, 624
Aggregate demand, 618
Below full-employment equilibrium, 625
Classical, 628
Disposable income, 620
Fiscal policy, 620
Full-employment equilibrium, 625
Inflationary gap, 624
Keynesian, 628
Long-run aggregate supply, 614
Long-run macroeconomic equilibrium, 622
Monetarist, 629
Monetary policy, 620
New classical, 628
New Keynesian, 629
Output gap, 624
Recessionary gap, 625
Short-run aggregate supply, 615
Short-run macroeconomic equilibrium, 622
Stagflation, 627

STUDY PLAN PROBLEMS AND APPLICATIONS

myeconlab You can work Problems 1 to 19 in MyEconLab Chapter 26 Study Plan and get instant feedback.

Aggregate Supply (Study Plan 26.1)

1 Explain the influence of each of the following events on the quantity of real GDP supplied and aggregate supply in India and use a graph to illustrate.

- ◆ UK firms move their call handling, IT and data functions to India.
- ◆ Petrol prices rise.
- ◆ Wal-Mart and Starbucks open in India.
- ◆ Universities in India increase the number of engineering graduates.
- ◆ The money wage rate rises.
- ◆ The price level in India increases.

2 Wages Could Hit Steepest Plunge in 18 Years

A bad economy is starting to drag down wages for millions of workers. The average weekly wage has fallen 1.4% this year through September. Colorado will become the first state to lower its minimum wage since the federal minimum wage law was passed in 1938, when the state cuts its rate by 4 cents an hour.

Source: *USA Today*, 16 October 2009

Explain how the fall in the average weekly wage and the minimum wage will influence aggregate supply.

3 Chinese Premier Wen Jiabao has warned Japan that its companies operating in China should raise pay for their workers. Explain how a rise in wages in China will influence the quantity of real GDP supplied and aggregate supply in China.

Aggregate Demand (Study Plan 26.2)

4 South Africa trades with the UK. Explain the effect of each of the following events on South Africa's aggregate demand.

- ◆ The government of South Africa cuts income taxes.
- ◆ The UK experiences strong economic growth.
- ◆ South Africa sets new environmental standards that require power utilities to upgrade their production facilities.

5 The Bank of England cuts the quantity of money and all other things remain the same. Explain the effect of the cut in the quantity of money on aggregate demand in the short run.

6 Kenya trades with the UK. Explain the effect of each of the following events on the quantity of real GDP demanded and aggregate demand in Kenya.

- ◆ The UK goes into a recession.
- ◆ The price level in Kenya rises.
- ◆ Kenya increases the quantity of money.

7 Durable Goods Orders Surge in May, New Home Sales Dip

The US government announced that demand for durable goods rose 1.8 per cent, while sales of new homes dropped 0.6 per cent in May. US companies suffered a sharp drop in exports as other countries struggle with recession.

Source: *USA Today*, 24 June 2009

Explain how the items in the news clip influence US aggregate demand.

Explaining Macroeconomic Trends and Fluctuations (Study Plan 26.3)

Use the following graph to work Problems 8 to 10.

Initially, the short-run aggregate supply curve is SAS_0 and the aggregate demand curve is AD_0.

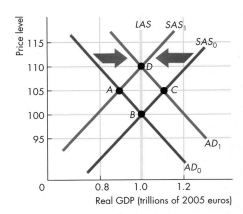

8 Some events change aggregate demand from AD_0 to AD_1. Describe two events that could have created this change in aggregate demand. What is the equilibrium after aggregate demand changed? If potential GDP is €1 trillion, the economy is at what type of macroeconomic equilibrium?

9 Some events change aggregate supply from SAS_0 to SAS_1. Describe two events that could have created this change in aggregate supply. What is the equilibrium after aggregate supply changed? If potential GDP is €1 trillion, does the economy have an inflationary gap, a recessionary gap or no output gap?

10 Some events change aggregate demand from AD_0 to AD_1 and aggregate supply from SAS_0 to SAS_1. What is the new macroeconomic equilibrium?

Use the following data to work Problems 11 to 13.

The following events have occurred in UK history:

◆ A deep recession hits the world economy.

◆ The world oil price rises sharply.

◆ UK businesses expect future profits to fall.

11 Explain for each event whether it changes short-run aggregate supply, long-run aggregate supply, aggregate demand or some combination of them.

12 Explain the separate effects of each event on UK real GDP and the price level, starting from a position of long-run equilibrium.

13 Explain the combined effects of these events on UK real GDP and the price level, starting from a position of long-run equilibrium.

Use the following data to work Problems 14 and 15.

The table shows the aggregate demand and short-run aggregate supply schedules of Mainland, a country in which potential GDP is €1,050 billion.

Price level	Real GDP demanded	Real GDP supplied in the short run
	(billions of 2005 euros)	
100	1,150	1,050
110	1,100	1,100
120	1,050	1,150
130	1,000	1,200
140	950	1,250
150	900	1,300
160	850	1,350

14 What is the short-run macroeconomic equilibrium real GDP and price level?

15 Does the country have an inflationary gap or a recessionary gap and what is its magnitude?

16 **Geithner Urges Action on Economy**

The US Treasury Secretary Timothy Geithner is reported as having said that the US can no longer rely on consumer spending to be the growth engine of recovery from recession. The government needs to sow the seeds for business investment and exports. 'We can't go back to a situation where we're depending on a near short-term boost in consumption to carry us forward,' he said.

Source: *The Wall Street Journal*, 12 September 2010

a Explain the effects of an increase in consumer spending on the short-run macroeconomic equilibrium.

b Explain the effects of an increase in business investment on the short-run macroeconomic equilibrium.

c Explain the effects of an increase in exports on the short-run macroeconomic equilibrium.

Macroeconomic Schools of Thought

(Study Plan 26.4)

17 Describe what a classical macroeconomist, a Keynesian, and a monetarist would want to do in response to each of the events listed in Problem 11.

18 **Adding Up the Cost of Obama's Agenda**

When campaigning, Barack Obama has made a long list of promises for new federal programmes costing tens of billions of dollars. Obama has said he would strengthen the nation's bridges and dams ($6 billion a year), extend health insurance to more people (part of a $65-billion-a-year health plan), develop cleaner energy sources ($15 billion a year), curb home foreclosures ($10 billion in one-time spending) and add $18 billion a year to education spending. In total a $50-billion plan to stimulate the economy through increased government spending. A different blueprint offered by McCain proposes relatively little new spending and tax cuts as a more effective means of solving problems.

Source: *Los Angeles Times*, 8 July 2008

a Based upon this news clip, explain what macroeconomic school of thought Barack Obama most likely follows.

b Based upon this news clip, explain what macroeconomic school of thought John McCain most likely follows.

19 Based upon the news clip in Problem 16, explain what macroeconomic school of thought US Treasury Secretary Timothy Geithner most likely follows.

ADDITIONAL PROBLEMS AND APPLICATIONS

myeconlab You can work these problems in MyEconLab if assigned by your lecturer.

Aggregate Supply

20 Explain for each event whether it changes the quantity of real GDP supplied, short-run aggregate supply, long-run aggregate supply or a combination of them.

   ◆ UK car producers switch to a new technology that raises productivity.

   ◆ Toyota and Honda build additional plants in the UK.

   ◆ The prices of car parts imported from China rise.

   ◆ Workers in UK car plants agree to a cut in the money wage rate.

   ◆ The UK price level rises.

Aggregate Demand

21 Explain for each event whether it changes the quantity of real GDP demanded or aggregate demand.

   ◆ UK car producers switch to a new technology that raises productivity.

   ◆ Toyota and Honda build new plants in Wales.

   ◆ The prices of car parts imported from China rise.

   ◆ Workers in UK car plants agree to a lower money wage rate.

   ◆ The UK price level rises.

22 Inventories Surge

The US Commerce Department reported that wholesale inventories rose 1.3 per cent in July, the best performance since July 2008. A major driver of the economy since late last year has been the restocking of depleted store shelves.

   Source: Associated Press, 13 September 2010

Explain how a surge in inventories influences current aggregate demand.

23 Low Spending Is Taking Toll on Economy

The US Commerce Department reported that the economy continued to stagnate during the first three months of the year, with a sharp pullback in consumer spending the primary factor at play. Consumer spending fell for a broad range of goods and services, including cars, auto parts, furniture, food and recreation, reflecting a growing inclination toward thrift.

   Source: *The New York Times*, 1 May 2008

Explain how a fall in consumer expenditure influences the quantity of real GDP demanded and aggregate demand.

Explaining Macroeconomic Trends and Fluctuations

Use the following information to work Problems 24 to 26.

The following events have occurred in UK history:

   ◆ The world economy goes into an expansion.

   ◆ UK businesses expect future profits to rise.

   ◆ The government increases its expenditure on goods and services in a time of war or increased international tension.

24 Explain for each event whether it changes short-run aggregate supply, long-run aggregate supply, aggregate demand or some combination of them.

25 Explain the separate effects of each event on UK real GDP and the price level, starting from a position of long-run equilibrium.

26 Explain the combined effects of these events on UK real GDP and the price level, starting from a position of long-run equilibrium.

Use the following data to work Problems 27 and 28.

In Japan, potential GDP is 600 trillion yen and the table shows the aggregate demand and short-run aggregate supply schedules.

Price level	Real GDP demanded	Real GDP supplied in the short run
	(billions of 2005 yen)	
75	600	400
85	550	450
95	500	500
105	450	550
115	400	600
125	350	650
135	300	700

27 **a** Draw a graph of the aggregate demand curve and the short-run aggregate supply curve.

   b What is the short-run equilibrium real GDP and price level?

28 Does Japan have an inflationary gap or a recessionary gap and what is its magnitude?

Use the following information to work Problems 29 to 31.

Spending by Women Jumps

The magazine Women of China reported that Chinese women in big cities spent 63% of their income on consumer goods last year, up from a meager 26% in 2007. Clothing accounted for the biggest chunk of that spending, at nearly 30%, followed by digital products such as mobile phones and cameras (11%) and travel (10%). Chinese consumption as a whole grew faster than the overall economy in the first half of the year and is expected to reach 42% of GDP by 2020, up from the current 36%.

Source: *The Wall Street Journal*, 27 August 2010

29 Explain the effect of a rise in consumption expenditure on real GDP and the price level in the short run.

30 If the economy had been operating at a full-employment equilibrium,

  a Describe the macroeconomic equilibrium after the rise in consumer spending.

  b Explain and draw a graph to illustrate how the economy can adjust in the long run to restore a full-employment equilibrium.

31 Why do changes in consumer spending play a large role in the business cycle?

32 **It's Pinching Everyone**

The current inflationary process is a global phenomenon, but emerging and developing countries have been growing significantly faster than the rest of the world. Because there is no reason to believe that world production will rise miraculously at least in the immediate future, many people expect that prices will keep on rising. These expectations in turn exacerbate the inflationary process. Households buy more of non-perishable goods than they need for their immediate consumption because they expect prices to go up even further. What is worse is that traders withhold stocks from the market in the hope of being able to sell these at higher prices later on. In other words, expectations of higher prices become self-fulfilling.

Source: *The Times of India*, 24 June 2008

Explain and draw a graph to illustrate how inflation and inflation expectations 'become self-fulfilling'.

Macroeconomic Schools of Thought

33 **Should Congress Pass a New Stimulus Bill? No, Cut Taxes and Curb Spending Instead**

The first stimulus was not too meager, but it was the wrong policy prescription. Anybody who studies economic history would know that government spending doesn't produce long-term, sustainable growth, and jobs. The only sure way to perk up the job market is to cut taxes permanently and rein in public spending and excessive regulation.

Source: sgvtribune.com, 11 September 2010

Economists from which macroeconomic school of thought would recommend a second spending stimulus and which a permanent tax cut?

Economics in the News

34 After you have studied *Reading Between the Lines* on pp. 630–631, answer the following questions.

  a Describe the growth of the German economy during 2010.

  b Did Germany have a recessionary gap, an inflationary gap or full employment at the end of 2010?

  c Use the *AS–AD* model to illustrate the German economy during 2010.

  d Suppose that aggregate demand continues to expand rapidly through 2011 and that the ECB does not act strongly enough to dampen the expansion. Use the *AS–AD* model to illustrate the state of the German economy at the end of 2011. Indicate whether there is full employment, a recessionary gap or an inflationary gap.

  e Suppose that aggregate demand continues to expand rapidly through 2011 but that the ECB acts strongly enough to halt the expansion. Use the *AS–AD* model to illustrate the state of the economy at the end of 2011. Indicate whether there is full employment, a recessionary gap or an inflationary gap.

CHAPTER
27

Expenditure Multipliers

After studying this chapter you will be able to:

◆ Explain how expenditure plans are determined

◆ Explain how equilibrium real GDP is determined when the price level is fixed

◆ Explain the expenditure multiplier when the price level is fixed

◆ Explain the relationship between aggregate expenditure and aggregate demand and explain the multiplier when the price level changes

Alicia Keys sings into a microphone in a barely audible whisper and through the magic of electronic amplification, her voice fills an auditorium. Sir Alan Sugar, entrepreneur, and his assistant are being driven along one of London's bumpy roads and thanks to the car's efficient shock absorbers, the assistant's notes are tapped into a BlackBerry without missing a keystroke.

Expenditure plans fluctuate like the volume of Alicia Keys' voice and the uneven surface of a London road. How does the economy react to those fluctuations? Does it behave like an amplifier or a shock absorber?

In *Reading Between the Lines* at the end of the chapter you will see the role played by fluctuations in consumption expenditure during 2009.

Fixed Prices and Expenditure Plans

In the Keynesian model that we study in this chapter, all the firms are like your grocery store: they set their prices and sell the quantities their customers are willing to buy. If they persistently sell a greater quantity than they plan to and are constantly running out of inventory, they eventually raise their prices. And if they persistently sell a smaller quantity than they plan to and have inventories piling up, they eventually cut their prices. But on any given day, their prices are fixed and the quantities they sell depend on demand, not supply.

Because each firm's prices are fixed, for the economy as a whole:

1 The *price level* is fixed and
2 *Aggregate demand* determines real GDP.

The Keynesian model explains fluctuations in aggregate demand at a fixed price level by identifying the forces that determine expenditure plans.

Expenditure Plans

Aggregate expenditure has four components: consumption expenditure, investment, government expenditure on goods and services and net exports (exports minus imports). These four components of aggregate expenditure sum to real GDP (see Chapter 20, pp. 461–462).

Aggregate planned expenditure is equal to the sum of the *planned* levels of consumption expenditure, investment, government expenditure on goods and services and exports minus imports. Two of these components of planned expenditure, consumption expenditure and imports, change when income changes and so they depend on real GDP.

A Two-Way Link Between Aggregate Expenditure and Real GDP

There is a two-way link between aggregate expenditure and real GDP. Other things remaining the same,

◆ An increase in real GDP increases aggregate expenditure and

◆ An increase in aggregate expenditure increases real GDP.

You are now going to study this two-way link starting with a review of the influences on consumption plans and saving plans.

Consumption and Saving Plans

Several factors influence consumption expenditure and saving plans. The more important ones are

1 Disposable income
2 Real interest rate
3 Wealth
4 Expected future income

Disposable income is aggregate income minus taxes plus transfer payments. Aggregate income equals real GDP, so disposable income depends on real GDP. To explore the two-way link between real GDP and planned consumption expenditure, we focus on the relationship between consumption expenditure and disposable income when the other three factors listed above are constant.

Consumption Expenditure and Saving

The table in Figure 27.1 lists the consumption expenditure and the saving that people plan at each level of disposable income. Households can only spend their disposable income on consumption or save it, so planned consumption expenditure plus planned saving always equals disposable income.

The relationship between consumption expenditure and disposable income, other things remaining the same, is called the **consumption function**. The relationship between saving and disposable income, other things remaining the same, is called the **saving function**.

Consumption Function

Figure 27.1(a) shows a consumption function. The *y*-axis measures consumption expenditure and the *x*-axis measures disposable income. Along the consumption function, the points labelled *A* to *F* correspond to the rows of the table. For example, point *E* shows that when disposable income is £800 billion, consumption expenditure is £750 billion. As disposable income increases, consumption expenditure also increases.

At point *A* on the consumption function, consumption expenditure is £150 billion even though disposable income is zero. This consumption expenditure is called autonomous consumption, and it is the amount of consumption expenditure that would take place in the short run even if people had no current income. Consumption expenditure in excess of this amount is called induced consumption, which is the consumption expenditure that is induced by an increase in disposable income.

45° Line

Figure 27.1(a) contains a 45° line, the height of which measures disposble income. At each point on this line, consumption expenditure equals disposable income. Between points *A* and *D*, consumption expenditure exceeds disposable income; between points *D* and *F* consumption expenditure is less than disposable income; and at point *D*, consumption expenditure equals disposable income.

Saving Function

Figure 27.1(b) shows a saving function. Again, the points *A* to *F* correspond to the rows of the table. For example, point *E* shows that when disposable income is £800 billion, saving is £50 billion. As disposable income increases, saving increases. Notice that when consumption expenditure exceeds disposable income in part (a), saving is negative in part (b). Negative saving is called *dissaving*.

Figure 27.1 Consumption Function and Saving Function

(a) Consumption function

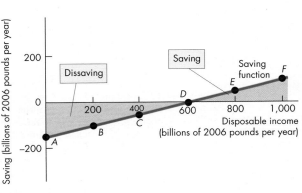

(b) Saving function

	Disposable income	Planned consumption expenditure	Planned saving
	(billions of 2006 pounds per year)		
A	0	150	−150
B	200	300	−100
C	400	450	−50
D	600	600	0
E	800	750	50
F	1,000	900	100

The table shows consumption expenditure and saving plans at various levels of disposable income. When disposable income is £800 (row *E*) planned consumption expenditure is £750 and planned saving is £50.

Part (a) of the figure shows the consumption function (the relationship between consumption expenditure and disposable income). The height of the consumption function measures consumption expenditure at each level of disposable income.

Part (b) shows the saving function (the relationship between saving and disposable income). The height of the saving function measures saving at each level of disposable income. Points *A* to *F* on the consumption and saving functions correspond to the rows in the table.

The height of the 45° line in part (a) measures disposable income. So along the 45° line, consumption expenditure equals disposable income. Consumption expenditure plus saving equals disposable income.

When the consumption function is above the 45° line, saving is negative (dissaving occurs). When the consumption function is below the 45° line, saving is positive. At the point where the consumption function intersects the 45° line, all disposable income is consumed and saving is zero.

Marginal Propensities

The **marginal propensity to consume** (*MPC*) is the fraction of a *change* in disposable income that is consumed. It is calculated as the *change* in consumption expenditure (Δ*C*) divided by the *change* in disposable income (Δ*YD*) that brought it about. That is:

$$MPC = \frac{\Delta C}{\Delta YD}$$

In the table in Figure 27.1, when disposable income increases from £600 billion to £800 billion, consumption expenditure increases from £600 billion to £750 billion. The *MPC* is £150 billion divided by £200 billion, which equals 0.75.

The **marginal propensity to save** (*MPS*) is the fraction of a *change* in disposable income that is saved. It is calculated as the *change* in saving (Δ*S*) divided by the *change* in disposable income (Δ*YD*) that brought it about. That is:

$$MPS = \frac{\Delta S}{\Delta YD}$$

In the table in Figure 27.1, when disposable income increases by £200 billion, saving increases by £50 billion. The *MPS* is £50 billion divided by £200 billion, which equals 0.25.

Because an increase in disposable income is either spent on consumption or saved, the marginal propensity to consume plus the marginal propensity to save equals 1. You can see why by using the equation:

$$\Delta C + \Delta S = \Delta YD.$$

Divide both sides of the equation by the change in disposable income to obtain:

$$\frac{\Delta C}{\Delta YD} + \frac{\Delta S}{\Delta YD} = 1$$

Δ*C*/Δ*YD* is the *marginal propensity to consume* (*MPC*) and Δ*S*/Δ*YD* is the *marginal propensity to save* (*MPS*), so:

$$MPC + MPS = 1$$

Slopes and Marginal Propensities

The slope of the consumption function is the marginal propensity to consume and the slope of the saving function is the marginal propensity to save.

Figure 27.2(a) shows the *MPC* as the slope of the consumption function. A £200 billion increase in disposable income, shown as the base of the red triangle, brings a £150 billion increase in consumption expenditure, shown as the height of the red triangle. The slope of the consumption function is given by the formula 'slope equals rise over run' and is £150 billion divided by £200 billion, which equals 0.75 – the *MPC*.

Figure 27.2(b) shows the *MPS* as the slope of the saving function. A £200 billion increase in disposable income, the base of the red triangle, increases saving by £50 billion, the height of the triangle. The slope of the saving function is £50 billion divided by £200 billion, which equals 0.25 – the *MPS* is 0.25.

Figure 27.2 Marginal Propensities to Consume and Save

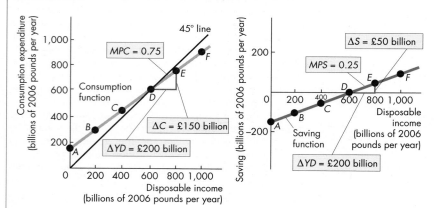

The *MPC* is equal to the change in consumption expenditure divided by the change in disposable income. It is measured by the slope of the consumption function. In part (a), the *MPC* is 0.75.

The marginal propensity to save, *MPS*, is equal to the change in saving divided by the change in disposable income. It is measured by the slope of the saving function. In part (b), the *MPS* is 0.25.

(a) Consumption function   **(b) Saving function**

myeconlab Animation

The UK Consumption Function

Figure 1 shows the UK consumption function. Each blue dot represents consumption expenditure and disposable income for a particular year. (The dots are for the years 1970 to 2010 and the dots of eight of the years are identified.)

The line CF_{70} is an estimate of the UK consumption function in 1970, and the line CF_{10} is an estimate of the UK consumption function in 2010.

The slope of the consumption function in the figure is 0.8, which means that a £100 billion increase in disposable income brings an £80 billion increase in consumption expenditure. This slope is an estimate of the marginal propensity to consume and it is the middle of the range of values that economists have estimated for the marginal propensity to consume.

The consumption function shifts upward over time as other influences on consumption expenditure change. Of these other influences, the real interest rate and wealth fluctuate and so bring upward *and* downward shifts in the consumption function.

But rising expected future disposable income brings a steady upward shift in the consumption function. As the consumption function shifts upward, autonomous consumption expenditure increases.

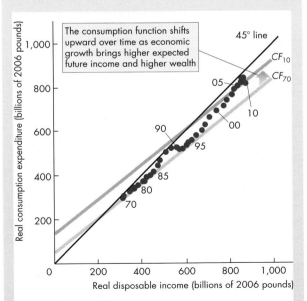

Figure 1 The UK Consumption Function

Source of data: Office for National Statistics.

Consumption and Real GDP

Consumption expenditure changes when disposable income changes and disposable income changes when real GDP changes. So consumption expenditure is a function of real GDP. An increase in real GDP increases disposable income, which increases consumption expenditure. We use this link between consumption expenditure and real GDP to determine equilibrium expenditure. But before we do so, we need to look at one other component of aggregate expenditure: imports. Like consumption expenditure, imports are influenced by real GDP.

Import Function

UK imports are determined by a number of factors, but in the short run with fixed prices, one factor dominates: UK real GDP. Other things remaining the same, the greater the UK real GDP, the larger is the quantity of UK imports. So an increase in UK real GDP brings an increase in UK imports.

The relationship between imports and real GDP is determined by the **marginal propensity to import** – the fraction of an increase in real GDP that is spent on imports. It is calculated as the change in imports divided by the change in real GDP that brought it about, other things remaining the same. For example, if a £100 billion increase in real GDP increases imports by £20 billion, the marginal propensity to import is 0.2.

1   Which components of aggregate planned expenditure are influenced by real GDP?
2   Define and explain how we calculate the marginal propensity to consume and the marginal propensity to save.
3   How do we calculate the effects of real GDP on consumption expenditure and imports by using the marginal propensity to consume and the marginal propensity to import?

You can work these questions in Study Plan 27.1 and get instant feedback.

Real GDP influences consumption expenditure and imports, which in turn influence real GDP. Your next task is to study the second piece of the two-way link between aggregate expenditure and real GDP and see how all the components of aggregate planned expenditure interact to determine real GDP.

Real GDP with a Fixed Price Level

You are now going to learn how expenditure plans determine real GDP when the price level is fixed. We begin by studying the relationship between aggregate planned expenditure and real GDP. We describe this relationship either by an aggregate expenditure schedule or by an aggregate expenditure curve. The *aggregate expenditure schedule* lists aggregate planned expenditure generated at each level of real GDP. The *aggregate expenditure curve* is a graph of the aggregate expenditure schedule.

Then we'll learn about the key distinction between *planned* expenditure and *actual* expenditure. And finally, we'll define and learn what determines equilibrium expenditure and real GDP.

Figure 27.3 Aggregate Expenditure

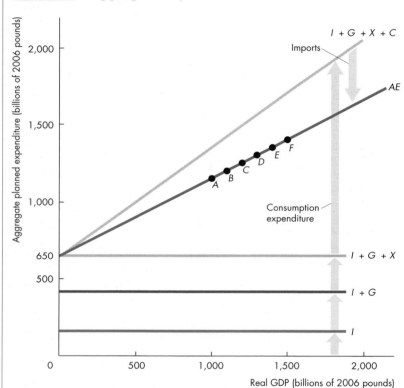

Aggregate planned expenditure is the sum of planned consumption expenditure, investment, government expenditure and exports minus imports. When real GDP is zero, aggregate planned expenditure is £650 billion. When real GDP is £1,000 billion, (row A of the table) planned consumption expenditure is £700 billion, planned investment is £150 billion, planned government expenditure is £260 billion, planned exports are £240 billion and planned imports are £200 billion, so aggregate planned expenditure is £1,150 billion.

The graph shows the relationship between the components of aggregate expenditure and real GDP. The green, blue and orange arrows show investment, government expenditure and exports – the expenditures that do not vary with real GDP. The red and purple arrows show consumption expenditure and imports – the expenditures that vary with real GDP. The red curve *AE* is the aggregate planned expenditure curve.

	Real GDP (Y)	**Consumption expenditure** (C)	**Investment** (I)	**Government expenditure** (G)	**Exports** (X)	**Imports** (M)	**Aggregate planned expenditure** (AE = C + I + G + X − M)
				(billions of 2006 pounds)			
	0	0	150	260	240	0	650
A	1,000	700	150	260	240	200	1,150
B	1,100	770	150	260	240	220	1,200
C	1,200	840	150	260	240	240	1,250
D	1,300	910	150	260	240	260	1,300
E	1,400	980	150	260	240	280	1,350
F	1,500	1,050	150	260	240	300	1,400

Aggregate Planned Expenditure and Real GDP

The table in Figure 27.3 sets out an aggregate expenditure schedule together with the components of aggregate planned expenditure. To calculate aggregate planned expenditure at a given real GDP, we add the various components together. The first column of the table shows real GDP and the second column shows the consumption expenditure generated by each level of real GDP. A £1,000 billion increase in real GDP generates a £700 billion increase in consumption expenditure – the *MPC* is 0.7.

The next two columns show investment and government expenditure on goods and services. Investment depends on factors such as the real interest rate and the expected future profit. But at a given point in time, these factors generate a particular level of investment. Suppose this level of investment is £150 billion. Also, suppose that government expenditure on goods and services is £260 billion.

The next two columns show exports and imports. Exports are influenced by income in the rest of the world, prices of foreign-produced goods and services relative to the prices of similar UK-produced goods and services and foreign exchange rates. But exports are not directly affected by UK real GDP. In the table, exports appear as a constant £240 billion. In contrast, imports increase as real GDP increases. A £100 billion increase in real GDP generates a £20 billion increase in imports – the marginal propensity to import is 0.2.

The final column of the table shows aggregate planned expenditure – the sum of planned consumption expenditure, investment, government expenditure and exports minus imports.

Figure 27.3 plots an aggregate expenditure curve. Real GDP is shown on the *x*-axis and aggregate planned expenditure on the *y*-axis. The aggregate expenditure curve is the red line *AE*. Points *A* to *F* on this curve correspond to the rows of the table. The *AE* curve is a graph of aggregate planned expenditure (the last column) plotted against real GDP (the first column).

Figure 27.3 also shows the components of aggregate expenditure. The constant components – investment (*I*), government expenditure (*G*) and exports (*X*) – are shown by the vertical gaps between the horizontal lines. Consumption expenditure (*C*) is the vertical gap between the lines labelled *I* + *G* + *X* + *C* and *I* + *G* + *X*.

To construct the *AE* curve, subtract imports (*M*) from the *I* + *G* + *X* + *C* line. Aggregate expenditure is

expenditure on UK-produced goods and services. But the components of aggregate expenditure, *C*, *I* and *G* include expenditure on imported goods and services. For example, if you buy a new mobile phone, your expenditure is part of consumption expenditure. But if the mobile phone is a Nokia made in Finland, your expenditure on it must be subtracted from consumption expenditure to find out how much is spent on goods and services produced in the UK – on UK real GDP. Money paid to Nokia for mobile phone imports from Finland does not add to aggregate expenditure in the UK.

Because imports are only a part of aggregate expenditure, when we subtract imports from the other components of aggregate expenditure, aggregate planned expenditure still increases as real GDP increases, as you can see in Figure 27.3.

Consumption expenditure minus imports, which varies with real GDP, is called **induced expenditure**. The sum of investment, government expenditure and exports, which does not vary with real GDP, is called **autonomous expenditure**. Consumption expenditure and imports can also have an autonomous component – a component that does not vary with real GDP. Another way of thinking about autonomous expenditure is that it would be the level of aggregate planned expenditure if real GDP were zero.

In Figure 27.3, autonomous expenditure is £650 billion – aggregate planned expenditure when real GDP is zero. For each £100 billion increase in real GDP, induced expenditure increases by £50 billion.

The aggregate expenditure curve summarizes the relationship between aggregate planned expenditure and real GDP. But what determines the point on the aggregate expenditure curve at which the economy operates? What determines *actual* aggregate expenditure?

Actual Expenditure, Planned Expenditure and Real GDP

Actual aggregate expenditure is always equal to real GDP, as we saw in Chapter 20 (p. 462). But aggregate *planned* expenditure does not necessarily equal actual aggregate expenditure and real GDP. How can actual expenditure and planned expenditure differ from each other? Why don't expenditure plans get implemented? The main reason is that firms might end up with greater inventories or with smaller inventories than planned. People carry out their consumption expenditure plans, the government implements its planned expenditure on goods and services and net exports are as planned. Firms carry out their plans to purchase new buildings, plant and equipment. But one component of investment is the increase in firms' inventories of goods. If aggregate planned expenditure is less than real GDP, firms don't sell all the goods and services they produce and they end up with more inventories than they had planned. They have unplanned inventories. If aggregate planned expenditure is greater than real GDP, firms sell more goods and services than they produce and inventories fall to below the level that firms had planned.

Equilibrium Expenditure

Equilibrium expenditure is the level of aggregate expenditure that occurs when aggregate *planned* expenditure equals real GDP. Equilibrium expenditure is a level of aggregate expenditure and real GDP at which everyone's spending plans are fulfilled. When the price level is fixed, equilibrium expenditure determines real GDP. When aggregate planned expenditure and actual aggregate expenditure are unequal, a process of convergence

Figure 27.4 Equilibrium Expenditure

(a) Equilibrium expenditure

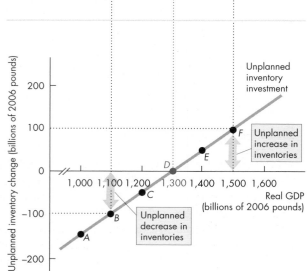

(b) Unplanned inventory change

	Real GDP (Y)	Aggregate planned expenditure (AE)	Unplanned inventory change (Y − AE)
	(billions of 2006 pounds)		
A	1,000	1,150	−150
B	1,100	1,200	−100
C	1,200	1,250	−50
D	**1,300**	**1,300**	**0**
E	1,400	1,350	50
F	1,500	1,400	100

The table shows expenditure plans at different levels of real GDP. When real GDP is £1,300 billion, aggregate planned expenditure equals real GDP.

Part (a) of the figure illustrates equilibrium expenditure, which occurs when aggregate planned expenditure equals real GDP at the intersection of the 45° line and the *AE* curve. Part (b) of the figure shows the forces that bring about equilibrium expenditure.

When aggregate planned expenditure exceeds real GDP, firms' inventories decrease – for example, point *B* in both parts of the figure. Firms have an unplanned decrease in inventories, so they increase production. Real GDP increases.

When aggregate planned expenditure is less than real GDP, firms' inventories increase – for example, point *F* in both parts of the figure. Firms have an unplanned increase in inventories, so they decrease production. Real GDP decreases.

When aggregate planned expenditure equals real GDP, there are no unplanned inventory changes and real GDP remains constant at equilibrium expenditure.

towards equilibrium expenditure occurs. And throughout this convergence process real GDP adjusts. Let's examine equilibrium expenditure and the process that brings it about.

Figure 27.4(a) illustrates equilibrium expenditure. The table sets out aggregate planned expenditure at various levels of real GDP. These values are plotted as points *A* through *F* along the *AE* curve. The 45° line shows all the points at which aggregate planned expenditure equals real GDP. So where the *AE* curve lies above the 45° line, aggregate planned expenditure exceeds real GDP; where the *AE* curve lies below the 45° line, aggregate planned expenditure is less than real GDP; and where the *AE* curve intersects the 45° line, aggregate planned expenditure equals real GDP. Point *D* illustrates equilibrium expenditure. At this point, real GDP is £1,300 billion.

Convergence to Equilibrium

What are the forces that move aggregate expenditure towards its equilibrium level? To answer this question, we must look at a situation in which aggregate expenditure is away from its equilibrium level. Suppose that in Figure 27.4, actual aggregate expenditure is £1,100 billion. But aggregate *planned* expenditure is £1,200 billion, point *B* in Figure 27.4(a). Aggregate planned expenditure exceeds *actual* expenditure. When people spend £1,200 billion and firms produce goods and services worth £1,100 billion, firms' inventories fall by £100 billion, point *B* in Figure 27.4(b). Because the change in inventories is part of investment, *actual* investment is £100 billion less than *planned* investment.

Real GDP doesn't remain at £1,100 billion for very long. Firms have inventory targets based on their sales. When inventories fall below target, firms increase production to restore inventories to their target levels. To increase inventories, firms hire additional labour and increase production.

Suppose that firms increase production in the next period by £100 billion. Real GDP increases by £100 billion to £1,200 billion. But again, aggregate planned expenditure exceeds real GDP. When real GDP is £1,200 billion, aggregate planned expenditure is £1,250 billion, point *C* in Figure 27.4(a). Again, inventories decrease, but this time by less than before. With real GDP of £1,200 billion and aggregate planned expenditure of £1,250 billion, inventories decrease by £50 billion, point *C* in Figure 27.4(b). Again, to restore inventories, firms hire additional labour and production increases; real GDP increases yet further.

The process that we have just described – planned expenditure exceeds real GDP, inventories (stocks) decrease and production increases to restore the inventories back to their target levels – ends when real GDP has reached £1,300 billion. At this real GDP, there is equilibrium expenditure. Unplanned inventory changes are zero. Firms do not change their production.

You can do a similar experiment to the one we've just done, but starting with a level of real GDP greater than equilibrium expenditure. In this case, planned expenditure is less than actual expenditure, inventories pile up and firms cut production. As before, real GDP keeps on changing (decreasing this time) until it reaches its equilibrium level of £1,300 billion.

This process of convergence to equilibrium is driven by changes in production and real GDP, not by changes in prices. Throughout the entire process the price level (and the price of every firm's output) remains fixed.

Review Quiz

1   Explain the relationship between aggregate planned expenditure and real GDP.
2   Distinguish between autonomous expenditure and induced expenditure.
3   What is the relationship between aggregate planned expenditure and real GDP at equilibrium expenditure?
4   What adjusts to achieve equilibrium expenditure?
5   If real GDP and aggregate expenditure are less than equilibrium expenditure, what happens to firms' inventories? How do firms change their production? What happens to real GDP?
6   If real GDP and aggregate expenditure are greater than equilibrium expenditure, what happens to firms' inventories? How do firms change their production? What happens to real GDP?

You can work these questions in Study Plan 27.2 and get instant feedback.

We've learned that when the price level is fixed, real GDP is determined by equilibrium expenditure. And we have seen how unplanned changes in inventories and the production response they generate bring a convergence towards equilibrium expenditure. We're now going to study *changes* in equilibrium expenditure and discover an economic amplifier called the *multiplier*.

The Multiplier

Investment and exports can change for many reasons. A fall in the real interest rate might induce firms to increase their planned investment. A wave of innovation, such as occurred with the spread of multimedia computers in the 1990s, might increase expected future profits and lead firms to increase their planned investment. An economic boom in the US and Canada might lead to a large increase in their expenditure on UK-produced goods and services – UK exports. These are all examples of increases in autonomous expenditure in the UK.

When autonomous expenditure increases, aggregate expenditure increases and so do equilibrium expenditure and real GDP. But the increase in equilibrium expenditure and real GDP is *larger* than the change in autonomous expenditure. The **multiplier** is the amount by which a change in autonomous expenditure is magnified or multiplied to determine the change in equilibrium expenditure and real GDP.

To understand the basic idea of the multiplier, we'll work with an example economy in which there are no income taxes and no imports. So we'll first assume that these factors are absent. Then, when you understand the basic idea, we'll bring these factors back into play and see what difference they make to the multiplier.

The Basic Idea of the Multiplier

Suppose that investment increases. The additional expenditure by businesses means that aggregate expenditure and real GDP increase. The increase in real GDP increases disposable income, and with no income taxes, real GDP and disposable income increase by the same amount. The increase in disposable income brings an increase in consumption expenditure. And the increased consumption expenditure adds even more to aggregate expenditure. Real GDP and disposable income increase further, and so does consumption expenditure. The initial increase in investment brings an even bigger increase in aggregate expenditure because it induces an increase in consumption expenditure. The magnitude of the increase in aggregate expenditure that results from an increase in autonomous expenditure is determined by the *multiplier*.

The table in Figure 27.5 sets out aggregate planned expenditure. When real GDP is £1,200 billion, aggregate planned expenditure is £1,225 billion. For each £100 billion increase in real GDP, aggregate planned

expenditure increases by £75 billion. This aggregate expenditure schedule is shown in the graph as the aggregate expenditure curve AE_0.

Initially, equilibrium expenditure is £1,300 billion. You can see this equilibrium in row B of the table, and in the graph where the curve AE_0 intersects the 45° line at the point marked B.

Now suppose that autonomous expenditure increases by £50 billion. What happens to equilibrium expenditure? You can see the answer in Figure 27.5. When this increase in autonomous expenditure is added to the original aggregate planned expenditure, aggregate planned expenditure increases by £50 billion at each level of real GDP. The new aggregate expenditure curve is AE_1. The new equilibrium expenditure, highlighted in the table (row D'), occurs where AE_1 intersects the 45° line and is £1,500 billion (point D'). At this point, aggregate planned expenditure equals real GDP. Equilibrium expenditure is £1,500 billion.

The Multiplier Effect

In Figure 27.5, the increase in autonomous expenditure of £50 billion increases equilibrium expenditure from £1,300 billion to £1,500 billion – an increase of £200 billion. That is, the change in autonomous expenditure leads, like Alicia Keys' electronic equipment, to an amplified change in equilibrium expenditure. This amplified change is the multiplier effect – equilibrium expenditure increases by more than the increase in autonomous expenditure. The multiplier is greater than 1.

Initially, when autonomous expenditure increases, aggregate planned expenditure exceeds real GDP. As a result, firm's inventories decrease. Firms respond by increasing production to restore their inventories to their target levels. As production increases, so does real GDP. With a higher level of real GDP, *induced expenditure* increases. So equilibrium expenditure increases by the sum of the initial increase in autonomous expenditure and the increase in induced expenditure. In this example, the initial increase in autonomous expenditure is £50 billion and induced expenditure increases by £150 billion, so equilibrium expenditure increases by £200 billion.

Although we have just analysed the effects of an *increase* in autonomous expenditure, the same analysis applies to a decrease in autonomous expenditure. If initially the aggregate expenditure curve is AE_1, equilibrium expenditure and real GDP are £1,500 billion. A decrease in autonomous expenditure of £50 billion shifts the aggregate expenditure curve downward by

Figure 27.5   The Multiplier

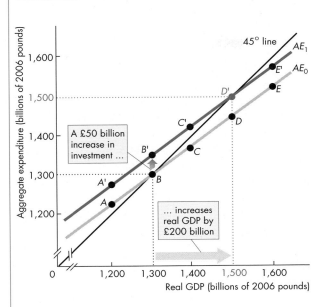

Real GDP (Y)	Aggregate planned expenditure			
	Original (AE₀)		New (AE₁)	
	(billions of 2006 pounds)			
1,200	A	1,225	A'	1,275
1,300	**B**	**1,300**	**B'**	**1,350**
1,400	C	1,375	C'	1,425
1,500	**D**	**1,450**	**D'**	**1,500**
1,600	E	1,525	E'	1,575

A £50 billion increase in autonomous expenditure shifts the *AE* curve upward by £50 billion from *AE₀* to *AE₁*. Equilibrium expenditure increases by £200 billion from £1,300 billion to £1,500 billion. The increase in equilibrium expenditure is 4 times the increase in autonomous expenditure, so the multiplier is 4.

£50 billion to AE_0. Equilibrium expenditure decreases from £1,500 billion to £1,300 billion. The decrease in equilibrium expenditure (£200 billion) is larger than the decrease in autonomous expenditure that brought it about (£50 billion).

Why Is the Multiplier Greater Than 1?

We've seen that equilibrium expenditure increases by more than the increase in autonomous expenditure. This makes the multiplier greater than 1. How come? Why does equilibrium expenditure increase by more than the increase in autonomous expenditure?

The multiplier is greater than 1 because of induced expenditure – an increase in autonomous expenditure *induces* further increases in expenditure. If Vodafone spends £10 million on a new telephone-video system, aggregate expenditure and real GDP immediately increase by £10 million. But that is not the end of the story. Electrical engineers and video-system designers now have more income and they spend part of the extra income on consumption goods and services.

Real GDP now increases by the initial £10 million plus the extra consumption expenditure induced by the £10 million increase in income. The producers of consumption goods and services now have increased incomes and they, in turn, spend part of the increase in their incomes on consumption goods and services. Additional income induces additional expenditure, which creates additional income.

The Size of the Multiplier

The economy is in a recession and now profit prospects start to look better. Firms are making plans for large increases in investment. The world economy is also heading towards expansion and exports are increasing. The question on everyone's lips is: how strong will the expansion be? This is a hard question to answer. But an important ingredient in the answer is working out the size of the multiplier.

The *multiplier* is the amount by which a change in autonomous expenditure is multiplied to determine the change in equilibrium expenditure that it generates. To calculate the multiplier, we divide the change in equilibrium expenditure by the change in autonomous expenditure. Let's calculate the multiplier for the example in Figure 27.5. Initially, equilibrium expenditure is £1,300 billion. Then autonomous expenditure increases by £50 billion and equilibrium expenditure increases by £200 billion to £1,500 billion. So:

$$\text{Multiplier} = \frac{\text{Change in equilibrium expenditure}}{\text{Change in autonomous expenditure}}$$

$$= \frac{£200 \text{ billion}}{£50 \text{ billion}} = 4$$

The Multiplier and the Slope of the *AE* Curve

The magnitude of the multiplier depends on the slope of the *AE* curve. In Figure 27.6, the *AE* curve in part (a) is steeper than the *AE* curve in part (b), and the multiplier is larger in part (a) than in part (b). To see why, let's do a calculation.

Aggregate expenditure and real GDP change because induced expenditure and autonomous expenditure change. The change in real GDP (ΔY) equals the change in induced expenditure (ΔN) plus the change in autonomous expenditure (ΔA). That is:

$$\Delta Y = \Delta N + \Delta A$$

But the change in induced expenditure is determined by the change in real GDP and the slope of the *AE* curve. To see why, begin with the fact that the slope of the *AE* curve equals the 'rise', ΔN, divided by the 'run', ΔY. That is:

$$\text{Slope of the } AE \text{ curve} = \Delta N \div \Delta Y$$

So:

$$\Delta N = \text{Slope of the } AE \text{ curve} \times \Delta Y$$

Now use this equation to replace ΔN in the first equation above to give:

$$\Delta Y = (\text{Slope of the } AE \text{ curve} \times \Delta Y) + \Delta A$$

Now, solve for ΔY as:

$$(1 - \text{Slope of the } AE \text{ curve}) \times \Delta Y = \Delta A$$

and rearrange to give:

$$\Delta Y = \frac{\Delta A}{1 - \text{Slope of the } AE \text{ curve}}$$

Finally, divide both sides of this equation by ΔA:

$$\text{Multiplier} = \frac{\Delta Y}{\Delta A} = \frac{1}{1 - \text{Slope of the } AE \text{ curve}}$$

Using the numbers for Figure 27.5, the slope of the *AE* curve is 0.75, so:

$$\text{Multiplier} = \frac{1}{1 - 0.75} = \frac{1}{0.25} = 4$$

When there are no income taxes and no imports, the slope of the *AE* curve equals the marginal propensity to consume (*MPC*). So the multiplier is:

$$\text{Multiplier} = \frac{1}{(1 - MPC)}$$

But $(1 - MPC)$ equals *MPS*. So another formula for the multiplier is:

$$\text{Multiplier} = \frac{1}{MPS}$$

Because the marginal propensity to save (*MPS*) is a fraction – a number between 0 and 1 – the multiplier is greater than 1.

Figure 27.6 The Multiplier and the Slope of the AE Curve

(a) Multiplier is 4

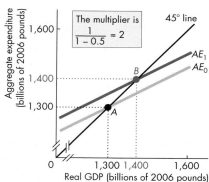

(b) Multiplier is 2

Imports and income taxes make the *AE* curve less steep and reduce the value of the multiplier. In part (a), with no imports and income taxes, the slope of the *AE* curve is 0.75 (the marginal propensity to consume) and the multiplier is 4.

But with imports and income taxes, the slope of the *AE* curve is less than the marginal propensity to consume. In part (b), the slope of the *AE* curve is 0.5. In this case, the multiplier is 2.

Imports and Income Taxes

Imports and income taxes influence the size of the multiplier and make it smaller than it otherwise would be.

To see why, think about what happens following an increase in UK investment. An increase in investment increases real GDP, which in turn increases consumption expenditure in the UK. But part of this increase in consumption expenditure is expenditure on imported goods and services, not expenditure on UK-produced good and services. Only expenditure on goods and services produced in the UK increases UK real GDP. The larger the marginal propensity to import, the smaller is the change in UK real GDP.

Income taxes also make the multiplier smaller than it otherwise would be. Again, think about what happens following an increase in investment. An increase in investment increases real GDP. But because income taxes increase, disposable income increases by less than the increase in real GDP. Consequently, consumption expenditure increases by less than it would if taxes had not changed. The larger the income tax rate, the smaller is the change in disposable income and real GDP.

The marginal propensity to import and the marginal tax rate together with the marginal propensity to consume determine the multiplier. And their combined influence determines the slope of the *AE* curve.

Over time, changes in the marginal propensity to consume, the marginal propensity to import and the income tax rate change the value of the multiplier. These changes make the multiplier hard to predict. But they do not alter the fundamental fact that an initial change in autonomous expenditure leads to a magnified change in aggregate expenditure and real GDP.

The Mathematical Note on pp. 658–661 shows the effects of taxes, imports and the *MPC* on the multiplier.

The Multiplier Process

The multiplier effect isn't a one-shot, overnight event. It is a process that plays out over a few months. Figure 27.7 illustrates the multiplier process. In round 1, autonomous expenditure increases by £50 billion. At this time, real GDP increase by £50 billion (the green bar in round 1). This increase in real GDP increases induced expenditure in round 2. With the slope of the *AE* curve equal to 0.75, induced expenditure increases by 0.75 times the increase in real GDP, so the increase in real GDP of £50 billion induces a further increase in

expenditure of £37.5 billion. This change in induced expenditure (the green bar in round 2), when added to the previous increase in expenditure (the blue bar in round 2), increases aggregate expenditure and real GDP by £87.5 billion. The round 2 increase in real GDP induces a round 3 increase in expenditure. The process repeats through successive rounds. Each increase in real GDP is 0.75 times the previous increase. The cumulative increase in real GDP gradually approaches £200 billion.

Figure 27.7 The Multiplier Process

Increase in real GDP (billions of 2006 pounds)

Expenditure round

■ Increase in current round
■ Cumulative increase from previous rounds

Autonomous expenditure increases by £50 billion. In round 1, real GDP increases by the same amount. With the slope of the *AE* curve equal to 0.75, each additional pound of real GDP induces an additional 0.75 of a pound of induced expenditure.

The round 1 increase in real GDP brings an increase in induced expenditure of £37.5 billion in round 2. At the end of round 2, real GDP has increased by £87.5 billion.

The extra £37.5 billion of real GDP in round 2 brings a further increase in induced expenditure of £28.1 billion in round 3. At the end of round 3, real GDP has increased to £115.6 billion.

This process continues with real GDP increasing by ever smaller amounts. When the process comes to an end, real GDP has increased by a total of £200 billion.

myeconlab Animation

The Multiplier in the Great Depression

The aggregate expenditure model and its multiplier were developed during the 1930s by John Maynard Keynes to understand the most traumatic event in economic history, the *Great Depression*.

In 1929, the global economies were booming. Real GDP had never been higher. By 1933, real GDP had fallen to 94 per cent of its 1929 level and unemployment had doubled from 1.25 million to 2.5 million.

Table 1 shows the GDP numbers and components of aggregate expenditure in 1929 and 1933.

Autonomous investment and exports fell sharply but autonomous consumption rose because a 14 per cent fall in the price level increased the real value of wealth. In all

however, autonomous expenditure fell from $17 billion to $3 billion and exports fell by a large amount. Government expenditure held steady.

The figure uses the *AE* model to illustrate the Great Depression. In 1929, with autonomous expenditure of £10.7 billion, the *AE* curve was AE_{29}. Equilibrium expenditure and real GDP were £15.1 billion. By 1933, autonomous expenditure had fallen to £10.1 billion – a fall of £0.6 billion and the *AE* curve had shifted downward to AE_{33}. Equilibrium expenditure and real GDP had fallen to £14.2 billion.

The decrease in autonomous expenditure of £0.6 billion brought a decrease in real GDP of £0.9 billion. The multiplier was £0.9/£0.6 = 1.5. The slope of the *AE* curve is 0.33 – the fall in induced expenditure, £0.3 billion, divided by the fall in real GDP, £0.9 billion. The multiplier formula, 1/(1 – Slope of the *AE* curve), delivers a multiplier of 1.5.

Table 1

Components of Expenditure

	1929	1933
	(billions of 1929 pounds)	
Induced consumption	8.4	7.9
Induced imports	−4.0	−3.8
Induced expenditure	**4.4**	**4.1**
Autonomous consumption	3.2	4.6
Investment	1.9	1.1
Government expenditure	1.8	1.9
Exports	3.8	2.5
Autonomous expenditure	**10.7**	**10.1**
GDP	**15.1**	**14.2**

Source of data: London & Cambridge Economic Service 1970.

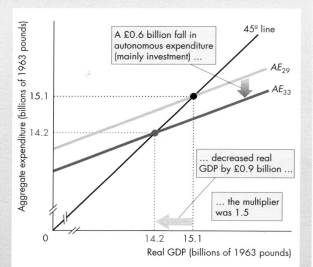

Figure 1 Aggregate Expenditure in the Great Depression

Business Cycle Turning Points

At business cycle turning points, the economy moves from expansion to recession or from recession to expansion. Economists understand these business cycle turning points like seismologists understand earthquakes. They know quite a lot about the forces and mechanisms that produce them, but they can't predict them. The forces that bring business cycle turning points are the swings in investment and exports. The multiplier is the mechanism that gives momentum to the economy's new direction.

The Multiplier and the Price Level

We have just considered adjustments in spending that occur in the very short run when the price level is fixed. In this time frame, the economy's potholes, which are changes in investment and exports, are not smoothed by shock absorbers like those on the car travelling along a country road. Instead, they are amplified like Alicia Keys' voice. But these outcomes occur only when the price level is fixed. We now investigate what happens after a long enough time lapse for the price level to change.

Adjusting Quantities and Prices

When firms can't keep up with sales and their inventories fall below target, they increase production, but at some point they raise their prices. Similarly, when firms find unwanted inventories piling up, they decrease production, but eventually they cut their prices.

So far, we've studied the macroeconomic consequences of firms changing their production levels when their sales change, but we've not looked at the effects of price changes. When individual firms change their prices, the economy's price level changes.

To study the simultaneous determination of real GDP and the price level, we use the *aggregate supply–aggregate demand model*, which is explained in Chapter 26. But to understand how aggregate demand adjusts, we need to work out the connection between the aggregate supply–aggregate demand model and the equilibrium expenditure model that we've used in this chapter. The key to understanding the relationship between these two models is the distinction between the aggregate *expenditure* and aggregate *demand* and the related distinction between the *aggregate expenditure curve* and the *aggregate demand curve*.

Aggregate Expenditure and Aggregate Demand

The aggregate expenditure curve is the relationship between the aggregate planned expenditure and real GDP, when all other influences on aggregate planned expenditure remain the same. The aggregate demand curve is the relationship between the aggregate quantity of goods and services demanded and the price level, when all other influences on aggregate demand remain the same. Let's explore the links between these two relationships.

Deriving the Aggregate Demand Curve

When the price level changes, aggregate planned expenditure changes and the quantity of real GDP demanded changes. The aggregate demand curve slopes downward. Why?

There are two main reasons:

◆ Wealth effect
◆ Substitution effects

Wealth Effect

Other things remaining the same, the higher the price level, the smaller is the purchasing power of people's real wealth. For example, suppose you have £100 in the bank and the price level is 105. If the price level rises to 125, your £100 will buy fewer goods and services. You are less wealthy. With less wealth, you will probably want to spend a bit less and save a bit more. The higher the price level, other things remaining the same, the higher is saving and the lower is consumption expenditure and aggregate planned expenditure.

Substitution Effects

For a given expected future price level, a rise in the price level today makes current goods and services more expensive relative to future goods and services and results in a delay in purchases – an *intertemporal substitution*. A rise in the UK price level, other things remaining the same, makes UK-produced goods and services more expensive relative to foreign-produced goods and services. As a result, UK imports increase and UK exports decrease – an *international substitution*.

When the price level rises, each of these effects reduces aggregate planned expenditure at each level of real GDP. As a result, when the price level *rises*, the aggregate expenditure curve shifts *downward*. A fall in the price level has the opposite effect. When the price level *falls*, the aggregate expenditure curve shifts *upward*.

Figure 27.8(a) shows the shifts of the *AE* curve. When the price level is 105, the aggregate expenditure curve is AE_0, which intersects the 45° line at point *B*. Equilibrium expenditure is £1,300 billion. If the price level increases to 125, the aggregate expenditure curve shifts downward to AE_1, which intersects the 45° line at point *A*. Equilibrium expenditure decreases to £1,200 billion. If the price level decreases to 85, the aggregate

Figure 27.8 Equilibrium Expenditure and Aggregate Demand

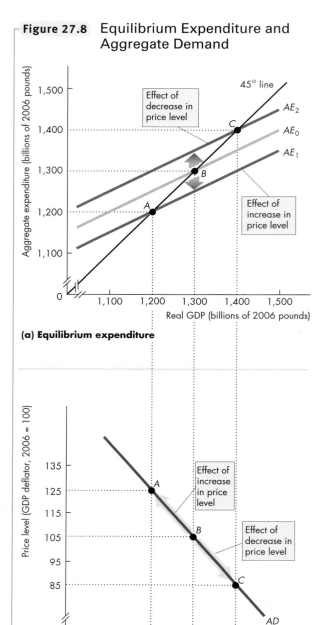

(a) Equilibrium expenditure

(b) Aggregate demand

When the price level is 105, the *AE* curve is AE_0 and equilibrium expenditure is £1,300 billion at point *B*. When the price level rises to 125, the *AE* curve shifts downward to AE_1 and equilibrium expenditure is £1,200 billion at point *A*. When the price level falls to 85, the *AE* curve shifts upward to AE_2 and equilibrium expenditure is £1,400 billion at point *C*. Points *A*, *B* and *C* on the *AD* curve correspond to the equilibrium expenditure points *A*, *B* and *C*.

expenditure curve shifts upward to AE_2, which intersects the 45° line at point *C*. Equilibrium expenditure increases to £1,400 billion.

We've just seen that when the price level changes, other things remaining the same, the aggregate expenditure curve shifts and the equilibrium expenditure changes. But when the price level changes, other things remaining the same, there is a movement along the aggregate demand curve.

Figure 27.8(b) shows the movements along the aggregate demand curve. At a price level of 105, the aggregate quantity of goods and services demanded is £1,300 billion – point *B* on the *AD* curve. If the price level rises to 125, the aggregate quantity of goods and services demanded decreases to £1,200 billion. There is a movement up along the aggregate demand curve to point *A*. If the price level falls to 85, the aggregate quantity of goods and services demanded increases to £1,400 billion. There is a movement down along the aggregate demand curve to point *C*.

Each point on the aggregate demand curve corresponds to a point of equilibrium expenditure. The equilibrium expenditure points *A*, *B* and *C* in Figure 27.8(a) correspond to the points *A*, *B* and *C* on the aggregate demand curve in Figure 27.8(b).

Changes in Aggregate Expenditure and Aggregate Demand

When any influence on aggregate planned expenditure other than the price level changes, both the aggregate expenditure curve and the aggregate demand curve shift. For example, an increase in investment or exports increases both aggregate planned expenditure and aggregate demand and shifts both the *AE* curve and the *AD* curve. Figure 27.9 illustrates the effect of such an increase.

Initially, the aggregate expenditure curve is AE_0 in part (a) and the aggregate demand curve is AD_0 in part (b). The price level is 105, real GDP is £1,300 billion and the economy is at point *A* in both parts of Figure 27.9.

Now suppose that investment increases by £100 billion. At a constant price level of 105, the aggregate expenditure curve shifts upward to AE_1. This curve intersects the 45° line at an equilibrium expenditure of £1,500 billion (point *B*). This equilibrium expenditure of £1,500 billion is the aggregate quantity of goods and services demanded at a price level of 105, as shown by point *B* in part (b). Point *B* lies on a new aggregate

Figure 27.9 A Change in Aggregate Demand

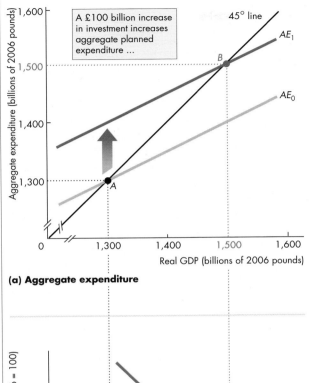

A £100 billion increase in investment increases aggregate planned expenditure ...

(a) Aggregate expenditure

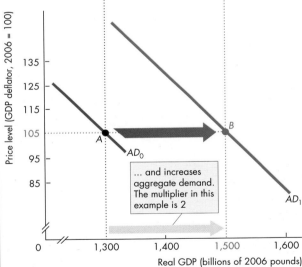

... and increases aggregate demand. The multiplier in this example is 2

(b) Aggregate demand

The price level is 105. When the aggregate expenditure curve is AE_0 in part (a), the aggregate demand curve is AD_0 in part (b). An increase in autonomous expenditure shifts the AE curve upward to AE_1. In the new equilibrium, real GDP is £1,500 billion (at point B). Because the quantity of real GDP demanded at a price level of 105 increases to £1,500 billion, the AD curve shifts rightward to AD_1.

demand curve. The aggregate demand curve has shifted rightward to AD_1.

But how do we know by how much the AD curve shifts? The multiplier determines the answer. The larger the multiplier, the larger is the shift in the aggregate demand curve that results from a given change in autonomous expenditure. In this example, the multiplier is 2. A £100 billion increase in investment produces a £200 billion increase in the aggregate quantity of goods and services demanded at each price level. That is, a £100 billion increase in autonomous expenditure shifts the aggregate demand curve rightward by £200 billion.

A decrease in autonomous expenditure shifts the aggregate expenditure curve downward and shifts the aggregate demand curve leftward. You can see these effects by reversing the change that we've just described. If the economy is initially at point B on the aggregate expenditure curve AE_1 and on the aggregate demand curve AD_1, a decrease in autonomous expenditure shifts the aggregate expenditure curve downward to AE_0. The aggregate quantity of goods and services demanded decreases from £1,500 billion to £1,300 billion, and the aggregate demand curve shifts leftward to AD_0.

Let's summarize what we have just discovered:

> **If some factor other than a change in the price level increases autonomous expenditure, the AE curve shifts upward and the AD curve shifts rightward. The size of the AD curve shift equals the change in autonomous expenditure multiplied by the multiplier.**

Equilibrium Real GDP and the Price Level

In Chapter 26, we learned that aggregate demand and short-run aggregate supply determine equilibrium real GDP and the price level. We've now put aggregate demand under a more powerful microscope and have discovered that a change in investment (or in any component of autonomous expenditure) changes aggregate demand and shifts the aggregate demand curve. The magnitude of the shift depends on the multiplier.

But whether a change in autonomous expenditure results ultimately in a change in real GDP, a change in the price level, or a combination of the two depends on aggregate supply. There are two time frames to consider: the short run and the long run. First we'll see what happens in the short run.

An Increase in Aggregate Demand in the Short Run

Figure 27.10 describes the economy. In part (a), the aggregate expenditure curve is AE_0 and equilibrium expenditure is £1,300 billion – point A. In part (b), aggregate demand is AD_0 and the short-run aggregate supply curve is SAS. (Chapter 26, pp. 615–617 explains the SAS curve.) Equilibrium is at point A, where the aggregate demand and short-run aggregate supply curves intersect. The price level is 105 and real GDP is £1,300 billion.

Now suppose that investment increases by £100 billion. With the price level fixed at 105, the aggregate expenditure curve shifts upward to AE_1. Equilibrium expenditure increases to £1,500 billion – point B in part (a). In part (b), the aggregate demand curve shifts rightward by £200 billion, from AD_0 to AD_1. How far the AD curve shifts is determined by the multiplier when the price level is fixed.

But with this new AD curve, the price level does not remain fixed. The price level rises and as it does so, the AE curve shifts downward. The short-run equilibrium occurs when the aggregate expenditure curve has shifted downward to AE_2 and the new aggregate demand curve, AD_1, intersects the short-run aggregate supply curve at point C. Real GDP is £1,430 billion and the price level is 118.

When the price level effects are taken into account, the increase in investment still has a multiplier effect on real GDP, but the multiplier effect is smaller than it would be if the price level were fixed. The steeper the slope of the SAS curve, the larger is the increase in the price level and the smaller is the multiplier effect on real GDP.

An Increase in Aggregate Demand in the Long Run

Figure 27.11 illustrates the effect of an increase in aggregate demand starting at full employment. Real GDP equals potential GDP, which is £1,300 billion. The long-run aggregate supply curve is LAS. Initially, the economy is at point A in part (a) and part (b).

Investment increases by £100 billion. The aggregate expenditure curve shifts upward to AE_1 and the aggregate demand curve shifts rightward to AD_1. With no change in the price level, the economy would move to point B and real GDP would increase to £1,500 billion. But in the short run, the price level rises to 118 and real GDP increases to £1,430 billion. With the higher price

Figure 27.10 The Multiplier in the Short Run

(a) Aggregate expenditure

(b) Aggregate demand

An increase in investment shifts the AE curve from AE_0 to AE_1 in part (a) and shifts the AD curve from AD_0 to AD_1 in part (b). The price level does not remain at 105 but rises, and the higher price level shifts the AE curve downward from AE_1 to AE_2. The economy moves to point C. In the short run, when prices are flexible, the multiplier is smaller than when the price level is fixed.

myeconlab Animation

Figure 27.11 The Multiplier in the Long Run

(a) Aggregate expenditure

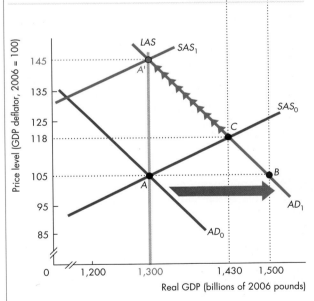

(b) Aggregate demand

Starting from point *A*, an increase in investment shifts the *AE* curve upward to AE_1 and shifts the *AD* curve rightward to AD_1. In the short run, the economy moves to point *C*. In the long run, the money wage rate rises, the *SAS* curve shifts to SAS_1, the price level rises, the *AE* curve shifts back to AE_0 and real GDP decreases. The economy moves to point *A'* and in the long run, the multiplier is zero.

Animation

level, the aggregate expenditure curve shifts from AE_1 to AE_2. The economy is now in a short-run equilibrium at point *C*.

But real GDP now exceeds potential GDP. The workforce is more than fully employed, and in the long run shortages of labour increase the money wage rate. The higher money wage rate increases costs, which decreases short-run aggregate supply. The *SAS* curve begins to shift leftward towards SAS_1. The price level rises further and real GDP decreases. There is a movement along AD_1, and the *AE* curve shifts downward from AE_2 towards AE_0. When the money wage rate and the price level have increased by the same percentage, real GDP again equals potential GDP and the economy is at point *A'*. In the long run, the multiplier is zero.

Review Quiz

1 How does a change in the price level influence the *AE* curve and the *AD* curve?
2 If autonomous expenditure increases with no change in the price level, what happens to the *AE* curve and the *AD* curve? Which curve shifts by an amount determined by the multiplier? Explain why.
3 How does an increase in autonomous expenditure change real GDP in the short run? Does real GDP change by the same amount as the change in aggregate demand? Why or why not?
4 How does real GDP change in the long run when autonomous expenditure increases? Does real GDP change by the same amount as the change in aggregate demand? Why or why not?

You can work these questions in Study Plan 27.4 and get instant feedback.

You are now ready to build on what you've learned about aggregate expenditure fluctuations. We'll study the business cycle and the roles of fiscal policy and monetary policy in smoothing the cycle while achieving price stability and sustained economic growth. In Chapter 28 we study the UK business cycle and inflation, and in Chapters 29 and 30 we study fiscal policy and monetary policy, respectively. But before you leave the current topic, *Reading Between the Lines* on pp. 656–657, looks at the effects of changes in the UK consumption function in the past few years.

Reading Between the Lines

Shifts in the UK Consumption Function

The Financial Times, 28 December 2010

Property Prices Link to Household Spending

Norma Cohen

With house prices set for a modest decline over the coming year, economists are pondering a related question: what effect is this likely to have on patterns of household spending?

The question has been hotly debated, particularly as the house price boom came to a head – not only in Britain but in other economies, including the US, Spain and Ireland, where surging house prices accompanied falling savings rates and rising levels of consumer indebtedness.

Certainly, as prices fell in 2008–09, consumer spending fell sharply. Surveying the economy, economists John Campbell and Joao Cocco concluded that there was indeed a correlation between the wealth that many older households had accumulated in their homes and spending.

'It is tempting to attribute the correlation between house prices and consumption to a direct housing wealth effect: increasing house prices increases wealth, which in turn increases consumption,' they wrote. . . .

Similarly, according to John Muellbauer, a professor of economics at Oxford University who has studied housing and credit trends, suggesting that 'feel-good' factors produce a correlation between rising house prices and rising consumption is to miss the point.

The main reason that consumption rises with house prices is because of what he terms the 'collateral effect' – that is, as housing values rise, the value of collateral which can be used to back a loan rises too. As the value of that collateral falls, lenders, fearing losses, withdraw credit. That leads to economic shocks. . . .

The Essence of the Story

◆ The article asks if there is a link between house prices and consumer spending.

◆ When house prices soared in the UK, US, Spain and Ireland, the saving rate fell.

◆ House prices in the UK fell during 2008 and 2009.

◆ Consumer spending fell in the same period as the fall in house prices.

Economic Analysis

◆ A household's wealth consists of all the assets that it owns minus all the liabilities that it owes.

◆ A household's *real* wealth is its wealth in terms of the goods and services that it can buy and is wealth (nominal wealth) deflated by the price level.

◆ For a household that owns its home, the value of the home minus the outstanding balance owed on a mortgage is part of the household's wealth.

◆ A household's wealth can increase for either of two reasons: the household saves or the assets the household owns rise in value.

◆ In a household's wealth accumulation plan, it doesn't matter for which of these two reasons wealth increases.

◆ If a household's wealth increases because the value of its home has increased, the household has an incentive to increase consumption and save less out of its current disposable income.

◆ The increase in consumption expenditure shifts the consumption function upward.

◆ A fall in house prices, other things remaining the same, decreases wealth and provides the opposite incentive to decrease consumption expenditure and increase saving. The consumption function shifts downward.

◆ Figure 1 shows the annual rate of increase of house prices in the UK (HP inflation) and the growth in real consumption expenditure between 2007 and 2010.

◆ House prices fell during 2008 and 2009 as the annual increase in house prices became negative and wealth decreased.

Figure 1   House prices and consumption expenditure

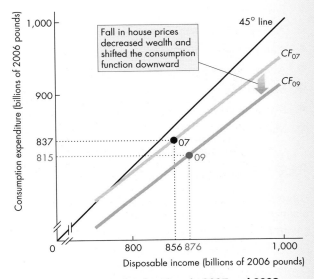

Figure 2   UK consumption functions in 2007 and 2009

◆ The figure also shows that in the third quarter of 2008 the annual growth in real consumer spending became negative, which means that real consumption expenditure fell over the same period as wealth declined.

◆ Figure 2 shows how the fall in the real value of wealth during 2008 and 2009 shifted the consumption function downward from CF_{07} to CF_{09}.

The Algebra of the Multiplier

This note explains the multiplier in greater detail. We begin by defining the symbols we need:

◆ Aggregate planned expenditure, AE

◆ Real GDP, Y

◆ Consumption expenditure, C

◆ Investment, I

◆ Government expenditure, G

◆ Exports, X

◆ Imports, M

◆ Net taxes, T

◆ Disposable income, YD

◆ Autonomous expenditure, A

◆ Autonomous consumption expenditure, a

◆ Autonomous taxes, T_a

◆ Marginal propensity to consume, b

◆ Marginal propensity to import, m

◆ Marginal tax rate, t

Aggregate Expenditure

Aggregate planned expenditure (AE) is the sum of planned consumption expenditure (C), investment (I), government expenditure (G) and exports (X) minus the planned amount of imports (M). That is:

$$AE = C + I + G + X - M$$

Consumption Function

Consumption expenditure (C) depends on disposable income (YD) and we write the consumption function as:

$$C = a + bYD$$

Disposable income (YD) equals real GDP minus net taxes ($Y - T$). So replacing YD with ($Y - T$), the consumption function becomes:

$$C = a + b(Y - T)$$

Net taxes equal autonomous taxes (that are independent of income), T_a, plus induced taxes (that vary with income), tY.

So we can write net taxes as

$$T = T_a + tY$$

Use this equation in the previous one to obtain:

$$C = a - bT_a + b(1 - t)Y$$

This equation describes consumption expenditure as a function of real GDP.

Import Function

Imports depend on real GDP and the import function is:

$$M = mY$$

Aggregate Expenditure Curve

Use the consumption function and the import function to replace C and M in the aggregate planned expenditure equation. That is:

$$AE = a - bT_a + b(1 - t)Y + I + G + X - mY$$

Collect the terms on the right-side of the equation that involve Y to obtain:

$$AE = [a - bT_a + I + G + X] + [b(1 - t) - m]Y$$

Autonomous expenditure (A) is $[a - bT_a + I + G + X]$ and the slope of the AE curve is $[b(1 - t) - m]$. So the equation for the AE curve, which is shown in Figure 1, is:

$$AE = A + [b(1 - t) - m]Y$$

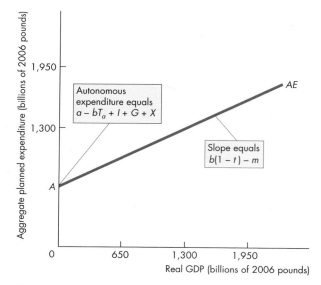

Figure 1 The *AE* Curve

Equilibrium Expenditure

Equilibrium expenditure occurs when aggregate planned expenditure (*AE*) equals real GDP (*Y*). That is:

$$AE = Y$$

In Figure 2, the scales of the *x*-axis (real GDP) and the *y*-axis (aggregate planned expenditure) are identical, so the 45° line shows the points at which aggregate planned expenditure equals real GDP. That is, along the 45° line, *AE* equals *Y*.

Figure 2 shows the point of equilibrium expenditure at the intersection of the *AE* curve and the 45° line.

To calculate equilibrium expenditure and real GDP, we solve the equations for the *AE* curve and the 45° line for the two unknown quantities *AE* and *Y*. So, starting with:

$$AE = A + [b(1 - t) - m]Y$$

$$AE = Y$$

replace *AE* with *Y* in the *AE* equation to obtain:

$$Y = A + [b(1 - t) - m]Y$$

The solution for *Y* is:

$$Y = \frac{1}{1 - [b(1 - t) - m]} A$$

The Multiplier

The *multiplier* equals the change in equilibrium expenditure and real GDP (*Y*) that results from a change in autonomous expenditure (*A*) divided by the change in autonomous expenditure. A change in autonomous expenditure (ΔA) changes equilibrium expenditure and real GDP (ΔY) by:

$$\Delta Y = \frac{1}{1 - [b(1 - t) - m]} \Delta A$$

$$\text{Multiplier} = \frac{1}{1 - [b(1 - t) - m]}$$

The size of the multiplier depends on the slope of the *AE* curve and the larger the slope, the larger is the multiplier. So the multiplier is larger:

1   The greater the marginal propensity to consume (*b*)

2   The smaller the marginal tax rate (*t*)

3   The smaller the marginal propensity to import (*m*)

An economy with no imports and no marginal taxes has *m* = 0 and *t* = 0. In this special case, the multiplier equals 1/(1 − *b*). If *b* is 0.75, the multiplier is 4 as shown in Figure 3.

In an economy with *b* = 0.75, *t* = 0.2 and *m* = 0.1, the multiplier is 1/[1 − 0.75(1 − 0.2) + 0.1], which equals 2.

Make up some more examples to show the effects of different values of *b*, *t* and *m* on the multiplier.

Figure 2 Equilibrium Expenditure

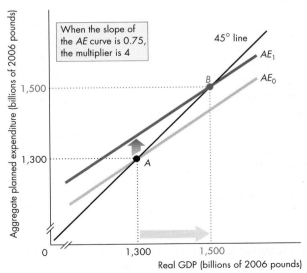

Figure 3 The Multiplier

Government Expenditure Multiplier

The **government expenditure multiplier** equals the change in equilibrium real GDP (Y) that results from a change in government expenditure (G) divided by the change in government expenditure. Because autonomous expenditure is equal to

$$A = a - bT_a + I + G + X$$

the change in autonomous expenditure equals the change in government expenditure. That is,

$$\Delta A = \Delta G$$

You can see from the solution for equilibrium expenditure Y that

$$\Delta Y = \frac{1}{1 - [b(1 - t) - m]} \Delta G$$

The government expenditure multiplier equals

$$\frac{1}{1 - [b(1 - t) - m]}$$

In an economy in which $t = 0$ and $m = 0$, the government expenditure multiplier is $1/(1 - b)$. With $b = 0.75$, the government expenditure multiplier is 4, as Figure 4 shows.

Make up some examples and use the above formula to show how b, m and t influence the government expenditure multiplier.

Autonomous Tax Multiplier

The **autonomous tax multiplier** equals the change in equilibrium expenditure (Y) that results from a change in autonomous taxes (T_a) divided by the change in autonomous taxes. Because autonomous expenditure is equal to

$$A = a - bT_a + I + G + X$$

the change in autonomous expenditure equals $-b$ multiplied by the change in autonomous taxes. That is,

$$\Delta A = -b\Delta T_a$$

You can see from the solution for equilibrium expenditure Y that

$$\Delta Y = \frac{-b}{1 - [b(1 - t) - m]} \Delta T_a$$

The autonomous tax multiplier equals

$$\frac{-b}{1 - [b(1 - t) - m]}$$

In an economy in which $t = 0$ and $m = 0$, the autonomous tax multiplier is $-b/(1 - b)$. In this special case, with $b = 0.75$, the autonomous tax multiplier equals -3, as Figure 5 shows.

Make up some examples and use the above formula to show how b, m and t influence the autonomous tax multiplier.

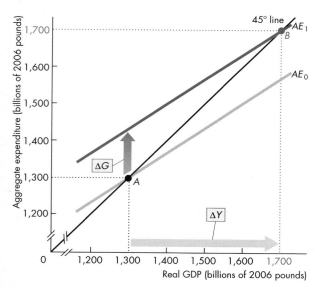

Figure 4 Government Expenditure Multiplier

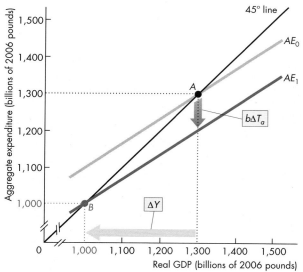

Figure 5 Autonomous Tax Multiplier

Balanced Budget Multiplier

The **balanced budget multiplier** equals the change in equilibrium expenditure (Y) that results from equal changes in government expenditure and autonomous taxes divided by the change in government expenditure. Because government expenditure and autonomous taxes change by the same amount, the budget balance does not change.

The change in equilibrium expenditure that results from the change in government expenditure is

$$\Delta Y = \frac{1}{1 - [b(1 - t) - m]} \Delta G$$

And the change in equilibrium expenditure that results from the change in autonomous taxes is

$$\Delta Y = \frac{-b}{1 - [b(1 - t) - m]} \Delta T_a$$

So the change in equilibrium expenditure resulting from the changes in government expenditure and autonomous taxes is

$$\Delta Y = \frac{1}{1 - [b(1 - t) - m]} \Delta G +$$

$$\frac{-b}{1 - [b(1 - t) - m]} \Delta T_a$$

Notice that

$$\frac{1}{1 - [b(1 - t) - m]}$$

is common to both terms on the right side. So we can rewrite the equation as

$$\Delta Y = \frac{-b}{1 - [b(1 - t) - m]} (\Delta G - \Delta T_a)$$

The AE curve shifts upward by $\Delta G - b\Delta T_a$, as shown in Figure 6.

But the change in government expenditure equals the change in autonomous taxes. That is,

$$\Delta G = \Delta T_a$$

So we can write the equation as

$$\Delta Y = \frac{1 - b}{1 - [b(1 - t) - m]} \Delta G$$

The balanced budget multiplier equals

$$\frac{1 - b}{1 - [b(1 - t) - m]}$$

In an economy in which $t = 0$ and $m = 0$, the balanced budget multiplier is $(1 - b)/(1 - b)$, which equals 1, as Figure 6 shows.

Make up some examples and use the above formula to show how b, m and t influence the balanced budget multiplier.

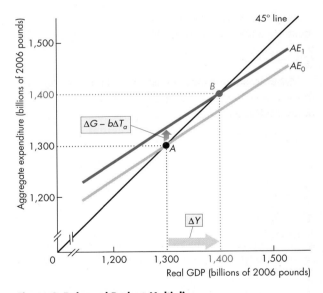

Figure 6 Balanced Budget Multiplier

SUMMARY

Key Points

Fixed Prices and Expenditure Plans
(pp. 638–641)

◆ When the price level is fixed, expenditure plans determine real GDP.

◆ Consumption expenditure is determined by disposable income, and the marginal propensity to consume (*MPC*) determines the change in consumption expenditure brought about by a change in disposable income. Real GDP is the main influence on disposable income.

◆ Imports are determined by real GDP, and the marginal propensity to import determines the change in imports brought about by a change in real GDP.

Working Problems 1 to 3 will give you a better understanding of fixed prices and expenditure plans.

Real GDP with a Fixed Price Level
(pp. 642–645)

◆ Aggregate *planned* expenditure depends on real GDP.

◆ Equilibrium expenditure occurs when aggregate planned expenditure equals actual expenditure and real GDP.

Working Problems 4 to 7 will give you a better understanding of real GDP with a fixed price level.

The Multiplier (pp. 646–650)

◆ The multiplier is the magnified effect of a change in autonomous expenditure on equilibrium expenditure and real GDP.

◆ The multiplier is determined by the slope of the *AE* curve.

◆ The slope of the *AE* curve is influenced by the marginal propensity to consume, the marginal propensity to import and the income tax rate.

Working Problems 8 to 11 will give you a better understanding of the multiplier.

The Multiplier and the Price Level
(pp. 651–655)

◆ The aggregate demand curve is the relationship between the quantity of real GDP demanded and the price level, other things remaining the same.

◆ The aggregate expenditure curve is the relationship between aggregate planned expenditure and real GDP, other things remaining the same.

◆ At a given price level, there is a given aggregate expenditure curve. A change in the price level changes aggregate planned expenditure and shifts the aggregate expenditure curve. A change in the price level also creates a movement along the aggregate demand curve.

◆ A change in autonomous expenditure that is not caused by a change in the price level shifts the aggregate expenditure curve and shifts the aggregate demand curve. The magnitude of the shift of the aggregate demand curve depends on the multiplier and the change in autonomous expenditure.

◆ The multiplier decreases as the price level changes. The multiplier in the long run is zero.

Working Problems 12 to 21 will give you a better understanding of the multiplier and the price level.

Key Terms

Aggregate planned expenditure, 638
Autonomous expenditure, 643
Autonomous tax multiplier, 660
Balance budget multiplier, 661
Consumption function, 638
Disposable income, 638
Equilibrium expenditure, 644
Government expenditure multiplier, 660
Induced expenditure, 643
Marginal propensity to consume, 640
Marginal propensity to import, 641
Marginal propensity to save, 640
Multiplier, 646
Saving function, 638

myeconlab You can work Problems 1 to 22 in MyEconLab Chapter 27 Study Plan and get instant feedback.

Fixed Prices and Expenditure Plans

(Study Plan 27.1)

Use the following data to work Problems 1 and 2.

You are given the following information about the US economy.

Disposable income	Consumption expenditure
(trillions of dollars per year)	
3	3.4
4	4.2
5	5.0
6	5.8
7	6.6

1 Calculate the marginal propensity to consume.

2 Calculate saving at each level of disposable income and calculate the marginal propensity to save.

3 **The US and China's Savings Problems**

Last year China saved about half of its gross domestic product while the US saved only 13 per cent of its national income. The contrast is even starker at the household level – a personal saving rate in China of about 30 per cent of household income, compared with a US rate that dipped into negative territory last year (–0.4% of after-tax household income). Similar extremes show up in the consumption shares of the two economies.

Source: *Fortune*, 8 March 2006

Compare the *MPC* and *MPS* in the US and China. Why might they differ?

Real GDP with a Fixed Price Level

(Study Plan 27.2)

Use the figure in the next column to work Problems 4 and 5.

The figure illustrates the components of aggregate planned expenditure on Turtle Island. Turtle Island has no imports or exports, no incomes taxes and the price level is fixed.

4 Calculate autonomous expenditure and the marginal propensity to consume.

5 **a** What is aggregate planned expenditure when real GDP is €6 billion?

   b If real GDP is €4 billion, what is happening to inventories?

   c If real GDP is €6 billion, what is happening to inventories?

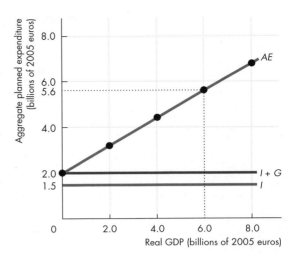

6 Explain the difference between induced consumption expenditure and autonomous consumption expenditure. Why isn't all consumption expenditure induced expenditure?

7 **US Recovery?**

In the second quarter, US businesses increased spending on equipment and software by 21.9 per cent, while a category that includes home building grew amid a rush by consumers to take advantage of tax credits for homes.

Source: *The Wall Street Journal*, 31 July 2010

Explain how an increase in business investment at a constant price level changes equilibrium expenditure.

The Multiplier (Study Plan 27.3)

Use the following data to work Problems 8 and 9.

An economy has a fixed price level, no imports and no income taxes. *MPC* is 0.80 and real GDP is £150 billion. Businesses increase investment by £5 billion.

8 Calculate the multiplier and the change in real GDP.

9 Calculate the new real GDP and explain why real GDP increases by more than £5 billion.

Use the following data to work Problems 10 and 11.

An economy has no imports and no income taxes. An increase in autonomous expenditure of £200 billion increases equilibrium expenditure by £800 billion.

10 Calculate the multiplier and the marginal propensity to consume.

11 What happens to the multiplier if an income tax is introduced?

The Multiplier and the Price Level

(Study Plan 27.4)

Use the following data to work Problems 12 to 16.

Suppose that the economy is at full employment, the price level is 100 and the multiplier is 2. Investment increases by £100 billion.

12 What is the change in equilibrium expenditure if the price level remains at 100?

13 **a** What is the immediate change in the quantity of real GDP demanded?

   b In the short run, does real GDP increase by more than, less than or the same amount as the immediate change in the quantity of real GDP demanded?

14 In the short run, does the price level remain at 100? Explain why or why not.

15 **a** In the long run, does real GDP increase by more than, less than or the same amount as the immediate increase in the quantity of real GDP demanded?

   b Explain how the price level changes in the long run.

16 Are the values of the multipliers in the short run and the long run larger or smaller than 2?

Use the following news clip to work Problems 17 and 18.

Cameron Wants Foreign Office to Make Export Drive a Priority

David Cameron vowed yesterday to put the Foreign Office in the vanguard of Britain's export drive, appointing a trade expert as its new permanent secretary and opening the door for business people to become ambassadors.

Source: *The Financial Times*, 22 July 2010

17 Will a £1 billion increase in UK exports increase aggregate expenditure by more than, less than or exactly £1 billion? Explain.

18 Explain and draw a graph to illustrate how an increase in exports will influence aggregate expenditure and aggregate demand in both the short run and the long run.

Use the following news clip to work Problems 19 to 21.

Working Poor More Pinched as Rich Cut Back

Cutbacks by the wealthy have a ripple effect across all consumer spending, said Michael P. Niemira, chief economist at the International Council of Shopping Centers. When shoppers splurge on $1,000 dinners and $300 limousine rides, that means fatter tips for the waiter and the driver. Sales clerks at upscale stores, who typically earn sales commissions, also depend on spending sprees of mink coats and jewelry.

Source: MSNBC, 28 January 2008

19 Explain and draw a graph to illustrate the process by which 'cutbacks by the wealthy have a ripple effect'.

20 Explain and draw a graph to illustrate how real GDP will be driven back to potential GDP in the long run.

21 Why is the multiplier only a short-run influence on real GDP?

Mathematical Note (Study Plan 27.MN)

22 You are given the following information about an economy: autonomous consumption expenditure is €50 billion, investment is €200 billion and government expenditure is €250 billion. The marginal propensity to consume is 0.7 and net taxes are €250 billion. Exports are €500 billion and imports are €450 billion. Assume that net taxes and imports are autonomous and the price level is fixed.

   a What is the consumption function?

   b What is the equation of the *AE* curve?

   c Calculate equilibrium expenditure.

   d Calculate the multiplier.

   e If investment decreases to €150 billion, what is the change in equilibrium expenditure?

   f Describe the process in part (e) that moves the economy to its new equilibrium expenditure.

Fixed Prices and Expenditure Plans

Use the following data to work Problems 23 and 24.

You are given the following information about the economy of Australia.

Disposable income	Saving
(billions of dollars per year)	
0	−5
100	20
200	45
300	70
400	95

23 Calculate the marginal propensity to save.

24 Calculate consumption at each level of disposable income. Calculate the marginal propensity to consume.

Use the following news clip to work Problems 25 to 27.

Americans $1.7 trillion Poorer

Americans saw their net worth decline by $1.7 trillion in the first quarter of 2008. Until then, net worth had been rising steadily since 2003. Michael Englund, senior economist with Action Economics said that the recent declines may not affect consumer spending. Americans have actually spent more in recent months – spending everything in their wallet and borrowing more. Household debt grew by 3.5 per cent with consumer credit rising at an annual rate of 5.75 per cent.

Source: CNN, 5 June 2008

25 Explain and draw a graph to illustrate how a decrease in household wealth theoretically influences the consumption function and saving function.

26 According to the news clip, how did consumption expenditure respond in the first quarter of 2008? What factors might explain why consumers' actual response differs from what the consumption function model predicts?

27 Draw a graph of a consumption function and show at what point consumers were actually operating in the first quarter. Explain your answer.

Real GDP with a Fixed Price Level

Use the following spreadsheet, which lists real GDP (Y) and the components of aggregate planned expenditure in billions of pounds, to work Problems 28 and 29.

	A	B	C	D	E	F	G
1		Y	C	I	G	X	M
2	A	100	110	50	60	60	15
3	B	200	170	50	60	60	30
4	C	300	230	50	60	60	45
5	D	400	290	50	60	60	60
6	E	500	350	50	60	60	75
7	F	600	410	50	60	60	90

28 Calculate autonomous expenditure. Calculate the marginal propensity to consume.

29 a What is aggregate planned expenditure when real GDP is £200 billion?

b If real GDP is £200 billion, explain the process that moves the economy towards equilibrium expenditure.

c If real GDP is £500 billion, explain the process that moves the economy towards equilibrium expenditure.

30 **UK Recovery Fears Remain Despite Growth**

Second quarter 2010 growth of the UK economy was at the fastest pace in 11 years. Despite this momentum, doubts remain over whether a strong recovery can be sustained. The two key components of demand that grew fastest were consumption expenditure and inventory investment. Inventory investment added 1 percentage point to growth and is at its highest since 1994.

With the effect of inventory investment likely to be short-lived and no other sources of stimulus, growth may slow.

Source: *The Financial Times*, 28 August 2010

Explain why a rise in inventories is associated with recovery and why the contribution of inventory investment to aggregate expenditure is likely to be short-lived.

The Multiplier

31 Darling's Risky Fiscal Stimulus

The government is taking a gamble. The Chancellor of the Exchequer is poised to unveil a short, sharp fiscal stimulus to boost consumption and stop the economy from sliding into a slump. The magnitude of the stimulus must be credible: something of the order of 1.5 per cent of gross domestic product.

Source: *The Financial Times*, 24 November 2008

If the slope of the *AE* curve in the UK is 0.6, calculate the immediate change in aggregate planned expenditure and the change in equilibrium expenditure if the price level doesn't change.

32 Cameron Bets On Northern Recipe For Growth

David Cameron has claimed that his 'northern alliance' with Nordic and Baltic states will become a driving force in 'the greenest region in the world' and 'avant-garde in delivering jobs and growth'. Mr Cameron announced that energy ministers would work on plans for an 'electricity super grid' to take green energy from one country to another and from offshore wind farms through sub-sea cables.

Source: *The Financial Times*, 21 January 2011

If, with high cyclical unemployment, the UK along with the Nordic and Baltic states spent £100 billion on green energy projects, how would equilibrium expenditure change, other things remaining the same?

The Multiplier and the Price Level

33 Stimulating Debate

Should the government hire people to bury banknotes down disused mineshafts, so that private firms can hire yet more people to dig them up again? Keynes said that there are circumstances in which government spending as wasteful as this could nevertheless be beneficial.

Source: *The Financial Times*, 30 October 2010

Explain and draw a graph to illustrate the effect of the activities described in the news clip on equilibrium expenditure, real GDP and the price level and contrast the outcomes for (i) an economy with considerable unemployment and (ii) an economy that is close to full employment.

Use the following news clip to work Problems 34 to 36.

Where Americans Will (and Won't) Cut Back

Consumer confidence has tumbled but even as consumers cut back on spending, there are some things they refuse to give up. Market research reports that Americans are demonstrating a strong reluctance to give up on everyday pleasures, but many are forced to prioritize and scale back some of their spending. Spending on dining out, out-of-the-home entertainment, clothes, vacations and buying lunch tend to be the first to be cut and many Americans are driving less and staying at home

more. A whopping 50 per cent of Americans plan to buy an HD or flat-panel TV in the next year. Cable and satellite TV subscriptions are also way down the list on cutbacks. Despite the expense, another thing consumers refuse to go without completely is travel. Even in these tough times, 59 per cent of Americans plan to take a trip in the next six months.

Source: CNN, 16 July 2008

34 Which of the expenditures listed in the news clip are part of induced consumption expenditure and which are part of autonomous consumption expenditure? Explain why all consumption expenditure is not induced expenditure.

35 Explain and draw a graph to illustrate how declining consumer confidence influences aggregate expenditure and aggregate demand in the short-run.

36 Explain and draw a graph to illustrate the long-run effect on aggregate expenditure and aggregate demand of the decline in consumer confidence.

Economics in the News

37 After you have studied *Reading Between the Lines* on pp. 656–657 answer the following questions.

a What happened to UK house prices during 2008 and 2009?

b Why might a fall in house prices be associated with a fall in consumption, 'other things remaining the same'?

c What happened to consumer spending in the UK in 2008 and 2009? Explain why.

d What 'other things' could have happened in the economy that might have led to a different outcome?

38 The Biggest Risk to Growth

The biggest risk to growth in the UK is that the economies of its trading partners suffer badly, slowing demand for exports.

Source: *The Financial Times*, 11 November 2010

a Does the decrease in UK exports bring a movement along the *AE* curve or a shift of the *AE* curve?

b Suppose that UK exports decrease by £120 billion in 2011 and the multiplier is 1.5. If other things remain the same, what is the decrease in real GDP?

c Suppose that the UK economy is at full employment in 2011 and exports increase by £120 billion. Will there still be a multiplier effect?

Mathematical Note

39 In an economy, autonomous spending is £20 billion and the slope of the *AE* curve is 0.6.

a What is the equation of the *AE* curve?

b Calculate equilibrium expenditure.

c Calculate the multiplier if the price level is fixed.

Inflation and Output Cycles

After studying this chapter you will be able to:

◆ Explain how demand-pull and cost-push forces bring cycles in inflation and output

◆ Explain the short-run and long-run trade-off between inflation and unemployment

◆ Explain the main theories of the business cycle

In the 1970s, Arthur M. Okun proposed what he called the 'misery index' – the sum of inflation and unemployment. Inflation and unemployment do make us miserable: inflation raises our cost of living and unemployment either takes our jobs or scares us into thinking that we might lose our jobs. Following the global financial crisis, both inflation and unemployment in the UK have risen and real income growth has fallen.

We want rapid income growth, low unemployment and low inflation, but can we have all three at the same time? Or do we face a trade-off among them? As this chapter explains, we face a trade-off in the short run but not in the long run. At the end of the chapter, in *Reading Between the Lines*, you will see how China is handling this short-run trade-off .

◈ Inflation Cycles

In the long run, inflation is a monetary phenomenon. It occurs if the quantity of money grows faster than potential GDP. But in the short run, many factors can start an inflation, and real GDP and the price level interact. To study these interactions, we distinguish between two sources of inflation:

◆ Demand-pull inflation

◆ Cost-push inflation

Demand-pull Inflation

An inflation that results from an initial increase in aggregate demand is called **demand-pull inflation**. Demand-pull inflation can be kicked off by any of the factors that change aggregate demand. Examples are a cut in the interest rate, an increase in the quantity of money, an increase in government expenditure, a tax cut, an increase in exports, or an increase in investment stimulated by an increase in expected future profits.

Initial Effect of an Increase in Aggregate Demand

Suppose that last year the price level was 110 and both real GDP and potential GDP were £1,300 billion. Figure 28.1(a) illustrates this situation. The aggregate demand curve is AD_0, the short-run aggregate supply curve is SAS_0 and the long-run aggregate supply curve is *LAS*.

Now aggregate demand increases and the aggregate demand curve shifts rightward to AD_1. Such a situation arises if, for example, the Bank of England lowers the interest rate or exports increase.

With no change in potential GDP and with no change in the money wage rate, the long-run aggregate supply curve and the short-run aggregate supply curve remain at *LAS* and SAS_0, respectively.

The price level rises to 113 and real GDP increases above potential GDP to £1,350 billion. The economy experiences a 2.7 per cent rise in the price level (a price level of 113 compared with 110 in the previous year) and a rapid expansion of real GDP. Unemployment falls below its natural rate. The next step in the unfolding story is a rise in the money wage rate.

Figure 28.1 A Demand-pull Rise in the Price Level

(a) Initial effect

(b) The money wage adjusts

In part (a), the aggregate demand curve is AD_0, the short-run aggregate supply curve is SAS_0 and the long-run aggregate supply curve is *LAS*. The price level is 110 and real GDP is £1,300 billion, which equals potential GDP. Aggregate demand increases to AD_1. The price level rises to 113 and real GDP increases to £1,350 billion.

In part (b), starting from above full employment, the money wage rate begins to rise and the short-run aggregate supply curve shifts leftward towards SAS_1. The price level rises further and real GDP returns to potential GDP.

Money Wage Response

Real GDP cannot remain above potential GDP forever. With unemployment below its natural rate, there is a shortage of labour. In this situation, the money wage rate begins to rise. As the money wage rate rises, short-run aggregate supply starts to decrease and the *SAS* curve starts to shift leftward. The price level rises further and real GDP begins to decrease.

With no further change in aggregate demand – the aggregate demand curve remains at AD_1 – this process comes to an end when the short-run aggregate supply curve has shifted to SAS_1 in Figure 28.1(b). At this time, the price level has increased to 121 and real GDP has returned to potential GDP of £1,300 billion, the level from which it started.

A Demand-pull Inflation Process

The events that we've just studied bring *a one-time rise in the price level*, not inflation. For inflation to occur, aggregate demand must persistently increase.

The only way in which aggregate demand can persistently increase is if the quantity of money persistently increases. Suppose the government has a budget deficit that it finances by selling bonds. Also suppose that the Bank of England buys these bonds. When the Bank of England buys bonds, it creates more money. If the Bank of England responds continually to the budget deficit, aggregate demand increases year after year. The aggregate demand curve keeps shifting rightward. This persistent increase in aggregate demand puts continual upward pressure on the price level. The economy now experiences demand-pull inflation.

Figure 28.2 illustrates the process of demand-pull inflation. The starting point is the same as that shown in Figure 28.1. The aggregate demand curve is AD_0 and the short-run aggregate supply curve is SAS_0. Real GDP is £1,300 billion and the price level is 110. Aggregate demand increases, shifting the aggregate demand curve to AD_1. Real GDP increases to £1,350 billion and the price level rises to 113. The economy is at an above full-employment equilibrium. There is a shortage of labour and the money wage rate rises. The short-run aggregate supply curve shifts leftward to SAS_1. The price level rises to 121 and real GDP returns to potential GDP.

But the Bank of England increases the quantity of money again and aggregate demand continues to increase. The aggregate demand curve shifts rightward to AD_2. The price level rises further to 125 and real GDP again exceeds potential GDP at £1,350 billion. Yet

Figure 28.2   A Demand-pull Inflation Spiral

Each time the quantity of money increases, aggregate demand increases and the aggregate demand curve shifts rightward from AD_0 to AD_1 to AD_2 and so on.

Each time real GDP goes above potential GDP, the money wage rate rises and the short-run aggregate supply curve shifts leftward from SAS_0 to SAS_1 to SAS_2 and so on.

The price level rises from 110 to 113, 121, 125, 133 and so on. There is a perpetual demand-pull inflation. Real GDP fluctuates between £1,300 billion and £1,350 billion.

myeconlab Animation ◆

again, the money wage rate rises and decreases short-run aggregate supply. The *SAS* curve shifts to SAS_2 and the price level rises further to 133. As the quantity of money continues to grow, aggregate demand increases and the price level rises in an ongoing demand-pull inflation process.

Demand-pull Inflation in Liverpool

You may better understand the inflation process that we've just described by considering what is going on in an individual part of the economy, such as a Liverpool soft drinks factory.

Initial Increase in Demand

Initially, when aggregate demand increases, the demand for soft drinks increases and the price of soft drinks rises. Faced with a higher price, the soft drinks factory works overtime and increases production. Conditions are good for workers in Liverpool and the soft drinks factory finds it hard to hang on to its best people. To do so it has to offer higher money wages. As money wages increase, so do the soft drinks factory's costs.

Aggregate Demand

What happens next depends on what happens to aggregate demand. If aggregate demand remains unchanged, the firm's costs are increasing but the price of soft drinks is not increasing as quickly as the factory's costs. Production is scaled back. Eventually, the money wage rate and costs increase by the same percentage as the price of soft drinks. In real terms, the soft drinks factory is in the same situation as it was initially – before the increase in aggregate demand. The soft drinks factory produces the same quantity of soft drinks and employs the same amount of labour as before the increase in aggregate demand.

But if aggregate demand continues to increase, so does the demand for soft drinks and the price of lemonade rises at the same rate as the money wage rate. The soft drinks factory continues to operate above full employment and there is a persistent shortage of labour. Prices and wages chase each other upward in an unending spiral.

Demand-pull Inflation in the UK

A demand-pull inflation like the one you've just studied occurred in the UK during the 1970s.

In 1972–1973, the government pursued an expansionary monetary and fiscal policy. Its goal was to lower the unemployment rate and boost the rate of economic growth. The aggregate demand curve shifted rightward, the price level increased quickly and real GDP moved above potential GDP. The money wage rate started to rise more quickly and the short-run aggregate supply curve shifted leftward.

The Bank of England responded with a further increase in the growth rate of the quantity of money. Aggregate demand increased even more quickly and a demand-pull inflation spiral unfolded.

By the mid-1970s, the inflation rate had reached more than 20 per cent a year. Contrary to the government's goal, the growth rate of real GDP didn't increase and the unemployment rate didn't decrease. On the contrary, the late 1970s were years of extremely high unemployment and slow real GDP growth.

You've seen how demand-pull inflation arises. Let's now see how an aggregate supply shock brings cost-push inflation.

Cost-push Inflation

An inflation that is kicked off by an increase in costs is called **cost-push inflation**. The two main sources of increases in costs are:

1 An increase in the money wage rate
2 An increase in the money prices of raw materials

At a given price level, the higher the cost of production, the smaller is the amount that firms are willing to produce. So if the money wage rate rises or if the prices of raw materials (for example, oil) rise, firms decrease their supply of goods and services. Aggregate supply decreases, and the short-run aggregate supply curve shifts leftward.[1]

Let's trace the effects of such a decrease in short-run aggregate supply on the price level and real GDP.

Initial Effect of a Decrease in Aggregate Supply

Suppose that last year the price level was 110 and real GDP was £1,300 billion. Potential real GDP was also £1,300 billion. Figure 28.3(a) illustrates this situation. The aggregate demand curve was AD_0, the short-run aggregate supply curve was SAS_0 and the long-run aggregate supply curve was LAS.

Now the world's oil producers form a price-fixing organization that strengthens their market power and increases the relative price of oil. They raise the price of oil, and this action decreases short-run aggregate supply. The short-run aggregate supply curve shifts leftward to SAS_1. The price level rises to 117 and real GDP decreases to £1,250 billion. The economy is at a below full-employment equilibrium and there is a recessionary gap.

The event that we've just described is a *one-time rise in the price level*. It is not inflation. In fact, a supply shock on its own cannot cause inflation. Something more must happen to enable a one-time supply shock, which causes a one-time rise in the price level, to be converted into a process of ongoing inflation. The quantity of money must persistently increase. Sometimes it does increase, as you will now see.

---

[1] Some cost-push forces, such as an increase in the price of oil accompanied by a decrease in the availability of oil, can also decrease long-run aggregate supply. We'll ignore such effects here and examine cost-push factors that change only short-run aggregate supply.

Figure 28.3   A Cost-push Rise in the Price Level

(a) Initial cost push

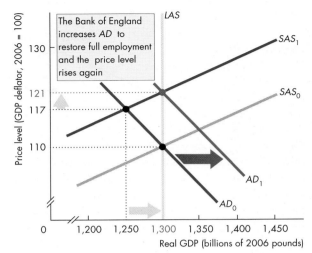

(b) The Bank of England responds

Initially, the aggregate demand curve is AD_0, the short-run aggregate supply curve is SAS_0 and the long-run aggregate supply curve is LAS. A decrease in aggregate supply shifts the short-run aggregate supply curve to SAS_1. The price level rises to 117 and real GDP decreases to £1,250 billion. The economy experiences a one-time rise in the price level.

In part (b), if the Bank responds by increasing aggregate demand to restore full employment, the aggregate demand curve shifts rightward to AD_1. The economy returns to full employment but the price level rises further to 121.

myeconlab Animation

Aggregate Demand Response

When real GDP decreases, unemployment rises above its natural rate. In such a situation, there is often an outcry of concern and a call for action to restore full employment. Suppose that the Bank of England cuts the interest rate and increases the quantity of money. Aggregate demand increases. In Figure 28.3(b), the aggregate demand curve shifts rightward to AD_1 and full employment is restored. But the price level rises further to 121.

A Cost-Push Inflation Process

The oil producers now see the prices of everything they buy increasing, so oil producers increase the price of oil again to restore its new high relative price. Figure 28.4 continues the story. The short-run aggregate supply curve now shifts to SAS_2. The price level rises and real GDP decreases.

The price level rises further, to 129, and real GDP decreases to £1,250 billion. Unemployment increases above its natural rate.

If the Bank of England responds yet again with an increase in the quantity of money, aggregate demand increases and the aggregate demand curve shifts to AD_2. The price level rises even higher – to 133 – and full employment is again restored. A cost-push inflation spiral results. The combination of a rising price level and falling real GDP is called **stagflation**.

You can see that the Bank of England has a dilemma. If it does not respond when producers raise the oil price, the economy remains below full employment. If it lowers the interest rate and increases the quantity of money to restore full employment, it invites another oil price hike that will call forth yet a further increase in the quantity of money.

If the Bank of England responds to each oil price hike by increasing the quantity of money, inflation will rage along at a rate decided by oil producers. But if it keeps the lid on money growth, the economy remains below full employment.

Figure 28.4 A Cost-push Inflation Spiral

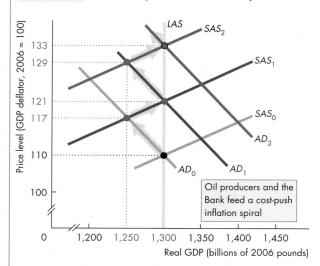

When a cost increase (for example, an increase in the world oil price) decreases short-run aggregate supply from SAS_0 to SAS_1, the price level rises to 117 and real GDP decreases to £1,250 billion. The central bank responds with an increase in the quantity of money that shifts the aggregate demand curve from AD_0 to AD_1. The price level rises again to 121 and real GDP returns to £1,300 billion. A further cost increase occurs, which shifts the short-run aggregate supply curve again, this time to SAS_2. Real GDP decreases again and the price level now rises to 129. The central bank responds again and the cost-push inflation spiral continues.

myeconlab Animation ————————————————◆

Cost-push Inflation in Liverpool

What is going on in the Liverpool soft drinks factory when the economy is experiencing cost-push inflation?

When the oil price increases, so do the costs of producing soft drinks. These higher costs decrease the supply of soft drinks, increase the price and decrease the quantity produced. The factory lays off some workers.

This situation persists until either the Bank of England increases aggregate demand or the price of oil falls. If the Bank increases aggregate demand, the demand for soft drinks increases and so does the price. The higher price of soft drinks brings higher profits and the factory increases its production. It rehires the laid-off workers.

Cost-push Inflation in the UK

A cost-push inflation like the one you've just studied occurred in the UK during the 1970s. In 1974 the Organization of the Petroleum Exporting Countries

(OPEC) raised the price of oil fourfold. The higher oil price decreased aggregate supply, which caused the price level to rise more quickly and real GDP to shrink. The Bank of England then faced a dilemma: would it increase the quantity of money and accommodate the cost-push forces or would it keep aggregate demand growth in check by limiting money growth?

In 1975, 1976 and 1977, the Bank of England repeatedly allowed the quantity of money to grow and inflation proceeded rapidly. In 1979 and 1980, OPEC was again able to push oil prices higher. On that occasion, the Bank of England decided not to respond to the oil price hike with an increase in the quantity of money. The result was a recession but also, eventually, a fall in inflation.

Expected Inflation

If inflation is expected, the fluctuations in real GDP that accompany demand-pull and cost-push inflation that you've just studied don't occur. Instead, inflation proceeds as it does in the long run, with real GDP equal to potential GDP and unemployment at its natural rate. Figure 28.5 explains why.

Suppose that last year the aggregate demand curve was AD_0, the aggregate supply curve was SAS_0 and the long-run aggregate supply curve was LAS. The price level was 110 and real GDP was £1,300 billion, which is also potential GDP.

To keep things as simple as possible, suppose that potential GDP does not change, so the LAS curve does not shift. Also suppose that aggregate demand *is expected to increase* to AD_1.

In anticipation of this increase in aggregate demand, the money wage rate rises and the short-run aggregate supply curve shifts leftward. If the money wage rate rises by the same percentage as the price level is expected to rise, the short-run aggregate supply curve for next year is SAS_1.

If aggregate demand turns out to be the same as expected, the aggregate demand curve is AD_1. The short-run aggregate supply curve, SAS_1, and AD_1 determine the actual price level at 121. Between last year and this year, the price level increased from 110 to 121 and the economy experienced an inflation rate equal to that expected. If this inflation is ongoing, aggregate demand increases (as expected) in the following year and the aggregate demand curve shifts to AD_2. The money wage rate rises to reflect the expected inflation and the short-run aggregate supply curve shifts to SAS_2. The price level rises, as expected, to 133.

Figure 28.5   Expected Inflation

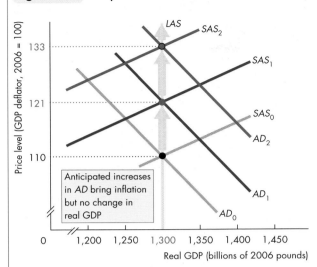

Potential real GDP is £1,300 billion. Last year, the aggregate demand curve was AD_0 and the short-run aggregate supply curve was SAS_0. The actual price level was the same as the expected price level – 110.

This year, aggregate demand is expected to increase to AD_1. The rational expectation of the price level changes from 110 to 121. As a result, the money wage rate rises and the short-run aggregate supply curve shifts to SAS_1.

If aggregate demand actually increases as expected, the actual aggregate demand curve AD_1 is the same as the expected aggregate demand curve. Real GDP is £1,300 billion and the actual price level is 121. The inflation is correctly expected.

Next year, the process continues with aggregate demand increasing as expected to AD_2 and the money wage rate rising to shift the short-run aggregate supply curve to SAS_2. Again, real GDP remains at £1,300 billion and the price level rises, as expected, to 133.

myeconlab Animation

What caused this inflation? The immediate answer is that because people expected inflation, the money wage rate increased and the price level increased. But the expectation was correct. Aggregate demand was expected to increase and it did increase. It is the actual and expected increase in aggregate demand that caused the inflation.

An expected inflation at full employment is exactly the process that the quantity theory of money predicts. To review the quantity theory of money, see Chapter 24, pp. 574–575.

This broader account of the inflation process and its short-run effects show why the quantity theory of money doesn't explain the fluctuations in inflation. The economy follows the course described in Figure 28.5, but as predicted by the quantity theory, only if aggregate demand growth is forecasted correctly.

Forecasting Inflation

To anticipate inflation, people must forecast it. Some economists who work for macroeconomic forecasting agencies, banks, insurance companies, trades unions and large companies specialize in inflation forecasting. The best forecast available is one that is based on all the relevant information and is called a **rational expectation**. A rational expectation is not necessarily a correct forecast. It is simply the best forecast with the information available. It will often turn out to be wrong, but no other forecast that could have been made with the information available could do better.

Inflation and the Business Cycle

When the inflation forecast is correct, the economy operates at full employment. If aggregate demand grows faster than expected, real GDP rises above potential GDP, the inflation rate exceeds its expected rate and the economy behaves like it does in a demand-pull inflation. If aggregate demand grows more slowly than expected, real GDP falls below potential GDP and the inflation rate slows.

Inflation and Unemployment: The Phillips Curve

Another way of studying inflation cycles focuses on the relationship and the short-run trade-off between inflation and unemployment, a relationship called the **Phillips curve** – so named because it was first suggested by New Zealand economist A.W. Phillips.

Why do we need another way of studying inflation? What is wrong with the *AS–AD* explanation of the fluctuations in inflation and real GDP? The first answer to both questions is that we often want to study changes in both the expected and actual inflation rates and for this purpose, the Phillips curve provides a simpler tool and clearer insights than the *AS–AD* model provides. The second answer to both questions is that we often want to study changes in the short-run trade-off between inflation and real economic activity (real GDP and unemployment) and again, the Phillips curve serves this purpose well.

To begin our explanation of the Phillips curve, we distinguish between two time frames (similar to the two aggregate supply time frames). We study

◆ The short-run Phillips curve
◆ The long-run Phillips curve

The Short-run Phillips Curve

The **short-run Phillips curve** shows the relationship between inflation and unemployment, holding constant:

1 The expected inflation rate
2 The natural unemployment rate

You've just seen in the previous section what determines the expected inflation rate. You learned about the natural unemployment rate and the factors that influence it in Chapter 21, pp. 489–490.

Figure 28.6 shows a short-run Phillips curve, *SRPC*. Suppose that the expected inflation rate is 10 per cent a year and the natural unemployment rate is 6 per cent, point *A*. A short-run Phillips curve passes through this point.

If inflation rises above its expected rate, the unemployment rate falls below its natural rate. This joint movement in the inflation rate and the unemployment rate is illustrated as a movement up the short-run Phillips curve from point *A* to point *B*. Similarly, if inflation falls below its expected rate, unemployment rises above the natural rate. In this case, there is

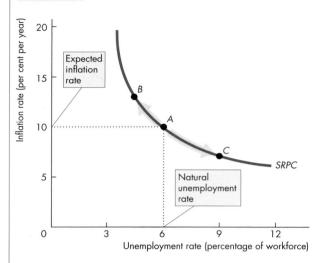

Figure 28.6 A Short-run Phillips Curve

The short-run Phillips curve, *SRPC*, shows the relationship between the inflation rate and the unemployment rate at a given expected inflation rate and given natural unemployment rate. With an expected inflation rate of 10 per cent a year and a natural unemployment rate of 6 per cent, the short-run Phillips curve passes through point *A*.

An unexpected increase in aggregate demand lowers the unemployment rate and increases the inflation rate – a movement up the short-run Phillips curve to point *B*. An unexpected decrease in aggregate demand increases the unemployment rate and lowers the inflation rate – a movement down the short-run Phillips curve to point *C*.

myeconlab Animation ◆

movement down the short-run Phillips curve from point *A* to point *C*.

The Short-run Phillips Curve and the Short-run Aggregate Supply Curve

The short-run Phillips curve is like the short-run aggregate supply curve. A movement along the *SAS* curve that brings a higher price level and an increase in real GDP is equivalent to a movement along the short-run Phillips curve from *A* to *B* that brings an increase in the inflation rate and a decrease in the unemployment rate.

Similarly, a movement along the *SAS* curve that brings a lower price level and a decrease in real GDP is equivalent to a movement along the short-run Phillips curve from *A* to *C* that brings a decrease in the inflation rate and an increase in the unemployment rate.

The Long-run Phillips Curve

The **long-run Phillips curve** is a curve that shows the relationship between inflation and unemployment, when the actual inflation rate equals the expected inflation rate. The long-run Phillips curve is vertical at the natural unemployment rate. It is shown in Figure 28.7 as the vertical line *LRPC*.

The long-run Phillips curve tells us that any expected inflation rate is possible at the natural unemployment rate. This proposition is the same as the one you discovered in the *AS–AD* model, which predicts that when inflation is expected, real GDP equals potential GDP and unemployment is at its natural rate.

Changes in the Expected Inflation Rate

The short-run Phillips curve intersects the long-run Phillips curve at the expected inflation rate. A change in the expected inflation rate shifts the short-run Phillips curve but it does not shift the long-run Phillips curve.

In Figure 28.7, if the expected inflation rate is 10 per cent a year, the short-run Phillips curve is $SRPC_0$. If the expected inflation rate falls to 7 per cent a year, the short-run Phillips curve shifts downward to $SRPC_1$. The vertical distance by which the short-run Phillips curve shifts from point A to point D is equal to the change in the expected inflation rate. If the actual inflation rate also falls from 10 per cent to 7 per cent, there is a movement down the long-run Phillips curve from A to D. An increase in the expected inflation rate has the opposite effect to that shown in Figure 28.7.

The other source of a shift in the Phillips curve is a change in the natural unemployment rate.

Changes in the Natural Unemployment Rate

The natural unemployment rate changes for many reasons that are explained in Chapter 21, pp. 489–490. A change in the natural unemployment rate shifts both the short-run and the long-run Phillips curves. Figure 28.8 illustrates such effects. If the natural unemployment rate increases from 6 per cent to 9 per cent, the long-run

Figure 28.7 Short-run and Long-run Phillips Curves

The long-run Phillips curve is *LRPC*, a vertical line at the natural unemployment rate. A fall in expected inflation shifts the short-run Phillips curve downward by the amount of the fall in the expected inflation rate.

For example, if the expected inflation rate falls from 10 per cent to 7 per cent a year, the short-run Phillips curve shifts downward from $SRPC_0$ to $SRPC_1$. The new short-run Phillips curve intersects the long-run Phillips curve at the new expected inflation rate – point D.

With the original expected inflation rate (10 per cent a year), an actual inflation rate of 7 per cent a year would occur at an unemployment rate of 9 per cent, at point C.

Figure 28.8 A Change in the Natural Unemployment Rate

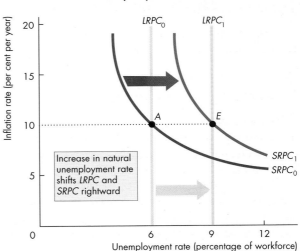

A change in the natural unemployment rate shifts both the short-run and long-run Phillips curves. Here the natural unemployment rate increases from 6 per cent to 9 per cent and the two Phillips curves shift rightward to $SRPC_1$ and $LRPC_1$. The new Phillips curves intersect at the expected inflation rate – point E.

ECONOMICS IN ACTION

The Shifting Short-run Trade-off

When A.W. (Bill) Phillips first discovered the curve that bears his name, he was looking at data on wage inflation and unemployment between 1861 and 1957. It was hard to see the Phillips curve in the data. The scatter diagram of data covering almost 100 years was more like a snowstorm than a neat inverse relationship.

Figure 1(a) continues the story that Phillips began by showing a scatter diagram of the UK inflation rate and the unemployment rate from 1960 to 2010. Each dot represents the inflation rate and unemployment rate in a particular year. We certainly cannot see a Phillips curve similar to that shown in Figure 28.6.

But we can interpret the data in terms of a shifting short-run Phillips curve like those in Figures 28.7 and 28.8. Three short-run Phillips curves appear in Figure 1(b). During the 1960s the expected inflation rate was 2 per cent a year and the natural unemployment rate was 2 per cent at point A, so the short-run Phillips curve was $SRPC_0$. From the mid-1970s to the mid-1980s the expected inflation rate averaged 12.5 per cent a year and the natural unemployment rate averaged 8 per cent at point B so the short-run Phillips curve was $SRPC_1$. During the 1990s the expected inflation rate was 2.5 per cent a year and the natural unemployment rate was 5 per cent at point C so the short-run Phillips curve was $SRPC_2$.

All the points in the graph are on short-run Phillips curves that lie between those shown.

(a) Time sequence

(b) Shifting Phillips curves

Figure 1 Phillips Curves in the UK

Source of data: Office for National Statistics.

Phillips curve shifts from $LRPC_0$ to $LRPC_1$. If expected inflation is constant at 10 per cent a year, the short-run Phillips curve shifts from $SRPC_0$ to $SRPC_1$. Because the expected inflation rate is constant, the short-run Phillips curve $SRPC_1$ intersects the long-run curve $LRPC_1$ (point E) at the same inflation rate as that at which the short-run Phillips curve $SRPC_0$ intersects the long-run curve $LRPC_0$ (point A).

Changes in both the expected inflation rate and the natural unemployment rate have shifted the UK Phillips curve but the expected inflation rate has had the greater effect.

Review Quiz

1 How would you use the Phillips curve to illustrate an unexpected change in the inflation rate?
2 If the expected inflation rate increases by 10 percentage points, how would the short-run Phillips curve and long-run Phillips curve change?
3 If the natural unemployment rate increases, what happens to the short-run Phillips curve and the long-run Phillips curve?
4 Does the UK have a stable short-run Phillips curve? Explain why or why not.

You can work these questions in Study Plan 28.2 and get instant feedback.

The Business Cycle

The business cycle is easy to describe but hard to explain and business cycle theory remains unsettled and a source of controversy. We'll look at two approaches to understanding the business cycle:

◆ Mainstream business cycle theory
◆ Real business cycle theory

Mainstream Business Cycle Theory

The mainstream business cycle theory is that potential GDP grows at a steady rate while aggregate demand grows at a fluctuating rate. Because the money wage rate is sticky, if aggregate demand grows faster than potential GDP, real GDP moves above potential GDP and an inflationary gap emerges. And if aggregate demand grows slower than potential GDP, real GDP moves below potential GDP and a recessionary gap emerges. If aggregate demand decreases, real GDP also decreases in a recession.

Figure 28.9 illustrates this business cycle theory. Initially, actual and potential GDP are £1,000 billion. The long-run aggregate supply curve is LAS_0, the aggregate demand curve is AD_0 and the price level is 100. The economy is at full employment at point A.

An expansion occurs when potential GDP increases and the LAS curve shifts rightward to LAS_1. During an expansion, aggregate demand also increases, and usually by more than potential GDP, so the price level rises. Assume that in the current expansion, the price level is expected to rise to 110 and the money wage rate has been set based on that expectation. The short-run aggregate supply curve is SAS_1.

If aggregate demand increases to AD_1, real GDP increases to £1,300 billion, the new level of potential GDP, and the price level rises, as expected, to 110. The economy remains at full employment but now at point B.

If aggregate demand increases more slowly to AD_2, real GDP grows by less than potential GDP and the economy moves to point C, with real GDP at £1,250 billion and the price level at 107. Real GDP growth is slower and inflation is lower than expected.

If aggregate demand increases more quickly to AD_3, real GDP grows by more than potential GDP and the economy moves to point D, with real GDP at £1,350 billion and the price level at 113. Real GDP growth is faster and inflation is higher than expected.

Growth, inflation and the business cycle arise from the relentless increases in potential GDP, faster (on average) increases in aggregate demand and fluctuations in the pace of aggregate demand growth.

Figure 28.9 The Mainstream Business Cycle Theory

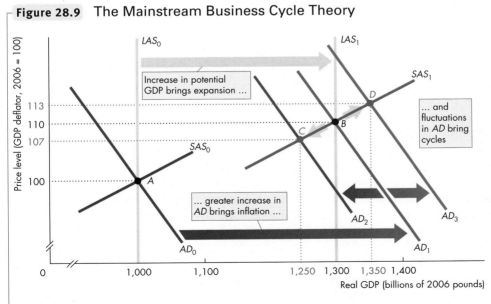

In a business cycle expansion, potential GDP increases and the LAS curve shifts rightward from LAS_0 to LAS_1. A greater than expected increase in aggregate demand brings inflation.

If the aggregate demand curve shifts to AD_1, the economy remains at full employment. If the aggregate demand curve shifts to AD_2, a recessionary gap arises. If the aggregate demand curve shifts to AD_3, an inflationary gap arises.

 myeconlab Animation

This mainstream theory comes in a number of special forms that differ regarding the source of fluctuations in aggregate demand growth and the source of money wage stickiness.

Keynesian Cycle Theory

In **Keynesian cycle theory**, fluctuations in investment driven by fluctuations in business confidence – summarized by the phrase 'animal spirits' – are the main source of fluctuations in aggregate demand.

Monetarist Cycle Theory

In **monetarist cycle theory**, fluctuations in both investment and consumption expenditure, driven by fluctuations in the growth rate of the quantity of money, are the main source of fluctuations in aggregate demand.

Both the Keynesian and monetarist cycle theories simply assume that the money wage rate is rigid and don't explain that rigidity.

Two newer theories seek to explain money wage rate rigidity and to be more careful about working out its consequences.

New Classical Cycle Theory

In **new classical cycle theory**, the rational expectation of the price level, which is determined by potential GDP and *expected* aggregate demand, determines the money wage rate and the position of the *SAS* curve. In this theory, only unexpected fluctuations in aggregate demand bring fluctuations in real GDP around potential GDP.

New Keynesian Cycle Theory

The **new Keynesian cycle theory** emphasizes the fact that today's money wage rates were negotiated at many past dates, which means that past rational expectations of the current price level influence the money wage rate and the position of the *SAS* curve. In this theory, both unexpected and currently expected fluctuations in aggregate demand bring fluctuations in real GDP around potential GDP.

The mainstream cycle theories don't rule out the possibility that occasionally an aggregate supply shock might occur. An oil price rise, a widespread drought, a major hurricane, or another natural disaster could, for example, bring a recession. But supply shocks are not the normal source of fluctuations in the mainstream theories. In contrast, real business cycle theory puts supply shocks at centre stage.

Real Business Cycle Theory

The newest theory of the business cycle, known as **real business cycle theory** (or RBC theory), regards random fluctuations in productivity as the main source of economic fluctuations. These productivity fluctuations are assumed to result mainly from fluctuations in the pace of technological change, but they might also have other sources, such as international disturbances, climate fluctuations, or natural disasters. The origins of RBC theory can be traced to the rational expectations revolution set off by Robert E. Lucas, Jr., but the first demonstrations of the power of this theory were given by Edward Prescott and Finn Kydland and by John Long and Charles Plosser. Today, RBC theory is part of a broad research agenda called dynamic general equilibrium analysis, and hundreds of young macroeconomists do research on this topic.

We'll explore RBC theory by looking first at its impulse and then at the mechanism that converts that impulse into a cycle in real GDP.

The RBC Impulse

The impulse in RBC theory is the growth rate of productivity that results from technological change. RBC theorists believe this impulse to be generated mainly by the process of research and development that leads to the creation and use of new technologies.

To isolate the RBC theory impulse, economists measure the change in the combined productivity of capital and labour. Figure 28.10 shows the RBC impulse for the UK from 1971 to 2010. You can see that fluctuations in productivity growth are closely correlated with real GDP fluctuations.

The pace of technological change and productivity growth is not constant. Sometimes productivity growth speeds up, sometimes it slows and occasionally it even *falls* – labour and capital become less productive, on average. A period of rapid productivity growth brings a business cycle expansion, and a slowdown or fall in productivity triggers a recession (as it did in 2009).

It is easy to understand why technological change brings productivity growth. But how does technological change decrease productivity? All technological change eventually increases productivity. But if, initially, technological change makes a sufficient amount of existing capital – especially human capital – obsolete, productivity can temporarily fall. At such a time, more jobs are destroyed than created and more businesses fail than start up.

Figure 28.10 The Real Business Cycle Impulse

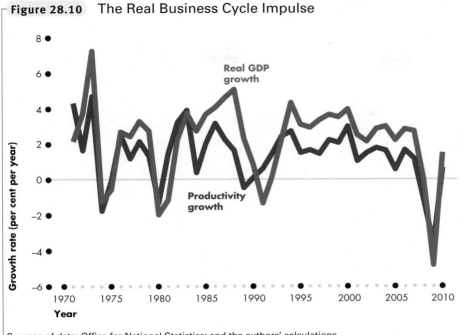

The real business cycle impulse is fluctuations in the growth rate of productivity that are caused by changes in technology. The fluctuations in productivity growth shown here are calculated by using growth accounting (the one-third rule) to remove the contribution of capital accumulation to productivity growth. Productivity fluctuations are correlated with real GDP fluctuations. Economists are not sure what the productivity variable actually measures or what causes it to fluctuate.

Sources of data: Office for National Statistics; and the authors' calculations.

The RBC Mechanism

Two effects follow from a change in productivity that sparks an expansion or a contraction:

1 Investment demand changes

2 The demand for labour changes

We'll study these effects and their consequences during a recession. In an expansion, they work in the direction opposite to what is described here.

Technological change makes some existing capital obsolete and temporarily decreases productivity. Firms expect the future profits to fall and see their labour productivity falling. With lower profit expectations, they cut back their purchases of new capital, and with lower labour productivity, they plan to lay off some workers. So the initial effect of a temporary fall in productivity is a decrease in investment demand and a decrease in the demand for labour.

Figure 28.11 illustrates these two initial effects of a decrease in productivity. Part (a) shows the effects of a decrease in investment demand in the loanable funds market. The demand for loanable funds curve is DLF and the supply of loanable funds curve is SLF (both of which are explained in Chapter 23, pp. 540–544).

Initially, the demand for loanable funds curve is DLF_0 and the equilibrium quantity of funds is £150 billion at a real interest rate of 6 per cent a year. A decrease in productivity decreases investment demand, and the demand for loanable funds curve shifts leftward from DLF_0 to DLF_1. The real interest rate falls to 4 per cent a year, and the equilibrium quantity of loanable funds decreases to £120 billion.

Figure 28.11(b) shows the demand for labour and supply of labour (which are explained in Chapter 22, pp. 513–514). Initially, the demand for labour curve is LD_0, the supply of labour curve is LS_0 and equilibrium employment is 50 billion hours a year at a real wage rate of £17.50 an hour. The decrease in productivity decreases the demand for labour, and the demand for labour curve shifts leftward from LD_0 to LD_1.

Before we can determine the new level of employment and real wage rate, we need to take a ripple effect into account – the key effect in RBC theory.

The Key Decision: When to Work?

According to RBC theory, people decide when to work by doing a cost–benefit calculation. They compare the return from working in the current period with the

Figure 28.11   The Loanable Funds and Labour Markets in a Real Business Cycle

(a) Loanable funds and interest rate

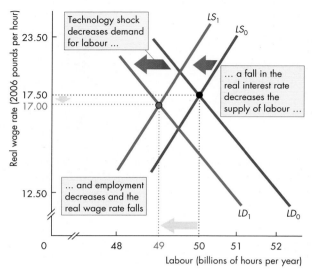

(b) Labour and wage rate

In part (a), the supply of loanable funds *SLF* and initial demand for loanable funds DLF_0 determine the real interest rate at 6 per cent a year. In part (b), the initial demand for labour, LD_0 and supply of labour, LS_0, determine the real wage rate at £17.50 an hour and employment at 50 billion hours a year.

A technological change temporarily decreases productivity, which decreases both the demand for loanable funds and the demand for labour. The demand curves shift leftward to DLF_1 and LD_1 respectively.

In part (a), the real interest rate falls to 4 per cent a year. In part (b), the fall in the real interest rate decreases the supply of labour (the when-to-work decision) and the supply curve shifts leftward to LS_1. Employment decreases to 49 billion hours and the real wage rate falls to £17 an hour. A recession is under way.

expected return from working in a later period. You make such a comparison every day at university. Suppose your goal in this course is to get an A. To achieve this goal, you work hard most of the time. But during the few days before the midterm and final exams, you work especially hard. Why? Because you believe that the return from studying close to the exam is greater than the return from studying when the exam is a long time away. So during the term, you take time off for the movies and other leisure pursuits, but at exam time, you study every evening and weekend.

RBC theory says that workers behave like you. They work fewer hours, sometimes zero hours, when the real wage rate is temporarily low, and they work more hours when the real wage rate is temporarily high. But to properly compare the current wage rate with the expected future wage rate, workers must use the real interest rate. If the real interest rate is 6 per cent a year, a real wage of £1 an hour earned this week will become £1.06 a year

from now. If the real wage rate is expected to be £1.05 an hour next year, today's real wage of £1 looks good. By working longer hours now and shorter hours a year from now, a person can get a 1 per cent higher real wage. But suppose the real interest rate is 4 per cent a year. In this case, £1 earned now is worth £1.04 next year. Working fewer hours now and more next year is the way to get a 1 per cent higher real wage.

So the when-to-work decision depends on the real interest rate. The lower the real interest rate, other things remaining the same, the smaller is the supply of labour today. Many economists believe this *intertemporal substitution effect* to be of negligible size. RBC theorists believe that the effect is large, and it is the key feature of the RBC mechanism.

You saw in Figure 28.11(a) that the decrease in the demand for loanable funds lowers the real interest rate. This fall in the real interest rate lowers the return to current work and decreases the supply of labour.

In Figure 28.11(b), the labour supply curve shifts leftward to LS_1. The effect of the decrease in productivity on the demand for labour is larger than the effect of the fall in the real interest rate on the supply of labour. That is, the demand curve shifts farther leftward than does the supply curve. As a result, the real wage rate falls to £17 an hour and employment decreases to 49 billion hours. A recession has begun and is intensifying.

What Happened to Money?

The name *real* business cycle theory is no accident. It reflects the central prediction of the theory. Real things, not nominal or monetary things, cause the business cycle. If the quantity of money changes, aggregate demand changes. But if there is no real change – with no change in the use of resources and no change in potential GDP – the change in the quantity of money changes only the price level. In RBC theory, this outcome occurs because the aggregate supply curve is the *LAS* curve, which pins real GDP down at potential GDP, so when aggregate demand changes, only the price level changes.

Cycles and Growth

The shock that drives the business cycle of RBC theory is the same as the force that generates economic growth: technological change. On average, as technology advances, productivity grows; but as you saw in Figure 28.10, it grows at an uneven pace. Economic growth arises from the upward trend in productivity growth and, according to RBC theory, the mostly positive but occasionally negative higher frequency shocks to productivity bring the business cycle.

Criticisms of RBC Theory

The three main criticisms of RBC theory are that (1) the money wage rate is sticky, and to assume otherwise is at odds with a clear fact; (2) intertemporal substitution is too weak a force to account for large fluctuations in labour supply and employment with small real wage rate changes; and (3) productivity shocks are as likely to be caused by changes in aggregate demand as by technological change.

If aggregate demand fluctuations cause the fluctuations in productivity, then the traditional aggregate demand theories are needed to explain them. Fluctuations in productivity do not cause the business cycle but are caused by it!

Building on this theme, the critics point out that the so-called productivity fluctuations that growth accounting measures are correlated with changes in the growth rate of money and other indicators of changes in aggregate demand.

In Defence of RBC Theory

The defenders of RBC theory claim that the theory explains the macroeconomic facts about the business cycle and is consistent with the facts about economic growth. In effect, a single theory explains *both growth and the business cycle*. The growth accounting exercise that explains slowly changing trends also explains the more frequent business cycle swings.

Its defenders also claim that RBC theory is consistent with a wide range of *micro*economic evidence about labour supply decisions, labour demand and investment demand decisions and information on the distribution of income between labour and capital.

The strongest defence of RBC theory is not its detailed explanation of the cycle and growth but its method, the *dynamic general equilibrium* approach to studying the aggregate economy that is employed today by new classical and new Keynesian researchers as they continue to gain a better understanding of the economy.

Review Quiz

1 Explain the mainstream theory of the business cycle.
2 What are the four special forms of the mainstream theory of the business cycle and how do they differ?
3 According to RBC theory, what is the source of the business cycle? What is the role of fluctuations in the rate of technological change?
4 According to RBC theory, how does a fall in productivity growth influence investment demand, the market for loanable funds, the real interest rate, the demand for labour, the supply of labour, employment and the real wage rate?
5 What are the main criticisms of RBC theory and how do its supporters defend it?

You can work these questions in Study Plan 28.3 and get instant feedback.

You can complete your study of inflation and economic fluctuations in *Reading Between the Lines* on pp. 682–683, which looks at inflationary pressures in China and the tough trade-off faced by that fast-changing economy.

Reading Between the Lines

China's Inflation–Growth Trade-off

The Financial Times, 21 November 2010

China's Twilight Economy Piles Pressure on Inflation Fight

FT

James Kynge

China has lambasted the US for its decision to launch another $600bn in monetary easing, fearing that this round of 'quantitative easing' may feed the flood of money rushing into mainland China from overseas. But while capital inflows are a problem for Beijing, there should be no doubt that China's swelling money supply and resurgent inflation are primarily 'Made in China'.

Bank lending . . . is looking increasingly likely to bust through the government's solemnly decreed 2010 target. . . . But more worrying . . . are the inflationary pressures springing from a subterranean world of informal finance. Although the size of China's underground financial system is uncertain, it is unlikely to be modest. . . .

Thus the total assets contained within China's twilight economy may well be in excess of Rmb6,000bn.

If this number is added to the 2010 official lending target of Rmb7,500bn, then it becomes clear that China's 2009 record lending splurge was no 'one-off' and may well be exceeded by this year's level.

It is pressures caused by such ballooning money supply, coupled with various structural influences inherent in the take-off of China's rural economy, that are the prime causes of inflation.

China knows that it cannot bring discipline to its huge, unregulated underground economy without sacrificing growth, and yet unless it grapples with the root causes of money supply, it may fail to tame inflation.

The Essence of the Story

- China's inflation rose throughout 2010.

- China criticizes the US for its policy of 'quantitative easing', which is flooding the world economy with money.

- Some of this money has gone to China and increased aggregate demand.

- Most of the increase in money in China comes from China's banks and its large informal banking system.

Economic Analysis

◆ China's inflation rate during 2010 was on an upward trend as you can see in Figure 1.

◆ Figure 2 shows the main source of the increase in inflation: a money growth rate that vastly exceeds the growth rate of real GDP.

◆ You can see in Figure 2 that the inflation rate and real GDP growth rate fluctuate in sympathy with the fluctuations in money growth but with a time lag.

◆ The news article notes that in addition to the growth of money there is a large growth in credit in the informal parts of China's economy.

◆ China is experiencing both demand-pull and cost-push inflation forces.

◆ Figure 3 illustrates these forces by showing what has been happening to China's aggregate demand and aggregate supply.

◆ In 2008, aggregate demand was AD_{08} and short-run aggregate supply was SAS_{08}. Real GDP was ¥26 trillion (in 2005 prices) and the price level was 120 (2005 = 100).

◆ In 2010, potential GDP was ¥31 trillion and the long-run aggregate supply curve was LAS_{10}.

◆ Between 2008 and 2010, the quantity of money increased, credit grew and a global expansion increased the demand for China's exports. Aggregate demand increased and the AD curve shifted rightward to AD_{10}.

◆ Commodity prices and the money wage rate increased, which decreased short-run aggregate supply and the SAS curve shifted leftward to SAS_{10}.

◆ To slow inflation, China must slow the money growth rate.

◆ This action will slow the rate of increase of aggregate demand and will temporarily slow the growth rate of real GDP.

Figure 1 China's inflation in 2010

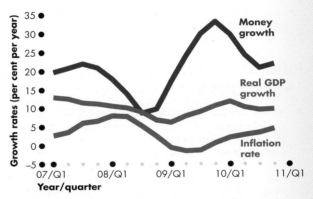

Figure 2 Money growth, real GDP growth and inflation

Figure 3 Changes in aggregate supply and aggregate demand

SUMMARY

Key Points

Inflation Cycles (pp. 668–673)

◆ Demand-pull inflation is triggered by an increase in aggregate demand and fuelled by ongoing money growth. Real GDP cycles above full employment.

◆ Cost-push inflation is triggered by an increase in the money wage rate or raw material prices and is fuelled by ongoing money growth. Real GDP cycles below full employment in a stagflation.

◆ When the forecast of inflation is correct, real GDP remains at potential GDP.

Working Problems 1 to 11 will give you a better understanding of inflation cycles.

Inflation and Unemployment: The Phillips Curve (pp. 674–676)

◆ The short-run Phillips curve shows the trade-off between inflation and unemployment when the expected inflation rate and the natural unemployment rate are constant.

◆ The long-run Phillips curve, which is vertical, shows that when the actual inflation rate equals the expected inflation rate, the unemployment rate equals the natural unemployment rate.

Working Problems 12 to 14 will give you a better understanding of inflation and unemployment: the Phillips curve.

The Business Cycle (pp. 677–681)

◆ The mainstream business cycle theory explains the business cycle as fluctuations of real GDP around potential GDP and as arising from a steady expansion of potential GDP combined with an expansion of aggregate demand at a fluctuating rate.

◆ Real business cycle theory explains the business cycle as fluctuations of potential GDP, which arise from fluctuations in the influence of technological change on productivity growth.

Working Problem 15 will give you a better understanding of the business cycle.

Key Terms

Cost-push inflation, 670
Demand-pull inflation, 668
Keynesian cycle theory, 678
Long-run Phillips curve, 675
Monetarist cycle theory, 678
New classical cycle theory, 678
New Keynesian cycle theory, 678
Phillips curve, 674
Rational expectation, 673
Real business cycle theory, 678
Short-run Phillips curve, 674
Stagflation, 671

myeconlab You can work Problems 1 to 15 in MyEconLab Chapter 28 Study Plan and get instant feedback.

Inflation Cycles (Study Plan 28.1)

1 Pakistan: Is it Cost-Push Inflation?

With CPI already spiking 11.8 per cent for the first ten months of the fiscal year, the average CPI inflation for the same period last year stood at 22.35 per cent. Some economists insist the current bout of inflationary pressures is spawned by increasing prices of fuel, food, raw materials, transportation, construction materials, elimination of energy subsidies, etc as indicated by the spike in the wholesale price index (WPI), which rose 21.99 per cent in April from a year earlier.

Source: *Daily the Pak Banker,* 22 May 2010

Explain what type of inflation Pakistan is experiencing.

Use the following figure to work Problems 2, 3, 4 and 5. In each question, the economy starts out on the curves labelled AD_0 and SAS_0.

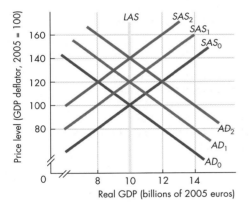

2 Some events occur and the economy experiences a demand-pull inflation.

a List the events that might cause a demand-pull inflation.

b Describe the initial effects of a demand-pull inflation.

c Describe what happens as a demand-pull inflation spiral proceeds.

3 Some events occur and the economy experiences a cost-push inflation.

a List the events that might cause a cost-push inflation.

b Describe the initial effects of a cost-push inflation.

c Describe what happens as a cost-push inflation spiral proceeds.

4 Some events occur and the economy is expected to experience inflation.

a List the events that might cause an expected inflation.

b Describe the initial effects of an expected inflation.

c Describe what happens as an expected inflation proceeds.

5 Suppose that people expect deflation (a falling price level), but aggregate demand remains at AD_0.

a What happens to the short-run and long-run aggregate supply curves? (Draw some new curves if you need to.)

b Describe the initial effects of an expected deflation.

c Describe what happens as it becomes obvious to everyone that the expected deflation is not going to occur.

Use the following news clip to work Problems 6 to 8.

Money's Too Loose to Mention

UK inflation at 3.7 per cent is above target and above forecasts. This inflation can't be blamed on temporary factors such as a rise in commodity prices or a tax increase, although these events did occur and will make inflation worse before it gets better. Rather, embedded inflation and inflation expectations seem to be rising and the UK now has higher inflation than any other developed economy.

Source: *The Financial Times,* 19 January 2011

6 Does the news clip describe a situation in which the UK is experiencing demand-pull inflation, cost-push inflation, or an expected inflation spiral? Explain.

7 Draw a graph to illustrate the effects of the temporary factors noted in the news clip.

8 Draw a graph to illustrate and explain how the UK might be experiencing an expected inflation spiral.

Use the following news clip to work Problems 9 to 11.

Tight Money Won't Slay Food, Energy Inflation

It's important to differentiate between a general increase in prices – a situation in which aggregate demand exceeds their aggregate supply – and a relative price shock. For example, a specific shock to energy prices can become generalized if producers are able to pass on the higher costs. So far, global competition has made that difficult for companies, while higher input costs have largely been neutralized by rising labour productivity. Since 2003, US core inflation has averaged less than 2 per cent a year in the 30 major economies. History also suggests the US central bank's gamble that slowing growth will shackle core inflation is a winning wager. The risk is that if US consumers don't believe price increases will slow, growing inflation expectations may become self-fulfilling.

Source: Bloomberg, 9 May 2008

9 **a** Explain the two types of inflation described in this news clip.

   b Explain why 'rising labour productivity' can neutralize the effect on inflation of 'higher input costs'.

10 Explain how 'slowing growth' can reduce inflationary pressure.

11 Draw a graph to illustrate and explain how 'growing inflation expectations may become self-fulfilling'.

Inflation and Unemployment: The Phillips Curve (Study Plan 28.2)

12 **Iran Postpones Cutting Petrol Subsidies**

   Inflation is about 10 per cent and the unemployment rate is about 14 per cent. Earlier this month Iran's main audit body slammed the government's plan to scrap petrol subsidies, warning that implementing such a reform might result in unrest. The government also intends to scrap subsidies on natural gas, which most Iranians use for cooking and heating, as well as electricity, but the new prices are still not known. However, in recent weeks some households have received electricity bills with nearly sevenfold price increases.

Source: AFP, 15 September 2010

   a If Iran unexpectedly removes the subsidies and consumers don't know what the higher prices will be, draw a graph to show the most likely path of inflation and unemployment.

   b If Iran removes the subsidies and announces the new prices so that consumers know what they are, draw a graph to show the most likely path of inflation and unemployment.

13 **Recession? Maybe. Depression? Get Real**

   The unemployment rate during the Great Depression peaked at nearly 25 per cent in 1933, after an initial spike from 3 per cent in 1929 to nearly 8.7 per cent in 1930. The unemployment rate is just 5 per cent, only up from 4.5 per cent a year ago. Also during the Great Depression there was deflation, which is not happening today.

Source: CNN, 28 May 2008

   a Can the inflation and unemployment trends during the Great Depression be explained by a movement along a short-run Phillips curve?

   b Can the inflation and unemployment trends during 2008 be explained by a movement along a short-run Phillips curve?

14 **Inflation Report Press Conference**

   Despite weak demand, inflation is above the 2 per cent target. The slack in the economy is likely to reduce inflationary pressure, but it is possible that rising import prices and commodity prices will push up inflation and inflation expectations.

Source: Bank of England, 10 November 2010

   Explain this report in terms of shifts and movements along a short-run and long-run Phillips curve.

The Business Cycle (Study Plan 28.3)

15 **Debate on Causes of Joblessness Grows**

   What is the cause of the high unemployment rate? One side says more government spending can reduce joblessness. The other says it's a structural problem – people who can't move to take new jobs because they are tied down to burdensome mortgages or firms that can't find workers with the requisite skills to fill job openings.

Source: *The Wall Street Journal*, 4 September 2010

   Which business cycle theory would say that the rise in unemployment is cyclical? Which would say it is an increase in the natural rate? Why?

ADDITIONAL PROBLEMS AND APPLICATIONS

 You can work these problems in MyEconLab if assigned by your lecturer.

Inflation Cycles

Use the following news clip to work Problems 16 and 17.

Bernanke Sees No Repeat of '70s-Style Inflation

There is little indication today that a 1970s-style cost-push spiral is about to begin. Then, as now, a serious oil price shock occurred, but today's economy is more flexible in responding to difficulties, Bernanke said. Also, today the US Federal Reserve monitors inflation expectations. If people believe inflation will keep going up, they will change their behaviour in ways that aggravate inflation – thus, a self-fulfilling prophecy. In the 1970s, people demanded (and received) higher wages in anticipation of rapidly rising prices; hence, the cost-push spiral began. The inflation rate has averaged about 3.5 per cent over the past four quarters. That is 'significantly higher' than the Federal Reserve would like but much lower than the double-digit inflation rates of the mid-1970s and 1980, said Bernanke.

Source: *USA Today*, 4 June 2008

16 Draw a graph to illustrate and explain the inflation spiral that the US experienced in the 1970s.

17 a Explain the role that inflation expectations play in creating a self-fulfilling prophecy.

  b Explain Bernanke's predictions about the impact of the 2008 oil price shock as compared to the 1970s shock.

Inflation and Unemployment: The Phillips Curve

Use the following information to work Problems 18 and 19.

The Reserve Bank of New Zealand (the central bank) signed an agreement with the New Zealand government in which the Bank agreed to maintain inflation inside a low target range. Failure to achieve the target would result in the governor of the Bank losing his job.

18 Explain how this arrangement might have influenced New Zealand's short-run Phillips curve.

19 Explain how this arrangement might have influenced New Zealand's long-run Phillips curve.

Use the following information and the figure in the next column to work Problems 20 and 21.

An economy has an unemployment rate of 4 per cent and an inflation rate of 5 per cent a year at point *A* in the figure. Some events occur that move the economy in a clockwise loop from *A* to *B* to *D* to *C* and back to *A*.

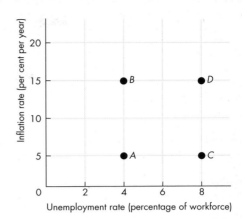

20 Describe the events that could create this sequence. Has the economy experienced demand-pull inflation, cost-push inflation, expected inflation, or none of these?

21 Draw in the figure the sequence of the economy's short-run and long-run Phillips curves.

Use the following news clip to work Problems 22 to 24.

Inflation in Brazil

Dilma Rouseff, Brazil's incoming president will face the challenge of consumer price inflation running well above the government's target of 4.5 per cent a year. Prices rose by 5.6 per cent in the 12 months to November and the rate is expected to reach 6 per cent by the year end. Price rises have spread to other sectors as the fast growth in Brazil's economy, expected to be about 7.5 per cent this year, puts pressure on supply.

Source: *The Financial Times*, 22 December 2010

22 Is Brazil experiencing demand-pull or cost-push inflation? Explain.

23 Draw a graph to illustrate the initial rise in the price level and the money wage rate response to a one-time rise in the price level.

24 Draw a graph to illustrate and explain how Brazil might experience an inflation spiral

Use the following information to work Problems 25 and 26.

Because the US Federal Reserve doubled the monetary base in 2008 and the government spent billions of dollars bailing out troubled banks, insurance companies and auto producers, some people are concerned that a serious upturn in the inflation rate will occur, not immediately but in a few years' time. At the same time, massive changes in the global economy might bring the need for structural change in the US.

25 Explain how the doubling of the monetary base and government bailouts might influence the short-run and long-run unemployment–inflation trade-offs. Will the influence come from changes in the expected inflation rate, the natural unemployment rate or both?

26 Explain how large-scale structural change might influence the short-run and long-run unemployment–inflation trade-offs. Will the influence come from changes in the expected inflation rate, the natural unemployment rate or both?

The Business Cycle

Use the following information to work Problems 27 to 29.

Suppose that the business cycle in the UK is best described by RBC theory and that a new technology increases productivity.

27 Draw a graph to show the effect of the new technology in the market for loanable funds.

28 Draw a graph to show the effect of the new technology in the labour market.

29 Explain the when-to-work decision when technology advances.

30 **Real Wages Fail to Match a Rise in Productivity**

For most of the last century, wages and productivity – the key measure of the economy's efficiency – have risen together, increasing rapidly through the 1950s and 1960s and far more slowly in the 1970s and 1980s. But in recent years, the productivity gains have continued while the pay increases have not kept up.

Source: *The New York Times*, 28 August 2006

Explain the relationship between wages and productivity in this news clip in terms of real business cycle theory.

Economics in the News

31 After you have studied *Reading Between the Lines* on pp. 682–683 answer the following questions.

a Given the money growth rate in China, why isn't real GDP growing at a faster pace?

b If the money growth rate in China remains at the levels of 2010, what do you expect to happen to inflation in 2011 and 2012?

c Use the *AS–AD* model to describe the inflationary process in China.

d What policies would you recommend to the Chinese government to reduce inflation? Explain why?

32 **Germany Leads Slowdown in Eurozone**

The pace of German economic growth has weakened 'markedly', but the reason is the weaker global prospects. Although German policymakers worry about the country's exposure to a fall in demand for its export goods, evidence is growing that the recovery is broadening with real wage rates rising and unemployment falling, which will lead into stronger consumer spending.

Source: *The Financial Times*, 23 September 2010

a How does 'exposure to a fall in demand for its export goods' influence Germany's aggregate demand, aggregate supply, unemployment and inflation?

b Use the *AS–AD* model to illustrate your answer to part (a).

c Use the Phillips curve model to illustrate your answer to part (a).

d What do you think the news clip means by 'the recovery is broadening with real wage rates rising and unemployment falling, which will lead into stronger consumer spending'?

e Use the *AS–AD* model to illustrate your answer to part (d).

f Use the Phillips curve model to illustrate your answer to part (d).

Macroeconomic Policy

Trade-offs and Free Lunches

A policy trade-off arises if, in taking an action to achieve one goal, some other goal must be forgone. The Bank of England wants to avoid a rise in the inflation rate and a rise in the unemployment rate. But if the Bank raises the interest rate to curb inflation, it might increase unemployment. The Bank faces a short-run trade-off between inflation and unemployment.

A policy 'free lunch' arises if in taking actions to pursue one goal, some other (intended or unintended) goal is also achieved. The Bank of England wants to keep inflation in check and, at the same time, to boost the economic growth rate. If lower inflation brings greater certainty about the future and stimulates saving and investment, the Bank gets both lower inflation and faster real GDP growth. It enjoys a free lunch.

The two chapters in this part describe the institutional framework in which fiscal policy (Chapter 29) and monetary policy (Chapter 30) are made, describes the instruments of policy and analyses the effects of policy. This exploration of economic policy draws on almost everything that you learned in previous chapters.

These policy chapters serve as a capstone on your knowledge of macroeconomics and draw together all the strands in your study of the previous chapters.

Understanding Macroeconomic Policy

The central challenges of fiscal policy and monetary policy are to contribute to achieving the fastest possible sustainable growth rate of real GDP, to maintain a stable price level and to minimize the volatility of fluctuations of real GDP around potential GDP and of unemployment around the natural unemployment rate.

All fiscal policy and monetary policy actions work by influencing the incentives that people and businesses face. And these incentives can be influenced either in a well-understood and predictable manner or in a poorly understood and capricious or surprising manner.

Does it matter whether policy is predictable or a surprise?

Economists are in agreement that it does matter and that predictable policy actions do a better job than policy surprises.

A government that commits to a tax and spending regime that is sustainable and predictable and not subject to capricious change creates an environment in which self-interested decisions can best serve the social interest.

A central bank that adopts a well-understoood target, sets its policy instrument to achieve that target and explains its policy choices in the framework of its target delivers a better outcome for all the goals of macroeconomic policy than does a central bank that acts capriciously and surprises financial markets by its actions.

But there remains much debate about just what the targets of policy should be. Should fiscal policy be aimed at achieveing long-term growth and equity across the generations, or should it be aimed at the short-run stabilization objective of smoothing the cycles in economic activity? Should monetary policy be governed by an explicit inflation target, a money stock growth target or some implicit targets that might include stabilizing output and employment?

There are no settled answers to these questions.

Milton Friedman was born into a poor immigrant family in New York City in 1912. He was an undergraduate at Rutgers and a graduate student at Columbia University during the Great Depression. From 1977 until his death in 2006, Professor Friedman was a Senior Fellow at the Hoover Institution at Stanford University. But his reputation was built between 1946 and 1983, when he was a leading member of the 'Chicago School', an approach to economics developed at the University of Chicago and based on the views that free markets allocate resources efficiently and that stable and low money supply growth delivers macroeconomic stability.

Friedman has advanced our understanding of the forces that determine macroeconomic performance and clarified the effects of the quantity of money. For this work, he was awarded the 1977 Nobel Prize for Economic Science.

By reasoning from basic economic principles, Friedman (along with Edmund S. Phelps, the 2006 Economics Nobel Laureate) predicted that persistent demand stimulation would not increase output but would cause inflation.

When output growth slowed and inflation broke out in the 1970s, Friedman seemed like a prophet, and for a time his policy prescription, known as monetarism, was embraced around the world.

'Inflation is always and everywhere a monetary phenomenon.'

MILTON FRIEDMAN
The Counter-Revolution in Monetary Theory

CHAPTER 29

Fiscal Policy

After studying this chapter you will be able to:

◆ Describe the UK government's recent budgets

◆ Explain the supply-side effects of fiscal policy

◆ Explain how fiscal policy redistributes benefits and costs across generations

◆ Understand and explain fiscal stimulus in recession

Every spring, the Chancellor of the Exchequer presents his budget. In 2010, UK governments (central and local) spent 47 pence of every pound earned and had a budget deficit of £149 billion. Does a pound spent by the government have the same effects as a pound spent by someone else? What happens if governments spend more than they receive in receipts and run into debt? Does government debt damage economic growth and the well-being of future generations? How do taxes affect the economy?

You will find some of the answers in this chapter. And in *Reading Between the Lines* at the end of the chapter, you can see how the government of Ireland is using fiscal policy in an attempt to restore confidence in its debt and stimulate a flagging economy.

◈ Government Budgets

A government's **budget** is an annual statement of projected outlays and receipts during the next year together with the laws and regulations that will support those outlays and receipts. The finance minister – the Chancellor of the Exchequer in the UK – presents the budget to Parliament in what is often a piece of political theatre and always a major media event.

A government's budget has three major purposes:

1   To state the scale and allocation of the government's outlays and its plans to finance its activities

2   To stabilize the economy

3   To encourage the economy's long-term growth and balanced regional development

Before the Second World War, the budget had only the first of these goals – to plan and finance the business of government.

But during the late 1940s and early 1950s, the budget began to assume its second purpose – stabilization of the economy.

In more recent years, the budget has assumed its third goal of helping to secure faster sustained economic growth and to seek balance across regions.

Today, the budget is the tool used by a government in pursuit of its fiscal policy. **Fiscal policy** is a government's use of its budget to achieve macroeconomic objectives such as full employment, sustained economic growth and price-level stability. It is the fiscal policy aspects of the budget that we focus on in this chapter.

Government budgets differ in size and detail, but they all have the same components. Here, we'll illustrate a government budget by looking at the UK.

Highlights of the UK Budget in 2010

Table 29.1 shows the main items in the UK government's budget. The numbers are projections for the fiscal year beginning in April 2010. The three main items in the budget are:

◆   Receipts

◆   Outlays

◆   Budget balance

Table 29.1

The Government Budget in 2010/11

Item		Projections (billions of pounds)
Receipts		**531**
Taxes on income and wealth		189
Taxes on expenditure		186
National Insurance contributions		97
Other receipts and royalties		59
Outlays		**695**
Expenditure on goods and services		388
Health	107	
Education	59	
Law and order	22	
Defence	46	
Other	154	
Transfer payments		265
Debt interest		42
Budget balance (surplus +/deficit −)		**−164**

Source of data: HM Treasury, Budget 2010.

Receipts

Receipts come from four sources:

1   Taxes on income and wealth

2   Taxes on expenditure

3   National Insurance contributions

4   Other receipts and royalties

The largest source of revenue is *taxes on income and wealth*, which were projected to be £189 billion in 2010/11. These are the taxes paid by individuals on their incomes and wealth and the taxes paid by businesses on their profits.

The second largest source of revenue is *taxes on expenditure*, which in 2010/2011 were projected at £186 billion. These taxes include VAT and special duties and taxes on gambling, alcoholic drinks, petrol, luxury items and imported goods.

Third in size are *National Insurance contributions*, projected to be £97 billion in 2010/11. This revenue comes from contributions paid by workers and employers to fund the welfare and healthcare programmes.

Fourth in size are *other receipts and royalties*. This item includes oil royalties, stamp duties, car taxes, miscellaneous rents, dividends from abroad and profits from nationalized industries.

Outlays

Outlays are classified in three broad categories:

1 Expenditure on goods and services
2 Transfer payments
3 Debt interest

Expenditure on goods and services are by far the largest item at £388 billion in 2010/11.

Table 29.1 lists some of the larger components of these expenditures. Health (expenditure on the National Health Service) took £107 billion and education took another £59 billion. The provision of law and order and defence, the two traditional roles of government, took only £68 billion between them.

Transfer payments – £265 billion in 2010/11 – are payments to individuals, businesses, other levels of government and the rest of the world. These payments include National Insurance benefits, healthcare benefits, unemployment benefits, welfare supplements, grants to local authorities and aid to developing countries.

Debt interest, which in 2010/11 is projected to be £42 billion, is the interest on the government debt minus interest received by the government on its own investments.

The bottom line of the government budget is the balance – the surplus or deficit.

Budget Balance

The government's budget balance is equal to its receipts minus its outlays. That is:

$$\text{Budget balance} = \text{Receipts} - \text{Outlays}$$

If receipts exceed outlays, the government has a **budget surplus**. If outlays exceed receipts, the government has a **budget deficit**. If receipts equal outlays, the government has a **balanced budget**. In fiscal year 2010/11, with projected outlays of £695 billion and revenue of £531 billion, the projected government deficit is £164 billion.

How typical is the budget of 2010/11? Let's look at its recent history.

The Budget in Historical Perspective

Figure 29.1 shows the government's receipts, outlays and budget balance since fiscal year 1970/71. The figure expresses the receipts, outlays and the budget balance as percentages of GDP. Expressing them in this way lets us see how large government is relative to the size of the

Figure 29.1 UK Government Receipts, Outlays and Budget Balance

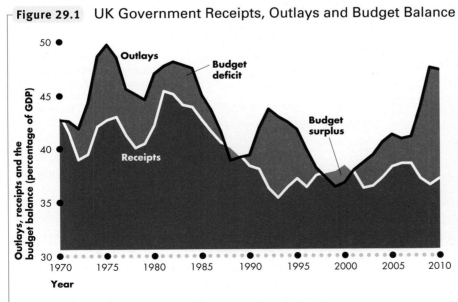

The figure records the UK government's receipts, outlays and budget deficit as percentages of GDP.

During the 1970s, the budget deficit became large and persisted well into the 1980s. A budget surplus appeared briefly in 1988, but income tax cuts and an increase in outlays turned the budget into a deficit again by 1990.

The budget returned to surplus at the end of the 1990s and in 2000 but for the rest of the 2000s, a large and growing deficit emerged.

Source of data: HM Treasury, *Budget 2010*.

economy, and it helps us to study *changes* in the scale of government over time. You may think of these percentages of GDP as telling you how many pence of each pound that we earn get paid to and spent by the government.

Throughout most of this period there was a budget deficit. The deficit increases in recessions and decreases in expansions. The budget was in surplus only at the end of the 1980s and again in 1998 to 2000. The deficit was large during a deep recession of the early 1970s but the deficit has trended upwards and the largest deficit occurred during 2009 and 2010 when it exceeded 10 per cent of GDP.

Why did the government deficit grow so sharply in recent years? The immediate answer is that outlays increased and receipts decreased. But which components of outlays increased and which sources of receipts decreased? Let's look at receipts and outlays in a bit more detail.

Receipts

Figure 29.2 shows the components of receipts received by the government as a percentage of GDP, from 1988 to 2010. Government receipts as a percentage of GDP decreased sharply from 1988 to 1993. This decrease occurred because the 1990–1992 recession decreased

tax revenues. Firms' profits fell, which lowered the taxes on business profits, and as the unemployment rate increased, the revenue from personal income taxes decreased.

Receipts trended upward from 1994 to 2000 as the economy settled into a long boom. They then settled to a plateau as the economy grew at a steady rate.

Receipts reached a peak in 2007 and then fell as the global recession took hold.

Outlays

Figure 29.3 shows the components of government outlays as percentages of GDP, between 1988 and 2010. Like receipts, outlays fluctuate over the business cycle. But unlike receipts, outlays have trended upwards. And the main source of increase is expenditure on goods and services, up from 20 per cent of GDP in 1990 to 27 per cent in 2010. Transfer payments have increased too, from 15 per cent of GDP in 1990 to 18 per cent in 2010.

Interest payment on government debt is a small component of government outlays. The amount of interest paid depends on the debt. In recent decades the ratio of debt to GDP fell so interest payments fell too. But in 2010 government debt jumped to become a large percentage of GDP and interest payments increased sharply.

Figure 29.2 UK Government Receipts

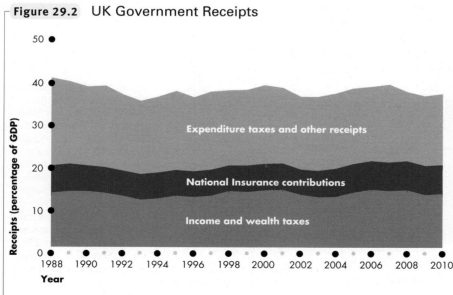

The figure shows the three components of government receipts: income and wealth taxes (including taxes on business profits), National Insurance contributions and expenditure taxes (including VAT).

Receipts from income and wealth fell during the recession of the early 1990s and 2008–2009.

Receipts increased during the strong expansion years from 1994 to 2001.

Source of data: HM Treasury, *Budget 2010*.

myeconlab Animation

Figure 29.3 UK Government Outlays

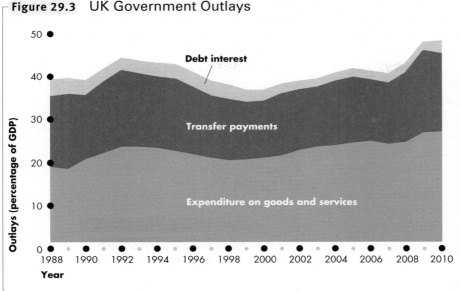

The figure shows three components of government outlays: expenditure on goods and services, transfer payments and debt interest.

Expenditure on goods and services has trended upward.

Transfer payments have also trended upward, but they are dominated by their cyclical changes.

Debt interest fell from 1996 to 2009 but then jumped in 2010.

Source of data: HM Treasury, *Budget 2010*.

Deficit, Debt and Capital

Government debt is the total amount of borrowing by the government. It is the sum of past deficits minus the sum of past surpluses plus payments to buy assets minus receipts from the sale of assets.

A budget deficit or the purchase of assets increases government debt and a budget surplus or the sale of state-owned assets reduces government debt.

Figure 29.4 shows the history of UK government debt from 1975 to 2010. In 1975, the debt–GDP ratio was just under 60 per cent. The debt–GDP ratio fell during the next 15 years and fell especially sharply during the 1980s as the government sold off state-owned assets such as British Rail and British Telecom. The debt increased spectacularly during 2009 and 2010 when the budget went into deficit and the government bought a large public stake in two troubled banks: the RBS and Lloyds.

Like individual and business debt, government debt is incurred to buy assets. Governments own public assets such as roads, bridges, schools and universities, public libraries and defence equipment. But the value of UK government assets is only £400 billion, which falls well short of its total debt.

How do the UK deficit and debt compare with deficits and debts in other major economies and the EU?

Figure 29.4 UK Government Debt

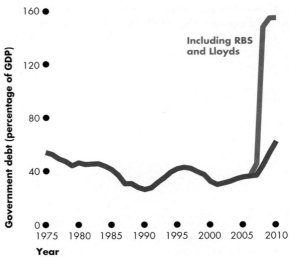

In 1975, UK government debt was 59 per cent of GDP. During the 1970s and 1980s the government reduced its debt by selling state assets such as British Rail and British Telecom. Government debt rose sharply after the 1990–1992 recession and fell from 1997 to 2002. In 2008–2010, a large budget deficit and the part-nationalisation of two banks, RBS and Lloyds, increased government debt astronomically.

Source of data: HM Treasury, *Budget 2010*.

◆▶ ECONOMICS IN ACTION

EU Government Budget Balances and Debts

The budget of each member state of the EU has similar categories of receipts and outlays to the UK budget. In addition to the national budgets, the Council of the EU draws up the EU budget, which the European Parliament approves.

The EU receives 89 per cent of its revenue from the member states and 11 per cent from EU tariffs on imports from non-member countries. Member states' contributions are based on VAT, which provides 13 per cent of revenue, and on gross national product, which produces 87 per cent of revenue. (A country's gross national product is equal to its gross domestic product plus net property income from the rest of the world.)

The total EU budget in 2010 was €141 billion – equivalent to less than 1 per cent of EU GDP. Figure 1 shows how the EU spends its resources. Structural measures – grants to weaker economic regions and expenditure on measures to improve competitiveness – take the largest slice at 45 per cent of total EU outlays. Agriculture – support for the Common Agricultural Policy (CAP) – and the environment take the next largest slice at 42 per cent of total EU outlays.

Despite its small size relative to GDP, the EU budget is hotly debated and contributes to economic life in many EU countries. For example, Ireland in the past has benefited from both the CAP and the EU structural programmes.

Most government revenue and outlays in the EU remain with the member states. The 27 members of the EU span a huge range of budgetary outcomes. Two aspects of these budgets are budget balances and government debt.

Figure 2 shows the budget balances of the 27 EU members in 2009. They range from a deficit of 15 per cent of GDP in Greece to 0.7 per cent in Luxembourg. The EU average is a deficit at 6.8 per cent of GDP. The UK has the third largest deficit.

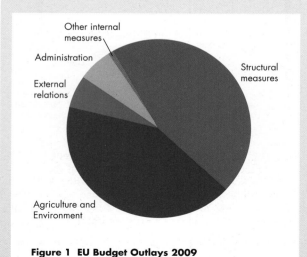

Figure 1 EU Budget Outlays 2009

Source of data for Figures 1, 2 and 3: Eurostat.

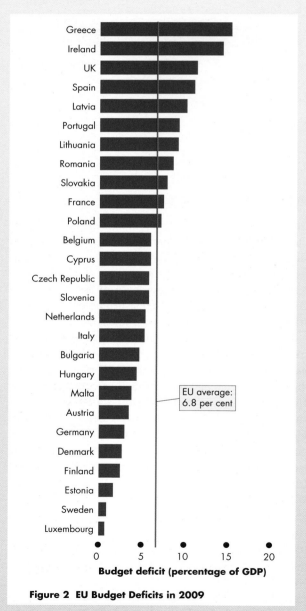

Figure 2 EU Budget Deficits in 2009

Figure 3 shows the EU government debt in 2009. It ranges from a high of 127 per cent of GDP in Greece to a low of 7 per cent in Estonia. The EU average debt is 74 per cent of GDP.

There is no significant correlation between debt and the budget balance. The UK has a budget deficit that is larger than the EU average and debt that is less than the EU average while Germany has a budget deficit that is below the EU average and debt equal to the EU average. Some EU countries with large debt such as Malta are running low deficits to bring the debt down, while others such as Greece have large deficits along with high debt–GDP ratios.

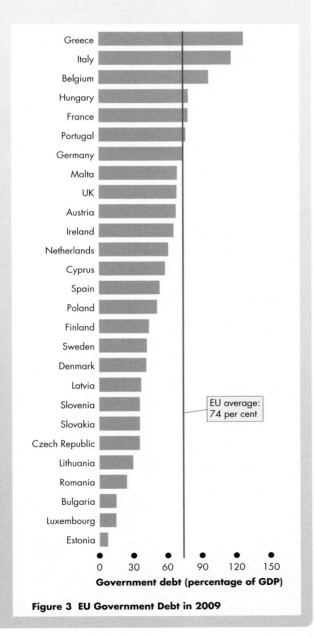

Figure 3 EU Government Debt in 2009

UK and EU Budget Balances and Debt in a Global Perspective

In *Economics in Action* (opposite), you can see that in 2009, the UK had a budget deficit of 11.4 per cent of GDP and the EU nations on average had a budget deficit of 6.8 per cent of EU GDP. How do these deficits compare with those in other advanced economies?

The answer is that the UK has one of the largest deficits and the EU average is in the middle of the pack. Only the US comes close to the UK with a deficit just below the UK's. Like the UK and US, Japan has a deficit greater than the EU's.

Among the countries that have smaller deficits than the EU average are the newly industrialized Asian economies (Hong Kong, Singapore, South Korea and Taiwan), Australia and Canada.

There is nothing inherently wrong with a government running a deficit, provided the resources are being used to add to the stock of social capital. There is also a case for a temporary government deficit to try to lift an economy from recession. We look more closely at using a deficit to stimulate the economy later in this chapter.

Review Quiz

1 What are the functions of a government's budget?
2 What are the goals of fiscal policy?
3 Describe the main sources of receipts and outlays in the budget of the UK government.
4 Under what circumstances does a government have a budget surplus?
5 Which members of the EU ran a budget deficit in 2009?
6 Which members of the EU had the largest debt levels in 2009?
7 Explain the connection between a government's budget deficit and its debt.

You can work these questions in Study Plan 29.1 and get instant feedback.

Now that you know what the main components of the government's budget are, it is time to study the *effects* of fiscal policy. We'll begin by learning about the effects of taxes on employment, aggregate supply and potential GDP. Then we'll study the effects of budget deficits and see how fiscal policy brings redistribution across generations. Finally, we'll look at fiscal stimulus and see how it might be used to speed recovery from recession and stabilize the business cycle.

Supply-side Effects of Fiscal Policy

How do taxes on personal and corporate income affect real GDP and employment? The answer to these questions is controversial. Some economists, known as supply-siders, believe these effects to be large and an accumulating body of evidence suggests that they are correct. To see why these effects might be large, we'll begin with a refresher on how full employment and potential GDP are determined in the absence of taxes. Then we'll introduce an income tax and see how it changes the economic outcome.

Full Employment and Potential GDP

You learned in Chapter 22 (pp. 513–515) how the full-employment quantity of labour and potential GDP are determined. At full employment, the real wage rate adjusts to make the quantity of labour demanded equal the quantity supplied. Potential GDP is the real GDP that the full-employment quantity of labour produces.

Figure 29.5 illustrates a full-employment situation. In part (a), the demand for labour curve is *LD*, and the supply of labour curve is *LS*. At a real wage rate of £15 an hour and 50 billion hours of labour a year employed, the economy is at full employment.

In Figure 29.5(b), the production function is *PF*. When 50 billion hours of labour are employed, real GDP – which is also potential GDP – is £1,300 billion.

Let's now see how an income tax changes potential GDP.

The Effects of the Income Tax

The tax on labour income influences potential GDP and aggregate supply by changing the full-employment quantity of labour. The income tax weakens the incentive to work and drives a wedge between the take-home wage of workers and the cost of labour to firms. The result is a smaller quantity of labour and a lower potential GDP.

Graphical Analysis and Illustration

Figure 29.5 shows the outcome we've just described. In the labour market, the income tax has no effect on the demand for labour, which remains at *LD*. The reason is that the quantity of labour that firms plan to hire depends only on how productive labour is and what it costs – its real wage rate.

Figure 29.5 The Effects of the Income Tax on Aggregate Supply

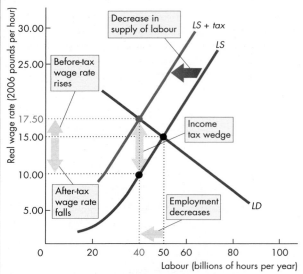

(a) Income tax and the labour market

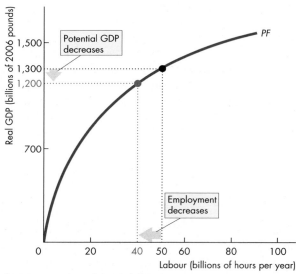

(b) Income tax and potential GDP

In part (a), with no income tax, the real wage rate is £15 an hour and employment is 50 billion hours. In part (b), potential GDP is £1,300 billion. An income tax shifts the supply of labour curve leftward to *LS + tax*. The before-tax wage rate rises to £17.50 an hour, the after-tax wage rate falls to £10 an hour, and the quantity of labour employed decreases to 40 billion hours. With less labour, potential GDP decreases to £1,200 billion.

myeconlab Animation

But the supply of labour does change. With no income tax, the real wage rate is £15 an hour and 50 billion hours of labour a year are employed. An income tax weakens the incentive to work and decreases the supply of labour. The reason is that for each pound of before-tax earnings, workers must pay the government an amount determined by the income tax code. So workers look at the after-tax wage rate when they decide how much labour to supply. An income tax shifts the supply curve leftward to *LS + tax*. The vertical distance between the *LS* curve and the *LS + tax* curve measures the amount of income tax. With the smaller supply of labour, the before-tax wage rate rises to £17.50 an hour but the after-tax wage rate falls to £10 an hour. The gap created between the before-tax and after-tax wage rates is called the **tax wedge**.

The new equilibrium quantity of labour employed is 40 billion hours a year – less than in the no-tax case. Because the full-employment quantity of labour decreases, so does potential GDP. And a decrease in potential GDP decreases aggregate supply.

In this example, the tax rate is high – £7.50 tax on a £17.50 wage rate is a tax rate of about 43 per cent. A lower tax rate would have a smaller effect on employment, which in turn would have a smaller effect on potential GDP.

An increase in the tax rate to above 43 per cent would decrease the supply of labour by more than the decrease shown in Figure 29.5. Equilibrium employment and potential GDP would also decrease still further. A tax cut would increase the supply of labour, increase equilibrium employment, and increase potential GDP.

Taxes on Expenditure and the Tax Wedge

The tax wedge that we've just considered is only a part of the wedge that affects labour-supply decisions. Taxes on consumption expenditure add to the wedge. The reason is that a tax on consumption raises the prices paid for consumption goods and services and is equivalent to a cut in the real wage rate.

The incentive to supply labour depends on the goods and services that an hour of labour can buy. The higher the taxes on goods and services and the lower the after-tax wage rate, the less is the incentive to supply labour. If the income tax rate is 25 per cent and the tax rate on consumption expenditure is 10 per cent, a pound earned buys only 65 pence worth of goods and services. The tax wedge is 35 per cent.

Some Real World Tax Wedges

Edward C. Prescott of Arizona State University, who shared the 2004 Nobel Prize for Economic Science, has estimated the tax wedges for a number of countries, among them the US, the UK and France.

The US Tax Wedge

The US tax wedge is a combination of 13 per cent tax on consumption and 32 per cent tax on incomes. The income tax component of the US tax wedge includes Social Security taxes and is the marginal tax rate – the tax rate paid on the marginal dollar earned.

France's Tax Wedge

Prescott estimates that in France, taxes on consumption are 33 per cent and taxes on incomes are 49 per cent.

The UK Tax Wedge

The estimates for the UK fall between those for the US and France. The figure shows these components of the tax wedges in the three countries.

Does the Tax Wedge Matter?

According to Prescott's estimates, the tax wedge has a powerful effect on employment and potential GDP. Potential GDP in France is 14 per cent below that of the US (per person), and the entire difference can be attributed to the difference in the tax wedge in the two countries.

Potential GDP in the UK is 41 per cent below that of the US (per person), and about a third of the difference arises from the different tax wedges. (The rest is due to different productivities.)

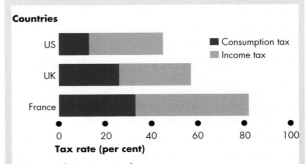

Figure 1 Three Tax Wedges

Source of data: Edward C. Prescott, *American Economic Review*, 2003.

Taxes and the Incentive to Save and Invest

A tax on interest income weakens the incentive to save and drives a wedge between the after-tax interest rate earned by savers and the interest rate paid by firms. These effects are analogous to those of a tax on labour income. But they are more serious for two reasons.

First, a tax on labour income lowers the quantity of labour employed and lowers potential GDP, while a tax on capital income lowers the quantity of saving and investment and slows the growth rate of real GDP.

Second, the true tax rate on interest income is much higher than that on labour income because of the way in which inflation and taxes on interest income interact. Let's examine this interaction.

Effect of Tax Rate on Real Interest Rate

The interest rate that influences investment and saving plans is the real after-tax interest rate. The real after-tax interest rate subtracts the income tax rate paid on interest income from the real interest rate. But the taxes depend on the nominal interest rate, not the real interest rate. So the higher the inflation rate, the higher is the true tax rate on interest income. Here is an example. Suppose the real interest rate is 4 per cent a year and the tax rate is 40 per cent.

If there is no inflation, the nominal interest rate equals the real interest rate. The tax on 4 per cent interest is 1.6 per cent (40 per cent of 4 per cent), so the real after-tax interest rate is 4 per cent minus 1.6 per cent, which equals 2.4 per cent.

If the inflation rate is 6 per cent a year, the nominal interest rate is 10 per cent. The tax on 10 per cent interest is 4 per cent (40 per cent of 10 per cent), so the real after-tax interest rate is 4 per cent minus 4 per cent, which equals zero. The true tax rate in this case is not 40 per cent but 100 per cent!

Effect of Income Tax on Saving and Investment

In Figure 29.6, initially there are no taxes. Also, the government has a balanced budget. The demand for loanable funds curve, which is also the investment demand curve, is *DLF*. The supply of loanable funds curve, which is also the saving supply curve, is *SLF*. The interest rate is 3 per cent a year, and the quantity of funds borrowed and lent is £200 billion a year.

A tax on interest income has no effect on the demand for loanable funds. The quantity of investment and

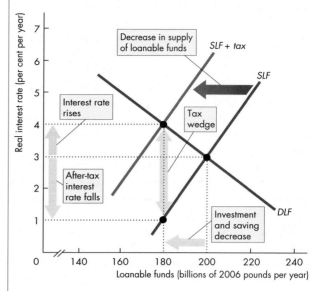

Figure 29.6 The Effects of a Tax on Capital Income

The demand for loanable funds and investment demand curve is *DLF*, and the supply of loanable funds and saving supply curve is *SLF*. With no income tax, the real interest rate is 3 per cent a year and investment is £200 billion. An income tax shifts the supply curve leftward to *SLF + tax*. The interest rate rises to 4 per cent a year, the after-tax interest rate falls to 1 per cent a year, and investment decreases to £180 billion. With less investment, the real GDP growth rate decreases.

myeconlab Animation

borrowing that firms plan to undertake depends only on how productive capital is and what it costs – its real interest rate. But a tax on interest income weakens the incentive to save and lend and decreases the supply of loanable funds. For each pound of before-tax interest, savers must pay the government an amount determined by the tax code. So savers look at the after-tax real interest rate when they decide how much to save.

When a tax is imposed, saving decreases and the supply of loanable funds curve shifts leftward to *SLF + tax*. The amount of tax payable is measured by the vertical distance between the *SLF* curve and the *SLF + tax* curve. With this smaller supply of loanable funds, the interest rate rises to 4 per cent a year but the after-tax interest rate falls to 1 per cent a year. A tax wedge is driven between the interest rate and the after-tax interest rate, and the equilibrium quantity of loanable funds decreases. Saving and investment also decrease.

Tax Revenues and the Laffer Curve

An interesting consequence of the effect of taxes on employment and saving is that a higher tax rate does not always bring greater tax revenue. A higher tax rate brings in more revenue per pound earned. But because a higher tax rate decreases the number of pounds earned, two forces operate in opposite directions on the tax revenue collected.

The relationship between the tax rate and the amount of tax revenue collected is called the **Laffer curve**. The curve is so named because Arthur B. Laffer, a member of US President Ronald Reagan's Economic Policy Advisory Board, drew such a curve on a table napkin and launched the idea that tax cuts could increase tax revenue.

Figure 29.7 shows a Laffer curve. The tax rate is on the *x*-axis, and total tax revenue is on the *y*-axis. For tax rates below T^*, an increase in the tax rate increases tax revenue; at T^*, tax revenue is maximized; and a tax rate increase above T^* decreases tax revenue.

Most people think that the UK is on the upward-sloping part of the Laffer curve; so is the US. But France might be close to the maximum point or perhaps even beyond it.

The Supply-side Debate

Before 1980, few economists paid attention to the supply-side effects of taxes on employment and potential GDP. Then, when Ronald Reagan took office as president, a group of supply-siders began to argue the virtues of cutting taxes. Arthur Laffer was one of them. Laffer and his supporters were not held in high esteem among mainstream economists, but they were influential for a period. They correctly argued that tax cuts would increase employment and increase output. But they incorrectly argued that tax cuts would increase tax revenues and decrease the budget deficit. For this prediction to be correct, the US would have had to be on the 'wrong' side of the Laffer curve. Given that US tax rates are among the lowest in the industrial world, it is unlikely that this condition was met. And when the Reagan administration did cut taxes, the budget deficit increased, a fact that reinforces this view.

Supply-side economics became tarnished because of its association with Laffer and came to be called 'voodoo economics'. But mainstream economists, including Martin Feldstein, a Harvard professor who was Reagan's chief economic advisor, recognized the power of tax cuts as incentives but took the standard

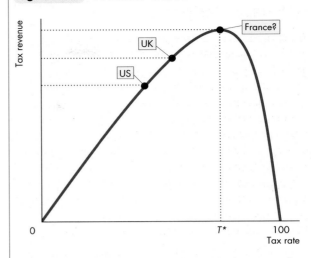

Figure 29.7   A Laffer Curve

A Laffer curve shows the relationship between the tax rate and tax revenues. For tax rates below T^*, an increase in the tax rate increases tax revenue. At the tax rate T^*, tax revenue is maximized. For tax rates above T^*, an increase in the tax rate decreases tax revenue.

myeconlab Animation

view that tax cuts without spending cuts would swell the budget deficit and bring serious further problems. This view is now widely accepted by economists of all political persuasions.

Review Quiz

1   How does a tax on labour income influence the equilibrium quantity of employment?
2   How does the tax wedge influence potential GDP?
3   Why are consumption taxes relevant for measuring the tax wedge?
4   Why are income taxes on capital income more powerful than those on labour income?
5   What is the Laffer curve and why is it unlikely that the UK is on the 'wrong' side of it?

You can work these questions in Study Plan 29.2 and get instant feedback.

You now know how taxes influence potential GDP and saving and investment. Next we look at the generational effects of fiscal policy.

Generational Effects of Fiscal Policy

Is a budget deficit a burden on future generations? If it is, how will the burden be borne? And is the budget deficit the only burden on future generations? What about the deficit in the state pension fund? Does it matter who owns the bonds that the government sells to finance its deficit? What about the bonds owned by foreigners? Won't repaying those bonds impose a bigger burden than repaying bonds owned by UK residents?

To answer questions like these, we use a tool called **generational accounting** – an accounting system that measures the lifetime tax burden and benefits of each generation. This accounting system was developed by Alan Auerbach of the University of Pennsylvania and Laurence Kotlikoff of Boston University. Generational accounts for the UK have been prepared by Roberto Cardarelli and James Sefton of the National Institute of Economic and Social Research in London and Laurence Kotlikoff (reported in the *Economic Journal*, November 2000).

Generational Accounting and Present Value

Income taxes and National Insurance contributions are paid by people who have jobs. Pensions are paid to people after they retire. Healthcare benefits are also provided on a larger scale to older retired people. So to compare taxes and benefits, we must compare the value of taxes paid by people during their working years with the benefits received in their retirement years. To compare the value of an amount of money at one date with that at a later date, we use the concept of present value. A **present value** is an amount of money that, if invested today, will grow to equal a given future amount when the interest that it earns is taken into account. We can compare pounds today with pounds in 2030 or any other future year by using present values.

For example, if the interest rate is 5 per cent a year, £1,000 invested today will grow, with interest, to £11,467 after 50 years. So the present value (in 2010) of £11,467 in 2060 is £1,000.

By using present values, we can assess the magnitude of the government's debts to older citizens in the form of state pensions and medical benefits.

But the assumed interest rate and growth rate of taxes and benefits critically influence the answers we get. For example, at an interest rate of 3 per cent a year, the present value (in 2010) of £11,467 in 2060 is £2,616.

The lower the interest rate, the greater is the present value of a given future amount.

Because there is uncertainty about the proper interest rate to use to calculate present values, plausible alternative numbers are used to estimate a range of present values.

Using generational accounting and present values, economists have studied the situation facing the governments arising from their pension and healthcare obligations, and they have found some time bombs!

The UK Welfare State and the Pensions Time Bomb

In 1942, as the Second World War was raging, William Beveridge (an economist and Director of the London School of Economics) envisaged a world in which the state provided social insurance that protected everyone from the five evils of 'want, disease, ignorance, squalor and idleness'. The *Beveridge Report* became the blueprint for the creation of the post-war welfare state, which provided universal pensions and health services as well as education and housing.

When state pensions and the National Health Service (NHS) were introduced, today's demographic situation was not foreseen. The age distribution of the UK population is dominated by a surge in the birth rate after the Second World War that created what is called the 'baby boom generation'. More than 12 million 'baby boomers' (almost 20 per cent of the population) are now retired or of retirement age. By 2033, more than 20 per cent of the population will have reached retirement age. Under today's arrangements, outlays on pensions and operating the NHS in 2033 will vastly exceed today's outlays. The obligation to make these outlays is a debt owed by the government and is just as real as the bonds that the government has issued to finance its budget deficits.

Fiscal Imbalance

To assess the government's obligations, economists use the concept of fiscal imbalance. **Fiscal imbalance** is the present value of the government's commitments to pay benefits minus the present value of its tax revenues. Fiscal imbalance is an attempt to measure the scale of the government's true liabilities – its true debt. The production of these accounts requires assumptions about future population trends, taxes, transfers and government expenditure, the initial value of government debt and the real rate of interest used in the present value discounting. The calculation of the fiscal imbalance is highly sensitive to these assumptions. For example, it matters very much whether pensions and unemployment benefits are linked to inflation or to earnings growth.

Estimates of UK and Other Fiscal Imbalances

On the assumption of strict control of government spending, Cardelli, Sefton and Kotlikoff reckon that the fiscal imbalance is 20 per cent of GDP. This figure is large but not an impossible one for the government to plan for. A more recent estimate is much less optimistic. Four economists at Freiburg University[1] estimate the UK's fiscal imbalance at a staggering 510 per cent of GDP. If this figure is correct, when added to the government's market debt in 2010, the total debt obligation of the UK government is 575 per cent of GDP – or £8.3 trillion (in 2010 prices).

Figure 29.8 shows the Freiburg economists' estimates of international fiscal imbalances for eight countries. The UK has the largest fiscal imbalance but the US, France and Germany also have sizeable fiscal imbalances.

Fiscal imbalance is an enormous obligation for many countries and it points to a catastrophic future. How can the UK government meet its pension and NHS obligations?

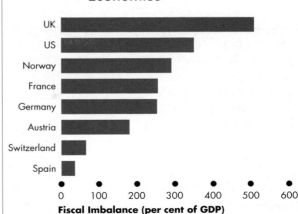

Figure 29.8   Fiscal Imbalances in Eight Economies

Fiscal imbalance is an enormous problem for many countries. On current tax and benefit rates, the UK government has a true debt of more than 5 years' GDP. The US government isn't far behind at almost 4 years' GDP. Even Norway and Germany, normally considered to have sound fiscal policies, owe almost 3 years' GDP to future citizens. Spain is at the other extreme with a fiscal imbalance of only a few months' GDP.

Source of data: Hagist, Moog, Raffelhüschen and Vatter (see footnote 1).

Coping With Fiscal Imbalances

There are five possible ways of coping with the fiscal imbalances:

1   Raise income taxes

2   Raise National Insurance contributions

3   Cut government discretionary spending

4   Cut unemployment and other welfare state benefits

5   Raise the state pension age

None of these measures is painless or free from political controversy. By combining the five measures, the pain from each could be lessened, but it would still be severe.

Raising income taxes or raising National Insurance contributions would have damaging supply-side effects.

[1] Christian Hagist, Stefan Moog, Bernd Raffelhüschen and Johannes Vatter, "Public Debt and Demography – An International Comparison Using Generational Accounting", Cesifo DICE Report 4 2009.

Either action would lower potential GDP and the growth rate of real GDP and lower the well-being of future generations. Government discretionary spending is just about impossible to cut and doing so presents challenges for national security and public health and safety. This leaves cutting benefits as the only viable option.

There is one further way of meeting these obligations and that is to pay for them by printing money. But the consequence of this solution is a seriously high inflation rate (see Chapter 24, pp. 574–575).

Generational Imbalance

A fiscal imbalance must eventually be corrected and when it is, people either pay higher taxes or receive lower benefits. The concept of generational imbalance tells us who will pay. **Generational imbalance** is the division of the fiscal imbalance between the current and future generations, assuming that the current generation will enjoy the existing levels of taxes and benefits.

The numbers produced by Cardarelli, Sefton and Kotlikoff (at the low end of the range of estimates) suggests that people born in 1972 (aged 25 in 1997) will pay 65 per cent more in taxes over their lifetime than those born in 1997.

Because the estimated fiscal imbalance is so large, it is not possible to predict how it will be resolved. But we can predict that the outcome will involve both lower benefits and higher taxes or paying bills with new money and creating inflation.

International Debt

You've seen that borrowing from the rest of the world is one source of loanable funds. What value of UK bonds are held abroad? Research by Adam Chester and Hann-Ju Ho of Lloyds-TSB suggests that 30 per cent or £284 billion of UK government bonds are held by foreign investors. This amount is well short of total UK foreign indebtedness because foreign investors own corporate bonds, shares and bank deposits.

The international debt of the UK is important because, when that debt is repaid, the UK will transfer real resources to the rest of the world. Instead of running a large net trade deficit, the UK will need a surplus of exports over imports. To make a surplus possible, UK saving must increase and consumption must decrease. Some tough choices lie ahead.

Review Quiz

1 What is a present value?
2 Distinguish between fiscal imbalance and generational imbalance.
3 How large was the estimated UK fiscal imbalance in 2010 and what is an indicator of how it divides between current and future generations?
4 What is the source of the UK fiscal imbalance and what are the painful choices that we face?
5 How much of UK government debt is held by the rest of the world?

You can work these questions in Study Plan 29.3 and get instant feedback.

myeconlab

You now know how the supply-side effects of fiscal policy work and you've seen the shocking scale of fiscal imbalance. We conclude this chapter by looking at fiscal policy as a tool for fighting a recession.

Fiscal Stimulus

The 2008–2009 recession brought Keynesian macro-economic ideas back into fashion and put a spotlight on **fiscal stimulus** – the use of fiscal policy to increase production and employment. But whether fiscal policy is truly stimulating, and if so, how stimulating, are questions that generate much discussion and disagreement. You're now going to explore these questions.

Fiscal stimulus can be either automatic or discretionary. A fiscal policy action that is triggered by the state of the economy with no action by government is called **automatic fiscal policy**. The increase in total unemployment benefits triggered by the massive rise in the unemployment rate through 2009 is an example of automatic fiscal policy.

A fiscal policy action initiated by government is called **discretionary fiscal policy**. It requires a change in a spending programme or in a tax law. A fiscal stimulus initiated by the Obama administration in the US in 2009 as a means of dealing with the recession is an example of discretionary fiscal policy.

Whether automatic or discretionary, an increase in government outlays or a decrease in government receipts can stimulate production and jobs. An increase in expenditure on goods and services directly increases aggregate expenditure. And an increase in transfer payments (such as unemployment benefits) or a decrease in tax revenues increases disposable income, which enables people to increase consumption expenditure. Lower taxes also strengthen the incentives to work and invest.

We'll begin by looking at automatic fiscal policy and the interaction between the business cycle and the budget balance.

Automatic Fiscal Policy and Cyclical and Structural Budget Balances

Two items in the government budget change automatically in response to the state of the economy. They are *tax revenues* and *means-tested spending*.

Automatic Changes in Tax Revenues

The tax laws that Parliament enacts don't legislate the number of pounds the government will raise. Rather they define the tax rates that people must pay. The number of pounds paid depend on tax rates and incomes. But incomes vary with real GDP, so tax revenues depend on real GDP. When real GDP increases in a business cycle expansion, wages and profits rise, so tax revenues from these incomes rise. When real GDP decreases in a recession, wages and profits fall, so tax revenues fall.

Means-tested Spending

The government creates programmes that pay benefits to qualified people and businesses. The spending on these programmes results in transfer payments that depend on the economic state of individual citizens and businesses. When the economy expands, unemployment falls, the number of people experiencing economic hardship decreases, so means-tested spending decreases. When the economy is in a recession, unemployment is high and the number of people experiencing economic hardship increases, so means-tested spending on unemployment benefits and food stamps increases.

Automatic Stimulus

Because government receipts fall and outlays increase in a recession, the budget provides automatic stimulus that helps to shrink the recessionary gap. Similarly, because receipts rise and outlays decrease in a boom, the budget provides automatic restraint to shrink an inflationary gap.

Cyclical and Structural Budget Balances

To identify the government budget deficit that arises from the business cycle, we distinguish between the **structural surplus or deficit**, which is the budget balance that would occur if the economy were at full employment, and the **cyclical surplus or deficit**, which is the actual budget balance *minus* the structural surplus or deficit.

Figure 29.9 illustrates these concepts. Outlays *decrease* as real GDP increases, so the outlays curve slopes downward; and receipts *increase* as real GDP increases, so the receipts curve slopes upward.

In Figure 29.9(a), potential GDP is £1,300 billion and if real GDP equals potential GDP, the government has a *balanced budget*. There is no structural surplus or deficit. But there might be a cyclical surplus or deficit. If real GDP is less than potential GDP at £1,200 billion, outlays exceed receipts and there is a *cyclical deficit*. If real GDP is greater than potential GDP at £1,400 billion, outlays are less than receipts and there is a *cyclical surplus*.

In Figure 29.9(b), if potential GDP equals £1,300 billion (line *B*), the structural balance is zero. But if potential

Figure 29.9 Cyclical and Structural Surpluses and Deficits

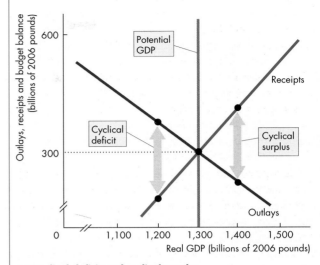

(a) Cyclical deficit and cyclical surplus

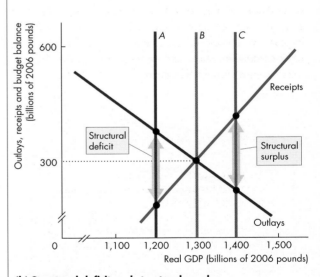

(b) Structural deficit and structural surplus

In part (a), potential GDP is £1,300 billion. When real GDP is less than potential GDP, the budget is in a cyclical deficit. When real GDP exceeds potential GDP, the budget is in a cyclical surplus. The government has a balanced budget when real GDP equals potential GDP.

In part (b), if potential GDP is £1,200 billion, there is a structural deficit and if potential GDP is £1,400 billion, there is a structural surplus. If potential GDP is £1,300 billion, the budget is in structural balance.

myeconlab Animation

GDP is £1,200 billion (line *A*), the government budget has a *structural deficit*. And if potential GDP is £1,400 billion (line *C*), the government budget has a *structural surplus*.

UK Structural Budget Balance

The UK budget deficit in 2010 was £131 billion. The recessionary gap (the gap between real GDP and potential GDP) was about 6 per cent of potential GDP. With a large recessionary gap, you would expect some of the deficit to be cyclical. But how much of the 2010 deficit was cyclical and how much was structural?

The International Monetary Fund estimates that the UK had a *structural deficit* of 7.6 per cent of potential GDP in 2010. Of the major developed economies, only the US is estimated to have a larger structural deficit than the UK.

Figure 29.10 shows the actual and cyclical deficits. The gap between the two shows the structural deficit. You can see that the cyclical deficit was small from 2004 to 2008. But it exploded in 2009 and 2010. When full employment returns, the cyclical deficit will vanish.

Figure 29.10   **UK Cyclical and Structural Budget Balance**

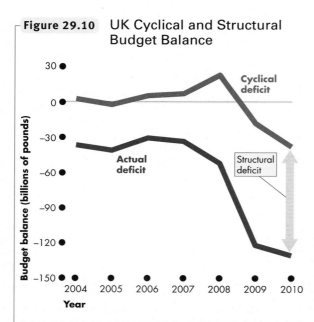

As real GDP shrank in the 2008–2009 recession, receipts fell, outlays increased, and the budget deficit increased. The cyclical deficit was small compared to the actual deficit; most of the 2010 deficit was structural.

Source of data: HM Treasury, *Budget 2010*.

myeconlab Animation

Fiscal Stimulus in the US Economy

In 2008, UK Prime Minister Gordon Brown called on all governments to cut taxes and increase spending to stimulate a flagging global economy. The world's largest economy came to Brown's party in grand style.

In February 2009 Barack Obama signed into law the American Recovery and Reinvestment Act at an economic forum he hosted in Denver. This act was the third and most ambitious in a series of stimulus packages aimed at increasing investment and consumer expenditure and leading to the creation of jobs.

The total package added $862 billion to the federal government's budget deficit: $288 billion from tax cuts and the rest from increased spending. The spending increases included payments to state and local governments ($144 billion), spending on infrastructure and science projects ($111 billion), programmes in healthcare ($59 billion), education and training ($53 billion), and energy ($43 billion).

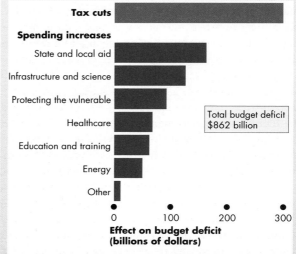

Figure 1 The Components of the 2009 Fiscal Stimulus Act

Obama signs the 2009 Fiscal Stimulus Act.

Discretionary Fiscal Stimulus

Most discussion of discretionary fiscal stimulus focuses on its effects on aggregate demand. But you've seen (on pp. 698–701) that taxes influence aggregate supply and that the balance of taxes and spending – the government budget deficit – can crowd out investment and slow the pace of economic growth. So discretionary fiscal stimulus has both supply-side and demand-side effects that end up determining its overall effectiveness.

We're going to begin our examination of discretionary fiscal stimulus by looking at its effects on aggregate demand.

Fiscal Stimulus and Aggregate Demand

An increase in government expenditure has a direct effect on aggregate demand. A tax cut influences aggregate demand by increasing disposable income and consumption expenditure. Both forms of fiscal stimulus have multiplier effects.

Let's look at the two main fiscal policy multipliers: the government expenditure and tax multipliers.

The **government expenditure multiplier** is the quantitative effect of a change in government expenditure on real GDP. Because government expenditure is a component of aggregate expenditure, an increase in government spending increases aggregate expenditure and real GDP. But does a £1 billion increase in government expenditure increase real GDP by £1 billion, or more than £1 billion, or less than £1 billion?

When an increase in government expenditure increases real GDP, incomes rise and the higher incomes bring an increase in consumption expenditure. If this were the only consequence of increased government expenditure, the government expenditure multiplier would be greater than 1.

But an increase in government expenditure increases government borrowing (or decreases government lending if there is a budget surplus) and raises the real interest rate. With a higher cost of borrowing, investment decreases, which partly offsets the increase in government spending. If this were the only consequence of increased government expenditure, the multiplier would be less than 1.

The actual multiplier depends on which of the above effects is stronger and the consensus is that the crowding-out effect is strong enough to make the government expenditure multiplier less than 1.

The **tax multiplier** is the quantitative effect of a change in taxes on real GDP. The demand-side effects of a tax cut are likely to be smaller than an equivalent increase in government expenditure. The reason is that a tax cut influences aggregate demand by increasing disposable income, only part of which gets spent. So the initial injection of expenditure from a £1 billion tax cut is less than a £1 billion.

A tax cut has similar crowding-out consequences to a spending increase. It increases government borrowing (or decreases government lending), raises the real interest rate and cuts investment.

The tax multiplier effect on aggregate demand depends on these two opposing effects and is probably quite small.

Figure 29.11 shows how fiscal stimulus is supposed to work if it is perfectly executed and has its desired effects.

Potential GDP is £1,400 billion and real GDP is below potential at £1,300 billion so the economy has a recessionary gap of £100 billion.

To restore full employment, the government passes a fiscal stimulus package. An increase in government

Figure 29.11   Expansionary Fiscal Policy

Potential GDP is £1,400 billion, real GDP is £1,300 billion, and there is a £100 billion recessionary gap. An increase in government expenditure and a tax cut increase aggregate expenditure by ΔE. The multiplier increases consumption expenditure. The *AD* curve shifts rightward to AD_1, the price level rises to 115, real GDP increases to £1,400 billion, and the recessionary gap is eliminated.

myeconlab   Animation

expenditure and a tax cut increase aggregate expenditure by ΔE. If this were the only change in spending plans, the AD curve would shift rightward to become the curve labelled $AD_0 + \Delta E$ in Figure 29.11. But if fiscal stimulus sets off a multiplier process that increases consumption expenditure, and does not crowd out much investment expenditure, aggregate demand increases further and the AD curve shifts to AD_1.

With no change in the price level, the economy would move from point A to point B on AD_1. But the increase in aggregate demand brings a rise in the price level along the upward-sloping SAS curve and the economy moves to point C.

At point C, the economy returns to full employment and the recessionary gap is eliminated.

Fiscal Stimulus and Aggregate Supply

You've seen earlier in this chapter that taxes influence aggregate supply. A tax on labour income (on wages) drives a wedge between the cost of labour and the take-home pay of workers and lowers employment and output (p. 698). A tax on capital income (on interest) drives a wedge between the cost of borrowing and the return to lending and lowers saving and investment (p. 700). With less saving and investment, the real GDP growth rate slows.

These negative effects of taxes on real GDP and its growth rate and on employment mean that tax cuts increase real GDP and its growth rate and increase employment.

These supply-side effects of tax cuts occur along with the demand-side effects and are probably much larger than the demand-side effects and make the overall tax multiplier much larger than the government expenditure multiplier – see *Economics in Action*.

An increase in government expenditure financed by borrowing increases the demand for loanable funds. The real interest rate rises, which decreases investment and private saving. This cut in investment is the main reason why the government expenditure multiplier is so small and why a deficit-financed increase in government spending ends up making only a small contribution to job creation. And because government expenditure crowds out investment, it lowers future real GDP.

So a fiscal stimulus package that is heavy on tax cuts and light on government spending works. But an increase in government expenditure alone is not an effective way to stimulate production and create jobs.

The description of the effects of discretionary fiscal stimulus and its graphical illustration in Figure 29.11 makes it look easy: calculate the recessionary gap and the multipliers, change government expenditure and taxes, and eliminate the gap. In reality, getting the magnitude and the timing right is difficult.

Magnitude of Stimulus

Economists have diverging views about the size of the government expenditure and tax multipliers. This fact makes it impossible for government to determine the amount of stimulus needed to close a given output gap. Further, the actual output gap is not known and can only be estimated with error. For these two reasons, discretionary fiscal policy is risky.

How Big Are the Fiscal Stimulus Multipliers?

When the US government cut taxes by $300 billion and increased government expenditure by almost $500 billion, by how much did aggregate expenditure and real GDP change? How big were the fiscal policy multipliers? Was the government expenditure multiplier larger than the tax multiplier? These questions are about the multiplier effects on *equilibrium real GDP*, not just on aggregate demand.

President Obama's economic adviser, Christina Romer, a University of California, Berkeley, professor, expected the multiplier to be about 1.5. She was expecting the spending increase of $500 billion to go a long way towards closing the $1 trillion output gap in 2010.

Robert Barro, a professor at Harvard University, says this multiplier number is not in line with previous experience. Based on his calculations, an additional $500 billion of government spending would increase aggregate expenditure by only $250 billion because it would lower private spending in a crowding-out effect by $250 billion – the multiplier is 0.5.

Patrick Minford, a professor at Cardiff University, says that the government expenditure multiplier on real GDP is even smaller and is 0.35. He arrives at this number based on 30 years of research on the UK economy. Harald Uhlig, a professor at the University of Chicago, agrees with Minford's assessment of the multiplier and says this number also applies to the US.

If Minford and Uhlig are correct, a $500 billion increase in government spending increases aggregate expenditure by between $150 billion and $200 billion.

Time Lags

Discretionary fiscal stimulus actions are also seriously hampered by three time lags:

◆ Recognition lag
◆ Law-making lag
◆ Impact lag

Recognition Lag

The recognition lag is the time it takes to figure out that fiscal policy actions are needed. This process involves assessing the current state of the economy and forecasting its future state.

Law-making Lag

The law-making lag is the time it takes to pass the laws needed to change taxes or spending. This process takes time because each MP has a different idea about what is the best tax or spending programme to change, so long debates and committee meetings are needed to reconcile conflicting views. The economy might benefit from fiscal stimulation today, but by the time the law has been passed, a different fiscal medicine might be needed.

Impact Lag

The impact lag is the time it takes from passing a tax or spending change to its effects on real GDP being felt. This lag depends partly on the speed with which government agencies can act and partly on the timing of changes in spending plans by households and businesses. These changes are spread out over a number of quarters and possibly a number of years.

Economic forecasting is steadily improving, but it remains inexact and subject to error. The range of uncertainty about the magnitudes of the government expenditure and tax multipliers make discretionary fiscal stimulus an imprecise tool for boosting production and jobs. Also the crowding-out consequences of fiscal stimulus raise serious questions about its effects on long-term economic growth.

There is greater agreement about tax multipliers. Because tax cuts strengthen the incentive to work and to invest, they increase aggregate supply as well as aggregate demand.

These multipliers get bigger as more time elapses. Harald Uhlig says that after one year, the tax multiplier is 0.5 so that the $300 billion tax cut would increase real GDP by about $150 billion by early 2010. But with two years to respond, real GDP would be $600 billion higher – a multiplier of 2. And after three years, the tax multiplier builds up to more than 6. Patrick Minford's research on the UK economy supports the findings of Uhlig.

The implications of the work of Barro, Uhlig and Minford are that tax cuts are a powerful way to stimulate real GDP and employment but spending increases are not effective.

Christine Romer agrees that the economy hasn't performed in line with a multiplier of 1.5 but says other factors deteriorated and without the fiscal stimulus, the outcome would have been even worse.

Christina Romer 1.5

Robert Barro 0.5

Patrick Minford 0.35

Review Quiz

1 What is the distinction between automatic and discretionary fiscal policy?
2 How do taxes and means-tested spending programmes work as automatic stabilizers to dampen the business cycle?
3 How do we tell whether a budget deficit needs discretionary action to remove it?
4 How can the government use discretionary fiscal policy to stimulate the economy?
5 Why might fiscal stimulus crowd out investment?

You can work these questions in Study Plan 29.4 and get instant feedback.

You've now seen the effects of fiscal policy, and *Reading Between the Lines* on pp. 710–711 applies what you've learned to the fiscal policy actions of the government of Ireland in the crisis of confidence that hit a number of EU economies in 2010.

Reading Between the Lines

Ireland's Fiscal Contraction

The Financial Times, 4 November 2010

Dublin Increases Budget Spending Cuts

FT

John Murray Brown and Alan Beattie

Ireland is facing budget cuts next month twice as savage as originally envisaged, as the embattled Fianna Fáil – led government seeks to reassure debt markets that its fiscal reduction plan is on track.

Officials said on Wednesday the December 7 budget would include a €6bn adjustment through cuts in public spending and tax increases, resulting in a deficit in 2011 of 9.25 – 9.5 per cent of gross domestic product.

This compares with 32 per cent this year, after including a one-off €30bn banks bail-out. . . .

The International Monetary Fund said Ireland's debt–GDP ratio in 2011 would be 21 percentage points higher than previously projected because of bailouts in the banking sector. Dublin on Thursday estimated that the debt would reach 105 per cent of GDP compared with 25 per cent before the crisis.

The fund calculated that Ireland's total financing needs in 2010 was the equivalent of 38.4 per cent of GDP.

Ireland's benchmark 10-year bond yields jumped to 7.67 per cent and the cost for Dublin to borrow compared with Germany, the Eurozone's biggest economy, also rose to a record 5.21 percentage points. . . .

The scale of next year's fiscal adjustment is twice the €3bn envisaged at the time of last year's budget and reflects the gloomier growth outlook where the government is now forecasting GDP to increase by 1.75 per cent next year, compared with a forecast of 3.3 per cent last December.

In 2010, growth is estimated at 0.25 per cent. The four-year plan to 2014 envisages savings of €15bn to bring the deficit below 3 per cent, the limit set for Eurozone members under the Maastricht treaty. . . .

The Essence of the Story

◆ Ireland has an unsustainably large government budget deficit.

◆ The government of Ireland is cutting expenditure and increasing taxes.

◆ The government's goal is to reduce the deficit from 32 per cent of GDP in 2010 to 3 per cent by 2014.

Economic Analysis

- The global financial crisis brought a banking crisis in Ireland, which the Irish government tackled by bailing out the banks.

- The bail-out drove the budget deficit and the debt–GDP ratio of the Irish government to levels never before experienced.

- Figure 1 shows the budget deficit and government debt as percentages of GDP in 2009 and 2010 and their projected values for 2011 and 2012 by a leading independent forecasting organization in Dublin.

- In 2010, the high deficits and debt increased the risk of default by the government of Ireland and drove the interest rate on its debt to more than 9 per cent a year.

- An increase in government spending that raises the interest rate crowds out private investment.

- The intent of the decrease in government spending and increase in taxes is to lower the default risk and lower the interest rate in Ireland.

- A fall in the interest rate will encourage private investment, which will eventually offset the fall in government spending.

- Figure 2 shows projected growth rates of government spending, private investment and real GDP for 2011 and 2012.

- Government spending is expected to fall, but private investment and real GDP are expected to increase.

- Figure 3 explains these changes. A fall in government spending decreases aggregate demand and shifts the AD curve leftward from AD_{10} to AD_{11}. Real GDP decreases.

- Eventually, the smaller deficit and debt diminishes the risk of default, the interest rate falls, and investment increases. The AD curve shifts rightward from AD_{11} to AD_{12}. Real GDP increases.

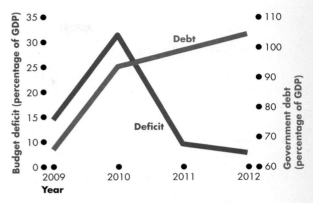

Figure 1 Ireland's government deficit and debt

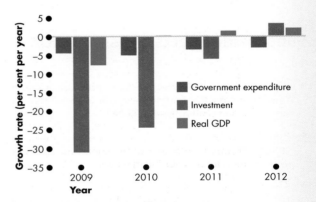

Figure 2 Past and projected growth rates

Figure 3 Ireland's aggregate supply and aggregate demand

SUMMARY

Key Points

Government Budgets (pp. 692–697)

◆ The government budget finances the activities of the government and is used to conduct fiscal policy.

◆ Government receipts come from taxes on income and wealth, taxes on expenditure and National Insurance contributions.

◆ When government outlays exceed receipts, the government has a budget deficit.

Working Problems 1 to 3 will give you a better understanding of government budgets.

Supply-side Effects of Fiscal Policy (pp. 698–701)

◆ Fiscal policy has supply-side effects because taxes weaken the incentive to work and decrease employment and potential GDP.

◆ Fiscal policy has supply-side effects because taxes weaken the incentive to save and invest, which lowers the growth rate of real GDP.

◆ The Laffer curve shows the relationship between the tax rate and the amount of tax revenue collected.

Working Problems 4 to 7 will give you a better understanding of the supply-side effects of fiscal policy.

Generational Effects of Fiscal Policy (pp. 702–704)

◆ Generational accounting measures the lifetime tax burden and benefits of each generation.

◆ One study estimates the UK fiscal imbalance to be 510 per cent of the value of one year's production.

◆ Future generations will pay for 65 per cent of the benefits of the current generation.

◆ About 30 per cent of UK government debt is held by the rest of the world.

Working Problems 8 and 9 will give you a better understanding of the generational effects of fiscal policy.

Fiscal Stimulus (pp. 704–709)

◆ Fiscal policy can be automatic or discretionary.

◆ Automatic fiscal policy might moderate the business cycle by stimulating demand in recession and restraining demand in a boom.

◆ Discretionary fiscal stimulus influences aggregate demand and aggregate supply.

◆ Discretionary changes in government expenditure or taxes have multiplier effects of uncertain magnitude but the tax multiplier is likely to be the larger one.

◆ Fiscal stimulus policies are hampered by uncertainty about multipliers and by time lags (law-making lags and the difficulty of correctly diagnosing and forecasting the state of the economy).

Working Problems 10 to 21 will give you a better understanding of fiscal stimulus.

Key Terms

Automatic fiscal policy, 704
Balanced budget, 693
Budget, 692
Budget deficit, 693
Budget surplus, 693
Cyclical surplus or deficit, 705
Discretionary fiscal policy, 704
Fiscal imbalance, 702
Fiscal policy, 692
Fiscal stimulus, 704
Generational accounting, 702
Generational imbalance, 703
Government debt, 695
Government expenditure multiplier, 707
Laffer curve, 701
Present value, 702
Structural surplus or deficit, 705
Tax multiplier, 707
Tax wedge, 699

STUDY PLAN PROBLEMS AND APPLICATIONS

 myeconlab You can work Problems 1 to 21 in MyEconLab Chapter 29 Study Plan and get instant feedback.

Government Budgets (Study Plan 29.1)

Use the following news clip to work Problems 1 and 2.

The Budget

George Osborne says he has little option but to push on with the harshest public spending cuts in living memory because a reversal would alarm the bond markets and plunge Britain into 'financial turmoil'. Responding to growing clamour for him to explore a 'plan B' for recovery, the chancellor insisted that there would be no weakening of the government's resolve in implementing austerity measures.

Source: *The Financial Times*, 30 January 2011

1 What is the UK government's plan for fiscal policy in the budget 2010?

2 What would be a 'plan B' for the government to adopt?

3 At the end of 2008, the government of China's debt was ¥4,700 billion. (¥ is yuan, the currency of China). In 2009, the government spent ¥6,000 billion and ended the year with a debt of ¥5,300 billion. How much did the government receive in tax revenue in 2009? How can you tell?

Supply-side Effects of Fiscal Policy

(Study Plan 29.2)

4 The government is considering raising the tax rate on labour income and asks you to report on the supply-side effects of such an action. Answer the following questions using appropriate graphs. You are being asked about *directions* of change, not exact magnitudes. What will happen to

a The supply of labour and why?

b The demand for labour and why?

c The equilibrium level of employment and why?

d The equilibrium before-tax wage rate and why?

e The equilibrium after-tax wage rate and why?

f Potential GDP?

5 What fiscal policy action might increase investment and speed economic growth? Explain how the policy action would work.

6 Suppose that instead of taxing *nominal* capital income, the government taxed real capital income. Use appropriate graphs to explain and illustrate the effect that this change would have on

a The tax rate on capital income.

b The supply of and demand for loanable funds.

c Investment and the real interest rate.

7 Suppose that in Sinoland, investment is £400 billion, saving is £400 billion, tax revenues are £500 billion, exports are £300 billion, and imports are £200 billion.

Calculate government expenditure and the government budget balance and explain the impact the government is exerting on investment: is the impact positive or negative?

Generational Effects of Fiscal Policy

(Study Plan 29.3)

8 The Office for Budget Responsibility projects that, under current policies, public debt will reach 233 per cent of GDP in 30 years and nearly 500 per cent in 50 years.

a What is a fiscal imbalance? How might the government reduce the fiscal imbalance?

b How would your answer to part (a) influence the generational imbalance?

9 **Increase in US Payroll Taxes Needed for Social Security**

US Social Security faces a $5.3 trillion shortfall over the next 75 years, but a congressional report says the massive gap could be erased by increasing payroll taxes paid by both employees and employers from 6.2 per cent to 7.3 per cent and by raising the retirement age to 70.

Source: *USA Today*, 21 May 2010

a Why is US Social Security facing a $5.3 trillion shortfall over the next 75 years?

b Explain how the suggestions in the news clip would reduce the shortfall.

c Would the suggestions in the news clip change the generational imbalance?

Fiscal Stimulus (Study Plan 29.4)

10 The economy is in a recession, and the recessionary gap is large.

a Describe the discretionary and automatic fiscal policy actions that might occur.

b Describe a discretionary fiscal stimulus package that could be used that would not bring an increase in the budget deficit.

c Explain the risks of discretionary fiscal policy in this situation.

Use the following news clip to work Problems 11 to 13.

Obama's Economic Recovery Plan

If the president is serious about focusing on jobs, a good start would be to freeze all tax rates and cut federal spending back to where it was before all the recent bailouts and stimulus spending.

Source: *USA Today*, 9 September 2010

11 What would be the effect on the budget deficit and real GDP of freezing tax rates and cutting government spending?

12 What would be the effect on jobs of freezing tax rates and cutting government spending?

13 If the government froze its current spending and instead cut taxes, what would be the effect on investment and jobs?

14 The economy is in a recession, the recessionary gap is large, and there is a budget deficit.

a Do we know whether the budget deficit is structural or cyclical? Explain your answer.

b Do we know whether automatic stabilizers are increasing or decreasing the output gap? Explain your answer.

c If a discretionary increase in government expenditure occurs, what happens to the structural deficit or surplus? Explain.

15 The research of economists Patrick Minford and Harald Uhlig suggests that tax cuts to stimulate the economy would pay for themselves in the long run.

a Explain what is meant by tax cuts paying for themselves. What does this statement imply about the tax multiplier?

b Why would tax cuts not pay for themselves?

Use the following news clip to work Problems 16 and 17.

Summers Calls for Infrastructure Spending

Larry Summers, the outgoing director of the White House National Economic Council, said the US must ramp up spending on domestic infrastructure to drive the economic recovery. He said that a combination of low borrowing costs, cheap building costs and high unemployment in the construction industry make this the ideal time to rebuild roads, bridges and airports.

Source: Ft.com, 7 October 2010

16 Is this infrastructure spending a fiscal stimulus? Would such spending be a discretionary or an automatic fiscal policy?

17 Explain how the rebuilding of roads, bridges and airports would drive the economic recovery.

Use the following news clip to work Problems 18 to 20.

Stimulus Debate Turns on Rebates

In 2008, as pressure built up on Washington to juice the economy, a one-time consumer rebate emerged as the likely centrepiece of a $150-billion stimulus programme. But who should actually get rebates? Everyone who pays income taxes? Or only lower- and middle-income households because they are more likely to spend more of their rebate than are higher-income households, spend it quickly, and every dollar spent on stimulus could generate a dollar in GDP?

Source: CNN, 22 January 2008

18 **a** Explain the intended effect of the $150 billion fiscal stimulus package. Draw a graph to illustrate the effect.

b Explain why the effect of this fiscal policy depends on who receives the tax rebates.

19 What would have a larger effect on aggregate demand: $150 billion worth of tax rebates or $150 billion worth of government spending?

20 Explain whether a stimulus package centred around a one-time consumer tax rebate is likely to have a small or a large supply-side effect.

21 Compare the impact on equilibrium real GDP of a same-sized decrease in taxes and increase in government expenditure.

ADDITIONAL PROBLEMS AND APPLICATIONS

myeconlab You can work these problems in MyEconLab if assigned by your lecturer.

Government Budgets

22 UK public sector net debt as a percentage of GDP in 2009/10 was 154.7 but excluding 'financial interventions' by the Bank of England, the net debt was 53.6 per cent of GDP.

Explain what accounts for this big difference in the two figures. What did the UK government do in 2008 to inflate the budget deficit and increase the debt–GDP ratio?

Supply-side Effects of Fiscal Policy

Use the following information to work Problems 23 and 24.

Suppose that in the UK, investment is £160 billion, saving is £140 billion, government expenditure on goods and services is £150 billion, exports are £200 billion and imports are £250 billion.

23 What is the amount of tax revenue? What is the government budget balance?

24 **a** Is the government's budget exerting a positive or negative impact on investment?

b What fiscal policy action might increase investment and speed economic growth? Explain how the policy action would work.

25 Suppose that capital income taxes are based (as they are in the UK and most countries) on nominal interest rates. And suppose that the inflation rate increases by 5 per cent. Use appropriate diagrams to explain and illustrate the effect that this change would have on

a The tax rate on capital income.

b The supply of loanable funds.

c The demand for loanable funds.

d Equilibrium investment.

e The equilibrium real interest rate.

Use the following news clip to work Problems 26 and 27.

Sir Richard Lambert, the outgoing head of the CBI, accused the government of failing to articulate a clear vision for economic growth. Commenting on the 50 per cent tax rate, he said that business investment in the UK will suffer if high paid individuals drifted elsewhere for tax reasons.

Source: *The Financial Times*, 25 January 2011

26 Why has the UK government raised the top rate of tax to 50 per cent?

27 What are the possible long-term consequences of such a tax rise on the supply-side of the economy, for tax revenues and the budget deficit?

Use the following news clip to work Problems 28 to 30.

Tax Hikes for Top Earners

750,000 more people will start to pay the 40% rate of tax as a result of forthcoming tax rises. However, 500,000 people will no longer be paying income tax because the point at which income tax starts to be paid will rise. The government has made the tax changes revenue neutral. The main gainers from the tax changes are lone parents and low income households.

Source: BBC, 31 January 2011

28 What do you think the term revenue neutral means?

29 Explain the potential demand-side effect of the tax changes.

30 Explain the potential supply-side effects of the tax changes.

Generational Effects of Fiscal Policy

31 **Push to Cut Deficit Collides With Politics as Usual**

So it goes in Campaign 2010 where cutting the deficit is a big issue but where support for doing some of the hard things to achieve that is running into politics as usual. Nowhere is that more apparent than in the debate – or lack thereof – on the nation's spending on big entitlement programs. According to the latest projections from the Congressional Budget Office, spending on the big three entitlement programs – Social Security, Medicare and Medicaid – is to rise by 70 per cent, 79 per cent, and 99 per cent, respectively, over the next 10 years.

Source: *The Wall Street Journal*, 5 October 2010

If politicians continue to avoid debating the projected increases in these three entitlement programmes, how do you think the fiscal imbalance will change? If Congress holds the budget deficit at $3.1 trillion, who will pay for the projected increases in expenditure?

Fiscal Stimulus

32 The economy is in a boom and the inflationary gap is large.

  a Describe the discretionary and automatic fiscal policy actions that might occur.

  b Describe a discretionary fiscal restraint package that could be used that would not produce serious negative supply-side effects.

  c Explain the risks of discretionary fiscal policy in this situation.

33 The economy is growing slowly, the inflationary gap is large, and there is a budget deficit.

  a Do we know whether the budget deficit is structural or cyclical? Explain your answer.

  b Do we know whether automatic stabilizers are increasing or decreasing aggregate demand? Explain your answer.

  c If a discretionary decrease in government expenditure occurs, what happens to the structural budget balance? Explain your answer.

Use the following news clip to work Problems 34 to 36.

Juicing the Economy Will Come at a Cost

The $150-billion stimulus plan will bump up the deficit, but not necessarily dollar for dollar. Here's why: if the stimulus works, the increased economic activity will generate federal tax revenue. But it isn't clear what the cost to the economy will be if a stimulus package comes too late – a real concern since legislation could get bogged down by politics.

Source: CNN, 23 January 2008

34 Explain why $150 billion of stimulus won't increase the budget deficit by $150 billion.

35 Is the budget deficit arising from the action described in the news clip structural or cyclical or a combination of the two? Explain.

36 Why might the stimulus package come 'too late'? What are the potential consequences of the stimulus package coming 'too late'?

Economics in the News

37 After you have studied *Reading Between the Lines* on pp. 710–711 answer the following questions.

  a What policy is the Irish government following in dealing with its budget deficit and rising debt–GDP ratio?

  b How does the Irish government plan to meet its target?

  c What is the reason for the sharp rise in the budget deficit?

  d What has happened to the Irish long-term bond rate as a result of the experience of high deficits and debt–GDP ratio?

  e How has the recent history of high deficits and debt affected private investment?

  f Why might a fiscal austerity programme lead to an expansion in private investment and reverse crowding out?

38 **US Financial Crisis Over? Not Really**

Economist Deepak Lal says the US financial crisis is not solved and contains the seeds of a more serious future crisis. For India and China, with no structural deficit, a temporary budget deficit above that resulting from automatic stabilizers makes sense. But it doesn't make sense for the US with its large structural deficit.

Source: rediff.com, 18 October 2010

More Fiscal Stimulus Needed

Economist Laura Tyson says there is a strong argument for more fiscal stimulus combined with a multi-year deficit reduction plan.

Source: marketwatch.com, 15 October 2010

  a How has the business cycle influenced the US federal budget in the 2008–2009 recession?

  b With which news clip opinion do you agree and why?

  c Why might Laura Tyson favour a multi-year deficit reduction plan and would that address the concerns of Deepak Lal?

CHAPTER
30

Monetary Policy

Every month, six eminent economists join the Governor and Deputy Governors of the Bank of England to analyse and deliberate on the state of the UK economy and to decide whether to change the interest rate. A similar meeting takes place each month in Frankfurt at the ECB. How do the Bank of England and ECB make their interest rate decisions? How do they get the interest rate to change? And how do a central bank's decisions influence the economy?

What special measures can a central bank take in a financial crisis like the one that engulfed the global economy in 2008?

This chapter explains monetary policy. And *Reading Between the Lines* at the end of the chapter looks at the Bank of England's policy dilemma at the beginning of 2011.

After studying this chapter you will be able to:

◆ Describe the objectives and framework of UK monetary policy

◆ Explain how the Bank of England influences interest rates

◆ Explain the transmission channels through which the Bank of England influences inflation and real GDP

◆ Explain the Bank of England's extraordinary policy actions in 2008–2010

Monetary Policy Objectives and Framework

A nation's monetary policy objectives and the framework for setting and achieving them stem from the relationship between the central bank and government. Monetary policy making involves two activities:

1   Setting the policy objectives
2   Achieving the policy objectives

In a few countries, the central bank sets the objectives and decides how to achieve them. And in some countries, the government makes all the monetary policy decisions and tells the central bank what actions to take. But in most countries, including the UK, the government sets the monetary policy objectives and the central bank decides how to achieve them.

Here, we'll describe the objectives of UK monetary policy and the framework and assignment of responsibility for achieving those objectives.

Monetary Policy Objectives

The objectives of monetary policy are ultimately political and are determined by government. But they are pursued by the actions of the central bank. The Bank of England Act of 1998 sets out the objectives of UK monetary policy.

Bank of England Act 1998

The 1998 Bank of England Act sets out the Bank's monetary policy objectives as being:

(a)   to maintain price stability, and

(b)   subject to that, to support the economic policy of Her Majesty's Government, including its objectives for growth and employment.[1]

The Act also requires the Chancellor of the Exchequer to specify annually in writing:

(a)   what price stability is to be taken to consist of, and

(b)   what the economic policy of Her Majesty's Government is to be taken to be.[2]

One of the most important innovations in the 1998 Act is its establishment of the Monetary Policy Committee

---

[1] Bank of England Act (1998) section 11.
[2] Bank of England Act (1998) section 12.

or MPC, an independent group of six experts who with the governor and two deputy governors make the monetary policy decisions. (See Chapter 24, p. 564 for more details on the composition of the MPC.)

Remit for the Monetary Policy Committee

The Chancellor renews and if necessary modifies the remit for the monetary policy committee at roughly annual intervals. This remit is stated in two parts corresponding to the two monetary policy objectives.

Price Stability Objective

The first part of the remit for the monetary policy committee is an operational definition of 'price stability'. Since the beginning of 2004, this objective has been specified as a target inflation rate of 2 per cent a year as measured by the 12-month increase in the Consumer Prices Index (CPI).

Although the inflation target is renewed annually, the intention is that inflation be locked in at a low and stable rate over the long term. To achieve long-term price stability, deviations from the inflation target in either direction that exceed 1 percentage point require the Governor of the Bank to write an open letter to the Chancellor explaining why the target has been missed and what steps will be taken to bring the inflation rate back to its target. And for every three months that the inflation rate misses its target by more than 1 percentage point, a further explanation must be provided.

Government Economic Policy Objectives

The government's economic policy objectives as they relate to monetary policy are to achieve high and stable levels of economic growth and employment.

Price stability is the key goal and a major contributor to achieving the other goals of government economic policy. Price stability provides the best available environment for households and firms to make the saving and investment decisions that bring economic growth. So price stability encourages the maximum sustainable growth rate of potential GDP.

But in the short run, the Bank of England faces a trade-off between inflation and economic growth and employment. Taking an action that is designed to lower the inflation rate and achieve stable prices might mean slowing the economic growth rate and lowering employment.

In both the primary objective of price stability and the consequential goal of high and stable growth and employment, monetary policy in the UK is similar to that in the rest of the EU (see *Economics in Action* on p. 720).

Actual Inflation and the Inflation Target

Figure 30.1 compares the CPI measure and target of 2 per cent a year since the beginning of 2004. January 2004 was the date the Bank of England was charged by the Chancellor of the Exchequer to switch from a target of 2.5 per cent a year inflation measured by the Retail Prices Index less mortgage interest payments (RPIX) to a target of 2 per cent a year measured by the Consumer Prices Index (CPI). During this period, the average rate of increase of the CPI was just above the target at 2.4 per cent a year.

The Bank of England was successful in keeping inflation within the target range of 1 per cent to 3 per cent a year for three years from the beginning of 2004. But during those years, the inflation rate moved from the bottom to the top of the target range. Inflation burst through the upper limit of the target range in March 2007. This event triggered an open letter from the Governor to the Chancellor as required by the Chancellor's remit for the Monetary Policy Committee. The 3 per cent a year upper bound was breached again from May 2008 to February 2009 and throughout 2010.

Rationale for an Inflation Target

Two main benefits flow from adopting an inflation target. The first is that the purpose of the Bank of England's policy actions are more clearly understood by financial market traders. A clearer understanding leads to fewer surprises and mistakes on the part of savers and investors.

The second benefit is that the target provides an anchor for expectations about future inflation. Firmly held expectations of low inflation make the short-run output–inflation (or unemployment–inflation) trade-off as favourable as possible – see Chapter 28, pp. 674–676. Also, firmly held (and correct) inflation expectations help individuals and firms to make better economic decisions, which in turn help to achieve a more efficient allocation of resources and a more stable economic growth rate.

Figure 30.1 Inflation Target and Outcomes

The MPC's inflation target is a range of 1 per cent to 3 per cent a year. Inflation was inside the target from 2004 until March 2007. From May 2008 to February 2009 and throughout 2010, inflation has been above the 3 per cent a year upper limit.

Source of data: Office for National Statistics.

myeconlab Animation

Controversy About Inflation Targeting

Not everyone agrees that the inflation targeting brings benefits. Critics argue that by focusing on inflation, the Bank of England sometimes permits the unemployment rate or real GDP growth rate to suffer.

The fear of these critics is that if the inflation rate begins to edge upward towards and perhaps beyond a full percentage point above target, the Bank of England might reign in aggregate demand and push the economy into recession. At the same time, the Bank might end up permitting the pound to rise on the foreign exchange market and making exports suffer.

One response of supporters of inflation targeting is that by keeping inflation low and stable, monetary policy makes its maximum possible contribution towards achieving full employment and sustained economic growth.

Another response is 'look at the growth and unemployment record'. From May 1997 when the Bank of England was made operationally independent and given the goal of price stability, until 2008, the UK economy was free from recession and had falling unemployment. Only when the entire global economy was reeling from financial crisis did the UK real GDP fall and unemployment begin to rise.

Monetary Policy in the Eurozone

The Eurozone is the 17 member states of the EU that use the euro as their currency. The European Central Bank (ECB), which was established in 1998, is the Eurozone's central bank.

The conduct of monetary policy in the Eurozone is very similar to that in the UK. In fact, today there has been a convergence of views on how monetary policy should be conducted and the central banks of most industrial countries pursue monetary policy using similar objectives, tools and decision-making frameworks.

The objectives of Eurozone monetary policy are laid out in Article 105 of the Treaty Establishing the European Community (the Treaty of Rome), which assigns overriding importance to price stability as the ECB's monetary policy goal. The Treaty also requires the ECB to support broader Community economic policies, which means supporting policies aimed at achieving sustained growth and high employment.

The ECB's Governing Council has defined price stability as 'a year-on-year increase in the Harmonised Index of Consumer Prices (HICP) for the euro area of . . . below, but close to, 2 per cent a year over the medium term.'

Like the Bank of England and most other central banks, the ECB recognizes 'that ensuring price stability is the most important contribution that monetary policy can make to achieve a favourable economic environment and a high level of employment'. In other words, price stability is the goal of monetary policy *because it contributes to the achievement of other economic objectives.*

Review Quiz

1 What are the objectives of monetary policy?
2 What is the rationale for setting an inflation target?
3 What is the Bank of England's record in achieving the inflation target?

You can work these questions in Study Plan 30.1 and get instant feedback.

You now know the objective of monetary policy and the Bank of England's record in achieving it. You're now going to see how the Bank conducts monetary policy.

The Conduct of Monetary Policy

How does the Bank of England conduct its monetary policy? This question has two parts:

◆ What is the monetary policy instrument?

◆ How does the Bank make its monetary policy decisions?

The Monetary Policy Instrument

A **monetary policy instrument** is a variable that a central bank can directly control or closely target. The Bank of England must choose between two possible instruments: the monetary base or an interest rate.

The Bank's choice of monetary policy instrument is an interest rate. The Bank sets Bank Rate (also known as the Bank of England Base Rate), which is linked to the interest rate that banks earn on reserves and pay on borrowed reserves. The Bank then trades in the repo market to make the **repo rate** – the interest rate in the repo market – equal to Bank Rate. Banks can borrow and lend reserves in the repo market. A bank that is short of reserves and a bank that has excess reserves can use a repo to move the reserves from one bank to the other. The Bank of England also trades in the repo market.

Figure 30.2 shows the Bank Rate since January 2004. Bank Rate is normally changed in steps of a quarter of a percentage point.[3] The rate reached a peak of 5.75 per cent a year in 2007 and then fell in rapid succession in much greater steps than a quarter of a per cent to a low of 0.5 per cent a year in April 2009. The sharp fall in the Bank Rate was a coordinated attempt by the central banks of the developed world to deal with the credit crunch and the global financial crisis.

Between 2004 and 2007, Bank Rate was on a rising trend. The reason is that the inflation rate had moved up from below target to above target and by 2007 the inflation rate was pushing against the upper limit of a 3 per cent a year rate of increase of the CPI.

Since 2007, the Bank Rate has been lowered, first in short steps and then in rapid steps as the full scale of the economic crisis became apparent. During 2010 the inflation rate has been above the upper bound of 3 per cent a year but the rate of interest has remained at the historically low level of 0.5 per cent a year.

---

[3] When you read about interest changes in the press, you might encounter the term 25 basis points. A basis point is 100th of 1 per cent, so 25 basis points is 0.25 percentage points.

Figure 30.2   **Bank Rate**

The Bank of England sets Bank Rate and then takes actions to ensure that the banking system is supplied with its desired level of reserves. When the inflation rate is above 2 per cent a year and the Bank wants to avoid going above target, it raises Bank Rate. When the inflation rate is below 2 per cent a year and the Bank wants to avoid going below target, it lowers Bank Rate.

Source of data: Bank of England.

 Animation

Figure 30.3   **The Market for Bank Reserves**

The demand curve for reserves is *RD*. The quantity of reserves demanded decreases as the repo rate rises because the repo rate is the opportunity cost of holding reserves. The supply curve of reserves is *RS*. The Bank of England uses open market operations to make the supply of reserves equal the quantity of reserves demanded (£20 billion in this case) at a repo rate equal to Bank Rate (5 per cent a year in this case).

 Animation

Having decided the appropriate level for Bank Rate, how does the Bank of England move the repo rate to its target level? The answer is by using open market operations (see Chapter 24, pp. 565–567) to adjust the quantity of monetary base.

To see how an open market operation changes the repo rate, we need to examine the repo market. The higher the repo rate, the greater is the quantity of overnight loans supplied on repurchase agreements and the smaller is the quantity of overnight loans demanded in the repo market. The equilibrium repo rate balances the quantities demanded and supplied.

An equivalent way of looking at the forces that determine the repo rate is to consider the demand for and supply of bank reserves. Banks hold reserves to meet their desired reserve ratio so that they can always make payments. But reserves are costly to hold. The alternative to holding reserves is to lend them in the repo market and earn the repo rate. The higher the repo rate, the higher is the opportunity cost of holding reserves and the greater is the incentive for banks to economize on the quantity of reserves held.

So the quantity of reserves demanded by banks depends on the repo rate. The higher the repo rate, other things remaining the same, the smaller is the quantity of reserves demanded.

Figure 30.3 illustrates the demand for bank reserves. The *x*-axis measures the quantity of reserves that banks hold on deposit at the Bank of England, and the *y*-axis measures the repo rate. The demand for reserves is the curve labelled *RD*.

The Bank's open market operations determine the supply of reserves shown by the supply curve *RS*. To decrease reserves, the Bank conducts an open market sale. To increase reserves, the Bank conducts an open market purchase.

Equilibrium in the market for bank reserves determines the repo rate where the quantity of reserves demanded by the commercial banks equals the quantity of reserves supplied by the Bank of England. By using open market operations, the Bank adjusts the supply of reserves to keep the repo rate equal to Bank Rate.

Next, we see how the Bank makes its policy decision.

ECONOMICS IN ACTION

Bank of England Decision Making

The MPC meets monthly to set the Bank Rate and throughout the month the committee gets an extensive briefing by the economists of the Bank of England where all the available industry, national and international data on economic performance, financial markets and inflation expectations are reviewed, discussed and weighed in a careful deliberative process.

The MPC meeting lasts two days and on the second day members explain their views as to what they think are the important factors in the economy and what they think the interest rate decision should be.

The Governor of the Bank then puts to the meeting the decision that he thinks will command a majority. Any member in a minority is asked to record what the interest rate should be and justify that decision formally in the minutes.

The interest rate decision is announced at 12 noon on the second day of the deliberations. After announcing a Bank Rate decision, the Bank engages in public communication to explain the reasons for the MPC's decision. The Bank of England's communication exercise is extremely thorough and includes a detailed and carefully researched *Inflation Report* and press conference with the Governor.

The Governor's press conference is recorded and a video placed on the Bank's website. (Take a look!)

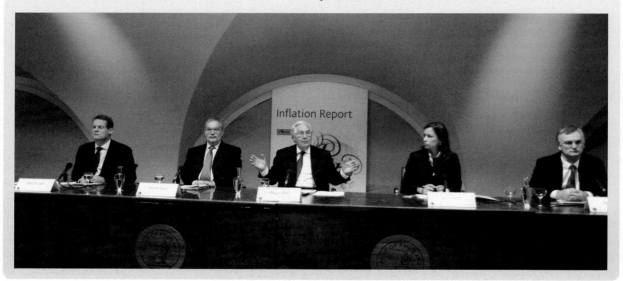

The Bank of England's Decision-making Strategy

The Bank of England (along with most other central banks) follows a process that uses an *inflation targeting rule*. To implement its inflation targeting rule, the Bank must gather and process a large amount of information about the economy, the way it responds to shocks and the way it responds to policy. The Bank must then process all this data and come to a judgement about the best level at which to set Bank Rate.

The process begins with an exercise that uses a model of the UK economy that you can think of as a sophisticated version of the *AS–AD* model (see Chapter 26). The Bank's economists provide the MPC with a variety of forecasts and scenarios running two years into the future. Crucially the inflation rate is forecasted with probabilities assigned to each scenario so that the MPC is aware of the uncertainty and risks that surround any particular forecast.

Review Quiz

1 What is the Bank of England's monetary policy instrument?
2 What is the main influence on the MPC's interest rate decision?
3 What happens when the Bank of England buys or sells securities in the open market?
4 How is the repo rate determined?

You can work these questions in Study Plan 30.2 and get instant feedback.

Monetary Policy Transmission

You've seen that the Bank of England's goal is to keep the price level stable (keep the CPI inflation rate at 2 per cent a year) and to achieve maximum growth and employment (keep the output gap close to zero). And you've seen how the Bank can use its power to set Bank Rate at its desired level. We're now going to trace the events that follow a change in Bank Rate and see how those events lead to the ultimate policy goal. We'll begin with a quick overview of the transmission process and then look at each step a bit more closely.

Quick Overview

When the Bank of England lowers Bank Rate, other short-term interest rates and the exchange rate also fall. The quantity of money and the supply of loanable funds increase. The long-term real interest rate falls. The lower real interest rate increases consumption expenditure and investment. And the lower exchange rate makes UK exports cheaper and imports more costly. So net exports increase. Easier bank loans reinforce the effect of lower interest rates on aggregate expenditure. Aggregate demand increases, which increases real GDP and the price level relative to what they would have been. Real GDP growth and inflation speed up.

When the Bank raises Bank Rate, the sequence of events that we've just reviewed plays out but the effects are in the opposite directions.

Figure 30.4 provides a schematic summary of these ripple effects for both a cut (on the left) and a rise (on the right) in Bank Rate.

The ripple effects summarized in Figure 30.4 stretch out over a period of between one and two years but the time lags involved and the strength of each of the effects are never quite the same and are unpredictable.

The interest rate and exchange rate effects are immediate. They occur on the same day that the MPC announces its decision. Sometimes they even anticipate the decision. The effects on money and bank loans follow in a few weeks and run for a few months. Real long-term interest rates change quickly and often in anticipation of the short-term rate changes. Spending plans change and real GDP growth changes after about one year. And the inflation rate changes between one year and two years after the change in Bank Rate. But these time lags are especially hard to predict and can be longer or shorter.

We're going to look at each stage in the transmission process, starting with the interest rate effects.

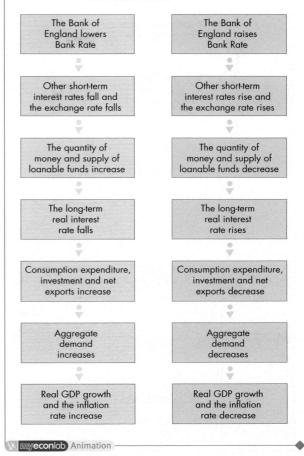

Figure 30.4 The Ripple Effects of a Change in Bank Rate

myeconlab Animation

Interest Rate Changes

The first effect of a monetary policy decision by the MPC is a change in Bank Rate. Other interest rates then change. Short-term interest rate effects occur quickly and predictably. Long-term interest rate effects occur more slowly and less predictably. Figure 30.5 shows the fluctuations in three interest rates: the repo rate, a short-term bill rate and a long-term bond rate.

Repo Rate

As soon as the MPC announces a new setting for Bank Rate, the Bank of England's bond dealers undertake the necessary open market operations to adjust reserves. There is little doubt about where the interest rate changes shown in Figure 30.5 are generated. They are driven by the Bank of England's monetary policy.

Figure 30.5 Three Interest Rates

The short-term interest rates – repo rate and the short-term bill rate – move closely together. The long-term bond rate fluctuates less than the short-term rates but long-term and short-term interest rates move in the same general direction.

Source of data: Bank of England.

 myeconlab Animation

The Short-term Bill Rate

The *short-term bill rate* is the interest rate paid by the UK government on 3-month Treasury bills. It is similar to the interest rate paid by UK businesses on short-term loans. Notice how closely the short-term bill rate follows the repo rate. The two rates are almost identical.

A powerful substitution effect keeps the 3-month Treasury bill rate and the repo rate close. Commercial banks have a choice about how to hold their short-term liquid assets. And an overnight loan to another bank is a close substitute for short-term securities such as 3-month Treasury bills. If the interest rate on the Treasury bill is higher than the repo rate, the quantity of overnight loans supplied decreases and the demand for Treasury bills increases. The price of a Treasury bill rises and the interest rate falls.

Similarly, if the interest rate on a Treasury bill is lower than the repo rate, the quantity of overnight loans supplied increases and the demand for Treasury bills decreases. The price of a Treasury bill falls, and the interest rate on Treasury bills rises.

When the interest rate on Treasury bills is close to the repo rate, there is no incentive for a bank to switch between making an overnight loan and buying Treasury bills. Both the Treasury bill market and the repo market are in equilibrium.

The Long-term Bond Rate

The *long-term bond rate* is the interest rate paid on bonds issued by large corporations. It is this interest rate that businesses pay on the loans that finance their purchase of new capital and that influences their investment decisions.

Two features of the long-term bond rate stand out: it does not track closely with the short-term rates, and it fluctuates less than the short-term rates so that in some years the long-term rate exceeds the short-term rate and in other years the gap is reversed.

A dominant effect on the long-term interest rate is the long-term expected inflation rate. In 1997, just before the Bank of England began inflation targeting, the expected inflation rate was high, so the long-term bond rate was also high, and much higher than the short-term rate. In an environment of uncertain long-term inflation, long-term loans are riskier than short-term loans. To provide the incentive that brings forth a supply of long-term loans, lenders must be compensated for the additional risk. Without compensation for the additional risk, only short-term loans would be supplied.

The long-term interest rate fluctuates less than the short-term rates because it is influenced by expectations about future short-term interest rates as well as current short-term interest rates. The alternative to borrowing or lending long term is to borrow or lend using a sequence of short-term securities. If the long-term interest rate exceeds the expected average of future short-term interest rates, people will lend long term and borrow short term. The long-term interest rate will fall. If the long-term interest rate is below the expected average of future short-term interest rates, people will borrow long term and lend short term. The long-term interest rate will rise.

These market forces keep the long-term interest rate close to the expected average of future short-term interest rates. And the expected average future short-term interest rate fluctuates less than the current short-term interest rate.

Exchange Rate Fluctuations

The exchange rate responds to changes in the interest rate in the UK relative to the interest rates in other countries – *the UK interest rate differential*. We explain this influence in Chapter 25 (see pp. 589–590).

When the Bank of England raises Bank Rate, the UK interest rate differential rises and, other things remaining the same, the pound appreciates. And when the Bank lowers Bank Rate, the UK interest rate differential falls and, other things remaining the same, the pound depreciates.

Many factors other than the UK interest rate differential influence the exchange rate, so when the Bank changes Bank Rate, the exchange rate does not usually change in exactly the way it would with other things remaining the same. So while monetary policy influences the exchange rate, many other factors also make the exchange rate change.

Money and Bank Loans

The quantity of money and bank loans change when the Bank of England changes Bank Rate. A rise in Bank Rate decreases the quantity of money and bank loans and a fall in Bank Rate increases the quantity of money and bank loans. These changes occur for two reasons: the quantity of money supplied by the banking system changes and the quantity of money demanded by households and firms changes.

You've seen that the Bank changes the quantity of bank reserves to keep the repo rate equal to Bank Rate. A change in the quantity of bank reserves changes the monetary base, which in turn changes the quantity of deposits and loans that the banking system can create. A rise in Bank Rate decreases reserves and decreases the quantity of deposits and bank loans created; and a fall in Bank Rate increases reserves and increases the quantity of deposits and bank loans created.

The quantity of money created by the banking system must be held by households and firms. The change in the interest rate changes the quantity of money demanded. A fall in the interest rate increases the quantity of money demanded and a rise in the interest rate decreases the quantity of money demanded.

A change in the quantity of money and the supply of bank loans directly affects consumption and investment plans. With more money and easier access to loans, consumers and firms spend more. With less money and loans harder to get, consumers and firms spend less.

The Long-term Real Interest Rate

Demand and supply in the market for loanable funds determine the long-term real interest rate, which equals the long-term nominal interest rate minus the expected inflation rate. The long-term real interest rate influences expenditure decisions.

In the long run, demand and supply in the loanable funds market depend only on real forces – on saving and investment decisions. But in the short run, when the price level is not fully flexible, the supply of loanable funds is influenced by the supply of bank loans. Changes in Bank Rate change the supply of bank loans, which changes the supply of loanable funds and changes the interest rate in the loanable funds market.

A fall in Bank Rate that increases the supply of bank loans increases the supply of loanable funds and lowers the equilibrium real interest rate. A rise in Bank Rate that decreases the supply of bank loans decreases the supply of loanable funds and raises the equilibrium real interest rate.

These changes in the real interest rate, along with the other factors we've just described, change expenditure plans.

Expenditure Plans

The ripple effects that follow a change in Bank Rate change three components of aggregate expenditure:

◆ Consumption expenditure
◆ Investment
◆ Net exports

Consumption Expenditure

Other things remaining the same, the lower the real interest rate, the greater is the amount of consumption expenditure and the smaller is the amount of saving.

Investment

Other things remaining the same, the lower the real interest rate, the greater is the amount of investment.

Net Exports

Other things remaining the same, the lower the interest rate, the lower is the exchange rate and the greater are exports and the smaller are imports.

So eventually, a cut in Bank Rate increases aggregate expenditure and a rise in Bank Rate curtails aggregate expenditure. These changes in aggregate expenditure plans change aggregate demand, real GDP and the price level.

Change in Aggregate Demand, Real GDP and the Price Level

The final link in the transmission chain is a change in aggregate demand and a resulting change in real GDP and the price level. By changing real GDP and the price level relative to what they would have been without a change in Bank Rate, the Bank influences its ultimate goals: the inflation rate and full employment.

The Bank Fights Recession

If inflation is low and real GDP is below potential GDP, the Bank takes actions that are designed to restore full employment. Figure 30.6 shows the effects of the Bank of England's actions, starting in the market for bank reserves and ending in the market for real GDP.

Market for Bank Reserves

In Figure 30.6(a), which shows the market for bank reserves, the MPC lowers Bank Rate from 5 per cent to

4 per cent a year. To keep the repo rate close to Bank Rate, the Bank of England buys securities and increases the supply of bank reserves from RS_0 to RS_1.

Money Market

With increased reserves, the banks create deposits by making loans and the supply of money increases. The short-term interest rate falls and the quantity of money demanded increases. In Figure 30.6(b), the increase in the supply of money shifts the supply of money curve from MS_0 to MS_1. The interest rate falls from 5 per cent to 4 per cent a year and the quantity of money increases from £1,400 billion to £1,500 billion. The interest rate in the money market and the repo rate are kept close to each other by the powerful substitution effect described on p. 724.

Loanable Funds Market

Banks create money by making loans. In the long run, an increase in the supply of bank loans is matched by a rise in the price level and the quantity of real loans is

---

Figure 30.6 The Bank of England Fights Recession

(a) The market for bank reserves

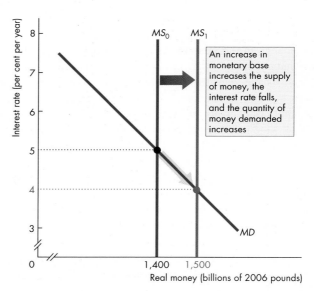

(b) Money market

In part (a), the MPC lowers Bank Rate target from 5 per cent to 4 per cent a year. To make the repo rate equal to Bank Rate, the Bank of England buys securities in an open market operation and increases the supply of reserves from RS_0 to RS_1.

In part (b), the increase in monetary base increases the supply of money from MS_0 to MS_1. The short-term interest rate falls and the quantity of money demanded increases. The short-term interest rate and Bank Rate change by similar amounts.

myeconlab Animation

unchanged. But in the short run, with a sticky price level, an increase in the supply of bank loans increases the supply of (real) loanable funds.

In Figure 30.6(c), the supply of loanable funds increases and the supply of loanable funds curve shifts rightward from SLF_0 to SLF_1. With the demand for loanable funds at DLF, the real interest rate falls from 6 per cent to 5.5 per cent a year. (Here, we assume a zero inflation rate so that the real interest rate equals the nominal interest rate.) The long-term interest rate changes by a smaller amount than the change in the short-term interest rate as described on p. 724.

The Market for Real GDP

Figure 30.6(d) shows aggregate demand and aggregate supply. Potential GDP is £1,300 billion, where LAS is located. The short-run aggregate supply curve is SAS, and initially, the aggregate demand curve is AD_0. Real GDP is £1,200 billion, which is less than potential GDP, so there is a recessionary gap. The Bank is reacting to this recessionary gap.

The increase in the supply of loans and the decrease in the real interest rate increase aggregate planned expenditure. (Not shown in the figure, a fall in the interest rate lowers the exchange rate, which increases net exports and also aggregate planned expenditure.) The increase in aggregate expenditure, ΔE, increases aggregate demand and also shifts the aggregate demand curve rightward to $AD_0 + \Delta E$. A multiplier process begins. The increase in expenditure increases income, which induces an increase in consumption expenditure. Aggregate demand increases further, and the aggregate demand curve eventually shifts rightward to AD_1.

The new equilibrium is at full employment. Real GDP is equal to potential GDP. The price level rises to 105 and then becomes stable at that level so after a one-time adjustment, there is price stability.

In this example, we have given the Bank a perfect hit at achieving full employment and keeping the price level stable. It is unlikely that the Bank would be able to achieve the precision of this example. A Bank Rate cut that is too little or too late leaves the economy in a recession and too big a cut sends inflation above target.

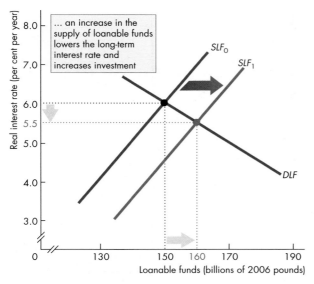

(c) The market for loanable funds

In part (c), an increase in the supply of bank loans increases the supply of loanable funds and shifts the supply of loanable funds curve from SLF_0 to SLF_1. The real interest rate falls and investment increases.

(d) Real GDP and the price level

In part (d), the increase in investment increases aggregate planned expenditure. The aggregate demand curve shifts to $AD_0 + \Delta E$ and eventually shifts rightward to AD_1. Real GDP increases to potential GDP and the price level rises.

The Bank Fights Inflation

If the inflation rate is too high and real GDP is above potential GDP, the Bank of England takes actions that are designed to lower the inflation rate and restore price stability. Figure 30.7 shows the effects of the Bank's actions starting in the market for reserves and ending in the market for real GDP.

Market for Bank Reserves

In Figure 30.7(a), which shows the market for bank reserves, the MPC raises Bank Rate from 5 per cent to 6 per cent a year. To keep the repo rate close to Bank Rate, the Bank sells securities and decreases the supply of reserves of the banking system from RS_0 to RS_1.

Money Market

With decreased reserves, the banks shrink deposits by decreasing loans and the supply of money decreases. The short-term interest rate rises and the quantity of money demanded decreases. In Figure 30.7(b), the supply of money decreases from MS_0 to MS_1, the interest

rate rises from 5 per cent to 6 per cent a year and the quantity of money decreases from £1,400 billion to £1,300 billion.

Loanable Funds Market

With a decrease in reserves, banks must decrease the supply of loans. The supply of (real) loanable funds decreases, and the supply of loanable funds curve shifts leftward in Figure 30.7(c) from SLF_0 to SLF_1. With the demand for loanable funds at DLF, the real interest rate rises from 6 per cent to 6.5 per cent a year. (Again, we're assuming a zero inflation rate so that the real interest rate equals the nominal interest rate.)

The Market for Real GDP

Figure 30.7(d) shows aggregate demand and aggregate supply in the market for real GDP. Potential GDP and LAS are £1,300 billion. The short-run aggregate supply curve is SAS and initially, the aggregate demand is AD_0. Now, real GDP is £1,400 billion, which is greater than potential GDP, so there is an inflationary gap. The Bank is reacting to this inflationary gap.

Figure 30.7 The Bank of England Fights Inflation

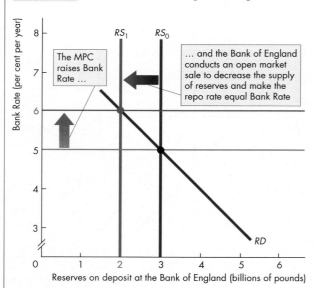

(a) The market for bank reserves

In part (a), the MPC raises Bank Rate from 5 per cent to 6 per cent. To make the repo rate equal to Bank Rate the Bank of England sells securities in an open market operation to decrease the supply of reserves from RS_0 to RS_1.

(b) Money market

In part (b), the supply of money decreases from MS_0 to MS_1, the short-term interest rate rises, and the quantity of money demanded decreases. The short-term interest rate and Bank Rate change by similar amounts.

The decrease in the supply of bank loans, and the increase in the real interest rate decrease aggregate planned expenditure. (Not shown in the figures, a rise in the interest rate raises the exchange rate, which decreases net exports and also aggregate planned expenditure.)

The decrease in aggregate expenditure, ΔE, decreases aggregate demand and the aggregate demand curve shifts to $AD_0 - \Delta E$. A multiplier process begins. The decrease in expenditure decreases income, which induces a decrease in consumption expenditure. Aggregate demand decreases further, and the aggregate demand curve eventually shifts leftward to AD_1.

The economy returns to full employment. Real GDP is equal to potential GDP. The price level falls to 105 and then becomes stable at that level so after a one-time adjustment, there is price stability.

Again, in this example, we have given the Bank a perfect hit at achieving full employment and keeping the price level stable. If the Bank raised Bank Rate by too little or too late, the economy would have remained with an inflationary gap and the inflation rate would have moved above the target. And if the Bank raised Bank Rate by too much it would push the economy from inflation to recession.

Loose Links and Long and Variable Lags

The ripple effects of monetary policy that we've just analysed with the precision of an economic model are, in reality, very hard to predict and anticipate.

To achieve its inflation target and its additional mandate to support the government's economic policy of keeping real GDP growing at the maximum sustainable rate and maintaining full employment, the Bank needs a combination of good judgement and good luck.

Too large an interest rate cut can bring inflation, as it did during the 1970s. And too large an interest rate rise in an inflationary economy can create unemployment, as it did in 1981 and 1991.

Loose links in the chain that runs from Bank Rate to the ultimate policy goals make unwanted policy outcomes inevitable. And time lags that are both long and variable add to the Bank of England's challenges.

(c) The market for loanable funds

In part (c), a decrease in the supply of bank loans decreases the supply of loanable funds and shifts the supply of loanable funds curve from SLF_0 to SLF_1. The real interest rate rises and investment decreases.

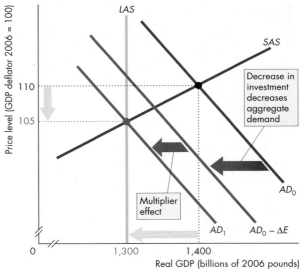

(d) Real GDP and the price level

In part (d), the decrease in investment decreases aggregate planned expenditure. The aggregate demand curve shifts to $AD_0 - \Delta E$ and eventually shifts leftward to AD_1. Real GDP decreases to potential GDP and the price level falls.

ECONOMICS IN ACTION

A Look at the Long and Variable Lag

You've studied the theory of monetary policy. Does it really work in the way we've described? It does, and Figure 1 provides some evidence to support this conclusion.

In Figure 1 the blue line shows Bank Rate that the Bank targets minus the long-term bond rate. You saw earlier (in Figure 30.5) that the short-term interest rates fluctuate more than the long-term rate. We can view the gap between the long-term bond rate and Bank Rate as a measure of how hard the Bank is trying to steer a change in course. When Bank Rate falls relative to the long-term bond rate, the Bank is cutting Bank Rate in an attempt to boost aggregate demand and stimulate real GDP growth. And when Bank Rate rises relative to the long-term bond rate, the Bank is raising Bank Rate in an attempt to decrease aggregate demand, restrain inflation and slow real GDP growth.

The red line in Figure 1 shows the real GDP growth rate one and a half years later.

You can see that when the MPC raises Bank Rate, the real GDP growth rate slows one and a half years later. And when the MPC lowers Bank Rate, the real GDP growth rate speeds up one and a half years later.

Not shown in this figure, with other things remaining the same, the inflation rate increases and decreases in line with the fluctuations in the real GDP growth rate. But the effects

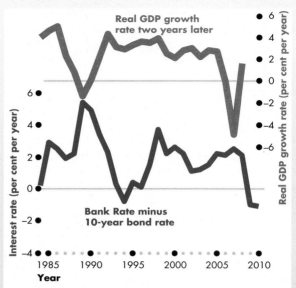

Figure 1   Interest Rates and Real GDP Growth

Sources of data: Bank of England and Office for National Statistics.

of an interest rate change on the inflation rate take even longer. Also, other influences on the inflation rate break the link between inflation and real GDP fluctuations.

Loose Link from Bank Rate to Spending

The real long-term interest rate that influences spending plans is linked only loosely to Bank Rate. Also, the response of the real long-term interest rate to a change in the nominal rate depends on how inflation expectations change. And the response of expenditure plans to changes in the real interest rate depends on many factors that make the response hard to predict.

Time Lags in the Adjustment Process

The Bank is especially handicapped by the fact that the monetary policy transmission process is long and drawn out. Also, the economy does not always respond in exactly the same way to a policy change. Further, many factors other than policy are constantly changing and bringing new situations to which policy must respond.

Review Quiz

1   Describe the channels by which monetary policy ripples through the economy and explain how each channel operates.
2   Do interest rates fluctuate in response to the Bank of England's actions?
3   How do the Bank of England's actions change the exchange rate?
4   How do the Bank of England's actions influence real GDP and how long does it take for real GDP to respond to the Bank's policy changes?
5   How do the Bank's actions influence the inflation rate and how long does it take for the inflation rate to respond to the Bank's policy changes?

You can work these questions in Study Plan 30.3 and get instant feedback.

Extraordinary Monetary Stimulus

During the financial crisis and recession of 2008–2009, the Bank of England lowered the Bank Rate to 0.5 per cent a year. Bank Rate cannot fall much further, so what can the Bank do to stimulate the economy? The Bank of England has answered this question with some extraordinary policy actions. To understand those actions, we need to dig a bit into the anatomy of the financial crisis to which the Bank is responding. That's what we'll now do. We'll look at the key elements in the financial crisis and then look at the Bank's response.

The Key Elements of the Crisis

We can describe the crisis by identifying the events that changed the values of the assets and liabilities of banks and other financial institutions. Figure 30.8 shows the stylized balance sheet of a bank: deposits plus own capital equals reserves plus loans and securities (see Chapter 24, p. 562). Deposits and own capital are the banks' sources of funds (other borrowing is ignored here).

Deposits are the funds loaned to the bank by households and firms. A bank's *own capital* is the funds provided by its shareholders and includes the bank's undistributed profits (and losses). A bank's reserves are currency and its deposit at the Bank of England. A bank's loans and securities are the loans made by the bank and government bonds, private bonds, asset-backed bonds, and other securities that the bank holds.

Three main events can put a bank under stress:

1   A widespread fall in asset prices

2   A significant currency drain

3   A run on the bank

Figure 30.8 summarizes the problems that each event presents to a bank. A widespread fall in asset prices means that the bank suffers a capital loss. It must write down the value of its assets and the value of the bank's own capital decreases by the same amount as the fall in the value of its securities. If the fall in asset prices is large enough, the value of a bank's own capital might fall to zero, in which case the bank is insolvent. It fails.

A significant currency drain means that depositors withdraw funds and the bank loses reserves. This event puts the bank in a liquidity crisis. It is short of cash reserves.

A run on the bank occurs when depositors lose confidence in the bank and massive withdrawals of deposits occur. The bank loses reserves and must call in loans and sell off securities at unfavourable prices. Its own capital shrinks.

The red arrows in Figure 30.8 summarize the effects of these events and the problems they brought in the 2007–2008 financial crisis. A widespread fall in asset prices was triggered by the bursting of a house-price bubble in the US that saw house prices switch from rapidly rising to falling. With falling house prices, subprime mortgage defaults occurred and the prices of mortgage-backed securities and derivatives whose values are based on these securities began to fall. Many of these mortgage backed securities were being held by banks and financial institutions around the world.

People with money market mutual fund deposits began to withdraw them, which created a fear of a massive withdrawal of these funds analagous to a bank run like the one experienced by Northern Rock.

With low reserves and even lower own capital, banks, in turn, called in loans. A lot of these loans were to other banks in the money market. The loanable funds market and money market dried up.

Because the loanable funds market is global, the same problems quickly spread to other economies, and foreign exchange markets became highly volatile.

Hard-to-get loans, market volatility and increased uncertainty transmitted the financial and monetary crisis to real expenditure decisions.

Figure 30.8   The Ingredients of a Financial and Banking Crisis

Event	Deposits	+	Own capital	=	Reserves	+	Loans and securities	Problem
Widespread fall in asset prices			▼				▼	Solvency
Currency drain	▼				▼			Liquidity
Run on bank	▼		▼		▼		▼	Liquidity and solvency

myeconlab Animation

The Policy Actions

Policy actions in response to the financial crisis on both sides of the Atlantic dribbled out over a period of more than a year. Here, we'll focus on the UK policy actions, which may be placed under four broad headings:

◆ Interest rate cuts
◆ Bank bailouts
◆ Quantitative easing
◆ Macro-prudential regulation

Interest Rate Cuts

The Bank of England's first and natural response to the 2007 financial crisis was to lower Bank Rate. But it acted slowly at first. In August 2007 when the initial shocks were felt, Bank Rate was at a relatively high 5.75 per cent. The Bank was more concerned about the risk that inflation would burst through the 3 per cent upper bound of its target than it was about the risk of recession so the Bank Rate cuts were timid: down to 5.5 per cent in December, 5.25 per cent in February 2008, and 5 per cent in April 2008.

It wasn't until the crisis deepened with massive bank failures in the US and tottering UK banks that interest rates fell steeply. But starting in October 2008, the fall was steep, down to 0.5 per cent by March 2009.

Bank Bailouts

The first signs that the financial crisis might be serious and need an extraordinary policy response was the run on Northern Rock. At first, the Bank of England hesitated to act. But in September 2007, it extended a deposit insurance guarantee to Northern Rock's depositors and provided emergency loans to the bank.

The serious risk of bank failure and massive bailouts didn't come until a year later, in October 2008, when the biggest banks, RBS, Lloyds TSB and HBOS were on the brink of collapse.

The policy response to this situation blurs the distinction between monetary policy and fiscal policy for it was the UK government, not the Bank of England, that made the bold moves. The government forced a merger between Lloyds and HBOS and injected £37 billion into RBS and the enlarged Lloyds TSB. These banks were now partly owned by the taxpayer – 60 per cent in the case of RBS and 40 per cent in the case of Lloyds.

The other two large commercial banks, Barclays and HSBC, raised additional capital without government help.

The bailed out RBS and Lloyds turned out to need a further injection of public funds in November 2009 when they received a further £31 billion. This injection of funds took the taxpayer stake in RBS to 84 per cent, making it virtually a nationalized firm.

The goal of these massive and unusual injections of public funds into large commercial banks was designed to ensure that the banks didn't fail. Failure would have had a ripple effect (a tsunami effect is perhaps a better metaphor) through the entire national and global financial system and would have brought an enormous crash in the quantity of money (bank deposits) in the UK economy.

Quantitative Easing

The Bank of England launched a programme of quantitative easing in March 2009. **Quantitative easing (QE)** occurs when the Bank of England creates an increase in the monetary base by buying government bonds and high grade corporate bonds in the open market. The sellers of these bonds might be commercial banks but they also are pension funds and insurance companies. The Bank set aside £200 billion for QE purchases.

You can see that QE is a type of *open market operation*. In normal times, the Bank of England performs open market operations by buying repurchase agreements, *repos*, and UK Treasury Bills. These open market operations (see p. 721) supply the quantity of reserves that enable the Bank of England to keep short-term interest rates close to Bank Rate.

With the large interest rate cuts after October 2008, open market operations were used on a massive scale to keep the banks well supplied with reserves. This action lowered bank holdings of securities and increased their reserves.

The Bank of England's QE open market operations take place in the market for loanable funds. With short-term interest rates as low as they can go, the goal of QE is to increase the monetary base and lower long-term interest rates.

The idea is that QE would make the banks flush with excess reserves, which they would lend to firms and households. The quantity of money would increase and asset prices would rise. With easier access to credit and greater wealth from higher asset prices, consumption expenditure and investment would increase aggregate demand and real GDP would grow more quickly.

Did QE succeed in achieving its goals? The final verdict is not yet in but a first look at the effects of QE is not encouraging.

QE did not lower long-term interest rates (although it might have prevented them from rising) and it did not bring a large increase in bank lending and the quantity of money.

Interest rates on long-term bonds had fallen from around 5 per cent in mid-2008 to around 3.25 per cent in March 2009 when QE began. From March 2009 to end 2010, interest rates on long-term bonds had no visible trend or change.

The commercial banks reserves swelled but rather than increasing loans to firms and households, the banks have sat on their excess reserves. Consumers have been using any spare cash to pay off debt (repay loans to the banks).

The overall outcome is that the monetary base has risen but the quantity of money has not. Figure 30.9 shows the growth of the M4 definition of money and the money multiplier. Both fell dramatically during 2009 and remained low during 2010.

Supporters of QE say that without it the recession would be even worse and if there is a fault it is that the Bank of England has been too timid and should have employed QE on a larger scale.

Macro-prudential Regulation

Macro-prudential regulation is regulation of the monetary financial institutions and other financial institutions and financial markets to lower the risk of crisis and failure of these institutions and markets.

We briefly described how monetary financial institutions are regulated in Chapter 24 (see p. 562). The key components of this regulation are the assignment of responsibility for oversight and monitoring of financial institutions and markets and rules governing the liquidity and scale of own funds for financial institutions.

UK macro-prudential regulation is evolving and will change over the next few years as the Bank of England plays an enhanced role along with the Treasury and the Financial Services Authority.

A debate will be ongoing about what it means for a bank to be 'too big to fail' and whether large banks should be broken up into smaller banks.

A further ongoing debate will consider the appropriate scale and cyclical characteristics of commercial banks' own funds and the appropriate composition of a bank's assets and liabilities.

Figure 30.9 QE, M4 Growth and the Money Multiplier

Before the Bank of England embarked on its QE policy, the money multiplier was falling and the growth rate of M4 was slowing. After QE began, the money multiplier crashed as the commercial banks sat on their excess reserves and M4 growth slowed even further as people paid off existing bank loans.

Source of data: Bank of England.

myeconlab Animation

While all the extraordinary measures evolve and respond to the changing situation, the Bank of England will need to keep a firm grip on its main policy objective: its inflation target.

To complete your study of monetary policy, take a look at *Reading Between the Lines* on pp. 734–735 and see how the Bank of England faced a monetary policy dilemma in 2011.

Reading Between the Lines

Monetary Policy Dilemma

The Financial Times, 1 February 2011

Conflicting Data Paint Picture of Two-speed Economy

FT

Norma Cohen

Conflicting data have presented a picture of a two-speed economy that is likely to sharpen the dilemma the Bank of England's policy setters face at their monthly meeting next week.

Output from the UK manufacturing sector surged to a record high in January according to a closely watched survey, with readings for new orders showing a particularly sharp rise. Offsetting that positive finding were new data showing that lending to businesses and households was very weak in December, coupled with news that the National House price survey showed a 0.1 per cent decline in January from a month earlier. . . .

The Markit/CIPS survey for the purchasing managers' index rose to 62 in January from 58.7 in December, the highest reading since the survey was created in 1992.

Underscoring the growth message – given the historical link between expansion and rising prices – the survey also flashed a danger signal on inflation. Input prices – the cost of goods the manufacturers need to assemble their products – registered their highest reading on record. Markit, which compiles the index said average purchase prices had risen at the steepest pace in the survey's history. . . .

In any case, offsetting the strong message from the manufacturing survey, were new data from the Bank showing that lending to private non-financial companies contracted again in December, that approvals for loans to buy homes fell to a 21 month low and that a key measure of money supply is contracting. . . .

Over all, the data suggest very sluggish lending to the household sector. The rate at which total net lending to households is growing, looked at over the previous six month or 12 month periods, is the slowest since the Bank began keeping records in 1988. On these measures net lending is expanding at rates of 0.4 and 0.7 per cent.

The Essence of the Story

- ◆ A survey of purchasing managers in the manufacturing sector indicates a fast recovering UK economy.

- ◆ Bank lending to businesses is weak and new mortgage loans and house prices have fallen.

- ◆ Other data suggest a build up of inflationary pressure with input prices rising rapidly.

- ◆ With conflicting information about different parts of the economy, the recovery remains fragile.

Economic Analysis

◆ The UK economy is sending conflicting signals that make it difficult to read the true strength of the recovery.

◆ Figure 1 shows the strong expansion of manufacturing output throughout 2010. This signal suggests a strong recovery.

◆ Inflationary pressure has been building up with input prices of the production industries rising at double-digit rates and CPI inflation is above the upper bound of the inflation target (see Figure 30.1, p. 719).

◆ Inflation expectations are also increasing. Figure 2 shows that inflation is expected to hit 4 per cent a year in 2011 and to be close to 3 per cent per year in five years.

◆ Both the manufacturing output and inflation data suggest a strong recovery that requires a a rise in Bank Rate and a reversal of quantitative easing (QE) to bring the inflation rate back into the target range.

◆ Other indicators point in the opposite direction. Figure 3 shows the rate of growth of bank lending to businesses and households, which fell throughout 2010.

◆ The dilemma for the Bank of England is whether it should raise Bank Rate to choke off rising inflation expectations or keep Bank Rate low and anticipate that a weakening recovery will remove the inflationary pressures.

◆ If the recovery really is fragile, raising Bank Rate might stop the recovery and send the economy into a double dip recession.

◆ If the recovery really is strong, not raising Bank Rate risks a permanent rise in the expected inflation rate, which will be costly to lower in the future.

◆ Making the wrong decision will increase the volatility of real GDP growth and inflation and delay the recovery. The outcome could be higher inflation or lower real GDP growth.

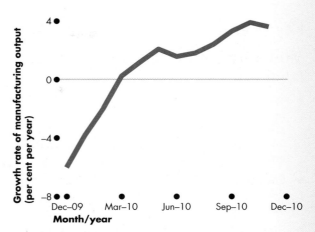

Figure 1   Growth rate of manufacturing output

Figure 2   Inflation expectations

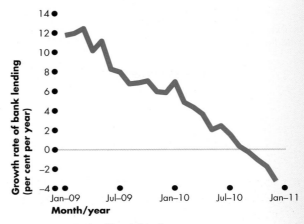

Figure 3   Growth of bank lending

SUMMARY

Key Points

Monetary Policy Objectives and Framework (pp. 718–720)

◆ The Bank of England Act 1998 requires the Bank to use monetary policy to achieve stable prices and to support the government's economic policies of high and stable economic growth and employment.

◆ Each year, the Chancellor of the Exchequer specifies the Bank's remit in terms of a numerical target for the inflation rate.

◆ Since 2004, the Bank has been required to achieve an inflation rate measured by the CPI of 2 per cent a year.

Working Problems 1 to 5 will give you a better understanding of monetary policy objectives and framework.

The Conduct of Monetary Policy

(pp. 720–722)

◆ The Bank's monetary policy instrument is Bank Rate.

◆ The Bank's Monetary Policy Committee (MPC) sets Bank Rate and announces any change at roughly monthly intervals.

◆ The Bank pushes the repo rate close to Bank Rate by using open market operations.

◆ By buying or selling securities in the open market, the Bank is able to change bank reserves and change the repo rate.

Working Problems 6 to 10 will give you a better understanding of the conduct of monetary policy.

Monetary Policy Transmission

(pp. 723–730)

◆ A change in Bank Rate changes other interest rates, the exchange rate, the quantity of money and loans, aggregate demand and eventually real GDP and the price level.

◆ A change in Bank Rate changes real GDP a year to 18 months later and changes the inflation rate with an even longer time lag.

Working Problems 11 to 20 will give you a better understanding of monetary policy transmission.

Extraordinary Monetary Stimulus

(pp. 731–733)

◆ A financial crisis has three ingredients: a widespread fall in asset prices, a currency drain and a run on banks.

◆ The Bank of England and Treasury responded to the financial crisis with four groups of measures: steep interest rate cuts, bank bailouts, quantitative easing and macro-prudential regulation.

Working Problems 21 to 26 will give you a better understanding of extraordinary monetary stimulus.

Key Terms

Macro-prudential regulation, 733
Monetary policy instrument, 720
Quantitative easing (QE), 732
Repo rate, 720

STUDY PLAN PROBLEMS AND APPLICATIONS

ⓧ myeconlab You can work Problems 1 to 26 in MyEconLab Chapter 30 Study Plan and get instant feedback.

Monetary Policy Objectives and Framework (Study Plan 30.1)

1 'Unemployment is a more serious economic problem than inflation and it should be the focus of the Bank of England's monetary policy.' Evaluate this statement and explain why the Bank's primary policy goal is price stability and not full employment.

2 'Because the CPI inflation rate includes the prices of food and fuel, which are volatile and influenced by global demand and supply, the Bank of England should strip these items from the index that it targets.' Explain why the Bank of England is required to target the CPI inflation rate.

3 'Monetary policy is too important to be left to the MPC. The government should be responsible for it.' How is responsibility for monetary policy allocated among the MPC, Parliament, and the government?

4 **Mervyn King Gives Warning over UK Public Deficit**

Mervyn King says the government must cut the public deficit.

Source: *BBC*, 20 January 2010

a Does the governor of the Bank of England have either authority or responsibility for the UK government budget deficit?

b How might a government budget deficit complicate the Bank's monetary policy? [Hint: Think about the effects of a deficit on interest rates.]

c How might the Bank's monetary policy complicate Parliament's deficit cutting? [Hint: Think about the effects of monetary policy on interest rates.]

5 **Inflation: Surging Fuel Costs Push CPI to 3.4 per cent**

At 3.4 per cent, consumer price inflation (CPI) is now way above the Bank of England's government-set target of 2 per cent, the highest since January and one of the steepest rates in Europe.

Source: *The Guardian*, 20 April 2010

a What does this news clip imply about the MPC's interest rate decisions?

b How can the 3.4 per cent inflation rate be reconciled with the Bank of England's obligations under the 1998 Bank of England Act?

The Conduct of Monetary Policy (Study Plan 30.2)

6 What are the two possible monetary policy instruments, which one does the Bank of England use, and how has its value behaved since 2004?

7 How does the Bank of England hit its repo rate target? Illustrate your answer with an appropriate graph.

8 What does the Bank of England do to determine whether Bank Rate should be raised, lowered or left unchanged?

Use the following news clip to work Problems 9 and 10.

Bank of England's Trade-off

When the Bank of England's MPC meets on Thursday, it will be shaping up for its first three-way vote, amid an intensifying debate on the trade-off between apparent signs of inflation and indications that the economy is sinking into stagnation.

Source: *The Financial Times*, 6 October 2010

9 Explain the dilemma faced by the Bank of England in October 2010.

10 a Why might the MPC have decided to cut Bank Rate in the months following the October 2010 meeting?

b Why might the MPC have decided to raise Bank Rate in the months following the October 2010 meeting?

Monetary Policy Transmission (Study Plan 30.3)

11 What are the roles of Bank Rate and the long-term interest rate in the monetary policy transmission process?

12 a Is it the long-term nominal interest rate or the long-term real interest rate that influences spending decisions? Explain why.

b How does the market determine the long-term nominal interest rate and why doesn't it move as much as the short-term rates?

Use the following news clip to work Problems 13 and 14.

The Pound's Sharp Fall

Masahiro Sakane, chairman of Komatsu, the Japanese maker of construction and mining equipment, says the company's plant in north-east England will benefit from the pound's sharp fall against the euro.

Source: *The Financial Times*, 5 March 2010

13 How does a lower sterling exchange rate influence monetary policy transmission?

14 Would a fall in the exchange rate mainly influence unemployment or inflation?

Use the following news clip to work Problems 15 to 17.

Economists Growth Forecasts

Economic recovery and job creation in the UK over the next few years will depend on growth in business investment.

Source: *The Financial Times*, 29 December 2010

15 Explain the effects of the Bank of England's low interest rates on business investment. Draw a graph to illustrate your explanation.

16 Explain the effects of business investment on aggregate demand. Would you expect it to have a multiplier effect? Why or why not?

17 What actions might the Bank of England take to stimulate business investment further?

Use the following news clip to work Problems 18 to 20.

Shrinking Economy Shock

The UK economy shrank in the final quarter of 2010, a shock contraction that casts doubt on the strength of growth in the industrialised world and the wisdom of early fiscal tightening.

Source: *The Financial Times*, 25 January 2011

18 If real GDP continues to shrink, what would most likely happen to the output gap and unemployment in 2011?

19 **a** What actions that the Bank of England had taken in 2009 and 2010 would you expect to influence UK real GDP growth in 2011? Explain how those policy actions would transmit to real GDP.

    b Draw a graph of aggregate demand and aggregate supply to illustrate your answer to part (a).

20 What further actions might the Bank of England take in 2011 to influence the real GDP growth rate in 2011? [Remember the time lags in the operation of monetary policy.]

Extraordinary Monetary Stimulus

(Study Plan 30.4)

Use the following news clip to work Problems 21 to 23.

UK Pound Weakens on QE Bets

The pound fell to the weakest level in almost seven months against the euro as mortgage approvals dropped to the least since March 2009, heightening speculation that the Bank of England may soon be pressed into quantitative easing.

Source: fxnonstop.com, 25 October 2010

21 What is the connection between actions that the Bank of England might take and the foreign exchange value of the pound?

22 What is the significance of falling mortgage approvals? How does that suggest further QE?

23 Why might the Bank contemplate further QE? What are the arguments for and against further quantitative easing at the beginning of 2011?

24 Suppose that the UK government had not bailed out RBS and Lloyds and instead had allowed them to fail.

    a How would the failure have changed the quantity of money and interest rates?

    b How would real GDP and the inflation rate have been different?

25 Suppose that the Bank of England had raised Bank Rate in 2010 as the inflation rate moved above the 3 per cent upper bound.

    a How would the repo rate have differed from its actual path?

    b How would real GDP and the inflation rate have been different?

26 **Prospects Rise for US Federal Reserve Easing Policy**

William Dudley, president of the New York Fed, raised the prospect of the Fed becoming more explicit about its inflation goal to 'help anchor inflation expectations at the desired rate.'

Source: ft.com, 1 October 2010

    a Why might inflation targeting be especially important in a financial crisis?

    b How does 'anchor[ing] inflation expectations at the desired rate' help to make QE work better?

ADDITIONAL PROBLEMS AND APPLICATIONS

 You can work these problems in MyEconLab if assigned by your lecturer.

Monetary Policy Objectives and Framework

Use the following information to work Problems 27 to 29.

The statutory role of the Bank of England is to maintain price stability, and subject to that, to support the economic policy of Her Majesty's Government, including its objectives for growth and employment.

27 Explain the harmony among these goals in the long run.

28 Explain the conflict among these goals in the short run.

29 Based on the performance of UK inflation and unemployment in 2010, which of the Bank's goals appears to have taken priority?

30 The deep 2008–2009 recession and the overshoot of inflation above the upper bound of the target suggests that the inflation target should be raised. Do you agree? Why or why not?

31 Suppose the Chancellor of the Exchequer decided to strip the Bank of England of its operational independence to meet a government specified inflation target and gave Cabinet the task of deciding interest rate changes. How would you expect the policy choices to change? Which arrangement would most likely provide price stability?

32 The European Central Bank (ECB) targets the Eurozone inflation rate to make it remain below but close to 2 per cent a year. To pursue this goal, the ECB sets the official ECB interest rate but pays close attention to the growth rate of the quantity of money.

  a Compare and contrast the policy objectives of the ECB and the Bank of England.

  b Compare and contrast the policy strategies of the ECB and the Bank of England.

Use the following news clip to work problems 33 and 34.

Government borrowing rose from £17.4 billion a year ago to £23.3 billion in November the highest total for a single month since records began in 1993, and much higher than the £17 billion that economists had predicted.

Source: *The Financial Times*, 21 December 2010

33 How would the government deficit change in 2011 and 2012 if the Bank of England raised interest rates?

34 How would the government deficit change in 2011 and 2012 if the Bank of England did not raise the rate of interest and the value of sterling depreciated sharply?

The Conduct of Monetary Policy

35 Looking at Bank Rate since 2000, identify periods during which, with the benefit of hindsight, the rate might have been kept too low. Identify periods during which it might have been too high.

36 Explain the dilemma that rising inflation and weakening growth poses for the Bank of England.

37 Why might the Bank of England decide to lower interest rates when inflation is rising and growth is weakening?

38 Why might the Bank of England decide to raise interest rates when inflation is rising and growth is weakening?

Monetary Policy Transmission

Use the following information to work problems 39 to 41.

From 2008 to 2010 the rate of interest on UK 10-year maturity bonds fell from 4.6 per cent a year to 3.6 per cent a year. During the same period, the Bank Rate fell from 4.7 per cent a year to 0.5 per cent a year.

39 What role does the long-term real interest rate play in the monetary policy transmission process?

40 How does the Bank Rate influence the long-term real interest rate?

41 What do you think happened to inflation expectations between 2008 and 2010 and why?

Use the following information to do problems 42 and 43.

Financial markets predict a 95 per cent or more certainty that rates will rise by a quarter of a percentage point in June, October and January over 2011 and 2012, leaping from 0.5 per cent to 1.25 per cent.

Source: *The Financial Times*, 24 January 2011

42 How do expectations of the future of the interest rate influence the exchange rate?

43 How does monetary policy influence the exchange rate?

44 **Dollar Tumbles to 15-year Low Against Yen**

The dollar tumbled to a fresh 15-year low on persistent fears over the US economic outlook.

Source: yahoo.com, 7 October 2010

  a How do 'fears over the US economic outlook' influence the exchange rate between the US dollar and the UK pound?

b How does US monetary policy influence the exchange rate between the US dollar and the UK pound?

c How does US monetary policy influence the UK economy?

Use the following news clip to work Problems 45 and 46.

Top Economist says America Could Plunge into Recession

Robert Shiller, Professor of Economics at Yale University, predicted that there was a very real possibility that the US would be plunged into a Japan-style slump, with house prices declining for years.

Source: timesonline.co.uk, 31 December 2007

45 What challenge do falling house prices pose for the conduct of monetary policy? How could monetary policy prevent house prices from falling?

46 Describe the time lags in the response of output and inflation to monetary policy actions designed to respond to falling house prices.

Use the following news clip to work Problems 47 and 48.

Greenspan Says Economy Strong

The US central bank chairman, Alan Greenspan, said inflation was low, consumer spending had held up well through the downturn, housing-market strength was likely to continue, and businesses appeared to have unloaded their glut of inventories, setting the stage for a rebound in production.

Source: cnn.com, July 16, 2002

47 What monetary policy actions would you expect to have created the situation described by Alan Greenspan?

48 What monetary policy actions would you expect a central bank to take in the situation described by Alan Greenspan?

Extraordinary Monetary Stimulus

49 Between August 2007 when the global financial crisis started and April 2008, Bank Rate was cut from 5.75 per cent to 5 per cent. Only when the shockwaves intensified in October 2008 did the Bank of England respond with extraordinary rate cuts, dropping Bank Rate to 0.5 per cent by March 2009.

a Why was the Bank of England so timid in its initial interest rate cuts in the first year of the global financial crisis?

b How would you expect the massive rate cuts between October 2008 and March 2009 to influence real GDP and the inflation rate in 2009, 2010 and 2011? Describe the transmission mechanisms and the time lags.

50 Explain how bailing out troubled banks and taking them into public ownership avoids the risk of a serious collapse of aggregate demand. Does the government borrowing to buy the troubled banks have any effect on aggregate demand?

51 Explain the key differences between QE and normal open market operations.

52 What are the three ingredients of a financial and banking crisis and how do the four extraordinary monetary policy actions address each of them?

53 The UK economy suffered a shock contraction in real GDP in the fourth quarter of 2010. Shadow chancellor Ed Balls said the figures were a matter of 'great concern' and due largely to the speed and scope of the coalition government's deficit reduction programme.

Source: BBC, 24 January 2011

a If the Bank of England had expected the economy to weaken in the fourth quarter, what policy actions might it have taken differently from what it did take?

b Describe the time lags in the response of output to the policy actions you have prescribed.

Economics in the News

54 After you have studied *Reading Between the Lines* on pp. 734–735 answer the following questions.

a Why does the Bank of England face a dilemma in setting monetary policy?

b What would be the short-term and long-term consequences of delaying a rise in the interest rate if inflation turned out to remain above the upper bound of the target throughout 2011?

c What would be the short-term and long-term consequences of raising interest rates immediately if the UK economy was weak during 2011?

d What is the role of expectations in determining what the Bank of England monetary policy should be in the current period?

55 The governor of the Bank of England Mervyn King said that inflation could reach 5 per cent a year within a few months and that this was of more concern than the surprise drop in GDP in the fourth quarter of 2010.

Source: *The Daily Telegraph*, 15 February 2011

a What was the Bank of England's monetary policy throughout 2010?

b Given the Governor's comments, what would you expect the Bank of England's monetary policy to be in 2011?

Glossary

Above full-employment equilibrium A macroeconomic equilibrium in which real GDP exceeds potential GDP. (p. 624)

Absolute advantage A person who is more productive than others. (p. 40)

Adverse selection The tendency for people to enter into agreements in which they can use their private information to their own advantage and to the disadvantage of the less-informed party. (p. 444)

Aggregate demand The relationship between the quantity of real GDP demanded and the price level. (p. 618)

Aggregate planned expenditure The expenditure that households, firms, governments and foreigners plan to undertake in given circumstances. It is the sum of planned consumption expenditure, planned investment, planned government expenditure on goods and services and planned exports minus planned imports. (p. 638)

Aggregate production function The relationship between real GDP and the quantity of labour when all other influences on production remain the same. (p. 513)

Allocative efficiency A situation in which goods and services are produced at the lowest possible cost and in quantities that provide the greatest benefit. We cannot produce more of any good without giving up some of another good that we *value more highly*. (p. 35)

Antitrust law A law that regulates oligopolies and prevents them from becoming monopolies or behaving like monopolies. (p. 332)

Asymmetric information A market in which buyers and sellers have private information. (p. 444)

Automatic fiscal policy A fiscal policy action that is triggered by the state of the economy with no action by the government. (p. 704)

Autonomous expenditure The sum of those components of aggregate planned expenditure that do not vary with real GDP. Autonomous expenditure equals the sum of investment, government expenditure, exports and the autonomous parts of consumption expenditure and imports. (p. 643)

Autonomous tax multiplier The magnification effect of a change in autonomous taxes on equilibrium expenditure and real GDP. (p. 660)

Average cost pricing rule A rule that sets price to cover cost including normal profit, which means setting the price equal to average total cost. (p. 290)

Average fixed cost Total fixed cost per unit of output. (p. 228)

Average product The average product of a factor of production. It equals total product divided by the quantity of the resource employed. (p. 223)

Average total cost Total cost per unit of output. (p. 228)

Average variable cost Total variable cost per unit of output. (p. 228)

Balanced budget A government budget in which revenues and expenditures are equal. (p. 693)

Balanced budget multiplier The multiplier that arises from a fiscal policy action that changes *both* government expenditure and taxes by the *same* amount so that the government's budget balance remains unchanged. (p. 661)

Balance of payments accounts A country's record of international trading and its borrowing and lending. (p. 600)

Bank of England The central bank of the UK. (p. 564)

Bank Rate The Bank of England's official interest rate. The interest rate that the Bank of England charges on secured overnight loans to the commercial banks. (p. 565)

Barrier to entry A legal or natural constraint that protects a firm from potential competitors. (p. 276)

Below full-employment equilibrium A macroeconomic equilibrium in which potential GDP exceeds real GDP. (p. 625)

Benefit The benefit of something is the gain or pleasure that it brings and is determined by preferences. (p. 10)

Big trade-off A trade-off between equity and efficiency. (pp. 117, 429)

Bilateral monopoly A situation in which a union (a monopoly seller) faces a monopsony buyer. (p. 397)

Black market An illegal trading arrangement in which the price exceeds the legally imposed price ceiling. (p. 128)

Bond A promise to make specified payments on specified dates. (p. 535)

Bond market The market in which bonds issued by firms and governments are traded. (p. 535)

Budget An annual statement of the government's projected outlays and receipts during the next year together with the laws and regulations that support those outlays and receipts. (p. 692)

Budget deficit A government's budget balance that is negative – outlays exceed receipts. (p. 693)

Budget line The limits to a household's consumption choices. (p. 176)

Budget surplus A government's budget balance that is positive – receipts exceed outlays. (p. 693)

Business cycle The periodic but irregular up-and-down movement of total production and other measures of economic activity. (p. 467)

Capital The tools, equipment, buildings, and other constructions that businesses now use to produce goods and services. (p. 6)

Capital and financial account A record of all UK investments abroad and foreigners' investments in the UK. (p. 600)

Capital accumulation The growth of capital resources. (p. 38)

Capture theory A theory of regulation that states that the regulation is in the self-interest of producers. (p. 289)

Cartel A group of firms that has entered into a collusive agreement to limit output and increase prices and profits. (p. 319)

Ceteris paribus Other things being equal – all other relevant things remaining the same. (p. 24)

Chain volume measure A measure that uses the prices of two adjacent years to calculate the real GDP growth rate. (p. 476)

Change in demand A change in buyers' plans that occurs when some influence on those plans other than the price of the good changes. It is illustrated by a shift of the demand curve. (p. 58)

Change in reserve assets The net increase or decrease in a country's holdings of foreign currency reserves that comes about from the official financing of the difference between the current account and capital and financial account balances. (p. 600)

Change in supply A change in sellers' plans that occurs when some influence on those plans other than the price of the good changes. It is illustrated by a shift of the supply curve. (p. 63)

Change in the quantity demanded A change in buyers' plans that occurs

when the price of a good changes but all other influences on buyers' plans remain unchanged. It is illustrated by a movement along the demand curve. (p. 61)

Change in the quantity supplied A change in sellers' plans that occurs when the price of a good changes but all other influences on sellers' plans remain unchanged. It is illustrated by a movement along the supply curve. (p. 65)

Classical A macroeconomist who believes that the economy is self-regulating and that it is always at full employment. (p. 628)

Classical growth theory A view that the growth of real GDP per person is temporary and that when it rises above the subsistence level, a population explosion brings it back to the subsistence level. (p. 521)

Coase theorem The proposition that if property rights exist, only a small number of parties are involved and transactions costs are low, then private transactions are efficient. (p. 371)

Collusive agreement An agreement between two (or more) producers to restrict output, raise the price, and increase profits. (p. 322)

Command system A method of organizing production that uses a managerial hierarchy. (pp. 106, 203)

Common resource A resource that is rival and non-excludable. (p. 348)

Comparative advantage A person or country has a comparative advantage in an activity if that person or country can perform the activity at a lower opportunity cost than anyone else or any other country. (p. 40)

Competitive market A market that has many buyers and many sellers, so no single buyer or seller can influence the price. (p. 56)

Complement A good that is used in conjunction with another good. (p. 59)

Compound interest The interest on an initial investment plus the interest on the interest that the investment has previously earned. (p. 406)

Constant returns to scale Features of a firm's technology that lead to constant long-run average cost as output increases. When constant returns to scale are present, the *LRAC* curve is horizontal. (p. 234)

Consumer Prices Index (CPI) An index that measures the average of the prices paid by consumers for a fixed 'basket' of consumer goods and services. (p. 493)

Consumer surplus The value of a good minus the price paid for it, summed over the quantity bought. (p. 109)

Consumption expenditure The total payment for consumer goods and services. (p. 461)

Consumption function The relationship between consumption expenditure and disposable income, other things remaining the same. (p. 638)

Contestable market A market in which firms can enter and leave so easily that firms in the market face competition from potential entrants. (p. 330)

Cooperative equilibrium The outcome of a game in which the players make and share the monopoly profit. (p. 329)

Cost-push inflation An inflation that results from an initial increase in costs. (p. 670)

Crawling peg An exchange rate that follows a path determined by a decision of the government or the central bank and is achieved in a similar way to a fixed exchange rate by central bank intervention in the foreign exchange market. (p. 597)

Creditor nation A country that during its entire history has invested more in the rest of the world than other countries have invested in it. (p. 602)

Credit risk The risk that a borrower, also known as a creditor, might not repay a loan. (p. 447)

Cross elasticity of demand The responsiveness of the demand for a good to a change in the price of a substitute or complement, other things remaining the same. It is calculated as the percentage change in the quantity demanded of the good divided by the percentage change in the price of the substitute or complement. (p. 91)

Crowding-out effect The tendency for the government budget deficit to raise the real interest rate and *decrease* investment. (p. 546)

Currency The notes and coins held by households and firms. (p. 559)

Currency drain ratio The ratio of currency to deposits. (p. 568)

Current account A record of the receipts from the sales of goods and services to foreigners, the payments for goods and services bought from foreigners, income and other transfers received from and paid to foreigners. (p. 600)

Cycle A tendency for a variable to alternate between upward and downward movements. (p. 475)

Cyclical surplus or deficit The actual budget balance minus the structural surplus or deficit. (p. 705)

Cyclical unemployment The fluctuations in unemployment over the business cycle. (p. 489)

Deadweight loss A measure of inefficiency. It is equal to the decrease in consumer surplus and producer surplus that results from an inefficient level of production. (p. 113)

Debtor nation A country that during its entire history has borrowed more from the rest of the world than it has lent to it. (p. 602)

Default risk The risk that a borrower, also known as a creditor, might not repay a loan. (p. 447)

Deflation A process in which the price level falls – a negative inflation. (p. 492)

Demand The relationship between the quantity of a good that consumers plan to buy and the price of the good when all other influences on buyers' plans remain the same. It is described by a demand schedule and illustrated by a demand curve. (p. 57)

Demand curve A curve that shows the relationship between the quantity demanded of a good and its price when

all other influences on consumers' planned purchases remain the same. (p. 58)

Demand for loanable funds The relationship between the quantity of loanable funds demanded and the real interest rate when all other influences on borrowing plans remain the same. (p. 540)

Demand for money The relationship between the quantity of real money demanded and the interest rate – the opportunity cost of holding money – when all other influences on the amount of money that people plan to hold remain the same. (p. 571)

Demand-pull inflation An inflation that results from an initial increase in aggregate demand. (p. 668)

Depreciation The decrease in the value of a firm's capital that results from wear and tear and obsolescence. (p. 462)

Deregulation The process of removing a previously imposed regulation. (p. 289)

Derived demand The demand for a factor of production, which is derived from the demand for the goods and services produced by the factor. (p. 391)

Desired reserve ratio The ratio of the reserves to deposits that banks consider prudent to hold. (p. 568)

Diminishing marginal rate of substitution The general tendency for the marginal rate of substitution to diminish as the consumer moves along an indifference curve, increasing consumption of the good on the *x*-axis and decreasing consumption of the good on the *y*-axis. (p. 180)

Diminishing marginal returns The tendency for the marginal product of an additional unit of a factor of production to be less than the marginal product of the previous unit of the factor. (p. 225)

Direct relationship A relationship between two variables that move in the same direction. (p. 18)

Discounting The conversion of a future amount of money to its present value. (p. 406)

Discouraged workers People who are available and willing to work but have stopped actively looking for jobs because he or she believes that no jobs are available. (p. 487)

Discretionary fiscal policy A fiscal policy action that is initiated by the government (Chancellor of the Exchequer in the UK). (p. 704)

Diseconomies of scale Features of a firm's technology that lead to rising long-run average cost as output increases. (p. 234)

Disposable income Aggregate income minus taxes plus transfer payments. (pp. 414, 620, 638)

Dominant-strategy equilibrium An equilibrium in which the best strategy of each player is to cheat *regardless of the strategy of the other player*. (p. 321)

Dumping The sale by a foreign firm of exports at a lower price than the cost of production. (p. 162)

Duopoly A market structure in which two producers of a good or service compete. (p. 318)

Economic activity rate The percentage of the working-age population who are economically active. (p. 487)

Economically active The people who have a job or are willing and able to take a job. (p. 485)

Economically inactive The people who do not want a job. (p. 485)

Economic depreciation The change in the market value of capital over a given period. (p. 199)

Economic efficiency A situation that occurs when the firm produces a given output at the least cost. (p. 201)

Economic growth The expansion of production possibilities that results from capital accumulation and technological change. (pp. 38, 508)

Economic growth rate The annual percentage change in real GDP. (p. 508)

Economic model A description of some aspect of the economic world that includes only those features of the world that are needed for the purpose at hand. (p. 12)

Economic profit A firm's total revenue minus total cost. (p. 198)

Economic rent Any surplus – consumer surplus, producer surplus or economic profit. It is also the income received by the owner of a factor of production over and above the amount required to induce that owner to offer the factor for use. (p. 284)

Economics The social science that studies the *choices* that individuals, businesses, governments, and entire societies make and how they cope with *scarcity* and the *incentives* that influence and reconcile those choices. (p. 4)

Economies of scale Features of a firm's technology that lead to a falling long-run average cost as output increases. (pp. 212, 234)

Economies of scope Decreases in average total cost that occur when a firm uses specialized resources to produce a range of goods and services. (p. 213)

Efficiency A situation in which the available resources are used to produce goods and services at the lowest possible cost and in quantities that give the greatest value or benefit. (p. 7)

Efficient scale The quantity at which average total cost is a minimum – the quantity at the bottom of the U-shaped *ATC* curve. (p. 304)

Elastic demand Demand with a price elasticity greater than 1; other things remaining the same, the percentage change in the quantity demanded exceeds the percentage change in price. (p. 87)

Elasticity of supply The responsiveness of the quantity supplied of a good to a change in its price, other things remaining the same. (p. 94)

Employment rate The percentage of people of working age who have jobs. (p. 486)

Entrepreneurship The human resource that organizes the other three factors of production: labour, land, and capital. (p. 6)

Equilibrium expenditure The level of aggregate expenditure that occurs when aggregate planned expenditure equals real GDP. (p. 644)

Equilibrium price The price at which the quantity demanded equals the quantity supplied. (p. 66)

Equilibrium quantity The quantity bought and sold at the equilibrium price. (p. 66)

European Central Bank (ECB) The central bank of the Eurozone – the members of the EU that use the euro as their currency. (p. 564)

Excess capacity A firm has excess capacity if it produces below its efficient scale. (p. 304)

Excess reserves A bank's actual reserves minus its desired reserves. (p. 568)

Exchange rate The price at which one currency exchanges for another currency in the foreign exchange market. (p. 586)

Excludable A good is excludable if it is possible to prevent someone from enjoying its benefits. (p. 348)

Expansion A business cycle phase between a trough and a peak – the phase in which real GDP increases. (p. 467)

Expected utility The utility value of what a person expects to own at a given point in time. (p. 439)

Expected wealth The money value of what a person expects to own at a given point in time. (p. 438)

Export subsidy A payment made by a government to a domestic producer of an exported good. (p. 161)

Exports The goods and services that we sell to people in other countries. (pp. 152, 462)

External diseconomies Factors outside the control of a firm that raise the firm's costs as the industry produces a larger output. (p. 263)

External economies Factors beyond the control of a firm that lower the

firm's costs as the industry produces a larger output. (p. 263)

Externality A cost or a benefit that arises from production and falls on someone other than the producer or a cost or a benefit that arises from consumption and falls on someone other than the consumer. (p. 348)

Factors of production The productive resources that businesses use to produce goods and services. (p. 5)

Final good An item that is bought by its final user during the specified time period. (p. 460)

Financial capital The funds that firms use to buy physical capital. (p. 534)

Financial institution A firm that operates on both sides of the market for financial capital. It is a borrower in one market and a lender in another. (p. 536)

Firm An economic unit that hires factors of production and organizes those factors to produce and sell goods and services. (pp. 43, 198)

Fiscal imbalance The present value of the government's commitments to pay benefits minus the present value of its tax revenues. (p. 702)

Fiscal policy The government's attempt to influence the economy by setting and changing taxes, making transfer payments, and purchasing goods and services. (pp. 620, 692)

Fiscal stimulus The use of fiscal policy to increase production and employment. (p. 704)

Five-firm concentration ratio A measure of market power that is calculated as the percentage of total revenue (the value of sales) in an industry accounted for by the five firms with the largest value of sales. (p. 208)

Fixed exchange rate A foreign exchange rate that is pegged at a value determined by the central bank and is achieved by central bank intervention in the foreign exchange market. (p. 596)

Flexible exchange rate A foreign exchange rate that is determined by market forces in the absence of central bank intervention. (p. 596)

Foreign currency The money of other countries regardless of whether that money is in the form of coins, notes or bank deposits. (p. 586)

Foreign exchange market The market in which the currency of one country is exchanged for the currency of another. (p. 586)

Free-rider problem The absence of an incentive for people to pay for what they consume. (p. 351)

Frictional unemployment The unemployment that arises from normal labour turnover – from people entering and leaving the workforce and from the ongoing creation and destruction of jobs. (p. 489)

Full employment A situation in which the unemployment rate equals the natural unemployment rate. At full employment, there is no cyclical unemployment – all unemployment is frictional and structural. (p. 489)

Full-employment equilibrium A macroeconomic equilibrium in which real GDP equals potential GDP. (p. 625)

Game theory A tool that economists use to analyse strategic behaviour – behaviour that takes into account the expected behaviour of others and the recognition of mutual interdependence. (p. 320)

GDP deflator One measure of the price level, which is an index of the prices of all the goods and services in GDP. It is calculated as nominal GDP divided by real GDP, multiplied by 100. (p. 496)

Generational accounting An accounting system that measures the lifetime tax burden and benefits of each generation. (p. 702)

Generational imbalance The division of the fiscal imbalance between the current and future generations, assuming that the current generation will enjoy the existing levels of taxes and benefits. (p. 703)

Gini coefficient The area between the line of equality and the Lorenz curve as a percentage of the entire area beneath the line of equality. (p. 417)

Goods and services The objects that people value and produce to satisfy their wants. (p. 5)

Government debt The total amount of borrowing by the government. It equals the sum of past budget deficits minus the sum of past budget surpluses minus plus payments to buy assets minus receipts from the sale of assets. (p. 695)

Government expenditure Goods and services bought by the government. (p. 462)

Government expenditure multiplier The magnification effect of a change in government expenditure on goods and services on equilibrium expenditure and real GDP. (pp. 660, 707)

Government failure A situation in which government actions lead to inefficiency – to either underprovision or overprovision. (p. 346)

Gross domestic product (GDP) The market value of all the final goods and services produced within a country during a given time period – usually a year. (p. 460)

Gross investment The total amount spent on purchases of new capital and on replacing depreciated capital. (pp. 462, 534)

Hotelling Principle The proposition that the price of a non-renewable natural resource is expected to rise at a rate equal to the interest rate. (p. 402)

Human capital The knowledge and skill that people obtain from education, on-the-job training, and work experience. (p. 5)

Hyperinflation An inflation rate that exceeds 50 per cent a month. (p. 492)

Implicit rental rate The firm's opportunity cost of using its own capital. (p. 198)

Import quota A restriction that limits the maximum quantity of a good that may be imported in a given period. (p. 160)

Imports The goods and services that we buy from people in other countries. (pp. 152, 462)

Incentive A reward that encourages an action or a penalty that discourages one. (p. 4)

Incentive system A method of organizing production that uses a market-like mechanism inside the firm. (p. 203)

Income effect The effect of a change in income on consumption, other things remaining the same. (p. 185)

Income elasticity of demand The responsiveness of demand to a change in income, other things remaining the same. It is calculated as the percentage change in the quantity demanded divided by the percentage change in income. (p. 92)

Indifference curve A line that shows combinations of goods among which a consumer is indifferent. (p. 179)

Individual transferable quota (ITQ) A production limit that is assigned to an individual who is free to transfer the quota to someone else. (p. 378)

Induced expenditure The sum of the components of aggregate planned expenditure that vary with real GDP. Induced expenditure equals consumption expenditure minus imports. (p. 643)

Inelastic demand A demand with a price elasticity between 0 and 1; the percentage change in the quantity demanded is less than the percentage change in price. (p. 87)

Infant-industry argument The argument that a new industry must be protected to enable it to grow into a mature industry that can compete in world markets. (p. 162)

Inferior good A good for which demand decreases as income increases. (p. 60)

Inflation A process in which the price level is rising and money is losing value. (p. 492)

Inflationary gap The amount by which real GDP exceeds potential GDP. (p. 624)

Inflation rate The annual percentage change in the price level. (p. 495)

Interest The income that capital earns. (p. 6)

Interest rate parity A situation in which the rates of return on assets in different currencies are equal. (p. 594)

Intermediate good An item that is produced by one firm, bought by another firm and used as a component of a final good or service. (p. 460)

Inverse relationship A relationship between variables that move in opposite directions. (p. 19)

Investment The purchase of new plant, equipment, and buildings and additions to inventories. (p. 461)

Isocost line A line that shows the combinations of labour and capital that can be bought for a given total cost and given factor prices. (p. 245)

Isocost map A series of isocost lines, each one of which represents a different total cost but for given prices of labour and capital. (p. 245)

Isoquant A curve that shows the different combinations of labour and capital required to produce a given quantity of output. (p. 243)

Isoquant map A series of isoquants, one for each different output level. (p. 243)

Job A contract for the trade of labour services. (p. 390)

Keynesian A macroeconomist who believes that left alone, the economy would rarely operate at full employment and that to achieve and maintain full employment, active help from fiscal policy and monetary policy is required. (p. 628)

Keynesian cycle theory The theory that fluctuations in investment driven by fluctuations in business confidence – summarized in the phrase 'animal spirits' – are the main source of

fluctuations in aggregate demand. (p. 678)

Labour The work time and work effort that people devote to producing goods and services. (p. 5)

Labour productivity The quantity of real GDP produced per hour of labour. (p. 517)

Laffer curve The relationship between the tax rate and the amount of tax revenue collected. (p. 701)

Land The gifts of nature that we use to produce goods and services. (p. 5)

Law of demand Other things remaining the same, the higher the price of a good, the smaller is the quantity demanded; the lower the price of a good, the larger is the quantity demanded. (p. 57)

Law of diminishing marginal rate of substitution The marginal rate of substitution of labour for capital diminishes as the amount of labour increases and the amount of capital decreases. (p. 244)

Law of diminishing returns As a firm uses more of a variable input, with a given quantity of other inputs (fixed inputs), the marginal product of the variable input eventually diminishes. (p. 225)

Law of supply Other things remaining the same, the higher the price of a good, the greater is the quantity supplied; the lower the price of a good, the smaller is the quantity supplied. (p. 62)

Least-cost technique The combination of labour and capital that minimizes the total cost of producing a given level of output. (p. 246)

Legal monopoly A market structure in which there is one firm and entry is restricted by the granting of a monopoly franchise, government licence, patent or copyright. (p. 276)

Lemon problem The problem that in a market in which it is not possible to distinguish reliable products from lemons, there are too many lemons and too few reliable products traded. (p. 444)

Lender of last resort The Bank of England is the lender of last resort in the UK – if all the banks are short of reserves they can borrow from the Bank of England. (p. 567)

Limit pricing The practice of setting the price at the highest level that inflicts a loss on an entrant. (p. 331)

Linear relationship A relationship between two variables that is illustrated by a straight line. (p. 18)

Loanable funds market The aggregate of all the individual markets in which households, firms, governments, banks and other financial institutions borrow and lend. (p. 538)

Long run A period of time in which the quantities of all factors of production can be varied. (p. 222)

Long-run aggregate supply The relationship between the quantity of real GDP supplied and the price level when the money wage rate changes in step with the price level to maintain full employment; real GDP equals potential GDP. (p. 614)

Long-run average cost curve The relationship between the lowest attainable average total cost and output when both capital and labour are varied. (p. 233)

Long-run market supply curve A curve that shows how the quantity supplied in a market varies as the market price varies after all the possible adjustments have been made, including changes in each firm's plant and the number of firms in the market. (p. 263)

Long-run macroeconomic equilibrium A situation that occurs when real GDP equals potential GDP – the economy is on its long-run aggregate supply curve. (p. 622)

Long-run Phillips curve A curve that shows the relationship between inflation and unemployment when the actual inflation rate equals the expected inflation rate. (p. 675)

Lorenz curve A curve that graphs the cumulative percentage of income or wealth against the cumulative percentage of households or population. (p. 415)

M4 A measure of money that consists of currency held by the public plus bank deposits and building society deposits. (p. 559)

Macroeconomics The study of the performance of the national economy and the global economy. (p. 4)

Macro-prudential regulation Regulation of the monetary financial institutions and other financial institutions and financial markets to lower the risk of crisis and failure of these institutions and markets. (p. 733)

Margin When a choice is changed by a small amount or by a little at a time, the choice is made at the margin. (p. 11)

Marginal benefit The benefit that a person receives from consuming one more unit of a good or service. It is measured as the maximum amount that a person is willing to pay for one more unit of the good or service. (pp. 11, 36)

Marginal benefit curve A curve that shows the relationship between the marginal benefit of a good and the quantity of that good consumed. (p. 36)

Marginal cost The *opportunity cost* of producing one more unit of a good or service. It is the best alternative forgone. It is calculated as the increase in total cost divided by the increase in output. (pp. 11, 35, 228)

Marginal cost pricing rule A rule that sets the price of a good or service equal to the marginal cost of producing it. (p. 289)

Marginal external benefit The benefit from an additional unit of a good or service that people other than the consumer enjoy. (p. 355)

Marginal external cost The cost of producing an additional unit of a good or service that falls on people other than the producer. (p. 369)

Marginal private benefit The benefit from an additional unit of a good or service that the consumer of that good or service receives. (p. 355)

Marginal private cost The cost of producing an additional unit of a good or service that is borne by the producer of that good or service. (p. 369)

Marginal product The increase in total product that results from a one-unit increase in the variable input, with all other inputs remaining the same. It is calculated as the increase in total product divided by the increase in the variable input employed, when the quantities of all other inputs are constant. (p. 223)

Marginal propensity to consume The fraction of a change in disposable income that is consumed. It is calculated as the change in consumption expenditure divided by the change in disposable income that brought it about. (p. 640)

Marginal propensity to import The fraction of an increase in real GDP that is spent on imports. (p. 641)

Marginal propensity to save The fraction of a change in disposable income that is saved. It is calculated as the change in saving divided by the change in disposable income that brought it about. (p. 640)

Marginal rate of substitution The rate at which a person will give up good y (the good measured on the y-axis) to get an additional unit of good x (the good measured on the x-axis) and at the same time remain indifferent (remain on the same indifference curve). (p. 180)

Marginal rate of substitution of labour for capital The increase in labour needed per unit decrease in capital to allow output to remain constant. (p. 243)

Marginal revenue The change in total revenue that results from a one-unit increase in the quantity sold. It is calculated as the change in total revenue divided by the change in quantity sold. (p. 250)

Marginal social benefit The marginal benefit enjoyed by society – by the consumer of a good or service (marginal private benefit) plus the marginal benefit enjoyed by others (marginal external benefit). (p. 355)

Marginal social cost The marginal cost incurred by the entire society – by the producer and by everyone else on whom the cost falls – and is the sum of marginal private cost and the marginal external cost. (p. 369)

Market Any arrangement that enables buyers and sellers to get information and to do business with each other. (p. 44)

Market failure A state in which the market does not allocate resources efficiently. (p. 113)

Markup The amount by which the firm's price exceeds its marginal cost. (p. 305)

Means of payment A method of settling a debt. (p. 558)

Microeconomics The study of the choices that individuals and businesses make, the way those choices interact in markets and the influence governments exert on them. (p. 4)

Minimum efficient scale The smallest quantity of output at which the long-run average cost curve reaches its lowest level. (p. 235)

Minimum wage A regulation that makes the hiring of labour below a specified wage rate illegal. The lowest wage rate at which a firm may legally hire labour. (p. 131)

Mixed good A private good the production or consumption of which creates an externality. (p. 348)

Monetarist A macroeconomist who believes that the economy is self-regulating and that it will normally operate at full employment, provided that monetary policy is not erratic and that the pace of money growth is kept steady. (p. 629)

Monetarist cycle theory A theory that regards fluctuations in both investment and consumption expenditure, driven by fluctuations in the growth rate of the quantity of money, as the main source of fluctuations in aggregate demand. (p. 678)

Monetary base The sum of the liabilities of the Bank of England plus coins issued by the Royal Mint. (p. 565)

Monetary financial institution A financial firm that takes deposits from households and firms. (p. 561)

Monetary policy The central bank conducts a nation's monetary policy by changing interest rates and adjusting the quantity of money. (p. 620)

Monetary Policy Committee (MPC) The committee in the Bank of England that has the responsibility for formulating monetary policy. (p. 564)

Monetary policy instrument A variable that the central bank can directly control or closely target. (p. 720)

Money Any commodity or token that is generally acceptable as a means of payment. (pp. 44, 558)

Money multiplier The ratio of the change in the quantity of money to the change in monetary base. (p. 569)

Money price The number of pounds or euros that must be given up in exchange for a good or service. (p. 56)

Monopolistic competition A market structure in which a large number of firms compete by making similar but slightly different products and compete on product quality, price, and marketing and are free to enter and exit the industry. (pp. 207, 300)

Monopoly A market structure in which there is one firm, which produces a good or service that has no close substitute and in which the firm is protected from competition by a barrier preventing the entry of new firms. (pp. 208, 276)

Monopsony A market in which there is a single buyer. (p. 397)

Moral hazard A situation in which one of the parties to an agreement has an incentive after the agreement is made to act in a manner that brings additional benefits to himself or herself at the expense of the other party. (p. 444)

Mortgage A legal contract that gives ownership of a home to the lender in the event that the borrower fails to meet the agreed loan payments (repayments and interest). (p. 535)

Mortgage-backed security A type of bond that entitles its holder to the income from a package of mortgages. (p. 536)

Multiplier The amount by which a change in autonomous expenditure is magnified or multiplied to determine the change in equilibrium expenditure and real GDP. (p. 646)

Nash equilibrium The outcome of a game that occurs when player A takes the best possible action given the action of player B and player B takes the best possible action given the action of player A. (p. 321)

National saving The sum of private saving (saving by households and businesses) and government saving (budget surplus). (p. 539)

Natural monopoly A market in which economies of scale enable one firm to supply the entire market at the lowest possible cost. (p. 276)

Natural monopoly good A good that is non-rival and excludable. When buyers can be excluded if they don't pay but the good is non-rival, marginal cost is zero. (p. 348)

Natural unemployment rate Natural unemployment as a percentage of the labour force. The unemployment rate when the economy is at full employment – all unemployment is frictional and structural. (p. 489)

Negative relationship A relationship between variables that move in opposite directions. (p. 19)

Neoclassical growth theory The proposition that real GDP grows because technological change induces saving and investment that make physical capital grow. (p. 521)

Net borrower A country that is borrowing more from the rest of the world than it is lending to it. (p. 602)

Net exports The value of exports minus the value of imports. (p. 462)

Net investment Net increase in the capital stock – gross investment minus depreciation. (pp. 462, 534)

Net lender A country that is lending more to the rest of the world than it is borrowing from it. (p. 602)

Net taxes Taxes paid to governments minus cash payments received from governments. (p. 538)

Net worth The market value of what a financial institutions has lent minus the market value of what it has borrowed. (p. 537)

New classical A macroeconomist who holds the view that business cycle fluctuations are the efficient responses of a well-functioning market economy bombarded by shocks that arise from the uneven pace of technological change. (p. 628)

New classical cycle theory A rational expectations theory of the business cycle in which the rational expectation of the price level, which is determined by potential GDP and expected aggregate demand, determines the money wage rate and the position of the *SAS* curve. (p. 678)

New growth theory A theory of economic growth based on the idea that real GDP per person grows because of the choices that people make in the pursuit of ever greater profit and that growth can persist indefinitely. (p. 522)

New Keynesian A Keynesian who holds the view that not only is the money wage rate sticky but that prices of goods and services are also sticky. (p. 629)

New Keynesian cycle theory A rational expectations theory of the business cycle that emphasizes the fact that today's money wage rates were negotiated at many past dates, which means that past rational expectations of the current price level influence the money wage rate and the position of the *SAS* curve. (p. 678)

Nominal GDP The value of the final goods and services produced in a given year valued at the prices that prevailed in that same year. It is a more precise name for GDP. (p. 465)

Nominal interest rate The number of pounds (or euros) that a unit of capital earns. (p. 539)

Non-excludable A good is non-excludable if everyone benefits from it regardless of whether they pay for it. (p. 348)

Non-renewable natural resources A natural resource that can be used only once and that cannot be replaced once it has been used. (p. 390)

Non-rival A good is non-rival if one person's use does not decrease the quantity available for someone else. (p. 348)

Normal good A good for which demand increases as income increases. (p. 60)

Normal profit The return that an entrepreneur can expect to receive on the average. (p. 199)

Offshoring A UK firm can either produce in another country or outsource to a firm in another country. (p. 164)

Oligopoly A market structure in which a small number of firms compete and natural or legal barriers prevent the entry of new firms. (pp. 207, 318)

Open market operation The purchase or sale of government bonds by the central bank in the loanable funds market. (p. 565)

Opportunity cost The highest-valued alternative that we give up to get something. (pp. 10, 33)

Optimal currency area A geographical area that is better served by a single currency than by several currencies. (p. 599)

Original income The wages, interest, rent and profit earned in factor markets and before paying income taxes. (p. 414)

Output gap Real GDP minus potential GDP. (pp. 490, 624)

Outsourcing A situation in which a firm buys finished goods, components or services from other firms. (p. 164)

Payoff matrix A table that shows the payoffs for every possible action by each player for every possible action by each other player. (p. 320)

Perfect competition A market in which there are many firms each selling an identical product; there are many buyers; there are no restrictions on entry into the industry; firms in the industry have no advantage over potential new entrants; and firms and buyers are well informed about the price of each firm's product. (pp. 207, 250)

Perfectly elastic demand Demand with an infinite price elasticity; the quantity demanded changes by an infinitely large percentage in response to a tiny price change. (p. 87)

Perfectly inelastic demand Demand with a price elasticity of zero; the quantity demanded remains constant when the price changes. (p. 86)

Perfect price discrimination Price discrimination that extracts the entire consumer surplus. (p. 287)

Phillips curve A curve that shows a relationship between inflation and unemployment. (p. 674)

Pigovian taxes Taxes that are used as an incentive for producers to cut back on an activity that creates an external cost. (p. 372)

Political equilibrium The outcome that results from the choices of voters, firms, politicians and civil servants. (p. 347)

Pooling equilibrium The equilibrium in a market when only one message is available and an uninformed person cannot determine quality. (p. 447)

Positive relationship A relationship between two variables that move in the same direction. (p. 18)

Potential GDP The quantity of real GDP at full employment – when all the economy's labour, capital, land and entrepreneurial ability are fully employed. (p. 466)

Poverty A situation in which a household's income is too low to be able to buy the quantities of food, shelter, and clothing that are deemed necessary. (p. 418)

Predatory pricing Setting a low price to drive competitors out of business with the intention of setting a monopoly price when the competition has gone. (p. 334)

Preferences A description of a person's likes and dislikes and the intensity of those feelings. (pp. 10, 36)

Present value The amount of money that, if invested today, will grow to be as large as a given future amount when the interest that it will earn is taken into account. (pp. 406, 702)

Price cap A government regulation that sets the maximum price that may legally be charged. (p. 128)

Price cap regulation A regulation that specifies the highest price that the firm is permitted to set. (p. 291)

Price ceiling A government regulation that sets the maximum price that may legally be charged. (p. 128)

Price discrimination The practice of selling different units of a good or service for different prices or of charging one customer different prices for different quantities bought. (p. 277)

Price effect The effect of a change in the price of a good on the quantity of the good consumed, other things remaining the same. (p. 183)

Price elasticity of demand A units-free measure of the responsiveness of the quantity demanded of a good to a change in its price, when all other influences on buyers' plans remain the same. (p. 84)

Price floor A regulation that makes it illegal to charge a price lower than a specified level. (p. 131)

Price level The average level of prices. (p. 492)

Price support A government guaranteed minimum price of a good. (p. 141)

Price taker A firm that cannot influence the price of the good or service it produces. (p. 250)

Principal–agent problem The problem of devising compensation rules that induce an agent to act in the best interest of a principal. (p. 203)

Principle of minimum differentiation The tendency for competitors to make themselves similar as they try to appeal to the maximum number of clients or voters. (p. 353)

Private good A good or service that is both rival and excludable. (p. 348)

Private information Information that is available to one person but is too costly for anyone else to obtain. (p. 444)

Producer surplus The price received for a good minus its minimum supply-price (or marginal cost) summed over the quantity sold. (p. 111)

Product differentiation Making a product slightly different from the product of a competing firm. (pp. 207, 300)

Production efficiency A situation in which the economy cannot produce more of one good without producing less of some other good. (p. 33)

Production possibilities frontier The boundary between the combinations of goods and services that can be produced and the combinations that cannot. (p. 32)

Production quota An upper limit to the quantity of a good that may be produced in a specified period. (p. 139)

Production subsidy A payment made by the government to a producer for each unit produced. (p. 140)

Productivity curve A relationship between labour productivity and physical capital per hour of labour, when human capital and the state of technology are fixed. (p. 520)

Profit The income earned by entrepreneurship. (p. 6)

Progressive income tax A tax on income at an average rate that increases with the level of income. (p. 427)

Property rights Legally established titles to the ownership, use and disposal of anything that people value, and which are enforceable in the courts. (pp. 44, 370)

Proportional income tax A tax on income at a constant average rate, regardless of the level of income. (p. 427)

Public choice A decision that has consequences for many people and perhaps for the entire society. (p. 346)

Public good A good or service that is both non-rival and non-excludable. It can be consumed simultaneously by everyone and no one can be excluded from enjoying its benefits. (p. 348)

Public production The production of a good or service by a public authority that receives its revenue from the government. (p. 357)

Purchasing power parity A situation in which the prices in two countries are equal when converted at the exchange rate. (p. 594)

Quantitative easing (QE) Lending on repurchase agreements to inject reserves into commercial banks. (pp. 567, 732)

Quantity demanded The amount of a good or service that consumers plan to buy during a given time period at a particular price. (p. 57)

Quantity supplied The amount of a good or service that producers plan to sell during a given time period at a particular price. (p. 62)

Quantity theory of money The proposition that in the long run, an increase in the quantity of money brings an equal percentage increase in the price level. (p. 574)

Rate of return regulation A regulation that requires the firm to justify its price by showing that the price enables it to earn a specified target per cent return on its capital. (p. 290)

Rational choice A choice that compares costs and benefits and achieves the greatest benefit over cost for the person making the choice. (p. 10)

Rational expectation The most accurate forecast possible – a forecast that uses all the available relevant information. (p. 673)

Real business cycle theory A theory that regards random fluctuations in productivity as the main source of economic fluctuations. (p. 678)

Real exchange rate The relative price of UK-produced goods and services to foreign-produced goods and services. (p. 595)

Real GDP The value of final goods and services produced in a given year when valued at the prices of a reference base year. (p. 465)

Real GDP per person Real GDP divided by the population. (pp. 466, 508)

Real income A household's income expressed as a quantity of goods that the household can afford to buy. (p. 177)

Real interest rate The quantity of goods and services that a unit of capital earns. It is the nominal interest rate adjusted for inflation and is approximately equal to the nominal interest rate minus the inflation rate. (p. 539)

Real wage rate The quantity of goods and services that an hour's work can buy. It is equal to the money wage rate divided by the price level. (p. 514)

Recession A business cycle phase in which real GDP decreases for at least two successive quarters. (p. 467)

Recessionary gap The amount by which potential GDP exceeds real GDP. (p. 625)

Reference base period The period in which the CPI or RPI is defined to be 100. (p. 493)

Regressive income tax A tax on income at an average rate that decreases with the level of income. (p. 427)

Regulation Rules administered by a government agency to influence prices, quantities, entry and other aspects of economic activity in a firm or industry. (p. 289)

Relative price The ratio of the price of one good or service to the price of another good or service. A relative price is an opportunity cost. (pp. 56, 177)

Rent The income that land earns. (p. 6)

Rent ceiling A regulation that makes it illegal to charge a rent higher than a specified level. (p. 128)

Rent seeking The pursuit of wealth – any attempt to capture a consumer surplus, a producer surplus, or an economic profit. (p. 284)

Repo A repurchase agreement in which a commercial bank sells a government bond to the Bank of England and simultaneously agrees to *repurchase* it (buy it back) usually two weeks later. (p. 564)

Repo rate The interest rate in the repo market. (p. 720)

Required reserve ratio The ratio of reserves to deposits that banks are required, by regulation, to hold. (p. 562)

Resale price maintenance A distributor's agreement with a manufacturer to resell a product *at or above a specified minimum price*. (p. 333)

Reserves Cash in a bank's vault plus its deposit at the central bank. (p. 561)

Retail Prices Index (RPI) An index that measures the average of the prices paid by consumers for a fixed "basket" of consumer goods and services. (p. 493)

Risk aversion The attitude towards risk. (p. 438)

Rival A good is rival if one person's use decreases the quantity available for someone else. (p. 348)

Rule of 70 A rule that states that the number of years it takes for the level of a variable to double is approximately 70 divided by the annual percentage growth rate of the variable. (p. 508)

Saving The amount of income that households have left after they have paid their taxes and bought their consumption goods and services. (p. 534)

Saving function The relationship between saving and disposable income, other things remaining the same. (p. 638)

Scarcity Our inability to satisfy all our wants. (p. 4)

Scatter diagram A diagram that plots the value of one economic variable against the value of another for a number of different values of each variable. (p. 16)

Screening Inducing an informed party to reveal private information. (p. 447)

Search activity The time spent looking for someone with whom to do business. (p. 128)

Self-interest The choices that you think are the best for you. (p. 7)

Separating equilibrium The equilibrium in a market when signalling provides full information to a previously uninformed person. (p. 447)

Short run The period of time in which the quantity of at least one factor of production is fixed and the quantities of the other factors can be varied. The fixed factor is usually capital – that is, the firm has a given plant size. (p. 222)

Short-run aggregate supply The relationship between the quantity of real GDP supplied and the price level when the money wage rate, the prices of other factors of production and potential GDP remain constant. (p. 615)

Short-run market supply curve A curve that shows how the quantity supplied in a market varies as the market price varies when the each firm's plant and the number of firms remain the same. (p. 256)

Short-run macroeconomic equilibrium A situation that occurs when the quantity of real GDP demanded equals the short-run quantity of real GDP supplied – at the point of intersection of the *AD* curve and the *SAS* curve. (p. 622)

Short-run Phillips curve A curve that shows the trade-off between inflation and unemployment, holding constant the expected inflation rate and the natural unemployment rate. (p. 674)

Shutdown point The output and price at which the firm just covers its total variable cost. In the short run, the firm is indifferent between producing the profit-maximizing output and shutting down temporarily. (p. 254)

Signal An action taken by an informed person (or firm) to send a message to uninformed people or an action taken outside a market that conveys information that can be used by that market. (p. 308)

Signalling A situation in which an informed person takes actions that send information to uninformed persons. (p. 446)

Single-price monopoly A monopoly that must sell each unit of its output for the same price to all its customers. (p. 277)

Slope The change in the value of the variable measured on the y-axis divided by the change in the value of the variable measured on the x-axis. (p. 22)

Social interest Choices that are the best for society as a whole. (p. 7)

Social interest theory A theory that politicians supply the regulation that achieves an efficient allocation of resources. (p. 289)

Stagflation The combination of inflation and recession. (pp. 627, 671)

Stock A certificate of ownership and claim to the firm's profits. (p. 536)

Stock market A financial market in which shares of stocks of corporations are traded. (p. 536)

Strategies All the possible actions of each player in a game. (p. 320)

Structural surplus or deficit The budget balance that would occur if the economy were at full employment and real GDP were equal to potential GDP. (p. 705)

Structural unemployment The unemployment that arises when changes in technology or international competition change the skills needed to perform jobs or change the locations of jobs. (p. 489)

Subsidy A payment made by the government to a domestic producer based on the quantity produced. (p. 357)

Substitute A good that can be used in place of another good. (p. 59)

Substitution effect The effect of a change in price of a good or service on the quantity bought when the consumer (hypothetically) remains indifferent between the original and the new consumption situations – that is, the consumer remains on the same indifference curve. (p. 186)

Sunk cost The past expenditure on a plant that has no resale value. (p. 222)

Supply The relationship between the quantity of a good that producers plan to sell and the price of the good when all other influences on sellers' plans remain the same. It is described by a supply schedule and illustrated by a supply curve. (p. 62)

Supply curve A curve that shows the relationship between the quantity supplied and the price of a good when all other influences on producers' planned sales remain the same. (p. 62)

Supply of loanable funds The relationship between the quantity of loanable funds supplied and the real interest rate when all other influences on lending plans remain the same. (p. 541)

Symmetry principle A requirement that people in similar situations be treated similarly. (p. 118)

Tariff A tax that is imposed by the importing country when an imported good crosses its international boundary. (p. 157)

Tax incidence The division of the burden of a tax between the buyer and the seller. (p. 133)

Tax multiplier The quantitative effect of a change in taxes on real GDP. (p. 707)

Tax wedge The gap between the before-tax and after-tax wage rates. (p. 699)

Technological change The development of new goods and better ways of producing goods and services. (p. 38)

Technological efficiency A situation that occurs when the firm produces a given output by using the least amount of inputs. (p. 201)

Technology Any method of producing a good or service. (p. 200)

Time-series graph A graph that measures time (for example, months or years) on the x-axis and the variable or variables in which we are interested on the y-axis. (p. 474)

Total cost The cost of all the factors of production that a firm uses. (p. 227)

Total fixed cost The cost of the firm's fixed inputs. (p. 227)

Total product The maximum output that a given quantity of factors of production can produce. (p. 223)

Total revenue The value of a firm's sales. It is calculated as the price of the good multiplied by the quantity sold. (pp. 88, 250)

Total revenue test A method of estimating the price elasticity of demand by observing the change in total revenue that results from a change in the price, when all other influences on the quantity sold remain the same. (p. 88)

Total surplus The sum of consumer surplus and producer surplus. (p. 112)

Total variable cost The cost of all the firm's variable inputs. (p. 227)

Trade-off An exchange – giving up one thing to get something else. (p. 10)

Trades union An organized group of workers whose purpose is to increase wages and to influence other job conditions. (p. 396)

Tragedy of the commons The absence of incentives to prevent the overuse and depletion of a common resource. (p. 374)

Transactions costs The costs that arise from finding someone with whom to do business, of reaching an agreement about the price and other aspects of the exchange, and of ensuring that the terms of the agreement are fulfilled. The opportunity costs of conducting a transaction. (pp. 115, 212, 371)

Trend The general tendency for a variable to move in one direction. (p. 475)

Tying arrangement An agreement to sell one product only if the buyer agrees to buy another, different product. (p. 333)

UK interest rate differential A gap equal to the UK interest rate minus the foreign interest rate. (p. 591)

Unemployment rate The percentage of the people in the labour force who are unemployed. (p. 486)

Unit elastic demand Demand with a price elasticity of 1; the percentage change in the quantity demanded equals the percentage change in price. (p. 86)

Utilitarianism A principle that states that we should strive to achieve "the greatest happiness for the greatest number of people". (p. 116)

Value of marginal product The value to the firm of hiring one more unit of a factor of production. (p. 391)

Velocity of circulation The average number of times a pound (or euro) of money is used annually to buy the goods and services that make up GDP. (p. 574)

Voucher A token that the government provides to households, which they can use to buy specified goods and services. (p. 357)

Wages The income that labour earns. (p. 6)

Wealth The market value of all the things that people own. (pp. 416, 534)

Workforce The sum of the people who are employed and who are unemployed. (p. 485)

Working-age population The total number of men aged 16 to 64 and women aged 16 to 59 who are not in prison, hospital or some other form of institutional care. (p. 485)

Index

Note: key terms and pages on which they are defined appear in **bold**.

Publisher's Acknowledgements

We are grateful to the following for permission to reproduce copyright material:

Cartoons

Cartoon on page 4 © Frank Modell/ The New Yorker Collection/www. cartoonbank.com; Cartoon on page 113 © Mike Twohy/The New Yorker Collection/www.cartoonbank.com; Cartoon on page 182 © Robert Weber/The New Yorker Collection/ www.cartoonbank.com; Cartoon on page 204 Funny Money cartoon by David Austin, *Financial Times, Weekend,* 13/11/1999, p. xxvi, © David Austin, Financial Times, with permission from Janet Slee; Cartoon on page 288 from *Voodoo Economics,* Chronicle Books (Hamilton, W. 1992) p. 3, with permission from William Hamilton.

Photographs

(Key: b-bottom; c-centre; l-left; r-right; t-top)

airbus.com: Airbus S.A.S 2010 43; **Alamy Images:** 67photo 353, ACE STOCK LIMITED 468l, Adrian Sherratt 469l, Alex Segre 459, Ashley Cooper 367, Big Pants productions 437, Caro 468r, Catchlight Visual Services 469r, 667, Catchlight Visual Services 469r, 667, Charles Polidano / Touch The Skies 221, China Images 507, Classic Image 174t, 458, Classic Image 174t, 458, david hancock 275, David Levenson 613, david pearson 207bl, DBURKE 151, Greg Balfour Evans 585, Imagestate Media Partners Limited – Impact Photos 261r, INTERFOTO 506, Janine Wiedel Photolibrary 413, Jeff Morgan 02 3, Jeffrey Blackler 207br, Johnny Greig 483, Juice Images

249, Julio Etchart 389, keith morris 184t, Kuttig – People 184b, Marc Hill 345, Mark Fagelson 259, oliver leedham 213, Pat Behnke 637, Peter Cavanagh 335, Philip Quirk 207tl, Picture Contact BV 121, Picturebank 105, Radius Images 197, Robert Clayton 317, RubberBall 387, Simon James 557, sportsphotographer.eu 299, Tim Graham 173, vario images GmbH & Co.KG 235, World History Archive 388; **Bridgeman Art Library Ltd:** A river valley with a swineherd resting under a tree in the foreground, a hamlet beyond (oil on panel), Ryckaert, Marten (1587–1631) / Private Collection / Photo © Christie's Images / The Bridgeman Art Library 374; **Corbis:** Bettmann 174b, Dave Reede / All Canada Photos 31; **Fotolia.com:** Chadaeva Tolkunay 69, Edyta Pawlowska 689, Gina Sanders 53, m.schuckart 457, Mike Shannon 349, Sabine 8l, terex 261l, Wally Stemberger 611; **Getty Images:** AFP 690, Alexey SAZONOV / AFP 71, BEN STANSALL / AFP 9, Bloomberg 537t, 717, 722, Charles Ommanney 706, Chris Ratcliffe / Bloomberg 175, Christopher Furlong 127, Fox Photos 484, Kevork Djansezian 55, NATALIA KOLESNIKOVA / AFP 83, Rama Lakshmi / TWP 7, Tomohiro Ohsumi / Bloomberg 587, Torn Williams 709t; **GNU Free Documentation License: Wikipedia:** 54; **John Tamblyn:** Prelims; **Patrick Minford:** 709b; **Pearson Education Ltd:** Photodisc. Photolink 8r; **Press Association Images:** Associated Press 344, Charles Dharapak 620l, Christian Lutz 620tr, J. Scott Applewhite 620tc, Johnny Green / PA Archive 533, 620bc, Johnny Green / PA Archive 533, 620bc, PA WIRE 343, The Canadian Press, Sean Kilpatrick 620br, Tophams 612; **Reuters:** Jason Reed 537b, Kevin

Lamarque 549, Paul Hackett 691; **Robert Barro, Harvard University:** 709c; **Science & Society Picture Library:** National Railway Museum 519; **Science Photo Library Ltd:** NASA 505; **Xavier Sala i Martin:** 1.

Figures

Figure 22.10 after *These Are the Good Old Days: A Report on US Living Standards,* Federal Reserve Bank of Dallas 1993 Annual Report. Reproduced with permission.

Text

Extract on page 46 after Crop switch worsens global food price crisis, *The Guardian,* 05/04/2008 (Vidal, J.), Copyright Guardian News & Media Ltd. 2008; Extract on page 98 after Fears of Social Unrest When Harvest Fails, *The Independent,* 27/08/2010 (Walker, S.), Copyright © 2010 The Independent; Extract on page 120 after Volcano cloud hangs over European Economy, 19/04/2010 (Odula, T.), used with permission of The Associated Press Copyright © 2010. All rights reserved; Extract on page 144 after OECD (2010) Government support to farmers rises slightly in OECD countries, News Release 01/07/2010, www.oecd.org/agriculture, with permission from OECD; Extract on page 190 after Amazon.com Says Kindle Sales Accelerated Last Quarter, *BloombergBusinessweek.com,* 19/07/2010 (Galante, J.), http:// www.businessweek.com/news/ 2010-07-19/amazon-com-says-kindle-sales-accelerated-last-quarter.html, used with permission of BloombergBusinessweek.com

The Financial Times